NORWICH CATHEDRAL

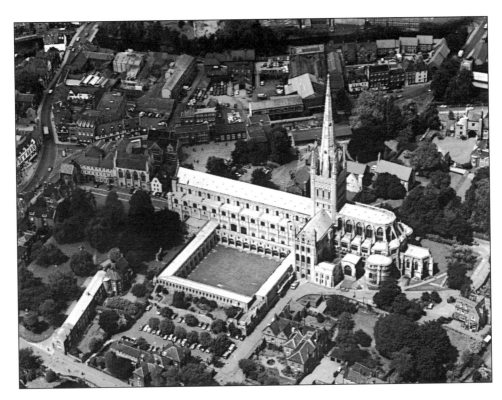

Norwich Cathedral from the air.

Norwich Cathedral

Church, City and Diocese, 1096–1996

EDITED BY
IAN ATHERTON, ERIC FERNIE,
CHRISTOPHER HARPER-BILL
AND HASSELL SMITH

THE HAMBLEDON PRESS

LONDON AND RIO GRANDE

Published by The Hambledon Press, 1996
102 Gloucester Avenue, London NW1 8HX (UK)
PO Box 162, Rio Grande, Ohio 45674 (USA)

ISBN 1 85285 134 1

A description of this book is available from
the British Library and from the Library of Congress

Typeset by Carnegie Publishing, 18 Maynard St, Preston

Printed on acid-free paper and bound in
Great Britain by Cambridge University Press

Contents

Foreword

by the Bishop of Norwich

Work on the first palace began at the same time as the building of the cathedral, and so bishops of Norwich have lived on the same site for nearly 900 years, under the shadow of our great cathedral. Our houses have been altered, enlarged, reduced, vandalised, Victorianised and, in 1958, built again from scratch, but still in the same beautiful setting. The view of Norwich Cathedral from the study window of the present bishop's house is a daily inspiration, as one marvels at the grace of the architecture and ponders its history. There is always a consciousness that one is but part of a long succession, privileged for a while to live in this place, and knowing that future generations of bishops will gaze on the same view and think similar thoughts.

Bishops may wonder at and be inspired by the building, but something more than episcopal contemplation is needed to do justice to the reality that is Norwich Cathedral, and that is the purpose of this book.

Our cathedral has occupied a central and influential position in the development of the city of Norwich, the county of Norfolk and the diocese of Norwich. Its history, archaeology and architecture in the context of the changes in social and ecclesiastical life of succeeding ages are complex and profoundly important. A definitive study of these subjects is a massive task, which the authors of this book have undertaken with great dedication and scholarly expertise.

This volume will surely rank as perhaps the most important and comprehensive volume ever produced about the cathedral. I am proud, as the seventieth successor of the first bishop of Norwich, Herbert de Losinga, to be in office at the time of this landmark in our history. This book is a most fitting offering as we celebrate the 900th anniversary of our foundation, for in charting the past it will, like its subject, stand as a work of great value for future generations.

Peter Norvic.

In Memory of

Arthur Bensley Whittingham (1901–1986)
and
Andrew Henry Robert Martindale (1932–1995)

Preface

Hassell Smith

Norwich, down to the eighteenth century, ranked with Bristol and York as one of the foremost regional capitals of England, only Bristol challenging its position as second city of the realm. Despite this preeminence, there is no comprehensive modern history of the city or of its magnificent cathedral – a cultural gap which, in part at least, *Norwich Cathedral: Church, City and Diocese, 1096–1996* is intended to fill. The cathedral is one of the most important Norman buildings in England, while its size, remarkable state of preservation and range of architectural features make it a significant structure among the great churches of western Europe.

The thirty-five scholars who have contributed to this volume realise that no series of essays can have the unity of a book created by one mind. They have, none the less, striven to achieve the greatest possible unity by mutual consultation during its preparation. They have written so as to make every chapter accessible to the non-specialist. The book has a clear and integrated structure. Part I deals with the events leading to the foundation of the cathedral; Part II focuses on the building itself. Part III describes life within the precinct during the medieval period and the priory's relations with the city, the diocese and the wider world. Part IV covers the cathedral's decoration and the variety of arts that have been used in its adornment. Finally, Part V traces the post-Reformation history of the cathedral to the present day.

Barbara Dodwell and Christopher Harper-Bill were the originators of this volume. In 1987 they visited me at the University of East Anglia to enquire whether the Centre of East Anglian Studies would prepare a collection of essays on the history of Norwich Cathedral to celebrate the 900th anniversary of its foundation. I readily responded to this request since such a project epitomised everything for which the Centre stood: it was interdisciplinary in that it embraced history, art history and archaeology; it could only be achieved through cooperation between members of the university and scholars living in the region or working in other universities and associated institutions; and the volume, when completed, would help the people of East Anglia to understand their cultural and spiritual inheritance better but would, at the same time, be of national and international significance.

All the essays have been written by experts who have incorporated a good deal of their own research as well as providing, where appropriate, a summation of the work of others. That said, each contributor has handled his or her topic differently. Some chapters are based on exhaustive research; others are exploratory essays which open up new aspects and point the way to further research. Two (from the former dean and the surveyor of the fabric) are based upon personal experience. Some are focused within the close; others are outward-looking and set the cathedral and those who served it in a wider context. We are proud of our achievement and offer it as our contribution for this year of celebrations to the dean and chapter, to the citizens of Norwich, to the Friends of Norwich Cathedral and to those throughout the diocese who look to the cathedral as their mother church.

The publication of this book has been made possible by grants from:

The Leverhulme Trust

The Alderman John Norman's Foundation

The Dean and Chapter of Norwich Cathedral

The Diocese of East Anglia

The editors and contributors gratefully acknowledge advice and encouragement from Professor Owen Chadwick OM, Professor Patrick Collinson and Professor Barrie Dobson. We have been privileged to draw upon their wisdom and experience. It was Owen Chadwick who advised us that we should seek funding for a research assistant. Without that advice this volume would not have been completed in time to celebrate the cathedral's 900th anniversary. On a personal note, we have greatly appreciated his encouragement while he served as chancellor of this university. We are also grateful to the bishop of Norwich (the Right Reverend Peter Nott) and to the former dean of Norwich (the Very Reverend Paul Burbridge) for giving their blessing and support to this volume.

The editors, the contributors and the publisher also thank Ian Atherton who, as our research assistant, has done so much, so well and so willingly to make this volume possible. There are, surely, few research assistants who are promoted to editor, but we have had no hesitation in inviting him to join the editorial team. I alone have experienced the depth of his commitment and I have found it inspiring. It remains for me, as convenor of the team, to thank the editors and contributors, all of whom have worked and written without remuneration. It is no small achievement to complete a project which, by any standards, must be deemed a large cooperative enterprise. Responsibility for that achievement rests principally with the contributors.

To produce a volume of this size is to incur many debts. Those who have helped particular contributors are acknowledged in the appropriate chapters. Here the editors wish to thank those who have assisted in the editorial processes. Maylis Baylé assisted with some difficult illustrations; Michael Brandon Jones did most of the photographic work, often at short notice; Christopher Brooke and Peter Lasko supported our applications for funding; Robert Ashton and Roberta Gilchrist participated in our colloquia and gave much support; Sam Hornor, clerk to the Trustees of the Alderman Norman's Foundation, has advised us and watched over our deliberations; Phillip Judge and Steven Ashley provided cartographic assistance; Jean Kennedy, Frank Meeres (curator of the Dean and Chapter Archive) and the entire staff of the Norfolk Record Office have given advice and excellent service, especially in making available the Dean and Chapter records after the disastrous fire in 1994; Jane Key did some specialist word-processing at a critical stage; Peter Martin has commented constructively on the final drafts of many chapters; Tom Mollard guided us to material in the dean and chapter's library; Colin Pordham, chapter clerk and administrator, has been a great enabler; Norman Scarfe solved at least one editorial problem with characteristic promptness; Norma Watt, assistant keeper of art at the Norwich Castle Museum, helped with the selection of illustrations from the collections in her care; Alan Webster gave valuable advice in the final stages; Mavis Wesley has looked after our finances and a good deal more as well.

Special thanks go to Martin Sheppard of Hambledon Press. He has been involved in the preparation of this volume from its early stages and has been both tolerant and creative throughout its production. Finally, we all thank Richard Wilson, Director of the Centre of East Anglian Studies, who has provided accommodation, specialist facilities and intellectual stimulation throughout this project.

Centre of East Anglian Studies
University of East Anglia

Illustration Acknowledgements

The editors and the publisher wish to thank the following for their kind permission to reproduce figures and plates:

S. J. Ashley 23, 25, 46, 56, 167–68, 173, 175; Ian Atherton 209–11, 213–14; James Austin 54, 62–63; Bayerische Staatsbibliothek 130; Bodleian Library, pl. IIb; British Library 115, 117, pl. IIa; British Museum 5, 65; Dean and Chapter of Canterbury Cathedral 164; Dean and Chapter of Norwich Cathedral 4, 6, 19, 118, 120, 137–38, 184–85, 195–96, 202, 206–8, 212, 216–218, 220–23, 226, 228, 230–31, pls Vb, c, VI, VII; Deutsches Archäologisches Institut 64; Eastern Daily Press 151; Richard Fawcett 100–13; Eric Fernie 12–16, 22, 28, 31; Jonathan Finch 178–83, 186–94, 204; Jill Franklin 48–50; Jane Geddes 154–58, 160–61; L. Grodecki 55, courtesy of Maylis Baylé; Ken Harvey, pl. IIIa; Julia Hedgecoe 123, 126, 128–29, pls IIIb–c; Stephen Heywood 11, 21, 26–27, 29–30, 32, 35, 38–40, 42–45, 51–53, 57–59, 61; Phillip Judge 1, 66–69, 71, 73, 84, 114, 116, 122, 125, 127, 131, 145, 177; Dennis King 146–50; Cliff Middleton, pl. I; National Portrait Gallery, London 203; Norfolk Museums Service (Norfolk Air Photographs Library) and Derek A. Edwards frontispiece, 2, 8; Norfolk Museums Service (Norwich Castle Museum) 7, 152, 199, 201, pls VIIIa, b; Norfolk Record Office 118, 137–38, 184, 217, 220–23, 226, 228, 230–31, pls VI, VII; Master and Fellows of Pembroke College, Cambridge 205; Mrs J. Philps 3; Royal Commission on the Historical Monuments of England 132, 134–35, 139–44, 224–25, 227, 229, pls IV, Va; Norman Scarfe 3; Scolar Press, Aldershot 130; Society of Antiquaries of London 17–18, 20, 33, 97, 162, 165–66, 219; Malcolm Thurlby 70, 72, 74–80; Master and Fellows of Trinity College, Cambridge 124; University of East Anglia 24, 34, 36–37, 41, 47, 81, 91–92, 96, 98–99, 119, 197–98, 215; Piers Wallace 9–10; Warburg Institute 60, 163; Francis Woodman 82–83, 85–90, 93–95.

Figs 12–16, 22, 28, 31 appear in E. C. Fernie, *An Architectural History of Norwich Cathedral* (Oxford, 1993), as figs 5, 24, 27, 25, 28, 8, 21 and 11; figs 17–18, 33, 219 appeared in S. R. Pierce, *J. A. Repton: Norwich Cathedral at the End of the Eighteenth Century* (Farnborough, 1968); fig. 20 first appeared in D. H. S. Cranage, 'Eastern Chapels in the Cathedral Church of Norwich', *Antiq. J.*, 12 (1932), pp. 117–36; figs 25 and 68 are redrawn from E. C. Fernie, *An Architectural History of Norwich Cathedral* (Oxford, 1993), figs 17, 21, 28; fig. 46 is based on a drawing made for E. C. Fernie which first appeared in A. B. Whittingham, 'The Bishop's Palace', *Programme of the Royal Archaeological Institute's Summer Meeting at Norwich* (1979), p. 90, fig. 19; fig. 64 is taken from E. von Mercklin, *Antike Figuralkapitelle* (Berlin, 1962); figs 69 and 73 are redrawn from B. Cherry, 'Romanesque Architecture in Eastern England', *JBAA*, 131 (1978), p. 14, fig. 6, and p. 12, figs 5e, 5f, 5g; fig. 91, an engraving by Henry Hulsburgh (d. 1729), copied from Daniel King's engraving of 1655, is from Sir Thomas Browne, *Repertorium* (London, 1725), facing p. 25; fig. 130 is taken from A. Henry, ed., *The Mirour of Mans Saluacioune* (Aldershot, 1986), p. 66; fig. 153 is from R. and J. Brandon, *Analysis of Gothic Architecture* (London, 1847), section 2, pl. 8; fig. 159 is from E. W. Tristram, *English Medieval Wall Painting*, 2 vols (London, 1950), ii, pl. 102; fig. 197, engraved by T. Barber from a sketch by T. Higham, is taken from T. K. Cromwell, *Excursions in the County of Norfolk*, 2 vols (Norwich, 1818), i, facing p. 22; fig. 200 is from Sir Thomas Browne, *Works*, ed. S. Wilkin, 4 vols (London, 1835–36), iv, frontispiece.

Abbreviations

Antiq. J.	*Antiquaries' Journal.*
Arch. J.	*Archaeological Journal.*
BAACT	British Archaeological Association Conference Transactions.
BL	British Library.
Blomefield, *Norfolk*	F. Blomefield and C. Parkin, *An Essay Towards a Topographical History of the County of Norfolk*, 11 vols (2nd edn, London, 1805–10).
CCR	*Calendar of Close Rolls*, 67 vols (London, 1902–).
Communar Rolls	E. C. Fernie and A. B. Whittingham, eds, *The Early Communar and Pitancer Rolls of Norwich Cathedral Priory with an Account of the Building of the Cloister* (NRS, 41, 1972).
CPL	*Calendar of Entries in the Papal Registers Relating to Great Britain*, 17 vols (London and Dublin, 1893–).
CPR	*Calendar of Patent Rolls*, 60 vols (London, 1901–).
CSPD	*Calendar of State Papers, Domestic*, 92 vols (London, 1856–).
DB	*Domesday Book.*
DNB	*Dictionary of National Biography.*
EEA, vi	C. Harper-Bill, ed., *English Episcopal Acta vi: Norwich, 1070–1214* (London, 1990).
EHR	*English Historical Review.*
Fernie, *NC*	E. C. Fernie, *An Architectural History of Norwich Cathedral* (Oxford, 1993).
First Register	H. W. Saunders, ed., *The First Register of Norwich Cathedral Priory* (NRS, 11, 1939).
GS	E. M. Goulburn and H. Symonds, *The Life, Letters and Sermons of Bishop Herbert de Losinga*, 2 vols (Oxford and London, 1878).
JBAA	*Journal of the British Archaeological Association.*
NA	*Norfolk Archaeology.*

NCC	B. Dodwell, ed., *The Charters of Norwich Cathedral Priory*, 2 vols (Pipe Roll Society, new series, 40, 46, 1974–85).
PRO	Public Record Office.
NRO	Norfolk Record Office.
NRS	Norfolk Record Society.
RS	Rolls Series.
TRHS	*Transactions of the Royal Historical Society*.
VCH	Victoria County History.

PART I

The Foundation

I

The East Anglian Sees
before the Conquest

James Campbell

Even to sketch the early history of the diocese of East Anglia is a loaves and fishes exercise.[1] Very little evidence has to be made to explain over four hundred years of development, doubtless complicated. Bede, writing in 731, starts us off on a fairly firm footing. His story of the church in East Anglia begins with the conversion of two of its kings, Rædwald in about 616, and his son Earpwald about a decade later. The former abandoned his faith, the latter perished soon after his conversion. The continuous history of our church begins with King Sigeberht. When Sigeberht became king, in about 630, he was already a Christian, for he had been converted while an exile in Gaul. He soon gained the help of a bishop from Burgundy, Felix, and a see was established at *Dommoc*. Under Felix and his immediate successors (of whom Bede tells us little more than their names) most or all of the East Angles probably became Christians, at some level. We are told of Bisi, who was bishop from about 669, that when illness prevented his exercising his office, two bishops, Æcce and Beaduwine, were appointed in his place. This probably happened in 673 or rather later and would have accorded with Archbishop Theodore of Canterbury's

1. The principal histories of the diocese are E. M. Goulburn, H. Symonds and E. Hailstone, *The Ancient Sculptures in the Roof of Norwich Cathedral . . . to Which is Added a History of the See of Norwich* (London and Norwich, 1876), A. Jessopp's contribution to the Diocesan Histories series, *Norwich* (London 1884), and D. H. S. Cranage, ed., *Thirteenth-Hundredth Anniversary of the Diocese of East Anglia* (Norwich, 1930). For the succession of pre-Conquest bishops, which can be but imperfectly established, E. B. Fryde, D. E. Greenway, S. Porter and I. Roy, eds, *Handbook of British Chronology* (3rd edn, London, 1986), pp. 216–17. P. Wade-Martins, *Excavations in North Elmham Park, 1967–72*, 2 vols (East Anglian Archaeology, 9, Gressenhall, 1980), i, pp. 3–11, surveys the history of the Anglo-Saxon dioceses in East Anglia. S. Rigold there provides biographical details of the bishops of the re-established see of Elmham (pp. 10–11); so too does F. E. Harmer in the apparatus to her *Anglo-Saxon Writs* (Manchester, 1952).

policy of dividing large sees.[2] Thereafter, for two centuries, East Anglia had two sees. One remained at *Dommoc*, the other was, by 803, and probably from the beginning, at Elmham.

Where was *Dommoc*? And was the Elmham see at North Elmham (Norfolk) or South Elmham (Suffolk)? These thorny questions have long vexed the learned.[3] Let us begin with *Dommoc*. It is agreed that Bede's description of the place as *civitas* shows that it was of Roman significance. It is commonly identified with Dunwich. This view is at least as old as the fifteenth century. It may originate in no more than an apparent verbal relationship between the two names. To the extent that philologists accept the significance of this relationship they do so uneasily.[4] There could have been a considerable Roman place near Dunwich; if so it is lost under the sea. Another late medieval source located *Dommoc* at Felixstowe. The name suggests a connection with Bishop Felix. There was a Roman fort there, now lost to sea-erosion. Both cases begin with a suggestive place-name and each is supported by plausible circumstantial evidence. Both places concerned are now fathoms deep in the North Sea. There is nothing for it but to keep an open mind on the matter. (See fig. 1 for the location of places mentioned in the text).

Furthermore, there are reasons for considering other possible sites. Here we must remember that *Dommoc* was not the only important place in early England knowledge of whose location has been lost. For example, *Clovesho* was the site of many important early Anglo-Saxon councils, but no one knows where it was. It is more likely that this place has changed its name than that it has completely disappeared. There is no doubt that places could change their names. Thus Peterborough was called *Medeshamstede* until the tenth century. Such changes may sometimes have been connected with places being known by more names than one; Bath was sometimes called *Akemanceastre*.[5] In short, sites should not be excluded from consideration because they now have names unconnected to that of *Dommoc*. This widens the range of possibilities to include Hoxne and Eye, both of which appear as significant

2. D. Whitelock, 'The Pre-Viking Age Church in East Anglia', *Anglo-Saxon England*, 1 (1972), pp. 1–22, provides an admirable and fully referenced account of the early history of the diocese.

3. The arguments are surveyed by Whitelock, 'Pre-Viking Age Church', p. 4n. The most recent contributions about the location of *Dommoc* are Fernie, *NC*, p. 201 (inclining towards Felixstowe) and J. Haslam, '*Dommoc* and Dunwich: A Reappraisal', *Anglo-Saxon Studies in Archaeology and History*, 5 (1992), pp. 41–46 (inclining towards Dunwich).

4. M. Förster, *Der Flussname Themse und seine Sippe* (Sitzungsberichte der Bayerischen Akademie der Wissenschaften Philosophisch-Historische Abteilung, Munich, 1941), part 1, p. 425n.; Whitelock, 'Pre-Viking Age Church', p. 4 n. 2; E. Ekwall, *The Concise Oxford Dictionary of Place Names* (4th edn, Oxford, 1960), s.v. 'Dunwich'.

5. C. Plummer and J. Earle, eds, *Two of the Saxon Chronicles Parallel*, 2 vols (Oxford, 1899), i, p. 117; E. Ekwall, *Concise Oxford Dictionary of Place Names*, s.v. 'Akeman Street'.

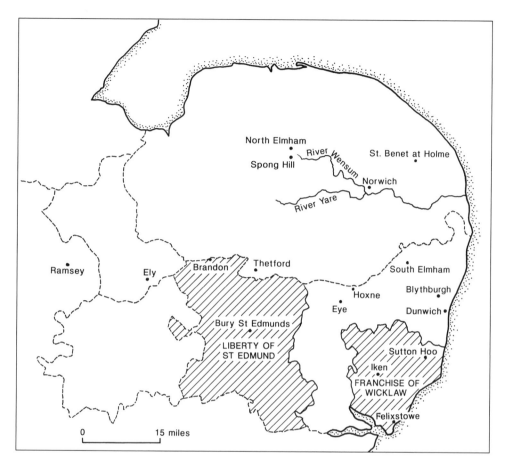

Fig. 1. Map locating places mentioned in the text.

ecclesiastical centres.[6] The discovery of rich late Roman treasures at both places suggests a Roman site somewhere near.[7] If a plausible Roman site could be found at Blythburgh it would be a strong candidate. This case is a variant on, rather than a substitute for, that for Dunwich. The 'wich' element in Dunwich could indicate that it was a trading centre associated with a centre of authority whose name had the same first element and a different termination, just as *Lundenwic* seems to have been a trading centre beside London.[8] There is evidence that Blythburgh, not

6. For Hoxne see pp. 6, 9, 14, 17 below. The discovery of a ninth-century episcopal seal-matrix at Eye (pp. 12–13 below) takes its ecclesiastical importance back before the foundation of the Benedictine priory in the eleventh century. Compare also Whitelock, 'Pre-Viking Age Church', p. 4 and n. 2.

7. R. I. Bland and C. Johns, *The Hoxne Treasure: An Illustrated Introduction* (London, 1993).

8. M. Biddle, 'A City in Transition; 400–800', in M. D. Lobel, ed., *The City of London from Prehistoric Times to c. 1520* (corrected edn, Oxford, 1991), pp. 26–28.

Dunwich, was the local centre of authority. The discovery of a probably eighth-century Anglo-Saxon writing tablet (suggested to be one for liturgical use) indicates an ecclesiastical site there, as does a late story that it was the burial place of a seventh-century king.[9]

The Elmham problem is less exercising, for only two sites fall under consideration. Both North Elmham and South Elmham were, by the eleventh century, centres of major estates of the East Anglian see. At each there is a ruined church, now strongly argued to be of late eleventh-century date though not with necessary conclusiveness.[10] County patriotism has fuelled the flames of a controversy over which Elmham was the *sedes* (episcopal seat), one in which balance has not always been maintained, nor even courtesy. Undoubtedly the *sedes* was at North Elmham in the tenth and eleventh centuries. Indeed, a ruin there has for long been regarded as that of the late Anglo-Saxon cathedral of Elmham (fig. 2). This identification has recently been brought seriously into doubt. However, extensive excavations on an adjacent site have discovered part of an important late Anglo-Saxon cemetery, and of settlement remains, from both before and after the Danish invasions; these could have been associated with an episcopal *sedes*. Furthermore that North, not South, Elmham was the episcopal seat in the late Anglo-Saxon period is put beyond doubt by there having been what Domesday calls '*ecclesia sedes episcopatus de Sudfolc*' ('a church [which was] the episcopal seat for Suffolk') from the tenth century at Hoxne.[11] It is incredible that there should have been another centre of episcopal authority at South Elmham seven miles away. The matter does not, however, end there. What may be the oldest evidence for ecclesiastical occupation on either site is a worn fragment of a ninth- or tenth-century tombstone built into the ruined 'Old Minster' at South Elmham.[12] The episcopal estate at South Elmham has a specially ancient air, not least because it seems originally to have consisted of a large rectangular bloc of land. One part of it, Homersfield, may take its name from Hunberht, the last known ninth-century bishop of Elmham.[13] The application of the term 'minster' to the church in the middle ages strengthens the case for the site having associations with something more than an episcopal

9. Haslam, '*Dommoc* and Dunwich', pp. 43–44. For the tablet, L. Webster and J. Backhouse, eds, *The Making of England, Anglo-Saxon Art and Culture, AD 600–900* (London, 1991), p. 81, no. 65.

10. S. Heywood, 'The Ruined Church at North Elmham', *JBAA*, 135 (1982), pp. 1–10; Fernie, *NC*, pp. 207–9; N. Batcock, 'The Parish Church in Norfolk in the 11th and 12th Centuries', in J. Blair, ed., *Minsters and Parish Churches: The Local Church in Transition, 950–1200* (Oxford, 1988), p. 179 n. 4, for argu-

ments against those of Heywood; S. Heywood, 'The Round Towers of East Anglia', in Blair, ed., *Minsters and Parish Churches*, p. 175 n. 7.

11. *DB Suffolk*, fo. 379a (no. 18/1); compare p. 14 below.

12. N. Smedley and E. Owles, 'Excavations at the Old Minster, South Elmham', *Proceedings of the Suffolk Institute of Archaeology*, 32 (1970), p. 10.

13. N. Scarfe, *The Suffolk Landscape* (London, 1972), pp. 123–24.

Fig. 2. The ruins at North Elmham, often regarded as the late Anglo-Saxon cathedral.

chapel.[14] So too does its being a quarter of a mile from the bishops' medieval manor house (though this may have moved its site). Recent investigation has suggested the possibility of there having been an important middle Saxon site not at the 'Old Minster' but near South Elmham Hall a mile away.[15] Although evidence for organised eighth- or ninth-century settlement has been detected at North Elmham, it is not by itself enough to prove the presence of the *sedes*.[16] If, as is likely, a tenth- or eleventh-century ivory carving, now at Cambridge, was found at North Elmham then this may be the earliest unambiguous physical evidence for an important ecclesiastical site there.[17] It is in any case odd that two major episcopal residences

14. J. Ridgard, 'References to South Elmham Minster in the Medieval Account Rolls of South Elmham Manor', *Proceedings of the Suffolk Institute of Archaeology*, 36 (1987), pp. 196–201.

15. Ridgard, 'References to South Elmham Minster', pp. 198–99; see also the report of the Suffolk Institute's excursion to South Elmham in 1987, *Proceedings of the Suffolk Institute of Archaeology*, 36 (1988), pp. 324–25,

and compare Scarfe, *Suffolk Landscape*, pp. 117–18.

16. Wade-Martins, *Excavations in North Elmham Park*, i, pp. 37–124.

17. J. Beckwith, *Ivory Carvings in Medieval England* (London, 1972), p. 121, no. 18; J. O'Reilly, 'Early Medieval Text and Image: The Wounded and Exalted Christ', *Peritia* (1987–88), pp. 71–118, especially pp. 74–75.

Fig. 3. The 'Old Minster' and its enclosure at South Elmham.

and estates should both be called Elmham. True, there are other pairs of places with the same names, one in Norfolk, the other in Suffolk.[18] But, while coincidence could explain there being two episcopal Elmhams, it seems more probable that while one gave its name to the see, the see gave its name to the other. It has been suggested that South Elmham was the early Elmham *sedes*, and that this was later moved to North Elmham.[19] Another possibility is that South Elmham was *Dommoc*. The *civitas* denomination could be accounted for by the site of the 'Old Minster' in an enclosure which may be Roman (fig. 3).[20]

The problems about the location of *Dommoc* and Elmham are indicative of how bad our sources are for the early history of the church in East Anglia. The absence

18. O. K. Schram, 'Place-Names', in F. Briers, ed., *Norwich and its Region* (British Association for the Advancement of Science, Norwich, 1961), pp. 141–49 at p. 144.

19. Scarfe, *Suffolk Landscape*, pp. 116–23.

20. Smedley and Owles, 'Excavations at the Old Minster, South Elmham', p. 14. Wade-Martins, *Excavations in North Elmham Park*, i, p. 5, reserves judgement since the Roman finds are scanty.

of records from the religious communities situated or owning land there is, in part, indicative of Viking destruction in the last decades of the ninth century. But, note, few pre–1066 records survive from any such post-Viking communities either, with the sole exceptions of the great Benedictine foundations of Ely and Bury. When the see moved to Norwich its bishops may have cherished their links to time-honoured Elmham. The stone episcopal throne in the cathedral is battered, weathered and hard to interpret (fig. 4). The best guess is that it is composed of components brought from Elmham.[21] Even if stones came from Elmham to Norwich, no records did, so far as we can tell. It is questionable whether more than the most minimal knowledge of the early history of the see survived. A good deal of what appears in post-Conquest sources is false. Thus the statement in an early Norwich document that the see had been located at Bury from the earliest times was a self-interested lie.[22] The Norwich story that King Edmund had been martyred at the episcopal centre of Hoxne was probably no better. This convenient tale first appears in a grant made by Bishop Herbert de Losinga to the cathedral in 1100 or 1101.[23] The likelihood is that Edmund met his death somewhere near Bury St Edmunds.[24] The list of bishops shows how thin our knowledge is. We cannot establish with accuracy the length of the episcopate of any Anglo-Saxon bishop of East Anglia; and there could well have been bishops entirely unknown to us.[25] The last Anglo-Saxon king of East Anglia was Edmund, killed by the Danes in 869. For about a century after this we hear of no bishops in East Anglia.

What can be learned about the East Anglian bishops and their sees in the ten obscure generations between Sigeberht and Edmund (from the 630s to the 860s)? The bishops' most frequent appearances to us are in the records of ecclesiastical councils, chiefly those held under the aegis of Mercian kings in the eighth and early ninth centuries. Some twenty-five documents show one or both of the East Anglian bishops as witnesses at these meetings between 673 and 845; only two such occasions are recorded after 827.[26] Sometimes these records tell us about something more than

21. C. A. R. Radford, 'The Bishop's Throne in Norwich Cathedral', *Arch. J.,* 116 (1959), pp. 115–32; A. B. Whittingham, 'Norwich Saxon Throne', *Arch. J.,* 136 (1979), pp. 60–68; Fernie, *NC,* p. 29 n. 20.

22. V. H. Galbraith, 'The East Anglian See and the Abbey of Bury St Edmunds', *EHR,* 40 (1925), pp. 222–24.

23. *NCC,* i, no. 112. M. Carey Evans, 'The Contribution of Hoxne to the Cult of St Edmund, King and Martyr, in the Middle Ages and Later', *Proceedings of the Suffolk Institute of Archaeology,* 36 (1987),

pp. 182–95, puts a moderate case for Hoxne.

24. S. E. West, 'A New Site for the Martyrdom of St Edmund?', *Proceedings of the Suffolk Institute of Archaeology,* 35 (1983), p. 223.

25. D. Whitelock, M. Brett and C. N. L. Brooke, eds, *Councils and Synods with other Documents relating to the English Church,* i, *AD, 871–1204,* 2 vols (Oxford, 1981), i, pp. 81–82.

26. These documents are printed by A. W. Haddan and W. Stubbs, eds, *Councils and Ecclesiastical Documents Relating to Great Britain and Ireland,* 3 vols in 4 (Oxford, 1869–78), iii.

Fig. 4. The remains of the bishop's throne, which may have come from North Elmham, installed at the head of the apse in Norwich Cathedral.

the fact of attendance. Thus the record of the *Clovesho* meeting of 803 lists and specifies the entourages brought by the bishops. Four priests and two deacons accompanied Alhheard of Elmham while his colleague of *Dommoc* brought four priests and two abbots. One of these abbots, Lull, shows up in a different context.[27] About 800 Alcuin, the great English court-scholar of Charlemagne, wrote to the bishops of East Anglia, jointly. With skilled Latin and unctuous piety, he sought their prayers and mentioned a recent conversation with Abbot Lull, very probably the same man.[28] This rare glimpse of the church life of East Anglia reminds us of the importance to it of monasteries and of continental connections; and of the possibility that it enjoyed a degree of learning and sophistication of which no more remains to us than fragments and echoes.

We have, remarkably, a life of the first known abbot in East Anglia, Fursey, an Irishman. Bede had this life, and also enough additional knowledge to fill out its East Anglian context a little. We are told that Fursey was eminent in birth and in learning. He left his native island to spend his life in foreign parts as a pilgrim for the love of Christ. He preached the gospel in East Anglia, where King Sigeberht (*c.* 635) gave him the site at *Cnobheresburg* (an unidentified place) for a noble monastery.[29] After a time he lived as a hermit and then, fearing the consequences of Mercian invasions, sailed to Gaul, where he founded a monastery at Lagny, on the Marne. Were it not for Fursey's *Vita* we should have known nothing about Irish influence on the East Anglian church. Irish missionaries may have added more than *Cnobheresburg* to the number of early East Anglian monasteries. A letter from Ælfwald, king of the East Angles, who died not later than 749, gives us a minimum for that number; he tells his correspondent, St Boniface, that prayers are being said for him in seven monasteries.[30] A most striking feature of the English church in the later seventh and earlier eighth century was the foundation of royal nunneries (generally in association with subordinated communities of monks). The East Anglian royal family was rich in holy women, and one of these, Æthelfryth, founded the great abbey of Ely in about 673.[31] (Ely at this period, but not later, was part of the kingdom of East Anglia).[32]

27. Whitelock, 'Pre-Viking Age Church', p. 17.
28. Whitelock, 'Pre-Viking Age Church', p. 17.
29. Bede, *Historia ecclesiastica*, book iii, chapter xix, in C. Plummer, ed., *Venerabilis Baedae opera historica*, 2 vols (Oxford, 1896). Camden's guess that *Cnobheresburg* was Burgh Castle, though endlessly repeated, has much to be said against it and precious little for it, J. Campbell, *Essays in Anglo-Saxon History* (London and Ronceverte, West Virginia, 1986), p. 101 and n. 14; S. Johnson, *Burgh Castle: Excavations by Charles Green* (East

Anglian Archaeology, 20, Gressenhall, 1983), pp. 119–21.
30. Whitelock, 'Pre-Viking Age Church', p. 16.
31. E. Miller, *The Abbey and Bishopric of Ely* (Cambridge, 1951), pp. 7–15.
32. Whitelock, 'Pre-Viking Age Church', p. 7. By the tenth century the Devil's Dyke seems to have marked the boundary of the kingdom, M. Winterbottom, ed., *Three Lives of English Saints* (Toronto, 1972), pp. 69–70. The boundary of the East Anglian diocese corresponded until altered in 1836 by a

Nothing does more to bring home to us the problems and possibilities associated with the early East Anglian church than does the strange case of St Botulf. There are only scraps of information about this saint and his monastery at *Icanho* (which recent work has established with reasonable certainty to have been at Iken).[33] The anonymous *Lives* of the abbots of Monkwearmouth/Jarrow, a contemporary and reliable source, states that the future abbot, Ceolfrith, went to East Anglia to study under Botulf, probably in the 670s. This proves that Botulf was, as the anonymous author says, widely known for his life and doctrine, and establishes the likelihood that *Icanho* was a centre of learning. It helps to explain why, to judge from the evidence of church dedications, Botulf became a widely regarded saint. At least sixty-one medieval English churches were dedicated to him.[34] Recent excavations at Brandon have revealed how likely it is that there were significant monasteries of which written sources tell us even less than they do about *Icanho*, that is to say, nothing. We can be sure that this major eighth- and ninth-century site was ecclesiastical, for several styluses (metal implements for writing on wax or marking parchment) have been found. One tiny fragment more than hints at wealth and importance; it is a piece of stamped gold, showing the eagle symbol of St John, probably part of a book cover.[35]

What of the bishops themselves in the period from 630 to 860? Very slight and patchy knowledge suggests more than it proves. We know that at least one bishop, Cuthwine, bishop of *Dommoc* for some period between 716 and 731, had been to Rome and there acquired an illuminated manuscript on the life of St Paul. A copy made from another such manuscript probably owned by the same bishop survives.[36] These fragments of information, like others, hint at elements of grandeur, sophistication and learning of which almost all trace has been lost. Perhaps the most remarkable survival from the early East Anglian bishops is a seal matrix, found at Eye, and almost certainly that of Æthelwold, a bishop of *Dommoc* known to have held office at some time between 845 and 870 (fig. 5).[37] It is the earliest such object

note 32 continued
statute of 6–7 William IV; it had not been affected by the creation of the see of Ely in 1109, A. H. Thompson, 'The Connection of Norwich with Contiguous Dioceses', in Cranage, ed., *Thirteen-Hundredth Anniversary of the Diocese of East Anglia*, pp. 28–29.

33. Whitelock, 'Pre-Viking Age Church', pp. 10–12; S. E. West, N. Scarfe and R. Cramp, 'Iken, St Botolph and the Coming of East Anglian Christianity', *Proceedings of the Suffolk Institute of Archaeology*, 35 (1984), pp. 279–301.

34. F. Arnold-Forster, *Studies in Church Dedications*, 3 vols (London, 1899), iii, pp. 343–44.

35. Webster and Backhouse, eds, *Making of England*, pp. 81–88, nos 66 a–y.

36. Whitelock, 'Pre-Viking Age Church', pp. 9–10.

37. T. A. Heslop, 'English Seals from the Mid Ninth Century to 1100', *JBAA*, 133 (1980), pp. 2–3. Rigold, in Wade-Martins, ed., *Excavations in North Elmham Park*, i, p. 10, for the possibility that the seal belonged to a tenth-century Bishop Æthelwold.

to be found in England. Scholars disagree
on the purposes for which a seal would
have been used in this period. It does
however strongly suggest that Bishop
Æthelwold's activities included some
which required easily replicated indications of authenticity. That may not seem
much, but actually it is rather a lot. It is
a striking instance of our ignorance of
ninth-century East Anglia that our only
other evidence for his existence is his
profession of obedience to the archbishop of Canterbury.[38] The last bishop
of *Dommoc* to appear on the ancient episcopal lists is Æthelwold's predecessor
Wilred. It may have been this which led
William of Malmesbury to allege that
the East Anglian dioceses were reunited
immediately after Wilred's pontificate.
Though William's account is demon-
strably imperfectly informed, his attri-
buting the reunion of the sees to
impoverishment due to Mercian invasions is not entirely negligible for, had
he been just guessing, one might have
supposed he would have blamed Danish
invasions, not Mercian.[39]

Fig. 5. Bishop Æthelwold's seal matrix (height
2¾ inches, 6.9 cm).

The Danish invasions destroyed the old East Anglian kingdom. It fell under
Danish rule for two generations after its last English king, Edmund, was killed in
869. The known history of its church in this period would not fill a postcard.
The Danes probably introduced a new pagan element, especially round the rivers,
estuaries and islands of north-east Suffolk and south-east Norfolk.[40] One place name
in this area, Ellough, probably derives from the Old Norse for 'temple'.[41] The great
majority of the East Anglian population was English and Christian. The first Danish
king, Guthrum (*c.* 870–90), became a Christian and it is probable that his immigrant

38. M. Richter and T. J. Brown, eds, *Canterbury
Professions* (Canterbury and York Society,
67, Torquay, 1972), p. 24, no. 28.
39. William of Malmesbury, *De gestis pontificum*

Anglorum, ed. N. E. S. A. Hamilton (RS,
1870), p. 148.
40. Schram, 'Place-Names', pp. 145–46.
41. Ekwall, *Concise Oxford Dictionary of English
Place-Names*, p. 164.

countrymen were fairly soon converted.[42] Who performed episcopal functions in East Anglia in this dark period? There could have been bishops of whom we know nothing. And what about church property? No ecclesiastical property which appears in Domesday Book for Norfolk and Suffolk can be proved to have been in church hands in the pre-Viking age, except to the extent that it is an unavoidable conclusion that at least one of the Elmhams must have been a church estate before the great catastrophe. Suppose, for the sake of illustrative argument, that South Elmham was an ancient episcopal endowment. What, in that case, happened to it between 870 and 918? Did it remain the property of bishops of whom we have no knowledge? Or was there a clerical community there which hung on, Danes or no Danes? Or did it pass into Danish hands, to be restored to the church when English kings conquered Danish East Anglia? A path signposted only by question marks is tedious indeed to tread. But it has to be trodden if we are to consider the possible relationship between the old East Anglia, of the independent kings, and the new, when it was brought under the rule of the conquering kings of the house of Wessex (917).

Our ignorance of East Anglian episcopacy is not lightened until we have the will of Bishop Theodred of London, made between 941 and 953. This refers to his *bishopriche* (translated by Dr Whitelock as 'bishopric') at Hoxne.[43] This reference together with that in Domesday makes it clear that there was a *sedes episcopatus* for Suffolk at Hoxne. Domesday shows also that Hoxne was one of the only two significant episcopal estates in Suffolk and the centre of jurisdiction for a whole hundred, 'Bishop's Hundred'.[44] Difficult questions arise. What was a bishop of London doing with episcopal authority in East Anglia? Perhaps the kings of the house of Wessex were exercising there a policy employed elsewhere in lands conquered from the Danes: that of keeping centres of episcopal authority as near as possible to the West Saxon heartland. Thus from 971 until after the Conquest a vast diocese extending from the Thames to the Humber had its *sedes* at Dorchester-on-Thames; and from the same year until 1016 the see of York was held in plurality with that of Worcester. A second question is that of whether Bishop Theodred's authority extended to Norfolk. Perhaps it did, or perhaps there was a separate diocese there held by one or more of the bishops found witnessing earlier tenth-century charters and whose sees are not known. Two other facts about Theodred should be mentioned. He was a fairly extensive landowner in Suffolk.

42. D. Whitelock, 'The Conversion of the Eastern Danelaw', *Saga-Book of the Viking Society*, 12 (1941), pp. 159–76.
43. Whitelock, Brett and Brooke, *Councils and Synods*, pp. 74–80. The will also mentions a minster at Hoxne and a church dedicated to St Ethelbert and served by a community there; it is unclear whether we have one institution here or two, compare pp. 18–19 below and p. 5 above.
44. *DB Suffolk*, fo. 379a (no. 18/1).

Possibly he was German, for his name is probably German and several of his clergy also bore German names.[45]

The known series of the bishops of Elmham recommences with Eadwulf (*alias* Athulf) who was in office by 955 or a little earlier, though he may have had a predecessor.[46] Two of Eadwulf's three immediate successors were said to have been called Theodred. It is not fully certain that there were two of them, nor whether there was a connection with Theodred, bishop of London.[47] With Æthelstan who held office for a few years before his death in 1001 the darkness lifts a little. This is because of Æthelstan's connection with the abbey of Ely. Ely was refounded in about 970 by Æthelwold, bishop of Winchester, under the aegis of King Edgar. Within a generation Ely became rich indeed, far richer than the bishops of East Anglia even if only its Norfolk and Suffolk estates are taken into account: Domesday's valuation of these for 1066 is about £279, as compared to about £157 for the lands of the see. Of some 1200 free dependents of the abbey, about 800 lived in Norfolk, about 270 in Suffolk.[48] The relation of the abbey to the East Anglian bishops and to East Anglia generally was intricate. Ely held not only extensive lands in Suffolk but also the great franchise of Wicklaw, five-and-a-half hundreds in the south east of the county. This area included a main focus of authority of the early East Anglian kings, including the burial-ground of Sutton Hoo. It is hard not to guess at some connection between Ely's position here and its original foundation by an East Anglian princess. Perhaps the coincidence was by chance. It is barely possible that it reflects institutional continuity. More probably it reflected historical consciousness.[49] The abbey of Ely not only became, rapidly, much richer than the East Anglian see, it also had at least as good a claim to enshrine East Anglian religious tradition.

One might have thought that the consequence would have been tension between Ely and Elmham. On the contrary, there was intimacy. In the twelfth century Bishop Æthelstan's memory was specially valued at Ely as *confessor Christi* and benefactor. He was believed to have given Ely not only an estate but also the furniture of his chapel. The account of the latter suggests great wealth: a cross, a pyx of gold and silver weighing 20 lb, a chalice and paten of 10 lb of silver, 40 mancuses of gold (a mancus represented just over four grams of gold), and other rich goods. There was a *quid pro quo* for this beneficence. We are told that Æthelstan

45. Whitelock, Brett and Brooke, *Councils and Synods*, p. 76; cf. also William of Malmesbury, *De gestis pontificum*, pp. 144, 154.
46. R. R. Darlington, 'Ecclesiastical Reform in the Late Old English Period', *EHR*, 51 (1936), p. 423.
47. Rigold in Wade-Martins, ed., *Excavations in North Elmham Park*, i, p. 10.
48. Miller, *Abbey and Bishopric of Ely*, p. 16 nn.

3 and 4.
49. Compare P. Warner, 'Pre-Conquest Territorial and Administrative Organisation in East Suffolk', in D. Hooke, ed., *Anglo-Saxon Settlements* (Oxford, 1988), pp. 17–21, where it is argued that major elements in the organisation and especially the boundaries of Wicklaw were older than the Danish invasions.

arranged, long before his death, to be buried at Ely.[50] Anglo-Saxons set great store on being buried in the right place. The grandeur of Ely was what Bishop Æthelstan wanted, not the humbler, and one may fairly guess less celibate, circumstances of whatever community there was at his North Elmham *sedes*.

A significant clue to the intimacy between Ely and Elmham was that we are told in the twelfth-century *Liber Eliensis* that the liberty of the abbey in the late Anglo-Saxon period was such that it could choose whichever bishop it pleased to exercise episcopal functions there.[51] We lack precise contemporary evidence for this; all the same, it is likely that an element in the Ely/Elmham nexus lay in Ely not lying in the Elmham diocese. The abbey founded by a bishop of Winchester in the diocese of Dorchester wished to use the bishop of Elmham as a guarantor of independence.

The connection grew closer with the next bishop, Ælfgar. There are two important stories about him. One shows that, at an early stage in his career, he was a member of the clerical household of the great Dunstan, archbishop of Canterbury.[52] The other tells that he retired from his see to Ely and then did that abbey yeoman service. Eadnoth, bishop of Dorchester, formerly abbot of Ramsey, was killed at the battle of *Assandun* (1016). As the monks of Ramsey brought his body home they stayed the night, unwisely as it proved, at Ely. Ælfgar, '*vir sanctus*' (holy man), made them drunk and stole Eadnoth's body to 'increase the dignity' of Ely.[53] We have the story only in a twelfth-century form, but many contemporary parallels suggest its authenticity and remind us how far apart medieval piety could be from modern.[54] In any case it is important that a bishop of Elmham retired to Ely and was warmly remembered there.

According to the *Liber Eliensis*, Bishop Ælfgar's successor, Ælfwine, another *sanctus confessor*, had been an Ely monk from childhood and had brought major estates with him to that monastery.[55] The most extraordinary thing about him, and something which is a warning against discussing the activities of eleventh-century ecclesiastics in terms too knowingly cynical, is that, by both Ely and Bury tradition, he played a major role in the foundation in about 1020 of the abbey of Bury St Edmunds.[56]

So, within a few decades, the ecclesiastical position in East Anglia had been transformed, in such a way that the bishop was outshone by the great abbots. One might have thought that, like some of their continental *confrères*, the bishops would

50. E. O. Blake, ed., *Liber Eliensis* (Camden Society, third series, 91, 1962), pp. xxxviii, 137–38.

51. Blake, *Liber Eliensis*, pp. 402–3.

52. Blake, *Liber Eliensis*, p. 142; W. Stubbs, ed., *Memorials of Saint Dunstan, Archbishop of Canterbury* (RS, 1874), pp. 120, 218, 317.

53. Blake, *Liber Eliensis*, p. 142.

54. P. J. Geary, *Furta Sacra: Thefts of Relics in the Middle Ages* (revised edn, Princeton, 1990).

55. Blake, *Liber Eliensis*, pp. 144–45.

56. Blake, *Liber Eliensis*, p. 155; M. K. Lawson, *Cnut: The Danes in England in the Early Eleventh Century* (London, 1993), p. 142.

have reacted with wounded aggression to the appearance of these cuckoos in the diocesan nest.[57] But not so. So far as our meagre sources (all monastically preserved) tell us, the episcopal attitude to the abbeys was one of involved benevolence. The continuance of this attitude emerges from our next major source for the East Anglian see. This is the will of Bishop Ælfric.[58] It is a characteristic inconvenience of these studies that there were two bishop Ælfrics (Ælfric II and Ælfric III) in succession and we do not know which one this was. Balance of probability somewhat favours Ælfric II, who died in 1038. He had been appointed by Cnut, and may have been one of his household clerics. He left important estates to Bury and gave cash legacies to Ely and to the other (and much lesser) local house, St Benet at Holme (which had been refounded *c.* 1019). He also made legacies to two communities of priests, one at Elmham, one at Hoxne. This provision reinforces what other sources imply. First, that the East Anglian see, though called Elmham, had two *sedes*, one for Norfolk at Elmham, the other at Hoxne for Suffolk. Secondly, it shows how even the bishop could regard the communities at those *sedes* as relatively small beer. Each community received a 'fen' (? a peat digging). One was stated to be worth 1000 pence. Probably the other was of comparable worth. Unless we assume that what was stated was income not capital value, the good bishop has left not only more to Bury, more to Ely, more to St Benet's at Holme, but more indeed to his tailor, than he left to the communities at his own *sedes*.

A secular landowner could take a comparable view. We have the will of such a man, Ælfric 'Modercope'.[59] He names 'Bishop Ælfric' as an executor. This is thought to have been Ælfric III (who died in 1042 or 1043 and was yet another bishop with an apparent Ely connection; he is said to have been prior there).[60] He naturally left something to the bishop: his tent, and good bedclothes. But to Bury and Ely he left landed estates (and £5 to St Benet at Holme – ever the poor sister).

After the death of Ælfric III things seem to have looked up for the see of East Anglia, though possibly more by accident than design. His successor was Stigand. Stigand had (probably) been an important priest in the service of King Cnut.[61] He was certainly close to Emma, Cnut's widow and mother of the new king, Edward the Confessor. In 1043 he had a bad experience. Edward turned against Emma, seized her property, and deposed her adviser, Stigand, from his see. But, next year, he got it back and held it until 1047. Then, proceeding to better

---

57. E.g., E. Amann and A. Dumas, *L'église au pouvoir des laiques, 888–1057* (n. p., 1940), p. 359.

58. Whitelock, Brett and Brooke, *Councils and Synods*, no. 66, pp. 513–14.

59. Whitelock, ed., *Anglo-Saxon Wills*, pp. 74–75.

60. Bartholomew Cotton, *Historia Anglicana*, ed. H. R. Luard (RS, 16, 1859), p. 388.

61. F. Barlow, *The English Church, 1000–1066* (2nd edn, London and New York, 1979), pp. 77–78.

things, as bishop of Winchester, he was happily, but we may reasonably suppose not accidentally, replaced in the East Anglian see by his brother Æthelmær.[62]

It rather looks as if Stigand was a local boy, perhaps from Norwich; certainly he made good. In an important way, he was the most successful cleric in the long history of the English church. Gaining the rich see of Winchester in 1047, he added to it Canterbury itself in 1052, held in plurality. As if that were not enough, he had his grip on several abbeys, including Ely.[63] What he did to gain, or earn, so much we do not know. Perhaps he ran the administration of the English state: no small thing. What is certain is that his wealth was vast and his patronage formidable.[64] He gave a great silver or silver-plated crucifix with a life-size statue of Jesus and other treasures to Ely.[65] Had they survived we would have a more substantial sense of his grandeur, something like that which Norwich Cathedral leaves of the generous energy of another church tycoon.

Æthelmær was deposed from his see in the Norman purge of the English episcopate in 1070. Until then, as Stigand's brother, he must have been a man to reckon with. Most of what we know of him comes from the Domesday survey. Both of Domesday's accounts of the lands of the see (that for Norfolk and that for Suffolk) are, remarkably, divided into two. Thus the Norfolk account begins with 'lands of the bishop of Thetford belonging to the see' and then goes on to 'lands of the same in fee' (*terra eiusdem de feodo*); in Suffolk there is a similar division between 'the lands of William, bishop of Thetford' and 'the fee (*feudum*) of the bishop of Thetford'.[66] It appears that the second sections relate to lands acquired by the see after 1066.[67] Much of interest emerges here. The pre-Conquest lands of the see in Norfolk were valued at £117 for 1066, £177 for 1086. Almost all lay in west and central Norfolk. Their wide distribution there suggests that at some stage it may have been intended to have an episcopal estate in every hundred in that area.[68] The lands acquired after the Conquest were somewhat more valuable than those acquired before, with a valuation of £186 for 1086. The distribution of the new lands was very different from that of the old, for they lay largely in the eastern part of the county. Lands in seventeen out of the twenty-one eastern hundreds were involved;

62. For Stigand's early career and the complications of the sources, Darlington, 'Ecclesiastical Reform', p. 400; Harmer, ed., *Anglo-Saxon Writs*, pp. 571–72.

63. Blake, *Liber Eliensis*, pp. 168, 425–26. The nature of his relationship with Ely is unclear; but he certainly had control of important Ely estates.

64. Barlow, *English Church, 1000–1066*, pp. 76–81.

65. Blake, *Liber Eliensis*, pp. 168, 196, 200–1,

293–94. (The descriptions of this gift are not fully consistent).

66. *DB Norfolk*, fos 191a–193b; *DB Suffolk*, fos 379a–381a.

67. This interpretation is that of B. Dodwell, 'The Honour of the Bishop of Thetford/Norwich in the Late Eleventh and Early Twelfth Centuries', *NA*, 33 (1962–65), pp. 186–87. For some further details and complications, see below, p. 19.

68. Scarfe, *Suffolk Landscape*, pp. 122–23.

previously the see had held land in only two of these. The pattern in Suffolk is different. There the lands in the first section consisted almost entirely of two complexes centred on Hoxne and South Elmham and valued at £40 10s. (1066) and £36 9s. (1086). The *feudum* apparently acquired since 1066 was valued (1086) at £26 7s. The lands concerned were largely in the vicinity of the two main episcopal estates. Thus Domesday indicates a sharp distinction between the patterns of episcopal lordship in Norfolk and Suffolk. In Norfolk the estates were by 1066 widely distributed in the west of the county and, by 1086, over the east as well. In Suffolk the episcopal lands remained concentrated round two centres in the north east of the county. The bishops held nothing within the liberty of St Edmund (the whole west of the county) and virtually nothing in the liberty of St Etheldreda (Wicklaw) in the south east. Thus their property was confined to the area where hundredal jurisdiction was kept by the king.

It is important that major additions to the lands of the see were made between 1066 and 1086. Many of these were associated with Bishop Æthelmær. In one instance Domesday tells us that he bought the land concerned 'for the see' (*ad episcopatum*).[69] In others it seems that what had been his personal lands had been associated with the endowment of the see after his deposition. The richest of the holdings concerned was Hemsby, valued at £26 in 1066. The Domesday account hints at something of the Stigand family's *modus operandi*. It says that Earl Ælgar had held it, Ailwi bought it, Stigand took it away (*abstulit*) and gave it to Æthelmær: the witnesses of the hundred said they did not know how this had come about, but that from that time it had been part of the episcopal estate.[70] Another Domesday entry casts a unique little shaft of light on one way in which a bishop might prosper. It says that Bishop Æthelmær had seized some land as a forfeiture (*invasit pro forisfactura*) because its owner had married within a year of the death of her husband.[71]

It is notable about Æthelmær's acquisitions that they frequently involved purchase. This is characteristic of East Anglian land transactions at this time and reflects the high level of economic activity there. It was a booming area. Not only was Norfolk the most populous shire in England, it also contained the most densely populated areas. Suffolk was not far behind. East Anglia's four major towns were among the most important in England. The greatest of them was Norwich. Not so very much of a place, it would seem, in the early tenth century, by William the Conqueror's reign it was a major town, with a population which could have been as high as 10,000. Not only an important centre of manufacture, it was also a major port with significant foreign trade. The Wensum and the Yare gave easy access to Yarmouth,

69. *DB Norfolk*, fo. 194a (no. 10/23).
70. *DB Norfolk*, fo. 195a (no. 10/30).
71. *DB Norfolk*, fo. 199a (no. 10/67). For a comparable instance, A. J. Robertson, ed., *Anglo-Saxon Charters* (Cambridge, 1939), p. 112.

whose herring fisheries may well already have ensured that more food came from there than from anywhere else in England. From Yarmouth the Ant and the Bure led to the most densely populated parts of England and to boundless supplies of fuel – peat. Here, as in East Anglia in general, density of population was accompanied by heavy rural capitalisation: thousands of plough-beasts, scores of watermills.[72]

An important element in investment in the countryside was ecclesiastical: beside the mills and the plough teams stood the parish churches and their priests. The crowning achievement of the English church in the tenth and eleventh centuries was the creation of a close network of parishes. Domesday notes the presence of over 400 churches in Suffolk;[73] and over 300 churches and chapels in Norfolk.[74] In 1291 the diocese of Norwich contained 1349 parishes, about 14 per cent of the English total. Lincoln contained more parishes, but only one other diocese, York, contained even half so many as Norwich.[75] Domesday did not seek to record all churches and it is demonstrable that, even in East Anglia, it by no means did so. That is to say that, while it is undoubted that the diocese had at least half its medieval complement of parishes by 1086, it may well have had far more. If so, it must have presented its bishop with something of an administrative nightmare, particularly since there were, before the Conquest, no archdeacons to provide an authority intermediate between the bishop and the parishes.

Suppose we imagine Æthelmær, last of the English bishops of Elmham, looking back over the hundred years since the reestablishment of his see. What problems and possibilities might have occupied his mind? He would have known that the rise of the great Benedictine abbeys had overset the balance of ecclesiastical wealth and regard in East Anglia. He would have been in no doubt that the solemn and celibate appeal of the monks far exceeded that of secular communities such as that of North Elmham. To assume that Æthelmær was not conscientious just because he was married and well-connected could be unjustly to impugn many later prelates of the Church of England. If he was conscientious he would have weighed the difficulties posed by the site of his *sedes* and the size of his diocese. In early days North Elmham may have been as suitable a site as any and better than most. It was a good route centre; and, importantly, less than a mile from the episcopal site lies a vast pagan Anglo-Saxon cemetery (Spong Hill), suggesting that a Christian

72. H. C. Darby, *The Domesday Geography of Eastern England* (3rd edn, Cambridge, 1971), esp. pp. 107–24, 161–79; J. Campbell, 'Norwich', in M. D. Lobel and W. H. Johns, eds, *Historic Towns*, 3 vols (Oxford and London, 1969–89), ii, pp. 5–8.

73. Scarfe, *Suffolk Landscape*, pp. 138–39.

74. G. Munford, *The Analysis of the Domesday Book of the County of Norfolk* (London, 1858),

pp. 79–112; D. Dymond, *The Norfolk Landscape* (London, 1985), pp. 81–87.

75. W. Hudson, 'The "Norwich Taxation" of 1254 so far as it relates to the Diocese of Norwich', *NA*, 17 (1908–10), pp. 69–70; E. L. Cutts, *Parish Priests and their People in the Middle Ages in England* (London, 1914), p. 394; J. R. H. Moorman, *Church Life in England in the Thirteenth Century* (Cambridge, 1946), pp. 4–5.

cult-centre succeeded a pagan one. (It is characteristic of the complications of these studies that evidence has now been found suggesting that there was a pagan cremation cemetery at South Elmham also.)[76] Even in the mid tenth century, though the urban take-off in East Anglia had begun, it may not have gone very far. By Æthelmær's time it certainly had. Possibly Æthelmær had some canon law collection in which he might have read that an episcopal *sedes* should be at a centre of population. Even if, as may well be, Æthelmær was not canonically informed, common sense would have shown that North Elmham would not do as a diocesan centre. Then, as now, it was essential for a bishop to keep contact with parishes and their priests. In a relatively small and manageable diocese, like Worcester, a bishop such as Æthelmær's contemporary Wulfstan could fairly easily travel round, doing good. But when the number of parishes in the diocese of Worcester was at its medieval maximum it did not reach 400.[77] Æthelmær's diocese had far more parishes than that by 1066. If the parishes and the people were too numerous for the bishop to get round to them, the only practical solution was for the priests and the people to come to the bishop. But suppose a bishop of East Anglia did try to get priests and people together from his diocese, one of the largest in the whole of the western church.[78] Where was the roof big enough to cover them? There is nothing anachronistic in imagining what Æthelmær's *desiderata* would have been. That is to say, a vast mother church, at a major centre of population and communication, rivalling the liturgical magnificence and popular appeal of the great Benedictine abbeys, and endowed on a scale commensurate with East Anglian wealth. To accomplish so much, an organiser, fund-raiser and prophet of some genius would seem to have been required.

76. C. Hills and K. Penn, *The Anglo-Saxon Cemetery at Spong Hill, North Elmham, Part ii* (East Anglian Archaeology, 11, Gressenhall, 1981); Ridgard, 'References to South Elmham Minster', p. 199.

77. Cutts, *Parish Priests and their People*, p. 385.
78. Darlington, 'Ecclesiastical Reform', p. 412, for the possibility of late Anglo-Saxon synods.

2

Herbert de Losinga

Deirdre Wollaston

A part from Anselm, whose life and thoughts are so vividly recorded by Eadmer and by his own writing, few early Anglo-Norman ecclesiastics are as familiar to us as Herbert de Losinga. In Herbert's case the biographical material is scant, but the fortunate survival of fifty-seven letters and fourteen sermons provides a unique insight into his character and intellect.[1] The second part of this chapter, based mainly on the letters, will deal thematically with Herbert's various roles as a courtier and diplomat, as a bishop, as a preacher and teacher, as a spiritual adviser to his monks, and as a patron of architecture. First it is necessary to outline the main events of his life up to the establishment of the see at Norwich, beginning with the debate on his origins and name.

Early Life

Many authors from the sixteenth century onwards have claimed Herbert as a native Englishman.[2] This tenacious myth seems to have originated with John Bale, who gave Suffolk as the bishop's birthplace.[3] In spite of these claims, the earliest and most reliable evidence, that of Bartholomew Cotton, is unequivocal: Herbert was born at Exmes in southern Normandy.[4]

1. The letters are in a seventeenth-century manuscript, Brussels, Royal Library, MS 3723 (7965–73); published in Latin by R. Anstruther, *Epistolae Herberti de Losinga* (Brussels, 1846). The sermons are in a twelfth-century manuscript, Cambridge, University Library, MS Ii. 2. 19 (s. xii). Letters and sermons are translated in GS.

2. GS, i, pp. 389–409; quotations from Bale, Pits, Godwin, Fuller, claiming English nationality for Herbert.

3. J. Bale, *Scriptorum illustrium maioris Britannie*, 2 parts (Basle, 1557), i, p. 171: 'Herbertus Losinga, ex pago Oxunensi in Sudevolgia Anglorum comitatu natus fertur . . .'

4. *First Register*, fo. 1: 'Herbertus Episcopus, qui Normannie in pago Oximensi natus . . .'; E. M. Beloe, 'Herbert de Losinga: An Enquiry as to his Cognomen and Birthplace', *NA*, 8 (1879), p. 283; Beloe also quotes Gerald of Wales, 'natus apud Exmes in pago Oximensi in Normannia', but I have not been able to trace this statement in Gerald's works.

The name Losinga is more puzzling. Florence of Worcester says the bishop was called Losinga on account of his skill in flattery, later adding that Herbert's father had the same name, an unacceptable inconsistency.[5] The ingenious attempts of Goulburn and Symonds to link Losinga with the hundreds of Loes and Lothingland in Suffolk can be dismissed since they started from a false premise.[6] More convincing is Beloe's theory that the name is a corruption of the Latin *Lotharingia* into French, which would mean Herbert's forebears were Lotharingians, from the area roughly corresponding to the Low Countries, who settled in Normandy.[7]

Herbert's early career is briefly summarised by Cotton, who says he was a monk of Fécamp, became an efficient prior of the house, and afterwards was brought to England by King William II.[8] Later letters reveal Herbert's deep affection for the Norman monastery where he took monastic vows and passed his youth.[9] When he established his own community of Benedictines at Norwich, the constitutions were closely modelled on those of Fécamp.[10]

Soon after William Rufus succeeded to the throne in 1087, Herbert was summoned to England and made abbot of Ramsey.[11] Secure in the royal favour, he no doubt hoped for promotion to a bishopric when a vacancy arose. In 1090 the bishop of Thetford, William Beaufai, died and Herbert saw his chance. Besides the bishopric, he also wanted to procure the abbacy of Winchester for his father, Robert.[12]

To secure these two preferments he paid Rufus £1000.[13] Herbert was therefore guilty of simony.[14] His judgement of Rufus was shrewd enough, but Herbert had

5. Florence of Worcester, *Chronicon ex chronicis*, ed. B. Thorpe, 2 vols (London, 1848–49), ii, p. 33: 'Hereberhtus, qui cognominabatur Losinga, quod ei ars adulationis nuper egerat . . . patre suo ejusdem cognominis'.
6. GS, i, pp. 3, 349–52; the authors were misled by Bale.
7. Beloe, 'Enquiry', pp. 282–89.
8. Bartholomew Cotton, *Historia Anglicana*, ed. H. Luard (RS, 16, 1859), p. 389: 'Fiscanni monachus, post ejus loci prioratum strenue administratum, translatus in Angliam a rege Willelmo . . .'; also *First Register*, fo. 1.
9. GS, i, pp. 64–66, letter xxxiv.
10. GS, i, pp. 64–6, letter xxxiv: 'Know ye that the uses and customs of the church of Fécamp are observed by our brethren at Norwich'. This evidence is corroborated by J. Tolhurst, *The Customs of the Cathedral Priory Church of Norwich* (Henry Bradshaw Society, 82, 1945–46), pp. xiv–xvi.
11. Florence, *Chronicon*, ii, p. 33; Cotton, *Historia*, p. 54; *First Register*, fo. 1; William of

Malmesbury, *De gestis regum Anglorum*, ed. W. Stubbs, 2 vols (RS, 90, 1887), ii, p. 385.
12. Florence, *Chronicon*, ii, p. 33; Malmesbury, *De gestis regum Anglorum*, ii, p. 385; Cotton, *Historia*, p. 389. While 'Wintonia' has usually been interpreted as referring to Hyde Abbey, this was not founded until 1109, after Robert's death. See J. Franklin, 'The Romanesque Sculpture of Norwich Cathedral' (unpublished University of East Anglia M.A. thesis, 1980), p. 25.
13. Simeon of Durham, *Historia regum*, in vol. 2 of his *Opera omnia*, ed. T. Arnold, 2 vols (RS, 75, 1882–85), ii, p. 223: 'pro episcopatu quem sibi, et abbatia quam patri suo Roberto, ab ipso rege Willelmo mille libris emerat . . .'
14. Florence, *Chronicon*, ii, p. 33; Malmesbury, *De gestis regum Anglorum*, ii, p. 385; Simeon, *Historia*, p. 223; Cotton, *Historia*, pp. 54, 391; even Cotton, while attempting to find excuses for Herbert's action, does not deny the simoniacal purchase of his see.

badly misjudged the current mood of the clergy. The Gregorian reform campaign was in full swing, with simony one of the main ecclesiastical malpractices the papacy was seeking to eradicate.[15] William of Malmesbury quotes a satirical jingle which conveys the sense of public outrage:

> A monster in the church from Losing rose
> Base Simon's sect the canons to oppose . . .
> Oh grief the church is let to sordid hire,
> The son a bishop, abbot is the sire . . .[16]

If contemporaries are to be believed, this dark episode acted as a catalyst in Herbert's life.[17] Modern historians have tended to dismiss the bishop's remorse as mere rhetoric. This may be partly true, but it would be uncharitable wholly to discredit Herbert's sincerity.

Herbert was consecrated bishop of Thetford in 1091.[18] There is little mention of his activities in the next few years.[19] As a member of the episcopate, he must have been affected by an important event in 1093: the appointment to the see of Canterbury, vacant since Lanfranc's death in 1089, of Anselm, whose consecration in December Herbert attended along with most English bishops.[20] A champion of the new reforms, Anselm was not prepared to make any concessions to the monarchy which undermined ecclesiastical authority. Almost immediately the archbishop and king fell out over a number of issues including which pope to support in the current papal schism; Anselm favouring Urban II, Rufus more inclined towards Clement III.[21] Possibly under Anselm's influence, Herbert decided on a highly risky undertaking which was bound to infuriate the king: to visit Pope Urban to seek absolution for the simoniacal purchase of his see. There is some disagreement amongst scholars about the dates and chronology of events.[22] What is clear from contemporary records is that Herbert carried out his intention, and that Rufus deprived him of his pastoral staff either

15. J. W. Alexander, 'Herbert of Norwich, 1091–1119: Studies in the History of Norman England', *Studies in Medieval and Renaissance History*, 6 (1969), pp. 123–25 n. 26.

16. Malmesbury, *De gestis regum Anglorum*, ii, pp. 386–87: translated in William of Malmesbury, *The History of the Kings of England*, trans. J. Sharpe, ed. J. Stevenson (Church Historians of England, Pre-Reformation Series, vol. iii, part 1, London, 1854), p. 290.

17. Malmesbury, *De gestis regum Anglorum*, ii, p. 387: 'prae se semper, ut aiunt, ferens Jeromini dictum, "Erravimus juvenes, emendemus senes".'

18. Cotton, *Historia*, p. 53: 'Anno gratiae MXCI Herbertus episcopus suscepit episcopatum Theofordensem'.

19. Alexander, 'Herbert', p. 127.

20. Eadmer, *Historia novorum in Anglia*, ed. M. Rule (RS, 81, 1884), p. 42.

21. Eadmer, *Historia*, pp. 40, 52–65; Eadmer discusses the papal schism and the conflict between Anselm and Rufus over it.

22. Alexander, 'Herbert', pp. 127–30, 150–53; Alexander ascribes Herbert's visit to the pope to 1093, before his disgrace in 1094. B. Dodwell, 'The Foundation of Norwich Cathedral', *TRHS*, 5th series, 7 (1957), p. 5; Dodwell prefers 1094 for both events.

before or after the journey to Rome.[23] The evidence, as I interpret it, favours a date in 1094 for both incidents.[24] More important is the significance one attaches to Herbert's uncharacteristic rashness on this occasion, which I would explain as a combination of guilt, worry about the security of his office, pressure from the archbishop and diplomatic cunning. Urban could hardly fail to welcome a double display of repentance and loyalty to himself, while the resignation of the episcopal insignia into the pope's own hands would be no less gratifying as a recognition of Rome's supreme power.[25] Although there is no record of a reconciliation, Rufus evidently forgave Herbert since he soon resumed the episcopal office.[26]

Shortly after Herbert's return from Rome, in 1094, the transfer of the episcopal seat from Thetford to Norwich was completed.[27] William of Malmesbury describes Norwich as 'a town celebrated for its trade and populousness', ascribing the change to Herbert's ambition.[28] This is hardly fair since it was Norman policy to resite cathedrals in thriving commercial centres; the king and archbishop must also have approved the scheme. Norwich had another advantage over Thetford: being on a navigable river it would be easier to transport materials for building a new cathedral. As Barbara Dodwell has made clear, there is no need to link an essentially practical move with the bishop's personal circumstances.[29] Nor can the necessary construction of the cathedral be seriously considered as an act of penance on Herbert's part, although this is the impression he chose to convey in his foundation charter: 'But God demanded the fruits of penitence; what fruits wilst thou bring forth, O tree, which art dried up and fit only to be cast into the fire? . . . Therefore for the redemption of my soul and the remission of all my sins, I am the first who have built at Norwich a church in the name and in the honour of the Holy and Undivided Trinity'.[30]

23. Florence, *Chronicon*, ii, p. 33; Malmesbury, *De gestis regum Anglorum*, ii, p. 386; Cotton, *Historia*, pp. 54, 391. All three record Herbert's penitential visit to Rome. The confiscation of Herbert's pastoral staff by Rufus is recorded under the year 1094 in the *Anglo-Saxon Chronicle*: C. Plummer, ed., *Two of the Saxon Chronicles Parallel*, 2 vols (Oxford, 1892–99), i, p. 229; also Simeon, *Historia*, p. 223.

24. Simeon, *Historia*, p. 223: 'latenter enim Urbanum papam adire . . . absolutionem quaerere voluit': i. e. the journey to Rome had not yet taken place. Dodwell, 'Foundation', p. 5; in support of Dodwell's arguments I would add that Herbert was unlikely to have chosen Urban before

coming into contact with Anselm.

25. Malmesbury, *De gestis regum Anglorum*, ii, p. 386; William's sly comment on Roman attitudes suggest that Herbert could be confident of success.

26. Dodwell, 'Foundation', p. 6.

27. Cotton, *Historia*, p. 54: 'Anno gratiae MXCIIII v idus Aprilis, episcopatus Theofordensis translatus est Norwycum ab Herberto episcopo'. Dodwell prefers 1095 for year of transfer, 'Foundation', p. 6.

28. Malmesbury, *De gestis regum Anglorum*, ii, pp. 385–86.

29. Dodwell, 'Foundation', pp. 1–18.

30. *First Register*, fo. 4. See Fernie, *NC*, pp. 14–15, on an earlier church of this dedication in Norwich.

This is conventional charter language up to a point, but Herbert was more ostentatious than most in advertising both sins and repentance. One could argue that, if his conscience had been clearer, he might have become a lesser patron of the arts. On the other hand, a less vain man might have been content with private penance. Herbert, in spite of his frequent assertions to the contrary, undoubtedly wished to be remembered on earth as well as in heaven.[31] Ecclesiastical architecture on a monumental scale was a perfect vehicle for achieving both these ends.

The building of the cathedral began in 1096.[32] With his own hands the bishop laid the first stone, which was evidently at the eastern extreme.[33] Work continued throughout Herbert's episcopate and the cathedral was finally completed under his successor, Bishop Eborard (1121–45).[34]

The Bishop and his Letters

Courtier and Diplomat

Orderic Vitalis took a cynical view of Herbert's relationship with the court in the reign of Rufus. Along with the infamous Ranulf Flambard, Herbert was included in a list of unworthy court favourites whom the king appointed 'looking less for piety in these men than for obsequiousness and willing service in secular affairs';[35] but Orderic acknowledged that some redeemed themselves later.[36] Herbert remained a loyal subject of the crown under Henry I. The single surviving letter addressed to Henry is somewhat unctuous,[37] but Herbert also mentioned incidentally his affection for the king when writing to a close friend, John.[38] He seems to have been especially fond of Henry's pious queen, Matilda, for whom he composed a prayer as well as corresponding with her.[39]

That Henry valued his diplomacy is illustrated by the fact that he chose Herbert as one of the three bishops sent on a delicate mission to Rome in 1101–2, to

31. GS, i, p. 85, letter i: 'I cannot think that . . . my past life, which alas! is darkened by many foul sins, should be recorded for my successors': one of many such statements belied by Herbert's actions.

32. Cotton, *Historia*, p. 54: 'Anno gratiae MXCVI Norwycensis ecclesia fundata est a Domino Herberto episcopo'.

33. *First Register*, fo. 8: 'Incepit autem opus ecclesie sue in loco nunc est capella beate Marie . . . et in opere suo primum lapidem primus apposuit'.

34. *First Register*, fo. 9v: 'Opus ecclesie Norwycensis ubi Herbertus episcopus predecessor suus dimiserat, incepit . . . ecclesiam integraliter consummavit'.

35. Orderic Vitalis, *The Ecclesiastical History*, v, ed. and trans. M. Chibnall, 6 vols (Oxford, 1969–80), v, pp. 202–3.

36. Orderic Vitalis, *Ecclesiastical History*, v, pp. 204–5.

37. GS, i, pp. 182–84, letter xi.

38. GS, i, p. 12, letter xlv.

39. GS, i, pp. 298–313, letters xviii and xxv.

Fig. 6. Norwich Cathedral from the south east, *c.* 1876.

represent the royal cause in the investiture conflict with Anselm.[40] The mission turned out to be a disaster in more ways than one. Herbert was captured en route by Count Guy of Lyon and held to ransom.[41] When the king's party finally reached Rome, Pope Paschal predictably gave his full support to the archbishop; but Herbert and his companions misinterpreted the pope's message on their return to England.[42] In order to resolve the confusion a second embassy had to be dispatched, which settled the matter in Anselm's favour.[43]

In the long-lasting controversy over the respective rights of Canterbury and York, which hinged on the York metropolitans' objection to professing obedience to the archbishops of Canterbury, the bishop of Norwich was twice chosen as mediator. In 1108 he went as Anselm's envoy to York, but failed to persuade the rival archbishop to make any concessions.[44] The dispute continued under Anselm's successor, Ralph d'Escures, who took the case to Rome in 1116, inviting Herbert to accompany him. This time illness contributed to the failure to win Paschal's approval; Herbert, who never reached the papal court, cannot be held responsible.[45]

Bishop

While Herbert may appear inconsistent in acting as spokesman for the king on one occasion, and for the archbishop on others, he remained a loyal member of the episcopate except where royal prerogatives were threatened. The king's man over investiture, Herbert nevertheless joined other bishops in complaining when Henry despoiled the church during Anselm's exile (1103–7).[46] There is no evidence that he opposed the archbishop in his energetic campaign for ecclesiastical reform. Herbert attended three major church councils, in 1102, 1108 and 1109, which passed decrees against clerical marriage, simony and involvement in secular justice, and deposed a number of guilty abbots.[47]

The relationship between the secular and monastic clergy, often strained, reached a low point after Anselm's death in 1109 over the question of who was going to succeed him. As a monk with moderate views, Herbert was evidently considered by some a possible candidate for the archbishopric. Abbot Richard of Ely ended a letter to Herbert, 'so in the heavenly rest . . . if not in the pontifical chair,

40. Eadmer, *Historia*, p. 132; Malmesbury, *De gestis pontificum Anglorum*, ed. N. E. S. A. Hamilton (RS, 52, 1870), pp. 106–7. See also p. 285.

41. Eadmer, *Historia*, p. 133; Malmesbury, *De gestis pontificum*, p. 108.

42. Eadmer, *Historia*, pp. 133–40; Malmesbury, *De gestis pontificum*, p. 108.

43. Malmesbury, *De gestis pontificum*, pp. 111–13.

44. Alexander, 'Herbert', p. 164 n. 73.

45. Eadmer, *Historia*, pp. 237–41, 289–91; Malmesbury, *De gestis pontificum*, pp. 129–30.

46. Eadmer, *Historia*, pp. 171–74.

47. Council of Westminster (1102): Eadmer, *Historia*, pp. 141–44; Malmesbury, *De gestis pontificum*, pp. 118–21; Simeon, *Historia*, pp. 234–35. Council of 1108: Simeon, *Historia*, pp. 240–41; Eadmer, *Historia*, p. 192.

Herbert may succeed Anselm'.[48] Richard, attacking the secular clergy, begged Herbert to write some work in defence of the superior virtues of the monastic life.[49] Herbert's reply was short and sharp and he sensibly refused to comply with Richard's request: 'Let reverence, then, be shown to the clerical order both among laymen and among monks, since both clerk and monk are on a level with one another in point of dignity, unless this natural equality is disturbed by dissimilarity of life and conduct'.[50]

Herbert liked being in complete control of his diocese, resenting the privileges enjoyed by certain monasteries which exempted them from episcopal control. Like his predecessors, he conducted a running battle with that richest and most splendid of East Anglian monasteries, Bury St Edmunds.[51] Eadmer maliciously suggests that the money Herbert was forced to pay Count Guy in 1101 had been intended for assisting his plea to the pope to bring Bury under diocesan control.[52] Whether true or not, Herbert lost his case.[53] Another potential threat to his authority was Thetford Priory, founded in 1107 by Roger Bigod, which as a Cluniac house was subject only to the abbot of Cluny and the papacy. In his letters to the monks of Thetford, Herbert adopted a decidedly cool tone, refusing to consecrate their churchyard unless they will restore to him 'absolutely and explicitly, without any quibble, the ancient episcopal dues'.[54] More high-handed was his insistence, possibly against the wishes of Earl Roger's family and certainly against those of the monks, that the founder's body should be buried in Norwich Cathedral instead of at Thetford.[55]

In general Herbert seems to have been an able and efficient administrator who conscientiously carried out the manifold duties of his office, which ranged from protecting episcopal rights to providing for the poor. While no doubt he enjoyed power, another side of his character hankered after the peace of the cloister. His own account of diocesan affairs is amusing:

> Here I am, that old and practised warrior, whose wrestling is not only with the powers of the air, and with spiritual wickedness in high places . . . but against flesh and blood, against viscounts, against county magistrates, against informers and apparitors, of whom there is such a multitude who live in our immediate neighbourhood, and against whom we watch by night, we exert ourselves to fight by day.[56]

48. GS, i, p. 265, letter lix.
49. GS, i, pp. 261–65, letter lix.
50. GS, i, p. 268, letter lx.
51. Eadmer, *Historia*, pp. 132–33; Malmesbury, *De gestis pontificum*, p. 107.
52. Eadmer, *Historia*, p. 133.
53. D. Knowles, *The Monastic Order in England* (Cambridge, 1950), p. 586.
54. GS, i, p. 169, letter ii.
55. GS, i, pp. 233–34, 166–67 note k. See also Alexander, 'Herbert', p. 143.
56. GS, i, pp. 24–25, letter xxx.

Preacher

Herbert's abilities as a preacher are best judged by his own sermons. These have been analysed in depth by Alexander, so a summary of his conclusion will suffice.[57] The sermons contain little original matter. Like most homilists, Herbert drew heavily on the writings of Augustine, Jerome and Gregory, as well as those of Isidore, Bede and Hrabanus Maurus. Whether he had read these authors in the original is hard to determine since the same material could be obtained from numerous *florilegia*, the popular collections of extracts from patristic writings. He was considered by contemporaries a learned man,[58] and his occasional requests in letters to borrow books,[59] along with his easy familiarity with patristic texts, would suggest a more than superficial knowledge at least of some authors. A number of his sermons reflect the growing cult of the Virgin Mary in this period; here the paucity of scriptural material inevitably encouraged the production of apocryphal legends, which Herbert used freely.[60] While he sometimes displayed awareness of recent doctrinal debate, for instance in his preaching on the eucharist, there is no evidence that he was involved in the great theological disputes of the time.[61] Nor did he share the scholastics' enthusiasm for applying philosophical argument to dogma.[62] For Herbert, faith was ultimately more important than reason: 'We seek a rational explanation, but the highest reason is to trust God's will and word'.[63] Herbert's skill in preaching is mentioned incidentally in an account of the translation of St Etheldreda at Ely in 1107; his moving sermon on this occasion apparently reduced the entire congregation to tears.[64]

Teacher

The most intimate and touching letters are those addressed to two boys, Otto and William, whose education in the monastery Herbert supervised with fatherly affection.[65] He took a lively interest in their studies, personally teaching them when in Norwich and, when absent, exhorting them to write to him frequently. In an early letter we catch a fleeting glimpse of the old bishop sitting uncomfortably on the low bench beside his pupils, patiently explaining the rules of Latin grammar.[66] The boys were to master their Donatus, he commanded, for on his return he would subject them to a stiff examination. Later they progressed to poetry: 'Write to me therefore in poetry, frame verses, compose odes . . . and rejoice the heart of your

57. Alexander, 'Herbert', pp. 80–213.
58. *First Register*, fo. 1: 'Erat quippe vir omni litterarum tam secularium quam divinarum inbutus sciencia'. Cotton, of course, is biased, but Malmesbury also praises his learning, *De gestis regum Anglorum*, ii, p. 387.
59. GS, i, p. 64, letter v; and p. 251, letter x.
60. Alexander, 'Herbert', pp. 204–8.
61. Alexander, 'Herbert', pp. 200–1.
62. H. O. Taylor, *The Medieval Mind* (London, 1911), pp. 338–77, on twelfth-century scholastics.
63. Alexander, 'Herbert', p. 201.
64. GS, i, pp. 372–78, extract from *Liber Eliensis*.
65. GS, i, pp. 19–51.
66. GS, i, p. 20, letter ix.

aged friend by cultivating the muses in every form'.[67] Herbert promised critical appraisal in return. Sometimes his criticisms seem unduly harsh, but he was sensitive to their reactions. When William failed to communicate, Herbert wrote anxiously to Otto: 'If he is hurt, let William open his heart; and as hitherto he has been to me another self in my affairs, so let him permit me to be another self in his'.[68] The reciprocity is pleasing and shows that Herbert, in spite of his high office, was not too pompous to listen to youthful opinions.

A theme which runs through several letters to his pupils is the tension between pagan literature and Christianity, which was the inevitable result of the medieval educational system. Herbert acknowledged that classical texts were an essential part of the curriculum in the formative stages: 'amidst playful little pieces of literature the tender minds of boys gradually but surely imbibe polished diction and the methods of tasteful composition'.[69] But the ultimate goal of education was spiritual wisdom; once they had served their purpose, classical texts were best discarded and forgotten. The bishop's guilt over his continuing enjoyment of profane literature emerges most forcefully in a remarkable letter, whose opening sentence provides a picture of Herbert at his most endearing: 'As not long ago I was musing in the silence of the night on your studies and . . . humming to myself some elegiac lines, sleep crept over me'.[70] He went on to describe a dream in which he was visited by an awesome female spectre, who rebuked him for forgetting his priestly office, saying, 'unseemly it is that Christ should be preached and Ovid recited by the same mouth . . .'[71] Whether an actual dream, or borrowed wholesale from Jerome and Boethius, the imagery powerfully illustrates the duality of medieval culture. It helps to explain why the twelfth-century renaissance never blossomed into full-blown classicism as happened in a later period.

Monastic Adviser

Herbert was a strict monastic disciplinarian. A number of his letters, such as the following one, were addressed to slack monks:

> You are, they say, seldom seen in the cloister, often in the parlours; slow in resorting to church, swift in resorting to the grange and the public roads which skirt it; you are constantly getting leave to have your blood let . . . [and] to have a bath. You are indulging your body, you are ruining your soul, and not only yours, but perchance also some of the souls which I had entrusted to your guidance.[72]

67. GS, i, p. 22, letter xlvii.
68. GS, i, p. 29, letter xxx.
69. GS, i, pp. 19–20, letter ix. See also pp. 134–5, 333.

70. GS, i, p. 43, letter xxviii.
71. GS, i, pp. 44–45, letter xxviii.
72. GS, i, pp. 105–9, letter xvi.

With runaway monks Herbert used stronger language, but he was prepared to forgive a young wanderer who returned penitent:

> I had intended to exclude Alexander from our society . . . but the persistency with which he begged me to remain softened my intention . . . Wherefore I pray you receive this brother once more into fellowship with you . . . for as the hardened folly of an old offender drives him naturally to despair, so on the other hand we may surely look for amendment from lenity shown to a youth.[73]

Authoritarian when he felt it was necessary, he was also understanding of youthful aberrations. It is in his letters to young monks and pupils in the monastic school that one sees Herbert at his best, as a wise and gentle counsellor thoroughly imbued with the spiritual values of St Benedict's Rule.

Patron of Architecture

In all of Herbert's writings there is not a single reference to architecture as such, although this is unfortunately entirely normal in a medieval context. The evidence for Herbert's obvious passion for architecture lies mainly in the buildings themselves, but his letters demonstrate at least his close involvement with the construction of the cathedral and monastery. When away from Norwich, the bishop wrote often to the prior and monks, sometimes expressing his anxiety over the slow progress of building operations. Building a church was, in Herbert's eyes, not just a means to an end, but a service to be rendered to God with the same unflagging devotion as the rest of the monastic routine required: 'Hold fast your rule, rear up your buildings, be constant in church, absent from none of the services, silent in the cloister, or in any other office within your precinct'.[74]

Sometimes Herbert was shamelessly manipulative. To be slow or sloppy in building, as in other tasks, posed a danger to their souls: 'I love you and am striving to deliver you, slow and indolent as you are, out of the hands of the divine severity. Often have I stirred you up in person . . . to apply yourselves fervently and diligently to the work of your church, and to show carefulness in that work, as done under the inspection of God's own eyes'.[75]

In spite of his entreaties, warnings and constant vigilance, Herbert was often exasperated by the lack of progress, grumbling,

> But alas the work drags on, and in providing materials you show no enthusiasm.
> Behold, the servants of the king and my own are really in earnest, gather

73. GS, i, pp. 138–39, letter li.
74. GS, i, p. 203, letter lvii.
75. GS, i, p. 132, letter xiv; although *opus*

ecclesiae is ambiguous, the context makes it clear here that Herbert means building the church since 'gathering stones' follows.

stones, carry them to the spot when gathered, and fill with them the fields and ways, the houses and courts; and you meanwhile are asleep with folded hands, numbed as it were, and frostbitten with a winter of negligence, shuffling and failing in your duty through a paltry love of ease.[76]

Besides conjuring up a vivid picture of the immense effort expended on transporting materials, the passage above begs a question: to what extent were the monks involved in the practical aspect of building? Probably the bishop was alluding only to unskilled labour, but it appears they were expected to do more than merely supervise the works. Also interesting is the mention of the king's servants. With his close court connections, it is in keeping that Herbert's work-force should include royal masons. The high quality of the work at Norwich, certainly cosmopolitan rather than provincial, bears this out.

Herbert's persistent 'stirring up' of the monks was evidently effective, as the cathedral advanced with remarkable speed in the first five years. Part of the church, possibly the whole eastern arm, was ready for use in 1101, when Henry I issued a charter there.[77] According to the *First Register*, by Herbert's death in 1119, the building had advanced 'as far as the altar of the Holy Cross'.[78] The location of this altar has been thoroughly investigated by Fernie, who concludes that it was in the fourth or fifth bay of the nave west of the crossing.[79]

Herbert's architectural patronage was by no means confined to the cathedral priory. As well as both the episcopal palace[80] and the chapel[81] alongside the cathedral, he built in Norwich a second monastery, St Leonard,[82] and a leper hospital, St Mary Magdalene.[83] At Great Yarmouth and King's Lynn he established two more Benedictine houses, St Nicholas and St Margaret, as cells of the cathedral priory.[84] He also built a new parish church at North Elmham.[85] These are the buildings recorded by the *First Register*, which is primarily concerned with the priory's own possessions.

76. GS, i, pp. 132–33, letter xiv.
77. *First Register*, fo. 3: 'in ecclesia Sancte Trinitatis de Norwyco donavi Deo et Herberto Episcopo et successoribus suis et monachis qui in eadem ecclesia deo serviunt . . . Facta est hec donatio ab Incarnatione domini MC primo'.
78. *First Register*, fo. 8: 'Perfecit autem idem Herbertus Ecclesiam Norwycensem suo tempore . . . usque ad altare Sancte Crucis . . .'
79. Fernie, *NC*, pp. 15–16.
80. *First Register*, fo. 8: 'Idem eciam domus episcopales excepta magna aula construxit'.
81. *First Register*, fo. 3v: 'unam ecclesiam apud Norwycum in curia sua . . . construxit'.
82. *First Register*, fo. 3: 'Ecclesiam Sancti Leonardi in quodam colle ejusdem silve . . . construxit . . .'
83. *First Register*, fo. 7: 'Herbertus vero Episcopus memoratus operibus misericordie sedulus insistens ad susceptionem leprosorum . . . ecclesie sue in honore beate Marie Magdalene fundavit'.
84. Cotton, *Historia*, p. 390: 'alias praeclari operis constituit ecclesias . . . tertiam apud Elmham; quartam Lenniae; quintam Gernemutae . . .'; also *First Register*, fo. 3v, on St Nicholas; and *First Register*, fo. 8, on St Margaret.
85. *First Register*, fo. 3v: 'aliam [ecclesiam] apud Elmham . . . de novo construxit . . .'

However, Stephen Heywood, using extensive archaeological and documentary evidence, has convincingly attributed to Herbert's patronage two more buildings, formerly believed to be Anglo-Saxon: the ruined churches at North and South Elmham, identified by Heywood as Norman episcopal chapels.[86] The enthusiasm for building which emerges in the bishop's letters is certainly borne out by his works: few Anglo-Norman patrons rival Herbert in the number, size and variety of the buildings he created.[87]

Some reference should be made to the funding of his buildings. William of Malmesbury was not entirely accurate when he claimed that the bishop purchased everything for the monks out of his own pocket.[88] Rufus may have donated lands and Henry I certainly did, The latter also provided rents and rights pertaining to fairs in Norwich, Lynn and Hoxne.[89] A number of feudal magnates contributed portions of their tithes,[90] and Herbert also imposed a tax on the population as a whole.[91] He even managed to persuade the monks of Bury to divert some of their own dues to Norwich.[92] Nevertheless, it is probably true to say that Herbert made a far more generous contribution to the building funds than most bishops; this is no doubt what impressed William of Malmesbury.[93] His final tribute to Herbert is a touching expression of faith in the redemptive powers of patronage:

> Finally, who can sufficiently extol his conduct, who, though not a very rich bishop, yet built so noble a monastery; in which nothing remains to be desired, either in the beauty of the lofty edifice, the elegance of its ornaments, or in the piety and universal charity of its monks. These things soothed him with joyful hope while he lived, and when dead, if repentance be not in vain, conducted him to heaven.[94]

Herbert de Losinga was a remarkable man, a complex and somewhat contradictory character combining many outstanding gifts with a few obvious failings. Certainly ambitious, and occasionally unscrupulous in realising his ambitions, he was at the

86. S. Heywood, 'The Ruined Church at North Elmham', *JBAA*, 135 (1982), pp. 1–10; see also Fernie, *NC*, pp. 208–9.
87. Fernie, *NC*, pp. 207–9.
88. Malmesbury, *De gestis regum Anglorum*, ii, p. 386.
89. Fernie, *NC*, pp. 11–12; *First Register*, fo. 7 for rights pertaining to fairs.
90. *First Register*, fo. 8: 'Plures etiam magnates de episcopatu duas partes decimarum dominicorum suorum nonnulli vero tertiam partem monasterio predicto contulerunt'.
91. *First Register*, fo. 8: 'Idem vero episcopus de quolibet mesuagio sue dyocese ad constructionem operis ecclesie Norwycensis instituit quoddam certum solvi'.
92. Fernie, *NC*, p. 13 and n. 39.
93. *First Register*, fo. 1v: 'Multa sibi locum Norwyci comparavit pecunia, primum a Regibus Willelmo Secundo et Henrico, deinde ab ipsius loci civibus'.
94. Malmesbury, *De gestis regum Anglorum*, p. 387.

same time deeply devout. Conscientious in carrying out his pastoral duties, he was particularly concerned with the spiritual and material welfare of his monks. If he sometimes misused his money, he was capable too of lavish generosity. As for his alleged skills in flattery, while I believe he had them and used them to advantage, his correspondence also shows that he was a loyal friend to a variety of people, regardless of social distinctions. Possibly Cotton overrated his scholarship when he described the bishop as 'a man imbued with every kind of learning, both secular and divine', but Herbert's letters and sermons reveal a lively and well-informed mind.[95] Most outstanding of Herbert's achievements is his extensive patronage of the visual arts, for which Norwich Cathedral and his other buildings provide ample testimony.

95. *First Register*, fo. 1. See above, n. 58.

3

Herbert de Losinga and the Foundation

Barbara Dodwell

I n medieval chronicles the establishment of a cathedral at Norwich is related to the simony of Bishop Herbert of Thetford and his subsequent repentance. For this sin he sought absolution in Rome and, on his return to England, moved the see to Norwich. There (and later writers have assumed that it was an act of penance) Herbert built and endowed a magnificent cathedral in which he installed monks in the place of secular priests. It is the purpose of the present chapter to examine this story and to add to it what is known of the foundation of the cathedral.[1]

The move to Norwich was, in fact, no sudden whim on the part of the bishop, but had its origin in events which went back to the early days of the Norman Conquest. As we have seen, for two centuries before 1066 there had been but one see covering East Anglia, that of Elmham, but there were two episcopal seats. In addition to the main seat of North Elmham in central Norfolk, there was for Suffolk a lesser seat at Hoxne,[2] a place which had associations with St Edmund. Neither North Elmham nor Hoxne was a place of any importance and in view of the Norman policy of transferring episcopal seats from rural to urban areas a change of seat was almost inevitable. The choice was not wide because, although East Anglia did not lack towns, few were entirely suitable. In practice the choice was restricted to the two larger Norfolk boroughs, Norwich, a growing commercial centre; and Thetford, once the chief town of East Anglia, but now outstripped by Norwich. The shift came with the appointment of a new bishop on the fall of Æthelmær in 1070. Herfast (1070–84), a Norman who had risen in royal service to the office of

---

1. This is an edited and abridged version of Barbara Dodwell, 'The Foundation of Norwich Cathedral', *TRHS*, 5th series, 7 (1957), pp. 1–18; the editors are grateful to the Royal Historical Society for permission to publish it here.

2. *DB*, ii, fo. 379; 'in hoc manerio est ecclesia sedes episcopatus de Sudfolc'.

chancellor, moved almost immediately to Thetford where the church of St Mary was taken over for the new cathedral. A St Benet chronicler assigns the transfer to 1071.[3] The date may well be correct for it was as bishop of Thetford that Herfast personally autographed a decree drawn up in the Easter of 1072.[4]

Although Herfast was to remain at Thetford, there are good reasons for doubting whether this move was intended to be permanent. His ambition was to fix his seat at Bury St Edmunds and to gain control of that rich abbey. Already in 1071 he was attempting to deprive St Edmunds of its exemption from episcopal control, and either then, or within a few years, he was endeavouring to move his seat there. The transfer to Thetford is, therefore, probably best understood as a preliminary move in the attack upon Bury. The bishop's proposals very naturally found no supporters at the abbey, and Herfast, although obstinate, was no match for Abbot Baldwin. After a prolonged struggle in which the abbot turned for support to both pope and king, Herfast was finally forced to abandon his claim in 1081.[5] Thwarted, he remained at Thetford. This is surprising because not only was the situation at Thetford unsatisfactory, and possibly irregular, but land in Norwich had been given by the king 'for the principal seat of the bishopric'.[6] Yet there is no evidence that Herfast moved his seat to Norwich. Both he and his successor William Beaufai (1085–c. 1090) are described as bishops of Thetford.[7] It was still as bishop of Thetford that Herbert Losinga was consecrated in 1091.

The seat of Canterbury being vacant, Herbert was consecrated by the archbishop of York,[8] probably at the same time as Ralf, bishop of Chichester, that is at Epiphany 1091.[9] A royal charter which may belong to 27 January 1091 is witnessed by both Herbert as bishop of Thetford and Ralf as bishop of Chichester.[10] Of Herbert's simony there is no doubt. At the price of £1000 Herbert bought preferment both

3. *Chronica minor Sancti Benedicti de Hulmo*, printed as an appendix to H. Ellis, ed., *Chronica Johannis de Oxnedes* (RS, 13, 1859), p. 431.

4. Paleographical Society, iii, plate 170.

5. T. Arnold, ed., *Memorials of St Edmund's Abbey*, 3 vols (RS, 96, 1890–96), i, pp. 60–67, 345, 347; see also D. Knowles, *The Monastic Order in England* (Cambridge, 1949), pp. 581–82.

6. *DB*, ii, fo. 117. The grant may have been made early in Herfast's episcopate, for he is reported to have attested the decrees of the council of 1075 as bishop of Norwich. D. Wilkins, *Concilia Magnae Britanniae et Hiberniae*, 4 vols (London, 1737), i, p. 364.

7. There is a story that after Herfast's death

William repeatedly endeavoured to make Baldwin, abbot of Bury, bishop and to fix his seat at Bury. V. H. Galbraith, 'The East Anglian See and the Abbey of Bury St Edmunds', *EHR*, 40 (1925), p. 227.

8. Hugh the Cantor, *The History of the Church of York, 1066–1127*, ed. C. Johnson (London, 1961), p. 7.

9. C. W. Foster, ed., *The Registrum Antiquissimum of the Cathedral Church of Lincoln*, i (Lincoln Record Society, 27, 1931), p. 10, note by Sir Frank Stenton.

10. H. W. C. Davis, C. Johnson and H. A. Cronne, eds, *Regesta regum Anglo-Normannorum, 1066–1154*, 3 vols (Oxford, 1913–68), i, no. 315.

for himself and for his father Robert, who now became abbot of Hyde.[11] The affair seems, curiously, to have shocked public opinion.[12] The sum was possibly unduly large and the purchase of preferment for both father and son may have been felt to go beyond the bounds of normal behaviour.

The events of the next few years are not so plain. According to the *Anglo-Saxon Chronicle* the bishop was deprived of his staff by the king in February 1094.[13] No reason is given in the *Chronicle*, but what seems to be an original annal of Florence of Worcester reports that it was because Herbert wanted to go secretly to Rome to seek absolution for the sin of simony from Pope Urban.[14] This is presumably to be connected with Malmesbury's story that the bishop repented and went to Rome, where he resigned his staff and ring to the pope and was reinstated; on his return to England he moved the see to Norwich.[15]

It can, I think, be fairly concluded that repentance was not long delayed and that Herbert decided to seek absolution from Urban. Permission to leave the country would almost certainly be refused. In any event England had not yet decided to recognise Urban as pope and was possibly inclining more towards Clement. Herbert, if he wished to go to Rome, had to do so secretly. Some writers have suggested that the bishop went to Rome in 1093 and that he was deprived by the king on his return.[16] Urban was, however, unable to enter Rome until Christmas 1093 and he remained there only until the summer of the next year. If Herbert did indeed go to Rome, the visit must have been made early in 1094.

Herbert was present at the consecration of Anselm early in December 1093,[17] then with other bishops attended the king at Gloucester over Christmas.[18] It is probable that on leaving the court he set out for Rome and that the king, arriving at Hastings in February, heard of the bishop's departure and immediately deprived him of his office. Herbert had committed an outrageous offence. Not only had he left England without permission, he had gone to a pope, as yet unrecognised, to

11. Florence of Worcester, *Chronicon ex chronicis*, ed. B. Thorpe, 2 vols (London, 1848), ii, p. 34n.

12. William of Malmesbury, *De gestis regum Anglorum*, ed. W. Stubbs, 2 vols (RS, 90, 1887), ii, pp. 385–86.

13. C. Plummer, ed., *Two of the Saxon Chronicles Parallel*, 2 vols (Oxford, 1892–99), i, p. 229.

14. Plummer, *Saxon Chronicles*, i, p. 229. The passage is from the Lambeth MS. It does not occur in the Corpus MS where, however, an entry has been erased and rewritten. I have to thank Professor

Darlington for this information.

15. William of Malmesbury, *De gestis pontificum Anglorum*, ed. N. E. S. A. Hamilton (RS, 52, 1870), p. 151.

16. For example, E. A. Freeman, *The Reign of William Rufus*, 2 vols (Oxford, 1882), i, pp. 355–56, 448.

17. Eadmer says that all the bishops, except two whose names are given, were present: Eadmer, *Historia novorum in Anglia*, ed. M. Rule (RS, 81, 1884), p. 42.

18. Davis, Johnson and Cronne, *Regesta regum Anglo-Normannorum*, i, no. 338.

seek absolution for an appointment made by the king. Yet he was not long out of office. Although no annalist mentions a reconciliation with the king, a writ by which William restores land to the bishop may mark Herbert's return to favour.[19] In any event Herbert was again acting as bishop of East Anglia in the spring of 1095, when he was claiming, in vain, the right to assist at the translation of the relics of St Edmund.[20]

Permission to move the episcopal seat to Norwich may have been obtained when the bishop made his peace with the king. A date for the removal of the see, 9 April 1094, is given by Matthew of Paris as one of his embellishments to Wendover's *Flores historiarum*.[21] It is repeated by Bartholomew Cotton, the only chronicler on a national scale to come from Norwich,[22] but since he borrowed largely from Wendover and Paris his work cannot be accepted as independent evidence of its accuracy. It is difficult to reconcile the date with Herbert's deprivation and his visit to Rome, for it is most unlikely that the bishop could have returned to England by the beginning of April.[23] If my timing of the sequence of events is correct, this date is clearly wrong as to its year. On the whole it is reasonable to suppose that Herbert had obtained from the king permission to move the see when he sought land on which to build a new cathedral in Norwich. That was in 1095 and the removal of the see may belong to that year.

The reason for the transfer lies not so much in the events of 1094 as in the situation at Thetford. It is generally supposed that the cathedral had been established in the church of St Mary, a small church and insignificant by Norman standards. There seems to have been no room for expansion, the site afterwards proving too cramped for the Cluniac monks established there by Roger Bigod; they, in their turn, moved away to a fresh site. More importantly, the cathedral did not, it seems, belong to the bishop; it was, as the Norwich chronicle describes it, 'of another person's possessions'.[24] Herfast had treated the church as private property and had left it to his sons. It was held by them in 1086, after his death;[25] according to a Thetford monk it was from Richard son of Herfast that Roger Bigod acquired the church.[26] The situation at Thetford was clearly highly irregular. It is not surprising therefore that the bishop should want to move his seat – what is surprising is that the move was so long delayed. If the reason for the move is to be explained, not

19. *NCC*, i, no. 69.
20. Arnold, *Memorials of St Edmund's Abbey*, i, p. 87.
21. H. R. Luard, ed., *Flores historiarum*, 3 vols (RS, 95, 1890), ii, p. 26.
22. Bartholomew Cotton, *Historia Anglicana*, ed. H. R. Luard (RS, 16, 1859), p. 54.
23. R. L. Poole has estimated that in the twelfth

century the usual time for a journey to Rome was seven weeks: *Studies in Chronology and History* (Oxford, 1934), p. 264.
24. *First Register*, p. 22.
25. *DB*, ii, fo. 118v.
26. W. Dugdale, *Monasticon Anglicanum*, ed. J. Caley, H. Ellis, and B. Bandinel, 6 vols (London, 1846), v, p. 152.

Fig. 7. St Luke's Chapel (as painted by John Sell Cotman in the early nineteenth century).

by Herbert's simony, but by the peculiar situation at Thetford, the timing may well have been the result of the penitential visit to Rome. The repentance for simony was the occasion but hardly the cause of the change.

The old cathedral at Thetford was, nevertheless, not immediately abandoned and for some years Herbert is described as bishop of either place. In 1100–1 he witnessed a charter to St-Martin of Troarn as bishop of Thetford; and in September 1101 a charter to the city of Bath as bishop of Norwich.[27] A letter from Anselm, seemingly written shortly after the council of 1102, addresses him still as bishop of Thetford.[28] It was about this time, however, that Herbert obtained a papal bull authorising the move to Norwich,[29] and in about 1103 the cathedral church at Thetford was given

27. Davis, Johnson and Cronne, *Regesta regum Anglo-Normannorum*, ii, nos 524, 544.
28. F. S. Schmitt, ed., *S. Anselmi Cantuariensis archiepiscopi opera omnia*, 6 vols (Seckau, London and Edinburgh, 1938–61), iv, no. 254.
29. Herbert is said to have gone to Rome to obtain confirmation from Pope Paschal for the move to Norwich. He did this in 1101–2 when he was sent to Rome. The bishop of Coventry who also went on this mission obtained a bull authorising his transfer to Coventry in April 1102.

up to Roger Bigod for his new foundation. Thereafter Herbert ceases to be described as bishop of Thetford.

At Norwich preparations for the building of the new cathedral began in 1095. It was usual for the new cathedrals of the late eleventh century to be established in churches in being, either, as at Chichester, in the church of a monastic community or, as at Lincoln, in the most important parish church of the town. At Norwich the bishop already possessed two churches and it was presumably one of these, the church of the Holy Trinity, that Herbert chose for his cathedral.[30] Neither the church nor yet the site on which it stood was adequate for his purpose, for the bishop had ambitious plans and an overwhelming desire for space. In order to rebuild the church on a fitting scale, to set on each side of it monastic offices and an episcopal palace and then to give an open space before the monastery gates, additional land had to be acquired from Norwich citizens, from Roger Bigod and above all from the king.[31] The land required lay on the edge of the town or even outside it; part of it contained buildings which were demolished but, according to later tradition, most of it was meadowland called Cowholme, which belonged not to the borough but to the royal village of Thorpe.[32] It was part of the hundred of Blofield and not until the Dissolution was it incorporated into the borough. The area to be handed over was determined by Ranulf Flambard, Bishop Walkelin of Winchester and Roger Bigod, who probably went to Norwich during 1095.[33]

Herbert wasted no time. 1096 is the year given in priory chronicles for the foundation of the cathedral.[34] The existing church was pulled down and rebuilding commenced at once.[35] Building operations began, as was usual, at the eastern end, where two foundation stones were laid. The bishop laid the first which bore the inscription 'In the name of the Father, and of the Son and of the Holy Spirit, Amen. I, Herbert the bishop, have placed this stone'.[36] The second stone was laid by Hubert de Rye, a benefactor of the church. Slowly the eastern arm of the great church was built. The stones for the facings came from both Caen and Barnack

30. The church had been held by twelve burgesses in 1066 and had been given to the bishop by William I. The bishop also held the church of SS. Simon and Jude and, in 1086, that of St Michael: *DB*, ii, fo. 116v. The church of St Michael later passed into the hands of Roger Bigod.

31. *First Register*, pp. 24–28.

32. NRO, DCN 40/4, pp. 1–4. This is also printed in Dugdale, *Monasticon*, iv, pp. 13–15, from a copy in the Binham Cartulary, BL, Cotton MS Claud. D. xiii.

33. *NCC*, i, no. 1. The writ can probably be dated January 1096.

34. NRO, DCN, 40/3, fo. 1; DCN 40/4, p. 2.

35. Professor Eric Fernie is of the opinion that a previous church may be connected with burials close to the northern transept. He refutes the thesis put forward by Dean Cranage in 1932 - that the foundations of a small apse were those of an earlier church - by arguing that they represent a false start in Herbert's own building programme. Fernie, *NC*, pp. 19–22.

36. *First Register*, p. 50. A slightly different version is given in NRO, DCN 40/4, p. 2.

and were (it seems) used indiscriminately, while that for the rubble core was collected locally. By the beginning of September 1101 Herbert could refer to the church of the Holy Trinity which he had built and consecrated.[37] He presumably meant that the eastern end, possibly the choir, had been completed and consecrated. If, as Blomefield has suggested, the thirteenth-century feast of dedication, 24 September, is indeed the anniversary of Herbert's consecration of the choir,[38] that ceremony must have taken place at latest in 1100.

After the first flush of enthusiasm the rate of building was probably reduced. For Herbert the work went too slowly: one of his extant letters reproves the monks for their apathy towards the work of construction.[39] Building a cathedral was, inevitably, a slow business. Although there are some examples of fairly rapid building, as for instance Lanfranc's rebuilding of Canterbury, the erection of even a small cathedral could take twenty years. With the larger cathedrals the work was spread over a much longer period and there might be intervals in which building lapsed altogether. At Norwich the great church was still unfinished at the time of Herbert's death in 1119. The founder is reputed to have completed the eastern half of the cathedral, that is the choir with its surrounding aisles and chapels, the transepts each with an eastern chapel, the central tower and four or five bays of the nave. The nave was finished by his successor, Eborard (1121–45), who also heightened the tower.[40] Unfortunately, within fifty years of its completion the cathedral was damaged by fire and the then bishop, William Turbe (1146/47–74), was forced to make extensive repairs.[41]

There was more than a great church to build. The bishop's residence was, except for the great hall, completed during Herbert's episcopate.[42] Although Herbert's reference to the huts of the monastery may only be rhetorical,[43] it is probable that, as at Rochester, the monastic buildings were only temporary structures at first. He was, it seems, unable to accommodate all the monks beside the cathedral at the beginning, so some were sent to St Leonard's, just outside Norwich.[44] The monastic buildings were not finished until late in the twelfth century. The last item, the infirmary, is attributed to John of Oxford, who became bishop of Norwich in 1175.[45] When completed the whole was a magnificent series of buildings. The church was remarkable for its size, and in particular for the length of the nave, which contained the abnormal number of fourteen bays. These were not the only buildings belonging

37. *NCC*, i, no. 112.

38. Blomefield, *Norfolk*, iv, p. 1.

39. R. Anstruther, ed., *Epistolae Herberti de Losinga* (Brussels and London, 1846), letter xiv; GS, i, pp. 132–33. See also above, pp. 32–33.

40. Herbert is said to have built as far as the altar

of the Holy Cross. *First Register*, pp. 50, 56.

41. *First Register*, p. 76.

42. *First Register*, p. 50.

43. Anstruther, *Epistolae*, letter xxix; GS, i, p. 101.

44. *First Register*, p. 30. St Leonard's was built by 1101.

45. *First Register*, p. 82.

to the cathedral priory. At a very early date three cells and their churches were in being. St Leonard near Norwich, St Mary Magdalen, St Margaret and All the Holy Virgins at Lynn, and St Nicholas at Yarmouth were all built by Herbert Losinga.

It must not be assumed that the bishops of Norwich, still less the founder, supplied all the money for the erection of the cathedral, priory and dependent cells. According to Norwich chronicles Herbert did, at great cost to himself, buy land in Norwich from William II.[46] Presumably he contributed largely to the expenses of building cathedral and monastery, although, as neither was complete on his death, his successors also bore their share of these costs. A good deal of the money, however, came from other sources. According to Herbert, Henry I gave him the manor of Thorpe expressly for the building of the cathedral.[47] There was also a building fund for which the monks may have sought contributions,[48] and after the disaster of 1171 the bishop himself sat in a chair at the door of the cathedral to receive gifts.[49] More valuable were the contributions made by way of diocesan taxation. From Bury St Edmunds sources we learn of a carucage, a recurrent tax at the rate of four pence a carucate, which traditionally had been given by Sweyn for the rebuilding of the church of St Edmund and was still being taken by the abbey at the end of the eleventh century. With the consent of the abbot the tax was largely, although not entirely, diverted to the building of the cathedral and was then retained by the priory.[50] It was presumably taken from both lay and ecclesiastical holdings and may be identical with an aid which, according to the Norwich chronicle, Herbert demanded of each messuage in the diocese.[51] There was also a regular payment made specifically by churches. A charter of Eborard, Herbert's successor, refers to a customary payment, due from priests at the two synods, which Herbert had instituted for the construction and upkeep of the cathedral.[52] This is presumably that exaction which under the name of the Easter customary payment (*consuetudo paschalis*) was due from all the churches of the diocese, and which was remitted by Bishop John at the end of the twelfth century when the cathedral and monastery were completed.[53]

By 1091 a new grand East Anglian cathedral at Norwich was an edifice waiting to be built, but it required the vision, drive and administrative skills of Herbert de Losinga to bring such plans to fruition. It may also have taken the prompting of Herbert's guilty conscience to get the project rolling. Without his simony, and subsequent repentance, the physical setting for so much of the story of East Anglia's cathedral that will unfold below might have been very different.

46. *First Register*, p. 24; NRO, DCN 4/4, p. 1.
47. Anstruther, *Epistolae*, letter xxvi; GS, i, p. 230.
48. Herbert writes to the monks telling them to collect money, Anstruther, *Epistolae*, letter xiv; GS, i, p. 133.
49. *First Register*, p. 76.
50. Arnold, *Memorials of St. Edmund's Abbey*, i, p. 362.
51. *First Register*, p. 82.
52. *NCC*, i, no. 119.
53. *NCC*, i, no. 141.

PART II

The Building of the Cathedral

4

The Building: An Introduction

Eric Fernie

The laying of the foundation stone in 1096 provides a formal starting date for the building of the cathedral, but it is likely that preparations were in hand for a considerable time before that. The decision to locate the see in Norwich could have been taken as early as 1081 when William the Conqueror ended, at least temporarily, attempts by Herfast, the bishop of East Anglia (1070–84), to adopt Bury St Edmunds Abbey as the location of the see. William also gave land in Norwich for the new church, as is recorded in Domesday in 1086, so that when Herbert de Losinga, who became bishop in 1091, formally moved the see to Norwich in 1094, the city had been the intended site for ten years or longer.[1]

When Herbert started work on the cathedral he must have known that he was condemning himself to spend the rest of his years as bishop of East Anglia living on a building site. Work proceeded quickly enough to permit Henry I in 1101 to make a gift, in the cathedral, to the bishop and the monks. The building was constructed in two main campaigns, the first ending at the east end of the nave just to the west of the choir screen. This would have been a convenient place for a pause, allowing the clergy's part of the church to be roofed and in use. Since the extent of the first campaign was clearly planned, there is no reason to link it to Herbert's death in 1119: it is entirely possible that he hoped to embark on the second phase himself if time and money permitted.

It is a misconception that medieval cathedrals took centuries to build, a view which has arisen largely because they were so frequently altered, with the addition or renewal of such features as chapels or spires. In this sense most great churches were under construction throughout the middle ages, but if we restrict ourselves to examining the original design then building periods tend to be measured in decades rather than centuries. Norwich is no exception to this as the church and even most of the monastery and the bishop's palace were completed in less than fifty years, during the episcopate of Herbert's successor Eborard, who resigned in 1145.

---

1.   On the site before 1096, see Ayers, chapter 5.

The Norman cathedral, which survives almost in its entirety, conforms to a layout common among buildings of its type in England in the period, with a long east arm (of four bays and an apse), a long nave (of fourteen bays), a transept forming a crossing with the main east-west axis, aisles and an ambulatory with three radiating chapels. In elevation it has a main arcade, a gallery almost as large as the arcade and a clerestory with a wall passage.

The arrangements for the liturgy are more unusual. The sanctuary in the apse and the next bay to the west contained, as today, the central element of the whole building: the high altar for the celebration of the eucharist symbolising the Last Supper and therefore the Crucifixion. Behind the altar stood the bishop's throne in the much earlier and now unusual position on the axis of the building at the head of the apse. The high status of the throne is indicated by the fact that it stands above an east-facing niche which was probably intended to house relics. The original choir stalls occupied the crossing and the first and second bays of the nave, so that the part of the choir under the crossing was associated both with the well of light descending from the lantern and with the bells in the tower above. To the west of the choir screen in the third and fourth bays from the crossing stood the nave altar for services for the laity, set in a space apparently singled out by four cylindrical piers with spiral grooves, of which two are still completely visible and a third partially so.

The north-east and south-east radiating chapels have apses which turn them towards the east. Given the English preference for orientation over the north-east and south-east directions of standard radiating chapels, one might have expected the apses to be used to align the altars to the east, but instead they overcorrect and lie at an angle substantially different from the east-west axis of the building. There is no obvious explanation for this, other than a liking for the complicated shapes which result.

Herbert's cathedral, with its main spaces covered with timber roofs, is in essence an ancient Roman basilica. The only parts to be vaulted were the aisles and ambulatory (with groins), the ground-floor chapels off the ambulatory and the transept arms (with groins and semi-domes and barrels and semi-domes respectively), and, probably, the main apse (a semi-dome possibly supplied with ribs). This mixture of types and their locations in aisles as well as chapels suggests that vaults had no special significance, except for the semi-domes over the apses which appear to be related to sanctuaries.

The pier types are characterised by variety, a variety which provides the basis for one of the most ingenious forms of the alternation of arcade supports in the Romanesque architecture of western Europe. The west front is surprisingly simple, yet there is no evidence that, except in a few details, it was intended to be substantially different from its present form. The crossing tower, the part of the building most

Fig. 8. Norwich Cathedral and Castle from the air.

clearly visible from the city, is both very tall and one of the most lavishly decorated in the country.[2]

Norman buildings in England of the 1070s and 1080s are almost devoid of architectural decoration. As an early example of the second generation after the Conquest, Norwich was one of the first churches to break with this tradition, as, in addition to the standard cushion and volute capitals, its design includes rolls on the angles and undersides of arches, mouldings in the form of chevron and billet, the four spiral columns in the nave arcade, interlaced arcading and some decorated shafts in the clerestory. None the less, the only part of the building in which sculpture plays a prominent role is the north arm of the transept, probably intended to mark it off as the bishop's entrance to the church. This is most specifically suggested by the relief of a bishop on the exterior over the north door.

Even this degree of decoration must, however, have appeared restrained in comparison with the lost cloister of the original building, as the few loose capitals which survive from it are among the richest and most complex of the period, in both form and iconography. Their decoration involves themes which can be associated with classical characters such as Dionysus and with the writings of Ovid and Virgil, subject matter which may have been used as a memory aid in the monastic school.[3]

The monastic buildings around the cloister followed the standard arrangement of a dormitory to the east, a refectory to the south and a range to the west, probably for guests. The palace lies to the north of the church, keeping its more public affairs separate from those of the priory. The main part of Herbert's palace is built like a miniature keep. It is also laid out not at right angles to the cathedral but at a little less than ten degrees off the north-south axis of the church, which is the same as the divergence of the radiating chapels from the east-west axis.

Herbert's church is a masterpiece of the masons' craft. This is evident in the great unbroken lengths of the courses, particularly noticeable where they are reduced in depth to accommodate small items such as the capitals and bases of the window openings, indicating advance planning on an almost industrial scale. The same sort of planning occurs in the imaginative rhomboid shape of the blocks of the western-most spiral piers in the nave, designed so that the masonry joints do not conflict with the sloping edges of the spiral grooves. The stone was brought up the River Wensum to the canal beginning at Pull's Ferry from the quarries of Caen in Normandy and Barnack in Northamptonshire (on what is called the Lincolnshire Limestone Belt). The two types are different in colour and texture, though this would not have been evident originally as the whole building would have been

---

2. On the Romanesque cathedral see Heywood, chapter 6.

3. On the sculpture and decoration see Franklin, chapter 7.

plastered and painted, certainly on the inside and probably on the outside as well. In addition it is likely that the Norman building was provided with stained glass, given the parallels existing or known to have existed at Augsburg and Canterbury in the eleventh and early twelfth centuries. The building would consequently have presented a riot of colour, to an extent which it is probably difficult for twentieth-century taste to appreciate.

The cathedral must have been a staggering sight in the context of contemporary buildings in Norfolk and Suffolk. In the mid 1090s the architectural landscape consisted mainly of wooden structures, whether houses or churches of high and low status, defences (such as the castle at Norwich, before the 1090s consisting of earthworks and timber and still without a masonry keep) and some small masonry churches. The only exception would have been the abbey at Bury St Edmunds in Suffolk, already under construction in the 1080s and in many ways a source of architectural ideas for the cathedral and an achievement against which it could be measured. The abbey and the cathedral were therefore almost certainly the first representatives in their respective counties of the new Romanesque style imported from Normandy and elsewhere in continental Europe. This impact has a relevance beyond a purely local level. The Gothic cathedrals of northern France of the later twelfth and thirteenth centuries have often been compared to skyscrapers or to American and Soviet spacecraft in their scale, their cost and their impact on the contemporary imagination. The parallels are apt, but they are equally applicable to the new large-scale Norman churches like Norwich being built in England in the late eleventh and early twelfth centuries. If anything it is likely that the amount of stone quarried for buildings in England in those years was even greater than that in France between 1150 and 1250.

The whole repertoire of East Anglian masonry building of this period can be found at the cathedral. Relevant monuments include the churches and monasteries at Castle Acre (probably early twelfth century, despite the documentary date of 1090), Binham (from *c.* 1100), Wymondham (from 1107) and Thetford (from 1107). These buildings share the decorative vocabulary of the cathedral, the variety of pier types and details like the triple arch design of the clerestory bays. One major difference is the absence of an ambulatory. This cannot be due to a difference of scale, as the main spans of the buildings in question are not markedly smaller than the width of the cathedral, though there is no other obvious explanation for it. The keeps of the castles at Norwich and Castle Rising also show connections with the cathedral, priory and palace in regard to masonry techniques, decorative forms and type of chimney. Along with this group of buildings the architectural patronage of Bishop Herbert at places other than the cathedral should be mentioned, namely the dependent cell of St Leonard and the Lazar hospital in Norwich, St Margaret at King's Lynn, St Nicholas at Great Yarmouth, the parish church at

North Elmham and in all likelihood the ruined churches at North and South Elmham as well.[4]

The prime purpose of the building, namely divine worship, is expressed in the yearly round of the liturgy. The liturgical customs of Norwich, introduced from Fécamp in Normandy by Herbert, are set out in the thirteenth-century Customary which provides a guide to ceremonial, with a level of detail which extends to prescribing the distance between those taking part in processions, and the speed and character with which certain passages should be sung. The customs of Fécamp were themselves derived from Cluny. The Norwich customs were thus an aspect of the great monastic reform movement of the tenth and eleventh centuries, as well as of the Norman cultural invasion of England.[5]

The Gothic Additions, Alterations and Reconstructions

The most important development in the architectural history of the middle ages was the replacement of the old Romanesque style with the new Gothic one, the style inaugurated in northern France in the middle of the twelfth century which dominated the architecture of western Europe until the sixteenth century. Building activity in the cathedral in this period can thus be seen in many ways as a series of attempts at bringing the building up to date, some instigated by the need for repairs but others apparently undertaken in the spirit of renewal.

The first sign of this wish to modernise was Bishop John of Oxford's new infirmary of around 1180, but Bishop Suffield's scheme for remodelling the east end in the middle of the thirteenth century was much more far-reaching as, if it had been completed, it would have destroyed the Romanesque ambulatory and radiating chapels. Of this work only fragments of the axial Lady Chapel survive. The next programme was undertaken as a result of the damage sustained in the riot of 1272. This led to the rebuilding of the free-standing bell tower to the west of the façade (*c.* 1300–10), the Ethelbert Gate (*c.* 1317), the chapter house (*c.* 1290–1300) and, extending over the fourteenth and early fifteenth centuries, the cloister. The walks of the cloister were constructed in a clockwise direction with tracery of varying designs offering a series of textbook examples of English tracery types over the period. In the early fourteenth century Bishop Salmon (1299–1325) renewed and added to parts of the palace and built the Carnary Chapel. After damage resulting from the fall of the spire in 1361 (or 1362, the year is disputed) the clerestory of the east arm was rebuilt to a dramatic new design, with a tall

4.   On the influence of the cathedral see   5.   On the Customary see Chadd, chapter 15.
Thurlby, chapter 8.

wall passage supported on thin columns, while the apse windows contain one of
the earliest examples of Perpendicular tracery in East Anglia.

The later thirteenth century also sees the start of the extensive collection of
monastic account rolls which has survived at Norwich and which, along with
collections of deeds and charters such as the *First Register*, provide a large part of
the dating and other evidence for building work at the cathedral, particularly after
1300 and especially from the rolls of the sacrists and communars.[6]

The next period of transformation began with the doorway added to the west
front by Bishop Alnwick (1426–36) and the great west window above it paid for
from his will after his death in 1449. In the course of the next seventy years the
four main vessels of the church were entirely covered with rib vaults, that over the
nave being built by Bishop Lyhart (1446–72), that over the east arm by Bishop
Goldwell (1472–99), and those over the transept arms by Bishop Nix (1501–35/36).
The spire was rebuilt and the main arcade of the east arm remodelled in the same
period, the first definitely and the second probably by Goldwell, an attribution
depending on detailed arguments concerning the Boleyn heraldry, and on the
observation that Goldwell's tomb is inserted into the arcade and therefore must be
later than it.

Although Lyhart's nave vault is usually assumed to have been built after and
because of the fire of 1463, it is noteworthy that a censing angel which formed part
of the liturgical furniture in the nave (and for which a hole is provided in the new
vault) was not used during the 1450s, implying some disruption and therefore the
possibility that Lyhart erected his vault before the fire. This reading of the documentary
evidence is supported by the fact that the fire of 1463 damaged the choir stalls in
the area under the crossing rather than those in the nave further west. There are,
however, no recorded examples of a medieval church being provided with a vault
over its nave and not over its east arm, so the building of the vault in the nave at
Norwich implies an intention to vault the east arm as well. If Lyhart's project arose
from a need to repair the nave after a fire the order of building would make sense,
but if he was embarking on the next stage of modernisation without any specific
need to repair, it is unclear why he did not start east of the crossing.[7]

What remains of the stone sculpture of the Gothic period is almost entirely
confined to doorways into the cathedral and the close. The most sophisticated is
that called the prior's door in the north-east corner of the cloister, which is decorated
with seven small almost free-standing figures representing Christ, angels, saints and
Old Testament figures forming a complex series of iconographic sets. The work
belongs with the carving of the adjacent vault bosses. The Ethelbert Gate has in

6. On the documents and the library see   7. On the buildings of the Gothic period see
   Dodwell, chapter 16.   Woodman, chapter 9.

the spandrels of its external face a representation of a man fighting a dragon, probably intended to rebuke the citizens for their part in the riot of 1272. The Carnary Chapel and the extension to the palace, both of the time of Bishop Salmon, were originally decorated with a number of figures in niches, of which only the corbels and canopies remain to indicate the quality of the work. Bishop Alnwick's west doorway to the cathedral originally had large-scale figures in its niches, while the contemporary Erpingham Gate contains finely cut figurated voussoirs.[8]

If in most respects Norwich Cathedral provides good, representative examples of Romanesque and Gothic architectural design, in one respect it is unique, namely in the number of bosses which decorate the points at which the ribs of the vaults intersect. There are more than a thousand of them, carved with foliage, heraldry, individual figures from wild men to musicians and, of course, religious imagery. The bosses in the cloister walks include all of these variants. Those on Lyhart's nave vault depict from east to west the Christian story from Creation to Doomsday, with many examples of Old Testament scenes paralleling and hence prefiguring scenes from the New, whereas by contrast the majority of the bosses in the presbytery are decorated with the gold well of Bishop Goldwell's rebus or signature, while the transept vaults have a small number of New Testament scenes repeated many times. There is no obvious explanation for this profusion, which is unmatched anywhere else in the medieval world.[9]

The influence exerted by the Gothic work at the cathedral is strong throughout the fourteenth and fifteenth centuries, especially in Norfolk though occasionally in Suffolk. There are strong links with Ely Cathedral, but the role of the abbey at Bury St Edmunds remains unclear as almost nothing of Gothic date survives. Norwich's influence is chiefly evident in window tracery and arch mouldings. Thus the decoration on the Ethelbert Gate, the tracery of the south and west walks of the cloister and, to a lesser extent, the clerestory windows in the east arm are the sources of some of the most popular designs in use in Norfolk, Suffolk and even Lincolnshire in the fourteenth century. The Perpendicular tracery in the north walk of the cloister (designed by Robert Wadhurst, who worked at Westminster before his time at Norwich and Ely) occurs at Hemsby in Norfolk and at Sudbury St Peter in Suffolk; the west doorway and the great west window are respectively related to work at Salle and Fakenham, both in Norfolk; while the Erpingham Gate of the 1420s can be related to work such as the nave of Wiveton in Norfolk and the porch of Beccles in Suffolk.[10]

While we tend to think of medieval cathedrals primarily in terms of their masonry,

8. On the sculpture of the Gothic period apart from the bosses see Sekules, chapter 10.

9. On the bosses see Rose, chapter 18.

10. On the influence of the Gothic work see Fawcett, chapter 11.

of equal importance were the roofs, doors, screens, shutters and furniture, the ironwork which accompanied the carpentry, the wall paintings, panel paintings, window glass, bells and heraldry. Wood carving is well represented by the choir stalls. These survive from two periods, the earlier of which, of the early fifteenth century, include the important return stalls flanking the doorway to the choir screen, which have extensive foliage carving as well as finely detailed lierne vaults above and misericords with varied subjects below. The later group, which appear to belong to repairs after the fire of 1463, have more extensively pierced tracery and more systematically arranged scenes on the misericords.[11]

Although nothing survives of the polychromy of the original Romanesque building there are numerous if fragmentary examples from later in the middle ages. The earliest are those of the late twelfth century in the south aisle of the nave depicting Bishop Herbert's simony and his consequent building of the cathedral. While the wall paintings of masonry and abstract patterns in the eastern arm and radiating chapels almost certainly belong to the refurbishment after the fire of 1272, the images including a bishop on the east side of the ante-reliquary chapel in the north aisle of the presbytery should be dated before that fire, especially because of their similarity to the related paintings at Horsham St Faith. This means a post-1272 date for the insertion of the chapel platform will have to be reconsidered. The paintings on the vault and west arch of this bay belong at the very end of the thirteenth century or early in the fourteenth and can be paralleled with the sculpture on the prior's door in the cloister, while their similarity with paintings at Little Wenham in Suffolk render explanations dependent on influence from Westminster unnecessary.

The documentary evidence indicates that the cathedral was filled with coloured images, on stone, wood and metal, and there are remains of paint on the sculptures of the Erpingham Gate, on the bosses of Goldwell's vault over the presbytery, on those of Nix's vaults over the transepts and, probably the latest pre-Reformation painting in the building, on his chantry in the south aisle of the nave.[12]

The altarpiece depicting five episodes from the Passion of Christ, now in St Luke's Chapel, is the only medieval panel in the cathedral which may have been made for the building. The heraldry connects it to those who were prominent in the suppression of the Peasants' Revolt in 1381, including the bishop after whom it has come to be called the Despenser retable. Its style has been connected with work from as far afield as Germany, Bohemia and France. Only fragments of the medieval glazing of the cathedral survive, and most of what is there is either from other sites or of post-medieval date.[13]

11. On the stalls see Sekules, chapter 10.
12. On the medieval polychromy see Park and Howard, chapter 19.
13. On the panel paintings and glass see King, chapter 20.

Ironwork of a very high quality survives in the cathedral, on the doors of the infirmary and the Carnary, on the great chest and in Prior Catton's lock, as well as in the form of examples in wall paintings. There was also a decorated clock of the early fourteenth century, now lost.[14] Frequent and often complex bell ringing played a central part in the running of the cathedral. The bells, which were the responsibility of the sacrist, ranged from the large ones of 50 to 60 cwt (2.5 to 3 tonnes) in the bell tower near the Erpingham Gate, intended to sound over great distances, to the smaller ones in the crossing tower used at the start of the daily offices.[15]

The evidence supplied by heraldry is of particular significance for the dating of buildings of the fifteenth and sixteenth centuries. Thus, for example, on the basis of the heraldic evidence the west doorway can be dated to the time of Bishop Alnwick (1426–36); a vault in the west walk of the cloister to *c.* 1420, shortly after the death of Sir Robert Knollys in 1407; the Erpingham Gate to the 1420s; the pulpitum to the time of Bishop Lyhart (1446–72); the vault added to the fourteenth-century Bauchun Chapel to the middle of the fifteenth century by the arms of William Seckington; the vaults of the nave, east arm and transept arms to the times of the respective bishops; and the reworking of the arcades of the presbytery to *c.* 1500.[16]

The earliest surviving tomb in the cathedral, consisting of a Purbeck slab on the south side of the presbytery, is that of Bishop Wakering, who contributed to work on the cloister and the choir stalls. Only one medieval brass survives but the number of indents suggests an original total of over a hundred. One of the most important tombs of all, that of Bishop Herbert before the high altar in the middle of the east arm, has suffered the greatest vicissitudes, acquiring its present form of an inscribed slab in the seventeenth century. There have also, however, been some surprising survivals, in particular the late fifteenth-century tomb of Bishop Goldwell, with its alabaster effigy and a canopy. Monuments to members of the laity include the raised stone tomb of Sir James Hobart (d. 1507) and the large Purbeck slab of Sir Thomas Windham (d. 1522), both in the north arcade of the nave.[17]

We know of two medieval seals of the priory. The earlier, probably made before 1145, is a hybrid of Anglo-Saxon and continental Norman types showing Christ's Resurrection. The later one, instituted in 1258, consists of an ecclesiastical building with a representation of Bishop Herbert as founder, and on the reverse Christ blessing, four monks' heads and, below, the Annunciation taking place in the doorway of a church. In both cases the buildings on the seals are based on the designs of earlier seals rather than on the architecture of the cathedral.[18]

---

14. On the ironwork see Geddes, chapter 21.
15. On the bells see Cattermole, chapter 25.
16. On the heraldry see Sims, chapter 23.

17. On the monuments see Finch, chapter 24.
18. On the seals see Heslop, chapter 22.

The Post-Medieval Additions

In his essay on this period Thomas Cocke refers to the cathedral as having been 'radically refashioned both inside and out', a statement which seems to conflict with the claim that Herbert's cathedral survives almost in its entirety, but both claims are justifiable from their two different perspectives. Compared with the state of most cathedrals of the Romanesque period in England, Norwich is indeed very well preserved, as even the parts which have been demolished or restored have left sufficient trace to permit an almost complete reconstruction of the original form. Conversely, Cocke is right to stress the extent of work carried out on the cathedral since the Reformation and the slight attention which has been paid to its significance, particularly in terms of social history.[19]

The years immediately following the Reformation saw almost nothing but neglect of the fabric and its consequent decay, from Dean Gardiner's stripping of the lead from the roof of Suffield's Lady Chapel to the destruction of the chapter house and the collapse of the free-standing bell tower. The seventeenth century saw the start of repair work and the building of a new bishop's chapel by Bishop Reynolds. In the time of Dean Bullock in the middle of the eighteenth century Matthew Brettingham erected a windlass for working in the crossing tower, made a model of the proposed scaffolding, underpinned the foundations on the north side of the building, laid a new pavement and impressed at least some of the clergy with his ability to save money. In the second half of the century structural work became more prominent, as for example in Dean Lloyd's refashioning of parts of the east arm, in the 1760s, and the insertion of timber framing into the spire.

The nineteenth century saw a concerted attempt to return the cathedral (so systematically Gothicised in the later middle ages) to its original Romanesque form, which of course resulted in parts of it assuming a Neo-Romanesque guise. Many parts are just that, attempts to restore what was thought to have been there in the original design, as, for instance, the pilasters and paired half shafts marking the chord of the main apse, with the strange stump of an arch springing west from the pier on the north side of the sanctuary. For the south face of the transept Anthony Salvin produced a completely new design, removing the east range of the claustral buildings to provide a second façade for the building, while in the 1840s Edward Blore remodelled the upper parts of the west front. Despite these 'relentless Neo-Romanesque' alterations, Norwich did not undergo a full-scale Victorian restoration like many other medieval cathedrals.

---

19. See Cocke, chapter 33. On the post-medieval tombs and glass see respectively Finch, chapter 24 and King, chapter 20.

In the late 1840s Robert Willis, the father of church archaeology, responded to questions put to him by the dean about various parts of the building, in the process setting standards of preservation which were later to become those of the Society for the Preservation of Ancient Buildings. Thus, when in the 1870s the floor of the sanctuary was lowered, the ragged bases were left exposed, as they remain today. These would certainly have been tidied up if the work had been carried out in an age before Willis and others had made people aware of the importance of such fragments of evidence. This change in attitude provides an introduction to the conflict in the twentieth century: between the church seen as a working building used for worship and the church seen as an historical document.

The most noteworthy addition of the twentieth century is the Regimental Chapel of 1930–32, which stands on the site of its predecessors, the axial chapel of Herbert's church and the Lady Chapel built by Bishop Suffield. This Neo-Gothic design was the work of Sir Charles Nicholson, the next architect of national standing to work on the cathedral after Salvin and Blore. Three foundation stones were laid at its inception, the first and second echoing those of the original ceremony in 1096, with the bishop using the words of Herbert de Losinga, and the person following him being like Hubert de Rye a prominent layman, namely the earl of Leicester, high steward of the cathedral.

Since the 1950s the cathedral has been in the care of two very different men who have both in their own way made a fundamental contribution to the building and its history: the late Arthur Whittingham, whose antiquarian knowledge of the fabric of all the buildings in the close was unsurpassed; and Sir Bernard Feilden, who has an international reputation in the conservation of ancient monuments. During the fifties, sixties and seventies Feilden carried out extensive work on the building. He began with the consolidation of the spire using grouting, concrete ties forming a polygon, new brickwork and timber-framing, and moved on to the strengthening of the crossing tower with steel chains and concrete. Then followed the remaking of the main roofs with fire-proof steel and concrete frames and of the gallery roofs in wood, the repair of the external masonry, and the cleaning of the vault in the east arm. Finally, he instituted quinquennial inspections and oversaw a rolling programme of repair.[20] As a result of this programme of restoration, made possible by the fund-raising activities of the Friends, the cathedral enters its tenth century in a good state of repair.

20. On the work of his stewardship, see Feilden, chapter 34.

5

The Cathedral Site before 1096

Brian S. Ayers

The cathedral church of the Holy and Undivided Trinity with its attendant medieval Benedictine priory, and the close within which both are situated, have long been thought to occupy a site which was already settled in some measure before 1096.* The *First Register* of Norwich Cathedral Priory suggests as much in its reference to the great cost of the land acquired for the seat of the bishopric.[1] Less explicitly, there is evidence that at least part of the close was previously in Blofield Hundred,[2] with an implication that settlement preceded the Conquest, while there are indications that a number of parish churches within the area probably originated in the pre-Conquest period. Settlement prior to 1096, therefore, seems probable; but the exact nature, chronology and extent of the occupation needs to be explored.

An analysis of pre-cathedral utilisation of the site has to be undertaken with an awareness of the limitations of the source materials. These limitations apply to all urban research at this period but, taken together, a variety of sources can provide considerable enlightenment when used with caution. Careful study of terrain, topography, place-names, churches, antiquarian observation, archaeological evidence and documentary sources permits a suggested framework for urban development in Norwich and some postulated detailing of the later Saxon and Saxo-Norman environment.[3]

1. *First Register*, p. 25.
2. J. Campbell, 'Norwich', in M. D. Lobel, ed., *Historic Towns* (London, 1975), p. 5 n. 45.
3. It should be emphasised, however, that many of these various types of evidence are in need of careful reassessment, although it is outside the scope of the present essay to explore such matters in detail.

* The writer is most grateful to his colleagues Phil Andrews, Barbara Green and Sue Margeson who kindly commented on aspects of this paper; to Hassell Smith and Ian Atherton for further comment; to Piers Wallace for the illustrations; and to his wife Lynn for help with the editing.

The site of the cathedral close lies to the south and west of the River Wensum, occupying an area of some forty-two acres (seventeen hectares) in the angle of the river (fig. 9). Much of the subsoil consists of sands and gravels, well-drained but, near the river, liable to flooding. Indeed, the eastern part of the site, known as Cowholme or cow pasture in the middle ages, was then, as now, too low-lying to permit many buildings. From the eastern side of the lower close, however, the land rises to the west, steepening considerably in the area of the upper close.

The river was fordable in at least two locations on the fringes of the site, where Fye Bridge and Bishop Bridge now stand. The latter is the lowest fording point on the Wensum and was probably used as the crossing for a Roman road from Brundall.[4] Sporadic finds of Roman material along its course and some topographical reconstruction suggest that this road was aligned on Bishopgate as it runs from the bridge to the Great Hospital site; then it veered slightly to pass beneath the cathedral church itself before leaving the area of the precinct in the approximate location of Erpingham Gate.[5] Such a Roman road would have needed a causeway for the length of Bishopgate, although thereafter it would have been situated on the gravel terrace. This gravel extends north of the close to a spur of land called *Bichil* in medieval documentation,[6] at the southern end of another early bridge, that of St Martin.[7] It has been suggested that this was the crossing for a north-to-south road which also ran through the site of the close, effecting a junction with the Roman road approximately where the central tower of the cathedral church now stands.[8] Such a north-to-south road may, however, be a late Saxon feature and cannot be discussed yet.

Evidence for prehistoric, Roman and early Saxon activity within the cathedral precinct can largely be discounted. Admittedly, Roman material is located occasionally within the close but in nearly all cases it derives from medieval robbing of Roman sites, as in the case of the Roman material used for core-work in the excavated Norman apse of the cathedral. Admittedly, too, possible early Saxon pottery sherds have been recovered within the cathedral close, from sites within the area of Norwich School.[9] These, together with similar finds at

4. B. Green and R. Young, *Norwich: The Growth of a City* (Norwich, 1981), p. 8.

5. See A. Carter, 'The Anglo-Saxon Origins of Norwich: The Problems and Approaches', *Anglo-Saxon England*, 7 (1978), pp. 175–204, fig. 7.

6. K. I. Sandred and B. Lindstrom, 'The Place-Names of Norfolk, i, The Place-Names of the City of Norwich', *English Place-Name Society*, 61 (1989), p. 138.

7. Recorded in 1106: C. Johnson and H. A. Cronne, eds, *Regesta regum Anglo-Normanno-*rum, *1066–1154*, ii, *Regesta Henrici Primi, 1100–1135* (Oxford, 1956), p. 55.

8. Carter, 'Anglo-Saxon Orgins', p. 193 and fig. 7.

9. Sites 45N and 46N excavated by Tony Baggs in 1956 and 1958: D. M. Wilson and J. G. Hurst, 'Medieval Britain in 1956', *Medieval Archaeology*, 1 (1957), p. 148; and D. M. Wilson and J. G. Hurst, 'Medieval Britain in 1958', *Medieval Archaeology*, 3 (1959), p. 298.

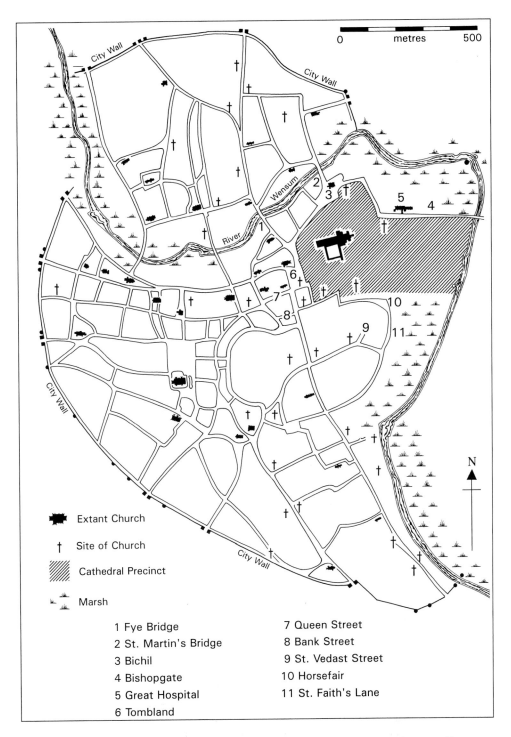

Fig. 9. Map of Norwich showing the medieval street pattern, existing churches, the sites of lost churches, the location of the cathedral close and street names mentioned in the text.

St Michael at Pleas, Redwell Street, are the only discoveries from this period within the walled area of the medieval city. They *may* indicate an early Saxon settlement but, despite the obvious advantages of a low-lying, well-drained and relatively flat site, the likelihood of such a settlement prior to the middle Saxon period remains slender.

The evidence for middle Saxon settlement (probably in the eighth century) within a limited area of the close is more positive. Excavations in 1956 and 1975 in the vicinity of Norwich School (45N, 46N: see fig. 10 for the location of such sites) produced Ipswich-type ware – a hard, grey pottery fabric found almost ubiquitously on sites of middle Saxon date in East Anglia. The material could not be associated with any features,[10] but the extent of the occupied area can be roughly postulated from negative evidence to the north at St Martin at Palace Plain (450N)[11] and to the south within the lower close (300N).[12] Recent excavation within the church of St Martin at Palace (584N), however, has unearthed a grave, the radiocarbon analysis for which also implies a possible middle Saxon date;[13] and middle Saxon pottery, again unassociated with features, was located beneath the Greyfriars precinct (845N), south of the close, in 1992–93. Currently, for the general area of the close, the evidence is thus equivocal; there is sufficient data to suggest some middle Saxon occupation, but not enough to indicate an embryonic urban settlement. Rather, the implication is of a small community of perhaps a few houses grouped on the gravel terrace close to a good ford over the Wensum.

Such a hamlet can possibly be identified with *Conesford*, a place-name which perhaps originated in the eighth century. Although as *Conesford* it is an Anglo-Scandinavian formation meaning 'King's Ford', and therefore of the ninth century or later, the Old Danish word '*kunung*' may have replaced the earlier Old English '*cyning*'.[14] It is not known to which ford the name refers; it could be either that at Fye Bridge or Bishop Bridge. The latter is perhaps more favoured, as the ford to the east allowed access to Thorpe where there may have been a royal (later episcopal) manor. Episcopal control of this manor in post-Conquest times led to the claim, referred to above, that parts of the city west of the river were historically in Thorpe (in Blofield Hundred) and the place-name could, therefore, be confirmatory evidence of early royal suzerainty.

Until the later ninth century it can, at best, be suggested that part of the close contained emerging settlement. Such occupation as can be inferred appears to have

10. M. W. Atkin and D. Evans, eds, *Excavations in Norwich: The Norwich Survey*, iii (East Anglian Archaeology), forthcoming.

11. B. S. Ayers, *Excavations at St Martin-at-Palace Plain, Norwich, 1981* (East Anglian Archaeology, 37, 1987).

12. Atkin and Evans, *Norwich Excavations*.

13. O. B. Beazley, *Excavations in the Church of St Martin-at-Palace, Norwich, 1987* (East Anglian Archaeology), forthcoming.

14. Sandred and Lindstrom, 'Place-Names of Norwich', p. 114.

lain north of the probable east-to-west Roman road, between it and the river. There is no evidence as yet that any occupation was at all urban in character. If urbanisation did take place in Saxon times it seems to have owed its origins to subsequent development in the last two centuries prior to the Norman Conquest. Study of this process needs to be undertaken in the context of the Anglo-Scandinavian and late Saxon town as a whole.

Evidence of early Norwich is sparse for urban historians. There is sufficient data to suggest some middle Saxon activity: both the town and the county had an Anglo-Scandinavian heritage that was clearly long and influential, as is shown by the number of its Anglo-Scandinavian street-name formations and late church dedications – for example Fishergate and Snaylgate (Calvert Street) and two churches dedicated to St Olaf. By the second quarter of the tenth century Norwich had a mint;[15] and as a settlement it was mentioned favourably in the *Liber Eliensis*.[16] The town was clearly well established by 1004 when, according to the Anglo-Saxon Chronicle, it was 'completely sacked' by Sweyn of Denmark.[17] This, and the mint and the Ely evidence, however, serve only to indicate that, by the second half of the tenth century at the latest, the town must have been growing considerably in importance. This importance is emphasised when it is considered that Norwich recovered from the Danish sack to such an extent that, by 1066, it was a major settlement,[18] and by 1086 probably the fourth largest borough in the country. The essential problem is that, despite this rapid late expansion, the location of the tenth-century town remains elusive.

In the current state of knowledge, it seems likely that initially it was centred on the north bank of the River Wensum (the probable site of a middle Saxon nucleus), within defences which may have been established during Anglo-Scandinavian rule of the Danelaw (i.e. before 917). Archaeological evidence for occupation on the south bank – from sites such as St Martin at Palace Plain (450N), Anglia Television (416N) and the nearby Castle Mall site – indicates that urban activity only started here in the eleventh century.[19] Once established, however, settlement increased dramatically in importance, shifting the focus from but not abandoning that on the north bank.

This migratory urban process is paralleled elsewhere: examples can be cited, from varying periods and for various reasons, from the ninth to the eleventh centuries, at York, London, Thetford, Southampton and Hedeby/Schleswig among

15. Green and Young, *Norwich*, p. 10.
16. Campbell, 'Norwich', p. 3.
17. G. N. Garmonsway, trans. and ed., *The Anglo-Saxon Chronicle* (London, 1953), p. 135.
18. P. Brown, ed., *Domesday Book: Norfolk* (Chichester, 1984), pp. 116–17.

19. Ayers, *Palace Plain*; B. S. Ayers, *Excavations in the North-East Bailey of Norwich Castle, 1979* (East Anglian Archaeology, 28, 1985); E. Shepherd, *Excavations South of Norwich Castle Mound, 1987–91*, forthcoming.

others.[20] The crucial question within the context of this volume is whether the cathedral site was central or peripheral to this eleventh-century expansion of Norwich. For some time a view has been held that the cathedral site was a prime focus of pre-Conquest urban settlement.[21] Recently, however, it has been argued that settlement within the close was sparse and peripheral before the Conquest and that the cathedral had been developed on a largely vacant site or that, at most, 'suburban' occupation took place 'just before the Norman Conquest'.[22] In part this revision is linked to the attempt to explain the rather equivocal results of several small exploratory archaeological excavations within the close which, inter alia, also established that there is no evidence to support any idea of a defended enclosure on the south bank of the river and that the only known pre-Conquest enclosure remains that to the north.

Despite this revision a strong case can still be made for the development of the cathedral site prior to 1066 as an area of primary urban occupation. Clearly parts of the site were peripheral to later Saxon urban development (site 300N is a salient case in point), but analysis of topography and parochial development, consideration of the apparent location of a market and possible institutional involvement in urban planning, together with archaeological observation, combine to suggest that an urban community of some size and importance developed during the eleventh century.

Topographically, the modern street pattern in the vicinity of the close is convoluted enough to suggest that the imposition of the cathedral precinct disrupted a pre-existing plan. The disposition of both east-to-west and north-to-south routes points to disruption rather than intentional layout. Indeed, leaving aside the probable alignment of the east-to-west Roman road referred to above (p. 60), an analysis of the city's street pattern within the close area, in concert with the known edge of the gravel terrace, is revealing.

Initially it is possible to suggest a pre-close road roughly following the line of the river by running along the gravel terrace which rises above the flood plain. It started at St Martin at Palace Plain, where excavation has demonstrated that the

20. R. A. Hall, 'York, 700–1050', in R. Hodges and B. Hobley, eds, *The Rebirth of Towns in the West, AD 700–1050* (Council for British Archaeology, research report no. 68, 1988), pp. 125–32; A. Vince, *Saxon London: An Archaeological Investigation* (London, 1988); P. Andrews, *Excavations in Thetford* (East Anglian Archaeology), forthcoming; M. Brisbane, 'Hamwic (Saxon Southampton): An Eighth-Century Port and Production Centre', in Hodges and Hobley, *Rebirth of Towns*, pp. 101–108; E. Roesdahl, *Viking Age Denmark* (London, 1982).

21. Carter, 'Anglo-Saxon Origins'; Atkin and Evans, *Norwich Excavations*; M. W. Atkin *et al.*, *Excavations in Norwich, 1971–1978, Part ii* (East Anglian Archaeology, 26, 1985); J. Bown, *Excavations on Calvert Street, 1989–90* (East Anglian Archaeology), forthcoming.

22. Atkin and Evans, *Norwich Excavations*.

existing road occupies the edge of the terrace.[23] The early alignment can be followed along the (now lost) line of World's End Lane before turning south along a lost section of Holmestreet (closed by 1550) to join the north-to-south section of Bishopgate.[24] It could then have continued southward to meet St Faith's Lane at Horsefair (hugging the edge of the terrace the entire way) before terminating at the junction of St Faith's Lane (now Mountergate) with King Street. It is possible, therefore, to postulate a curving riverine, or at least marsh-edge, road which effectively delimited the settlement to its east and south.

The existence of such a road does not, of course, necessarily indicate occupation within the area which it bounded (including the area of the close west of Hook's Walk). It does, however, provide a basic framework within which more detailed occupation can be suggested. There are sufficient surviving topographical elements (St Vedast Street; St Faith's Lane; St Martin at Palace Plain) to suggest the possibility of north-to-south streets while a connecting grid of east-to-west streets can be implied from the Roman road and relict streets (Queen Street, Bank Street) still extant to the west of Tombland. The resulting 'gridiron' plan of a settlement may look fanciful (fig. 10) but it can, of course, be paralleled in other English towns. Wessex provides some obvious examples,[25] but others can be cited from areas closer to Norwich such as Bedford.[26]

The probability of the existence of this grid layout is strengthened by the location of other topographical features. Chief amongst these are the open areas of Tombland and Palace Plain or *Bichil*. Both sites retain much in common. Each was almost certainly rectangular in form, although parts have been eroded by development in subsequent centuries. The church of St George Tombland is an obvious, probably twelfth-century, encroachment on Tombland, while it could be argued that the block of property east of St Martin at Palace (and which was partially excavated in 1972) represents encroachment on open space there. Frontages at both locations have been extended, narrowing the width of space.[27] Each site had a substantial church within it, located centrally but towards one end. That of St Martin at Palace survives; that of St Michael Tombland was destroyed after 1096. Each site was probably a market. The location of *Bichil* and the name of Tombland would suggest this,[28]

23. B. S. Ayers and P. Murphy, 'A Waterfront Excavation at Whitefriars Street Car Park, Norwich, 1979', in *Waterfront Excavation and Thetford Ware Production, Norwich* (East Anglian Archaeology, 17, 1983), pp. 1–60; Ayers, *Palace Plain*.

24. Ayers, *Palace Plain*; the location is indicated on fig. 97.

25. M. Biddle and D. Hill, 'Late Saxon Planned Towns', *Antiq. J.*, 51 (1971), pp. 70–85.

26. Here Haslam suggests a plantation as early as the eighth century: J. Haslam, 'The Origin and Plan of Bedford', *Bedfordshire Archaeological Journal*, 16 (1983), pp. 29–36.

27. Atkin and Evans, *Norwich Excavations*.

28. Sandred and Lindstrom, 'Place-Names of Norwich', p. 148, where it is noted that 'tom' means 'free from' or 'empty'.

although a reference of *c.* 1300 in the *First Register* of Norwich Cathedral Priory speaks of 'terra vocabatur terra Sancti Michaelis *et nunc* est ibi le Tombland' ('land called the land of St Michael and now is the Tombland'), implying that the name could be quite late.[29] The importance of Tombland is suggested further by the reputed location of the earl's palace at its southern end.[30]

The number and location of probable pre-Conquest churches is also indicative of urban growth. Estimates of eleventh-century church numbers vary, but there is general agreement that between twenty-three and twenty-five churches existed in Norwich at the time of the Conquest.[31] Only nine of these are mentioned by name in either pre-Conquest documentation (two) or Domesday Book (seven) but, significantly, three are or were on the fringes of the close (St Michael Tombland, St Martin at Palace and, a little further away, SS. Simon and Jude) and two were within the close (St Mary in the Marsh and Christ Church alias Holy Trinity).[32] A late twelfth-century document reiterates the early origins of St Mary in the Marsh (although allowance for special pleading should perhaps be made) when it states that 'within the said place called Cowholm was situated a church of St Mary which was founded long before the Conquest . . .'[33]

The situation of these churches also tends to confirm a pre-Conquest grid layout of what was to become the cathedral site. The location of St Mary in the Marsh is known (fig. 10) and, indeed, it has been suggested that much of No. 10 The Close contains fabric of this building. The site of Christ Church/Holy Trinity (fig. 10) can also be inferred. Observation of burials below the north wall of the bishop's palace in 1960, and the excavation in 1987–88 of further burials (792N), suggest that the church and graveyard may have been located close to the present north transept of the cathedral church.[34] The evidence remains equivocal but location here would site the foundation on a crossroads formed by the east-to-west Roman road and a north-to-south road extending from a river crossing at *Bichil* to St Vedast Street (fig. 10). The line of this road was suggested by the late Alan Carter.[35] Although evidence for it remains slender, the hypothesis is fortified by a lack of contradictory data and considerable circumstantial evidence. The existence of a

29. *First Register*, p. 26; my italics.
30. See below, pp. 70–71.
31. Carter, 'Anglo-Saxon Origins', pp. 194–95, where the arguments are summarised.
32. The evidence for Christ Church comes from Sifflead's will (*c.* 990–1066) and for Holy Trinity from Domesday Book: D. Whitelock, ed., *Anglo-Saxon Wills* (London, 1930), no. xxxviii; Brown, *Domesday Book*. Current thinking suggests that they were one and the same foundation.

Campbell, 'Norwich', appendix ii.
33. W. Hudson and J. C. Tingey, *The Records of the City of Norwich*, 2 vols (Norwich, 1906–10), i, p. 52.
34. A. Whittingham, 'The Foundation of Norwich Cathedral', *Arch. J.*, 137 (1980), p. 313; J. Bown, 'Excavations next to the North Transept of Norwich Cathedral, 1987', *NA*, forthcoming.
35. Carter, 'Anglo-Saxon Origins', p. 193 and fig. 7.

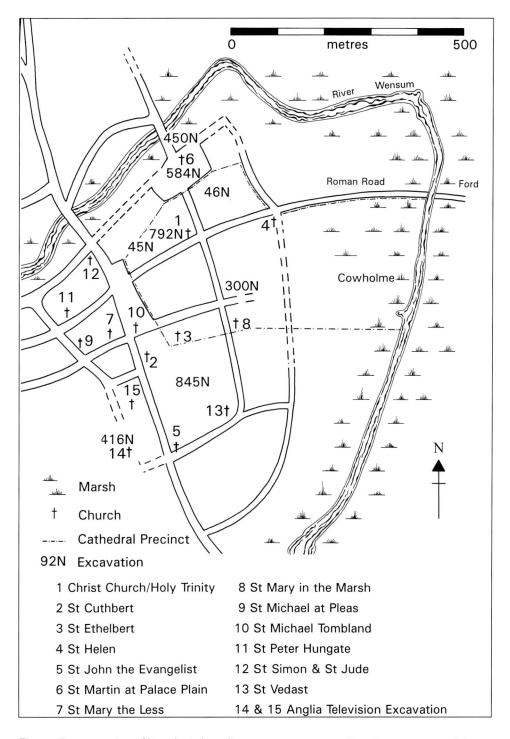

Fig. 10. Reconstruction of hypothetical rectilinear street pattern preceding the construction of the close. Churches and excavation sites mentioned in the text are marked.

north-to-south route would link the pre-Conquest churches of St Martin at Palace
and (the presumed site of) Christ Church; it would proceed southward to the
(reputedly) pre-Conquest church of St Mary in the Marsh and thence to the site
of the church of St Vedast. The latter is not known from documentation as
pre-Conquest and may be later in origin, notwithstanding James Campbell's suggestion that it acted as a focus for an early (i.e. pre-Conquest) Flemish community,[36]
and the discovery here of a pre-Conquest cross shaft.[37] Should all these churches
be pre-Conquest foundations, however, at least three of them could have stood at
road intersections (fig. 10). The extraordinary number of early and presumed early
churches in the city which are or were located in a similar topographical situation
is obvious from fig. 10 where the churches of St Cuthbert, St Mary the Less, St
Michael at Pleas, St Peter Hungate and SS. Simon and Jude all occupy corner sites.

It thus becomes possible, by locating the sites of other possible pre-Conquest
churches (such as St Ethelbert and St Helen) and extending alignments of existing
streets, to construct a grid system for late Saxon urban development as outlined
above (p. 65). Such an exercise is partly based on the premise that all the churches
are pre-Conquest foundations, but there is some internal consistency in that known
and postulated elements combine to suggest a settlement area centred on Tombland
with established north-to-south and east-to-west links.

It can be objected that there is, as yet, little archaeological or structural evidence
to support this hypothesis; that the proposed area is excessively large; and that the
formation of such a cohesive, rectilinear settlement implies centralised planning on
too grand a scale. Each argument can, however, be countered.

Archaeological material certainly remains scanty, although excavation within the
area of the close has hardly been extensive. Vestigial elements of Saxo-Norman
structures were identified by excavation in the area of Norwich School;[38] evidence
from St Martin at Palace Plain also suggests eleventh-century occupation;[39] and a
possible 'late Saxon' pit has been observed below the foundations south east of the
cathedral church crossing.[40] Most recently, excavations in 1993 beneath the site of
the Franciscan friary (845N), which stood to the south of the cathedral close, have
not only located structures of Saxo-Norman date but have also uncovered part of
a north-to-south road or lane. This feature, metalled in its final, fourteenth-century
phase, by flint with ruts or drain runs at either side, seems to have originated in

36. Campbell, 'Norwich', p. 6.
37. W. Hudson, 'On a Sculpted Stone Recently
     Removed from a House on the Site of the
     Church of St Vedast, Norwich', *NA*, 13

(1898), pp. 116–24. This could have come
     from another building.
38. Atkin and Evans, *Norwich Excavations*.
39. Ayers, *Palace Plain*.
40. Whittingham, 'Norwich Cathedral', p. 313.

the post-Conquest period as an addition to the relict street pattern south of the close; it is clearly overlain by an early wall of the friary precinct.[41]

Nearly all sites investigated within the close have, additionally, produced pottery material of Thetford-type ware. This fabric is notoriously difficult to date precisely and is frequently found on twelfth-century sites as well as eleventh-century ones. Nevertheless, there is sufficient material to suggest that eleventh-century growth was at least on the scale envisaged by the hypothesis. That such expansion occurred in the tenth century seems unlikely given the lack of other corroborative material; a very late eleventh- to twelfth-century date seems even more unrealistic, given the probable disruption of the Conquest period (especially that engendered by the revolt of Earl Ralph de Guader in 1075 which occasioned depredation and fire) and the foundation of the cathedral and priory in 1096. It is, however, quite likely that any occupation was very late in the Anglo-Saxon period. The St Martin at Palace Plain material, while including a number of artifacts in early contexts which are clearly pre-Conquest in date, suggests that activity did not necessarily predate 1066 by a great deal.[42]

Structural evidence has been cited for evidence of pre-Conquest activity but can be dealt with summarily. The most frequently-quoted example is that of supposedly Anglo-Saxon fabric in the west wall of the cloister; recent scholarship has, however, demolished suggestions that it predates the cathedral.[43] The other example is that of foundations excavated by Dean Cranage at the east end of the church in 1930.[44] These he interpreted, probably incorrectly, as an apse for a pre-Conquest church. Recently Eric Fernie has advanced convincing arguments that the uncovered features formed part of the Norman cathedral. No other potential structural evidence for Anglo-Saxon buildings has been recovered within the close but it is clear that a local Anglo-Scandinavian tradition was preserved in early Norman work at the site (the 'Urnes'-style capital discovered in the cloister is a case in point),[45] while late Saxon work is known from the vicinity (notably at the church of St Martin at Palace, which has long-and-short work in the east wall and where recent excavations have uncovered fragments of a cross shaft and a grave-cover of tenth- to eleventh century date).[46]

The excessive size of the postulated settlement does not necessarily weaken the hypothesis, since one of the more remarkable discoveries made when six acres of the castle bailey were excavated was that pre-Conquest or, at least, Saxo-Norman

41. The road is illustrated in B. S. Ayers, *Norwich* (London, 1994), p. 33. Excavation report forthcoming as J. Bown and P. Emery, *Norwich Greyfriars* (East Anglian Archaeology).

42. Ayers, *Palace Plain*, table 1.

43. Fernie, *NC*, pp. 22–23.

44. D. H. S. Cranage, 'Eastern Chapels in the Cathedral Church of Norwich', *Antiq. J.,* 12 (1932), pp. 117–26.

45. A. Borg *et al.*, *Medieval Sculpture from Norwich Cathedral* (Norwich, 1980), p. 12.

46. Beazley, *St Martin-at-Palace Church.*

occupation appears to have extended across the entire area.[47] Settlement in Norwich was clearly extensive in the era of the Conquest and it is likely to have been most marked on the prime site adjacent to the river with easy access to water and level ground for building.

The creation of such a large and apparently rectilinear area of Norwich south of the river (as fig. 10) may have been a deliberate result of institutional policy, a form of 'urban development plan' which could reflect ambitious planning on the eve of the Conquest rather than the achievement of a densely settled urban community. It would not be appropriate to explore reasons for such a development here (although the sacking of Norwich by the Danes in 1004 can be noted in passing) but it seems evident that there were powerful ecclesiastical and lay influences in Norwich in the first half of the eleventh century which could have contributed substantially to urban growth. Foremost among these was an episcopal estate which, by 1066, was held by Stigand, archbishop of Canterbury. Stigand, besides holding the churches of St Martin at Palace and St Michael, also had 'full jurisdiction and patronage over fifty [burgesses]' while 'a woman, Stigand's sister' (*una mulier soror Stigandi*) held some thirty-two acres of land.[48] In fact, Stigand's land-holding would have been considerably larger since the church of St Michael alone had 112 acres attached, although not all of this need have been in the area of the later medieval city. Stigand was not the only magnate landholder. The church of SS. Simon and Jude was held privately by the bishop, both before and after the Conquest, while the earl of East Anglia had extensive property and, with the king, held 180 acres of land. The text of Domesday Book implies that the settlement of Norwich was effectively carved up between the king, the earl and Stigand, these three controlling the total of 1320 burgesses. This triumvirate could have developed a rectilinear town on a practically virgin site with comparative ease in the eleventh century. Such a development might explain the apparent dichotomy of a remarkably successful and densely-populated atypical town of 1066, compared to the provincial settlement of the later tenth century which was distinguished by a mint but apparently little else. This explanation cannot be overplayed, however; when Herbert de Losinga acquired the site for his foundation, he bought it from the king, by exchange with Roger Bigod, *and from the citizens*.[49]

Development of the site of the close prior to 1096 can, accepting the above model, be readily understood in the context of current knowledge of Anglo-Saxon Norwich as a whole. Urban occupation was limited prior to the eleventh century, with most nucleated settlement probably located on the north bank of the River Wensum. Expansion on the south bank seems to have been largely a phenomenon

---

47. Shepherd, *Excavations South of Norwich Castle.*

48. Brown, *Domesday Book*, p. 116a, b.

49. *First Register*, p. 24; my italics.

of the eleventh century, possibly encouraged by powerful institutions. Such a development captured a central importance for the area of Tombland. This importance is underlined by the proximity of the church of St Michael at Pleas *de Motstowe* (the 'place where assemblies are held',[50] although these need not have been pre-Conquest assemblies); the assertion that Roger Bigod had a *palatium* on Tombland, perhaps the site of the palace of the Saxon earls;[51] the similar assertion that the bishop had a 'palace' there too,[52] reputedly on the site of the Maid's Head Hotel; and the undoubted wealth and importance of the church of St Michael Tombland. It ought to be noted also that the finest piece of pre-Conquest art recovered from the city is a fragment of a walrus ivory pectoral cross of tenth-century date, found during excavations for the Tombland public lavatories in 1878 and now in the Victoria and Albert Museum.[53] The area of the close, immediately east of Tombland and near to the river, was almost certainly of similar significance.

Further indications of the possible density of Anglo-Saxon settlement within the cathedral precinct might have been derived from analysis of post-Conquest *hawgavel* or landgable rents (a type of ground rent) for the close area, had these survived. Such an analysis, undertaken for much of the rest of the city, tends to suggest the relative density of population of the Anglo-Saxon town, but the work is not possible within the close where the collection and recording of rents was the responsibility of the prior. Records have largely been lost, although it is known that the parish of St Mary in the Marsh was held 'solely of the church of the Holy Trinity to which they pay landgable'.[54] Recently a list of prior's landgable, which predates any known city list, was discovered in the cellarer's cartulary for part of the prior's fee or liberty outside the close at St Martin at Palace Plain.[55] There is a suggestion in this list, however, that the prior reallocated rents to redefined properties in the twelfth century, thus undermining the value of the list for historical reconstruction of the late Saxon town. As new planning was clearly even more prevalent within the close than outside, it is likely that any further landgable evidence that may be found will be similarly restricted in its usefulness.

It can be argued that the creation of the close, together with the establishment of the castle and the French Borough, formed part of an intended band of Norman settlement across the pre-existing town. The effect was certainly devastating in the short term, although the overall intention may have been less considered. Acquisition

50. Sandred and Lindstrom, 'Place-Names of Norwich', p. 85.
51. Campbell, 'Norwich', p. 6 n. 5.
52. Carter, 'Anglo-Saxon Origins', p. 191 n. 4.
53. J. Beckwith, 'An Ivory Relief of the Crucifixion', *Burlington Magazine*, 103 (1961), pp. 434–37. The cross is illustrated in Ayers, *Norwich*, p. 31.
54. Hudson and Tingey, *Records of Norwich*, i, p. 56.
55. M. Tillyard, 'The Documentary Background', in Ayers, *Palace Plain*, pp. 137–40 and plate xliii.

of the area of the prior's fee seems to have been piecemeal, with the bishop perhaps holding part of the area as early as 1081;[56] and certainly the major eastern and northern parts of the liberty were not acquired until 1101 and 1106.[57]

The case for extensive Anglo-Saxon and Saxo-Norman settlement beneath the site of the cathedral close must remain unproven. The balance of probability seems, however, to this writer at least, weighted towards considerable eleventh-century expansion (over an area as far east as Hook's Walk and beyond the precinct wall to both the north and the south) rather than towards post-1096 development on largely open space. The clearance or incorporation into the close of at least one known Anglo-Saxon church and three probable ones seems to endorse this. The site was low-lying, relatively flat and well-served by both land and water routes. In short it was as ideally situated for an urban settlement as it clearly proved to be for the succeeding ecclesiastical precinct.

56. William I granted property to Herfast, bishop of Thetford, according to Domesday Book: 'Fourteen dwellings which King William gave to E[rfast] for the principal seat of the bishopric', Brown, *Domesday Book*, p. 117a; see also below, p. 73.

57. Bishop Herbert received the manor of Thorpe in 1101 and additional land 'from the bishop's land to the water, and from the bridge of St Martin to the land of St Michael': Johnson and Cronne, *Regesta regum Anglo-Normannorum*, p. 55. A map illustrating the suggested growth of the prior's fee (within which lay the close) is given as fig. 96 in Ayers, *Palace Plain*, p. 135.

6

The Romanesque Building

Stephen Heywood

This chapter will attempt to reconstruct, according to the available evidence, those parts of the Romanesque cathedral and priory buildings which have been obscured or demolished. A brief look at the documentary evidence is followed by a general description of the Romanesque buildings. A more detailed examination of different parts of the church, the conventual and episcopal buildings is undertaken, investigating aspects of the design and archaeology. The chapter finishes with an assessment of the architectural importance and context of Norwich Cathedral.[1]

The Documentary Evidence

The principal source for the early history of the cathedral is the *First Register* of Norwich Cathedral Priory compiled towards the end of the thirteenth century.[2] The writer recounts the laying of the foundation stone by Bishop Herbert de Losinga (1091–1119) in the easternmost chapel dedicated to the Holy Saviour.[3] The year, 1096, is not mentioned in the *First Register* but the *Historia Anglicana* by Bartholomew Cotton gives the date.[4] Preparations were being made at least as early as *c.* 1084 because Domesday Book refers to a gift of fourteen houses in Norwich to Bishop Herfast (1070–84) by King William 'for the principal seat of the bishopric'.[5] Bishop Herbert acquired more land during the 1090s through donations and other transactions.[6] However, the only firm reference to building works is that of the

1. Acknowledgement is made to Fernie, *NC*. Whilst there are some divergent or complimentary interpretations in this chapter, it is in large part similar to the main views expressed in the book. References will be limited to important additional material and illustrations.

2. *First Register.* fos 1v–14v.

3. *First Register*, fo. 8r.

4. B. Cotton, *Historia Anglicana*, ed. H. R. Luard (RS, 16, 1859), p. 54.

5. *DB Norfolk*, ii, fo. 117a.

6. B. Dodwell, 'The Foundation of Norwich Cathedral', *TRHS*, fifth series, 7 (1957), pp. 1–18; Fernie, *NC*, pp. 9–13.

foundation ceremony in 1096 which may post-date by as much as five years
the digging of the foundations and other preliminary site works. It will be seen
that the fabric reveals evidence of works which may have preceded the foundation
date.[7]

The author of the *First Register*, with an apparent concern for accuracy, says that
'according to the stories of old men, spoken but not written down' Herbert had
built 'as far as the altar of the Holy Cross' when he died in 1119.[8] Holy Cross was
the standard dedication for the altar which stood in the nave immediately west of
the choir screen or pulpitum. It will be seen that the fabric reveals a break at this
point, although it seems likely that a pause in building was predetermined and that
the point was reached before Herbert's death.[9] There was an interregnum of two
years during which time we can assume building ceased until the appointment of
Bishop Eborard in 1121. The *First Register* indicates that the building was completed
by Eborard who retired to Normandy in 1145.[10] Within fifty years the church as
well as the conventual buildings around the cloister to the south and the bishop's
palace to the north were in place.

A series of disasters is recorded following the completion of the cathedral. Major
fires occurred in 1171, 1272 and 1463.[11] The effect of the fires can be seen where
the limestone has turned pink, but in some cases the damage was so severe that
refacing was required. All the Romanesque roofs have been replaced. The fire of
1463 resulted in the building of a vault over the nave by Bishop Lyhart[12] and the
subsequent decisions to vault the transepts and eastern arm may have been influenced
by the risk of fire. A tempest in 1361/62 blew down the spire, damaging the
Romanesque clerestory which was rebuilt as a result.[13]

Other major alterations affecting the Romanesque fabric were the rebuilding of
the cloister following the riot of 1272, the replacement of the axial chapel by Bishop
Walter Suffield (1244–57) during the thirteenth century, the demolition of the south
transept chapels, the reshaping of the west front by the insertion of Bishop Alnwick's
window and portal during the fifteenth century and by late nineteenth-century

7.   See below, pp. 82–84, 107.
8.   *First Register*, fo. 8r.
9.   See below, pp. 99–104.
10. *First Register*, fos 9v, 13r.
11. 1171 fire: *First Register*, fo. 14v; Cotton,
     Historia Anglicana, p. 77, and for 1272 riot
     pp. 146–54; T. Stapleton, ed., *Liber de
     antiquis legibus* (Camden Society, old series,
     34, 1846), pp. 145–48; relevant parts of latter
     two transcribed in Fernie, *NC*, appendix 5,
     pp. 211–12; W. Rye, 'The Riot between

the Monks and the Citizens of Norwich in
1272', *Norfolk Antiquarian Miscellany*, 2
(1883), pp. 17–89. 1463 fire: Sir R. Baker,
A Chronicle of The Kings of England (London,
1670), p. 217.

12. Compare below, p. 187.
13. H. Wharton, *Anglia sacra* 2 vols (London,
     1691), i, p. 415; D. J. Stewart, 'Notes on
     Norwich Cathedral', *Arch. J.*, 32 (1875), p.
     37; Blomefield, *Norfolk*, iii, p. 514. See also
     below, p. 171 n. 8.

Fig. 11. East wall of crossing.

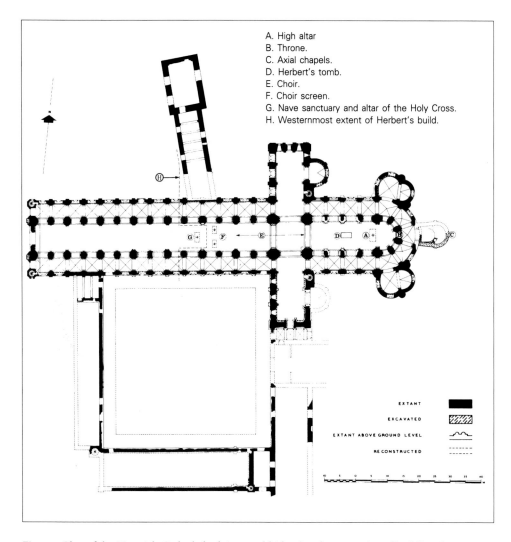

A. High altar
B. Throne.
C. Axial chapels.
D. Herbert's tomb.
E. Choir.
F. Choir screen.
G. Nave sanctuary and altar of the Holy Cross.
H. Westernmost extent of Herbert's build.

EXTANT

EXCAVATED

EXTANT ABOVE GROUND LEVEL

RECONSTRUCTED

Fig. 12. Plan of the Norwich Cathedral, cloister and bishop's palace; remains of buildings between 1091 and 1145.

restorers, the heightening of all the gallery roofs during the later middle ages, the reshaping of two nave bays to form Bishop Nix's chantry chapel and the refacing of the main arcades in the eastern arm by Bishop Goldwell.[14] During the post-medieval period the principal events were the demolition of the east and west ranges of the cloister and enthusiastic restorations by a number of architects during the nineteenth and twentieth centuries.[15]

14. See below, pp. 158–96.

15. Fernie, *NC*, pp. 157–99. See also below, pp. 705–27.

Description

Despite this alarming catalogue of demolitions and alterations Norwich Cathedral is one of the best preserved Romanesque cathedrals in Europe, with almost all the original fabric of the church surviving. This fabric consists of flint rubble and mortar faced with limestone ashlar. East Anglia has virtually no local source of freestone and the stone was imported from Caen in Normandy and Barnack (Northants.) near Stamford. In the main arcade elevations the two sorts can easily be distinguished: the grey, rough and fossil-filled stone is Barnack whilst the Caen stone is of a lighter colour and smoother texture.[16] The two types of stone alternate in a fairly regular manner. This is the simple result of the good building practice of distributing equally the different properties of two types of material. No decorative effect was intended, as all the internal surfaces were thinly plastered and painted. Some painted areas survive at the east end; in order to imagine the appearance of the building towards the middle of the twelfth century it is necessary to reconstruct painted imitation masonry throughout.

The rectangular blocks of ashlar are distinctively tooled with rough diagonal grooves made with an axe; the shafts and mouldings are similarly tooled with vertical strokes. Ashlar is used more sparingly in the conventual buildings and the bishop's palace, where the wall surfaces are faced with neat courses of large broken flint pebbles with only the openings and angles dressed with limestone.

The ground plan of the Romanesque cathedral consists of an exceptionally long aisled nave of fourteen bays, aisleless transepts and an eastern arm, each of four bays, emanating from the crossing (fig. 12). The eastern arm has in addition an arcaded apse terminating the main space of the building. The aisles continue around the back of the apse to form the ambulatory from which the radiating chapels are entered. The two-storey lateral radiating chapels have curious and complex shapes each consisting of two intersecting segments of a circle, a smaller semicircle on the eastern side forming the sanctuary and a larger irregular segment forming the nave. The angles where the segments meet and where they adjoin the ambulatory are filled externally with further circular segments forming quadrant pilasters.

The original axial chapel has been lost, except for some of its foundations which can still be seen beneath the floor of the present memorial chapel. It had a distinct horseshoe plan. Two-storey apsidal chapels also projected from the east walls of the transepts. Only the ground floor northern chapel survives. However, the arches which opened from the demolished chapels into the transepts exist, as do the roof

---

16. B. S. Ayers, 'Building a Fine City: The Provision of Flint, Mortar and Freestone in Medieval Norwich', in D. Parsons, ed., *Stone: Quarrying and Building in England, AD 43–1525* (Chichester, 1990), pp. 223–25.

lines on the exterior. The aisles and ambulatory are groin-vaulted and the radiating chapels have groin-vaulted naves with semi-domes over their apsidal sanctuaries. The north transept chapel has a barrel vault terminating in a semi-dome.

The plan and elevations of the building, along with the adjoining conventual buildings, are designed according to a system of proportions based on the relationship of the side of a square to its diagonal or in arithmetical terms one to the square root of two, or 1:1.4142 (fig. 13). The proportion is used to determine sizes from the smallest detail to the overall relationships between the main architectural spaces. For example, the diagonal of the square aisle bay is equal to the thickness of the main arcade wall plus the side of the square (fig. 14). Thus the difference between the side of the square and its diagonal determines the thickness of the arcade wall.

Similarly, if the side of the aisle square plus the thickness of the arcade wall is read as the side of a square its diagonal produces the width of the nave. The actual dimensions are 14 ft 11 in. (4.54 m.) for the width of the aisle bay, this number multiplied by the square root of two produces 21 ft 1 in. (6.42 m.), which is the thickness of the arcade wall plus the aisle width. This number multiplied by the square root of two equals the width of the nave: 29 ft 10 in. (9.1 m.). This sum is also equal to

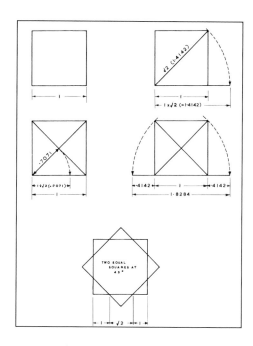

Fig. 13. The square root of two established by means of the square.

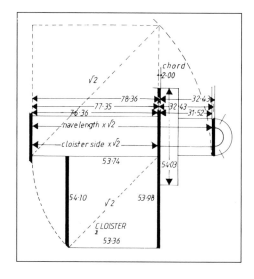

Fig. 15. Plan of church and cloister with overall dimensions.

twice the aisle width. The proportion is also used to determine the relationship between the length of the nave and the cloister dimensions, the nave length from the western crossing piers being equal to the diagonal of the cloister square. Similarly,

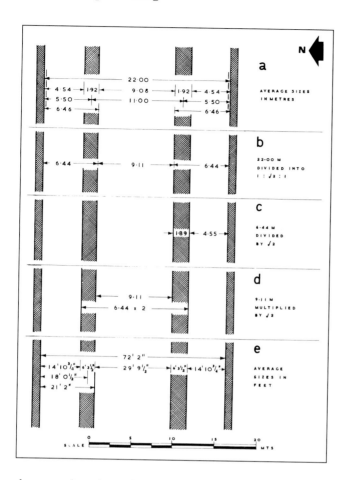

Fig. 14. Width of nave and aisles.

the nave length multiplied by the square root of two produces the length of the eastern arm to the chord of the apse (fig. 15). The ratio is also found in the elevations. For example, the width of the aisle bay is the same as the height of the piers and this dimension plus the width of the arcade wall equals the distance from the floor to the foot of the gallery. The height of the lantern ceiling multiplied by the square root of two also produces the height of the lantern tower.[17]

The medieval church was divided into two distinct parts. The eastern part was the domain of the priory, the western that of the lay public. The division between the two areas was at the third pier west of the crossing where the pulpitum still stands today. The nave altar, dedicated to the Holy Cross, stood immediately west of the pulpitum. Four circular piers, different from all the others in the nave and decorated with helical grooves, mark its position and accentuate the division. Their prominence is emphasised by a deliberate misalignment, in relation to the other piers in the main arcades, by which they project into the nave one foot off the axis

17. For a full account of proportional system see Fernie, *NC*, pp. 94–100.

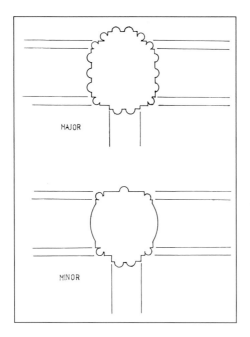

Fig. 16. Plan of major and minor pier.

of each arcade. The four piers, of which the two easternmost were encased after the 1463 fire, form a square.

The main arcades of the building are supported on two different alternating types of pier (figs 16, 41). The major pier consists of a square core with attached pilasters and shafts, whilst the minor has a circular core with fewer attached shafts. The major pier has triple half shafts on a pilaster responding to the soffit of the main arcade and nook shafts supporting the outer order. A pilaster with two half shafts and flanked by nook shafts projects into the nave and rises to the base of the clerestory, with the nook shafts stopping off to support the outer order of the gallery storey.

The minor pier has segments of its circular core responding to the soffit of the main arcade, nook shafts supporting the outer order and a single half shaft projecting into the nave space rising to support the outer order of the gallery storey. On the aisle sides both types of pier have a pilaster with two half shafts responding to the transverse arch. Finally, the shafts and pilasters which project into the nave space rose to the tops of the walls aligned to elements of the roof structure. They have since been replaced by fifteenth-century wall shafts supporting the vaults.

The Romanesque internal elevations, best appreciated in the nave, are of three storeys (fig. 17). The middle or gallery storey is of the same dimensions as the main arcade. It differs from it in so far as all the piers have square or rectangular cores and the arches are of three orders instead of two. The only alternation is that determined by the main piers below. The clerestory provides a direct source of light to the nave. Each bay consists of a central arch corresponding to the window and flanked by smaller arches which are supported on free-standing columns. The window is on the outside surface of the wall whilst the tripartite arrangement is on the inside, divided by a wall passage replacing the core of the wall. The area of wall between each clerestory bay is decorated with blind arcading, most units of which were filled in when the vaults were erected (fig. 21).

There is a final important point concerning the original appearance of the interior. The nave, transepts and eastern arm (except for the apse and aisles) were originally without stone vaults, having instead a simple timber roof probably without a ceiling.

Fig. 17. Longitudinal section looking north as in 1799, by J. A. Repton.

The Romanesque external elevations survive in a somewhat restored and altered state (fig. 18). They reflect the internal bay and storey divisions with pilasters and string courses. At ground floor level nearly all the original windows have been widened during the later middle ages. At gallery level single windows, mostly blocked, are flanked by single blind arches. The level in between the two storeys is enlivened with blind arcading which encircled the entire building. At clerestory level the windows and blind arches survive for the most part unaltered and reflect the tripartite internal arrangement. The crossing tower is Romanesque up to the base of the spire and to the eaves of the four corner turrets (fig. 19). Although a lot of the ashlar facing has been renewed during the last two centuries, the elevations most probably replicate the original as shown in the drawings of 1799 by J. A. Repton which preceded the major restorations.[18] The four corner buttresses, decorated with half

18. S. R. Pierce, *J. A. Repton: Norwich Cathedral at the End of the Eighteenth Century* (Farnborough, 1968), pls 3 and 7. Sir Bernard Feilden has suggested that the Romanesque crossing tower originally rose some 15 ft (4.6 m.) higher. This theory is based on the rough surfaces shown in Repton's sections (figs 17 and 18) on the sides of the corner turrets. For a discussion see Fernie, *NC*, pp. 42–44.

Fig. 18. South elevation and section through locutory, cloister walks and slype as in 1799, by J. A Repton.

shafts, rise above eaves level to form turrets. The surfaces in between are covered with decorative motifs. The lowest storey lights the lantern above the crossing with three windows on each face and blind arches in between. The decoration becomes more varied above this storey and new motifs are introduced. These consist of lozenges and circles enclosed in the blind arcades between the bell openings and two rows of oculi encircled by double roll mouldings to the top storey.

Eastern Arm

The eastern arm of the Romanesque church has lost its original clerestory, its roofs have been replaced, the original axial chapel has gone and the main arcades have been remodelled. There are, none the less, several clues in the surviving fabric which allow the reconstruction of its appearance in the twelfth century.

When the foundations of the present axial chapel were being excavated in 1930 those of the southern half of Herbert's chapel of St Saviour were uncovered. The remains of a still earlier smaller chapel were found, underlying the walls of the one

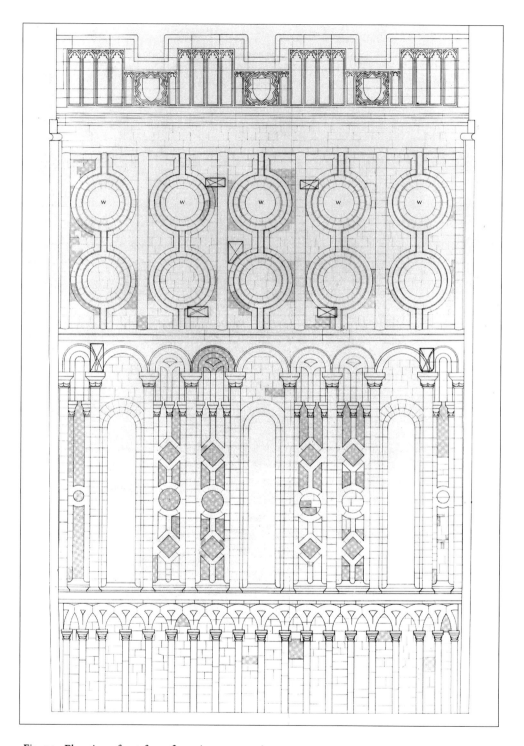

Fig. 19. Elevation of east face of crossing tower as in 1994.

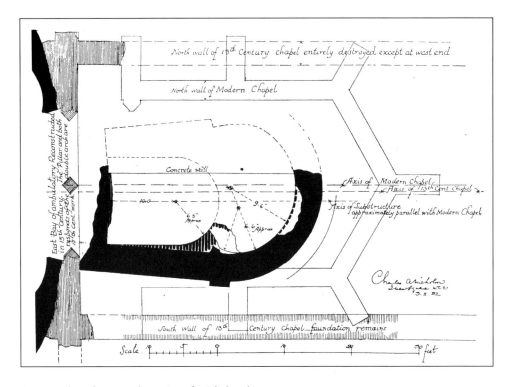

North wall of 13ᵗʰ Century chapel entirely destroyed except at west end

North wall of Modern Chapel

East Bay of ambulatory Reconstructed in 13ᵗʰ Century. The Pillar and both responds of the double arch are 13ᵗʰ Cent. work

Concrete mill

Axis of Modern Chapel
Axis of 13ᵗʰ Cent Chapel
Axis of Substructure approximately parallel with Modern Chapel

6.3 Approx
6.6 Approx

Charles Nicholson

South Wall of 13ᵈ Century chapel foundation remains

Scale. ␣␣␣␣␣␣␣␣␣␣ *feet*

Fig. 20. Plan of excavated remains of axial chapels.

that was eventually built (fig. 20). This has led to some wild speculation about the date of the earlier chapel. However, examination reveals that the fabric of these two chapels is indistinguishable, both consisting of large flint courses with similar joint widths and mortar. This suggests that there was little time between the two builds and tends to confirm the statement in the *First Register* that the building was constructed from the 'lowest foundations'.[19] The smaller chapel implies a different axis for the complete church and its plan is different from that of its successor not only in scale but also in shape, as it lacks the distinct horseshoe plan and the apse appears to have been semicircular only on the inside with a flat wall externally.[20] This leads to the conclusion that a different smaller building was originally projected and that a radical change of plan took place soon after it was begun. It is reasonable to suppose that the earlier scheme corresponds to the indications in the documents of works before the formal foundation and that when, in 1096, Herbert laid the foundation stone in this chapel the final scheme had been established.

19. *First Register*, fo. 9r.
20. D. H. S. Cranage, 'Eastern Chapels in the

Cathedral Church of Norwich', *Antiq. J.*, 12 (1932), pp. 117–36; Fernie, *NC*, fig. 6.

In 1361/62 a great wind blew down the spire which fell onto the roof of the eastern arm damaging the clerestory, which was subsequently rebuilt. Half shafts relating to the original clerestory remain in situ beside the springing points of the eastern crossing arch, a base relating to the westernmost south clerestory window survives and the imprint of the Romanesque wall passage vault is visible to the north. These features are precisely comparable to the surviving Romanesque clerestory in the rest of the building and justify its reconstruction on the same lines (fig. 21).

The reconstruction of the arrangement around the main apse and in particular its covering is not so straightforward (fig. 22). The floor of the wall passage is considerably lower in the apse and a pair of bases survive at this level indicating that arcading continued around the apse. A pair of responds at the chord

Fig. 21. South transept, west wall: northernmost bay of clerestorey.

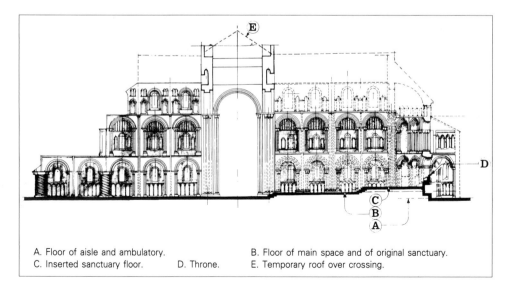

A. Floor of aisle and ambulatory.
C. Inserted sanctuary floor.   D. Throne.
B. Floor of main space and of original sanctuary.
E. Temporary roof over crossing.

Fig. 22. Longitudinal section looking north as in 1121.

of the apse, reconstructed on the original bases in the nineteenth century, supported an arch with a diaphragm wall above it. The scars of the continuation of this diaphragm wall survive at gallery level. All these indicate that the original covering of the apse was a masonry semi-dome with a row of windows at its base. The lower level of the wall passage around the apse enabled windows to be introduced which barely penetrated the fabric of the vault itself. The chord arch with diaphragm wall and the lower wall passage would have been unnecessary if the covering had been of timber. Semi-domes are used elsewhere in the building and do not represent an unpractised technique. Even the small local parish church of Fritton in Suffolk has a vaulted semi-dome with penetrating windows similar in principle to the main apse at Norwich.[21]

The row of windows along the base of the semi-dome would not have imitated the tripartite system of the clerestory elsewhere in the building, as there was simply not enough room to do so. It is probable that they were based on the smaller arches of the standard clerestory bay. It has been suggested that the shafts which divide the apse bays supported ribs.[22] This would be very plausible if the building had other examples of rib vaulting. However, the provision of ribs would give a visual function to the shafts and appropriate added emphasis to the main apse. Furthermore, rib vaults had been introduced at Durham in 1093 and there is no reason to believe the architect at Norwich would have been unaware of the new technique. The apse of Cerisy-la-Forêt (*c.* 1080) in Normandy gives a good impression of the probable original arrangement at Norwich.[23] The parallel is especially appropriate because the apse wall passage at Cerisy is at a lower level as at Norwich.

The covering of the main space of the eastern arm was of timber. Although this roof has been lost, there are indications of its shape on the eastern face of the east wall of the crossing tower (fig. 11). There is an area on this wall of painted masonry pattern which, although heavily restored, delimits the shape of the Romanesque roof. Corresponding to the edges of the painted section there is disturbed masonry which clearly reflects the line of the original roof timbers. The horizontal edge at the top of the masonry pattern probably corresponds to the collar of the Romanesque roof truss. Also of relevance to the original roof structure are the two pairs of decorative blind arches and a doorway leading from the tower wall passage into thin air. The existence of decoration within the roof space suggests that it was visible from below and that there was therefore no ceiling. However, the doorway must have originally led somewhere and its presence is often regarded as proof that there was a usable roof space and consequently a ceiling. The space could only have been lit by roof lights of some sort and seems unworthy of the decoration it received.

21. N. Pevsner and E. Radcliffe, *Suffolk* (Buildings of England, Harmondsworth, 1974), p. 225.

22. Fernie, *NC*, p. 38.

23. R. Liess, *Der Frühromanische Kirchenbau des* *11ten Jahrhunderts in der Normandie* (Munich, 1967), pp. 204–15, fig. 53; L. Musset, *Normandie Romane*, 2 vols (La-Pierre-qui-Vire, 1967), i, pp. 155–60.

The doorway may have provided access to a balcony or catwalk which would have left the decoration visible from below. The former possibility is supported by surviving slots in the masonry of the south wall of the tower corresponding to the south transept where there is a similar doorway. These holes, similar to putlog holes, are precisely on the level of the sill of the doorway and could have carried timber joists for a simple balcony. The existence of a catwalk is an equal possibility and implies that the roof had tie beams which is probable for a roof of *circa* 1100.

A comparison with surviving Romanesque roofs enables a fair idea of the original appearance at Norwich to be formed (fig. 23). It can be surmised that the wall plates were double with sole pieces and ashlar struts. The existence of at least one collar beam is suggested by the horizontal top edge to the painted area mentioned above and the absence of soulaces renders the use of tie beams unavoidable. Each truss may have had a tie beam but, given the necessity for the decorated area to be visible from below, it is more likely that only the trusses corresponding to the bay divisions had

Fig. 23. Perspective drawing of eastern arm looking west showing tentative reconstruction of the original roof.

tie beams. The half shafts and pilasters which articulate the main elevations would have provided a visual support for the tie beams. This reconstruction resembles no other known roof in detail but it does have elements based on the roofs at Waltham Abbey, Peterborough Norman Hall and Soignies Abbey, Belgium.[24]

24. For Waltham and Peterborough Norman Hall: C. A. Hewett, *English Cathedral and Monastic Carpentry* (Chichester, 1985), pp. 2–4. Soignies: R. Maere and L. Delferière, 'La Collégiale St-Vincent de Soignies', *Revue Belge d'archéologie et d'histoire de l'art*, 8 (1938), pp. 5–48; J. Fletcher, 'Medieval Timberwork at Ely', in BAACT, 2, *Ely, 1979*, ed. N. Coldstream and P. Draper (1979), fig. 2, p. 62.

At gallery level there are various indications of the original appearance. The original height of the external walls can be established by identifying the surviving Romanesque splayed windows and the imprints of the steeply pitched lean-to roofs visible on the eastern faces of the transepts (fig. 24). The responds which now support the flying buttresses originally carried half arches which traversed the gallery to reply to the taller responds against the piers. The same arrangement of half arches existed in the nave. The two arches at the chord of the apse were full semicircles and they supported diaphragm walls, the remains of which are easily identified. The upper storeys of the radiating chapels are entered from the gallery ambulatory. The former large archways at their entrances have been reduced to simple doorways but the shape of the arches can be seen. The eaves level of the original external wall is marked by a distinct offset and the arches in question rose well above this level. This indicates that the lean-to roof could not have continued around the ambulatory without being interrupted by the tops of the entrances to the radiating chapels. This apparent problem can be overcome by reconstructing double-pitched roofs at right angles to the lean-to roof of the ambulatory, thus accommodating the entrance arches (fig. 25).

Fig. 24. North gallery of eastern arm looking west.

This leads to the question of how the radiating chapels were roofed. They certainly rose at least to the height of the ridge of the roofs accommodating the entrance arches, which in turn is determined by the upper wall plate of the lean-to ambulatory roof. There is no further evidence in the fabric itself and one can only speculate whether the roofs rose to single apices higher than the ridges of the adjoining roofs; or whether the apse part of each chapel had a separate lower roof as the span is less than that of the nave part. This latter configuration has the advantage of being similar to the only earlier example of the curious double-circle radiating chapel at Méhun-sur-Yèvre near Bourges.[25] However, in this case the eaves are also at a lower level.

Fig. 25. Hypothetical axonometric reconstruction of the ambulatory and radiating chapels from the north east.

The quadrant pilasters pose an interesting question. This detail is unique to East Anglia and is commonly found on the round-towered churches which are also particular to the region. In addition they are used on Herbert's chapel at North Elmham and on the radiating chapels of Bury St Edmunds Abbey.[26] Is their use on parish churches in imitation of Bury St Edmunds Abbey and the cathedral or vice-versa? The feature is too distinctive for the occurrence to be coincidental and the former explanation is the most plausible. The question of how they were treated at roof level remains. Given the delight at Norwich in pinnacles and turrets, and the unfinished appearance of them, it is probable that the quadrant pilasters were finished off as turrets with steeply pitched conical stone summits (figs 25, 26). Support for this interpretation may be found at the small Norfolk round-towered church of Haddiscoe Thorpe

25. M. Deshoulières, 'Méhun-sur-Yèvre: église collégiale Notre-Dame', *Congrès archéologique de France*, 94 (1931), pp. 329–38.

26. S. Heywood, 'The Ruined Church at North Elmham', *JBAA*, 135 (1982), pp. 1–10; S. Heywood, 'The Round Towers of East Anglia', in J. Blair, ed., *Minsters and Parish Churches: The Local Church in Transition, 950–1200* (Oxford, 1988), p. 169.

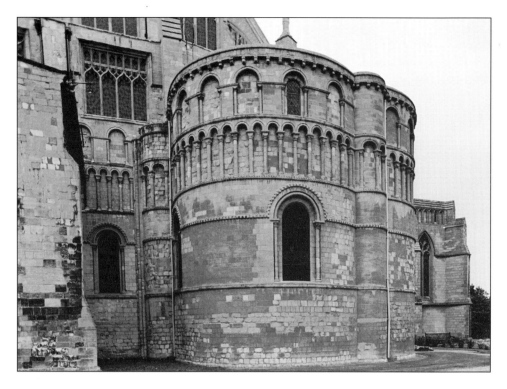

Fig. 26. South radiating chapel.

where the quadrant pilasters rise above the level of the nave roof and are capped with conical pieces of limestone (fig. 27).[27]

A distinctive characteristic of the eastern arm is that the floor level of the main space is raised markedly in relation to that of the aisles and ambulatory (fig. 22). The original bases in the sanctuary and the survival of chamfered plinths in the aisles corresponding to the raised central space show that the difference in levels is part of the original design.

The aisles in the eastern arm slope downwards markedly towards the east. The positioning of the bases indicate that this is quite deliberate and not the result of settlement or alteration. This odd sloping effect and the difference in floor levels may derive from the semi-subterranean origins of ambulatories. The precursors of the Romanesque ambulatory are Carolingian outer crypts which consisted of low corridors around the main apse beside relics placed beneath the sanctuary. They were specifically designed for the circulation of pilgrims and it was only at the end of the tenth century that the ambulatory was incorporated into the main

27. H. M. and J. Taylor, *Anglo-Saxon Architecture*, 3 vols (Cambridge, 1965–78), i, pp. 271–72.

church. In the centre of the outer face of the main apse arcade at Norwich there is a deep niche which probably housed relics. It is from this position that relics are normally viewed in crypts. Thus it is suggested that the arrangement at Norwich is a deliberate reference to the traditional or archaic positioning of relics.

This attachment to traditional forms is also reflected in the positioning of the bishop's throne in the apse on the axis above and physically attached to the relic chamber. This is clearly a reference to early Christian practice and follows the dictates of the *Testamentum Domini*, the fifth-century rule book on the correct form and ordering of Christian chur-ches.[28] By the eleventh century the prac-tice had been dropped in north-western Europe and its use at Norwich must be deliberately anachronistic. The modern throne incorporates pieces of damaged stone with traces of possible Anglo-Saxon decoration. It is believed that these stones are the remains of the throne of the first bishop of the East Angles, St Felix.[29] By the twelfth century

Fig. 27. Round tower with quadrant pilaster at church of St Matthias, Haddiscoe Thorpe, Norfolk.

the seventh-century throne would have been regarded as a holy relic in its own right and it might have appeared appropriate that it should be placed in the same position as it probably held in Felix's church.

The deliberate adoption of archaic forms may also be explained as an attempt to give the building an air of antiquity to compensate for the new cathedral being built on a virgin site without the cachet of it being placed over or adjacent to an ancient foundation. Most contemporary cathedrals and abbey churches were being rebuilt at established sites; Bishop Herbert was certainly aware of Winchester,

28. C. A. R. Radford, 'The Bishop's Throne of Norwich Cathedral', *Arch. J.*, 116 (1959), pp. 121–28; E. C. Fernie, 'An Architectural and Archaeological Analysis of the Sanctuary of Norwich Cathedral', *NA*, 39 (1986), pp. 296–305; *Testamentum domini*, I, xix, in C. Mango, *The Art of the Byzantine Empire, 312–1453* (Sources and Documents Series; Englewood Cliffs, NJ, 1972), p. 25.

29. See also above, fig. 4 and p. 9.

Canterbury, Ely and his arch rival at Bury St Edmunds, which all had this advantage over Norwich.

The erection of the throne and the associated blind arcaded screens filling each flanking bay represent an early alteration to the original build. The masonry of the screens is not bonded into the adjacent piers and its decoration, although Romanesque, is of a later character than that of the original work. The throne is at present perched unnecessarily high at the head of a long flight of steps. This is because during the nineteenth century the floor of the sanctuary was lowered, revealing the original bases of the chord piers and those on the eastern faces of the piers immediately west of them (fig. 22). The heightening of the floor in the sanctuary was undoubtedly part of the alterations associated with the installation of the throne, as the arrangement had the throne at the head of a flight of three steps, the number prescribed in the *Testamentum Domini*. Furthermore, the revealed bases are not damaged by fire, whilst the apse piers immediately above the level of the raised floor are. As Herbert de Losinga was enthroned bishop in Thetford before the transfer of the see, a fitting date for all these changes is 1121, the year of the enthronement of Eborard, Herbert's successor and the first bishop to be enthroned at Norwich.

The main arcades in the eastern arm have undergone major alteration since their initial construction. Despite this, their original appearance can be ascertained. By observing the gallery piers it is easy to recognise that the three westernmost pairs of piers followed the same system of alternation as the nave (figs 17, 22). Where the shafts which projected into the main space have been removed the remaining scars leave little doubt that they were the same as in the nave. At the chord of the apse each pier has a projecting pilaster with shafts which supported the chord arch and diaphragm wall. The chord piers have circular cores, which is a departure from the alternating system. The apse arcade piers are also minor and the columnar form is a deliberate choice – being a reference to the standard iconographic practice of apse arcades being supported on columns. Interestingly, at the western end of the church, the main arcade responds again depart from the alternating system with the minor pier form. This suggests that the device had the added function of emphasising the first and last bays of the building.

The apse arcade survives unaltered except that large areas of fire-damaged facing have been renewed in recent times. The arcade bays are much narrower than in the normal arcade and, in order to maintain the correct height at gallery level, they spring from a higher level and are stilted.

The Crossing and Transepts

In structural terms the crossing is the centre of the building where four arms of equal height and width abut a square structure pierced by four arches of equal size and carried up to form a massive tower. In functional or liturgical terms, however, the crossroads aspect of the space is denied as it simply forms the eastern part of the choir. The stalls originally passed in front of the north and south crossing arches as if they did not exist. Thus the furniture accentuated the east-west axis and relegated the transepts to subsidiary adjuncts. The design of the crossing piers reflects this use in the subtle treatment of the shafting. Although each face of the pier under a crossing arch has exactly the same function, the faces which correspond to the transepts are provided with pairs of half shafts whilst those to the nave are provided with sets of three, thus stressing the east-west axis. The axis is further emphasised by the responds to the east-west crossing arches being 1 ft (30 cm.) deeper than their north-south counterparts, reducing the span by 2 ft (60 cm.) The difference in spans is imperceptible to the naked eye but an effect is achieved by introducing an extra half shaft against the side of the deeper responds, thereby adding to the rhythm created by the triple half shafts. Thus the function of this space is clearly reflected in the details of its design (fig. 28).

Although the crossing tower apart from the spire is essentially of the Romanesque period, it appears that it was built in three phases corresponding to three levels below the lantern ceiling. The pauses in construction are suggested by the differences in style and the introduction of different decorative motifs. The lower wall passage

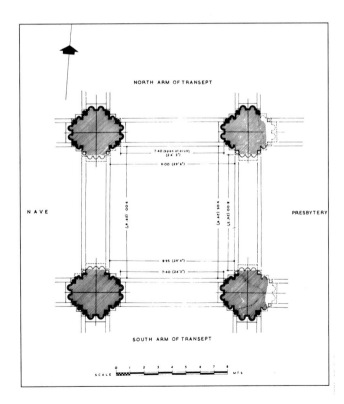

Fig. 28. Plan of crossing.

Fig. 29. Blind arcade capitals at middle storey of interior elevation of lantern tower.

Fig. 30. Blind arcade capitals on the bishop's throne screen.

is obviously part of the first phase and contemporary with the crossing arches. The second phase corresponds to the row of blind arcading which has capitals by the same workshop as that responsible for the arcaded screens beside the bishop's throne (figs 29, 30).[30] The third phase is represented by the clerestory and the rest of the lantern tower. It can be described as mannered with tightly grouped shafts and absurdly narrow side arches to the internal clerestory bays and, on the exterior of the tower, the introduction of roundels and lozenges surrounded by triple roll mouldings (fig. 19). The evidence suggests a date around the middle of the first campaign for the first phase (1100–10). The second phase is associated with the installation of the bishop's throne and the enthronement of Bishop Eborard in 1121. It is possible that the work took place during the interregnum after Eborard's appointment yet before the official ceremony. It is interesting to note that the main roofs would have risen well above the top of phase one, suggesting that some form

30. I am grateful to Jill Franklin for having brought this observation to my attention.

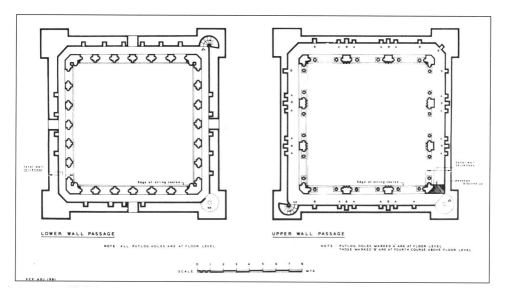

Fig. 31. Plans of lantern tower wall passages.

of temporary protection would have been required. The third phase probably took place about twenty years later, towards the end of the second campaign (*c.* 1140). A close examination of the putlog holes in the lantern tower reveals further evidence of this division into separate phases (fig. 31). At floor level in the lower wall passage there are putlog holes on each side of the tower. Each hole is opposite an arched opening and most of them correspond to a similar hole on the other side of the tower. It is clear that these holes carried a scaffolding platform which enabled masons to construct an arcade unimpeded by the putlogs. On the upper wall passage similar putlog holes exist; as they are opposite the arcade supports, they could only have served a purpose before the construction of the arcades. It is probable therefore that they served as housings for a temporary roof structure which was removed when work recommenced towards the end of the second campaign.

The pauses in construction arose from good building practice. By allowing a few years between each level the structure had the chance to settle before more weight was piled on. It is perhaps due to this practice that the lantern at Norwich is one of the few major Norman crossing towers which have not suffered serious collapse.[31]

The transept arms are aisleless, with former two-storey chapels projecting to the east from each arm and two stair turrets housed between the chapels and the aisles of the eastern arm. Circulation from the nave at gallery level is continued through

31. Problems occurred with the crossing towers at Winchester, Bury St Edmunds, Evesham, Lincoln, Ely and Peterborough.

wall passages, which also provided access to the upper chapels. The south transept was connected to the conventual buildings on the eastern side of the cloister, according to the standard monastic layout, and the north transept provided access for the bishop and his retinue. Each arm is divided into four bays by pilasters.

The outermost bays of each transept caused a number of problems for the builders. The gable ends needed to be of three bays for reasons of basic symmetry. The windows also needed to be of the same size as elsewhere. The space was limited because the width of the internal elevations was reduced by the thicknesses of the east and west walls. An ingenious solution to the problem was found by changing the profiles of the window reveals of the inner skin at middle and clerestory levels. The normal reveal consists of a nook shaft supporting an angle roll. This technique is used consistently throughout the building except in the end bays of the transepts, where the system is changed to a half shaft supporting a soffit roll. This has the advantage of maximising the width of the opening without having to reduce the overall width of the supports, which are predetermined by the pilasters dividing the elevation into bays (fig. 32).

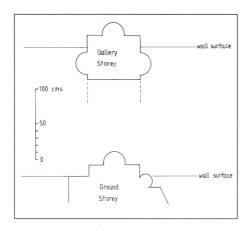

Fig. 32. Horizontal sections of gallery level pier and ground level window reveal in north transept gable end.

The harmonious treatment of these end bays is further inhibited by their narrowness and by having to accommodate on the east wall at ground and middle levels the thickness of the chapel walls (fig. 33). In the south transept the method chosen was untidy. It consisted of making the west wall bay wide enough to accommodate tripartite openings at middle and clerestory levels, whilst having to reduce the width on the east wall in order to leave room for the chapel entrance. The fenestration in the east wall is misaligned with the middle storey window offset to the south, accommodating the chapel wall, and the clerestory window recovering the centre of the bay unencumbered by the chapel wall which is only of two storeys. The result is a very irregular bay. The solution chosen for the north transept is more successful and leads one to think that the builders had learnt by their mistakes. The bay is of regular dimensions and the problem of the east wall is solved by using two thirds of the tripartite system. This allows the window to be offset, with the rest of the bay filled by the small adjoining arch. The arrangement is repeated at clerestory level maintaining vertical alignment.

Fig. 33. Cross section of transepts, looking east, as in 1799, by J. A. Repton.

The north transept is distinguished by the provision of lavish decoration. The bishop's doorway in the north wall is announced on the exterior by a near life-size relief carving of a bishop housed in a niche directly above the door.[32] On the interior the doorway is surmounted by a blind arcade with finely carved capitals and twinned triangular arches of billet moulding above. The end wall is further decorated with three projecting grotesque heads. Similar heads may have projected from the bases of the blind arcade above the stair doorway in the east wall. The doorway itself has a lavishly decorated tympanum and carved hood mould. Finally, some of the clerestory and middle storey columns are polygonal and some are adorned with a variety of surface motifs.[33]

There is a final feature which greatly affects the impression of the original appearance of the cathedral. The staircases which are fitted into the angles between the transepts and the eastern arm rose up to form towers decorated with three storeys of blind arcading. Similarly there were tall turrets flanking the gable ends of the transepts. These towers had been dismantled by the early nineteenth century but they are represented in early engravings and are clearly shown on the detail of the cathedral on James Corbridge's map of Norwich of 1727.[34]

The Ending of the First Campaign

The *First Register* of Norwich Cathedral tells us that when Herbert de Losinga died in 1119 building had reached the altar dedicated to the Holy Cross, that is, the nave altar which stood to the west of the pulpitum. The present pulpitum is a heavily restored late medieval version built after the fire of 1463. It is very probable that it stands in the same position as the Romanesque pulpitum because the four decorated round piers marked the position of the nave altar. Furthermore, the easternmost pair of decorated piers were so badly cracked and eroded by the fire that they had to be encased in masonry (fig. 34). The four piers east of this line were also badly damaged, but not so severely, whilst those to the west were only slightly damaged. This shows that there was more wooden furniture in the eastern part of the nave because the fire had more inflammable material to fuel it. It was particularly intense at the westernmost point of the choir where the encased decorated piers are situated and where, it can be inferred, the Romanesque timber screen stood with choir stalls east of it.

A departure from the standard ground plan of the main arcade piers occurs in the second bay of the south arcade (fig. 35). The three half shafts on the eastern

32. The relief in the niche is a glass fibre fac-simile of the original which has been moved into the ambulatory.

33. For the Romanesque sculpture see also below, pp. 116–35.

34. For illustration of this detail see Fernie, *NC*, pl. 12 p. 37.

Fig. 35. Nave: south pier 2 seen from the east.

Fig. 34. Nave: north pier 3 seen from the
north east.

face of the second pier rise from an arched corbel table at approximately six feet
from ground level. This is not the result of an alteration: because the masonry
courses perfectly and there is no sign of the half shafts having been cut back in
any way. The surface of the minor pier which faces this also has a flat section of
wall rather than the standard segmental shape, although the thin joints between
the ashlar blocks and the smooth tooling suggest that it is a late medieval alteration.
The deliberate variation to the form of the second pier relates to the use of the
Romanesque choir. The lack of any further evidence only allows vague speculation
but it occurs in the area where the first campaign ended and may be interpreted
as a processional entrance to the new choir or possibly as provision for a small
chapel.

There is evidence in the fabric for a pause in building in this vicinity. Whether
the pause was directly caused by the death of Herbert is open to debate, as the
completion of the monks' choir allowed the church to come into use and was the
natural place to pause and take stock. Breaks at this point in other major monastic

Fig. 36. Nave: south aisle
blind arcading in bay 2.

churches were commonly observed and the likelihood that it was predetermined
suggests that Herbert's death in 1119 should be regarded as a *terminus ante quem* for
the first campaign.

Changes of decorative detail and minor errors occur all over the building. Some
of these changes have been regarded as building breaks or indications of a change
of plan, of mason or of a campaign. Building breaks occur not only at the end of
a campaign but also after a year's work and even a day's work. Indeed progress
in the building of a wall can sometimes be followed in minute detail by detecting
the hairline joints which occur at the end of each 'lift', thereby identifying a
pause in building of as little as a day to allow the mortar to set.[35] The break which
occurs at the completion of the monks' choir can be identified as a major break
because of numerous changes occurring at the same point. Each change might
be seen in itself as immaterial but their accumulation leads to a more definite
conclusion.

The evidence for the break is stepped, with indications in bays five and six at
ground level, three and four at gallery level and bay three in the clerestory. At
ground level an excavation which took place in 1899 revealed a rubble bed extending
from the east to a straight line corresponding to the eastern faces of the fourth pair
of piers (fig. 12). Its eastern extent is not known. At the level of the main arcades,
eighteenth-century drawings by J. A. Repton and W. Wilkins show that billet-
moulded hoods are absent in the first four bays on the north side and the first three

35. For an illustration and discussion of 'lifts'
see W. J. Rodwell, 'Anglo-Saxon Church
Building: Design and Construction', in L.
A. S. Butler and R. K. Morris, eds, *The*
Anglo-Saxon Church: Papers on History Archi-
tecture and Archaeology in Honour of Dr H. M.
Taylor (CBA Research Report no. 60,
1986), pp. 159–61.

Fig. 37. Nave: south aisle
blind arcading in bay 4.

Fig. 38. Nave: south gallery
pier 3 from the north.

on the south.[36] The hoods which now exist are modern. In the south aisle wall the blind arcading in bays four and six (bay five arcading has been replaced) is of an inferior quality. The voussoirs have no cavettos and the bases are roughly squared without any moulding (figs 36, 37). The impression gained is that materials were in short supply, as might be expected towards the end of a campaign. The decorated fifth pier in the south arcade produces the same impression, as the top three courses of ashlar have been laid as plain blocks, without the grooving. The evidence suggests that the break at main arcade level occurs in bays four and five, the west pair of decorated piers having then been built.

At gallery level the principal evidence for a break is the third pair of piers, where each pier is markedly wider to the west of the half shaft than to the east (fig. 38). This has the effect of making the outer order of the arch springing from its western side eccentric in relation to the other orders. This unhappy mistake is repeated and accentuated along the entire north gallery arcade, west of the pier in question. Although the same initial mistake is made on the south arcade, it is almost immediately corrected. This suggests that all the gallery piers west of the break on the north side were built before those on the south; when the arches were thrown the mistake was recognized in time for the design of the south gallery piers to be adjusted. The pair of piers which caused this error were the last gallery piers to be built towards the end of the programme. As precisely the same irregularity occurs on both piers, it is fitting to ask whether or not it was deliberate. Could it have had something to do with provision for a temporary roof? Or might plans for the pulpitum which was situated here have a bearing? There is not enough evidence for more than speculation, but it is clear that if it was deliberate the fact was forgotten by the time building recommenced.

At clerestory level the evidence for a pause in building can be recognized by a distinct change in design on the north side. In bay 4 the vault over the central arch is altered in order to accommodate blind arches which had been introduced on each side of the opening (fig. 39). This complicated design is repeated in a slightly simpler form in bays five, six and seven, whereupon the following bay reverts to the original form. On both sides of the nave, bays one, two and three have a mixture of volute and cushion capitals whilst cushion capitals are used exclusively in all the remaining clerestory bays westwards (figs 39, 40).

---

36. For the rubble bed see W. St John Hope and W. T. Bensly, 'Recent Discoveries in the Cathedral Church of Norwich', *NA*, 14 (1901), pp. 115, 126, with plan facing p. 125; Pierce, *Repton*, pl. 5; W. Wilkins, London, Society of Antiquaries, MS 766.

Fig. 39. Nave: north clerestory bays 4 and 5 from the south-east.

Fig. 40. Nave: north clerestory bay 3.

The Completion of the Church

Bishop Eborard was appointed in 1121 and we are told that he had completed the construction of the church and the immediate conventual buildings by the time of his retirement in 1145.

The nave bays are the most complete of the Romanesque building and they provide an almost uninterrupted view of the original internal elevation (fig. 41). Despite the impression of perfect balance there are some radical departures from symmetry. The principal one is the difference between the two gallery arcades. The eccentric shape of the order decorated with chevron on the north side has already been discussed above. The mistake and its correction on the south side also have the effect of rendering the minor piers on the north side much wider than their counterparts on the south. Consequently the major piers on the south side are noticeably wider than those on the north.

Fig. 41. Nave interior:
north elevation looking east.

Fig. 42. Nave interior: west wall.

There is a further difference between the two galleries in that they are at different levels. This would be imperceptible if the builders had not returned the string courses marking the floor levels onto the west wall. The string courses become the abaci of narrow two-bay blind arcades which are at markedly different levels. It is a mystery why the builders chose to underline their error (fig. 42).

There are several other changes of detail which occur at various intervals along the nave. These may indicate pauses, changes of masons or simply a taste for variety. It would be inappropriate to enumerate these here.

The Conventual Buildings

The Romanesque conventual buildings have suffered considerably from alteration and destruction since the Reformation, but some still remain, like the locutory, with barrel vault and transverse arches, at the northern end of the west range. On the south side of the cloister the barrel-vaulted dark entry survives with the roofless refectory beside it.

Enough remains of the refectory in order to see that it was one of the most splendid in Europe (fig. 43). The lower level of the interior was decorated with

Fig. 43. Refectory: interior of north wall from the south east.

Fig. 44. Refectory: single surviving bay of blind arcading in south-east corner.

interlaced blind arcading of which only one bay survives in the south-east corner and with fragmentary indications in the north-west corner (fig. 44). The blind arcades were divided into bays by pilasters which rose up to form the supports of a wall passage which ran around the full extent of the building. Access was gained by stairs at the north-west and south-east corners. The passage passed in front of the clerestory which survives only on the north side and consists of twenty-four closely spaced windows with the springings of the wall passage arches in between. Towards the eastern end of the north wall there is a shallow depression at wall passage level. Immediately behind this on the external face is a buttress which presumably counteracted the thrust of a two- or three-bay arcade which defined the dais end of the refectory. The depression exists in order to allow for circulation behind a respond encroaching on the passage.

Fig. 45. West range of
cloister: interior of east wall
from the north west.

Despite the wholesale refacing of the Romanesque walls at cloister level during
the later medieval reconstruction, there are areas of original walling to be seen in
the rooms above the east, west and south walks. These walls were, of course,
originally external and have been protected from the weather since the construction
of the rooms above the cloister during the late middle ages. Above the east walk
the wall retains some blind arcading and indications of the dormitory fenestration.
The refectory windows, although heavily restored, can be seen in the library above
the south walk and the remains of the interlaced arcading with the double-splayed
windows can be appreciated in the room above the west walk.

These round double-splayed windows have been the subject of much discussion
due to the archaic technique employed in their construction (fig. 45).[37] They are
not dressed with ashlar and wickerwork centring was used. This technique is
considered by some to indicate Anglo-Saxon workmanship and for this reason the
wall has been regarded as belonging to the earliest phase of construction, contemporary with the earliest documentary evidence of land acquisition during the 1080s.
It is highly unlikely that the east wall of the west range could have been the first
part of the integrated and proportioned design of the whole cathedral complex, as
the wall does not deviate from the plan in any way. The double-splay technique
is undoubtedly indigenous, particularly suited to building with flint rubble in a
region with practically no local source of freestone. However, there is no evidence
to support the view that the use of double-splayed windows discontinued soon after
the Norman Conquest. There are several twelfth-century examples of double-splayed
windows in East Anglian parish churches. The church at Hales in Norfolk is a good
case where the building is abundantly decorated with mature Romanesque sculpture

37. J. Gunn, 'Saxon Remains in the Cloisters of
　　Norwich Cathedral', *NA*, 8 (1879), pp. 1–9;
　　Taylor, *Anglo-Saxon Architecture*, i, pp. 470–
　　71; Heywood, 'Round Towers', p. 170.

of *c.* 1130 and the tower, which is a later addition, has round double-splayed windows.[38] It is not unusual to find late examples of the double-splayed technique in parish churches, but to find a row of such rustic windows in a principal claustral building of the cathedral church of East Anglia is perhaps surprising. However, as both surfaces of the wall were plastered it is probable that the lack of quality was imperceptible. The row of interlaced arcading forming the eaves may be a later adornment but there is no reason to suppose that it cannot be contemporary with the circular windows – this form of decorative arcading was first used at Norwich on the north transept in *c.* 1100.[39]

An examination of the surviving wall of the west range reveals the imprint of former groin vaults, subsequently patched with rubble and tile. These vaults were at a higher level than those forming the dormitory undercroft and therefore the first floor rooms were considerably lower. This may be the reason for using circular windows to light these spaces. It certainly corroborates the probable function of the west range as principally a warehouse, possibly without much living accommodation. The building may have been converted into the guests' range at a later date.[40]

Parts of the east range stood until the early nineteenth century when they were demolished in order to form the present roadway. There are indications of the dormitory undercroft vaults in the surviving west wall and in the boundary walls of the prior's hall which formed its eastern wall. The Romanesque chapter house had an apsidal east end which was revealed by excavation in 1889.[41] The slype was the last part of the east range to be demolished and it was recorded by J. A. Repton (figs 18, 33). It consisted of three groin-vaulted bays and served as a passageway from the cloister to the eastern parts of the monastic precinct. It had doorways to the east and west and the centre bay accommodated an entrance into the south transept and the west bay a doorway to the chapter house.

38. Heywood, 'Round Towers', figs 55 and 56, p. 171.

39. The spandrels of the arcading have recently been rendered, giving the impression that it consists of a row of two-centred arches.

40. Franklin and Fernie suggest that double-splayed windows may have been used in order to restrict the view into the cloister of guests and other lay people. See J. A. Franklin, 'The Romanesque Cloister Sculpture of Norwich Cathedral' (unpublished University of East Anglia M. A. thesis, 1980), p. 66, n. 12; Fernie, *NC*, p. 23. This assumes that the west range contained the hostry

originally. It is not mentioned in documents until 1319 when the hostelers' rolls begin. See R. Gilchrist, 'An Archaeological Desk-Based Assessment of Three Areas of Proposed New Development at Norwich Cathedral' (Report for Dean and Chapter of Norwich Cathedral, 1994), pp. 4–12; a copy is available in the Sites and Monuments Record for Norfolk, Gressenhall.

41. For the 1889 excavation see W. T. Bensly, 'The Diocese and Cathedral Church of Norwich', in H. J. (Dunkinfield) Astley, ed., *Memorials of Old Norfolk* (London, 1908), p. 44.

The Bishop's Palace

The Romanesque palace, completed before Herbert de Losinga's death, consists of a wide, two-storey, passageway leading to a slightly wider and taller, rectangular hall, resembling a small keep. Until 1858 the passageway was connected to the church at the fourth and fifth bays of the nave (fig. 46).[42] The lower storey of the passage is barrel vaulted with transverse arches. Entry to the church was gained at gallery level, where the blocked doorway can be seen. The ground floor aisle wall accommodates a doorway of modern date and, as J. A. Repton's plan gives no indication of a doorway, it is probable that passage was restricted to the upper level only.

The fabric of the former palace has been extensively altered including a complete refacing of the west façade. However, two blocked, ashlar-dressed, Romanesque windows can be seen on the eastern side, as well as a mutilated string course and indications of two large blind arches with robbed dressings. At the point where the linking passageway was demolished a surviving Romanesque impost suggests that a large opening existed at ground level; it may represent the remains of a gatehouse accommodated beneath the bishop's walkway at the entrance to an enclosed episcopal court.

Herbert de Losinga also built a chapel in his court which was replaced in the fourteenth century by Bishop Salmon's chapel;[43] this was demolished in the seventeenth century. Excavations in 1859 revealed an apse within Bishop Salmon's east end and it may be assumed that the fourteenth-century chapel was either built on the foundations of Herbert's or that it was simply a modernization of the original.[44] In the late seventeenth century Bishop Salmon's chapel was described by Thomas Browne as having been 30 ft (9 m.) wide and 130 ft (40 m.) long.[45] The width probably reflects that of Herbert's chapel as well, but it is less acceptable to assume that it had the same length.

The *First Register* tells us that Herbert completed the palace except for the great hall.[46] The doorway at the eastern end of the great hall is the one recognizable early feature surviving and shows that the building is of Romanesque date. However, the arch profiles have undercut chevron ornament on the same plane as the angle

42. *Norwich Mercury*, 5 May 1858.
43. Mentioned in the Customary of the cathedral. See J. B. Tolhurst, ed., *The Customary of the Cathedral Priory Church of Norwich* (Henry Bradshaw Society, 82, 1948), p. 169.
44. H. Harrod, 'Excavations Made in the Gardens of the Bishop's Palace, Norwich,

April, 1859', *NA*, 6 (1864), p. 36.
45. T. Browne, *Repertorium* (1712), p. 15, and *Antiquitates Capellae D. Iohannis Evangelistae* (1712), pp. 5–6, both in *Posthumous Works of Sir Thomas Browne, 1680–1712* (London, 1712).
46. *First Register*, fo. 8r.

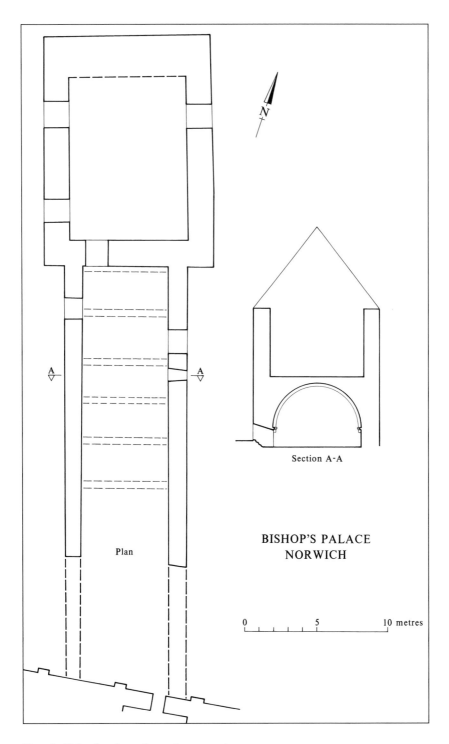

Fig. 46. Bishop's palace: plan and cross section.

roll (which is of a later character than those in the cathedral church) and confirm the statement in the *First Register*. Bishop Eborard's successor William Turbe (1146/47–74) appears to have been the most likely patron, although the register does not refer to his authorship.

The Importance of Norwich Cathedral

Norwich Cathedral is a major European building and should be seen in this context. In terms of size alone its overall length (433 ft or 132 m.) is the same as that of Emperor Constantine's church of St Peter in Rome. Amongst contemporary churches it is exceeded only by Bury St Edmunds Abbey (487 ft 4 ins or 148.57 m.), Winchester Cathedral (*c.* 515 ft or 157 m.) and Cluny Abbey (565 ft 1 in. or 172.27 m.). It is thus rendered comparable with the imperial foundations at Mainz and Speyer; it leaves the major foundations of Normandy to a lesser league altogether with the Conqueror's church of St Étienne in Caen a mere 275 ft 6 ins (84 m.) in total length.

A departure from purely Norman models characterises architecture in England from *c.* 1080. Not only are churches on a far grander scale but they also draw from a wider field of influence and forms are adapted and developed far beyond the level reached in Normandy before the Conquest. Norwich Cathedral played its part in this process and this chapter will indicate the main innovative features of the design without attempting to cover those aspects which characterise other major buildings of the same generation.

In general terms the cathedral has a predictable place in the development of Anglo-Norman architecture in eastern England. As regards the alternation of supports Norwich takes its cue from Ely Cathedral (begun 1083): the piers of the main arcades in both buildings alternate between circular and square cores (fig. 16). The principal difference at Norwich is that the elements of the piers which project into the main space of the nave alternate and articulate the elevation by connecting to the orders of the gallery arches. At Ely each pier has a pilaster with half shaft simply emphasising the division into bays. The degree of complexity in the Norwich design and its integration with the whole elevation is innovative and one of the most sophisticated in Europe.

The tripartite clerestory arrangement at Norwich has its immediate source at Ely again, which in turn is a development of its first use at Winchester Cathedral (begun 1079). The treatment at Norwich is remarkable in that each bay is a composition in its own right where every wall is transformed into an articulate part of a self-contained architectural unit (figs 21, 39, 40). In comparison with the clerestory at Ely (fig. 47), the Norwich clerestory has shorter colonnettes with a stilted central arch above furnished with nook shafts replying to the angle roll. The area of walling above the smaller arches is decorated with blind arcades and some of the clerestory

Fig. 47. Ely Cathedral:
clerestory bay in north wall
of north transept from the
south west.

bays have groin-vaulted central arches which accommodate tiny blind arches. The clerestory aedicule, as it could be termed, reaches its zenith at Norwich and remains unsurpassed in Romanesque architecture.

A striking aspect of the design at Norwich, which requires some explanation, is the use of the four decorated columns marking the position of the nave altar.[47] It was standard practice in monastic churches until the thirteenth century to have the division between the choir and the liturgical nave a few bays west of the crossing. At Norwich the division formed by the pulpitum is emphasised by the four columns around the nave altar directly in front of the pulpitum. A number of other churches emphasise this division in a variety of ways. Within the Anglo-Norman context the first pair of piers west of the crossing at Peterborough Cathedral are of a different, more prominent, design than all the other nave piers. At Tewkesbury Abbey the first pair of piers have square bases, the second pair of bases are square on their

47. For a discussion of the subject see E. C.
    Fernie 'The Use of Varied Nave Supports

    in Romanesque and Early Gothic Chur-
    ches', *Gesta*, 22 (1984), pp. 107–17.

eastern sides and circular to the west and the remaining piers have circular bases. At Romsey Abbey the first pair of piers from the crossing are giant order columns while the remaining piers are compound. In a wider context the first pair of piers at the early twelfth-century Alpirsbach Abbey in Germany (Baden-Württemberg) are square piers whilst the others are all columns. The same device is used at the nearby abbey of Hirsau and at the related church of Paulinzelle (Thuringia).[48] In the twelfth-century brick church at Bad Segeberg in north Germany the column-pier alternating system is interrupted towards the eastern end of the nave by a compound minor pier.[49] The closest parallel to Norwich in terms of having two pairs of different piers, with a standard pair in between, marking the former position of the nave altar is the early Gothic cathedral at Laon (*c.* 1160–90), which has arcades supported on columns except for the second and fourth pair which are adorned with colonnettes.

There is no precise source for the arrangement of the decorated columns at Norwich but the helical grooves which adorn them can be shown to have a special significance which can be traced back to antiquity.[50] The shrine at Old St Peter's in Rome was surrounded by twelve spiral columns of which one survives in the treasury of St Peter's and which undoubtedly inspired Bernini to use similar columns for his baldacchino in the new church of St Peter. There are several medieval examples of spiral columns being used to mark sanctuaries, following the example of Constantine's fourth-century basilica. The mid ninth- or early tenth-century crypt at Repton has four spiral columns marking the position of St Wystan's tomb; and the eleventh-century crypts at Deventer, St Peter at Utrecht and Canterbury Cathedral use spiral columns to mark the positions of altars or similar features.[51] The spiral columns at Durham Cathedral (1093) in the eastern arm and transepts are similar to those at Norwich and may also have had an analogous function.[52] The specific source for the form of the columns at Norwich may be Durham while the use of spiral decoration was an established way of marking a position of liturgical importance.

Norwich Cathedral's East Anglian sisters at Ely and Bury St Edmunds are related in many ways and both have western transepts. It is often remarked that these transepts are a reference to the buildings of the Holy Roman Empire, such as Speyer

48. For the latter three churches see P. Héliot, 'Sur les tours de transept dans l'architecture du moyen âge', *Revue Archéologique* (1965), i, pp. 171–76.

49. J. Habich, *Handbuch der Deutschen Kunstdenkmäler: Hamburg, Schleswig-Holstein* (Deutscher Kunstverlag, 1971), p. 107.

50. E. C. Fernie, 'The Romanesque Piers of Norwich Cathedral', *NA*, 36 (1977), pp. 383–86.

51. E. C. Fernie, 'St Anselm's Crypt', in BAACT, 5, *Canterbury, 1979*, ed. N. Coldstream and P. Draper (1982), pp. 31–32; E. C. Fernie, *The Architecture of the Anglo-Saxons* (London, 1983), pp. 116–21; Fernie, *NC*, pp. 130–33.

52. E. C. Fernie, 'The Spiral Piers of Durham Cathedral', in BAACT, 3, *Durham (1977)*, ed. N. Coldstream and P. Draper (1980), pp. 50–58.

Cathedral (Rhineland Palatinate) and St Michael at Hildesheim (Lower Saxony) where the Carolingian westwork commonly survives in a more integrated, Romanesque form. Nineteenth-century restorers convinced themselves that a western transept was originally intended at Norwich and consequently built massive responds against the façade in imitation of the crossing piers.[53] It has been shown beyond doubt that there was never an intention to build a western transept yet this does not lessen the influence of the imperial churches of northern Europe on the design of Norwich Cathedral. This can be seen in the profusion of towers and turrets which originally bedecked the cathedral. James Corbridge's representation of the cathedral on the map of Norwich of 1727 shows that the stair turrets in the corners between the transept and the eastern arm originally rose up to form towers decorated with three levels of blind arcading. Similarly the turrets on the external corners of the transepts were much taller. Turrets also rise from the corners of the crossing tower and the west façade had tall turrets above the four staircases. Additionally, it is possible that the quadrant pilasters in the angles of the radiating chapels continued upwards to form circular turrets (fig. 25). This taste for towers and pinnacles had its origins in the Carolingian period with Saint-Riquier (Somme) and Fulda (Hesse), for example. It continued under the Ottonian and Salian dynasties with such churches as Metz (Moselle) and Speyer, with 'shoulder' towers as at Norwich and circular towers at Gernrode (Saxony), St Michael at Hildesheim and Möllenbeck (Lower Saxony) as purely random examples of an almost universal liking for turrets and pinnacles.

The curious double-circle radiating chapels at Norwich are almost without precedent. The sole surviving earlier example is at Méhun-sur-Yèvre (Cher). The design is so distinctive and rare that it is difficult to believe that the Norwich architect was unaware of it or at least of a lost common source. Despite this, Anglo-Norman designers had a definite predilection for unusual radiating chapels. At Winchester the east end is an apse echelon design with an ambulatory; the radiating chapels at Worcester are of an unique polygonal design; and those at Canterbury are based on the plan of the chapels at St Maria-im-Kapitol in Cologne yet stand outside the ambulatory and were surmounted by towers.

Bury St Edmunds Abbey was the wealthiest and probably the most powerful institution in East Anglia during the eleventh and twelfth centuries. The Romanesque church was begun in 1081 and the eastern arm was completed by 1095. The church

53. Excavations which took place during the early 1970s show that a western transept was never intended. See E. C. Fernie, 'Excavations on the Façade of Norwich Cathedral', *NA*, 36 (1974), pp. 72–75; J. P. McAleer, 'The Romanesque Façade of Norwich Cathedral', *Journal of the Society of Architectural Historians of Great Britain*, 25 (1966), pp. 136–40; J. P. McAleer, 'The Façade of Norwich Cathedral: The Nineteenth-Century Restorations', *NA*, 41 (1993), pls I–XI, pp. 392–97.

consisted of a four-bay eastern arm with an ambulatory and radiating chapels and a crypt extending beneath the entire area, a transept with eastern aisle and four apsidal chapels and a long nave with a western transept which had single apsidal chapels and octagonal towers at its extremities. Unfortunately the building was almost completely destroyed after the Dissolution and the remaining foundations are very scanty. However, enough remains for general similarities with Norwich to be pointed out, such as both having ambulatories and being of a similar scale. There are two minor features which show a specific connection with Norwich: the radiating chapels had quadrant pilasters; and the north-east presbytery pier is of the same profile as the Norwich crossing piers.[54] While at present it is not possible to make any further firm comparisons, it can be surmised that Bury was an important factor in the formation of the design for Norwich Cathedral.

The design of Norwich Cathedral draws from a large number of sources. The angle roll with cavetto and the wall passage are the only specifically Norman contributions. The three-storey elevation with the gallery as large as the main arcade, the ambulatory with radiating chapels, the compound pier, the alternation of supports, the regular crossing with lantern and the standard monastic layout of the conventual buildings around a square cloister are all elements introduced and developed in central France (and to a lesser extent in the Holy Roman Empire) around the year 1000.[55] They were adopted in Normandy towards the middle of the eleventh century, culminating in William the Conqueror's church of St Étienne in Caen of the 1060s where the innovative Norman roll moulding and clerestory wall passage are in evidence. At Norwich the clerestory aedicule and the spiral pier are attributable to post-Conquest developments in England and the turreted skyline to the Empire. The position of the bishop's throne is, with the crypt-like treatment of the ambulatory, deliberately archaic and may be the result of the desire to emulate contemporary churches which had the distinct advantage over Norwich of being built on already well-established religious sites.

Norwich Cathedral is not a building of innovation; it is an expression of the well-assimilated ideals of Romanesque architecture, where the individual spaces are defined yet integrated with each other. This is achieved through the use of alternating compound supports whose shafts and pilasters divide into bays yet link the storeys by replying to the orders of the gallery arcade. Each clerestory aedicule is a masterpiece of articulation, every one a miniature temple. The remarkable state of preservation means that it requires only a small effort of the imagination to see the Romanesque building with wooden ceilings, steeply pitched roofs at the east end and a skyline of towers and pinnacles.

54. Fernie, *NC*, pp. 138–40.
55. For a description of the development of Romanesque architecture, see Fernie, *Anglo-Saxons*, pp. 74–89.

7

The Romanesque Sculpture

Jill A. Franklin

Norwich Cathedral is not endowed with elaborate architectural sculpture. In the main, its arch mouldings have a thoroughly standard late eleventh- or early twelfth-century profile, namely an angle roll edged by a single or double hollow roll. Soffit rolls occur in the transepts but beyond that, the only types of ornament found on the voussoirs, unelaborated in all cases, are single or double billet in the presbytery, transepts and nave, and chevron in the nave alone.[1] None of the surviving Romanesque doorways has any figural or foliate ornament. There is restrained use of blank arcading, sometimes intersected, throughout the building. Originally there were two pairs of cylindrical piers in the nave bearing carved spirals. Decorated shafts occur sporadically at clerestory and tribune gallery level. Only in the north arm of the transept, on the twelfth-century screen inserted into the apse arcade and in the crossing tower, is the picture at all different. In those locations more original carving is concentrated than anywhere else in the building. The crossing tower, for example, contains a staggering 344 twelfth-century capitals. The overall impression, neverthe-less, is of a building that is sparely decorated. The Romanesque cloister lying to the south of it must have appeared ornate by comparison.

Within the eastern arm, transept and crossing tower there are something in the region of 1200 surviving Romanesque capitals.[2] The vast majority, approximately

---

1. Chevron is restricted to the tribune arcades of the nave. Double billet occurs at main arcade level. Single billet is used on the tripartite arcading of the nave clerestory. A change is discernible in the ornament of the nave, in the tribune from bay 9 and in the clerestory from bay 8. The chevron in the tribune is of one type consistently along the south side and up to bay 9 on the north side, namely a single order lying parallel to the plane, on an arch of square section. In the remaining six north bays, however, the

arch on which the chevrons sit has a cham-fered edge. In bay 8 of the clerestory only two of the triple arches have billet and thereafter only the central arch has; see J. A. Franklin, 'The Romanesque Cloister Sculpture of Norwich Cathedral' (unpub-lished University of East Anglia M.A. disser-tation, 1980), p. 68 n. 10.

2. I have recorded a total of 1239 capitals, including some 120 in the transept which are now largely concealed by subsequent vaulting.

76 per cent, are derived from the cushion capital. Some 167 are volute capitals, over one third of which are concentrated in the presbytery. A mere three capitals from this huge total bear figural ornament of any kind; two have masks and the third a pair of dragon-like creatures. West of the crossing, the ratio of volute to cushion-derived capitals is even lower. There are only some fifty-two original volute capitals in the western arm. Whatever this preponderance of cushion and scallop capitals indicates, it is not merely chronological development. Along the entire length of the nave, the wall shafts rising to the springing of the tribune gallery arches all carry a volute capital, bar the westernmost pair. Moreover, at the extreme western end of the nave, presumably part of the final building campaign under Bishop Eborard (1121–45), there is on the interior façade a cushion-volute capital, that strange Anglo-Norman hybrid form which occurs as early as *c.* 1070 in the crypt at Lastingham (Yorkshire).[3]

The Bishop's Effigy and the Decoration of the North Transept

On the external north wall of the north transept, above the portal, is a niche containing a figure carved in relief (fig. 48).[4] The figure is tonsured, vested in alb, stole, chasuble and amice, and carries a staff. It evidently represents a bishop since the right hand is raised in blessing.[5] He is flanked by a pair of spiral-fluted colonnettes supported on beast masks. The latter have bulging eyes, upright pointed ears and deeply grooved muzzles. The colonnettes are surmounted by capitals. One of these is foliate, the other bears a dragon-like creature with a coiled tail. Sitting within a niche and carved on a single slab which tapers toward the base, this configuration of effigy, shafts and arch has prompted the suggestion that the relief is in fact the lid of a tomb, relocated to the niche in the north transept wall.[6] This theory was attributed to Sir Alfred Clapham by Canon Boston of Norwich, who examined the figure in the company of Sir Alfred, with the aid of a ladder. According to Canon Boston, Clapham decided that the slab was indeed the lid of a tomb, probably that

3. For the Lastingham capital, see M. Baylé, *Les origines et les premiers développements de la sculpture romane en Normandie: art de Basse Normandie* (C bis, Caen 1992), pl. 649.
4. The relief panel now in the niche is a cast replica, the original having been relocated to the ambulatory in 1967: see Fernie, *NC*, p. 84 n. 23.
5. My thanks to Sandy Heslop for this observation. He knows of no figure represented in the act of blessing which can certainly be identified as an abbot, rather than a bishop:

see T. A. Heslop, *Image and Authority: English Seals of the Eleventh and Twelfth Centuries* (forthcoming).
6. At its widest point, the slab measures 26 in. (66 cm.), narrowing to 24. 2 in. (61. 5 cm.) at its base. It is 64 in. (162 cm.) tall and 11 in. (27 cm.) deep. The figure is shod in enormous boots which project unconvincingly 1 in. (3 cm.) beyond the front plane of the slab and are thus likely to be modern additions.

Fig. 48. Norwich Cathedral:
effigy of bishop from the
exterior of the north transept.

of the founding bishop, Herbert de Losinga.[7] Clapham's original verdict, published
earlier, was rather more circumspect: he pronounced the rendering of the figure
'similar' to that of a monumental effigy but the slab apparently *in situ*, rather than
relocated.[8] At the top of a ladder, Sir Alfred was perhaps swayed by the canon's
enthusiasm for the identification of the relief as the tomb of the first bishop, an
idea which can in fact be refuted. Clapham's own view, more cautiously expressed,
that the figure resembles a funerary effigy but bears no sign of ever having been
situated elsewhere, contains the germ of another idea.

Herbert de Losinga died in 1119 and was buried before the high altar.[9] A new

7.   N. Boston, 'The Founder's Tomb in Nor-   *tecture after the Conquest* (Oxford, 1934),
     wich Cathedral', *NA*, 32 (1961), p. 4.   p. 156 n. 3.
8.   A. W. Clapham, *English Romanesque Archi-* 9.   *First Register*, p. 56 (fo. 9v).

monument to him was erected in the fifteenth century and was itself replaced in 1682.[10] Whatever the fate of the original tomb, the theory that it found its way into the north transept niche can be discounted. It has been demonstrated that both niche and relief are part of one and the same structure.[11] In all probability, the two are coeval, although it is conceivable that relief could predate niche. What is *not* feasible is the notion that the relief postdates the niche, as would have to be the case if it were Herbert's tomb slab and ever used as such. Herbert had completed the church as far as the nave altar – including the transept where niche and relief are situated – before his death in 1119. The relief is not therefore the founder's redeployed tomb slab. It can reasonably be dated to *c.* 1100 on stylistic grounds.[12] Thus, if not his tomb, the effigy could well be Herbert's commission. Precluding the unlikely idea of his having placed an image of himself on his newly-constructed cathedral, who else might Herbert have chosen to represent on the slab and why is it, the only figural relief sculpture on the entire building, located where it is?

Fig. 49. Norwich Cathedral: north arm of transept, north wall, interior.

The north transept doorway, above which the figure stands, can only have been used to pass to and from the episcopal complex lying to the north of the cathedral. Thus is it popularly referred to as the bishop's door. Within the north transept itself is concentrated more sculptural ornament than anywhere else in the building. Here, too, occurs what Pevsner describes as 'an anomaly . . . corresponding to the effigy outside'.[13] For above the door, on the inside, is a most unexpected motif: a pair of triangular-headed arches linked by a third, smaller arch, all three composed of strips of billet moulding. In the middle of this composition is a small carved beast head (fig. 49). This in

10. For a discussion of Bishop Herbert's successive funerary monuments, see below, pp. 483–85.
11. Fernie, *NC*, pp. 83–84.
12. Fernie, *NC*, p. 84; G. Zarnecki, 'The Chi-

chester Reliefs', *Arch. J.*, 110 (1953), pp. 106–19.
13. N. Pevsner, *The Buildings of England: North-East Norfolk and Norwich* (Harmondsworth, 1962; reprinted 1979), p. 218.

fact looks reset, as do two further heads above the windows flanking the portal. Nowhere else in the building do triangular-headed, or gabled, arches occur. While examples can be found in eleventh-century France, in England they are not a feature of mature Romanesque architecture but are part of the vocabulary of Anglo-Saxon ornament.[14] Thus at St Andrew's, Great Dunham (Norfolk), probably of the second half of the eleventh century, the west door is surrounded by a gabled stone strip, notched in a manner that resembles the Norman billet motif.[15] Gabled stripwork decorated with billet can be found on a number of the round-towered parish churches of Norfolk. Although it has now been established that all but a handful of these towers are post-Conquest structures, rather than Anglo-Saxon as long believed, the use of gabled arches on them may be seen as an example of Anglo-Saxon survival.[16]

The isolated use of gabled billet in a prestigious Anglo-Norman cathedral begun three decades after the Conquest surely points to some specific reference. What might have provoked this apparent piece of atavism? Eric Fernie has suggested that the figure depicted in the niche is not Herbert, first bishop of Norwich in the late eleventh century, but Felix, first bishop of East Anglia in the seventh. How better for Bishop Herbert to proclaim his somewhat hard-won title than by establishing a link with his illustrious predecessors, placing an image of him above the portal connecting episcopal complex and church? As Clapham appeared to imply, the relief may have been intended to evoke for the beholder the lid of a tomb, perhaps indeed an ancient one. If Fernie's identification is correct, the use of the archaising gabled arch above the inner face of that portal would seem entirely appropriate. Further support for the view that this figure represents Felix, evangeliser of East Anglia, can be derived from a relief, also of the late eleventh century, of St Saturninus, evangeliser of the Languedoc, of similar size and shape and placed in the centre above the entrance in the south wall of the transept of Saint-Sernin, Toulouse.[17]

Elsewhere within the north transept there are other indications that sculpture has been used to dignify this particular part of the church. In the east wall is a doorway leading to one of the building's four spiral staircases. This is the only surviving Romanesque portal in the cathedral with a carved tympanum (fig. 50).[18] It bears a

14. E. C. Fernie, *The Architecture of the Anglo-Saxons* (London, 1983), pls 79, 81, 84.
15. H. M. and J. Taylor, *Anglo-Saxon Architecture*, 3 vols (Cambridge, 1965–78), ii, pl. 454.
16. S. Heywood, 'The Round Towers of East Anglia', in J. Blair, ed., *Minsters and Parish Churches: The Local Church in Transition*

(Oxford University Committee for Archaeology, monograph no. 17, 1988), p. 170.
17. Fernie, *NC*, pp. 85–87, and personal communication.
18. The motif on the tympanum of the north doorway at Marham is identical. There is only one other decorated tympanum surviving *in situ* in the county, at Tottenhill.

Fig. 50. Norwich Cathedral: north arm of transept, detail of portal in east wall.

complex, quincunx motif, rotated through 45 degrees, prefabricated and slightly misassembled.[19] The reason for the doorway's distinctive treatment had presumably to do with the fact that it gave access from the transept to the presbytery tribune gallery and the upper storeys of the radiating and axial chapels.[20] It was thus perhaps very much the bishop's door, just as the north transept itself was particularly associated with him. This doorway is flanked by blank arcading and is surmounted by still more, the bases of which just clear the apex of the tympanum. Some of these bases, it has only very recently been observed, are damaged and were evidently decorated originally with projecting carved elements which were subsequently hacked away (fig. 51).[21] Judging from what survives, this lost carving may have been figural, conceivably representing beasts or beast masks. In this same tier of blank arcading, supported by the damaged bases, is the only capital in the church itself to have significant figural ornament, namely a pair of dragon-like creatures with coiled tails (fig. 52). The entrance to the upper levels of the presbytery, perhaps used by the bishop or the prior, would thus have been surmounted by colonnettes ostensibly

19. The unit of the design is a rotated square, some 4 × 4 in. (10 × 10 cm.) Its surface is subdivided into the nine (i. e. five plus four) compartments of a quincunx. In some cases, the cardinal compartments of the square are in relief and read like the five on dice. In others, these five compartments are cut away. The subtlety of this design has been distorted by the inconsistent assembly of the squares.

20. All five of the Romanesque apsidal chapels including, probably, the axial chapel were originally two-storeyed. It is an assumption, unsupported by documentary evidence, that these upper chambers had a liturgical function. Judging from their architectural sculpture, it would certainly seem that they served more than a merely utilitarian purpose. The interiors of those which survive are embellished with blank arcading and capitals, some decorated. The galleries giving access to them are likewise distinguished with architectural sculpture. See also Fernie, *NC*, p. 73.

21. Stephen Heywood observed this hitherto unremarked phenomenon in 1993. For other previously unpublished features of the building see Heywood's contribution to this volume.

Fig. 51. Norwich Cathedral: north arm of
transept, detail of arcading on east wall.

Fig. 52. Norwich Cathedral: north arm of
transept, capital on arcading of east wall.

resting on the heads of beasts. This in effect would mirror the setting of the sculpted
bishop above the north portal, one of whose flanking capitals, moreover, also bears
a dragon with a serpentine tail. Blank arcading supported on beast corbels is an
uncommon architectural motif but it can be found on the façade of Rochester
Cathedral (Kent) of the second half of the twelfth century. It occurs there in
conjunction with two episcopal effigies which are themselves modern but probably
replace Romanesque originals.[22]

While considering the rich sculptural decoration of the north transept, it is worth
recording that the only spur bases in the building are both located there, in the wall
passage at tribune level; and that, of the six decorated colonnettes within the church,
five are situated in the north transept. Other examples of the use of sculpture to
emphasise an architectural hierarchy elsewhere in the building include the four spiral
piers in the nave demarcating the area of the nave altar, the chip-carved imposts,
unique in the building, flanking the opening of the axial chapel and the arch to the
north transeptal chapel which has a moulded profile on its entrance face alone.

The Carved Heads in the Presbytery: Connections with Normandy

In this comparatively unadorned building, the few sculpted elements, grouped or
isolated, are particularly evident. It is tempting to see them as invested with special

22. Who the original effigies represented is
unknown but the two obvious seventh-
century candidates are Bishops Justus and
Paulinus.

Fig. 53a. Norwich Cathedral: corbel head, presbytery tribune gallery, north side.

Fig. 53b. Norwich Cathedral: corbel head, presbytery tribune gallery, south side.

significance. The pair of carved male heads (figs 53a and 53b), which face each other in the presbytery across the chord of the apse at the springing of the tribune arcade are a case in point, but precisely who or what they represent remains unknown. Almost as intractable is the question of their authenticity. They sit, slightly awkwardly, where one expects to see a capital, at the point at which the tribune gallery arcade abuts the west face of the chord piers. Each head is carved on a concave ground. The upper edge of this cavetto neatly aligns with the impost above, which in turn supports a hood moulding. Both impost and hood moulding are unquestionably Romanesque. The lower edge of the curve, however, does not meet its supporting pilaster at all tidily, being set back too far. The curve is greater than necessary, as if intended for a pilaster of shallower projection.

The capital zone, of which the corbel heads are an integral part, is evidently Romanesque. Moreover, corbel heads and adjacent capitals, together with their accompanying imposts, betray in their reddened colour damage by fire. Any scorched masonry in this part of the cathedral which has the quality of Romanesque work will be original, rather than Victorian restoration, there having been no recorded fire here in the building's post-medieval history.[23] It seems reasonable therefore to propose that the heads are both pristine and *in situ*.

How then to account for their rather uncomfortable disposition? They might at some stage have been dislodged and reinserted, given the degree of nineteenth-century restoration in the sanctuary, but it is hard to imagine they would ever have looked any more at home than they do now; they simply do not fit the space they were meant to occupy. A corbel head used instead of a capital is an unusual enough substitution. It could simply be that the misalignment at Norwich was the result of this uncommonness. In fact, the heads have been quite radically recut at some stage, presumably in the nineteenth century, which alone probably accounts for their incongruities.

Many of the corbel heads beneath the eaves on the outside of the cathedral are replacements.[24] Some originals, displaced, are stored inside the building, but in all cases these are grotesque in character, unlike the pair under discussion which are almost naturalistic by comparison. They are secular in appearance, rather than manifestly hieratic or religious. They bear no distinguishing attributes of kingship or divinity. One of the pair, that to the north, is clean-shaven while his counter-part to the south sports a beard and unusually jaunty, upturned moustaches. In this distribution of facial hair, if in no other respect, the Norwich heads resemble the somewhat later pair on the prior's doorway at Ely Cathedral.[25] The two twelfth-century marble

23. Fernie, *NC*, p. 28.

24. J. A. Franklin in A. Borg *et al.*, *Medieval Sculpture from Norwich Cathedral* (Norwich,

1980), p. 23.

25. G. Zarnecki, *The Early Sculpture of Ely Cathedral* (London, 1958), pls 54, 56.

corbel heads supporting the lintel of the portal of Maguelone Cathedral (Hérault) have been cited in connection with the pair of heads at Ely.[26] At Maguelone, as on the portal at Ely and in the sanctuary at Norwich, one of the heads is clean-shaven and the other has moustache and beard. With good reason, the Maguelone heads have been identified as, respectively, St Peter and St Paul.[27] A similar identification seems likely at Ely and conceivable at Norwich too.

Corbel heads supporting arches within a building are far from common at this period. They do occur, however, in a small group of minor Romanesque churches in Normandy, moreover in the choir. At Tollevast for example, in the Cotentin, corbels, sometimes in the form of moustachioed human heads, carry the ribs in the vaulted choir bays.[28]

Within three decades of the Conquest, Anglo-Norman architecture had responded with an astonishing variety of solutions to the liturgical, political, technological and aesthetic imperatives of the age. The germinal buildings in Normandy in this process, the abbeys at Jumièges and Caen begun in the 1040s–1060s, lay at a considerable remove; by the late eleventh century, when Norwich Cathedral was being designed, much in English architecture had been absorbed from other quarters, such as the German Empire, or was quite simply unprecedented. In the realm of architectural sculpture, the cushion capital was already in use in English buildings by the 1070s, even though it was equally alien to both Normandy and pre-Conquest England.[29] It is all the more striking, therefore, to observe in a major late eleventh-century English cathedral such as Norwich an enduring affiliation with capital sculpture in Normandy.

The connection is seen at its strongest at the abbey of Cerisy-la-Forêt, also located in the Cotentin, a building probably of the 1080s. Points of comparison between Norwich and Cerisy have already been noted by scholars, including the occurrence at both of a type of volute capital decorated with criss-crossed straps.[30] On another volute capital at Cerisy, a seated figure in a tunic clasps a stem of foliage in either outstretched hand (fig. 54). This brings to mind the image on a cushion capital probably from the twelfth-century cloister at Norwich where, however, as we shall see, the theme was more elaborately treated (fig. 59). The motif of a manikin

26. Zarnecki, *Early Sculpture of Ely Cathedral*, pl. 30.
27. R. Saint-Jean in J. Lugand *et al.*, *Languedoc Roman* (La Pierre-qui-Vire, 1975), p. 236, pl. 79.
28. L. Musset, *Normandie Romane*, 2 vols (3rd edn, La Pierre-qui-Vire, 1987), i, pls 72, 73.
29. Fernie, *NC*, pp. 142–44.
30. The comparable, capitals at Norwich and Cerisy are illustrated in G. Zarnecki, '1066

and Architectural Sculpture', *Proceedings of the British Academy*, 52 (1966), pls xiv a and b. For other points of comparison between the two buildings see Franklin, 'Romanesque Cloister Sculpture of Norwich Cathedral', p. 43; J. A. Franklin, 'The Romanesque Cloister Sculpture of Norwich Cathedral Priory', in F. H. Thompson, ed., *Studies in Medieval Sculpture* (London, 1983), p. 67; Fernie, *NC*, p. 117.

Fig. 54. Cerisy-la-Forêt: capital in nave.   Fig. 55. Lion-sur-Mer: capital fragment no. 3.

straddling and clasping symmetrical coiled stems also occurs in Normandy on a volute capital from Lion-sur-Mer, north of Caen, probably of the late eleventh century (fig. 55) and again on a nave arcade capital at Ryes, near Bayeux, of *c.* 1100.[31]

The Cloister

Fourteen damaged Romanesque capitals, together with some twenty-five voussoir fragments, have come to light at the cathedral since the beginning of this century, having been reused as masonry in the construction of the existing Gothic cloister.[32] The voussoirs came from openings some six to ten feet (two to three metres) wide, perhaps those of the lost Romanesque chapter house.[33] They bear foliate motifs set within keeled billet and are related to the decorated portals of a group of parish churches in the south east of the county.[34] The capitals are believed to have come from the arcades of the dismantled twelfth-century cloister for which there is no documented date. They are double capitals. Only one member of each pair has carved ornament, the other having been left plain. Presumably they were disposed so that the carved capital faced the cloister walk. The carving in some cases is of very high quality.[35] On a number of the capitals there are unmistakable elements of narrative, indicated both by the subject matter – albeit now vestigial – and even

31. For Lion-sur-Mer, see Baylé, *Origines*, pl. 654. For Ryes, J. -J. Bertaux, 'Contribution a l'etude de l'art Roman en Normandie', ii, 'Le décor sculpté des églises paroissiales romanes de l'ancien doyenné de Creully', *Annales de Normandie*, 19 (1969), fig. 5.

32. For a catalogue of the fragments reused in the cloister, see Franklin in Borg *et al.*, *Medieval Sculpture from Norwich Cathedral*, pp. 5–21.

33. Franklin, 'Romanesque Cloister Sculpture of Norwich Cathedral Priory', pp. 58–67.

34. Franklin in Borg *et al.*, *Medieval Sculpture from Norwich Cathedral*, pp. 23–26.

35. Eight of the finest capitals appear to be the work of a single sculptor, Franklin, 'Romanesque Cloister Sculpture of Norwich Cathedral Priory', p. 57.

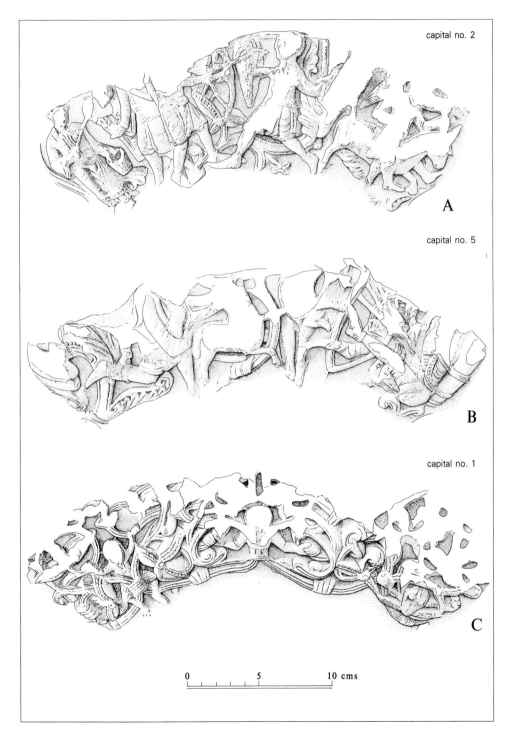

capital no. 2

A

capital no. 5

B

capital no. 1

C

0   5   10 cms

Fig. 56. Norwich Cathedral: capitals, probably from the Romanesque cloister, with the decoration drawn as if unwrapped. (Drawings by Steven Ashley.)

a

b

c

Fig. 57a, b, c
Norwich Cathedral: capital no. 2, probably
from the Romanesque cloister.

a

b

c

Fig. 58a, b, c
Norwich Cathedral: capital no. 5, probably
from the Romanesque cloister.

more by the organisation of the figural decoration itself. In most cases, the ornament fails to respect the geometry of its cushion capital, being wrapped around the latter's three exposed faces in the manner of a frieze. It was this observation which led to the drawings of three of the capitals in figures 56a, 56b and 56c. The three represented in the drawings are among the most intriguing of the group in terms of their iconography (compare figs 57, 58 and 59). It is on them also that the continuous character of the ornament is best seen. On one capital (figs 56a and 57), for example, one figure physically overlaps another, suggesting narrative continuity and perhaps two sequential representations of a single personage.

On at least one of the capitals (number 5) the decoration, though badly damaged, is markedly classicising in character. On one of its faces a creature, which might be a centaur or perhaps a deer, recoils from an assault by a naked figure bearing a long-handled weapon (figs 56b and 58).[36] Another of the three carved faces of this capital is entirely taken up by the remains of a remarkable carving of an archer, using his feet to shoot three arrows simultaneously from a long bow. This appears to be a unique image, without visual parallel in antiquity or medieval Europe. There are depictions of archers using a knee or foot to string a bow, or shooting an arrow from a kneeling position.[37] There are also descriptions by classical authors of bowmen using their feet to operate a foot bow.[38] What is altogether exceptional about the Norwich archer is the fact of his being seated. The posture he adopts is presumably a sign of his own might, or conceivably that of his bow. Two of the great archers of Greek mythology had occasion to shoot from a seated position. Odysseus did so when using his powerful bow, in order to demonstrate effortless superiority over Penelope's suitors.[39] Apollo settled himself down before showering Agamemnon's army with a relentless hail of arrows for nine days.[40]

The scenes carved on capital 2 (figs 56a and 57) have eluded satisfactory interpretation.[41] There are no biblical or other religious themes which correspond to the episodes depicted. The most distinctive and puzzling of them includes two figures, one of which inclines toward the other, the latter dressed in a long robe and holding a vessel and a rod of some sort. On the remaining faces of the capital are a scene of combat and a mounted figure accompanied by a boar. Referring again to classical mythology, the incident in which the sorceress Circe, with wand and magic potion,

36. Franklin in Borg *et al.*, *Medieval Sculpture from Norwich Cathedral*, p. 12.
37. E. H. Minns, *Scythians and Greeks* (Cambridge, 1913), fig. 93.
38. Arrian, *Indica*, book xvi.
39. *Odyssey*, xxi, line 420. Such a suggestion, however, poses problems: in the episode in question, Odysseus notably shot a single arrow rather than three. Above all, how would one account for the reference to this passage from the Odyssey in an English monastery at a date as early perhaps as the second decade of the twelfth century?
40. *Iliad*, i, line 42ff.
41. Franklin in Borg *et al.*, *Medieval Sculpture from Norwich Cathedral*, pp. 9–11.

a

b

c

Fig. 59a, b, c
Norwich Cathedral: capital no. 1, probably
from the Romanesque cloister.

transforms the companions of Odysseus into pigs supplies some of the imagery on the Norwich capital (fig. 60).[42]

On capital 1 (figs 56c and 59), the dynamic of the narrative is more evident.[43] It is also possible again to infer a classical allusion from the subject matter. On one face is a figure set within foliage, ostensibly a familiar enough theme from the Romanesque repertory (fig. 59a). Here, though, is something more than is conveyed by the standard term 'inhabited scroll'. Neither is this one of the numerous contemporary depictions unquestionably to be found in various media of 'frail, naked humanity . . . for ever caught in the coils [of the tanglewood]'[44] 'striving to free [itself] from the world of sensual temptation . . .'[45] The Norwich figure is neither naked nor struggling; he is suspended amid the encircling stems, rather than enmeshed in them.

42. Ovid, *Metamorphoses*, xiv, lines 276–97. The struggle depicted in the scene of combat is an unequal one, between an archer and a swordsman. When Odysseus fought Eurymachos and the other suitors, they were armed with swords and he with a bow, *Odyssey*, xxii, lines 79–88.

43. Franklin in Borg *et al.*, *Medieval Sculpture from Norwich Cathedral*, p. 9.

44. T. S. R. Boase, *English Art, 1100–1216* (Oxford, 1953), p. 89.

45. T. A. Heslop, 'Brief in Words but Heavy in the Weight of its Mysteries', in N. Stratford, ed., *Romanesque and Gothic: Essays for George Zarnecki* (Woodbridge, 1987), p. 117.

Fig. 60. Circe changing the companions of Odysseus into pigs.

Ulysfis focij a Circe in porcos.

On the third face of the same capital (fig. 59c), the foliage seen on the first face is repeated but this time without the figure. Between these two opposing sides of the capital there is, on the intermediate face, yet again a figure in a similar pose to the first but with the essential difference that the lower half of his body has been replaced by scrolled stems (fig. 59b). Because of the continuous nature of the decoration on the Norwich capitals, these three scenes are visually interconnected. It appears that a process of transformation has been represented here, shown in three successive stages. Walking around the capital when it was still *in situ*, one might have perceived the gradual emergence of the manikin from the foliage, like fruit on a bough, or conversely his disappearance into it. A condensed and neatly inverted version of this theme also occurs on a twelfth-century capital in the chapter house entrance at Horsham St Faith Priory in Norfolk, where the figure has materialised only below the waist (fig. 61). A similar metamorphosis may be depicted

Fig. 61. Horsham St Faith: capital of entrance to chapter house.

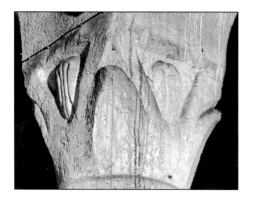

Fig. 62. Dijon, Saint-Bénigne: crypt capital.   Fig. 63. Dijon, Saint-Bénigne: crypt capital.

in sculpture of the early eleventh century at Saint-Bénigne, Dijon (figs 62 and 63). There, on the well-known pair of capitals in the rotunda which are sometimes referred to, surely erroneously, as 'unfinished',[46] foliate forms gradually anthropomorphise into bearded 'orants'. At Dijon the process of transformation takes place on a pair of capitals, rather than on the successive faces of a single one, as on the Norwich cloister capital.

Precisely what such 'foliage figures' represent is unclear but again a classical allusion seems possible. The version of the motif found on the Norwich capital, wherein the figure clasps symmetrical foliate scrolls, these or some other foliage replacing the figure's lower limbs, occurs in sculpture variously throughout antiquity. Illustrated here is an example on a capital from the Palaestra at Aphrodisias (fig. 64) and another on a relief of the Augustan period (fig. 65). The childlike figure on the Roman terracotta has been identified as the god Zagreus (Orphic homonym for Dionysus) flanked by the giant Titans by whom he was beguiled before being dismembered, devoured and eventually reborn.[47] The boy Dionysus was transformed into a goat by Zeus to protect him from Hera's wrath or from the giants who were pursuing him.[48] 'Horned Dionysus' reappeared in many different guises thereafter.[49] On the capital in the nave at Ryes in Normandy, mentioned above, the manikin in foliage has small pointed horns or beast's ears, as does the 'foliage figure' on another capital

46. They are described thus by various authorities, e. g. M. Durand-Lefebvre, *Art Gallo-Romaine et sculpture Romaine* (Paris, 1937), pp. 275–76; M. F. Hearn, *Romanesque Sculpture* (Oxford, 1981), p. 42.

47. V. Macchioro, *Zagreus* (Florence, 1930), p. 72; E. Simon, 'Zagreus: Uber orphische Motive in Campanareliefs', in M. Renard, ed., *Hommages à Albert Grenier*, 3 parts (Brussels, 1962), iii, pp. 1425–26; C. Gasparri in *Lexicon Iconographicum Mythologiae Classicae* (Zurich, 1986), iii, p. 559. The alternative identification as Ampelos seems less likely, given the latter's relative obscurity.

48. Apollodorus, *Bibliotheca*, iii, 4. 3; Ovid, *Metamorphoses*, v, line 329.

49. Nonnus, *Dionysiaca*, vi, lines 170ff, 210.

at Saint-Bénigne, Dijon, in the crypt.[50]
The figure in foliage on the Norwich
capital had its face sheared off in the
fourteenth century but, just discernible,
once one looks for them, are tiny pro-
jections on either side of his head (fig.
59a). The foliage itself, according to the
interpretation offered here, will be the
vine from which Dionysus sprang.[51]

Fig. 64. Capital from the Exedra of the
Palaestra at Aphrodisias.

The pagan themes tentatively identified on these Norwich cloister capitals
might represent random borrowings
from the classical repertory, or they
might have been selected for their allegorical properties. Equally there may have
been a more practical reason for their inclusion. The vitality of the classical literary
tradition within twelfth-century monasticism is well attested. The possible occurrence

50. R. Oursel, *Bourgogne Romane* (5th edn, La
Pierre-qui-Vire, 1968), pl. 7.
51. According to myth, Dionysus was born

once from the earth, again from the vine
and yet again having been torn to pieces by
the Titans, *Diodorus Siculus*, iii, 62, 3–9.

Fig. 65. Dionysus/Zagreus beguiled by Titans. Roman terracotta.

of pagan imagery at the heart of a monastic cathedral, on the capitals of its conventual cloister, however, gives rise to a certain unease. The relative dearth of pagan imagery in Romanesque manuscript painting perhaps contributes to this concern, although there was certainly a strong tradition of graphic representation of pagan iconography in the twelfth century. This is demonstrated by the series of bronze bowls produced at various northern European centres, bearing engraved depictions of mythological cycles.[52] The lacuna in terms of illustrated texts is nevertheless remarkable, given that classical authors were copied, studied and committed to memory as a matter of course in Benedictine houses during the twelfth century. The legends surrounding Dionysus, for example, were recounted by Ovid and other *auctores* familiar to the middle ages. It may be that we need look no further than this for an explanation of his possible presence in a Romanesque monastic cloister.

At Norwich, in the first two decades of the twelfth century, Bishop Herbert's own letters are shot through with classical references.[53] This was perhaps less the manifestation of exceptional erudition than the surfacing willy-nilly of the schooling absorbed in his youth. Classical culture lay at the heart of monastic education, the cardinal factor being Latin; thanks largely to historical accident, the Anglo-Norman monk and his semitic deity addressed one another in the tongue of Ovid and Virgil. The child in a monastic school had to be able to articulate the language of the illogical and capricious Greco-Roman pantheon in order to apprehend the Word of God. Of the large numbers of classical texts housed in monastic libraries, the majority are apparently recorded in the inventory of the cloister school, rather than in that of the community in general.[54] Herbert de Losinga certainly exhorted young brethren at Norwich to pursue their study of Ovid with increased vigour.[55]

Seen in this context, the adoption of pagan motifs for a monastic cloister, skilfully executed in stone at doubtless considerable cost, need be seen neither as a faintly sacrilegious conceit nor as at all incongruous. Boys in a monastic school would have spent considerable periods of time in the cloister alleys.[56] Cloister capitals carved

52. J. Weizmann-Fiedler, *Romanische gravierte Bronzeschalen* (Berlin, 1981).
53. GS, i, pp. 10, 12, 15, 21, 23, 28, 32–33, 39, 44–45, 54, 64, 156–57, 243–44, 249. Also, Franklin, 'Romanesque Cloister Sculpture of Norwich Cathedral', p. 16. For a discussion of this theme see above, p. 31.
54. J. Leclercq, *The Love of Learning and the Desire for God* (3rd edn, London, 1982), p. 114. No source is given for this assertion.
55. GS, i, p. 23.
56. At Canterbury, after daybreak, the community retired to the cloister where the children were to read aloud, D. Knowles, ed., *The Monastic Constitutions of Lanfranc* (London, 1951), p. 4. At Cluny the pupils were installed along the length of the cloister walk, facing the masters who were thus able to oversee them, P. Riché, *Écoles et enseignement dans la haut moyen âge* (Paris, 1989), p. 221. There was evidently a monastic school at Norwich Cathedral in the time of Herbert de Losinga, R. H. Harries, P. Cattermole and P. Mackintosh, *A History of Norwich School* (Norwich, 1991), p. 5.

with dramatic or mythological themes may conceivably have served some pedagogical, perhaps mnemonic function. In their respective treatises on artificial memory, both Hugh of St-Victor in the twelfth century and Thomas Bradwardine in the fourteenth allude in passing to the image of the architectural cloister. Both discuss mnemonic systems wherein information is logged in some form of visualised grid in the mind's eye. Writing *c.* 1130 for the edification of young boys, Hugh of St Victor begins by stressing the need to sort information in an orderly way. A money-changer's purse, says Hugh, is divided into a number of compartments, 'just as a cloister embraces many cells'. For ease of retrieval, knowledge, like coins, must be stored in discrete compartments, equivalent in the eye of the mind to the divisions in the money-changer's pouch.[57] In *De memoria artificiale adquirenda* Bradwardine states that information can be memorised by association with vivid images, lodged in a firm location conjured up by the mind. This location, he says, should be real and familiar, rather than imagined. It should be four-sided and graspable at a single glance, as is a garden or a cloister.[58] Whether or not the boys in the cloister at Norwich were subjected to memory drills of the kind advocated by Hugh of St-Victor, it is likely that Herbert de Losinga would have concurred with him in the view that 'the whole usefulness of education consists only in the memory of it'.[59] Herbert himself was certainly conversant with the work of 'Tully',[60] author of the seminal classical text on memory, the *Rhetorica ad Herennium*.[61]

This observation on the role that cloister sculpture might have played in monastic life casts yet another light on Bernard of Clairvaux's endlessly citable *Apologia*.[62] His rhetorical railing against the 'monstrous centaurs' and other fabulous creatures carved in marble in twelfth-century Cluniac cloisters is based on their being in his view distracting, pointless and expensive. Given that, in his day, Cistercian houses accommodated only adult men and did not incorporate schools, Bernard's objection to elaborate and captivating cloister carving might thus seem entirely reasonable.

57. Hugh's text is the preface to his *Chronica*, composed *c.* 1130, M. Carruthers, *The Book of Memory* (Cambridge, 1990, reprinted 1993), p. 80ff, appendix A, p. 261.

58. Carruthers, *Book of Memory*, appendix C, p. 281. See also 'Thomas Bradwardine "De memoria artificiale adquirenda"', *Journal of Medieval Latin* 2 (1992), pp. 25–43, for Dr Carruthers' revised reading of Bradwardine's treatise.

59. Carruthers, *Book of Memory*, p. 82.

60. GS, i, p. 10.

61. Carruthers, *Book of Memory*, p. 307 n. 116.

62. C. Rudolph, 'The Things of Greater Importance': *Bernard of Clairvaux's Apologia and the Medieval Attitude toward Art* (Philadelphia, 1990), pp. 11–12.

8

The Influence of the Cathedral on Romanesque Architecture

Malcolm Thurlby

In the Romanesque period Ely Cathedral (after 1081), Bury St Edmunds Abbey (after 1081) and Norwich Cathedral (1096 to before 1145) were hubs of architectural activity in East Anglia (see fig. 66 for the location of places mentioned in the text). While it is sometimes possible to pinpoint early affiliates of Ely, the subsequent influence of Norwich on the nave and south-west transept at Ely makes it difficult to be positive about the relative direct impact of each church on others in the region. Furthermore, the ruined state of Bury St Edmunds makes it equally hard to gauge the relative influence of Norwich and Bury, especially in buildings in the Norfolk – Suffolk border region. Some of the buildings discussed in this chapter may therefore have been immediately influenced by Ely or Bury rather than Norwich. Be that as it may, specific stylistic motifs and technical details show a Norwich affiliation and in the main geographical proximity make Norwich influence probable.

The influence of Norwich Cathedral on Romanesque architecture in East Anglia and further afield is evident at a number of different levels.[1] In the first place there are works commissioned by Bishop Herbert de Losinga (1091–1119). Secondly, similarities between Norwich Cathedral, the priory churches of Castle Acre, Binham, Wymondham and Thetford, and the cathedrals of Ely and Peterborough, are strong enough to suggest the involvement of Norwich masons. In certain parish churches some architectural details, such as tower and chancel arches or doorways, suggest the work of cathedral-trained craftsmen. In others, local artisans attempted to incorporate motifs from the cathedral into a traditional repertoire.

1. R. Gem, 'The English Parish Church in the 11th and Early 12th Centuries: A Great Rebuilding?', in J. Blair, ed., *Minsters and Parish Churches: The Local Church in Transition, 950–1200* (Oxford, 1988), pp. 21–30.

Fig. 66. Map showing the location of places mentioned in the text.

The Architectural Patronage of Bishop Herbert de Losinga

Of the churches and chapels founded by Herbert only fragments survive.[2] At St Margaret's, King's Lynn (Norfolk), the surviving Romanesque fabric in the western towers post-dates Herbert's work on the church, but provides evidence for a nave elevation of main arcade, gallery and clerestory which was based on the cathedral. The clustered shafts on the clasping buttresses of the south-west tower evolve from the cathedral crossing tower. Of Herbert's aisleless cruciform church of St Nicholas, Great Yarmouth, there remains the richly-articulated crossing tower. One range of the Lazar Hospital, 219 Sprowston Road, Norwich, survives with

2.   For documentation and discussion, see Fernie, *NC*, pp. 207–9.

Romanesque west and south doorways, the features of which are allied to the cathedral. At St Mary's, North Elmham (Norfolk), the east responds of the nave arcades reflect the cathedral with paired shafts, bulbous, 'tectonic' capitals and scalloped capitals with incised edges. The ruined churches of North Elmham (Norfolk) and South Elmham (Suffolk), formerly believed to be respectively the Anglo-Saxon cathedral and the Old Minster, are more likely to be bishop's chapels erected by Herbert.[3] The dimensions of the main body from the apse to the west wall at North Elmham are the same as those reported for Herbert's palace chapel at Norwich, while the quadrant pilasters and 'tectonic' bases relate to the cathedral.[4] At South Elmham the stilted apse, short rectangular nave and west tower of the same width reflect the proportions of the sanctuary, presbytery and the crossing tower of the cathedral.[5]

Castle Acre

Castle Acre Priory (founded *c.* 1087–89) may have been commenced before Norwich Cathedral, but its construction progressed at a considerably slower pace and the pointed arches with continuous roll mouldings on the south-west tower are not likely before 1160 and may be as late as *c.* 1190.[6] Therefore it would be difficult to think of Castle Acre as a major centre of architectural activity in the manner of Norwich.

The juxtaposition of Barnack and Carstone stone in the eastern arm at Castle Acre may be allied to that of Barnack and Caen stone at the cathedral. It is possible that in both cases a permanent polychrome was intended but, if that was the case, it would have to be argued that the deviations from regular patterning were aesthetically acceptable and that the walls were intended to remain unpainted.[7]

3. S. Heywood, 'The Ruined Church at North Elmham', *JBAA*, 135 (1982), pp. 1–10; Fernie, *NC*, pp. 208–9. See above, figs 2–3.
4. Fernie, *NC*, p. 209.
5. Fernie, *NC*, p. 209.
6. W. H. St J. Hope, 'Castleacre Priory', *NA*, 12 (1895), pp. 105–57; E. P. Willins, *Castle Acre Priory, Norfolk* (London, [1878]); F. H. Fairweather, 'Additions to the Plans of Norman Priory Churches in Norfolk', in C. R. Ingleby, ed., *A Supplement to Blomefield's Norfolk* (London, 1929), pp. 318–24; F. J. E. Raby and P. K. B. Reynolds, *Castle Acre Priory* (2nd edn, London, 1952).

7. Fairweather, 'Norman Priory Churches', p. 323, and B. Cherry, 'Romanesque Architecture in Eastern England', *JBAA*, 131 (1978), pp. 12, refer to red and grey sandstone in the eastern arm of Castle Acre; they suggest that it was arranged in an ornamental pattern. However, Fernie, *NC*, p. 149, observes the lack of strict alternation of the two kinds of stone and that the Carstone peters out in the transept, and suggests that 'the stones were mixed for economy's sake, and mixed relatively regularly in order to distribute their different properties as evenly as possible'.

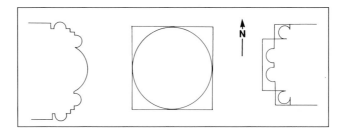

Fig. 67. Castle Acre Priory,
south presbytery arcade piers.

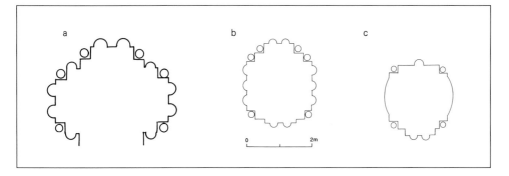

Fig. 68.
a. Norwich Cathedral, north-west crossing pier.   b. Norwich Cathedral, nave arcade, major pier.
c. Norwich Cathedral, nave arcade, minor pier.

The variety in pier design at Castle Acre is more pronounced than at Norwich.[8] In the presbytery main arcades the east responds have paired parallel shafts to carry the inner order and nook shafts for the outer order, the free-standing second pier is cylindrical and the west respond has a segmental face flanked by single nook shafts, forms all related to Norwich (fig. 67). The paired parallel shafts appear on the north and south crossing arches (fig. 68a), and the east responds of the nave arcades.[9] The cylindrical pier is a plain version of those articulating the altar of the Holy Cross in Norwich nave.[10] The segmental face is found on the minor nave and apse piers,

8.   On the Norwich piers, see E. C. Fernie, 'The Romanesque Piers of Norwich Cathedral', *NA*, 36 (1977), pp. 383–86; Fernie, *NC*, pp. 63, 76, 96; for Castle Acre, Cherry, 'Romanesque Architecture in Eastern England', pp. 12–14. See also, L. R. Hoey, 'Pier Form and Vertical Wall Articulation in English Romanesque Architecture', *Journal of the Society of Architectural Historians*, 48 (1989), pp. 258–83, at pp. 276–78.

9.   The same form is also used at Norwich for the responds of the arches from the transepts

to the aisles, and the transept and radiating chapel entrances. At Bury St Edmunds it appears on the east faces of the eastern crossing piers and on the west face of the adjacent pier to the east in the north arcade: Cherry, 'Romanesque Architecture in Eastern England', pl. VIa.

10. Fernie, 'Romanesque Piers', pp. 384–85; E. C. Fernie, 'The Use of Varied Nave Supports in Romanesque and Early Gothic Churches', *Gesta*, 23 (1984), pp. 107–17 at p. 111.

and the east respond of the north presbytery arcade (fig. 68c).[11] As at Norwich, the responds of the arches from the transepts to the presbytery aisles have paired parallel shafts flanked by nook shafts; this motif recurs on the west face of the eastern crossing piers. This creates an asymmetry between the east and west faces of the crossing piers. Paired parallel shafts, without nook shafts, articulate the east and aisle faces of the west crossing piers. On the west face there is a single shaft for the inner order and nook shafts for the second order. This form is then repeated on the east face of the second arcade pier. Thus once again there is asymmetry to the design of the crossing pier but symmetry is now created around the design of the first nave bay. An interesting analogue for this is provided in the west bay of Norwich nave where the segmental face of the penultimate pier is repeated on the west respond.[12] The asymmetrical pier/symmetrical bay-design principle continues throughout the nave at Castle Acre to culminate with an oversized penultimate pier for the support of the twin western towers (fig. 69).[13] The east face of these piers repeats the Norwich minor-pier format (fig. 68c) with the addition of incised spirals on the segmental face which may be based on the Norwich spiral piers.[14] Triple parallel shafts and nook shafts articulate the west face of this pier and the west respond in the manner of the Norwich major piers (fig. 68b).[15] Throughout the nave aisles the responds change according to the pier design; on the evidence of the three extant cases the same would be true for the vertical articulation.[16]

Evidence for the articulation of the gallery arches is found in the nave in the south-west bay, the east face of the penultimate south pier and on the west respond on the north-west tower (fig. 70). The arches had two orders each carried on nook shafts. The presbytery gallery arches have gone but the respond of the arch from the north transept to the north presbytery gallery is only articulated with a chamfered string at the springing of the arch.

---

11. Fernie, 'Romanesque Piers', p. 384, suggests that the major piers in the presbytery and the east face of the eastern crossing piers may have used the same segmental form.
12. E. C. Fernie, 'Excavations at the Façade of Norwich Cathedral', *NA*, 36 (1974), pp. 75.
13. Cherry, 'Romanesque Architecture in Eastern England', p. 14, figs 6 and 7.
14. The west face of nave pier five and the east face of pier six have incised lozenges similar to Durham Cathedral nave and affiliates at Selby Abbey and Kirkby Lonsdale (Cumbria).
15. Triple parallel shafts are also used in the dormitory undercroft doorway, flanked by

two nook shafts, and on the respond on the middle of the north wall, flanked by single nook shafts.
16. It can no longer be determined whether vertical articulation was used in the presbytery, but in the transept only the north-west angle of the north transept and the south-west angle of the south transept are articulated. In this connection it is worth noting the lack of vertical articulation in the south transept of Ely Cathedral, especially in view of the similarity in the clerestory design in both places with tall, narrow side arches springing from the same level as the window arches.

Intersecting blind arcading is used on the west wall of the north transept at both Castle Acre and Norwich, while the single blind arches flanking the aisle windows on the second and third north nave aisle bays at Castle Acre relate to the exterior nave gallery walls at Norwich. The Castle Acre west front follows the sectional

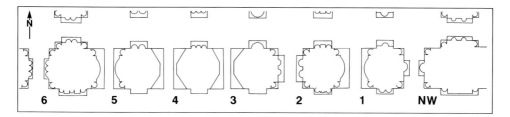

Fig. 69. Castle Acre Priory, nave arcade piers. Respond opposite north-west crossing pier and pier 4 deduced from south aisle; pier 3 and east face of pier 5 hypothetical, deduced from adjacent piers and responds.

Fig. 70. Castle Acre Priory, nave, interior to south west.

mode of Norwich with the addition of towers over the aisle bays.[17] Both façades have three doorways with blind arcading above the aisle doorways and single windows flanked by blind arches.[18] The reticulated masonry behind the blind arches flanking the main west window at Castle Acre may be compared with this motif above the north aisle façade window at Norwich. Even the unusual detail of small flints in the mortar at the top of the plinth course on the Castle Acre façade is paralleled at Norwich.[19]

Binham

Binham Priory was founded by Peter de Valoines as a daughter house of the great Benedictine abbey of St Albans. Matthew Paris mentions that the cell existed in the time of Abbot Paul (d. 1093), but the foundation charter and endowment were not completed until *c.* 1104.[20] Building progressed slowly and, according to Matthew Paris, Prior Richard de Parco (1226–44) 'built the front of the church from the foundation to the roof'.[21]

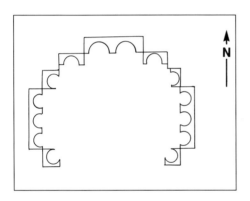

Fig. 71. Binham Priory, presbytery arcade pier.

The piers of the crossing, main arcade and gallery, and the nook-shafted buttress on the south presbytery aisle at Binham are all based on their counterparts at Norwich. The Binham crossing has triple parallel shafts to carry the soffits, like the east and west crossing arches at Norwich. The presbytery arcade piers at Binham also have triple parallel shafts to carry the inner order of the arch and nook shafts for the second order (fig. 71). There follows a second set of nook shafts and paired parallel shafts on the face of the pier. The second set of nook shafts is matched on the north-east and south-east crossing piers, where the shaft continues above the main arcade to the gallery in the manner of Norwich nave major piers (fig. 68b). While at Norwich these shafts carry the

17. Fernie, 'Excavations', relates Castle Acre façade to Norwich.
18. The intersecting arcade above the south aisle doorway at Norwich is the product of nineteenth-century restoration and does not agree with pre-restoration representations of the façade: J. P. McAleer, 'The Romanesque Façade of Norwich Cathedral', *Journal of the*

Society of Architectural Historians, 25 (1966), pp. 136–140.
19. Fernie, 'Excavations', p. 72.
20. W. Dugdale, *Monasticon Anglicanum*, 6 vols in 8 (London, 1817–30), iii, p. 341; *VCH Norfolk*, ii, p. 343.
21. M. Paris, *Chronica majora*, ed. H. R. Luard, 7 vols (RS, 57, 1872–84), vi, p. 90.

outer order of the gallery arch, at Binham the continuation of the shaft above this level on the south-east crossing pier precludes this arrangement. This second set of nook shafts may have carried an extra order of the eastern crossing arch but, given the use of identical nook shafts on the presbytery arcade piers, they may have articulated a high groin or rib vault.[22] This is unusual in East Anglian Romanesque architecture, where the preference was for wood-roofed main spans. However, it is likely that the apses of the major churches, including Norwich Cathedral, were vaulted; in incorporating a high stone vault in the presbytery Binham may reflect its mother house of St Albans.[23]

The presbytery gallery piers repeat the main arcade design minus the second set of nook shafts and, as such, conform to the gallery piers at Norwich. The cushion capitals of the gallery west responds have incised edges, a detail used at Norwich in one set of apse gallery capitals.[24]

The transepts at Binham were not vaulted; the wall shafts next to the south-east and south-west crossing piers continue above the level of what would be an appropriate springing point of a high vault. Next to the south-west crossing pier there remains a minor arch of the clerestory with a small nook shaft flanking the arch above the free-standing column. The same design is fully preserved in the nave, where the affiliation to the Norwich clerestory is obvious, even though the Binham version omits the shafted wall arch for the window that is a consistent feature at Norwich.[25]

On the north-west and south-west crossing piers the triple shafts to the nave aisle soffits follow the presbytery but at gallery level they are omitted. This plain design continues down the nave and contrasts with the richness of the liturgically more important eastern arm. Vertical articulation remains the same as in the presbytery, with paired shafts on an impost block continuing in the nave to the roof, a form derived from the major piers at Norwich.

22. The paired front shafts and the adjacent set of nook shafts are absent from the east presbytery piers at Binham. It may be that they were removed when the apse was rebuilt. Fairweather, 'Norman Priory Churches', p. 326, talks of a fracture between the east respond of the south arcade and the springing of the apse, but it is not clear exactly how to interpret this in relation to the Romanesque fabric.

23. The case for a rib-vaulted apse at Norwich is made by C. Wilson, 'Abbot Serlo's Church at Gloucester (1089–1100): Its Place in Romanesque Architecture', in BAACT, 7, *Gloucester and Tewkesbury, 1981*, ed. T. A. Heslop and V. A. Sekules (1985), pp. 64 and 80 n. 75. On the former high groin vault in the Romanesque presbytery of St Albans, see C. R. Peers and W. Page, eds, *VCH Hertfordshire*, ii (London, 1908), pp. 484, 490.

24. Incised-edge cushion capitals were later used at Norwich Cathedral, inside the west front on the right blind arcade and in the clerestory of the crossing lantern, in the nave of Wymondham Priory, the crossing at Attleborough and elsewhere.

25. For the context of the Norwich clerestory design, see L. Hoey, 'The Design of Romanesque Clerestories with Wall Passages in Normandy and England', *Gesta*, 28 (1989), pp. 78–101.

The ornamentation of the outer order of the nave arcades changes from bay to bay. On the one hand, this reflects the long building programme; on the other, it admirably illustrates the twelfth-century love of design variety, something that can also be experienced in the related nave of Wymondham Priory.[26]

Wymondham

Wymondham Priory was founded in 1107 as a cell of St Albans by William d'Albini.

26. On design variety in English Romanesque ornament, see M. Thurlby and Y. Kusaba, 'The Nave of Saint Andrew at Steyning: A Study of Variety in Design in Twelfth-Century Architecture in Britain', *Gesta*, 30 (1991), pp. 163–75.

Fig. 72. Wymondham Priory, nave, interior to north west.

It was richly endowed by him and his wife, Maud, daughter of Roger Bigod, earl of Norfolk.[27]

Nine bays of the original twelve-bay Romanesque nave are preserved in modified form (fig. 72) The two-order arches of the main arcades are extant but, with the exception of the west responds and the penultimate piers, the piers have been reworked into irregular octagons in the fifteenth century. However, details of capitals and vertical articulation are preserved to show that the pier form would have been the same as in the gallery, with paired parallel shafts to carry the soffit and nook shafts for the outer order. The paired parallel shafts reflect the east and west arches of the crossing at Norwich and the east respond of the nave arcade. An alternation of paired and single shafts ran from floor to roof in the manner of Norwich nave. The penultimate west piers are larger than those to the east and are articulated with three parallel shafts on each face, those towards the nave originally continuing to the roof plate. The west respond is similarly articulated and together they indicate twin western towers in the manner of Castle Acre. Only the west minor arch of the west clerestory bay survives but, in view of the other similarities with Norwich, an analogous clerestory may be reconstructed.

Thetford

Roger Bigod founded a Cluniac priory of Thetford in 1104 which was moved to the present site where the sod was turned by Bishop Herbert de Losinga in 1107. The monks moved into the new church on St Martin's Day, 1114.[28]

The presbytery arcade piers at Thetford are based on the minor piers at Norwich (figs 68c, 73 and 74).[29] The crossing piers have paired parallel shafts for the north and south arches and triple parallel shafts for the east and west arches as at Norwich. The segmental face of the east side of the east crossing piers reflects the design of the presbytery arcade piers; this design may also have been used at Norwich.[30] The triumphal arch shares the twin parallel shafts with its counterpart at Norwich and preserves the springing of the arch itself which is now missing at Norwich. The dado arcade in the presbytery aisles and transept chapels may also be equated with Norwich, although this feature may possibly have derived from Ely.[31]

The nave is poorly preserved. There remains the west respond of the north nave

27. *VCH Norfolk*, ii, p. 336; Fairweather, 'Norman Priory Churches', pp. 328–34.
28. *VCH Norfolk*, ii, p. 363; H. Harrod, 'Observations on the History and Present State of Thetford Priory', *NA*, 3 (1852), pp. 105–24; Fairweather, 'Norman Priory Churches', pp. 334–39; F. Raby and P.

K. B. Reynolds, *Thetford Priory* (London, 1979).

29. Hoey, 'Pier Form', p. 278 n. 107.
30. Fernie, 'Romanesque Piers', p. 384.
31. Half-shaft buttresses like those at Thetford are used on the south nave aisle of Ely Cathedral.

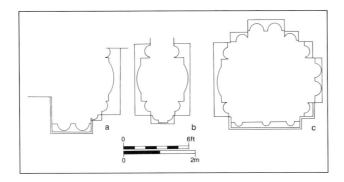

Fig. 73. Thetford Priory,
presbytery arcade piers;
a: east respond;
b: presbytery pier;
c: crossing pier.

arcade with nook shafts flanking an angled core; and the north aisle respond of the
penultimate pier with a large central shaft flanked by two lesser ones and two nook
shafts. The variety in the design of these responds is analogous to the nave of Castle
Acre which suggests that, like Castle Acre, other piers in the Thetford nave may
have changed form in each bay. The scale of the Thetford responds, plus the
thickening of the walls of the westernmost aisle bays, shows that there were twin
west towers in the manner of Castle Acre. The west front at Thetford had three
doorways, like Norwich and Castle Acre, and the bases of a blind arcade on the
north face of the north-west tower at Thetford imply that the Thetford façade was
richly arcaded like Castle Acre.

Details of the monastic buildings at Thetford have affiliations with Norwich. In
the slype there are bases like inverted cushion capitals, as in the transept and nave
clerestories at Norwich.[32] Harrod records two mouldings found near the chapter
house entrance: a double cone like the north transept west clerestory at Norwich;
and a double cheese, a multiplied version of the single cheese above the blind arcade
at the back of the bishop's throne at Norwich.[33]

Of the four priory churches influenced by Norwich none adopts the apse –
ambulatory plan with radiating chapels. Instead, the three-apse termination is

32. S. E. Rigold, 'Romanesque Bases in the
    South-East of the Limestone Belt', in M.
    R. Apted, R. Gilyard-Beer and A. D.
    Saunders, eds, *Ancient Monuments and their
    Interpretation: Essays Presented to A. J. Taylor*
    (London and Chichester, 1977), p. 108, ob-
    serves that 'upturned cushion-capitals are
    common in East Anglia under small shafts
    of portals, fonts, wall-arcades, etc . . .' He
    cites examples on the portals of Haddiscoe
    (Norfolk), Southoe (Hunts.), Great Wy-
    mondley (Herts.), the frater at Horsham St
    Faith (Norfolk), the slype at Thetford, the

presbytery at Carrow (Norfolk), and the
west range at Binham. To these may be
added the south doorways at Burgh St Margaret (Norfolk), Ormesby (Norfolk) and
Kenninghall (Norfolk); Kilverstone (Norfolk), bell opening; Chedgrave (Norfolk),
north doorway; East Winch (Norfolk), pis-
cina; Hales (Norfolk), south nave window;
Wissett (Suffolk), north doorway and other
sites discussed below.
33. Harrod, 'Thetford', p. 121, refers to similar
    mouldings on the west face of the tower
    arch at Attleborough.

preferred for the two-bay eastern arms at Binham and Castle Acre, and in the three-bay presbyteries at Thetford and Wymondham.[34] In other respects these churches are close to Norwich. All have unaisled transepts with a single apsidal chapel to each arm which, at least at Binham and Castle Acre, had two storeys like Norwich.[35] Elevations comprise main arcade, gallery and clerestory with wall passage, although relative proportions vary. Thetford comes closest to Norwich, with an approximately one-to-one proportion between main arcade and gallery. At Wymondham the gallery is slightly lower, at Castle Acre lower still and at Binham it is further diminished and lacks direct lighting.[36] Like Norwich, gallery arches are not sub-divided, except in the north nave and north transept bays adjacent to the crossing at Wymondham where sub-arches of the gallery are preserved. Pier forms and vertical articulation are related to, or evolve from, Norwich. Similarly, arch mouldings follow Norwich with angle rolls, shallow hollows

Fig. 74. Thetford Priory, presbytery, interior from north transept.

and rolls on the face of the arch, some or all of which may be set off by quirks. Aisles are groin-vaulted in the manner of the cathedral.

Ely Cathedral

Ely was begun early in the abbacy of Simeon (1081–93), and the eastern arm, crossing and transepts were probably completed by 1106 when the relics of St Etheldreda were translated. In 1109 papal approval was given for its conversion to an episcopal see. Work on the upper parts of the western transept was completed

---

34. For plans, see Fernie, *NC*, Castle Acre, fig. 53; Binham, fig. 54; Wymondham, fig. 55.
35. The walls of the Thetford transept chapels do not stand high enough to determine whether or not they had two storeys. The

Wymondham chapels are only known from excavation.

36. The line of the Binham gallery roof is preserved on the section of wall to the left of the south nave aisle west window.

Fig. 75. Ely Cathedral,
south nave aisle interior.

by Bishop Ridel (1173–89), while the western transept and galilee porch are the
work of Bishop Eustace (1197–1215).[37]

The nave of Ely Cathedral is more richly articulated than the transepts and almost
certainly reveals the influence of Norwich. In the nave aisles dado arcades are
introduced on the model of Norwich and they are topped with a stringcourse
enriched with the same chevron as on the Norwich nave gallery arches (fig. 75).
Mouldings of the same family as Norwich are used on all arches in the nave at Ely
except the middle order of the four eastern bays. Several details in the south-west
transept at Ely betray a close knowledge of Norwich (fig. 76); the stepped form of
the third level of blind arcade on the west wall relates to the first level arcade in the

37. L. F. Salzman, ed., *VCH Cambridgeshire*, ii (London, 1948), pp. 202–3.

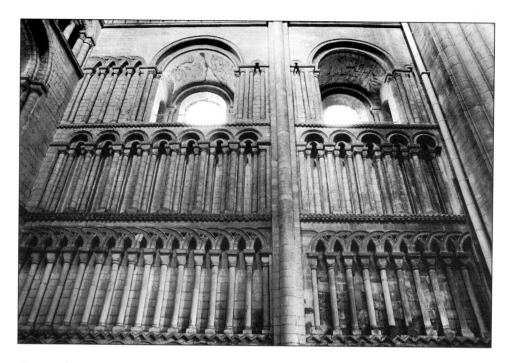

Fig. 76. Ely Cathedral, south-west transept, interior west wall.

lantern at Norwich; the superposed blind arches next to the gallery arches on the east wall reflect the blind arches above the minor arches of the Norwich clerestory; constructional details of the west wall passage and the south windows, including a moulded wall arch carried on shafts with cushion capitals and transverse barrel vaults with partial groins intruding from the sides, recall the Norwich north nave clerestory.

Peterborough Cathedral

The Benedictine abbey church, now the cathedral, of Peterborough was commenced in 1117 or 1118. It was ready for services by 1143 but work on the nave was not completed until the time of Abbot Benedict (1177–94).[38]

Elements from Norwich Cathedral play a significant, although far from exclusive, role in the design of Peterborough Cathedral.[39] The clerestory follows the Norwich

38. R. M. Serjeantson and W. R. D. Adkins, eds, *VCH Northamptonshire*, ii (London, 1906), pp. 431–47.
39. For instance, the three-apse east end, the sub-divided gallery openings and possibly the stair vices at the apse chord that link

the gallery and clerestory reflect Ely Cathedral; see J. P. McAleer, 'Some Observations about the Romanesque Choir of Ely Cathedral', *Journal of the Society of Architectural Historians*, 53 (1994), pp. 80–94.

stepped rhythm, incorporating the window wall arch on columns as well as the small nook shafts above the intermediate columns to raise the springing of the central arch. The soffits of the east and west crossing arches are carried on triple parallel shafts, while the aisle face of the north-east and south-east crossing piers is segmental in the manner of the Norwich minor piers. The aisleless west wall and terminal walls of the transepts come close to Norwich in their use of superposed large round-headed windows in hollow walls (fig. 77).

There is clear evidence that the Peterborough apse was rib-vaulted: in this regard it may have followed Norwich, where the half shafts on the front of the apse piers would logically have continued as ribs in the apse vault. The form of the Peterborough vault, with three radiating ribs in the apse preceded by a quadripartite vault in the next bay to the west, would have been more elaborate than Norwich, but the iconographic form of a permanent canopy over the high altar is the same.[40]

Waltham Abbey

Many details of Waltham Abbey nave (begun *c.* 1120) betray a detailed knowledge of East Anglian churches.[41] The use of groin vaults in the aisles reflects all major East Anglian churches before Peterborough. The moulding of the south aisle east arch with angle roll and a hollow on the wall face compares with Norwich and Ely. Most specifically in connection with Norwich, the first two bays of the north clerestory and the entire south clerestory have the stepped design with minor nook shafts above the columns. As in the Binham clerestory, the window wall arch is not repeated at Waltham.

Norwich Castle

On the basis of the similarity with Henry I's castle at Falaise (Normandy), Norwich Castle is generally attributed to his reign (1100–35).[42] The rich external arcading marks a new departure in castle architecture and may be explained through the

40. M. Thurlby, 'The Romanesque Apse Vault at Peterborough Cathedral', in D. Buckton and T. A. Heslop, eds, *Studies in Medieval Art and Architecture Presented to Peter Lasko* (Stroud, 1994), pp. 171–86.

41. E. C. Fernie, 'The Romanesque Church of Waltham Abbey', *JBAA*, 138 (1985), pp. 48–78.

42. H. M. Colvin *et al.*, eds, *History of the King's Works*, 6 vols (London, 1963–76), i, p. 39;

ii, p. 754, fig. 8, compares the north elevations of Norwich and Falaise. See also, W. Wilkins, 'An Essay towards a History of the Venta Icenorum of the Romans and of Norwich Castle: with Remarks on the Architecture of the Anglo-Saxons and Normans', *Archaeologia*, 12 (1796), pp. 132–80; A. Hartshorne, 'Norwich Castle', *Arch. J.*, 46 (1889), pp. 260–68; A. B. Whittingham, 'Norwich Castle', *Arch. J.*, 106 (1949), p. 77.

Fig. 77. Peterborough Cathedral, transept, interior to north east.

influence of the cathedral. Although the castle exterior was completely refaced by Salvin between 1833 and 1839, reference to pre-restoration drawings shows that the details may be trusted.[43] The forms of the blind arcades, the mouldings and cushion capitals, and (in the top arcade on the west face) the reticulated stonework at the back of the arcade, all find parallels at the cathedral. Similarly, the blind arches flanking the windows at the castle reflect the cathedral clerestory.

Castle Rising

Castle Rising was commenced in 1138 by William d'Albini, founder of Wymondham Priory.[44] It is related in plan and other respects to Norwich Castle, although it is not totally encrusted with exterior arcading. Many features betray a knowledge of the cathedral and other Norfolk churches. The great staircase has nook-shafted buttresses, as at the cathedral, and nook shafts are also used on angle buttresses. The plinth on the exterior of the staircase is the same as on the exterior of the south presbytery aisle at Binham.[45] The blind arcading, whether plain, intersecting or with reticulated masonry behind, relates to Norwich Castle and Cathedral. The simple chevron string on the exterior of the staircase is related to the nave gallery arches at the cathedral. The roundels recall the cathedral crossing tower and are now inhabited with various heads. In the vestibule the cushion capitals and bases for the windows and the doorway to the great hall repeat these motifs in the clerestory of the cathedral. The barrel vaults of the window heads of the vestibule with partially intruding side groins are the same as the cathedral nave clerestory west of the third bay.

Orford (Suffolk)

Of the parish church traditionally believed to have been begun by Wimar, chaplain to Henry II, *c.* 1166–70, there remain the ruined presbytery arcades, the eastern crossing piers and the north respond of the arch to the former north transept chapel.[46] The square-ended, six-bay presbytery projected one bay beyond the aisles. The elaborate arcade piers change on the east-west axis but match north-south except in the third piers, which on the north is an angle-set octagon with angle shafts and

43. Wilkins, 'Norwich Castle', pls xxiv–xxvi, xxxviii–xli. For Salvin at Norwich, see J. Allibone, *Anthony Salvin: Pioneer of Gothic Revival Architecture, 1799–1881* (Columbia, Missouri, 1987), pp. 95–97, 160.

44. R. A. Brown, *Castle Rising* (London, 1983).

45. Cherry, 'Romanesque Architecture in Eastern England', p. 17 n. 37. The same moulding is used below the north nave aisle windows at Castle Acre.

46. F. H. Fairweather, 'Excavations in the Ruined Choir of the Church of St Bartholomew, Orford, Suffolk', *Antiq. J.,* 14 (1934), pp. 170–76.

on the south is cylindrical with raised lozenges.[47] Although the multi-scalloped capitals, arch mouldings and chevron ornament are later than Norwich Cathedral, several details betray reference to the cathedral. The east and west responds of the presbytery arcades have triple parallel shafts for the inner order flanked by nook shafts for the outer order.[48] The segmental face of the Norwich minor pier is reflected in the south respond to the north transept chapel. The north and south crossing arches have paired parallel shafts flanked by nook shafts in the manner of their counterparts at Norwich. The north re-spond of the arch from the north trans-ept to the north presbytery aisle has triple parallel shafts with intervening wedges, a design most closely allied to the nave faces of the tower piers at St Margaret's, King's Lynn.

Fig. 78. Attleborough, crossing, interior to south west.

Attleborough

The low crossing arches of the parish church (*c.* 1140) each have two orders and the soffit carried on triple parallel shafts (fig. 78).[49] The stylised foliage on the underside of the cushion capitals is related to Norwich south presbytery gallery and the south-west tower pier at Wymondham. The superposed wall pas-sages in the tower recall their counter-parts at the cathedral, while the openings from these passages towards the nave with twin-shafted responds without capitals or bases are handled in the manner of Norwich lantern. In the ruins of the former eastern arm there are north-west and south-west nook shafts with volute capitals.

47. The raised spiral design on the penultimate north arcade pier is paralleled in the north nave arcade at Pittington (Co. Durham) and Compton Martin (Somerset). N. Pevsner and E. Williamson, *The Buildings of England: County Durham* (2nd rev. edn, Harmonds-worth, 1983), pp. 380–81, pl. 30; N. Pev-sner, *The Buildings of England: North Somerset*

and Bristol (Harmondsworth, 1958), pl. 7 printed in reverse.
48. Hoey, 'Pier Form', p. 278 n. 107.
49. E. Fernie, *Architecture of the Anglo-Saxons* (London, 1983), p. 169, relates the low crossing arches at Attleborough to Mel-bourne (Derbyshire), Melton Constable (Norfolk) and Oulton (Suffolk).

They are set too far from the eastern arch to be related to its articulation and therefore they were probably used in connection with a rib-vaulted chancel.

The Influence of the Cathedral on Minor Church Building

Certain motifs at Norwich Cathedral are traditionally associated with Anglo-Saxon architecture, including circular double-splay windows, quadrant pilasters and triangular arches.[50] While the triangular-headed arch is certainly Anglo-Saxon, it may well be that the double-splay windows and quadrant pilasters were disseminated from the cathedral.[51] Inside the cathedral, above the blind arcade above the doorway in the north wall of the north transept, are blind triangular hoods with a central *prokrossos* (projecting hood). In contrast to Anglo-Saxon triangular arches, the hoods are ornamented with billet.[52] Such juxtapositions of Anglo-Saxon and Norman motifs occur in many East Anglian minor churches. At Haddiscoe (Norfolk) the bell openings are carved with billet and have triangular heads surmounted by *prokrossoi*. The mid-wall shafts are renewed but may repeat the original design with octagonal shafts and scalloped capitals as in the north transept clerestory of the cathedral. The horizontal divisions of the tower with chamfered string courses reflect such articulation at the cathedral; it may well be that the quadrant pilaster in the angles between the tower and the nave west wall were inspired by those in the radiating chapels at the cathedral.[53]

In the round tower at Herringfleet (Suffolk) the triangular bell opening arches with mid-wall shafts are paired and enclosed in a round-headed arch with angle roll and single billet as in the cathedral. Double billet flanks the nook shafts with cushion capitals and there is a chamfered string beneath the bell chamber level. The tower side of the arch communicating with the nave is enriched with a row of billet down the jambs.

Billet ornament on a triangular arch appears on a more monumental scale in the west doorway at Great Dunham (Norfolk). Here the question of the continuity of Anglo-Saxon motifs after the Conquest is especially interesting because the quoins

50. H. M. and J. Taylor, *Anglo-Saxon Architecture*, 3 vols (Cambridge, 1965–78), i, pp. 5, 244, 271; ii, p. 524; iii, pp. 807–10, 838, 853–54.

51. S. Heywood, 'The Round Towers of East Anglia', in Blair, *Minsters and Parish Churches*, pp. 169–70, discusses the theory of the dissemination of the quadrant pilaster from the cathedral versus their representing a local Anglo-Saxon building tradition.

52. Billet ornament is used, for example, on the west towers at Jumièges and St Étienne at Caen. It seems to have been introduced into England from Normandy after the Conquest as in the string courses and window hoods of Winchester Cathedral transepts. However, an interesting example of the motif occurs above the north respond of the chancel arch at Great Paxton (Hunts.), a building traditionally dated about 1050.

53. See above, n. 51; Heywood, 'North Elmham,' pp. 2–3.

Fig. 79. Great Dunham, nave, interior to north west.

Fig. 80. Norwich Cathedral, apse gallery to north west.

of the nave and the axial tower are treated in long-and-short fashion. Yet a date before the early twelfth century is unlikely because the internal nave wall arcading must surely derive from the presbytery gallery at the cathedral (figs 79 and 80). Mid-wall shafts with cushion capitals are used in the bell openings; above this are circular, double-splay openings of the type used in the west wall of the cloister at Norwich.[54]

Another clear post-Conquest use of the double-splayed roundel is in the round tower added to the nave at Hales (Norfolk).[55] Given that the blocked Romanesque window with nook shafts and cushion capitals in the south nave wall and the various blind arches in the apse depend on the cathedral, the west tower must date from well into the twelfth century.

Double-splay roundels also appear in the chancel at Framingham Earl (Norfolk),

54. For the west wall of Norwich cloister, Fernie, *NC*, pp. 22–23.

55. Heywood, 'Round Towers', p. 170.

where the seemingly strange angle of the side walls can be allied to the angle of the bishop's chapel to the nave at Norwich Cathedral, in that it conforms to the one to the square root of two proportional system employed throughout the Romanesque cathedral.[56]

Several parish churches preserve doorways related to the cathedral. In each case they have two orders with a plain inner order interrupted only by a chamfered impost block; and a second order with columns and moulded arch.[57] Designs are based on the north transept and nave aisle west doorways plus the imposts from the aisle wall arches and are often accompanied by other cathedral-related details. The north doorway at Quidenham (Norfolk) has the second order carried on volute capitals and an angle roll, hollow and front roll on the arch. This work is contemporary with the round west tower with quadrant buttresses. The north doorway at Old Buckenham (Norfolk) conforms to the basic type but with incised-edge cushion capitals and richer forms in the arch. At Fundenhall (Norfolk) the south doorway has volute capitals and mouldings compatible with the cathedral in the second order. Most interestingly the nook-shafted jambs of the west arch of the axial tower there are mainly of Caen stone but with Barnack interspersed as at the cathedral. At Marham (Norfolk) the north doorway has reticulated masonry in the tympanum in the manner of the tympanum of the doorway to the stair vice in the cathedral north transept. At Gillingham (Norfolk) the outer order of the west doorway has an angle roll, angle fillet and face roll plus a billet hood. On the north doorway a billet hood, volute capitals and the same simple chevron as in the Norwich nave gallery. This chevron is repeated in the sub-arcuation of the north bell chamber of the axial tower. Here there are paired bell openings under enclosing arches. The details are different on all four faces in keeping with the variety of ornamentation in the nave arcades at Binham and Wymondham.

At South Lopham (Norfolk) the north nave doorway is a rich example of the group, with incised-edge cushion capitals and a double-cheese hood. Interestingly, next to the doorway there is a circular double-splay window. The angle roll and hollow mouldings of the west faces of the east and west arches of the axial tower relate to the cathedral. The inner order is carried on ill-formed cushion capitals which are paralleled in some of the gallery responds in the Norwich presbytery. The quirked-chamfer abaci also relate to the cathedral. The axial tower has rich ashlar arcading on a rubble core with some volute but mainly cushion capitals. The bell stage has paired openings with angle rolls and quirked hollows and roundels which can be read as rustic versions of those on the Norwich crossing tower.

56. Fernie, *NC*, pp. 94–100.
57. J. A. Franklin, 'The Romanesque Cloister Sculpture of Norwich Cathedral' (un-   published University of East Anglia M.A. thesis, 1980).

Further references to provincial reflections of Norwich Cathedral would add little to the thesis that the cathedral was of prime importance for the development of Romanesque architecture in East Anglia. As the major architectural undertaking in Norfolk in the fifty years after its inception in 1096, Norwich Cathedral would have been both a home for skilled masons and a major centre for training young craftsmen. The direct impact of these men has been traced in many buildings, while the aesthetic aspects of design details are also felt in more rustic efforts of local artisans trying to keep abreast of the current architectural fashions.

9

The Gothic Campaigns

Francis Woodman

Bishop Suffield and the New East End

Thirteenth-century England experienced a mania for extending its major churches eastwards. Her cathedrals were already long by continental standards, in part a consequence of the peculiar provision in many for both bishops and monks. Most post-Conquest cathedrals offered inadequate liturgical space, hence few English Romanesque eastern terminations survive intact. That at Norwich remains, but only just. Canterbury set the fashion in the 1180s, sparking an explosion of new east ends – Chichester, Lincoln, Winchester, Hereford, Rochester among others. Becket brought Canterbury astonishing fame, and now every English saint was sought out, rehabilitated and rehoused. Saintless cathedrals like Norwich could exploit the rising cult of the Virgin Mary but, whatever the excuse, eastern extensions dominated English architecture for nearly a century. In the case of Salisbury and eventually Westminster, twice rethought in thirty years, wholly new churches were seen as the only answer. Yet it was not entirely a matter of status. Norman eastern plan-types were not only too short, many provided for a liturgy that did not suit the English. Pre-Conquest England had favoured many Germanic liturgical ideas, especially a strict orientation of altars most easily accommodated within a square or stepped plan. Apse, ambulatory and radiating chapels offered subsidiary altars facing north east and south east, evidently no problem for the French but resisted by the English from the outset. Winchester, Canterbury and Norwich had attempted a squaring of the circle – radiating chapels skewed eastwards with strange and even bizarre consequences. The new desire for a separate axial Lady Chapel also reflects the popularity of new liturgical rites such as the Use of Sarum. These often required a distinct Virgin sanctuary for Marian rites and sometimes, as in the case of Winchester, led to two axial chapels in tandem: first the saint, then the Virgin.

Norwich entered the race rather late and apparently with little lasting enthusiasm. Bishop Walter Suffield (1244–57), demolished Losinga's eastern axial chapel for a longer, square-ended Lady Chapel.[1] Though demolished after the Dissolution, its outline remains with lumps and fragments visible in the grass. It measured nearly 36 ft by 72 ft (11 m. by 22 m.) and was nearly 7 ft (2 m.) wider than the presbytery. What is less immediately clear is evidence for the intended connection between Lady Chapel and ambulatory. Here, considerable standing remains were incorporated into the modern axial chapel. On either side, what appear to be buttresses project north and south immediately adjoining the Romanesque aisle. The northern 'buttress' actually contains the jamb of an intended east-facing window, part of a new, square-plan or stepped eastern termination. Had the plan proceeded, the new window bay would have replaced at least the curved section of the Romanesque ambulatory wall between the northern radial chapel and the entrance to the new Lady Chapel. No evidence remains to suggest the extent of this scheme though, unless the proposed window was to be virtually a single lancet, it could only have proceeded at the expense of the radial chapels. At the very least, square bays with sufficient space for small altars would terminate the presbytery aisles, replacing the curved sections of the ambulatory. Possibly, the original concept included merely a restructuring of the existing radial chapels, either squaring them or, in some way breaking through to join more directly with the new work. More likely, the whole Romanesque ambulatory scheme was destined to disappear. The model may well have been Salisbury, where the new cathedral had a highly developed stepped plan, though any retention of the main apse at Norwich would have forced considerable compromise. At St Bartholomew's, Smithfield, London, a similar scheme was undertaken; but there part of the Romanesque apse was sacrificed and the new stepped east end connected up in a somewhat ungainly fashion. Winchester provides another potential model, though the continued existence of the Romanesque apse within the early thirteenth-century stepped east end is debatable. Both Smithfield and Winchester possessed Romanesque ambulatory radial chapels of unusual plan, those at St Bartholomew's being modelled upon Norwich. One final possibility is the intended destruction of the main apse, providing a square-end upon the chord piers, with a double aisled square ambulatory in the manner of Southwark and Salisbury.

The axial Lady Chapel was probably four bays long with angle buttresses. No further evidence for buttresses, and hence potential vaulting, has yet been uncovered. The roof scars visible before the addition of the current axial chapel (fig. 81) suggest that the Romanesque gallery door/window might have given access to a roof space above a vault. The main ambulatory entrance survives, though the present jambs and central trumeau are fifteenth-century replacements. The earlier tympanum has twin openings from the ambulatory, with complex mouldings and pronounced dog-tooth decoration. The spandrel is cut through by a large quatrefoil enclosed

1. B. Cotton, *Historia Anglicana*, ed. H. R. Luard (RS, 16, 1859), p. 394. See also above, fig. 20.

Fig. 81. Norwich Cathedral from the east, a nineteenth-century engraving, showing the roof scar left by the removal of Suffield's Lady Chapel in the later sixteenth century.

within a circle, recalling St Hugh's choir at Lincoln and de Lucy's Lady Chapel at Winchester. The reverse side within the chapel shows no sign of vault scars. For some reason, the jambs and trumeau of the Lady Chapel entry were replaced in the late middle ages with new work in the Perpendicular style. These have moulded capitals rather too large for their role. Additional mouldings can be seen buried within the plaster setting of the jambs. The purpose of replacing the lower elements of the entry while leaving the thirteenth-century tympanum can only be guessed at – perhaps the previous jambs were damaged in one of the fires or possibly the whole building was updated *c.* 1450. If so, why not the tympanum? Suffield died in May 1257 and was buried in a standing tomb placed in the centre of his chapel. His saintly life doubtless raised expectations of canonisation but it was not to be.

The Ethelbert Gate

A structure of modest size but considerable elaboration, the Ethelbert Gate was the principal entrance to the priory from the city until the fifteenth century. Traces of an earlier gateway remain towards the inner arch. The gate was rebuilt after the riots of 1272. The new work dates from *c.* 1310–17; the doors were made in the latter year.[2] It is two-storeyed, the upper level left blank externally for defence. The amount of restoration has left little original facing but the overall design can be confirmed from early nineteenth-century illustrations.

The exterior entrance is flanked by flat pilaster buttresses, containing gabled figure niches, rising through the upper storey and ending with a horizontal cornice. The squat entrance arch is decorated with square foliate designs. The spandrels are filled with copies of great sculptures of a man (left) hunting a dragon (right), entangled in branching vines containing other animals. This is a rare use of large-scale architectural sculpture on the outside of a gate.

The internal floor division is marked by a chequerwork band of alternating flint and stone, one of several purely regional elements in the façade. The upper storey, severely restored since 1945, represents a more solid and angular version of the earlier Fyndon Gate in St Augustine's Canterbury, completed *c.* 1310, with a continuous row of gabled niches of varying widths, all blinded, resembling a series of triptych altarpieces. The background infill is of squared flints, once polished to suggest glazing. Only the wider niches have figure pedestals. The result is distinctly uneven, nine gabled niches spread across the gate, with four different widths creating a quirky and angular asymmetry.

2. For details of the riots and repairs see Fernie, *NC*, pp. 163–81, 211–12, and also below, pp. 259–61. For the sculpture of the gate see V. Sekules, 'The Fourteenth Century', in A. Borg *et al.*, *Medieval Sculpture from Norwich Cathedral*, (Norwich, 1980), pp. 30–35, and below, pp. 199–202.

The parapet and gable are executed in flushwork now consisting of wheel designs and tracery designs, all by William Wilkins in 1815, following an earlier restoration of 1809 by Repton and Fayerman. The original flushwork was less prosaic. The side circles were infilled with three trefoils upturned and stacked one above two, a design based upon the east cloister walk. The intervening 'windows' were two-light, but with cusped pointed heads and possibly a cusped apex light. The large central circle contained six cusped hexafoils arranged radially, plus six cusped lobes forming a central rosette. There was evidence of battlements or at least pedestals in series along the horizontal stretches of the parapet.

The whole roof-scape of the Ethelbert Gate is notably at odds with the rest and it may post-date 1317. Flushwork was very popular in East Anglia. Butley Abbey Gatehouse, 1320–25, is commonly cited as the progenitor. Benet Hulme Gatehouse (partially surviving) also includes flushwork and, notably, large sculptured panels within the main arch spandrels. But the briefest inspection of the rest of the Ethelbert Gate reveals that flushwork was a major component from the outset, its use predating Butley by perhaps a decade.

A sawn-off north-side turret with alternating stone and flint stripes gives access to the upper chamber, formerly St Ethelbert's Chapel, replacing the city church burnt in the riots. The southern flank of the gate, visible from the close, is decorated at first-floor level with three restored two-light windows, alternating with flushwork versions of themselves.

The inner east façade has a strongly framed entry arch, more sharply pointed than its pair. The whole ensemble recalls the Walsingham Slipper Chapel. A broad band of flushwork quatrefoils divides the two levels. The upper façade is a giant essay in flushwork based upon three equal windows, two in flushwork flanking one glazed. The three-light windows have ogees and 'wire-netting' designs, while other tracery recalls the south cloister walk.

A date for the vault of *c.* 1330 is suggested by the lierne pattern and the structure of the webs. The pattern copies the cloister, established *c.* 1297, plus additional tiercerons for each ridge. Liernes then form circles, with extra bosses as they pass through the diagonals. The arrangement resembles the north presbytery aisle of Ely Cathedral, 1323–24. In the earliest bays of the cloister vault (designed *c.* 1297, executed 1316–19), the diagonals at the springers adopt their true arcature and thus project further than the rest – each rib has a different length to achieve, and should properly express these differences with varying curves. As the diagonals reach furthest their overall arcature should be the flattest, thus breaking the line of the all other shorter ribs. The cloister vaults of *c.* 1320 modify this feature by distorting the diagonal so that it rises more steeply and flattens more suddenly. The Ethelbert Gate attempts something of the same, with the diagonals staying close to the others above the springing. Hence the diagonals are not stressed as much as they would be in true geometry. The webbing within the gate is very advanced, with single stone planks where possible. The longer curve of the diagonals causes the webbing to fold, eliminating any tendency to 'cone'. The contemporary high stone vaults of the Ely presbytery and the wooden vault within the octagon adopt a similar folded web construction, each panel of the webbing cutting back behind the following rib.

The Chapter House

Nothing remains of this most important monastic office save the entry bays in the east cloister walk (fig. 82). The new chapter house was built after the events of 1272, with the tracery ironwork purchased in 1288–89.[3] It was roofed in 1291–92 and glazing began in 1292–93, six years prior to the commencement of the new cloister. The plan was a rectangular hall with a polygonal apse, all probably built upon the foundations of its Romanesque predecessor. Presumably the seven un-obstructed bays had windows, with some additional lighting from the west (cloister) gable, though the later upper story of the cloister would have proved limiting. The dormitory night entry crossed the western bay of the chapter house, possibly traversing the wood-partitioned vestibule.

3. *Communar Rolls*, pp. 29–30.

Fig. 82. The chapter house entrance from the east walk of the cloister.

The entry from the cloister has three uniform arches, only the central opening being practical. It seems Cistercian in character, though other Gothic chapter houses, most notably Westminster, had similar approaches. The arches are of the 1280s though not the traceried infill which dates from the 1320s. The arches entered an open vestibule, the actual door being set back one bay. The east face above the entry still shows evidence of a flat ceiling, which was lined with green buckram in 1478–79.[4] The passage above within the chapter house had a wall arcade, now lost, but no other architectural features of the building are known.

The entry tracery infill has caused much comment as it is so aggressively ogeed. It is best seen from the exposed eastern side where even the overarches have tiny flip-top ogees with foliate finials. These, and the ogeed cusped lobes in the spandrels, are almost certainly additions of the 1320s, contemporary with the Decorated doors of the east walk.

The cloister side makes clear the intention to front the entry with some vaulted structure, though not necessarily a new cloister. Westminster Abbey has a three-bay vaulted section fronting the chapter house vestibule quite different from the rest of the cloister later built round it. Perhaps Norwich intended the same, only later deciding upon a complete rebuild. Certainly, the reconstruction of the cloister began at the chapter house, the bay dimensions being wider than the rest. The eventual vaulting along this section, executed in *c.* 1316–19, proved too short by about one inch (2 cm.). A filler can be seen above each springer of the entry arches.

One curious though sadly no longer obvious feature of the entry was the 'foundation' stone beneath the jamb of the northern arch, inscribed 'Richard Uppehalle, the beginner of this work, laid me' ('Ricardus Uppehalle hujus operis inceptor me posuit') in four lines.[5] Subsequently, this inscription has been complicated with the commencement of the cloister campaign in 1297 under Bishop Walpole (1288–99), though the reference appears to refer to Uppehalle as founder of the chapter house. The inscription dates to before 1289. Uppehalle was a local landowner from Tasburgh whose connection with the priory is unclear, though he made of loan of £20 to the cellarer in the early 1290s. His position seems one of benefactor rather than officer or employee. He was certainly not a mason, nor the designer of the new work. The master mason of Norwich Cathedral in the mid 1280s was one Richard le Machun, also named Richard of the King's Bed and 'king's servant'.[6] Such a title might indicate that Richard was 'given' by the king to Norwich after the fire of 1272. He was later granted a corrody or retirement support by the priory at the request of the king. Richard is possibly identical with Richard Curteys, father of the brothers John Ramsey I and William Ramsey I. John Ramsey I was master of the Norwich cloister

4.   *Communar Rolls*, p. 30.   6.   *Communar Rolls*, p. 30.
5.   Fernie, *NC*, pp. 166–67.

c. 1323. William Ramsey I, mason at Westminster, was founder of the Norwich masonic dynasty of the early fourteenth century: his two sons, William Ramsey II and John Ramsey II, were successive masters of the cloister between 1326 and 1349. It was they who would have supplied the ogee tracery within the entries. Thus the two campaigns of the entries, arches and tracery, may be by grandfather and grandsons.

The Cloister

The cloister of Norwich Cathedral was rebuilt between 1297 and 1430.[7] Damage in 1272 had been slight, the Romanesque lean-to roof being made good while work proceeded elsewhere. The chapter house was rebuilt before any decision was reached over the cloister, leaving the builders of the latter with a spacing problem along the east walk. The rebuilt cloister is square though the number of bays differs, with twelve eastern bays but only eleven on the others, plus angle bays. Construction was at best in fits and starts and was complicated by the sequence of campaigns.

The cloister consists of a perimeter wall common to various claustral buildings and consequently of many periods. Only that along the west walk (fig. 83) was

7.   All references are from *Communar Rolls*.

Fig. 83. The west walk of the cloister showing the vault and perimeter wall.

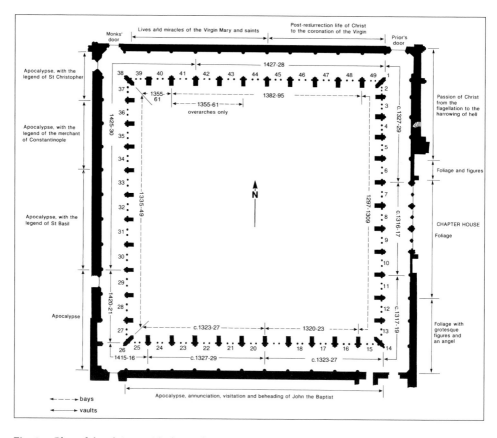

Fig. 84. Plan of the cloister with dates of construction of bays and vaults and with iconographical themes of the main series of bosses.

substantially rebuilt, though the entire perimeter received vault support shafts of uniform design. The inner or tracery wall fronts the cloister garth and could be built quite separately from the rest. The basic design is a rectangular elevation defined by stepped buttresses, with a large overarch containing glazed tracery supported on slender colonnettes. An upper storey exists all round, with a simple single-light window per bay. The interior of the tracery wall has clustered Purbeck marble shafts dividing each bay, with individual groups for the transverse and wall arches of the intended vault. The forty-nine vault bays could be built at any time and in any sequence once the appropriate supports were prepared (see fig. 84 for the sequence of construction). The initial vault design was strictly maintained, though structural changes occur.

Remarkably for such a long and bitty campaign, much documentation survives, offering a full history of the work. Building began in 1297 under Bishop Walpole. He was elevated to Ely in 1299 and John Salmon, the prior of Ely, came to Norwich in his place. Relations between Norwich and Ely were evidently good. The

Fig. 85. The east walk of the cloister.

contemporary camera rolls reveal that Salmon pressed ahead with the eastern tracery wall (fig. 85) plus the first bay of the south walk (bay 15) and northwards towards the church, incorporating the angle bay 49, all built by 1308–9. The corner bays provided bracing once the vault campaigns began. The original tracery remains in bay 49, while that in bay 15 had been lost by the eighteenth century. No vaults were constructed at this time, only the tracery walls, though the vault springers were part of the first build, their base-courses bonded into the walls.

Payment for the cloister campaign was transferred to the communar in 1313–14 and, fortunately, most of the relevant expenditure rolls survive. The Norwich communar was a sort of general dogsbody, making payments for work not covered by the other monastic officers. In grander houses the cloister might be scheduled as a 'new work' (*novum opus*) and put into the hands of a major official but, at Norwich, the piecemeal work made that unnecessary. Nevertheless, the communar rolls are an unusually rich source of architectural information, plus providing evidence of a first-class monastic row.

In 1313–14 the communar, Nicholas Hindolveston, purchased stone and marble worth £21 intended for the new south walk, confirming that the tracery walls of the east walk were finished. Yet no construction occurred and, by the next year, his money was diverted to the Ethelbert Gate, then nearing completion. In all,

Fig. 86. The south walk of the cloister, bays 17 and 18.

Hindolveston provided over £115 for the gate, leaving nothing for the cloister. When work recommenced, probably in 1316–17, some vaults were erected along the east walk. It appears that the three chapter house bays were tackled first, perhaps because their different width from all others made mass production impossible. The southern bays followed, the whole work spanning from 1316–17 to 1319. The northernmost bays (bays 1–6), were built later, well after the vaults in the south walk were under way.

Between 1320 and 1322 over £22 was provided by the communar, with masons cutting and preparing materials already in store. In 1322–23, this material became the tracery walls for bays 16–19 (fig. 86). In three rolls John Ramsey is called 'master', that is master mason for the work. In 1326–27 William Ramsey replaced his brother John as master; although John returned briefly to the work, he then retired, leaving William once again in charge. During this campaign, John Worstead became communar and pressed ahead at a faster rate. In his first year, the large marble block necessary to construct the south-west angle of the cloister arrived; in 1324–25, £69 was spent, £40 alone on wages. The number of workmen is occasionally specified, beginning with fifteen, dropping to ten or eleven, then fewer. The declining number does not mean less activity as construction may utilise less men than cutting and preparing.

Evidence for the progress of the south walk comes with the vaulting of bays 15–19 by 1327. In 1324–25 brick arrived for the vaults, indeed the upper surfaces of these vaults have brick packing over the webs. Before these bays were completed, attention returned to the east walk, where between 1325 and 1327 bays 1–6 were vaulted. Thus the east walk contains tracery walls of the 1290s and vaults of the late 1320s. While this progressed, the rest of the south walk was vaulted, stopping two bays short (bay 24) of the south-west angle, bay 26. The intervening tracery bay, 25, must have stood in order to abut the vault of bay 24. It was at this point that work suddenly stopped and the cloister campaign ran into local difficulties.

Prior Robert Langley died before 29 August 1362 and was replaced by William Claxton, whose views on the cloister project and its management by communar John Worstead differed greatly from his predecessor. Worstead was suspended from his office and called to account for the monies spent. At issue was the calculation that the east walk had cost considerably less per bay than those of the south, seen to be Worstead's personal responsibility. That the comparison was unfair is highlighted by the need to complete the east walk during Worstead's period of office, but the communar did not ease the situation when he provided an apologia, a justification, which was seriously flawed. A figure of £11 per bay was suggested for the east walk compared with £34 in the south. Apart from mathematical errors, it is unclear whether the east walk price included the vault – the fact that one tracery bay of the later west walk would cost £18 without a vault would suggest not. Worstead tried several tacks to justify his stewardship, including the claim that his work was more sumptuous, perhaps a reference to the greater provision of figured bosses. That the south walk bays are larger than their fellows to the east is obvious, eleven tracery bays making up the distance of twelve. This alone affected the cost per bay. However, the evident hostility of the prior coupled with some rather vague accounting left Worstead in monastic limbo, out of favour and out of office. The consequence was a five-year halt.

Inexplicably, when work began again in 1335 it was once more under the control of Worstead, this time as pitancer, an office he had previously combined with communar. An account headed 'Cloister Work', 29 September 1335 to 1 August 1336, records a rather desultory gift of £3 6s. 8d. from Bishop Ayremynne, who died on 27 March 1336. Included in this roll are robes for Master William and his brother, who were also paid 16s. 8d. for a return trip from London. The two Ramseys were nephews of the previous master John. They provided new templates for the work costing 6s. 8d., while Worstead claimed 7s. 8d. for his own trip to London, returning with further new templates. A purchase of marble confirms that the west walk was projected, the work to commence in 1336–37. Suddenly Worstead was deprived yet again of responsibility, the subprior taking control. In his first year, 1336–37, the sub-prior acquired sufficient material for two tracery bays. John atte Grene of

Tasburgh was mason-in-charge, though he soon departed for Ely. Financial control continued to swing back and forth, Worstead being reinstated as communar by 1338–39. The constant shifting of monetary authority probably reflects the continuing hostility between Worstead and Prior Claxton.

Perhaps not surprisingly, the expenditure rolls of this period are a bit patchy. In 1338–39 Worstead spent £13 on the west walk, though there is no evidence of actual construction. A robe worth 16s. 8d. was purchased for Master John Ramsey, who received an annual retainer of £1 1s. Materials include Purbeck marble from Corfe and lead for bonding it together. In the following year, Worstead finally relinquished control of the cloister campaign. Nothing further can be gleaned until 1343–44, when Master John Ramsey is mentioned again, and a fur-trimmed robe bought for John Lilie, mason, presumably a new resident warden. The upper storey of the south walk was in hand in 1344–45. Prospects for more rapid progress on the cloister proper seemed brighter in August 1344 with the death of Prior Claxton. Almost immediately preparations were made to utilise all the stored and prepared materials. Clipsham and Purbeck were purchased, while in 1345–46 enough marble parts were delivered from Yarmouth for eight tracery bays. It is mentioned that the Purbeck shafts arrived ready polished, whereas Purbeck moulded sections such as capitals and bases were merely ready-carved. One delivery of stone arrived from Dublin with 76s. 3d. carriage costs, another boat-load of Caen stone cost 80s. 6d., while five masons, their mates and boys were paid a total of £20 14s. 8d. Yet still no construction appeared to be in hand, merely preparation.

Actual building work began in 1346–47, the masons receiving a reward on the laying of the first stone of the west walk, a decade after the templates and initial materials had been purchased. In the next three years the eleven tracery bays of the west walk were erected (fig. 87), but no upper levels nor vaults. Clipsham stone continued to arrive, while other purchases included scaffolding, thatch for frost protection, lead for marble setting and 9 cwt (457 kg.) of iron for tracery tiebars. Perhaps the most interesting purchase at this time was an illustrated Apocalypse Book, the theme chosen for the vault bosses in the new work.

Throughout 1348–49 stone continued to arrive from Caen and Clipsham but then, on 25 June 1349, everything stopped. The money in hand was split up for safe-keeping, 159 great voussoirs were sold off and everyone went home. Everyone still alive that is. Both Ramseys were dead, along with about one third of the population of England. The Black Death had arrived.

The plague caused serious economic and agricultural difficulties. By 1350–51 the communar's annual income had fallen from over £50 to less than £9. Inflation rocketed. Some urgent cloister work was done to prevent frost and water damage, carpenters making tight the temporary roof over the west walk. It was 1355–56 before Norwich could contemplate new construction. Over the following five years

Fig. 87. The west walk of the cloister.

the north walk began to take shape: seven piers were built, with five tracery arches and two tracery units at the north-west angle, bays 39–40. The master mason of Ely, John Attegrene the Younger, was mentioned in 1357–58 as holding twenty shillings 'of the balance in hand', suggesting that he was now master of the cloister. Difficulties mounted, the spire blew down in 1361/62, seriously damaging the presbytery.[8] Little productive work upon the cloister was done for another two decades.

In 1381–82 the promise of a £100 legacy from Walter Bernay encouraged yet another campaign, aimed at completing the tracery walls of the north walk. Bernay, a Londoner, was buried in the cloister in 1379 and, between 1381 and 1385, his executors provided some £50 for the work. In the latter year three masons were employed, fed by the cellarer. Another £32 followed from Bernay's estate in 1385–86,

8. The date of the collapse of the spire is disputed between 1361 and 1362. Blomefield, *Norfolk*, iii, p. 514, says that 'in 1361, on the 15th of January, the cathedral steeple being blown down, and the choir much damaged, he [Bishop Percy] gave £400 out of his own purse, and obtained an aid of nine-pence in the pound of the clergy of his diocese to repair it'. Even if 15 January 1361 was the date of the storm rather than the bishop's donation, it is not clear if Blomefield was using the old style year which ran from 25 March, in which case the date would now be given as 15 January 1362.

Fig. 88. The north walk of the cloister.

13s. 4d. going on a robe for Master Robert Wadhurst, apparently another new master of the work. It is clear that the master received an annual stipend plus pay for work actually performed, the preferred method of employment for master masons of Norwich at this time. Work in this phase included completing the tracery bays from 44 to 48 and inserting the tracery within bays 41–48 (fig. 88). By 1394–95 a temporary roof covered the north walk and the cloister was generally cleaned up.

The opening of the fifteenth century saw an odd situation in the cloister at Norwich. Both the east and south walks stood much as they are now – upper storeys built and vaults complete, all except bays 25 and 26 which were still unvaulted. The west and north walks stood one storey high, all the tracery erected but with temporary roof and no vaults. To date, the work had taken a century. When the next and final campaign commenced, everything was to be achieved in a mere eighteen years.

Preparatory work began in 1411–12 following another legacy of £100, this time from the rector of St Mary in the Marsh, Geoffrey Symond. The money was to pay for vaulting the bays from 'where the towels hang' adjoining the refectory door to the guest house door (bays 25–29). Materials arrived and masons started work. Hervey Lyng and his son worked for eleven weeks at 6s. 8d. a week, while John Bale was paid 3s. weekly. Between 1412 and 1414 another £35 was spent, with stone arriving from Quarr (Isle of Wight), new templates bought and robes purchased for Lyng and others. Lyng and his son worked over thirty weeks during 1413–14. Costs rose in 1414–15, reaching £26, and rose again in 1415–16 when vault construction actually began. The south-west corner vaults, bays 25–26, cost £33 9s. 9d. John Watlington, presumably an important carver, was housed at considerable expense by the priory, though his weekly pay over twenty-two weeks, 2s. 4d., suggests that his living expenses were met by the cathedral. Watlington's pay was equalled by that of another carver, Brice the Dutchman. He worked over a similar period, taking approximately two weeks to carve each boss. The two vault bays were erected by 1417, after which a three year gap is evident.

When work started again in 1420–21 a new master of the cloister appears, working on a fixed-price contract. This more modern approach to construction was much favoured in the fifteenth century, gradually replacing the older form of life-tenured master masonship. The contract system worked better for a monastery like Norwich with limited building requirements, the size of Norwich ensuring a constant flow of architectural talent. The contract of 1420–21 went to James and John Woderofe who constructed three bays of the cloister vault, bays 27–29, at a cost of £16, representing the last part of Symond's bequest. Half the money went directly to the Woderofes as fee, plus robes worth £1 5s. 6d. as 'reward'. Templates and timber centring were purchased, with 3500 bricks to back the webbing. John Horn, gravour, carved the bosses, he and 'two masons' receiving silk belts as reward while the Woderofes received one extra mark. The work was evidently satisfactory and on schedule. One particular boss in bay 29, outside the guesthouse door, carries the arms of Sir Robert Knollys and his wife Constance Beverley, a rare donor commemoration within the scheme.

The upper storey over these bays may have been built concurrently, though the north walk seems to have been given priority. Timber was bought for the complicated roof that formerly covered the first floor of the north walk, sloping steeply to clear the aisle windows of the nave. Brother John Ellingham, communar from 1414–15 until 1420–21, agreed to pay any money over the £5 outlay, and the roof was leaded in 1423–24. If this represents the whole of the roof, then the north walk received its upper storey and roof with only half the vaults built, whereas the west walk seems to have progressed with vault, upper storey and roof in sequence.

The Woderofes were certainly paid for work on the north walk in 1423–24, receiving £28 1s. 11d. for twenty-four weeks. This may have been taken from the £40 donated to the work by Henry Wells, archdeacon of Lincoln. It is interesting that the personal patronage attracted to Norwich by the cloister campaign is almost entirely ecclesiastical, running counter to the contemporary norms. A good example occurs in 1425–26, when the upper storey of the west walk was completed, partly from a gift of 23s. 6d. from Master John Hancock, rector of St Mary in the Marsh.

At this time, work proceeded on both the west and north walks, the priory paying for the latter, while the executors of Bishop Wakering, who died 1425, paid for the vaults from bay 30 to the nave door in bay 38 (fig. 83). Details of this work are scarce, but it was definitely completed by 1430.

One set of unspecified vaults were completed in 1426–27 while, in the next year, £5 was paid to John Horn for fifteen weeks (4s. per week) and another 'gravour', William Reppys, was paid for six 'keystones' at 6s. 8d. each. These were for the last vaults at the east end of the north walk, thus completing the circuit.

In 1430–31 the priory cleared the cloister of earth and rubbish and declared the work done, 133 years after the *fundatio*. Some minor work remained: the upper west windows were glazed with 'histories' in 1437–38; the washing 'lavers' (bays 26–27) were made by the Woderofes in 1443–44; and a frame was made next to the prior's door to rehouse the ancient Bigod memorial. The years 1450–53 saw the repaving of the west walk and the final glazing work in the upper windows of the north walk.

The cloister reconstruction is a sorry tale of inadequate financing and sluggish management. For much of the time the priory lacked the will to proceed. The last campaign illustrates what could be done with a bit of pushing. The scarcity of secular donations is notable. Either Norwich did not express sufficient public confidence in the work to attract outside interest, or it consciously avoided it. It cannot be that the Norfolk gentry were poor.

The Architecture of the Cloister

Each walk has tracery bays in three lights set within moulded overarches. The tracery is supported upon colonnettes, with moulded capitals and bases, all executed in Purbeck marble. The outer supports are tripled. The continuity of these forms is extraordinary given the stylistic span of the cloister, more so as the tracery changes in every walk, providing a tracery survey covering almost a century.

The east walk tracery of *c.* 1297 is set within a double-chamfered overarch (fig. 85). The main lights have spherical triangles stacked two and one. The lights are subcusped, the apices pinched into the smallest of ogees, the first appearance of this important decorative motif in Norwich. The early tracery bay on the north walk, bay 49, varies this pattern, with the stacked trefoils replaced by three elongated quatrefoils in a spray.

The late thirteenth-century scheme retains the rigidity of the Geometrical period, with almost everything based upon circles or arcs. Spherical triangles appeared first as windows at Westminster Abbey, entering tracery almost immediately, while other motifs present at Norwich relate to St Paul's choir, London, dating from 1258. Ogee arches were very new in 1297, first appearing in Canterbury *c.* 1285–90 and in London work after 1290. Clearly, the designer of the east walk tracery was in close touch with the royal workshops, which were the first to promote this most radical motif. The moulded bases in the east walk are also very advanced, resembling those from the upper chapel at St Stephen's Westminster. The work at Norwich was by Master Richard 'le Machun'. He was probably Richard Curteys, progenitor of the Ramsey dynasty of London and Norwich masons. It is clear that from the start the cloister at Norwich was in London, one might almost say dynastic, hands. This fact would explain the modernity of the work until 1330.

In the south walk, from 1322, the overarches are more elaborate, while the tracery introduces two new themes, dominant ogees and alternation (fig. 86). The main lights are emphatically ogeed, the extensions forming twin lobes within the tracery. In one pattern, the lobes are softer and more rounded, in the other more angular.

The south walk is undoubtedly the work of John Ramsey, nephew of Richard (le Machun) Curteys. John had worked at Norwich from *c.* 1304. The walk contains flowing patterns of the new Decorated style, including the four-lobe cluster, soon to spread throughout East Anglia and occurring in frillier form at the galleries of the new choir of Ely *c.* 1330. Its origin is unclear, possibly John Ramsey invented it. One might read the alternative open quatrefoil theme of the south walk as being a wavy line diagonal grid, similar though simpler to the cloister bay fronting the Westminster Abbey chapter house. It certainly has the angularity of the crypt windows of St Stephen's Westminster, *c.* 1292.

The west walk tracery, erected 1345–50, also alternates (fig. 87), with one design varying a south walk motif, the other echoing the isolated 1290s design in bay 49. The west walk was by William Ramsey, nephew of John of the south walk. William became an important London master, designing the new chapter house and cloister of St Paul's from 1331, and later taking control of St Stephen's Westminster. Norwich had made a wise investment in the Ramsey family. Tracery similar to the west walk appeared in the Ely Lady Chapel, from 1322 and again at gallery level in the Ely choir. However, the Norwich tracery reveals its age, designed around 1330 but not built until 1344. By then London tracery had become more rectilinear, with straight sided lozenges and crisper reticulation. The contemporary cloister of the London Greyfriars, *c.* 1346, looked very like Ramsey's Norwich scheme 'Perped' up.

The north walk displays the most dramatic changes of all and marks the transition from Decorated to Perpendicular. The first two bays, 39 and 40, erected in 1352–60, are quite at odds with all the others, and with each other. Bay 39 introduces a flatter ogee main light, while the upper tracery has large ogeed reticulation. Bay 40 has clearly been altered, the original design being somewhat similar to the 'collapsed' pattern in the west walk. At some stage vertical mullions have been intruded into the design, making it more Perpendicular and closer to what follows eastwards.

These two bays are stylistically most odd. Bay 39 is an attempt to reticulate and update the west walk design without losing the basic flowing formation. Bay 40 is a mess, a crude conversion of something to Perpendicular But what? The documents suggest this as the work of John Attegrene, concurrently master mason of Ely Cathedral. Attegrene can have designed little at Ely, his father having been master until *c.* 1350. If the Norwich work represents his style it is more modern than anything currently at Ely.

The last designs along the north walk, executed between 1382 and 1394, again alternate closely related schemes (fig. 88). The first has straight-up mullions rising rather oddly from moulded capitals, providing the only rectilinear triple division within the cloister tracery. In the first pattern, the main lights alternate segmental, depressed ogee and segmental. The tracery contains miniature two-light windows, inverted dagger-lights, mouchettes and supertransoms. The alternate design repeats some elements but the middle light has also a segmental head, from which rise intersecting subarcs, their curvature not exactly corresponding with those of the side-lights. The main overarches along the north walk are of a piece including bay 49, whose tracery dates from *c.* 1300.

The tracery of the north walk is probably by Robert Wadhurst, called master in 1385–86. It is all deliberately confusing if not muddled. Related tracery patterns occurred in the Norwich presbytery clerestory windows (*c.* 1365) and Swanton Morley (*c.* 1380).

The vault design remains constant throughout, with only minor constructional differences. The vaults rest on Purbeck responds, each consisting of a marble column core-post, plus smaller detached columns as required, usually groups of three, expanded to five on the three-quarter angle turns. The responds support springer blocks generally set into the wall and consequently part of the mural campaigns. Pre-existing late thirteenth-century springers could dictate the abandonment of current vault techniques during later vault construction, as happened most obviously in the last northern bays 48 and 49, where the responds are *c.* 1308, the vaults *c.* 1428.

The rib pattern is subdued even by the standards of the 1290s. It has transverse and diagonal ribs, plus axial and cross-axial, each rib having one additional pair of tierceron ribs. In all the vaults to bay 41 the diagonals and transverse ribs are given greater prominence with extra moulding profiles. In addition, in the earliest vaults, bays 6–10, the diagonals take up their true arcature, hence their longer reach emphasises the turn from axial to cross-axial. This abrupt fold was eliminated gradually by a series of adjustments to the arcature of the diagonal, at first pushing it up out of the way, causing the webbing to buckle over it; then from bay 42 adopting the true cone, where all ribs are equal, the webbing geometrically smooth and rounded, and laid plank-style, commonly a single block wide. A transitional stage existed in the period *c.* 1325–29, manipulating the arcature of the tierceron so as to neutralize further the awkward presence of the longer diagonals. These subtle changes allow the vaults to be dated in sequence with some accuracy as follows:

c. 1316–17	Bays 7–10
c. 1317–19	Bays 11–14
c. 1323–27	Bays 15–19
c. 1327–29	Bays 20–24, bays 1–6
c. 1415–16	Bays 25–26
c. 1420–21	Bays 27–29
c. 1425–30	Bays 30–41
c. 1427–28	Bays 42–49

Throughout the campaign, the vault responds and patterns remain remarkably consistent, with only slight and almost imperceptible changes occurring in the rib profiles in the fourteenth-century campaigns.

The outer walls of the cloister give access to all the major monastic offices; each was given appropriate doorways. Curiously, each new door reflects the current architectural style so that while the cloister interior proceeds in harmony, the succession of doors trumpet their stylistic differences.

The earliest doors lead to the chapter house, already described. The vaults over these doors, built some twenty years later, have had to be lifted one inch (2 cm.) by means of fillers, evidently correcting a workshop mistake. The period around 1330 saw the insertion of a set of doors and niches strewn along the east walk. First and foremost is the so-called prior's door, one of the most unusual designs of its day. The jambs are simple enough, four shafts per splay, outlined by deep scooped trough mouldings. All the capitals and bases are moulded and rounded, rather archaic but in keeping with the adjoining vault responds. The arch-head has standard mouldings but laid over them, spread in the manner of an oriental fan, is arranged a series of crocketed triangular and ogeed gables, pinned down at the springers with half arches. The seven complete gables contain figures identified as Christ, two angels, St Peter, St Edmund, St John the Baptist and Moses, all in good condition, the colour recently restored. The survival of such quality sculpture is one thing, the arrangement quite another. The figures sprawl across the voussoirs, their feet on the inner mouldings, their heads towards the outer. This radiality is peculiarly Decorated in feeling and conjures ideas of the Ely Lady Chapel executed by the designer of the Bristol Cathedral tomb recesses. It is hard to credit the prior's door as a work of William Ramsey, who in 1331 was to design that most rectilinear chapter house at Old St Paul's Cathedral. Bay 1 also contains two ogeed tabernacles formerly housing the memorial to Roger Bigod, who died in 1107. Two other contemporary doors occur, in bay 6, to the tresaunce, and bay 14 to the infirmary passage. Both have ogeed heads, the former with elaborate cusping and subcusping, gilded crockets and an oversized foliate finial. Perpendicular doors and fixtures occur from bay 26 onwards, commencing with a moulded door to the refectory, with further moulded doors in bays 29 to the guesthouse and 38 to the nave. Bays 26 and 27 contain the refectory washing tanks, decoratively treated with curling vines and with internal figure niches. They are the work of James Woderofe, who was paid £2 10s. for 10 tons (10 tonnes) of stone. He remitted the rest due, perhaps 30s., in memory of his brother John's soul.

The Carnary Chapel

The Carnary Chapel (from 'charnel' or bone-house, the original use of the crypt), was built after 1316 by Bishop Salmon (1299–1325).[9] The two-storeyed building, now caught up in the school, was once almost free-standing. Much restored, it was Norwich's answer to St Stephen's Westminster, with a vaulted vestibule and crypt, and a raised unvaulted chapel. There was a north-west stair turret, a big east window (now lost) and a later west window. It was served separately by priests, whose house stood further west. Probably the work of the Ramseys, the style is linked with earlier work at St Augustine's Canterbury. The surviving interest centres on the dumpy entrance, the porthole crypt windows and the original lateral tracery, unrestored on the north flank, often seen as proto-Perpendicular with their stacked lights hinting at the rectilinear.

Additions to Losinga's Palace

Bishop Salmon added a great hall beside the Romanesque structure *c.* 1320; although demolished in 1662, segments survive.[10] The vaulted, two-storeyed eastern porch has steep arched ground-floor openings and tracery and other details related to the octagon at Ely, where Salmon had been prior before his elevation to Norwich. The porch entry is flanked by the remains of figures in ogee-headed niches. The tierceron vault springs from foliate capitals. Ghost sections of the hall proper remain against the porch and indicate the presence of blank wall arcades.

The dais end was reused as the base of the present Restoration chapel built by Bishop Reynolds (1661–76). This displays a selection of Decorated windows, very fancy and flowing, though awkwardly reused. They are said to come from Bishop Salmon's chapel (demolished in the mid seventeenth century) south of the hall. Again, they are not dissimilar from tracery in the octagon campaign at Ely.

Salmon appropriately rebuilt the kitchens within the base of the main tower, with

9.   Fernie, *NC*, pp. 181–82.   Norwich', *Arch. J.*, 137 (1980), pp. 365–68.
10. A. B. Whittingham, 'The Bishop's Palace,

big brick vaults upon a central column, while Bishop Lyhart (1446–72) fashioned a great chamber above *c.* 1450, with Perpendicular windows (since blocked) and a wooden ceiling, now concealed. The early Renaissance panelling is said to have been brought from Benet Hulme Abbey in 1536. It has characteristic roundel heads.

The Presbytery Chapels

Projecting square-planned chapels were added to the presbytery in the years *c.* 1325–30, probably as chantry foundations.[11] The southern, Bauchun Chapel survives, now with a Perpendicular window and topped by an elaborate tierceron vault (both *c.* 1460). The ungainly entry arch is matched by another to a demolished chapel off the north aisle directly opposite, perhaps an attempt to emulate the new plan of Wells.

The Presbytery Clerestory

In 1361/62 a great storm blew down the spire of Norwich Cathedral, demolishing the presbytery roof and Romanesque clerestory. The new presbytery clerestory, 1364–86, presents several architectural and archaeological problems.[12] The plan follows that of the Romanesque presbytery, with four straight bays and five canted bays turning the apse, and it was designed to have an exposed wooden roof. The existing vault dates from 1472–99. Thus the two campaigns are a century apart, the latter remarkably sympathetic in style to the former (fig. 89). That fact, plus extensive restorations – late nineteenth-century photographs show at least six bays recently refaced externally – make the whole work difficult to unpick.

Fig. 89. The late fourteenth-century presbytery clerestory and the late fifteenth-century presbytery vault, north side.

The scale of the windows plus the present dramatic flyers suggest a fragile mural

11. Fernie, *NC*, p. 183.
12. H. Wharton, *Anglia Sacra*, 2 vols (London, 1691), i, p. 415, and Blomefield, *Norfolk*, iii, p. 514.

construction. The structure is extremely top-heavy. The internal arrangement of the clerestory wall converts a basically thick-walled structure into a skeletal system of passages and open-work tabernacles. The wall retains virtually all the thickness of its Romanesque forebear, though raised higher, and the internal passage becomes the principal architectural device. The straight bays have tall four-light windows set into the outer skin of the wall (fig. 90), framed by correspondingly tall inner arches that in turn define the intervening wall piers. The piers are totally voided away for almost the full height of the window jambs, becoming tall, vaulted, open-sided, ogee-topped tabernacles. The full wall thickness only returns above and would have given the elevation an even more pro-nounced top-heavy feeling prior to the addition of the high vault. The taber-nacles support pedestals, later employed to carry the vault spring. Whatever stood on them formerly must have risen to the height of the window arch-spring, otherwise the scheme would have been even more wavy than at present. The variety of levels within the wall piers is only one of the late Decorated elements within the scheme. The intention be-hind the voided piers is to create unex-pected and unnerving cross-vistas of the large windows and to suggest that both the original roof and the thick upper walls are supported by the slenderest of means. All the mouldings retain the sof-ter rounder fashions of the Decorated style.

Fig. 90. The presbytery clerestory, west bay, south side.

The apse bays have even less solidity than those further west. The space be-tween windows is reduced by half. The dividing wall pier is cut away to an even greater height, the total wall thickness appearing only at the level of the window arch-spring. The wedge-shape plan of the canted bays means that the inner support for the upper wall becomes a single clustered pier. The slight external pilaster buttresses and the spindly interior support create a very unstable window wall, excessively overhung with masonry and with a real threat of warping, if not a complete cork-screwing of the structure. Add the strong winds at such a height, of which Norwich had had a recent and calamitous reminder, and the stability of the clerestory structure is called in question. The elevated transoms within the apse windows are one stiffening element but, alone, insufficient. The original scheme must have utilised the roof frame plus external flying buttresses to render the brittle fabric viable. Flyers must have existed from the start, first as an essential engineering part of the straight bays, then to stiffen the canted bays against the wind, and finally to support the top-heavy structure of the upper walls.

If we think of the unvaulted clerestory as a collapsing building, and English medieval builders certainly give the impression that that is how they did regard their buildings, then flyers act like wooden shoring actively pushing the walls inwards, while the roof frame, here later replaced by the vault, acted as a strainer stopping the walls from imploding. The fragile piers of the clerestory passage are probably sufficient themselves to uphold the total weight of the thick upper wall and roof but not to resist sudden side gusts or roof pressures. In reality they did not have to, they merely balanced the load. It is the difference between underpinning and carrying. The idea of a buttressing system pushing the clerestory walls inward, while the roof or vault acts as a strainer, seems to lie behind the design of many English vault systems within thick walled elevations from the Durham nave onwards. The Norwich presbytery clerestory, both with and without the vault, is merely a sophisticated version of a centuries-old technology.

The existing flyers are probably late fifteenth-century reconstructions. The diagonal pilasters rising from the buttress tops crash through the panelled roof battlements in an arbitrary fashion.[13] The battlements proceed at odds with the bay system below, only in the canted bays do merlons occupy the angles, with a centrally placed embrasure; otherwise, the rhythm simply does not fit. This irregularity appears totally wilful and intentional. The physical evidence suggests that the pilaster mouldings have always collided quite blatantly through the conflicting panelling and cusping. Perhaps it is a piece of 1360s late Decorated fancy?

The clerestory mixes five basic tracery patterns over thirteen windows, matching only north with south, another Decorated notion. The first against the tower (fig. 90) is positively Decorated in its flowing arrangements. The three other windows of the straight presbytery bays have the distinctive four-petal design of the cloister south walk, though contained within straight mullions. The apse windows are more modern, with the earliest Perpendicular details in East Anglia. They give the impression of being designed by another hand. The axial and outer windows have aggressively sharp lozenges, with an obscured central lozenge 'Gloucester-style'.[14]

13. Daniel King's overall elevation of the 1650s shows pronounced pinnacles above the parapets: See Fernie, *NC*, p. 86, pl. 29.

14. The closest parallel may be the lost, mid century windows of St Katherine by the Tower, London.

The intervening pair have similar tracery though retaining softer forms within the apex.

The whole concept of the clerestory internal elevation derives from the Lady Chapel at Ely, completed around the mid fourteenth century. Ely has huge windows set into deep splays, with every available surface gouged out into elaborate niches and tabernacles. What Norwich has done is to void the lower half of each wall pier, replacing the Ely figure niches with peep-show views of stained glass, and releasing the embedded clustered angle piers of Ely by making them free-standing, thus emphasising and exploiting the wall thickness. This is very much in the tradition of late Decorated architecture, recalling Wells rather than Gloucester.

The Norwich clerestory shows familiarity with both Ely and contemporary London designs. Robert Wodehirst, first mentioned in London, is usually credited with the Norwich work. He had worked at Westminster in the 1350s, though not as master mason.[15] The Norwich attribution depends upon the closeness of the names Robert Wodehirst with Robert Wadhurst, master of the work on the great cloister at Norwich from at least 1385, where his pay was good but not overgenerous. Wadhurst and his family lived in Pockthorpe, Norwich, where he died in 1401. The last years of his life were clearly active, for he worked at Ely Cathedral between 1387 and 1393, after the building of the Norwich clerestory. Whether the London Wodehirst and the Norwich Wadhurst are one and the same is unclear; Wadhurst is a village in East Sussex, Woodhurst is near Ely.

The Alnwick Work

Bishop William Alnwick (1426–36) initiated a scheme that would eventually transform the cathedral. His major contribution was to modernise the central section of the west front. While Alnwick left the lowest section of the nave wall intact, merely fronting it with a shallow porch, all else was swept away for one of the most ambitious west windows of its day (fig. 91). The porch was evidently begun during Alnwick's episcopacy, the window after his death in 1449 at Lincoln, whence he had been translated. His executors were to erect a great window at the west end of Norwich and to find stone, iron, glass, workmen and everything else necessary from his estate. The porch is not mentioned.[16]

Combination porch and great windows were a fashion in English late-medieval architecture: prototypes for Norwich include Winchester, Westminster Abbey and Canterbury. Each favoured a low porch flanked by niches, sufficient depth within

15. For reference to Wodehirst, see J. Harvey, *English Medieval Architects* (2nd edn, Gloucester, 1984), pp. 342–43.

16. Blomefield, *Norfolk*, iii, p. 531 n. 6. Perhaps the hole was ready and only the tracery and glazing awaited.

the splays for a shallow vault and the maximum possible area of glazing above. The window apex at Norwich rises comparatively higher than any other, the nave being still unvaulted, thus freeing the window to soar as far as structural prudence would permit.

The present appearance is distinctly odd. The window dominates, its layout clashing with virtually every other element of the façade. Pre-Victorian illustrations show a different balance: the side pilasters rise as substantial turrets almost equalling the gable. The pilaster façades are treated with tall blank arches, perhaps eighteenth-century, while the porch below occupies the full width of the central façade. What has happened subsequently is the restoration of Romanesque features on the pilasters,

Fig. 91. The earliest representation of the west front, as it appeared in the mid seventeenth century after Bishop Alnwick's remodelling two centuries earlier.

removing some of Alnwick's work, the lowering of the turrets and the shifting of sections of the porch. It is little wonder if the result is haphazard.

The original design of the porch survived until 1875. It was a standard layout, a screen-like façade projecting from the main elevation, with a central outer-arch set within a square frame, steeply raked jambs with blind tracery and a mock-up vault with ribs, liernes and bosses, preceding a lower inner door set within moulded jambs and voussoirs. The outer spandrels contain demi-angels and the arms of Norwich and Alnwick; around the former is the motto 'Pray for the soul of Lord William Alnwick' ('Orate pro anima Domini Willelmi Alnwyk'). By this time he was evidently dead. The flanking elevation consisted of pairs of canopied figure-niches, with tall pedestal bases and dividing buttresses and, above each niche, a panel containing kneeling or demi-figures. The main niches once contained figures of bishops and a king with a kneeling bishop.[17] The Victorian 'restoration' needed the end-space then occupied by the outer niches in order to reconstruct the tall half shafts of the Romanesque design. The intruding niches were sliced off and turned through ninety degrees, thus forming new niched 'sides' where previously none had existed, and narrowing considerably the whole façade.[18] Though no original work was lost, the design has suffered severely, the porch no longer forming a firm and long enough base for the great void above.[19]

The great west window followed after 1449, Alnwick making a rare exception to the rule that bishops of Norwich, once translated, forgot their previous cathedral. The model was the west window of Westminster Hall, built *c.* 1394, an unusual choice being both old and domestic. Walter Lyhart, then bishop, had connections at court, being confessor to Queen Margaret. A London architect may therefore have been responsible. Equally, any one of the masons named as working for the cathedral in the mid fifteenth century might have designed the window, though details within the tracery do not appear local. The obvious Norwich candidate would have been James Woderofe, who worked intermittently for the cathedral from 1415 to 1451. While other masons worked for the cathedral concurrently, Woderofe appears the most important. In April 1449 he and a John Jakes received expenses and a reward of £7 from Henry VI for going to Eton with their gear.[20] The reason is unknown though Henry generally irritated all concerned with the Eton project by his constant changes of mind. Woderofe died in Norwich in 1453, by which date the great window was probably finished.

The main lines of the Westminster window are copied faithfully at Norwich. A

17. D. J. Stewart, 'Notes on Norwich Cathedral', *Arch. J.*, 32 (1875), p. 39.
18. See below, figs 225, 227–29.
19. The present doors date from Lyhart's episcopacy, 1446–72.
20. D. Knoop and G. P. Jones, 'The Building of Eton College', *Ars quatuor coronatorum*, 46 (1933), p. 105.

single transom divides the window into two tall tiers of lights, nine across, equally divided into three groups. Within the tracery head, the three groups are subarcuated, the returning arcs helping to support the great overarch. Similarly, the major dividing mullions proceed to the arch-head unbroken, clarifying the design and propping the gable wall above. The tracery is standard London Perpendicular though some of the superlights contain the most curious and original feature of all – ogeed main light arch-heads finishing with a moulded pedestal standing proud of the glazing. Either they supported sculpture set against the glass or glazed figures 'stood' on stone pedestals. They do not occur at Westminster, where the equivalent side-lights contain lozenges and dagger-lights.

Internally, the lower Romanesque work survives, though a new four-centred doorway has been crudely inserted within the earlier frame. Higher up, small figures of Bishop Alnwick decorate the jambs and commemorate his gift. The existing junction between window and high vault is unfortunate, the vault forced up to avoid cutting the tracery head.

Alnwick began another work within the close, a new gate to the bishop's palace, again completed by Lyhart. The brick-built gate has stone and flint facing. The two-storeyed exterior façade has major and minor entries, and twin windows above set rather too close together and squashing a central canopied niche with a figure of the Virgin. The principal entrance arch is framed by slender pilaster posts and heraldic spandrels, the frieze above has shields alternating with the MARIA cipher. The internal vault has stone ribs and brick webbing, unfortunately plastered over. The tierceron pattern is straightforward yet all but the diagonals are bossless, the ribs merely interconnecting. Similar vaults occur in the west tower of St Peter Mancroft, *c.* 1450? The centre boss contains the figure of Alnwick.

The Erpingham Gate

This new entrance to the close was a mid fifteenth-century gift of the Erpingham family in memory of Sir Thomas, hero of Agincourt.[21] The design resembles a canopied tomb, blown out of proportion (fig. 92). The great arch has finely executed sculpture with the kneeling figure of Sir Thomas in the gable. The internal barrel vault once boasted a network of ribs.

The High Vaults

Norwich Cathedral is quintessentially an Anglo-Norman building of the first order. What little post-Romanesque reconstruction did occur has hardly altered this overall

---

21. Fernie, *NC*, p. 187.

Fig. 92. The Erpingham Gate, west façade, in the later nineteenth century.

feeling. The one major addition, the high vaults, have if anything enhanced the quality of the architecture, blending the toughness of the elevation with the soft flow of lierne vaulting. Yet the reason lying behind this comprehensive building campaign was not aesthetic but practical. Open-roofed interiors suffered fires and other roof collapses throughout the middle ages, none more so than Norwich, whose wooden spire burnt, fell or simply blew down. A stone vault intervening between roof and church was the obvious solution. How to fit one upon an existing elevation unprepared to accommodate such lateral pressures determined much of the present appearance.

The nave vault (fig. 93) was built by Bishop Walter Lyhart (1446–72), his heraldry and punning rebus, a hart lying in water, forming sculptured corbels alternating throughout. Traditionally, the vault is dated after the fire of 1463, though no supporting evidence exists. Secondary references in the sacrists' rolls suggest that the nave was inoperative over the years 1454–60, when no payments occur for the mechanical festive angel swung from the nave roof.[22] Furthermore, the raising and refenestration of the nave galleries, with their roofs and battlements, occurred between 1454 and 1462; it is hard to dissociate this work from the nave vault campaign.[23] Indeed, the new galleries and near-flat roofs probably act as box-girder supports, strengthening the nave elevation and resisting the thrust of the new high vault. Lyhart's new pulpitum, surviving in form if not substance, was also erected and decorated before the disaster of 1463, Thomas Growt being paid 13s. 4d. for work upon the 'perk' in 1462.[24] A date before 1463 would make sense of other references, for example, Robert Everard was paid in 1465–66 for repairing 'two panels' of the vault near the bishop's oratory, north of the nave altar.[25] Even the exposed wooden nave roof needed only minimal attention after the fire, 1000 nails being used in 1469 to repair two southern sections.[26] In the absence of substantive documentary evidence to the contrary, it must be accepted that Lyhart built the nave vault before 1463, and that such fire-proofing saved the nave and most of its fittings.

The vault pattern (fig. 93) is rich and decorative. Each bay is divided by transverse arches plus axial and cross-axial ridges, with five additional pairs of tiercerons. While the diagonals are slightly enhanced, the net effect is of a continuous flowing cone of thirteen members plus wall ribs. Short liernes form a stellar pattern around each centre, while further liernes form triangles linking up the transverse arches. All intersections are marked by large sculptured bosses. The clarity of the pattern contrasts with the contemporary and more deliberately perverse vault of Winchester.

The construction is rib and panel, an attempt being made to keep the web spacing

22. NRO, DCN 1/4/84 and DCN 1/4/87.
23. NRO, DCN 1/4/87.
24. NRO, DCN 1/4/88.

25. NRO, DCN 1/4/90.
26. NRO, DCN 1/4/91.

Fig. 93. The nave vault.

sufficiently narrow as to allow single 'planks' of stone spanning the ribs. Where the geometry inevitably leads to a widening gap, liernes intervene and give further support to the webs. This apparent structural use of liernes is innovative though entirely logical, the English always looking for shortcuts in rib-vault construction. Another ploy involves the notable arcing of the cross-axial vault profile. The outline of the vault is distinctly humped across the nave, rising from the apices of the Romanesque clerestory windows to a high centre and then falling again. Thus the profile resembles a segmental barrel pierced by the lunettes of the clerestory windows. The thrust of this vault hits the nave elevations nearer the vertical than one with a flat east-west crown. It gains the added benefit in that the weight and thrust of the vault is accommodated nearer to the base of the Romanesque clerestory without overall loss of absolute height. In this way, the builders avoided exterior flying buttresses, indeed the elevated and flattened gallery roof provides the required stiffening to the whole cross-section. The higher crown also helped the vault to get over the tall west window. Above the vault lies a rubble packing approximately three feet (one metre) deep. This dead weight clamps the vault tight and prevents slippage, though its main role is that of a sacrificial fire-barrier.

The western bay of the vault lifts dramatically in order to clear the Perpendicular west window, inserted after 1449 but apparently before the decision to build a stone vault. Other problems were handled by the vault builders in a rather more summary fashion. The open roof had rested upon twin half shafts in alternate bays. These were cut down to clerestory sill level and replaced by bundles of shafts with contemporary capitals and bases. Similar bundles of shafts were added to the intervening bays, though here they descend to the Romanesque capitals at gallery springing level with corbels carrying the Lyhart rebus. Throughout much of the nave elevation it is possible to see further Romanesque blind arcading above the lateral arches of the clerestory ensemble.

The vaulting of the choir (fig. 94), built by Lyhart's successor James Goldwell (1472–99), presented different problems though the solution appears the same. Indeed it is possible that the nave design was chosen for its suitability for the choir. The fourteenth-century choir clerestory looks remarkably spindly and unstable, yet it appears to carry a heavy stone vault with ease. To the French this would appear unexceptional, but to the English, used to thick walls, mural interiors and solidity, the perforated spaces and relatively large windows of the choir clerestory might have been expected to crumble beneath the added weight of a stone vault. The addition of a vault over so much glass must have seemed special indeed. So perfect is the combination of fourteenth-century elevation and late fifteenth-century vault that it is hard to imagine the former without the latter. The thickness of the upper clerestory wall, the high-cut passage and open-work tabernacle effect of the wall piers all conspire to float the vault free of the window wall, effectively suspending

Fig. 94. The vault of the presbytery with the clerestory of the apse.

the 'weight' over the passage. The engineering truth is very different. The thrust of the vault, again made more vertical by the arcing of the cross-axial profile, passes through the thickness of the upper clerestory wall above the passage vaults to be met directly by the flyers outside. Their presence would not be so obvious from inside were the clerestory still fitted throughout with stained glass. The flyers and their buttresses form the counter-balance to the vault, the open-work tabernacled 'vault-supports' merely acting as pivotal points of balance.

The designer of the choir vault knew perfectly how to exploit the construction of the earlier elevation. Equally, he blended the new with the old quite seemlessly. The ogee gabled tops across the open-work mural passages provide the perfect visual support for the new vault springers in all the bays, except the most westerly one against the tower. Here, the ogee canopy stands away from the corner where logic and construction must site the vault springer. The solution? Ignore it and put the springer where it must go. The structure of the choir vault follows that of the nave including the rubble barrier above. The greater uniformity of the vault bosses – the Goldwell rebus – and the luminous quality of the lighting create a stunning effect, making the Norwich choir one of the finest and most interesting interiors of the English middle ages.

The transepts received their vaults only in the sixteenth century, following a fire in 1509. They feature the arms of Bishop Richard Nix (1501–35/36). Their design follows the established pattern with a few short-cuts, such as the block springers.

Identifying the designer of the vault scheme is complicated by the number of named masons active in the cathedral in the period 1450–1500. Robert Everard appears constantly and was connected with the post-fire reconstruction. William of Worcester's mention of Everard and the spire project does not preclude two teams working at once. Repairing a vault and designing one are different matters. No large-scale vault campaign is known in Norwich prior to the cathedral nave. Everard, a mason contractor and builder of parish churches, may have had neither the expertise nor experience necessary to engineer so great a project. A specialist may well have been imported from elsewhere. In the 1460s two major vault campaigns were in progress in East Anglia, at Bury St Edmunds and King's College Chapel Cambridge. Bury post-dates Norwich though the problems were analogous – a comprehensive high-vault built over an existing Romanesque structure. King's Cambridge was to be vaulted according to a design of 1448 by the architect, Reginald Ely from Coltishall near Norwich. All work stopped at King's in 1461. John Auntell, mason, appears in Norwich as a freeman in 1469–70, having worked previously at King's under Reginald Ely.[27] Auntell was Everard's neighbour in Palace Plain.[28] This, and

27. Harvey, *English Medieval Architects*, p. 8.   28. NRO, Norwich City Records, case 1, roll 20, m. 12.

the presence of both men in the cathedral in the 1480s, has suggested a senior-junior partnership. Auntell also received a bonus in the form of a robe from the sacrist in 1484–85. Robes from the sacrist, responsible for the cathedral fabric, would not denote such rank as one from the prior. Nor was the value that great, but it is notable that even as late as the mid 1480s, Everard and Auntell received robes of the same value. Of course, other than the structural problems unique to the choir, the vault design copies the nave. Auntell may have had experience of high vault construction elsewhere, or at least have been privy to the 1448 project for King's, Cambridge, undoubtedly a rib and lierne vault.

The Spire

A spire was erected over the central tower of Norwich Cathedral between 1291 and 1297. It had a wooden frame and was covered in lead.[29] In 1361/62 a great storm brought it down with sufficient force to destroy the presbytery clerestory.[30] It is generally assumed that its replacement was wooden and that it burnt in the fire of 1463, which was evidently caused by lightning. The present spire was nearing completion in 1482, when eight wind-vanes were purchased to surmount the pinnacles near the base. The scaffolding and 'dirt' were finally cleared away in 1492, perhaps after the completion of the high vaults of the presbytery.[31] In about 1478 William of Worcester, who knew Norwich well, made his famous marginal memo to ask Robert Everard 'how many inches does the Norwich spire batter in six feet?'[32]

The spire rises about 315 feet (96 metres) and is the second highest to survive from the English middle ages. The design is straight-up with no broaching or staging, though the profile changes slightly at about half-height. The complete structure is contained within the parapets of the older tower, the eight stepped buttresses at the base once topped with wind-vanes. The buttresses assist the stability by dead-weighting the base, preventing any tendency to spread. Two-light, unglazed 'windows' alternate around four of the eight sides, thus reducing the overall wind resistance. There is a degree of linear crocketing, which intensifies nearer the top. In the fifteenth century, the Romanesque angle turrets were given additional crocketed spirelets to complete the group and further dead-weight the corners of the tower.

The main spire is a finely coursed brick structure covered with a thin coat of Weldon stone. The basic construction is an eight-sided brick cone with bands of

29. *Communar Rolls*, p. 28.
30. Stewart, 'Notes on Norwich Cathedral', p. 37.
31. Personal correspondence from Paul Cattermole.
32. Harvey, *English Medieval Architects*, p. 1103. The 1471–72 reference to the *campanile* and

Robert Everard refers to the free-standing belfry. The central tower was called the *campanile in choro*. Further, the Goldwell Register mentions an indulgence offered for donations towards the rebuilding after the fire. Personal correspondance from Paul Cattermole.

flint rubble about every six brick courses. Norwich has a considerable stock of fifteenth-century brick structures, though the bricks in the spire are amongst the largest found – up to 14 in. (36 cm.) in length. The lowest parts of the stone skin are not bonded or pegged into the brick fabric as they are in the upper three sections, but 'lean' on the gradient of the slope. The whole structure was stiffened by an internal wooden frame, renewed with plentiful use of old timbers in the eighteenth century. Beneath the spire, and within the top stage of the Romanesque tower, a massive four-part squinch construction was inserted to carry the weight, estimated at some 500 tons (500 tonnes). The squinches cut across the four corners of the tower with ever expanding brick arches, so transforming the square plan into an octagon. The heavy structure of the Romanesque work and the launching of the spire well within the tower assure stability.[33]

As a stone-clad brick structure, the spire of Norwich Cathedral joins that exclusive club of top quality East Anglian products – Bury St Edmunds west tower, the upper sections of King's College Chapel and the central tower of Canterbury Cathedral by John Wastell of Bury.

The Redressing of the Presbytery

England's cathedrals in the late middle ages either attracted major private patronage or they did not. Norwich did not. Even significant burials such as the Hobarts and Erpinghams found no expression in architectural modernisation. One problem was a lack of major local patrons: the interests of the dukes of Norfolk lay at Thetford, the dukes of Suffolk built at Wingfield and Ewelme, while other regional money was spirited away by the Norwich mendicant houses, widely popular with the Norfolk gentry. What Norwich Cathedral needed was a major dynasty. But who? The emergent family was Boleyn. The Boleyns had been minor Norfolk gentry – the Victorians would have called them 'Trade' – but they rose spectacularly by skilful marriages. In the late fifteenth century Norwich attracted the patronage of both Anne, widow of Sir Geoffrey Boleyn (d. 1463), and of their son, Sir William (d. 1505), grandfather of Queen Anne Boleyn.

To tempt such patrons almost the whole presbytery was on offer. It already contained the tomb of the founder plus that of Roger Bigod, earl of Norfolk and founder of Thetford Priory. He was well remembered, having helped to settle the cathedral boundaries, and his cloister memorial was renewed in 1443–44.[34] Association with so great a patron must have seemed most attractive to the ascendant Boleyns. The presbytery also needed attention. Scorching from the fire of 1463 can be seen on the clerestory arcades, increasing in severity as it progresses eastwards. If the

33. Similar to Wymondham Abbey, undated. The mid height tracery suggests it is earlier than Norwich spire.

34. *Communar Rolls*, p. 43.

damage was this bad at such a height, the conflagration below must have been fearsome. Furnishings and fittings would have added to the flames and the old Romanesque structure must have been seriously injured. Doubtless the fabric required more than a coat of paint; resurfacing was the only option. The attractiveness of this unique opportunity brought in the Boleyns – their arms could decorate the sanctuary, their tombs could grace the most sacred area of the church, their remains could borrow the Bigod ancestral bones.

The precise date of the Tudorisation of the presbytery is unclear, despite the mass of heraldic evidence, much of which is commemorative and inaccurate. There are some architectural guidelines. The first aisle bay south contains the chantry tomb of Prior Thomas Bozoun (1471–80). While there is no precedent for a standing monument and chapel built by a Norwich prior, the structure presumably dates from around his death.[35] The chapel stands at aisle level, its flat-topped canopy providing a platform floor within the main arcade. The west wall of the chapel was built against one side of the Romanesque pier now partly exposed. Hence it predates the Tudor transformation of the presbytery. The east side stops short of either work and must have left a gap before another tomb was inserted *c.* 1500.

The tomb of Bishop Goldwell (1472–99), two bays along, is clearly a workshop import from elsewhere; it represents an insert into the presbytery after the Tudor redressing.[36] The newly fashioned side walls encasing the Romanesque piers already stood and the intrados vault was already executed. The tomb fits badly into the space and is clumsily assembled, particularly the redundant canopy. The end-posts are designed for a flat-backed setting, not to collide with the Perpendicular half columns of the transformed arches. Plaster has been added liberally to convert rounded half shafts into flat planes. Below and out of sight, the Tudor corner shafts have been cut off within the voided canopy top.

The Goldwell tomb is unfortunately undated. Generally, given the promotional prospects of the English hierarchy, only archbishops of Canterbury built their tombs in their lifetimes, papal election being thought unlikely. By the late middle ages, however, attitudes changed universally. Either through age, ill-health or dynastic disfavour, some bishops abandoned thoughts of upward translation and built tombs and chantries in their current cathedrals. Sometimes they were caught out. Bishop Audley of Hereford built his chantry-tomb between 1492 and 1502, only to be translated to Salisbury, where he built another. Bishop West built one in Putney and then another at Ely after 1525. Goldwell, a Yorkist, found little favour from the Tudor Henry VII, and his tomb may well post-date 1485. It might coincide with the completion of his high vault scheme *c.* 1491, which alone demonstrates his dedication to Norwich.

35. See also below, pp. 482–83 and fig. 186.   36. See also below, pp. 472 and fig. 180.

Fig. 95. Presbytery, north
arcade, bays 3 and 4.

The tomb evidence would therefore suggest a date for the Tudor work of *c.* 1480–90, though even this dating must take into account the spasmodic sequence of the work. The refacing was clearly executed in a series of short campaigns. The bonding throughout is erratic but some obvious vertical breaks occur. On the north side, bay 1 came first, followed by bays 2 and 3 together, then bay 4. The short stretch of wall between bay 4 and the north-east crossing pier was apparently refaced last (fig. 95). On the south side, each bay may well be a separate build, progressing arch by arch to the crossing. While the interior was then limewashed over, the intermittent work suggests either irregular payments or personal, tailor-made accommodation.

The Boleyn interest seems to have been present from the outset. Both sides of the easternmost bay make structural provision for the additional family shields. The shield of Anne and Geoffrey occurs seven times, but the extensive appearance of Anne's ancestry makes plain her patronage.[37] Her date of death is unknown. The

37. See below, p. 462.

arms of Sir William Boleyn (d. 1505) occur once, in bay 2 south, providing the latest date for the work as no reference appears to his heirs.

The architectural transformation was simplicity itself. Take a four bay Romanesque presbytery, strip all the projecting architectural elements from the wall, insert a new floor level in both apse and sanctuary bay, square off the arcade piers, recast the arches with modern, four-centred designs, insert fancy vaults, resurface the walls with smooth masonry leaving plenty of blank shields for donors' arms and add tall canopied figure-niches to taste. Top the work with diamond-plan cresting and wait for the money to roll in. The cost cannot have been great, for the Romanesque core continues to carry the structure. What was achieved was a kind of stage-effect transformation, similar to many English Perpendicular modernizations such as Sherborne and Winchester, with the added bonus that the top storey already existed. The Boleyns were clearly satisfied, witness the plethora of their brightly painted arms, the chaotic quarterings amply revealing their tortuous climb to respectability.

The architecture of the new campaign suffers from a certain mechanical blandness. It stands no qualitative comparison with contemporary work such as Windsor or King's Cambridge. The frames, spandrels and general detailing seem merely etched into the surface, the whole elevation looking more Gothick than Tudor. Perhaps coloured and befigured, the scheme took life. The most successful features are the internal arch vaults. The eight arches contain no less than six different designs, a characteristic mix of straight-laced Perpendicular with more flouncy continental inspirations. Bay 1 south contains a net vault yet there follow two bays of flowing curvilinear designs of lobes and circles. Bay 4 south has the only vault to match its opposite number, with circles infilled with flamboyant motifs. The northern series begins with a sober criss-cross pattern which is quickly abandoned in the second bay for lots of cusped lobes arranged within triangles. The last design, bay 3 north, displays the only quasi-fan vault in the group. The combination of Perpendicular correctness and more Flamboyant designs finds its closest parallel in the canopy vaults of the jamb niches at King's, Cambridge, where the second campaign is contemporary with Norwich. Cambridge is an obvious source for the architect here with John Auntell, the likely candidate, having worked at King's.

Ultimately the Boleyn gamble did not pay off. The rapid rise in the family's fortunes took their interests elsewhere, for they had no roots in Norwich, and the descendants of Sir William suffered unhappy fates. Doubtless, had the Norwich scheme borne fruit, a second stage was envisaged as the gallery level seems to have been prepared for a similar fate. The whole presbytery was clearly to be transformed into a new guise, with Tudor arches and internal vaults at both Romanesque levels, reaching up to the Perpendicular clerestory and vault. Norwich would become a Perpendicular Ely choir or another Gloucester, free of descending tracery.

10

The Gothic Sculpture

Veronica Sekules

At first sight, Norwich Cathedral is notable for the restraint of its architectural decoration from the period from the thirteenth to the fifteenth centuries. It never had a major screen façade such as those of Salisbury, Wells, Lichfield or Exeter, on which sculpted figures make a dramatic impact as the visitor first approaches the building. It lacks buttresses or pinnacles which may have been adorned by niches for figures and gablets for corbels such as existed at York or Lincoln. Norwich has also suffered many losses. Bishop Suffield's mid thirteenth-century Lady Chapel, which might have afforded scope for sculptural ornament, no longer exists. Liturgical furnishings, such as the pulpitum commissioned by Bishop Walter Lyhart, survive in a very altered state. Elaborate image niches in Bishop Goldwell's presbytery have been stripped of figures. Carved, gilded and bejewelled altar retables, reredoses and images, in as far as they ever existed in quantity at Norwich, have almost entirely disappeared. Even tombs of the medieval period are not numerous and there is no evidence to suggest that the shrines to St William and the venerated bishops Walter Suffield and John Salmon had ornate settings with sculptural bases or canopies. These shrines had in any case declined in power by the height of the period under consideration here.[1]

The attitude towards Gothic sculpture at Norwich seems to have been consistent with that of the twelfth century, in that its impact was either intentionally or by default confined to the periphery of the building. In this period the principal sites for sculpture were the gateways and doorways and the upper parts of the church. Images are immensely numerous and tend towards the small-scale. Life-size figures are few in number. The great glory of Norwich is the vault bosses of the nave, presbytery, transept, Bauchun Chapel and cloister, and here dramatic impact is

---

1. J. R. Shinners, 'The Veneration of Saints at Norwich Cathedral in the Fourteenth Century', *NA*, 40 (1988), pp. 134–35.

Fig. 96. The prior's doorway of 1297–1314.

created by multiplicity and repetition. This body of sculpture was surely intended to inspire awe and admiration for its sheer quantity and virtuosity of execution.[2]

Of the same period as the earliest of the cloister bosses, that is 1297–1314, is the doorway (usually known as the prior's doorway) leading from the north-east corner of the cloister into the south aisle of the nave (fig. 96). Its inventive design, with alternating triangular and ogee canopies straddling the mouldings of the arch and the correspondingly alternating standing and seated figures beneath them, has justifiably earned it a place among the finest examples of English carving of its date. The design is full of subtlety, as the alternations enhance the relationships between the figures. There are seven figures in all, representing Christ at the apex flanked by standing angels, who are in turn flanked by St Peter and St Edmund, king and martyr, Moses and St John the Baptist. The figures, as has been pointed out, are arranged in three pairs either side of Christ, facing each other across the arch.[3] But the arch figures can also be read in a number of other configurations, appearing to make three groups of three as well as a group of three and a group of four. Thus on the one hand we have Christ displaying his wounds flanked by angels holding instruments of the Passion, as a discrete group representing the suffering of the Passion. Accompanying them are the four saintly figures trampling on their adversaries. On the other hand, the three seated figures, Christ, St Peter and St Edmund, appear as a group representing spiritual and temporal authority. Christ, with St John the Baptist and Moses facing him, can also be read as a group representing the old and the new law. The figures manage at the same time to achieve a delicacy and elegance, and a slightly eccentric vigour, whereby their relationships to one another in these groupings are accentuated. However, the entire doorway is conceived in a small-scale and decorative mode, perhaps owing to the fact that the sculpture has without doubt the same authorship as the cloister bosses immediately to the south.

The gateways of the priory precinct form an extraordinarily interesting series and two of them, the Ethelbert Gate and the Erpingham Gate, must be among the most elaborate known, and certainly unrivalled for the quality of their sculpture.[4] The Ethelbert or Great Gate (fig. 97) was originally the main ceremonial entrance into the south-west corner of the monastic precinct from Tombland. Its twelfth-century

2. On the bosses see below, pp. 363–78.
3. The doorway is discussed in Fernie, *NC*, p. 175.
4. Very few comparable gateways survive. A notable example is at St Augustine's Abbey, Canterbury, discussed in P. Binski and J. Alexander, *Age of Chivalry* (London, 1987), cat. 327. Aspects of the function of gateways are discussed by P. Fergusson in '"Porta

Patens Esto": Notes on Early Cistercian Gatehouses in the North of England', in E. C. Fernie and P. Crossley, eds, *Medieval Architecture and its Intellectual Context* (London, 1990), pp. 47–59. I am grateful to Lynne Broughton for allowing me to read her unpublished article 'Lincoln Minster: Exchange Gate' and for discussing the Norwich gateways with me *in situ*.

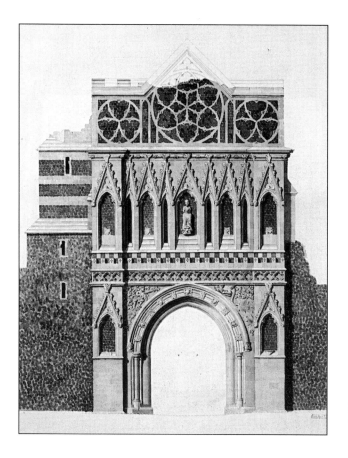

Fig. 97. The Ethelbert Gate
prior to restoration, a drawing by John Adey Repton of
1803.

predecessor had been severely damaged by fire in the riots of 1272, but was probably
still serviceable enough for rebuilding to be put off until after work on the church
had been completed and the cloister rebuilding was well under way.[5] It has been
generally accepted, as Arthur Whittingham first suggested, that the date of its building
corresponds to the entry in the communar's roll for 1316 for *expensis circa portas*
(expenses about the gate) of £115 8s. 5¼ d., although a number of authorities have
suggested that the lierne vault of the interior and the east façade date a few years
later into the 1320s.[6] The principal, west façade is designed in three registers. The
ground storey entrance arch, studded with large foliate voussoirs, is flanked by two
gabled image niches on the buttresses and, in the spandrels above, a relief carving
of a man drawing his sword against a dragon. Above this is the façade for the upper
chamber, a chapel dedicated to St Ethelbert in recollection of the chapel of the same
dedication which formerly existed outside the gate. It is decorated with three gabled

5. J. T. Macnaughton-Jones, 'St Ethelbert's
    Gate, Norwich', *NA*, 34 (1966), pp. 74–84.
6. *Communar Rolls*, pp. 33, 90; P. Lindley, 'The

Arminghall Arch and Contemporary Sculpture in Norwich', *NA*, 40 (1987), p. 25;
Fernie, *NC*, pp. 180–81.

image niches, flanked by narrower, gabled arches containing windows with a further two gabled niches, possibly also for images on the outer buttresses, corresponding to those on the floor below. Eric Fernie has remarked on the subtlety of this design, which indeed, with its complex alternation patterns, has echoes of the cloister prior's doorway tympanum.[7] The top register hides the roof line and consists of a gable façade decorated with what must have been one of the earliest examples of knapped flint and ashlar tracery flushwork. The Ethelbert Gate has undergone radical restorations. The attic storey was repaired and the flushwork tracery patterns altered by William Wilkins in 1815 (fig. 97). In 1964, during a restoration undertaken by Feilden and Mawson, the spandrel carvings were totally replaced by replicas and most of the gabled niches of the upper storey were also renewed. The Virgin and Child at the

centre is a replacement for the only original figure which then remained from this level, another image of Christ displaying his wounds. Panels of original sculpture from the spandrels were saved and these, together with early photographs and drawings, give some indication of the character and quality of the carving (fig. 98).[8]

Fig. 98. The head of a dragon, an original panel of sculpture from the Ethelbert Gate, *c.* 1316.

In its original state, the Ethelbert Gate would have been a highly decorative building presenting a façade rich in images which the cathedral otherwise lacked. In a sense it would have operated as a principal façade and, in as far as one can glean from the remaining images, it communicated a strong message designating the gate as the opening to the hallowed ground beyond. The rebuilding of the gate had been necessitated by the results of the conflict of 1272 between the townspeople and the priory. The scene of conflict between man and dragon on the spandrel of the main arch opening is surely intended to recall this. The dispute here is enacted against a background of vine scroll foliage, emanating from broken roots at the base of the spandrels. A lion stands upon the root below the man and on the side of the dragon in a similar position is a crested bird with a serpent-like tail. This recalls a passage from Isaiah's prophecies (14:29–31) concerning the overthrow of Babylon:

> Rejoice not thou, whole Palestina, because the rod of him that smote thee is broken; for out of the serpent's root shall come forth a cockatrice, and his

7.   Fernie, *NC*, p. 180.
8.   A. Borg *et al.*, *Medieval Sculpture from Norwich*   *Cathedral* (Norwich, 1980), pp. 30–34.

fruit shall be a fiery flying serpent. And the first-born of the poor shall feed, and the needy shall lie down in safety; and I will kill thy root with famine, and he shall slay thy remnant. Howl, O gate; cry, O city; thou, whole Palestina, art dissolved: for there shall come from the north a smoke, and none shall be alone in his appointed times. What shall one then answer the messengers of the nation? That the Lord hath founded Zion, and the poor of his people shall trust in it.[9]

The figure of Christ displaying his wounds in the central niche of the upper storey may well have been flanked in neighbouring niches by SS. Mary and John, and perhaps by angels bearing instruments of the Passion, thus reinforcing the message of salvation from evil forces through Christ. While it is possible to find numerous examples of principal façades and doorways from the twelfth century onwards ornamented with sculpture emphasising the triumph of divine authority over mortal strife, it is very rare on a gateway, monastic or secular: one may infer that at Norwich it was inspired by the particular circumstances which led to the 1272 riots. The closest parallel for part of the imagery is probably a copy, at the early fourteenth-century gatehouse to St Benet's Abbey at Holme in Norfolk, where a man is wielding a spear against a winged dragon, also against a background of vine scroll in the spandrels of the main arch.

The first two or three decades of the fourteenth century were fruitful times for the commissioning of sculptural decoration on the buildings of the precinct. This was largely due to building activity instigated by Bishop Salmon, which included the east walk of the cloister with the prior's doorway discussed above, the Carnary College and the bishop's palace. The Carnary College is situated to the northwest of the west façade of the cathedral and incorporated Bishop Salmon's chantry foundation. Its entrance porch and west and east exterior walls were originally encrusted with sculpture in the form of large images resting on corbels within gabled, finialled and pinnacled niches on the buttresses. The taste for sculptural embellishment seems to have extended to the palace, the only remaining sculpted portion of which is the east porch now within the boundaries of Norwich School. Decorating its vault are remarkably well-preserved vault bosses, one depicting a scene of a devil perched behind a male and a female figure holding hands. Other fragments of capitals and decorative carvings survive and can be associated with these works, providing a poignant testimony to the riches that have been lost.

9.   I am grateful to T. A. Heslop for bringing to my attention a passage from Guibert of Nogent, *De vita sua*, where he quotes from Isaiah 14:29 in the context of a description of civil strife between Godfrey, count of Namur, and Enguerrand de Boves at Tournus: *Patrologia Latina*, vol. 156, col. 910d; Guibert of Nogent, *The Autobiography of Guibert Abbot of Nogent-sous-Coucy*, trans. C. C. S. Bland (London and New York, 1925), book iii, ch. 3, p. 133.

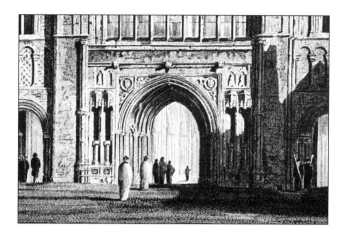

Fig. 99. The west doorway
of Norwich Cathedral, an
engraving by John Britton,
1816.

A campaign of works in the early fifteenth century addressed the west portal in
the façade of the cathedral and the related western precinct gateway. The central
portal and great window in the west façade of the cathedral were commissioned by
Bishop Alnwick, according to the continuation of Cotton's chronicle: 'Lord William
Alnwick . . . caused the great west door with the window above to be made at
his own cost'.[10] An inscription in a scroll in the spandrels over the entrance arch
calls the onlooker to 'Orate pro anima Domini Willelmi Alnewyk' (pray for the
soul of Lord William Alnwick). The porch has been narrowed as a result of
nineteenth-century additions to the turrets flanking it. It is clear from the engraving
by Hulsbergh reproduced in Sir Thomas Browne's *Repertorium* of 1712 (above,
fig. 91), and from John Britton's engraving of 1816 (fig. 99), that there were formerly
two niches for statues either side of the entrance arch and correspondingly four
smaller images in niches above, alongside the spandrels containing the inscription.[11] The large niches apparently contained figures of two bishops and two other
male ecclesiastics, possibly cardinals. The smaller ones above contained, on the south,
Alnwick receiving the instrument of his confirmation from King Henry VI, according
to Blomefield.[12] The surviving image of the Virgin Mary on the north side suggests
that this pair might have represented an Annunciation. Alnwick left Norwich in
1436 to become bishop of Lincoln, where he died in 1449. The invocation on this
doorway to pray for his soul has led most scholars to assume that the whole
commission was executed posthumously in the middle of the century, rather than

10. H. Wharton, *Anglia sacra*, 2 vols (London,
    1691), i, p. 417: 'Magister Willelmus
    Anewyk . . . fieri fecit ex sua gratia majus
    hostium Occidentale cum fenestra supere-
    minenti . . .' Blomefield, *Norfolk,*, iii, pp.
    531–32; C. J. Evans, 'The Heraldry of Nor-
    wich Cathedral', *NA*, 8 (1879), p. 83;
    Fernie, *NC*, p. 186.

11. T. Browne, *Repertorium: or, Some Account of
    the Tombs and Monuments in the Cathedral
    Church of Norwich* (London, 1712), p. 24.

12. Blomefield, *Norfolk*, iii, p. 532.

while he was still resident at Norwich. However, his will mentions only a bequest for the window, implying that the doorway was already paid for. If the two elements of the façade were constructed separately, Alnwick's commissioning of the doorway between 1425 and 1436, as a means of giving thanks for his institution to Norwich, is a distinct possibility.

The design of the west doorway has been convincingly related by Richard Fawcett to that of the north door of Westminster Hall and the closely related west door of Westminster Abbey, both dating from the late 1390s and designed by the king's master mason, Henry Yeveley.[13] Fawcett also attributed the west doorway to the same mason as that of the Erpingham Gate and identified work of a similar nature at a number of churches in Norwich and Norfolk, including Norwich St George Colegate, Wiveton, Great Cressingham, Walpole St Peter, Blakeney and Hingham. The similarities have mainly appeared in the form of moulding profiles, tracery patterns and some other masonry details.[14] Generally, there is little sculpture in these buildings and even when there is, there is no demonstrable relationship equivalent to that of the masonry details. For example, Fawcett draws attention to the undeniably close similarity of design between the tomb of Lord Morley at Hingham and the Erpingham Gate (figs 107, 109, 110), yet the sculpture, profuse on both monuments, is unrelated.[15] It may be that a pattern of working which has been observed elsewhere also operated among these buildings – that a number of masons with access to a common stock of moulding profiles, tracery designs and other architectural components, were involved in constructing them. The masons would have worked essentially collaboratively, combining in different permutations for different commissions, hence the possibility of mouldings being identical while other details, such as sculptural style, differ.[16] In cases such as this it is also likely that either a specialist image carver was brought in on site, or the sculpture was commissioned quite separately from the main construction and supplied from a centre specialising in fine image carving.

13. R. Fawcett, 'Later Gothic Architecture in Norfolk' (unpublished University of East Anglia Ph. D. thesis, 1975), p. 387.
14. Fawcett, 'Later Gothic Architecture', pp. 326–93; R. Fawcett, 'St Mary at Wiveton in Norfolk, and a Group of Churches Attributed to its Mason', *Antiq. J.*, 62 (1982), pp. 35–56.
15. Fawcett, 'Later Gothic Architecture', pp. 378–82; Fawcett, 'St Mary at Wiveton', pp. 51–52.
16. For accounts of collaborative masonry practice see S. Murray, *Building Troyes Cathedral* (Bloomington, 1987); J. White, 'The Reliefs on the FaÇade of the Duomo at Or-

vieto' *Journal of the Warburg and Courtauld Institutes*, 22 (1959), pp. 254–302; J. C. Bonne, 'Organisation architectonique et composition plastique des tympans romans: Les modèles de Conques et d'Autun', in X. Barral i Altet, ed., *Artistes, artisans et production artistique au moyen âge*, 3 vols (Paris, 1986–90), ii, pp. 185–202; V. Sekules, 'The Sculpture and Liturgical Furnishings of Heckington Church and Related Monuments: Masons and Benefactors in Early Fourteenth- Century Lincolnshire' (unpublished University of London Ph. D. thesis, 1990), pp. 129–47.

John Harvey attributed the Erpingham Gate and the west door to James Woderofe, a mason actively working on the cathedral between 1415 and 1451.[17] Among other tasks, he was in charge of the last phase of work on the cloister and, with John Jakes, was paid in 1444–45 for making the *lavatorium* in the west walk. The surviving detail of the *lavatorium* shows it to be only slightly related to work on the west front and Erpingham Gate. Unfortunately there are no medieval figures left in its niches, but its framework is highly ornate by comparison, with much richer foliate carving on lengthier finials, more complex vaults beneath niche gablets, and panels of intricate blind tracery which are unlike anything found on the two façades.

Another point of view about the authorship of the gateway is expressed by Frank Woodman, who attributes its design to the St Peter Mancroft workshop associated with Reginald Ely, later master mason of King's College Chapel, Cambridge. He suggests a date bracket of 1430–50.[18] Again this attribution has been made with reference to the architecture and the moulding detail: there is nothing strikingly similar in the oeuvre with any of the fine decorative carving or image work. The style of the sculpture on the Alnwick porch and Erpingham Gate is hard to parallel locally. One again needs to look to Westminster Abbey for the aesthetic tendency it seems to espouse, to Henry V's chantry designed *c.* 1437 by the master mason of the abbey, John Thirsk. Henry V's chantry is a much grander commission and more richly decorated. By comparison the Norwich monuments are provincial, but they contain distinct echoes of the designs of its canopy-work, mouldings decorated with formalised leaf patterns and figure style with carefully arranged broad-fold drapery.

The Erpingham Gate, like the Ethelbert Gate a century earlier, acts in effect like a principal façade and is larger and more elaborately decorated than the west door of the cathedral, the design of which it partly echoes, being basically an arch framed by a rectangular panel with decorated spandrels, between two faceted turrets (above, fig. 92). The turret façades feature the heraldry of Sir Thomas Erpingham prominently and repeatedly. Each one has Erpingham at the centre, with Clopton from his first wife Joan to the south, and Walton from his second wife Joan to the north.[19] Sir Thomas Erpingham has therefore been assumed as the principal benefactor. He had been chamberlain to Henry IV, warden of the Cinque Ports, steward of the royal household, marshal of England and was responsible for persuading the king to give Norwich its charter in 1404. In his later years he was a generous benefactor to the

17. J. Harvey, *English Medieval Architects: A Bio-graphical Dictionary down to 1550* (rev. edn, Gloucester, 1984), p. 343.

18. F. Woodman, *The Architectural history of King's College Chapel and its Place in the De-velopment of Late Gothic Architecture in England and France* (London, 1986), pp. 18–19, 84–87.

19. A. P. Sims, 'The Church Gate of Norwich Cathedral Priory' (unpublished University of East Anglia B. A. thesis, 1990); E. W. Tristram, 'The Erpingham Gate', in Friends of Norwich Cathedral, *Ninth Annual Report* (Norwich, 1938), pp. 40–46.

cathedral as well as to the Norwich Blackfriars church and to churches on his manors. He died without issue in 1428 and was buried in the cathedral, where he also established a chantry.[20]

Most scholars have assumed on stylistic grounds that the gateway was executed towards the middle of the fifteenth century, that is some time after Erpingham's death. There is no documentary evidence for this. Indeed, the contents of his will, made in 1427, are known and it is not mentioned.[21] Tony Sims argues that the gateway is likely to date from the early 1420s and suggests that, because of relationships between the careers and devotional interests of Sir Thomas Erpingham and Sir John Wodehouse, its building coincided with the foundation in 1421 of Wodehouse's chantry in the crypt of the Carnary Chapel, dedicated to the Trinity and the five wounds.[22] While this is an attractive proposition, there are problems stylistically with such an early dating for the gate. The relative dating of the Erpingham Gate and the Alnwick porch should perhaps be reconsidered in the light of the possibility that both were paid for during Alnwick's episcopate, in Erpingham's case perhaps shortly before he made his will, although neither need have been completed until the mid 1430s.

The main jambs of the gateway arch include two rows of figured voussoirs. The outer series are all female saints and seem to be virgin martyrs accompanied by saints of local importance; the inner are most likely to be the twelve apostles. Two large standing male figures, apparently tonsured and holding books, appear at the summits of the turrets at the base of the gable storey. At the centre of the gable is a single niche containing the kneeling figure of Sir Thomas Erpingham flanked by two shields, originally for the see and the priory, set in relief panels. In the spandrels are shields to the Trinity, Crucifixion and eucharist. Early engravings and photographs show four pedestals for figures of the four evangelists rising from the edge of the gable roof.[23] Apart from this, the gable is unadorned and faced with rough flints, although originally it probably had an ashlar facing as is suggested in Britton's engraving. Tony Sims has observed that the figure of Sir Thomas fits ill into the central niche and that it is more likely to have been moved there much later from his tomb; and that the original inhabitant of the niche was probably a Trinity.[24]

Monastic gateways ornamented with the heraldry of secular donors are well known, for example at Butley Priory in Suffolk, with a multitude of shields covering its façade; or at Castle Acre in Norfolk, where arms of the Warennes are prominent in the centre of the gable. Erpingham took this tradition a stage further, in that he

20. T. John, 'Sir Thomas Erpingham, East Anglian Society and the Dynastic Revolution of 1399', *NA*, 35 (1970–72), pp. 96–108; Blomefield, *Norfolk*, iv, pp. 38–39, 344.
21. Blomefield, *Norfolk*, iv, p. 39.

22. Sims, 'Church Gate', p. 24.
23. J. Britton, *Architectural and Antiquarian Guide to the Cathedral of Norwich* (London, 1817), frontispiece.
24. Sims, 'Church Gate', pp. 16–18.

and his wives symbolised by their heraldry appear together in carefully arranged and ordered registers with representations of the monastery and the episcopate, the Trinity, Christ and symbols of his sacrifice, and Christ's immediate followers: apostles, disciples and early saints and martyrs. It has the appearance of a personal memorial, emphasising partnership in a benign order of fellowship and community.

An interesting theory concerning the gate's origins is recorded by Francis Blomefield, according to which the gate was paid for by Sir Thomas as penance for Lollardy. In the course of reprimanding him for his Wycliffite sympathies, Bishop Henry Despenser allegedly 'enjoined him to build the gate at the entrance of the precinct'. The dispute between the two men was resolved before the king and Erpingham was, according to Blomefield, publicly pardoned in 1400.[25] However, Erpingham was clearly a pillar of the establishment who rigorously supported the cathedral authorities; he would have been a very unlikely Lollard. It has been shown that the disagreement between Despenser and Erpingham was more likely to have concerned the deposition of Richard II and succession of Henry Bolingbroke as Henry IV, of which Erpingham was an influential facilitator and Despenser an opponent.[26] The king's intervention was to encourage a public reconciliation following Erpingham's bringing of charges to him against Despenser. While Blomefield's interpretation of these events might have been creative, the coincidence in date between Lollard persecutions and the building of the gate might still be significant. Bishop Alnwick's campaign against heresy began in 1428.[27] As a major element in the heresy was the rejection of the doctrine of transubstantiation, the appearance on the gate of symbols denoting the sacrament is important. Lollards also rejected any form of material magnificence, decoration and images, and they did not approve of worship of saints. The imagery of Erpingham's gate is thus openly defiant of their cause. It does not appear likely that it is the work of a reformed heretic, as Blomefield supposes, but of a zealot intent on asserting an orthodoxy. In a curious way its function echoes that of the Ethelbert Gate. In the face of an opposing force challenging the authority of the church, its imagery reinforces the church's hierarchy and doctrine.[28]

Possibly related to the campaign of works at the west end of the cathedral was the systematic refurbishment to its east of the liturgical furnishings and their setting, including the pulpitum and the choir stalls. Some of this renewal was necessitated by a storm of 1361/62 which caused major damage to the choir and more by the

25. Blomefield, *Norfolk*, iii, p. 524, iv, p. 45.
26. John, 'Sir Thomas Erpingham', pp. 96–108.
27. N. P. Tanner, *Heresy Trials in the Diocese of Norwich, 1428–31* (Camden Society, fourth series, 20, 1977).
28. The role of imagery in reinforcing church

doctrine in opposition to the Lollard threat is a major thrust of the argument in A. E. Nichols, *Seeable Signs: The Iconography of the Seven Sacraments, 1350–1544* (Woodbridge, 1994).

fire caused by lightning which struck the cathedral in 1463. The pulpitum itself was built after the later fire at the behest of Bishop Walter Lyhart, who was buried before it.[29] The choir stalls were probably funded by bequests and donations from numerous prominent local benefactors, Sir Thomas Erpingham among them. Charles Tracy asserts in his study of the Norwich stalls that this may be one of the earliest examples of lay involvement in the commissioning of choir stalls for a monastic cathedral.[30] The history of the building of the choir stalls was first outlined by Arthur Whittingham and his account is that relied upon by all later scholars, although some of his identifications of heraldry and subject matter are being reconsidered.[31] The first period of rebuilding is believed to have been delayed until Bishop Wakering's episcopate (1415–25). There was a second phase after the 1463 fire, during the time of Bishop Goldwell (1472–99). The quality of the carving of the canopies of both phases, but particularly of the misericords, is of a very high order and all writers on the subject have commented on this. Tracy compares the earlier canopy carvings with woodwork of metropolitan character at Gloucester and Winchester Cathedrals; and the later carvings with Prior Rahere's tomb at St Bartholomew the Great, London, and the tomb of John Tiptoft, earl of Worcester, at Ely Cathedral.[32] Details of the carving on the canopies, the supporters and the arm rests, relate to the stalls at St Margaret, King's Lynn, and Salle church, both in Norfolk. Tracy also makes comparisons with work in Suffolk at Fressingfield, Southwold and Wingfield. There is a strong possibility that the workshop that made these stalls was based in East Anglia. Further research may indeed identify more examples of its work.

The disciples of Christ appeared once more in a prominent position on the cathedral, as large-scale seated figures as supports to the flying buttresses of the presbytery. The originals were replaced by copies in the later nineteenth century but, in origin, this work dates from after 1472 and is contemporary with Bishop Goldwell's vault.[33] Figures occupying this position are rare, as flying buttresses are normally surmounted by pinnacles and finials. Seated figures of heraldic beasts are placed on top of finials surmounting the parapet of St George's Chapel, Windsor, dating from 1475 to 1511. These may or may not predate those at Norwich, but

29. Fernie, *NC*, pp. 187–88.
30. C. Tracy, *English Gothic Choir Stalls, 1400–1540* (Woodbridge, 1990), p. 32.
31. A. B. Whittingham, *The Stalls of Norwich Cathedral* (Norwich, 1961); A. B. Whittingham, *Norwich Cathedral Bosses and Misericords* (Norwich, 1981). M. Rose, *The Misericords of Norwich Cathedral* (Dereham, 1994) has made some additions to Whittingham's identifications of subject matter.
32. Tracy, *Choir Stalls*, pp. 35–36.

33. I am grateful to Keith Darby, surveyor to the fabric, for assisting me with tracing the original figures from the presbytery buttresses. They are mentioned in N. Pevsner and P. Metcalf, *The Cathedrals of England*, 2 vols (Harmondsworth, 1985), ii, p. 256, as 'in a nearby garden' and 'near the visitors' centre'. Mr Darby has confirmed that there are four in the grounds of the former archdeaconry (no. 57 The Close) and three near the ruined gateway to the hostry.

they demonstrate that the idea was current in the royal workshops. Very similar, and probably a copy, is the retrochoir of Peterborough, where flying buttresses are also crowned by disciple figures, though this work may postdate Norwich by some twenty years. At Norwich, the twelve piers of the presbytery had long been in place before flying buttresses were added, but the placing of the disciples upon them made explicit their symbolic significance. It is characteristic of Norwich that the sculpture here acts very much in service to the building. It may be physically peripheral, but it is certainly not so in terms of its function, which is to beautify and, more importantly, to give spiritual meaning to a particular architectural feature.

11

The Influence of the Gothic Parts
of the Cathedral on Church
Building in Norfolk

Richard Fawcett

Architectural ideas found in one building tend to be disseminated to others in two main ways. The most direct way is if a mason from one building goes on to work at others when, particularly if he was the designing mason, there is a clear possibility of identifiable kinship between all of the structures concerned. Less directly, parts of one building may serve as models for the patrons or masons of others, and be copied more or less closely, albeit with an admixture of ideas from other sources. As might be expected, the architectural evidence suggests that Norwich Cathedral influenced, or was related to, other churches within the diocese in both of these ways.

Although parish churches represented a greater proportion of architectural production in later medieval East Anglia than had previously been the case, Norwich Cathedral and Priory continued to provide first-rate architectural patronage up to the Reformation. Outstanding among the various operations in this period were the reconstruction of the cloister, the presbytery clerestory and the precinct gateways, and the progressive vaulting of the main spaces of the cathedral itself. The services of high calibre masons were secured for several of these prestigious works, which naturally provided stimuli for patrons of building operations elsewhere. Yet the scale and complexity of the cathedral works meant that the lessons they had to offer to those involved in lesser building campaigns might be of limited application. Even the most splendidly endowed parish churches did not require cloister walks or precinct gateways, and there was little requirement for stone vaulting, except occasionally in porches. As a consequence, in many cases we probably should not expect influences from the cathedral to be revealed in more than either a generalised similarity, or in the repetition of the most striking details, such as tracery patterns.

So far as cases of the same designing masons being at work in both the cathedral and lesser churches are concerned, it is probably also true to say that the clearest indications of this will be found where the relevant cathedral works are of a relatively small scale. In such cases there would be no reason for the mason to adopt an approach to his task different from that of working on a parish church. Conversely, the greater the disparity in scale and complexity, the more limited may be the range of parallels. Nevertheless, if the idea of an identifiable personal approach to design is to have any validity, we must assume that we should be able to detect this approach through the details of a mason's work.

A number of cases where the evidence strongly points to a cathedral mason having also been involved at a parish church will be discussed in the second part of this chapter. However, many of the parallels between the architectural features in the cathedral and those in parish churches of the diocese can only be offered as likely illustrations of one influencing the other. These parallels will be discussed first.[1]

The Cathedral as a Source of Architectural Ideas

Probably the first occasion, in the period covered by this chapter, when cathedral building provided a stimulus for significant numbers of churches throughout the diocese occurred when the traceried arcading of the south cloister walk was started to the designs of John and William Ramsey in the 1320s.[2] One of the tracery designs, with diagonally-placed daggers set out like the leaves of a four-petalled flower, foreshadows the fashion for one of the most popular window types to be used in the area in the fourteenth century (fig. 100a). Among examples of the type in Norfolk are two-light windows at Rockland All Saints, and three-light windows at Beetley, Norwich St Michael Coslany, Attleborough and Hevingham. Closely related variants are at Hingham, Gresham, Acle, Taverham, Hickling, Weasenham St Peter, Aylmerton, Postwick, Norwich St Helen, Hethersett and Swannington. Other variants are to be found in Suffolk, as at SS. Peter and Paul, Wangford (near Southwold), Laxfield and Heveningham, and in Cambridgeshire at Sutton in the Isle of Ely (figs 100c to 100h). The same motif was also to be used as a subordinate element in much larger windows, as at Attleborough.

This basic design was not limited to Norfolk and Suffolk. A more richly curvilinear variant was employed in the choir at Ely Cathedral (fig. 100b) when it was rebuilt after the collapse of the tower in 1322, and where the Ramseys were involved in at least some of the earlier fourteenth-century work, if not necessarily the choir

1. This chapter is largely based on research undertaken for the author's 'Later Gothic Architecture in Norfolk' (unpublished University of East Anglia Ph. D. thesis, 1975).

2. *Communar Rolls*, p. 34.

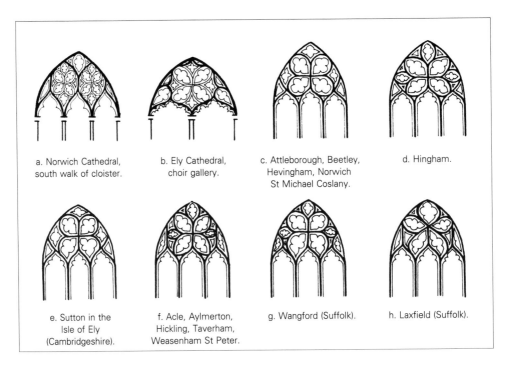

a. Norwich Cathedral,
south walk of cloister.

b. Ely Cathedral,
choir gallery.

c. Attleborough, Beetley,
Hevingham, Norwich
St Michael Coslany.

d. Hingham.

e. Sutton in the
Isle of Ely
(Cambridgeshire).

f. Acle, Aylmerton,
Hickling, Taverham,
Weasenham St Peter.

g. Wangford (Suffolk).

h. Laxfield (Suffolk).

Fig. 100. Tracery of diagonally-disposed four-petal flower type.

itself.[3] The type also enjoyed a limited vogue elsewhere in Britain, though it was certainly most common in Norfolk, and it is difficult not to conclude that it was Norwich Cathedral which provided the main model for those churches in the diocese which display similar designs. Although relatively few of these are securely dated, it is worthy of note that the idea was to remain current over an extended period. The nave of Attleborough, for example, where this tracery figures prominently, is unlikely to have been built before the third quarter of the fourteenth century.[4]

To varying extents, the tracery designs used in the other cloister walks also furnished a pool of ideas for the designers of East Anglian churches. After a long pause, reconstruction of the west walk began in 1346–47, probably to designs provided eleven years earlier by William and John Ramsey.[5] The tracery of this walk involved two alternating variants which are related to the type in the south walk already discussed. In one the groups of four daggers were set on vertical and horizontal axes; the other was very similar, except that the lateral daggers were

3. A. B. Whittingham, 'The Ramsey Family of Norwich', *Arch. J.,* 137 (1980), pp. 285–89, at pp. 285–86.

4. R. Fawcett, 'Sutton in the Isle of Ely and its Architectural Context', in BAACT, 2, *Ely, 1978,* ed. N. Coldstream and P. Draper (1982), pp. 80–81.

5. *Communar Rolls,* p. 38.

deflected downwards to the apices of the equilateral arches of the main openings. With a possible exception at Hevingham, the latter type does not seem to have inspired much of a following, although the vitality of links along the 'Norwich–Ely axis' are again demonstrated by the way a more complex development on that theme was employed within the sub-arches of the four-light windows along the flanks of the Ely Lady Chapel.

The former type, with horizontal and vertical daggers, was to find a wide following, and was even more popular than the version with the diagonally-set daggers in the south walk. Among derivatives are two-light windows at Wramplingham, Walcott, Starston, Yelverton, Felthorpe, Tottington, Watlington, Houghton-le-Dale Slipper Chapel, Westwick, Hindringham, Costessey, Weston Longville, Bramerton, Norwich St Mary Coslany, Carleton-Rode, Forncett St Peter, Poringland, Colney, Erpingham, Trunch, Wroxham, Swanton Abbott and Framingham Earl. There are three-light versions at Ingham, Norwich St George Tombland, Aylsham, Beeston St Lawrence, Tuttington, Castle Acre, Weston Longville and Acle. As with the diagonal-dagger arrangement, this design was also to figure in larger compositions, as at Aylsham, Banningham, Weston Longville and Worstead.

The question of derivation of this type from the cathedral is complicated by its relatively wide currency elsewhere. There are known to have been examples in the London cloister of the Greyfriars, often thought to be very early fourteenth century, but perhaps more likely to date from work recorded on the cloister in 1346,[6] in which case they may themselves be a direct reflection of the influence of the Ramsey family of masons in the capital. The problem is also complicated because, once again, we find a different – and in this case earlier – version of the same idea in the choir of Ely, started after 1322. It was indeed the more lavish convolutions of the Ely version which must have inspired examples in western Norfolk at Snettisham and Heacham, an area where the influence of Norwich so often seems to have been subordinate to that of Ely. Despite these caveats it seems reasonable to conclude that it was Norwich which inspired the great majority of the Norfolk examples, especially since most of them are concentrated in the centre and east of the county.

The start of work on the western bays of the north cloister walk in the 1350s introduced two further tracery types, in which subordinated curvilinear forms are placed within pairs of reticulation units.[7] (The net-like reticulation pattern is indicated on fig. 101 by the stronger lines). That in bay 40 (fig. 101a) seems to have been the more influential, although its present appearance has probably been distorted by eccentric restoration, as a result of which the vertical form pieces separating the two curved mouchettes at the base of the reticulation units are simply carried straight

6. M. Hastings, *St Stephen's Chapel and its Place in the Development of Perpendicular Style*   (Cambridge, 1955), p. 150 and pl. 55.

7. *Communar Rolls*, pp. 38–39.

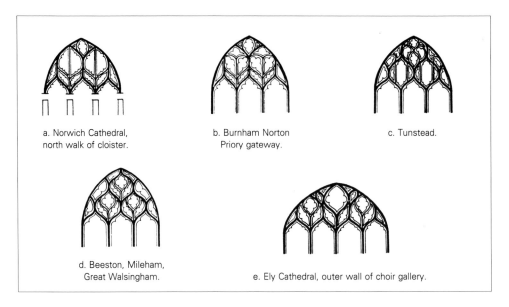

a. Norwich Cathedral,
north walk of cloister.

b. Burnham Norton
Priory gateway.

c. Tunstead.

d. Beeston, Mileham,
Great Walsingham.

e. Ely Cathedral, outer wall of choir gallery.

Fig. 101. Tracery with subordinate tracery within reticulation units.

up to the apices of those units in a way that is most unlikely to reflect the designer's intention. The original arrangement cannot be known with certainty, although it seems likely to have been similar to the tracery in the upper floor of the gateway at the Carmelite friary of Burnham Norton, where the central vertical in each unit continues up between two larger daggers before bifurcating above those daggers (fig. 101b). The date of the friary gateway is unknown, although its construction may have followed the acquisition of extra land for new buildings in 1353.[8] In view of this connection between Burnham Norton and Norwich, it is interesting to note that the master of works at Norwich in 1352–53 was one William de Norton, though this may be no more than coincidental.[9]

The continuing common currency of ideas between Norwich and Ely at this period is demonstrated by the use of tracery with lesser forms contained by reticulation units in one pair of windows in the Ely choir gallery (fig. 101e); but, as always at Ely, there is greater incidental enrichment. Since the high outer walls of the gallery may represent a modification of the original design, it is likely that the Ely examples of the type are closer to the finishing date of the choir of 1338 than the starting date of 1322. In this case the parallels between the two cathedrals could be attributable to the movements of masons of the Attegrene family. The younger John, who may have been responsible for these tracery designs at Norwich, had

8.   T. H. Bryant, *The Churches of Norfolk: Hun-*
     dred of Brothercross (Norwich, 1914), p. 21.

9.   *Communar Rolls*, p. 39.

been earlier at Ely with his father; he was, incidentally, to return there as master mason in 1357–58.[10]

Windows having sub-tracery within shapes approximating to reticulation units related to those in the north walk of the cathedral cloister were not entirely new in Norfolk. One of the earliest, rather tentative, explorations of the idea may have been at the bishop's palace, in the porch of the hall built by Bishop Salmon between 1318 and 1325. Other examples which could be earlier than those at the cathedral are to be seen at Hingham and Elsing; it is thus by no means certain how far the cathedral examples simply reflected, rather than directed, a local fashion. One closely interrelated group of buildings which consistently used tracery of this type, and is almost certainly attributable to a single designing mason, includes parts of the churches at Great Walsingham, Beeston St Mary, Tunstead, Beetley, Little Fransham, Houghton-le-Dale Slipper Chapel, Rougham, Narborough and Mileham (figs 101c and 101d). A related sub-group of churches includes Ashill, Caston and Thompson.[11]

Among other Norfolk churches with windows which show variants on the same themes are Trowse, Seething, North Pickenham, Taverham, Weybourne, Corpusty, Great Witchingham, Wood Dalling, Starston, West Barsham, Great Ryburgh, Colney, Mundford and Colton. Related windows are to be seen at Attleborough, Great Ellingham, Snetterton, Tottington, Banham and South Lopham. The basic motif of a sub-traceried reticulation unit was also to be employed as one element in larger compositions like those found at Heydon, Narborough, and Fakenham. It should be said, however, that in a number of these examples the clarity of relationships is forfeited through the way the lesser forms are not strictly subordinated to the containing forms.

The collapse of the cathedral spire in 1361/62 led to the diversion of building activity from the cloister to the more urgent needs of the presbytery clerestory. The precise dates of the rebuilding are unknown, although it is likely that reconstruction started immediately and there are references to work in 1364 and 1369. For our present purposes, the new and enlarged clerestory is chiefly remarkable for the design of its windows, in which – apart from the western bay – rectilinear designs were first used consistently at the cathedral (fig. 102a).

The sequence of the building operation is uncertain, though it may not be simplistic to assume that the bay adjacent to the tower, with its rather stereotyped curvilinear forms, was rebuilt first. The contrast between the windows of that bay and those of three of the faces of the apse, which seem to have been ultimately inspired by windows in the south transept and choir at Gloucester Cathedral, is

10. J. Harvey, *English Medieval Architects* (London, 1954), p. 119.
11. R. Fawcett, 'A Group of Churches by the Architect of Great Walsingham', *NA*, 37 (1980), pp. 277–94.

quite striking.[12] Whoever was in charge of the design of this part of the cathedral was clearly well aware of developments at the most advanced centres, although he could not resist embellishing his work in a way which might have surprised the designer of Gloucester.

The most 'correct' of these windows, those in the east face and the westernmost of the canted faces of the apse, had little impact in the diocese. It is true that all the clerestory windows were of a scale that could only have been emulated in the most lavishly funded operations, but these particular windows were perhaps also just too austere to be immediately comprehensible in an area which, outside Norwich, tended to be architecturally rather conservative. One of the few cases of this design being repeated is at the cathedral itself, where the leaves of the west door are decorated with a closely similar pattern, albeit at a considerably later date, and probably with no direct debt to the clerestory.

The other windows of the new clerestory, despite their size and complexity, did attract a limited following in a small number of the more ambitious churches of the diocese. Those of the easternmost canted faces of the apse and of three of the bays of the south flank had the basic 'Gloucester matrix', embellished by a cross-shaped arrangement of figures at the head of the window, with related groupings within the sub-arches. These windows must have been the inspiration for the imposing north transept window at Aylsham, which shows a similar tendency to gild the lily in its overenrichment. The work at Aylsham is traditionally said to date from after Edward III's gift of the manor to his son, John of Gaunt, in 1371; a rather firmer basis for dating could be a bequest of 1377 for the furnishing of the chapel of the Holy Trinity on the north side of the church.[13]

A similar design is employed in the blind tracery decorating the splayed flanks of the west doorway of the priory church of St Margaret at King's Lynn. However, as was so often the case in the west of the county, there the design is closer to a variant found at Ely Cathedral, where the west window of the Lady Chapel has this pattern within its two main sub-arches. This apparent debt to Ely is perhaps all the more remarkable since King's Lynn was a dependent of Norwich Cathedral Priory; it may simply be that by that stage the design had become part of the common stock of ideas rather than that it was a direct borrowing from Ely.

12. The debts of the cathedral clerestory tracery to Gloucester, and its links with a number of churches in the diocese, were discussed by R. Wain-Heapy in 'The Spread of Perpendicular', *Architectural Review*, 148 (1970), p. 319. It was speculated there that the work might be attributable to the mason John of Tyrington.

13. NRO (Shirehall), MF 22, Norwich Consistory Court, register of wills, vol. 1 (Heydon), fo. 143. Details of bequests relating to operations on Norfolk churches are to be found in P. Cattermole and S. Cotton, 'Medieval Church Building in Norfolk', *NA*, 38 (1983), p. 237.

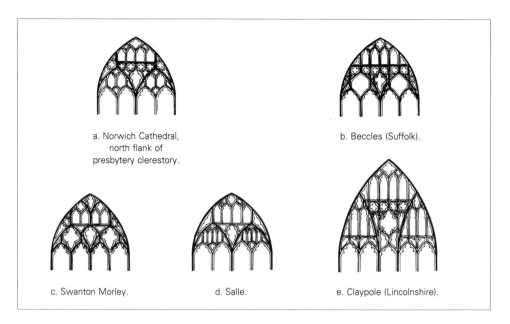

a. Norwich Cathedral,
north flank of
presbytery clerestory.

b. Beccles (Suffolk).

c. Swanton Morley.

d. Salle.

e. Claypole (Lincolnshire).

Fig. 102. Tracery related to Norwich Cathedral presbytery clerestory.

The clerestory window type which had the most significant following was that in three of the bays along the north flank (fig. 102a). While the basic matrix of this design was essentially like that in the other windows, the main elements contained subordinate lights defined by super-mullions, with further enrichment in the form of a row of circular quatrefoils below a transom running above the heads of the two main sub-arches. The most precise copy of this window is in the south chapel at Beccles (fig. 102b), which may belong to a building campaign for which funds were being donated in 1369.[14] Unfortunately, the subordinate tracery of the sub-arches there appears to have been lost. Another example, albeit outside the diocese, which may have been inspired by the work at the cathedral is the five-light window inserted into the east wall of the chancel at Claypole in Lincolnshire (fig. 102e).

Within Norfolk, tracery inspired by this type at the cathedral is to be found at the eastern ends of the aisles of Swanton Morley; and in the western window of Salle, in the ground floor stage of the tower (figs 102c and 102d). Although in neither case is the band of quatrefoils below a transom repeated within the main tracery field, at Swanton Morley this family trait is reflected in a band of quatrefoils below the transom which sub-divides the main lights at half height. At that church

14. NRO (Shirehall), MF 22, Norwich Consistory Court, register of wills, vol. 1 (Heydon), fo. 17r: Robert Botild de Mutford 3s. 4d. 'ad fabricam novae eccliae [sic] Bekles'. (My thanks to Dr Simon Cotton for this reference.)

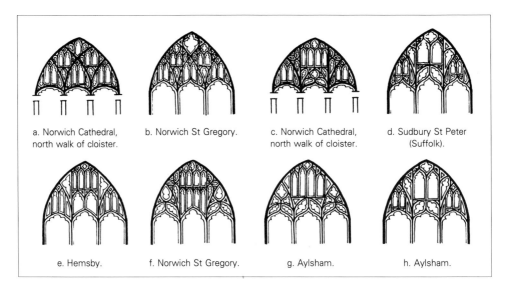

a. Norwich Cathedral,   b. Norwich St Gregory.   c. Norwich Cathedral,   d. Sudbury St Peter
north walk of cloister.   north walk of cloister.   (Suffolk).

e. Hemsby.   f. Norwich St Gregory.   g. Aylsham.   h. Aylsham.

Fig. 103. Tracery with tight concentrations of forms.

the debt to the cathedral is probably a close one, since the work is known to have
been underway in 1379.[15] Salle was a little later, the nave being started in the last
years of the fourteenth century, with the lower part of the tower having heraldry
indicating dates of between 1405 and about 1420.[16] This is certainly not an excessive
period of time for work of such high prestige as that at the cathedral to exercise
its influence.

A significant feature of the windows around the cathedral apse clerestory, as
opposed to those along the flanks of the presbytery, is the treatment of the transom
which divides the main lights into two parts. Between these transoms and the lower
light heads is a tight concentration of miniature lights, four corresponding to each
of the main lights, the ultimate inspiration for which could have been the blind
tracery across the walls between gallery and clerestory levels at Gloucester. The same
treatment of the transom is found in the west window of Salle, and a similar
concentration of lesser lights was also used within the sub-arches of the tracery there.

Tracery with an even greater concentration of forms is found in the two types
which were designed for the remaining eight bays of the north cloister walk at the
cathedral, where work was resumed in the 1380s (fig. 104).[17] Robert Wadhurst was
recorded as master mason; he had earlier worked at the palace and abbey of

15. NRO (Shirehall), MF 22, Norwich Con-   16. W. L. E. Parsons, *Salle* (Norwich, 1937),
    sistory Court, register of wills, vol. 1 (Hey-   pp. 22–23.
    don), fo. 161.   17. *Communar Rolls*, p. 39.

Fig. 104.
Norwich Cathedral, tracery
in north walk of cloister.

Westminster and was later to go on to work at Ely.[18] In one of these new cloister tracery types the field has a basic matrix of intersecting arcs (fig. 103a); in the other the articulation is by means of sub-arches embracing the side lights and with super-mullions rising from the supporting shafts (fig. 103c). The concentration of tracery within this matrix creates a rather screen-like appearance. It is perhaps not surprising that a similar approach was to become common in church furnishings such as rood screens − although no direct debts to the cloister tracery are here suggested for such decorative work. Other Norfolk windows which appear to show identifiable debts to the tracery of the north cloister walk are at Aylsham and in the nave at Hemsby, while in Suffolk the aisle windows at Sudbury St Peter may also have taken their lead from the cathedral (figs 103d, e, g and h). Examples even closer to those at the cathedral will be discussed below (p. 221).

One rather later feature of the cathedral which may have had a limited impact within Norfolk was the west doorway, with the window above it, paid for by Bishop William Alnwick. He was translated from Norwich to Lincoln in 1436 and,

18. Harvey, *English Medieval Architects*, p. 299.

at his death in 1449, left money for the window; inscriptions in the spandrels of the doorway request prayers for his soul. The designs of both the window (which will be discussed later) and of the doorway were closely modelled on those of Westminster Hall, which date from the 1390s. As first built the doorway was deeply recessed within a framework enriched by elaborate flanking tabernacles (there were originally two pairs of tabernacles, but one on each side was turned through ninety degrees in the 1875 restoration). The whole composition was too ambitious to have found precise followers in the churches of the diocese but, in the doorways opening into the magnificent twin towers of Southrepps and Fakenham, we find designs which appear to have modelled themselves on it in the way tabernacles flank the doorway. That at Fakenham is probably the closer in spirit to Norwich, since the carved frieze of its base course has shields within octofoiled squares, rather like those beneath the cathedral tabernacles.

The dates of none of these doorways can be fixed with certainty. That at the cathedral would appear to date from after Alnwick's death in 1449, in view of the inscribed request for prayers for his soul, though unlike the window above it is not mentioned in his will. At Southrepps there were bequests for work on the tower in 1431, 1448 and 1467, while at Fakenham there were bequests in 1447, 1449, 1465 and 1511.[19] It should be remembered, however, that towers called for protracted building operations; the first bequests may simply indicate that funds were being gathered in anticipation of the work.

19. Cattermole and Cotton, 'Medieval Church Building in Norfolk', pp. 262 and 247.

Fig. 105.
Norwich St Gregory,
window tracery.

Cathedral Masons whose Work may be Identified Elsewhere

One of the earliest instances of a particular mason possibly working both at the cathedral and elsewhere concerns the designer of the St Ethelbert Gate. The outer face of this gateway probably dates to about 1316–17, and a case has been made for it being the work of the older John Ramsey. He has also been proposed as the mason responsible for the opulent additions to the nave at Cley church.[20] Certainly, there is a marked similarity in the way the arch mouldings emerge from broadly-curved jambs in the outer archway at the former and in the south doorway at the latter. Beyond this, there are other tricks of design at Cley which show detailed parallels with contemporary work at the cathedral. Nevertheless, without full discussion of the works of the Ramsey family in Norwich, Ely and London, there must be some doubt about the specific attribution at Cley, although it can hardly be in doubt that the works at the cathedral were a major source of ideas for it.

Moving onto rather firmer ground, we have already seen how most of the succession of tracery in the cloister of Norwich Cathedral provided a fertile source of inspiration within and beyond the diocese. However, in the crudely restored aisle windows of Norwich St Gregory (fig. 105), there are signs of a much closer kinship with work at the cathedral. Of the two types seen at St Gregory's one is copied almost exactly from Robert Wadhurst's north cloister walk, while the second of Wadhurst's designs provides the starting point for a closely related variant (figs 103b and 103f). The fact that St Gregory's was appropriated to the cathedral priory, combined with a tradition that it was rebuilt by the priory in 1394 and the existence of a bequest of that year, strongly support the idea that the designer of the cloister windows was also responsible for the nearby church.[21]

Another early case of close architectural kinship is seen in the doorway at the outer entrance to the cloister dark entry; the mouldings of this doorway are so precisely repeated in the porch of Norwich St Laurence that there seems little doubt

---

20. *Communar Rolls*, p. 33, and Whittingham, 'Ramsey Family', p. 285.

21. The bequest is in NRO, DCN 1/10/9. In addition, and despite a thirty-year gap, there are some similarities between the piers and bases of the arcades at St Gregory's, and those of the wall passage inside the cathedral presbytery clerestory. The bases of both have a pair of ogees below a roll, with a flat soffit, although at the cathedral the top ogee has a returned curve below the top roll. At both the piers are of quatrefoil form, with the shafts connected by curved intermediate sections; however, at St Gregory's those curves emerge unbroken from the shafts and are separated by a reentrant angle, whereas at the cathedral the shafts are separated by a double-curved member which is distinctly separated from the shafts. Such slight differences do not detract from a potentially significant kinship of type.

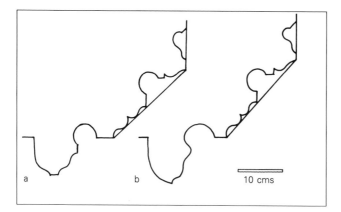

Fig. 106. Mouldings related to Norwich Cathedral cloister dark entry doorway: a; Norwich Cathedral, dark entry.
b: Norwich St Lawrence, south porch arch.

Fig. 107. Norwich Cathedral, Erpingham Gateway.

Fig. 108. Beccles (Suffolk), south porch.

that one mason was using the same template on two occasions (figs 106a and 106b). Neither of these can be securely dated, although it is possible that the St Laurence doorway dates from about 1388 when a grant of land was made for the rebuilding of the south porch.[22]

22. Blomefield, *Norfolk*, iv, p. 262, records that in 1388 the rector was infeoffed in land which was to be sold for funds to build a new south porch.

The dark entry doorway is a relatively minor piece of architecture. There is much more impressive evidence of masons working both at the cathedral and on other churches within the county in the first half of the fifteenth century.[23] The starting-point for looking at these is the great Erpingham Gate (fig. 107). On heraldic evidence the work was started no sooner than 1410, when the first husband of Sir Thomas Erpingham's second wife died. The work was presumably largely finished by 1428, when Erpingham himself died, although the plainness of the surmounting gable by comparison with the extraordinary richness of the archway may indicate that the work was never fully completed. Analysis and comparison of both the overall approach to design and, in particular, of the singularly elaborate mouldings indicate that the designer of the gateway almost certainly must have been responsible for a number of other major building operations. These included the lower stages of the west tower at Wymondham Abbey, for which land was granted in 1445; the south porch of Beccles church in Suffolk, towards which there was a bequest in 1455 (fig. 108); and the tomb in Hingham church of Thomas, Lord Morley, who died in 1435, although his tomb was only painted as late as 1462 (fig. 109).

All of these works were conceived in the grand manner. Their interrelationship is particularly marked by the prominent use of octagonal corner buttresses, which in most cases are lavishly tabernacled. But the clearest indications of their common authorship are to be seen in their highly sophisticated mouldings, which depend on a refined and highly individual balance between concentrations of delicate and often asymmetrical elements in alternating continuous and supported orders (fig. 110). These mouldings are sufficiently distinctive to permit ascription of a number of smaller-scale works to the same mason, since several formations are reused so regularly and with such precision that the same templates must have been repeatedly reapplied. The clearest link between the major works, on one hand, and the lesser works, on the other, is observable in the use of a particular formation at both Wymondham and Wiveton. Among these other works are the nave of Wiveton church, under construction in 1437; the arcades of Norwich St John Maddermarket, which was ready for roofing in 1452; the south porch of Great Cressingham, to which there was a bequest in 1439, and the tower door of the same church (fig. 111). Porches at the churches of Hilborough, Norwich St Mary Coslany, Norwich St Margaret, Westwick, Walpole St Peter and Blakeney must also be included in the list. It may be added that the reuse of moulding templates at different churches is frequently within contexts that are so closely comparable that there is no case for speculating that the mouldings might simply have been bought ready-cut from the quarry.

---

23. Details of all the structures related to the Erpingham Gate are given in R. Fawcett, 'St Mary at Wiveton in Norfolk, and a Group of Churches Attributed to its Mason', *Antiq. J.*, 62 (1982), pp. 35–56.

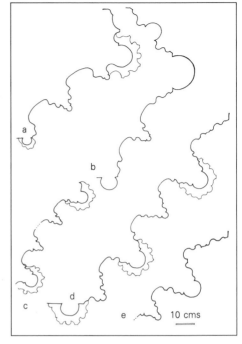

Fig. 109. Hingham, tomb of Thomas, Lord Morley.

Fig. 110. Mouldings related to Norwich Cathedral Erpingham Gateway:

a. Beccles (Suffolk), south porch.
b. Norwich Cathedral Erpingham Gateway, jamb of inner arch.
c. Hingham Morley tomb, part of jamb.
d. Wymondham Abbey, west doorway.
e. Norwich Cathedral Erpingham Gateway, part of jamb of outer arch.

In addition to these buildings, it is at least a possibility that the west doorway of the cathedral, which has been discussed above, was also the work of the same mason, since it shows a number of significant similarities with the other works. There are, however, less grounds for certainty in this case because the overall debt of the doorway to that at Westminster Hall so completely conditioned the design in other respects. The suggestion has been made by Harvey that the designer of the Erpingham Gate and the west doorway was James Woderofe, a master mason who is known to have worked at the cathedral between 1415 and 1451, albeit with no specifically recorded involvement in those particular works.[24] This must certainly be a possibility, although it should not be assumed that he was the only master of importance

24. Harvey, *English Medieval Architects*, pp. 299–300.

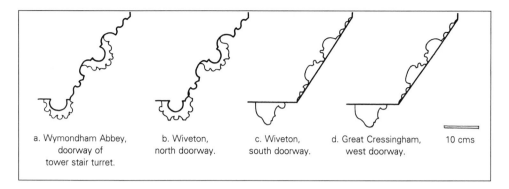

a. Wymondham Abbey, doorway of tower stair turret.

b. Wiveton, north doorway.

c. Wiveton, south doorway.

d. Great Cressingham, west doorway.

10 cms

Fig. 111. Lesser mouldings used by mason of Norwich Cathedral Erpingham Gateway.

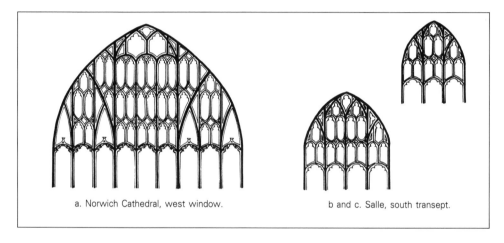

a. Norwich Cathedral, west window.

b and c. Salle, south transept.

Fig. 112. Tracery related to Norwich Cathedral west window.

working at the cathedral in those years, particularly since the works considered above bear no certain relationship with the vault bosses in the final bays of the cloister walks, or with the extensions to the reliquary arch inside the cathedral, which are the only surviving works at the cathedral firmly documented to Woderofe.

The vast nine-light west window of the cathedral, which was itself closely modelled on the much earlier gable wall windows of Westminster Hall (dating from the 1390s), had a limited impact within the diocese (fig. 112a). As already said, the Norwich window, together with the processional doorway beneath it, were built with funds provided by Bishop William Alnwick, who died in 1449. Although money for the window was left in his will,[25] some time may have elapsed before

25. E. M. Goulburn *et al.*, *The Ancient Sculptures in the Roof of Norwich Cathedral* (London, 1876), pp. 466–67.

construction began, since its internal reveals appear to be coursed in with the wall shafts for the vaulting which was built by Bishop Lyhart after the fire of 1463. Among the refinements of this window copied from the Westminster prototypes are such details as the sub-arch framing the central lights immediately below the main arch apex, and the latticed transoms formed by giving the upper tracery lights reversed arches at their bases above the lower tracery light arches.

These details are closely reflected in two strikingly handsome windows in the south transept at Salle church (fig. 112). The Salle windows belong to a remodelling of the transept to form a chapel for Thomas Brigg; he died in 1494 but the remodelling may have been somewhat earlier than that, since a date for the glass in the last third of the century has been suggested.[26] The links are sufficiently close for one to suspect that the Salle windows could be by the mason responsible for the west window of the cathedral.

Other highly creative masons were also working at the cathedral in the fifteenth century. Apart from the works already discussed, the finest single piece of this period is the monks' doorway into the cathedral nave, at the northwest corner of the cloister. With its jambs and arches of attenuated orders framing a central row of tabernacles, this doorway displayed a high level of finesse on the part of its designer (fig. 113a). The same mason was perhaps also re-

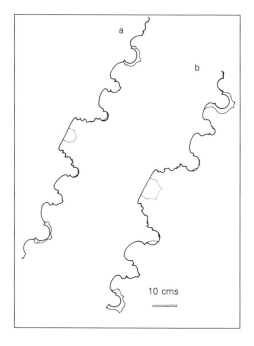

Fig. 113. Mouldings related to Norwich Cathedral monks' doorway:
a: Norwich Cathedral monks' doorway.
b: Beccles (Suffolk) south doorway.

sponsible for the doorway of the pulpitum, built by Bishop Lyhart after the fire of 1463, which reveals similar tricks of detail in the mouldings, with a row of tabernacles at the centre of the formation.

Whether or not the pulpitum doorway was the work of the mason of the monks' doorway, the mason of the latter was almost certainly the designer of the south doorway at the church of Beccles, a church which has already been shown to have had close relationships with the cathedral in other respects. The designs of the two doorways are as close as would be possible without the same templates having been

26. D. King, 'Salle Church: the Glazing', *Arch. J.,* 137 (1980), pp. 333–35.

used, while the formations are of such complexity that this must surely mean that the same mason was responsible for both (fig. 113b).

It has already been pointed out that the porch which embraces this doorway at Beccles must be the work of the designer of the Erpingham Gate. Yet the highly distinctive details of the two sets of work must mean that there is little likelihood that the designer of the Erpingham Gate was the same mason who designed the monks' doorway; and by the same token the south porch and the south doorway at Beccles can hardly be other than the work of two different masons. On this evidence it is clear that not only might there be more than one high-calibre mason working at the cathedral at any one time, but that those masons might then go on together to work at other places. Since James Woderofe is known to have had a brother, John, who was also working at the cathedral, this certainly makes it attractive to see those names as being behind the two specific groups of linked works under discussion. However, this is not the place to attempt a detailed consideration of the evidence for the names of the masons whose work is briefly considered here, and in any case this possibility would seem to be vitiated by the absence of references to James after 1451 and the apparent death of John in 1443.

All that can be attempted within the scope of this chapter is to offer some of the cases in which the cathedral and its satellite buildings appear to be significantly related to other buildings within the diocese. Inevitably it has been necessary to present an oversimplified picture of what is only too evidently a highly complex story: in particular, without giving fuller thought to the interaction of ideas between Norwich and Ely, much of the work carried out in the two central quarters of the fourteenth century is only partly comprehensible. Nevertheless, it is hoped that the parallels and relationships discussed will give at least some indication of how the cathedral continued to play a seminal role in the spread of ideas well into the period when the parish churches represented by far the highest proportion of architectural effort within the diocese.

PART III

The Cathedral
and the Priory
1096–1538

12

The Monastic Community

Barbara Dodwell

When Herbert de Losinga moved the cathedral from Thetford to Norwich he
did more than site his *cathedra*, his chair, in another if more important town:
in place of secular clerks he instituted monks. While this is understandable, for he
was himself a monk, it is perhaps surprising that he had such grandiose ideas. He
is credited with establishing a community of sixty monks – a foundation that would
equal the older cathedral priories of Worcester and Winchester – with a church to
match. In addition five cells were established: one across the river from Norwich,
at St Leonard's where monks were reputed to have lived while the monastery was
being built;[1] one each at Lynn and Yarmouth; and two others associated with
donations by lay people, one by Agnes wife of Hubert de Rye at Aldeby,[2] the other
by Ralf *dapifer* (steward) of the abbey of Bury St Edmunds and Edith his wife at
Hoxne in Suffolk.[3] It is not until the fourteenth century that numbers can be checked
and then we do indeed find rather more than sixty monks, no less than sixty-seven
monks being reported in 1348–49 by the communar.[4] Plague then took its toll and
numbers were halved. Yet around 1453 there were about sixty monks again, although
fifty was a more typical figure and there were periods when it was considerably
lower. However there was always recovery. Even immediately before the translation
of the prior and monks into the dean and chapter there were still thirty-eight
monks.[5]

1. *First Register*, p. 30.
2. *NCC*, i, no. 20.
3. P. M. Barnes and C. F. Slade, eds, *A Medieval Miscellany for Doris Mary Stenton* (Pipe Roll Society, 36, 1962), p. 160.
4. NRO, DCN 1/12/27. John Salmon's visitation report seems to confirm the presence of sixty or more monks in 1308. E. H. Carter, ed., *Studies in Norwich Cathedral History* (Norwich, 1935), p. 20.
5. Dr Greatrex thought that these figures excluded the monks in the five cells, numbering twelve to fifteen, but they would still need to be provided with clothing or money in lieu and might well have been counted. Nor is there any reason why they should be excluded from the pittance paid by the prior of St Leonard since, except for the priors, their stay in the cells was always regarded as a temporary matter. J. Greatrex,

The monks must have formed one of the smallest elements of those resident at the priory. Dr Saunders, working from the distribution of bread grains in the late thirteenth and early fourteenth centuries, argued for a total community of about 270 people. He put the number of monks resident at Norwich at fifty, and the staffs of the departmental offices at 150, a figure which includes the clerks of the church as well as cooks, grooms and other servants. Apart from the steward, it does not include the men who received fees, such as auditors and attorneys, nor indeed any of the labour force brought in to work on the fabric. This figure, which at first sight may seem unduly large, can however be justified, since the servants are listed in the account rolls. Finally, Saunders allowed for about fifty transients in the guest hall; these would have included mainly servants whose masters were entertained by the prior, messengers from the manors and other low-class visitors.[6]

By the early thirteenth century recruitment through the donation of children brought by their parents to the monastery had practically disappeared and was in 1215 pronounced unlawful. The round of services demanded that would-be recruits had already acquired a knowledge of Latin grammar and, where possible, had some acquaintance with chanting. In practice this meant that they came from families, either rural or urban, who could afford some education for their children. The normal procedure was for a young man, probably still in his late teens, to spend a probationary year of instruction. Latin would figure largely and in addition the young man would be taught to memorise the psalms. He would receive instruction in the Benedictine Rule and in the customs of the house, including the form of service. He would also be taught the chants. At the end of that year, assuming a satisfactory report, and at the minimum age of nineteen, he would be professed a monk. In the early middle ages many set their sights no higher, but by the thirteenth century it became usual for all monks who had entered while still young to aim at ordination. This would entail further instruction in the Rule and further scholastic education. First the monk was presented to the bishop for appointment as a subdeacon. He then became available to take special duties in the services. A year later he might be appointed a deacon and play a rather more important role in the

note 5 continued
'Monk Students from Norwich Cathedral Priory at Oxford and Cambridge, *c.* 1300 to 1530', *EHR*, 106 (1991), pp. 559–60. She was of the opinion that the pension from the prior of St Leonard was paid only to the monks in the mother house. See also H. W. Saunders, *An Introduction to the Obedientiary and Manor Rolls of Norwich Cathedral Priory* (Norwich, 1930), pp. 160–62.

6.   Saunders, *Obedientiary Rolls*, pp. 90–91, 160–62. These low-class visitors, together with the 150 staff in the departmental offices, would have eaten second- and third-class bread. Since four times more grain was supplied for these types of bread than for the first class bread, he reckoned that visitors and support staff outnumbered monks by four to one. This calculation suggested an average of fifty guests.

services. Finally, after further study and at the minimum age of twenty-five, came ordination to the priesthood and the right to play a full part in the liturgy.

The monks at Norwich followed the customs of Herbert's own monastery of Fécamp. Among his letters is one written to the abbot of Fécamp saying that the usages of that abbey were observed at Norwich so far as he could recollect them but, since his memory was imperfect, asking whether it might be possible to send one or two monks to stay at Fécamp to learn their usages.[7] Either such a visit took place, or a copy of the customs was sent, for in the mid thirteenth century the connection was plainly visible, as in the Norwich observance of the feasts of two French saints. Moreover, some adaptation had become necessary for, unlike Fécamp, Norwich was a cathedral. The bishop had to be fitted into the liturgical routine and, when present played, for example, an important part in the Easter ceremonies.[8]

In general the round of daily worship was that of any Benedictine monastery. By the mid thirteenth century manual labour was no longer required. Instead, the monks spent their time, when not in church, in reading in the cloister or in work in the scriptorium. Their day began early. Rising still in their night slippers, around two o'clock in winter and earlier in summer, the monks assembled in the church for a series of services, consisting largely of prayers and psalms, whose timing depended on the seasons. After a period of private prayer, nocturnes in winter began at about 3 am, followed by a time for reading, since the next service, matins, might not begin until daybreak, and the next, prime, not until full daylight. After prime much of the morning was spent in prayer or reading, although there was an interlude for washing and changing into day shoes, while those monks who had been ordained said their private masses. Thereafter, the two main services were terce and the said mass. There followed a gathering of a different kind, a meeting of the whole convent in the chapter house where not only did the monks confess their faults and receive correction but much of the priory business was transacted. Finally came a sung high mass. Only after this did the monks eat. In winter this meal might not take place before two o'clock and until around 1300 it was the only meal of the day. In summer the meal was earlier, around midday, with a second meal served in the evening. In summer, too, the monks were allowed a siesta. The rest of the afternoon was occupied by work in cloister, scriptorium or office, followed by prayers and in winter by a drink in the refectory or in summer by supper. Their day ended early – the last service, compline, taking place before 7 pm in winter and not much later in summer.

This was the usual round observed by all monasteries in the early period. But

7. GS, i, pp. 164–66.
8. J. B. Tolhurst, ed., *The Customary of the Cathedral Priory Church of Norwich* (Henry Bradshaw Society, 82, 1943), pp. xvi–xvii. See also below, pp. 314–24.

during the fourteenth and fifteenth centuries changes were multiplying, with the general aim of making life easier for the monks. The first service of the day came to take place at midnight, after which the monks went back to bed, rising again at 7 am. The morning devotions and times for readings were altered to allow for an earlier dinner, now generally at 11 or 11.30 am, and a supper was introduced for the winter months, with the exception of Lent and Advent. To what extent the monks of Norwich followed the new pattern is uncertain. They did not, however, accept the new clock-time arrangement of a 7 am rising, for at the 1520 visitation they were told to rise at dawn.[9] On the other hand they probably did accept the earlier dinner time and the winter supper.

On Sundays and the many feast days a more elaborate liturgy was performed, with extra prayers, psalms and lessons. We can get some idea of the flavour of these occasions from the Norwich Customary, that product of about 1260 which, while not a service book, gives directions for the ordering of the services and principally for the sung high mass.[10] It was a world of ceremonial and, since barely a week passed without the observation of one or more saints' days, the monks' daily round was frequently marked by additional elements. There were in all six grades of feasts, ranging from the principal feasts down to those saints marked merely by commemoration.[11]

There were ten principal feasts. These comprised the nine main feasts of the church – Christmas, Epiphany (6 January), Easter, Ascension, Pentecost (or Whit Sunday), Trinity, the Assumption and Nativity of our Lady (15 August and 8 September respectively) and All Saints (1 November) – plus the day of dedication (24 September), a feast not observed until after 1279, and fixed then perhaps in an arbitrary fashion.[12] At these feasts and at the three quasi main feasts, Circumcision (1 January), Purification (2 February) and the octave of Easter, the community was vested in copes for the high mass and twelve lessons were read at matins instead of the usual three in winter and one in summer. In addition there was extra lighting and on occasion, principally Palm Sunday and at Easter, the church was decorated.[13]

There was no special saint's day to celebrate. The cathedral was dedicated to the Holy Trinity and that day became part of the Whitsun activities. In the mid twelfth century an attempt was made to adopt the Norwich boy, William, who was alleged

9. A. Jessopp, ed., *Visitations of the Diocese of Norwich, AD 1492–1532* (Camden Society, new series, 43, 1888), p. 194.
10. See pp. 314–24.
11. J. B. L. Tolhurst, 'The Monastic Customary of Norwich', in D. H. S. Cranage, ed., *Thirteen-Hundredth Anniversary of the Diocese of East Anglia: Official Handbook* (Norwich, 1930), p. 79.
12. J. B. Tolhurst, 'The Date of Consecration of the Cathedral Church', in Friends of Norwich Cathedral, *Sixteenth Annual Report, 1945* (Norwich, 1946), p. 18.
13. Tolhurst, *Customary*, pp. xxvi, 31, 75, 90–91.

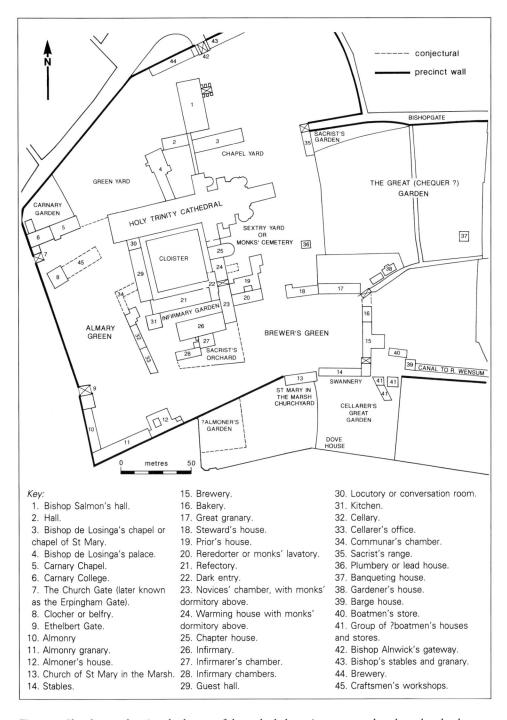

Key:
1. Bishop Salmon's hall.
2. Hall.
3. Bishop de Losinga's chapel or chapel of St Mary.
4. Bishop de Losinga's palace.
5. Carnary Chapel.
6. Carnary College.
7. The Church Gate (later known as the Erpingham Gate).
8. Clocher or belfry.
9. Ethelbert Gate.
10. Almonry
11. Almonry granary.
12. Almoner's house.
13. Church of St Mary in the Marsh.
14. Stables.
15. Brewery.
16. Bakery.
17. Great granary.
18. Steward's house.
19. Prior's house.
20. Reredorter or monks' lavatory.
21. Refectory.
22. Dark entry.
23. Novices' chamber, with monks' dormitory above.
24. Warming house with monks' dormitory above.
25. Chapter house.
26. Infirmary.
27. Infirmarer's chamber.
28. Infirmary chambers.
29. Guest hall.
30. Locutory or conversation room.
31. Kitchen.
32. Cellary.
33. Cellarer's office.
34. Communar's chamber.
35. Sacrist's range.
36. Plumbery or lead house.
37. Banqueting house.
38. Gardener's house.
39. Barge house.
40. Boatmen's store.
41. Group of ?boatmen's houses and stores.
42. Bishop Alnwick's gateway.
43. Bishop's stables and granary.
44. Brewery.
45. Craftsmen's workshops.

Fig. 114. Sketch map showing the layout of the cathedral precincts *c.* 1500, based on the plan by A. B. Whittingham published in *Arch. J.* 106 (1949) and that in G. A. Metters, ed., *The Parliamentary Survey of Dean and Chapter Properties in and around Norwich in 1649* (NRS, 51, 1985), pp. 116-17.

to have been killed by the Jews, as a child saint. There was initial success, the boy's body being brought into the monastery, first to the chapter house and later to the eastern end of the great church. If the motives were mixed (and certainly the offerings at his tomb played their part), the immediate response was to draw pilgrims from the diocese and to enhance the prestige of the cathedral.[14] Yet by 1363 the yearly offerings at his tomb had fallen to only two pence. A limited revival came when the furriers' guild took up the cult: for a while substantial offerings were reported, only to disappear in the fifteenth century.[15] The attempt to establish a local saint cannot be said to have succeeded.

Processions were a regular feature of the monks' worship. On Sundays they left their places in the choir, sprinkled with holy water all the altars at the eastern end of the church, then went into and round the cloisters, returning to the nave by the western door and up the nave to those altars before the choir screen. At the greater festivals the processional route was often longer, with the monks, having dealt with altars at the eastern end, then leaving by the door in the north transept to visit the chapel in the court of the episcopal palace and returning to the cloister via the monks' cemetery (for this route see fig. 114).

How soon outsiders were introduced to assist with the additional singing required at the major festivals is uncertain. The Customary does not suggest that they were employed in the mid thirteenth century and those entries in the fourteenth-century rolls to the effect that singers should be rewarded for their work at Christmas and Easter with wine and refreshment do not make it clear that they were not monks. Nevertheless, by the fifteenth century there are explicit references to lay singers such as 'to Thomas Borrell and other singers of the Lord Suffolk for wine nine pence', and William of Gloucester was paid for singing in the choir and at the mass of the Blessed Virgin Mary for a fortnight at Christmas in 1480.[16] By contrast choir boys had become a regular part of the cathedral choir by the mid thirteenth century, being then assigned particular duties such as opening the daily litany on the vigil of the feast of St John the Baptist.[17] In the time of Prior William Kirby (1272–89) the choir school was organised with thirteen boys, poor and able to learn, under a master.[18] The song school under the general charge of the almoner continued until

14. Thomas of Monmouth, *The Life and Miracles of St William of Norwich*, ed. A. Jessopp and M. R. James (Cambridge, 1896), tells the story.

15. J. R. Shinners, 'The Veneration of Saints at Norwich Cathedral in the Fourteenth Century', *NA*, 40 (1988), pp. 135–37.

16. NRO, DCN 1/9/76, 1/9/78. From the late thirteenth century minstrels were employed

at the cathedral on feast days but this was probably for entertainment.

17. Tolhurst, *Customary*, p. 135.

18. Worcester Cathedral, MS B 680. J. Greatrex, 'The Almonry School of Norwich Cathedral Priory in the Thirteenth and Fourteenth Centuries', in D. Wood, ed., *The Church and Childhood* (Studies in Church History, 31, 1994), pp. 169–81.

the time of the Dissolution.[19] Perhaps one of the greatest of the fifteenth-century innovations, even though it was only temporary, came with the appointment of a lay choir master. This was one John Scarlet, a noted minstrel and described as a singer, who in 1443–44 was paid for his work in the choir and at the mass for the previous two years. He is generally described as organising the mass of the Blessed Virgin Mary, a particularly difficult mass to sing.[20] Within a few years he was also placed in charge of the cathedral choir school, a position which he seems to have held until his death or retirement, possibly in 1468.[21] John Scarlet was clearly an exceptional man and found no immediate successor, although paid singers were still employed.

By 1333 the priory had acquired an organ, for in that year there were two references to an organist, one for the provision of his robe, the other for his victuals.[22] Forty years later there is a reference to two organs, a small one in the chapel of St Mary and what the scribe called a great organ; immediately we read of payments made to organ blowers, presumably for the great organ. It was, it seems, not in daily use since blowers were paid only for work at the great feasts, once specified as Christmas, Easter and Whitsun.[23]

The dietary regime had also changed by the fourteenth century. Most notable was the gradual erosion of that part of the Rule of St Benedict which banned the eating of meat except in the infirmary. The Rule was evaded with some ingenuity since it continued to be observed generally in the refectory, but by the end of the twelfth century the refectory ceased to be the only place in which the monks ate. At Bury St Edmunds, for instance, meat dishes were regularly laid before Abbot Sampson (1182–1211). Although he did not himself partake of them, he could invite any monks he wished to dine with him in his own lodgings.[24] During the thirteenth century a second dining room was generally being provided in which irregular food like roast or stewed meats could be eaten. The refectory was, however, never abandoned. In 1336 Pope Benedict XII regularised the situation by ordering that half the monks must eat there and this came to mean half the community on any given day, after allowing for those monks necessarily absent on business or at

19. R. Harries, P. Cattermole and P. Mackin-tosh, *A History of Norwich School* (Norwich, 1991), pp. 6–10.

20. NRO, DCN 2/3/54 and 1/6/68. The term is *pro custodia*. Among the injunctions of Bishop Bateman is one ordering that no monk shall put his name down to sing at the mass of St Mary unless he was suffi-ciently skilled. C. R. Cheney, 'Norwich Cathedral Priory in the Fourteenth

Century', *Bulletin of the John Rylands Library*, 20 (1936), p. 116.

21. NRO, DCN 1/6/88, fo. 62. The last pay-ment for the mass occurs in 1468–69, al-though his name is not mentioned: NRO, DCN 2/3/79.

22. NRO, DCN 1/4/27.

23. NRO, DCN 1/9/23 and 1/9/44–47.

24. H. E. Butler, ed., *The Chronicle of Jocelin of Brakelond* (London, 1949), p. 40.

university. Moreover, on fast days during the week and during Advent and Lent the whole convent were required to dine in the refectory.[25]

While there is no architectural evidence that Norwich possessed such a second dining room, one can only assume that the refectory was divided in some way so as to provide one. Certainly, by the end of the thirteenth century, pork, mutton and beef were being bought for the monks at Norwich for the four meat days: Sundays, Mondays, Tuesdays and Thursdays. On these days even the refectory could provide made-up meat dishes and offals as well as chickens, pigeons and the like. The remaining three days, Wednesday, Friday and Saturday, were fish days on which herring, whiting, cod, roach and eels predominated, with the occasional luxury of conger eel, oysters and salmon. Except during Lent and Advent this community of upwards of 300 persons appears to have eaten prodigious numbers of eggs. These, the only commodity whose purchase was recorded on a weekly basis, totalled between 7000 and 13,000 thousand a week.[26] Throughout, bread remained the basic constituent of the diet. Of the three kinds produced by the bakery the greater part of the best bread was eaten by the monks, the allowance being a 2 lb. (0.9 kg.) loaf of bread a day, to be divided between dinner and supper.[27] It is not possible on the Norwich evidence to work out how much meat each monk consumed, although it is worth noting that for the monks of Westminster the average allowance on a meat day was a little under two pounds, an amount which in our eyes might seem excessive but which would be normal for the gentry of the period.[28] In any event the monks did not eat everything put before them, for it was their custom to leave food uneaten which in due course was given to the poor. For the rest the monks ate vegetables produced in their own gardens, onions, leeks, beans and peas, all probably used in potage. Their food was heavily spiced, for the cellarer regularly bought pepper, cloves, cinnamon and cumin and occasionally ginger. Herbs were provided from the priory gardens (for their location see fig. 114) which also produced nuts and fruit: apples, pears and even cherries are frequently mentioned in the priory accounts.[29]

It is generally assumed that within a monastic cathedral the monks, set apart from the world, worshipped and prayed in the choir and presbytery and that services for the laity were confined to the nave. The reality appears to have been more complicated at Norwich where, for a variety of reasons and on a number of occasions, the laity had access to the presbytery. The cathedral was, after all, the mother church of the diocese. In the mid twelfth century we are told that the throng of pilgrims

25. B. Harvey, *Living and Dying in England, 1100–1540: The Monastic Experience* (Oxford, 1993), pp. 40–41.
26. NRO, DCN 1/2/1, 8, 10, 14, 15.
27. Saunders, *Obedientiary Rolls*, p. 91.
28. Harvey, *Living and Dying*, p. 55.
29. As in NRO, DCN 1/11/10.

to the shrine of St William, then at the south side of the high altar, had so interrupted the monks' services that the body had to be moved to an altar on the north side of the presbytery – now the Jesus Chapel.[30] There is plenty of evidence that the public visited the chapels of the apse. Pilgrimages to the shrine of St William were encouraged. Later, in 1376, the furriers' guild adopted St William as its patron saint and members were required to attend a requiem mass at his tomb there.[31] Two other guilds are known to have been accorded chapels at the east end of the cathedral. One, that for the plumbers, glaziers and bell founders, had the chapel opposite the Jesus Chapel, which thereby changed its dedication from St John the Baptist to St Luke, the guild's patron saint.[32] The second was the prestigious guild of St George which had a small chapel dedicated to that saint just below the high altar.[33] There is other evidence that the priory authorities encouraged the laity to visit the presbytery chapels. To attract and to stimulate oblations, new images were made for various altars and new shrines were erected at the east end. In the twenty-five years after the gales which damaged the presbytery roof in 1361/62 new saints were introduced – Petronilla, Theobald, Anthony and Leger – whose chapels in all probability were erected in the north presbytery.[34] Moreover, the laity entered the presbytery in the course of attending some services. Thus, in the mid thirteenth century, the bishop, or in his absence the prior, regularly preached to the populace from the high altar during Lent and Holy Week.[35]

The initial constitution of the cathedral priory was that of a community headed by a bishop who played an active part in its life, in fact acting as its abbot (fig. 115). While this is certainly true of Herbert's episcopate, it still pertained under the third bishop, William Turbe (1146/47–74), who had been both a monk and prior of Norwich. During his time the monks still regularly attested episcopal *acta* and the bishop, an enthusiastic supporter of the cult of St William, himself decreed that the relics should be removed to the chapter house and later into the church itself. Moreover, possibly late in his episcopate, he appointed a new prior to reform the state of religion and supported him against a minority of rebellious monks.[36] This close relationship was broken at the appointment of the next bishop, the careerist John of Oxford (1175–1200), whom the monks even accused of doing them injury.[37]

30. Thomas of Monmouth, *Life of St William*, pp. 220–21.
31. Shinners, 'Veneration of Saints', p. 136.
32. E. Sansbury, *An Historical Guide to Norwich Cathedral* (Norwich, 1986), p. 34.
33. M. Grace, ed., *Records of the Gild of St George in Norwich, 1389–1547* (NRS, 9, 1937), p. 15.
34. Shinners, 'Veneration of Saints', p. 140. See also pp. 179–82, 401–04.
35. Tolhurst, *Customary*, pp. 64, 81.
36. C. Harper-Bill, 'Bishop William Turbe and the Diocese of Norwich, 1146–74', *Anglo-Norman Studies*, 7 (1984), pp. 152–53.
37. *First Register*, p. 82.

Fig. 115. One of the monks
(left) receives from Bishop
John Salmon a confirmation
of the grants to St Paul's
Hospital (1302). The prior
appears on the right
(BL, Cotton Charter ii 19).

From then on the prior came to have complete day to day control. Although
relations with the bishop might on occasion deteriorate, as during the time of Henry
Despenser (1369–1406), generally speaking the bishops were in close contact with
the priory and prepared to come to its aid in the time of disaster in the fifteenth
century. Three of them had previously been priors and a fourth was elected but
rejected by the king.[38]

The prior had control over discipline; he presided at chapter meetings and as
head of a council of seniors dealt with much administrative detail. It was probably
this body that decided which monks should be sent to university and which were
to be recalled for duties at home.[39] He came to have overall financial control: he
could pardon a deficit and he could order payments to be made for a particular
purpose. It was probably the prior who decreed that certain expenses should be

38. William Turbe, Roger Scarning and Alex-
    ander Tottington. The prior rejected was
    Simon Elmham. For further details con-

cerning the relations between the bishop
and priory see pp. 281–300.
39. Greatrex, 'Monk Students', p. 263.

shared by all departments, not equally but according to some predetermined scale. These included royal taxation, the cost of lawsuits and that of sending monks to university.[40]

It was normal in a Benedictine monastery for a decentralized system of administration to be set up. At Norwich the emergence of the full set of departmental officers, known as obedientiaries, was not complete until the end of the thirteenth century. For the twelfth century the *Life of St William* provides references to a sacrist and precentor and a charter of Bishop John of Oxford to an almoner, while the existence of a cellarer and possibly also a hosteler can be assumed.[41] The cellarer was the most important of these officials, for originally he had control of all income. His main task was to provide the community with its food and at one time his charge seems to have extended to the provision of cutlery, cups and even table cloths. In the second half of the thirteenth century his empire was crumbling. In 1270 he was relieved of his duties in the dining room by the institution of a refectorer to take charge of that department.[42] Soon a superior official appeared, the master of the cellar, who had charge of the prior's chamber (*camera prioris*). Although the title is not accorded him on the heading of his account roll until 1293, there is a reference to a master of the cellar in the text of an earlier roll.[43] He was to be the most important of the obedientiaries. He ran the prior's office, looking after his chamber and chapel. As well as supplying the luxuries for the prior and his guests, he came to pay the salaries and expenses of the priory's lay officials, to hand out rings and money gifts to a whole host of local officials, to pay tips to those men bringing messages and letters, to pay for minstrels hired for the entertainment of the prior and his guests and so on and so forth. He also looked after the buildings in which he himself worked, as well as the kitchen, brewhouse and stables. In addition he was responsible for the provision of corn for the whole community. He therefore needed cash for general expenses and special purchases, and estates for the production of grain. It is not surprising to find that he held almost all the early endowment – the manors given by the king, by Bishop Herbert and other early benefactors.[44]

The cellarer, who may originally have held these properties, came to take a subordinate position. He was left with responsibility for all foodstuffs other than corn, and in particular those bought in the market. While he was not responsible for the kitchen buildings, he paid the cooks and brewers and saw that their utensils

40. See below, pp. 244–46, 306–07, 310–11.

41. Thomas of Monmouth, *Life of St William*, sacrist, pp. 114, 145, 165, 174–75, 186, 213; precentor, p. 214. For an almoner, *NCC*, i, no. 144.

42. *NCC*, i, nos 220–21.

43. NRO, DCN 1/1/10. The title occurs under small expenses in shoes for the master of the cellar 2s., in 1283. NRO, DCN 1/1/6.

44. For the administration of the estates see pp. 339–59.

were kept in good repair. A third official connected with the procurement of food was the gardener, a very minor official who looked after the vegetable garden and orchard. Three officials supervised the housekeeping side of the monastery: one, the chamberlain, was responsible for the monks' clothing and bedding; the second, the infirmarer, looked after the sick, seeing that their quarters were warm, buying medicines and paying those called in to attend them; the third, the hosteler, saw that the guest house was properly furnished and lit.

The cathedral church and its services were under the care of the precentor and sacrist, the former responsible for the organisation of services and the provision of choir books, the latter looking after the altars and their decoration and, costing considerably more, the upkeep of the church. It was he who paid for the frequent mending of broken windows and for the new and elaborate clock erected in the fourteenth century;[45] after the fires of 1272 and 1463 many of the subsequent rebuilding expenses passed through his accounts. There was, however, no one official in charge of *all* repairs and rebuilding. Although each obedientiary was regarded as responsible for all the expenses of his department, not all building expenses could be so neatly assigned and the communar seems to have dealt with minor repairs, especially those arising in the dormitory, library and school, while the pitancer, in theory responsible for extra dishes available at anniversaries and other feast days, came to deal with the rebuilding of the cloister.[46]

Philanthropic work was handled by two offices. One was the almonry which, besides distributing bread and money to the poor, was concerned also with the education of thirteen boys attending the almonry school, with regard to both their lodging and the wages of their master. The other was the hospital of St Paul, apparently set up independently for the care of the poor in the first half of the twelfth century.[47] It was, however, under the control of the priory, one of whose monks acted as its warden, and came to be regarded as a charitable department, sharing in the financial responsibilities of the whole monastery.

Such was the departmental organization on which the priory relied throughout the period between 1280 and 1540 – a period in which it embellished its church, rebuilt its monastic buildings, improved its educational standards and gave patronage to cultural pursuits. The occasion for an extensive rebuilding programme was provided by the townsmen in 1272, when a dispute with the priory culminated in their

45. See pp. 441–42, 503.
46. *Communar Rolls*, pp. 12–13.
47. For the almonry school see Harries, Cattermole and Mackintosh, *History of Norwich School*, pp. 6–10. The hospital was founded

to sustain the poor. *NCC*, i, nos 98 and 254; see also R. Gilchrist and M. Oliva, *Religious Women in Medieval East Anglia* (Norwich, 1994), p. 70.

sacking it and causing extensive damage to both the cathedral and its associated buildings.[48] Immediately after this riot, Prior William Kirby (1272–89) set about cleansing and repairing the cathedral church, the kitchens, refectory, dormitory, guest house – the list must have seemed endless. By 1278 there had been major repairs to the church, with the roof mended, glass windows repaired and much repainting. The old service books were replaced by new ones, possibly including a lavishly decorated psalter with much gold leaf.[49] All was made ready for a great occasion: the enthronement of a new bishop and the dedication of the cathedral in the presence of the king and queen and a great crowd of notables.[50] Kirby went on to initiate the building of a new chapter house, in all probability larger and more elaborate than its predecessor.[51] His successors carried on the work. By 1300 not only had the spire been repaired but plans were also afoot for the building of a new cloister. A new substantial stone belfry had been begun under the aegis of the sacrist.[52] Moreover, the same official was made responsible for the provision of a new clock. This may not have been strictly necessary, for a clock they already had, but its reliability seems to have been in doubt, since Bishop Salmon (1299–1325), on his visitation in 1308, complained about their timekeeping and demanded a new and goodly clock.[53] What was erected was indeed no ordinary clock. It was a magnificent astrological one which took about three years to install.[54] Meanwhile, the prior had decided to enlarge his own accommodation, mainly by the provision of a new private chapel.

None of this building work was done on the cheap. Expensive stone, Caen or Barnack, was used, experienced architects were employed and a specialist smith was deputed to make and erect the doors to the chapter house.[55] The clock required outside expertise from both London and Canterbury, while paints for the prior's chapel had to be procured in London.[56] The only parts of this work still extant show that it was done to a high artistic standard. In the cloister there was the notable achievement of the prior's doorway, while the main bosses in the south walk show scenes from the Apocalypse which bear a marked resemblance to manuscript illustration, a choice which would appear to involve a priory official, perhaps the prior himself.[57]

The priory's enthusiasm for architectural embellishment was surpassed by that for education. In the 1270s there had been great debate in monastic circles concerning higher education for monks. Already the larger monasteries were required to provide

48. See pp. 259–62.
49. London, Lambeth Palace Library, MS 368.
50. Bartholomew Cotton, *Historia Anglicana*, ed. H. R. Luard (RS, 1859), p. 157.
51. See pp. 163–65.
52. NRO, DCN 1/4/13. See also pp. 192, 501–02..

53. Carter, *Studies in Cathedral History*, p. 22.
54. NRO, DCN 1/4/21–23. See also pp. 441–42, 503.
55. *Communar Rolls*, p. 85.
56. NRO, DCN 1/1/30.
57. See also pp. 199, 365–68.

a daily lecture in theology or canon law for their abler monks. Norwich was certainly one of the larger monasteries but whether it could provide these lectures is unknown. It is, however, probable that the monks used as their teachers secular clerks who had attended university. In an early account roll there is note of a payment of 13s. 4d. to one Master William le Parcheminer when he *incepit artem* (incepted in arts); he may have been one of their teachers.[58] It is also likely that monks received instruction from the Franciscans, who had successfully established one of their main *studia* in Norwich; this attracted scholars and had established itself as a minor intellectual centre. On the artistic side workshops had been established in Norwich which produced books of high quality and, which may have been more important, books of lesser value but of greater use to the would-be scholar. Moreover the city also provided a class of professional scribes whose expertise, as we shall see, could be exploited for work within the priory.

Meanwhile educational provision for the monks was being tackled by the Benedictines at a national level. The main problem was how to establish a base, a house to which monks could be sent and in which they could live under supervision. This problem was solved when Gloucester Abbey was prepared to hand over a site it possessed in Oxford. Norwich Priory was enthusiastic from the beginning, making a financial contribution towards the necessary extra building as early as 1278–79.[59] At the meeting in 1291 which made the final decision to establish Gloucester College the new prior of Norwich, Henry Lakenham (1289–1310), played a decisive part.[60] He had an interest in learning; he even owned a book on the education of the religious;[61] and he sent monks from Norwich as soon as the college was opened.[62] The original plan did not specify the number of students, simply proposing that at least one monk should attend from each monastery.

The cathedral priory at Norwich could well be proud of its response since it sent more than the basic requirement. In the late thirteenth and early fourteenth centuries, when one monk student a year might have been expected, more than one went to Oxford. Although initially we do not know the number sent annually, since the account rolls only specify 'for our fellows at Oxford', it must have been at least two since the noun is in the plural. Later in the fourteenth century the pope fixed a ratio of one student from every twenty monks. Again Norwich responded enthusiastically since, when the rolls begin to name these students, we find the usual

58. NRO, DCN 1/1/1.
59. NRO, DCN 1/1/4.
60. W. A. Pantin, ed., *Documents Illustrating the Activities of the General and Provincial Chapters of the English Black Monks*, 3 vols (Camden Society, third series, 45, 47, 54, 1931–37), i, pp. 129–30.
61. N. R. Ker, 'Medieval MSS from Norwich Cathedral Priory', *Transactions of the Cambridge Bibliographical Society*, 1 (1949), p. 14. It was the *Liber de eruditionis religiosorum*.
62. Payments to scholars at Oxford occur in 1292 and 1293. NRO, DCN 1/13/11 and 1/4/11.

number to be two or three and sometimes even more, although we do not know if all were there together or some for only part of the year.[63] The Norwich monks did well at Oxford. While some seem to have stayed for only a few years, others stayed for a minimum of six to seven years, long enough to have obtained a degree. Yet others even stayed the seventeen years or so required for the higher courses in theology and canon law.[64] The prior and senior monks were sympathetic to men of ability. It was they who decided which monks should become students, what courses they should take and how long they would remain at university. Up to the end of the fourteenth century, at least six men stayed the course to obtain their doctorate, among them some noted scholars, including John Stukle, Adam Easton and Thomas Brinton. Both the latter left Norwich to find a career elsewhere, Adam Easton at the papal court of Rome, eventually becoming a cardinal, and Thomas Brinton as bishop of Rochester.[65] While at Oxford Norwich monks stood out as able scholars, playing a prominent part in university life and ranking closely behind those from the larger and much richer cathedral priories of Canterbury and Durham. Some became leading scholars of their day.[66]

This concern for the academic achievement of Norwich monks might be viewed simply as evidence of devotion to scholarship for its own sake. However, since men such as Easton and Brinton desired to leave the parent house, it is more likely to reflect a severely practical consideration: the aim being to equip men for service to the mother house. In the late thirteenth century there were two crying needs. One was for men with knowledge of canon law, since ecclesiastical disputes were multiplying and heads of religious houses were being increasingly used by popes to act as judges; the other was for men who could preach, not only in Latin at the main festivals in the cathedral but also in English to local communities. In a course in theology at Oxford the monks received an official vocational training in preaching, based on a thorough knowledge of the scriptures, plus some philosophy, including Aristotle and the Arabic scholars. The course in canon law had an even more practical component, for besides teaching the law of the church it gave a training in public speaking. The priory did not expect its monk students to become original thinkers but good preachers and reasonable administrators.

Intellectual standards were maintained in the fifteenth century and the monastery remained determined to continue sending monks to university. For most of the fourteenth and fifteenth centuries Oxford was the place of first choice. The problem of providing suitable accommodation was the determining factor in the first half of the fourteenth century, but in 1350 William Bateman, the then bishop of Norwich, founded Trinity Hall at Cambridge, to be known as the College of the Scholars of

63. Greatrex, 'Monk Students', p. 557.
64. Greatrex, 'Monk Students', p. 564.
65. *DNB*, *s.n.* Brinton; Easton.
66. Pantin, *English Black Monks*, i, pp. 23–29.

the Holy Trinity of Norwich. For a few years, 1353–57, Cambridge became the preferred university but then the monk scholars returned to Oxford. About a century later, however, Cambridge gradually came back to favour and almost all of the scholars to be named in the rolls after 1485 studied at the nearer university.[67] The number of monk students generally remained two, although sometimes it might rise to three or even four. In times of financial crisis only one monk might be sent to university. After 1463 none at all was, as pensions were temporarily withdrawn.[68] It was also reported at a visitation enquiry in 1492, though as a great scandal, that there were no monks at university.[69] Yet on the whole Norwich seems to have sent more students to college than other monasteries of comparable size. Dr Greatrex has suggested that over the period from 1292 to 1538 Norwich maintained a ratio of university students to total monastic population of one in seven. Out of eighty-six monks to have been students, twenty-eight took degrees while another fourteen studied for a period long enough to have allowed them to supplicate for a degree.[70] It is a record of which to be proud.

How did the monk students perform at the end of their courses? As at other cathedral monasteries they supplied the bulk of the priors. Of the ten elected after 1400, seven had been university educated and these included some active and able men. William Worsted, for instance, prior from 1427 to 1436, played a prominent part at the provincial chapters of the Benedictines and was appointed as one of the delegates to represent the chapter at the Council of Basle.[71] The monk students were also well represented as priors of the dependent cells, some appointed soon after coming down from university. Below that level they seem to have played little part in general administration. They do not provide the masters of the cellar or the cellarers, nor even many of the precentors who, incidentally and inter alia, were the men in charge of the monastic library. As Dr Greatrex has stated, 'under one third of the university group can be identified as office holders'.[72] For most university-trained monks administration was not their forte.

They may perhaps have provided much of the preaching, the ostensible reason for sending men to college, but this cannot be proved. At that time sermons were given at two levels: the one prestigious, as at the triennial meetings of the English chapters of the Benedictines and, at a somewhat lower level, at the main feasts in the cathedral; the other popular, to the people of Norwich. In both the fourteenth and fifteenth centuries Norwich monks were invited to preach at the provincial

67. Greatrex, 'Monk Students', p. 562.

68. The scholars' pensions were reassigned to the building of the church, as in NRO, DCN 1/5/98.

69. Jessopp, *Visitations*, p. 4.

70. Greatrex, 'Monk Students', p. 564.

71. Pantin, *English Black Monks*, iii, p. 105.

72. That is for periods of more than two years, Greatrex, 'Monk Students', p. 569.

chapters and some were praised for their preaching.[73] In the mid fourteenth century monk students had been recalled from Oxford to preach at festivals, as were both Thomas Brinton and Adam Easton,[74] and the latter was later kept in Norwich to preach against the friars whose views were then regarded as subversive.[75] This preaching may have been at the popular level but there is no clear evidence for popular preaching until the fifteenth century, when wine for the preachers became an annual expense.[76] The sermons could have been given within the cathedral, for there is a record of payment for a new pulpit in the church in 1440.[77] By that time, however, there was another venue, a preaching yard, called the green yard, lying to the north of the cathedral and close to the Carnary Chapel; this too had a pulpit.[78] The green yard was to become the place for public sermons, its popularity lasting well into the seventeenth century.[79] Here there were special seats for both cathedral and city dignitaries. The aldermen's seating goes back to the time of Elizabeth Woodville's visit to the city in 1469. After her visit some of the structures used in the welcoming ceremonies, as well as the material for covering the seats, were reused in the green yard.[80] The preaching yard may have been used only in the summer months, in which case the sermons established by Bishop Lyhart (1446–72) in his will to be given every Sunday in Advent and Lent would have taken place within the cathedral. They were certainly intended for the people of the diocese.[81] The monks themselves probably received lectures on theology. The evidence for this is late: a mid sixteenth-century contract with Dr John Barret required him to expound Holy Scripture every Tuesday and Thursday.[82] This was, however, not a new contract but the renewal of an old one, for the said John Barret had been employed as a *lector* before the Dissolution.[83]

Sending monks to college, if only for a few years, made demands upon the monastic library.[84] This was true for all Benedictine houses at this time and most amassed large collections of books. At Norwich the need may have been greater because of possible losses in the 1272 riot. From the late thirteenth century the normal practice was for individual monks to buy books which in due course passed into the library collection. This is known by the custom of placing an inscription, usually on the flyleaf or first folio, naming the donor and assigning a pressmark. As

73. For instance John Dereham. Pantin, *English Black Monks*, ii, p. 155.
74. NRO, DCN 1/12/29.
75. Pantin, *English Black Monks*, iii, pp. 28–29.
76. Wine for the preachers is recorded from 1421–22. NRO, DCN 1/10/14–38.
77. NRO, DCN 1/4/78.
78. NRO, DCN 1/1/82. Under foreign receipts the master of the cellar sells timber to the sacrist for a pulpit in the preaching yard.
79. See below, pp. 541–42, 547.
80. NRO, NCR, chamberlain's accounts, 1470–1490, fo. 8.
81. Blomefield, *Norfolk*, iii, p. 537.
82. NRO, DCN 47/1, fo. 23v.
83. NRO, DCN 29/3, fo. 113.
84. For the library see below, pp. 332–38.

elsewhere the library was arranged according to donor.[85] The book buyers were not only those who had gone to university, for three of them had held high office before Gloucester College was opened. The earliest of these, Ralf of Frettenham, had been master of the cellar immediately after the riot. He gave three books which are still extant and, judging by their pressmarks (which range from C3 to C12), possibly twelve. The other two, John of Cawston and Ralf of Illingham, each gave at least one book. Not much later, Henry Lakenham, prior between 1289 and 1310, who did so much to promote the sending of monks to university, gave at least four books; again judging by the pressmarks which range between F31 and F47, probably as many as seventeen and possibly even more. The survivals, which include devotional works and a *Liber de eruditione religiosorum*, possibly by Humbert de Romanis, reflect the interests of an intelligent monastic superior interested in higher education.[86]

In the mid fourteenth century the library benefited from the collection of another bibliophile. This was Prior Simon Bozoun (1344–52), another monk who did not go to Oxford. He has left us a catalogue of his library consisting of thirty-one volumes and showing a wide range of interests: history, travel, law, philosophy and even a copy of the Koran.[87] About fifty years later an even larger collection of books was bequeathed to the cathedral priory. This was the personal library of the scholar and writer Adam Easton (d. 1397), who had left Norwich for the papal curia. His bequest, packed into six barrels, eventually arrived in 1407 and was merged with the priory library. It was assigned the letter X and one of the books bearing that letter which still survives is numbered 228. On only three of these is there an inscription giving the name, the task seeming too much for the monk librarian.[88]

Another way of acquiring books was by in-house production. Skins were prepared, professional scriptors and even some illuminators employed, and binders put to work, all the latter apparently paid by piece-work. These books included historical works, Bibles and legal texts. Even the almoner had his own copy of the *Sext* of Boniface VIII.[89] It has been reckoned that in all the monastic library contained 400 to 500 works by 1325, well before the substantial bequests of Bozoun and Easton.[90] Most of the extant volumes are of the text-book variety. There is no reason, for instance, why office copies of legal texts should be illustrated, nor the texts studied by theological students. A reasonable lay out, a clear hand, with perhaps the highlighting of those initials starting a new section, was the most that could be expected.

85. Ker, 'Medieval MSS', p. 6.
86. Dodwell, 'History and Monks', p. 41; Ker, 'Medieval MSS', p. 14.
87. J. C. Brewer, ed., *The Works of Giraldus*

Cambrensis (RS, 5, 1867), pp. xxxix–xl.
88. Ker, 'Medieval MSS', p. 17.
89. NRO, DCN 1/6/9.
90. Ker, 'Medieval MSS', p. 6.

Professional scribes soon penetrated into the offices of all the obedientiaries. Each official came to have a personal clerk who wrote out business documents, including his account rolls. These professionals may also have had a hand in the organisation of the archive. Around 1300 the prior and senior monks decided to reorganise their muniments.[91] For all monasteries it was essential to keep title deeds and royal and episcopal charters in orderly fashion, so that they could be quickly produced when required; and to enter these documents into registers or cartularies for speedier consultation. At Norwich all charters, except those of the almoner and chamberlain, were rearranged and assigned pressmarks, the royal and episcopal documents and final concords each being separately grouped while the rest were arranged topographically as though for a general cartulary.[92] An inventory was indeed made but never a general cartulary. Instead some obedientiaries made particular collections for their own offices.[93] The master of the cellar commissioned a new cartulary which not only reflected the changes but shows a great advance on earlier registers. It is a large folio volume, well laid out with the initial letters of each deed decorated in scroll work in red and blue ink. For some reason a less elaborate duplicate was also made.[94] Even more attractive was the next cartulary to appear, that of the almoner. Its layout and the use of coloured inks for the headlines proclaims the skill of its scriptor.

Paid clerks or scribes may also have been employed to transcribe the manorial surveys, made at the behest of Prior William Kirby, which were written in book form as a fine copy. Such hired professionals could provide the skills required for books that needed the use of coloured inks, but for first- class work the monks probably went to the Norwich workshops. The fine copy of the chronicle of the Norwich monk Bartholomew Cotton, a thoroughly professional piece of work, may have been an in-house product, certainly more than one scribe and one illuminator were employed, but more likely it was a workshop piece.[95] As to the Ormesby Psalter there is no doubt. It was a work of high quality. Throughout all of its four stages the decoration was sumptuous. After being abandoned by a knightly family it was recommissioned by the monk, Robert of Ormesby, who probably came of the wealthy family of that name.[96] The expense of this work was presumably borne by the family and not by the priory, but this may not be true of another magnificent psalter, again the product of a Norwich workshop of the early fourteenth century. The Gorleston Psalter (plate IIa) yet again was not made for the cathedral but for the parish of that name. When, how and why it came into the hands of the priory

91. See below, p. 327.
92. See below, pp. 327–30.
93. NRO, DCN 40/12.
94. NRO, DCN 40/1 and 40/2/2.

95. BL, Royal MS 14 C 1 contains book one, Cotton MS Nero C V the other two books.
96. Bodleian Library, MS Douce 366.

is unknown.[97] It too could have arrived as a gift but, if purchased, the date is likely to have been in the second quarter of the fourteenth century.

The repairs and rebuilding, the sending of monks to university, the employment of scriptors and the purchase of books all cost money. They were all heads of expenditure for which there was no regular income, since they were not the responsibility of a named obedientiary. How did the priory deal with this situation? Initially, as we have seen, the costs of these activities were divided among all the offices. For instance, the burden of sending monks to Oxford was so divided. The largest contributions came, not unnaturally, from the richest departments with the master of the cellar and the cellarer each usually paying annually 53s. 4d.; the smallest, from the meagre resources of the gardener, only amounted to 1s. Even the hard-pressed communar was making payments of a pound or more to individual scholars.[98] For the rebuilding after the riot of 1272 there were, of course, the reparations forced on the city and an indulgence of forty days granted by the pope for all who made contributions to the repair of the cathedral, although just how much this produced is not recorded. As for the contribution from the city, the £2000 was to be paid in twelve half-yearly instalments, each of £166 13s. 4d. The communar received what was probably the last instalment in 1282–83 and may also have received some of the earlier ones, although the prior seems to have held the purse strings.[99] William Kirby, the prior elected after the riot, stands out as a purchaser of property and rents; in other words he may have invested some of that money in land. In any event, a policy decision was soon made that the building work on the chapter house and cloister should not come out of ordinary income but from donations and bequests, both lay and ecclesiastical, from gifts from individual monks and from the giving up of certain dietary luxuries.

There were a few benefactors of substance. Three were remembered by inscriptions placed at or near the buildings with which they were associated. One such stone recorded the gift of the landowner Richard Uphall, regarded as the founder of the chapter house; another recorded the generosity of the merchant William Bauchun, who paid for the building of two chapels in the presbytery; a third stone was erected to show the part played by Bishop Ralph Walpole (1288–99), cofounder of the chapter house. To these should be added a few other rich benefactors. Some time between 1310 and 1326 Prior Robert Langley (1310–26) acknowledged a bequest of £102.[100] At what seems to be a time of crisis in 1326, Master Adam

97. BL, Additional MS 49622.
98. As in NRO, DCN 1/1/35, 1/2/15, 1/12/18. The amounts however tended to vary. See
Greatrex, 'Monk Students', pp. 566–68.
99. *Communar Rolls*, p. 45.
100. NRO, DCN 40/9, fo. 35v.

Flitcham provided the communar with £98, which in fact was not put into the cloister fund but used to buy rents.[101] There were also a number of small gifts and legacies. In the late thirteenth century most of them were channelled in the direction of the sacrist. In 1279 his accounts show £24 coming from this source and in 1285–86 one entry shows John le Turner paying over to the sacrist £6 12s. 4d. given to the fabric and to the repair of the church.[102] The stirring of emotions tended, however, to diminish and the figures, always erratic, soon fell off. In spite of these gifts the sacrist was generally overspent. The clock in its second year cost only £6 13s. 9½ d., yet even this small figure amounted to a third of his overspending for that year. In the last year of the clock expenses his deficit of £39 odd was entirely due to the clock account. If we reckon that the provision of a clock was a legitimate expense we might well query why he should also have been burdened with the costs of the new belfry.[103] When we turn to the situation of the communar and pitancer the inadequacy of donations and legacies is painfully apparent.[104]

As gifts and legacies, never generous, dried up, the monks increasingly overspent. Although by and large the first half of the fourteenth century was a time of prosperity, and for a while their incomes were steady, almost every department overspent, sometimes hugely, deficits being carried forward to be the first charge on the next account. This meant that unless income was increased or expenditure reduced the indebtedness would mount. This is what tended to happen. In 1321 the master of the cellar had spent £715 against an income of £595. Six years later that £120 deficit had grown to over £400.[105] These early fourteenth-century administrators seem to have been incurably optimistic. At some point, they seemed to think, income and expenditure would balance. Meanwhile confidence allowed them to continue spending as though there was no problem. No overall figures are available until 1363 and 1364 when they were running deficits of £513 and £608 respectively.[106] Eventually their finances were brought under control, mainly by a great contraction in expenditure. The main culprits, the master of the cellar and the cellarer, drastically pruned their outgoings: the master of the cellar no longer gave expensive presents, and gold rings no longer figure in his accounts, while the cellarer spent far less per head on food. In 1471–72 there was a credit balance.[107] Income had dropped but expenditure had dropped even more sharply; it was less than half that of 1363. The fall continued, income being a little over £1000 in 1531, yet control had prevented runaway expenditure.[108] In one sense these figures represent an achievement. The optimism of the early fourteenth century had been replaced by sober realism.

---

101. *Communar Rolls*, p. 111.
102. NRO, DCN 1/4/4 and 1/4/6.
103. NRO, DCN 1/4/22–23.
104. *Communar Rolls*, pp. 27–43.

105. NRO, DCN 1/1/28–29.
106. NRO, DCN 1/13/1.
107. NRO, DCN 1/13/3.
108. NRO, DCN 1/13/6.

What then did this deficit mean for building work in the cloister, as yet unfinished in the mid fourteenth century? The monks did not abandon their desire to modernise and beautify and there was no great lowering of standards. The priory was obviously content to operate on a stop-start basis and there was no sense of urgency. Benefactors were still to be found. Early in the fifteenth century £100 came from the will of Geoffrey Symond, rector of St Mary in the Marsh and a man with property in the city; and a little later Henry of Wells, archdeacon of Lincoln, gave at least £40.[109] Eventually the cloister was finished, having taken about 130 years.

The priory could not, however, afford to cope with disaster. In 1463 the spire, struck by lightning, fell and burned the roof of the nave. Repairs were immediately put in hand and for the next ten years were a major item of expenditure.[110] As after the riot of 1272, the priory deemed it an occasion to improve and beautify rather than just to restore but, even more than in 1272 it needed an extraordinary injection of cash to do so. Again the burden was beyond their own resources. Once more the king came to their aid. Since there was no culprit to fine this time he let them off some taxation, ostensibly for repairs. As before, the pope granted an indulgence, from the proceeds of which stone was bought from the Northamptonshire quarries.[111] As before the monks appealed for benefactions: £20 came immediately for the repair of the southern part of the church.[112] But thereafter no great amount of money seems to have come this way: a little over £5 in 1465–66 and under £2 in 1468–69.[113] Clearly they needed a wealthy benefactor. They found one in the person of the bishop, in fact of two successive bishops, Walter Lyhart (1446–72) and James Goldwell (1472–99). The first is to be thanked for the lovely vaulting in the nave, the second for that in the presbytery. It was not a case of the bishop providing the money and the priory appointing the architect and paying for the materials and workmen. Rather it would seem that the bishop was in charge throughout, perhaps choosing the architect and even deciding on the sophisticated plan for the nave bosses. This is not to say that the priory handed over all responsibility. The sacrist was engaged in repair and renewal for ten years. He appointed good architects, John and Robert Everard, who saw to repairs to the aisles and the organ loft and undertook some work on the roof. Robert Everard was also paid for a new west window and there were new windows in the presbytery.[114]

109. *Communar Rolls*, pp. 41, 43.
110. NRO, DCN 1/4/89–93.
111. NRO, DCN 1/4/94.
112. NRO, DCN 1/4/88.
113. NRO, DCN 1/4/90: gifts and legacies for the rebuilding of the church 75s. 5d.; from the office of the prior of St Leonard for the same work 26s. 8d.; from Brother John Thetford for the same work 10s. NRO, DCN 1/4/91: gifts and legacies for the rebuilding of the church 36s. 8d.
114. NRO, DCN 1/4/91. For these works see also pp. 182–96.

There is no doubt that over the centuries the monks maintained the fabric of the cathedral, if with episcopal help; they developed the idea of the popular sermon; they kept up their round of services, admittedly with the aid of paid singing men. But were the monks so busy with administration and building that their religious life suffered? Long ago Professor Knowles made the point that half the members of any monastic community came to be fully engaged in administration at some level. This is even more applicable in the case of a cathedral community.[115] Every few years the bishop visited the monasteries in his diocese to see whether the monks led a godly life, divine services were performed with due dignity and the finances were in good order. Very few of these findings are now extant. For Norwich there are only two for the fourteenth century, one in 1308 and the other probably in 1347. At the first John Salmon found no serious lapses but was extremely critical of the excuses made for non-attendance at services because of pressure of adminis-trative work. He decreed that two-thirds of the convent should always be present in the choir at divine service and that at the festivals all monks, unless unwell, should be present with the exception of a few officials.[116] At the second visitation William Bateman (1344–55) was critical of their financial arrangements; annual accounts, he recorded, were not coming in as they should and there ought to be a reserve fund. When he came to deal with the monks' behaviour he felt that they were too ready to eat meat and to go into the city to dine with friends.[117]

There is a gap of about 150 years before the next available visitation report. In this interval the offerings at the altars had fallen greatly. At the beginning of the fifteenth century the oblations at the high altar were generally in the region of £70 a year and sometimes considerably more,[118] but by 1450 the offerings had halved and shortly before the disaster to the nave roof were under £30.[119] It was as though the cathedral had ceased to be a popular venue for the great feasts. By the beginning of the sixteenth century the shortfall seems to have been even greater, but it may be exaggerated by a different method of accounting.[120]

If the fortunes of the mother house were falling, those of St Leonard's, the cell across the river, were enjoying a remarkable, if temporary, upturn. St Leonard's had become a place of pilgrimage. In a letter dated 28 September 1443 Margaret Paston told her husband, who had been ill, that she had promised to go on pilgrimages to Walsingham and to St Leonard's on his behalf.[121] The word pilgrim, however, is hardly ever used in the St Leonard's account rolls, although there are plenty of

115. D. Knowles, *The Monastic Order in England* (Cambridge, 1949), p. 429.
116. Carter, *Studies in Cathedral History*, p. 20.
117. Cheney, 'Norwich Cathedral Priory in the Fourteenth Century', pp. 106–8, 114–15.
118. NRO, DCN 1/4/46–67.
119. NRO, DCN 1/4/87.
120. NRO, DCN 1/4/108.
121. N. Davis, *Paston Letters and Papers of the Fifteenth Century*, 2 vols (Oxford, 1971–76), i, p. 218.

references to *hospitibus* (? visitors).[122] In its chapel stood a bejewelled image of St Leonard.[123] The oblations at his altar, around £25 annually in the mid fourteenth century, had dropped to under £10 by 1425.[124] Then came a marked revival: the offerings were over £25 by 1436 and even rose to £43 in 1454–55, much the same as the offerings received at the high altar at the cathedral at this time.[125] The chapel was also embellished with a new reredos, a new red carpet and even new windows.[126] Pilgrimages were, however, subject to the vagaries of fashion and St Leonard's popularity waned. By the 1490s the offerings had again fallen to under £10 a year, in spite of the introduction of a painting of the miracles of St Leonard.[127]

For the mother house the reports of the four visitations of the sixteenth century tell a sorry story. The general picture is one of a community at war with itself. There were accusations of insubordination, of divisions between juniors and seniors, the latter accused of abusing their position, the former of idleness; a group of younger monks protested that memorising the psalms, antiphons and responses was a waste of time. Undoubtedly there was much back-biting and too little concern over reform, but the picture may have been exaggerated.[128] The last set of accounts shows a community still at work and keeping to its old routines, even buying service books from some dissolved monasteries.[129] When the end came almost all the monks were considered worthy of being translated into canons.[130]

122. The term *peregrinus* (pilgrim) occurs in connection with a payment for ale. NRO, DCN 2/3/54.
123. NRO, DCN 2/3/41.
124. NRO, DCN 2/3/2–5 and 40.
125. NRO, DCN 2/3/50 and 66.
126. NRO, DCN 2/3/54.
127. NRO, DCN 2/3/97 (1493–94); DCN 2/3/100 onward (1496 onward). The painting comes under small expenses, DCN 2/3/90.
128. Jessopp, *Visitations*, pp. 71–79, 192–93, 196–206, 262–70.
129. NRO, DCN 29/3, p. 136.
130. Three monks were not included in the new foundation, for reasons that are not known.

13

The Cathedral and the City

Norman Tanner

We have a remarkable story to tell. That is to say, the relations during almost four and a half centuries – from the foundation of the cathedral and priory in 1096 to the transformation in 1538 of the cathedral priory into the dean and chapter – between the inhabitants of one of medieval England's three or four most important cities, a major provincial capital and a city of European standing, on the one hand, and the cathedral church with its attached priory community, on the other.[1] How did these two formidable bodies coexist? The relationship was fraught with considerable tension and it is to this side of the story that I shall turn first. Afterwards we shall look at other aspects of the relationship.

The Conflict between the Cathedral Priory and the Citizens

From 1096 to 1272

The origins of the cathedral and priory provide the key to understanding later developments.[2] The effects upon the city of the foundation of the cathedral church and priory have been described well by James Campbell. So I shall quote at some length from him:

1. Regarding the population of Norwich, estimates vary considerably. Previous estimates suggested figures somewhere between 5000 and 12,000 inhabitants, with the number rising to a peak in the late thirteenth or early fourteenth century, a sharp fall with the Black Death plague of 1348–49 and its recurrences, followed by a gradual recovery in the fifteenth and early sixteenth centuries: see J. Campbell, 'Norwich', in M. D. Lobel and W. H. Johns, eds, *Historic Towns*, 3 vols (London, 1969-), ii, pp. 9, 16–17. Recently

E. Rutledge has suggested a much higher figure for the peak before the Black Death, around 25,000 inhabitants in 1333; 'Immigration and Population Growth in Early Fourteenth-Century Norwich: Evidence from the Tithing Roll', *Urban History Yearbook*, 15 (1988), p. 27.

2. For the early period see: B. Dodwell, 'The Foundation of Norwich Cathedral', *TRHS*, 5th series, 7 (1957), pp. 1–18; *First Register*, pp. 3–57; Campbell, 'Norwich', pp. 8–9; Fernie, *NC*, pp. 5–17; *EEA*, vi, pp. 9–16.

The building of the Norman cathedral transformed another large part of Norwich. Herbert de Losinga . . . began to build a great cathedral and a cathedral priory for sixty monks in the area immediately to the south and west of the bend in the Wensum. The monastic buildings lay to the south of the cathedral, to the north de Losinga built a palace for himself, which included a small stone keep . . . It looks rather as if de Losinga was concerned to carve out a *cité episcopale* of a kind familiar on the Continent since Carolingian times, and the site he acquired was very large. It came from several sources. Part already belonged to the see. Tombland with part of the adjoining area [*terra Sancti Michaelis*] was obtained from Roger Bigod by exchange. The eastern part of the site was part of Thorpe and given by Henry I. The remainder, the land 'from the bishop's land to the water and from St Martin's bridge to the land of St Michael' was obtained, in form, from the king, probably in fact from others. Much of the site was meadow but the western part was already built up and at least two churches there had to be demolished: St Michael's [the most important in the city] and another [probably Christ Church]. Not all the urban area which de Losinga acquired was incorporated into the monastic precinct. Holme Street, Tombland and Ratton Row formed throughout the Middle Ages a built-up fringe to the close, distinct from the rest of the city chiefly in that their inhabitants lived under a different jurisdiction [i.e. the priory's; see fig. 116].

The consequences of his success for Norwich were lasting. Besides establishing a powerful monastery with franchisal jurisdiction within the city, he acquired the greater part of the rural environment of Norwich for the church. In the Anglo-Saxon period Norwich had only one ecclesiastical neighbour, the abbot of St Benet's of Holme, who owned Heigham. Otherwise the lands surrounding the city were mainly either royal demesne or in the hands of relatively small proprietors. This may have done much to explain the ease with which it seems to have expanded into the surrounding countryside. But de Losinga acquired for the cathedral priory and for the see Eaton, Newton, and Thorpe with its members [Arminghall, Lakenham and Catton]. Furthermore in about 1146 King Stephen founded the Benedictine nunnery of Carrow actually within the city fields immediately to the south of Norwich. Thereafter it was only in the northwest that the city was not edged by the lands of a monastery. The Norman period saw Norwich well and truly folded into the bosom of the church.[3]

It is not difficult to detect the potential for possible grievances in these arrangements. The surviving evidence is somewhat unbalanced inasmuch as most of it was

---

3.   Campbell, 'Norwich', pp. 8–9.

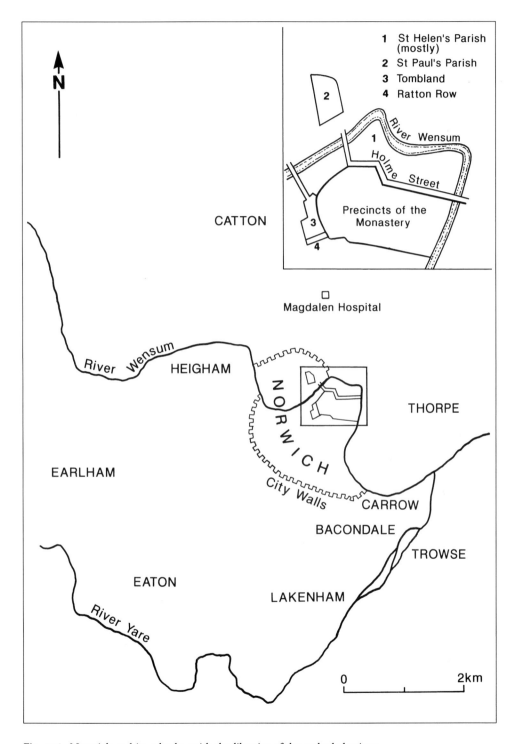

N

1   St Helen's Parish (mostly)
2   St Paul's Parish
3   Tombland
4   Ratton Row

River Wensum

Holme Street

Precincts of the Monastery

CATTON

□
Magdalen Hospital

River Wensum   HEIGHAM

N O R W I C H

THORPE

EARLHAM

City Walls   CARROW

BACONDALE

TROWSE

EATON

LAKENHAM

River Yare

0   2km

Fig. 116. Norwich and its suburbs, with the liberties of the cathedral priory.

written by monks of the cathedral priory, notably in the *First Register* of the priory, which was probably compiled in the early fourteenth century, perhaps by Bartholomew Cotton:[4] the evidence tends to emphasise the brighter side of things from the monastic viewpoint. Therefore some imagination and reading between the lines is necessary.

Herbert de Losinga, a Norman by birth and upbringing, doubtless incurred some of the hostility and resentment that members of that people, clergy as well a laity, met with in post-Conquest England. In the case of his foundation of the cathedral and priory, however, there is the important point that he was not pulling down an existing cathedral building or reforming a monastic community – moves that certainly caused opposition in various parts of Norman England – but rather founding a new cathedral and monastery for the city. We know, moreover, that although some of the early monks were Normans, others came from Norwich and elsewhere in East Anglia, so the community had some local roots.[5]

There was probably more substance in the feeling that much of the land given for the establishment of the cathedral and priory, as outlined above, had been removed in various ways from the city's control. This would have been wounding for Norwich, which was already a large and prosperous town. The transfer to the priory's jurisdiction of Tombland (or Tomlond, Danish for an open space), which appears to have been the centre of the late Anglo-Saxon borough, a market and a meeting-place,[6] may have been particularly painful. In examining in more detail the original grants of land and those of the following years, Miss Dodwell found that few of them were made by citizens of Norwich or by the free peasantry of the locality.[7] There is little to suggest that the building of the cathedral and priory was borne along on a wave of popular enthusiasm such as occurred in, for example, the building of Chartres Cathedral half a century later. The impression is of a somewhat self-contained and defensive world which regarded itself, rather than the city, as the centre of life in the area.

The period after the foundation until the disturbance of 1272 is obscure regarding relations between the cathedral priory and the city, largely on account of scarcity of evidence. It is unclear whether it should be seen as a time of mounting tension or of relatively harmonious relations. A succession of royal charters granted to the city, notably that of 1194, strengthened its corporate identity and rights of self-government and thereby, surely, increased its unease with the priory's extensive rights and privileges in the city and its suburbs. On the other hand, an apparently

4. *First Register*, pp. 7–11; NCC, i, pp. xxv–
    xxvii; Fernie, *NC*, pp. 1–2.
5. Dodwell, 'Foundation', p. 12.
6. W. Hudson and J. C. Tingey, *The Records*

    of the City of Norwich, 2 vols (Norwich,
    1906–10), i, p. v; Fernie, *NC*, p. 5.
7. Dodwell, 'Foundation', pp. 8, 14–15.

important agreement was reached between the prior and the citizens in 1205. The agreement regulated the citizens' rights of pasture in the suburbs of Lakenham and Eaton, which de Losinga had acquired for the priory at its foundation, as mentioned earlier. This may have removed, or at least diminished, one significant source of tension for a time. From the 1240s onwards, however, a number of lesser disputes between the priory and the citizens are known to have occurred, mostly involving their respective jurisdictions. They may have been precursors of the dramatic events now to be described.[8]

The Assault of 1272 and Afterwards

In the year 1272 matters came to a head in what turned out to be one of the most violent assaults on a religious institution in medieval England.[9] The attack on the cathedral and priory appears to have escalated from a scuffle between townsmen and servants or tenants of the priory at a quintain (a jousting-post) on or around the feast of the Trinity (19 June in that year) on Tombland, the contentious area which lay outside the monastic precincts but was subject to the priory's jurisdiction. In the ensuing days and weeks further acts of provocation were committed by both sides, though chiefly it seems by the priory. These acts included the prior bringing in men from Yarmouth, who allegedly fortified the bell tower of the monastery and joined the prior's men in various assaults upon the city. Finally on 11 August the citizens attacked the cathedral and priory. There are many contemporary and later accounts of this assault, all partial in their sympathies. We must limit ourselves to quoting two of them. The London-based chronicle, written into the *Liber de antiquis legibus*, which provides an extended account of the disturbance, one representing the citizens' viewpoint, saw the attack as a legitimate response to the violence perpetrated by the men from Yarmouth and to various assaults by men from the priory. But the attack got out of hand and went sadly wrong:

> On seeing this violence [of the men from Yarmouth] the citizens reckoned these evildoers were clearly acting contrary to the king's peace, inasmuch as they had set up an illegal fortress in the city. The citizens assembled together and decided to arrest them and bring them before the king's justice. So they armed themselves and approached the gate into the monastic precincts. The

8. Hudson and Tingey, *Records* i, pp. xxv–xxx, 11–18, ii, pp. 212–14; Campbell, 'Norwich', pp. 9, 13; B. Dodwell, ed., *Feet of Fines for the County of Norfolk for the Reign of King John, 1201–1215* (Pipe Roll Society, new series, 32, 1958), no. 68; W. Rye, 'The Riot between the Monks and Citizens of Norwich in 1272', *Norfolk Antiquarian Miscellany*, 2 (1883), pp. 18–19.

9. Most of the surviving records of the disturbance are edited with an introduction in Rye, 'Riot in 1272', pp. 17–89. See also, Hudson and Tingey, *Records*, i, pp. xxx–xxxi, 269–71; A. Gransden, *The Chronicle of Bury St Edmunds, 1212–1301* (London, 1964), pp. 50–52.

gate, however, was defended by armed men and the citizens were not able
to enter in. So they set fire to it and burned it down. The fire spread, burning
the bell tower and all the monastic buildings and even, as some say, the
cathedral church, alas, together with all the saints' relics, books and ornaments
in the church. Thus whatever could be burned was reduced to ashes, except
one chapel which remained unharmed. The monks and all who could do so
escaped by flight. Some from both sides, however, were killed.[10]

The second account comes from the *Historia Anglicana* of Bartholomew Cotton,
a monk of the cathedral priory, possibly at the time of the disturbance, who compiled
his record some years after the event, probably in the 1290s.[11] Not surprisingly, he
defended the priory and laid the blame with the citizens. Ignoring the events leading
up to the assault, he wrote:

> In the year 1272, on the day following the feast of St Laurence [i.e. on 11
> August], the citizens of Norwich laid siege around the precincts of the mon-
> astery. When their insults failed to gain them admittance, they set fire to the
> main gate into the monastery, beyond which lay a certain parish church [St
> Ethelbert's]. They burned the gate and the church together with all its orna-
> ments, books, images and contents. At the same time they set fire to the
> almonry, to the gate of the [cathedral] church and to the great bell tower, all
> of which, together with the bells, immediately caught fire. Some citizens
> launched fiery missiles from the tower [of the parish church] of St George [at
> Tombland] into the great-belfry situated beyond the choir. The fire consumed
> the whole [cathedral] church except the chapel of the blessed Mary, which
> was miraculously preserved.[12] Moreover, they burned the dormitory, the re-
> fectory, the guest hall, the infirmary with its chapel, and indeed almost all the
> buildings within the precincts of the monastery. They killed many members
> of the monastery's household, some subdeacons and clerics, and some lay
> people, in the cloister and within the precincts of the monastery. Others they
> dragged off and put to death in the city, others they imprisoned. After they
> had gained entry into the buildings, they looted all the sacred vessels, books,
> gold and silver, and everything else that the fire had spared. All the monks
> except two or three fled from the monastery. Not content with this iniquity,
> the citizens continued their burning, killing and plundering for three days.[13]

10. T. Stapleton, ed., *De antiquis legibus liber*
(Camden Society, old series, 34, 1846),
p. 146; Rye, 'Riot in 1272', p. 74.
11. B. Cotton, *Historia Anglicana*, ed. H. R.
Luard (RS, 16, 1859), pp. xvii, liv-lv; *First
Register*, pp. 7–8.

12. For the translation of this sentence see D. J.
Stewart, 'Notes on Norwich Cathedral',
Arch. J., 32 (1875), pp. 27–28.
13. Cotton, *Historia Anglicana*, pp. 146–47; Rye,
'Riot in 1272', pp. 75–76.

We know that some thirteen people were killed on the priory side, though no monk is known to have perished. The damage caused by the fire must have been extensive, though the surviving Norman stonework shows that the basic structure of the cathedral remained intact. The reprisals were correspondingly severe. The bishop of Norwich and later the pope excommunicated the citizens involved in the attack and laid Norwich under an interdict. The liberties of the city were taken into the king's hand for some years. The city was condemned to pay the huge sum of £2000 towards repairing the damage done to the cathedral and about thirty citizens are known to have been hanged in punishment.[14]

Thereafter, until the early sixteenth century, tension between the two sides was never far below the surface.[15] The crux of the problem was that the exempt liberties of the priory within the city, and the jurisdiction of the city government in the suburbs, which contained extensive grazing lands of the priory, had been defined in incompatible terms by royal charters granted to both parties. On the one hand, charters granted to the citizens, including the charter of 1404 which made the city into a county and gave it a mayor, had given them jurisdiction within the city and its suburbs without explicitly exempting the priory's lands from this jurisdiction. On the other hand, the priory rightly claimed that the late eleventh and early twelfth century charters, giving it lands and liberties in Norwich and its suburbs, antedated the charters granted to the citizens and had not been revoked by them. The crown was still confirming the priory's liberties in the fifteenth century.

The citizens never tried seriously to abolish the priory's franchises altogether. In practice the disputes centred on three points. The first was about whether the following areas lay within the priory's exempt liberties: Tombland, Ratton Row and Holme Street (the small pieces of land lying just outside the precincts of the priory); St Paul's parish, sometimes called Normansland or Spiteland, which was a separate enclave in the northern ward of the city and included St Paul's Hospital; and Magdalen Hospital, situated in the northern suburb of the city. The second concerned the prior's rights in holding an annual fair on Tombland over Pentecost, from which the priory, not the city government, received the tolls and at which the priory held its own court. The third was over the extent of the rights of the

14. Rye, 'Riot in 1272', pp. 23–29; Hudson and Tingey, *Records*, i, pp. xxx–xxxi; Fernie, *NC*, pp. 163–81, 211–12.

15. The following account, up to the dissolution of the priory, is largely taken, except where other references are given, from N. Tanner, *The Church in Late Medieval Norwich, 1370–1532* (Toronto, 1984), pp. 144–54. References to the sources are given there. The extracts are reproduced by permission of the publisher, the Pontifical Institute of Mediaeval Studies, Toronto. For the Reformation period see also M. C. McClendon, 'The Quiet Reformation: Norwich Magistrates and the Coming of Protestantism, 1520–1525' (unpublished Stanford University Ph. D. thesis, 1990), pp. 16–48.

priory and of the citizens in the grazing lands of Eaton and Lakenham. Neither side appears to have denied to the other all rights of grazing in these lands, at least after the settlement of 1205 mentioned above: the issues appear to have been a combination of where the boundaries between their respective areas lay, the number of animals that each party was allowed to pasture, and the payments due to the priory from the citizens for the right to graze.

These unresolved issues, on top of the more general rivalry, provided endless opportunities for friction. It may be that most of the fourteenth century was a period of relative quiet, due in part to an agreement reached between the two parties in 1306 regarding the prior's view of frankpledge in his fee.[16] In this respect it is noticeable that although Norwich was a centre of disturbance in the Peasants' Revolt of 1381, and in other places the revolt provided an occasion for attacks on ecclesiastics and religious institutions, there does not appear to have been an attack on the cathedral and priory at that time.[17] From the late fourteenth century onwards, however, when records become more abundant, scarcely a decade passed for which there is not evidence of some clash between the two sides.

From Gladman's Insurrection to 1538

The most serious clash occurred in 1443.[18] That it occurred then and not in 1381 or in Cade's rebellion of 1450, just as the most violent clash of all had occurred in 1272 and not during the preceding baronial wars, illustrates how local and comparatively unconnected with national events the conflict was. For several reasons relations between the cathedral priory and the municipality became more than usually strained in the late 1430s and early 1440s. The citizens came to resent as too generous to the priory an agreement reached with the city government in 1429. Two of the terms, in particular, appear to have rankled with the citizens: an annual rent of four shillings to be paid by the city to the priory; and recognition of the priory's liberties in the suburbs. The crown, moreover, had exacerbated matters between the two parties by fining the mayor and various citizens for much earlier breaches of its own rights and those of the priory in the suburbs, and by upholding

16. Campbell, 'Norwich', p. 13. Frankpledge was the system of preserving the peace by the compulsory association of men into groups of ten, each member of which was surety for the others. The view of frankpledge was the duty of seeing that these associations were kept in perfect order and number, and in the areas of the priory's jurisdiction was vested in the prior.

17. E. Powell, *The Rising in East Anglia in 1381*

(Cambridge, 1896), pp. 28–31; R. B. Dobson, *The Peasants' Revolt of 1381* (2nd edn, London, 1983), pp. 256–59.

18. See note 15 above. See also P. Maddern, *Violence and Social Order: East Anglia, 1422–1442* (Oxford, 1992), pp. 175–205; B. R. McRee, 'Religious Gilds and Civic Order: The Case of Norwich in the Late Middle Ages', *Speculum*, 67 (1992), pp. 86–89.

against the city government the more extreme claims of the priory to jurisdiction in parts of the city and its suburbs. Finally, the priory had in John Heverlond, its prior from 1436 until his death in 1453/44, a man who was noted for his confrontational style in a wide range of issues.

The priory allied itself to a variety of parties with grievances against the city government and this alliance was the main reason why matters came to a head in 1443. First, the king, who, in addition to the actions just mentioned, was angered by the request made by the citizens in 1440 that £100 lent to him by the city be repaid, and by their refusal of a further loan in the following year. Secondly, Thomas Wetherby, a very wealthy man who had been mayor in 1427 and 1432 and who, having tried unsuccessfully to get his nominees elected to the same office in subsequent years, led a minority faction in the city into increasingly bitter opposition to the majority. This group was joined by a number of East Anglian magnates with old scores to settle with the city, including the earl of Suffolk and the duke of Norfolk, and they gained the support of the bishop of Norwich, Thomas Brouns. In addition, there were the abbots of St Benet of Holme and of Wendling in Norfolk: the former in dispute with the city regarding the detrimental effects of its newly-built mills upon his mills and lands in the suburb of Heigham; the latter regarding various rents due to him from the city on various pieces of property in Norwich, notably a quay on the River Wensum.

The grievances of the two abbots, together with Prior Heverlond's claim that the city government had violated various rights of the priory in its liberties and during its Whitsun fair, were first heard by a commission of oyer and terminer at Thetford in July 1441. These disputes, and some obscure complaints of the bishop of Norwich against the citizens, were then submitted by the parties concerned to the arbitration of the earl of Suffolk. The earl made his award sometime in 1442. The whole of it is not known but it evidently went in favour of the ecclesiastics. Part of it ordered the citizens to destroy their new mills and to give bonds of £100, £50 and £50 to the abbot of St Benet's, Prior Heverlond and Bishop Brouns respectively, presumably as pledges that they would carry out the award.

The city government refused to accept the award, despite considerable pressure from its opponents to do so, and its refusal finally erupted in 1443 into what is known as Gladman's Insurrection. There are three rather different reports relevant to this remarkable disturbance. Defending the conduct of the citizens some five years after the event, the city government claimed that there had not been a riot but only a 'disport as is and ever has been the custom in any city or borough through all this realm on Fastyngong [Shrove] Tuesday', in which a certain John Gladman rode through the city on a horse, crowned as king of Christmas, with representations of the season carried before and after him. A second account, which covers the events immediately before and after the disturbance but not the event

itself, was written into the city's official chronicle, the *Liber albus*, in 1482. This
report says that Wetherby and the 'council' of the abbot of St Benet of Holme, in
their efforts to get the bond of £100 sealed for the abbot with the city's common
seal, persuaded the mayor on 25 January to call an assembly, but the 'commons' of
the city came to the assembly in great numbers and removed the common seal in
order to prevent the bond being sealed. The third report is that of a presentment
made by a jury of twelve men from Norfolk before an inquisition held at Thetford
on 28 February 1443. The jury appears to have been packed with Wetherby's
supporters and the account may exaggerate the scale of the disturbance and the
extent to which it was premeditated. It seems, however, closer to the truth than
the first account (that of the city government) for several reasons. It is the earliest
of the three reports, coming little more than a month after the disturbance; it gets
the date right, on or around 25 January, whereas the city government offered no
explanation why a 'disport' such as was customary on Shrove Tuesday (5 March in
1443) took place more than a month earlier; and it correlates better with the version
in the *Liber albus*. The jury's reported description of the events is as follows, which
I quote at length on account of its interest:

> William Hempstead [the mayor] of the city of Norwich, merchant of the
> same, and the commonalty of the city, on Tuesday 22 January 1443, in the
> said city, planned to make a common insurrection and disturbance of all the
> liege subjects of the lord king in the said city and surrounding country. They
> believed that by this insurrection and disturbance they would be sufficiently
> powerful, in the said city and surrounding country, as to be able to force
> Thomas, bishop of Norwich, John, abbot of St Benedict of Holme, and John,
> prior of the church of the Holy Trinity [i.e. the cathedral] in Norwich, by
> threats of burning, killing and plundering, to surrender various actions of theirs
> which they possessed against the said mayor and commonalty and many others
> of the same city. They believed too that, because the city formed a county
> of its own, separated from the county of Norfolk by letters patent of King
> Henry IV [i.e. the charter of 1404], and because of their strength and the
> large number of people who would gather round them, the king would neither
> dare nor be able to punish them by his law for the aforesaid transgressions.
>   Accordingly, they then and there arranged for John Gladman of the said
> city, merchant, to ride in the city on a horse, like a crowned king, with a
> sceptre and sword carried before him by three unknown men; and Robert
> Suger of Norwich, souter, Robert Hennyng of the same, hosteler, Richard
> Dallyng, cutler, and twenty-four other persons likewise to ride on horseback,
> before the said John Gladman, with a crown upon their arms and carrying
> bows and arrows, as if they were valets of the crown of the lord king; and a

hundred other unknown persons, some on horseback and some on foot, to follow the same John Gladman, carrying bows and arrows and swords.

They went around urging people in the city to come together and to make an insurrection and riots there. On 25 January 1443 they were able, thanks to the lack of good government there, to ring and have rung in turn various bells in the city. Thereupon the mayor and commonalty, with many other unknown persons from the said city to the number of 3000, having been summoned by the said ringing of bells, were able, thanks to the lack of good government in the city, to come together in bands and to make a violent insurrection throughout the entire city; that is to say, they were armed with swords, bows and arrows, hauberks and coats of armour, and with other weapons collected for a warlike purpose. They were able to cross over to the priory of the cathedral church of the Holy Trinity of Norwich, in the county of Norfolk. There they shouted, 'Let us burn the priory and kill the prior and monks', and immediately they dug under the gates of the priory so as to enter in, they brought wood to burn the priory and placed cannons – that is, guns – pointing towards the priory.

From that day until four o'clock in the afternoon on the following day they broke the peace by attacking the priory in order to burn it, and they plotted to kill the prior and monks. They continued their insurrection until Richard Walsham and John Wychyngham, fellow monks of the prior, due to these threats and assaults, surrendered to them a certain evidence belonging to the prior which was sealed with the city's common seal [i.e. the agreement of 1429, see above p. 262]. In this evidence it was stated, among other things, that Robert Baxter, formerly mayor of the city, John Sypater and William Iselham, former sheriffs, and the commonalty of the city granted by the said document to William Worsted, predecessor of the present prior, and to his successors for ever an annual rent of four shillings, which was to be paid in Norwich by the mayor and sheriffs and their successors each year on the feast of St Michael for ever; and also that neither the then mayor and commonalty nor their successors would ever hold any court dealing with persons or real estate, whether arising from a suit or from a writ of the king, or any court of the sheriff dealing with any lands, tenements or rents, whether it concerned a contract or any actual, possible or future matter, in the meadows called Conisford Meadows or the fields, heath lands, meadows and pasture lands in Bracondale, Eaton, Lakenham and Earlham. Thus they forcibly removed the aforesaid evidences belonging to the prior which had been kept in the priory.

They kept the city with closed gates and in a state of arms, like a city at war with the lord king, from Monday 28 January to Monday 4 February 1443. They kept John, duke of Norfolk, outside the city for a whole week from

Tuesday 29 January 1443 and John Vere, earl of Oxford, and other ministers of the lord king from Monday 26 to Wednesday 28 September 1442[19] – whom the lord king had appointed, by his letters patent of commission, to deal with the insurrection and riots, to arrest, to restore peace in the city and to restore good government to it – and they would not allow the said duke and earl to enter the city during this time.[20]

As in 1272 both the church and the crown struck back. The archbishop of Canterbury excommunicated the citizens involved, though the bishop of Norwich claimed to have tried to defer execution of the sentence and refused to lay the city under an interdict. William Hempstead, the mayor, was imprisoned 'on the king's counsel' in the Fleet in London for six weeks from 13 February and was fined £50. During the mayor's imprisonment Wetherby and his faction appear to have controlled the city and carried out the earl of Suffolk's award. According to the *Liber albus* they wrecked the city's new mills to such an extent that they were useless for many years; and Wetherby sealed the three bonds of £100, £50 and £50 with the city's common seal and gave them to the abbot of St Benet of Holme, Prior Heverlond and Bishop Brouns. Finally, in March 1443 a commission appointed to inquire into the disturbance declared the city's liberties forfeit and imposed very heavy fines: a collective fine of £2000 on the city and sums totalling over £1500 on individual rioters. The liberties of the city were only restored in November 1447, by which time the collective fine, reduced to 1000 marks (£666 6s. 8d.), had been paid.

There are obvious similarities between the assault of 1272 and Gladman's Insurrection. In the latter, indeed, there may well have been some conscious imitation of the former. In Gladman's Insurrection, however, nobody is known to have been killed, either in the disturbance or in punishment for it, and the damage caused by fire and plundering was much less. The monks showed more prudence and the citizens more restraint.[21]

The conflict continued after 1443 but it was never again so fierce. The broad alliance of interests hostile to the city slowly dissolved. Thomas Wetherby died a year or two later and there was never again such a powerful 'pro-priory faction' within the city government. The city's disputes with the abbots of St Benet's of Holme and Wendling were gradually resolved, largely in its favour. Perhaps of most importance was the change of attitude on the part of the crown. Until the 1440s

---

19. The last dates are obviously wrong, but the correct dates are unknown.
20. NRO, NCR, case 17b, book of pleas, fos 17v–18r (new fos 40v–41r). The translation of the passage in Hudson and Tingey, *Records*, i, pp. 340–41, is much abbreviated

and sometimes inaccurate.
21. Maddern, *Violence and Social Order*, p. 198; A. King, 'The Merchant Class and Borough Finances in Later Medieval Norwich' (unpublished Oxford University D. Phil. thesis, 1989), p. 29.

it always seems, in the last resort, to have supported the priory against the citizens. Later it was less willing to do so. The change began in Edward IV's reign and may have been in return for support given by people of Norwich to the Yorkist cause on several occasions.[22] Thus in 1482 one of the citizens' grievances against the priory was removed when Edward IV granted them the right to hold two fairs each year, though these appear not to have prospered and the priory continued to hold its annual fair over Pentecost. In the early 1490s the central government began to put pressure on both parties to reach a lasting settlement to all the matters in dispute. The attempt failed because both sides refused to compromise on certain issues. Efforts were renewed in 1517 by Cardinal Wolsey, who was determined that the priory, as well as the citizens, should make concessions.

After long and costly negotiations agreement was reached in 1524. The city government reluctantly made the greater concessions over grazing lands in the suburbs. The priory gave the city eighty acres of land in Eaton and Lakenham, subsequently called the Town Close, for which it was to receive £13 6s. 8d. a year from the city. In return the city surrendered its claims to grazing rights elsewhere in the two suburbs. The other concessions came from the priory. It surrendered to the city its right to hold a fair over Pentecost and the profits and jurisdiction stemming from it; and its claims to jurisdiction in Tombland, Ratton Row and Holme Street and in all its other liberties within the 'county of Norwich', except within the precincts of the monastery. The agreement was ratified by two royal charters of 1524 and 1525. As a result the dispute appears to have eased considerably until the dissolution of the priory in 1538.

The period after Gladman's Insurrection, the eve of the Reformation, therefore saw a relaxation of tensions and the gradual weakening of the priory's position in relation to the citizens. The settlement of 1524–25 gave the city much of what it wanted. In this respect the dissolution of the priory may be seen as largely unnecessary rather than as the inevitable culmination of mounting conflict. Nevertheless the dispute resurfaced in the post-Reformation period, when the prior and monks had been succeeded by the dean and chapter.[23]

There was this long-running saga of tension between the cathedral priory and the inhabitants of Norwich, centring around their respective rights in the city and its suburbs. It is a comparatively well-documented story and has considerable continuity, lasting throughout the period treated in this chapter.

Norwich was, of course, by no means unique in having the kind of difficulties

22. R. Storey, *The End of the House of Lancaster* (London, 1966), p. 225.

23. See below, pp. 524–26, 549–51, 557.

that have been outlined. Such tensions were normal, indeed virtually inevitable, in towns with large, property-owning monasteries. In many other towns they boiled over at times into open violence. We may think of St Albans and Bury St Edmunds during the Peasants' Revolt in 1381, to mention only two others, though it is true that the events in Norwich in 1272 were on an unusually violent and bloody scale by any standards. The disputes in Norwich were largely about temporal matters – jurisdiction and the financial emoluments associated with it – but since a monastery and cathedral church represented so clearly the 'church on earth' such disputes must have influenced people's religious outlook.

Did the events of 1272 and 1443 express, albeit at an unusually high level of intensity, the normal attitude of the people of Norwich towards the cathedral priory or were they, rather, quite abnormal happenings? This is a difficult question and no doubt the answer lies somewhere in the middle. The rest of this chapter should provide some further clues. Here it must suffice to say that, on the one hand, there is nothing to suggest that tensions were continuously at the feverish level of those two years, as if such outbreaks might have happened at any time. Both disturbances were caused by an exceptional conjuncture of various factors. Matters at other times were evidently much quieter. On the other hand, the events of 1272 and 1443 cannot be dismissed as entirely untypical. We have seen that there was a succession of lesser clashes and that the grievances underlying all the incidents remained unresolved and potential sources of friction, at least until the early sixteenth century. Another point is that the disturbances of 1272 and 1443 were not caused by small and unrepresentative groups of people. It is impossible to know the precise numbers involved on either occasion. Three thousand people were mentioned for 1443 and figures for 1272 vary from 32,000 mentioned by some chroniclers to Rye's figure of fewer than 173 identifiable assailants.[24] The highest figure surely represents the exaggeration of chroniclers, exceeding even the largest estimates of the total population of the city,[25] nevertheless the evidence suggests that both attacks had quite a wide measure of popular support. In this respect it is noticeable that the Bury St Edmunds chronicler says that women joined in the assault in 1272 and that a woman was among those hanged in punishment.[26] We also find secular priests among the assailants.[27] So, while the disputes were chiefly with the freemen of the city – the citizens in the narrower sense of that word – and concerned principally their rights and prerogatives, the conflict was not confined to them and involved, at least to some extent, the wider population of the city.

24. See above p. 265; Rye, 'Riot in 1272', pp. 23, 78; Gransden, *Chronicle of Bury*, p. 51.
25. For the city's population, see above, p. 255 n. 1.
26. Gransden, *Chronicle of Bury*, pp. 51–52; see also Rye, 'Riot in 1272', p. 21 n. 1.
27. Rye, 'Riot in 1272', pp. 22.

Despite all the problems and opposition, was there at the same time a fair measure of devotion to and respect for the cathedral church and priory, even civic pride in them, as is often the case with large and important institutions that we find in our midst?

Social and Spiritual Relations

Economic, Social and Charitable Roles

One thing is certain: everybody in Norwich would have felt the presence of the cathedral priory. The cathedral church and the monastic buildings formed much the largest and most imposing complex of buildings in the city, with the possible exception of the castle. The priory's extensive property and jurisdictions in the city and its suburbs would have impinged on the daily life of the population, not just at the times of open conflict that have been mentioned above. The priory must have been much the largest employer in Norwich. H. W. Saunders calculated that, from the late thirteenth century onwards, when the surviving obedientiary rolls commence, a minimum of 150 men and women, in addition to the monks themselves, were engaged in regular employment in or around the monastery.[28] There must have been, moreover, a considerable number of other people who were employed on a casual basis or whose employment was affected in an indirect way by the priory. These are sizeable figures in view of the total population of the city.[29] The numbers would have increased when special building projects or decorative or repair works were being undertaken. These and other aspects of the priory's role as an employer in the city will be apparent from many pages of this book.

Many of the inhabitants would have owed their tithes and various other dues to the cathedral priory. Approaching half of the fifty or so parish churches in the city were appropriated to the priory; in such cases parishioners paid their tithes and other dues to the religious house rather than to the parish priest. The obligation may have contributed to the tension between the townspeople and the priory, though in fact the surviving evidence (admittedly rather scarce) does not suggest that it created a major problem.[30]

At the level of institutional charity, the priory was responsible for St Paul's Hospital in the northern ward of the city. It was one of the two largest (the other being St Giles's) of the dozen or so hospitals in the city and its suburbs. Founded in the early twelfth century, it acted as an almshouse for between a dozen and about

28. H. W. Saunders, *An Introduction to the Obedientiary and Manor Rolls of Norwich Cathedral Priory* (Norwich, 1930), pp. 162–63. On the priory as landlord see E. Rutledge, 'Landlords and Tenants: Housing and the Rented Property Market in Early Fourteenth-Century Norwich', *Urban History*, 22 (1995), pp. 7–24.

29. See above, p. 255 n. 1.

30. Tanner, *Church in Norwich*, pp. 5–7.

twenty persons, both men and women until the early fifteenth century and thereafter only women, as well as providing temporary relief to other needy people. One of the monks acted as master of the hospital and the priory had overall responsibility, financial and otherwise, for the institution. Two other hospitals – St Giles's and Magdalen – lay within liberties of the priory. Although they were independent institutions, the priory seems to have offered them its protection and occasionally more direct support. In addition, there were the distributions made to the poor, mostly in the form of food, by the officials (obedientiaries) of the monastery, chiefly the almoner. These alms, recorded in the account rolls of the obedientiaries from the late thirteenth century onwards, almost certainly continued throughout the priory's existence. Even if prudence seems at times to have got the better of generosity, with a decline in alms apparently setting in after about 1350, the distributions must have formed an important source of poor relief in the city.[31]

The account rolls of the priory's cellarer indicate a different form of charity. In 1431–32 payments were made to 'minstrels of the city and other players performing before the lord prior, the mayor of the city and others on the day of the banquet at Christmas'. A century earlier, before Norwich had a mayor, similar payments were made to minstrels performing at a banquet which the prior held for the bailiffs. Whether the feast was an annual event is not clear but the celebrations – although the records give only a fleeting glimpse of them – provide a pleasant corrective to the tensions mentioned in the earlier part of this chapter.[32]

Education and Learning

Norwich was one of the most important intellectual and cultural centres in medieval England. Of all the institutions in the city, the cathedral priory almost certainly made the most important single contribution to the work of education. The education of the monks has been discussed by Barbara Dodwell.[33] Here it must suffice to say something about the schools administered by the priory for persons other than its own monks and to add a few remarks of a general nature.

The history of these schools has been told recently by Paul Cattermole and Joan Greatrex.[34] In the early years of its existence the priory conducted a school for

31. VCH Norfolk, ii, pp. 322, 442–50; E. H. Carter, 'The Constitutions of the Hospital of St Paul (Normanspitel) in Norwich', NA, 25 (1935), pp. 342–53; First Register, p. 66; Saunders, Obedientiary Rolls, pp. 122–27, 169–71.

32. NRO, DCN 1/1/30, 33 and 80. I am indebted to Miss Barbara Dodwell for this information. See also Saunders, Obedientiary Rolls, pp. 182–83.

33. See pp. 232–33, 243–48.

34. R. Harries, P. Cattermole and P. Mackintosh, A History of Norwich School (Norwich, 1991), pp. 5–21; J. Greatrex, 'The Almonry School of Norwich Cathedral Priory in the Thirteenth and Fourteenth Centuries', in D. Wood, ed., The Church and Childhood (Studies in Church History, 31, 1994), pp. 169–81. What follows draws extensively on their accounts.

oblates (boys given to the monastery by their parents with a view to their becoming monks). While such a school would have been largely internal to the monastery, it is possible that some boys from the city who were not oblates attended the school. Doubtless, too, some oblates eventually exercised their right not to become monks and went on to lead their lives in the city. Thus the distinction between oblates and city (and country) students may have been somewhat fluid. The practice of receiving child-oblates declined in the Benedictine Order from the middle of the twelfth century. So it seems likely that this school within the cathedral priory, which disappears from record, was gradually transformed into the almonry school. The latter, the earliest known example of its kind in England, certainly existed in the late thirteenth century. Thereafter it had a continuous existence until the dissolution of the priory. It formed part of the almonry of the monastery and it seems to have flourished, with around twenty students at its height. Most of them were alms-boys, who were supported by the priory; of the remaining fee-paying students, a few were young clerics in minor orders. The majority of them probably came from Norwich, though from the late fourteenth to the early fifteenth century there were some boarders from outside the city. This school, too, was partly monastic in character in that the students had singing (it was sometimes called the song school) and other duties in the cathedral and priory, but it provided an education for boys of the city, both those intending to be priests and those not so intending. In this sense it was outward-looking towards the city. Although the school formed an integral part of the monastery and was supported by it, the teaching appears to have been done by secular priests, not by monks.

The other school for which the priory had some responsibility was the grammar school, sometimes called the episcopal school. The links were various. The school had been founded at an early date, quite likely by the first bishop of Norwich, Herbert de Losinga. By 1156, in the earliest clear reference to its existence, it was listed as a possession of the cathedral priory. Charters show that the priory appointed the master of the school until the late thirteenth century, when the appointment was taken over by the bishop. The school was situated within a liberty of the priory, in Holme Street. It had various links with the almonry school. Its size and purpose, moreover, seem to have been similar to those of the almonry school, though its liturgical functions were directed towards the church of St Giles's Hospital – the hospital supported some of the students – rather than to the cathedral. Its teaching, too, seems to have been done by secular priests, not monks. There may have been some form of an amalgamation of the two schools in the early sixteenth century.

Norwich contained a number of other schools. Each of the four friaries (Franciscan, Dominican, Carmelite and Augustinian) had a *studium*: there appear to have been, in the late middle ages, two or three 'song schools' attached to other religious institutions. There may have been a school for girls at Carrow Nunnery in the suburbs of the city. The *studia*, however, were for young friars of the four orders, not for outside students, so far as we know. The song schools were almost certainly smaller institutions than the schools connected with the cathedral priory. The *studia* and the song schools, moreover, were later on the scene, the four friaries dating from the thirteenth century.[35] So it may well be that for over a century the cathedral priory was running, or had some responsibility for, the only schools in the city and environs, at least for boys; and for the rest of the middle ages the schools with which the priory was connected were probably doing more for the school-room education of the inhabitants of Norwich than were any other institutions in the city.

There was also the wider contribution of the cathedral priory to learning and culture in medieval Norwich.[36] Before the thirteenth century the priory must have enjoyed an unrivalled position as a centre of learning in the city. Thereafter the scene changed considerably with the establishment of four friaries, the growth of a literate laity and parish priests with university degrees. For the later period, in medieval Christendom as a whole, most historians have compared unfavourably the academic attainments of Benedictine monks with those of the orders of friars. In Norwich the evidence shows there to have been intellectually active friaries but not that the cathedral priory was eclipsed. A number of monks of the priory feature in the catalogue of renowned British writers, *Scriptorum illustrium maioris Britannie catalogus*, which was compiled in the sixteenth century by John Bale, himself a former member of the Carmelite friary in Norwich who must have known the local scene. They include Thomas of Monmouth, the author of the life of St William of Norwich, who will be mentioned later, and the learned fourteenth-century monks Adam Easton and Thomas Brinton, who ended their lives as a cardinal and the bishop of Rochester respectively. There was also Bartholomew Cotton, author of *Historia Anglicana*, mentioned earlier. The monastic library, which appears to have contained at least 1350 volumes at the dissolution of the priory, almost certainly formed the largest collection in Norwich and was one of the finest libraries in medieval England.[37] It is an intriguing but as yet unanswered question whether the townspeople had access to the books of this library or could borrow them (there is no clear evidence to suggest that either possibility was open to them). In all sorts of other ways the cathedral was an educational and intellectual treasure-house open to the people: in architecture, sculpture, roof bosses, paintings, stained glass and

35. Harries, Cattermole and Mackintosh, *Norwich School*, pp. 3–4; N. Orme, *English Schools in the Middle Ages* (London, 1973), pp. 30–32; Tanner, *Church in Norwich*, pp. 33–34; *VCH Norfolk*, ii, p. 352; W. Rye, *Carrow Abbey* (Norwich, 1889), p. 4; W. J.

Courtenay, *Schools and Scholars in Fourteenth-Century England* (Princeton, New Jersey, 1987), pp. 106–11.

36. For this paragraph see Tanner, *Church in Norwich*, pp. 28–32, 35, 110–12.

37. See below, pp. 332–38.

misericords. These features are discussed elsewhere in this book. Many other fine churches stood in Norwich – those of the friaries and some parish churches especially – but none could surpass the cathedral.

Religious Activities

When we speak here of 'religious activities' we should remember that for medieval people life was less compartmentalized: its religious and secular aspects were more integrated than they are for most of us today. Several topics that have already been mentioned, for example learning and charity, were inseparable from religion. For medieval people the subjects now to be discussed formed only a part of religious activity, on the whole what might be called its more spiritual and other-worldly dimensions: other aspects have been covered (however inadequately) by what has been said earlier.

A very influential role of the cathedral priory, at least potentially so, was the appointment of a large proportion of the parish priests of Norwich.[38] Approaching half of the fifty or so parish churches in the city were 'appropriated' to the priory, as mentioned earlier, and for these churches the priory had the right to appoint the priest in charge and probably any other priests who were attached to them. Many of the parishes in question were among the smaller ones in terms of population. Nevertheless for a large proportion of the inhabitants the priests who had the official 'care of souls' would have been appointed by the priory. Did the priory have any policy regarding the appointments and what were the effects upon the parishioners? In the present state of research these important questions remain largely unanswered. In most cases we do not know even the name of the priest in question, since most of them appear to have been appointed as 'untenured' parish chaplains or stipendiary priests: it is only the 'tenured' rectors and vicars whose appointments were recorded in the episcopal registers. Many of the benefices, moreover, were among the poorer ones in the city. It may well be that they did not attract the better, or at least the better educated, candidates. Could the priory have improved the situation? These are questions that merit further investigation.

Regarding the religious functions of the cathedral church itself, it is quite difficult to assess how medieval people envisaged the purpose of a cathedral. In Norwich, as in most cathedral cities, there were many other churches – those of parishes and friaries, and others – in which a wide range of religious activities took place. In a sense, therefore, the cathedral church was an 'added extra'. We should probably think first of the regular round of liturgical services, especially the eucharist and the hours (matins, lauds, vespers, etc.) of the divine office. In theory these services formed the 'heart and soul' of any cathedral and especially of those, such as Norwich,

---

38. For this paragraph see Tanner, *Church in Norwich*, pp. 173–78.

to which a monastic community was attached.[39] How many of the townspeople attended them is impossible to know and it may not have been regarded as an important matter anyway, especially in view of the abundance of other churches in the city: the important thing was that they were being performed by the monks. Preaching has been discussed by Barbara Dodwell.[40]

Norwich Cathedral was a pilgrimage centre of some importance, though never one of the first rank.[41] Our earliest evidence comes from the cult of St William, the twelve year-old apprentice to a skinner of Norwich who was alleged to have been crucified by Jews of the city during the Passover of 1144. His body, having been discovered in Thorpe Wood outside the city, was buried first in the cemetery of the priory and subsequently in several places in the cathedral, finally in 1154 in what is now the Jesus Chapel there (at least until 1436 when it may have been moved again). Our information comes almost exclusively from Thomas of Monmouth. He came to Norwich and became a monk of the cathedral priory shortly after the alleged martyrdom; subsequently he wrote an account of the life and miracles of William. To a considerable extent his account was a promotional exercise but it gives us some basis for assessing the cult. It suggests there was a fair amount of interest, especially within the city, in the years immediately after Thomas began to promote the boy's cult. In the peak years of 1150–51 two-thirds of pilgrims reporting miracles at his shrine were from Norwich. During the next two decades interest in him, especially among the inhabitants of the city, appears to have declined. Perhaps there was a healthy unease with a cult that easily gave scope to antisemitism and was based on tenuous credentials.

During the next hundred years there is a gap in the records regarding pilgrim shrines in the cathedral, no doubt partly due to the destruction of records in the attack on the priory in 1272. From that year until the Reformation the account rolls of the sacrist, recording inter alia offerings to a number of shrines and altars in the cathedral, survive for many years. Much the largest offerings were made 'to the high altar'. They totalled each year £20–£50 between the late thirteenth and the late fourteenth century, £55–£85 from the 1390s to the 1440s, except for a peak of about £120 for each of three successive years around 1400, when they were bolstered by a special indulgence probably connected with the Jubilee year of 1400, then declined in the 1450s and 1460s to around £20. They remained at this level until the decade or so before the dissolution of the priory, when they fell to about

39. See pp. 233–37.
40. See above, pp. 239, 246–47.
41. For pilgrimages see Thomas of Monmouth, *The Life and Miracles of William of Norwich*, ed. A. Jessopp and M. R. James (Cambridge,

1896), passim; J. R. Shinners, 'The Veneration of Saints at Norwich Cathedral in the Fourteenth Century', *NA*, 40 (1987–89), pp. 133–44; Tanner, *Church in Norwich*, pp. 88–90.

£5 a year. These are substantial sums.[42] Offerings to the shrine of St William lagged far behind. They rarely totalled more than £1 a year, though there was an exceptional year in 1386–87 when they amounted to nearly £20. This burst of generosity may well have been connected with the peltiers' guild, founded in 1376, which was dedicated to the saint and held various devotions in his honour. There were a number of other shrines in the cathedral as well as in the priory's cell of St Leonard in the suburbs of the city. All of them received significant sums of money for periods of time though none revealed a large-scale devotion: an image of St Leonard at the cell; and in the cathedral three shrines of St Mary, an image of St Sitha of Lucca, the tombs of two bishops of Norwich, Walter Suffield (1244–57) and John Salmon (1299–1325), a cross, an unspecified collection of relics, and various others.

Unfortunately the sacrists' account rolls provide no details about the number and provenance of donors – just the total amount of money given each year. We can only assume that a proportion of them were from Norwich. It is difficult, too, to estimate how far the particular shrines represented genuine popular devotion and how far, instead, they were promoted by the priory as potential sources of income. No doubt both factors usually entered in. What is clear is that there was a marked decline in the offerings over a long period before the dissolution of the priory. In this sense the cathedral anticipated the reaction against pilgrimages and the cult of saints that set in with the Reformation. On the part of the inhabitants of Norwich, however, there does not appear to have been any general decline in these kinds of devotion during the later period: it is just that they focused (mainly) on other churches and shrines in the city and outside it.[43] Whether this represented a turning-away from the cathedral on the part of the inhabitants depends on how many of the pilgrims and donors in the earlier period came from Norwich rather than from outside it. Regardless of where the pilgrims came from, we can say that in the earlier period, that is to say before about 1450, the cathedral had a significant role in the city as a centre of pilgrimage. It never acquired a saint of great popularity but it looks as though people came to the cathedral in substantial numbers. Margery Kempe, the devout burgess of Lynn, who came to Norwich to 'offer' at the cathedral before and after her journey to the Holy Land, was just one example.[44]

Guilds, both those of crafts and trades and those with various other affiliations, provided another opportunity for contacts between the townspeople and the cathedral

42. By way of comparison, the average annual wage of a building labourer in southern England in the fifteenth century amounted to about £5: E. H. P. Brown and S. V. Hoskins, 'Seven Centuries of Building Wages', in E. M. Carus-Wilson, ed., *Essays in Economic History*, 3 vols (London, 1954–62), ii, p. 177.

43. Tanner, *Church in Norwich*, pp. 83–87.

44. M. Kempe, *The Book of Margery Kempe*, ed. S. B. Meech and H. E. Allen (Early English Text Society, old series, 212, 1940), book i, chapters 26, 43, pp. 60 and 102.

and priory.[45] A good proportion of the ones known to us chose the cathedral for some of their religious activities. Most of the evidence comes from the later middle ages. An ordinance issued by the king in 1388 ordered all guilds in England to report their activities to the central government. Of the nineteen guilds (sometimes called 'confraternities' or 'mysteries') of Norwich that made returns, five said they held various of their religious activities in the cathedral, principally an annual mass. They were the peltiers' guild, mentioned earlier, the carpenters' guild and the guilds of the Holy Trinity, St George, and Holy Trinity and St Mary. All of them claimed to be relatively recent foundations, within the previous quarter of a century, and all of them except the last named survived into the sixteenth century (assuming the guild recorded later as the skinners' was the same as the peltiers'). We also know of a guild 'of the mass [of the name] of Jesus' held in the cathedral from the 1460s to the 1520s. The cathedral was also the place chosen by the city government for the various religious activities of the crafts and trades of the city. An ordinance of the city government in 1449 made the cathedral the destination of processions on the feasts of All Saints (1 November), Christmas (25 December) and Epiphany (6 January). On these feasts the guild members were to be ready to process in their livery to the cathedral, together with the mayor, sheriffs and aldermen, or to such other place as the mayor might direct. As late as 1543 the cathedral was assigned as the place for the annual guild-mass of at least nine crafts and trades.

St George's, the most famous guild in medieval Norwich and the best recorded, had close links with the cathedral. According to its return to the ordinance of 1388, it had been founded in 1385 as 'the fraternity of St George the martyr in the cathedral church . . . of Norwich'. It celebrated a mass in the cathedral on its annual 'guild day', the feast of St George (23 April). In 1417 it became the only guild in Norwich to acquire a royal charter; hence it claimed King Henry V as its founder. As the guild grew in size and prestige, its guild day became a grand occasion. By 1420 at the latest the mass in the cathedral was preceded by an elaborate procession through the city by the members of the guild and various notables, together with an accompanying pageant about the saint. A banquet followed the mass. After the meal and on the following morning, the members of the guild were supposed to return to the cathedral for further services, this time for their founder, benefactors and deceased members. Among its other activities the guild maintained a chantry priest in the cathedral to say mass and pray for the living and dead members and various other persons. The pre-eminence of the guild was sealed in 1452 when it was, in effect, united to the city government. Its known membership totalled at

45. For guilds see M. Grace, ed., *Records of the Gild of St George in Norwich, 1389–1547* (NRS, 9, 1937), pp. 6–27; McRee, 'Religious Gilds', pp. 74–97; Tanner, *Church in Norwich*, pp. 68–71, 74, 78–81, 205–6, 208, 212.

times over 200 persons, including some women. Among them we know of two priors of the cathedral priory, John Mollet (1454–71) and Robert Catton (1504–29).

An unusually large number of hermits and anchorites lived in medieval Norwich; some fifty being identifiable from the earliest in 1250 to the last in the 1540s. The cathedral priory played a small role in supporting them. It gave some form of patronage to a hermitage at Bishopsgate, which lay at the edge of the monastic precincts. It was the patron or appropriator of the church of several parishes in which other hermits and anchorites lived, but in these cases, with the possible exception of a hermitage in St Mary at Newbridge parish, there is no evidence of direct support or formal patronage.[46]

Perpetual chantries – the saying (or sometimes 'chanting') of a mass and other prayers by a priest, daily in perpetuity, for the souls of various persons – were a characteristic feature of late medieval religion throughout western Christendom. Cathedrals were a natural location for them. Norwich Cathedral had a good number of them but only two, belonging to guilds, had links with the townspeople (other than bishops of Norwich). They were the chantry of St George's guild and the 'mass of the name of Jesus' maintained by the chantry of that name (in the second case the mass may have been said only once a week). Most of the other founders were members of prominent East Anglian families or bishops of Norwich. Wealthy citizens founded a fair number of perpetual chantries in the city but they chose to locate them in other institutions: the friaries or parish churches or colleges of secular priests. Their preference for these places is noticeable. They may have felt that such institutions needed the money given for the chantry services more than the relatively wealthy cathedral priory. There is some evidence to suggest, moreover, that the priory at times was remiss in maintaining the chantries entrusted to it. Sharp-eyed citizens may have been more discerning than status-conscious county families and bishops.[47]

Burial and the Evidence of Wills

Wills provide another insight into relations between the people of Norwich and the cathedral priory.[48] They survive in large numbers from 1370 onwards. Between that year and 1532, the beginning of the English Reformation, over 1500 wills of

46. R. Clay, *The Hermits and Anchorites of England* (London, 1914), p. 235; Blomefield, *Norfolk*, iv, pp. 402, 474; Tanner, *Church in Norwich*, pp. 58–59, 173–78, 198–202; NRO, DCN 1/11/3, 16 and 18.

47. Tanner, *Church in Norwich*, pp. 92–98, 107. The chantry probably established by William Bauchun (of Norwich?) appears not to have been a perpetual one: B. Dodwell, 'William Bauchun and his Connection with the Cathedral Priory at Norwich', *NA*, 36 (1975), pp. 113–16.

48. For this section see, except where other references are given, Tanner, *Church in Norwich*, pp. 12–13, 114–17, 120–21, 126, 189, 222.

the laity of the city survive, men outnumbering women by slightly more than three to one, and approaching 300 of the clergy (all of the secular clergy). There are various difficulties in interpreting this evidence. The lay people in question came disproportionately from the wealthier ranks of the community. It is difficult, too, to assess how far custom and other factors limited the testator's freedom of action as well as the extent to which possible beneficiaries and the phraseology of the will were suggested to the testator by the scribe or other professional person who wrote down the will. Despite these limitations, testators enjoyed a considerable measure of freedom and the choices made by those from Norwich are revealing of their attitude towards the cathedral priory.

One choice regarded the place of burial. The large majority of the laity chose to be buried in a parish church or its cemetery. Of the approximately 10 per cent who preferred a religious house, most asked to be buried in the church or cemetery of one of the four friaries in the city. Altogether only six lay people – less than a half per cent of the total – asked to be buried in the cathedral church or its cemetery. This small number may represent awe of or distance from the cathedral priory rather than hostility to it, but it is significant none the less. Most of the six were prominent citizens who left substantial bequests to the priory. John de Berney, who made his will in 1374, is a good example. He was a very wealthy merchant who had been a member of parliament for the city and was probably steward of the priory in his later years.[49] He left over £10 to the cathedral and the monks of the priory, yet even he feared that his request for burial might be refused. He asked to be buried in the cathedral church, in St Anne's Chapel, where one of his wives already lay buried, if the prior and monks would allow it: if not, he wanted to be buried in the parish church of Burgh. In fact his wish was granted. Of the clerical testators, however, almost 5 per cent asked to be buried in the cathedral or its cemetery.

Evidence other than wills also suggests that relatively few of the laity of the city chose the cathedral for burial. In the late middle ages, however, the bones of rather more of them – we do not know how many – are likely to have found their final resting-place close to the cathedral: in the Carnary, founded by Bishop Salmon in 1316 as a place for storing 'the bones of persons buried in the city of Norwich', which lay within the precincts of the cathedral priory as well as being under its patronage.[50]

Many more testators left bequests to the cathedral priory than looked to it for burial. Just over a third of the laity left a bequest to the cathedral church or to the priory. This figure, however, is still below those for the four friaries, to each of

49. Dodwell, 'William Bauchun', p. 112.
50. Blomefield, *Norfolk*, iv, pp. 6–46; H. W. Saunders, *A History of the Norwich Grammar*   *School* (Norwich, 1932), pp. 3–17, 43–48; Fernie, *NC*, pp. 181–82.

which almost half of the laity left something, and it compares with 95 per cent who gave to one or more parish churches. Bequests to the cathedral priory differed from those to the friaries in that the majority of the former were left to the cathedral church rather than to the priory, whereas the latter were almost invariably left to the friaries or individual friars rather than to their churches. The distinction may seem insignificant since bequests to the cathedral church went to, or were administered by, the priory. But the wills give the impression that it was primarily the church – often referred to as 'my mother church' – rather than the monks that the testators wanted to support. Most bequests were within the range of 3s. 4d. (quarter of a mark) to £1, though a fair number after around 1490 were smaller sums, sometimes only a few pennies. Large bequests, such as John Berney's, were rare. It seems likely that, once again, the relatively wealthy priory was felt to be less in need of bequests than the friaries and parish churches of the city. Around the middle of the fifteenth century, however, the proportion of testators giving to the cathedral priory doubled, from below a quarter to almost half. Much of the increase was accounted for by small bequests, many of which may have been little more than conventional gestures inserted at the suggestion of the scribe of the will. Nevertheless the rise may reflect the better relations that appear to have existed between the citizens and the priory after about 1450. Among clerical testators, the proportion giving to the priory was somewhat higher than among the laity.

How do we conclude this long and complex story? Attitudes towards the cathedral and priory among so many people, during the course of almost four and a half centuries, must have varied widely. We are limited in our answers, of course, by the evidence that happens to survive. There is plenty of room, moreover, for further research into various topics, some of which have already been indicated. We would like to know more about the attitude of the townspeople towards the priory in the 1530s, the decade in which it was dissolved.[51]

Nevertheless there appears to have been much continuity in the general situation. In terms of the long-standing conflict between the two parties, the only major change occurred after about 1450, when the city gradually gained the upper hand in its relationship with the priory. The central question is the familiar one facing students of the middle ages: how did people regard large and wealthy religious institutions in their midst? It is a difficult question and we must be careful not to project our own value-judgements back into that age. On the one hand, there existed the considerable tension outlined in the first half of the chapter. There was, too, a

---

51. For some information see McClendon, 'The Quiet Reformation', pp. 48, 155.

continuous tradition throughout medieval Christendom of criticism of excessive ecclesiastical wealth and outward display. For this criticism we need to look no further than Francis of Assisi or Chaucer or Langland. On the other hand, cathedrals and monasteries stood for values that were respected. Most people, moreover, recognised that wealth and outward splendour could be used for God's glory and the service of others, not just for personal aggrandisement. We have seen that the cathedral priory performed a wide range of religious, social, economic, charitable and educational roles in Norwich. Cathedral and priory together formed quite an outward-looking institution, one that was active in the city. Much of this activity seems to have been appreciated and supported, often indeed initiated, by the inhabitants. The cathedral priory may not have been as close to the people as the parish churches, friaries and some other religious institutions. It probably never enjoyed much immediate popularity in the ordinary sense of the word. People, however, expected different roles for various religious institutions: some were expected to be more formal than others. Outward appearances suggest that the cathedral and priory formed the most important religious institution in medieval Norwich and that it made a major contribution to Norwich's position as an unusually religious city,[52] as well as to many other aspects of the city's fame.

52. Tanner, *Church in Norwich*, pp. 167–71.

14

The Medieval Church
and the Wider World

Christopher Harper-Bill

The Cathedral Priory and the Bishop: Mutual Support, 1096–1175

The actions of Bishop Herbert de Losinga (1091–1119) in transferring the see of the bishops of East Anglia to Norwich and founding a new cathedral church, staffed by a community of Benedictine monks rather than by secular prebendaries, were in accordance with the programme of the Norman hierarchy which sought to reform the Old English Church, of which the organisation and practices were, to their eyes, lax and outmoded. The Council of London of 1075, with the approval of William the Conqueror, had authorized the transfer or relocation of the bishoprics of Lichfield, Selsey and Sherborne to Chester, Chichester and Old Sarum, and decreed that other transfers from small towns to cities should await the approval of the king, currently campaigning on the continent.[1] It is interesting that in the strictly contemporary list of those present at this council Bishop Herfast (1070–84), who had moved the East Anglian see from North Elmham to Thetford in the early 1070s, is described as bishop of Norwich.[2] This is perhaps an indication of intent, although Herfast was simultaneously engaged on a campaign to annex to the bishopric the abbey of Bury St Edmunds, which was only ended in 1081 by a royal judgement in favour of the abbey's independence. Indeed, after Herfast's death the Conqueror

1. D. Whitelock, M. Brett and C. N. L. Brooke, eds, *Councils and Synods, with Other Documents relating to the English Church*, i, *AD 871–1204*, 2 vols (Oxford, 1981), ii, p. 613. This chapter could not have been written without the painstaking editorial work on the cathedral priory's charters up to *c.* 1300 accomplished by Miss Barbara Dod-

well. I am extremely grateful to Dr Ian Atherton for his searches in the calendars of late medieval governmental records and to Professor Hassell Smith for much constructive criticism.

2. Whitelock, Brett and Brooke, *Councils and Synods*, ii, p. 615.

reputedly tried to persuade Abbot Baldwin of Bury to accept the bishopric and move the see there.[3]

The monastic cathedral was a uniquely English institution, the product of the dynamic leadership of the tenth-century reform movement by St Dunstan and other distinguished religious. The primatial church of Canterbury, and also those of Winchester and Worcester, were monastic communities. The Norman bishops, who had witnessed the impetus given to religious revival in Normandy by the Benedictines, for once approved of what they found: monks were installed at Rochester in 1080 and at Durham in 1083, while in 1090 the see of Wells was moved to the abbey of Bath.[4] It was therefore perfectly natural that Bishop Herbert, himself a monk, should wish to have a Benedictine cathedral chapter when he established a new mother church for his diocese.

There is no reason to believe the tradition that Herbert de Losinga founded Norwich Cathedral as spectacular atonement for his sin of simony in buying the East Anglian see from William Rufus, or that the task was imposed upon him by Pope Urban II as a penance after his repentance and offer of resignation.[5] His actions were entirely in accord with royal and ecclesiastical policy and in tune with the religious spirit of an age dominated by the monastic tradition. A monk himself, raised from Fécamp in Normandy to the abbacy of Ramsey, Herbert would certainly have envisaged his fellow-monks at Norwich as partners, albeit unequal ones, in the governance of his diocese. Primarily, of course, the cathedral was to be a spiritual centre, a model for the liturgical life of the diocese, dedicated to the Holy Trinity rather than to any mere saint, into which the bishop introduced the rites of the monastery of his own profession. The prior and convent were also to be fellow trustees of the estates of the church. Their ratification was required for many of the bishop's acts and, under the founder and his two immediate successors, they provided assistance in diocesan administration, not least in providing a writing-office and episcopal chaplains and clerks.[6]

They were also given a role in Losinga's attempts to emphasise the authority of his church. It has been said of him that 'through a policy which one can only call "episcopal imperialism" he firmly imprinted the stamp of his authority through county and diocese'.[7] The latter was large, comprising the two prosperous counties

3. V. H. Galbraith, 'The East Anglian See and the Abbey of Bury St Edmunds', *EHR*, 40 (1925), pp. 222–8; B. Dodwell, 'The Foundation of Norwich Cathedral', *TRHS*, 5th series, 7 (1957), pp 1–18, at pp. 2–3.

4. M. D. Knowles, *The Monastic Order in England* (Cambridge, 1940), pp. 129–34.

5. For Herbert's career, see above, pp. 22–35, and especially the full study by J. W. Alexander, 'Herbert of Norwich, 1091–119:

Studies in the History of Norman England', *Studies in Medieval and Renaissance History*, 6 (1969), pp. 115–232.

6. *EEA*, vi, pp. xliii–xliv.

7. N. Batcock, 'The Parish Church in Norfolk in the Eleventh and Twelfth Centuries', in J. Blair, ed., *Minsters and Parish Churches: The Local Church in Transition, 950–1200* (Oxford University Committee for Archaeology, Monograph no. 17, 1988), p. 188.

of Norfolk and Suffolk, and also a group of parishes in the half-hundred of Exning in Cambridgeshire. The establishment of village churches, which is one of the main features of the history of the English church in the period between the late tenth and the late twelfth centuries, proceeded more swiftly here than in some other regions. The listing of Suffolk churches in Domesday Book is unusually full, and estimates of those recorded here vary from 364 to 422; for Norfolk the information is less comprehensive, but churches are listed in connection with 217 villages, and there were almost certainly many more. At the end of the thirteenth century the *Taxatio ecclesiastica* of 1291 lists 1165 parishes in the diocese, although it has been suggested that this is a severe underestimate and that the true total was in fact 1349.[8] In common with other Norman bishops, Herbert appointed archdeacons to assist him in the administration of this extensive diocese and to act as his agents for the enforcement of good discipline; there were certainly two such officers by 1107 and three by his death in 1119.[9]

He also worked through his convent to imprint the stamp of his authority by establishing four dependent cells. St Leonard's was just across the river from the cathedral. The house at Yarmouth, whose rights against the local inhabitants were staunchly defended, later provided a recreational centre for the Norwich community. Another cell, founded at Lynn, participated in the growing prosperity of that flourishing port. When Aldeby church was given to the cathedral priory, Herbert established a priory cell there too. Some years after his death a fifth dependent priory was founded at Hoxne, where the church had originally been given to the monks by their founder.[10] Most later bishops were rather less confident of the identity of episcopal and monastic interests.

In the next few years the bishop allocated to the monks substantial estates both on the outskirts of Norwich and further afield in the diocese. A clear division was made, as was the practice in other monastic cathedrals, between the estates of the bishop and those of the chapter, so as to minimise royal interference and profiteering during vacancies of the see, and also to eliminate tension between diocesan and convent, which in the long term proved inevitably to be a forlorn hope.[11] Many of Herbert de Losinga's letters, of which a remarkable collection survives, testify to

8. For these figures, see R. V. Lennard, *Rural England, 1066–1135* (Oxford, 1959), p. 288; H. C. Darby, *The Domesday Geography of Eastern England* (3rd edn, Cambridge, 1971), pp. 138, 190–92; W. Hudson, 'The "Norwich Taxation" so far as it relates to the Diocese of Norwich', *NA*, 17 (1910), pp. 69–70.

9. *EEA*, vi, pp. xxvi–xxvii, xxxix–xliii.

10. Knowles and Hadcock, *Medieval Religious Houses*, pp. 58, 68, 72, 82; for Lynn, see D. M. Owen, 'Bishop's Lynn: The First Century of a New Town?', in R. A. Brown, ed., *Proceedings of the Battle Conference on Anglo-Norman Studies, ii, 1979* (Woodbridge, 1980), pp. 141–53.

11. For Bishop Herbert's charters for the cathedral priory, see *NCC*, i, nos 106–15; *EEA*, vi, nos 11–18; for the division of property, see *First Register*, pp. 24–25.

his concern both for the welfare and for the good discipline of his community.[12] His rule over the convent was genuinely that of the abbot as delineated in the Rule of St Benedict; in this relationship few of his successors, by reason of their provenance and appointment, were able to emulate him.

In his foundation of the new cathedral, Bishop Herbert was careful to obtain the support of both king and pope, in which at a time of conflict between royal power and papal authority, he was remarkably successful. The implementation of the project was achieved soon after the reconciliation between Herbert and William Rufus following the bishop's unauthorised visit to Pope Urban II, not yet recognised by the king, to confess his sin of simony. In 1094–95 Rufus restored the confiscated lands of the bishopric, releasing Herbert and all his men from actions brought against them by his notorious agent, Ranulf Flambard.[13] Among the properties restored were the church of Holy Trinity. The *First Register* records that the bishop at great expense also acquired from Rufus land around that church.[14] The high price demanded may be characteristic of the king's ecclesiastical policy, although it should be noted that Rufus made notable benefactions of East Anglian churches to his own favourite monastery of Battle.[15]

The earliest dealings of Henry I with the new cathedral church are a reflection of his desire to win support for his regime by renouncing the exactions practised by his brother, as much as of Losinga's desire to gain royal support for the priory. It was probably at Christmas 1100 that he remitted the twenty-five shillings annual rent retained by Rufus when he gave the land at Norwich and also restored, for a price, the estate at Eccles which Ranulf Flambard had held, probably by coercion, of the bishop. Henry I, throughout his reign, confirmed various grants made by his subjects to the church and also conceded the exemption of certain estates from royal exactions. His own major gift was the manor of Thorpe by Norwich which, according to one of Herbert's letters, was donated specifically to finance the building of the church.[16] It was on this occasion, at a great royal council at Windsor on 3 September 1101, that Bishop Herbert issued, in the presence of an august company of witnesses, his most solemn charter recording his foundation and its endowment.[17] The king subsequently granted further royal land at Norwich and, of equal

---

12. For an English translation of his literary remains, see GS.
13. *NCC*, i, no. 69; for Flambard's ecclesiastical exactions, see R. W. Southern, 'Ranulf Flambard', in his *Medieval Humanism and Other Studies* (Oxford, 1970), pp. 183–205.
14. *DB Norfolk*, fo. 116v; *First Register*, pp. 24–25.
15. E. Searle, ed., *The Chronicle of Battle Abbey* (Oxford, 1980), pp. 98–99.
16. For Henry I's charters and writs in favour of the cathedral priory, see *NCC*, i, nos 3–22, 70–78.
17. *NCC*, i, no. 113; *EEA*, vi, no. 12; *First Register*, pp. 38–40.

importance, extended the monks' Whitsun fair to ten days and granted them the right to three-day fairs at Lynn and Hoxne.[18]

As to Losinga's success in harnessing support from the papacy, the earliest papal document in the Norwich archives is a bull of Pope Paschal II, issued on 28 April 1102, when Herbert was in Rome.[19] This confirmed the founder's own intentions: that a community of monks should forever be established in the church of Norwich; and that none of the bishop's successors should eject them or infringe the rights and possessions granted to them by King Henry I and others of the faithful.

Losinga's successors, Eborard of Calne and William Turbe, continued this close relationship between bishop and priory. Eborard of Calne, appointed second bishop of Norwich in 1121, was a royal chaplain who fathered children and was surrounded by a multitude of nephews while bishop.[20] Yet despite the hostility of many of the secular clergy to the Benedictines in the early twelfth century, he appears to have enjoyed a good relationship with his monks. He supervised the completion of the cathedral, confirmed to the convent two-thirds of the levy from the churches of the diocese, known as *caritas*, which the founder had granted to it for the building fund, and he responded favourably to their petition against the heavy exactions of his own officials.

During his episcopate further papal privileges were obtained for the priory. In 1126 Honorius II confirmed that Norwich should be the mother church of the diocese of Norfolk and Suffolk; in 1142 Innocent II confirmed to the monks offerings made at the cathedral priory's dependent churches; and between 1150 and 1153 Eugenius III ratified two specific grants of land.[21] Such papal confirmations are entirely typical of the increasing contact between England and Rome in the first half of the twelfth century, which was not impeded by the king unless royal interests were threatened, and of the desire of ecclesiastical corporations across western Europe for apostolic ratification of their rights and possessions.[22]

---

18. After Henry I's death little more was to come to the monks by way of royal donation. Stephen, Henry II and John all issued confirmation charters in the early years of their reigns (*NCC*, i, nos 23, 35–36). Stephen granted the churches of Bracon Ash and St Sepulchre, Norwich, which had been held by Richard de Bellofago before his promotion to the bishopric of Avranches, and also conceded free customs in their land at Yarmouth. (*NCC*, i, nos 24–25). Henry II issued several confirmations of various estates, but himself gave only the church of Witton, on the condition that it was granted by the monks to one of his royal clerks. More importantly, perhaps, he conceded that the prior and convent might not be brought to court except before the king himself or his justiciar (*NCC*, i, nos 26–34, 79).

19. *NCC*, i, no. 274.
20. For a summary of his career, see *EEA*, vi, pp. xxxi–xxxiii.
21. *NCC*, i, nos 275–77.
22. For the context, see M. Brett, *The Church under Henry I* (Oxford, 1975), pp. 34–62.

Despite his reluctance to support the nascent cult of St William (allegedly the victim of ritual murder by the Jews just outside Norwich in the 1140s),[23] and despite his alienation of two estates, the communal memory of the monks recorded that Eborard had shown them much affection.

William Turbe, a protégé of the founder, had been prior at Norwich before his election as bishop and after his elevation he maintained a close relationship with his cathedral chapter.[24] In the early years of his episcopate monks frequently attested his charters. At a moment of crisis during the Becket conflict he retired for safety to the cloister, and when the cathedral was damaged by fire in 1171 he devoted himself, although now a very old man, to its repair and is reputed to have sat at the door personally collecting alms. He issued the already customary episcopal confirmation of all the possessions of the prior and convent, to which he made modest additions, but he showed particular concern for the cell at Lynn, to which he made significant benefactions.

Turbe endeavoured to extend even further the close relationship between bishop and priory. In 1155 he obtained additional privileges for the cathedral priory from the English pope, Adrian IV.[25] Adrian confirmed the bulls of previous popes and commanded that the churches of Bury St Edmunds should answer to the bishop for the cure of souls, thus establishing that the immunity secured by the cathedral's great rival should not extend to spiritual autonomy within its annexed parishes. Moreover, he decreed that the prior and convent of Norwich should have the right to elect their own bishop. Turbe had himself been freely elected during the vacuum of royal authority during Stephen's reign, in contrast to the first two bishops of Norwich, who were clearly royal nominees. This papal privilege was seldom to be observed in the future. Shortly after Turbe's death, Pope Alexander III ordered that parish churches within the diocese in the gift of the great abbeys of Ramsey and St Albans and of Cluniac monasteries should also be subject to the mother church of Norwich, thus ensuring the integrity of the diocese in the face of monastic claims to exemption. A further bull of Alexander III, granted to Bishop John of Oxford (1175–1200) while he was attending the Third Lateran Council of

23. For the cult of St William, see Thomas of Monmouth, *The Life and Miracles of St William of Norwich*, ed. A. Jessopp and M. R. James (Cambridge, 1896); discussion by R. C. Finucane, *Miracles and Pilgrims: Popular Beliefs in Medieval England* (London, 1977), pp. 118–21, 161–62; and B. Ward, *Miracles and the Medieval Mind* (rev. edn, Aldershot, 1987), pp. 68–76.

24. C. Harper-Bill, 'Bishop William Turbe and the Diocese of Norwich, 1146–74', in R. A. Brown, ed., *Anglo-Norman Studies*, 7 (Woodbridge, 1985), pp. 142–60. There is, however, some evidence of factionalism within the community. Certain monks physically assaulted the prior appointed by the bishop with the specific intention of effecting reform. The malefactors were excommunicated.

25. *NCC*, i, no. 278; see also no. 279.

1179, confirmed episcopal rights in all churches of the diocese, of which the boundaries were fixed by papal decree at the extent at which they were to remain until the Reformation.[26]

By the end of the twelfth century this intimate relationship between bishop and priory had begun to break down and the concept of bishop/abbot to fade. Probably it had never been as clearly articulated as the above account suggests and the seeds of discontent between bishop and priory had been sown by Losinga himself when he established separate estates for bishop and convent. But the factor which most affected this relationship was the interests of crown and papacy in the affairs of the convent and the election of bishops.

The Cathedral Priory and the Bishop: Episcopal Appointment, 1175–1538

The transfer of the site of the mother church of the shires of Norfolk and Suffolk had of necessity involved negotiation with the papacy and the English crown. It was impossible, at the turn of the eleventh and twelfth centuries, to ignore either the authority of the vicar of St Peter, which recent popes had transformed from a vague aspiration into an ever more intrusive reality, or the practical power of the Anglo-Norman monarchy, whose servants were fashioning methods of interventionist bureaucratic government which were to become a model for other western European states. From the foundation of the cathedral priory, papal and royal interests were to play a key role in its relationship with the bishop. The potential for conflict between pope and king was most evident when there was the need to select a new bishop. Since the conversion of the new barbarian kingdoms of western Europe to Catholic Christianity between the sixth and eighth centuries, tribal rulers had expected to appoint the leaders of the church within their dominions. The assertion by Pope Gregory VII (1073–85) and his circle that the church at all levels should be free from secular domination, and that bishops and abbots should be canonically elected by those clergy over whom they were to preside, was quite revolutionary; it was fiercely resisted by kings across the continent. In 1106 a compromise was reached in the Anglo-Norman realm, whereby Henry I conceded free election of prelates but retained the right to homage for the lands of bishoprics and monasteries. An election free in theory might, however, be something very different in practice, since no king could afford in reality to sacrifice control over the composition of the episcopate. It would therefore have been a brave cathedral chapter prepared to

---

26. *NCC*, i, nos 281–83.

defy the will of Henry I or Henry II when required to elect their new pastor in the royal presence.

After the election of William Turbe by the priory, for the remainder of the middle ages, here as in other sees, it was normally the will of the king and the English government, albeit occasionally mitigated by papal initiative, which was the vital factor in the making of a bishop. After Turbe's death a delegation of Norwich monks was summoned in 1175 by Henry II to Woodstock to 'elect' a bishop in his presence. The successful candidate was John of Oxford, royal servant and diplomat, who had masterminded the king's propaganda campaign against Thomas Becket.[27] In 1200 the royal nominee was John de Gray (1200–14), King John's most trusted servant: the monks on whom he was imposed could have had little idea then that he would turn out to be one of their most beneficent pastors.[28]

After King John's submission to Pope Innocent III in 1213, and after the accession of Henry III who, when he grew to manhood, was inclined both by personal piety and by political expediency to be the most pro-papal of English kings, the influence of Rome on episcopal appointments was at its high point. Yet even now royal interests were not neglected. Pandulf (1215–26), the papal chamberlain, elected to Norwich in 1215 while serving as Innocent's envoy to King John, acted subsequently as papal legate, but he was also one of the most active and influential members of the regency government during the minority of Henry III.[29] Of five bishops of Norwich appointed during Henry's reign (1216–72), three were men who had risen to eminence through royal service, as king's clerks or justices. In 1236 the monks elected as bishop their own prior, Simon of Elmham, but the crown appealed to Rome and, after investigation by the legate Otto, the election was quashed in June 1239. The convent was then coerced into accepting the appointment of the royal judge, William Raleigh (1239–43). When four years later he was translated, against the king's will, to Winchester, the convent proceeded to the election of Walter Suffield (1244–57), who was a local man but was also, as a distinguished theologian in the university of Paris, exactly the type of candidate favoured by the papacy for elevation to the episcopate. It is rather surprising that the three bishops appointed in the reign of Edward I (1272–1307), a king notoriously assertive of royal rights, were all 'ecclesiastical candidates' rather than civil servants: William Middleton (1278–88) had been Official of the court of Canterbury; Ralph Walpole (1288–99) was a theologian who supported Archbishop Winchelsey in his conflict with the king over royal taxation of the church; and John Salmon (1299–1325) was the Benedictine

---

27. *EEA*, vi, p. xxxv, and references there given.
28. *EEA*, vi, p. xxxvii, and references there given.

29. For the identification and appointment, see N. Vincent, 'The Election of Pandulph Verracio as Bishop of Norwich, 1215', *Historical Research*, 68 (1995), pp. 143–63.

Fig. 117. Herbert's foundation charter, a copy made in the late twelfth or early thirteenth century (BL, Cotton MS Augustus II, fo. 103).

prior of Ely.[30] In the thirteenth century, therefore, the influence of crown and papacy appears evenly balanced, but the interests of the convent (even if it was normally supine) were not entirely disregarded.

In the next century, papal intervention was rather more pronounced than in many other dioceses.[31] In 1325 King Edward II engineered the election of his chancellor, Robert Baldock, but he failed to obtain the bishopric because the royal emissary to the pope at Avignon, William Ayremynne, also a king's clerk, persuaded the pope to appoint him to Norwich. On Ayremynne's death in 1336 the convent again elected one of their number, Thomas of Hempnall, but the election was quashed because the pope had reserved the see to himself and appointed Anthony Bek, a member of an ecclesiastical dynasty whose fortunes were built on service to the crown. In 1343 the convent's election was again invalidated because the pope appointed William Bateman, a distinguished papal diplomat whose elevation was in fact welcome to the convent, because he was a local man, and to the king (although he objected to its manner), because he knew him well as the pope's ambassador. In 1355 Thomas Percy was appointed by the pope, although he was not yet twenty-three years old, at the express wish of Henry, earl of Lancaster, one of Edward III's most trusted lieutenants. Percy's successor, Henry Despenser, likewise a member of an English noble family, came to the notice of the pope through his military activities in Italy (in which he displayed a propensity for belligerence he was later to indulge in his suppression of the peasants' rising and in a 'crusade' to Flanders); he was consecrated at Rome in 1370.

In the opening years of the fifteenth century the convent's election was for once upheld by the pope in the face of royal opposition. Alexander Tottington (1406–13), the former prior, was imprisoned by Henry IV after his election in September 1406, but was appointed by the pope in January 1407. A final example of papal intervention occurred in 1445–46, when Henry VI's nominee for the see, his Carmelite confessor John Stanbury, was rejected by the pope in favour of Walter Lyhart (1446–72), the nominee of the earl of Suffolk; Stanbury was, however, subsequently appointed by the pope to Hereford.

Thus, throughout its existence, despite Pope Adrian IV's privilege of free election,

---

30. For thirteenth-century appointments and references thereto, see J. Le Neve, *Fasti ecclesiae Anglicanae, 1066–1300*, ii, *Monastic Cathedrals* ed. D. E. Greenway (London, 1971), pp. 56–58; also M. Gibbs and J. Lang, *Bishops and Reform, 1215–72* (Oxford, 1934), app. C.

31. For fourteenth- and fifteenth-century appointments, see John Le Neve, *Fasti ecclesiae Anglicanae, 1300–1540*, iv, *Monastic Cathedrals* ed. B. Jones (London, 1963), pp. 23–25. For brief biographies, see *DNB, sub nomine*, and for those who were graduates, A. B. Emden, *Biographical Register of the University of Oxford to AD 1500*, 3 vols (Oxford, 1957–59); and *Biographical Register of the University of Cambridge to AD 1500* (Cambridge, 1963).

the convent only very occasionally obtained its way. Yet although only two bishops in the two centuries before the Reformation were themselves monks, many of those imposed upon the community proved to be perfectly acceptable. Papal influence appears to have been more effective than in some other sees yet, even when a royal nomination was unsuccessful, no candidate was imposed by the pope who was unacceptable to the English government. Normally the royal will was the decisive factor. The only two non-graduates in this later period (apart from the monk Tottington) were the royal clerks William Ayremynne (1325–36) and John Wakering (1415–25). Bishops Thomas Percy, Henry Despenser and Richard Courtenay (1413–15) were all scions of noble families in the court circle and had no connection with East Anglia. In the fifteenth century, Bishop William Alnwick (1426–36) had been keeper of the privy seal; James Goldwell (1471–99) the king's secretary; Thomas Jane (1499–1500) dean of the chapel royal; and Richard Nix (1501–35/36) registrar of the Order of the Garter. Even Thomas Brouns (1436–45), although a professional canon lawyer, was also an experienced royal diplomat.

The Cathedral Priory and the Bishop: Discord, 1175–1538

The episcopate of John of Oxford (1175–1200) witnessed a period of bitter conflict between convent and bishop.[32] Bartholomew Cotton, writing a century later, remembered John in his *Chronicle* as the bishop who finally completed Herbert de Losinga's church and the conventual buildings, but from contemporary records it appears that a more accurate picture is given in the *First Register*: 'on account of divers injuries and burdens which he caused to the convent of Norwich a discord arose between him and the convent in 1183, which continued throughout his whole episcopate'.[33] The main complaint detailed in this source was of the financial losses which John of Oxford caused the monks. Although it is not absolutely clear what the cathedral priory was forced to sacrifice, the *First Register* states that he remitted to all the diocese the financial aid which Bishop Herbert had imposed on every property for the building of the cathedral, and abolished too that custom of the church of Norwich known as the 'Paschal Custom', also due to the monks. Whatever the precise details, it is certain that the monks lost major sources of revenue and that the bishop gave them little in compensation. His only substantial concession was the annexation of the revenues of the churches of Ormesby to the cathedral's dependent hospital of St Paul.[34]

---

32. For what follows, see C. Harper-Bill, 'John of Oxford, Diplomat and Bishop', in M. Franklin and C. Harper-Bill, eds, *Medieval Ecclesiastical Studies in Honour of D. M. Owen* (Woodbridge, 1995), pp. 83–105.

33. H. R. Luard, ed., *Bartholomei de Cotton historia Anglicana* (RS, 1859), p. 393; *First Register*, pp. 82–83.

34. NCC, i, no. 259 (ii); *EEA*, vi, no. 269.

Another issue of conflict was the right of presentation of clergy to the parish churches of which Norwich Cathedral held the patronage. This was a perennial problem for the bishops of monastic cathedrals, who lacked the lucrative prebends with which the bishops of Lincoln, London or Salisbury could reward their own clerks. A few years later, in 1220, Pope Honorius III recognised the problem, granting the bishop-elect of Norwich an indult or licence to appoint his clerks to more than one benefice, because those in his gift were few and of little value.[35] One dispute of which details survive concerned the church of Martham, to which Bishop John unilaterally instituted Geoffrey, the dean of the city of Norwich. The monks' complaint that he should not act in such matters without their consent was heard by Archbishop Hubert Walter between July 1197 and June 1198.[36] The immediate result was that Geoffrey resigned his church and was readmitted at the presentation of the prior and convent. In the wider context, it was agreed that the bishop would grant those churches in the cathedral's gift only with the advice and consent of the monks. Excepted from this arrangement were the churches of the episcopal manors, of which the bishop was to have sole disposal, and those churches whose revenues were received in whole by the convent, where the monks might choose suitable vicars. An agreement reached under John of Oxford's successor, however, suggests that this settlement was far from conclusive and that presentation to churches remained a matter of contention.[37]

The issues at stake were, however, wider than patronage or specific revenues. A bull of Pope Celestine III, dated 29 October 1194, states that he had heard (obviously from the monks' appeal to Rome) that the bishop had deprived the convent of its possessions, had ejected certain learned brethren who had opposed him on the community's behalf and had forbidden appeal to superior authority against the enormities he had committed.[38] The pope granted them an indult that the monks might freely come to his court or any other to defend their case. He also forbade the bishop to confiscate the priory's possessions, to expel any brother or to pronounce sentence of excommunication or interdict against them without manifest and reasonable cause.[39] This was far from the end of the matter. A mandate of Pope Innocent III to Bishop John of Oxford, dispatched around 30 March 1200 and again certainly elicited by the monks, reflects their fear of episcopal aggression in other areas.[40] The bishop was forbidden to force the prior and convent to receive into

35. *CPL, 1198–1304*, p. 71.
36. *NCC*, i, nos 263–64; *EEA*, vi, nos 558–59.
37. *NCC*, i, nos 177–78; *EEA*, vi, nos 390–91.
38. *NCC*, i, no. 285.
39. This, just like the previous privileges of Popes Alexander III and Lucius III that no judicial sentence was to be promulgated against the convent without just cause (*NCC*, i, nos 283–84), was sufficiently vague to allow endless obfuscation in any dispute with diocesan or metropolitan.

40. C. R. and M. G. Cheney, eds, *The Letters of Pope Innocent III (1198–1216) concerning England and Wales* (Oxford, 1967), nos 205–6.

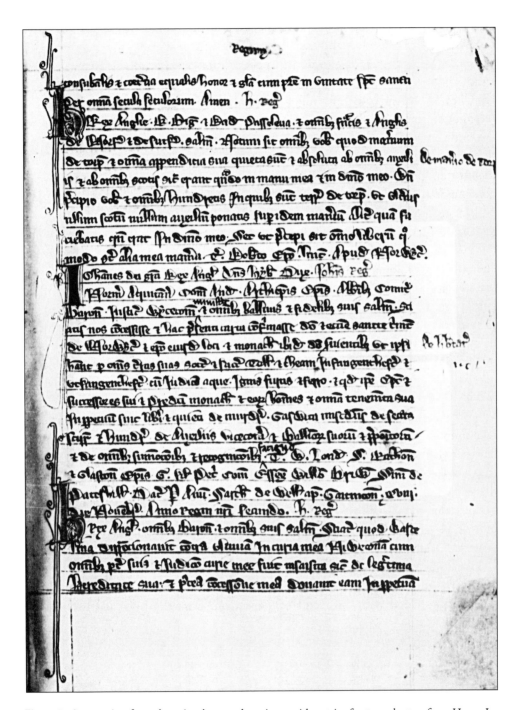

Fig. 118. An opening from the priory's seventh register, with entries for two charters from Henry I and one from King John.

their community persons not examined by them according to ancient custom; to appoint a prior from outside the convent without the monks' consent; or to expel one whom they had elected; or to remove perfectly acceptable superiors from the cathedral's dependent cells in order to appoint priors who were less suitable. At the same time the archdeacons and their officials were forbidden to charge the monks' churches for chrism and holy oil; to suspend from office their clerks; to impose interdict on their churches; or to interfere with the monks' ancient right to receive the body of anyone who might choose to be buried amongst them. It is obvious that the convent, used for almost a century to benevolent episcopal rule, feared for their autonomy in the face of John of Oxford's perceived aggression. In view of contemporary developments in other dioceses with monastic cathedrals, they were perhaps right to do so.[41]

John of Oxford's successor, John de Gray, came from the same stable. Trained in the royal administration, he had been chancellor to Prince John before his accession and has been described as the only man consistently trusted by that ruler throughout his troubled reign.[42] He was constantly in the royal entourage, except for a long period when he was justiciar of Ireland, and was hence seldom at Norwich. Despite, or probably because of this, his relations with his cathedral chapter were excellent, in marked contrast to those of his predecessor. He was considered by the compiler of the *First Register* to have been, with the exception of the founder, 'beyond all others favourable and gracious to the monks of Norwich, to whom he extended many benefits'.[43]

His concessions to the monks were of two kinds.[44] First, in 1205, he reached a compromise with the cathedral chapter concerning numerous matters of contention between them. Most importantly, he negotiated an agreement with the monks about their respective rights of presentation to the numerous parish churches of which the cathedral held the patronage, 'in order to resolve various conflicts between bishops and monks which had lasted from the foundation of the church to the present, so that peace might be restored between them'.[45] He also rationalised the respective rights of bishop and chapter at Lynn, confirmed the monks' dues in the episcopal manor of North Elmham, remitted the exaction of twenty marks worth of herrings imposed on them by his predecessors and resolved (albeit temporarily) the priory's quarrel with the rector of Thornham about the lands and revenues of

41. For a summary of the conflict at Canterbury, with references to that at Coventry, see C. R. Cheney, *Hubert Walter* (London, 1967), pp. 135–57.
42. *EEA*, vi, pp. xxxvii–xxxix; S. Painter, *The Reign of King John* (Baltimore, Maryland,

1949), p. 79.
43. *First Register*, pp. 88–89.
44. For Gray's charters for the cathedral priory, see *NCC*, i, nos 143–79; *EEA*, vi, nos 373–410.
45. *NCC*, i, no. 178; *EEA*, vi, no. 391.

that church. Six years later, in 1211, bishop and monks also settled the long-standing dispute about their respective rights in Thorpe Wood.

Secondly, Bishop Gray also granted to the monks numerous churches *in proprios usus*, that is, he appropriated them, allowing the convent to become the corporate rector and to receive the revenue of these churches, rather than merely having the right to choose the parish priest.[46] Whereas the bishops of Norwich, like all their English episcopal colleagues, normally insisted, in accordance with canon law, that monasteries to which parish churches were appropriated should present to the bishop vicars, who would receive a fixed portion of the church's revenues and have security of tenure, Gray allowed the monks of Norwich to have their churches served by chaplains who might be appointed and dismissed at will without reference to the bishop – a concession which certainly increased the profitability of the churches to the convent but which was hardly conducive to effective pastoral care. His generosity to the monks was probably regretted by his successors, who in 1228 and 1245 obtained papal permission to investigate and rectify the situation in those parish churches held by religious in which vicarages had not been established or had been inadequately endowed.[47]

The relations between the convent and the thirteenth-century bishops, be they papal officials, royal clerks or academic theologians, were generally cordial. All of them were adequate diocesans, who when absent from their diocese made provision for its efficient governance by deputies of high calibre. The most notable amongst them was Walter Suffield, a Paris theologian appointed in 1244, who achieved the remarkable feat of acting as a papal tax assessor and also winning a popular reputation for sanctity.[48] Most of these bishops issued general confirmations of their predecessors' donations, and throughout the century a number of parish churches were appropriated to the monks. Blickling, for example, was granted in 1265 specifically to increase provision for the priory's guests; St Etheldreda's Norwich in 1270 to provide cutlery, dishes and napkins for the refectory; and St Gregory's Norwich in 1276 to improve the care of sick monks.[49] Bishop Suffield in 1246 confirmed the exempt jurisdiction of the prior and convent in their own manors, reserving to the bishop only criminal and matrimonial cases and faults detected in visitation.[50] Middleton in

46. For the profitability of parish churches, see generally B. R. Kemp, 'Monastic Possession of Parish Churches in England in the Twelfth Century', *Journal of Ecclesiastical History*, 31 (1980), pp. 133–60; for the diocese of Norwich, C. Harper-Bill, 'The Struggle for Benefices in Twelfth-Century East Anglia', in R. A. Brown, ed., *Anglo-Norman Studies*, 11 (Woodbridge, 1989), pp. 113–32.

47. *NCC*, i, nos 292, 299; both Suffield and Walton, however, themselves appropriated to the monks churches which were to be served by removeable chaplains (*NCC*, i, nos 206, 217).

48. See articles in *DNB* and Emden, *Biographical Register of Oxford*.

49. *NCC*, i, nos 217, 220, 224.

50. *NCC*, i, no. 210.

1278 settled a dispute between the monks and the rector of North Elmham about maintenance of the chancel there, and Walpole in 1297 similarly arbitrated in a quarrel between the convent and the parson of North Cressingham.[51] The bishops appear to have conscientiously balanced their roles of titular abbot, bound to defend their monks, and diocesan obliged to maintain parochial rights. The only conflict, and that a very minor one, between bishop and chapter concerned suit of court of the episcopal manor of Thorpe: this was resolved by a composition of 1290 whereby the bishop relaxed his rights in return for a small money payment.[52]

The complexity of the relationship between the bishop and his monks is once again apparent in the fourteenth century. The first extant episcopal injunctions for the cathedral priory were issued after a visitation in 1309 by Bishop John Salmon, formerly prior of Ely.[53] They concentrate on performance of the divine office and, if at first glance they appear critical of the monks, are in fact a reflection of the concern of a bishop, himself schooled in the cloister, about the inevitable secular preoccupations of many monks engaged in the administration of the house and its extensive estates. Salmon insisted that at least two-thirds of the community of about sixty monks should be present at every celebration of the divine office, which was of course the priory's *raison d'être*. Mass books should be standardised, new vestments purchased as necessary and a clock provided for the regulation of the monastic life. He emphasised the urgency of his instructions, since the cathedral should be seen as the model for the liturgical life of the diocese as a whole.

After the episcopate of Anthony Bek (1337–43), when relations between diocesan and chapter were somewhat strained, the rule of William Bateman (1344–55) demonstrated once more that a secular bishop could live harmoniously with a monastic chapter.[54] A local man, he undoubtedly endeared himself to the community by his vigorous attempt to assert the jurisdiction of the church of Norwich over the exempt abbey of St Edmund (in which his eleventh- and twelfth-century predecessors had lamentably failed). When Bury's protest to the king resulted in the confiscation of his lands and the imprisonment of his agents, Bateman took refuge in the monastic precinct. During his enforced residence he too issued injunctions to the monks, very different from those of Salmon in that they concentrated on the financial administration of the house. The observations on the decline of monastic discipline are purely rhetorical. The bishop was concerned to ensure the production of inventories by the obedientiaries and the return of annual accounts by the priors of the dependent cells. This was the attempt of a practical man to guarantee sound

51. *NCC*, i, nos 231, 235.
52. *NCC*, i, no. 233.
53. E. H. Carter, *Studies in Norwich Cathedral History* (Norwich, 1935), pp. 19–24.
54. A. H. Thompson, 'William Bateman,

Bishop of Norwich, 1344–55', *NA*, 25, i (1933), pp. 102–37; for his injunctions, see C. R. Cheney, 'Norwich Cathedral Priory in the Fourteenth Century', *Bulletin of the John Rylands Library*, 20 (1936), pp. 93–120.

financial administration at a time of declining economic fortunes. That he was in no way hostile to the monks is shown by his appointment of three priors in succession as his vicars-general for the diocese – an unusual step in an age when episcopal government was normally entrusted to graduate lawyers from the universities.

In the 1380s there began a long and complex dispute between the cathedral and Bishop Despenser.[55] The conflict came to a head in the mid 1390s. The central issues were the nature and extent of the jurisdiction of the prior and convent in their own manors; the right of the bishop to intervene in the internal affairs of the community; and the discipline of the priory and its dependent cells. There was no matter of substance which had not been in dispute in the time of John of Oxford two centuries before. When an appeal was lodged by the monks at the papal court, for the first of many times in 1394, Boniface IX confirmed various twelfth- and thirteenth-century bulls in their favour. The following year the pope ordered the archbishop of Canterbury and the bishop of Hereford to negotiate an amicable composition between bishop and chapter, or, if they failed in this, to remit the case to Rome. At the bishop's instigation, however, King Richard II intervened, ordering both parties to appear before the archbishop and the royal council. Here a compromise began to emerge but, before it could be finalised, Archbishop Courtenay died and dissension broke out again. After a further appeal, the pope in May 1397 commissioned the new archbishop, Thomas Arundel, to finalise the agreement. Before this could be done, he had been translated because of the king's personal indignation against him to St Andrews. In the end, it was a royal commission which decided matters, largely in favour of the bishop, in March 1398. The convent again appealed to Rome, where the pope declared the proceedings and 'pretended sentence' to be null and void, recalling the case to himself. Later, in September 1401, Boniface IX prohibited Archbishop Arundel, now restored to Canterbury after the Lancastrian 'revolution' of 1399, from visitation of Norwich Cathedral, because he had learned that he was prejudiced in favour of the bishop. Eventually, although the verdict of the judge appointed by the pope was far more favourable to the convent, the bishop almost immediately controverted its terms. Despite another papal sentence in their favour, later in 1401 the monks agreed to submit to Archbishop Arundel's arbitration, which did little more than repeat the ruling of the royal commission of 1398. The convent then decided to make the best of things and compounded with Bishop Despenser for the exercise of their previous privileges.

---

55. The main stages of this convoluted dispute are summarized in *CPR, 1391–96*, pp. 703–4, 712; *CCR, 1392–96*, pp. 513–14; *CPR, 1396–99*, p. 107; *CPL, 1362–1404*, pp. 477, 518–20, 522, 525; *CPL, 1396–1404*, pp. 11–12, 187–88, 195, 273–74, 318–19, 369, 380, 495–96, 526–27, 586–87; *CPL, 1404–15*, p. 139. There are numerous documents in the dean and chapter archives in the Norfolk Record Office which amplify these in terms of minor detail.

The stages of this dispute have been detailed at some length because it reveals the difficulties encountered by ecclesiastical bodies caught between the conflicting claims of papal and royal jurisdiction; it also shows the extent both of the effort and revenue which might be expended by prelates and corporations in the defence of rights and privileges perceived to be rightfully theirs. Most revealing of all is the sequel to the dispute between Despenser and the monks. Prior Alexander Tottington had been the most determined defender of monastic autonomy against his diocesan but, after he was eventually accepted as the new bishop in 1407, he was equally insistent on episcopal rights, renewing the conflict with the monks and insisting on the full implementation of Archbishop Arundel's adjudication. Tottington saw his new office as a sacred trust, just as previously he had believed he would answer to the Holy Trinity for his preservation of the rights of the community. It was only in 1411 that this dispute, which had rumbled on for a quarter of a century, was finally settled by a far more comprehensive arbitration by Archbishop Arundel.[56]

There was further altercation in the mid fifteenth century, this time between the convent and Bishop Thomas Brouns (1436–45).[57] This concerned *reverencialia*, marks of respect demanded by the diocesan. Brouns objected to any inferior, especially the prior, wearing full pontifical vestments or giving benediction when he was present and obtained from Pope Eugenius IV an indult that none should presume so to do. He insisted that when he conducted a visitation of the cathedral he should be met in solemn procession at the west door and that the bells should be rung. In any procession on great occasions the prior should walk behind him at his right, holding the hem of his cope, and he should be censed by the prior or a senior monk. When agreement had been reached on these matters, the bishop also complained that the prior had refused him the kiss of peace; on this issue in October 1443 he appealed to Rome. Eventually it was agreed that this mark of respect and concord should be rendered to the bishop only when he returned to the cathedral after an absence of two months or more. That such liturgical minutiae should lead to conflict and litigation may today seem absurd, indeed, contrary to the spirit of religion, but this dispute again reveals the intense importance attached to status and office in the middle ages.

The final evidence for the relationship of bishop and monastic chapter is provided by the visitation injunctions issued by Bishops Goldwell and Nix between 1492 and 1532.[58] The findings at these enquiries have been interpreted very differently, the

56. Carter, *Norwich Cathedral History*, pp. 35–72.

57. E. F. Jacob, 'Thomas Brouns, Bishop of Norwich, 1436–45', in H. R. Trevor-Roper, ed., *Essays in British History Presented to Sir Keith Feiling* (London, 1964), pp. 61–84, at pp. 77–78.

58. A. Jessopp, *Visitations of the Diocese of Norwich, 1492–1532* (Camden Society, new series 43, 1888), pp. 1–8, 71–79, 192–94, 196–206, 262–70; for criticism, see M. D. Knowles, *The Religious Orders in England*, iii (Cambridge, 1959), pp. 73–75.

charitable observer considering it to be inevitable that in a community of forty or so monks there should be some backbiting and the occasional minor misdemeanour; the more austere critic presenting them as a revelation of a sad state of affairs in an institution devoted to observance of the Rule of St Benedict and to the service of God. In the present context, what is notable is the comprehensive nature of the episcopal injunctions. Goldwell in 1492, for example, legislated about the proper celebration of masses for benefactors, the care of the sick in the infirmary, the provision of wholesome and sufficient food, the separation of monks and laymen in the refectory, office-holding in the community and the upkeep of monks at university. In 1520, after visitation by his commissaries, Nix ordered that sheep should not be pastured in the cloister garth and pronounced on the manner of procession from dormitory to church for the celebration of the night office. In the last years of the old order, these injunctions indicate a concern on the bishop's part for his monastic cathedral chapter which was far from perfunctory.

From what has been written above, it would be easy to suppose that the relationship of bishop and monks at Norwich was characterised by almost perennial tension. Just as historians of medieval English politics tend to concentrate on the great constitutional crises, so ecclesiastical historians are led by the nature of their sources to focus upon conflict within the church. In fact, the disputes which have been described were ripples on the surface of a normally harmonious relationship. Later medieval bishops were seldom present at Norwich; even when in the diocese, they usually resided at one of their manor houses outside the city.[59] Yet several of them contributed handsomely to the repair and embellishment of the cathedral.[60] The prior and convent commonly issued confirmations of episcopal acts, even when their own property rights were not directly affected.[61] When appropriating parish churches to other monasteries the bishop normally stipulated that an annual pension should be paid to the cathedral community; and by the end of the fifteenth century the list of such payments was substantial.[62] The bishop's consistory court held its sessions in one of the chapels of the cathedral and, from the 1450s, the diocesan or his suffragan celebrated ordinations in the Lady Chapel.[63] Against all the odds (in

59. Thirteenth-century episcopal documents were commonly dated at Gaywood or Hoxne.

60. For the contributions of Percy, Lyhart, Goldwell and Nix, see Emden, *Biographical Register of Oxford, s.n.* See also below, pp. 182–96.

61. See the various volumes of *Suffolk Charters* (Suffolk Records Society, 1979-), indices, *s.v.* Norwich, prior and convent. Such con-

firmations are recorded more regularly than in some other dioceses.

62. See the list of such pensions in 1499 in C. Harper-Bill, ed., *The Register of John Morton, Archbishop of Canterbury, 1486–1500*, iii (Canterbury and York Society, forthcoming).

63. B. Burnham, 'The Episcopal Administration of the Diocese of Norwich in the Later Middle Ages' (unpublished Oxford University B. Litt. thesis, 1971), pp. 36–39. The

view of the conflicting external interests which determined episcopal appointments and the anomalous position of the usually secular prelate of a monastic church), bishops and monks, although always intensely conscious of their respective rights, normally managed to work in cooperation as head and members of the mother church of the diocese.

The Cathedral Priory and the Laity

If the new cathedral of the 1090s was essentially the creation of the first bishop of Norwich, it served until the Reformation as an architectural model for the lay patrons of numerous local churches.[64] It also provided a channel for the religious devotion of many men and women from all social classes, even if the mother church of the diocese was secondary in their affections to the monasteries patronised by the knightly benefactors of the twelfth century or the parish churches which were so lavishly embellished in the later middle ages.

Throughout the medieval centuries there was near-universal conviction that the path to eternal beatitude might be negotiated by the granting of property or money to God's servants. This did not signify the exclusion from heaven of the poor, who might by their very presence at some holy site attain remission of their sins. Rather it was a recognition that the acquisition of wealth normally entailed guilt, which could be expiated by charity.[65] 'Alms extinguish sin as water does fire', insisted Bishop Herbert de Losinga in one of his sermons. Perhaps responding to this exhortation, Alan son of Flaald in the early twelfth century, in the preamble of his charter granting the manor of Eaton to the priory, allowed his scribe to expand upon the generosity of God to mankind and upon the obligation upon men to return some at least of His gifts to His service.[66] From the lavish donations of the

note 63 continued

consistory court usually sat in the Bauchun Chapel; rolls of wills proved therein are extant from 1370. The number of wills proved there rises from about 50 p. a. in the 1370s to about 200 p. a. by 1500. Other judicial records are extant only from the early sixteenth century, for which see E. Stone and B. Cozens-Hardy, eds, *Norwich Consistory Court Depositions, 1499–1512 and 1518–30* (NRS, 10, 1938). In 1510–11 the consistory court was convened on sixty-five occasions, when 261 cases were heard, of which only forty-nine were *ex officio*, or disciplinary. Probate and litigation thus brought many people into contact with the

cathedral church. For ordinations, see Burnham, 'Episcopal Administration', p. 126, and J. F. Williams, 'Ordinations in the Norwich Diocese during the Fifteenth Century', *NA*, 31 (1955–57), pp. 299–346.

64. See pp. 137–57, 210–28.

65. For general discussion of religious motivation, see C. Harper-Bill, 'The Piety of the Anglo-Norman Knightly Class', in Brown, ed., *Proceedings of the Battle Conference*, 2, pp. 63–77; C. J. Holdsworth, *The Piper and the Tune: Medieval Patrons and Monks* (Stenton Lecture 1990, Reading 1991).

66. GS, ii, p. 26; *NCC*, ii, no. 364; *First Register*, pp. 42–44 (1107 x 14).

aristocracy to the widow's mite, no better spiritual investment could be envisaged than the purchase of the prayers of monks, those knights of Christ who waged a continual liturgical battle against the forces of Satan. When in the mid twelfth century Roger de Munteny granted his mill at Plumstead to the monks of Norwich, he did so 'for the salvation of my soul and that of my wife, and for the souls of William my father and Rahesia my mother and of Siwat the priest of Plumstead'.[67] The contractual element of grants in free alms – that is, free from secular rent or service – is on occasion explicitly stated. Shortly after the foundation Eudo *dapifer* (the steward) and his wife, granting the manor of Postwick, begged that in return for this the monks should receive them into their spiritual benefits and that after their deaths they should commemorate them as if they were brethren of the house.[68] In 1130, Maurice of Windsor and his wife granted the church of St Edmund at Hoxne; the monks gave them in return full confraternity of their house, with the benefit of their prayers before and after their deaths, and also the option of entering themselves into the monastic life.[69]

It is therefore surprising to find that early lay donations to the cathedral were not lavish. To the four manors given by Bishop Herbert and to Thorpe, acquired by him from the king, were added Newton, granted by Godric *dapifer* in 1101, and a few years later Eaton, the donation of Alan son of Flaald.[70] Hubert de Rye, who laid the second foundation stone after the bishop, followed the fashion of the new Norman lords of England by granting two-thirds of the tithes of all his East Anglian manors to the cathedral.[71] His example was followed by others and there was a further trickle of grants by the leaders of local society later in the twelfth century: for example, Roger of Gunton, who held four knights' fees of the bishop, gave the church of Martham.[72] One alleged grant is of particular interest. After the death of Roger Bigod in 1107, Bishop Herbert successfully defended in the king's court his claim that before Roger's foundation of Thetford Priory, which claimed his corpse, he had granted his body to be buried in the cathedral: therein at Norwich in fact he remained, one of the few laymen to be buried there in the middle ages.[73] It must be that the bishop hoped that Roger's burial would bring attendant benefactions

67. *NCC*, ii, no. 202 (1146 x 74).
68. *NCC*, ii, no. 220 (1101 x 19).
69. *First Register*, pp. 68–69; B. Dodwell, 'Some Charters relating to the Honour of Bacton', in *A Medieval Miscellany for D. M. Stenton* (Pipe Roll Society, new series, 36, 1962), pp. 147–65, no. 6.
70. *NCC*, ii, nos 364, 371.
71. *First Register*, p. 51. For grants of tithes, see G. Constable, *Monastic Tithes from their Origins to the Twelfth Century* (Cambridge, 1964), especially p. 82.
72. *NCC*, i, no. 129 (1146 x 49).
73. B. Golding, 'Anglo-Norman Knightly Burials', in C. Harper-Bill and R. Harvey, eds, *The Ideals and Practice of Medieval Knighthood*, 1 (Woodbridge, 1986), pp. 35–36; compare *EEA*, vi, nos 21–22. It is only from the sixty or so years before the Reformation that there is any physical evidence of gentry burials within the cathedral church: see pp. 467–75, 479–81.

from his family and his tenants. These do not appear to have materialised, and indeed the paucity of endowments by such great families may have been to the long-term advantage of the monks of Norwich. If it diminished their financial resources, so that economically they could never rival such great corporations as St Albans and Bury St Edmunds, they nevertheless escaped the overwhelming burden of hospitality to the living and liturgical commemoration of the dead which pressed so heavily on houses with a plethora of influential lay benefactors.

To understand this relative paucity of lay investment, it is necessary to set the foundation of Norwich Cathedral Priory in the context of remarkable monastic expansion in East Anglia in the late eleventh century. Before the Conquest, in a region which is better described as Anglo-Scandinavian than Anglo-Saxon, there had been only St Benet of Holme, refounded by King Cnut as a Benedictine community in 1019, from which the next year a group of monks were sent to Bury St Edmunds and a few years later a small cell was established at Rumburgh.[74] The new Norman aristocrats, amongst whom the Conqueror divided East Anglia and who imposed their feudal honours on the substructure of native social organisation, were enthusiastic supporters of the Benedictine ideal; most of them were eager to establish communities on their own estates in imitation of those which flourished across the Channel. Monasteries were founded by William Malet at Eye *c.* 1080, by William de Warenne at Castle Acre in 1089, by Richard Fitz Gilbert at Clare in 1090 and by Peter de Valognes at Binham before 1093. Soon after the foundation of Norwich itself, Robert Fitz Walter endowed a community at Horsham St Faith in 1103 and William d'Albini at Wymondham in 1107, while in 1103 Roger Bigod planted Cluniac monks in the now abandoned site of the cathedral at Thetford.[75] These foundations transformed the ecclesiastical geography and the landscape of East Anglia, but the munificence of the founders to their own monks certainly diverted funds which might otherwise have been available for the endowment and building of the new cathedral. It is this large group of baronial houses, and the rival attractions of the cult of St Edmund eagerly promoted by the monks of Bury, rather than lack of enthusiasm for the monastic order which explain why the bulk of the cathedral church's revenues were granted by the bishop himself from the episcopal estates.

There were few grants either, in the twelfth century, from the free peasant farmers who contributed a multitude of donations to many of the religious houses of East Anglia and the Danelaw.[76] Rather more such gifts (or sales) materialised in the

74. M. D. Knowles and R. N. Hadcock, *Medieval Religious Houses: England and Wales* (2nd edn, London, 1971), pp. 61, 74–75.

75. Knowles and Hadcock, *Medieval Religious Houses*, pp. 59, 65, 68, 81, 83, 98, 103.

76. See the charters collected by F. M. Stenton in *Danelaw Charters* (Oxford, 1920) and *The Free Peasantry of the Northern Danelaw* (Oxford, 1969).

thirteenth century in those vills where the cathedral priory had already established territorial interests. Spiritual considerations remained important to vendors, even when a transaction was obviously commercial. Thus, for example, around 1200, William son of Roger of Cringleford sold to the priory's almoner for four marks an annual rent of four shillings in Shottesham; he was received in return by the monks into their society and into participation in all their good works.[77] A concern for the liturgical life of the cathedral is indicated by a small group of late thirteenth-century grants specifically made to finance the lighting of the high altar.[78] The situation in and around the priory's manor of Newton may be taken as typical of thirteenth-century trends. The monks were attempting to consolidate their holdings here and in adjacent Trowse. While there were still a few small gifts in free alms, far more common were 'grants' or quitclaims of land and rent made for a financial consideration, either an entry-fine or annual rent or both, as when Ralph Jobbe of Trowse granted an acre of meadow for twenty-six shillings down and two pence annual rent.[79] Such transactions were occurring on every priory manor.

Below the social level of those who were buried in the cathedral, or who made even modest grants or sold small parcels of land to the cathedral priory, many others across the diocese must have come into contact with their mother church and its monastic community. All those within the jurisdiction of the bishop throughout the counties of Norfolk and Suffolk were also exhorted to visit the cathedral once a year; allegedly this obligation was imposed by Bishop Eborard in the early twelfth century – although the text is spurious, it probably encapsulates a genuine episcopal mandate.[80] Certainly Bishop William Raleigh (1239–43) ordered all parish priests of the diocese to join in solemn processions to the cathedral in Easter week, and to encourage their parishioners to join them.[81] Failure so to do would result in a fine of two shillings for the incumbent, but there is no way of knowing how many lay people responded to the injunction.

The cathedral church was replete with images designed to excite the devotion and elicit the alms of the faithful. The most important was certainly that of the Holy Trinity, the patron of the church and the most universal of dedications.[82] It was surely, however, the desire of the monks of Norwich to have their own local saint, particularly associated with their community, which lay at the root of the extremely dubious cult of little St William, allegedly the victim of ritual murder by the Jews in the 1140s. The cult appealed initially to the citizens of Norwich, although

77. *NCC*, ii, no. 482.
78. *NCC*, ii, nos 248–50, 252.
79. *NCC*, ii, nos 371–454, especially no. 436.
80. F. M. Powicke and C. R. Cheney eds, *Councils and Synods, with other Documents relating to the English Church*, ii, AD 1205– 1313, 2 vols (Oxford, 1964), i, p. 363; compare i, p. 344; *EEA*, vi, p. 360 (app. i, no. 23).
81. Powicke and Cheney, *Councils and Synods*, ii, part i, p. 364.
82. For the images, see *VCH Norfolk*, ii, p. 321.

it was a member of the East Anglian aristocracy, Mabel de Bec, who paid for the shrine. Within a few years of the 'martyrdom', the tomb was attracting as many pilgrims from the hinterland as from the city. From the late middle ages there are extant representations of the boy-saint at Worstead, Litcham and Loddon in Norfolk and at Eye in Suffolk. In 1325 the monks thought it worthwhile to reembellish his shrine, the last recorded offering at the chapel in the wood, the site of his death, occurring in 1506. Yet William, a beneficent and miracle-working saint, was never able to provide the focus of local piety and solidarity achieved by the cult of St Edmund in the southern part of the diocese; no more, despite his evident sanctity, did the revered thirteenth-century bishop, Walter Suffield, at whose tombs offerings were also made.[83]

Pilgrims certainly came, attracted not only by the shrines but by the papal indulgences acquired by the monks. Following that offered in 1400 to those visiting the three main altars of the church during the feast of Holy Trinity, almost £50 was given, while a further £62 was donated at the high altar during the remainder of the year; this was comparable to the income from a large manor.[84] Perhaps the investment of the laity in the cathedral was, in view of its status as mother church of the diocese, disappointing, far less than in the other Benedictine foundations of the post-Conquest period, in the major pilgrimage centres of Bury St Edmunds, Bromholm and Walsingham, or in the burgeoning Perpendicular parish churches of the fifteenth century. Yet in view of all that was given elsewhere, the donations to Norwich were far from negligible.[85]

The Cathedral Priory and Extra-Diocesan Relations

The cathedral priory's interaction with the metropolitan, the archbishop of Canterbury, was naturally less intense than its relationship with the diocesan, the bishop of Norwich. In the early years the monks received an impressively solemn charter from St Anselm (1093–1109). In 1281 from Archbishop Pecham (1279–92) they obtained a comprehensive confirmation of all their ecclesiastical revenues and an exemplification of their title deeds damaged in the disturbance of 1272.[86] Archbishop Winchelsey (1293–1313) in 1304 pronounced excommunication against all those who had robbed or defrauded the priory of its possessions.[87] From the thirteenth century the prior was obliged to attend, in person or by proxy, the increasingly

83. H. W. Saunders, *An Introduction to the Obedientiary and Manor Rolls of Norwich Cathedral Priory* (Norwich, 1930), p. 103.
84. *VCH Norfolk*, ii, p. 322.
85. For lay devotion, especially in the parochial context, see E. Duffy, *The Stripping of the Altars: Traditional Religion in England, 1400–1580* (New Haven and London, 1992), pp. 1–376. This is replete with East Anglian material.
86. *NCC*, i, nos 260, 266.
87. *NCC*, i, no. 268.

frequent provincial assemblies presided over by the metropolitan, which developed into the convocation of Canterbury, the main business of which, rather than the discussion of reform, became the granting of taxation to the king.[88] Less frequently the convent was subject to archiepiscopal visitation, such as those conducted by Pecham and Winchelsey.[89]

In the first half of the fourteenth century this normally harmonious relationship was disrupted by two jurisdictional disputes. The first concerned the respective rights and revenues of metropolitan and convent during vacancies of the see of Norwich. This was a common cause of dissension between archbishop and cathedral chapters. The dispute arose from the appointment by Archbishop Reynolds (1313–27) of an official for the vacant see in September 1325, when Robert Baldock, elected and conformed by the king, resigned because of the papal appointment of William Ayremynne.[90] The prior and convent appealed to the pope against the scope of the jurisdiction and the financial rights claimed by the archbishop during vacancies. After Reynolds's death, the monks arrived at a compromise in 1330 with his successor, Archbishop Meopham (1327–33).[91] The jurisdiction of Canterbury during vacancies was admitted but the archbishop's official was to be prohibited from visitation; rather, the monks were to nominate three persons to the archbishop, from whom he should choose the visitor. Of the profits of visitation, largely the procuration fees for the expenses of the visitor paid by religious houses and parishes, two-thirds were to go to the archbishop and a third to the cathedral priory. Although this agreement was not as favourable to the chapter as similar thirteenth-century compositions at some other cathedrals, it did emphasise the continuing rights of the monks of Holy Trinity in the diocese, even when deprived of their head.

The second dispute involved the attempt of Archbishop Stratford (1333–48) in the autumn of 1343 to conduct an archiepiscopal visitation of Norwich diocese.[92] The bishop and prior both appealed against this to the papal court at Avignon, alleging that the archbishop was not observing correct canonical procedure. The cathedral precinct and the episcopal palace were put in a state of defence to repel intruders. Stratford excommunicated bishop and prior, placed the diocese under interdict and obtained writs ordering 'disturbers of the peace' to appear before a royal commission. Tension was reduced by the death of Bishop Bek but litigation nevertheless continued at Avignon. There the archbishop's sentences were quashed, because they had been issued after appeal to the papal court, but no definitive ruling

88. For the history of convocation, see E. W. Kemp, *Counsel and Consent* (London, 1961), chapters 3–5.
89. *NCC*, i, nos 265, 269.
90. J. R. Wright, *The Church and the English Crown, 1305–1334* (Toronto, 1980), pp. 329–30.
91. I. J. Churchill, *Canterbury Administration*, 2 vols (London, 1933), i, pp. 194–207; ii, pp. 61–78.
92. R. M. Haines, *Archbishop John Stratford* (Toronto, 1986), pp. 67–68.

appears to have been given on this issue. Like conflict between bishop and chapter, such dramatic confrontation was far from the norm. Despite some tension because of his stand in the Despenser affair, Archbishop Thomas Arundel appears to have conducted his visitation perfectly peacefully in 1411.

Like all other Benedictine houses, Norwich Cathedral Priory after 1215 became subject to the authority of the provincial chapter of the Order established for Canterbury, as for all other provinces of the western church, by Pope Innocent III. Compulsory membership of this body involved financial expenditure.[93] Not only did the convent have to meet the expenses of its proctor attending the triennial assembly (these amounted in 1298–99, for example, to 32s. 0¼ d.); it also had to pay an income tax which was levied by the provincial chapter on all Benedictine houses, at rates varying from ¼ d. to 1d. in the pound. The contribution for 1414–17, for instance, was £7 3s. 3d., and in 1492 (at the rate of ½ d. in the mark) £17 13s. 7½ d. At the turn of the thirteenth and fourteenth centuries contributions were raised by the chapter for the construction of the Benedictine college at Oxford: in 1319–20 Norwich paid £3 9s. 9¾ d. for a three-year period. Extra expense was incurred when there were exceptional needs. In 1311 Norwich contributed £5 19s. 2d. to the expenses of the English Benedictine delegates at the general council of the church held at Vienne, where it was particularly important that they were well represented because of attacks by the friars on the monastic way of life. In 1435 Prior William Worsted of Norwich (1427–36) was himself appointed one of the four representatives of the Benedictine province of Canterbury at the Council of Basle.

The individual houses both obtained advantages and incurred obligations by membership of the provincial chapter. A proctor was maintained at the court of Rome to represent the interests of English Benedictines – the Norwich convent must have used his services a great deal in their sporadic disputes in the fourteenth century with archbishop and bishop. In the 1360s this role, now at Avignon, was fulfilled by Thomas Brinton, a monk of Norwich and later bishop of Rochester. At home, the prior of Norwich was commissioned by the chapter to conduct visitations of other Benedictine houses. In 1318–19, for example, with the abbot of Ramsey, he was appointed to visit all communities in the diocese of Lincoln and in 1423 to conduct a visitation of all Black Monk houses in the dioceses of Ely and Norwich; these duties were normally conducted by deputy. Paradoxically, in view

93. W. A. Pantin, ed., *Documents Illustrating the Activities of the General and Provincial Chapters of the English Black Monks, 1215–1540*, 3 vols (Camden Society, third series, 45, 47, 54, 1931–37); for what follows, see i, pp. 61, 172–74, 177, 278–80; ii, p. 248; iii, pp. 105, 164, 174, 194, 227, 236–37, 240–41. For educational activities associated with the provincial chapter, see pp. 244–48.

of the long struggle for exemption from the bishop of Norwich, Bury St Edmunds submitted to visitation by the prior in 1390, 1411 and 1441. In return, Norwich itself had to submit to the enquiries of the chapter's delegates, for example in 1423 by the commissary of the abbot of Colchester, who reported that he had found at the cathedral priory excellent observance of the Rule.

The relationship between the church of Norwich and the church of Rome has already been mentioned many times, with regard to the early privileges obtained for the recently founded cathedral, to the papal claims to the right of appointment of bishops and to the appeals lodged at the court of Rome against the alleged aggression of bishops and archbishops. The pope, as the Vicar of Christ, claimed to exercise the plenitude of power within the universal church, and the monks of Norwich, like all ecclesiastical corporations in England and throughout western Christendom, were eager to invoke papal authority when they found it to be in their own best interests.[94] Contact with the papacy was normal and regular from the early twelfth to the early sixteenth centuries, even while for seventy years in the fourteenth century the pope's residence at Avignon made him suspect in England as an ally of the French, and thereafter from 1378 to 1415 while the papal schism disfigured the unity of the church. Privileges, confirmations and favourable judicial decisions obtained from Rome were balanced by numerous obligations imposed by papal government on the convent, most particularly upon the prior.

During the thirteenth century the monks of Norwich elicited general confirmations of their rights and privileges from Innocent III (1202), Honorius III (1217), Gregory IX (1230), Urban IV (1262), Gregory X (1272 x 74) and Nicholas IV (1291).[95] The most comprehensive, however, was that issued by Pope Innocent IV in 1249.[96] In addition to listing in detail the cathedral priory's possessions, the pope granted exemption from tithe on its newly-cultivated lands, freedom to receive into the community whomsoever the monks wished, free right of burial within their cemetery, and prohibition of the establishment within their parishes of any chapels and of any unprecedented exaction by diocesan or metropolitan. Other more specific confirmations were obtained when the cathedral community felt that its rights were threatened. In 1206, for example, Innocent III confirmed the monks' right to bury in their cemetery anyone drowned off the coast at Lynn; in 1230 Gregory IX recognised the danger to the monks' possessions during vacancies of the see, granting them an indult that they might excommunicate invaders of their estates; and Gregory X in 1273 added his support to the action taken by bishop and king against the Norwich rioters, appointing the bishops of London and Ely as his agents to act

---

94. For a convenient and incisive summary of medieval papal history, see R. W. Southern, *Western Society and the Church in the Middle Ages* (Harmondsworth, 1970), pp. 91–169.

95. *NCC*, i, nos 287, 290, 293, 307–8, 310–11, 313.

96. *NCC*, i, no. 302.

on the monks' behalf.[97] The readiness of the prior and convent to seek the support of the papacy on any pretext is well illustrated by two examples. In 1223 they alleged that Bishop John de Gray, while not in his right mind, had alienated some of their ecclesiastical revenues; Pope Honorius III granted them permission to reoccupy. In 1291 they successfully petitioned that they might take advantage of papal privileges which their predecessors, because of their simplicity and ignorance of the law, had failed to utilise; this claim seems quite remarkable given their litigiousness throughout the thirteenth century.[98]

The papal court acted on behalf of the monks in a wide range of matters. Innocent III in 1214, for example, commissioned judges-delegate to hear in England their appeal against the rector of Swanton concerning tithes in his parish; and in 1300 Boniface VIII commissioned the prior of neighbouring Horsham St Faith to ensure the return to the cathedral of tithes and rents misappropriated by certain 'sons of Belial'.[99] In the next century, the prior received various indults designed to facilitate the administration of the monastery by circumventing the strict provisions of the canon law. In 1378 and 1401 he was authorised to grant dispensation for monks in their twentieth year – below the legal age – to be ordained to the priesthood; this was a reflection of the shortage of priests in the years following the Black Death.[100] In 1471 the pope allowed monks of Norwich Cathedral Priory to study at the two Cambridge colleges founded by Bishop Bateman.[101] In the later middle ages, too, numerous indults were issued by the papacy to individual monks. In the fifteenth century at least six Norwich monks were licensed by Rome to receive secular benefices, that is, to act as the parsons of parish churches,[102] while from the 1350s seven monks, including three priors, were granted papal permission to choose their own confessors, who might at the hour of their death grant them full remission from their sins.[103]

This was the greatest benefit which the pope could bestow, and it was dispensed widely, not only on named individuals. The court of Rome was a source of spiritual

97. NCC, i, nos 289, 294, 309.
98. NCC, i, nos 291, 315. There is no evidence to substantiate the assertion against Bishop Gray.
99. Cheney and Cheney, *Letters of Innocent III*, no. 955 (compare no. 696); NCC, i, no. 383. For the papal judicial system in the localities, see J. E. Sayers, *Papal Judges Delegate in the Province of Canterbury, 1198–1254* (Oxford, 1954).
100. CPL, *Petitions, 1342–1419*, p. 345; CPL, *1362–1404*, p. 33; CPL, *1396–1404*, p. 357.
101. CPL, *1471–84*, p. 900.

102. CPL, *1404–15*, pp. 282, 380; CPL, *1458–71*, p. 190; CPL, *1471–84*, pp. 290, 802; CPL, *1481–92* (xv), no. 113; CPL, *1502–13*, no. 699. Two of these monks had left the cloister without permission, but both were absolved by the pope and allowed to retain both their monastic habit and their parish church (CPL, *1404–15*, p. 380; CPL, *1471–84*, p. 714).
103. CPL, *Petitions, 1342–1419*, p. 345; CPL, *1342–62*, pp. 408, 506; CPL, *1396–1404*, pp. 47, 147, 216; CPL, *1427–47*, p. 392.

benefits eagerly exploited by ecclesiastical institutions throughout western Europe; it was seen as 'the well of grace'.[104] The monks of Norwich acquired papal indulgences to speed the souls of benefactors and pilgrims through purgatory. Innocent IV in 1249 and Nicholas IV in 1291 both granted one year and forty days' remission to those confessed and contrite who visited the cathedral on various feast days.[105] In 1317 visitors to the chapel of St John the Evangelist there were rewarded with an indulgence of one hundred days. In 1363 remission of seven years and seven Lents was granted to those who, within the next ten years, made a contribution to the cathedral's fabric, which had recently suffered from storm damage.[106] In 1473 Pope Sixtus IV granted twelve years and twelve Lents to those visitors who gave alms. Only for a very brief period did such a pilgrimage bring the greatest benefit which the papacy could confer, a plenary remission of all penalties due for sin. On 23 March 1398 Boniface IX granted to Norwich the same indulgence as the Portiuncula of Assisi, also given to Bury St Edmunds two months later.[107] The St Albans chronicler comments with acerbity on the rivalry between these two houses and Ely to obtain the greatest spiritual benefits. In December 1402, however, the pope revoked all such grants of plenary indulgence. In the forgiveness of sin, as in other matters, the cathedral had no monopoly: it had to face competition within the diocese from other great ecclesiastical corporations.[108]

The reverse of the coin was that, in return for all the benefits received from Rome, the prior and convent owed various obligations to the apostolic see. From the beginning of the thirteenth century the prior was occasionally called upon to act as a papal judge-delegate, a local agent of a universal system of justice; in 1221, for example, he was one of the judges in an important suit between St Botolph's Colchester and Holy Trinity Aldgate.[109] He might be mandated by Rome to fulfil other commissions – for instance, in 1223, to conduct with the bishop and prior of Ely a papal visitation of Westminster Abbey, or in 1402 to act as local guardian of the rights of Eye Priory in Suffolk.[110]

104. J. A. F. Thomson, '"The Well of Grace": Englishmen and Rome in the Fifteenth Century', in R. B. Dobson, ed., *The Church, Politics and Patronage in the Fifteenth Century* (Gloucester, 1984), pp. 99–114. The phrase was used by Sir John Paston in a letter of 1473.

105. *NCC*, i, nos 301, 314.

106. *CPL, 1305–42*, p. 142; *CPL, Petitions, 1342–1419*, pp. 418, 445.

107. W. E. Lunt, *The Financial Relations of the Papacy with England, 1327–1534* (Medieval Academy of America Publications, 74, Cambridge, Massachusetts, 1962), p. 488.

108. For commentary on indulgences, see Southern, *Western Society*, pp. 136–43.

109. J. E. Sayers, *Papal Government in England during the Pontificate of Honorius III (1216–1227)* (Cambridge, 1984), p. 226; see also Cheney and Cheney, *Letters of Innocent III*, nos 250, 270.

110. *CPL, 1198–1304*, p. 133; *CPL, 1396–1404*, p. 293. For other instances of the prior as papal mandatory, see *CPL, 1198–1304*, p. 353; *CPL, 1342–62*, pp. 515, 549; *CPL, 1396–1404*, pp. 80, 423; *CPL, 1404–15*, p. 126; *CPL, 1417–31*, p. 517.

The convent, like all ecclesiastical corporations, was also subject to papal incursions on its rights of patronage. Just as the popes claimed the right to appoint (or, to use the technical term, to 'provide') to all bishoprics, so, despite numerous complaints in parliament and elsewhere, did they insist on their power to reserve to themselves appointment to an ever-widening category of lesser livings. Such papal demands reached their height in the fourteenth century.[111] Between 1342 and 1404 fourteen petitioners were rewarded by the pope with the concession that the next ecclesiastical living in the gift of the prior and convent of Norwich should be reserved to them.[112] Despite the constant allegations in the Commons and elsewhere that such reservations benefited foreigners and resulted in the export of revenue from the realm, all these grants were, in fact, in favour of Englishmen sufficiently well-placed to exploit the system of papal patronage. Many of the successful candidates were graduates. Indeed the universities petitioned actively for their members: in 1363, for example, Michael de Causton, chancellor of Cambridge, was granted by the pope reservation of a Norwich church.[113] Despite loudly expressed lay hostility to papal provisions, great lords too in reality were prepared to exploit the system: in 1357, for instance, the Black Prince petitioned the pope to grant to one of his clerks a benefice in the gift of the monks of Norwich.[114]

The most onerous burden, in the thirteenth and early fourteenth century, was the obligation to payment of papal taxation which was levied on all the local churches of western Europe, but collected most effectively in strong centralised monarchies such as England, where the crown took an increasingly large proportion of the receipts. The last of three papal assessments of ecclesiastical revenue in the thirteenth century, the *Taxatio ecclesiastica* of Pope Nicholas IV (1291), in fact served as the basis of royal taxation of the English church in the later middle ages. In the *Taxatio* the total revenues of the cathedral priory were calculated at £830 12s. 8d., so that whenever a tenth was levied by the pope or, far more frequently in the long run by the king, £83 1s. 3¼d. was payable.[115] In addition to the burden of payment,

111. For discussion, see W. A. Pantin, *The English Church and the Papacy in the Fourteenth Century* (Cambridge, 1955), chapters 3–5.
112. *CPL, 1342–62*, pp. 61, 207–8; *CPL, 1396–1404*, pp. 129, 250–51, 417; *CPL, Petitions, 1342–1419*, pp. 95–96, 292, 345, 404, 408, 430–31, 449.
113. *CPL, Petitions, 1342–1419*, pp. 404, 408.
114. *CPL, Petitions, 1342–1419*, p. 292.
115. For this calculation, see Saunders, *Obedientiary Rolls*, pp. 26–33. Temporalities were valued at £431 8s. 8d., of which £8 0s. 1½d. came from Suffolk properties, the rest

from Norfolk. Spiritual revenues (churches, pensions, tithes, etc.) were valued at £399 4s. For comparison, the value of Westminster Abbey's possessions were calculated in 1291 at £1294: B. Harvey, *Westminster Abbey and its Estates in the Middle Ages* (Oxford, 1977), p. 62. In the *Valor Ecclesiasticus* of 1535, however, while Norwich's income was calculated at £1061 14s. 3½d. (less £186 19s. 8¾d. allowable expenses), that of Westminster was assessed at £2827 (Saunders, *Obedientiary Rolls*, p. 27; Harvey, *Westminster Abbey*, p. 63).

the monks of Norwich were often also saddled with the responsibility of collection. The function of deputy papal collectors for the diocese, or at least for the two northern archdeaconries, was imposed upon them five times between 1267 and 1319.[116]

The relationship of the cathedral priory with the English crown was not dissimilar to that with the papacy, although in the later middle ages more was demanded of them. From the reign of Edward I the burden of royal taxation fell heavily on Norwich, as on all the great churches of England. In September 1294 the king levied a moiety of all benefices and goods: the cellarer of Norwich alone paid £161 7s. 6d. as half of the revenue of his office, based on the papal assessment.[117] Thereafter in the fourteenth century, and increasingly after the outbreak of the Hundred Years War in 1337, regular royal taxation became the norm, usually levied as a tenth calculated on the basis of the 1291 survey.[118] There were other miscellaneous royal impositions: in 1332 the monks contributed to the subsidy for the marriage of the king's sister to the count of Guelders; two years later they were ordered to send a cart to Durham for the king's Scottish expedition.[119] As late as 1522 the priory made a grant of £200 towards Henry VIII's personal expenses while in France to recover his rightful crown.[120] Indeed, it has been clearly demonstrated that in the period 1485 to 1529 the English church contributed two and a half times more to the crown than to the papacy.[121] The situation was little different for Norwich, as for all other cathedral and monastic churches, from the middle of the fourteenth century. As with taxes previously destined in theory for Rome, the prior and convent not only had to pay but also frequently bore the considerable burden of collection within the diocese.[122] In addition to direct taxation, the monks were also frequently solicited to provide loans in cash, victuals or wool in order to support ailing royal finances.[123] Again the prior was often among those commissioned to raise such loans throughout the county of Norfolk.[124]

116. Lunt, *Financial Relations*, pp. 627, 633, 636–38.
117. *CPR, 1292–1301*, p. 91; Saunders, *Obedientiary Rolls*, p. 173.
118. For a convenient summary of such grants made in the province of Canterbury, see D. B. Weske, *Convocation of the Clergy* (London, 1937), app. C.
119. *CCR, 1330–33*, p. 590; *CCR, 1333–37*, p. 100.
120. *Letters and Papers, Foreign and Domestic, of the Reign of Henry VIII*, 21 vols in 35 (London, 1880–91), iii (2), no. 2483.
121. J. J. Scarisbrick, 'Clerical Taxation in England, 1485 to 1547', *Journal of Ecclesiastical History*, 11 (1960), pp. 41–54.
122. W. A. Morris and J. B. Strayer, *The English Government at Work 1327–36*, ii, *Fiscal Administration* (Cambridge, Massachusetts, 1947), p. 234; for examples, see *CPR, 1321–24*, p. 28; *CCR, 1337–39*, pp. 17, 34, 51, 80, 91; *CCR, 1402–05*, pp. 349–50, 414.
123. For example, *CCR, 1307–13*, p. 260; *CCR, 1313–18*, p. 130; *CPR, 1313–17*, pp. 158, 203, 205, 368, 441; *CCR, 1341–43*, p. 684; *CPR, 1345–48*, p. 341; *CCR, 1346–49*, p. 266; *CPR, 1377–81*, pp. 29–30; *CPR, 1396–99*, p. 181.
124. For example, *CPR, 1436–41*, p. 249; *CPR, 1441–46*, pp. 61, 430.

The resources of the church of Norwich were also tapped by frequent royal demands that the monks should provide a corrody, or lifetime maintenance, for retired servants of the crown. Those who benefited in the fourteenth and fifteenth centuries included king's sergeants and yeomen, a chancery clerk and the usher of the queen's chamber.[125] There is evidence from 1321 and 1338 of resistance to such impositions, because of the heavy burden of taxation upon the church, but the government regarded the excuses as feigned and frivolous.[126] In 1337 and again in 1447 the cathedral priory was granted exemption from such burdens, but in fact corrodians continued to be appointed. Even after a third statement of exemption, given for a price in 1482, the monks were still complaining against this exaction in 1488.[127] Quite apart from the financial cost of these corrodies, it is quite certain that they represented a major intrusion of the world into the cloister.

In recompense for these exactions, however, the priory did receive various benefits from the crown. Most notably, the king supported the priory in the wake of the assault upon it in 1272. Edward I visited draconian penalties on the ringleaders of the riot, fined the city and enforced the payment of compensation to the monks.[128] Long before this moment of crisis, however, almost from the time of their foundation, the monks of Norwich had learned the benefits of utilising the royal courts, whose ever-increasing scope in the twelfth and thirteenth centuries exceeded that even of the papal judicial system. Many of Henry I's writs in favour of the cathedral priory were probably issued in response to the monks' appeals to the royal court, as in the case of his instruction that they were to hold their land at Taverham in peace.[129] It was certainly only after litigation before the king himself at Norwich, possibly in May 1108, that they recovered possession of Newton by Trowse.[130]

It is only from the end of the twelfth century, however, with the beginning of the systematic keeping of royal records, that it is possible to gauge the extent to which Norwich Cathedral Priory, like all great ecclesiastical corporations, was constantly engaged in litigation to protect or recover its lands and rights. The volume of cases, which normally concerned relatively small parcels of land or the right of presentation to parish churches, may best be indicated by the number of final

125. *CCR, 1302–7*, p. 77; *CCR, 1307–13*, pp. 238, 347; *CCR, 1313–18*, pp. 452, 571; *CCR, 1327–30*, pp. 392, 417; *CCR, 1333–37*, p. 324; *CCR, 1337–39*, pp. 256, 662–63; *CPR, 1338–40*, p. 546; *CCR, 1339–41*, p. 482; *CCR, 1343–46*, p. 353; *CCR, 1392–96*, p. 240; *CCR, 1399–1402*, p. 99; *CCR, 1422–29*, pp. 71, 382; *CCR, 1461–68*, p. 164.

126. *CCR, 1318–23*, pp. 408–9; *CCR, 1337–39*, p. 663.

127. *CPR, 1345–48*, p. 539; *CPR, 1446–52*, p. 134; *CPR, 1476–85*, p. 307; NRO, DCN 41/87.

128. A. Gransden, ed., *The Chronicle of Bury St Edmunds, 1212–1301* (London, 1964), p. 52; for the king's subsequent arbitration in November 1275, see *CCR, 1272–79*, pp. 217–18.

129. *NCC*, i, no. 22 (1115 x 27).

130. *NCC*, i, no. 10.

concords (agreements made before the king's justices sitting either at Westminster or on circuit in the locality) to which the monks were party. Forty-nine such documents are extant for the period 1191 to 1303.[131] In other words, the prior and convent appeared, through their attorneys, before the royal justices on average at least once every twenty-seven months throughout the thirteenth century. The monks were in court more often as plaintiffs than as defendants (twenty-nine to twenty cases). Although by their nature these final concords recorded compromises, in fact the convent seldom sacrificed much. In 1205, for example, the monks recognised that a disputed common pasture near Norwich was by right the citizens', but it was agreed that it should be held of the cathedral priory for a fixed sum for each animal grazed, and the monks themselves were to have the use of forty acres of it.[132] In 1242 the monks surrendered the right of presentation to the church of Kirk Oswald in Cumbria, but acquired in return the church and land at Denham in Suffolk; and in 1286, although they abandoned their claim to the manor of Aldeby, where they had a dependent cell, they received in recompense a cash payment of £200.[133] It is interesting, too, that one element of these legal proceedings was often the reception, as part of the settlement, of the monks' adversaries into the confraternity of the cathedral; in other words, a spiritual element entered even into hard-headed legalistic negotiations over revenue.

The medieval church of Norwich was an influential corporation, a major landlord in the region and a participator in the great affairs of the kingdom and of the universal church. After a catalogue of jurisdictional disputes, of rights and privileges fiercely contested and of tax demands by pope and king designed in large measure for the financing of warfare, it is easy to forget, but it must never be forgotten, that the primary reason for the foundation and continued existence of the cathedral priory was the salvation of souls. While offerings can be counted, it is of course impossible to estimate the impression made in the fifteenth century on the large congregations gathered in the nave when a great angel, newly decorated each year with silver foil, descended from the roof of the cathedral to cense the people.[134] Such a demonstration of Christian unity has little in common with the jurisdictional disputes detailed above, or with the violent conflicts between the monks and the citizens of Norwich described elsewhere in this volume. Yet it was the *raison d'être* of the cathedral church and the monastic community.

---

131. *NCC*, i, nos 318–81 passim. The bishop entered into other concords on behalf of the church of Norwich.

132. *NCC*, i, no. 324.

133. *NCC*, i, nos 336, 365.

134. *VCH Norfolk*, ii, p. 322.

15

The Medieval Customary
of the Cathedral Priory

David Chadd

To the founder and first occupants of the cathedral priory its structures and organisation had one primary purpose – to be an efficient environment for the life of a community following the Rule of St Benedict. That Rule, straightforward enough for a small group in the seventh century, had by the eleventh become a complex web of accreted tradition in which the elements of work, study and liturgy were bound closely together. In so far as these strands of the Rule can be separated – and they are, of course, ultimately inextricable – it is the last which would have loomed largest in the life of any medieval monk, the one whose intricacies would have required the highest degree of organisation and whose demands would have impinged upon almost every other aspect of the community's life. No new house could have hoped successfully to arrange the yearly round of liturgical observance – the *Opus Dei* – on a blank sheet, and none, even when like the first Cistercians they were bent upon radical reform, seems to have tried to do so. The detailed governance of almost any Benedictine house was therefore based on some kind of critical edition of existent customs.[1]

Answers to the attendant questions of how and why this selective process occurred are in the vast majority of cases plagued by the absence of sources. In the case of Norwich, however, we have a copy of the house's Customary, dating from the second half of the thirteenth century, and a letter from Bishop Herbert, the contents of which promise clarification of that book's source. Both of these texts are

1. For monastic customaries in general, see K. Hallinger, 'Consuetudo: Begriff, Formen, Forschungsgeschichte, Inhalt', in *Untersuchungen zu Kloster und Stift* (Veröffentlichungen des Max-Planck-Instituts für Geschichte, 68, Göttingen, 1980), pp. 140– 66; and L. Donnat, 'Les coutumes monastiques autour de l'an Mil', in D. Iogna-Prat and J.-C. Picard, eds, *Religion et culture autour de l'an Mil* (Paris, 1990), pp. 17–24.

published.[2] To take the letter first, we have Herbert writing to Prior Roger of Fécamp (which puts the letter in the period between Roger's accession in December 1109 and Herbert's death in July 1119), telling him that the customs of the Normandy house have been followed at Norwich in so far as they have been able to get them from 'Lord Baldwin' (a figure otherwise unidentified – possibly the Baldwin, bishop of Dol, who was a great friend to Fécamp), or in as much as Herbert has been able to recall them; and effectively asking permission to send one or two monks to observe Fécamp liturgy with a view to importing elements of it to Norwich. An examination of the history suggested by this letter will come when we look at the Customary itself, but it is worth noting here the implication that it was not necessarily upon written sources alone that even something so huge and complicated as a liturgical Use depended for its transmission in the central middle ages; that memory and personal observation coupled with note-taking were also factors in play.

To a certain extent it is possible to see the role of Fécamp in this picture as resulting simply from a mixture of convenience and Herbert's personal homage to the house in which, having made his profession, he rose to the office of prior before his translation to Ramsey in 1087. Fécamp had, however, a wider importance than just this and one which would have made its observances particularly attractive as a model. Duke Richard II of Normandy had in 1001 summoned William of Volpiano to superintend the reform of Fécamp. The abbey, situated alongside one of the most favoured palaces of the dukes of Normandy, had long enjoyed ducal attention and patronage, and Richard had nominated it as the place of his burial.[3] William, son of an aristocratic Piedmontese family and protégé of the sainted Majolus, abbot of Cluny, had already acquired a reputation for thorough and efficient reform which was to leave an indelible mark on the history of western monasticism, and to earn him the sobriquet of '*Supra-regula*' ('Beyond-the-Rule'). At the time of this, his first reforming venture in Normandy (where his influence was to be profound), he was abbot of St-Bénigne at Dijon, a house whose reform he had undertaken in 989.

2. J. B. L. Tolhurst, ed., *The Customary of the Cathedral Priory Church of Norwich* (Henry Bradshaw Society, 82, London, 1948). The manuscript is now Cambridge, Corpus Christi College, MS 465. Herbert's letter is numbered xxxiv in R. Anstruther, ed., *Epistolae Herberti de Losinga, primi episcopi Norwicensis, Osberti de Clara et Elmeri, prioris Cantuariensis* (Publications of the Caxton Society, Brussels and London, 1846), p. 68, with an English translation in GS, i, p. 64.

3. For the key role played by Fécamp in the development of Norman government, see J.-F. Lemarignier, *Étude sur les Privilèges d'exemption et de juridiction ecclésiastique des abbayes Normandes depuis les origines jusqu'en 1140* (Archives de la France Monastique, 44, Paris, 1937), especially ch. II; and J.-F. Lemarignier, 'Le monachisme et l'encadrement religieux des campagnes du royaume de France situées au nord de la Loire, de la fin du Xe à la fin du XIe siècle', in *Le istituzioni ecclesiastiche della 'Societas Christiana' dei secoli XI–XII: diocesi, pievi E Parrochie. Atti della sesta Settimana Internazionale di Studio, Milano, 1–7 Settembre 1974* (Miscellanea del Centro di Studi Medioevali, 8, Milan, 1978), pp. 357–94.

Only a few months before receiving the commission to reform Fécamp he had embarked upon the foundation of the house of Fruttuaria on his family estate in the Canavese (Piedmont), with whose organisation he remained intimately involved.[4] The scope of William's reforming activities was wide, from church building, through monastic schooling, to the content and execution of liturgical observance. It is the latter which concerns us here. His own disciple and biographer, Rodulf Glaber, tells us specifically of his reputation in liturgical work and of his profound knowledge of chant and skill in teaching it.[5] Something of this sort might be expected from a scion of Cluny, the great Burgundian house famous for its splendid and elaborate liturgy. William seems to have been responsible for compiling customaries for houses with whose organisation he was involved; those which survive share familial characteristics which derive some of their elements from Cluny without being in any way wholly dependent upon it. Where we have sources from which to deduce the musical constituents of these customs, it would seem that William was responsible for systematic editing and rearrangement of the inherited corpus of chant, and probably for the addition of a sizeable repertory of newly-composed items, producing an idiosyncratic repertory (*cursus*) of antiphons and responds.[6]

Seen in this light, Fécamp must have had for Herbert resonances more far-reaching than those occasioned by personal circumstance. It was an institution whose recent history distilled a characteristically symbiotic blend of temporal and spiritual power. Its organisation had been, with ducal support, subject less than a century earlier to the thoroughgoing attentions of William of Volpiano, the most renowned monastic

4.   There is a readable account of William's work in W. Williams, *Monastic Studies* (Manchester, 1938), pp. 99–120; and, in great detail, in N. Bulst, *Untersuchungen zu den Klosterreformen Wilhelms von Dijon (962–1031)* (Pariser Historische Studien, 11, Bonn, 1973), with an account of the Fécamp reforms at pp. 147–61. See also, stressing the continuity of William's work after his death, N. Bulst, 'La réforme monastique en Normandie: étude prosopographique sur la diffusion et l'implantation de le réforme de Guillaume de Dijon', in R. Foreville, ed., *Les mutations socio-culturelles au tournant des XIe–XIIe siècles. Actes du colloque international du CNRS: études Anselmiennes IVe session* (Spicilegium Beccense, 2, Paris, 1984), pp. 317–30. For a general review of Fécamp's insular connections see M. Chibnall, 'Fécamp and England', in *L'Abbaye Bénédictine de Fécamp: ouvrage scientifique du XIIIe centenaire, 658–*

1958, 3 vols (Fécamp, 1959), i, pp. 127–35, 375–78.

5.   J. France, N. Bulst, P. Reynolds, eds, *Rodulfus Glaber opera* (Oxford, 1989), p. 288. For suggestions about William's specific work in this area see F. Hansen, *H 159 Montpellier: Tonary of St-Bénigne of Dijon* (Copenhagen, 1974), p. 21; and R. Steiner, 'Marian Antiphons at Cluny and Lewes', in S. Rankin and D. Hiley, eds, *Music in the Mediæval English Liturgy: Plainsong and Mediæval Music Society Centennial Essays* (Oxford, 1993), pp. 175–204 at pp. 200–1.

6.   For some of the characteristics of customaries associated with William's reform, see below. The fundamental study of the chant elements of William's work is R. Le Roux, 'Guillaume de Volpiano: son cursus liturgique au Mont-Saint-Michel et dans les abbayes Normandes', in J. Laporte, ed., *Histoire et vie monastiques* (Millénaire monastique du Mont-Saint-Michel, 1, Paris, 1966), pp. 417–72.

Fig. 119. Norwich
Cathedral cloister, *c.* 1876.

reformer of his time, attentions which (in the ritual sphere at least) had about them
the unmistakable aroma of Cluny-derived authority, efficiency and splendour. In
this complex of things there lay a cultural statement whose echoes reached out to
almost every corner of life. If the building of a cathedral such as Norwich was
'intended to impress the English with the power of the Norman conquerors and
the divine favour reflected in the majesty of their churches', then that intention
was realised daily and visibly in liturgical ritual.[7] The compelling meaning of all this
for an entrepreneurial Norman bishop engaged in establishing a new monastic
cathedral in England needs no emphasis.[8]

7. The quotation is from C. N. L. Brooke,
    'Princes and Kings as Patrons of Monasteries:
    Normandy and England', in *Il monachesimo
    e la riforma ecclesiastica, 1049–1122: atti della
    quarta settimana internazionale de studio, Men-
    dola, 23–29 Agosto 1968* (Miscellanea del cen-
    tro di studi medioevali, 6, Milan, 1971), pp.
    125–52 at p. 132.

8. For the Cluniac components of the liturgy
    introduced to Canterbury by Lanfranc, see
    D. Knowles, *Decreta Lanfranci monachis Can-
    tuariensibus transmissa* (Corpus consuetudi-
    num monasticarum, 3, Siegburg, 1967),
    passim and especially pp. xvii–xix; and M.
    Gibson, *Lanfranc of Bec* (Oxford, 1978), pp.
    170–76.

At the point at which Tolhurst published his edition of the Norwich Customary he seems not to have consulted in detail the one surviving custom-book of Fécamp, a text which to this day stubbornly remains unprinted.[9] He came, however, to the opinion – one in which he has been followed by other writers – that Norwich had indeed drawn its customs from Fécamp.[10] That general view was expressed with characteristic caution, based as it largely was upon internal evidence, but from it the present writer will not differ. It is not only, however, a collation of the Fécamp books which may help us to give some precision to the picture. In the half century since Tolhurst's work a mass of material has been published on 'Cluny' ritual, including most notably new critical editions of the texts deriving ultimately from the customs of Dijon and Fruttuaria, with which William of Volpiano was concerned at the time of his Fécamp project.[11] We may therefore ask again of this material whether it demonstrates that the Norwich book consistently transmits customs characteristic of what might be called William's 'dialect' of Cluny ritual; and whether we are in a position to assess how such a process might have come about. Full answers to these questions can of course be given only as part of a systematic – and necessarily prolix – reassessment of all the texts involved. In a shorter essay it may, however, be possible to outline the broad picture, giving some idea of the nature and richness of the ritual with which the first monks of Norwich Priory adorned their services.

Some initial notes of caution should be sounded. The main text of the Norwich book as we have it dates from at least 150 years after Herbert's letter; whatever its origin, it must incorporate the results of continuous emendation.[12] It is the same for the Fécamp ordinal, which is a half-century or so older. Both books carry numerous marginal emendations, made over the course of time, as no doubt their ancestors did; the eventual incorporation of these into the main text of a new edition would keep the process going. They are therefore primarily documents of their time – as evidence for older practices they must be treated with care. This is especially so when discrepance between sources occurs, as it does very frequently between the

9. Fécamp, Musée de la Bénédictine, MS 186 (s. xii ex.). An edition of this text is in the publication programme of the Henry Bradshaw Society. For the discussion below, reference has also been made to a noted Breviary (s. xiii) of the house, Rouen, Bibliothèque Municipal, MS 205.

10. Tolhurst, *Customary*, pp. xiv–xvii, and J. B. L. Tolhurst, 'The Monastic Customary of Norwich', in D. H. S. Cranage, ed., *Thirteen-Hundredth Anniversary of the Diocese of East Anglia: Official Handbook* (Norwich 1930), pp. 79–82.

11. The Dijon text (with the siglum B²) is in

K. Hallinger, *Consuetudines Cluniacensium antiquiores cum redactionibus derivatis* (Corpus consuetudinum monasticarum 7/2, Siegburg, 1983). The Fruttuaria text is in L. Spätling and P. Dintner, *Consuetudines Fructuarienses-Sanblasianae*, 2 vols (Corpus consuetudinum monasticarum 12/1 and 12/2, Siegburg, 1985–87). There is an extensive discussion of the sources and their interrelationship in K. Hallinger, *Consuetudinum saeculi X/XI/XII monumenta: introductiones* (Corpus consuetudinum monasticarum 7/1, Siegburg, 1984).

12. Tolhurst, *Customary*, pp. xiv–xv.

Fécamp and Norwich books. Similarly, the texts which convey Fruttuaria liturgy are not manuscripts from that house itself but rather editions made at (or for) other centres which wished – or needed – to derive their liturgy from that source.[13]

The nature of the Norwich book itself must also be taken into account. It is essentially a directory of ceremonial, with excursions into other related aspects of the community's life, intended probably for the use of the master of ceremonies – the man to whom the first emender of the book (Tolhurst's 'Hand A') refers as *custos ecclesie* or *custos ordinis*.[14] The scope of his duties will have dictated its contents. He does not (for instance) seem to have had anything to do with the details of the 'drama' of the *Visitatio Sepulchri* (*Visit to the Sepulchre*) which formed part of matins on Easter Day; his book simply tells him that the monks who are to play the parts of the three Marys visiting the sepulchre should prepare themselves and enter the choir after the third responsory.[15] On the other hand, pertinent matters are treated with considerable care. The antiphon *O mundi domina* (*O mistress of the world*), sung at matins on Christmas morning, is specifically directed to be sung slowly (*morose*) because of its brevity, with the repeat of its last clause likewise *morose*.[16] With processions, care is to be taken that there is always a space of four or five paces between the participants.[17] The book contains many such vignettes of the very practical business of organising liturgical ritual. What it does not do is to detail all constituent chants and prayers of a given service. It assumes the existence of such information in the various books used in choir, none of which has survived. It is therefore difficult to deduce from this book the details of the sacramentary and the *cursus* of chant material in use at Norwich. With regard to the latter, although there are certainly elements which belong to William's *cursus*, there are many items which do not. As an instance, the history – that is, the ensemble of chants and lessons – for St Mary Magdalene (22 July) in the Fécamp books is that known from the opening of its first responsory as *Gloriosa diei huius sollempnia* (*The glorious solemnity of this day*). That which can be inferred from the Norwich Customary is the distinctly different history *Gloriosa es Maria Magdalena* (*Thou art glorious O Mary Magdalene*).[18] To restate the point, there can be no guarantee that distinctions such as this

13. Spätling and Dintner, *Consuetudines*, p. xiv ('Sie wurden vielmehr in den *armaria* des reformierten Tochter-Klöster pietätvoll deponiert . . .'); Donnat, 'Les coutumes', pp. 18–19. None of the Cluny 'antiquiores' sources are from the Burgundian house itself.

14. Tolhurst, *Customary*, pp. 88, 90.

15. Tolhurst, *Customary*, p. 94

16. Tolhurst, *Customary*, p. 32.

17. Tolhurst, *Customary*, p. 58.

18. Tolhurst, *Customary*, p. 151, with the cue for the distinctive antiphon sequence for second vespers *Adest praeclara* which belongs to this history. For Fécamp, see the breviary, Rouen, Bibliothèque Municipale, MS 205, fos 285ff. For a general treatment of the Magdalene's histories, see D. Chadd, 'An English Noted Breviary of *circa* 1200', in Rankin and Hiley, *Music in the Mediæval English Liturgy*, pp. 205–38 at pp. 215–16, with references.

stem from the original book in use at Norwich rather than from emendations subsequently made to it. In some cases, indeed, it may be possible to infer from our book such emendation actually under way. An illustrative case is the office for the feast of SS. John and Paul on 26 June. In William's *cursus*, as it is shown by the Fécamp sources, the office for this feast is given a proper history in which both the overall arrangement and some of the individual chant elements are quite distinctive. In the Norwich book, the material which came after the rubric *Ad matutinas; lectiones proprie et responsoria* (*At matins; proper lessons and responsories*) has been erased and in palimpsest has been added the cues for the responsories of the first nocturn from the common of saints; that is to say, a history which is not at all (as the rubric has led us to believe it would be) 'proper'.[19] Although there can be, once again, no guarantee that there was original agreement between the Norwich and Fécamp sources, there can be little doubt that in our book chants from the common were substituted for those of some proper history or other. The nature of this emendation will point to the sort of changes which can be seen even within the text as we have it, and with the sort of problems which necessarily ensue.

If that leaves us unable to be categorical about the liturgical (strictly speaking) pedigree of our book, the situation is rather better if we turn to the ritual, even if the same caveats must apply. If we take as a benchmark the seventeen points in which Dom Hallinger has isolated non-Cluny characteristics of St-Bénigne ritual, we shall find that the Norwich book, where its contents allow a comparison, tends to follow them.[20] If we then bring into play the books from Fécamp and Fruttuaria, we shall see how the ritual of Norwich belongs clearly in this family. Some brief examples must suffice. The first is of the strikingly ceremonious performance of the antiphon *Nolite timere* (*Be not afraid*) with the canticle *Benedictus* after lauds on the feast of St Thomas the Apostle, five days before Christmas.[21] Appendix 1 contains the texts of this ceremony from the books of Norwich, Fécamp, Mont-St-Michel, St-Bénigne at Dijon and Fruttuaria. Between these there is an obvious familial relationship. At the end of lauds, two monks move to the centre of the church, in front of the altar step, and sing the whole of the antiphon with 'raised voices'. They and the choir, the latter beginning the psalm *Benedictus*, genuflect. The psalm is

19. Rouen, Bibliothèque Municipale, MS 261, fol. 227v, and Tolhurst, *Customary*, p. 139. I would differ from Tolhurst's judgement that the new material was added by his 'Hand A'. It seems to me that the emendations to matins and lauds material are one long - and very neat - palimpsest in the original hand.

20. Hallinger, *Introductiones*, pp. 242–43.

21. The *Benedictus*, normally referred to as 'psalm', is the canticle of Zacharias from Luke 1:68 ('Blessed be the Lord God of Israel; for he hath visited and redeemed his people'). It is the regular 'psalm' of lauds, and its use in this ceremony means that it has two proximate performances in the liturgy of this day.

then sung by the choir, alternate sides of which take alternate verses, and the performance of this is interspersed and concluded with repetitions of the antiphon – as many as six in the very prolix version from Mont-St-Michel. This extensive use of an unabbreviated psalm-antiphon makes it very 'special' in medieval liturgical terms.[22]

The account given above is a synthesised one, for the relationship between the versions in the manuscripts is highly complex and obscure, as no two of them agree in detail. None the less, the coincidence of elements binds them all together in a group which also includes Jumièges and St-Epvre at Toul, both of which houses – like the continental ones whose sources are given in the appendix – were reformed by William.[23] This ceremony was not used at Cluny until later and its distribution can leave no doubt that it was a part of the repertory associated with the reform work of William of Volpiano.[24] Two points may be made about the Norwich version. First, it is difficult to see how the form in which we have it could be derived from a Fécamp book, so dissimilar are the versions that we have from the two centres. Secondly, it is hard to imagine that a successful performance would have been possible from it – the omission of some key words makes the directions virtually impenetrable, certainly when compared with the precision of the analogues. The complete lack of indications about the points within the psalm where the antiphon is to be repeated lead one to suspect that a whole sentence has been lost from it. Might we here take Herbert's letter at its face value and suppose a ceremony imperfectly recalled from memory, never used in its fullest possible form and consequently never subjected to correction?

Elsewhere there are instances in which it seems highly likely that the Norwich and Fécamp books show clear textual relationship. An example is the procession after terce and before mass on the feast of the raising of the cross (15 September).[25] Once again, the ensemble of ritual elements in the Norwich book confines this ceremony to the milieu of houses which received customs from William, but between the Norwich and Fécamp versions there are particularly close ties. Their texts are given in parallel columns in Appendix 2. The essence of the ceremony is the carrying of the cross by a priest, dressed in alb and golden stole, in procession

22. For a succinct account of the usual form of the psalm-antiphon, see F. Ll. Harrison, *Music in Medieval Britain* (London 1958), pp. 58–61.

23. The ordinal of Jumièges is Rouen, Bibliothèque Municipale, MS 398, and that of Toul is Paris, Bibliothèque National, MS lat. 975. On the work of William of Volpiano at these houses, see Bulst, *Unter-*

suchungen, pp. 163–67 and 90–98 respectively.

24. For the later incorporation into Cluny ritual see K. Hallinger, 'Herkunft und Überlieferung der Consuetudo Sigiberti', *Zeitschrift der Savigny-Stiftung für Rechtsgeschichte* 87 (Kanonistische Abteilung, 56, 1970), pp. 194–242, at pp. 203 and 206.

25. Tolhurst, *Customary*, p. 172.

around the precincts, with two phylacteries (presumably containing holy relics) suspended from the arms of the cross. The cross is accompanied by carriers of holy water and candelabra, and followed by the whole community in order. Upon the return to the choir of the church, the priest sets up the cross upon a prepared seat before the altar, and the community in order, one by one and starting with the bishop and prior, genuflect before it and venerate it with a kiss. What is striking about the Norwich and Fécamp versions is the high incidence of exact verbal correspondence between them, indicated in Appendix 2 by the passages in bold type. In each of these cases, the sources from Dijon and Fruttuaria are either silent about these details or express them in quite different words. It is very probable that we have here an instance of the Norwich book literally copying its prescriptions from a Fécamp source.

It is unlikely that Norwich was the only Benedictine house in Norman England which used ceremonial derived from William of Volpiano's reforms, mediated through the abbeys of Normandy. The breviary of Winchcombe is in fact one of the oldest surviving witnesses of the liturgical Use associated with him, and elements of it can be found also in the service books of the abbeys of Gloucester, Evesham, Hyde (Winchester) and Peterborough. None of these houses however has left us a customary or other directory of ceremonial comparable with that of Norwich, and about the ritual elements of their liturgy we can therefore know nothing. It is only with the Norwich book that we can see, through the eyes of the late thirteenth century, the legacy of one important facet of the Normans' cultural invasion of this island.

Appendix 1

NORWICH (Tolhurst, *Customary*, p. 22)
Post *Benedicamus domino* venient duo fratres in medio chori et cantabunt alta voce *Nolite timere* totam qua cantata flectent genua ibidem. Deinde cantetur [psalmum *Benedictus*] a choro flectendo genua in stationibus suis. Postea incipiat cantor *Gloria patri* et iterum [antiphona] cantetur post *Gloria*.

FÉCAMP (Fécamp, Musée de la Bénédictine, MS 168, fo. 9)
Post *Benedicamus domino* a duobus monachis ad gradum cantetur tota antiphona *Nolite timere** et subiugente cantore psalmus *Benedictus* flectens omnes genua. Post primum et secundum psalmi versum repetatur a dextro et a sinistro choro singillatim decantanda. Similiter et post penultimum et ultimum in fine psalmi versum, eo ordine quo supra distinctum est cantetur antiphona. Post *Gloria patri* antiphona iterum decantata dicatur a sacerdote sine cuiuslibet versiculum sed tantum *Dominus vobiscum* . . .

MONT-ST-MICHEL (Avranches, Bibliothèque Municipale, MS 216, fo. 102v)
Post *Benedicamus Domino* duo cantores in superiori parte chori stantes, scilicet ante altare chori, cantent antiphonam *Nolite timere* et genibus flexis revertatur uterque in locum suum. Qua antiphona ab utroque choro simul cantata incipiet cantor *Benedictus* et post primum uersum repetetur antiphona semper altius cantando. Tunc subcentor incipiet secundum uersum *Et erexit*. Deinde antiphona. Tunc cantor incipiet uersum *Sicut locutus* et sic dicatur psalmus. Et post penultimum uersum repetatur antiphona semper altius cantando ab illo choro qui dicit uersum, et post ultimum uersum similiter ab alio choro, et post *Gloria* ab omnibus sine neupma. Mox sacerdos subiungat *Dominus uobiscum*, or' *Concede quesumus omnipotens Deus ut magne festiuitatis*.

ST-BÉNIGNE, DIJON (Hallinger, *Consuetudines Cluniacensium*, p. 24)
Finitis autem matutinis pergant duo fratres ante gradum altare dicere antiphonam *Nolite timere* complentes eam. Hac finita flectant genua sua cum ceteris omnibus. Tunc incipiatur psalmus *Benedictus*. Repetatur autem haec eadem antiphona quatuor vicibus, duabus in initio psalmi et duabus ad consummationem eiusdem psalmi. Novissime dicatur a sacerdote *Dominus vobiscum*.

FRUTTUARIA (Spätling and Dintner, *Consuetudines Fructuarienses*, p. 107)
Finitis matutinis laudibus post *Benedicamus domino* respondentibus omnibus *Deo gratias* eant duo fratres in medio ante altare et inchoent excelsa voce antiphonam *Nolite timere* usque *Dominus vester*. Tunc inchoet abbas psalmum *Benedictus dominus* et flectant omnes genua. Post primum versum repetant antiphonam, similiter post ultimum versum *Illuminare*, iterum post *Gloria patri*. *Sicut erat*.

---

* A contemporary hand adds in margin: 'et prosternant se ad gradum revertent ad sedilibus suis'.

Appendix 2

NORWICH (Tolhurst, *Customary*, p. 172)

Post terciam preparatur processio. Hic sacerdos **in alba et aurea stola** accipiet crucem **cum duobus philateriis suspensis in brachiis ipsius** et eo stante ante gradum in choro cum converso tenente aquam benedictam et aliis tenentibus duo candelabra. Incipiet cantor antiphonam *Sanctifica nos* et procedant conversi et sacerdos, deinde ceteri ut sunt novicii. Post antiphona cantentur responsoria *Dulce lignum, O crux benedicta, Hoc signum, Nos autem,* et fiet processio circa choream. Revertente vero processione, fiet statio ante crucem donec finiatur antiphona vel responsorium quod tunc cantabitur. Deinde ad introitum chori incipiet cantor antiphonam *O crux splendidior.* Sacerdos vero cum cruce accedens versus altare inveniet ante ipsum sedem preparatam, **et vertens tergum [ad] sanctuarium tenebit depositam crucem et erectam super sedem ante se [ad] fratribus adorandum**. Tunc episcopus et prior et ceteri omnes in ordine accedentes, **et facta una tantum ante eam flexione genuum osculabuntur eam**. Quod cum fecerint omnes, erigatur a sacerdote ponenda in loco suo. Deinde pulsentur omnia signa ad missam.

FÉCAMP (Fécamp, Musée de la Bénédictine, MS 168, fo. 148r)

Post terciam fiat processio per claustrum in navem ecclesie sacerdote cantaturo ea die missam **in alba et in aurea stola** sanctam crucem deferente **cum duobus philicteriis suspensis a brachiis ipsius** qui et ipse post eos qui candelabra et aquam benedicta et thuribulum portant debet procedere. Deinde abbas, pueri, priores, aliique in suo ordine et eat processio per claustrum cantans. In primis vero cantatur antiphona *Sanctifica nos domine* deinde responsorium *O crux benedicta* V' *O crux gloriosa,* reponsorium *Nos autem gloriari*; ad introitum chori antiphona *O crux splendidior.* Introgressus chorum sacerdos cum cruce accedet ad preparatum apud altare cum pallio et tapeto sedem **et vertens tergum ad sanctuarium tenebit depositam crucem et erectam super sedem ante [se] ad adorandum fratribus**. Tunc abbas et alii incipientes a prioribus accedentes **facta una tantum ante eam flexione genuum** adorabunt et **osculabunt eam** cantantes has antiphonas; *O crux benedicta, O crux viride lignum, Crux fidelis, Adoramus te christe, O crux benedicta.* Adorata sancta cruce antiphona a sacerdote incipienda *Super omnia ligna cedrorum.*

16

The Muniments
and the Library

Barbara Dodwell

The Muniments

The archives of the dean and chapter of Norwich (moved to the Norfolk Record Office in 1975) consist of two elements, the first being a large number of medieval manuscripts and the second being the records of the post-Reformation cathedral.

For the historian of today the most important part of the medieval manuscripts comprises the obedientiary rolls. They are important because of their rarity: most monastic houses fell into the hands of laymen in the sixteenth century and their obedientiary rolls, having no relevance for that time, have been lost. Even that handful of monastic cathedrals whose fate was different, with the exception of Durham and Norwich, seems not to have preserved these documents carefully. At Norwich, however, there are nearly 1400 individual rolls. Some are duplicates, for the obedientiary was required to send a copy to the sub-prior while keeping another in his own office; some cover only part of the year, for when a new official took over a new roll was required. Some indeed cover several years, with the annual rolls being sewn together, and some were even entered into books. Despite considerable gaps in the series, this collection of rolls is one of the best in the country.

The obedientiary roll is an account roll. Every year each official (or obedientiary), including the warden of the hospital of St Paul and the prior of each cell, was required to provide his superior with a set of accounts showing first his income from all sources, be they farm profits, rents, oblations from churches (and in the case of the sacrist, from particular altars within the cathedral), legacies and gifts, or sales of any commodities such as wax, stone or timber being surplus to immediate requirements. Having set out and totalled his income, he then detailed his expenses, which in large part depended on his responsibilities and also in lesser part on the need to repair the mills, manor houses, rectories, urban properties and churches in his charge. Moreover, this being a decentralized institution,[1] he had to pay his share of communal burdens: the cost of sending monks to university, the cost of lawsuits, expenses involved in the election of a new prior and the payment of taxes of various kinds – the list was long. We cannot be sure when these account rolls were first issued. The earliest to survive is a roll for the prior's chamber (*camera prioris*) of 1263–64, although it cannot have been the first of the series.[2] The earlier rolls are full of detail, but changes occurred during the fifteenth century. It becomes increasingly obvious that in many cases there are totals behind which lie other documents which have not survived. By the sixteenth century the details of the costs of repairs are no longer given, instead there is reference to a book of accounts.[3] Similarly the sacrist no longer supplies details of legacies, instead the scribe refers to a red book belonging to his office.[4] It was normal practice to keep past rolls, both by the office and by the sub-prior, although there are many gaps and in the main there are more rolls for the fifteenth century than for any other period.[5]

If historians today attach special importance to the run of obedientiary rolls, the main concern of the medieval monks was to preserve their title deeds and grants of privileges. There survive over 1800, although by no means all of these were grants to the priory.[6] Many of the late thirteenth-century grants, be they donations or sales, came with attendant proofs of possession – the grantor's title deeds. These could not be discarded but were of secondary importance. Of greater interest were those grants and confirmations transferring properties and rents to the cathedral priory. It was necessary not only to preserve these but also to put them in some kind of order, so that (should the need arise) any document could be easily located. But here there was a clash of interests – should there be one central collection or should each obedientiary have charge of the grants and title deeds for the properties assigned to his office? This can only have become an issue towards the end of the thirteenth century when the full complement of offices had been arrived at.[7] I suspect that compromise prevailed and that all the documents relating to the foundation of the cathedral priory, be they from king, pope or bishop, were at first kept as a single group while the later grants were handed over to the obedientiaries for safe-keeping in their offices.

1. See above, pp 241–42.
2. NRO, DCN 1/1/1. It records arrears for the previous year.
3. NRO, DCN 1/4/12.
4. NRO, DCN 1/4/11.
5. A general description of the obedientiary rolls has been given by H. W. Saunders, *An Introduction to the Obedientiary and Manor Rolls of Norwich Cathedral Priory* (Norwich, 1930). The only rolls to have been printed are the early rolls of the communar and pitancer: *Communar Rolls*.
6. As yet only two volumes of Norwich Priory deeds have been printed, *NCC*, i and ii. H. W. Saunders also edited that part of *Registrum primum* containing the chronicle, *First Register*.
7. For the development of the obedientiaries, see pp. 241–42, 348–49.

Around 1300 there came a general rearrangement of the muniments. This is known to us by an inventory of which a fair copy made in book form was written soon after 1327. This reorganisation set the pattern for the rest of the middle ages. The notion of keeping a separate group of foundation documents, while allowing departmental heads to keep deeds and later grants relating to their properties, would appear to have been abandoned in favour of a centralised muniment room.[8] The plan was to create three specialised collections: one of royal *acta*, another of episcopal *acta* and a third of legal compromises, known as final concords, were each to be presented in roughly chronological order. A fourth collection was to include the bulk of the title deeds and was to be arranged largely but not exclusively on the basis of the office to which they related. Each of these collections was assigned a set of letters, the royal *acta* taking A to C, the episcopal D to F, while G was the letter given to the final concords. In the title deed collection the letters J to Q covered the estates of the master of the cellar, R to T those of the cellarer and X and Y those of the sacrist. Norwich properties held by a variety of offices were assigned the letter U (or V), while Z was given over to sundry oddments. Within the confines of each letter the documents were then assigned numbers so that each document could be easily identified.[9]

Comprehensive as this arrangement might seem at first glance, in no way did it include the whole archive. No provision seems to have been made for the inclusion of papal privileges and archiepiscopal confirmations. Although the former are entered into the *First Register*, which otherwise follows the order of the inventory, these documents are not there provided with the informative rubrics which in all other cases the compiler based on inventory entries.[10] It is as though these documents had been deliberately excluded. The same appears to be true of archiepiscopal confirmations. These are not entered in the inventory and those still extant bear a pressmark unlike any other. There were, also, other omissions. The title deeds of the five cells were not entered, nor indeed did all the obedientiaries participate in the reorganisation. The most obvious absentee is the almoner, who kept his title deeds, including final concords and some of his royal *acta*, apart from the main collection. Another absentee, although in lesser degree, was the chamberlain. The inventory therefore never included all the title deeds and presumably was not intended to. Nor can we assume that all the material contained within it was, in fact, kept centrally. The absentees noted here were probably not the only officials to retain control of their

8. In the inventory Herbert de Losinga's foundation charter seems to be an addition, distinguished not by a number but by a symbol, as though it had been added to the list of his deeds. NRO, DCN 40/12, p. 10.

9. A later reorganisation changed both the letter and the numbering of royal and episcopal charters. *NCC*, i, p. xvii.

10. Most of the papal documents are provided with brief rubrics while some have no rubric at all.

own title deeds. The contents of this inventory suggest that around 1300 there was a plan to preserve the priory's grants and title deeds in a central archive which was well ordered to facilitate the location of documents. Its omissions, however, suggest that the convenience of some of the obedientiaries eroded if not actually thwarted the full implementation of this plan.

This incomplete implementation of the move towards a centralised archive is reflected in the Norwich cartularies. These were volumes into which grants and deeds were transcribed in order to facilitate speed of reference. Some Benedictine houses produced a single large general cartulary which opened with separate sections of royal and episcopal *acta* before presenting copies of title deeds. In East Anglia, Ely followed this pattern, although it also produced a separate cartulary for the almoner. By contrast Norwich produced no general cartulary; instead separate volumes were compiled for each of the main officers. The cellarer's cartulary, we are told, was begun in 1282.[11] Thereafter specialist registers for other departments followed. Before 1300 the sacrist had produced one and an early attempt had been made to compile one by the master of the cellar. In the early fourteenth century a second cartulary was made for this same official. This, like the first, contained additional matter, such as royal and episcopal deeds, papal privileges and final concords: it also included an early chronicle, but it was not a general cartulary, for it contained no title deeds for any other office.[12]

This large volume is an indication of the advent of the professional scribe. It shows a great advance on the three earlier registers. Not only is it well laid out but initial letters are decorated with scroll work in red and blue ink. Even more attractive was the next cartulary to appear, that of the almoner.[13] Its layout and the use of coloured inks for the headlines proclaim the skill of its scriptor. Later in the fourteenth century came the last of the office cartularies, a small volume recording the chamberlain's title deeds, less beautiful but again a professional piece. Throughout the later centuries additional material was added to the existing cartularies, but grants and purchases of new properties were few, curtailed by the restraints of the Statute of Mortmain. The fifteenth century saw the production of two more specialist cartularies. One, made in the middle of the century, was of episcopal *acta*; the other, of royal deeds, ran to the reign of Henry VII, with a few later additions. They were probably in-house productions made for the use of the prior.[14]

The transcription of title deeds into books was apparently only thought necessary for the major offices. The less important, such as the precentor, infirmarer, hosteler and gardener, all relied on income from city properties. Their title deeds were,

11. NRO, DCN 40/5, fo. 2.
12. NRO, DCN 40/1.
13. NRO, DCN 40/2.

14. The Italianate script of *Registrum tertium* has been spotted amongst the obedientiary rolls.

Fig. 120. The cloister garth, showing the graveyard and one of the houses abutting the cloister and south transept, in a 1785 painting by William Wilkins.

according to the inventory, stored with the central muniments and the documents endorsed with the name of the office. A small roll would have sufficed for their needs. Similarly, a roll was probably all that was necessary for the refectorer who held property in Bracondale, a suburb to the south of Norwich, as well as in the city itself. But all this is conjecture, as no such rolls have survived. Whether the priory's cells, at St Leonard's, Yarmouth, Lynn, Hoxne and Aldeby, and the hospital of St Paul ever compiled registers is problematical. All that survive are an elegant roll for the hospital, made when Bishop John Salmon (1299–1325) confirmed its grants, and a rather untidy cartulary for Hoxne.[15]

The administration of the priory estates of itself generated records. The least bulky were those for their urban properties, some requiring no more than rentals which, however, would need updating. Tithes associated with urban churches necessarily created records, including memoranda showing the location of the land thus tithed and the names of its tenants. By contrast, country estates produced a mass of material,

15. Bishop Salmon's roll is now BL, Cotton Charter ii 19. The Hoxne cartulary is now in the Suffolk Record Office, Ipswich.

some appearing only occasionally but much of it coming in on an annual basis; all of it requiring attention and most of it housing. The most obvious to us now are the court and account rolls of the priory's manors. These begin in 1255–56, a date too late to be the first year of their production, although it might conceivably be the year in which the monks decided to retain them. While they were not preserved with great regularity they form an important element of the archive. Less common are rentals, surveys and related documents. Here it is only necessary to refer to one manuscript, a survey of manors assigned to the master of the cellar. It was ordered by Prior William Kirby on his election in 1272 and it took about twenty years to complete. It was then written up in book form as a fine copy and, perhaps because it was a fine copy, retained.[16] Many religious houses, among them Ramsey Abbey, produced similar surveys a little earlier in the mid thirteenth century.

Occasionally we find material that relates to the priory as a whole. Most notable are the *status obedientiariorum* which provide an overall conspectus of the income of the priory, and the *proficia maneriorum* which, between 1295 and 1340, attempt to establish, manor by manor, the profitability of its demesne farming.[17]

There remains the question of where the muniments were kept. In all religious houses the normal place for the safe-keeping of important documents was the treasury, and so it was at Norwich. Here the treasury was an upper room over the slype to the south of the south transept. As the building has long since disappeared we cannot tell whether it contained built-in cupboards and hutches. It did however contain chests and it is very probable that royal charters were kept in long chests divided into compartments.[18] Such compartments would be a very practical way of storing documents, royal, episcopal or papal, which came in a number of different shapes and sizes; as did their seals, which could present additional complications.[19] For the ordinary title deeds, all manorial documents, and obedientiary rolls the normal place of storage seems to have been the office of the official concerned. While the rolls could have been kept in hutches, the title deeds were probably stored in chests, several of which have survived to this day. They are long and thin and divided by series of short notched pegs protruding from the inner sides on which probably hung bags, perhaps of linen, containing deeds, carefully folded so as to enclose the seal.[20] In their offices too the major obedientiaries probably kept their own cartularies.

The new foundation, and more particularly the refoundation of Edward VI,

---

16. Now BL, Stowe MS 936.

17. See pp. 349–51, 353, 356–58.

18. The clue lies in a note in the inventory that two versions of a royal charter (A31) that existed in triplicate were to be found in the next compartment, B. NRO, DCN 40/12, p. 2.

19. Some early twelfth-century charters written in the scriptorium of the beneficiary were long and thin. *NCC*, i, plate 3.

20. Two chests are illustrated in *NCC*, i, plate 1.

brought a change from a decentralised to a centralised institution. There seems to have been no destruction of old records. In fact, the central collection was increased by the return of records from the cells to the mother house. Of the old records, the title deeds and royal and episcopal *acta* were necessarily preserved.[21] Most papal privileges were, however, discarded, either around 1538 or later in the seventeenth century. Such of the obedientiary rolls as had survived were retained. Similarly the administrative records, the surveys and rentals, manor and court rolls were kept, although most of them can have had little relevance for the new state of affairs.

Once set up as a secular cathedral the archive material changed markedly. Constitutionally it was necessary to preserve the charters of Henry VIII and Edward VI and the early statutes.[22] Accounts were presented more simply, one roll for income, another for expenditure, a system which lasted into the seventeenth century. Audit papers, not preserved in the monastic period, survive for part of the seventeenth century in the form of receipts acknowledging payments made, on the one hand to the high steward (an important personage well able to sign his name), and on the other to bedesmen who could only make their marks. One new feature was the systematic registration of leases, the series of volumes beginning in 1538. Another was the recording of the minutes of chapter meetings. The extant series begins in 1566, although it must have been initiated earlier, and is of course still in progress. Records of ecclesiastical administration are also there. On the economic side the dean and chapter as landlord required the tenants of large estates to pay special attention to court rolls and rentals and to send in copies regularly; similarly, every twenty years tenants were to provide them with fresh surveys, rentals and terriers. These are reinforced by the parliamentary surveys prepared for the sale of capitular estates following the abolition of deans and chapters in 1649.[23]

With centralisation there could be only one place where muniments were kept – the treasury. The statutes laid down that the chests in which records were kept were to be housed in the treasury, and this may have applied to past records as well as to the current lease counterparts. This was probably not the medieval treasury, for a house with an inner and outer room was specified,[24] and in 1567 a petty canon

---

21. Almost all the royal deeds were still extant in the late fifteenth century, for the scribe of *Registrum tertium* copied directly from the documents and noted their absence where necessary.

22. For the problems surrounding the statutes in the sixteenth century, see pp. 530–33. What purport to be the Henrician statutes were copied into *Liber miscellaneorum*, no. 2, NRO, DCN 29/2, p. 23 onwards. Those seemingly of Elizabeth are in BL, Stowe MS 128. A seventeenth-century copy of the 1620 statutes is in NRO, DCN 113/1, a modern copy is NRO, DCN 28/1.

23. The parliamentary survey of dean and chapter properties in and around Norwich has been edited by G. A. Metters and published by the NRS, vol. 51 (1985).

24. NRO, DCN 29/2, p. 50, chapter 33.

was appointed to have charge of the evidences in the treasury house.[25] Perhaps there was already disorder, for in 1568 it was alleged that the 'register books are ill kept, [and] the counterpanes of leases either not received or lost'.[26] How the records were kept in the early seventeenth century we do not know but in mid century came the blow of sequestration. In April 1649 the lands of deans and chapters were confiscated for sale by the government and their records, even the medieval ones, transported to London. Although in November 1660 parliament declared such sales to be void, the new dean had not only to negotiate the return of properties so sold but also to redeem the title deeds and other records still held in London.[27] It is not surprising that not all documents were returned to their rightful owners. The documents, when returned, were probably not well sorted, for when Dr Prideaux was appointed prebendary in 1681 he found the old records in a parlous state 'lying in a very confused and disorderly manner on the floor of a room which was unpaved and covered in dirt and the windows broken'.[28] This room was known as the treasury. Blomefield writing in the 1740s identified it as that room over the chapel of St Luke where the muniments remained until their removal to the Norfolk Record Office in 1975.[29] The records of the new foundation seem, however, to have been kept elsewhere. During the late seventeenth and part of the eighteenth centuries they were in the charge of the chapter clerk and stored in his office, although by 1766 some had been deposited in the audit room.[30] They were later to be added to the medieval manuscripts in the treasury.

The Library

The basis for any monastic collection of books was primarily those necessary for the conduct of services: the psalters and missals, plus the books of the Old and New Testaments. To this can be added the homiletic literature, the devotional reading of the monks and then those grammatical works used for the education of novices. The movement for the opening of Oxford University to the Benedictines in 1292 enlarged their horizons;[31] commentaries on the Bible, philosophical works, legal works, all found their way into monastic libraries. In the background, an abiding

25. J. F. Williams and B. Cozens-Hardy, eds, *Extracts from the Two Earliest Minute Books of the Dean and Chapter of Norwich Cathedral, 1566–1649* (NRS, 24, 1953), p. 25.
26. W. H. Frere and W. P. M. Kennedy, eds, *Visitation Articles and Injunctions of the Period of the Reformation*, 3 vols (Alcuin Club Publications, 14–16, 1910), iii, p. 218.
27. D. Owen, 'Bringing Home the Records:

The Recovery of the Ely Chapter Muniments at the Restoration', *Archives*, 8 (1967–68), p. 123.
28. Anonymous, *The Life of the Reverend Humphrey Prideaux, DD* (London, 1748), p. 21.
29. Blomefield, *Norfolk*, iii, p. 9.
30. NRO, DCN 40/23, p. 25.
31. See pp. 244–47.

interest in the past, in the history of one's country and, more particularly, in the history of one's house took a firm hold. These elements are certainly to be found at Norwich, but it is not easy to determine the size and scope of its monastic library. As with other monastic cathedrals the monks' secular successors disposed of their inherited book collections. Bishop Bale, who toured England in search of the remnants of monastic libraries, listed some fifty-eight books that can definitely be associated with the pre-Reformation library at Norwich,[32] thereby providing us with a catalogue of a small part of the monastic book collection, especially valuable in that no medieval catalogue is now extant, although the monks had made a catalogue in 1315 and possibly updated it in the fifteenth century.[33] All that we have are book lists from four cells: St Leonard's, Yarmouth, Lynn and Hoxne.[34] Apart from this we are left with chance references and survivals.

Nevertheless occasional references in Herbert de Losinga's letters give some idea of the beginning of the cathedral library. With the emphasis on the need to study grammar and logic, and with the mention of Donatus and the *Categories* of Aristotle, it seems that the collection was well supplied on that side. It is also clear that Herbert's references to the study of sacred writing meant more than the study of the Old and New Testaments, for the young men were recommended to look to the Fathers, Jerome, Augustine, Ambrose and Gregory.[35] By the thirteenth century new writers such as Anselm in England, Hugh of St-Victor in Paris and Bernard of Clairvaux had come forward and some of their works would presumably have found their way into the monastic library. Yet the only indication that this might be so comes from the flyleaf of the Norwich Customary. This is probably part of a book list although it has been described as a collection of sayings, written at different times. Authors include Seneca and Augustine, and of the newer authors, Anselm and Bernard.[36] This may have been part of a Norwich book list, but the flyleaf has been cut from a larger sheet and might, thereby, have no direct connection with the cathedral priory.

We have no real idea of the range of interest, still less of the number of books contained in the priory at the time of the riot of 1272. According to the chronicle of Bartholomew Cotton books and ornaments were destroyed, either by fire or by

32. H. C. Beeching, 'The Library of the Cathedral Church of Norwich', *NA*, 19 (1915), p. 85.

33. NRO, DCN 1/9/3, for six skins to make a catalogue. For the fifteenth century, NRO, DCN 1/9/75 and 77.

34. The St Leonard's, Yarmouth and Lynn book lists occur in inventories. NRO, DCN 2/3/41 and 65 and DCN 3/3. The Lynn in-ventory, now at Canterbury, has been noted by D. M. Owen, *The Making of King's Lynn* (London, 1984), p. 123. The Hoxne book list, only partly legible, is written on the dorse of an account roll. NRO, DCN 2/6.

35. GS, i, pp. 20, 30 and 35.

36. J. B. Tolhurst, ed., *The Customary of the Cathedral Priory Church of Norwich* (Henry Bradshaw Society, 82, 1948), p. v.

looters.[37] But while this would have applied to books forming part of the altar furnishings, did it apply to their library? Such books were normally kept in cupboards in the cloister and the cloister was apparently not damaged. This is not to say that looters did not penetrate there. They could have opened the cupboards and flung down and destroyed their contents. Certainly not everything was destroyed. A twelfth-century copy of the sermons of Herbert de Losinga, bearing a Norwich pressmark, has survived, as have homilies of Pope Gregory.[38] Moreover, an early chronicle, later to be incorporated into that in the *First Register*, has survived.[39] Finally, the Norwich Customary, which relates to the 1260s, is another book to have come through the riot unscathed.[40] But this is not a sufficient basis for the argument that the book collection was not seriously damaged.

The period immediately after the riot was one in which the Norwich book collection grew rapidly, as indeed did most monastic libraries. As elsewhere the influx was due to the gifts, or more probably bequests, of individual monks. This, the first spell of intensive book collecting, probably gave a library of between 400 and 500 books.[41] Thereafter growth, though steady, was slower, although a change in the form of inscription may make Norwich books more difficult to spot. While most donors are associated with but a single volume, two large donations are known. The first came from Prior Simon Bozoun (1344–52), who was not it seems a graduate, the second from Adam Easton, who was a doctor of theology and a considerable scholar and writer.[42]

As a whole the collection fell into two parts. In the first category came the service books required in the choir and private chapels, not only at the monastery itself but also in the cells. These would carry no pressmark. Two of the important psalters used at the mother church come into this group. The earlier is a lavish but thoroughly provincial book, perhaps produced immediately after the 1272 riot in preparation for the dedication of the church in 1278.[43] The second, a magnificent volume, the product of a Norwich workshop of the early fourteenth century, is in no sense a provincial piece (plate IIa). This, the Gorleston Psalter, was not originally made for the cathedral church but for the parish of that name. When, why and how it came into the hands of the priory is unknown but, if purchased by the priory, the date is likely to be in the second quarter of the fourteenth century. On the other hand it could well have arrived at the priory as a gift.[44]

37. Bartholomew Cotton, *Historia Anglicana*, ed. H. R. Luard (RS, 16, 1859), p. 147.

38. N. R. Ker, 'Medieval Manuscripts from Norwich Cathedral Library', *Transactions of the Cambridge Bibliographical Society*, 1 (1949), pp. 12–13.

39. B. Dodwell, 'History and the Monks of Norwich Cathedral Priory', *Reading*

Medieval Studies, 5 (1979), pp. 43–44.

40. Ker, 'Norwich MSS', p. 15, no. 25.

41. Ker, 'Norwich MSS', pp. 6–7.

42. See also p. 248.

43. London, Lambeth Palace Library, MS 368.

44. P. Lasko and N. J. Morgan, eds, *Medieval Art in East Anglia, 1300–1520* (Norwich, 1973), p. 18.

There are other books of this kind that do bear pressmarks and thereby seem to have found their way into the library. Although primarily arranged by donor, the letters A and B were reserved for books of a particular kind. Pressmark A took in psalters, presumably those used for private devotion, as well as homilies, including the sermons of Herbert de Losinga. B seems to have been used for portable breviaries, perhaps those that had belonged to individuals, and if so, again for private use. Neil Ker listed three small psalters with A pressmarks,[45] presumably those having a devotional rather than a public use, and it could be that the great psalter listed in the inventory of the cell of Yarmouth came into the same category.[46] But what does one make of the Ormesby Psalter? That was given by Robert of Ormesby, perhaps sometime in the 1330s, to lie on the desk of the subprior in the choir of the cathedral. Yet it came to bear the pressmark A1, and so was part of the library and not of the choir collection (plate IIb).[47] It certainly was a work of high quality. Throughout all its stages, and apparently there were four, the decoration was sumptuous. How long it lay on the sub-prior's desk is unknown, the pressmark, A1, presumably coming from a late reorganisation of the library, when it would have replaced an earlier volume; for A1 must have been assigned when the catalogue was first made in 1315–16. Perhaps it came to be regarded as a devotional work.

The lists of surviving works prepared by Neil Ker may or may not be representative of the medieval library. It must be noted that a number of volumes are of a composite nature in that they consist of several booklets bound together. Neil Ker when preparing his lists noted only the first of the booklets.[48] As might be expected, there were books intended for devotional use: the Bibles, the homilies of St Gregory and St Augustine, the sermons of SS. Bernard and Bonaventura, the penitential of Grosseteste. The sending of monks to Gloucester College to read theology, and with that an extension of in-house education, undoubtedly increased the range of the library, producing glossed Bibles and biblical commentaries, as well as philosophical works from Aristotle to Aquinas and Avicenna.[49] There were legal texts such as the *Decretum* of Gratian, the *Decretals* of Gregory IX and the *Sext* of Boniface VIII, necessary for the canon law course and essential reference works for the main offices.[50] As befitted a community in which the main purpose of university education was the provision of training for preaching, there were sermons, including those of

45. Ker, 'Norwich MSS', p. 13.
46. NRO, DCN 3/3. *Psalterium magnum*, A xlvj.
47. Bodleian Library, MS Douce 366.
48. N. R. Ker, *Medieval Libraries of Great Britain* (2nd edn, London, 1964), pp. 136–37.
49. Peter Lombard's work on the Psalms as well as his *Sentences*, an essential text book for

the course in theology, are there. Aquinas does not appear in Ker's lists, being contained in a composite volume.
50. Their presence is known from in-house production. Dodwell, 'History and Monks', pp. 40–41.

Thomas Brinton, the Norwich monk and a noted preacher who became bishop of Rochester (1373–89).[51] There were also a number of preaching manuals. Prior Simon Elmham (1235–57) had a copy of Alan de Lille's *Summa de arte predicandi* and Simon Bozoun had bought a copy of John Bromyard's *Summa predicantium*.[52] The friars had used the myths and fables of antiquity for moral ends in their sermons; so too did the monks, since the Norwich library contained Vincent de Beauvais' *De eruditione filiorum nobilium* with its collection of fables.[53] The same purpose might be attributed to the presence at the cell at Hoxne of the *Song of Roland* (in Latin), but whether the same could be said of that cell's copy of the *Gesta* of Sir Gawain with its story of violence and lust is problematical.[54]

Another class of books which seems to have been immensely popular was that dealing with the past. This was something that all monks could appreciate, university educated or not. In this Norwich was but following a common development. Religious houses were producing both national histories, often no more than compilations of the works of others, and original works relating to the past of the particular house. St Albans, with its chronicles by Roger of Wendover and Matthew Paris, might have led the way in history writing but in the thirteenth century few houses were without some kind of chronicle, be it national or local. The priory had begun to produce a chronicle in the twelfth century with an account of its foundation. This was used as the vehicle for the citing of early grants. Its first section, which probably ran to the death of Herbert in 1119, was possibly compiled in the first half of the twelfth century; it was later incorporated into a chronicle running to about 1300 but one which degenerated into a mere transcription of episcopal deeds.[55] It seems to have survived the riot of 1272, for it was later written into the *First Register* of the early fourteenth century. A second twelfth-century work produced at Norwich was Thomas of Monmouth's *Life of St William*. This told the story of the alleged martyrdom of a Norwich boy at the hands of the Jews and of the subsequent miracles worked at his tomb. It seems to have been compiled in 1172–73 and has survived in a single early copy, albeit not the original, probably written before 1200.[56] Since it carries no pressmark, it is not reckoned to be a Norwich library book. Yet both Leland and Bale saw a copy at Norwich in the sixteenth century. Either the priory copy survived the riot or was replaced.[57]

51. M. A. Devlin, ed., *The Sermons of Thomas Brinton, Bishop of Rochester* 2 vols (Camden Society, 3rd series, 85–86, 1954), i, p. xviii.

52. The first is bound up with J. Beleth etc., Cambridge University Library, Ff. 5. 28.

53. It had belonged to John of Stratton. Cambridge, Corpus Christi College, MS 325.

54. NRO, DCN 2/6. These occur at the end of the list. The books themselves have not survived.

55. Dodwell, 'History and Monks', pp. 43–44.

56. Cambridge University Library, Additional MS 3037.

57. Dodwell, 'History and Monks', pp. 42–43.

In the late 1260s the monks began to show an interest in national history. They bought historical works and even joined the ranks of those religious houses which produced a general chronicle. This was the usual mixture of borrowings from other chroniclers with a period of original composition and seems to have been written up in stages, the first perhaps in 1269, the second in 1272 and the third in 1284. This last was yet again followed by original composition in a variety of hands and ran from 1285 to 1291.[58] At some stage it became the property of Ralf of Frettenham, who was master of the cellar in 1272–73. This monk was also the owner of another historical work, a roll which combined historical and topographical information and which stopped shortly before 1272.[59] In 1292 the monk Bartholomew Cotton began to put together his chronicle under the title of the *Historia Anglicana*. This was a three-part piece of work, the first of which was an unacknowledged copy of Geoffrey of Monmouth's *Liber Britonum*, the second an extended version of the existing Norwich chronicle and the third part a topographical account of the dioceses of England together with a list of their respective bishops. In the early fourteenth century this was copied out professionally, and probably very expensively, for the illuminator was highly skilled, and he and the scriptor produced a fine copy.[60] The monks of this period also owned other historical works. Roger of Blickling owned a copy of Geoffrey of Monmouth's *Liber Britonum*, which may be the one copied in the priory in 1294–95, and John of Cawston owned a copy of the fourth book of Vincent de Beauvais' *Speculum historiale*. This historical interest lasted throughout the fourteenth century. Simon Bozoun, who died in 1352, owned a number of historical books, including Bede's *Ecclesiastical History* plus the most popular of the thirteenth-century chroniclers, the *Flores historiarum* of Matthew Paris, and a very recent piece of historical writing, Higden's *Polychronicon* in its 1327 version.[61] And at the end of the century the monks were still collecting chronicles.

Where the monks kept their books in the twelfth and thirteenth centuries is not known. Those used for services were probably in cupboards or presses in the choir, as they were in a later period. The other books were likely to have been placed in cupboards in the cloister. However, in 1382–83 there is a reference to books lying in common and, very soon after, in 1386–87, the word library is used. It seems that a specially designed book-room existed at Norwich, rather earlier than at Durham or Canterbury.[62] A similar set-up existed at the cell of St Leonard where, according to the inventory of 1422, books held in common lay in an upper chapel, later described as being next to the dormitory.[63] In both places the books were held

58. Dodwell, 'History and Monks', pp. 46–47.
59. BL, Additional MS 30079.
60. BL, Royal MS 14 C1 and Cotton MS Nero C V.
61. Dodwell, 'History and Monks', pp. 48–49.
62. NRO, DCN 1/9/20 and 1/9/22.
63. NRO, DCN 2/41.

on chains.[64] There are no references to books being kept in the cloister, but various books may have been shelved there: those belonging to individual monks, as well as those for the use of novices and those for reading in the refectory. The chaplains of the Carnary Chapel which stood by the Erpingham Gate also had their own library, to which Bishop Goldwell (1472–99) bequeathed a commentary on the *Decretals* to be kept chained for the use of those clerics working in the consistory court.[65]

The monks maintained their stock of books until the Dissolution. Their immediate successors seem to have taken reasonable care of the library but after the death of Robert Talbot (prebendary 1547–58) there was downright neglect. Bishop Bale was particularly scathing of Norwich: 'there all the library monuments are turned to the use of their grossers, candlemakers, soap sellers and other worldly occupiers';[66] and in 1574 the chapter agreed to demolish the old library.[67] The neglect ran into the seventeenth century and the library probably suffered during the Commonwealth. In 1673 the establishment of a new library in the audit chamber was ordered. Initially little may have been achieved, for in 1681, presumably under the guidance of Dr Prideaux, the newly appointed prebendary, it was agreed and ordered that a library be prepared for the receipt of books; that the dean should contribute £20 and each prebendary £10, either in books or money; and that the audit chamber be the room set apart for that purpose.[68] This seems to have given the library a new lease of life. Books came in – so many that in 1721 the library was declared to be 'too straightened conveniently to contain the books already placed there' and an order made that it should be enlarged.[69] This enlargement was to be necessary, for in 1745 Prebendary Nicholas Penny bequeathed a large collection of books.[70] During the eighteenth and nineteenth centuries several manuscript catalogues were made which show continued growth. By 1913 the collection had outstripped its accommodation and it was moved to the room over the south walk of the cloister where it is still housed. There have, however, been losses. In the 1930s some of its finest treasures were sold to pay for the repainting of the cloister bosses.[71] Less drastically, a number of volumes of historical interest have been placed on permanent loan in the library of the University of East Anglia. The collection now comprises some 8000 volumes and pamphlets.

64. NRO, DCN 1/9/15 and 2/3/75.
65. Blomefield, *Norfolk*, iii, p. 541.
66. J. Bale, *Index Britanniae scriptorum*, ed. R. L. Poole and M. Bateson (Oxford, 1902), p. xx.
67. Williams and Cozens-Hardy, *Extracts*, p. 31.

68. NRO, DCN 24/3, fo. 170.
69. NRO, DCN 115/3, p. 92.
70. A. J. Beck, *Norwich Cathedral Library* (Norwich, 1992), appendix F.
71. NRO, DCN 40/27.

17

The Estates of Norwich Cathedral Priory, 1101–1538

Roger Virgoe

The establishment and maintenance of a large Benedictine monastery at the new seat of the bishopric necessarily involved an endowment separate from that of the bishop. A substantial income from permanent sources, including landed estates, would be needed to provide for the building and maintenance of the cathedral and the monastic quarters and for the food, clothing and other needs of a large community of monks. The great Benedictine houses founded before or soon after the Norman Conquest were throughout the middle ages some of the greatest landowners in the country and Norwich Cathedral Priory soon fell within the same category.[1]

Great landed estates demanded sophisticated administration and increasingly from the early thirteenth century this was recorded in written documents. Because of their continuity as institutions, the comparative security of their muniment rooms, and perhaps also because of the higher educational standards of the monks, the estate and financial records kept by many monastic houses have been far more fully preserved than those of lay landowners. Although the Dissolution of the Monasteries in the 1530s dispersed and in some cases annihilated their records, the documents were often transferred as working archives and evidences of title to the new lay lords of their estates. In the case of the monastic cathedrals like Canterbury, Winchester, Ely, Durham and Norwich, they remained in the custody of the new secular chapters. Of course, there have been many losses over time, but the dean and chapter archive at Norwich has preserved a vast accumulation of medieval estate records, both those relating to the central administration of the

---

1. For general discussion of the estates of the monasteries, including the cathedral priories, in the eleventh and twelfth centuries see D. Knowles, *The Monastic Order in England* (Cambridge, 1950), pp. 59–136, 625–26.

estates and also the deeds, court rolls, accounts and surveys relating to individual properties.[2]

Such accumulations of records by the greater monastic houses have provided the basis for much of the economic and social history of England in the middle ages – from the studies of large-scale economic and demographic change to the recently more fashionable studies of the social structure of village communities. For Norwich Cathedral Priory Dr Eric Stone provided a thorough but unfortunately never published study of the estates to 1300, and more recently Dr Bruce Campbell has used some of the records in his studies of Norfolk agriculture,[3] but the Norwich Priory records have not been employed so extensively as, for instance, those of similar houses at Canterbury and Durham, or of many other monasteries.[4] Although much work remains to be done on the administrative, economic and social history of those estates, parishes and churches which came under the control of the priory, the patterns of change during the middle ages, largely derived from the study of the records of other religious houses, do allow their history to be set in a general context.

2. The archive is now deposited almost entirely in Norfolk Record Office, where there is an excellent handlist. Part of it was described, not always very accurately, by H. W. Saunders in his *An Introduction to the Obedientiary and Manor Rolls of Norwich Cathedral Priory* (Norwich, 1930). The early charters, taken mainly from registers, have been printed or calendared in *First Register*, NCC and EEA, vi.

3. E. Stone, 'The Estates of Norwich Cathedral Priory, 1100–1300' (unpublished Oxford University D. Phil. thesis, 1956): one aspect is dealt with in E. Stone, 'Profit and Loss Accountancy at Norwich Cathedral Priory', *TRHS*, 5th series, 12 (1962), pp. 25–48; B. M. S. Campbell, 'Arable Productivity in Medieval England: Some Evidence from Norfolk', *Journal of Economic History*, 43 (1983), pp. 379–404; B. M. S. Campbell, 'Agricultural Progress in Medieval England: Some Evidence from Eastern Norfolk', *Economic History Review*, 2nd series, 36 (1983), pp. 26–46. I am grateful to Dr Campbell

for allowing me to use his unpublished graphs and tables on the agricultural economy of the priory estates. I am, of course, responsible for any errors made in using this information.

4. For Canterbury, see R. A. L. Smith, *Canterbury Cathedral Priory* (Cambridge, 1943) and a number of articles by Mavis Mate, including 'The Farming Out of Manors; A New Look at the Evidence from Canterbury Cathedral Priory', *Journal of Medieval History*, 9 (1983), pp. 331–34, and 'Agrarian Economy after the Black Death: The Manors of Canterbury Cathedral Priory, 1348–91', *Economic History Review*, 2nd series, 37 (1984), pp. 341–54. For Durham, see D. Knowles, *The Religious Orders in England*, 3 vols (Cambridge, 1948–59), ii, pp. 313–19, and references given there. Among many similar studies of monasteries and their estates are J. A. Raftis, *The Estates of Ramsey Abbey* (Toronto, 1957); B. Harvey, *Westminster Abbey* (Oxford, 1977); E. Searle, *Lordship and Community: Battle Abbey* (Toronto, 1974).

The Building of the Estates

Although it must have been hoped that the newly-founded monastery would receive from members of the lay aristocracy gifts of landed property in return for intercessory prayers, it was inevitable that, as at Canterbury, the core of the priory's endowment would come from the property of the bishopric.[5] The division of the episcopal estates might have been seen initially as a purely formal one, as the bishop, himself a monk, was theoretically abbot of the cathedral monastery, but the separation was implicit in the initial charter by which Herbert de Losinga endowed the new monastery in 1101. 'For my redemption and absolution from sins' he granted to the monks in perpetuity for their victuals and clothing lands and privileges which, he enjoined, no future bishop was to disturb.[6]

King William II had in 1096 granted or confirmed to the bishop the site of the new house and added to it the lands of the church of St Michael in Norwich, with its lands in Taverham. On 3 September 1101 Henry I granted to the bishop and monks jointly his valuable manor of Thorpe next Norwich, with its appurtenant holdings at Catton, Lakenham and Arminghall, for the benefit of his soul and those of his father and mother, his brother, William, and all his ancestors and successors.[7] On the same day Bishop Herbert's charter to the monks was witnessed and sealed. Many of the lands of the bishopric described in Domesday Book were either in the hands of sub-tenants or consisted of commendations – comprising various rights of lordship – of various free tenants, but they included around a dozen manors and a good many smaller holdings held directly in demesne with a total value of around £240 p.a. Losinga added to these during the first decade of his episcopate. It was mainly from these lands that the priory was first endowed in 1101.[8]

The chief lands granted to the priory by Bishop Herbert's charter were manors at Hindolveston and Hindringham in north Norfolk, Martham and Hemsby in the east, and lands in the Norwich area comprising Catton, Lakenham and Arminghall, all appurtenant to the king's grant of Thorpe, together with half of Thorpe Wood and land at Plumstead and in Norwich itself. Properties at East Beckham, Gaywood and Hilgay were also included in the charter. Manors and other 'temporal' possessions were not the only sources of revenue for monasteries, and Losinga also included in his grant the advowson or rights of patronage and the tithes of the churches of Hoxne, Yarmouth, Lynn and Helmingham, and the chapel of St Leonard that he

5. Smith, *Canterbury*, pp. 1–14.
6. *First Register*, pp. 32–36.
7. *First Register*, pp. 28–30; *NCC*, i, nos 1–3.
8. *VCH Norfolk*, ii, pp. 114–23; B. Dodwell,

'The Honor of the Bishop of Thetford/Norwich in the Late Eleventh and Early Twelfth Centuries', *NA*, 33 (1965), pp. 185–200.

had recently built just outside Norwich. All of these named churches, except Helmingham, were quickly to become the sites of dependent houses or 'cells' attached to the priory.[9] He also gave to the priory the tithes from all other churches in the bishop's possession except those which he had already granted to a chaplain. The monks were also to receive the offerings made in the cathedral and had already been granted by the king the profits from fairs to be held in Norwich and Lynn.[10] Losinga, mindful of possible concern by his successors about the impoverishment of episcopal revenues, noted that he had bought in manors at South Elmham, Colkirk and Eccles and had improved Thorpe Manor to compensate for the grants to the priory.

During the remaining eighteen years of his episcopate Losinga made further gifts to the priory, notably a valuable estate at 'Gnatingdon' in Ringstead and property at Mintlyn, Fring and Gaywood in north-west Norfolk, together with half a dozen more churches.[11] Certain lay benefactors also added to the priory's estates: Godric the deacon granted to the monks the land he held at Great Cressingham; Alan son of Flaald the manor of Eaton and Agnes de Bellofago the church at Aldeby which became another cell of the priory.[12] It is impossible to put any accurate valuation on these endowments, as no surveys or accounts survive from such an early period; but, although certainly considerably less valuable than those of Bury St Edmunds Abbey, the estates were sufficient to support, from the produce of their demesne, from food-rents and money-rents, mills, tolls and market profits, sale of timber, tithes and offerings, a substantial community of up to sixty monks.

Bishop de Losinga's death in 1119 ended the first phase of the development of the priory's estates. No future bishop was to be so generous and the priory did not receive the endowments from lay magnates that might have been hoped for: great families like the Bigods, Warennes and Albini were more concerned with their own private foundations at Thetford, Castle Acre, Wymondham and elsewhere. Nevertheless the estates and other sources of income continued to grow. The foundation of the hospital of St Paul, closely associated with the priory, led not only to the diversion of some of the minor holdings to support it but also, probably during the 1120s, to grants from Richard de Bellofago of four valuable churches at Ormesby with their attached lands and tithes and from the king of the tithes owed by his hall at Ormesby.[13] From Bishop Eborard (1121–45) came some lands at Beckham, Hempstead and Plumstead, several churches and parts of the tithes of others; and from Bishop Turbe (1146/47–74) came three other churches and the very profitable

---

9. For brief histories of these cells see *VCH Norfolk*, ii, pp. 328–30; for their finances Saunders, *Obedientiary Rolls*, pp. 145–48.
10. *First Register*, p. 44.
11. *First Register*, pp. 49–50; *NCC*, i, nos 107–11.

12. *NCC*, i, nos 17, 20, 106.
13. *First Register*, pp. 63–67; *NCC*, nos 35, 100–2; C. Rawcliffe, *The Hospitals of Medieval Norwich* (Studies in East Anglian History, forthcoming).

manor of Sedgeford at a fee-farm rent of £20 p.a.[14] During the twelfth century the priory also acquired the control of some dozen or more Norwich parish churches, the tithes from a number of county parishes and – its only properties outside East Anglia – land at Scampton, Lincolnshire, and East Chalk in Kent.[15]

The large number of exchanges, grants and confirmations made by Bishop John de Gray (1200–14) mark the culmination of the second period of the priory's acquisitions. The charters granted by him in 1205 settled differences between the monks and their bishop. The most important new grants of that year were the bishop's manor (but not the church) at Great Cressingham and the release of the £20 rent from Sedgeford. In exchange the priory released its rights in the lay fee at Lynn and most of the possessions at Gaywood granted to the priory by Losinga. A number of other churches also were appropriated to the priory.[16]

The main age of grants of land had now come to an end. Most donations to the priory in the thirteenth century from bishops and others were in the form of tithes, pensions from churches and licences to appropriate churches where the priory already held the advowson – that is to receive all the rectorial tithes, while appointing a vicar to serve the parish. These rights were often valuable and they were efficiently exploited to bring in considerable income to the priory, though many of the Norwich churches which came under its patronage brought in little revenue.[17] Lands and associated property such as judicial rights, mills, markets and the like now came mainly through purchase. Some earlier acquisitions may, of course, have involved money payments but, as with so many other monasteries, it is the thirteenth century that saw the priory make a determined effort to extend its landed holdings in this way. Most of the numerous conveyances of which records survive were of fairly small amounts of land, acquired to extend demesne and rents in villages where the priory already held a manor or church. Other purchases were considerably larger. In 1248, for instance, Sir Walter de Mauteby was given 200 marks and the priory's lands at Beckham, in exchange for more lands in the very productive villages of Hemsby and Martham; and in 1286 300 marks were paid to William Roscelyn for the manor of Aldeby.[18]

The Statute of Mortmain, enacted in 1279 in response to the concern of the king and nobility at the constant extension of monastic landed property, forbade all future acquisitions of land by religious houses.[19] The priory continued to acquire some

---

14. *NCC*, i, nos 116, 119, 127–28, 131–32.
15. *NCC*, i, nos 27, 35, 177; Stone, 'Estates', pp. 65–73.
16. *NCC*, i, nos 144–78; *EEA*, vi, pp. xxx–xxxi, lviii, nos 377–410.
17. *NCC*, i, nos 180–230; Stone, 'Estates', pp.

61–66, 183–201, 214–20.
18. *NCC*, i, nos 333, 365; Stone, 'Estates', pp. 133–43.
19. For the statute and its effects see S. Raban, *Mortmain Legislation and the English Church, 1279–1500* (Cambridge, 1982).

properties afterwards, sometimes by royal licence, sometimes without, but few were of any great significance.[20]

Thus it was the late thirteenth century when the estates of the priory reached the shape and size they were to retain for the remaining 250 years of its existence. The period coincides, of course, with the rapid expansion of the working documents of the priory, which allow the listing of its possessions and income; and also with the two great clerical taxation assessments – the 'Norwich Taxation' of 1254 and the 'Taxation of Pope Nicholas' of 1291, which provide at least a partial listing of the possessions and their values and which were to remain the basis of clerical taxation assessments down to 1535.[21] Fig. 121 lists the main holdings of the priory at the end of the thirteenth century; these are plotted on the accompanying map (fig. 122). The priory had smaller sources of income – such as lands and tithes – in many other parishes, of course.

Estate and Financial Administration, 1101–1349

The overall demographic and economic changes of medieval England are now well established. From the time of the Norman Conquest and no doubt for some time before there was a substantial increase in the population of England (as of western Europe as a whole), probably accelerating during the thirteenth century to reach around 1300 a peak of perhaps five to six million – a density not to be reached again until the late seventeenth century. During this time Norfolk was certainly one of the most heavily populated counties. Whether or not population began to decline from its peak during the first half of the fourteenth century, there is no doubt of the decisive effect of the Black Death of 1348–49 which, with subsequent outbreaks of epidemic disease, produced a massive mortality that during the next hundred years more than halved the population. Only from around 1500 did a new increase begin.

The rise and fall of population was by no means the only determinant of the rhythm of economic change in medieval England but the latter did roughly coincide with the phases described above. Population rise during the twelfth and thirteenth centuries coincided with a substantial extension of land under the plough, while more intensive and extensive cultivation of cereals and livestock provided the basis

20. For licences see *NCC*, i, nos 49–52, 57 etc., and for comment see Stone, 'Estates', pp. 144–63. The largest post-1279 acquisition was from Sir Walter de Norwich at Great Cressingham, which was licensed by the crown in 1316: *CPR*, *1313–17*, p. 389.
21. *Taxatio ecclesiastica Angliae et Walliae* . . .

(Record Commission, 1802); W. E. Lunt, ed., *The Valuation of Norwich* (Oxford, 1926). Lunt prints the 1254 assessments from a Norwich Cathedral Priory register and compares them with some of those of 1291 and also with some contemporary accounts (pp. 501–6).

for the rapid expansion of markets and towns, which were further stimulated by the growth of trade in other raw materials and in manufactured goods, particularly cloth. Prices rose in response to greater demand and also to the expansion of the money supply with the exploitation of new silver deposits in Europe, producing a much more monetary economy. New levels of wealth and standards of living were generated for those who could take advantage of the opportunities. Among these were the greater landowners, both spiritual and temporal; as a consequence major changes in the methods of exploiting their estates occurred during the thirteenth century.

During the eleventh and twelfth centuries the widespread practice among monastic as well as other large landowners was to let most of their manors and other holdings to farm, receiving from some farmers rent in kind, which provided the massive quantities of grain needed to feed a large monastic community and its servants; and from others cash-rents used to purchase other necessities and to pay for building and the other expenses of the community.[22] Ely Priory, for instance, seems to have used its Cambridgeshire estates for food-rents, its more distant lands in East Suffolk for cash.[23] Unfortunately the evidence for Norwich Priory is slight from this period, but it seems as though similar if less systematic variations were the practice on their estates – some lands being granted at hereditary fee-farms, others at annual or short-term farms for food-rents or cash.[24] There is, unfortunately, very little evidence of how the priory's estates were administered during the first century of its existence, but it is reasonable to assume that, as at other monasteries, the cellarer, a monk appointed to supply food and drink to the community, had the prime administrative responsibility.

The expanding markets and inflationary trends of the thirteenth century made direct exploitation of landed estates, producing and selling grain for profit, much more lucrative to landowners than were fixed rents. Inevitably, some monasteries caught on to this trend earlier than others, but during the century there was a fairly consistent move towards bringing back leased land into direct exploitation, buying up freehold and villein land dependent on the lord's manors and, where possible, acquiring other lands by purchase – all with the intention of profiting from the direct cultivation and sale of the products of the lord's demesnes.[25] As with Norwich Cathedral Priory, the estates of many monasteries grew substantially during this period. The Statute of Mortmain restricted rather than ended this trend for some houses – at Battle Abbey, for instance, the last decades of the thirteenth century seem to have seen a further surge in the acquisition of land.[26]

22. Knowles, *Religious Orders*, i, pp. 32–54; compare Raftis, *Ramsey Abbey*, pp. 56–60.
23. E. Miller, *The Abbey and Bishopric of Ely* (Cambridge, 1951), p. 76.
24. Stone, 'Estates', pp. 328–30.

25. Knowles, *Religious Orders*, i, pp. 35–48; Smith, *Canterbury Priory*, pp. 113–45; Harvey, *Westminster Abbey*, pp. 131–4, 164–75; Raftis, *Ramsey Abbey*, pp. 97–112.
26. Searle, *Lordship and Community*, pp. 234–45.

Appropriated Churches

East Norfolk

Aldeby	£11
Hempstead	£3
Hemsby	£11
Martham	£17
Ormesby (4)	£21
Scratby	£5
Worstead	£13
Yarmouth	£38

Norwich Region

Arminghall	£3
Attlebridge	£6
Barford (½)	£1
Bawburgh	£8
Catton	£8
Eaton	£4
Great Plumstead	£4
Hemblington	£2
Lakenham	£6
Newton Trowse	£3
Sprowston	£5

Stoke Holy Cross	£2
Wicklewood	£11

Central and West Norfolk

Beckham	£3
Hindolveston	£5
Hindringham	£22
North Elmham	£13
Wighton	£14

West and North-West Norfolk

Fordham (½)	£1
Fring	£13
Lynn	£38
Riston	£3
Sedgeford	£11
Wiggenhall St Germans	£9

Suffolk

Denham	£2

Henley	£4
Hopton	£3

Norwich Churches

All Saints, Fye Bridge
St Cross
St Cuthbert
St Devast
St Etheldreda
St George Colegate
St Giles
St Gregory
St James
St John Ber Street
St John Sepulchre
St Martin Coslany
St Martin at Palace Plain
St Mary the Less
St Paul
St Peter Permountergate
St Saviour, Fye Bridge
Total value £21

Manors and Other Substantial Landed Estates

East Norfolk

Aldeby	£14
Dilham	£6
Hemsby	£52
Thurlton	£11
Martham	£59

Norwich Region

Arminghall	£17
Catton	£11
Eaton	£18
Great Plumstead	£16
Lakenham	£33
Monks' Grange, Pockthorpe	£6

Newton	£31
Norwich	£30
Taverham	£7
Thorpe	£10
Trowse	£13

Central and North Norfolk

Field Dalling	£13
Hindolveston	£43
Hindringham	£41

West and North-West Norfolk

Gaywood	£9

Great Cressingham	£13
Lynn	£6
Sedgeford & Gnatingdon	£61
Thornham	£7

Suffolk

Hopton	£4
Hoxne	£10
Yaxley	£10

Other Counties

Chalk (Kent)	£16
Scampton (Lincs)	£6

Fig. 121. The main properties of Norwich Cathedral Priory, *c.* 1300-1538. The values given are those of the *Valor Ecclesiasticus* of 1535. They are mostly far lower than the real income of the thirteenth and fourteenth centuries but provide a guide to the comparative values of the properties. These are rounded here to the nearest pound.

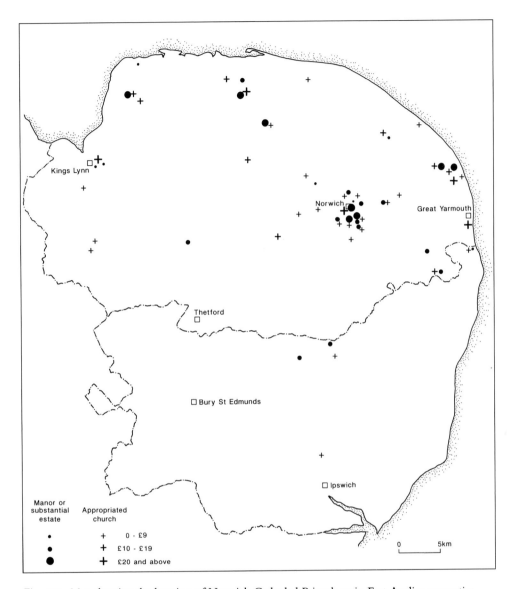

Fig. 122. Map showing the location of Norwich Cathedral Priory's main East Anglian properties, *c.* 1300–1538.

It is partly as a result of this new system of direct exploitation that the keeping of written records increased enormously, particularly those of the estates of bishops and religious houses. Much closer supervision both of individual manors and of the overall finances of monasteries was now needed. The consequent documentation survives in profusion and in increasingly standardized forms from the middle of the thirteenth century. The documents show how almost everywhere demesnes were exploited and rents, dues and services collected by local officials, most of them laymen, who produced accounts which were audited under the supervision of senior members of the monastic communities.[27]

Local administration of estates became fairly standardised but central administrative practice varied a good deal; among the greater monastic houses clear differences of practice and methods of making decisions become apparent. A large monastic community like Norwich, with many functions and varied forms of revenue, needed a number of different officers subordinate to the prior to undertake these duties and account for them to the community. Although many of the practical duties were carried out by servants and officials, their supervision and the final responsibility rested upon individual monks – the obedientiaries – chosen by the prior and the community.[28] Among the major religious houses responsibilities were organized in a variety of ways: although some offices, such as that of cellarer, were essential and almost universal, their independent responsibility for gathering income as well as dispensing supplies varied greatly among the religious houses.[29]

At Norwich the cells at Yarmouth, Lynn, Aldeby, Hoxne and St Leonard's and the hospital of St Paul had possessed from very early on their own independent sources of revenue. It was natural enough that the priory, faced in the thirteenth century with the administrative and financial complications that went with the direct exploitation of its lands, should allocate specific sources of revenue to the various obedientiaries who became responsible for both collection and distribution of income.

During the early thirteenth century responsibility for the supply of bread and ale to the monks was removed from the cellarer and hived off, being given to another obedientiary, the 'master of the cellar', who had a variety of other duties on behalf of the prior and the community as a whole.[30] Major sources of revenue were allotted

27. See Saunders, *Obedientiary Rolls*, for an analysis of these as they relate to Norwich Priory; J. Titow, *English Rural Society, 1200– 1350* (London, 1969), pp. 15–33, for more general discussion of their nature; Smith, *Canterbury*, pp. 100–150, for a description of administration of a priory's estates.

28. Knowles, *Religious Orders*, i, pp. 55–63. See also pp. 241–42.

29. Stone, 'Estates', pp. 271–73. For the duties of the cellarer in Benedictine monasteries see Knowles, *Monastic Order*, pp. 427–39.

30. Saunders, *Obedientiary Rolls*, pp. 68–73, puts the change later – but see Stone, 'Estates', pp. 271–73.

to both these officials, much smaller ones to the growing number of other obedientiaries. For some, such sources might include pensions or rents payable by their
colleagues – the cellarer, for instance, received regular payments from the priors of
Yarmouth, Lynn and Aldeby, the sacrist, infirmarer and gardener. Some, such as
the prior of Yarmouth, received more than three-quarters of their income from
offerings and fees and personal tithes from members of their parish.[31] But those with
larger responsibilities needed a substantial steady income from lands, churches and
tithes.

Apart from the specific endowments of the hospital and cells already referred to,
the first clear evidence of this system of allocating revenues to specific obedientiaries
comes from a charter of Bishop John of Oxford in the late twelfth century in
which he granted the church of St Saviour, Norwich, to the priory 'to the use of
the almonry'.[32] The series of grants and exchanges made by Bishop de Gray in
1205 nearly all specify the office to which the source of income is given – the
cellarer, for instance, received the Norfolk churches of Wiggenhall St Germans,
Sedgeford, Witton and Blickling (these two were later granted away), and the
church of Hopton in Suffolk; the chamberlain Arminghall manor and St Stephen's
church, Norwich.[33] Further such grants were made during the course of the
thirteenth century, mostly to the almonry.[34] These were grants for particular
purposes rather than to specific office- holders, so the shuffling around of duties,
as in the case of the cellarer, could have moved income around as well, but it is
only from the 1270s that such details become clear. By that time the allocation of
sources of income to the different obedientiaries had become more or less stabilised
in the form it would retain until 1538.[35]

The bulk of the expenditure of the priory and therefore most of its income fell
upon the master of the cellar and the cellarer. When we have the first comprehensive
figures of the income of the priory in the *status obedientiariorum* of 1363–64 – a
conspectus of each obedientiary's income and expenditure for the year on the lines
of a modern spread-sheet – the master of the cellar received about 20 per cent of
the total, the cellarer about 22 per cent. The proportion of the other obedientiaries
varied from the chamberlain's 7 per cent to less than 1 per cent to the gardener
and others. The cells had much more, of course: 12 per cent going to Lynn Priory,
10 per cent to Yarmouth, 3 per cent to St Paul's Hospital and about 8 per cent to
the other three. These proportions had probably remained fairly stable for many
years but the later middle ages was to see a sharp reduction in the proportion

---

31. Saunders, *Obedientiary Rolls*; Stone, 'Estates',
    pp. 273–84.
32. *NCC*, i, no. 142.
33. *NCC*, i, nos 144–70.

34. For example, *NCC*, i, nos 182, 185, 189.
35. Early account rolls of the obedientiaries
    show sources of income not greatly different
    from those of the early sixteenth century.

enjoyed by the cells and most of the obedientiaries and a rise to something like 40 per cent in the share of the master of the cellar.[36]

Thus the landed estates or 'temporalities' of the priory were mainly under the control of the master of the cellar and the cellarer. It was they who provided the essential foodstuffs for the monks and a considerable part of this came from demesne production of these estates and from food-rents. A far higher proportion of the income of the other obedientiaries and cells derived from 'spiritualities' – the profits of appropriated churches, separated tithes, pensions from beneficed clergy – and from more purely religious sources such as offerings, payments for masses and ceremonies, and legacies. Thus it is the master of the cellar and the cellarer who were most directly concerned with the exploitation of demesnes, though other smaller areas of arable land and also the land belonging to appropriated churches were also exploited, so the other obedientiaries were not shielded from the demands of the market.[37]

The division of the monastery's income proportionately to the responsibilities of the officers of the house, with very little central supervision, was a widely practised system among the large Benedictine houses of England in the twelfth and thirteenth centuries. During the thirteenth century, however, there was a general move towards more effective central supervision and auditing of accounts, partly under pressure from the popes, the ecclesiastical hierarchy and the Benedictine triennial assemblies or 'chapters' and partly owing to the demands of large-scale farming, which allowed more opportunities for peculation and waste, as well as profit.[38] Different houses adopted different methods, sometimes no doubt owing to the personality of the abbot or prior. At Canterbury Cathedral Priory, for example, a very centralised system was set up at the end of the thirteenth century under the formidable Abbot Henry of Eastry. Revenues from all the estates of the priory came to treasurers appointed by the prior and senior monks and were by them allotted to the different obedientiaries who were thus responsible for expenditure but not for income.[39] Similar centralising policies were adopted by Ely and Durham priories.[40] Other houses, such as Ramsey Abbey, though increasing central supervision of accounts, retained separately administered sources of revenue under the direct control of their main obedientiaries.[41] This was the practice followed by Norwich Cathedral Priory.

From the 1270s onwards there survive a large number of accounts of almost all the obedientiaries and cells of the priory, though very many have been lost and

---

36. NRO, DCN 1/13/1–4.
37. Stone, 'Estates', pp. 333–35.
38. Knowles, *Religious Orders*, i, pp. 57–63.
39. Smith, *Canterbury*, pp. 15–112. For Henry

of Eastry, see Knowles, *Religious Orders*, i, pp. 49–54.
40. Knowles, *Religious Orders*, i, p. 63; ii, pp. 313–19.
41. Raftis, *Ramsey Abbey*, pp. 99–114.

there are few years for which all survive.[42] From the 1290s there also survive central accounts which show how the main sources of landed and agricultural income were divided among the main obedientiaries.[43] It is clear that, however autonomous the Norwich obedientiaries were compared with their contemporaries at Canterbury and elsewhere, there was during this period, particularly under Prior Henry Laken-ham (1289–1310), a centrally directed policy to expand the income of the priory through efficient exploitation of their possessions.

The best illustration of this is the register of accounts of *proficua maneriorum* (profits of the manors) which, between 1295 and 1340, make a serious attempt to measure 'profit and loss' over all the main estates of the priory (including those churches with attached land) held by the more important obedientiaries – though it does not include the holdings of the cells.[44] Although the main purpose may have been to assess the profitability of 'wainage' (the net returns from arable farming of the demesne), the summary for each holding lists all other forms of revenue, such as rents, profits of manorial courts and the sale of stock; though after 1310 the accounts list only the holdings of the master of the cellar.[45] Many years ago Eric Stone analysed these accounts in detail and showed how elaborate and sophisticated the accounting methods were compared with the usual medieval 'charge and discharge' accounts which were primarily concerned to check the honesty of the accounting official.[46] They extended the earlier habit of noting profit at the end of some manorial accounts to cover the whole of the priory's landed estates and sought to answer the questions: 'Had the manors or demesnes paid as well as expected?' and 'Could better management have improved profit?' Norwich Cathedral Priory was probably among the pioneers of profit and loss accounting in England. The register, however, ends in 1340 and the system may then have been abandoned as economic circumstances changed.

There is little evidence of how this common policy was formulated and managed and no accounts of a common treasury survive, if one ever existed at this time. Large-scale financial activities were undertaken, it would seem, by coalescing the activities of various of the obedientiaries, as for instance in the allocation to the communar and pitancer of responsibility for the building of the cloister in the late thirteenth century.[47] But there is, in the fourteenth century and later, indication of the existence of a common treasury and occasional references to economic decisions

---

42. See handlist in NRO and Saunders, *Obedientiary Rolls*, pp. 68–73.

43. NRO, DCN 66/1–20, 40/13.

44. NRO, DCN 40/13; the rolls from which the register of *proficua* was compiled survive as DCN 66/1–20.

45. NRO, DCN 40/13.

46. Stone, 'Estates', pp. 366–87; Stone, 'Profit and Loss Accountancy'.

47. *Communar Rolls*. Stone, 'Estates', pp. 284–96, is sceptical about the existence of any serious central control during the thirteenth century.

made by the prior and the senior monks of the priory. It seems unlikely that in this close community in which many of the senior monks, including the prior, would have filled a number of administrative roles, their involvement in the economic activities of the obedientiaries would have only taken the role of auditing their accounts.[48]

Wherever the initiative for more direct management came from, the period between the 1260s and 1300 saw a very substantial increase in the acreage of demesne land under the plough: probably this was continuing an earlier trend, but the records are not available to prove this.[49] While forms of cultivation varied throughout the estates, which were strung out over most of the farming regions of Norfolk, barley was, and was to remain, much the largest crop almost everywhere, comprising consistently some 60 per cent of all demesne produce. Wheat production certainly increased substantially on the eastern and central manors of the priory. Sheep-flocks were kept, mainly on the north-western manors, no doubt partly for reasons of good husbandry since their profitability did not compare with that of grain.[50] Although intensive demesne cultivation often led to conflict with unfree tenants over demands for labour services and restrictions on transfer of land there is no evidence that the priory's policy brought the monks into serious conflict with their tenants. Labour services were fairly light on all the manors and probably were mostly commuted for money payments: it was usually easier and cheaper to employ paid labour in an overpopulated England, when wages were very low.

Until the mid thirteenth century there is no means of accurately assessing the income of the priory. From that time there survive both clerical taxation assessments and, in increasingly large quantities, manorial and obedientiaries' accounts and some central digests of income and expenditure. These sources are far from easy to interpret exactly, as at different times and for different purposes various forms of assessing gross and net income were employed, making comparisons, let alone precise valuations, difficult.[51] Nevertheless, the combination of the Taxation of Pope Nicholas of 1291 and the *proficua maneriorum* register of the 1290s does at least provide fairly full information on what contemporaries thought the income of the priory was and what were its main sources. The taxation commissioners assessed the taxable income at just under £1000 p.a., of which rather less than half came from 'temporalities' – landed revenues, rents, mills, markets; the rest from spiritualities – churches, tithes,

48. In 1346–47 a visitation of the priory by the bishop includes a reference to a central treasury but it was not then being properly used: C. R. Cheney, 'Norwich Cathedral Priory in the Fourteenth Century', *Bulletin of the John Rylands Library*, 20 (1936), pp. 93–120.
49. Dr Campbell's tables.

50. Dr Campbell's tables; Stone, 'Estates', pp. 328–65.
51. Stone analyses these problems fully in 'Estates', pp. 302–27, 366–87. He shows the defects in Saunders's methods of aggregating and comparing income and expenditure.

offerings and the like.[52] Although much more comprehensive than the Valuation of Norwich of 1254 it still considerably understated the real income of the priory.

Very close in time to this assessment was the first surviving account of the *proficua maneriorum* for 1294–95. It is clear that in almost every case the net income from the estate was much larger than that of the assessment of 1291. Hemsby, for instance, assessed at under £42 p.a., brought in £155 in 1294–95 and similar sums in subsequent years.[53] The sixteen 'manors' listed under the master of the cellar's control brought in a total of over £800. The cellarer held only two manors, at Great Cressingham and Hopton in Suffolk, but he also had a number of churches producing demesne profits as well as tithes and his total income from these sources in 1295–96 was over £248 – though this was only about half of his total receipts. Large incomes were similarly drawn from the chamberlain's manors at Lakenham and Arminghall and from churches held by the sacrist, almoner and the hospital. Of course, much of the income was dependent on sale of grain and prices fluctuated with the harvests, so these were not fixed sums – the cellarer's income from Great Cressingham, for instance, fluctuated over the next seven years between £43 and £20. But the total income listed in the *proficua* of 1295–96 is over £1571 and to that must be added the income from spiritualities (which were also efficiently exploited), rents and other issues from property in Norwich itself and the income of the cells. The net income of the priory around the end of the thirteenth century must have approached £2500, almost certainly the biggest income of any Norfolk lord, except possibly the bishop.

'The Age of High Farming', as historians have styled the thirteenth century, thus brought in a massive income for the monks of the priory, but the pressures must have been intense on the administrators and expenses were also high: it is not totally surprising that by the 1330s they were experimenting again with letting out some of the estates to farm. There was a slight downturn in the acreage of demesne under the prior's cultivation during the first half of the fourteenth century, partly no doubt owing to the leasing out of parts of the land. On some manors there was a decline in the number of livestock on the demesnes, presumably also because of leasing, though there was a substantial rise in cattle-farming on the estates in the Norwich area.[54] The real change was ushered in by the events of 1349.

52. Lunt, *Valuation of Norwich*, pp. 106–62, shows that the 1291 assessment is substantially closer to reality than that of 1254, mainly because more sources of income were now assessed.

53. Lunt, *Valuation of Norwich*, p. 567; NRO, DCN 40/13, 53; Stone, 'Estates', pp. 271–84.

54. Dr Campbell's notes; the *proficua* entries for several years in the late 1330s show that the manors of Hindringham and Hindolveston were let to farm: NRO, DCN 40/13.

Estate and Financial Administration, 1349–1538

The drastic fall in population from 1349 did not have an immediate effect on the estate policy of many religious houses. A number even made an attempt to extend direct control of their lands and to economise on rising labour costs by enforcing traditional labour services.[55] A series of poor harvests kept grain prices quite high for another twenty-five years and, although there was a considerable drop in the sown acreage on priory demesnes between the 1340s and 1350s, this was followed by two decades of stability.[56] The late 1370s, however, began the era of radical change in estate management that was to alter the whole nature of the relationship between the priory and its estates. Continuing decline in population, together with a series of good harvests, caused grain prices to plummet: they were not permanently to recover for over a century. Low prices were combined with considerably higher wages, in spite of the attempts to enforce the 1351 Statute of Labourers which aimed to maintain wages at 1347 levels. There was increasing difficulty, also, as shown most dramatically by the Peasants' Revolt of 1381, in enforcing labour services. Thus the late fourteenth century saw traditional villein holdings being increasingly replaced by contractual tenancies. It soon became clear to most lords, ecclesiastical and lay, that direct demesne farming was no longer profitable: there was consequently widespread leasing out of the demesnes and a withdrawal from direct cultivation.

As with the changes of the thirteenth century there were considerable variations in the pace and scale of leasing. The changes on the estates of Canterbury Cathedral Priory were rapid and decisive: between 1390 and 1400 virtually all of the demesnes of the priory were leased out.[57] Other houses were more hesitant, uncertain about the future and unwilling to discard completely a long tradition of direct exploitation of their demesnes, which had for long proved so profitable. Norwich Cathedral Priory seems to have fallen into this category.[58] There was certainly a drastic fall in sown acreage on the demesnes of the priory's manors during the 1380s, presumably due partly to the leasing out of much of the land – this is particularly noticeable at Hindolveston, Hindringham, Plumstead and Taverham. But it is clear that many of these were short-term leases and in the early fifteenth century there seems to have

---

55. For example on the estates of the monks of Westminster, at Ramsey and Winchester. For a brief survey of seigneurial responses see J. L. Bolton, *The Medieval English Economy, 1150–1500* (London, 1980), pp. 210–12.

56. Dr Campbell's tables.

57. Smith, *Canterbury*, p. 190.

58. The surviving records for the late middle ages are much less satisfactory and still await intensive analysis of the sort that Stone provided for the earlier period.

been a renewal of demesne arable farming on a substantial scale.[59] The policy did not work, however, and in the late 1420s a decision was made to farm out all remaining demesnes, even those like Sedgeford and Hemsby and Martham which seem never to have been leased before. By 1430 the sown acreage on the priory demesnes had dropped from nearly 3000 acres at the 1300 peak and 2000 acres in the early fifteenth century to twenty-seven acres.[60] Like nearly all other landlords, Norwich Cathedral Priory was now drawing almost all of its income from rents.

At Norwich Cathedral Priory wool had by the end of the fifteenth century become the only real source of income from sales, except for the occasional sale of timber. Unfortunately the relevant accounts tell us little about the growth of that activity between 1380 and 1480, by which time the priory already had some 4000 sheep – a very large increase from the fourteenth century. During the following fifty years the flocks grew bigger and more numerous, the priory possessing by 1520 some 8000 sheep in seven or eight flocks, thus rivalling the great flocks of the gentry sheep-farmers: the Fermours and Townshends and Southwells. Most of the priory's sheep were in the north west of the county, the classic 'sheep-corn' region, or around Norwich – there were almost none on the eastern manors.[61] Surviving accounts are mostly concerned with noting changes in the numbers of sheep, so the profit gained from the sale of wool, which obviously fluctuated from year to year, is difficult to estimate.[62] When they appear on the master of the cellar's rolls wool sales brought in substantial net sums – £35 in 1473–74, about £52 in 1483–84, £46 in 1535–36.[63] Wool was normally sold to the wool-broggers who abounded in central Norfolk, but in 1535–36 the whole wool-clip was sold directly to the Springs, the great clothiers of Lavenham.[64]

The end of demesne farming produced changes in administrative practices, though the forms of record-keeping altered comparatively little on most monastic estates. Each of the Benedictine houses was a separate institution, of course, and different decisions were made at different times about, for instance, length of leases: some – and this appears to have been true of Norwich – continued short-term for most of the century, in the hope perhaps that circumstances would allow the revival of direct farming; others were quickly extended to terms of lives or longer specified periods.[65] At some monasteries the fifteenth century seems to have seen an extension

59. Dr Campbell's tables. The cellarer's manor of Great Cressingham, for instance, was farmed out for a fixed sum of £20–£21 from the early 1380s until about 1412, when its demesnes were taken back into hand for a few years; from the early 1420s it was leased out again and this time the change was permanent: NRO DCN 1/2/25–45; MC 212/14.

60. Dr Campbell's tables.

61. Dr Campbell's tables.

62. NRO, DCN 64/1–12.

63. DCN 1/1/93, 94, 108.

64. NRO, DCN 1/1/108; K. Allison, 'Flock Management in the Sixteenth and Seventeenth Centuries', *Economic History Review*, 2nd series, 11 (1958–59), pp. 98–112.

65. Harvey, *Westminster*, pp. 150–60; Searle, *Lordship and Community*, pp. 324–36 etc.

in the authority of the abbot or prior over the obedientiaries' sources of income.[66] Some movement in this direction may help to explain the great increase in the proportion of the revenues for which the master of the cellar at Norwich was responsible, but there is no other evidence of substantial administrative change at the priory. Each obedientiary continued to be responsible for his allotted properties and for the production of annual accounts.

Studies of various monasteries seem to suggest a decline in vigour and the profit-making mentality among most of the older religious houses. By the end of the fifteenth century most were certainly much less actively engaged in running their estates, responsibilities being mainly in the hands of laymen. When the population and economy began to expand again in the early sixteenth century there seems to have been no attempt anywhere to revert to earlier practices by repossessing demesne lands and cultivating them for profit. The only direct form of agriculture that Norwich, like most early sixteenth-century monasteries, engaged in was sheep-farming.[67]

How did the economic and administrative changes described above affect the overall income and expenditure of the priory? Some rents were still in the form of specific amounts of grain or malt, but most foodstuffs were now purchased on the open market. With the exception of one or two short periods, particularly in the late 1430s, prices remained low for much of the fifteenth century and most monasteries managed to maintain a reasonably stable economic position. Of course, unlike lay lords who might increase their landed income by inheritance, marriage or royal patronage, religious houses were not in a position to expand their holdings to compensate for the fall in demesne and rent income. Few had the capital to purchase land, even if royal licences to do so were available, and the older houses had long ceased to be the recipients of landed endowments or indeed of substantial gifts of cash. So most religious houses saw a considerable drop in income during this period.[68] Estimates of income at Norwich after the early 1300s are only possible either by putting together the totals of the various obedientiary accounts, which rarely are all available for a single year, or by using the *status obedientiariorum* which are extant only for eleven years between 1363 and 1534.[69] These documents, which

66. Knowles, *Religious Orders*, ii, pp. 328–30.
67. Harvey, *Westminster*, pp. 160–64; Searle, *Lordship and Community*, pp. 260–66; Joyce Youings, 'Monasteries', in C. Clay, ed., *Rural Society: Land-Owners, Peasants and Labourers* (Cambridge, 1990), pp. 76–78.
68. R. B. Dobson, *Durham Priory, 1400–1450* (Cambridge, 1973), pp. 250–96; though Durham retained much of its magnificence and authority.
69. NRO, DCN 1/13/1–6. The dating of

these documents by Saunders (*Obedientiary Rolls*, p. 17) is very inaccurate. That in the NRO handlist is correct except for DCN 1/13/5, listed as 1505–6 but in fact 1409–10: it is dated as '2 Prior Robert' - who has been interpreted as Robert Catton (1504–30) but is, in fact, Robert Burnham (1407–27). I am grateful to Paul Rutledge for confirming that the handwriting as well as the contents date it to the early fifteenth century.

are also found at Durham Cathedral Priory and Ramsey Abbey and no doubt existed elsewhere, tabulate the receipts and expenditure of each obedientiary and cell, with the consequent surplus or deficit, and produce a total of all of these at the end to show the overall state of the priory's finances. The accounting basis is quite different from the *proficua* and, because of the inclusion of arrears among the receipts and the previous year's deficit among the expenses, it is not easy to estimate the actual income and expenditure for any particular year. Even so, they do provide a useful guide to the changing financial situation of the institution.

The first surviving accounts from 1363 and 1364 show that receipts were over £2200 p.a., showing as mentioned above, that a good recovery had been made from the onslaught of the Black Death. Expenditure, however, greatly exceeded receipts for almost all the major obedientiaries and the annual deficit moved from £500 to £600 in those two years. It is difficult to know what sort of problems this meant for the monastery, and certainly the deficit did not become any smaller over the next twenty years. The cellarers' accounts, for instance, show that though their income remained quite high, reaching £569 in 1370–71, their expenses also rose to produce a deficit of over £400 in 1382–83. Over the next twenty years, however, this was whittled away, even though income was declining, and by the time of the next surviving *status* in 1408–9 the deficit had become £86.[70] The overall income for the priory remained in that year at just over £2000 and the deficit had also been reduced to some £232. The financial difficulties that led to the leasing out of all demesnes in the late 1420s are clearly seen in the *status* of 1434 when the priory's total income had dropped to £1610 and the deficit risen to £350.[71]

The economic factors mentioned above, the sensible decision to farm out the demesnes and substantial economies led to much greater financial stability over the next fifty years. For much of that time the cellarer, for instance, was in surplus and the next surviving *status* – three from the 1470s – show that this was true of nearly all the obedientiaries (though not of the cells), even though there had been a further slump in income, which was down to around £1500 in these years.[72] Unfortunately no further *status* survives until 1531, so the financial developments of the intervening half-century have to be gleaned from the obedientiaries' accounts. These would suggest that the stability of the 1470s lasted well into the sixteenth century, even though income was continuing to decline.[73] Considerable economies must have

70. NRO, DCN 1/13/1, 2, 5; 1/2/24–50.
71. NRO, DCN 1/13/2.
72. NRO, DCN 1/13/3, 4.
73. The accounts of the master of the cellar change their character, so comparisons are not easy to make, but gross receipts grew to £629 p. a. in 1501–2, after which they fell away steadily; the cellarer's income remained fairly steady at between £200 and £250 p. a. and he usually had a slight surplus: NRO, DCN 1/1/93–108; Lestrange MS ND 17; DCN 1/2/82–99.

been made or unknown reserves drawn upon. The last four *status* accounts, running from 1531 to 1534, show a deteriorating situation in the first three years. Total income was dropping to under £1000 p.a. and the deficit rose in 1533 to £173. The last account of 1534 shows a marked improvement, due partly to a small rise in income, but much more to severe cutbacks in expenditure, which reduced the deficit to £10.[74]

This was the last surviving account of the priory. In the following year, however, came the great survey of ecclesiastical property throughout the realm to provide a new basis for clerical taxation which resulted in the *Valor Ecclesiasticus*.[75] The *Valor* lists in detail all the sources of income of all ecclesiastical persons and institutions. Its listing of the priory's temporalities and spiritualities confirms that there had been very little change in their character since the early fourteenth century but, of course, a big decline in the value of most of them. The *Valor* is not necessarily totally accurate but its overall assessment for Norwich Cathedral Priory at £1061 14s. 3½d. p.a., from which are deducted various pensions, rents, fees, wages and alms to produce a clear annual value of £874 14s. 6¼d., is close enough to the last surviving *status* accounts.

In spite of the absolute decline in income over the previous two centuries, particularly in the previous thirty years, Norwich Cathedral Priory in 1535 was still a great landowner. In Norfolk its income was still larger than that of any other institution or individual except the bishop, whose net income was some £979.[76] Its estates and religious and secular patronage still gave it a potentially important role in the society of East Anglia. As H. W. Saunders wrote, 'like some octopus with its head and heart in Norwich the monastery stretched its tentacles over the length and breadth of this big county, drawing from some one hundred and fifty villages'.[77] In terms of secular authority, however, it had never had the impact that priories like Ely and Durham had possessed. Some of these held 'liberties' which exempted part or all of their estates from the normal jurisdiction of the king's local officers – Bury St Edmunds in west Suffolk is the prime East Anglian example – and these houses were necessarily involved in major regional and national political affairs. Norwich Cathedral Priory had no such great privileged 'liberties', except over its own cathedral precinct, though it possessed minor jurisdictions over its manors. Its ecclesiastical jurisdiction, too, was limited to its estates. There is plenty of evidence to show that as a manorial lord it was actively involved in the lives of its tenants, at least until the 1420s – and even after that the prior or obedientiary continued to

74. NRO, DCN 1/13/6.
75. J. Caley and J. Hunter, eds, *Valor Ecclesiasticus*, 6 vols (1810–34). The priory's resources are listed in vol. iii, pp. 489–94.
76. Youings, 'Monasteries', estimates that over

the country as a whole religious houses still held more than one-fifth of the gross value of landed and other property.
77. Saunders, *Obedientiary Rolls*, p. 3.

attend manorial courts on occasion.[78] But there is little evidence of any direct involvement in county politics or of major litigation with laymen outside Norwich, at least after the thirteenth century. Although a great lordship, the priory's estates had essentially an economic function only. They existed to support the monastic community, its religious, charitable and educational functions in the cathedral and the buildings associated with that great edifice which the monks controlled for 450 years. For most of that period the estates were sufficiently well organised and administered to provide an income sufficient for these purposes; not even at the end of that time had the monks fallen into the penury and disorder which affected some religious houses. The priory died in 1538 as a result of extraneous pressure, not from internal disintegration. The redistribution of the estates among the dean, prebendaries and canons of the new secular chapter created in 1538 cut right across the old divisions among the obedientiaries and greatly weakened central control over them.[79] But until the nineteenth century villages like Sedgeford, Trowse and Catton continued to lie partly in the economic and social, as well as the religious, ambit of the cathedral, as they had done since 1101.

78. The prior, for instance, was present at a manor court in Great Cressingham in 1489: H. W. Chandler, ed., *Five Court Rolls of Great Cressingham* (London, 1885), p. 52.

79. NRO, DCN 29/3, fos 144–149, lists the sources of income given to each prebendary and the canons. Their valuation is taken from the *Valor* assessments.

PART IV

Decoration
and Function

18

The Vault Bosses

Martial Rose

In Norwich Cathedral there are over 1000 stone roof bosses. Of these about 700 are historiated, that is they either tell a story in themselves or are part of a story told in a sequence of bosses. Such a profusion of story-telling bosses is unique. Within this country, and indeed throughout Europe, there are very few historiated bosses. Apart from Norwich the highest number appears in the fourteenth-century vaulting of the nave of Tewkesbury Abbey, where fifteen such bosses in groups of five depict the Nativity, the Passion and the Ressurection of Christ. The numerical disparity in this field between Tewkesbury and Norwich must pose the question why such a phenomenon occurred in Norwich Cathedral on such a large scale and nowhere else.

Stone bosses are the keystones that hold in place ribbed vaulting. In Norwich Cathedral the incidence of such vaulting is extensive: in the cloister, the nave, the transepts, the presbytery and the Bauchun Chapel. The size of the bosses varies from eight inches in diameter to two feet (20 cm. to 61 cm.) Their quality is sometimes exquisite, sometimes crude. The workmanship dates from the very early part of the fourteenth century to the second decade of the sixteenth century. The subject matter extends from folklore to the lives of the saints, the representation of the Apocalypse, the story of the much wronged empress (a version of whose adventures Chaucer relates in his Man of Law's Tale), and, in the nave, from the Creation of the world to the Last Judgement.

The Cloister Bosses

To what extent the riots of 1272 damaged the Norman cloister is unknown, but in 1297 the prior and monks began to rebuild their cloister. Their series of campaigns, frequently interrupted by the need for more urgent work to other parts of the cathedral and monastery, extend down to 1453.[1]

---

1. *Communar Rolls*, p. 43.

It is possible that the cloister area had not been too severely affected by the fire of 1272. When, at the beginning of the twentieth century, some of the twelfth-century Romanesque double capitals were discovered in the cloister, concealed beneath later masonry, it was observed that they showed no evidence of having been scorched in a great conflagration.[2] The earlier cloister arcades, with their carved capitals, may well have been left standing until the walk in which they stood was ready for that particular phase of the rebuilding programme. The sculptors of the fourteenth century would in that case have had before them the carvings on the Romanesque capitals, which included representations of men, beasts and foliage.

Each cloister walk has eleven bays except the east walk, which has twelve. In addition there are four corner bays, making a total of forty-nine. Each bay, with two exceptions, has eight bosses. In all there are 394 bosses in the cloister. The subjects of the carving are: foliage; animals, real and imaginary; hybrid creatures; woodwose men or 'green men'; musicians with a wide variety of instruments; reflections of folklore with men in combat with beasts, with women and with each other; separate carvings of kings, bishops, priors and saints; the lives of the saints and martyrs; and an extensive representation of biblical themes. Of particular interest is the comparison between the first storied bosses at Norwich (in the east walk and executed in the first years of the fourteenth century) and the magnificent roof bosses in the Lady Chapel and the presbytery in Exeter Cathedral (carved in the last quarter of the thirteenth century and at the beginning of the fourteenth). These Exeter roof bosses do not present a continuous storied sequence such as we see in the Norwich cloister, which are the very first series of storied bosses in the history of church architecture.

The construction of the cloister vaulting began in the east walk with the four central bays which formed the entrance to the chapter house (above, fig. 84, bays 7, 8, 9, 10). The work was undertaken in the second decade of the fourteenth century. All thirty-six bosses in these bays are of foliage. There is no figure work, neither animal nor human. The next three bays to be completed were to the south. Here foliate carving predominates but human and animal figures begin to emerge. A dragon is to be seen eating an acorn; a 'green man' peers out from behind a frond of hawthorn leaves; and there is a hybrid creature sprouting two heads from one neck. This creature has clawed feet but no body.

The first series of storied bosses comprises the centre bosses of the five bays to the south of the prior's door (bays 1–5). From south to north they represent: the Flagellation; Carrying the Cross; the Crucifixion; the Ressurection; and the Harrowing of Hell. A common feature is that this Passion sequence is carved against a wreath of foliage. In the Flagellation, for instance, the vine leaves not only circle

2.   A. Borg *et al.*, *Medieval Sculpture from Norwich Cathedral* (Norwich, 1980), p. 6.

the main carving in which Christ himself is bound to the trunk of the vine, but bunches of grapes appear between the scourgers and Christ, and leaves partly cover the scourgers' tunics. In the Crucifixion leaves sprout from the arms of the cross, oak at the top, hawthorn at the base. In the Ressurection, behind Christ's partially damaged head, is a deeply carved oak leaf. It is as though the figured carving has had to emerge from the foliage and has not quite succeeded in shaking itself free. Nearby many other non-scriptural figures also appear in wreaths of foliage, as for instance the dragon eating hawthorn berries in bay 3 (fig. 123).

The work on the south walk began in 1323 under the supervision of John Ramsey, continuing later under that of his nephew William. The main feature in this walk, as indeed in the west walk, is the series of carvings of the Apocalypse – the revelation of St John the Divine. There are 102 in all, thirty-eight in the south walk and sixty-four in the west walk. It is possible that the initial plan for this task was to place about thirty such carvings along the central

Fig. 123. Cloister, east walk (bay 3). Dragon eating hawthorn berries.

longitudinal ridge in each of the three unbuilt walks. This plan was probably abandoned after the first four bays had been completed in the west walk. From this point carvings of the Apocalypse appear either side of the main ridge, and there was a concerted endeavour to complete the series just before the end of the walk at the monks' door. In church iconography there are very few examples of complete representations of the Apocalypse. The most interesting comparisons are with the fourteenth-century wall paintings in the chapter house of Westminster Abbey, of which there were originally perhaps a hundred; the east window of York Minster (1405–8), which contains eighty-one lights on the theme; the Angers tapestry (1375–79), which had ninety illustrations; and the eighty-five lights of the fifteenth-century rose window of the Sainte-Chapelle, Paris. There were, however, a great number of illuminated manuscripts devoted to the Apocalypse, and it is reasonable to suppose that the priory had access to some of these (compare plate IIIa and fig. 124).[3] When the west walk was under construction (1346–47), we learn

3.   M. R. James, *The Apocalypse in Art* (London, 1931), p. 78.

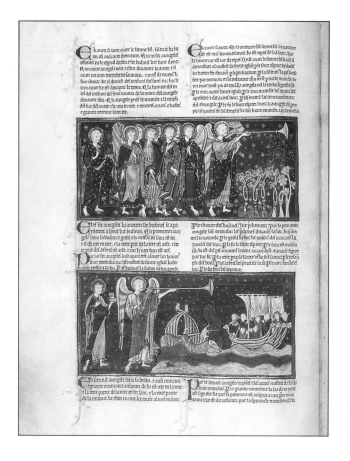

Fig. 124. Angels sound the first and second trumpets (Cambridge, Trinity College, MS R.16.2, fo. 8v).

from the communar rolls of Norwich Priory that a history of the Apocalypse, no doubt illuminated, was bought for use in carving the bosses.[4] It was M.R. James's contention that it was from one of a group of East Anglian thirteenth-century manuscripts that the Norwich carvers took their models. There is no doubt that East Anglia was the source of some of the very finest illuminated manuscripts in the early years of the fourteenth century. The priory would have had access to illuminated Apocalypse manuscripts and also to such psalters as those of Ormesby, Gorleston and Bromholm. Indeed, it may already have possessed the Ormesby and Gorleston manuscripts.[5]

The south walk, apart from the Apocalypse series, has its 'green men' bosses, lions lurking in the foliage and hybrid musicians. There are also three biblical carvings set over the window arches: John the Baptist about to be beheaded; the Annunciation; and the visit of Mary to Elizabeth. Over the refectory door is a carving of Adam and Eve tempted by the serpent, with his tail entwined around

4.　*Communar Rolls*, p. 39.　　　　　　　5.　See pp. 249–50, 334–35.

the tree. The image of the Fall in this position might have served as a caution to the monks, as they passed under the arch into the refectory, not to succumb to the deadly sin of gluttony. In the west walk the bosses over the nine north-ward wall arches (bays 29–37) depict the events in the life of St Basil in which the Virgin Mary intercedes on his behalf (bays 29–32), the Virgin Mary interceding on behalf of the merchant of Constantinople (bays 33–35); and aspects of the life of St Christopher (bays 36, 37). This treatment of the saints and the blessed intervention of the Virgin Mary is extended into the north walk and, because the carvings of the Apocalypse had been completed within the west walk, given greater prominence.

The first series of historiated or illustrative bosses of the Passion of Christ had been completed in the east walk by 1329 with the carving of the Harrowing of Hell. Over a hundred years later this series was continued into the north walk with a further thirteen bosses on post-Ressurection themes, followed by a series on the death, assumption and coronation of the Virgin, and a series of three bosses associated with St John the Evangelist, concluding with his assumption. Events from the lives of other saints are depicted as the north walk progresses westward, sometimes within a single boss (St Laurence on his gridiron; or St Martin on horseback cutting his cloak in half with his sword to share it with a peasant), sometimes by a pair of bosses (St Clement and St Nicholas), sometimes by a larger group, five bosses, for instance, telling the story of St Thomas of Canterbury. The last of these shows Henry II, having taken off all his clothes apart from his drawers, kneeling penitently at the shrine of St Thomas. His courtiers stand behind him holding his garments. Before him on the ground is his crown. Three monks lean over the shrine and beat the king with their scourges. At the west end of the north walk are two bosses telling part of the story of St Theophilus. As mentioned previously, the story of St Basil is told in four of the west walk bosses; and that of St John in three of the north walk bosses. Among the extant illuminated manuscripts of the Apocalypse it is common to find illustrations of the life of St John. In the Lambeth Palace Apocalypse (MS 209) there are also illustrations of the lives of St John, St Basil and St Theophilus.

Stone from quarries at Caen in Normandy was used for the cloister bosses, carved mostly by Norfolk craftsmen. For instance, James and John Woderofe were brothers and master masons working on the cloister's west and south walks from 1415 until the carving was completed in 1436. For ten weeks' work in 1415–16 they were paid 2s. 4d. a week plus food. Between 1420 and 1422 they vaulted three bays of the cloister for £16, with gratuities of 13s. 4d. It is thought that they were the carvers of the finest bosses in the west and north walks. Other carvers worked under them. John Horn was paid 4s. a week for fifteen weeks and William Reppys 6s. 8d. for carving each of six keystones. It has been suggested that these might be the post-Ressurection bosses in the north walk from the sealing of the tomb to the Ascension.[6]

The cloister was repaired and repainted under Professor Tristram's direction between 1936 and 1938. Fifty years later further repair and repainting had to be undertaken. The bosses had suffered badly from weathering and from moisture trapped by the paint of the 1930s; there is no longer any discernible trace of medieval paint.

The Nave Bosses

In 1463, only ten years after the paving of the cloister had been completed, the roof of the nave of the cathedral was consumed by fire. Bishop Walter Lyhart (1446–72) decided to replace the old wooden ceiling with a stone-vaulted one. In this vaulting more than 250 bosses tell the story of the history of the world in biblical terms, from Creation to Doomsday. Moving from the cloister to the nave the visitor, examining the roof bosses, will notice a change of style and content and will be confronted by one of the unique achievements of medieval art in the latter part of the fifteenth century.

Here, in contrast to the evolving style and layout of the cloister bosses, is a manifestation of late medieval religious iconography unique in conception and planned and executed on a grand scale. When the first foliate bosses were carved in the east walk of the cloister no overall scheme can have been set out for the master masons; but when work began on the nave roof a master plan and the story it was to depict had been carefully prepared. The themes had been established for each bay although some scope was left for the sculptor's invention, as for example the off-duty soldier quaffing wine in the bay of the Crucifixion (bay 12, no. 5).

The plan for reroofing the nave entailed the introduction of a stellar lierne pattern of stone vaulting above the fourteen Norman bays stretching from the crossing to the west window. The vaulting requires twenty-four keystones in each bay (fig. 125). Three additional bosses above the west window bring the number of nave bosses to 339. Of these, six in each bay (three to the south and three to the north above the windows) are invariably foliate and not part of the storied scheme (fig. 125, nos 19–24). The basis of the scheme is to devote seven of the bays, beginning above the choir, to stories of the Old Testament; and seven of the bays, ending at the west window, to stories of the New Testament. The main subjects of the first seven bays are: the creation of the world and the fall of Adam and Eve; Noah and the flood; Abraham and Isaac; Jacob (for example fig. 126); Joseph; Moses; David. The

6.   *Communar Rolls*, pp. 14, 42–43; J. Harvey, *English Medieval Architects* (London, 1954), pp. 343–44.

I. Norwich Cathedral from the air.

IIa. The Gorleston Psalter of the early fourteenth century. The initial introducing psalm 101 encloses a figure of Ecclesia carrying a church. The psalter is one of the great masterpieces of the East Anglian school of illumination (BL, Additional MS 49622, fo. 128v).

IIb. Detail from the Ormesby Psalter. The historiated initial shows Samuel anointing David. The psalter was given by Robert of Ormesby to the cathedral, probably in the 1330s (Bodleian Library, MS Douce 366, fo. 38r).

III. Carved bosses from the vaults of Norwich Cathedral.

a. The Apocalypse: the angel sounds the second trumpet (Revelation 8:8). Cloister, south walk, bay 21.

c. The Magi offer their gifts. North transept.

b. Christ enthroned at the Last Judgement, with a king and a pope at his feet, rising from their graves. Nave, bay 14, no. 10.

d. John the Baptist preaching. South transept.

IV. Roundel with the scene of the simony of Herbert de Losinga, a wall painting from the south
nave aisle.

Va. Wall painting of the Virgin and Child flanked by St Margaret and St Catherine, in the western segment of the vault of the ante-reliquary chapel.

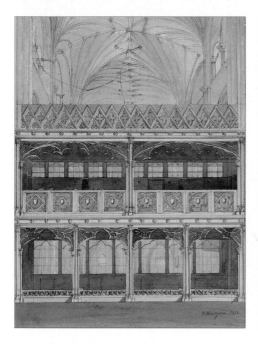

Vb. David Hodgson's watercolour of the front of the gallery across the north transept, with the closets above, in 1832 (NRO, DCN 128/3).

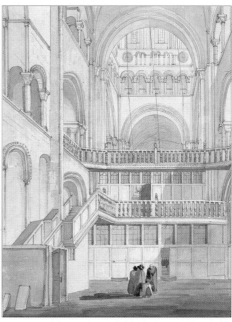

Vc. The back view of the 'closets' in the north transept, by David Hodgson, 1832 (NRO, DCN 128/4).

VI. The exterior of the south transept, with the deanery to the right; houses adjoining the cloister to the left. This watercolour was painted by David Hodgson shortly before the extensive alterations of Anthony Salvin remodelled and exposed the south face (NRO, DCN 128/1).

VII. The interior of the south transept, showing the quarter-jacks and also the different cross-walls and levels shortly before Anthony Salvin's alterations; by David Hodgson (NRO, DCN 128/2).

VIIIa. Norwich Cathedral from the ruins of the cell of St Leonard on Mousehold Heath, a Dutch-school painting of the early eighteenth century. The skyline is dominated by the cathedral and the towers of the city's many parish churches.

VIIIb. Norwich Cathedral from Pull's Ferry, by Edward Dayes (1763–1804).

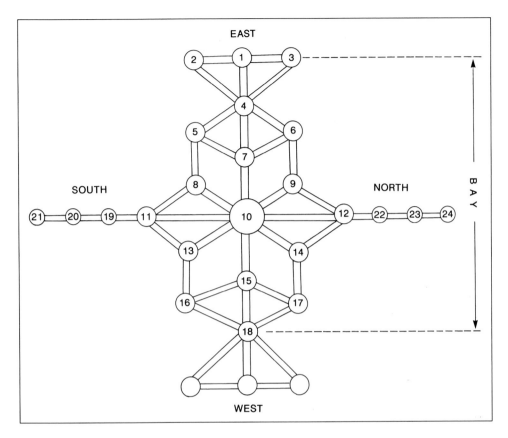

EAST

SOUTH   NORTH

B A Y

WEST

Fig. 125. Nave vault. Location of bosses within a sample bay. This plan should be read as if viewed from below.

Fig. 126. Nave (bay 3, no. 17). Jacob kills a kid on a table in front of his house (Genesis 27:6-14).

next seven bays are wholly concerned with the story of Christ: the Nativity; the Baptism; the Last Supper; Christ's arrest; the Crucifixion; the Ascension; the Last Judgement (fig. 127).

In each bay a central boss establishes the main subject and seventeen satellite ones contribute to the story. The latter are not placed in any linear chronological order, nor are they wholly devoted to the main story of the bay. For instance, the last boss on bay one (the Creation and the Fall) depicts the death of Cain (no. 18), while the first boss in the second bay shows Cain holding the

East							South						West
Creation and Fall	Noah and Flood	Abraham and Isaac	Jacob	Joseph	Moses	David	Nativity	Baptism	Last Supper	Christ arrested	Crucif- ixion	Ascension	Last Judgement
Bay 1	2	3	4	5	6	7	8	9	10	11	12	13	14

Fig. 127. Nave vault. The sequence of Old and New Testament stories.

jaw-bone of an ass as though he had just murdered Abel (bay 2, no. 1). This suggests that the last boss or bosses in one bay could look forward to the subject of the next bay. In this case it is the corruptness of man that brings about the flood.

Despite these irregularities there is no doubt that the bosses in each bay depict a particular biblical story. A consideration of the possible sources of inspiration for this particular sequence may help in appreciating the basis of selection.

Fig. 128. Nave (bay 7, no. 18). Solomon enthroned as judge and king, carrying in his hands the sword and temple.

The general planning of the themes deliberately illustrates how the Old Testament stories are fulfilled in the New Testament. Such patterning inheres in much medieval iconography and is best exemplified in the *Biblia pauperum* and the *Speculum humanae salvationis*, instructional picture books of the thirteenth and fourteenth centuries respectively. In these works the types of the Old Testament prefigure the anti-types of the New. In a limited manner such ideas can be detected in the Norwich layout. Thus the flood and Noah's ark in the second bay are a type of Christ's baptism in the ninth. Similarly Solomon sitting in judgement in bay seven is a type of Christ enthroned at the Last Judgement in bay fourteen (compare figs 128 and plate IIIb). But the scheme of the layout of the nave bosses, although clearly divided between Old and New Testament themes, does not follow in any detail the patterns inherent in either the *Biblia pauperum*, in which there are two Old Testament types to prefigure each New Testament anti-type, or the *Speculum humanae salvationis* where three Old Testament types prefigure each New Testament anti-type.

Both sources, however, appear to have provided patterns for individual bosses.

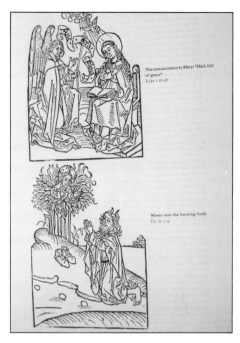

Fig. 129. Nave (bay 6). God speaking to
Moses from the burning bush
(Exodus 3:2).

Fig. 130. God speaking to Moses from the
burning bush. From the *Speculum Humanae
Salvationis*.

For instance, the carving of God speaking to Moses from the burning bush (bay 6,
no. 7) – which is a type of the immaculate conception – is very close to both these
sources where they show God with a beard and a cruciform nimbus rather than the
angel that speaks to Moses from the burning bush in the biblical version (compare
figs 129 and 130). There are two bosses depicting Abraham about to sacrifice his
son Isaac, one (bay 3, no. 10) apparently drawn from the *Biblia pauperum*, the other
(bay 3, no. 7) from the *Speculum humanae salvationis*. It would seem therefore that these
two popular pattern books were influential in fashioning many of the carvings in
the nave, though they did not determine the overall scheme that was adopted.

The selection of subjects within this scheme was possibly governed by the church
festal offices and the readings associated with them. These very often reinforced the
balance of Old and New Testament themes where each of the central Old Testament
figures is a type of Christ. Yet the New Testament bosses are strangely lacking in
certain key areas of iconography. For instance, they give no emphasis to the adoration
of either the shepherds or the kings at the Nativity.[7] Moreover, a complete omission

7.   This deficiency was amply compensated for
     forty years later when seventy-five bosses in
     the north transept were devoted to an ex-
     tended treatment of the Nativity.

in the cycle of carving is the death, assumption and coronation of the Blessed Virgin. Although Mary is prominent in the nave carvings of Pentecost and the Ascension it is somewhat surprising not to have representations of her death, assumption and coronation. An interesting comparison is with the stained glass windows in King's College Chapel in Cambridge (1515–47) which portray more systematically than the Norwich nave a type/anti-type scheme, much of it also directly derived from the *Biblia pauperum* and *Speculum humanae salvationis*; here, however, the whole is set within the framework of the life of the Virgin, beginning with the meeting of her parents and concluding with her coronation in heaven.

Clearly, the overarching scheme which governed the iconography in each bay of the cathedral nave was not derived directly from any of the obvious iconographical sources with their emphasis upon types. Rather, the scheme that was adopted, possibly under Bishop Lyhart's direction, was that of the ages of the world before Christ, set out in the first seven bays – Adam, Noah, Abraham, Jacob, Joseph, Moses, David, each a type of Christ – leading to the age of Christ, set out in the second set of seven bays, culminating in the end of the world and the Last Judgement (plate IIIb). The patriarchs of the Old Testament as precursors of Christ had frequently been represented in medieval art as part of a greater iconographic pattern of Christian theology, as in the east window of York Minster, or the north-east transept window of Canterbury Cathedral or the windows of Bourges or Chartres, or the sculpted figures in the north porch of Chartres. Most of these patriarchs also featured as main characters in the section of the mystery plays concerned with the Old Testament. But whereas the mystery plays would have given at least twice as much emphasis to the New Testament as to the Old, the iconography in the nave vaulting is evenly balanced between the two testaments.

The inspiration for creating this great cycle of historiated bosses most probably stemmed from the Apocalypse cycle completed only a few years earlier in the cloister. The composition of the nave cycle owed much in detail to the instructional pattern books, such as the *Biblia pauperum*, and a great deal thematically to the medieval notion of the lives of the patriarchs being fulfilled in that of Christ. Furthermore, the mystery plays, flourishing in East Anglia in the middle of the fifteenth century, would almost certainly have been influential in helping to deter-mine choice of subject and, in many instances, its treatment.

Pictorially, as has been shown, the masons may have followed examples from printed pattern books as earlier they had used illustrations from illuminated manu-scripts. But, as was common at the time, there was also a firm intention to depict many characters in contemporary style just as fifty or sixty years later the designers of the King's College Chapel windows were concerned with early sixteenth-century fashions. For instance, Pharaoh drowning in the Red Sea is costumed as a mid fifteenth-century English king, clad in gold-plated armour, while his chariot is shaped like a Yarmouth farm-cart. Rebecca and Joseph are set against a background of the house in which they live; this house looks remarkably like one which a fifteenth-century Norwich merchant might have owned. In addition, the flourishing of vernacular drama in East Anglia during the fifteenth century,[8] with the substance of the mystery plays following so closely the themes set out in the nave carvings, must have given an intense feeling of contemporaneity to both the work and the faith that underpinned it, especially as the craftsmen involved in the creation of the vaulting, and in the carving and painting of its bosses would in all likelihood have also been concerned with the acting and presentation of the plays.

The Bauchun Chapel

The fourteenth-century Bauchun Chapel received its present vaulting in the latter part of the fifteenth century.[9] The chapel had been used as the consistory court and William Seckington, one of the court's advocates, died in 1460 leaving a bequest for the work to be carried out. The vaulting in the chapel is divided into two bays. The bosses in each appear in the form of an ellipse (fig. 131). That the Virgin Mary is especially venerated in this chapel is immediately apparent by a glance at the two most prominent bosses: the central boss of the south bay portrays her assumption, that in the north bay her coronation (fig. 131, nos 12 and 36). Apart from angels with shields and musical instruments which are located towards the ribs' extremities (for example nos 8, 9, 15, 16), the remaining thirty-two bosses are devoted to a version of the medieval story of the calumniated empress found in the *Gesta Romanorum* and retold in a series of murals behind the choir stalls of Eton College.[10] Their haphazard ordering makes it difficult for each of the salient events to be identified, but the story is as follows: the emperor and the empress are married (no. 17); the emperor on leaving his realm hands over his authority to the empress; the emperor's brother makes advances to the empress which she rejects (no. 3); the emperor's brother, on the return of the emperor, maligns her and is believed (no. 13). The emperor orders her to be killed in the depths of a forest (no. 18); here she is rescued by a passing knight who, not knowing that she is the empress, takes her home and employs her as a nurse to his infant son (no. 25). The knight's brother's offer of love is rejected by the empress; the brother therefore murders his young nephew at night and places the dagger in the hand of the sleeping empress (no. 22).

8. R. Beadle, 'The Medieval Drama of East Anglia: Studies in Dialect, Documentary Records and Stagecraft' (unpublished University of York Ph. D. thesis, 1977).

9. Arthur Whittingham suggested the date of 1475: A. B. Whittingham, *Norwich Cathedral Bosses and Misericords* (Norwich, 1981), p. 13.

10. M. R. James, *The Sculptured Bosses in the Roof of the Bauchun Chapel of Our Lady of Pity* (Norwich, 1908), p. 1.

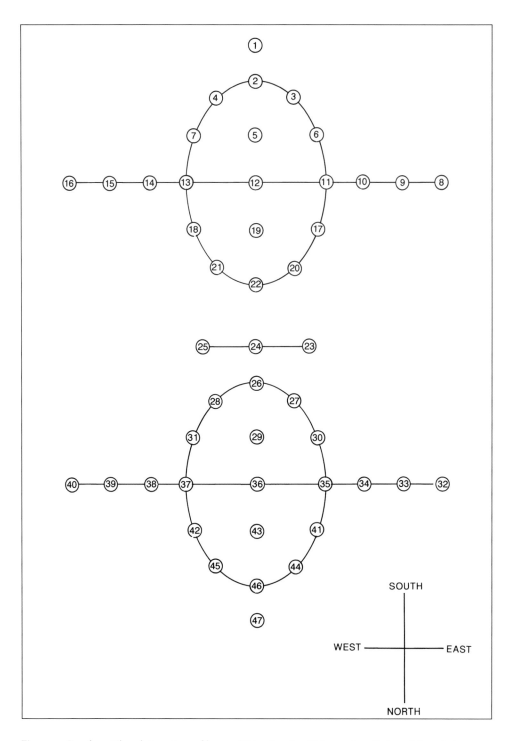

Fig. 131. Bauchun Chapel. Location of bosses. This plan should be read as if viewed from below.

She is accused of murder and left on a desert island to die (no. 6). She prays to the Virgin Mary, who shows her a plant on the island which has the power of curing leprosy (no. 7). The empress is taken off the island by a passing ship and cures, among many others, both her former traducers, who have become lepers. They have to confess their sins before they are cured. She returns to the emperor and kneels at his feet (no. 46). Frances Barasch argues that the story depicted by the bosses was gleaned from a variety of sources apart from the *Gesta Romanorum*,[11] but the compilation from which the sculptors must have worked remains to be identified.

Throughout, the empress wears her tall triple crown, even when she takes the role of nurse-maid. Much attention is given to the details of her dress. For example, at her marriage she stands with her head inclined towards the emperor, her tall crown, surmounted with a cross, far overtopping the emperor's. She is dressed in a v-neck gown of gold with a dark bodice showing beneath. In her left hand she holds a golden orb. She wears deep cuffs, perhaps of ermine. With her right hand she holds up her skirt as though she and the emperor are taking part in the wedding procession.

Most of the larger bosses in which the empress appears are carved with some care and considerable skill, but others are of poorer work. This discrepancy in the quality of the carving points to an apprentice working alongside a master mason, as does the apparently random placing of the bosses, apart from the two of the Virgin Mary.

The work was carried out during the episcopate of James Goldwell (1472–99). He had been consecrated bishop of Norwich in Rome, where he had been acting as Edward IV's secretary of state. The Italianate romance of the falsely accused empress of Rome would have been familiar to Goldwell. He clearly did not share Bishop Lyhart's view that the bosses should depict a unified scheme with a biblical foundation.

The Presbytery Bosses

Goldwell's reroofing and revaulting of the presbytery resulted in a work of great beauty, but thematically it was even further removed from the historiated design principles inherent in Lyhart's nave, since the bosses mainly depict neither religious nor secular story material.

Of the 128 bosses, ninety-four are of gold wells, a rebus or pun on the bishop's name, and twenty-nine are floral, mostly roses. Of the other five, coming at the intersection of the transverse rib and the main ridge, three bear Goldwell's crest or

---

11. F. K. Barasch, 'Norwich Cathedral: The Bauchun Chapel Legend of the Accused Queen', *The Early Drama, Art and Music Review*, 15 (1993), pp. 63–75.

coat of arms, one represents the Virgin Mary in glory and one shows God the Father supporting the crucified Christ; each of these five is slightly larger than the other presbytery bosses. Many of the presbytery bosses are surrounded by foliage painted onto the vaulting. The gold wells often have carved leaves sprouting from their top. The subject of these bosses trumpets out the bishop's ostentation and self-indulgence. Yet to the viewer the artistic achievement of the presbytery vaulting and the aesthetic satisfaction to be derived from it are supreme.

The Transept Bosses

In 1509, during Bishop Nix's episcopate (1501–35/36), fire destroyed the roofs of the transepts. The bishop decided to follow the pattern of the nave and presbytery and cover the transept arms with stellar lierne vaults.

There are four bays in each transept. As in the nave there are twenty-four bosses in each bay, but there are three additional bosses above the southern arch in each transept. The six lower bosses in each bay depict Bishop Nix's arms: azure with three mitres gold (the arms of the see), and gold with a chevron between three leopards' heads gules.[12] The subjects of the other bosses in each transept are as follows:

North Transept	Bay 1	The birth of John the Baptist
		The preparation in heaven for the Annunciation
		The Annunciation
	Bay 2	The Nativity
		The shepherds follow the star
	Bay 3	The adoration of the shepherds
		The adoration of the kings
	Bay 4	The flight into Egypt
		The massacre of the innocents
		The death of Herod
South Transept	Bay 1	The early life of Christ
		Christ in the temple
	Bay 2	The temptations
		Calling the disciples
	Bay 3	The first miracle
		John the Baptist and Herod
	Bay 4	Christ's ministry of healing

12. E. E. Dorling, 'Medieval Heraldry Remaining in the Cathedral Church of Norwich', Friends of the Cathedral Church of Norwich, *Fourth Annual Report* (Norwich, 1933), p. 12.

As in the nave these bosses do not tell their story by linear progression, but in accord with the stellar pattern as a series of satellites around a central star. Here the similarity ends. In contrast to the nave bosses those in the transepts can appear repetitious. For instance, the flight into Egypt occurs eight times, albeit in varied forms. But this apparent repetition is at the very core of the method of exposition. Unlike the nave, in which Old and New Testament subjects are dealt with in broad outline, the transepts take a more limited subject and deal with it in stage by stage detail. The method is not dissimilar to an artist compiling a sequence of drawings for an animated cartoon. For example, in the northernmost bay of the north transept there are nine bosses, all of which deal with the Annunciation. They depict a continuous action beginning with God instructing Gabriel in heaven to visit Mary; Gabriel leaves heaven's gates and approaches a doorway above which is a four-pointed star. At the Annunciation scene Mary is at a reading-desk upon which is an open book; the angel stands beneath an arch on the left; a pot of lilies stands between them. The sequence continues with Mary, still reading, framed in an archway, while to the right the angel speaks to Joseph, assuring him of Mary's purity and admonishing him for his suspicions. Five further bosses on the Annunciation adopt this incremental mode. Similar treatment is given to the shepherds, the three kings, and to Herod.

It cannot be claimed that the quality of the carving in the transepts is as energetic as that of the nave or the cloister. A number of hands were responsible for the work, and the execution of some of the carving is stiff, formalised and cramped. This is particularly true of the many bosses portraying feasts in the south transept. Yet there is much that is full of charm. The bosses depicting the three kings in their various journeyings are attractive in the detail of differentiation and the delicacy with which the three are shown on the smallest of bosses, mounted and bearing their gifts. Above all, in their approach to the Holy Family and in the offering of their gifts (plate IIIc) the workmanship is of a high order. In the south transept a number of scenes with boats are carved by a sculptor with a sharp sense of composition and, it would seem, with an intimate knowledge of vessels and their tackle. Perhaps these carvers at the beginning of the sixteenth century, when manuscripts were being replaced by printed books, felt less reliant on either source and were using their own observation and inventiveness more. This is certainly evident in the somewhat later painting of St Paul's ship in one of the south-western windows of King's College Chapel. Such precision and attention to realistic detail is exemplified in the south transept in the carving of John the Baptist preaching from a pulpit (plate IIId). The boss in its clarity and vitality, knitting the auditors to the preacher, seems to be making a statement about the contemporary stress on preaching, which was certainly a plank in the reformists' platform. An analogy is to be found in the late fifteenth-century east window of St Peter Mancroft, Norwich, where St Peter is to be seen preaching from a contemporary pulpit. The same hand that carved John the Baptist preaching probably carved Jesus with the doctors in the temple, another highly skilled work. It contrasts the young boy, simply dressed, his hair short-cropped, but seated in a raised high-backed chair, with the doctors in their patterned gowns and furred tippets, gathered close about him. Each doctor, bar one, appears to be disputing some religious text drawn from the open book which each holds. Only one of the doctors looks directly at Christ; in his right hand is a closed book.

The roof bosses of the transepts were the last to be carved in Norwich Cathedral. They returned to the historiated tradition which had begun 200 years earlier in the cloister. The uniqueness of this development stemmed from the first Passion sequence in the east walk and the major representation of the Apocalypse in the south and west walks. Nave, Bauchun Chapel and transept carvings followed with differing themes and styles, but each with major historiated cycles of carvings. The bishop who had instructed the work to be undertaken in the transepts was shortly to be imprisoned and disgraced; and within thirty years of the fire in the south transept the priory itself was dissolved. The day of the cathedral craftsmen seemed past, especially as they viewed the destruction of their work in the shrines dedicated to the Virgin Mary and the saints, and of those images on reredoses, retables, in niches and in chantry chapels. But desecrating the roof bosses seventy or eighty feet up (21 or 24 m.) was a more daunting task. It is for that inaccessibility that posterity has much to be thankful.

19

The Medieval Polychromy

David Park and Helen Howard

While the stunning paintings of Bishop Losinga and the sumptuous scheme of the ante-reliquary chapel are perhaps now the most celebrated wall paintings in the cathedral, they represent only a fraction of what is known of the painted decoration of the cathedral priory as a whole, comprising not only wall paintings but also architectural and sculptural polychromy, and panel paintings.* For the period from the late twelfth century to the Reformation, the evidence for this decoration is threefold: the surviving paintings themselves; antiquarian records of destroyed or obscured paintings; and abundant and richly informative medieval documents. This evidence has been shaped by the normal forces of destruction – rebuilding, redecoration, iconoclasm, restoration – though the fire of 1272 itself engendered significant renewal. The effects of iconoclasm on the wall paintings seem to have been largely confined to obliteration rather than destruction, but sculpture and panel painting fared far worse. Indeed, of the panel paintings only the Despenser retable survives from the original medieval furnishings. It, together with others now in the cathedral, are discussed elsewhere in this volume.[1]

Erratic survival inevitably obscures the historical record. Although a significant range of subjects is known – christological, hagiographical and historical, in addition to purely decorative painting – only limited conclusions can be drawn regarding developments in function, disposition or patronage. Piecing together the strands of evidence chronologically can at least provide a reasonable history of the decoration;

1. See below, pp. 410–15.

* For help of various kinds, we are especially grateful to Ian Atherton, Sharon Cather, Keith Darby, Jill Franklin, Miriam Gill, Sandy Heslop, Caroline Hull, David King and Tony Sims. Particular thanks are due to Eric Fernie, both for his advice and for his superhuman patience.

in this the documents are invaluable in the wealth of information they contain from the late thirteenth century onward, in particular for the painting of sculptures. But to begin this history is to begin with very little, for the one period from which no wall painting appears to be known is that of the original Romanesque construction. Although this may seem surprising, examination of other great churches of the period in England suggests that their polychromy was typically very limited: none at all has been found at Durham Cathedral or Winchester Cathedral, and only simple masonry pattern in the late eleventh-century minster at York.[2] Particular elements such as capitals may well have been elaborately painted, and in fact polychromy survives on a number of twelfth-century voussoirs and nook shaft capitals probably from doorways or other openings in the cloister.[3] But it seems that wall paintings with figure-subjects would normally have been confined to important locations such as altars. Doubtless, in such churches, there was less need – and indeed less architectural scope, given their large windows and massive arcades – for the type of extensive didactic programme employed at this time in the ordinary parish church.

Appropriately, among all the surviving or recorded schemes of wall painting in the cathedral, that which shows its foundation by Bishop Herbert de Losinga is both the earliest and the finest.[4] Three roundels in the nave south aisle, on the soffit of the transverse arch to the west of the fourth bay from the east, are unique in showing the story of Losinga, who bought the see (then of Thetford) from William Rufus in a notorious act of simony in 1091 (fig. 132). In the uppermost roundel, Losinga hands over money to a figure who may well be intended for Rufus's agent, Ranulf Flambard (plate IV and fig. 132). In the next, Losinga is shown as bishop, but now repentant with hands clasped in grief; the lowest roundel is entirely occupied by a depiction of the cathedral itself. Although modern commentators have preferred to stress the sound practical reasons for the move from Thetford, these paintings provide important evidence that Losinga's building of the cathedral was perceived from an early date as a direct penance for his simony. The

2. See, for example, D. Park and P. Welford, 'The Medieval Polychromy of Winchester Cathedral', in J. Crook, ed., *Winchester Cathedral: Nine Hundred Years, 1093–1993* (Chichester and Winchester, 1993), p. 125. At Norwich, masonry pattern above the crossing arch at the east end of the nave is recorded by E. W. Tristram, *English Medieval Wall Painting: The Twelfth Century* (Oxford, 1944), p. 139, but is more likely to have formed part of the extensive late thirteenth-century scheme discussed below.

3. See the catalogue entries by Jill Franklin, nos 14–18 and 25, in A. Borg *et al.*, *Medieval Sculpture from Norwich Cathedral* (Norwich, 1980).

4. This painting is fully discussed by D. Park, 'Simony and Sanctity: Herbert Losinga, St Wulfstan of Worcester and Wall-Paintings in Norwich Cathedral', in D. Buckton and T. A. Heslop, eds, *Studies in Medieval Art and Architecture Presented to Peter Lasko* (Stroud and London, 1994), pp. 157–70.

depiction of the cathedral is the earliest attempt to portray it with some degree of realism, showing its central tower with the low wooden spire subsequently destroyed in the riot of 1272.

These roundels are part of a scheme that originally extended throughout the fourth bay from the east in this aisle. Although woefully fragmentary, enough still survives of this scheme to reconstruct its extent and to attest to the quality and sumptuousness of the painting. The adjacent northern half of the western segment of the groin vault is occupied by a fragmentary scene, showing one or more figures facing a seated king, with attendant figures standing behind the throne. This subject probably belonged to another hagiographical, or perhaps biblical, cycle. From the fact that it occupies one half-segment, and from other slight remains of painting on the vault, it may be concluded that originally eight subjects were shown here. It also appears that there must have been a further three roundels on the western arch, and probably a similar series on the corresponding arch to the east (where only fragments survive): overall, therefore, the programme on the vault and arches of this one bay seems likely to have comprised no fewer than twenty subjects. It is tragic that so much has been lost, given their superlative quality. Their calm, monumental style, with relatively naturalistic facial modelling and drapery folds, is characteristic of the 'transitional' period between late Romanesque and early Gothic, and they can be confidently dated to *c.* 1190–1200.

Fig. 132. Scenes of Herbert de Losinga and the foundation of the cathedral: soffit of an arch in the south nave aisle.

On the south wall of the next bay to the west in the south aisle, other figures were discovered in 1862 during the construction of a monument to the Wodehouse

Fig. 133. Painting of St Wulfstan and other figures discovered in 1862 on the south wall of the fifth bay from the east: south nave aisle (drawing: F. B. Russel).

family. They were described and drawn at that time (fig. 133).[5] It was found then that the original Romanesque blind arcade had been removed at some time, and the entire width of the bay then plastered and painted on a single plane (the remains of the arcade shown in the drawing are thus behind this plane). At a later date, the painting had been covered over by plaster and/or whitewash; subsequently a crude replica of the original arcade was built against it. After about a week's exposure in 1862, it was again covered over by another recreation of the Romanesque arcade, with the arches filled by memorial tablets. This painting must, therefore, still exist.[6]

At present, all discussion of the painting must be conducted in the past tense, relying on the somewhat conflicting evidence provided by the nineteenth-century antiquaries. It showed, at left, St Wulfstan of Worcester (labelled SCS WVLSTANVS) holding a crozier and facing a king. In the centre was another figure, apparently kneeling, and to the right a further standing bishop. Since the painting was executed on a continuous plaster surface, uninterrupted by arches, it would be tempting to assume that all the figures belonged to a single representation of Wulfstan's most celebrated miracle, concerning the crozier given him by Edward the Confessor.

5.   They are also discussed in detail by Park, 'Simony and Sanctity', following the account of their discovery by F. C. Husenbeth, 'Mural Paintings in Norwich Cathedral', *NA*, 6 (1864), pp. 272–76. However, the present discussion has been revised in the light of the much more accurate descriptions of their physical context provided by 'A.', 'Frescoes Discovered in Norwich Cathedral in December, 1862', *The East Anglian*, 1 (1864), pp. 287–88, and T. Jeckell, 'Frescoes in Norwich Cathedral', *The East Anglian*, 1 (1864), p. 302. David King has kindly drawn our attention to yet another brief account, in the *Gentleman's Magazine*, 133 (1863), part 1, p. 317.

6.   'A.', 'Frescoes', p. 288: '[they] have again been hidden from view, perhaps at some future day to be again uncovered and to form the subject of speculation to unborn antiquaries who . . . will I should think, be very glad to find something to speculate about'.

The last of the Anglo-Saxon bishops, Wulfstan was supposedly ordered to relinquish his bishopric by William the Conqueror at a council at Westminster; he refused, thrusting his crozier into the Confessor's tomb. Since neither Lanfranc nor Bishop Gundulf of Rochester was able to retrieve it, but only Wulfstan, he was by this sign allowed to retain the bishopric. In the wall painting, some aspect of this story must have been illustrated by the figures of Wulfstan and the king, while in the only other surviving representation of the miracle – in a later fourteenth-century manuscript, almost certainly illuminated at Westminster – Wulfstan is first shown thrusting his staff into the Confessor's tomb (at Norwich, the sloping feature beneath Wulfstan?) and then with William and Lanfranc kneeling before him. It must be admitted, however, that such an interpretation of the wall painting does not seem to fit the available evidence: for instance, the central 'kneeling' figure was also labelled as a saint; and two of the nineteenth-century accounts described Wulfstan as 'receiving' the crozier from the king. One can only wish that the painting itself were still visible: thus the feature at Wulfstan's feet is variously described by the antiquaries as foliage or scrollwork, or 'a pavement of encaustic tiles'!

It would also be tempting to date this painting to the same period as the adjacent Losinga scenes, since both illustrate stories concerning the validity of royal appointments to bishoprics. However, so far as can be judged from the drawing, the style of the painting – and, in particular, the Lombardic lettering of the two most complete inscriptions – indicate a dating in the thirteenth century or possibly early fourteenth century. To complicate matters further, certain features such as Wulfstan's mitre appear to be of later date: indeed one of the nineteenth-century accounts records that the painting 'appear[s] at a subsequent period to have been repainted'.[7] Although St Wulfstan of Worcester may seem an unlikely saint to have been commemorated at Norwich, it is known that the cathedral priory possessed a relic of him by 1234 (when it was loaned to Henry III). In more general terms, both the Wulfstan and Losinga paintings may be seen as belonging to the trend, characteristic from the late twelfth-century onwards, of promoting 'saintly' bishops of the period immediately following the Conquest.[8]

The Wulfstan and adjacent figures may have been contemporary with a fragment of decoration still extant on the arch of the main arcade in the same bay. This painting, consisting of a riband pattern and fleurs-de-lys, belongs to a thirteenth-century scheme of decoration that survives throughout much of the eastern half of the cathedral: notably in the presbytery, ambulatory and eastern radiating chapels (figs 134–135), but also with remains in both transepts and in the eastern bays of the nave south aisle.[9] Much of this decoration is of an imitative nature, comprising

7.   'A.', 'Frescoes', p. 288.

8.   See below, p. 448.

9.   E. W. Tristram, *English Medieval Wall Paint-*

ing: The Thirteenth Century (Oxford, 1950), pp. 355–59, 583–85, pls. 201–203b, 203d, 204, supp. pls. 52, 56a–e, g.

Fig. 134. Decoration in the south aisle of the ambulatory, and on the entrance arch to St Luke's Chapel.

Fig. 135. Masonry pattern and other decoration on the arch leading to the apse of St Luke's Chapel.

masonry patterns of various kinds, fictive voussoirs and marbling, imitation vault ribs and bosses, and even trompe-l'oeil doors with 'metalwork' fittings in two arched recesses in the ambulatory.[10] Heraldic ornament also plays an important part in the scheme, with vair pattern in the form of painted ribs on the vault of the Jesus Chapel, and with a lion rampant in a lozenge frame surviving from the decoration of the entrance arch to St Luke's Chapel. The scheme serves both to enliven and to articulate the severe Romanesque architecture: groin vaults are transformed into rib vaults, and plain cushion capitals are enhanced with rosettes and chevron ornament.[11] The decoration in the Jesus

10. These are now rather difficult to decipher, but see Tristram's drawing reproduced below, fig. 159.
11. See the comments by Fernie, *NC*, p. 105,

where it is observed that 'the architectural sculpture in the building is little more than a handmaid to the painting'.

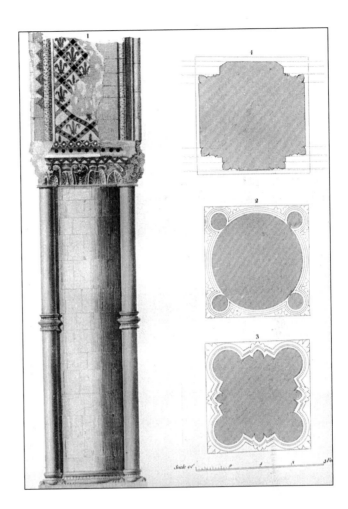

Fig. 136. Decoration
formerly existing in the
infirmary
(drawing: J. A. Repton).

Chapel was repainted in the 1870s, and some other parts of the scheme have also been completely renovated, including the masonry pattern and other decoration on the east face of the wall over the eastern crossing arch – whose outline, nevertheless, provides important evidence for the form of the original roof.[12] There is no doubt that all the decoration belongs to a single scheme, with such unmistakable motifs as the chevron or 'sawtooth' ornament occurring throughout.[13]

12. Fernie, *NC*, pp. 39, 41, pl. 14.
13. It is not clear, however, to what extent the scheme may have extended into the western part of the church. Masonry pattern enriched with rosettes, like some of that at the east end, has been recorded in the nave south aisle in the sixth bay from the crossing, and also on the fifth pier of the south arcade:

F. R. Horlbeck, 'Decorative Painting in English Medieval Architecture' (unpublished University of London Ph. D. thesis, 1957), p. 58. A surviving fragment of painting on the north wall of the north aisle, cut into by a Decorated window, is difficult to interpret, but is described by Tristram, *Thirteenth Century*, p. 584, as part 'of a square

The scheme has generally been dated to the period immediately following the 1272 fire, though there appears to be no evidence that it extends over fire-damaged masonry.[14] In fact, painted 'face-lifts' of Romanesque buildings were by no means uncommon in the thirteenth century – other examples are provided by the cathedrals at Ely, Peterborough and Durham[15] – and may in part be attributable precisely to the relative lack of original polychromy. Whether a dating in the 1270s is acceptable for the Norwich scheme depends primarily on its relationship to other paintings in the cathedral and the monastic complex (which was severely damaged by the fire), and indeed elsewhere.[16] Tristram regarded some of the decoration in the south aisle of the presbytery as contemporary with the paintings formerly visible in the adjacent

note 13 continued
cusped panel, framed within a medallion'. Although he associates it with the eastern decoration, it is different in colouring and design. Some scrollwork at the head of the west door of the nave, surviving above the inserted fifteenth-century doorway, seems likely to be of fourteenth-century date; although Tristram at first associated it with the other decoration, he later assigned it to after 1350: E. W. Tristram, 'The Paintings of Norwich Cathedral', in Friends of Norwich Cathedral, *Sixth Annual Report, 1935*, p. 7; E. W. Tristram, *English Wall Painting of the Fourteenth Century* (London, 1955), p. 229.

14. See Tristram, *Thirteenth Century*, p. 358.
15. Tristram, *Thirteenth Century*, pp. 363–67, 377, pls. 209–13, supp. pls 22b, 53, 57; for Durham, see also D. Park, 'The Interior Decoration of the Cathedral', in D. Pocock, ed., *Durham Cathedral: A Celebration* (Durham, 1993), pp. 58–59, pl. 1.
16. Other factors which should be mentioned are the heraldic decoration and fictive metalwork included in the scheme. The ornament of lozengy gules and vair employed on the vault of the Jesus Chapel has been interpreted by Tony Sims as the arms of Hubert de Burgh, justiciar of England from 1215 to 1232, while it has also been suggested that the lion at the entrance to St Luke's Chapel may be the arms of Hubert's third wife, Margaret; consequently it has been argued that these chapels contain two examples of the earliest heraldic wall painting in the country: below, pp. 451–52. However, the

earliest surviving example of heraldry in English wall painting is probably that in the chancel of Silchester (Hants.), of *c.* 1230(?). In general the decorative use of heraldry only became popular in the mid and second half of the thirteenth century: J. Cherry, 'Heraldry as Decoration in the Thirteenth Century', in W. M. Ormrod, ed., *England in the Thirteenth Century* (Proceedings of the 1989 Harlaxton Symposium, Harlaxton Medieval Studies, 1, Stamford, 1991), especially pp. 130–31. The lozenge frame of the lion at Norwich, moreover, points to a later rather than earlier dating (compare an early example of similar framing on the Valence casket, dating probably from the beginning of the fourteenth century: Cherry, 'Heraldry as Decoration', pl. 33). Vair itself was commonly used decoratively – see N. Morgan, *The Lambeth Apocalypse* (London, 1990), p. 74 and n. 5 – and is combined with red, as in the Jesus Chapel, in the border of the wall painting of St Christopher at Little Wenham (Suffolk), dating from *c.* 1300 (for the paintings of this church, see below, pp. 398–400). By contrast, Jane Geddes has argued that the fictive metalwork points to an early fourteenth-century date; it has been compared with the ironwork on the Carnary College door (1316–37), particularly in the use of a bar at the base of the fleurs-de-lys (below, pp. 434–38). But such bars are also used in the fleurs-de-lys in the scrollwork (albeit repainted) on the apsidal arch of the Jesus Chapel, so are more likely a stylistic device of little significance for dating.

Bauchun Chapel (dating from not earlier than the late 1320s), apparently because of their similar colouring;[17] this can be discounted, since the black and yellow used in this part of the aisle are standard colours throughout the thirteenth-century scheme.

On the other hand, he was undoubtedly correct in associating the scheme with several examples of painting, now lost, in the priory buildings. Decoration recorded in the infirmary in the early nineteenth century (fig. 136) showed the same sawtooth ornament, marbling and dotted banding as the cathedral scheme (fig. 135).[18] Following the fire, new doors were made for the infirmary as early as 1273–74,[19] and the painted decoration may well have dated from about the same time. Two further examples of decorative painting were recorded in the 1870s, in the chamber above the dark entry and in the adjacent chamber above the southeast angle of the cloister.[20] The former painting, on the south wall, comprising masonry pattern above a dado band of marbling with dotted borders (fig. 137), was clearly by the same workshop as the cathedral and infirmary paintings. In the chamber over the cloister the decoration, once again surviving on the south wall, consisted of a fictive textile hanging ornamented with roundels, one still containing the lower half of a lion guardant (fig. 138). Although this decoration is not paralleled in the cathedral scheme, it can scarcely be

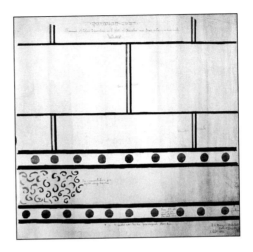

Fig. 137. Masonry pattern, marbling and other decoration formerly existing on the south wall of the chamber above the dark entry (drawing: J. H. Brown).

17. Tristram, *Fourteenth Century*, p. 229; for the Bauchun Chapel, see below, pp. 400–1.
18. For the decoration of the infirmary, sometimes confused with the dormitory, see F. Sayers, 'Notices concerning the Dormitory of the Cathedral-Monastery of Norwich', *Archaeologia*, 15 (1806), p. 314; and, in the same volume, W. Gibson, 'Observations on the Remains of the Dormitory and Refectory . . .', p. 327; and especially J. A. Repton, 'Description of the Ancient Building at Norwich, Which is the Subject of the Preceding Paper', pp. 334, 336–37, pl. XV. Although Repton mentions gilding on the capitals, it is unlikely that this was anything

more than yellow pigment; gilding does not occur in the cathedral scheme and is not mentioned by Gibson or Sayers.
19. *Communar Rolls*, p. 28.
20. *NA*, 8 (1879), p. 330; and annotated, full-size watercolour copies by J. H. Brown, NRO, DCN 131/121/1–2 (both dated 1 September 1873). Tristram, *Thirteenth Century*, p. 356, mistakenly regarded both areas of painting as having been in the chamber above the cloister, but also records decoration in the dark entry itself: 'relics of a plain masonry pattern are still visible on a jamb . . . and there is evidence to show that it once also covered the walls and vaulting'.

doubted that it belonged to the same period – its colouring was similar, and it showed the same love of imitating other materials. Regarding the architectural evidence for dating these paintings, the dark entry itself forms part of the original priory buildings;

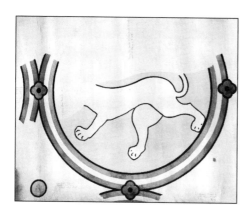

the chamber above it – next to the east end of the high Romanesque refectory – must have belonged to the same period. There is no reason that there could not have been a room over the adjacent corner of the cloister at that time, even though in general the original cloister was single-storeyed. Consequently, there is no reason to date the paintings to as late as the rebuilding of the cloister as a double-storeyed structure from 1297 onward.[21]

Fig. 138. Fictive textile hanging formerly existing on the south wall of the chamber above the south-east angle of the cloister (drawing: J. H. Brown).

Particularly valuable dating evidence for all these paintings is provided by some of the decoration in the Benedictine priory of Horsham St Faith, just to the north of Norwich. The surviving paintings here are all in the refectory range, which was converted into a house at the Reformation. The most celebrated are close in style to the illumination of Matthew Paris and therefore datable to *c.* 1250, though they were partially repainted in the fifteenth century. These paintings decorate the east wall of the refectory and comprise an enormous representation of the Crucifixion flanked by a male and female saint, above a series of scenes illustrating the foundation of the priory, with blank arcading at dado level.[22] At the east end of the south wall, however, a much more elaborate arch is painted in the dado, with a foliate border above and with traces of masonry pattern enriched by scrollwork higher up on the wall. This decoration was painted on a separate layer of plaster over another border and simpler masonry pattern coeval with the *c.* 1250 scheme on the east wall. The later decoration is immediately reminiscent of the Norwich paintings, in the characteristic dotted band at the base of the border and in the marbling around the arch. Further

21. We are grateful to Eric Fernie and Keith Darby for discussing this point with us.
22. Tristram, *Thirteenth Century*, pp. 360–61, 554, pls. 205–7; D. Purcell, 'The Priory of Horsham St Faith and its Wall Paintings', *NA*, 35 (1973), pp. 469–73; J. Alexander

and P. Binski, eds, *Age of Chivalry: Art in Plantagenet England, 1200–1400* (London, 1987), pp. 127, 313. For the architecture of the refectory range, see particularly D. Sherlock, 'Discoveries at Horsham St Faith Priory, 1970–1973', *NA*, 36 (1976), pp. 202–23.

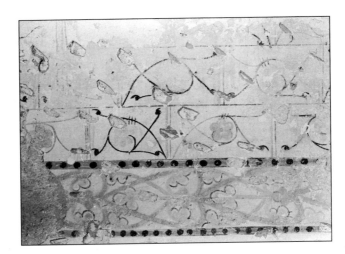

Fig. 139. Horsham St Faith Priory (Norfolk): masonry pattern and dado border on the west wall of the 'prior's chamber'.

decoration of the same phase still exists in the slype to the east of the refectory, where a fragmentary painted arch displays the sawtooth ornament so typical of the Norwich paintings; and also in the room above the slype – perhaps the prior's chamber – where the west wall retains masonry pattern enriched with scrollwork and rosettes, very like some of the cathedral decoration, above a dado band once again ornamented with dotted borders (fig. 139). As in the refectory, the decoration in this room was painted over an earlier thirteenth-century layer.[23] All the secondary decoration at Horsham St Faith is so close to the Norwich paintings that there can be no doubt that it is by the same workshop. From the evidence of the layers, it must be later than *c.* 1250, though on stylistic grounds not much later: the crocketed canopy of the refectory arch, for instance, may be compared in a general way to an example in the Carrow Psalter, a Norwich manuscript of *c.* 1250–60.[24] This evidence points clearly to a dating in the second half of the thirteenth century for the Norwich paintings. As we have seen, nothing in the latter painting contradicts this. Since the 1272 fire is likely to have provided the reason for redecorating at least some of the priory buildings, this lengthy analysis of the dating leads inexorably to the conclusion that the traditional dating in the 1270s is very likely to be correct. This would be further supported if the paintings were coeval with the set of holes for an attached (presumably metal) consecration cross on the external face of the

23. C. Babington, J. James and S. Rickerby, 'Horsham St Faith Priory: Report on Conservation Treatment of the Wall Paintings . . .' (unpublished report, Courtauld Institute/English Heritage, August 1989), p. 4.

24. Baltimore, Walters Art Gallery, MS W 34, fo. 22v; N. J. Morgan, *Early Gothic Manuscripts*, ii, *1250–1285* (A Survey of Manuscripts Illuminated in the British Isles, iv, part 2, London, 1988), p. 88, ill. 102.

nave north aisle of the cathedral, which presumably dates from the consecration in 1278.[25]

Also customarily assigned to the 1270s is the so-called ante-reliquary chapel itself, containing the most important wall paintings in the cathedral (figs 140–142). It occupies the space above a platform or bridge of two bays of quadripartite vaulting built over the fourth bay from the crossing of the north aisle of the presbytery. By 1424–25 it was certainly used to display relics, since work on the platform at that time is described as *sub reliquiis*.[26] In the 1420s campaign the platform was extended to east and west by James Woderofe and other masons, and the chapel paved with tiles.[27] Very likely it was at this time that the 'Relick Chapell' itself was built to the north, but this has long since disappeared. The blocking of the large Perpendicular arch through which it was entered from the ante-reliquary chapel now functions as the outer wall of the aisle at this point.[28] Still surviving in fragmentary condition, however, is a painted shield in the southern spandrel of the western extension of the platform, showing the arms of Bishop Wakering (1416–25). These are not Wakering's normal arms of three hawk's lures, seen elsewhere in the cathedral, but the device of a pelican in her piety used on his personal seal.[29] This symbol of Christ's sacrifice would have been particularly appropriate if, as has been recently strongly argued, the space beneath the platform was used as a temporary Easter sepulchre.[30]

In the past, two or more different phases of decoration in the ante-reliquary chapel have been identified on stylistic grounds. The paintings on the eastern side appear

25. Evidence for only one cross now appears to survive, though presumably there was a complete set originally. A comparison may be made with the more elaborate indents for metal inlay crosses at Salisbury Cathedral, which seem more likely to belong to the consecration of 1258 than to the reconsecration of 1280 as suggested by J. Blair, 'The Consecration-Cross Indents of Salisbury Cathedral', *Transactions of the Monumental Brass Society*, 12 (1975–79), pp. 16–20.
26. H. C. Beeching, 'The Chapels and Altars of Norwich Cathedral', *Architect and Contract Reporter*, 3 (1915), p. 452.
27. For a document referring both to the work on the platform and to paving in 1424–25, see J. Harvey, *English Mediaeval Architects: A Biographical Dictionary Down to 1550* (2nd edn, Gloucester, 1984), p. 343 n. 3; for a description of tiles of this period in the ante-reliquary chapel, see E. M. Goulburn, 'The

Confessio or Relic Chapel, an Ancient Chamber in Norwich Cathedral', *NA*, 9 (1884), p. 279.
28. See Goulburn, 'Confessio or Relic Chapel', p. 280, for a document of 1586 referring to the relic chapel. Some of the fifteenth-century tiles were found beneath the blocking of the interconnecting arch (Goulburn, 'Confessio or Relic Chapel', p. 279), strongly suggesting that this chapel was contemporary with the alterations to the ante-reliquary chapel.
29. See below, pp. 453–54; and see also *NA*, 3 (1852), pl. opposite p. 156.
30. T. A. Heslop, 'The Easter Sepulchre in Norwich Cathedral: Ritual, Transience, and Archaeology', in C. Smith, ed., *Echoes, Mainly Musical, from Norwich and Around: Local Studies for Michael Nicholas, Organist at Norwich Cathedral 1971–1994* (Norwich, 1994), pp. 17–20.

somewhat earlier than the rest and have been considered coeval with the construction of the chapel (thought to be in the 1270s). Regarding the paintings on the western arch and vault, they have been assigned to as much as half a century later,[31] though from slight differences of style there has been speculation that they too are of different periods – perhaps *c.* 1300 and *c.* 1325 respectively. Scientific examination has now proved that the eastern paintings are indeed earlier, but that the remaining decoration was undertaken in a single phase.[32]

The earlier paintings comprise the following elements: two censing angels on the west face of the eastern arch, the southern angel surviving more completely (fig. 140); a head of a bishop framed by a medallion, on the capital below the southern angel;[33] and foliate borders on the abacus of this capital and on an adjoining string course, and also on the arch itself. The censing angels must have flanked a central image; indeed it is clear from cuts in the masonry on either side that a screen – presumably the reredos for an altar – originally occupied this arch.[34] These paintings, with their striking primary palette, are in a very different technique to the later decoration. The pigments employed – ultramarine, red lead, lead white, yellow ochre, carbon black and lime white – are dense and opaque, and generally unmixed, though the highly expensive ultramarine is (as often elsewhere) both extended and bound with lime white. By contrast, the painters of the later scheme aimed to achieve translucent effects through the application of pigment mixtures and glazes over a reflective lead white ground. One sample, taken from the earlier painting at the top of the eastern arch, showed only a single pigment layer applied over a coarse plaster substrate, though evidence of a more complex preparatory technique was found elsewhere on the arch. Here the stone was first sealed with a proteinaceous material – probably animal glue – to reduce absorption of the binding medium from the ground and paint layers. In some samples two grounds

31. Tristram, *Fourteenth Century*, p. 230, dates them to *c.* 1325.

32. The examination was undertaken in 1993–94 by Helen Howard. It included on-site inspection in normal, raking and ultra-violet light; and examination of a small number of minute samples in cross-section and dispersion forms. A scanning electron microscope (SEM), used with energy-dispersive X-ray (EDX) analysis, was employed to confirm identifications made with polarised light microscopy and microchemical tests. Binding media were analysed through histochemical tests and Fourier transform infra-red (FTIR) microspectroscopy. We are indebted to Dr Richard Murphy of Im-

perial College, London, for access to the FTIR facilities; and to English Heritage for sponsoring this part of the analysis. Thanks are also due to Dr Arie Wallert of the Getty Conservation Institute for undertaking fluorescence spectrometry of the lake pigment in the second phase of painting.

33. Slight remains of painting on the capital on the north side suggest that it was similarly painted with a framed head, though nothing of the head itself survives.

34. Goulburn, 'Confessio or Relic Chapel', p. 284, refers to 'many plaster fragments discovered in the flooring of the chamber', which he considered were remains of the reredos.

Fig. 140. Censing angel on the south side of the eastern arch: ante-reliquary chapel.

can be distinguished: first calcium carbonate, then a layer of lead white which was sometimes tinted with yellow ochre, perhaps to provide a warmer cast to the subsequent paint layers. Analytical results suggested that the lead white was applied in an oil medium. Of particular significance is clear evidence that the later decoration extended over this scheme: a sample taken from the draperies of the southern angel indicates that a copper green pigment mixed with lead white was applied on a lead-based ground over the top; in other areas, madder lake – which is typical of the later decoration – has also been found over the earlier paintings. It may well be that this earlier painting extended over the vault itself, where much may still be hidden by the later scheme. In the eastern part of the north segment of the vault, adjacent to the eastern arch, a fragment of blue foliage is not only different stylistically to the other foliage on the vault, but is in ultramarine mixed with lime white like the painting on the arch, but unlike the azurite employed exclusively in the later scheme.

On stylistic grounds, it would be very difficult to date this first scheme in the chapel to as late as the 1270s. Moreover, in its colouring and ornamental motifs it is very different from the general decorative scheme in the cathedral (already discussed), which probably does date from that period and is clearly by a different workshop. In fact, the style of these ante-reliquary chapel paintings is immediately reminiscent of mid thirteenth-century works, such as the first scheme at Horsham St Faith.[35] The severely frontal head of the bishop, with its arched eyebrows and staring eyes with solid black pupils, may be compared to the head of the male saint

35. See above, pp. 388–89.

beside the Crucifixion at St Faith's, itself so close to the illumination of Matthew Paris. Convincing parallels for both the shape and expression of the face of the southern censing angel (fig. 140), and even for such details as its tiny pursed mouth, are provided by the Carrow Psalter (*c.* 1250–60).[36] The chapel paintings are nevertheless much superior in quality, and is certainly unlikely that such cathedral wall paintings would be any more backward than illumination which has been described as 'energetic and inventive but decidedly provincial'.[37] Further afield, general stylistic comparisons are provided by the famous roundel of the Virgin and Child in the bishop's palace at Chichester,[38] again of *c.* 1250–60, and where the symmetrical foliage sprays in the frame afford a close parallel to the foliage around the bishop's head at Norwich. Presumably there was originally more than one such head at this level on the eastern side of the chapel, and the very device of a row of heads bordering the dado zone – the bishop's head is only about 4 ft (1.22 m.) above floor level – has earlier parallels. Thus, in 1246, Henry III ordered that his lower chamber at Clarendon Palace should be wainscoted, with the wainscot painted green and bordered with a series of heads of kings and queens.[39] Even the border above the bishop's head and on the adjoining string course, of foliage arranged in repeated heart-shaped motifs, is of a type which suggests an earlier rather than a later dating; a similar border appears for example in the wall paintings of Ashampstead (Herts.) of *c.* 1230.[40] While it has been observed that the features of the architectural platform itself which forms the ante-reliquary chapel are 'low grade, and virtually undatable',[41] the style of the paintings indicates a dating of *c.* 1250–60. As has been seen, the space below the platform may have been used as an Easter sepulchre; it may be that the platform itself only acquired its function of displaying relics after the 1272 fire, when it was indeed painted with no fewer than twenty-four saints.

In this later scheme, the twelve apostles are depicted in pairs on the soffit of the western arch, standing under canopies and alternately holding a book or a scroll (fig. 141). On the vault, a further twelve saints are arranged in groups of three, one group to each segment, and with each figure identified by an inscription. These groups are divided by fictive ribs at the intersections of the groins, while at the crown of the vault a painted imitation of a carved boss shows Christ seated on a vine, which spreads out in great coils to surround the other figures. Each group of saints is of a particular type: virgins (Margaret and Catherine flanking the Virgin

---

36. See p. 389 and note 24.
37. Morgan, *Early Gothic Manuscripts*, ii, p. 88.
38. Tristram, *Thirteenth Century*, pp. 301–6, supp. pl. 43.
39. *Calendar of Liberate Rolls, 1245–51*, p. 63; Tristram, *Thirteenth Century*, p. 528. An earlier example is provided by the late twelfth-

century wall paintings of Barfreston (Kent), now mostly destroyed, where a series of framed heads (probably of apostles) bordered fictive dado draperies in the chancel; Tristram, *Twelfth Century*, supp. pl. 8b.
40. Tristram, *Thirteenth Century*, pl. 75.
41. Fernie, *NC*, p. 165.

Fig. 141. Apostles, on the south side of the western arch: ante-reliquary chapel.

Fig. 142. Virgin and Child flanked by St Margaret and St Catherine, in the western segment of the vault: ante-reliquary chapel.

with the Christ Child) in the western segment (pl. Va and fig. 142); apostles (Peter, Andrew, and Paul as apostle of the gentiles) to the east; martyrs (much damaged, but showing Stephen or Lawrence with Thomas Becket(?) and Edmund(?) to the south; and, finally, confessors (Martin, Nicholas, and Richard of Chichester) to the north. Probably the vine scroll itself is iconographically significant in this case, expressing the relationship between Christ and his different types of representative on earth: 'I am the vine, ye are the branches . . . Herein is my Father glorified, that ye bear much fruit; so shall ye be my disciples' (John 15: 5, 8).[42] This carefully considered programme is thus highly reminiscent of the equally logical arrangement of carved figures at the head of the 'prior's door' (between 1297 and 1314), where pairs of prophets, martyrs and angels culminate in the Christ of the Last Judgement at the apex.[43] It will be observed, however, that in the very nature of the painted programme, with its mostly standard saints, there appears to be little direct reflection

42. Oddly, however, in the north-west corner of the vault the scrollwork is shown with oak leaves (an observation for which we are indebted to Christian Binder).

43. Fernie, *NC*, p. 175, pl. 55.

of any relics that may have been displayed in the chapel, though St Catherine, for instance, had her own altar elsewhere in the cathedral.[44] The only unusual choice of saint is Richard of Chichester (canonised 1262), who may be present because of his relations with Norwich's own saintly Bishop Walter Suffield, to whom he bequeathed his 'serpents' tongues' – a warning device against poison, and an exceptional relic by any standards.[45]

It is clear from the recent scientific examination that the paintings on the vault and western arch belong to a single phase of decoration. On the vault, they were executed on a thin plaster ground, while only a fine lime skim was necessary on the ashlar masonry of the arch. In both cases, the surfaces were prepared with a lead white ground applied in broad brushstrokes, giving a very distinctive texture. The stratigraphy and materials of the paint layers are also identical. Samples taken from the purple draperies of St Andrew on the vault and of an apostle on the arch show exactly the same mixture of natural azurite and madder lake over the lead white ground. The palette of this scheme is more extensive than that of the earlier paintings: it includes azurite, verdigris, vermilion, madder lake, lead white, yellow ochre, carbon black and lime white. Although media analysis is compromised by past conservation treatments, examination of a sample from the arch firmly established the use of oil. In addition, analysis of the binding medium used to apply azurite on the vault indicated the presence of a proteinaceous component.[46] The present rather strange appearance of parts of the scheme is due to the alteration of some of the original materials; for example, that of vermilion to its dark form metacinnabar, as in the draperies of St Paul on the vault. It might be expected that, similarly, the dark flesh areas on the vault result from the alteration of the lead white pigment that was employed to form lead dioxide (plattnerite), which is particularly characteristic of wall paintings dating from about the first half of the fourteenth century, with some notable examples in East Anglia – for instance, at Little Wenham in Suffolk.[47]

44. J. R. Shinners, 'The Veneration of Saints at Norwich Cathedral in the Fourteenth Century', *NA*, 40 (1988), p. 138.

45. E. F. Jacob, 'St Richard of Chichester', *Journal of Ecclesiastical History*, 7 (1956), p. 187; see also Goulburn, 'Confessio or Relic Chapel', p. 278. Beeching, 'Chapels and Altars', p. 455, mentions 'negligible' oblations to St Richard recorded in the account rolls from 1386 onward.

46. See Tristram, *Fourteenth Century*, p. 65, for the belief that the paintings were 'carried out in oil colour, or perhaps an emulsion of oil'. The evidence of protein was found in the azurite of the Virgin's robe. Since the refractive index of oil and azurite is very similar, the pigment loses its intensity and is therefore normally applied in another medium; however, recent analysis by Raymond White (National Gallery) has shown that this problem was overcome, in the late thirteenth-century wall paintings executed in an oil medium at Angers Cathedral, by first coating the azurite particles with a proteinaceous medium.

47. P. Welford, 'An Investigation into the Phenomenon of Dark Flesh Areas in English Medieval Wall Paintings' (unpublished Courtauld Institute diploma dissertation, 1991), pp. 4, 6, 19, pls 2, 25–27.

However, no evidence of this has been found in the analysis, and at least some of the darkened appearance of the paintings – of the draperies as well as of the flesh areas – is explained by the only partial removal of past surface coatings and accretions.[48]

While few wall paintings of this period have been subjected to detailed scientific examination, the techniques of this scheme at Norwich are closely comparable – in layer structure, pigments and medium – to painting recently examined in the feretory of St Albans Abbey, dating probably from the first decade of the fourteenth century.[49] Although the Norwich paintings were assigned by Tristram to *c.* 1325,[50] and have been compared to the Thornham Parva retable, now dated to *c.* 1335,[51] close analysis of their style – at once both more mannered and more naturalistic than that of the earlier paintings in the chapel – clearly indicates a dating around 1300.[52] This self-consciously elegant style is best seen in the apostles on the western arch (fig. 141), where the figures, improbably attenuated, are balanced pose against pose. Faces, nearly all in three-quarter view, are long and thin, with bulging foreheads, sunken cheeks and meticulously delineated irises. In contrast to the linear parallel folds of the mid thirteenth century, the draperies here are angular and bulky, the folds modelled with heavy shading, accentuating the swaying poses. This elegant 'broad-fold' style was introduced from France into court painting at Westminster in the third quarter of the thirteenth century. Seen at its finest in the Westminster retable of *c.* 1270–80, it also appears elsewhere in the abbey – in the wall paintings in the south transept and St Faith's Chapel, dating probably from *c.* 1280–90 though possibly from the very beginning of the fourteenth century.[53] Where comparisons can be made with the ante-reliquary chapel paintings, for example between the head of St Thomas in the transept at Westminster and the more linear version of the same

---

48. According to E. Baker, the paintings had been treated with a preservative containing egg and had subsequently been coated with wax; E. Baker, 'The Ante-Reliquary Chapel, Norwich Cathedral', unpublished report for the Council for the Care of Churches (undated, but probably 1965). The earlier coating was probably applied in the nineteenth century; the wax by Professor Tristram in the 1930s. The Baker workshop partially cleaned the paintings during the 1960s. We are most grateful to Dr Christine Bläuer Böhm (Fachhochschule, Cologne) and Ms Jilleen Nadolny (National Gallery) for undertaking X-ray diffraction (XRD) analysis of the darkened flesh areas.

49. H. Howard, 'Workshop Practices and Identification of Hands: Gothic Wall Paint-

ings at St Albans', *Conservator*, 17 (1993), pp. 34–45.

50. See note 31 above.

51. For the comparison, see P. Lasko and N. Morgan, eds, *Medieval Art in East Anglia, 1300–1520* (Norwich, 1973), p. 26; and for the dating of the retable, C. Norton, D. Park and P. Binski, *Dominican Painting in East Anglia: The Thornham Parva Retable and the Museé de Cluny Frontal* (Woodbridge, 1987).

52. Norton *et al.*, *Dominican Painting*, p. 73, where Binski observes that the style 'seems to suit a date in the late thirteenth or very early fourteenth centuries'.

53. Norton *et al.*, *Dominican Painting*, pp. 68–69, for a discussion of the style and dating of the Westminster paintings.

Fig. 143. Little Wenham
(Suffolk): Saints Margaret,
Catherine and Mary
Magdalen, on the chancel
east wall.

head type in the apostle at lower left on the arch at Norwich (fig. 141), the similarities
are striking. Such close parallels are not surprising in view of the connections between
painting in Norfolk and at the court in this period: two Norfolk painters are recorded
as working in Westminster Palace in 1292; a further three in 1307.[54]

Yet there is no compelling need to posit a direct connection with Westminster
for the style of the ante-reliquary chapel paintings. One of the earliest examples of
the broad-fold style in East Anglian illumination is in a psalter of *c.* 1270–90, whose
calendar indicates a patron in the Norwich diocese,[55] and whose miniature showing
three female saints beneath slender canopies is immediately reminiscent of the chapel

54. Tristram, *Thirteenth Century*, pp. 115, 355;   55. Morgan, *Early Gothic Manuscripts*, ii, pp.
Tristram, *Fourteenth Century*, pp. 206, 288–   186–88, ills. 393–94.
89.

paintings. It is, however, somewhat cruder, and its architectural canopies – with their still-rounded arches and old-fashioned turrets and roofs – are retardataire compared with the continuous superstructure over the paired apostles in the chapel. No exact stylistic parallels for the wall paintings are provided by such celebrated later East Anglian manuscripts as the Gorleston Psalter. The same is true of wall paintings in the region,[56] though useful comparisons can be drawn with the superb paintings of Little Wenham, normally dated to the first quarter of the fourteenth century.[57] Perhaps surprisingly, the painting of three female saints on the chancel east wall at Little Wenham (fig. 143) is strikingly higher in quality, more ambitious in its illusionism and far more blatantly mannered. The poses of the Little Wenham figures are altogether more exaggerated (only the Virgin, at Norwich, shows a true S-curve), this extreme mannerism extending even to their delicately, almost impossibly curving fingers, while the illusionism is enhanced as the saints burst the confines of their niches. By contrast, the Norwich figures are unimaginatively posed: the paired apostles easily confined in their arches and the vault subjects responding to the shape imposed by the architecture only with awkwardly bent heads, leaving the surrounding areas to be filled with vinescroll. The convoluted, persuasively self-generating drapery folds at Little Wenham have an energy absent in the bulky, pendulous draperies of the Norwich figures. The canopy above the Little Wenham figures – perhaps the most elaborate of its date in England – is similar to the Norwich examples in being a single building, but shows far more clearly the origins of this style in such prime examples of French court art as the St Louis Psalter (between 1252 and 1270).[58] The quality of these parish church paintings is doubtless explained by patronage from the equally fine late thirteenth-century manor house immediately adjacent. The architectural details of the church itself – clearly contemporary with its decoration – suggest that the paintings may date from no later than the end of the thirteenth century.[59]

Closer in quality to the ante-reliquary chapel paintings are the diminutive figures painted on the lid of the chest at Newport (Essex) – a Christ on the cross flanked

---

56. The comparison by G. G. Callahan, 'Re-valuation of the Refectory Retable from the Cathedral at Pamplona', *Art Bulletin*, 35 (1953), p. 192 n. 40, with the now-destroyed wall paintings in Gorleston Church can be dismissed; it is clear from a copy of the painting of the three living and three dead, for which see W. F. Storck, 'Aspects of Death in English Art and Poetry – II', *Burlington Magazine*, 21 (1912), p. 315, that this painting at least dated from the mid fourteenth century. Nor is Callahan's asso-

ciation of the ante-reliquary chapel paintings, and other East Anglian and English 'court' painting, with the wall painting at Pamplona convincing.

57. For example, Alexander and Binski, *Age of Chivalry*, p. 128.

58. Paris, Bibliothèque Nationale, MS lat. 10525; R. Branner, *Manuscript Painting in Paris during the Reign of Saint Louis* (Berkeley and London, 1977), figs. 395–400.

59. For the manor house, which is assigned to the period *c.* 1270–80, see, for example,

by four saints, each neatly disposed in a separate panel beneath a canopy – dating probably from the end of the thirteenth century.[60] Although stylistic comparisons with this modest work must rely on essentials, it shares with the Norwich paintings a similar emphasis on horizontally bunched folds, tentative S-curves (each of the figures swaying predictably toward the centre), and an unimaginative simplicity in the rendering of the architecture of the canopies. In common with the ante-reliquary chapel and Little Wenham paintings, the chest displays the delicate naturalistic foliage so typical of the period around 1300. The arches framing the Newport figures are austere trefoils and, though the Little Wenham canopies are vastly more elaborate, they lack ogees, which are also absent in the ante-reliquary chapel. However, at Norwich, ogees are already prominent in the 'prior's door', of between 1297 and 1314,[61] providing further evidence that the ante-reliquary chapel paintings are relatively early, and may as easily be late thirteenth-century as early fourteenth-century.

Painting that most likely dated from *c.* 1330, or perhaps a few years later, was formerly visible in the Bauchun Chapel. The building of this chapel, off the south side of the presbytery, was being undertaken in 1327–29 at the expense of William Bauchun and the master of the cellar, though it may not have been entirely completed at that time.[62] Since the paintings were clearly of considerable importance, it is worth quoting Tristram's description in full, recording the

> remains of a scheme of painting executed, in all probability, soon after . . . [the chapel] was built, and carried out entirely in black, except for some yellow, sparingly used. Around a later window in the south wall is a scroll pattern enriched with five-petalled flowers and buds; and below the level of the window bottom masonry pattern of diamond form, executed in yellow line about an inch in width, with small squares in black at the intersections, each diamond having a quatrefoil in black in the centre. On the north wall, over the arch leading into the aisle, fragments survive of a subject framed within a large quatrefoil, and, below this, of a masonry pattern in black line,

note 59 continued

R. A. Brown, *Castles from the Air* (Cambridge, 1989), pp. 226–27. The church is briefly described by N. Pevsner, *Suffolk* (The Buildings of England, 2nd edn, Harmondsworth, 1974), pp. 340–41. Its stone rood screen, largely taken down in the early nineteenth century, seems to have been of particularly early appearance, with eight elementary trefoil arches flanking the central doorway; see D. E. Davy, *A Journal of Excursions through the County of Suffolk, 1823–1844*, ed. J. Blatchly (Suffolk Records

Society, 24, 1982), p. 106 and n. 231, and the reconstruction drawing on p. 107.

60. Alexander and Binski, *Age of Chivalry*, p. 347.

61. Fernie, *NC*, p. 175, pl. 55.

62. Fernie, *NC*, p. 183 and n. 75, and B. Dodwell, 'William Bauchun and his Connection with the Cathedral Priory at Norwich', *NA*, 36 (1974–75), pp. 111–18, who notes (p. 112) that it is 'difficult to be quite sure that the chapel was completed by the time of Bauchun's death in 1335–6'.

enriched with flowers like those on the south wall. Remains of a large subject, comprising four saints depicted under canopies, these and the heads of the figures alone, are visible on the east wall.[63]

Two watercolours by Tristram show the diamond pattern and the scrollwork around the window;[64] although the window itself is a fifteenth-century insertion, the decoration does appear to be of fourteenth-century type. The 'saints' may well have reflected the original dedication, which, from a carved inscription formerly set in the outside wall of the chapel, appears to have been to the Virgin and All Saints.[65] Although Tristram's account, published in 1955, describes the paintings as still visible, they were in fact already painted over by 1936.[66] Presumably they still exist, and an investigation would seem well worthwhile.

From the late thirteenth century onwards, the obedientiary rolls contain many references to painting of various types in the cathedral priory, though unfortunately these almost never relate to paintings that still survive. Nevertheless, they not only allow useful insights into works now lost, but are also extremely valuable in the copious evidence they provide for painters' names and wages, and also materials – the latter of exactly the same type as now identified by analysis of the ante-reliquary chapel paintings.[67] The sacrists' rolls are an invaluable source for painting in the cathedral itself. For example, in 1276–77, for work that seems at least partly to have concerned polychromed sculpture, payment is recorded for blue (*azur*), vermilion, verdigris, silver, gold, saffron (*croco*), lead white, oil, varnish, and stones (*petris*).[68] In 1287–88 John le Noreis and other painters were paid for work on an altarpiece (*tabula*).[69] The shrine of St William was decorated in 1304–5: forty leaves of gold were bought, as well as silver, lead white, vermilion, orpiment and oil; and Simon the painter and his apprentice (*garcionis*) were paid 25s. 6d. for their wages and board.[70] In 1316–17 the communar's rolls include a payment for lead white, red lead, oil and whitewash for images in the choir.[71] From the sacrists' rolls, again, we learn that a considerable amount was spent decorating the astonishingly elaborate new clock, with its astronomical dial and various automata. Payment is recorded for, among other things, gilding the sun and moon, painting a procession of monks

63. Tristram, *Fourteenth Century*, pp. 229–30.
64. London, Victoria and Albert Museum, Prints and Drawings, E483–1915.
65. Dodwell, 'William Bauchun', p. 111.
66. London, Courtauld Institute, Tristram Archive, unpublished note by M. D. Whinney, August 1936.
67. We are extremely grateful to Caroline Hull, of the University of Manchester, for much help with the documentary evidence and,

in particular, for various unpublished references.
68. NRO, DCN 1/4/3; *VCH Norfolk*, ii, p. 551 and n. 3.
69. NRO, DCN 1/4/7; *VCH Norfolk*, ii, p. 551 and n. 5.
70. NRO, DCN 1/4/16; *VCH Norfolk*, ii, p. 551 and n. 6.
71. NRO, DCN 1/12/13; *Communar Rolls*, pp. 13, 93.

(*chorea monachorum*) and for 500 leaves of gold brought from London. The wages of the painter and his assistant for fourteen weeks are recorded as 9s. 6d. per week, 'and not more, because they stayed at the table of our lord [prior]'.[72] In 1363–64 the sacrist paid 20s. for the making and painting of an image of St Catherine,[73] and £2 6s. 7d. for the gilding of two archangels at the high altar.[74] Painting was not only confined to stone, wood or metal. From the guild certificates submitted to parliament in 1389, we learn that the peltiers and 'other good men' were in the custom of offering candles decorated with flowers at St William's shrine;[75] these were probably painted with flowers like two early fourteenth-century candlestocks that still survive, one of which is said to have been found in Norfolk.[76]

The 1272 fire, as we have seen, necessitated a great deal of renovation work on the monastic buildings. Various entries in the refectorers' rolls refer to painting in the huge Romanesque refectory: for example, to the purchase of boards, colours, oil and lead white, and the payment of a painter's stipend, in 1290–91.[77] In 1296–97 ten pence was paid '*in pictur porticar[?] de refector*';[78] and despite the small sum involved, this presumably refers to painting in the arcaded wall passage that apparently extended around all four walls of the room.[79] In 1313–14 two shillings were paid for painting a cross,[80] which must surely have been on or against the east wall, since the Crucifixion was a standard subject in this location in refectories – the over-life-size example at Horsham St Faith is not only the nearest but also one of the most splendid examples to survive from the middle ages.[81] Elsewhere in the monastic complex, the communar rolls record expenditure in 1316–17 on lead white, oil and other materials for what appears to have been work on the Ethelbert Gate, at the south-west corner of the close.[82]

Various references to painting occur in the rolls of the master of the cellar with respect to the *camera prioris*; the dating of these rolls is somewhat uncertain but they may well fall within the period 1289–90 to 1294–95. In 1290–91(?), for example, payment is recorded for materials including vermilion, verdigris, orpiment and oil, as well as for the painters' stipend.[83] Such references are evidently to work

---

72. Sacrist's roll for 1324–25, NRO, DCN 1/4/23; H. Harrod, *Gleanings among the Castles and Convents of Norfolk* (Norwich, 1857), pp. 299–300, 339–41.

73. NRO, DCN 1/4/35; Shinners, 'Veneration of Saints', pp. 138 and 143 n. 33.

74. *VCH Norfolk*, ii, p. 321.

75. Shinners, 'Veneration of Saints', p. 136.

76. Alexander and Binski, *Age of Chivalry*, nos. 127–28, pp. 243–44.

77. NRO, DCN 1/8/3.

78. NRO, DCN 1/8/9.

79. For this passage, see Fernie, *NC*, p. 90.

80. NRO, DCN 1/8/23.

81. For this refectory iconography, see D. Park, 'Cistercian Wall Painting and Panel Painting', in C. Norton and D. Park, eds, *Cistercian Art and Architecture in the British Isles* (Cambridge, 1986), p. 206, and references.

82. *Communar Rolls*, pp. 12–13, 91.

83. NRO, DCN 1/1/10. The other rolls are DCN 1/1/9 (dated by the NRO to 1289–90? or 1267–68?), and DCN 1/1/11–12.

in the prior's lodgings, converted into the deanery at the Reformation. However, they need not refer specifically to his 'chamber', since the same overall heading is used for the prior's personal expenses generally.[84] Indeed, one or more may relate to the surviving decoration of beams in the prior's hall, for which a late thirteenth-century dating would be appropriate on stylistic grounds. The beams were discovered in 1889 above a sixteenth-century panelled ceiling, by which they are still hidden.[85] They must have formed the rafters of a flat ceiling. Their sides are decorated with chevrons, quatrefoils, heraldic devices such as lions and eagles, and quatrefoils containing male busts. Doubtless their undersides are also painted, but these cannot be examined because of the later ceiling. Although the beams are a very rare survival of domestic decoration of the period, comparison may be made with, for example, the recorded scheme of coats of arms on the rafters of the 'knight's chamber' at Peterborough, dating perhaps from the first decade of the fourteenth century.[86] Of the two surviving busts, one points ostentatiously at his eyes, while the other drinks from a cup. They may therefore have belonged to a series of the five senses, a subject particularly appropriate to their context. In the main survival of medieval secular painting in England, in the great chamber of Longthorpe Tower, the senses are shown in zoomorphic form,[87] though in an earlier French illustration they are represented by young men performing activities such as eating.[88] Further decoration of the prior's quarters was undertaken in the later 1320s and early 1330s, when payments were made for the painting of his new chapel. From these we learn that the colours were obtained from Norwich and London, and also from William Bauchun who seems to have been acting as a kind of 'builder's merchant' for the priory.[89]

The rolls continue to supply us with much information about painting in the later middle ages. In 1401 the sacrists' rolls record a payment of 2s. 6d. 'pro pictura super parientem ante magnam ymaginem beate Marie' ('for the picture on the wall before the great image of the Blessed [Virgin] Mary').[90] The image of St Petronilla was

84. See H. W. Saunders, *An Introduction to the Obedientiary and Manor Rolls of Norwich Cathedral Priory* (Norwich, 1930), p. 80.

85. G. E. Fox, 'A Note on the Discovery of Painted Beams at the Deanery, Norwich', *NA*, 11 (1892), pp. 179–81, and pls opposite pp. 179 and 180.

86. S. Gunton and S. Patrick, *The History of the Church of Peterburgh* (London, 1686), p. 40.

87. E. C. Rouse and A. Baker, 'The Wall-Paintings at Longthorpe Tower, near Peterborough, Northants.', *Archaeologia*, 96 (1955), pp. 44–47, pl. XVII.

88. Geneva, Bibliothèque Publique et Universitaire, MS Lat. 76, fo. 246 (thirteenth century); C. Nordenfalk, 'Les cinq sens dans l'art du moyen âge', *Revue de l'art*, 34 (1976), p. 21, fig. 8.

89. NRO, DCN 1/1/29, 31; see also Dodwell, 'William Bauchun', pp. 114–15.

90. 'Extracts from the Account-Rolls of Norwich Priory: Illustrative of Painting, Pigments &c', *Proceedings of the Archaeological Institute, Norwich, 1847* (London, 1851), p. 208.

painted at a cost of 5s. 6d. in 1404.[91] In 1414, 8s. 10d. was paid for painting carved images of St Gacian and St John of Bridlington; the bracket for the latter statue, painted with his name, was discovered during excavations in the nave in 1889.[92] The enormous sum of 117s. was spent in 1427 on an image of St Thomas Becket, including its painting and adornment with precious stones.[93] In the same year there is an intriguing reference to a payment of 3s. 4d. to John Virley 'pro factura et pictura de lez story sanguinis xpi in Anglic' ('for making and painting the story of the blood of Christ in English').[94] In 1444 John Jeckys was paid for placing images of St Barbara and St John the Evangelist in the chapter house and for painting them.[95] Recently, colouring has been found on the Erpingham Gate, the impressive entrance to the close paid for by Sir Thomas Erpingham, but perhaps built after his death in 1428.[96] This colour seems to be original and includes red pigment on the lips of some of the carved prophets and on the shield of Christ's wounds at the apex of the outer arch, as well as green pigment on the armorial surcoat of the figure of Erpingham himself in the pediment niche.[97] Various other examples of fifteenth-century painting are known only from antiquarian records. In his account of the bishop's palace, published in 1864, Harrod mentions a boss that had recently been removed from one of the apartments, carved with the arms of Bishop Lyhart (1446–72) and 'painted and gilt'.[98] Lyhart was responsible for the new vault of the nave, probably constructed after the fire of 1463 and decorated with 252 bosses carved with 'the whole of the Christian history of the world' from the Creation to the Last Judgement.[99] The colouring of these bosses would have been vital to their legibility from floor level, and indeed the existence of polychromy before they were overpainted is referred to by Philip Browne in 1807.[100] Their colouring is again mentioned in the 1890s, when a wash of stone colour applied in 1806 was removed.[101] The bosses were then

91. 'Extracts from the Account-Rolls of Norwich', p. 208. For offerings in the cathedral to St Petronilla, first mentioned in 1386, see Shinners, 'Veneration of Saints', p. 138 and nn. 38–39.

92. W. H. St J. Hope and W. T. Bensly, 'Recent Discoveries in the Cathedral Church of Norwich', *NA*, 14 (1901), p. 121.

93. Beeching, 'Chapels and Altars', p. 455.

94. 'Extracts from the Account-Rolls of Norwich', p. 208.

95. D. J. Stewart, 'Notes on Norwich Cathedral', *Arch. J.*, 32 (1875), p. 20.

96. Fernie, *NC*, p. 187.

97. D. A. Carthy, 'Erpingham Gate, Norwich' (unpublished report, Conservation Specialists Ltd, 1990), p. 6, and site notes, pp. 27,

29, 30, 32, etc. See also below, pp. 454–56.

98. H. Harrod, 'Excavations Made in the Gardens of the Bishop's Palace, Norwich, April, 1859', *NA*, 6 (1864), p. 29. He suggests that it belonged to alterations made before Henry VI's visit in 1449.

99. See Fernie, *NC*, pp. 188–90.

100. P. Browne, *An Account and Description of the Cathedral Church of the Holy Trinity, Norwich* (2nd edn, Norwich, 1807), p. 15.

101. C. H. B. Quennell, *The Cathedral Church of Norwich: A Description of its Fabric and a Brief History of the Episcopal See* (Bell's Cathedral Series, London, 1898), pp. 11, 67; and for the colour-washing in 1806, Harrod, *Gleanings*, p. 270.

're-coloured where necessary' in the 1930s.[102] A large hole in one of the eastern bays of the vault must have been used for the image of a censing angel, which was suspended over the congregation at the feast of the Holy Trinity from as early as 1401. The effect must have been dramatic, particularly since, as the sacrists' rolls tell us, the angel was regularly brightened with silver foil.[103]

The vault of the eastern arm was rebuilt by Lyhart's successor, Bishop Goldwell (1472–99). When all its original polychromy was in pristine condition, including the gilding of ninety-seven of its 132 bosses with the bishop's rebus of a gold well, it must have presented a stunning sight. In fact, the vault still retains much painted decoration, though the extent to which it is original is unclear.[104] The manner in which the bosses are emphasised by surrounding rays or foliage painted on the ribs and vault is certainly typical of the later middle ages; it is paralleled by the rather simpler decoration on the fifteenth-century vault of the Bauchun Chapel.[105] Goldwell was also responsible for the arches of the main arcade of the presbytery, whose carved shields have all been repainted, and his own tomb is set within two of the arches on the south side. Although the canopy and tomb chest were repainted under Tristram's direction in 1936,[106] it is likely that some of the elaborate painting and gilding of the alabaster effigy itself is original: it certainly deserves detailed investigation.[107]

Much the most interesting painting of this date, however, is the so-called 'Erpingham reredos' (fig. 144) in the north arcade of the presbytery, on the east pier of the bay opposite Goldwell's tomb.[108] It is painted over Goldwell's encasing of the original arcade, and cannot be earlier than his period, but its name derives from the belief that Sir Thomas Erpingham – who paid for the Erpingham Gate and died in 1428 – was buried in this bay.[109] Whether Erpingham was indeed buried here has

102. Friends of Norwich Cathedral, *Ninth Annual Report, 1938*, p. 4.

103. *VCH Norfolk*, ii, p. 322.

104. The colouring is described as 'mostly original' by A. B. Whittingham, *Norwich Cathedral: Bosses and Misericords* (Norwich, 1981), p. 14; but according to P. T. Jones, *The Story of the Cathedral Church of Norwich*, rev. by A. B. Whittingham (Gloucester, n. d.), p. 22, the painting around the bosses 'is Victorian, though traces of more extensive medieval decoration survive'.

105. See the first two plates in M. R. James and W. T. Bensly, *The Sculptured Bosses in the Roof of the Bauchun Chapel of Our Lady of Pity in Norwich Cathedral* (Norwich, 1908).

106. 'J. B. H.', 'James Goldwell: Bishop of Norwich; 1472–98', Friends of Norwich Cathedral, *Seventh Annual Report, 1936*, pp. 22, 24–25. A watercolour by G. E. Fox shows the colouring of the carved crest on the canopy before the repainting: London, Society of Antiquaries, Fox Collection, box 23, no. 25.

107. The rich colouring of the effigy was referred to by Dawson Turner: see C. E. Keyser, *A List of Buildings in Great Britain and Ireland having Mural and Other Painted Decorations* (3rd edn, London, 1883), p. 318; it is described by Harrod, *Gleanings*, p. 294, as 'painted and gilt'.

108. A. B. Whittingham, 'The Erpingham Retable or Reredos in Norwich Cathedral', *NA*, 39 (1985), pp. 202–6.

109. Whittingham, 'Erpingham Retable', p. 202.

Fig. 144. The 'Erpingham reredos', on the east pier of the second bay from the west: north arcade of the presbytery.

recently been questioned, and is indeed unclear partly because of the confusing nature of the evidence provided by Sir Thomas Browne's account of 1680. Browne wrote as follows:

> On the north side of the choir, between the two arches, next to Queen Elizabeth's seat, were buried Sir Thomas Erpingham, and his wives the Lady Joan, etc. whose pictures were in the painted glass windows, next unto this place, with the arms of the Erpinghams. The insides of both the pillars were painted in red colours, with divers figures and inscriptions, from the top almost to the bottom, which are now washed out by the late whiting of the pillars. He was a knight of the garter in the time of Henry IV . . .[110]

What can be made of this? Browne appears to be the earliest authority to refer to Queen Elizabeth's seat, which seems to have been directly in front (i.e. to the south) of the ante-reliquary chapel; his wording would therefore at first seem to indicate that Erpingham was buried in the bay between that chapel and the bay with the painting (which is the next to the west). On the other hand, it seems that the glass he describes must have been in the Perpendicular window of the same bay as the existing painting (since there is no window that it could have occupied in the other bay); his description of the painting also tallies exactly with that now visible (though none now survives on the western pier). The manner in which he then proceeds, without interruption, to provide biographical details of Erpingham might seem to suggest that this is with reference to the bay with the paintings – and, therefore, that this is in fact where Erpingham was buried.[111]

The complex iconography of the surviving painting is difficult to follow, since no more than fragments or 'ghosts' survive of many of the figures, particularly in the upper half. Severe damage was caused by the erection of a memorial tablet in the eighteenth century. Although this has since been removed, its painted border still confuses the earlier image. Nevertheless, the elements of the original programme – divided compositionally and iconographically between an upper and a lower half – are for the most part still reasonably clear.[112] The figures in the lower half surround a large cross, once attached but now lost, and are set against a red diapered background. Flanking the cross are the Virgin and St John with, above and below

110. T. Browne, *Repertorium: or, Some Account of the Tombs and Monuments in the Cathedral Church of Norwich* (London, 1712), pp. 7–8. The stained glass depicting Erpingham and his wives is illustrated in Browne's plate opposite p. 8.

111. We are very grateful to Tony Sims for corresponding with us about this problem. He has argued strongly that Erpingham was buried in the other bay – that next to the ante-reliquary chapel – in a recent unpublished report submitted to the dean and chapter.

112. A useful, if not entirely accurate, coloured reconstruction of the painting was made in the late 1960s, for which see Whittingham, 'Erpingham Retable', p. 202.

the cross-arm respectively, the four evangelists and four doctors, all depicted with scrolls. In the upper half of the painting, a figure of God the Father, with the Holy Spirit below, is surrounded by the nine orders of angels, their scrolls with inscriptions from the *Te Deum*. In general terms, the composition – crowded with small figures and fluttering inscribed scrolls – is not untypical of late medieval wall painting; perhaps the best parallel is provided by a late fifteenth-century painting of the assumption and coronation of the Virgin, surrounded by the nine orders of angels, in Exeter Cathedral.[113]

More relevant, however, are the parallels provided by various late medieval paintings in Norfolk. The use of an attached cross is paralleled by various rood paintings, as at Cawston, while the elaborate painted rood composition at Attleborough includes various figures grouped around the cross, including four prophets with scrolls above the horizontal arm.[114] The four doctors are represented on the fifteenth-century painted pulpits of Castle Acre and Burnham Norton, and also on various rood screens and in stained glass of the period, sometimes together with the four evangelists. But the deliberate hierarchy of their grouping on the pulpits and screens – where the pope (Gregory) and cardinal (Jerome) are placed centrally, flanked by the bishops[115] – is not paralleled in the Erpingham reredos, where Gregory and Jerome are on the outside. Again, the nine orders of angels are found in Norfolk glass, as at Salle, and on screens such as that at Barton Turf; while angels with sentences from the *Te Deum* also occur, as formerly at Ringland.[116] The particular manner in which the angelic order Powers is depicted in the reredos – chastising a devil with a scourge – is typically East Anglian; on the screens at Barton Turf and Southwold (Suffolk), for example, the angel is shown subduing the devil with a birch rod, whereas elsewhere it is normally shown with a sword.[117] With its particular emphasis on the Crucifixion, the iconography of the reredos may well reflect Erpingham's bequest of 300 marks to found a chantry at the altar of the Holy Cross in the cathedral.[118]

113. G. McN. Rushforth, 'Late Medieval Paintings in Exeter Cathedral', *Devon and Cornwall Notes and Queries*, 17 (1932–33), pp. 99–104.

114. E. T. Long, 'Recently Discovered Wall Painting in England – II', *Burlington Magazine*, 76 (1940), pp. 156–62, pl. A. See also B. Camm, 'Some Norfolk Rood-Screens', in C. Ingleby, ed., *A Supplement to Blomefield's Norfolk* (London, 1929), p. 249, for the suggestion that a wooden rood was originally placed in front of the existing painted cross at Attleborough.

115. J. Alexander, 'The Pulpit with the Four Doctors at St James's, Castle Acre, Norfolk', in N. Rogers, ed., *England in the Fifteenth Century* (Proceedings of the 1992 Harlaxton Symposium, Harlaxton Medieval Studies, 4, Stamford, 1994), pp. 198–206.

116. C. Woodforde, *The Norwich School of Glass-Painting in the Fifteenth Century* (Oxford, 1950), pp. 68, 130, 136.

117. Woodforde, *Norwich School*, p. 137.

118. Blomefield, *Norfolk*, iv, p. 39; and for the location of the altar of the Holy Cross, see Fernie, *NC*, pp. 15–16 and p. 20, fig. 5G. Our account of the reredos was kindly read in draft by David King, who sent us detailed

The latest pre-Reformation painting in the cathedral is connected with Bishop Nix (1501–35/36), responsible for the vaulting of the transepts after the fire of 1509, where much colour and gilding on the bosses was recorded in the 1930s.[119] Similar polychromy was found during cleaning of Nix's own chantry in the nave south aisle, particularly on the carved shields,[120] though these have since been entirely repainted. Naturally, painting in the cathedral did not entirely cease at the Reformation. To commemorate Queen Elizabeth's visit in 1578, a series of eleven large coats of arms was painted on the north wall of the cloister, though they had disappeared by the 1930s when they were replaced by new coats of arms during the overall restoration of the cloister.[121] A most unusual painted memorial on the east respond of the nave north arcade commemorates the organist William Inglott: within an elaborate strapwork surround, figures of Art and Age crown a recumbent effigy of Inglott, above an inscription recording that the memorial was 'erected' on 15 June 1622 (see below, fig. 178).[122]

Among the surviving wall paintings there is little evidence of direct iconoclasm in the Reformation or later periods, though in the Erpingham reredos it is notable that some faces have been deliberately scratched, including those of Gregory and Jerome, particularly obvious targets as pope and cardinal.[123] In general, however, paintings were simply obliterated with colourwash to be revealed once more in the modern period. Although much has been recovered in the last two centuries, much has also been concealed or damaged through restoration work and repainting. Now a more rigorous approach to recording and examination prevails – exemplified by the recent detailed analysis of the cloister bosses (repainted by Tristram in the 1930s).[124] Restraint in treatment, and recognition of the limitations of our knowledge and skills, should preserve what remains.

note 118 continued
comments. He very plausibly interprets it as, in essence, a representation of the Trinity, 'to which have been added as many extra elements as could be fitted in, thus rather obscuring the original purpose'. He refers to partial parallels for the iconography in stained glass, as formerly at Tottington (Norfolk), emphasises the relevance of the wording of the *Te Deum* to a representation of the Trinity, and cites Whittingham's suggestion that the choir altar near the painting was dedicated to the Holy Trinity (Whittingham, 'Erpingham Retable', p. 202).

119. C. J. P. Cave, 'The Roof Bosses in the Transepts of Norwich Cathedral Church',
Archaeologia, 83 (1933), pp. 45–65. Repainting was undertaken in the 1930s.

120. Hope and Bensly, 'Recent Discoveries', p. 113.

121. M. Colthorpe, 'Queen Elizabeth I and Norwich Cathedral', *NA*, 40 (1989), pp. 318–23.

122. Blomefield, *Norfolk*, iv, pp. 28–29; Friends of Norwich Cathedral, *Tenth Annual Report, 1939*, p. 69 and plate (showing the painting before subsequent substantial retouching).

123. Whittingham, 'Erpingham Retable', p. 202.

124. T. Curteis, S. Paine and Courtauld Institute, 'The Polychromy of the Norwich Cathedral Cloister Bosses' (unpublished report for the dean and chapter, 1992).

20

The Panel Paintings and Stained Glass

David J. King

As this chapter is concerned with a large number of works of art of two different media and of varying date and provenance, a uniform treatment has not been possible. The panel paintings made for the cathedral and the nearby church of St Michael at Plea have been discussed in greater details than the imported painting in the Jesus Chapel. The stained glass of the medieval and post-Reformation period up to 1700, which mainly consists of glass acquired from elsewhere, has been described, after a short introduction, window by window. The nineteenth- and twentieth-century glass, which was for the most part made for the cathedral and is to be found in over thirty windows, has had to be dealt with in a much more summary way, focusing mainly on the more interesting windows and attempting to set it in its context in the historical development of the medium.

The Panel Paintings

The Despenser Retable

The Despenser retable or altarpiece now in St Luke's Chapel is a highly important object because of the rarity of its survival and the quality of its painting.[1] There

1. A. Way, 'Notice of a Painting of the 14th Century, Part of the Decorations of an Altar: Discovered in Norwich Cathedral', *Proceedings of the Archaeological Institute, Norwich, 1847* (London, 1851), pp. 198–206; W. H. St J. Hope, 'On a Painted Table or Reredos of the Fourteenth Century in the Cathedral Church of Norwich', *NA*, 13 (1898), pp. 293–314; J. G. Waller, 'On the Retable in

Norwich Cathedral and the Paintings in St Michael at Plea', *NA*, 13 (1898), pp. 315–42; M. Rickert, *Painting in Britain: The Middle Ages* (Harmondsworth, 1954), pp. 176–77, pl. 159a; P. Plummer, 'Restoration of a Retable in Norwich Cathedral', *Studies in Conservation*, 4 (1959), pp. 106–15; A. G. G. Thurlow, *The Medieval Painted Retables in Norwich Cathedral* (Norwich, 1967), pp. 1–6;

are, however, many uncertainties as to its date, provenance and donors. It was discovered in 1847 used as a table in an upper room in the cathedral. It had been truncated at the top and the four corners had been cut out to enable legs to be inserted. Fortunately, the painting was on the underneath and had survived reasonably well. It depicted five scenes from the Passion of Christ: the Flagellation, Carrying of the Cross, Crucifixion, Resurrection and Ascension. The only serious loss to these scenes appears to have been the upper part of the figure of Christ in the central Crucifixion and in the Ascension. The damage to the frame is possibly more significant. The first problem is that nothing is known of the original shape of the retable, although the meagre surviving comparative material suggests that the present restoration as a rectangle is probably correct. A more serious problem is the loss of any heraldic plaques which may have continued along the top edge in the same way as on the other three sides. There could have been up to thirty of these in all. All those missing along the top may have borne the arms of the most significant people associated with the retable.

It has been said that the evidence of the surviving shields points to the association of the altarpiece with people who took part in the suppression of the Peasants' Revolt in 1381 in Norfolk, the most prominent of them being Henry Despenser, bishop of Norwich (1369–1406).[2] Hope's careful examination of the heraldic plaques enabled him to suggest identifications for seven of the banners of arms with varying degrees of certainty. A reexamination of the heraldry, in close conjunction with the lists of those known to have been involved in the suppression of the revolt in East Anglia, mainly three commissions of the peace recorded in 1381 and 1382, suggests that a number of amendments to Hope's list can be made: these may connect the retable even more closely with the revolt.[3]

The photograph published by Hope in 1898 shows no sign of the Despenser coat which he gives as the first and most important coat identifiable, nor was it mentioned by Way in the initial publication of the retable in 1847.[4] However, we have to rely on him when he says that 'clear traces' of the coat were visible. Despenser was the leader of the opposition to the rebels in Norfolk and took a notable part in the fight against them. Sir Stephen Hales was captured by the rebels and it is therefore

note 1 continued

J. Symonds, 'A Study of the Painted Altarpiece now in St Luke's Chapel, Norwich Cathedral' (unpublished University of East Anglia M. A. thesis, 1970); A. H. R. Martindale in P. Lasko and N. J. Morgan, eds, *Medieval Art in East Anglia, 1300–1520* (Norwich, 1973), pp. 36–37, 39; P. Tudor-Craig in J. Alexander and P. Binski, eds, *Age of Chivalry: Art in Plantagenet England,* 1200–1400 (London, 1987), pp. 516–17, pl. 711.

2. Hope, 'Painted Table', p. 302. Thurlow, *Retables*, p. 3.

3. *CPR, 1381–85*, commissions for peace, 14 December 1381, p. 84; 8 March 1382, p. 141; 21 December 1382, p. 247.

4. Hope, 'Painted Table', pp. 300–2. See also London, Victoria and Albert Museum, neg. 63244.

probable that his coat was present, as Hope suggests, and also that of Sir Thomas Morieux, who took part in Suffolk.[5] Hope thought that the traces of a chequy coat with a thin fess were probably the arms of the Clifford family, but they are more likely to have been from the coat of Sir Oliver de Calthorpe (chequy or and azur a fess ermine), who was on one of the commissions of peace.[6] The Kerdiston coat is not for Sir William Kerdiston, who died in 1361, as Hope suggests, but for the Sir William Kerdiston who was sheriff of Norfolk and Suffolk in 1381–82, and as such would have played an important part in the maintenance of order.[7] The paly nebuly argent/or coat which was identified as probably for Sir Nicholas Gernon is much more likely to have been argent three piles wavy gules two from the chief and one from the base reversed, either for John de Cavendish, chief justice of the court of the king's bench, who was killed by the rebels in Bury St Edmunds in June 1381, or for his son John Cavendish, knighted and awarded a pension by the king for his zeal in killing Wat Tyler, one of the rebel leaders.[8] Hope's attribution of the Howard coat to Sir John Howard of Fersfield cannot be supported, as his son Robert Howard was an assiduous member of commissions of peace and array well before and during the revolt, and would certainly have been represented in any heraldic roll of those who suppressed the rebels.[9] In view of this reinterpretation of the surviving heraldry on the frame, the tradition that the stimulus for the gift of the retable was to honour those involved locally in putting down the Peasants' Revolt receives more support, although it needs to be borne in mind that the series is incomplete and those represented were important local people who could have been represented in the heraldry for other reasons. As Pamela Tudor-Craig has pointed out, the need for a new retable may have been brought about by the damage to the presbytery caused by the fall of the spire in 1361/62, repairs for which continued for some time afterwards.[10]

One possible date for the completion of the retable could have been the visit to Norwich of King Richard II and his queen, Anne of Bohemia, in 1383. Royal visits are associated with refurbishment and renewal: the king and queen may have been taken to see the retable in the cathedral together with the new building of the presbytery (the cellarer's roll for 1382–83 mentions expenses incurred during their visit, and the chronicles say that they visited several 'abbeys' including Norwich)

5.   Blomefield, *Norfolk*, iii, p. 108; *CPR, 1381–85*, pp. 84, 141, 247. Sir Stephen Hales was also sheriff of Norfolk and Suffolk in 1378–79 and Thomas Morieux in 1366–69: H. Le Strange, *Norfolk Official Lists from the Earliest Period to the Present Day* (Norwich, 1890), p. 14.

6.   *CPR, 1381–85*, pp. 141, 247. Oliver de Cal-

thorpe was also sheriff of Norfolk and Suffolk in 1375–76: Le Strange, *Lists*, p. 14.

7.   Le Strange, *Lists*, p. 15.

8.   *DNB*; W. Copinger, *The Manors of Suffolk*, 7 vols (London, 1905–11), iii, pp. 60–61.

9.   *CPR, 1381–85*, pp. 84, 141, 151.

10.   Tudor-Craig in Alexander and Binski, *Chivalry*, p. 516.

and also the new choir in St Giles' Hospital, whose ceiling was painted with the imperial eagle, in honour of the queen, Anne of Bohemia, whose father was Holy Roman Emperor Charles IV.[11]

The question remains as to who paid for the retable, but its incomplete nature prevents any certainty on this point. It has been pointed out that its costs do not appear in the surviving sacrists' rolls for 1364–1400, where other items for the new building are mentioned, although in 1401 an entry appears to indicate that a new antependium was added to the high altar.[12] This does not necessarily point to a lay donation for the main altarpiece, as it could have been a private gift of the bishop. Certainly what was probably the preceding altarpiece for the high altar had been an episcopal donation. In 1314 Bishop Salmon gave a tabula for the high altar which, as is revealed by a letter of thanks from the prior to the bishop, was made ready in London.[13] On balance, however, a collective donation by those represented in the heraldry is the most probable.

The style of the retable has led different writers to draw different conclusions. Albert Way in 1847 thought that it was Italian work, and north German, French and Bohemian influences have been more reasonably suggested by modern writers. The stylistic similarity of the Betrayal and Crucifixion panels from the nearby church of St Michael at Plea has led to the conclusion that local craftsmen were responsible for both works, but it has also been pointed out that all these works could themselves have been made elsewhere.[14] Painters were at work at this time in both Norwich and London who could have been responsible: John Frenge, a Norwich painter, is recorded as restoring an altarpiece at St Vedast's church near the cathedral in 1384; and in early 1383 Gilbert Prince, the king's painter in London, was relieved of all obligations of jury and other civic duties, perhaps as a privilege, but possibly also to give him time to work.[15] The only conclusion to be drawn is that there was such a variety of stylistic experiment and influence in the second half of the fourteenth century, and so much comparable material has been lost, that it is impossible to make categorical statements concerning the provenance of this work of art based on style alone.

11. Thomas of Walsingham, *Historia Anglicana*, ed. H. T. Riley, 2 vols (London, 1863–64), in H. T. Riley, ed., *Chronica monasterii S. Albani*, 12 parts (RS, 28, 1863–76), part 1, vol. ii, p. 97. C. B. Jewson, *History of the Great Hospital* (Norwich, 1980), p. 9.

12. Hope, 'Painted Table', p. 302; 'Extracts from the Account-Rolls of Norwich Priory: Illustrative of Painting, Pigments

&c', *Proceedings of the Archaeological Institute, Norwich, 1847*, p. 208.

13. C. Norton, D. Park and P. Binski, *Dominican Painting in East Anglia* (Woodbridge, 1987), p. 79 n. 87.

14. A. H. R. Martindale in Lasko and Morgan, *Medieval Art in East Anglia*, pp. 36–37.

15. NRO, DCN, almoner's roll for 1383–84. *CPR, 1381–85*, 6 Jan. 1383, p. 216.

Panel Paintings from the Church of St Michael at Plea

Mention has already been made of the two panels showing the Betrayal of Christ (Visitors' Centre) and the Crucifixion with the Virgin Mary and St John and a pair of donors (St Andrew's Chapel). These were part of a disparate group of panels from the church of St Michael at Plea, some of which were described as being in the church in the eighteenth century.[16] They show signs of the type of token iconoclasm frequently seen on screen paintings where the faces are scratched, suggesting that they may have survived the Reformation and seventeenth-century iconoclastic period *in situ*. The two late fourteenth-century panels come from a retable which may have been similar to the Despenser retable in that it was a Passion series of five scenes, but with a different choice of iconography: Betrayal, Flagellation, Crucifixion, Entombment and Ascension. The lack of a Resurrection scene would be surprising, however, suggesting that when the panels were listed as above in the eighteenth century, further panels had already been lost. The two surviving panels have been cut off at the bottom and the two donors in the Crucifixion panel reveal nothing of their identity except that they were a secular pair. The amount of modern repainting on the St Michael at Plea panels is more than on the Despenser retable and it is essential to look at pre-restoration photographs to make an assessment of style, which is made harder by the damage to faces mentioned above.[17] The poses and drapery are less angular than on the Despenser retable and, although the heads of the soldiers in the Betrayal are similar in type to those of the Despenser Resurrection, they are softer in their manner of painting. The head of Christ in the Betrayal is also softer in style, without the high arched eyebrows seen on the Despenser retable and in the Litlyngton Missal Crucifixion.[18] If the Despenser retable is *c.* 1382–83, these panels could be a little later; in the absence of documentation a date range of *c.* 1380–90 should be given.

The remaining panels from St Michael at Plea are of fifteenth-century date. Five of them have been restored and placed in a modern frame to form a retable in St Saviour's Chapel; the sixth is in the Visitors' Centre. They consist of an Annunciation with subsidiary Visitation, a Crucifixion with the Virgin Mary and St John, a Resurrection, St Erasmus, an archbishop saint, and St Margaret of Antioch with the dragon, the latter panel being in the Visitors' Centre. Although different styles

---

16. Blomefield, *Norfolk*, iv, p. 321; Hope, 'Painted Table', pp. 312–14; Waller, 'Retable', pp. 315–42; P. Tudor-Craig, 'Medieval Panel Paintings from Norwich, St Michael at Plea', *Burlington Magazine*, 98 (1956), pp. 333–34; P. Tudor-Craig, *Exhibition of Medieval Paintings from St Michael at Plea, Norwich* (Victoria and Albert Museum, London, 1956); M. Rickert, *Painting in Britain: The Middle Ages* (2nd edn, Harmondsworth, 1965), p. 162; Symonds, 'Study'; N. J. Morgan in Lasko and Morgan, *Medieval Art in East Anglia*, pp. 37–38.

17. Hope, 'Painted Table', pls vii–viii.

18. Rickert, *Painting in Britain* (2nd edn, 1965), pl. 158.

are visible, all except the Resurrection, which is larger in format and later in date, may well have come from a screen with parcloses such as that at Ranworth.[19] Although the two male saints' panels were originally larger, as shown by the truncated demi-angels holding hangings behind the figures, they could have come from large floor-level parclose panels. A date of *c.* 1420–40 for the five earlier panels is suggested by the iconography and would also fit the drapery, which is less flowing than the apostles on the Castle Acre screen of *c.* 1412 and the head types, which retain the broad forehead and small chin of early fifteenth-century painting but are more precise in their technique.[20] The Resurrection panel, with its naturalistic setting and realistic detail, appears to be later in style and shows links with north German art. It should be dated to *c.* 1450–60.

In the Jesus Chapel is the central panel of an early sixteenth-century triptych. It depicts the adoration of the magi and has been attributed to Martin Schwarz. He was a German painter who lived in Rothenburg and was active from *c.* 1480 to 1522.[21] The Jesus Chapel painting is dated 1480 on the frame. However, the shape of the panel is typical of Antwerp work of the early sixteenth century and the style of the painting, which has been retouched in places, is closer to the many Flemish altarpieces painted at that time. Also, while some of the faces still show the influence of fifteenth-century Flemish art, the Renaissance ornament on the ruins in the background suggests a sixteenth-century date.

The Medieval and Renaissance Stained Glass

The earliest possible reference to a glazier in Norfolk is to a monk called Daniel from St Benet's Abbey who died in 1155 and was called *vitrearius*.[22] In view of the close links between Norwich Cathedral and St Benet's Abbey, it is possible that Daniel may have worked on the second phase of the Norman cathedral under Bishop Eborard (1121–45). In 1279–80 the son of Nicholas Vitriarius was paid for taking down painted glass shields (*scuta vitrea*) in the cathedral and in 1283–84 Nicholas, now called Fayerchild, and son, were provided with a robe by the sacrist.[23] While the names of several other glaziers occur in the cathedral accounts in the medieval period, this employment must have been largely for maintenance rather than extensive new glazing schemes. In the sacrist's roll for 1436 is an inventory of

19. N. J. Morgan in Lasko and Morgan, *Medieval Art in East Anglia*, pp. 49, 59.
20. S. Cotton, 'Mediaeval Roodscreens in Norfolk: Their Construction and Painting Dates', *NA*, 40 (1987), p. 47.
21. U. Thieme and F. Becker, *Allgemeines Lexikon der bildenen Künstler*, 37 vols (Leipzig, 1907–50), xxx, p. 365.
22. S. Brown and D. O'Connor, *Medieval Craftsmen: Glass-Painters* (London, 1991), p. 21.
23. C. Woodforde, *The Norwich School of Glass Painting in the Fifteenth Century* (Oxford, 1950), p. 9.

the cathedral glazier's hut which lists precisely the tools required for carrying out such a function: a large pair of compasses for setting out, a hammer, five grozing irons for cutting different thicknesses of glass, thirty-six closing nails, one soldering iron, two chisels, one working board, one stool, six pieces of lead and three pounds of solder.[24] No equipment for glass painting was kept there and new windows would have been put out to contract to local glaziers, who up to the fourteenth century lived in the area between the castle and the cathedral.[25]

Almost all of the medieval painted glass made for the cathedral has disappeared and the bulk of that which will be described has been acquired in recent years. The comparative dearth of antiquarian descriptions of glass painting in the cathedral suggests that the losses were early, and this is supported by the historical record of iconoclasm.[26] It is of course impossible to tell how much painted glass was in the cathedral just before the Reformation. Bishop Alnwick's will, proved in December 1449, provided for the building and glazing of the great west window, but is not clear whether it was glazed with painted glass.[27] The accounts and legacies for the building of the cloister also fail to indicate whether the glazing of the traceries there involved more than the heraldic glass recorded by Blomefield.[28] There was certainly a large amount of this type of glazing in other parts of the cathedral, mainly the arms of local nobility, bishops and royalty, as might be expected. One antiquarian suggests that the cathedral may also originally have been provided with extensive painted glass decoration. In 1815 the Rev. David Powell visited the cathedral and wrote in his notes: 'though now the remains of painted glass in this church are insignificant and scarcely worth describing yet sufficient remain plainly to shew that all the windows were once adorned with it even those which give light to the inside of the vaultings or second tier of arches . . .'[29]

The medieval and Renaissance glass which is now to be seen in the cathedral consists of one medieval shield of arms, some later heraldry and a few small pieces, all from the original glazing; glass brought in from other cathedral buildings; and several panels which have been acquired in recent years from various churches and collections in Norfolk and beyond. The glass will be described starting from the west in the north nave aisle, using the *Corpus vitrearum* system of numbering the windows within the church and, where appropriate, the panels within the windows (fig. 145).[30]

24. NRO, DCN, sacrist's roll for 1436.
25. W. Rye, *A Short Calendar of the Deeds Relating to Norwich Enrolled in the Court Rolls of the City, 1285–1306* (Norwich, 1903), pp. 31, 34; W. Rye, *A Calendar of Norwich Deeds Enrolled in the Court Rolls of the City, 1307–1341* (Norwich, 1915), pp. 29, 49, 58, 75, 77, 129.
26. Woodforde, *Norwich School*, pp. 208–10.

27. Blomefield, *Norfolk*, iii, pp. 531–32.
28. *Communar Rolls*, pp. 39, 116.
29. BL, Additional MS 17462, fo. 300 (Powell's topographical collections).
30. See for example P. A. Newton, *The County of Oxford: A Catalogue of Medieval Stained Glass* (*Corpus vitrearum medii aevi* Great Britain I, London, 1979), p. xx.

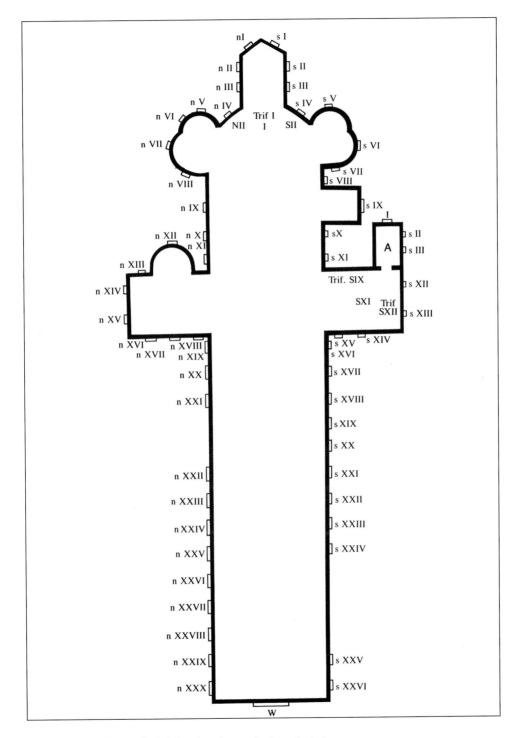

Fig. 145. Plan of the cathedral showing the numbering of windows.
St Catherine's Chapel (marked A) is separately numbered.

North Nave Aisle

The first five windows from the west each contain in the central light an heraldic panel: nXXX arms of Henry VII (the Mortimer quartering on the queen's impalement was omitted when the glass was restored); nXXIX arms of James I; nXXVIII arms of Charles I; nXXVII garter and arms of the earl of Shrewsbury, *c.* 1500; nXXVI badges and motto of the Emperor Charles V, sixteenth-century. All these panels, except the last, have been subject to restoration and have been moved from other nave windows.

St Andrew's Chapel, North Transept: East Window nXII

The glass here is mainly from the deanery, but the roundels in the third light showing at the top St John the Evangelist with the eagle and writing the gospel, seventeenth-century, and below, St Godelva, a female martyr, being strangled by two soldiers, sixteenth-century, are from the Baron Ash collection.[31] The three large heraldic panels in light two are for Dean Gardiner (bottom), 1573–89, Dean Montgomery, 1603–14, and Dean Suckling, 1614–28, respectively. The two remaining roundels in the first light depict St Francis of Assisi receiving the stigmata, sixteenth-century (bottom left), and the baptism of Christ, seventeenth-century (top left). The four Tudor panels from the deanery showing angels supporting shields may have been made to mark the occasion of the visit to Norwich and the cathedral in 1520 of Queen Catherine and Cardinal Wolsey during the episcopacy of Bishop Nix.[32] Panel 2a shows the royal arms surmounted by a crown; 2c, the arms of Cardinal Wolsey with his cardinal's hat; and 3c those of Bishop Nix and his mitre. The fourth panel is problematical. The coat shown is gules a cross flory argent, but no hat is held by the angel, which is, however, a restoration. If there was no hat, this would suggest that the fourth coat was for a lay person associated with the royal visit. It was assigned to the family of Walsham in a fifteenth-century Norfolk armorial manuscript. A very similar coat, gules a cross flory party per cross argent and sable, was to be found on the font of the local church of St Mary Coslany, along with those of England, France, Scotland, Ireland, St George and the city of Norwich.[33] These four panels are an example of local glass painting of the period, as is shown by decorative detail, but stylistic analysis is difficult as none of the heads are original. That on the angel in the last-mentioned panel is in fact a German

31. For the Flemish roundels in this window and in windows nVII, sXVI and sXX, see W. Cole, *A Catalogue of Netherlandish and North European Roundels in Britain* (London, 1993), pp. 162–63.

32. Blomefield, *Norfolk*, iii, p. 194; *Letters and Papers, Foreign and Domestic, of the Reign of Henry*, 21 vols in 35 (London, 1880–91), iii (i), p. 407.

33. J. Corder, *A Dictionary of Suffolk Arms* (Suffolk Records Society, 7, 1965), col. 259; Blomefield, *Norfolk*, iv, p. 491.

sixteenth-century head and that of the angel holding the Wolsey arms has a graffito: JRS 1822, possibly the date when it was made.

North Ambulatory

The memorial window to Arnold Kent (d. 1976), nXI, contains a sixteenth-century heraldic fleur-de-lys and a truncated mid sixteenth-century French panel from the trefoil head of a light showing the descent of the Holy Spirit onto the Virgin Mary and apostles at Pentecost.

The Erpingham window, nX, is so-called as it used to contain the figures of Sir Thomas Erpingham (d. 1428), and his two wives.[34] In 1963 the present window was assembled, made up from a few fragments of medieval glass extant in other windows of the cathedral, plus a large number of pieces collected over a number of years from other sources. The window was made by G. King and Son of Norwich, who were responsible for glazing several other windows in the church with glass acquired from elsewhere.[35] The borders of the window are filled with medieval fragments and will not be described in detail. The assembled pieces are set against plain and patterned quarries, some of which are from the north-west clerestory windows. Where known, the provenance is given in brackets.

Fig. 146. Head of Moses, Norwich glass painting, *c.* 1450–60. Erpingham Window, nX.

Main Lights (starting bottom left):

1a. Fifteenth-century roundel with evangelist symbol of St Matthew (bishop's palace, great drawing room).

2a. Fifteenth-century roundel with IHC monogram (unidentified cathedral window).

34. Sir T. Browne, *Repertorium: or, Some Account of the Tombs and Monuments in the Cathedral Church of Norwich in 1680* (London, 1712), pp. 7–8 and plate; Blomefield, *Norfolk*, iv, p. 39; BL, Additional MS 17462, fos 273, 275 (Powell's topographical collections).

35. A. B. Whittingham, 'The Erpingham Window', Friends of Norwich Cathedral, *Thirty-Fourth Annual Report* (Norwich, 1967), pp. 9–10; A. G. G. Thurlow and J. P. Burbridge, *Norwich Cathedral* (Andover, 1990), pl. p. 4.

3a.   Two fifteenth-century foliage eyelets (Hill House, East Dereham).

4a.   *c.* 1450–60 Norwich School head of main-light figure of Moses with rays of light shining from his ears (fig. 146; Hill House, East Dereham).

5a.   Two elaborate fifteenth-century roundels with initials; grotesque.

6a.   *c.* 1440–60 Norwich School head of main-light figure of bearded man, surrounded by sun-bursts from border (Hill House, East Dereham).

7a.   Fifteenth-century fragmentary arms of Delapole, azure a fess between three leopards' faces or.

8/9a.   Fifteenth-century fragmentary canopy top (some of the four canopy tops in this window are from the collection of Canon Gordon Roe).

1b.   Fifteenth-century roundel with evangelist symbol of St Mark (Mr Baron Ash).

2b.   Fifteenth-century apostle's head, fragment of baptism of Christ (Mr Baron Ash), angel's head (?).

3/4b.   Fifteenth-century standing angel holding shield, argent three piles in point gules, possibly for Guildesburgh (Mr Baron Ash).

5b.   Fifteenth-century shield with azure three mitres or, for the bishopric of Norwich (unidentified window in cathedral).

6b.   Sixteenth-century shield with merchant's mark between initials RD.

7b.   Fifteenth-century shield with arms of Lord Morley, argent a lion rampant sable crowned or (north-east clerestory window).

8/9b.   Fifteenth-century fragmentary canopy top.

1c.   *c.* 1330–40 roundel with grotesque figure playing bagpipes (bishop's palace, great drawing room).

2c.   Fifteenth-century composite quatrefoil: part of feathered angel carrying bowl, young male head, part of saint carrying sword (St Catherine?) (south-east clerestory window), wheel, from figure of seraph.

3/4c.   *c.* 1430–40 seated figure of God the Father from coronation of the Virgin, ex tracery light (Mr Richard Winch).

5c.   Fifteenth-century roundel with IHU monogram on shield in rod-and-leaf border (unidentified cathedral window).

6c.   Fifteenth-century roundel with crowned Tudor rose on twig between initials RH, presumably for *Rex Henricus*.

7c.   Sixteenth-century large heraldic crown.

8/9c.   Fifteenth-century fragmentary canopy top.

1d.   Late fifteenth-century roundel with St Catherine standing on Emperor Maxentius (Canon Gordon Roe, ex Jesus Chapel).

2d.   Fifteenth-century small angel's (?) head set on foliage.

3d.   Fifteenth-century fragments of pedestals including part of mantle.

4d.   Fifteenth-century fragmentary roundel of Resurrection (Mr Richard

Winch).

5d.   Fifteenth-century IHC monogram (unidentified cathedral window) set on fragments.

6d.   Fourteenth-century shield with azure three mitres or, for the bishopric of Norwich, set on fragments including sunbursts.

7d.   Quatrefoil of fragments. Fifteenth-century young head and part of St Peter with keys and inscription. 1528 head of St Hildegund of Meer, with almost illegible inscription on nimbus, here given in its complete form: S. HILDEGUNDIS REGINA FUNDATRIX ECCLESIAE MERENSIS (abbey of Steinfeld, cloister, window VIII, J. C. Hampp of Norwich).[36]

8/9d.   Fourteenth- and fifteenth-century canopy fragments.

Tracery:

A1–A8. Fifteenth-century foliage and Maria monograms (the latter from unidentified cathedral windows).

B1.   Fragment with rose on bird.

C1 and C3. Fifteenth-century foliage quatrefoils (C3 Hill House, East Dereham).

C2.   Fifteenth-century shield with azure a cross flory between four martlets or for Edward the Confessor (Mr Baron Ash).

The Calthorpe Window, nIX, contains a collection of twelve painted quarries, mainly heraldic. They come from the old bishop's palace and the collection of Mr Baron Ash, who gave the two central quarries which are evidently from a long sixteenth-century series of impalements of the Calthorpe family, who owned a house near the bishop's palace gates.[37] The coats here are for Calthorpe impaling St Omer and Calthorpe with a crescent for difference impaling Astley and are numbered 20 and 23 respectively. The two central quarries in the bottom row have the arms of the Worshipful Company of Grocers, and the same impaling the initials DWG.

The Jesus Chapel

The Bacon Memorial Window, nVII, to Sir Edmund Bacon, high steward of the cathedral from 1956 to 1979, was made by G. King and Son of Norwich. In the centre light is a modern heraldic achievement of Sir Edmund and an inscription to him. The rest of the glazing consists of reused medieval glass, mainly from the church of St Andrew, Tottington, Norfolk, and from Nowton Court, Suffolk. In

---

36. J. and W. Kurthen, 'Der Kreuzgang der Abtei Steinfeld und sein ehemalige Bildfensterschmuck', in W. Neuss, ed., *Die Glasmalereien aus dem Steinfelder Kreuzgang* (München Gladbach, 1955), pp. 135, 224; D. J. King, *Stained Glass Tours around Norfolk Churches* (Norwich, 1974), pp. 16–17.

37. Blomefield, *Norfolk*, vi, p. 517.

the bottom part of the window in the first and third lights (2a, 2c) are two fine representations of evangelist symbols, the lion of St Mark, bearing on a scroll *ecce sp[iri]c[us] s[an]c[tu]s*, and the young winged man of St Matthew, bearing the

inscription *ecce filius* (fig. 147). These were originally in the lower two main tracery lights of the east window of the north aisle (nIII) at Tottington.[38] The canopy tops now in the present window (7a, 6/7b, 7c) are also from this window, as is the small censing angel in 6b. Although the head types and drapery of the St Matthew symbol and the censing angel are very similar to a Peterborough psalter dated *c.* 1320, the use of smear shading and the three-dimensional elements in the canopy tops suggest that a slightly later date of *c.* 1330–40 is probable.[39] Between the two evangelist symbols in the centre light is a beautiful fragment of a Virgin and Child, of roughly similar date. This is of unknown origin, but was previously placed in this window. Above the two evangelist symbols are two figures of apostles, bearing scrolls with s[ANCTUS] MATHEUS and s[ANCTUS] THOMAS. They stand under simple canopies with stiff-leaf capitals

Fig. 147. Evangelist symbol of Saint Matthew, *c.* 1330–40. Bacon Memorial Window, nVII, ex church of St Andrew, Tottington, Norfolk.

and are set against a background of vine leaves and strapwork. Both heads have been replaced by fifteenth-century ones; and both panels are surmounted by additional canopy work of a slightly later date than the figures, which are *c.* 1300. They are clearly part of the same set of apostles as another figure in the tower window of the church of St Edmund, Downham Market, Norfolk.[40] The space between these two panels and the Tottington canopies has been filled with fragments including parts of a fourteenth-century border made of alternating vine leaves with stems and squirrels. In the tracery is some fifteenth-century eyelet foliage from another window at Tottington.

38. D. J. King in Lasko and Morgan, *Medieval Art in East Anglia*, p. 27.

39. N. J. Morgan in Lasko and Morgan, *Medieval Art in East Anglia*, pp. 14, 21.

40. D. J. King, *Tours*, p. 4.

The north-east window of the Jesus Chapel, nVI, contains a Flemish roundel of *c.* 1540–50 set in a cartouche, showing St Peter preaching. This was previously in the marble hall of the Norwich Union, Surrey Street.

Apse

Window nIV is a two-light window divided by a transom. Above the transom are set some modern patterned quarries and two sixteenth-century quarries with the arms of Norwich Cathedral hanging from a bishop's staff surmounted by a mitre. Below are several heraldic quarries and panels; the top left and bottom right of the larger panels are from the nearby church of SS Simon and Jude, where they were recorded in a south window in the eighteenth century. They are the arms of Bacon quartering Quaplode and Cecil quartering Castle.[41] Other glass is from the deanery, including the arms of Bishop Parkhurst (1560–75), Dean Gardiner (1573–89) and Dean Suckling (1614–28). One quarry has an inscription on a cartouche bearing 'D Gardiner 1575', but also the initials 'GI G', which probably refer to John Goglee (using the Italian 'Giovanni'), a glazier who became a freeman of Norwich in 1539/40 and died soon after this piece was made.[42] The glass was installed here in 1951.

Window sIV contains a large standing figure of an archbishop saint holding a cross staff in his left hand and live coals in his right. This is St Brice and is Rouen glass of *c.* 1600 (fig. 148). It was found by Dennis King, the Norwich glazier, at Langley Hall, Norfolk, the residence of the Beauchamp family, who are

Fig. 148. St Brice, Rouen, *c.* 1600, sIV.

41. Blomefield, *Norfolk*, iv, p. 356.

42. Woodforde, *Norwich School*, p. 13.

known to have bought French glass from J. C. Hampp, the well-known early nineteenth- century Norwich dealer in continental glass. The St Brice panel needed only slight modification to fit this opening and was installed here in 1957.[43]

St Luke's Chapel

Window sVI contains a panel of fifteenth-century glass recorded as being from the church of St Peter, Ringland, Norfolk, where there is still a series of figures of glass of *c.* 1460–70 in the north clerestory, to which this panel belongs. It originally depicted the Virgin and Child, but the Child has been lost except for an arm, from which hangs a string attached to a bird. Both figures are set against a glory.[44] This panel, which was for a time in Strangers' Hall, Norwich, then owned by the Bolingbroke family, who presented it to the cathedral, was installed here some time after 1929.[45]

St Catherine's Chapel, South Transept: Window sII

A Flemish roundel, sixteenth-century, showing St Catherine kneeling before the wheel on which she was tortured.

South Nave Aisle

The George King Memorial Window, sXVII, was installed by G. King and Son, glaziers, as a memorial to the cofounder of the firm which did much work here; he died in 1965. The old glass consists of several standard Norwich fifteenth-century patterned quarries spread across the main lights and in the first and third lights a pair of fine sixteenth-century Flemish roundels from a set of the four doctors of the church. They depict St Gregory (fig. 149) and St Augustine and are dated 1538. In the centre light is a head of St John the Evangelist with an eagle, surrounded by rod-and-leaf border; this is fifteenth-century Norwich work. Below in black letter is an inscription from Ecclesiasticus 1:27, *Timor D[o]m[ini] expellit peccatu[m] n[a]m*. The last two pieces are from St Etheldreda's church, Norwich.

The Elizabeth Graham Hunt Memorial Window, sXXI, was paid for by the Rev. Canon Stather Hunt in 1965 and installed by G. King and Son and consists mainly of a modern figure of St Elizabeth surrounded by Renaissance and later roundels, local medieval patterned quarries and fragments.[46] Only the complete pieces will be mentioned here (all are round or oval unless mentioned and are Flemish).

43. D. G. King, 'St Brice Bishop of Tours', Friends of Norwich Cathedral, *Twenty-Eighth Annual Report* (Norwich, 1957), pp. 6–7, plate inside front cover.
44. Woodforde, *Norwich School*, pp. 69–70, pl. xxi; D. J. King, *Tours*, pp. 19–20.
45. A MS report on the cathedral glass in 1929

by Eric Milner-White does not mention the Ringland panel.
46. P. V. Howes, 'Report for the Year Ending 31st December 1965', Friends of Norwich Cathedral, *Thirty-Second Annual Report* (Norwich 1965), p. 9.

Fig. 149. Roundel, St Gregory, Flemish, 1538. George King Memorial Window, sXVII.

1a. Sixteenth-century. Joseph being put down the well by his brothers.

3a. Seventeenth-century. A lay male donor kneeling before an altar, presented to St Sebastian by St John the Baptist.

5a. Sixteenth-century. A lay male donor kneeling before St Apollonia. Beside him from a tree hangs a shield bearing three roses and the initials WA.

6a. A rectangular seventeenth-century panel depicting St Agnes with lamb and palm branch.

1b. Seventeenth-century. A nimbed Dominican friar standing outside a door with two other friars is greeted by a group of laymen bearing two mitres.

5b. Seventeenth-century. A figure of God the Father standing in the clouds holding an orb.

6b. Seventeenth-century. A figure of St Augustine with heart, mitre and bishop's staff.

1c. Sixteenth-century. A fine roundel, a partner to 1a, of Joseph interpreting dreams.

3c. Seventeenth-century. St Anthony of Padua and another monk with plates of fish, set in a landscape by a waterfall.

5c. Sixteenth-century. St Gertrude as an abbess with black rats at her feet.

6c. A panel like 6a, with St Christina having an arrow in her neck and carrying a palm and book.

Fig. 150. Roundel, with
tree of Jesse, English, *c.* 1500.
Visitors' centre, light box.

Visitors' Centre

Six panels are on display in a light box. The four fragmentary upright rectangular
panels are of the second half of the fifteenth century, possibly from Suffolk, and
show scenes from the corporal acts of mercy. The other two panels are roundels,
that at the top being English, *c.* 1500, depicting the tree of Jesse (fig. 150), and the
other is Flemish, *c.* 1525 (partly restored), and depicts the Nativity of Christ.

The Modern Windows

All the windows in the cathedral have been reglazed in modern times.[47] Much of
the nineteenth- and early twentieth-century glass was restored under the War
Damage scheme which continued until the 1960s.[48] What has been described so far
is mainly the medieval and later glass up to *c.* 1700 which has been inserted since
the last war, often with glass of several different dates in the same window. What
follows after a short introduction is a very brief survey of the complete nineteenth-
and twentieth-century windows made for the cathedral or acquired from elsewhere.

47. The best account of the modern cathedral
glazing is in B. Haward, *Nineteenth Century
Norfolk Stained Glass* (Norwich, 1984), pp.
3, 194, 209, 220, 223–25, and gazetteer.

48. Details of this work can be found in the
various *Annual Reports* of the Friends of
Norwich Cathedral.

The iconoclasm of the Reformation dealt a serious blow to the art of glass painting in Norwich as elsewhere. Although there was an initial surge in work for glaziers to replace with plain glass the many painted windows which were destroyed, by 1570 glaziers appear in the lists of the poor in the city, including Richard, son of John Goglee, suggested above as the painter of the piece dated 1575 in window nIV.[49] Heraldic glass painting did continue in considerable quantity and is mentioned specifically in the new list of by-laws drawn up in 1618 to govern the glaziers' craft in the city.[50] Some examples of post-Reformation heraldic glass painting are extant in the cathedral and have been described above,[51] but apart from this the only seventeenth-century glass now in the cathedral is that which has been brought from elsewhere and has already been described. Although large figured windows of this century and the next do exist in other cathedrals such as Oxford and York, they are not known to have been made for this building, except possibly for the east window of the gallery in the apse, Trif.I, which contained a depiction of the transfiguration based on a design by Raphael and painted by the wife of Dean Lloyd,[52] whose tenure of this office was from 1765–1790, although Birkin Haward says that it dated from the early years of the next century. This window, however, appears to have been made with 'varnished colours' which were not fired and, not surprisingly, did not last long. It was remade in *c.* 1826 by the glass painter Zobel, working for the Norwich firm of Yarington and was a picture window, presumably painted in enamels, where the lead-lines formed an arbitrary grid which made no attempt to follow the design; it was based on a design by Giulio Romano. By 1847 it had fallen out of favour and was moved to the south transept, where it was destroyed by a bomb blast in 1942. Most of Zobel's other work has now been lost but, according to Birkin Haward, the painted quarries in the top part of window nIV are by him. The replacement for Zobel's window in the apse was by the firm of William Warrington, which painted the two axis clerestory windows on either side of the axis window and reset the central one by Yarington of Norwich, but it was again replaced in 1892 by the present window made by Clayton and Bell.[53]

The three eastern clerestory windows (clerestory I, NII, SII) were the gift of Bishop Stanley in 1846, presumably to commemorate the 750th anniversary of the

---

49. Woodforde, *Norwich School*, p. 206.
50. NRO, Norwich Glaziers, by-laws 1618, case 10.
51. See windows nXXIX, nXXVIII, nXII, nIX, nIV.
52. Dean Lloyd is recorded in 1767 as having persuaded the mayor and aldermen of the city to let him have for the cathedral three painted windows with kings and saints which he had seen in an old disused town

hall in the city, presumably the Guildhall. What happened to this glass is not known. This is in an extract from a letter from Ducarel to Loveday on 5 November 1767, written from the Doctors' Commons, noted by Dennis King in his papers. The original is Bodleian Library, MS Eng. lett. c. 6, fos 64–65.
53. Haward, *Nineteenth Century Norfolk Stained Glass*, p. 224 and gazetteer.

foundation of the cathedral. The axis window is signed with Warrington's monogram and rebus, and all three windows have main lights divided horizontally by a transom. The upper register has a series of the twelve apostles and the lower has in the central window the four evangelists with their symbols and in the two outer a series of historical figures connected with the founding of the see and building of the cathedral of Norwich. The northern window has St Felix, Bishop Bisi, St Humbertus and Herbert de Losinga; the southern window Bishop John of Oxford, Bishop Middleton, King Edward I and King Henry VII.

Warrington's work is more easily seen in window nXXII in the north nave aisle. It dates from the middle of the nineteenth century and consists of three main-light figurative scenes of the visit of the magi, the Crucifixion and the twelve-year-old Christ in the temple, surmounted by canopies containing small figures, with angels in the tracery. This window demonstrates very clearly the change which took place in nineteenth-century glass painting as a result of the Gothic Revival promoted by Pugin, for whom Warrington made windows, as it is a conscious attempt to reproduce the style of the fourteenth century. It was described in 1923 by Milner-White, later dean of York, as 'utterly despicable',[54] but can be seen now as a fine example of this style, with strong and clear design, well-balanced colours and sophisticated technique using abraded ruby and delicate drapery diapers.

The strong colours and medieval style of the Gothic Revival can also be seen in two windows in the south nave aisle, sXXIV, of *c.* 1852 by William Wailes, with the saviour of the world flanked by St Paul and St James the Less, and sXX, of *c.* 1862, by Hardman depicting faith, hope and charity. Other windows of 1860–90 also show a continuing medieval approach based on the thirteenth-century medallion window, such as those in the Jesus Chapel by J. Powell and Son of *c.* 1868 (nVIII) and in St Luke's Chapel by J. Hardman and Co. of *c.* 1873 (sV) and *c.* 1881 (sVII), but an opposing stylistic tendency is seen in the large Crucifixion window in the south transept (fig. 151, Trif.SIX), brought in after 1946 to replace the Zobel window mentioned above. This is French nineteenth-century glass in sixteenth-century Renaissance style and shows that, in the hands of a strong designer and painter, the 'picture window' style could still make a clear and powerful impact, even if the colours are rather strong.

A compromise between the Renaissance picture window and the Gothic Revival is seen in the huge west window of 1854 by George Hedgeland in memory of Bishop Stanley. Here, the six main scenes each extend across three lights, but in the manner of German sixteenth-century glass they are surmounted by Gothic canopies supported on columns. The lower tier of main lights has Old Testament scenes, the discovery of Moses in the rushes, Moses and the brazen serpent and

---

54. Manuscript notes in the possession of Dennis King.

Fig. 151. Crucifixion,
French, nineteenth century,
Trif.SIX.

Moses and the tablets; and the upper tier has the Nativity, Ascension and Christ preaching from the New Testament. The colours of this window are very strong, too much so for some tastes, and the painting is cruder than in most of the other nineteenth-century windows, but it cannot be denied that the window has considerable presence and a very clear design.

There are several windows in the cathedral which date from the 1890s and early

1900s, many being military memorials to the dead of the Boer Wars and First World War. Although the technique of the glass painting is competent in most of them, as a whole they are a disappointing group, with much repetition of subject matter involving St George and St Michael. Even window nXVIII by William Morris and Co. is misjudged in its colouring, with a very dark blue and green background which seems to negate the essence of a glass painting as a transmitter of image and light. Many of them are by Clayton and Bell, a firm capable of technically excellent glass, such as the two windows depicting Gideon, nXIV, and Joshua, nXV, in the north wall of the north transept, but the subject matter is often tedious and unimaginative. Window nXVI is not a war memorial, but illustrates Luke 5:31: 'They that are whole need not a physician but they that are sick', being a memorial to a local surgeon who died in 1903. It suffers from the other fault of many windows of this period of oversentimentality. One attractive window of this period is nXXIII of c. 1909 by the Whitefriars firm of J. Powell and Sons. It depicts various scenes from the life of St Paul. The drawing is competent, although the figured panels are rather dark.

Some nineteenth-century glass in addition to that mentioned above has been removed from the cathedral, for example certain upper windows in the north transept, and what may have been interesting glass of 1864 by O'Connor in sXXII. This latter has been replaced by scenes from the life of St Paul of c. 1880 by J. Hardman and Co. which were originally made for the church of St Margaret of Antioch, Burton on Trent.[55]

More modern military glass is in St Saviour's Chapel, where there are four windows by A.K. Nicholson of some time after 1930. These are better in colour and design, although still rather bland. The largest twentieth-century window is to be found in the Bauchun Chapel. The south window there, sIX, which is by Moira Forsyth and was made by G. King and Son in 1964, depicts the story of the Benedictines in England and is in what has been called the 'scratch and scribble' style of painting. The painting and design are clear and effective, but the colours may not be to everybody's taste.[56]

55. They were acquired by G. King and Son in 1968 and installed in the cathedral in the same year (correspondence in files of G. King and Son). In his report Milner-White described the original O'Connor window as 'wholly bad, vulgar, noxious' (manuscript notes in possession of Dennis King).

56. M. Forsyth, 'The Benedictines in England: Window in Norwich Cathedral', *Journal of the British Society of Master Glass Painters*, 14 (1965), p. 126.

21

The Medieval Decorative Ironwork

Jane Geddes

The surviving decorative ironwork in the cathedral and precincts is of very high quality and in some cases has the significant advantage that it can be dated quite closely by documentary sources. This is especially important because the designs were influential and can be used to date other examples. The items to be discussed below are the doors from the infirmary, the lost doors from the chapter house and the door at the Carnary College (St John's Chapel, in the precinct). There is also a wall painting of a door on the south wall of the ambulatory, by the chapel of St Luke. The great chest in the gallery, Prior Catton's lock and Bishop Nix's sacring bell bracket are mentioned. The cathedral also had an astonishing clock made between 1322 and 1325. Although it has disappeared, the sacrists' rolls give some idea of its complexity. At this stage of the middle ages, most working parts of clocks were made of iron and this one was certainly decorated.

The doors from the cathedral infirmary were salvaged when the infirmary was demolished in 1804 (fig. 152) and erected in Bracondale Woods, Norwich, by Dr Philip Martineau. They were bought by J. and J. Coleman in 1877 and donated to Norwich Museum in 1940. They now hang in Norwich Castle Museum.[1] The woodwork on the front of the doors is original and preserves traces of some lost iron, but the rear framing has been replaced. The doors are decorated with five horizontal rows of scrolls, with traces of a sixth row visible on the wood at the bottom. The semicircular area at the top is filled with two affronted dragons whose wings turn into scrolls. All the scroll terminals are stamped with tiny leaves and rosettes. The overall effect is one of great delicacy and grace. The design of these doors remains unique but the device of two affronted dragons at the top is also

---

1. Norwich Castle Museum records, Inv. no. 102. 940(1). Accounts contemporary with its demolition mistakenly call the infirmary the 'dormitory': J. Alexander and P. Binski, eds, *The Age of Chivalry* (London, 1987), p. 360, no. 336.

Fig. 152. Doors from Norwich Cathedral infirmary, now in Norwich Castle Museum.

found at York chapter house (*c.* 1280s), while stamps of a similar delicacy are found both on the York chapter house doors and on the York cope chest.[2]

The precise original location of the Norwich infirmary doors is not known. The infirmary was built by John of Oxford, bishop of Norwich (1175–1200), which presumably accounts for the Romanesque rounded top to the doors, but the style and technique of the ironwork suggests that they were made at least a century later.[3] After a fire in 1272 the cloister area had to be repaired. In 1297 Bishop John Salmon (1299–1325) paid for building in the cloister, including 'the residue towards the church, together with the door thereof and towards the door leading to the infirmary'.[4] This documentation from the *Itinerary* of William of Worcester is not specific about the ironwork but it does indicate that repair work was being undertaken in the appropriate place at the end of the thirteenth century. The chapter house also received new doors after the fire but they do not survive. They cost £4 6s. 8d. The hinges were made in Dereham where presumably the smith and his boy (*garcione*) lived. It cost 2s. 6d. to bring the doors to Norwich and the smith required four further assistants to install them. The total cost came to £5 3s. 1d.[5] This compares with the £12 paid to Thomas of Leighton for making, transporting and installing the grille over Queen Eleanor's tomb at Westminster in 1293–94.[6]

The original west door to St John's Chapel, Carnary College, now Norwich School, remains in use (fig. 153). The chapel was built by Bishop John Salmon in 1316, who appropriated the income from the church of Westhale to pay for four serving priests. More funds were raised in 1319 to find and maintain ornaments, lamps and other necessaries. By 1337 the furnishing was still incomplete so more funds were raised to pay for 'ornaments' and lights for the chapel.[7] The ironwork was either paid for on completion of the building in 1316, when some kind of door was certainly necessary, or out of the extra funds raised between 1319 and 1337. In either case, the Norwich door provides an approximate date for related ironwork in the surrounding parishes. The iron hinges of St John's Chapel consist of scrolls ending in stamped foliage terminals. These terminals are made with a carved mould

2. E. A. Gee, 'Architectural History until 1290', in G. Aylmer and R. Cant, eds, *A History of York Minster* (Oxford, 1977), p. 136.

3. D. J. Stewart and R. Willis, 'Notes on Norwich Cathedral', *Arch. J.*, 32 (1875), pp. 25–26; D. J. Stewart. 'Notes on Norwich Cathedral: The Cloisters', *Arch. J.*, 32 (1875), p. 176; A. B. Whittingham, 'The Monastic Buildings of Norwich Cathedral', *Arch. J.*, 106 (1949), pp. 86–87, plan.

4. Stewart, 'Notes on Norwich Cathedral: The Cloisters', p. 166. The camera rolls of 1273

mention the infirmary doors: *Communar Rolls*, p. 28.

5. *Communar Rolls*, p. 85.

6. B. Botfield, *Manners and Household Expenses* (Roxburgh Club, 57, 1841), pp. 35, 38.

7. *CPL, 1305–42*, pp. 140–41; *CPR, 1334–38*, p. 523; illustrated in R. and J. Brandon, *Analysis of Gothic Architecture* (London, 1847), section 2, pl. 8; Ecclesiological Society, ed., *Instrumenta ecclesiastica* (London, 1847), p. xxii; R. Bordeaux, *Serrurerie du moyen âge* (Oxford, 1858), p. 29.

Fig. 153. St John's Chapel,
Carnary College (from
Brandon, *Analysis of Gothic
Architecture*, 1847).

or swage and it is possible to trace the work of an individual blacksmith by matching the terminals made with the same stamp. In order to make an accurate comparison, plaster casts were made of all the stamped terminals, using a plasticine impression of the mould.

The hinges at St John's are formed by pairs of scrolls springing from a thick horizontal strap with raised square seatings for nail holes. The triangular area at the top of the door, always awkward to fill,[8] has a vertical stalk springing inorganically from the scroll below. The motif surrounding the door ring was the design most frequently used in the outlying parishes. The raised boss is surrounded by a moulded ring with four straight stalks springing from it, horizontally and vertically. The join between the ring and stalks is covered by a folded leaf and from the stalks spring pairs of leaves and scrolls. On the back of the door, irregular headed nails are used to spell out the letters T: F'rosc. The date or meaning of this inscription is not known although it looks like a name.

8.   For instance at Reepham (Norfolk) and Turvey (Bedfordshire).

The ring plates at Wickhampton and Filby in Norfolk (figs 154 and 155) are simplified versions of this, having the stalks and pairs of leaves but no scrolls. The ring plate at Stokesby (Norfolk) is based on a concave-sided diamond; stalks radiate from the boss diagonally as well as horizontally and vertically (fig. 156). These ring plates have exactly the same stamps as the St John's hinges, although differences in weathering, filing and haphazard repairs tend to obscure this. The three churches of Wickhampton, Filby and Stokesby, all near Great Yarmouth, were built in the first half of the fourteenth century, Stokesby (*c.* 1330–50) being the latest.[9] The small ring plates may all have been sent to these rural districts from a Norwich workshop because examples at Alderford (Norfolk) and Irstead (Norfolk), much more rustic in character, seem to be poorer local imitations.

Fig. 154. Wickhampton, Norfolk.

A fifth example of iron from this workshop may be a reproduction. The hinges at Crostwick (Norfolk) are on an exposed, new, north door and are in better condition than the four other pieces which are all deep inside porches (fig. 157). However, an undated drawing from the nineteenth century by Buckler shows the hinges as they are today, so if there are copies, they are certainly accurate imitations of medieval work.[10] Like the hinges at St John's, they have raised square seatings for nails on the profiled scrolls. The cinquefoil is the same size and type as those in the Norwich group but it is not from the same die.[11] The asymmetrical leaf at Crostwick is exactly like one type in the Norwich group but the rest of the stamps, fleurs-de-lys and trefoils are different. Allowing for the fact that the Crostwick hinges could be recent copies, their basic design shows that they are related to the Norwich group, but are probably later than the rest

---

9. I would like to thank Dr Christopher Wilson for his views on these churches.
10. J. Buckler, BL, Additional MS 36433, fo. 625.

11. At Wickhampton and Norwich there is a slight irregularity on the lower right edge of the central lobe but at Crostwick the stamp is perfectly symmetrical.

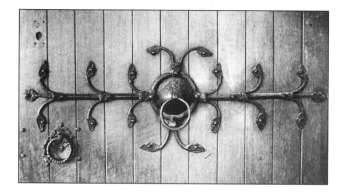

Fig. 155. Filby, Norfolk.

Fig. 156. Stokesby, Norfolk.

Fig. 157. Crostwick,
Norfolk.

Fig. 158. Orton Longueville,
Cambridgeshire.

and are datable *c.* 1340–60. Perhaps the replacement stamps and designs were made when the old set wore out.

A distant outlier at Orton Longueville by Peterborough is work of the same period and quality but by a different smith (fig. 158). The hinges on the chancel door have erroneously been attributed to Thomas of Leighton, the maker of the grille over Queen Eleanor's tomb in Westminster Abbey.[12] The cinquefoil stamp at the centre of the short scrolls is of the same type and size as used in the Norwich group, but the arrangement of veins between the lobes is different. There are also obvious technical differences between the nail seatings. At Orton Longueville they are elongated, flat and curved at one end, while on the Norwich work they are square. They bear no resemblance to Thomas of Leighton's work.

12. *VCH Huntingdonshire* (London, 1936), iii, p. 193; P. Royston, 'Orton Longville Church', *JBAA*, new series, 5 (1899), p. 100.

In 1950 Professor Tristram drew in considerable detail the remains of a painted door on the wall at the south end of the ambulatory in the cathedral (fig. 159).[13] Hardly any of this survives today so his illustration is the main evidence for its design. Scant traces of a cluster of ironwork scrolls are painted in the recess above

Fig. 159. Norwich Cathedral, wall painting on south side of ambulatory (from Tristram, *English Medieval Wall Paintings*, 1950).

the Losinga effigy, now moved to the south ambulatory from the exterior of the transept. The design on Tristram's illustration shows bold stamped terminals and a central circular ring boss. This is not unlike the ironwork on the Carnary College door. In particular they share a small detail in stamp design: the pronounced bar at the base of the fleurs-de-lys. This is not found on any other surviving examples of iron stamps and may suggest a direct connection between the wall painter and the smith. Another local example of painted iron hinges is at Horsham St Faith, just outside Norwich. Here the hinge design of paired scrolls is quite similar to the Norwich painting, but no attempt is made to depict the detail of stamped terminals. Most painted illustrations of decorative ironwork, usually found in manuscripts depicting chests or door hinges, tend to be somewhat schematic as at Horsham St Faith. This is why the wall painting at Norwich Cathedral seems unusually detailed, illustrating a specific metal-working technique, namely the bold stamp designs. Tristram dates the painting to 1272–78. However, a comparison between the delicate work of the infirmary doors (made after the fire, in the last quarter of the thirteenth century) and the bold design of those at Carnary College (1316–37) indicates that the painting is closer in concept to the later work (figs 152, 153, 159).

A substantial medieval chest survives in the north gallery of the presbytery (fig. 160).[14] Its ironwork is fairly plain and, unfortunately, dendrochronological

13. E. W. Tristram, *English Medieval Wall Painting*, 2 vols (London, 1950), ii, p. 355, pl. 102.

14. 30 in. × 69 in. × 28 in. (76 cm. high, 176 cm. long, 68 cm. wide).

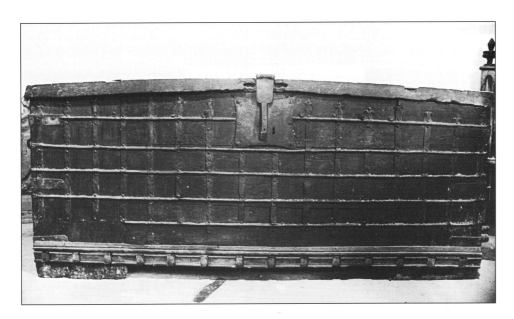

Fig. 160. Norwich Cathedral, chest in gallery.

examination by Dr John Fletcher suggested its tree rings were unsuitable for dating purposes. The woodwork indicates it is a composite piece. The base has four broad styles (vertical planks) forming the front and back corners. Three horizontal boards join each pair of styles with tongue and groove joints. The ends are held by an external ladder frame fixed to the front and back by iron corner brackets. The framing is a later addition because the brackets overlie the decorative iron bars on the front. The billet moulding across the bottom front of the chest is later still as it partially covers the corner brackets. The top edge of the front and back of the chest is bowed upwards. The flanges at the ends of the lid are reused from a pin-hinge chest (an early medieval design using only a wooden swivel to support the lid). Tenon joints projecting from the front of the flanges suggest they were once attached to another type of lid bracing. The lid itself is made of simple wooden tracery panels. Inside, there is a shelf all around the top edge of the chest and several wooden pegs project inwards from the front and back faces. This sort of chest could have been used to store documents, plate or vestments.

The original ironwork of the chest consists of five slender horizontal bars of irregular section crossed by sixteen thin vertical bands ending in simple, cut fleurs-de-lys. The back has thin plain horizontal bands. The lid is held by four thick plain strap hinges, contemporary with the central hasp and lock plate. The square lock plate has concave sides and two ribs to provide a seating for the hasp. On the lid are four further locks set into the wood, covered by plain rotating discs. The chest

161a. Norwich Cathedral, the Catton lock, west side, showing part of the door handle below.

161b. Norwich Cathedral, the Catton lock, east side.

is a unique piece and consequently hard to date. However, the front and back of the base are probably fourteenth century. The chest was apparently remade or extensively repaired in the fifteenth century: the side framing and corner brackets were added; and the lid was constructed from fifteenth-century tracery panels supported by twelfth- or thirteenth-century pin-hinge flanges. The billet moulding, possibly also a salvaged piece, was put on after the corner brackets.

Prior Catton (1504–29) produced his distinctive lock plates for the door in the south transept leading to the south aisle of the presbytery (figs 161a and 161b). On the west side a raised cable pattern makes a rim and horizontal division across the rectangular plate. The upper panel has the initials RC linked by scrollwork. The lower panel has the initials PN and the keyhole scutcheon. The initials stand for Robert Catton, Prior of Norwich. On the east face the keyhole is surrounded by a raised heart-shaped rim from which sprouts an elaborate foliage design.

Lock plates identifying their patron appear at the very end of the fifteenth century. Bishop Edmund Audley of Hereford (1492–1502) began his chantry there before he was translated to Salisbury and the building was completed by his successor.[15] Audley's lock plate at Hereford has his initials in Lombardic lettering and an interlocking grid above the keyhole. Sir Reginald Bray helped to complete the nave and transepts of St George's Windsor between 1503 and 1509. He had his rebus of the hemp bray or crushing tool carved on the stone work and also used his device on the lock plate at the entrance to his chapel.[16]

Immediately below Catton's lock plate is a medieval door handle fixed on by a

15. Royal Commission on Historical Monuments, *Herefordshire*, 3 vols (London, 1931–37), i, p. 107.

16. W. H. St J. Hope, *Windsor Castle: An Architectural History* (London, 1913), p. 451.

bracket of two flat rosettes (fig. 161a). They are attached to the door with rough, hand-made nails. The rosettes and nails contrast noticeably with the precise work-manship of the Catton lock above and appear to be about a century earlier in date. Flat rosettes chiselled in this way are found on the remarkably well-preserved cupboard doors of the Zouche Chapel, York Minster. These have been dated 1395–1410 by dendrochronology, which ties in well with the surrounding archi-tecture. Rosettes are also found on the large cupboard in the muniment room at Westminster Abbey, dated by dendrochronology to 'after 1390'. The cupboard is painted with white stars, matching those on the wall painting immediately behind. The painting depicts a white hart, the emblem of King Richard II (1377–99). So, it is likely that the rosette door handle in Norwich was made around 1400, but it is not known when the door was made or the handle attached.[17] As the vaulting of the south transept was completed by Bishop Nix (1501–35/36), it is likely that Prior Catton's lock was installed at this time in the preexisting doorway as part of the works in the south transept area.

Bishop Nix provided a small and unusual iron survivor from the middle ages. His chantry, situated seven bays west of the crossing between the piers of the south arcade, still has the bracket for supporting the sacring bell. It is placed above the capitals of the western pier. The rectangular bracket supports a swivel which would have linked the rope and bell. The bell was rung at the elevation of the host. Very few sacring bells survived the Reformation but similar brackets are found at Milton Abbey (Dorset) and Salhouse (Norfolk).[18]

Norwich Cathedral, according to Beeson, was one of the earliest in Britain to have a mechanical clock.[19] The first recorded *horologium* was made at Dunstable Priory in 1283, but already by 1290–91 Norwich was repairing its clock. By 1322 its cord was being replaced, proving that it was a weight-driven machine. At that date it is called *antiquum horologium* (the old clock) because the great new astronomical clock was being made. Expenses for the astronomical clock are recorded on the sacrists' rolls between 1322 and 1325 and they provide the earliest detailed account of clock making in England.[20] Its construction clearly represented state-of-the-art

17. J. M. Fletcher and M. C. Tapper, 'Medieval Artefacts and Structures Dated by Dendro-chronology', *Medieval Archaeology*, 35 (1984), pp. 123–24.

18. A. G. G. Thurlow, *Church Bells and Ringers of Norwich* (Norwich, 1948), p. 42. I would like to thank Paul Cattermole for providing me with this reference.

19. C. F. C. Beeson, *English Church Clocks, 1280–1850* (London, 1971), pp. 15–18, 104.

20. The sacrists' rolls extract is printed in F. Madden, 'Original Documents', *Arch. J.*, 12 (1855), pp. 175–77; H. W. Saunders, *Intro-duction to the Obedientiary and Manor Rolls of Norwich Cathedral Priory* (Norwich, 1930); and translated in H. Harrod, *Gleanings among the Castles and Convents of Norfolk* (Norwich, 1857), appendix C, pp. 339–42. I would like to thank Barbara Dodwell for pointing out the chapter house door and clock accounts.

technology: Robert de Turri and his successors twice wrecked the 87 lb. (39 kg.) engraved dial. The work could only be completed when Master Roger the clock-maker came from London in 1325. Wages and fur robes were dispensed to three clockmakers, Master Roger de Stoke for two years eleven weeks, Laurence for two years and Robert for four terms. Smiths, carpenters, masons and plasterers were also paid. Materials included iron bars and sheets, brass, copper, latten and small bells from Canterbury. The clock had a gilded sun and moon and automata including fifty-nine images and a choir of monks. White and red lead, silver foil, oil and other colours were used for the images. Adam the woodcarver, and the painter who did the colouring and gilding, worked in Norwich and dined at the prior's table. The whole project cost £52 9s. 6d. Tillett states that this mechanical wonder is said to have been burnt in the seventeenth century.[21]

Norwich Cathedral preserves a broad selection of medieval ironwork, and the rare occurrence of documentary evidence, even though the manuscripts and iron do not directly relate to each other. Objects missing from the list are any remains of Romanesque doors, hinges and chests, to complement the twelfth-century archi-tecture. In this respect local parish churches have proved more fortunate in preserving their Romanesque fittings, with splendid ironwork still surviving at Raveningham, Haddiscoe (much restored), Kirby Bedon, Runhall and Quidenham. The designs of ironwork at these churches are very varied and it would be unwise to assume that they necessarily reflect the superior craftwork commissioned for the cathedral. Most medieval cathedrals had some form of iron grille work around the choir ambulatory. This only survives *in situ* at Lincoln, but fragments are found at Canterbury and Winchester. Holes in the stonework of the choir piers at Norwich show that some form of barrier has been removed. Episcopal tombs, such as those of Bishop Beckynton at Wells and Archbishops Courtenay and Chichele at Canter-bury, all made in the fifteenth century, are guarded with magnificent railings. No medieval tomb railings, from ecclesiastics or laymen, survive at Norwich. Very few British cathedrals, apart from Canterbury, preserve a complete spectrum of decorative ironwork to complement all phases of the architecture. Norwich Cathedral, with its high quality examples which can be dated with reasonable accuracy, provides a valuable yardstick for dating and assessing more parochial work.

21. Norwich Central Library, Norfolk Studies Collection, Tillett MS 376, vol. 1, part 2, p. 88. Quoted in Thurlow, *Church Bells*, p. 42.

22

The Medieval
Conventual Seals

T. A. Heslop

The corporate seals of religious houses in the middle ages provided a perfect vehicle for disseminating the self-image of the institution. Charters and letters issued by the chapter circulated widely: indeed (since their primary function was to secure the validity of the text they accompanied) their seals needed to be well known so that the authenticity of impressions could be verified. While it would perhaps be overstating the case to call them inevitable sites of propaganda, they none the less had a real potential for conveying visual and verbal messages which left the viewer in little doubt about the 'personality' that the church wished to convey to the world.

In the late eleventh and early twelfth centuries in England there were essentially two options open to a religious corporation ordering a seal matrix. A native, Anglo-Saxon tradition favoured the ideographic representation of a church sur-rounded by a legend which stressed the institutional character of the object by including the word *ecclesia* (church). By contrast, the scheme which was widespread on the continent preferred a depiction of the dedicatory saint and a legend that claimed that this was his or her own personal seal.[1] So whereas the English pre-Conquest type gained its authority from association with the place, its buildings and corporation, the alternative, which became widespread in the British Isles after the Conquest, and may be seen as in some sense a Norman import, stressed instead the power of a holy patron. In both cases the aim was to encourage those who received sealed documents from the chapter to take them very seriously because of

---

1. T. A. Heslop, 'English Seals from the Mid Ninth Century to 1100', *JBAA*, 133 (1980), pp. 1–16, esp. pp. 7–9 and 13–14; G. Zar-necki, J. Holt and T. Holland, eds, *English* Romanesque Art, 1066–1100 (Arts Council of Great Britain, London, 1984), cat. 347–52, 356, 360.

their association with a potency greater than just the group of individuals who had drawn up the text. It was not long before those who were unable to decide between these alternatives, or who wanted the best of both worlds, hit on the idea of combining these two types so that hybrid formulae appear, showing the dedicatee in association with a building. The earliest known conventual seal of Norwich Cathedral is a remarkable and precocious instance of this new, hybrid genre (fig. 162).[2]

Fig. 162. First conventual seal of Norwich Cathedral Priory, *c.* 1125–40, 60 mm. diameter. Cast at the Society of Antiquaries, London, from an original on Canterbury Cathedral Archives, Ch. Ant. D12, of 1227.

Elsewhere in the twelfth century a dedication to Christ (as St Saviour or Christ Church) or to the Holy Trinity occasioned rather predictable responses. The phrase 'Christ Church' could stimulate the schematic image of a church, but much the most common iconography was Christ in Majesty, seated on a rainbow, raising his right hand in blessing and holding a book in his other hand.[3] This awesome reminder of final judgement would have encouraged recipients of documents verified with such a seal to heed the ultimate sanction against those who set at naught the will of God – or of his church. At Norwich, however, this appropriate and ubiquitous formula was disregarded and a very unexpected alternative was adopted. This was the virtual copying of the design on the reverse of the gold bulls of contemporary German kings and emperors.[4]

In its native context this image, which had been developed gradually over about a century, represented the emperor within the walls of Rome. He dominates the city but he also protects it, and his authority is manifest in his crown, orb and sceptre. On early versions of the type the city wall is quite strongly angled in the

2.   The Norwich seal is W. de G. Birch, *Catalogue of Seals in the Department of Manuscripts in the British Museum*, 6 vols (London, 1887), i, nos 2091–92. For another hybrid type of the same period, see Birch, *Catalogue*, i, nos 1963–65, and illustration in Zarnecki, Holt and Holland, *English Romanesque Art*, cat. 353.

3.   Majesty seals of this kind appear at, for example, Lenton (Notts.), Kirkham (Yorks.), Faversham (Kent) and Markyate (Beds.): Birch, *Catalogue*, i, nos 3456, 3360, 3147 and 3632. For a 'topographical' seal for this dedication at Christchurch (Hants.), see Birch, *Catalogue*, i, no. 4220.

4.   O. Posse, *Die Siegel der Deutschen Kaiser und Könige von 751 bis 1913*, 5 vols (Dresden, 1909–13), i, passim.

centre, but by the date of the imperial bull of Frederick Barbarossa (1154/55) the wall has become more nearly horizontal, with its three towers spread out almost in a line across the base of the seal (fig. 163).[5] This is most like the version used at Norwich Cathedral, but a straightforward derivation of it from the German prototype is complicated by the fact that the earliest known use of the Norwich seal, of 1145 at the latest, predates Frederick's by about a decade.[6] We are forced to suppose that the form used at Norwich took an earlier model even though the only surviving candidate, the bull of the Emperor Lothar datable to 1133 or soon afterwards, does not look so similar. We can also infer that enlarging and straightening out the city wall, into a form more closely resembling an ecclesiastical edifice, was a deliberate alteration made at Norwich so as to adjust the civic and temporal meaning of the bull of a secular ruler to local expectations about ecclesiastical seals. This motive is supported by the character of the legend, which has *ecclesia* as its final word, just as though it were in the Anglo-Saxon 'topographi-

Fig. 163. Imperial gold bull of Frederick Barbarossa, 1154/55, based on his royal bull of 1152, 60 mm. diameter. Cast in the Archives Nationales, Paris.

cal' tradition. Equally important changes were made to the figure. To begin with he was provided with a cruciform halo, to identify him as Christ. Though the sceptre was retained in his right hand, the orb was removed from his left, the hand being raised and its fingers extended and the open palm turned to face the spectator. The elevation of the hand and the position of his head, which breaks through the legend rim to touch the very top of the seal, both convey the impression of ascent.

These alterations raise the question: what did the chapter of Norwich intend their seal to represent? For several reasons it is unlikely to have been Christ's Ascension, which would anyway normally require the presence of the apostles. Perhaps, then, it is the Resurrection. Depictions of Christ rising from his tomb are rare before the thirteenth century, but of the handful that are known several have features in common with Norwich Cathedral's first seal. A good example is the plaque on the

5. Posse, *Siegel der Kaiser*, i, 22, 3–4 and R. Haussherr, ed., *Die Zeit der Staufer*, 4 vols (Würtembergisches Landesmuseum, Stuttgart, 1977), i, cat. 31.

6. On BL, Campbell Charter XII. 2, Birch, *Catalogue*, i, no. 2091; and *English Episcopal Acta*, vi, *Norwich, 1070–1214*, ed. C. Harper-Bell (Oxford, 1990), no. 37.

left arm of the front of the so-called 'Bury St Edmunds Cross', an elaborate walrus ivory carving covered with scenes, figures and inscriptions, and dating to about 1170. On it we see Christ, holding a short cross in his right hand and raising his open left palm upwards as he ascends from the sarcophagus.[7] On this analogy there can be little doubting that the subject matter of the seal is the same.

The significance of this choice is rather more difficult to assess. The usual way of alluding visually to the Resurrection at this period was simply by a representation of the Maries' visit to the sepulchre and their conversation with the angel. The unusual decision at Norwich to show Christ himself places the emphasis very clearly on the corporeality of the miracle. This may have been done for doctrinal reasons, for example to support the idea of the real presence of his living flesh in the transubstantiated eucharistic bread.

Fig. 164. Counterseal, early thirteenth century, 35 mm. by 25 mm., on Canterbury Cathedral Archives, Ch. Ant. D12, of 1227.

Another way of looking at it is, though, that it stresses a central mystery of the faith in an event that clearly links the bodily and the spiritual, the earthly and the heavenly. One of the surviving impressions of this seal bears a small counterseal showing a figure seated at a desk writing. The legend around its perimeter reads QUARE CELESTIA PER TERRESTRIA (seek heavenly things through earthly things) (fig. 164).[8] Although more overtly Neo-Platonic in its stress on revelation through the contemplation of divine history and creation, it is a parallel for the interest in moments of transcendence which also underlies the image on the large seal. Although we do not know whether the counterseal belonged to the chapter as a whole rather than to, for example, the prior, there is a good chance that the two seals were seen as complementing each other; indeed that the counterseal was made specifically as an extension of, or commentary on, the image of the Resurrection. As such it was an invitation to the

7.   E. Parker and C. Little, *The Cloisters Cross* (London, 1994), col. pl. VI, ill. 56.

8.   The counterseal appears on Canterbury, Cathedral Archives, Ch. Ant. D12 of 1227, which is the source of the casts of the obverse and reverse catalogued by Birch, *Catalogue*, i, as his no. 2091.

Fig. 165. Second conventual seal of Norwich Cathedral Priory, 1258, 80 mm. diameter, a) obverse, b) reverse. Casts at the Society of Antiquaries, London.

individual Christian whose body was locked in this world to allow his spirit the freedom to transcend.

In 1258 the seal we have been discussing was replaced by one that was substantially larger and had a double matrix which impressed both front and back of the wax with images of the same size (fig. 165).[9] At 3.1 inches (80 mm.) in diameter there was ample space on the two sides for the minute detail in which the best engravers of the day specialised. The format is closely derived from the two-sided seal then in use at Canterbury Cathedral in that it shows very similar schematic ecclesiastical edifices, though the various openings in the façades are occupied by different characters (fig. 166).[10] On its main face the new Norwich seal carries the legend +SIGILLUM ECCLESIE SANCTE TRINITATIS NORWICI (the seal of the church of Holy Trinity, Norwich), but very surprisingly makes no attempt to depict the Trinity or any of its members (Canterbury had shown Christ). Instead there is a full-length figure of a bishop, and inscribed beneath his feet the identification HERBERTUS FUNDATOR (Herbert the founder). To each side of him are three heads of other bishops and above are two angels with censers, descending from heaven and apparently directed towards Herbert (whereas at Canterbury the angels had censed Christ).

9. Birch, *Catalogue*, i, nos 2093–2101.
10. They are reproduced side by side in Birch, *Catalogue*, i, plate ix, and discussed by H. S. Kingsford, 'Some Medieval English Seal Engravers', *Arch. J.*, 97 (1940), pp. 155–79, who suggests a common authorship. In my view this is unlikely. For Canterbury see further T. A. Heslop, 'The Conventual Seals of Canterbury Cathedral, 1066–1232', in BAACT, 5, *Canterbury, 1979*, ed. N. Coldstream and P. Draper (1982), pp. 94–100.

Fig. 166. Third conventual seal of Canterbury Cathedral Priory, 1232, 93 mm. diameter, a) obverse, b) reverse. Casts at the Society of Antiquaries, London.

This image needs to be seen in the context of the thirteenth-century enthusiasm for early Norman bishops who 'refounded' their sees, of which the contemporary 'cults' of Osmund at Salisbury and Remigius at Lincoln are the clearest examples. There was, though, a general sense that the early post-Conquest period had been an age of episcopal saints. Wulfstan was already canonised, and Lanfranc and Anselm were held in very high regard, various attempts having been made to acquire papal approval for the latter's sanctification. It may well be that the failure of St William of Norwich to attract serious attention was causing the community to look for another cult focus, and in this clerical age Losinga would anyway have been far more to the chapter's tastes.

It is on the reverse that we find what might have been expected on the front: an image of Christ blessing. He is placed centrally, his half-length figure emerging from cloud. In a lower register beneath him, shown taking place in a double doorway in the façade, is the Annunciation. This pairing, of the celestial Christ with the moment of the incarnation, is another example of the ideas we encountered on the first seal and counterseal, of juxtaposing spirit and flesh, heaven and earth. It is one of many examples from religious houses of the way in which an iconography promulgated on an early seal is perpetuated in slightly different guise on a later replacement. To either side of this christological axis is a pair of tonsured heads, presumably designating this side of the seal as the 'conventual' face whereas the other had been relentlessly episcopal.

As though to express the piety and learning of the monks, the surrounding legend comprises a complicated pair of Leonine verses:

+EST MICHI NUMEN IDEM TRIBUS UNI LAUS HONOR IDEM
ET BENEDICO GREGI FAMULATUR QUI MICHI REGI

Such compositions are rarely susceptible of very satisfactory translation. Literally these lines may be interpreted in the following way: 'The same divine will is to me [Christ] as to the three [the Holy Trinity], the praise and honour of one is the same [i.e. it passes to all three]; and I bless the flock which serves me as king'. The stress on the function of the monastic chapter to praise and honour Christ and the Trinity is, of course, highly appropriate. The blessing that they receive in return would seem equally straightforward were it not for the conjunction of its wording, emphasising that Christ is king, and the date of the matrix, 1258.

In common with a few other houses, Norwich chose to place a date on its new matrix. It does not appear on either face, but on the edge of the impressions at ninety degrees to the main images. Edge inscriptions of any sort are pretentious because they imply a kind of seal even more intricate and complex than this one. Some seals, such as that from Canterbury Cathedral referred to above, employed four matrices which produced two separate discs of wax which had to be glued together after they had been impressed. To mask and secure the join between the two laminae a fifth matrix was lightly heated and turned around the edge to weld over the crack. At one level, then, the dating inscription implies that Norwich had a four-part matrix. By a small miracle we know that it did not. The miracle is that one face of the matrix of 1258 (the obverse) still survives at the cathedral, although it has been broken in half to cancel its validity. It was only ever part of a pair, not of a four-part matrix.[11]

It may be uncharitable to suppose a deliberate intention to deceive on the part of the chapter, for there are several reasons for wanting to date a matrix and they may have been at a loss to know where else to place the information. One reason is legal. In general the currency of one matrix takes over from that of another. So this dated matrix is a way of saying that after 1258 the old seal is invalid. This recourse would be particularly important if there was a forged matrix of the old seal in circulation. But there was perhaps also a political reason for including the information. 1258 was a tumultuous year in England. It saw the nadir of Henry III's fortunes: ignominious capitulation to Louis of France; the end of his cherished ambitions to gain the throne of Sicily for his son Edmund; and his submission to rule by council which is now taken as the origin of parliamentary government. There is, then, a real possibility that the legend of the new seal should be read as emphasising service to the King of Heaven because the temporal monarch has proved so unreliable. It is certainly quite difficult to imagine anyone in public life

---

11. NRO, DCN 129.

in England during 1258 who was capable of construing the Latin verse failing to see that this was a possible interpretation. It was a period of intense political comment and satire at virtually all levels of society. It is but a short step from that observation to the view that the monks of Norwich were taking advantage of King Henry's misfortunes to remind people that there was a higher authority who, in return for praise and honour, bestowed an eternal and unshakable reward on those who served him. The monastic community of Norwich were the faithful courtiers of this King of Kings. Even if the political circumstances did not themselves provoke the making of a new seal at the cathedral, having decided for whatever reason to commission this grand double matrix the chapter was not going to let the opportunity pass by without commenting to its own advantage on the nation's affairs.

Of course the message on the seal had an enduring validity; it is no surprise that it continued in use until the Reformation. Indeed, in many respects it persisted longer, for though the matrix with the depictions of Christ and the Annunciation was remade so as to omit imagery which had become offensive to the authorities, the old legend of the reverse was retained. So too, more surprisingly was the edge inscription with its reference to the year 1258.

23

Aspects of Heraldry and Patronage

Tony Sims

The armorial material will be dealt with chronologically, where possible, and blazoned unless published material can be referred to.

The ground floor radiating chapels contain two of the earliest examples of heraldic wall painting in the country, both dated to the thirteenth century. The first relates to Hubert de Burgh, justiciar (1215–31) to King John and Henry III. He bore lozengy gules and vair (fig. 167). This design, when extended into linear form, runs each side of the groin vault ridges of the Jesus Chapel. The design, albeit now restored, is ideally suited for this type of decoration as it readily retains its heraldic identity.[1] Vair, an heraldic fur, derives from cutting patterns for cloak linings using the winter coat of the Siberian squirrel; the white and blue of the back and underside when placed side by side give an overall alternating effect.

It has been suggested either that the chapel was decorated by the great justiciar, perhaps as a compliment to his nephew Bishop Thomas Blundeville (1226–36), or that Hubert's son John (d. before 1274) restored the chapel after the great fire of 1272.[2] The former suggestion seems more likely, since during his nephew's episcopate Hubert was constable of Norwich Castle (where the present museum

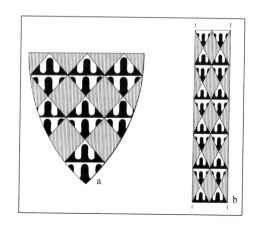

Fig. 167. The arms of Hubert de Burgh:
a) shield; b) section of groin-vault ridge
in the Jesus Chapel.

1. Another example of this design used in linear decoration is a border around a St Christopher wall painting at Little Wenham church, Suffolk; Hubert held the honour of Eye, only a few miles away.

2. H. C. Beeching, 'The Chapels and Altars of Norwich Cathedral', *Architect and Contract Reporter*, 3 (December 1915).

has a harness pendant of his arms). There is no evidence that fire spread to this section of cathedral when it was sacked in 1272.

The second example of early heraldic wall painting is to be found on the soffit of the entrance arch to the southern radiating chapel (St Luke's). It depicts a red lion rampant facing the sinister (in deference to the chapel altar) set in a lozenge with a whitish field, the latter probably the ground for the gold of the Scottish coat (fig. 168). The indented border simply fits the overall chapel decoration and is not relevant to the shield, but the lozenge denoting female arms is thirteenth-century painting.[3] Since Hubert de Burgh's third wife was Margaret, sister of Alexander II, king of Scotland, this heraldry could be hers. It may be then, that there is husband and wife patronage of these two chapels.

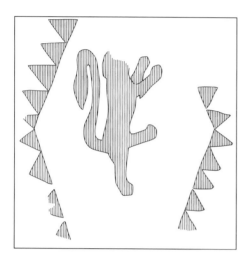

Fig. 168. Lion from a wall painting in St Luke's Chapel.

One of the great treasures of the fourteenth-century cathedral must have been the Ormesby Psalter, named after the monk Robert of Ormesby who donated it to the priory, perhaps in the 1330s.[4] The psalter was, however, commissioned earlier, and not by the Ormesbys, whose heraldry is not to be found in the volume. The heart-shaped shields within coral-coloured medallions decorating the fore edges of the book can tell us something about the date and provenance of the psalter. On the top edge nearest the spine appear the earliest recorded example of the priory arms, argent, a cross sable, followed by Ufford, sable, a cross engrailed or. The only coat discernible on the long edge (near the top) is the arms of the see, azure, three mitres or. The bottom edge nearest the spine has Ufford and the next coat appears to be England, the three gold lions on a red field. Cockerell mentions the quartered shield of England with England in the first quarter, dating this shield to between 1327 and 1339.[5] The absence of

3. Transcription by Keith Darby from E. W. Tristram's notebooks on the wall paintings in the Victoria and Albert Museum, London.

4. It is now Bodleian Library, MS Douce 366.

5. S. C. Cockerell and M. R. James, *Two East Anglian Psalters at the Bodleian Library Oxford* (Roxburghe Club, London, 1926), p. 3. The edges are so uneven now that this identification is, however, unreliable. M. Michael, 'The Little Land of England is Preferred before the Great Kingdom of France: The Quartering of The Royal Arms by Edward III', in D. Buckton and T. A. Heslop, eds, *Studies in Medieval Art and Architecture* (Stroud, 1994), p. 113.

marks of difference of bends sinister and dexter on the Ufford arms shows that this shield belongs either to the first Ufford earl of Suffolk, created in 1336, or the second and last Ufford earl, created in *c.* 1369. The heraldry may, therefore, indicate that the volume was owned by, or designed for, the Ufford family shortly before it was acquired by Robert of Ormesby and donated to Norwich Cathedral Priory.

Unique heraldry appears in the historiated initial on fo. 38r (plate IIb). This is the beginning of Psalm 27 'Dominus illuminatio mea et salus mea' (the Lord is my light and my salvation). It illustrates the anointing of David by Samuel and Our Lord handing down a shield to David, azure, on a cross argent, the sprouting tree of life. This shield would seem to be a unique attribution and it is used to allude to 'the Spirit of the Lord coming upon David' (Samuel 16:13). A knight on the left, representing Goliath, clearly bears, on surcoat and shield, the Foliot arms, but with gold bend probably to difference a branch of the family.[6]

The private seal of Bishop Henry Despenser (1369–1406) carries his shield à couché (on the side) from a large mantled helm surmounted by a mitre supporting the crest of a silver griffin head of ample size (fig. 169). On the dexter side of his shield are the arms of the see, which was its first use on a seal; and on the sinister, uniquely, the arms of his mother, Anne, daughter of William Lord Ferrers of Groby, gules, seven mascles voided, or.[7] Despenser's arms also appear on the so-called Despenser retable in St Luke's Chapel, dated to the years of his episcopate.[8]

Fig. 169. Privy seal of Bishop Henry Despenser.

The arms of Bishop Wakering (1415–25) appear in the spandrels of the stone doorway arch to the present clergy vestry, which was originally built as his chapel off the south ambulatory. The stonework has been reerected so that the armorial spandrels now face inwards. They contain Wakering impaling the priory, and those of the see impaling Wakering, argent, three hawks' lures stringed sable, a crescent for difference, and what appears to be a carved representation of the Blessed Virgin Mary in splendour at the arch apex. Wakering

6. Cockerell and James, *Two East Anglian Psalters*, p. 16.

7. C. Boutell, *English Heraldry* (London, 1899), p. 189.

8. See above, pp. 410–13.

sealed with a pelican vulning (wounding its own breast to feed its young on the blood, an allusion to the redemption of mankind through Christ's self- sacrificing death) and this appears in painted shield form in the south spandrel of the west face of the reliquary arch, much worn, but the drops of blood can be clearly seen.[9]

Nearby, in the now demolished reliquary chapel, a number of paving tiles, both four-and-a-half and nine inches square, were found in the nineteenth century. The latter are incised with the arms of Morley impaling Despenser (fig. 170).[10] Apparently tiles of both sizes remain under the wall of the blocked-up arch on the north side. A recently examined 9 in. (23 cm.) tile with these arms using both counter-relief

Fig. 170. Tile with the arms of Morley impaling Despenser, from the reliquary chapel.

and incised methods is probably the only patterned tile extant in Norwich Cathedral.[11] Thomas, Lord Morley (d. 1417), married secondly Anne (d. 1426), daughter of Edward, Lord Despenser, and niece of Bishop Henry Despenser of Norwich. It seems likely, therefore, that Lord and Lady Morley contributed to the cost of the chapel when it was extended east and west in 1424.

The panelling of the clergy vestry is from St Benet's Abbey and shows the abbey arms, sable, a crozier in pale between two ducal coronets or, the hand of God issuant from the dexter corner; this shield is also to be seen in the window of the vestment room except that the hand is from the sinister. Wakering and the priory are the two other shields in the same window all in coloured glass.

The Erpingham or 'Church' Gate, as it was called until the eighteenth century, was built as a memorial to Sir Thomas Erpingham (1357–1428).[12] Whether it was completed before or after his death is uncertain, but the heraldry leaves no doubt that it cannot have been started earlier than 1410. The columnar decoration and spandrels on the western face are covered with ecclesiastical and Erpingham heraldry. This includes his devices of the forget-me-not, the crowned falcon rising, his motto

9. T. G. Bayfield, 'A Descriptive Catalogue of the Seals of the Bishops of Norwich', *NA*, 1 (1847), p. 319.

10. E. M. Goulburn, 'The Confessio or Relic Chapel, an Ancient Chamber in Norwich Cathedral', *NA*, 9 (1884), p. 279.

11. Christopher Norton, Centre for Medieval Studies, University of York: letter of 18 April 1994.

12. A. P. Sims, 'The Church Gate of Norwich Cathedral Priory' (unpublished University of East Anglia B.A. thesis, 1990).

'Yenk' (think or remember), and the arms of his two wives, Joan Clopton (d. 1404) sable, a bend argent cotised indented or; and Joan Walton (d. 1424) argent, on a chief indented sable, three bezants. The pediment niche now contains a kneeling

figure of Sir Thomas Erpingham in armour and armorial surcoat (fig. 171), vert around an escutcheon, an orle of eight martlets argent and around the neck a collar of Esses with the Garter of that Most Noble Order below the left knee (awarded in 1401) and iron spur at the ankle. This figure was not originally in the niche. An early eighteenth-century illustration does not show it and Francis Blomefield, writing in the 1740s, is the first to describe its presence in the niche.[13] Moreover, recent inspection shows the niche to have been broken through to enable the base of the figure to fit on this plinth. What originally occupied this niche is a matter of conjecture, but the shield at the main arch head may provide the clue. It shows the five wounds of Christ still with some original colour. This suggests a connection with the crypt of Bishop Salmon's Carnary Chapel, just inside the gate. In 1421 Sir John Wodehouse, a comrade-in-arms with Erpingham at Agincourt, was granted a charter

Fig. 171. Effigy of Sir Thomas Erpingham.

to found an Agincourt chantry there dedicated to the five wounds of Christ.[14] The gate may have honoured that dedication by placing the shield displaying the same theme in the ultimate position of honour.[15] This, with the four evangelists originally

---

13. T. Browne, *Repertorium: or, Some Account of the Tombs and Monuments in the Cathedral Church of Norwich in 1680*, in *Posthumous Works of the Learned Sir Thomas Browne* (London 1712), facing p. 24; Blomefield, *Norfolk*, iv, p. 54.

14. Wodehouse is reputed to have gained an augmentation of honour at Agincourt. He originally bore an ermine chevron and three ermine cinquefoils on black, but after this

battle the chevron was gilded and scattered with drops of blood (goutee de sang). C. W. S. Giles, *The Romance of Heraldry* (London, 1951), p. 106, fig. 124. These arms can be seen borne by a nineteenth-century member of the family on a wall plaque in the south nave aisle.

15. M. Rubin, *Corpus Christi: The Eucharist in Late Medieval Culture* (Cambridge, 1991), pp. 304–5.

on the gable, probably with a representative of the Trinity in the niche, and with the emblems of the Passion emblazoned across the top tiers of the columnar decoration, created the composition for the 'image of pity' or the '*arma Christi*'.[16] The eastern face of the gate carries the full Erpingham achievement of shield, helmet and crest, falcon supporters and motto, carved in the 1950s in the same configuration as his seal.[17] The tinctures used in the repainting of 1990 are taken from Erpingham's original Garter stall plate in St George's chapel, Windsor.[18] On either side of the cross orphrey on the back of the Erpingham chasuble, as on the gate, are his arms: the forget-me-not, the crowned falcon rising, and his motto.[19] The so-called 'Erpingham' window in the north ambulatory aisle still contains a small quarry of the falcon rising on which is superimposed the forget-me-not with the letters of the motto 'Yenk' inscribed on each petal after the style of the chasuble.[20]

Bishop Alnwick (1426–36) probably began his alterations to the west front of the cathedral when the Erpingham Gate was nearing completion. The outer spandrels of the porch contain demi-angels and the arms of the see and of Alnwick, argent, a cross moline sable. By the time Alnwick was translated to Lincoln work had begun on the vaults of the west walk of the cloister. Here, in front of the guest hall door, are the only two armorial bosses in the whole of the claustral scheme. One shows an open door, above which are the arms of the priory and the see; the other shows the arms of Sir Robert Knollys and his wife Constance Beverley (fig. 172). He wears an armorial surcoat, gules, on a chevron argent three roses gules, seeded or. The rose charges were probably painted on and are not now visible.[21] Below is his shield and ram's head crest. His wife wears her armorial mantle, argent, a fess danceté between three leopards' heads sable.[22] Between them is a representation of the Trinity with censing angels above. This is probably not unlike the Trinity that may have been in the niche of the Erpingham gate. Knollys had been one of the first leaders of the 'companies' of free lances and freebooters plundering in Normandy and beyond at the end of the fourteenth century. His ravages were so terrible that the charred gables marking his route were called

16. E. Duffy, *The Stripping of the Altars* (London, 1992), p. 237.
17. NRO, Colman and Rye, no. 6816, fig. 3.
18. W. H. St J. Hope, *Stall Plates of the Knights of the Garter, 1348 to 1485* (Westminster, 1901), pl. xlii.
19. C. Lamb, R. M. Collins and C. J. Holyoake, *English Heraldic Embroidery and Textiles at the Victoria and Albert Museum* (London, 1976), p. 19.
20. Dennis King, photograph. Actual glass now broken.

21. A red rose was paid as a summer quit rent service on houses in London owned by Knollys. A rose is still presented to the lord mayor of London at midsummer, carried on a velvet cushion by a churchwarden of All Hallows by the Tower. Knollys's rose device would seem to refer to this custom or vice-versa. C. Hole, *A Dictionary of Folk Customs* (London, 1978), pp. 174–75.
22. BL, Harleian MS 901, Robert Kemp's collections, *c.* 1575, fo. 59r, Sculthorpe church.

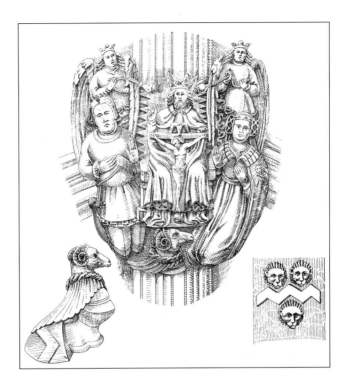

Fig. 172. Cloister boss with the arms of Sir Robert Knollys and Constance Beverley (after Goulburn).

'Knollys's mitres'.[23] How his arms came to be in the cloister is not certain. He bestowed much of the riches from his plundering expeditions on ecclesiastical institutions, but there is no record of any beneficence to the cathedral. He did however rebuild the churches at Harpley and Sculthorpe (west Norfolk) where much of his property lay. The communar rolls for 1421–22 record the receipt of £5 'from the rector of Harpley for the soul of Sir Robert de Knollys, knight'.[24]

A number of Knollys's comrades-in-arms are represented armorially and pictorially on the splendid misericords and armrests of the choir stalls, including Sir Thomas Morley, Sir Thomas Hoo, Sir Thomas Erpingham, William Ufford, earl of Suffolk, and Michael de la Pole, second earl of Suffolk. They are among prominent military and lay patrons remembered in the heraldry of the choir stalls in what must be the largest display of patronage of any scheme in the cathedral. For purposes of recognition, and to avoid repetition, figure 173 shows the sixteen families represented.[25] There are also three impersonal shields on the stalls: those of the priory,

23. *DNB*; G. Uden, *A Dictionary of Chivalry* (Ipswich, 1968), p. 165.
24. *Communar Rolls*, p. 42.
25. To avoid repetition the arms of alliance are precluded where the two families of the marriage are on one shield. The only

exception to this are the two Ufford shields with their marks of difference denoting (in one case, wrongly) different branches of the family. The whole scheme can be seen in M. Rose, *The Misericords of Norwich Cathedral* (Dereham, 1994).

MORLEY   CLERE   WITCHINGHAM   UFFORD

HOO   FELTON   ST OMER   ERPINGHAM

KERDISTON   BERNEY   HAVILE   DE LA POLE

UFFORD   STRANGE   ILLEY   WINGFIELD

BOVILLE   PRIORY

Fig. 173. Heraldry to be found on the choir stalls.

a shield of crossed staves and another with three shoes, the last two probably denoting the subject of pilgrimage.[26]

It is noteworthy that the families represented comprised a largely Lancastrian group. Most of them had members who were retainers of John of Gaunt or of his son Henry Bolingbroke, or who had connections with duchy of Lancaster lands in the county. On misericord S6 are two initials, interpreted by a number of writers as R.C. for Richard Courtenay, bishop of Norwich 1413–15.[27] Close inspection, however, suggests that the initials may be R.T., for Roger Turston, sacrist between 1364 and 1369, whose office would have included charge of the furnishings.[28] The fall of the spire in 1361/62 would almost certainly have damaged the earlier stalls and so Turston's period of office would have been an apt time to instigate a new scheme. Moreover, the heraldry suggests the possibility of legacies from that time. Alternatively, the carving of the stalls may suggest the hand of John Wakering, bishop of Norwich from 1415 to 1425, who in 1399 had been appointed chancellor of the county palatine of Lancaster and keeper of its privy seal. It is equally possible to detect the patronage of Sir Thomas Erpingham. He was responsible for a similar heraldic display in the east chancel window of the Austin friary in Norwich, which depicted all the knights of Norfolk and Suffolk who, since the time of Edward III, had died without male issue.[29] The heraldic display on the cathedral stalls may represent the arms of families with whose members Erpingham had campaigned in France during the late fourteenth and early fifteenth centuries. Sir Thomas Morley and Sir Thomas Hoo had been at Agincourt with him and Michael de la Pole died before the siege of Harfleur. Such speculation is tempting, but the real story behind this extensive heraldic scheme remains to be discovered.

There are two examples of canting arms or those whose devices play on the family name. On the arms of Wingfield on the left support of N7,[30] argent on a bend cotised sable, three pairs of wings conjoined in lure argent, the devices are hawks' wings or lures strung together in three pairs (much like the modern stunt kite) and used to train birds of prey for the hunt.[31] Bishop Wakering also bore

26. A. B. Whittingham, 'The Stalls of Norwich Cathedral', in Friends of Norwich Cathedral, *Nineteenth Annual Report, 1948*, p. 20.

27. Whittingham, 'Stalls of Norwich Cathedral', p. 17; C. Tracy, *English Gothic Choir Stalls, 1400–1540* (Woodbridge, 1990), p. 32.

28. H. W. Saunders, *An Introduction to the Obedientiary and Manor Rolls of Norwich Cathedral Priory* (Norwich, 1930), pp. 195–96. Turston had been refectorer in 1349–50.

29. Blomefield, *Norfolk*, iv, pp. 86–88.

30. The stalls on the north and the south are numbered from the west.

31. Cotising is the use of a narrow band of colour either side of the bend. This is missing here, one of several carvers' errors in the stalls. On the Hoo shield (the left supporter of S8) quarterly sable and argent, the central point of the label was not carved. Another mistake is on the left supporter of N3 showing the Ufford arms sable, a cross engrailed or, with a bend sinister (to the left) purporting to denote William, Lord Ufford, second earl of Suffolk. This is incorrect as the main line of the earls bore no marks of difference.

hawks' lures in a different configuration and he may have instigated the carving of the falcons that decorate the tracery of two choir-stall canopies on the north and south side exactly opposite each other. Falcons were a popular Lancastrian device: they appear on John of Gaunt's shield on his seal; they also support Erpingham's shield on the elbow of stall S7.

The second canting example is the family of de la Pole, whose usual blazon is azure, a bend between three leopards' heads or. But here, as in the de la Pole arms in stained glass both at Wingfield and Huntingfield churches, Suffolk, the charges are obviously polecats.

Cognate arms (those adopted by one family from the arms of another to whom they are connected by blood or feudal tenure), are illustrated by L'Estrange, the right supporter of N3, gules two lions passant argent, and the left supporter of S8 and N4, the arms of Felton, gules two lions passant ermine (very similar but differenced by her father, Sir Thomas Felton, who bore his lions crowned). The Felton whence the family took its name was Felton by Knockin in the march of Wales, which was in the liberty of John L'Estrange of Knockin.[32]

Henry VI visited the cathedral in 1449. It was perhaps in time for his visit that William Seckington, advocate in the consistory court and corrector of crime to

Fig. 174. The arms of Henry VI, formerly on top of the pulpitum.

Bishop Alnwick, paid for the stone vaulting and bosses in the Bauchun Chapel. Seckington's arms are on the south wall corbels; they appear to consist of three chevronnels on a bend with a star in the sinister chief.

There is an unusual boss to Bishop Walter Lyhart (1446–1472) in the porch to Bishop Salmon's chapel; his arms have hart supporters wrapped around the shield with water beneath them. The choir screen or pulpitum was started by Lyhart whose arms and rebus are in the spandrels of the arches on the west face, argent, a bull passant sable, armed unguled and tufted argent, a bordure sable bezanty and his rebus – a hart lying in water. Until the turn of this century a beautifully carved achievement of Henry VI's arms stood atop the pulpitum with golden crown, antelope supporters and the

32. H. Bedingfield and P. Gwynne-Jones, *Her-aldry* (Leicester, 1993), p. 56; G. E. Cokayne, *The Complete Peerage*, ed. V. Gibbs *et al.*, 13 vols in 14 (2nd edn, London, 1910–40), v, p. 289.

motto 'God save the king' in Latin (fig. 174). This sculpture is at present in store. In 1901 Lyhart's tomb was discovered, to the west of the pulpitum, complete with vestments and crozier. A gilt bronze ring of late fifteenth-century style with a small device of a bird on the signet was found in a grave alongside (fig. 175). This ring has not previously been identified, but probably belonged to Prior William Spynk (1488–1503);[33] his arms, which appear with those of Lyhart on the spandrels of the chapter house entrance in the eastern walk of the Great Hospital cloister, show three small birds.

Fig. 175. Impression from a late fifteenth-century signet ring.

Uniquely among English cathedrals, the patronage of all the high vaults at Norwich can be identified by their heraldry. Lyhart's responsibility for the splendid nave vault is acknowledged with his arms, but he may not have been its only patron. Less easily seen than his arms, there are two bosses in the first bay above the choir which portray a swan with a crown about its neck (also carved as the right supporter on misericord S16) and an antelope. Both were connected with Henry VI as royal badges, the antelope as his supporter. The swan was also a supporter of the Courtenay family (Richard Courtenay was bishop of Norwich 1413–15) and the crest of the Bourchier family (Thomas Bourchier was archbishop of Canterbury 1454–86 and a cardinal from 1461; his bust as cardinal is to be seen on the north corbel of the great west window).

The gold well rebuses which adorn the presbytery lierne vaulting testify to the generosity of Bishop Goldwell (1472–99). In addition, along the ridge rib are five different bosses. Starting from the east, the first three depict the assumption of the Blessed Virgin Mary, the Trinity and the arms of the see. The fourth and fifth shields are less easy to identify. The fourth displays a shield with a hat above; it must surely be that of Nicholas Goldwell (d. 1505), brother of the bishop, and master of the Great Hospital, since an identical shield decorates a nave pier in the Great Hospital. Nicholas was also dean of the college of St Mary in the Fields from 1498; archdeacon of Sudbury (1479–83), of Norwich (1483–97) and of Suffolk

33. John Cherry, personal communication.

(1497–1505); and vicar-general.[34] The hat or cap of maintenance may well have been used for one of these offices.[35]

The patronage of the alterations to the presbytery is shown by the magnificent heraldic scheme of seventeen shields depicting the Boleyns of Salle and Blickling. The scheme accompanies the tombs of Sir William Boleyn (d. 1505) and his mother Anne; the latter has subsequently been removed. At first glance the shields appear rather complex, but only seven families are represented: Boleyn, Bracton, Hoo, St Leger, St Omer, Witchingham and Butler – and only five shields combining their quarterings. These are the Boleyn coat, Sir William's parents,ʼhis paternal grandparents, his maternal grandparents and finally his own coat impaling his wife, Margaret Butler, argent, a chevron gules between three bulls' heads couped sable for Boleyn and or, a chief indented azure for Butler. It is his tomb to which the whole scheme is dedicated. His mother Anne Hoo, wife of Sir Geoffrey, lord mayor of London in 1457 and 1473, was daughter and coheiress of Sir John Hoo of Luton Hoo and Mulbarton, who was created Lord Hoo in 1448 and died in 1455. Sir Thomas Browne recorded Sir William's arms from the tomb together with a second set from a nearby stone; although Browne does not identify the latter, 'as the inscription was defaced', they are the arms of Sir William's mother Anne Hoo.[36]

The presbytery also contained the chantry of Elizabeth Clere (d. 1492) wife of Robert Clere; there is now no trace of it. The foundation charter of this chantry shows that income from the manors of Tharston in Norfolk and Claydon in Suffolk was used to endow it. There is now no evidence of this chantry but, to the north side of Sir William Boleyn's tomb, Blomefield described another stone with the Clere arms, argent on a fess azure three eagles displayed or, and Clere impaling Dovedale sable, a cross moline gules, pierced argent.[37] This is almost certainly the site of the chantry.

The presbytery floor area was not always as open as it is today. In the eighteenth century the founder's tomb, taken down in the Civil War and reerected in 1682, still stood on the site marked by the present floor slab before the rails of the high altar.[38] All that remains of this monument are five stone shields that once adorned the sides: two (prebendaries William Smith and Richard Kidder) built into the garden wall immediately to the south east of the axial chapel; the other four, the see and three other prebends (Joseph Loveland, Nathaniel Hodges and William Hawkins), are on display in the visitors' centre.

34. My thanks to Dr Carole Rawcliffe for this information.
35. That it is certainly not a cardinal's hat, as described in earlier accounts, is proved by comparison with the corbel of Cardinal Bourchier.
36. Browne, *Repertorium*, facing p. 14.
37. Blomefield, *Norfolk*, iv, p. 35.
38. N. Boston, 'The Founder's Tomb in Norwich Cathedral', *NA* 32 (1961), pp. 1–11. See also below, pp. 483–85.

After the fire of 1509, Bishop Nix (1501–1535/36) completed the fireproofing of the building by constructing the transept vaults in stone. His arms are on the vault-springing corbels as well as those of the see and the pelican vulning. Nix's splendid chantry tomb and vaults in the south nave aisle also show his arms, in one instance arrogantly impaling those of the see. Of interest are the examples of the Tudor rose, both open and closed and also quartered red and white. The Nix arms, argent, a chevron between three lions' heads gules, repeat themselves in the eastern string course of the chantry just above where the altar would have been, red lions' heads alternating with gold mitres. The north transept ground floor St Andrew's Chapel also shows his arms with those of Cardinal Wolsey in the south-east light of the eastern window. The centre light has Dean Suckling, Dean Montgomery and Dean Gardiner. The north-east light has Henry VIII's arms with, at the top, an as yet unidentified coat: gules, a cross flory argent.[39]

The antechoir under the pulpitum contained from 1510 the chapel of Our Lady of Pity and until the mid nineteenth century had two monuments which were moved to accommodate the sacrist's office.[40] The first, to Elizabeth Calthorpe née Berney (d. 1582), is the only Elizabethan tomb to show the correct lozenge shape for a lady's arms, here together with the arms of her two husbands. Daughter of Ralph Berney of Gunton, Norfolk, she married first Sir Francis Calthorpe and secondly John Culpepper of Suffolk. This monument is now in the north presbytery aisle just to the north west of the reliquary arch. The window above contains Calthorpe heraldry, probably from a house they owned, Berney's Inn, near the bishop's palace.[41] The second monument was to Dean John Croftes (1660–1670), chaplain to Charles I and II. The carved stone achievement of arms remains and is in storage; the tomb slab, showing the deanery impaling Croftes, or, three bulls' heads couped sable, a crescent for difference, was removed to the north nave aisle.[42] John Croftes was the son of Sir Henry Croftes of Tattingstone, Suffolk, and brother to William, Lord Croftes. He was appointed dean at the Restoration by Charles II.

To the north west of the pulpitum the Hobart chantry was situated in bay 5.[43] Only the altar tomb with reredos against the fifth pier and the Hobart achievement of arms high up on the west of the fourth pier now remain. Sir James Hobart (d. 1507), was attorney general to Henry VII and Henry VIII and married Margaret Naunton whose bird device is opposite the Hobart bull on the reredos. Between the ninth and tenth piers on the north of the nave stands the tomb of Sir Thomas Windham and his two wives, Eleanor, daughter and coheir of Richard Scroop of Upsall, and Elizabeth, daughter of Sir Henry Wentworth of Letheringham, Suffolk;

39. See also above, pp. 418.
40. Beeching, 'Chapels and Altars', p. 437; Blomefield, *Norfolk*, iv, pp. 29–31.
41. See above, pp. 421.

42. C. J. Evans, 'The Heraldry of Norwich Cathedral', *NA*, 8 (1879), pp. 77–78.
43. Browne, *Repertorium*, p. 4 and plate. See also below, pp. 479–80 and fig. 184.

the two shields of the marriage are recorded. The tomb was originally located in the earlier axial chapel of Our Lady but was moved to the Jesus Chapel and thence to its present position.[44]

Twentieth-century vestments and a crozier have unexpectedly pre-Reformation iconography and styling. Bishop Pollock (1910–42) recalled the scene at the coronation of George VI: 'the spectacle of uniforms and bishops' copes was very fine. I was wearing one specially beautiful, which had been presented to the cathedral church of Norwich for the bishop by Mr W. J. Birkbeck in his year as high sheriff of Norfolk' (1916).[45] William Birkbeck, a Norfolk man, banker and traveller, had visited Russia and become influenced by the Orthodox church; he brought back the last pieces of cloth of gold to be made there before the Revolution. He donated two sets of vestments, one for the bishop and the other for the dean (fig. 176). Both were designed by Sir Ninian Comper and embroidered by the Sisters of Bethany in London.[46] The dean's vestments have red velvet orphreys. Down one side are the royal arms and those of Bishop Pollock; azure, a boar passant between three fleurs de lys or, on a border engrailed or, four mitres azure, overall on a canton ermine a portcullis or. (The canton is worked using mouse pelt and minute black silk trails to represent ermine.) Lastly, Dean Wakefield, later bishop of Birmingham, argent, three bars sable on a chief of the second three owls of the first. The other side has the see, the priory and Birkbeck; argent between a fess compony or and azure, cotised azure, three lions' heads passant erased gules and tongued azure, a longbow azure stringed or, at the honour point. This shield impales Gurney,[47] argent, a cross engrailed gules. As the priors at Norwich were mitred from 1519, there is a mitre with these vestments.[48] The morse, or fastening, by Markentin and Krall of London contains a relic from the brow of Edward the Peacemaker, Edward VII. The morse of the bishop's vestments depicts the later patron saint of England, St George, killing the dragon.

The crozier was designed by the Norwich diocesan surveyor, Mr J. Arthur Reeve, and is very Gothic in style.[49] The head of the stave is silver-plated and carries four shields, representing the seats of the diocese – Dunwich, Elmham, Thetford and Norwich. Attached to the head is a central traceried octagonal knop of wood, with shields on the four square sides and four pinnacled buttresses on the other sides, squaring the whole architectural design. The arms are Pollock with mitre above, the

44. Blomefield, *Norfolk*, iv, pp. 7–8. See also below, pp. 480–81.
45. B. Pollock, *A Twentieth-Century Bishop: Recollections and Reflections* (London, 1944), p. 85.
46. S. Berry, *Victorian Treasures from English Churches* (London, 1967).
47. R. K. Birkbeck, *The Life and Letters of W. J. Birkbeck* (London, 1922), p. 257; H. Adderley, 'The Birkbeck Copes', in D. H. S.

Cranage, ed., *The Thirteen-Hundredth Anniversary of the Diocese of East Anglia: Official Handbook* (Norwich, 1930), pp. 66–68.
48. H. C. Beeching, 'The Library of the Cathedral of Norwich', *NA*, 19 (1917) p. 80 n. 1.
49. St Peter Hungate Ecclesiastical Museum, Norwich.

Fig. 176. The dean's
vestment's, worn by Dean
Burbridge (1983–95),
designed by Sir Ninian
Comper.

doctrine of the Blessed Trinity with crown, the dove of peace with dove crown and
the Passion emblems with crown, the arch of which is thorned and the rim of a
crown of thorns. The mounting for the crook is a mitre with broken chalice designs
thereon, alluding to the inscription around its base: MITRA:ABBATIS:SANCTI BENETI:
(The abbot's mitre of St Benet's Abbey). The silver crook itself is abundantly inscribed
and terminates clasping an heraldic crown ancient. Bishops of Norwich are today
still titular abbots of St Benet's, as the abbey was never officially dissolved.

From 1935 to 1938 a restoration scheme of the cathedral cloister bays took place:
the donors' arms, both mural and glass, and the royal scheme in the lavatory bays
were recorded by the then Dean Cranage.[50] Two large painted panels contain the

---

50. D. H. S. Cranage, 'Norwich Cathedral
     Cloisters', in Friends of the Cathedral
     Church of Norwich, *Eighth Annual Report*
     (Norwich, 1937), pp. 57–58.

coloured arms of the bishops and priors/deans of Norwich Cathedral; the bishops' panel hangs in the bishop's palace buildings and the deans' panel is to be seen in the deanery. The most modern heraldry is to be seen in the western shields alongside the Boleyn scheme in the presbytery. These are emblazoned with the present high steward of the cathedral and the two previous holders of the office: the blue shield with ermine cinquefoil for Lord Hastings (1948–56); the red shield with two mullets on silver for Sir Edmund Bacon (1956–79);[51] and finally the gold and blue shield with ermine canton, for Shirley, of the present high steward, Earl Ferrers.

51. There is also a memorial window to him on the north side of the Jesus Chapel: A. P. Sims, 'Bacon Memorial Window', *Norfolk* *Standard*, 3 (4, March 1984), p. 108, and above, p. 421.

24

The Monuments

Jonathan Finch

The cathedral contains over 300 monuments which span six centuries of commemorative art and exemplify most monumental forms, ranging from the simple ledger slab laid in the floor to the huge medieval chantry-tomb of Bishop Goldwell with its alabaster effigy and vaulted canopy. (For the location of monuments mentioned in the text, see fig. 177). Some, such as Chantrey's monument to Bishop Bathurst (fig. 177:16), are already recognised as being important within the national picture of monumental sculpture whilst others form a unique corpus of work by the much neglected eighteenth-century sculptors of Norwich. In order to understand the importance of the monuments they must be seen within a number of contexts such as the wider patterns of commemoration in the churches of the city and the county, and the 900 year history of internal alterations within the cathedral which have resulted in monuments being lost or moved.

Before we begin to examine the monuments we must ascertain who was commemorated within the walls of the cathedral. Although the privilege of burial and commemoration within Christian churches was originally restricted to high-ranking ecclesiastics, the financial importance of the substantial benefactions which accompanied aristocratic burials led to major lay patrons, such as John Berney (d. 1374) merchant and MP for Norwich and John Heydon (d. 1480) of Baconsthorpe, being buried and commemorated within Norwich Cathedral.[1] The monks faced direct competition for such lucrative burials from the other religious orders, particularly from the friars who were notoriously successful at attracting prestigious burials to their churches. Sir Thomas Browne, writing in the seventeenth century, was explicit in his belief that the lack of substantial medieval monuments to the region's 'noble and ancient' families in the cathedral was the result of the friars' success in this field.[2]

---

1.   N. P. Tanner, *The Church in Late Medieval Norwich, 1370–1532* (Toronto, 1984), pp. 12–13.

2.   Sir Thomas Browne cites the examples of the Uffords, Hastings, Radcliffes, Morleys, Windhams, Cliftons and Pigots buried else-

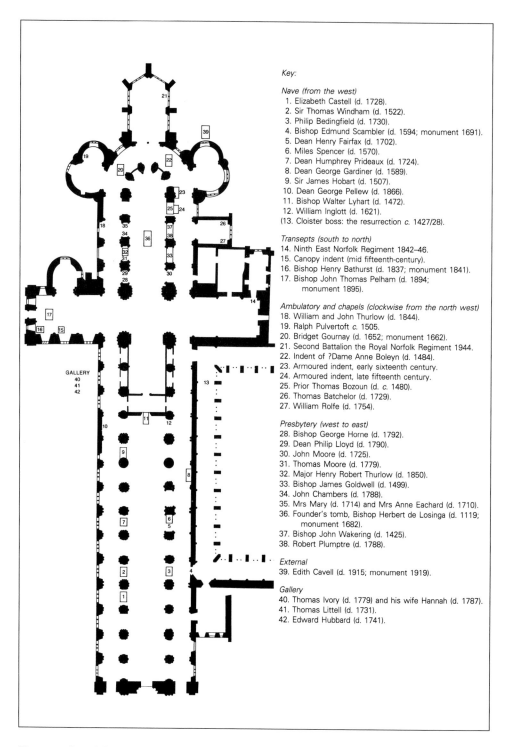

Key:

Nave (from the west)
1. Elizabeth Castell (d. 1728).
2. Sir Thomas Windham (d. 1522).
3. Philip Bedingfield (d. 1730).
4. Bishop Edmund Scambler (d. 1594; monument 1691).
5. Dean Henry Fairfax (d. 1702).
6. Miles Spencer (d. 1570).
7. Dean Humphrey Prideaux (d. 1724).
8. Dean George Gardiner (d. 1589).
9. Sir James Hobart (d. 1507).
10. Dean George Pellew (d. 1866).
11. Bishop Walter Lyhart (d. 1472).
12. William Inglott (d. 1621).
(13. Cloister boss: the resurrection *c.* 1427/28).

Transepts (south to north)
14. Ninth East Norfolk Regiment 1842–46.
15. Canopy indent (mid fifteenth-century).
16. Bishop Henry Bathurst (d. 1837; monument 1841).
17. Bishop John Thomas Pelham (d. 1894;
        monument 1895).

Ambulatory and chapels (clockwise from the north west)
18. William and John Thurlow (d. 1844).
19. Ralph Pulvertoft *c.* 1505.
20. Bridget Gournay (d. 1652; monument 1662).
21. Second Battalion the Royal Norfolk Regiment 1944.
22. Indent of ?Dame Anne Boleyn (d. 1484).
23. Armoured indent, early sixteenth century.
24. Armoured indent, late fifteenth century.
25. Prior Thomas Bozoun (d. *c.* 1480).
26. Thomas Batchelor (d. 1729).
27. William Rolfe (d. 1754).

Presbytery (west to east)
28. Bishop George Horne (d. 1792).
29. Dean Philip Lloyd (d. 1790).
30. John Moore (d. 1725).
31. Thomas Moore (d. 1779).
32. Major Henry Robert Thurlow (d. 1850).
33. Bishop James Goldwell (d. 1499).
34. John Chambers (d. 1788).
35. Mrs Mary (d. 1714) and Mrs Anne Eachard (d. 1710).
36. Founder's tomb, Bishop Herbert de Losinga (d. 1119;
        monument 1682).
37. Bishop John Wakering (d. 1425).
38. Robert Plumptre (d. 1788).

External
39. Edith Cavell (d. 1915; monument 1919).

Gallery
40. Thomas Ivory (d. 1779) and his wife Hannah (d. 1787).
41. Thomas Littell (d. 1731).
42. Edward Hubbard (d. 1741).

Fig. 177. Plan of the cathedral showing the location of monuments mentioned in the text.

In addition, the priory's long-running dispute with the city may have prejudiced wealthy citizens against being buried in the cathedral.[3] It is noticeable, for instance, that there are few monuments to civic dignitaries; they preferred instead to be commemorated within the thriving parish churches which grew with the mercantile wealth of the city. Only three mayors are known to have been commemorated within the cathedral, compared with at least eleven in St Peter Mancroft.[4] An analysis of medieval wills clearly shows that although the cathedral attracted small monetary donations from most wealthy Norwich citizens, it was rarely considered as a place of burial. The patrons who were commemorated within the cathedral tended to be county magnates rather than members of the city elite.[5] After the Dissolution the pattern of burials in the cathedral scarcely changed, with the parish churches of the city and county acquiring the burials which would once have been made in the churches of the religious orders.

The largest group of people commemorated within the cathedral is made up of those who served it during their lives. They range from bishops, priors and deans to lay people such as William Inglott (d. 1621), lay clerk and organist, whose monument is painted on the south pier adjacent to the pulpitum (figs 177:12 and 178). Their memorials pave the uneven floors and adorn the ancient walls. There is evidence from the beginning of the eighteenth century that certain areas were set aside for the burial of cathedral officers. The minor canons and their families were to be buried in the south transept, whilst the lay clerks 'and all other cathedral officers' were to be buried in the north transept.[6]

The collection of monuments seen within the cathedral today is the unique result of many different factors interacting over the centuries. Some led to monuments

note 2 continued

where in Norwich, the Bigods, Mowbrayes and Howards who were buried at Thetford Priory, the Mortimers at Attleborough and the Aubeneys at Wymondham, see *Repertorium: or, Some Account of the Tombs and Monuments in the Cathedrall Church of Norwich, 1680*, in G. Keynes, ed., *The Works of Sir Thomas Browne*, 6 vols (London, 1928), iii, p. 135.

3. For relations between the city and the priory, see pp. 255–80.

4. In the cathedral: John Manning (mayor 1415), d. 1430, lost brass; Jeremy Vynn (mayor 1690), d. 1705, ledger slab in ambulatory; and John Press (mayor 1753), d. 1773, mural monument moved from north transept now in gallery. In St Peter Mancroft: Thomas Elys (mayor 1460, 1465,

1474), d. 1487; Richard Aylmer (mayor 1511), d. 1512; Edward Coleburne (mayor 1720), d. 1730; Thomas Harwood (mayor 1728), d. 1746; John Patterson (mayor 1766), d. 1774; Thomas Starling (mayor 1767), d. 1788; Nathanial Roe (mayor 1777), d. 1795; James Hudson (mayor 1794), d. 1807; John Stainforth Patterson (mayor 1823), d. 1832; Sir John Harrison Yallop (mayor 1815, 1831), d. 1835; Robert Hawkes (mayor 1822), d. 1836.

5. Of the 1515 lay wills from Norwich dated between 1370 and 1532, only six request burial in the cathedral compared to forty-five requesting burial in the Dominican friary; see Tanner, *Church in Late Medieval Norwich*, pp. 12–13, 120–21 and appendix 3.

6. NRO, DCN 24/4, fo. 113r (6 June 1704).

Fig. 178. Monument to William Inglott
(d. 1621) in the nave. The painting shows two
members of the choir holding a wreath of bay,
a song book and an hourglass, standing by Inglott's effigy. The skulls and Fame blowing her
trumpet, which adorn the top of the strapwork
border, continue the themes of the inscription.

being erected and some, such as accidental damage or iconoclasm, have resulted
in their removal. Despite the cathedral's
apparent sense of timeless permanence
this restless process has not ceased and
even today monuments are at risk from
accidental damage or the cumulative
effects of decay over time. This chapter
will take a roughly chronological look
at some of the monuments within the
cathedral as well as those which have
long since been lost. The aim is to illustrate both the development of commemoration within the cathedral and to
place the monuments within wider historical contexts which were felt far beyond the walls of the precinct.

The earliest references to a monument in the cathedral are from the
twelfth century when the body of the
boy-saint William of Norwich (d. 1144)
was moved twice in three years because
the large crowds attracted by its mira-
culous reputation were disturbing services.[7] It has been estimated that in 1150 at
the peak of the cult a miracle was reported at the tomb every ten days.[8] The
tomb-shrines of William of Norwich, Bishop Suffield (d. 1256) and Bishop Salmon
(d. 1325), all now gone, attracted monetary offerings well into the fourteenth century
and were valuable assets to the priory. In order to maintain their popularity these
monuments had to be periodically embellished. In 1305, for example, a painter and
his assistant were employed for nine weeks in the costly process of painting and
gilding the tomb of William of Norwich.[9]

The earliest surviving monument, if the Romanesque carving of a figure on the
north wall of the north transept is excluded, is the indent and tomb-chest of Bishop
Wakering (d. 1425) on the south side of the presbytery (fig. 177:37).[10] The badly

7. See pp. 238–39, 274.

8. R. C. Finucane, *Miracles and Pilgrims* (London, 1977), p. 162; J. R. Shinners, 'The
   Veneration of Saints in Norwich Cathedral
   in the Fourteenth Century', *NA*, 40 (1989),
   pp. 133–44.

9. Shinners, 'Veneration of Saints', p. 135;
   William's shrine was finally dismantled *c.*
   1538: NRO, DCN 29/3, fo. 139r.

10. For a discussion of the Romanesque effigy,
    see above, pp. 117–20.

eroded Purbeck slab shows traces of an indent for a single effigy under a canopy with three finials and two shields either side of the head and another two above the canopy. There is no sign of an inscription though several sources speak of a circumscription which survived into the seventeenth century. The brass seems to have been complete at the beginning of the seventeenth century and was enclosed by iron railings until the middle of the eighteenth century.[11] From the south ambulatory the tomb-chest can be seen with shields in cusped circles and seven original figures holding symbols of the Passion (fig. 179). The stocky figures lack the graceful swaying posture of fourteenth-century weepers but share some similarities with the minor figure sculpture of fifteenth-century East Anglian fonts, such as that at Sloley (Norfolk). The most easterly panel, showing figures holding a mitre, book and crozier, is an early nineteenth-century addition to cover steps into the presbytery, supposedly restoring the tomb to its original length, although the

Fig. 179. Tomb of Bishop Wakering (d. 1425). Two of the seven surviving original figures on the side of his tomb-chest, one holding a crown of thorns and a staff, the other with two scourges and a sponge on a long reed, which has been recut as a skull.

authority for this and the accuracy of the symbols they hold are not known. All the panels seem to have been subjected to 'restoration' at this time; this included

11. In her introduction to the records of the guild of St George, Mary Grace states that the monument was erected in 1449, but I have been unable to trace the original reference; see M. Grace, ed., *Records of the Gild of St George in Norwich, 1389–1547* (NRS, 9, 1937), p. 24. The brass was still in place when described by Henry Chittings (*c.* 1600–20), Chester herald, who gives the arms as St George's; England and France quartered; the see of Norwich; and Wakering, and the circumscription as 'Orate pro a[n]i[m]a Reverendi p[at]ris

d[omi]ni Johannis Wakeringe quonda[m] Norwicen[sis] Ep[iscopi] qui obiit xxvi die Aprilis MCCCC xxv, [cuius anime propicietur Deus, Amen]'. The iron railings surrounded the slab when Mackerell recorded it in 1737. The manuscript collections of Chittings, an unpaginated transcription of 'Visitation of Churches in Norff', NRO, MC 186/346 650x4; Benjamin Mackerell, 'History of the City of Norwich both Ancient and Modern', 2 vols (1737) (NRO, MSS 78 and 79), i, p. 50; Blomefield, *Norfolk*, iv, p. 36.

the sponge carried by one figure being erroneously, or mischievously, recut as a skull.[12]

To the west of Wakering's tomb is the elaborate monument to Bishop Goldwell (d. 1499) with an alabaster effigy lying under a huge canopy with Perpendicular tracery (figs. 177:33 and 180). This effigy is notable as a rare pre-Reformation example of the processional cope, rather than the chasuble, being worn as the outer vestment. The monument formed the spectacular centrepiece to a network of bequests which spread across the county and beyond, for which the bishop made provision to ensure continuing intercessory prayers for his soul. Three stipendiary priests, supported from an endowment of £400, were attached to this perpetual chantry whilst another £146 was spent on a chantry at All Souls' College, Oxford, which also received £50 for the ornamentation of its chapel and altar. Another £38 was spent on securing prayers at various monastic churches, and 6s. 8d. was to be paid every Sunday for three years to twenty poor men to pray for his soul at the cathedral. In all Goldwell spent £636 on the endowment of intercessory prayers to speed his soul through purgatory.[13]

The only brass which survives from the medieval period is that of Ralph Pulvertoft, master of the charnel, in the Jesus Chapel (fig. 177:19); it is thought to be *c.* 1505. It is often stated that Norwich Cathedral 'has suffered grievously in the loss of its early monumental brasses', but it is not peculiar in this respect; cathedrals suffered the attentions of iconoclasts to a much greater degree than parish churches: only the cathedrals of Exeter, Oxford, Salisbury and Wells now retain as many as two medieval brasses apiece.[14]

12. NRO, DCN 112/2, 'Monumental Inscriptions and Monuments in the Cathedral Church of Norwich' collected by the National Society for Preserving the Memorials of the Dead, iii, p. 62; J. F. Williams, 'The Brasses of Norwich Cathedral', *Transactions of the Monumental Brass Society*, 9 (1960), p. 369; H. Harrod, *Gleanings among the Castles and Convents of Norfolk* (Norwich, 1857), p. 295.

13. W. K. Jordan, *The Charities of Rural England, 1480–1660* (London, 1961), p. 178. *Pace* Woodman (above, p. 194), the Goldwell monument is an expensive and elaborate monument of the highest quality. The canopy was an integral part of the late medieval monument, and originally signified the gateway through which the soul would pass into heaven. To describe a canopy as 'redundant' fails to grasp the symbolic role

that all medieval monuments played in the continuing relationship between the living and the souls of the dead. The chantry priests and the poor were paid to stand within the physical structure formed by the monument and pray for the soul of the deceased. The canopy embraced not only the tomb-chest and its effigy, but the altar and the people who served it and prayed at it. The tomb-chest and the canopy, with its elaborate traceried panels and end-posts, fits exactly into the new Tudor bay. Such a monument could not have been conceived within the narrow bays of the Romanesque presbytery. The Hobart monument is a far better example of a clumsily assembled monument (see below, pp. 479–80).

14. Williams, 'Brasses of Norwich Cathedral', p. 366.

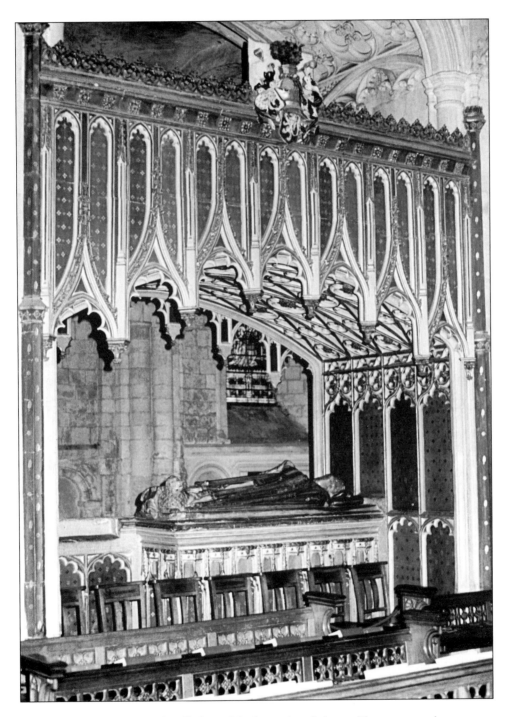

Fig. 180. Tomb of Bishop Goldwell (d. 1499) in the south ambulatory. The monument leaves room under the huge canopy for an altar at which the three priests celebrated mass and prayed for the bishop's soul. The colouring is not original.

One of the lost brasses is that of Bishop Lyhart (d. 1472) whose large slab was returned to its original place in front of the pulpitum which he built, after the excavation of what was thought to be his grave in 1899 (fig. 177:11).[15] The indent has been worn smooth and only a constellation of brass plugs, which once fastened the brass plates to the stone, now remains to give any idea of the size and complexity of the brass.

Several other brass indents are of interest. One huge slab, now in the south ambulatory, shows the figure of a lady wearing a veiled head-dress and a mantle, surrounded by ten heraldic shields; it probably dates from the last quarter of the fifteenth century (fig. 177:22). Arthur Whittingham has suggested that the slab commemorates Dame Anne Boleyn (d. 1484), great-great-grandmother of Queen Elizabeth I. Although the indent is of roughly the right date and in the right area of the cathedral, close to the site of the former monument to her son Sir William Boleyn on the south side of the presbytery immediately above Prior Bouzon's chantry chapel (fig. 177:25), it is impossible to be certain whom it commemorates.[16]

Also in the south ambulatory are two slabs with indents of men in armour. The earlier of the two wears plate armour with a sallet helmet (a light helmet with a neck-guard), probably dating from the late fifteenth century (figs 177:24 and 181a). The brass of Sir Peter Rede in St Peter Mancroft copies this style of armour although it was made almost a century later.[17] The other indent, from the beginning of the sixteenth century, shows a bare-headed man in armour with long hair (figs 177:23 and 181b). Finally, in the north transept there is a Purbeck slab cut diagonally from a larger, unidentified, slab which shows the indent of a mid fifteenth-century canopy with heraldic shields above (fig. 177:15).[18]

The destruction of medieval monuments, and brasses in particular, is usually attributed to Cromwellian troops in the 1640s and 1650s. The account of iconoclasm left by Bishop Hall and Sir Thomas Browne's comment that 'about a hundred brass inscriptions' were 'torn and taken away from gravestones and tombs' have both served to strengthen this belief.[19] An examination of the references in antiquarian sources such as Chittings's notes, however, makes it clear that much of the damage was done in the sixteenth century, probably during the Edwardian bouts of iconoclasm.

15. W. H. St J. Hope and W. T. Bensly, 'Recent Discoveries in the Cathedral Church of Norwich', *NA*, 14 (1901), p. 119.
16. NRO, MC 186/166 649x2; Williams, 'Brasses of Norwich Cathedral', p. 373; I am grateful to Malcolm Norris and William Lack for their comments on the indent.
17. The effigy survived when Chittings wrote, between 1600 and 1620, and may have served as a model for Rede's deliberately

antiquated brass. The slab has an eighteenth-century inscription to Judith Ellet at the top.
18. Williams, 'Brasses of Norwich Cathedral', p. 373.
19. J. Hall, *Hard Measure*, in P. Hall, ed., *The Works of Joseph Hall, DD*, 12 vols (Oxford, 1837), i, p. lv; Browne, *Repertorium*, p. 123. See also below, pp. 552–54.

Fig. 181. Brass indents of men in armour in the south ambulatory. (a) Plate armour and a sallet helmet, standing on a beast. Underneath, a large rectangular inscription and heraldry, *c.* 1470. (b) Armoured man, bare-headed with long hair, *c.* 1500.

Of the fifteen brasses mentioned by Chittings at the beginning of the seventeenth century (before the upheavals of the English Revolution), six were already damaged. The iconoclasm of the seventeenth century seems to have been little more than mopping up what remained. The brass of Bishop Lyhart, for example, was described as 'maimed' in 1631, after which it came loose from its stone and was nailed to the pulpitum door before it was finally lost in the late seventeenth century.[20]

Some destruction was motivated by grievances other than religious dogma. The treatment of Miles Spencer's monument (*c.* 1570) shows how 'iconoclasm' was not always a matter of removing religious icons. The economic role of the church also stirred resentment: 'the topstone was entire' Sir Thomas Browne tells us, 'but now broken, split and depressed by blows: more special notice being taken of this stone,

20. Chittings, NRO, MC 186/346 650x4; J. Weever, *Ancient Funerall Monuments within the United Monarchie of Great Britaine* (London, 1631), p. 795; Browne, *Repertorium*, p. 125.

because men used to try their money upon it, and because the chapter demanded their rents at this tomb'.[21]

The monument stands between the seventh and eighth piers of the south aisle (fig. 177:6). The freestone chest is surmounted by a huge slab, which Williams refers to as Tournai marble, with an indent showing a quatrefoil at each corner, which would have shown the symbols of the evangelists, and a prayer-scroll at the effigy's mouth.[22]

The monument to Bishop Scambler (d. 1594) was one of the greatest losses. Also on the south arcade of the nave, the monument was 'above a yard and a half high, with his effigies in alabaster lying upon it, and enclosed with a high iron grate'. The epitaph was composed from 'divine sentences . . . engraven in gold in a rich black stone'.[23] In his history of Norwich Cathedral, written in 1659 soon after the monument was destroyed, Thomas Searle claims that the monument was attacked on account of two verses of the inscription which read, 'Hinc abeat mortis terror; tibi vivo Redemptor, Mors mihi iam Lucrum est; tu pie Christe, salus' ('The terror of death departs; I live for you Redeemer, Death to me is now gain; thou pious Christ are salvation'), although it is difficult to see why the verses should have caused such offence to the reformers.[24] It is one of the few examples of iconoclasm that can be unequivocally attributed to the 1640s. Stripped down to the inner brickwork during the Civil War, zealously 'reformed quite away to the bricks', as Searle puts it, the remaining rubble was cleared away soon after. In 1691 James Scambler, the bishop's great-grandson, erected a mural monument to his memory (now above the monks' door into the cloister, fig. 177:4), with four verses of Latin, including two which are almost identical to those given above, suggesting that all four may have been taken from the original monument.[25]

21. Browne, *Repertorium*, p. 123. Thomas Haxey's monument in York Minster was used for rental payments by tenants of the dean and chapter until the nineteenth century, see G. E. Aylmer, 'Funeral Monuments and other Post-Medieval Sculpture', in G. E. Aylmer and R. Cant, eds, *A History of York Minster* (Oxford, 1977), p. 443.

22. The symbols of the evangelists and prayer-scrolls are rarely found on brasses after *c.* 1540–60: M. Norris, *Monumental Brasses: The Memorials* (London, 1977), p. 173; Williams, 'Brasses of Norwich Cathedral', p. 372. The brass may have been made some time before Spencer's death or, as he was a religious conservative (see below, p. 511), he may have chosen an antiquated style of

brass. The other possibility is that this may not be the original slab.

23. Browne, *Repertorium*, p. 124; Mackerell says it was 5 ft (1. 5 m.) high, NRO, MS 78 T136 A, p. 41; Thomas Searle, 'A Catalogue of all the Bishops of Norwich', London, Lambeth Palace Library, MS 593, pp. 268–69; I am indebted to Ian Atherton for this and other references.

24. London, Lambeth Palace Library, MS 593, p. 269.

25. London, Lambeth Palace Library, MS 593, p. 268: 'I live for you and wait for you; to you Christ, I shall rise / Since I shall justify you, Christ, by claiming faith. / The terror of death will depart; Christ, you are my Redeemer. / Death to me is now gain; you,

The complete destruction of Scambler's monument, perhaps motivated by fresh memories of his episcopacy as much as by the inscription, stands in stark contrast to the survival of Bishop Goldwell's. This serves as a reminder that the iconoclasm of the sixteenth and seventeenth centuries appears to have been selective and was rarely the wild fury or mindless vandalism that it is so often portrayed as being.

The legacy of the mid seventeenth-century revolution and the civil wars continued to affect patterns of commemoration long after the Restoration. There was a surge in retrospective commemoration during the 1660s, exemplified by the ledger-slab to Bridget Gournay in the northern part of the ambulatory (fig. 177:20). She died in 1652 but was not commemorated until 1662 when greater security for monuments could be assured, as the epitaph explains:

> King Charles 2nd having been restored
> By whose return not only the sleeping places of the living
> but also those of the dead
> As well as the sacred shrines themselves are preserved
> from the violations of fanatics.

When the monument to Dean Fairfax (d. 1702) was erected the dean and chapter found the epitaph, with its laudatory descriptions of his parliamentarian uncle and his role in the victory over the king at Naseby (1645), so offensive that the monument was covered with a cloak until two offending words had been erased (figs 177:5 and 182).[26] Dean Prideaux felt that the references were tantamount to 'bragging of rebellion and the victory w[hi]ch brought K[ing] Charles the First to the block'. Prideaux justified his own censorious actions by suggesting that adverse and violent public reactions to the epitaph could not be ruled out,

> no place could be more improper for the putting up of it in than the city of Norwich at this time, for Toryism to the height being now the prevailing humour of the place, should the dean and chapter permit this inscription to stand in our church it would provoke the rabble to break in upon us and tear it down and . . . execute other violences upon us; and what could we say for ourselves if they should, as long as such an occasion is given for it?[27]

note 25 continued
pious Christ, are salvation'. This and other translations from the Latin are by Dr Roger Virgoe. The mural monument was originally placed on the north side of the sixth pier in the southern arcade, but was moved to its current position in 1832: NRO, DCN 120/1/2, fo. 14.

26. The monument is by the famous London statuary William Stanton (1639–1705), for whom see A. Esdaile, 'The Stantons of Holborn', *Arch. J.*, 85 (1928), pp. 149–69. The two words, '*Nasebiani*' and '*Pii*', can still just be made out despite the heavy erasure.

27. Dean Prideaux's diary, 25 September 1703, NRO, DCN 115/1, pp. 222–24.

Fig. 182. Mural monument
to Dean Fairfax (d. 1702), in
the nave by William Stan-
ton, showing gaps were
words have been erased by
the dean and chapter.

Prideaux also drew attention to mistakes in the Latin inscription and the discrepance between the date of death given on the monument and the ledger slab over
his grave, which suggests that the well-known antagonism between the successive
deans also played a part in this incident.[28] Epitaphs have often been a source of
discomfort for the dean and chapter. In 1737 Richard Deere's ledger slab was 'not
permitted to be laid down, *on account of the inscription*' which suggested that he had
deserved higher office than that of a minor canon.[29]

28. See below, pp. 568–69.   29. Blomefield, *Norfolk*, iv, pp. 25–26.

The destruction of monuments did not cease in the seventeenth century. There have been three thorough surveys of the monuments since Sir Thomas Browne's *Repertorium* of 1680: Blomefield's in the mid eighteenth century (*c.* 1741); one, by the National Society for Preserving the Memorials of the Dead, in the late nineteenth century (*c.* 1884–93); and one made by F. Cross in 1914.[30] By comparing these surveys with the monuments that survive today it is possible to chart the continuing losses of the monuments. Ninety-four had been lost by 1884 and a further thirty-one by 1914; thirty-three more have either been lost or have become illegible since 1914. Those monuments which have been fortunate enough to survive continue

to decay and will eventually be lost forever, unless urgently needed conservation work is carried out. The monument to Dean Gardiner (d. 1589) on the south wall of the nave, for example, has deteriorated so much over the last century that the inscription, which was incised into the freestone and filled with pitch, is now completely illegible (figs 177:8 and 183).[31]

Two of the most important pre-Reformation monuments to members of the laity, both having suffered through the remodelling of the cathedral fabric, are to be found in the north arcade of the nave. The earliest is the monument to Sir James Hobart, who died in 1507 (figs 177:9 and 184). The raised chest-tomb of freestone, with cusped panels on the north side and more intricate work on the south, is surmounted by a well-defined brass indent of two effigies under a double canopy with two escutcheons at their feet. On closer inspection, however, it

Fig. 183. Monument to Dean Gardiner (d. 1589), in the nave. A simple architectural monument of freestone showing the three panels with the inscription incised in pitch. The panel on the front of the chest once took a brass inscription.

is noticeable that the monument has been assembled rather badly. The bases of the side shafts of the canopy have been laid out at different levels and the escutcheons have been arranged asymmetrically.

30. Blomefield, *Norfolk*, iv, pp. 7–46; NRO, DCN 112/2; DCN 112/1.

31. The long Latin inscription is recorded in Blomefield, *Norfolk*, iii, p. 624.

Fig. 184. Tomb of Sir James Hobart (d. 1507) in the nave. The drawing on the left (from Sir Thomas Browne's *Repertorium*, 1712) shows the chantry chapel which originally contained the monument. The view on the right (NRO, DCN 125/1) shows the exposed monument following the removal of the screen *c.* 1740.

The most striking feature of the monument, however, is its diminutive size.[32] The monument originally derived its scale from the stone screen which enclosed it within a chantry chapel. The chapel and monument were integral parts of one design: a private chapel in which to pray for the souls of the Hobart family within the greater architectural and spiritual context of the cathedral church. The screen around the monument, which may originally have formed part of the screen associated with the nave altar, was removed during the alterations of *c.* 1740.[33] The removal of the chapel destroyed the original spatial context of the monument and now the monument stands dwarfed by the lofty nave, robbed of its brasses and denuded of its screen.[34]

The monument to Sir Thomas Windham (d. 1522) and his two wives, which now

32. It measures only 2 ft 11 in. by 6 ft 1 in. by 2 ft 11 in. (90 cm. × 186 cm. × 90 cm.).
33. For these alterations see pp. 598, 708–09.
34. Blomefield, *Norfolk*, iv, p. 28, describes the monument as 'enclosed till the late repairs, and then laid open'; Harrod erroneously attributes the screen's destruction to the 'rebellion', *Gleanings*, p. 273.

Fig. 185. Tomb of Sir Thomas Windham (d. 1522). This unsigned nineteenth-century watercolour shows the large Purbeck monument in the Jesus Chapel before it was removed to the nave in 1872.

stands in the fifth bay of the north arcade of the nave (fig. 177:2), is one of the largest monuments in the county made entirely from Purbeck marble.[35] It had three large brass effigies and elaborate heraldic decoration also in brass and probably inlaid with coloured tinctures. The whole lavish monument was an emphatic statement of the power and status which Sir Thomas had so rapidly reestablished for his family after his father had been executed for treason in 1502.[36] The monument was originally placed in the Lady Chapel which, despite Windham leaving money for its repair, became ruinous and was pulled down before the end of the sixteenth century. The monument was then moved to the Jesus Chapel (fig. 185) where it remained in front of the altar until 1872 when it was again moved, this time to the position it occupies today.

Although the migration of this monument from the east to the west of the cathedral church is remarkable, few of the others survive in their original places. The cathedral was extensively repaved in 1740 resulting in the rearrangement of virtually all of those which were set in the floor; then nineteenth-century liturgical changes, such as changes in the level of the presbytery floor, were accompanied by further rearrangements.

35. The base of the monument is not Purbeck and may be restoration work from when the monument was removed from the Jesus Chapel in 1872.

36. R. W. Ketton-Cremer, *Felbrigg: The Story of a House* (London, 1982 edn), p. 13.

Fig. 186. Prior Bozoun's chantry chapel
(*c.* 1480) in the south ambulatory.

The only certain way to prevent such movement was to integrate one's monument into the very fabric of the church. Perhaps the best example of this is the chantry chapel of Prior Bosville or Bozoun (*c.* 1480) in the south ambulatory (figs 177:25 and 186). This delightful chapel, entered through a low four-centred arch, is set into the higher level of the presbytery. Before the bays in the presbytery were enlarged during the early Tudor remodelling, Prior Bozoun's chapel fitted neatly between two Romanesque piers.[37] The canopy has fine traceried panels, and a plain rectangular frame at the eastern end must once have taken a painted reredos for the altar. The inscription, which may originally have been painted on the ornamented panel at the back of the chapel, was recorded by Chittings as, 'O, you who pass by, man, woman or child, look at the top pictures, read, recognize the figures, and be mindful of yourself: thus well learn of death'. The traces of three skulls and the inscription 'morieris, morieris, morieris' (thou wilt die) can still be seen across the entablature above the arch.[38] On close examination the three skulls can be seen to be in varying states of decay. Blomefield

37. This interpretation differs from that of Dr Woodman (above, pp. 194–96). The relationship between the Bozoun Chapel and the presbytery is of great interest. The chapel does predate the Tudor remodelling as the base of the Romanesque pier, which could be seen behind the reredos panel at the eastern end of the chapel, clearly showed before it was recently covered. The position of this Romanesque pier also shows that the Tudorisation of the presbytery involved far more than simply refacing the Romanesque structure; the Romanesque piers were in fact cut back in order to widen the space within each bay substantially. Bozoun's chapel sat neatly, without gaps, between the bases of the Romanesque piers within the

smaller bay. That the pier at the west end of the monument was also cut back is suggested by the exposed Tudor shaft. William Boleyn's monument, which was a raised chest-tomb, was situated directly above the Bozoun Chapel, and not in the bay to the west, which contains the brass indent of Bishop Wakering (above, pp. 470–72).

38. Chittings has 'with this inscription on the upper part of the arch, O tu qui transis vir aut mulier puer ansis Respice picturas apices, lege, cerne figuras Et memor esto tui, sic bene disce mori under it three pictures of dead skulls . . .' If accurate, the reference to the skulls being below the inscription suggests a different arrangement. NRO, MC 186/346 650x4.

suggests this is to represent death in youth, middle and old age, but it may simply depict the fate of the body, a popular theme in medieval art.[39]

The three monuments which have marked the grave of Bishop Herbert de Losinga (fig. 177:36) illustrate the pressures on a monument, particularly from changes in the use of church space. It is also perhaps appropriate to review the evidence which Canon Boston produced detailing the various monuments which have been erected over the founder.[40] The earliest, presumably erected *c.* 1119, is referred to in the *First Register* (1290) as a 'sarcophagus [*sarcofago*] worthy of the burial of such a man'.[41] A description of the rituals performed at the tomb at the vigil of St Mary Magdalene, written in the mid thirteenth century, recounts that the monument was covered with a pall during the vigil and implies that it was located in the middle of the presbytery, rather than under the arcade which is considered to be the traditional site reserved for the burial of early bishops and founders (as can be seen, for example, at Chichester Cathedral).[42] Further details of this monument are unclear. It is now considered unlikely that the episcopal effigy over the door of the north transept was the original lid of the sarcophagus, as Boston believed it to be,[43] but the tomb may have included an effigy in low-relief or, more probably, a simple cross design. It is interesting to note that two bosses in the cathedral cloister, one of which depicts the sealing of Christ's tomb (a scene unique to the Norwich cycle of mystery plays), the other the resurrection, both show a sarcophagus decorated with a floriated cross with a stepped base. On one boss the lid is shown on a raised base decorated with quatrefoils around the sides (figs 177:13 and 187). This type of monument is not contemporary with the bosses (*c.* 1427–28) and the mason must have used a model of what an important ancient monument looked like. Perhaps the most obvious model was the founder's monument in the presbytery.[44]

This original monument must have been replaced during the episcopate of Walter Lyhart (1446–72), since the 'fair tomb of alabaster', described by Henry Chittings at the beginning of the seventeenth century, was adorned with eleven heraldic

39. See K. Cohen, *The Metamorphosis of a Death Symbol* (London, 1973).
40. N. Boston, 'The Founder's Tomb in Norwich Cathedral', *NA*, 32 (1961), pp. 1–12.
41. *First Register*, p. 57.
42. Blomefield, *Norfolk*, iii, p. 471. H. A. Tummers, 'Church Monuments', in M. Hobbs, ed., *Chichester Cathedral: An Historical Survey* (Chichester, 1994), p. 205.
43. See above, pp. 117–20.
44. In the gallery there are the remains of two medieval cross slabs. One fragment shows the crudely incised arms of a cross head, whilst another more complete slab has a cross head with four round-leafed bracelets in high relief. There is also some trace of decoration half way down the cross shaft but the slab is broken off at this point. There were two medieval cross slabs in St Luke's Chapel until it was reseated in 1721 (NRO, DCN 115/3, p. 90), one of which was probably the fine Purbeck slab with an engrailed cross (i. e. bordered with semicircular indents) on a stepped base, currently placed on the north side of the presbytery in the second bay.

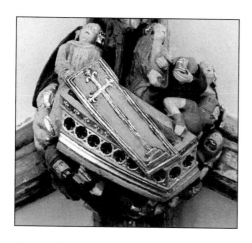

Fig. 187. Boss (*c.* 1427–28) from the north range of the cloister showing the resurrection and the empty tomb.

escutcheons including the arms of Bishop Lyhart together with those of the Windhams and the Cleres.[45] Whittingham suggested that the monument was erected after the fire of 1463, which damaged the presbytery, but the heraldic evidence provided by Chittings (which Whittingham does note refer to) suggests that the monument could have been erected in the first part of Lyhart's episcopacy; in which case the fire may not have been as devastating as some commentators have implied.[46] Very little else is known about this monument. Weever gives the text of a brass inscription which can be dated on stylistic grounds no more definitely than to the fifteenth century. References to changes in the arrangement of the presbytery during the 1640s give some indication that this was a large monument. These rearrangements involved placing the pulpit against the pier on the south of the presbytery, where Bishop Overall's monument is now sited, and seating the aldermen and mayor around the east end of the presbytery. It appears that the founder's monument in the middle of the presbytery obscured both the preacher and civic dignitaries from general view and, although somewhat surprisingly described as only being 'above an ell high', it was lowered or scaled down to a less imposing form which it retained until 1682.[47]

Attempting to recreate the design of the monument is difficult. The heraldic

45. NRO, MC 186/346 650x4; Blomefield, *Norfolk*, iv, p. 4.

46. Chittings lists the escutcheons as the church, the see of Norwich, Windham and Braunche impaled, the see of Norwich again, and Lyhart; then, 'on the north side of his tomb are six escutcheons', three of the see of Norwich, one of his own, one of the Trinity, one of Cleres and Braunche. NRO, MC 186/346 650x4. Dr R. Virgoe suggests that Clere impaling Braunche must refer to John Clere of Ormesby (d. by 1420) with Elizabeth, daughter of Sir Philip Braunche and mother of Robert Clere. The arms of Windham impaling Braunche are more obscure, but John Windham I (d.

1475) is called 'Jn Windham esq *alias* John Braunche of Bokenham, esquire' in 1440 (ref. Dr R. Virgoe). These two matches suggest a date earlier than 1463, perhaps at the beginning of Lyhart's episcopacy. Whittingham's views on the date of the monument are mentioned in Boston, 'Founder's Tomb', p. 4.

47. Browne, *Repertorium*, p. 128. An ell was roughly 45 in. (112 cm.), *OED*. In 1680 Browne wrote that 'in the late confusion' it had been 'taken down unto such a lowness as it now remaineth in'. Overall's monument is on the eastern pier of the bay which contains Wakering's tomb (fig 177:37).

escutcheons would have been arranged around the sides of a raised tomb-chest, which would have been relatively large to accommodate all eleven escutcheons. One would expect to find an effigy on such a tomb-chest and a canopy, particularly since it apparently obscured the east end of the church, but none of the references to the monument mention either of these. Chittings's reference to alabaster makes it tempting to suggest, however, that the monument did originally include an effigy, as these were the speciality of the alabaster workshops.

The remains of the fifteenth-century monument were replaced in 1682 by a monument commissioned by the dean and chapter from one Mr Brigstock for the princely sum of £30. The freestone monument had seven escutcheons emblazoned with the arms of the dean and the six prebendaries, including those of Humphrey Prideaux (later to be dean) who was the prime mover in erecting the new monument. It was topped with a black marble slab carrying a long Latin inscription. All that can be added to Boston's excellent account is that two years after the monument was completed, Mr Bubbins, blacksmith, was paid £20 4s. 7d. 'for iron to defend the founder's monument and other things'. Ironically, and despite Mr Bubbins's services, the monument shared the fate of its predecessor: in 1862 the freestone base was dismantled and the top slab was set into the floor as a ledger slab, where it can be seen today.[48]

The cathedral boasts a fine collection of work by some distinguished local sculptors of the eighteenth century, who represented one of the foremost provincial schools in England. Robert Singleton (fl. 1706–37) and George Bottomley (fl. 1728–35) went into partnership in 1729, the same year that they executed the monument to Thomas Batchelor in the Bauchun Chapel (figs 177:26 and 188). The monument features reclining putti, an urn and two skulls as well as a fine heraldic cartouche and a Latin inscription composed by the then chancellor of the diocese, Dr Thomas Tanner. In 1737 the *Norwich Mercury* carried an advertisement stating that the 'stock in trade late Messieurs Singleton and Bottomley' had been bought up by another Norwich statuary, Robert Page (d. 1778).[49]

Page's earliest known work is the monument to John Moore (d. 1725) in the third bay on the south side of the presbytery (figs 177:30 and 189). He came to be regarded as probably the best of the Norwich statuaries, whose sculpture could rival the finest London work of contemporaries such as John Cheere. Such was his

48. Dean and chapter audit book, 1680–90, NRO, DCN 11/3; Boston, 'Founder's Tomb', p. 10.
49. Blomefield, *Norfolk*, iv, pp. 14–15; R.

Gunnis, *Dictionary of British Sculptors, 1660–1851* (London, revised edition 1968), p. 353; *Norwich Mercury*, 31 December 1737.

Fig. 188. Mural monument
to Thomas Batchelor
(d. 1729), in the Bauchun
Chapel. By Robert Single-
ton and George Bottomley.

reputation, that when Page died on a visit to Battersea his remains were brought back to Norwich 'in a hearse, attended by two mourning coaches . . . and were interred with great solemnity in St John's Timberhill church' where he and his family are commemorated with a fine monument which he executed on the death of his wife.[50]

Page's talent was closely rivalled by that of Thomas Rawlins the younger (fl. 1747–81). The son of a mason-sculptor, he was trained in London and is certainly 'in the front rank of Norfolk statuaries'. His monument to William Rolfe (d. 1754), now in the Bauchun Chapel, shows all his flair and confidence (figs 177:27 and 190). A putto reclines on a skull in front of a large obelisk of coloured marble flanked by urns. Below an ornately decorated sarcophagus which bears the inscription are two winged cherub heads. The unveiling of the monument in the south transept in

---

50. Gunnis, *Dictionary*, p. 286; *Norfolk Chronicle*, 18 July 1778.

Fig. 189. Mural monument
to John Moore (d. 1725), in
the south ambulatory. The
earliest known work by
Robert Page.

1756 was announced in the *Norwich Mercury*, which reported that it 'is esteemed by many judges to be a very neat piece of workmanship'.[51]

John Ivory (d. 1805), nephew of the Norfolk architect Thomas Ivory, was apprenticed to Robert Page before being granted his freedom in 1752. He signs four monuments in the cathedral. The first, to Dr Thomas Moore (d. 1779), is one of three monuments in the county signed jointly with John DeCarle who had been

51. Gunnis, *Dictionary*, p. 315; C. L. S. Linnell
    and S. Wearing, *Norfolk Church Monuments*
    (Ipswich, 1952), p. 15; *Norwich Mercury*, 26

    June 1756. The monument was moved to
    the Bauchun Chapel in 1893.

Fig. 190. Mural monument
to William Rolfe (d. 1754),
in the Bauchun Chapel.
By Thomas Rawlins the
younger.

his apprentice and who went on to flourish in his own right (figs 177:31 and 191).
On the north side of the presbytery, it is an elaborate composition featuring a
weeping putto, and an extinguished torch symbolising mortality. Behind the putto
is a fine portrait of Moore. This composition, full of symbolism and detail, stands in
direct contrast to Ivory's monument for his uncle Thomas Ivory (d. 1779). Although
the latter monument was executed less than ten years later it shows a complete change
of style, to elegant and restrained Neo-Classicism (figs 177:40 and 192).[52] The two
very similar monuments by Ivory to John Chambers (d. 1788) and Dean Philip
Lloyd (d. 1790), both in the north arcade of the presbytery (fig. 177:34, 177:29),

52. Now in the gallery of the nave but originally in the north transept.

Fig. 192. Mural monument to Thomas and Hannah Ivory (d. 1779 and 1787). Now in the nave gallery, by John Ivory.

Fig. 191. Mural monument to Thomas Moore (d. 1779), in the north ambulatory. Including a portrait of the deceased, by John Ivory and John DeCarle.

show how quickly the simple elements of Neo-Classical design were adapted to mass production in the late eighteenth and nineteenth centuries.

Although no monuments in the cathedral are signed or currently attributed to the Norwich statuary Francis Stafford (fl. 1712–44), an advertisement in the *Norwich Mercury* (16 September 1732) states that 'specimens of his performance may be seen in the cathedral church of Norwich and many other places in the city and county'. Sculptured monuments which are of the right date include the mural monuments to the Mrs Mary and Mrs Anne Eachard (d. 1710 and 1714) in the north arcade of the presbytery (fig. 177:35), to prebendaries Thomas Littell (d. 1731) and Edward Hubbard (d. 1741) which are now in the gallery (fig. 177:41, 177:42), as well as numerous ledger slabs with armorial bearings such as those to Elizabeth Castell (d. 1728) and Dean Prideaux (d. 1724) in the north aisle floor, and to Philip Bedingfield (d. 1730) in the south aisle (fig.177:1, 177:7, 177:3).

The final partnership of Norwich statuaries is that of T. Stafford, son of Francis

Stafford, and G. Athow who signed two monuments in the cathedral, the first to Prebendary Robert Plumptre, who died in 1788, and the second to Bishop George Horne, who died in 1792 (fig. 177:38, 177:28). Stafford and Athow had a workshop near the cathedral, possibly in the close. Although the completion of their 'handsome monument' to Bishop Horne was announced in the *Norwich Mercury* their work leans towards the standardised simplicity of the nineteenth century and lacks the creativity and flair of their predecessors.[53]

The most prolific early nineteenth-century manufacturers in Norwich were the Watsons (whose firm flourished 1793–1851), who had a workshop in St Stephen's. They mass-produced white marble tablets (usually in the shape of sarcophagi) on black surrounds which can be found in many local churches. In the cathedral they sign monuments to William and John Thurlow (1844) in the north ambulatory (fig. 177:18), and a more unusual scroll above the prior's door to the cloister.[54]

Other nineteenth-century monumental sculpture did continue in a grand fashion, including Sir Francis Chantrey's monument to Bishop Bathurst (d. 1837). Erected in 1841, the year Chantrey died, it was the last of many episcopal monuments he executed. Unlike his episcopal monuments to Bishop Ryder (d. 1836) at Lichfield and Bishop Heber (d. 1826, monument erected 1835) at St Paul's, London, who were depicted kneeling at prayer, Chantrey returned to his earlier and more traditional style by depicting the strong-minded Whig sitting down (figs 177:16 and 204).

Chantrey's unique blend of realism and Neo-Classicism was not universally admired: Harrod's criticism that the monument 'might figure well in a college or hall or a museum vestibule; but it is not a fitting memorial for a church or chapel' does not overstate the case.[55] The problem is one of context, for while the statue shows all of Chantrey's naturalistic skills, the bishop appears to sit awkwardly, upon a high pedestal, amongst the Romanesque and Perpendicular interior. This unease is reflected in the fact that the monument has been moved, presumably with considerable difficulty, three times since it was first erected.[56]

53. Gunnis, *Dictionary*, p. 365; Linnell and Wearing, *Norfolk Church Monuments*, p. 16; *Norwich Mercury*, 27 October 1792.

54. The scroll commemorates the donation by the architect John Brown of a window to the dean and chapter in memory of the Rev. Samuel Stone.

55. Harrod, *Gleanings*, p. 295. See also M. Whinney, *Sculpture in Britain, 1530 to 1830* (London, 2nd edn revised by J. Physick, 1988), p. 408, for Chantrey's many public statues; N. Penny, *Church Monuments in Romantic England* (Yale, 1977), p. 74, for Chan-

trey's monuments being suitable for inside or outside churches.

56. Harrod knew the monument north of the high altar in the bay of the reliquary arch in 1857; by 1914 it was in the south transept and it is now in the north-west corner of the north transept: Harrod, *Gleanings*, p. 293, and NRO, DCN 112/1. Chantrey's most successful seated monument, to James Watt (1824) at Handsworth (West Midlands), is by contrast enhanced by being placed in a purpose-built Gothic chapel by Rickman. Penny, *Romantic England*, p. 198–99; Whinney, *Sculpture in Britain*, pp. 404–6.

Fig. 193. Tomb of Bishop Pelham (d. 1894), in the north transept. Recumbent effigy on a chest of coloured marble in the Gothic style by James Nesfield Forsyth.

The change in nineteenth-century tastes, from Neo-Classical to Gothic, is demonstrated by the monument to Bishop Pelham (d. 1894), also in the north transept, which was unveiled by the prince of Wales in 1895 (figs 177:17 and 193). The plain white marble preferred by Neo-Classical sculptors such as Chantrey has given way to the use of coloured marbles, the recumbent effigy is favoured over the kneeling, seated or standing posture, and 'Gothic' detailing such as individual brass lettering and heraldic escutcheons adorn the tomb. The sculptor was James Nesfield Forsyth of London, who was also responsible for the monuments to Dean Elliot (d. 1891) in Bristol Cathedral and Bishop Fraser (d. 1885) in Manchester Cathedral.[57]

The most successful monumental form to be revived during the late nineteenth century, in quantity at least, was the brass. Typical examples of commemorative brass inscriptions with Gothic 'black lettering', cover the walls of the cathedral, but two of the Victorian brasses do deserve special mention. The first, in the north arcade of the presbytery (fig. 177:32), is a cross brass to members of the Thurlow family including Major Henry Robert Thurlow (d. 1850). Unlike some of the later examples this brass still bears a close resemblance to its fourteenth-century antecedents. By contrast, although equally successful in its own right, the brass to Dean

57. B. Read, *Victorian Sculpture* (London, 1982), pp. 79, 359.

Fig. 194. War memorial in
the south transept by E. H.
Baily to members of the
Ninth East Norfolk Regi-
ment killed in Afghanistan in
1842. The brass beneath
commemorates those killed
in India in 1845–46.

Pellew (d. 1866) in the northern arcade of the nave (fig. 177:10) shows how the
revival brasses developed their own iconography, for although the detailing is Gothic
the brass depicts the effigy of the dean recumbent upon a chest-tomb, something
never seen on medieval brasses.[58]

The most significant group of late nineteenth- and twentieth-century memorials
in the cathedral are the war memorials mainly commemorating soldiers of the
Norfolk Regiment and the Seventh Royal Dragoon Guards. The earliest of these
war memorials is in the south transept and commemorates the officers and men of
the Ninth East Norfolk Regiment killed in the Afghan campaign of 1842 and in
India in 1845–46 (figs 177:14 and 194). This monument, featuring Britannia mourning at a sarcophagus surrounded by regimental colours, is signed by E. H. Baily of
London (d. 1867), one-time pupil of the sculptor John Flaxman. Unlike Flaxman

---

58. Pellew's brass is signed by T. J. Gawthorp   *Memorial Brasses* (London, 1983), p. 73 and
    & Son, London; see D. Meara, *Victorian*   plate 46.

and Chantrey, Baily is not often remembered, despite being one of the most successful sculptors of the nineteenth century; his statue of Nelson (1842), which stands high above Trafalgar Square, must be one of the most familiar pieces of sculpture in the country.[59] There are also memorials to those who lost their lives in China and Japan (1865–68), Egypt (1882) and South Africa (1900–2), as well as in both World Wars.

Another war memorial of interest is the bronze panel, on the south wall of the Regimental Chapel, to members of the Second Battalion, The Royal Norfolk Regiment, killed at Kohima in Assam in 1944 (fig. 177:21). The panel was originally erected at Kohima but was subsequently brought to the Regimental Chapel for safe-keeping; a stone memorial at Kohima now commemorates those who died there.[60]

Outside the cathedral, on Life's Green to the east of St Luke's Chapel, is a plain cross which commemorates Nurse Edith Cavell (fig. 177:39) who was shot in 1915 for aiding the escape of French and English soldiers from Brussels while it was under German occupation. Her hasty execution after she was found guilty by a military court, and despite pleas for clemency, caused public uproar and made her a national heroine. On 13 May 1919 her body was exhumed and brought with full military honours from Tir National, where she had been shot, to London. After a memorial service at St Paul's her body was carried in a special train from Liverpool Street Station to Norwich, where she was reburied at the cathedral.[61]

The hundreds of monuments which grace the cathedral provide a unique record of the people who have worshipped in and served the cathedral over its nine hundred year history. They provide unique evidence about changing religious beliefs, and the way attitudes to commemoration have changed over the centuries. The collection of monuments that we are able to enjoy today is the product of a wide range of forces, some responsible for adding monuments, whilst other forces have eroded their numbers. It is important to realize that those forces continue to exert an influence upon the surviving monuments today and that they will only survive for another 900 years if proper and prompt measures are taken to preserve them.

59. Gunnis, *Dictionary*, pp. 32–36. For other monuments by Baily, see Penny, *Romantic England*, pp. 6, 39, 73, 97, 103–5, 123.
60. I am grateful to Sam Horner for the benefit of his knowledge about the Regimental Chapel.
61. 'The Edith Cavell File. A transcript of documents, newspaper reports, official statements, etc., relating to the trial, sentence and execution of Nurse Edith Cavell'. Norwich, dean and chapter library, compiler and date unknown; A. E. Clark-Kennedy, *Edith Cavell: Pioneer and Patriot* (London, 1955).

25

The Bells

Paul Cattermole

The Norman cathedral at Norwich was designed to have a central tower; and whilst the windows above the crossing would light an important focal point within the church, its primary purpose was to house bells, which were essential for the smooth running of the monastic and cathedral church. The Norwich Customary of *c.* 1260 tells us how the cathedral bells were used in the thirteenth century, and it is perhaps surprising to discover how much daily ringing was needed to regulate the domestic and religious programme of the priory. Monks needed to be reminded of chapter meetings and services, while lay servants, who might be working at a distance, needed to know when to return for meals or other domestic occasions.[1] A pair of small bells was usually rung before the daily offices, but festivals were marked by special styles of ringing. On solemn occasions, such as Maundy Thursday, a single large bell might be used before the hour of absolution; and three small bells were rung for vespers on feast days, such as St John the Baptist or SS. Peter and Paul. More elaborate ringing is suggested by an instruction to sound 'all the bells' before services on the principal festivals, when the ringing was sometimes *festive* (joyfully), and at other times the bells were to be rung *ut classicum* (like a war-trumpet), suggesting that they were clashed together instead of being rung in sequence. The bells were also rung at significant moments in the liturgy on certain occasions. On Easter Eve the bells were rung during the *Gloria*, at the moment when the words *et in terra pax* (and on earth peace) were sung; and again on the eve of Pentecost, when the bishop approached the altar *cum festiva processione* (in festal procession). Proper ringing for the dead was important, both on the day of the funeral and at intervals afterwards: there are directions for ringing all the bells at *placebo* and *dirige* (office for the dead), on the anniversary of Bishop Herbert and on All Saints' Day.

---

1. References to the way the bells were used are scattered throughout J. L. B. Tolhurst, ed., *The Customary of the Cathedral Priory* *Church of Norwich* (Henry Bradshaw Society, 82, 1948).

Instructions sometimes differentiate between the 'bells in the choir' and the 'greater' bells, leaving no doubt that the former hung in the central tower, while the latter were in the detached clocher which stood west of the cathedral church. The two sets of bells had distinctive voices. Those in the central tower were used for the regular services, while the heavy bells were reserved for ringing on the most important festivals, such as the anniversary of Bishop Herbert, when the master of the cellar was charged with supplying food and drink for the ringers in the great steeple.

These few examples show how different combinations of bells were used for different purposes. It is not surprising that it needed a specialist to organise the complicated schedule of ringing detailed in the Customary. John Rudham, who is named in a master of cellar's roll of 1273–74,[2] appears as *campanarius* in a property transaction that he made in 1290,[3] suggesting that one of his duties was to organise ringing.[4] He must have had successors. Among sixteenth-century cathedral documents is a grant to John Flowerdew of the 'appointment of two clerks, commonly called *le Belleryngers*'. Flowerdew had paid £20 for the right to nominate two bell ringers (presumably the subsacrists), who were to receive a small annual salary and a robe from the sacrist. As the rectory manor of Bawburgh was security for the salaries, one wonders what benefit Flowerdew gained from this piece of patronage.[5]

Other large churches had more than one tower. For example, the 'leaden steeple' at Worcester contained bells, as well as the central tower, and there was a detached tower at Salisbury. Lincoln had bells in all three of its towers, while Shrewsbury Abbey had two rings of five bells: the larger with a tenor of 30 cwt (1.5 tonnes), while the smaller had a tenor of 11 cwt (550 kg). The Norwich rolls, which name some of the bells, reveal that the full complement in the clocher was five, of which the largest bell was called 'Lakenham'. It is not clear where the bells called 'Stratton' and 'Stockton' hung, but the bell called 'Blessed Mary' hung in the central tower with four companions.[6]

The Sacrist's Responsibility

The sacrist was responsible for providing the bells, and maintaining them in a fit condition to be rung; it is from his rolls that we are able to glean most information about bells in the pre-Reformation cathedral. Although there is no record of any special payment for ringing, it is probable that the fourteenth-century ringers were

2. NRO, DCN 1/1/3.
3. NRO, NCR, case 1, shelf a, roll 2, membrane 28.
4. H. B. Walters, *Church Bells of England* (London, 1912), p. 176, citing Ducange,

Promptorium Parvulorum.
5. NRO, DCN 38/4.
6. J. L'Estrange, *Church Bells of Norfolk* (Norwich, 1874), pp. 169–70, derived from the sacrists' rolls.

Fig. 195. The cathedral and lower close meadows from the south east, *c.* 1870–90.

among the 'servants of the church' who appear on the sacrist's payroll. A set of statutes, probably late Henrician, give details of how the subsacrists operated *c.* 1540.[7] Their duties included preparing the altars, attending to the candles, sweeping the church and keeping the glass windows clean; they were also required to ring the bells as directed by the dean and chapter. When more ringers were needed for special occasions, they could call on the services of as many of the bedesmen as were required. These sixteenth-century arrangements were probably a direct continuation of earlier practice.

The sacrists' rolls contain many references to oil, ropes and tallow, together with carpenters' bills for new headstocks and smiths' bills for ironwork. Until the fifteenth century, bell hanging was relatively crude. Bells were fixed to short timber headstocks (usually made of elm to prevent splitting) by iron bands, which were secured by nails. A pair of stout axles, driven into endgrain, rested in brass bearings fixed to the bell frame.[8] The bell rope was attached to a spar which projected far enough to give sufficient leverage to swing the bell, and a heavy iron clapper hung from a buckled

7.   NRO, DCN 29/2, fo. 23.

8.   P. Cattermole, *Church Bells and Bellringing:*

A Norfolk Profile (Woodbridge, 1990), see diagram p. 89.

leather strap or baldrick attached to an iron staple inside the bell. A typical repair entry occurs in 1427–28 when the sacrist paid a total of 43s. 4d. to 'William Coppyng for hanging the bell called Lakenham and trussing the great bells', and 'William Smyth of Nedeham for making one clapper for the bell called Lakenham with winding bands and nails'.[9] The stresses caused by swinging the bells, together with seasonal changes in the timber, made the iron bands work loose; 'trussing' involved jacking the bells up and refixing the ironwork, by withdrawing the old nails and hammering in new ones. Frequent ringing also meant that the clapper baldricks were constantly wearing out, hence the regular references in the rolls to repairing them.

The bells were usually swung through an angle of about thirty degrees on either side of the vertical. While it was relatively easy to chime the bells in a pre-determined sequence, it was not easy to change the sequence in any orderly fashion. During the fifteenth century English ringers discovered that bells could be swung much higher if a half-wheel was fitted in place of the lever. This process made them sound much more resonant and impressive: over a period of perhaps half a century the method known as full-circle ringing developed, which enabled ringers to change the sequence of the bells relatively easily. The great weight of moving metal put a strain on the bell gear (particularly the nailed iron bands), and the sacrist's roll for 1438–39 shows that improvements were made in both towers.[10] Stephen Carpenter was paid £6 13s. 4d. for a contract described as 'new hanging, stocking and wheeling the bells'. New bell irons costing 107s. 8d. are detailed as 'keys, bolts, gudgeons and nails', leaving no doubt that the bells were rehung with slotted bolts, secured by keys instead of the nailed bands which were so difficult to maintain.[11] New wheels are significant in the context of moves towards full-circle ringing in the fifteenth century.

The Bells in the Central Tower

The Customary assumes that the bells in the central tower would be used for most purposes, since they were conveniently placed for daily and liturgical use. When bells are swing-chimed the ropes do not move very quickly, so the ringers could easily stand on the church floor and the ropes could fall discretely in the corners of the crossing. With a more vigorous style, culminating in full-circle ringing, shorter ropes were essential. The response to this problem can be seen in the sacrists' rolls: in 1405–6 timber costing £8 was purchased for making a floor (*solarium*) in the great tower above the choir, which was built in the following year.[12] The term 'ringing solar' is commonly used for the platform where the bell ringers stand; it

9. NRO, DCN 1/4/63.
10. NRO, DCN 1/4/76.

11. Cattermole, *Church Bells*, see diagram p. 91.
12. NRO, DCN, 1/4/48 and 1/4/49.

seems probable that the chapter decided to remove the ringers from the crossing to a place where they could more easily control their bells.

Fire following a lightning strike gutted the tower in 1463, and the bells must have been cracked, if not melted. Although precise details of the new bells cannot be discovered, an entry in the roll for 1468–69 for torches at the funeral of Robert Brethenham provides a *terminus post quem*, for the tenor bell. New bell ropes, together with horse hide for baldricks, were bought in the same year.[13] It is most likely that five bells were cast in 1469. Details of the present occupants of the central tower are as follows.

Treble:
Diameter 28½ in. (72 cm.) Note C sharp
Weight 4 cwt (215 kg) approximately
'+ Fac Margareta : Nobis Hec Munera Leta'
('Margaret, make these duties joyful to us')

No. 2:
Diameter 30½ in. (77 cm.) Note B
Weight 5 cwt (250 kg) approximately
'+ Quesumus Andrea : Famulorum Suscipe Vota'
('We pray you Andrew, raise up the gifts of your servants')

No. 3:
Diameter 33 in. (84 cm.) Note A
Weight 5 cwt 2 qr 6 lbs (285 kg)
'ANNO DOMINI 1635 I B'

No. 4:
Diameter 37½ in. (95 cm.) Note G sharp
Weight 9½ cwt (450 kg) approximately
'+ Subueniat Digna : Donantibus Hanc Katerina'
('May the worthy Katherine send aid to those giving this [bell]')

Tenor:
Diameter 41½ in. (105 cm.) Note F sharp
Weight 12 cwt (600 kg) approximately
'+ Sum Rosa Pulsata : Mundi Maria Vocata
Orate Pro Aia Roberti Brethenham Monachi Norwici'
('When rung I am called Mary, Rose of the World
Pray for the soul of Robert Brethenham, monk of Norwich')

13. NRO, DCN 1/4/91.

Four fifteenth-century bells survive. Whilst three of them are of similar design, suggesting that they were part of a complete ring cast in 1469 by Richard Brasyer I at the Norwich bell foundry, the lettering on the treble differs, suggesting that it is the recast bell which the sacrist paid for in 1472.[14] The third bell, bearing the initials of John Brend II of Norwich, was purchased secondhand from Edward Tooke, a Norwich founder in 1678. A receipt for £30 survives for a bell 'being the third or middle bell of the five bells now hanging in the steeple of the cathedral church'.[15] In common with several other ancient rings, the five bells are tuned to one of the plainsong modes, in this case the Dorian. Sir Thomas Browne (*c.* 1680) describes heraldry painted 'inside the steeple over the choir', there being 'twenty-four escutcheons . . . six on each side'.[16] These can probably be identified with the eight panels containing arms that were painted in 1481–82 at a cost of fifty-two shillings.[17] If the decoration was visible from below, the bells must have been rung from a balcony which left the lantern stage of the tower open (perhaps like that at Merton College, Oxford); in which case the arms might have hung like hatchments on the front of the balustrade.

Before 1600 the cathedral bells were as good as almost any in Norwich (only St Andrew's church had six bells) and it is clear that five-bell ringing was a popular secular pastime until the eighteenth century.[18] The first ring of eight bells in Norwich was created at St Peter Mancroft in 1672. By 1740 the four eight-bell towers (St Peter Mancroft, St Andrew, St Michael at Coslany and St Giles) were the most popular with ringers. Although the five bells at the cathedral were less exciting, the Norwich Scholars probably supplied a team when required, but there was never a notable company of ringers attached permanently to the cathedral.[19] The *Norwich Mercury* records that the cathedral bells were rung for guild days during the early years of the eighteenth century, and the chapter accounts record regular payments to the ringers who performed on special occasions through to 1761.[20]

A chapter minute of 1766, which relates to the reordering of the choir, refers to the 'balustrades before the belfry'. These were to be 'taken away and made to range even with those below', when the stalls were reconstructed.[21] Repton's section of the cathedral shows balconies above the two-tiered box pews (known as 'the closets') that filled the arches opening into the transepts.[22] Level with the gallery, the balconies

14. NRO, DCN 1/4/93.
15. Bodleian Library, MS Tanner 133, fo. 174.
16. Sir Thomas Browne, *Repertorium*, in *Posthumous Works of the Learned Sir Thomas Browne* (London, 1712), p. 22.
17. NRO, DCN 1/4/97.
18. Cattermole, *Church Bells*, p. 16.
19. For an account of the Norwich Scholars, one of the earliest societies of change-ringers, see A. G. G. Thurlow, *Church Bells and Ringers of Norwich* (Norwich, 1948), pp. 23–33.
20. Thurlow, *Church Bells*, p. 40, confirmed in NRO, DCN 11/11.
21. NRO, DCN 24/5, fos 104–105.
22. S. R. Pierce, ed., *John Adey Repton and Norwich Cathedral at the End of the Eighteenth Century* (Farnborough, 1965), plate 5.

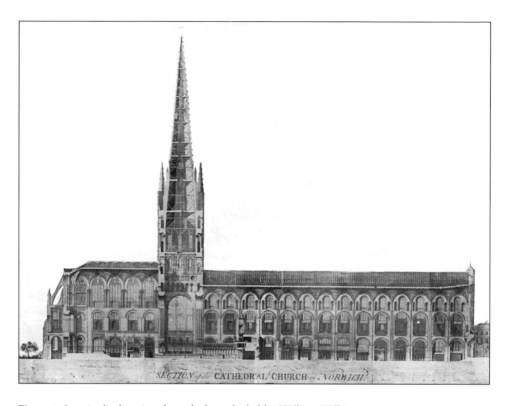

Fig. 196. Longitudinal section through the cathedral by William Wilkins, 1781.

had balustraded backs (facing the transepts) with low parapets in front, matching the cresting on the stalls beneath. This suggests that eighteenth-century ringers rang from two parallel platforms, which projected far enough into the choir to allow the bell ropes to fall vertically; but after 1766 the space was so restricted that it was impossible to do more than swing-chime the bells. A section of the central tower by Wilkins (fig. 196), dated 1781, shows a massive bell frame with 'scissors-braced' trusses, almost certainly installed in the fifteenth century.[23] Two bells, fitted with proper wheels for full-circle ringing, are ranged along the south tower wall; and if the other bells were in a similar frame on the north side, all five could have been rung from a pair of parallel balconies.

The bell chamber had been altered by the time John Adey Repton drew his section of the central tower in the 1790s, when bells (still furnished with wheels) were hung in four arches behind the sound-windows, with the fifth (which was largest) in an independent frame.[24] Parts of the fifteenth-century bell frame survive, used as vertical posts to support the bearings when the bells were rehung; a small

23. Framed drawing, hanging in the Chapter   24. Pierce, *Repton*, plates 5–6.
     Office, 12, The Close, 1993.

section of the independent frame can still be found in the north-east corner of the bell chamber. Careful examination of the surviving timber shows no sign of the stay and slider arrangement which would have been needed if the bells were to be rung in full circles after 1766, making it hard to substantiate the persistent tradition that Samuel Thurston and Charles Payne, prominent members of the Norwich Scholars, were in the last band that rang the cathedral bells,[25] although there is an entry in Payne's notebook which records that he rang at 'Christchurch' (a name sometimes used for the cathedral) *c.* 1820.[26]

Thomas Hurry, a Norwich ringer and bell hanger, wrote to the chapter in 1820 offering to exchange the three largest bells for 'such a tenor as no cathedral should be without'.[27] He had 'at command a most excellent bell for the purpose, rich in tone and similar in key to St Peter's tenor', which he recommended that the clock should strike on. He presumed 'it is desirable to remove those dangling ropes from the belfry which are at present such a diminution from the beauty of the choir'. Hurry's proposal was not accepted, and David Hodgson's watercolour (1832) shows the chiming ropes still in position.[28]

There was a move to have a ringing peal in 1888, when the Reverend Nathaniel Bolingbroke was asked to report to the dean and chapter. His recommendation for a heavy ring of eight bells did not find favour, and the bells remain as he saw them.[29] All five are fixed for stationary chiming in a pine bell frame which dates from the nineteenth century. Until 1970 the bells were chimed manually from a rack in the gallery behind the north-east pier of the central tower, but they are now connected to a mechanical chiming apparatus which, by repetition of notes, produces an eight-bell rhythm from five bells. They are also used for the chiming clock.

The Greater Bells in the Clocher

The clocher, or tower to the west of the cathedral, was of Norman origin. Its bells were an important status symbol, being reserved for use on major festivals.[30] Detailed accounts for its rebuilding after the 1272 riot provide an excellent insight into the workings of the masons' yard, as well as an indication of the importance of reinstating the bells.[31] The building campaign, costing more than £60 in some years, seems to have been in progress from 1299–1300 (when the masons' lodge was set up), through

25. T. E. Slater, 'Famous Norwich Ringers: Charles Payne', *Ringing World*, 14 March 1941, p. 123.
26. Norwich Diocesan Association of Ringers Library, Nolan Golden papers.
27. NRO, DCN 26/9/25.
28. Thurlow, *Church Bells*, frontispiece. NRO, DCN 128/4.
29. Norwich Diocesan Association of Ringers Library, *Annual Report* (1877–88), pp. 17–18.
30. Tolhurst, *Customary*.
31. NRO, DCN 1/4/13–1/4/17.

to 1306–7 and later. The sacrists' rolls provide us with the picture of a stocky detached tower built of limestone mainly from Barnack and Caen, surmounted by a leaded spire with a weather vane. The purchase of 180 ft (55.9 m.) of 'tablement' suggests that the tower was about 45 ft (14 m.) square (a figure confirmed by excavation in 1881).[32] The construction was under the supervision of John Ramsey, who himself cut the limestone for eight round windows. The great timbers erected in the 'berfrey', in 1306–7 were probably the basis of the spire; the tower must have been complete by 1309–10, when Prior Lakenham gave the sum of £40 to have a bell made.[33] The accounts show that metal was fetched from London, presumably to complement metal rescued from the fire of 1272, and that a bell was cast in the following year at a cost of £12 9s. 2d. A slightly later account at Ely, where the cost of preparing moulds and casting bells is detailed, suggests that Prior Lakenham's new bell weighed at least 50 cwt (2.5 tonnes).[34] Although this sounds huge by modern standards, it should be remembered that most large churches had swinging bells of that size in pre-Reformation times, of which the most impressive survivor is Great Peter at Gloucester weighing 60 cwt (3 tonnes).[35]

The clocher bells were kept in good repair down to the sixteenth century. They were claimed to be still in use in 1561, when a commendation from the earl of Leicester accompanied Mr William Huggins' request for a grant of 'certain vacant houses within your house, as the clocher, the old hostry hall, the library, the granary, which be houses of no use for you'.[36] The dean and chapter were not to be persuaded and stated that:

> the said clocher is so builded, and standeth so, before the cathedral church that the want thereof would be an occasion of great ruin and sudden decay of the said church by the south-west wind. Also the bells to ring to common sermons do hang in the same, and no other place meet for the same but that. And likewise the decaying thereof should be a blemish not only to the said church but also to the city.[37]

32. J. J. Raven, 'The Church Bells of Norfolk', in R. H. Mason, *History of the County of Norfolk* (London, 1884), p. 589. The excavation is mentioned and an internal dimension of 36½ ft (11.1m.) is given. See also *NA*, 19 (1915), p. xiii, where an external dimension of 50 ft (15.2 m.) is given. There is a plan in Thurlow, *Church Bells*, p. 38.

33. NRO, DCN 1/1/21. The bell was cast and the surplus metal was sold the following year (DCN 1/1/22).

34. F. R. Chapman, *Sacrist Rolls of Ely*, 2 vols (Cambridge, 1907), ii, pp. 138–39, discussed in C. J. Pickford and P. Cattermole, 'Ely Cathedral Bells', unpublished typescript, 1993. The draft of a text, which will form part of a projected publication by C. J. Pickford on Ely Cathedral bells, is deposited in the library of the dean and chapter at Ely.

35. M. Bliss and F. Sharpe, *Church Bells of Gloucestershire* (Gloucester, 1986), pp. 324–26.

36. NRO, DCN 47/2, fo. 41v.

37. NRO, DCN 47/2, fos 41v–42r.

It appears that the great bells in the clocher were used to summon those who came to hear sermons in the green yard, and doubtless for other important occasions. Despite these protestations the bells had been sold within a decade.

The receiver's account roll for 1569–70 shows that the chapter was under financial stress: vast numbers of oaks from outlying estates were turned into cash; and materials from redundant buildings in the close, such as the chapter house, were sold off in convenient parcels.[38] As the clocher bells were also deemed surplus to requirements, the dean and prebendaries entered into an agreement with Clement Paston of Oxnead for 'so many hundredweight of good and sufficient bell metal after the price of 28s. the hundred, and so many fothers of good and sufficient lead, shot in sows, after the rate of 20 cwt to the fother and after the price of £8 10s. the fother as do and shall in all amount to £200'.[39] The lead, already melted and cast into pigs, and the bell metal, doubtless broken up, were to be delivered to Paston at the clocher. There is no doubt that the building was abandoned and treated as a quarry for building materials, since the Great Hospital accounts record payments for paving stone and sand, collected from the clocher in 1576 and 1580.[40] A conveyance dated 1582 included 'the great clocher as the same is now very ruinous, decayed, uncovered and defaced', and the purchaser had all the remaining stone and timber at his disposal.[41] Thus it appears that the bells were taken down *c.* 1569 and that the clocher was reduced to rubble by *c.* 1580. Apart from foundations excavated in 1881, and the early building accounts, the only evidence for the design of the detached bell tower is contained in engravings published in 1558 and 1583.[42]

The Quarter-Jacks

The sacrist's rolls for 1322–24 record the construction of an elaborate clock, which appears to have been fitted with sun and moon dials, as well as ornamental figures to represent the hours. This clock, which stood in the south transept, was apparently burnt out in the seventeenth century. The pair of small metal figures now standing above the doorway in the south transept appear to have formed part of a Jacobean clock which replaced the fourteenth-century mechanism.[43]

Since the destruction of the clocher in the sixteenth century, the bells have not been perceived as an important element in the ceremonial life of the cathedral, as

38. NRO, DCN 10/1/26.
39. NRO, DCN 47/2 chapter minutes 15 June 1569. Also DCN 47/3, fo. 38v.
40. NRO, NCR, case 24, shelf a, Great Hospital account rolls, 1570–79, membranes 35 and 62.
41. NRO, DCN 47/3, fo. 387.
42. The engravings form part of two early maps that are described in T. Chubb and G. A. Stephen, *A Descriptive List of the Printed Maps of Norfolk, 1574–1916* (Norwich, 1928), pp. 193–96, plates xviii–xix.
43. Thurlow, *Church Bells*, p. 42.

they are at places such as York, Canterbury and Worcester. By the time the old ringing balconies at Norwich were removed in the eighteenth century, the focus of bell ringing in the city had shifted to St Peter Mancroft, whose bells, rather than those at the cathedral, were used in conjunction with important civic and national occasions. Only three English cathedrals (Norwich, Ely and Salisbury) lack a proper ring of bells hung for change-ringing. The main problem at Norwich would be to provide a floor for the ringers without reducing the lighting of the crossing space under the central tower.[44] Even if the cathedral bells are not the most exciting for twentieth-century bell ringers, the survival of four ancient bells is significant. Few English towers contain as many as four pre-Reformation bells; only two (Ipswich, St Lawrence, and London, St Bartholomew Smithfield) contain five.[45]

44. The problem has been solved at Merton College, Oxford, and at Pershore Abbey, Worcestershire.

45. Only two Norfolk churches have four pre-Reformation bells: Banham and St George Tombland, Norwich.

PART V

The Cathedral and the Dean and Chapter 1538–1996

26

Refoundation and Reformation, 1538–1628

Ralph Houlbrooke

In May 1538, nearly half way through its 900 year span, occurred the most important event in the history of the cathedral of the Holy Trinity since its foundation.[*] The Benedictine priory, one of the greatest monastic houses in East Anglia, was transformed into a secular community under the control of a dean and chapter. The principal author of the cathedral's first effective set of post-Reformation statutes, Edmund Suckling, the tenth dean of the new foundation, died in 1628. The ninety years between the transformation and Suckling's death were years of uncertainty and change during which the cathedral faced religious, jurisdictional, financial and constitutional problems. Suckling was an energetic churchman who had a clear view of the cathedral's character and purposes. But not long after his death his vision was to be temporarily extinguished by the storms of civil war and revolution.

Norwich was the first monastic cathedral to be refounded. The prior and convent made humble suit to Henry VIII and his council for their 'transposition'. The transformation was carried out by a charter granted on 2 May 1538. Its provisions were very conservative. The last prior and twenty-one monks, with another Benedictine drafted in from outside, were translated into a dean, six prebendaries and sixteen canons. All were dispensed from the habit and Rule of their Order, and were given the duties of serving God in the church and praying for the king and his ancestors. The priory's property was transferred to the new dean and chapter, who were empowered to allot salaries and stipends from their revenues to each chapter member. The exceptionally favourable provisions of the translation charter

[*] I am most grateful to Professor Claire Cross, Professor Patrick Collinson and Dr Diarmaid MacCulloch for reading, and commenting upon, earlier drafts of this chapter, and to Dr Ian Atherton for checking some of the references.

do not tell the full story. The cathedral's own accounts for 1538 show that three monks were not included in the new foundation. They also list enormous payments incurred 'by reason of the alteration and mutation' of the cathedral. On 1 April, just over a month before the translation, the prior and convent received licence to alienate lands to an annual value of over £48, including their cell of Hoxne. Two of those who purchased priory lands, Sir Richard Gresham and Sir Nicholas Hare, were entrusted with the delivery of substantial sums to the king's use. Henry clearly took his cut when he sanctioned the transformation. Further expenses were incurred in buying a new organ and service books, and choir vestments apparently modelled on those in use at St Paul's.[1]

Commissioners appointed by the crown in July 1538 recorded the cathedral properties and revenues as apportioned to the dean, six prebendaries and a fund for the payment of the canons' salaries. The first four prebends – chancellor's, precentor's, treasurer's and archdeacon's – were named from the office-holders whose income they provided. The last two were those of Lynn and Yarmouth. All but the last bore sundry reprises and charges: among those carried by the first prebend, for example, were the fees of the high steward, auditor, understeward and receiver-general. The clear value of the dean's endowment was just over £102. Just over £50 of revenue was earmarked for the stipends and household expenses of each of the first four prebendaries; the clear values of the other two prebends were just under £44 and just under £32 respectively. The salaries of the sixteen canons ranged from £11 3s. 11½d. to £10 8s. 4d. (the sum received by ten of them). The subdean and succentor were the two highest paid.[2]

Between December 1540 and September 1542 seven monastic cathedrals were refounded and six new cathedrals were established. But the translation of Norwich remained unique. All the other Henrician cathedrals were clearly new royal foundations: in every case there had been an interval between the dissolution of the previous monastery and the establishment of the new cathedral. There was far less

---

1. *Letters and Papers, Foreign and Domestic, of the Reign of Henry VIII*, 21 vols in 35 (London, 1880–91), xiii (i), nos 652, 878, 1115 (4); NRO, DCN 29/3, fos 113–114, 132r, 134–136; DCN 113/1, pp. 1–4; DCN 115/9, p. 4 (second series of pagination); J. Strype, *Annals of the Reformation . . . during Queen Elizabeth's Happy Reign*, 4 vols (Oxford, 1824), iii (2), p. 376. The three monks not included were John Wells (later a minor canon), William Wodehous (a cathedral almsman by *c.* 1547) and Robert Smyth. Of the prebendaries, Edmund Drake had been

prior of the cell of Aldeby, Nicholas Thurkyll prior of the cell of Hoxne. The list headed 'Custus & Expense ratione Alteracionis & mutacionis Religionis monasticalis Ecclesie Cathedralis Norwici in Decanum prebendarios et canonicos seculares' includes payments of £568 for expenses and £440 to the king's use (NRO, DCN 29/3, fo. 132r).

2. J. Caley and J. Hunter, eds, *Valor Ecclesiasticus*, 6 vols (London, 1810–34), iii, pp. 489–94.

continuity of personnel than at Norwich. The king's letters patent made high-flown declarations of reforming intent quite absent from the Norwich charter of 1538.[3]

On 26 May 1547 the Protector Somerset and other privy councillors required the Norwich chapter to surrender their church to royal commissioners. During his lifetime (they said) Henry VIII had decided on an alteration of Norwich Cathedral similar to that which other cathedrals of his foundation had undergone. The commissioners were instructed to see that the chapter, canons and all other officers of the cathedral remained there and continued to perform their functions until the alteration was perfected. The dean and chapter complied on 3 June. The charter of refoundation issued on 7 November declared the king's purpose that true religion and worship should be restored, the young educated in letters, the old (especially faithful servants of the king) sustained, and that alms and other pious duties might abound there. This time, only the dean and six prebendaries were mentioned in the letters patent of foundation; these constituted the chapter thereafter.[4] Some of the cathedral's previous possessions were excepted from the new grant of lands made on 9 November. According to official valuations, the endowment of £895 14s. 6¼ d. recorded in 1538 had been reduced to £798 6s. 3d. When the chapter tried to recover these lost possessions in Mary's reign they attributed the whole Edwardian refoundation to the insatiable appetite of 'greedy and subtile persons'.[5]

At the time of the refoundation or soon afterwards, Sir Edward North, chancellor of the court of augmentations, signed a 'proportion' listing the members of the cathedral body in some detail. The cathedral is here described as 'Christ's church in Norwich of the foundation of King Edward the vjth'. Never officially confirmed, this document must be treated with caution, but it offers the best available guide to the structure of the new establishment. The dean and six prebendaries, eight petty canons, gospeller and epistoler were all named. No one retained a 'corps' of lands and revenues such as had been recorded in 1538. The annual incomes envisaged for the dean and petty canons (previously canons) were almost the same as those of 1538, but the prebendaries had been sharply reduced to £20 each, though the first three prebendaries were also assigned additional life pensions. There were also six singing men, two sextons, eight choristers and their master, two vergers and six almsmen. Lay staff active outside the church included the high steward of the lands,

3. S. E. Lehmberg, *The Reformation of Cathedrals: Cathedrals in English Society, 1485–1603* (Princeton, 1988), pp. 81–91; A. Hamilton Thompson, ed., *The Statutes of the Cathedral Church of Durham* (Surtees Society, 143, 1929), pp. xxvi–xxxi.

4. NRO, DCN 115/9, pp. 2–4 (second series of pagination); DCN 29/2, pp. 79–89; DCN 28/1, *The Statutes of the Cathedral Church of Norwich* (n.p., n.d.), pp. ix–xiii; *CPR, 1547–48*, pp. 58–61. The dean and prebendaries were to be priests.

5. Caley and Hunter, *Valor Ecclesiasticus*, iii, p. 494; NRO, DCN 29/1, fos 30r, 35v; DCN 115/9, p. 4 (second series of pagination).

understeward, auditor, two butlers, a porter, two cooks and a cater to purchase food. The reader of the divinity lecture was listed separately. The same man, Dr John Barret, had been *lector conuentus* on the eve of the 1538 transformation. Over the following eighty years this establishment underwent only minor changes. By 1613 the number of minor canons had fallen to six, that of lay singing men had increased to eight. An organist had been added. The readership of the divinity lecture seems to have been discontinued. Changes in the body of lay staff included the addition of a chapter clerk and a ferryman.[6]

The two refoundations greatly changed the structure of the cathedral community. The distinction between chapter and minor canons had not existed within the medieval priory. The chapter now governed the rest of the cathedral body. The dean was appointed by the crown from the start. In 1538 the election of prebendaries was granted to the chapter, but in 1547 their nomination was reserved to the crown. (Mary I granted this patronage to Bishop Hopton in 1557, but he died the following year).[7] After the first generation had died out, the minor canons were appointed by the dean as were other members of the choir also.

The most important member of the cathedral corporation was the man whom one ex-monk canon called 'my sovereign and head the dean'.[8] Ten men were deans during the ninety years after the refoundation of 1538; of those, five (John Salisbury, George Gardiner, Thomas Dove, George Montgomery and Edmund Suckling) held office for eighty-one.[9] William Castleton, the last prior and first dean, resigned little over a year after the refoundation.

John Salisbury (*c.* 1502–73), scion of an old Denbighshire family, who succeeded Castleton in August 1539, had also been a Benedictine monk, though he had joined Norwich Cathedral as a prebendary only the year before. He seems to have owed his prebend to Thomas Wriothesley, Thomas Cromwell's patronage manager. His inclusion and subsequent rapid promotion suggest that he may well have been appointed as Cromwell's watchdog in the cathedral. Suspected of heresy while at Oxford in the 1520s, he had suffered a year's imprisonment followed by five years' confinement which had been, he later recalled, little better than imprisonment. Thereafter, he seems to have left radicalism behind him and to have accepted most policies of successive mid-Tudor governments without much difficulty. He had the unusual distinction of having led the surrender of two religious houses to the crown

6. NRO, DCN 113/1, pp. 41–43; DCN 29/2, p. 129. The charter stated clearly that the cathedral had been founded to the honour of the Holy Trinity.
7. *CPR, 1555–57*, p. 359.
8. NRO, Norwich Consistory Court, register

of wills (Attmere), fo. 370r (will of Francis at Mere).

9. J. Le Neve, *Fasti Ecclesiae Anglicanae, 1541–1857*, vii, *Ely, Norwich and Westminster Dioceses*, comp. J. M. Horn (London, 1992), pp. 42–43.

Fig. 197. The Carnary Chapel, taken over by the city corporation during the reign of Edward VI and used as the grammar school. This is an early nineteenth-century engraving.

and had become suffragan bishop of Thetford in 1536. His marriage caused his deprivation in 1554 and a sharp but short check to his career.[10]

Three staunch supporters of Queen Mary then held the deanery in rapid succession: John Christopherson (1554–57), John Boxall (1557–58) and John Harpsfield (1558–59). They were too busy elsewhere, and remained in office too short a time, to leave a deep imprint upon Norwich Cathedral. Salisbury returned to the deanery in 1559. But his last years, especially from about 1565, were to be darkened by illness and controversy. During the winter of 1568–69 the commissioners entrusted with a special royal visitation received testimony that Salisbury, his wife, Dr Miles Spencer (holder of the first prebend), the chapter's clerk and its receiver, John Hoo, who was widely believed to be Mrs Salisbury's lover, were cooperating in the plunder of the cathedral estates by means of irregular leases. Hoo and Spencer also belonged to a network of religious conservatives and recusants. But his affability,

10. *DNB*; A. B. Emden, *A Biographical Register of the University of Oxford, 1501–1540* (Oxford, 1974); London, Lambeth Palace Library, MS 113, fo. 79v; *Letters and Papers of the Reign of Henry VIII*, xiii (i), no. 867. Titchfield Abbey, which Salisbury had surrendered in 1537, became Wriothesley's mansion: see R. Graham and S. E. Rigold, *Titchfield Abbey, Hampshire* (London, 1969), p. 8.

pliancy and complaisance had helped to win Salisbury powerful friends; in 1569 he claimed that when certain individuals had sought to deprive him of his livings, he had been defended by noble and honourable men. He did not say who they were. But the support of the duke of Norfolk and the earl of Sussex had assisted his swift rehabilitation in 1554, and the earl of Derby presented him to the bishopric of Man in 1570.[11]

George Gardiner, who succeeded Salisbury after the latter's death in the autumn of 1573, was a very different character. A vigorous and skilful self-promoter, he set his sails to the prevailing winds of policy, pushed aside without scruple those who stood in his way, and used a well-publicised zeal for reform to further his own advancement. He had been born in Berwick and his Cambridge career had spanned the religious changes of the 1550s. He became a minor canon of Norwich Cathedral in about 1562, as well as minister of St Andrew's, a parish already associated with religious reform. Lord Robert Dudley was believed to have been his most important patron from soon after Elizabeth's accession, but it was at the request of Bishops Parkhurst of Norwich and Grindal of London that the lord keeper, Sir Nicholas Bacon, nominated him to the fifth prebend in Norwich Cathedral in 1565.[12] He soon made his mark, bringing about improvements in record keeping: a register of leases and a minute book of chapter meetings, begun in 1566. During the metropolitical visitation of 1567 Gardiner made serious charges concerning the lax standard of discipline at the cathedral. Next year, perhaps dissatisfied with the meagre results of the archbishop's visitation, he brought about through Sir William Cecil's influence a royal visitation by a commission headed by Bishop Parkhurst. It was Gardiner who presented the commissioners with the most detailed and damning testimony about the parlous state of the cathedral's affairs.[13] But some time after the metropolitical visitation of 1567, accusations were also made against Gardiner himself before Thomas Yale, Archbishop Parker's vicar-general. For most of the past sixteen years he had been 'a man very unquiet, troublesome, dissembling, setting debate betwixt man and man, an evil speaker, breaker of quiet, peace and charity'. At Cambridge he had busily prosecuted Protestants during Mary's reign. After coming to Norwich he had, among other things, been involved in a bloody brawl with John Toller, an ex-monk and petty canon of the cathedral; had sought by undue means to oust Dr John Stokes, 'a very old man', his predecessor in the fifth prebend

11. NRO, DCN 29/1, fos 36, 38r; London, Lambeth Palace Library, MS 113, fo. 83; Blomefield, *Norfolk*, iii, p. 618; D. MacCulloch, *Suffolk and the Tudors: Politics and Religion in an English County, 1500–1600* (Oxford, 1986), pp. 185–87, 214; *CPR, 1569–72*, p. 119. See pp. 475–76, for the possibility that Spencer chose an antiquated style of monumental brass.

12. Blomefield, *Norfolk*, iii, p. 621; *DNB*; BL, Lansdowne MS 443, fo. 144.

13. J. Strype, *The Life and Acts of Matthew Parker*, 2 vols (Oxford, 1821), ii, pp. 159–61; NRO, DCN 24/1; DCN 29/1, fos 35r–38v.

in the cathedral; and had finally agreed to give him an annual pension if he would resign it.[14] On Advent Sunday 1569, perhaps emboldened by the proceedings against Gardiner, John Salisbury delivered a sermon in the cathedral which included a stinging rebuke to those who sought to supplant men in their livings and practised simony – both things of which Gardiner might have been thought guilty. Parkhurst angrily called on Salisbury to explain himself.[15] Gardiner survived and prospered, despite the sentence given against him by Yale in February 1570 and (perhaps more important) involvement in an ill-judged puritan demonstration in the cathedral later in the year. In November 1573, with the support of both Leicester and Burghley, he was presented to the deanery. When dean, he skilfully avoided involvement in the religious conflicts of the later 1570s only to find himself engaged during the 1580s in an exhausting struggle over the cathedral lands. This was still unresolved on his death in 1589.[16]

Thomas Dove, Gardiner's successor, who allegedly owed his preferment to Queen Elizabeth's admiration of his eloquence as a preacher, was dean from 1589 to 1601. These years saw a successful outcome to the battle over the cathedral lands but also, less happily, jurisdictional disputes between the chapter and the city of Norwich. He was promoted to the see of Peterborough in 1601. Seven of the leading gentry of Norfolk liked him well enough to write to Robert Cecil in 1602 urging that he be translated from Peterborough to the newly vacant see of Norwich. They praised Dove's 'gifts and worthiness in every degree', and claimed that their experience of him left them unable to think of any man whom they more wished to be preferred to the place both for the glory of God and the quiet government of the county.[17] Dove was succeeded in July 1601 by John Jegon, a firm believer in uniformity and strong government who was after a short term of office made bishop of Norwich in January 1603.[18]

George Montgomery (1603–14), one of James I's early nominees for ecclesiastical preferment, was installed in June 1603. It is difficult to improve on Dean Prideaux's acid statement that 'he was a Scot by birth and very ill filled his place in this church being mostly absent from it'. Montgomery was also incumbent of Chedzoy in Somerset and held two or three Irish bishoprics during most of his time as dean of Norwich. He seems to have visited Norwich only three times after his installation,

14. W. H. Frere, ed., *Registrum Matthei Parker*, 3 vols (Canterbury and York Society, 35–36, 39, 1928–33), ii, pp. 762–64. Stokes may well have been the Augustinian friar of the same name who had been a conservative rival preacher to Matthew Parker in Suffolk in 1537: see Emden, *Biographical Register of Oxford, 1501–40*.

15. London, Lambeth Palace Library, MS 113,

fos 69–83; R. A. Houlbrooke, ed., *The Letter Book of John Parkhurst, Bishop of Norwich* (NRS, 43, 1974–75), pp. 91–92.

16. Frere, *Registrum Matthei Parker*, ii, pp. 764–66; PRO, SP12/73, fo. 171; BL, Lansdowne MS 443, fo. 43r; *DNB*.

17. *DNB*; Bodleian Library, MS Tanner 135, fo. 144.

18. *DNB*.

in September 1605, from February to June 1611, and from March to May 1614. Never were recorded chapter meetings less frequent or more poorly attended than in his time. His absence allegedly prevented the due completion of annual accounts. It was also a ground for reproach at a time when the chapter was engaged in quarrels with the city. Especially damaging, in the prebendaries' view, was a payment of £400 which they agreed to make to Montgomery as a 'farewell', or golden handshake, in the hope that he would then resign his place. He did not do so and the payment aggravated the cathedral's already precarious financial position.[19]

One man who anticipated Montgomery's departure with particular eagerness was Dr Edmund Suckling. Son of a mayor of Norwich, Suckling, appointed to the third prebend in 1587, was by the time of Montgomery's installation the second longest serving member of chapter. He assumed the chief administrative burdens in Montgomery's absence. In April 1604, less than a year after Montgomery's arrival, Suckling received a grant of the deanery in reversion. In May 1611 royal letters of commendam empowering Montgomery to hold the deanery for life, notwithstanding any grant to Suckling, were openly read in chapter at the dean's request. Suckling protested the nullity of the letters, and dissented from the chapter's decision that Montgomery should continue to hold the deanery with all its profits. Furthermore, he angrily resigned his office of receiver.[20]

Headstrong and imperious, regarded in some quarters as a stirrer of quarrels between cathedral and city, Suckling (1614–28) had a grand project: the issue of royal statutes for the cathedral. In 1620 he achieved his goal when James I granted a set, largely of Suckling's devising. But complaints by men whose interests had been damaged led to the appointment by Charles I of referees to investigate the points at issue. The beleaguered dean, who lost his sight in 1626–27, did not live to hear the ultimate outcome. The statutes received new royal approval in May 1629, but only after some important revisions.[21]

Some fifty men were appointed to the six prebends in Norwich Cathedral either on its translation or during the following ninety years. Thirty-six, almost three-quarters of the total, were installed during the first half of the period. The first generation were ex-monks, some of whom had already served several years: five of

19. NRO, DCN 115/9 (3), Dean Prideaux's Annals of the Cathedral from 1538 to 1677 (unfoliated), under years 1603, 1605, 1610, 1613; DCN 24/1, fos 155v–158v, 165v–174r, 180v–186v; DCN 29/2, pp. 130–31.
20. *CSPD, 1603–10*, p. 102; J. F. Williams and B. Cozens-Hardy, eds, *Extracts from the Two*

Earliest Minute Books of the Dean and Chapter of Norwich Cathedral, 1566–1649 (NRS, 24, 1953), p. 44.
21. Bodleian Library, MS Tanner 228, fo. 140v; NRO, DCN 115/9 (3), under years 1620, 1626, 1627; below, pp. 531–33; PRO, PCC wills 154 Barrington.

them had been replaced by 1550. The relatively turbulent years before 1580 saw at least five deprivations and a number of resignations. On the whole, tenures were longer, continuity greater, in the more stable later Elizabethan and Jacobean years, when three men were each members of the chapter for forty years or thereabouts.[22]

Norwich was one of the smaller and more poorly endowed cathedrals; after 1547 its prebends were not very attractive pieces of preferment. Many of its prebendaries nevertheless came from outside the diocese, the majority being well qualified, at least on paper. Half the first generation of prebendaries were named after places in Norfolk and all but one probably came from within the diocese. Of the men installed between 1538 and 1628 whose places of origin are known (about 60 per cent), some three-quarters had been born outside the diocese, though some of them had already put down roots within it. But as the result of a series of appointments made during the middle and later years of James I's reign, the majority of the chapter were Norfolk men in 1628. Three of the six ex-monk prebendaries of 1538 had degrees, two of them in canon law, one in theology. Nearly all the men appointed after 1538 were graduates at the time of their installation. The majority (some 60 per cent) gained degrees in divinity, in most cases before or around the time of their nomination to Norwich prebends; half of these theologians attained doctorates. On the face of it, the Norwich chapter was equipped to meet the challenges of an age of doctrinal controversy, though some of the best-qualified men seldom or never entered the close.

Over half of the prebendaries were probably in their thirties when they were appointed, a few in their twenties. The majority were therefore young enough to look forward to further preferment. But only one became a bishop (of Man, at the end of his life); six became deans, three of them at Norwich. Others moved on to archdeaconries or wealthier canonries, or held them with their Norwich prebends. One, William Whitaker (1578–95), was an outstanding theologian and controversialist who became regius professor of divinity at Cambridge and master of St John's College. Others, Percival Wiborne (1560–62) and John Walker (1570–74), were chosen official spokesmen to confer with captured Catholic priests in the early 1580s. Robert Johnson (1570–75) was a noted founder of schools and hospitals in the county of Rutland. John Beacon (1575–c. 1587), erstwhile public orator of Cambridge University and writer of Greek and Latin verses, served as chancellor in two dioceses. Apart from these Elizabethan appointees, Robert Talbot (1547–58) was a famous antiquary. Some others, such as John Barret (c. 1558–63), Fulk Roberts (1616–50) and Edmund Porter (1628–70), published sermons or controversial treatises. But the

---

22. Le Neve, *Fasti*, vii, pp. 51–60.

majority of these relatively well-known men played little part in the life of the cathedral.[23]

Crown appointments were to a great extent in the hands of successive lords chancellor and keepers of the great seal. Of these, Sir Nicholas Bacon (1558–79) had by far the largest opportunities of influencing the composition of the chapter. A number of the men nominated during his time were moderate puritans. Some were his own chaplains. He was certainly not a uniformly conscientious patron, however. Archbishop Parker was greatly distressed to discover in 1567 that the non-resident layman Thomas Smith (1562–c. 1570) stood bound to pay £5 a year out of his salary to a nephew of Bacon's studying at Cambridge.[24] Kinship probably played some part in the choice of prebendaries: Thomas Puckering (1595–1616) was related to a lord keeper; John Freake (1581–1604) and Thomas Jegon (1605–18) were respectively the son and the brother of bishops of Norwich; and John Spendlove (1616–66) was a dean's son-in-law. Edmund Suckling (1587–1614, dean 1614–28) was the son of a mayor of Norwich and brother of Sir John Suckling, later comptroller of the royal household, who also allegedly helped John Hassall (prebendary 1615–28) to become dean in 1628.[25]

It seems unlikely that many of the prebendaries of this period saw the cathedral as the centre of their lives. The great majority had other benefices. In 1567, according to George Gardiner, only half the prebendaries were resident. The other three, he claimed, never came to the cathedral except to claim their money. In 1613 only

23. The foregoing analysis is based on C. H. and T. Cooper, *Athenae Cantabrigienses*, 3 vols (Cambridge, 1858–1913); J. and J. A. Venn, *Alumni Cantabrigienses*, i, 4 vols (Cambridge, 1922–27); J. Foster, *Alumni Oxonienses, 1500–1714*, 4 vols (Oxford, 1891–92); Emden, *Biographical Register of Oxford, 1501–1540*; *DNB*; and Blomefield, *Norfolk*, iii, pp. 662–71. Compare the much larger scale analysis of chapter members' origins, qualifications, achievements and career patterns in Lehmberg, *Reformation of Cathedrals*, pp. 226–66.

24. R. O'Day, 'The Ecclesiastical Patronage of the Lord Keeper, 1558–1642', *TRHS*, 5th series, 23 (1973), pp. 89–109. During Bacon's time crown presentations and lord keeper's nominations were listed separately; yet Thomas Smith appears on the crown list: see BL, Lansdowne MS 443, fo. 21. For Smith see also J. Bruce, ed., *Correspondence of Matthew Parker* (Parker Society, 1853), pp.

312–13. Edmund Chapman, Jeffrey and Robert Johnson, John Walker, William Whitaker and Percival Wiborne were all moderate puritans. Thomas Fowle, Robert Johnson and Percival Wiborne were Bacon's chaplains, John Pedder rector of Redgrave, the parish containing his Suffolk residence. Besides Blomefield, *Norfolk*, iii, pp. 662–71, see *DNB* for Robert Johnson, Pedder, Walker, Whitaker and Wiborne; Cooper, *Athenae Cantabrigienses* for Chapman and Fowle; Venn, *Alumni Cantabrigienses* for Jeffrey Johnson.

25. See Cooper, *Athenae Cantabrigienses* and Blomefield, *Norfolk*, iii, pp. 662–71 for Freake, Jegon, Puckering, Spendlove and Suckling. For the possible role of Sir John Suckling in Hassall's appointment see *CSPD, 1623–25*, p. 404 (though at the time the deanery was not yet vacant, and Suckling died before Hassall became dean).

Fig. 198. The former monastic infirmary, converted to houses at the Reformation. This drawing, by R. Ladbrooke, shows it around the time when it was demolished, in 1804.

one prebendary kept house at the cathedral, another five miles away, a third twenty. Those three alone met and dealt with cathedral business; the rest, they said, 'are far off and seldom or never come amongst us'. Nor was there anything wrong in this state of affairs, the prebendaries argued in about 1627. No prebendary could maintain himself and his family without at least one additional benefice. So for discharge of their consciences and in order that they might content their parishioners by residing among them, they asked that the necessity of cathedral residence might be imposed on only one prebendary at a time, as was the case elsewhere. The presence of one would, they claimed, be quite sufficient to govern Norwich Cathedral.[26]

Attendance at most of the chapter meetings held between 1566 and 1628 was recorded in the first two chapter books.[27] During that period, there were thirty-two members. Of those, eighteen attended fewer than a third of the meetings convened while they belonged to the chapter. Only thirteen attended more than two-thirds. So nearly all the prebendaries fell into one of two fairly clearly defined groups. The frequent attenders, those who took a major part in cathedral administration, were nearly all men who held other benefices or offices within the diocese, many of them in Norfolk. While two of them were future deans of Norwich, few of them were to be remembered either for outstanding learning or distinctive churchmanship.

A development which fundamentally changed the character of the cathedral

26. Strype, *Parker*, ii, p. 159; NRO, DCN 29/2, pp. 130, 135–36.
27. NRO, DCN 24/1, 24/2; Williams and

Cozens-Hardy, *Extracts*, does not include the minutes of attendance.

community was the acceptance of clerical marriage between 1549 and 1553 and again after 1558. In 1554 the dean and two of the prebendaries were deprived of their benefices on account of their marriages, but from the 1560s onwards the chapter always included married men. In so far as Elizabeth I's notorious order of 1561 excluding the wives and children of cathedral clergy from the precincts was effective, it can only have discouraged married men from keeping residence.[28]

The wills made by the prebendaries reflect the diminishing cohesion of the cathedral community. Most of the men appointed under Henry or Mary who died at Norwich showed their attachment to the cathedral by requesting burial within it, by leaving money to all members of the chapter and choir who might participate in their funeral, by making gifts of money, books or vestments to the church, by personal legacies to valued friends within the close and by choosing executors from among their cathedral colleagues. In addition some, former monks in particular, began their wills with a solemn invocation of the Trinity to whom their church was dedicated. Henry Mannell or Manuel, who died between October 1569 and January 1570, was the last survivor of former monks of Norwich among the prebendaries. He left £10 to cathedral repairs and the paving of the choir. His legacies to those present at his burial ranged from 20s. to the dean to 1s. to each choir boy. He left 40s. to the petty canons' house for the purchase of wood and further small bequests to their cook and undercook. To Osbert Parsley, the most celebrated of Norwich singing men, his erstwhile servant, he made a personal bequest of 40s. His two executors were both petty canons who had been priory monks till 1538.[29] In later years, however, under Elizabeth and the early Stuarts, a number of prebendaries made wills which were almost entirely taken up with bequests to their wives and families. One of these was Nicholas Bate, the third longest serving member of the chapter, a man described in 1613 as being one of the only three prebendaries who attended to cathedral business. In the will which he made in 1627 he described himself simply as 'clerk' of Swaffham.[30] Most of it is concerned with the division of his property among his family. The only signs of any connection with the cathedral are references to leases from it and to the catership, by now a sinecure, left to his son Nicholas. His wife was his sole executrix.

The minor canons, singing men, and other choir members who maintained the round of cathedral services formed the true heart of the community. Though more important than the prebendaries in the cathedral's day to day life, the minor canons remain much more shadowy figures. Some of them had degrees. One, John Hallibred

28. *DNB* (for Salisbury); Blomefield, *Norfolk*, iii, pp. 618, 666, 669; G. R. Baskerville, 'Married Clergy and Pensioned Religious in Norwich Diocese, 1555', *EHR*, 48 (1933), pp. 52, 55; NRO, DCN 29/2, p. 55.

29. NRO, Archdeaconry of Norwich, register of wills (Busbye), fos 2r–3r; Le Neve, *Fasti*, vii, p. 54.

30. NRO, Norwich Consistory Court, original wills, no. 426.

alias Stokes, a doctor of theology (a quite exceptional case), had been a prebendary, but seems to have been prevailed upon by George Gardiner to resign his benefice in 1565. Gardiner is the only petty canon known to have become a prebendary. Most petty canons had negligible prospects of further advancement in the cathedral hierarchy. Some remained in post for a considerable time. Thomas Sadlington's death in 1638 terminated fifty-nine years' service.[31]

It was probably among the minor canons that the sense of a quasi-monastic community survived longest. At least four ex-monks of Norwich were still minor canons in 1559, twenty-one years after the dissolution. The last of them, Robert Stanton, did not die until 1576. Stanton, despite his comparatively low official status, enjoyed the special trust and respect of other survivors, a number of whom named him executor. In his own will Stanton followed the old pattern of leaving bequests to all members of the establishment, from the dean to choir boys and bedesmen, who attended his funeral. He requested burial in the cathedral and left a substantial legacy towards the repair of its windows.[32]

Like the prebendaries, the petty canons were allowed to take benefices outside the cathedral, but in their case any extramural responsibilities they assumed had to be compatible with the discharge of their choir duties. The 1586 puritan survey of the ministry described Thomas Thwaites, incumbent of Reymerston and SS. Simon and Jude in Norwich, as non-resident upon either of his benefices. Reymerston was certainly too far from Norwich to be served properly by a man who also had substantial cathedral duties. Other minor canons besides Thwaites served in one of the numerous benefices or curacies in the chapter's gift in the city or its suburbs. One of them, William Fugill, curate of St George's Tombland, was presented in the episcopal visitation of 1627 for neglecting parochial duties, including the reading of homilies, the provision of monthly sermons and the catechising of youth, as well as for frequenting alehouses. Fugill's serious personal inadequacy was already well known in the cathedral, where he had been in trouble for notorious drunkenness and for neglecting his sabbath and holy day duties.[33]

The minor canons, like the prebendaries, took to marriage, though they did so more slowly – only two of them were deprived for marriage in 1554.[34] The wills

31. A. H. Smith and G. M. Baker, eds, *The Papers of Nathaniel Bacon of Stiffkey*, iii, *1586–1595* (NRS 53, 1987 and 1988), p. 239; Frere, *Registrum Matthei Parker*, ii, p. 764; Blomefield, *Norfolk*, iii, pp. 620–21; Williams and Cozens-Hardy, *Extracts*, p. 21.

32. H. Gee, *The Elizabethan Clergy and the Settlement of Religion, 1558–1564* (Oxford, 1898), pp. 109–116; NRO, DCN 29/3, fos 113–14;

AN wills Bussell, fos 639–641v.

33. A. Peel, ed., *The Seconde Parte of a Register: Being a Calendar of Manuscripts . . . now in Dr Williams's Library* (Cambridge, 1915), ii, pp. 148, 155; NRO, DN/VIS 5/3/2, fo. 9; Williams and Cozens-Hardy, *Extracts*, pp. 57, 61, 64.

34. Baskerville, 'Married Clergy', p. 52.

later made by married petty canons show the same tendencies as those seen in prebendaries' wills: a transfer of loyalties and emotional bonds from the cathedral community to their families and (to some extent) the parishes where they served. Marriage undermined the arrangements for eating together which at first played an important part in cathedral life. Various members of the cathedral community made bequests to the 'canons' house' or 'common house' during the early years. But when Robert Stanton drew up his will in 1576 he was uncertain whether the petty canons would still be keeping house in their common hall at the day of his burial. In James I's reign it was alleged by a hostile critic that the posts of two butlers, a cater and two cooks provided for in the Edwardian 'proportion' had all become sinecures. In 1627 the prebendaries claimed that the old arrangements had caused such discontent between husbands and wives that the chapter had decided to convert the charges of meals into supplementary stipends. This disappearance of the Norwich common table followed a widespread pattern: similar arrangements came to an end during Elizabeth's reign at many other cathedrals.[35]

The gospeller, epistoler, singing men, organists, and the eight choristers and their master, were the remaining members of the choir. Family connections may have been helpful in starting a career in the choir. In 1569 the choir boys, under the tuition of Edmund Inglott, their master, included Edmund Inglott junior and William Inglott, who later became organist. John Carlton was singing man in 1566, Richard Carlton a petty canon in 1589. In 1620 no fewer than four Carltons were listed as epistoler and singing men. But skill was also necessary. In 1608 the singing man William Syar was first put on probation and then dismissed because of his insufficiency. There seem to have been reasonable security of tenure and some prospects of advancement for the able and conscientious singing man, who might become gospeller, epistoler or petty canon. Osbert Parsley, most expert of Norwich Cathedral singing men, probably served at Norwich for fifty years before his death in 1585. He not only sang but also composed sacred music, some of which survives. In 1569, when there were three levels of pay for singing men, he received half as much again as the basic rate and more than a petty canon's salary. His elegant monument in the cathedral, with its eloquent epitaph, testifies to the especially high esteem in which he was held. Two organists, William Cobbold and William Inglott (d. 1621), were distinguished composers of secular and sacred music.[36]

35. NRO, AN wills Bussell, fo. 640v; Bodleian Library, MS Tanner 228, fo. 140v; NRO, DCN 29/2, p. 142; Lehmberg, *Reformation of Cathedrals*, pp. 187–90.

36. NRO, DCN 29/1, fos 28r, 32r; Williams and Cozens-Hardy, *Extracts*, pp. 20–21, 24, 30, 43, 55; N. Boston, *The Musical History of Norwich Cathedral* (Norwich, 1963), pp. 30–34, 68–70.

The internal politics and external relations of Norwich Cathedral during this period hinged above all on some key problems and issues of religion and churchmanship, jurisdiction, finance and management, and on the constitution of the corporation itself. The role of the cathedrals in the Protestant church was from the start an uncertain and controversial one, as some reformers looked on them with suspicion and dislike. Norwich Cathedral, described in its own chapter book as 'this monastery' as late as 1567, a foundation with especially strong links with the past, might have been expected to face particular difficulties of adjustment.[37] Yet some members of the community were ready to embrace reform. In May 1548, nine years after his resignation, William Castleton, last prior and first dean, made a will which bears the very strong imprint of Protestant influences. His successor, John Salisbury, had suffered earlier for his reforming views. Two men who were still prebendaries, both former monks, made wills early in Edward VI's reign which suggest a ready acceptance of Protestant doctrines. Loye Ferrers (February 1548) expressed his faith that he was one of the elect by the passion and death of Christ. Castleton was one of his legatees. Edmund Drake (February 1549) looked forward to inheriting the kingdom of heaven prepared for God's elect from the beginning of the world. He left £4 for the preaching of sermons by the former Carmelite Dr John Barret, the cathedral divinity lecturer and a man regarded as a reformer under Edward VI.[38] Robert Watson, a well-known Protestant and controversial preacher, was nominated to Drake's prebend in 1549, despite his being a layman, but resigned it a little over two years later.[39]

The first signs of religious controversy within the cathedral community came early in 1549, with the appearance of a number of supposedly seditious rhymes and bills. Interrogatories administered to five petty canons (three of them ex-monks) and two singing men sought to uncover the source of suspected 'popish' inspiration and the authorship of libels against the mayor of Norwich and the Protestant preacher Thomas Rose. The enquiry discovered little. A bill entitled 'Eccho', which two of the canons had copied, contained the line 'I thought to have gone a furlong and yet I ran a mile', which could conceivably have referred to the speed of religious change under Edward VI. But the bills circulating around the cathedral were certainly not all on one side: one, found inside the church itself, criticised the Latin service which was soon to disappear.[40]

37. C. Cross, '"Dens of Loitering Lubbers": Protestant Protest against Cathedral Foundations, 1540–1640', in D. Baker, ed., *Schism, Heresy and Religious Protest* (Studies in Church History, 9, 1972), pp. 231–37; Williams and Cozens-Hardy, *Extracts*, p. 24.

38. NRO, Norwich Consistory Court wills Wellman, fos 75r–78r; Wymer, fos 260r–2r;

PRO, PCC wills 17 Populwell. See *DNB* for Salisbury and Barret.

39. Le Neve, *Fasti*, vii, p. 55; S. T. Bindoff, ed., *The House of Commons, 1509–58*, 3 vols (London, 1982), iii, pp. 560–61.

40. *Eastern Counties Collectanea*, I (1872–73), pp. 171–75.

The chapter seems if anything to have been rather more conservative early in Elizabeth I's reign than it had been in Edward VI's. Only one chapter member, Dean Harpsfield, lost his place, compared with three in 1554.[41] He made way for the return of John Salisbury, who had conformed under Mary. The core of the chapter, its most active members, were conservative conformists: the former Norwich monk Henry Manuel, John Stokes, Miles Spencer, a long serving chancellor of the diocese, and John Barret, former supporter of religious reform, whose ultimately sincere acceptance of the Marian settlement had been rewarded with a prebend, probably in 1558.[42]

The appointment of George Gardiner in 1565 was the harbinger of more dramatic changes. Early in 1569, answering the royal commissioners' enquiries, Gardiner portrayed the cathedral as a sick and useless institution. Preaching was neglected. Most members of the community received communion but once a year, some (he had heard) had not done so since the queen's accession. The dean and chapter themselves admitted that Bibles and Paraphrases had not been set up in the cathedral according to the queen's injunctions because when copies had been placed there they had been 'cut, spoiled and abused'.[43] John Salisbury used his 1569 Advent sermon to hit back at Gardiner. But for the fact that the queen was more merciful than many of those who professed Christ (he said), cruelty would have been as great as in the days of fire and faggot. It is hardly surprising that the sermon caused him to be accused of popish sympathies.[44]

In 1570 the complexion of the Norwich chapter was changed in a way not seen since its foundation. No fewer than four new prebendaries were installed (two on the deaths of long-serving conservatives, two on the deprivation of non-residents), all of them men of a strongly Protestant or puritan outlook. The reformers seem to have carried out some demonstration to mark their newly won ascendancy. They went too far. On 25 September 1570 the queen wrote to Bishop Parkhurst to enquire into certain innovations attempted by George Gardiner and three colleagues, John Walker, Thomas Fowle and Edmund Chapman. They had allegedly broken down the organs and committed 'other outrages'. The earl of Leicester, supposedly Gardiner's patron, criticised the prebendaries' action in a letter to Matthew Parker.[45]

41. Le Neve, *Fasti*, vii, pp. 42, 51, 53–55, 57, 59.
42. For Stokes's conservative views see Cambridge, Corpus Christi College, MS 102, fo. 247. The wills of these prebendaries are also revealing: see PRO, PCC wills 8 Lyon (Spencer); NRO, Norwich Consistory Court wills Knightes, fos 119v–122v (Barret), Archdeaconry of Norwich wills

Busbye, fos 2–3r, 215 (Manuel and Stokes). See also MacCulloch, *Suffolk and the Tudors*, pp. 185–87.
43. NRO, DCN 29/1, fos 33r, 34r, 37.
44. London, Lambeth Palace Library, MS 113, fos 73, 79.
45. Edmund Chapman, John Walker, Robert Johnson and Jeffrey Johnson succeeded

Gardiner seems to have had a shock which he never forgot; as dean he put radicalism behind him. When at the very end of 1574 Gardiner's erstwhile ally Edmund Chapman and two others openly inveighed against the manner of singing in the cathedral, Gardiner 'very pithily confuted certain of their reasons'. He also had another 'busy fellow' imprisoned for attempting liturgical innovation.[46] The mirage of a puritan cathedral soon disappeared. All the men appointed in 1570 had gone by 1579, the most militant of them, Edmund Chapman, deprived of his prebend. The cathedral played little part in the great struggle which developed in the later 1570s between Bishop Edmund Freake (1575–84) and the puritans of his diocese. A minor canon, Richard Crick or Creke, was one of the six ministers of Norwich who petitioned Lord Burghley against ceremonies in September 1576, though it was not long before he departed for the more congenial surroundings of East Bergholt. The leading Norwich puritan, John More, visited Nathaniel Bacon's house in the close and catechised there. When Gardiner threatened to complain to the privy council in the spring of 1578, it was John Beacon, since 1575 both prebendary and chancellor to Bishop Freake, who told Bacon. Beacon acknowledged that his sympathy with moderate nonconformists had led to his being calumniated as a 'favourer of puritans'. This sympathy was the main reason for a bitter quarrel between him and the bishop, who was intent on enforcing conformity. Freake wrote to Gardiner as to a trusted confidant, ridiculing his chancellor and seeking the dean's help in keeping track of Beacon's dealings at court.[47] After 1578, no known puritans or supporters of puritan aims joined the ring of regular attenders at the Norwich chapter. Hugh Castleton, one of the longest serving and most diligent prebendaries of the period (1577–1616) was described by a hostile observer as one of the 'principal solicitors and instruments' of Bishop Freake; John Freake, an intermittent participant in chapter business (1581–1604), was the bishop's son. Thomas Dove, Gardiner's successor as dean (1589–1601) was a conformist, though one sufficiently cautious and tactful to win the respect of leading Norfolk gentlemen. John Jegon, the next dean (1601–3) was recommended by both John Whitgift

note 45 continued
Miles Spencer, Henry Manuel, Nicholas Wendon and Thomas Smith (Le Neve, *Fasti*, vii, pp. 51, 54, 57, 59; Blomefield, *Norfolk*, iii, pp. 666, 669). See also PRO, SP12/73, fo. 171; Historical Manuscripts Commission, *Report on the Pepys Manuscripts, Preserved at Magdalene College, Cambridge* (London, 1911), pp. 174–76.

46. Houlbrooke, *Letter Book of Parkhurst*, pp. 254–55.

47. Le Neve, *Fasti*, vii, pp. 51, 54, 57, 59; Peel, *Seconde Parte of a Register*, pp. 143–46; P. Collinson, *The Elizabethan Puritan Movement* (London, 1967), p. 223; A. H. Smith and G. M. Baker, eds, *The Papers of Nathaniel Bacon of Stiffkey*, ii, *1578–1585* (NRS, 49, 1982 and 1983), pp. 8–9; A. H. Smith, *County and Court: Government and Politics in Norfolk, 1558–1603* (Oxford, 1974), pp. 208–25; NRO, DCN 29/2, p. 101.

and Robert Cecil, who described him as 'of good government' and 'capable of direction'.[48]

Cathedrals provided a natural habitat for the more confident high churchmanship which developed in the early seventeenth century. Its main elements included an emphasis on the value of formal and beautiful worship in an environment favourable to devotion; an insistence on hierarchy, conformity and order within the church; and the assertion of its jurisdiction and rights against outside challenge. All these elements existed or were taking shape at Norwich long before the end of our period. One component, which some would regard as the keystone, an explicit anti-Calvinism, if less readily detectable in the chapter itself before 1628, was supplied by Bishop Samuel Harsnett (1619–28), Dean Suckling's close ally. In 1624, the committee of grievances of the House of Commons heard a complaint that Harsnett was trying to give the cathedral a monopoly of Sunday morning preaching in Norwich. Suckling, probably the effective leader of the chapter well before 1614, when he at last became dean, energetically sought to defend the cathedral's jurisdiction. The statutes which crowned his life's work were designed above all to reinvigorate the cathedral community, conserve and exploit its property, and ensure the seemly celebration of divine services. William Laud, who knew the statutes well, referred in 1634 to Suckling with warm approval as 'the good old dean'. In 1616 Fulk Roberts, rector of St Clement's in Norwich since 1602, joined the chapter as Hugh Castleton's successor. He had already published, in 1613, *The Revenue of the Gospel is Tithes*, which attacked the diversion of tithes away from the parish ministry by appropriation, and insisted that an exact tenth be paid. His assertion that citizens should pay just as much tithe as countrymen was not one likely endear him to his fellow inhabitants of Norwich. In 1639 Roberts was to publish *God's Holy Hovse and Service*, with an introduction fulsomely praising William Laud's pursuit of decorum in church interiors and ritual. Edmund Porter, a theologian of some note who joined the chapter in 1628, was another prebendary whose views aroused the dislike of the puritans.[49]

The issue of jurisdiction, another long term problem in the cathedral's history, was connected with that of churchmanship. Shortly after Henry VIII's refoundation of the cathedral, in April 1539, its precincts were placed within the county of the city of Norwich by letters patent. The cathedral and the city entered into an agreement about the exercise of their respective jurisdictions which seems to have succeeded for some decades in preventing serious disputes between them. By about

48. *CSPD, Addenda, 1566–79*, p. 551; Bodleian Library, MS Tanner 135, fo. 144; *CSPD, 1601–3*, p. 55.

49. *DNB* for Harsnett and Roberts; K. Fincham, *Prelate as Pastor: The Episcopate of James I* (Oxford, 1990), pp. 243–46, 248–49, 279–88; *CSPD, 1623–25*, pp. 238, 246; W. Laud, *Works*, ed. J. Bliss and W. Scott, 7 vols (Oxford, 1847–60), vi, p. 403; Blomefield, *Norfolk*, iii, pp. 666–67.

1581, however, relations had been soured by the chapter's challenging the city's title to various properties, and its demands for sundry arrears of rent. Military preparations during the following decade placed further strains on the relationship. In 1588, 1596 and 1597 the chapter defended against the corporation the right of the able-bodied men of their liberty to be mustered only before their high steward (the earl of Leicester till 1588, then Sir Christopher Heydon). In 1597, following a complaint by Heydon, the privy council sent the corporation a sharp reprimand and ordered it to desist from similar action in future. Another cause of dispute arose in 1595, when Edmund Suckling resisted an attempt by the sheriffs of Norwich to arrest a butcher's wife and servant for slaughtering animals and selling meat in Lent within the cathedral liberty. The privy council told the dean and chapter that they had acted illegally in granting a licence to the butcher, demanding that he and anybody whom he had employed should be handed over to the mayor. Yet in November 1597 the chapter licensed another butcher to cater for people who had received dispensations to eat meat during Lent, at the request of Sir John Fortescue and Lord North. During the previous month the chapter had laid claim to jurisdiction over Ratton Row and Tombland, two small areas just outside the precinct which had long been bones of contention between cathedral and city in the later middle ages.[50]

The disagreements grew worse early in James I's reign. In 1605 the chapter commenced a suit against the city concerning the levying of poor rates. This dispute was settled in 1614 by a decision obliging the precinct to maintain its own poor but exempting it from paying towards city poor relief.[51] Meanwhile, an even more important jurisdictional dispute had come to a head. At issue was the authority of the city's justices of the peace within the precinct and those areas outside it, Tombland, Ratton Row, Holme Street and Normansland, over which the chapter claimed jurisdiction. The dean and chapter sought their own commission of the peace for their liberties. The corporation's numerous objections, set out in an anonymous memorandum drawn up during the dispute, can be reduced to four main heads: failures of duty on the chapter's part; the problem of disorder within the close; the prospect of damaging economic consequences for the city; and the danger of exacerbating jurisdictional strife. The second argument was the most persuasive. The memorandum painted a picture of a place very different from the quiet and sequestered close of today, one full of lively but disorderly activity. Inns,

50. *Letters and Papers of the Reign of Henry VIII*, xiv (i), no. 904 (5); Blomefield, *Norfolk*, iii, pp. 210–12; NRO, DCN 39/16; 41/103; 113/1, pp. 5–9; DCN 115/9 (3), 1582, 1588, 1594, 1595 and 1597, and pp. 18–20 (2nd series of pagination); NRO, NCR 9i (demands of Dean Gardiner) and 9k (pleas between city and dean and chapter, wrongly dated 1602 in a later hand, really *c.* 1581); above, pp. 255–69.

51. Blomefield, *Norfolk*, iii, pp. 360–61.

alehouses and victualling houses received all sorts of people; there, during divine service, men's servants spent their time and their masters' money wastefully. If the chapter's commission were to extend to those areas of the city outside the precinct over which it claimed jurisdiction, the memorandum pointed out, it would be easy for offenders to escape punishment by 'leaping' from one liberty to the other. The whole project of an independent commission was designed to 'give countenance to the church' and was inspired by 'the stirring motion of one man', Edmund Suckling.[52]

The objections, some of them cogent ones, were of no avail. On 13 June 1610, the earl of Northampton and four other commissioners were authorised to arbitrate in the dispute. On 19 September 1610 a royal charter was granted empowering six justices (the dean, vice-dean, treasurer, high steward or receiver, understeward and principal coroner) to hold sessions of peace within the close. The chapter allegedly owed its success to the influence of Suckling's brother Sir John. It was a success gained only at the cost of stoking up resentment for the future.[53]

Of all the problems confronting the dean and chapter during this period the most persistent were those involved in the management of their revenues and estates. In part these were due to pressures from outside, but they were exacerbated by the greed and incompetence of chapter members. Powerful laymen looked hungrily at the cathedral estates after the Henrician refoundation. One of the most importunate was the proud and headstrong earl of Surrey. In 1542 and 1545 he gained ninety-nine year leases of the former dependent cell of St Leonard's, which he converted into the mansion of Mount Surrey, later notorious as the rendezvous of Ket's rebels in 1549, and the cathedral's share of Thorpe Wood. Both these properties passed permanently out of the chapter's hands.[54]

In 1547 the government divested the cathedral of some of its choicest properties, including the manors of Hemsby, Martham, Lakenham, Plumstead and Wicklewood. The official value of its endowments was reduced by nearly a hundred pounds, from £895 14s. 6¼ d. to £798 6s. 3d. Yet the chapter was charged with an annual rent of £89 11s. 5½ d., exactly the same as the tenth calculated by the commissioners appointed in 1538. This rent was never paid to the crown, the discovery of this fact being probably an important reason for the royal visitation of the cathedral in 1568–69. The visitors were instructed to enquire about the 'decays' of the cathedral

---

52. Bodleian Library, MS Tanner 228, fo. 140v. Some of the points made here had been anticipated in complaints of the city against the dean and prebends dated 3 September 1598 (NRO, NCR 9i).

53. NRO, DCN 115/9 (3), 1610; DCN 41/115;

DCN 113/1, pp. 33–36; Bodleian Library, MS Tanner 228, fo. 140v.

54. NRO, DCN 115/9 (3), 1542, 1544; DCN 47/1, fos 18–20, 44–45; *Letters and Papers of the Reign of Henry VIII*, xxi (ii), no. 287.

and 'coloured' leases made to its prejudice. George Gardiner answered questions bearing on these points especially fully. He claimed that the true yearly income from the cathedral estates even in 1547 had been only £672 10s. 8d., partly because a number of properties had been let out on long leases below their true value before that date. The current clear annual revenue of the cathedral, according to Gardiner, stood at £658 18s. 8d., nearly £140 less than that envisaged in 1547. Within the last twelve years there had been great spoil of timber. The practice of making leases far below the real values of properties had continued. Lessees included the dean and Mrs Salisbury, Miles Spencer, John Debney, the understeward and chapter clerk, and John Hoo the receiver, Mrs Salisbury's alleged lover. Leases to the use of the dean and his wife had been made out to other ostensible lessees. Almost no order had been observed in making leases. The receiver had been given such large discretion that the chapter had become, as Gardiner put it, servants to their servant. Apart from the mismanagement of the chapter estates, the then very large sum of £200 had been 'lost' by Henry Manuel, the last monk prebendary, over three quarters of it, apparently, when he had been receiver. Gardiner also described the failure to account properly for materials, especially lead, from demolished buildings. It was a sorry state of affairs. As if the prebendaries' own covetousness and fecklessness were not enough, they faced continuing pressure for favours from the local gentry. The visitation had one good result. Shortly afterwards, on 7 May 1569, the outstanding debt to the crown of £1970 12s. 1d. was written off, at the humble petition of the dean and chapter, and their future annual payment reduced to £50. This favourable outcome was attributed in large part to the influence of Robert Dudley, earl of Leicester, the cathedral's high steward, who received a fine silver gilt cup for his pains.[55]

In 1573 George Gardiner became dean himself and now had the chance to practise the tighter and more effective management for which he had called. Yet ironically enough, the deanship of this would-be reformer was marked by some of the most obscure manoeuvres and complicated disputes in the history of the cathedral. In February 1579, June 1580 and August 1581 three leases of one hundred years each were made out to the queen covering between them the greater part of the chapter estates. Dean Prideaux (1702-24), the most eminent historian of the cathedral, believed that it 'was intended by the knavery of Gardiner to curry favour with the earl of Leicester to whom it was intended the queen should assign this grant'. According to Prideaux's story, the queen fully understood Gardiner's intention and the ruinous effect it would have on the cathedral. As a result, she refused to accept

55. Caley and Hunter, *Valor Ecclesiasticus*, iii, p. 494; *CPR, 1547-48*, i, pp. 59-61; NRO, DCN 29/1, fos 26v, 30, 33v, 35v-37v; DCN 113/1, p. 41; 115/9 (3), 1569; *CPR, 1566-69*, pp. 205-6, 363.

the leases, gave Gardiner a box on the ear, called him knave, and 'told him that she did not make him dean to betray his church'. The leases, Prideaux was sure, did not take effect. It is an appealing story, like so many of those told about Elizabeth. Yet it cannot be trusted. Elizabeth certainly assigned the third lease to Henry Ryce, a gentleman usher. Furthermore, litigation arising out of the leases was still going on in James I's reign. In 1617, for instance, Dean Suckling was still trying to oust Dru Drury from the manor and rectory of Catton, which had been covered by the 1579 lease. Gardiner's purpose in making out these leases remains obscure. Might they have been designed to forestall a more fundamental threat to the cathedral's title to its lands?[56]

Just such a threat soon materialised. In 1570 Lord Wentworth had been granted a patent authorising him to seek out lands in Norfolk and Suffolk formerly devoted to superstitious uses whose existence had been 'concealed' from the crown. His assignees, Theophilus and Robert Adams, challenged the chapter's title to all its lands. The 1538 translation of the cathedral priory into a dean and chapter had, it was claimed, been invalid. Henry VIII could not have carried it out without the consent of the bishop as the founder's representative. The priory, therefore, had never been dissolved in law. Nor could the surrender of 1547, carried out in the name of a legally non-existent dean and chapter, have set this right.[57]

In July 1583 judgement was given in the exchequer court for the assignees of Lord Wentworth's patent for concealed lands. They then leased much of the property involved to Sir Thomas Shirley, a notorious projector and adventurer, to William Downing and others. Shirley thereby insured his earlier purchase of the 1581 lease from Henry Ryce, to whom it had been assigned by the queen. A bill to establish the cathedral's title failed in the 1584–85 parliament. During the next few years, the hopes of the main parties were pinned on a settlement to be worked out by the law-officers of the crown at Lord Burghley's request. A scheme was ready by January 1587, but it was far from advantageous to the cathedral chapter, who would have received only their old rents for ninety-nine years. Gardiner, who accepted the most important elements of this plan in August 1587, protested in October 1588 that the detailed scheme which had by then been drawn up was contrary to the

56. NRO, DCN 47/3, fos 124r–127r, 133r–134r; DCN 24/1, fos 56r, 61r, 66r. I am grateful to Dr Ian Atherton for supplying copies of the first and third leases and references to all three leases from the chapter books. It appears that the second lease included North Elmham, but no copy of it has yet been discovered. See also NRO, DCN 41/111, DCN 90/2, 90/7, and DCN 115/9 (3), 1581; Strype, *Annals*, iii (2), p.

577. Prideaux claimed that the leases covered all the estates. Sir Ralph Shelton, Sir Henry Woodhouse and other gentlemen of the county had already complained about the first lease before 7 August 1580: J. R. Dasent, ed., *Acts of the Privy Council of England, 1580–81* (new series, London, 1890–1907), pp. 134–35.

57. Smith, *County and Court*, p. 266; Strype, *Annals*, iii (1), pp. 488–91; iii (2), pp. 376–78.

earlier agreement and quite unacceptable to the chapter. Next year, in 1589, a second attempt to secure their title by statute failed. Perhaps it was this setback which killed George Gardiner. Whatever his aims in this extraordinary affair, he left behind him an unenviable if perhaps ill-deserved reputation for crooked dealing which survived in chapter tradition during the seventeenth century.[58]

After his death, litigation in common law and prerogative courts, punctuated by the intermittent use of force, focused in particular on Martham parsonage, continued over the next few years. The patentees had the support of the exchequer court, but in Norfolk, where many of the gentry were chapter tenants, feeling ran high against them, and a number of justices refused to help them. Then, in 1593, at a lucky third attempt, the long hoped for statute was achieved, with the crucial help of Edward Coke, MP for Norfolk and Speaker of the House of Commons. It confirmed the validity of Henry VIII's possession of all the monastic lands which had come into his hands, as also that of his foundation of deans and chapters. An attempt to exploit a flaw in Edward VI's regrant of the cathedral properties was finally defeated in 1598. The struggle for the chapter lands had one beneficial result if it made the chapter and many of the Norfolk gentry allies in a struggle with the hated patentees. Thomas Dove, his reputation untarnished by Gardiner's manoeuvres, was able to enjoy the satisfaction of final victory, the approbation of some of the leading men of Norfolk and (a mark of trust never enjoyed by Gardiner) a seat on the county bench.[59]

The cathedral's economic troubles were by no means at an end after 1598. In 1613 the active prebendaries put their yearly revenue at between £700 and £800. They were at least £1600 in debt 'in the eye of the world', largely because they had forfeited bonds by failing to pay debts by the due day. £400 had been borrowed in order to pay Dean Montgomery for 'his pains and charges in church business', though he had never explained this claim.[60]

The parlous state of the cathedral's finances made it more difficult to maintain its buildings. In the thirty years after the first refoundation sundry losses occurred through fire and dilapidation, including the Lady Chapel and the church of St Mary in the Marsh, over and above the deliberate demolition or adaptation of monastic buildings. In 1601, after the steeple and other parts of the cathedral had suffered serious storm damage, the bishop's vicar-general raised a grant towards their repair from the clergy of the diocese meeting in their synods. The Suffolk clergy (who

58. Smith, *County and Court*, p. 267; *DNB*, s.v. Shirley, Thomas; Strype, *Annals*, iii (2), pp. 56–62, 574–79, and pp. 58–59, for Gardiner's hope in 1587 that a new endowment of the cathedral would include all the lands possessed by the priory in 1538. For his

seventeenth-century reputation, see, for example, NRO, DCN 90/7/3.

59. Smith, *County and Court*, pp. 267–75, 358; 35 Elizabeth I c. 3; Bodleian Library, MS Tanner 135, fo. 144.

60. NRO, DCN 29/2, pp. 130–31.

seem to have needed some persuading) were told that the costs could not be met out of the cathedral's own income. It had fallen into the greatest poverty and want through the fraud and malice of sundry persons who had sought to strip the church of its property and turn it to their own use.[61]

Suckling's more energetic management seems to have brought a substantial improvement in the cathedral's financial position after 1614. In 1627 he claimed that the only debts he knew of amounted to £125, the consequence of recent lawsuits. Some of the litigation undertaken in Suckling's time resulted from leases prejudicial to the chapter, including those of 1579 and 1581 to Elizabeth I, which the chapter regarded as invalid. In 1620 some members of the chapter agreed to forgo money due to them. The new statutes granted the same year provided that part of the cathedral's rents should be paid in kind or at the best current market value of the produce in future. All these are pointers to a vigorous determination to place the chapter's finances on a sounder footing, though only a study of rentals and accounts could show how and when this goal was achieved.[62]

Suckling's chief ambition was to gain the grant of authoritative statutes for the cathedral. Henry VIII's letters patent of 1538 empowered the chapter to make their own. In 1569 the dean and chapter claimed that they had made statutes in King Henry's time, which they had given to Archbishop Parker's visitors in 1567. A nearly complete set of Henrician statutes certainly survives at Norwich. They are a variant of a draft code of about forty chapters sent to most of the new cathedrals in 1544. But the establishment which they envisaged differed in various respects from the one which actually existed at Norwich after the refoundation of 1538. It is difficult to see how they could have been properly enforced there, and it seems unlikely that they were drafted by the Norwich chapter. In any event, Edward VI's refoundation of Norwich Cathedral in November 1547 seriously weakened the legal basis of any Henrician statutes. He undertook to issue new ones but this pledge was never fulfilled. Hence George Gardiner's statement in answer to the royal commissioners in 1569 that the cathedral had no statutes at all, which he regarded as the prime cause of all its disorders. The commissioners bluntly reported that there were 'no statutes to govern the house withal'.[63]

---

61. For a rosier view of these developments, see G. A. Metters and A. Whittingham, eds, *The Parliamentary Survey of Dean and Chapter Properties in and around Norwich in 1649* (NRS, 51, 1985), pp. 102–3. But compare NRO, DCN 29/1, fo. 36r; DCN 92/4 (extracts relating to the episcopal visitation of 1601).

62. NRO, DCN 115/9, p. 57 (2nd series of pagination); DCN 90/2, 90/7; Williams and Cozens-Hardy, *Extracts*, p. 56; DCN 28/1, p. 24 (cap. 25). See also pp. 665–73, 685–86.

63. NRO, DCN 113/1, p. 2; DCN 29/1, fos 30v, 34r, 37r; DCN 29/2, pp. 24–53; Thompson, *Statutes of Durham Cathedral*, pp. xxxviii–xl; DCN 28/1, p. x; W. H. Frere and W. P. M. Kennedy, eds, *Visitation Articles and Injunctions of the Period of the Reformation*, 3 vols (Alcuin Club Publications, 14–16, 1910), iii, p. 217.

Gardiner made an eloquent request for statutes and probably took part in drafting a code of fifty chapters which was drawn up around this time. Although prefaced by a declaration that the queen issued it at the request of the dean and chapter, there is in truth no evidence on the patent rolls or elsewhere that it was ever ratified; and there are no references to it in the answers and submissions concerning the state of the cathedral made in 1613 and 1627. The code of 1569 would have implemented certain reforms which Gardiner certainly thought important. It is distinguished in particular by its very strong emphasis on preaching, which may not have been to the queen's taste. It laid down an annual rota of sixty-four cathedral sermons, of which the dean and six prebendaries were to preach twenty-eight. Six preachers were to be added to the cathedral body, each bound to preach at least four sermons a year in the cathedral and eight elsewhere. This provision was probably modelled on the institution at Canterbury Cathedral. Another entirely new provision was that six scholars at any one time were to be supported for up to five years at Cambridge, chosen from among those boys at the common grammar school in Norwich who had previously been choristers at the cathedral. The chapter about leases stipulated that lessees for terms over twenty-one years should bear the cost of repairs (something about which Gardiner was particularly concerned), and directed that future leases should where possible include provision for rents in kind.[64]

The fact that the cathedral lacked authoritative statutes between 1547 and 1620 did not mean that it was completely without guidance in running its affairs. Injunctions were given by the commissioners for the royal visitation of 1559. A detailed set of injunctions issued by Bishop Parkhurst in 1570 dealt among other things with the admission and qualifications of various members of the cathedral body, the duties of the divinity lecturer, the conduct of and attendance at services, the safe-keeping of money and muniments, the use of the common seal and the regulation of victualling within the precinct. The chancellor of the diocese, visiting the cathedral in 1596, required improvements in the conduct of services and the control of alehouses in the precinct. The chapter bound itself from time to time by resolutions concerning such matters as the granting of leases, the conduct of services and the duties of choir members. In January 1602 the dean and chapter summoned the whole choir before them and published certain orders extracted from 'the old statutes', though is not clear exactly which statutes these were.[65]

In drafting the statutes granted by James I in 1620, Edmund Suckling drew

---

64. BL, Stowe MS 128, fos 17r, 19v–20r, 21v, 25v; compare NRO, DCN 115/9, pp. 43–60 (2nd series of pagination); DCN 29/1, fo. 36; DCN 29/2, pp. 129–31, 135–43. I am grateful to Professor Collinson for pointing out that the provision for six preachers was probably inspired by the Canterbury institution.

65. *Eastern Counties Collectanea*, 1 (1872–73), pp. 18–21; Williams and Cozens-Hardy, *Extracts*, pp. 23, 29, 31, 38, 40, 45; NRO, DCN 47/1, fo. 65.

principally upon the Henrician code of *c.* 1544, though he almost certainly made use of the abortive Elizabethan set as well. In many respects the Jacobean statutes no doubt confirmed existing practice. They dealt among other things with the election, duties and emoluments of the members of the cathedral body, the conduct of services, the management of the cathedral's property, residence requirements, the holding of chapters, the appointment and responsibilities of a vice-dean, receiver, and treasurer chosen annually from among the prebendaries, and the powers of the bishop as arbiter and visitor. One very important stipulation (cap. 25) was that a proportion of the rents should in future be paid in kind or at the best current price in Norwich market of the provisions concerned.[66]

The statutes were granted by James I at Bishop Harsnett's petition and received in the cathedral with great pomp on 5 September 1620. But they were not to survive without alteration. A number of people felt that their interests had been damaged by them. The most important of these was Sir John Suckling, who became comptroller of the royal household in 1622, the dean's brother and previously his influential ally in securing the commission of the peace for the cathedral liberty. It seems that he provided for one of his sons by means of a lease of the valuable chapter properties of Newton manor and Trowse parsonage. Yet chapter 25 of the 1620 statutes reserved these very properties to be the 'corps' of the deanery, forbidding their demise in future, except from year to year, and thus barring Sir John and his sons from renewing the lease. He asked that the matter be referred to the consideration of two peers and two bishops. His petition, probably made after the death of James I, grantor of the statutes, was renewed by his sons after his own death in 1627. Sir John Suckling complained too of the great prejudice done to the rest of the chapter. In their own declaration (1627?), the prebendaries said that only two of them had been consulted about the code. They particularly objected to what they thought excessively generous provision for the dean, including the unique allocation of the 'corps' of specified property; inadequate provision for the prebendaries; unduly stringent residence requirements; and the attempt to revive the long-defunct common table. This last was an impractical scheme, they claimed. 'And the plain English is', they later pointed out, 'that thirty-one persons must be fed with meat and drink and not with mathematical speculations'. But they made clear their hope that the king would alter rather than altogether revoke the statutes, for the cathedral had been like a ship without tackle when it had none. They did not believe that the statutes were injurious to the chapter's farmers, as had been suggested to the king.[67]

66. NRO, DCN 28/1.
67. Williams and Cozens-Hardy, *Extracts*, pp. 54–55; PRO, SP16/44/49; NRO, DCN

115/9, pp. 58–60 (2nd series of pagination); DCN 29/2, pp. 135–37, 142; DCN 28/1, p. 25. The referees were Archbishop Abbot,

During 1627 there took place events extraordinary even by the standards of Norwich Cathedral's history. In February, after Edmund Suckling had failed to heed three commands to bring or send up his cherished statutes, Charles I ordered him committed to the custody of the sheriff of Norwich and suspended from his decanal office. He died, blind, in the late spring or early summer of 1628. Yet the greater part of his principal achievement survived him. Some of the referees who considered them seem to have taken a harsh view of his statutes. But William Laud, one of the referees, and the rising star of the Caroline church, wanted some of the harsh language of a draft report toned down. Although he agreed with some of the criticisms of the statutes, he thought that Suckling had meant honestly, recommending that a description of them as 'partially and unadvisedly framed and thus surreptitiously gotten from his late majesty' should be left out. The referees' report recommended that the statues be reformed. In May 1629 Charles finally confirmed his father's statutes by letters patent, but with revisions which met the prebendaries' most serious complaints. Their required period of residence was reduced from five months to four, with the proviso that there must always be at least one prebendary living in the precinct. Suckling's attempt to reestablish the common table was abandoned, on the ground that it no longer suited a cathedral of slender revenues, most of whose minor canons and other ministers were married. The manor of Newton and rectory of Trowse were placed on the same footing as the rest of the cathedral's possessions. A few other changes were made but, apart from these alterations, the Jacobean code was confirmed. At last Norwich Cathedral had a secure and comprehensive set of statutes.[68]

How far were the aims of the foundation achieved during the years covered by this chapter? The restoration of true religion and worship was the first aim set out in Edward VI's letters patent of 1547. (The preface to his father's draft statutes of 1544 had spoken of the maintenance of divine service and the preaching of the gospel). The others were the education of the young, the assistance of the old, especially those who had served the king or the realm, and the giving of alms.

The celebration of daily services was the most important function of the cathedral community. In late medieval secular cathedrals the daily round commonly consisted

---

note 67 continued
the earl of Manchester, George Montaigne (bishop of London), William Laud (bishop of Bath and Wells) and Sir Humphrey May, chancellor of the duchy. Bishop Harsnett and Dean Suckling answered the prebendaries' first 'suggestions' in their own 'humble manifestation' to the referees: DCN 115/9, pp. 56–58 (2nd series of pagination). Sir John Suckling's career is described in *DNB* entry for his son Sir John, the poet (1609–42).

68. PRO, SP16/55/51, 68/45; PCC wills 154 Barrington; NRO DCN 24/2, fos 71v–2r; DCN 28/1, pp. 45–49.

of three masses and eight other offices. In Mary's reign the dean and chapter recalled that a pretext for the 1547 refoundation had been the need to bring Norwich's order of service into line with that observed in Henry's other new foundations. The Norwich dean and chapter 'followed not the same rule and order but kept their order and time of their service as then was used in the church of Paul's and other cathedral churches within this realm'. The surviving Henrician draft statutes envisaged the continuance of daily masses and offices, but said that the latter need not be chanted at night. Between the issuing of the first Prayer Book in 1549 and the accession of Mary in 1553, daily matins and evensong were probably the main services at Norwich. Communion would have been celebrated far less often than mass had been under the old order. Mary's reign presumably brought the restoration of whatever arrangements had been in force early in 1549.[69]

The cathedral statutes and a series of orders, the most detailed of which were issued in 1605, give us a much fuller picture of the conduct of Norwich services during the reigns of Elizabeth I and James I than we have for the years before 1559. During this period, it is clear, matins and evensong were supposed to be celebrated every day by the choir members, clad in their surplices (graduates, chapter 16 of 1620 specified, with hoods appropriate to their degrees). An order issued by the dean and chapter in 1566 specifically mentioned petty canons, gospeller, epistoler and singing men; draft statute 39 of *c.* 1569 the choristers and almsmen as well. This statute provided that morning prayer was to begin at latest at 8 am, if there was a sermon or lecture, otherwise at 9 am; evening prayer at 4 pm. On working days (it stipulated), service might be sung 'in plain note', without any parts, but with a psalm in metre at the beginning and the end. The inclusion of the Litany, which the Book of Common Prayer required after morning prayer on Sunday, Wednesday and Friday, is confirmed by the orders of 1605. Communion was infrequent. The prebendaries claimed in 1627 that they had never had more than four communions a year in the cathedral (on Palm Sunday, Easter Day, Whitsunday and Christmas Day) within the memory of man. Communicants had usually numbered twenty or thirty, but sometimes as few as twelve or fourteen, scarcely more than forty even on Easter Day. This, they pointed out, was because the inhabitants of the precinct communicated in their own church, St Luke's chapel. But chapter 16 of the 1620 statutes envisaged more frequent communion.[70]

69. Lehmberg, *Reformation of Cathedrals*, pp. 9–10; NRO, DCN 115/9, p. 5 (2nd series of pagination); DCN 29/2, pp. 32, 34.
70. NRO, DCN/28/I, pp. 10–12, 13–14; Williams and Cozens-Hardy, *Extracts*, p. 23; BL, Stowe MS 128, fo. 24r; DCN 29/2, pp. 109, 143. The 1620 statutes specify eleven 'double' feasts on which communion was to be celebrated; and seem to include certain other days of solemn celebration (Coronation Day and Gunpowder Plot Day are particularly mentioned) in the same category.

The maintenance and development of dignified liturgy and sacred music may have been the cathedral's greatest achievement during this period, one whose detailed history has yet to be written. It was in choir that the unity of the cathedral community was most visibly and audibly expressed. The maintenance of discipline and decorum during services was a perennial concern of successive deans and chapter meetings. Disquiet was expressed from time to time about slackness, scrambling for places or noise during services. The worst problems seem to have arisen during the time of the absentee Dean Montgomery. Some singing men were abusive when prebendaries tried to correct their faults, and a singing men's strike was attempted in 1608. But the very frequency of orders concerning the choir shows how high it ranked in the chapter's order of priorities.[71]

In 1569 George Gardiner disapprovingly observed that cathedral music marred the 'ditty' (obscured the words?), and that the choir would not sing Geneva psalms. The following year he is supposed to have been one of the prebendaries who attacked the organs. But the sort of cathedral music which he disliked, at any rate during his phase of reforming fervour, survived and flourished. Two or three new organs were provided during this period. The number of lay singing men increased from six to eight between 1569 and 1613. The draft statutes of 1569 required the singing men to be expert in plainsong, pricking and descant. Those of 1620 stipulated that the adult choir must include equal numbers of basses, tenors and counter-tenors (altos). Finally, the cathedral nurtured a series of notable composers of church music: Osbert Parsley, William Cobbold and William Inglott.[72]

The cathedral's record in providing effective preaching was probably much less distinguished than its achievements as a centre of musical excellence. The mayor and other citizens of Norwich had attended 'solemn' sermons at the cathedral before the Reformation. A pulpit and seats for the mayor and aldermen to use whenever sermons were delivered at the cathedral existed in the green yard north of the cathedral in 1546, and had probably been set up long before. In June 1542 Dr John Barret, erstwhile *lector conuentus*, was appointed divinity lecturer for life, with the duty of lecturing on the scriptures in the chapter house on most Tuesdays and Thursdays throughout the year. George Gardiner claimed in 1569 that there was no divinity lecture in the cathedral like that in other cathedral churches, though a ledger book list of December 1568 names Henry Byrd as reader of the lecture. Other men may have lectured in the cathedral from time to time without a formal appointment. Bishop Parkhurst mentioned in 1573 that the puritan minor canon

71. Williams and Cozens-Hardy, *Extracts*, pp. 23, 35–36, 38–43, 45, 47, 50, 52–53, 57–58, 61, 64.
72. NRO, DCN 28/1, p. 12; DCN 29/1, fos 28r, 34v, 37; DCN 29/2, p. 129; DCN 29/3,

fos 134–136; PRO, SP12/73, fo. 171; BL, Stowe MS 128, fo. 21r; Boston, *Musical History*, pp. 7, 30–34, 68–70. For these and other composers, see below, pp. 689–93.

Richard Crick had done so. But no lecturer was included in the 1613 list of cathedral personnel or provided for in the statutes of 1620.[73]

George Gardiner also alleged in 1569 that he alone of the prebendaries was a resident preacher. In the sermon he gave the following Advent, Dean Salisbury admitted his own neglect of this duty. From about 1570, most if not all the prebendaries were preachers, but some of them seldom or never came near the cathedral, while others devoted most of their pastoral effort to their Norfolk benefices. Failing the addition of extra preachers along the lines envisaged in the draft statutes of *c.* 1569, the cathedral community did not contain enough qualified men to provide regular sermons throughout the year. Yet in 1578 John Beacon, the bishop's chancellor, could refer to the 'solemn order of long time commonly observed' by which a public sermon was preached every Sunday in the green yard. It seems that the qualified clergy of the diocese had to fill the gap left by the cathedral's inadequate resources.

At some stage a scheme was introduced whereby the bishop or his vicar-general chose at the Easter synod at Ipswich and the Michaelmas synod at Norwich ministers to preach at the cathedral in turn on the Sundays not covered by other arrangements. It must have been introduced before 1614, because between then and 1626 four Norwich benefactors, Sir John Pettus, Sir John Suckling, Henry Fawcett and Edward Nutting, provided in their wills endowments to pay the preachers on the annual diocesan rota or 'combination'. Archbishop Parker had, as early as 1567, endowed an annual sermon to be given by the master of Corpus Christi College in Cambridge on the Sunday after Ascension Day. Under the Jacobean statutes, the duty of preaching fell to the bishop on Easter Day, Whitsunday and Christmas Day, to the dean on Trinity Sunday and the Sunday after Easter. The Sundays of Advent and Lent were to be covered by the four archdeacons and the six prebendaries respectively. It is remarkable how few sermons the chapter provided. The draft statutes of 1544 had envisaged that the dean and prebendaries would contribute twenty-seven sermons, those of 1569 twenty-eight, in each case over three times as many as the eight laid down in 1620.[74]

Education was another field in which ultimate achievement fell somewhat short of early aspirations. The cathedral priory had helped to support a grammar school

73. NRO, NCR 9h, 'Right of the citizens to attend the cathedral, 1526'; DCN 115/9 (3), 1542; DCN 29/3, fo 113r (I am grateful to Miss Barbara Dodwell for pointing out to me that Barret had been *lector conuentus*); DCN 29/1, fo. 37r; DCN 47/1, fos 395–396; Houlbrooke, *Letter Book of Parkhurst*, p. 215.

74. NRO, DCN 29/1, fo. 37r; DCN 28/1, p.

15; DCN 29/2, p. 32; London, Lambeth Palace, MS 113, fo. 72r; Historical Manuscripts Commission, *Calendar of the Manuscripts of the Most Honourable the Marquis of Salisbury*, 24 vols (London, 1883–1976), ii, p. 196; Blomefield, *Norfolk*, iii, pp. 312–13; Bodleian Library, MS Tanner 134, fos 31–32; BL, Stowe MS 128, fos 19v–20r.

and had usually maintained between one and four monks at one of the universities. Under Henry VIII's draft statutes of 1544, the cathedral would have chosen a master and undermaster to teach grammar to twenty carefully selected poor boys maintained at its expense. Payments to a master and undermaster appear in the cathedral's accounts for 1545. The 'proportion' of 1547 allocated £88 to the salaries of a master, usher and twenty boys, yet at the same time excused the chapter from making these payments until sufficient money had become available. In the event, that day never arrived, and the only grammar school maintained after this date appears to have been supported by the city of Norwich. The chapter's failure to set up the school planned in 1547 and its alleged conversion of the endowments to private gain were the subjects of sharp complaint in an anonymous Norwich memorandum of James I's reign. Meanwhile, however, the chapter had instituted the practice of granting exhibitions to university students. But of the fifteen grants so far noticed, nine went to the sons or relatives of prebendaries, a tenth to the son of a chapter clerk. One went to a poor scholar, but he received only half the standard grant of forty shillings.[75]

The relief of old age and poverty was the last of the major aims announced by the founding kings. The survey ordered in 1538 had recorded sundry alms payments amounting to over £35 a year, the biggest of which were the daily provision of alms for poor men sitting at dinner and supper in the common hall (£12 a year) and a Maundy Thursday distribution of bread, herrings, drink and money (£10). A dole for the soul of the founder, Bishop Herbert, worth ten marks a year, was still being maintained. Payments were also made to the hospital of St Paul, or Norman's, whose masters had been appointed by the priory. In 1565 the corporation of Norwich took over responsibility for this hospital, which they leased from the chapter for 500 years.[76]

The draft Henrician statutes provided for the maintenance of six poor bedesmen, aged or war-wounded, to be named by the crown, who were to attend services as far as they were capable and perform sundry tasks in and around the church. In 1547 the six poor men were assigned £6 each rather than the ten marks envisaged in 1544. Three of the men listed were former canons of the cathedral, the fourth a former monk. Nominations were regularly made thereafter. They included a number of maimed war veterans. Many places were granted before they fell vacant, so at times there may have been a queue of expectant poor men. At least one poor man sold his patent, though this was highly irregular. The Henrician statutes and

75. H. W. Saunders, *An Introduction to the Obedientiary and Manor Rolls of Norwich Cathedral Priory* (Norwich, 1930), pp. 169, 184–85; R. Harris, P. Cattermole and P. Mackintosh, *A History of Norwich School* (Norwich, 1991), p. 24; NRO, DCN 29/2, pp. 42–44, 49; DCN 113/1, pp. 41–43; Bodleian Library, MS Tanner 228, fo. 140v; Williams and Cozens-Hardy, *Extracts*, pp. 13–14, 22

76. Caley and Hunter, *Valor Ecclesiasticus*, iii, pp. 490–93; NRO, DCN 47/2, fos. 148v–149r.

the 1547 'proportion' also set aside £20 a year for charitable distributions, but payment was suspended until the cathedral was able to meet this obligation. It is uncertain whether such distributions were ever made: in James I's reign it was claimed that nothing was done. In 1581 the chapter book recorded the deposit of £20 to be a perpetual stock for the poor people of St Giles, one of the chapter's livings in Norwich. But this seems to have been an ad hoc payment. The conclusion seems inescapable that the cathedral's contribution to poor relief was smaller after the refoundation than it had been before, and that far fewer indigent people benefited from its alms.[77]

The story of Norwich Cathedral between 1538 and 1628 has many sad aspects. It only partly fulfilled its founders' declared purposes. Its historian is tempted to adapt Dean Acheson's famous dictum and say that it had lost its vocation but failed to find a role. Perhaps it would be truer to say that it did have roles, but that its activities were not informed by a single coherent vision, such as, however obscured, had guided the cathedral priory in its later years. Wholehearted Protestant reform was hard to reconcile with the majestic formality and the appeal to the senses which cathedral liturgy, music and architecture embodied. The failure of the short-lived attempt to create a puritan cathedral is not surprising. Not until Dean Suckling's time did there develop an energetic churchmanship which was thoroughly at home in the close. Then (once the dust thrown up by the struggle over the Jacobean statutes had settled) the cathedral community may have gained greater internal cohesion only to make more external enemies.

What might be called the cathedral's management structure was badly flawed. It fell to an always largely absentee chapter to supervise the other choir members who constituted the true core of the community. The lack of authoritative governing statutes created a situation in which, as George Gardiner said, every man knew what money he was entitled to but not what he should do for it. Vulnerable to would-be predators, sometimes mismanaged by timid, incompetent or greedy chapter members, the Elizabethan cathedral's income, which may have been inadequate to start with, failed to keep pace with inflation.

In 1569 George Gardiner eloquently expressed his hope that the cathedral might become a true mother to the diocese to minister to her children the food of God's word and an example of holy life. This vision was never fully realised either at Norwich or elsewhere. Instead, even in the best run cathedrals, attachment to old

77. NRO, DCN 29/2, pp. 44, 49, 53; DCN   394, 402v; DCN 24/1, fo. 66r; Bodleian
    113/1, p. 42; DCN 47/1, fos 288–292,   Library, MS Tanner 228, fo. 140v.
    319v–320v, 324v, 341r, 346r, 383v, 393–

ways helped frustrate the achievement of a thoroughgoing Protestant Reformation and contributed powerfully to the emergence of a different conception of the church in the seventeenth century. To some extent, developments at Norwich can be seen to have conformed to a pattern discernible in other cathedrals.[78] But nowhere, perhaps, does this pattern appear in a more dramatically accentuated form, or the stage of cathedral history support a more colourful cast of contrasting characters.

78. NRO, DCN 29/1, fo. 38v. At both York and Durham there was a determined but brief effort to make the cathedral an active centre of Protestantism early in Elizabeth's reign, followed by a conservative reaction or loss of momentum and the advent of 'Arminianism' in the early seventeenth century. At York there were jurisdictional clashes between city and minster early in Charles I's reign. Cathedrals generally suffered a stagnation of income. These developments are described by D. Marcombe in 'The Durham Dean and Chapter: Old Abbey Writ Large?', in R. O'Day and F. Heal, eds, *Continuity and Change: Personnel and Administration of the Church in England 1500–1642* (Leicester, 1972); C. Cross, 'From the Reformation to the Restoration', in G. Aylmer and R. Cant, eds, *A History of York Minster* (Oxford, 1977); Lehmberg, *Reformation of Cathedrals*; D. Marcombe and C. S. Knighton, eds, *Close Encounters: English Cathedrals and Society since 1540* (Nottingham, 1991). Studies of Lincoln and Canterbury cathedrals during this period have recently been completed by M. Bowker and Prof. P. Collinson.

27

Revolution and Retrenchment: The Cathedral, 1630–1720

Ian Atherton and Victor Morgan

For the best part of a hundred years, from before the civil wars to the early eighteenth century, Norwich Cathedral, its clergy and officers, were tossed about on the waves of national strife.* The violence done to the cathedral in 1643, when the organ, service books and vestments were burned, did not match the riot of 1272 either in fury or damage, but this period does have a claim to be the most turbulent in the cathedral's history. Uniquely in its 900-year history, for eleven years from 1649 to 1660 Norwich Cathedral (in common with all the others) was effectively liquidated. Bishops were abolished in October 1646, deans and chapters followed in 1649 and their lands were sold. The cathedral building remained, although there were even proposals to pull that down.[1] Nor was the restoration of crown, church and cathedrals in 1660 the end of the dean and chapter's troubles: two generations of party rage and faction-fighting lay ahead. Indeed, few of the cathedral's problems arose solely within the close itself. Consequently, its history can only be understood within the wider context of the politics and religion of Stuart England.

1. J. S. Morrill, *The Nature of the English Revolution* (Harlow, 1993), pp. 154–55; Histori- cal Manuscripts Commission, *Ninth Report: Part I* (London, 1883), p. 320.

* The authors would like to thank the staff of the Norfolk Record Office for their patience and assistance, especially in supplying documents after the fire in the Norwich Library building. Thanks are due too to Norma Watt of the Norwich Castle Museum Art Department; and to Professor Hassell Smith, Dr Richard Wilson, Dr Jane Tillier, Jeff Atherton and James Saunders who read and corrected drafts of this chapter; none the less, any mistakes or infelicities are the responsibility of the authors.

The 1630s, Liturgy and Worship

Even before the disputes over the new statutes had died down, the cathedral was embroiled in a conflict played out in Norwich between two increasingly polarised forces.[2] On one side stood the city corporation and the radical religious groups within the city led by some of its chief magistrates; on the other were ranged the bishop, dean and prebendaries at the apex of the official, established church. Both sides controlled substantial ecclesiastical patronage in Norwich. The dean and chapter appointed the ministers to twenty or so city parishes, using these livings to subsidise their minor canons whose main duties were in the cathedral.[3] This left many of the city's increasingly populous parishes with the desultory services of ill-paid and frequently changing curates. This did not always endear the cathedral to a lay magistracy increasingly concerned with its own spiritual sustenance and that of the populace of the city as a whole. In addition, the more zealous Protestants tended to see cathedrals as the 'fountain of superstition', spearheading moves to introduce more ceremonial into church worship and so lead England back to the arms of Rome and the papal antichrist. Cathedrals could be seen as the superfluous detritus of a church not yet fully reformed.[4]

Such views spurred on developments which had first taken root in the 1570s, whereby the city corporation became in effect the overseer of an 'unestablished', parallel form of religious provision within its walls. It funded or managed preachers, lectureships and sermon series.[5] In some parishes it had power over the presentation of the minister, or provided or supplemented his income.[6] In 1608 it founded, for the edification of the city's preachers, what has become known as the 'Old City Library' in the room over the porch of New Hall (now known as St Andrew's Hall).[7] The choice of this site for the library was deliberate: across the open space from the hall was the church of St Andrew, since the 1570s a shining beacon of forward Protestantism.[8] The intervening space, adjacent to the hall, was converted into an open-air preaching yard known as the 'green yard'. As such it was a very

2. For the new statutes, see above, pp. 531–33.
3. N. P. Tanner, *The Church in Late Medieval Norwich, 1370–1532* (Toronto, 1984), pp. 173–78. The demolition of churches, uniting of benefices and granting away of advowsons gradually reduced this figure somewhat.
4. Oxford, Corpus Christi College, MS 206.
5. NRO, NCR, chamberlains' accounts, 1558–1648, press E, case 18, shelf a, passim, and swordbearers' accounts, press E, case 18,

shelf d, passim. Over time the chamberlains' accounts introduce payments for sermons as a separate category.
6. Blomefield, *Norfolk*, iv, pp. 187–88.
7. NRO, MSS 4227–4228 (T 137 F).
8. V. Morgan, 'Cambridge University and "The Country", 1560–1640', in L. Stone, ed., *The University in Society*, 2 vols (Princeton and London, 1975), i, p. 241; John More, *Three Godly and Fruitful Sermons* (London, 1594), 'Epistle Dedicatory'.

evident challenge to the green yard in the close (in the angle between the bishop's palace and the nave) where the cathedral provided preaching in the summer months.[9]

There is no doubt that cathedrals had become anomalies at the Reformation. Their clergy were left like cuckoos, inhabiting a building designed for a different species of user. Stripped of the sacrifice of the mass for the dead, much of their architecture and space were left with little or no meaning. At Norwich many parts were now useless – virtually all liturgical functions were crammed into the choir and presbytery. The nave, no longer needed to keep monks and laity apart, became little more than a thoroughfare and covered exercise yard. Indeed, until the 1740s it provided a back way into the bishop's palace.[10] The dean and chapter were constantly complaining that the noise of people walking and playing in the nave and aisles interrupted divine service.[11] The rest of the building was put to other uses. Two chapels (St Anne's and St Andrew's) became a private house; St Luke's Chapel became the parish church for the close; the Jesus Chapel was used as the new chapter house and vestry, the room above it as a plumber's workshop.[12] The belfry, Lady Chapel and chapter house were all demolished or allowed to fall down.[13] The galleries filled with rubbish.[14]

The three generations after the Reformation had seen the cathedral struggling, and failing, to find a new role for itself. Attempts had even been made early in Elizabeth's reign to mould it to the services of puritan worship, but they had failed.[15] From the 1620s, however, it began to find that new role, as a bastion of a new type of church of England orthodoxy, albeit an orthodoxy that many elements of the church continued to doubt. In particular the cathedral did this in three ways: by bolstering the political order, holding services for special occasions and providing preaching. While these developments were not confined to the 1630s, they can best be introduced here, since it was in this decade that they caused the greatest controversy, markedly intensifying political tensions within Norwich.

9. D. J. Coby, 'St Andrew's, Norwich (1550–1730): Parochial Prestige in an Urban Context' (unpublished University of East Anglia M. A. thesis, 1992); H. Sutermeister, *The Norwich Blackfriars* (Norwich, 1977), pp. 15–16.

10. BL, Additional MS 5828, fo. 125r.

11. *CSPD, 1635*, pp. xxx–xxxi; Bodleian Library, MS Tanner 133, fo. 182; NRO, DCN 24/4, fos 44v–45r; DCN 115/2, p. 283. This was a problem in nearly every cathedral in the land: G. Cobb, *English Cathedrals* ([London], 1980), pp. 9, 19–20, 23 n. 45. The nave at Norwich was not again used for services until 1831, and then only

briefly while the choir was renovated: NRO, DCN 120/1/2, fo. 12v.

12. G. A. Metters, ed., *The Parliamentary Survey of Dean and Chapter Properties in and around Norwich in 1649* (NRS, 51, 1985), pp. 102–3, 108; NRO, DCN 24/3, fo. 108r; DCN 24/4, fo. 183r.

13. See pp. 502–3, 529.

14. Bodleian Library, MS Rawlinson C. 368, fo. 3r.

15. See above, pp. 522–23, and J. Saunders, 'Darkness or Enlightenment? The Role of the Early Elizabethan Cathedral', unpublished paper given at the Tudor seminar in Cambridge, 2 November 1994.

Liturgically, the reforms were associated with the names of Archbishop Laud (1633–45) and Bishop Matthew Wren (1635–38). As Archbishop Laud argued, 'the external worship of God in his church is the great witness to the world, that our heart stands right in that service of God'; ceremonial is 'the hedge that fences the substance of religion from all the indignities which profaneness and sacrilege too commonly put upon it'.[16] The cathedral service was meant as a glimpse of the divine order and was, in part, modelled on the worship in the court of heaven depicted in the Revelation of St John. It aimed at creating a true inward religion by reflecting the glories, beauty and order of God and heaven.

There thus began a deliberate long-term attempt to create an opulent setting for the worship in the choir. Such practices offended many who feared that a stress on the outward forms of religious services led to idolatry and popery, but they also found their lay supporters, as the list of benefactions to the cathedral shows. While in 1635 the hangings of the choir were described as 'naught', by the early eighteenth century the cathedral inventories boasted yards of red damask, red carpet cloths for the altar, damask napkins, purple velvet altar hangings and cushions, red silk damask-fringed pulpit cloths and tapestry hangings for the choir, many of these given by lay donors. The altar was further adorned with two massive silver-gilt candlesticks, bought with money from the corporation, and a large prayer book and Bible with gilt clasps and bosses.[17] The choir boys wore purple gowns and white surplices, the lay clerks and minor canons surplices (the latter with square caps), while the bishop and dean had scarlet robes (as did the aldermen).[18] Before the Civil War there were richly embroidered (but somewhat threadbare) copes for the celebrant, epistoler and gospeller.[19]

Integral to the cathedral service was the musical rendering of psalms, anthems and hymns.[20] Several members of the choir composed music to be sung in the cathedral.[21] Like other aspects of ceremonious worship, the music of cathedrals was

16. W. Laud, *A Relation of the Conference betweene William Lawd . . . and Mr Fisher the Jesuite* (London, 1639), sig. *3.

17. *CSPD 1635*, p. xxx. NRO, DCN 11/6 (1720); DCN 111/1 (1704 and 1726); C. R. Manning, 'Church Plate in the Deanery of Norwich', *NA*, 10 (1888), pp. 68–70.

18. NRO, DCN 11/1 (1662); DCN 11/2 (1676); DCN 24/4, fos 44v–45r; W. Laud, *Works*, ed. W. Scott and P. Bliss, 7 vols (Oxford, 1847–60), v, p. 483; W. J. Thomas, ed., *Anecdotes and Traditions, Illustrative of Early English History* (Camden Society, 5, 1839), p. 21.

19. *CSPD, 1635*, p. xxx; G. Keynes, ed., *The*

Works of Sir Thomas Browne, 6 vols (London, 1928–31), v, p. 167; H. L'Estrange, *The Alliance of Divine Offices* (Oxford, 1846; 1st published 1659), p. 104; NRO, DCN 29/2, pp. 312–15. The copes were destroyed in 1643 and replaced by only one, in gold and red, the gift of Philip Harbord: it is illustrated in BL, Additional MS 23037, fo. 153 and NRO, DCN 125/2.

20. NRO, DCN 24/4, fo. 179r.

21. See pp. 690–93. However, the destruction of the music books in 1643 means that we only know for certain what was sung in the cathedral after 1660, when the choir's repertoire included anthems by famous composers

a contentious issue, many of the more zealous Protestants seeing the playing of organs and singing of anthems as standing in the way of the right worship of God.[22] Its supporters at Norwich, however, saw in music a means of 'quickening and heightening' devotions, stirring up Christian affection and 'a sweet settlement and composure' of 'mind and affections': 'the artificial contrivance of various notes into one harmony and consent' was a glimpse of the divine order and 'the properest emblem and expression of that charitable consent and agreement of minds and affections which should be amongst Christians'.[23] These were the desired effects. How far they were achieved is hard to gauge, but one source, hostile to the cathedral and its services, records the (possibly apocryphal) reactions of one Atkins to the service at Norwich Cathedral: he is alleged to have said 'if I do but go into church and say my prayers, and hear the organs go, they make the water run down my cheeks, they are so good and so sweet a music'. The critic remained unmoved: 'thus are many lulled asleep in Romish ignorance'.[24]

The Act of Uniformity had imposed the Book of Common Prayer on all churches in the kingdom; this uniformity was itself meant to represent the divine harmony and constancy. Yet it should not be assumed that the services in all churches were exactly alike. There was still some scope for variation within the set pattern and it was in this area that Norwich, like all cathedrals, excelled. The Norwich arrangement followed that of other cathedrals. The basic routine on ordinary days was early morning prayers between 6 am and 7.30 am (depending on the season), matins at 9 am with an anthem, and evening prayer with another anthem at 4 pm.[25] When there was a sermon a psalm would be sung before and after.[26] The service was more elaborate on Sundays, feast days and all days of solemnity such as 5 November.[27] On Christmas Day the Norwich waits (the city band) may have played in the

note 21 continued

such as Thomas Morley, Henry Purcell and Orlando Gibbons, as well as compositions by the Norwich choir members Anthony Beck, James Cooper, Richard Ayleward and Richard Blagrave. Bodleian Library, MS Tanner 401; R. T. Daniel and P. Le Huray, 'The Sources of English Church Music, 1549–1660', *Early English Church Music Supplementary*, i, *Parts 1 and 2* (London, 1972), i, p. 1; ii, pp. 74, 80, 82–83, 95, 99, 104–5, 107–8, 113, 117–18, 123–24, 129, 133, 137.

22. P. Le Huray, *Music and the Reformation in England, 1549–1660* (Cambridge, 1978, 1st published 1967), chap. 2; London, Lambeth

Palace Library, MS 3507, fos 115–116r.

23. Bodleian Library, MS Tanner 134, fo. 207r; F. Roberts, *Gods Holy Hovse and Service* (London, 1639), p. 54.

24. T. L., *Trve Newes from Norwich* (London, 1641), p. 5.

25. Bodleian Library, MSS Tanner 133, fo. 165, Rawlinson C. 368, fo. 3r; NRO, DCN 24/3, fos 57v, 69v, 90v–91r; DCN 24/4, fos 105v–106r, 134r; DCN 11/3 (1681); DCN 33/22 (19 and 21 August 1702); BL, Stowe MS 128, fo. 11r.

26. NRO, DCN 24/2, fo. 16r.

27. *The Statutes of the Cathedral Church of Norwich* (privately printed, n.d.), chap. xiv (there is a copy at NRO, DCN 28/1).

cathedral.[28] Double-feast days were supposed to see the celebration of the eucharist but for many years this did not happen. In 1627 the prebendaries stated that they could only ever remember four communions a year, each with a very small congregation of between twelve and thirty.[29] Pressure from high churchmen for more frequent communions was somewhat ineffective; change was slow, in part because many laity did not wish to receive more often.[30] Even by 1676 there were only monthly communions in the cathedral, while a weekly celebration was not introduced until about 1684.[31] The story of the cathedral liturgy, paralleling that elsewhere, is of a slow increase in ceremonial, decorum and order, throughout the seventeenth century, punctuated by the Civil War.

The regular daily pattern of worship formed the bulk of the choir's work and had for centuries been the métier of cathedrals but, in the three centuries after the Reformation, Norwich, in common with other cathedrals, found renewed vigour as a provider of services for special occasions. On days of public fasting or public celebration the cathedral was the focus of the city's religious devotions. The city corporation would attend in full regalia and on all days of celebration the bells would be rung and there might even be a bonfire in the close.[32] On fast days there would be a sermon at the cathedral; every Whitmonday the Weavers' Company had their own service and sermon; by 1700, if not earlier, a special service before the judges was a highlight of the summer assize week.[33] Perhaps the greatest annual event in the cathedral's calendar was the mayor's guild service, when there was a service for the corporation and new mayor; a long streamer might adorn the top of the spire.[34] When Charles II visited Norwich in 1671 he was sung into the

28. G. A. Stephen, *The Waits of the City of Norwich* (Norwich, 1930), p. 59; NRO, DCN 11/1.

29. *Statutes*, chap. xvi. NRO, DCN 29/2, p. 143. Double-feast days were: Christmas Day; Circumcision of Christ (1 January); Epiphany (6 January); Purification (2 February); Easter Day; Ascension Day; Pentecost; Trinity Sunday; St John the Baptist (24 June); Michaelmas (29 September); All Saints (1 November).

30. I. J. Atherton, 'Viscount Scudamore's "Laudianism"', *Historical Journal*, 34 (1991), pp. 582–83. Archbishop Sheldon ordered weekly communions in cathedrals in 1670, but to little immediate effect: E. Cardwell, ed., *Documentary Annals of the Reformed Church of England*, 2 vols (new edn, Oxford, 1844), ii, p. 332; D. Granville, *Remains*

(Surtees Society, 47, 1865), p. 71.

31. Bodleian Library, MS Tanner 133, fo. 162r; Historical Manuscripts Commission, *Report on the Manuscripts of the Marquess of Downshire*, i, *Papers of Sir William Trumbull*, 2 parts (London, 1924), i, p. 27.

32. In 1692, for example, the bells sounded out on 23 and 29 May (for a naval victory against the French and in remembrance of the restoration of Charles II respectively); 19 October (King William's landing at Yarmouth); 4, 5 and 10 November (the king's birthday, Gunpowder Plot and a thanksgiving day): NRO, DCN 11/4.

33. NRO, DCN 24/2, fos 88v, 159r; DCN 115/1, p. 112; DCN 11/5 (1701). J. Jeffery, *The Duty and Encouragement of Religious Artificers* (Cambridge, 1693).

34. Browne, *Works*, v, pp. 168–69.

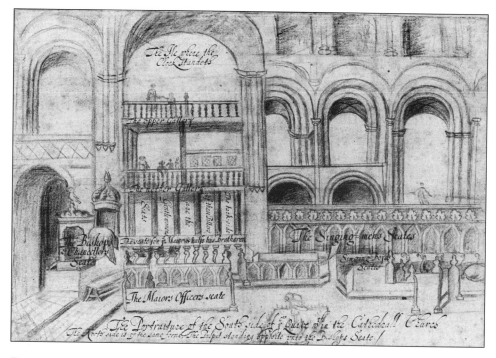

Fig. 199. Drawing of the south side of the choir, c. 1630. This, the earliest known drawing of the interior of the cathedral, shows the two-tier 'closets' and the position of some of the seating for the corporation and choir. (Norwich Castle Museum, Bolingbroke Collection 135.22).

cathedral with an anthem before dining on 'choice wine and sweetmeats' at the bishop's palace.[35] The first visit of a new bishop to his cathedral was also a time of great festivities. After the celebrations and processions to and through the cathedral at the first visit of Bishop Charles Trimnell (1708–21), Dean Humphrey Prideaux gratefully recorded that 'a great multitude of people attended the church. No bishop has been received with better respects since the memory of any alive'.[36]

The order and ceremony also served to buttress the political order of a hierarchical society. The Sunday morning service became the visible embodiment of the conception of order. The seating in the choir of the cathedral was fixed by the dean to reflect the hierarchy here on earth which was itself an image of the fixed divine order of creation.[37] The position, style and type of seat, the route to that seat, even the size, quality and binding of the prayer books in those seats, reflected this hierarchy

35. NRO, MS 453, Chronicle of Norwich, 1671; R. H. Hill, ed., *The Correspondence of Thomas Corie* (NRS, 27, 1956), p. 34.
36. NRO, DCN 115/2, pp. 225–26. See also

the record of the first visit of Bishop Butts in 1733 in NRO, DCN 25/3.
37. NRO, DCN 24/4, fos 48r, 81, 102v–103r; Bodleian Library, MS Tanner 133, fo. 50v.

and the dignity of the persons sitting there.[38] Much of this is clearly reflected in a drawing of the choir (*c.* 1630) showing the position and style of some of the seats (fig. 199). The same principles held true for the outdoor sermons in the green yard where, once again, the position and type of seat was carefully ordered, from the better sort in their individual covered seats built gallery-wise against the nave to lesser mortals paying a halfpenny to sit on benches on the grass (fig. 200).[39]

Norwich Cathedral was to become a bulwark of orthodoxy against the alternative religious provisions available in the city. It was one of the few places in Norwich firmly in ecclesiastical control with regular, weekly sermons. Other preaching in the city tended, as we have seen, to be in lay hands and so less amenable to the influence of the church's hierarchy. When, under James I and Charles I, there emerged a cadre of bishops who wished to assert a more ceremonial orthodoxy against the radicals, Norwich, along with other cathedrals, was well prepared for the task.

The high church Samuel Harsnett (1619–28), denounced as a formalist and favourer of papists by his enemies, came to the see of Norwich from Chichester where he had reformed the lax standards of the cathedral there.[40] At Norwich he attempted to put down the alternative preachers by granting a monopoly to the cathedral sermon. All parish Sunday services in the city were to end by 9.30 am so that everyone could attend the cathedral sermon.[41] The cathedral was placed in the front line in the battle against heterodoxy, religious and political, but Harsnett's attempt failed. Powerful laity resented his actions, particularly if they had to travel from the other side of the city. There was nothing like enough room for all of Norwich's 20,000 or so inhabitants, even in summer when the sermon was preached outside in the green yard. So, while the elite attended the service of God their apprentices and servants went to the service of mammon, gambling and drinking in taverns.

A decade later Bishop Matthew Wren (1635–38) was forced to change tack and order Sunday morning sermons in all city churches. None the less, the role of the cathedral as Norwich's main provider of sermons, particularly by more learned

38. Bodleian Library, MSS Tanner 133, fos 5r, 13r, 15r, Tanner 134, fos 3–15, 37–39, 118–119, 149–150; NRO, DCN 24/3, fos 100r, 108r, 148v; DCN 24/4, fos 102v–103r, 141r; DCN 115/1, p. 112; DCN 115/2, p. 241; DCN 115/3, p. 2; DCN 111/1 (1704 and 1726 inventories).

39. Browne, *Works*, v, pp. 167–68; NRO, DCN 24/2, fos 109r, 112r; PRO, SP16/188/3, fo. 3r. The outdoor pulpit and all the seats were destroyed in the civil wars;

thereafter all the sermons, winter and summer, were preached in the choir.

40. *DNB*; A. Foster, 'The Dean and Chapter 1570–1660', in M. Hobbs, ed., *Chichester Cathedral: An Historical Survey* (Chichester, 1994), pp. 91–92.

41. A similar practice had been tried in London with the Paul's Cross sermons: F. Heal and R. O'Day, eds, *Church and Society in England: Henry VIII to James I* (London, 1977), pp. 151–52.

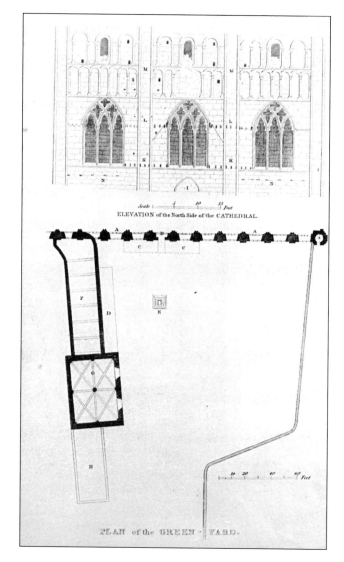

ELEVATION of the North Side of the CATHEDRAL.

PLAN of the GREEN-YARD.

Fig. 200. Conjectural plan of the green yard. The elevation of the nave north wall records the scars left by the joists which supported the two-tiered covered stands.

Key:
A. North aisle of the cathedral.
B. Entrance to the green yard.
C. Dean and chapter gallery.
D. Gallery of the mayor and corporation.
E. Pulpit.
F–H. Bishop's palace.
I. Entrance to the green yard.
K. First-floor joist holes.
L. Second-floor joist holes
M. Presumed height of the roof.
N. Series of holes, 4 inches by 3.

preachers, continued.[42] Wren's appointment, and Laud's elevation to Canterbury two years earlier, gave fresh impetus to the new churchmanship and its assertive clericalism. They found willing adherents among the clergy of Norwich Cathedral. Despite the chapter's traditional jealousy of its rights and opposition to interference from outside, two visitations in two years – by Nathaniel Brent, the archbishop's agent, in 1635 and by Wren himself the following year – passed smoothly.[43] Brent

42. Bodleian Library, MSS Tanner 68, fos 316r, 336r, Tanner 114, fos 205–206, 217–218.
43. *CSPD, 1635*, pp. xxx–xxx; Bodleian Library, MSS Tanner 68, fos 86r, 167r, Rawlinson C. 368, fos 2r, 3r. An attempt to visit the cathedral in 1618 had provoked the chapter to defend its rights vigorously: NRO, DCN 29/2, p. 129; Lambeth, MS 942, no. 11.

made some recommendations for the improvement of the cathedral's fabric but addressed his principal criticism to the civic authorities, admonishing them for their irreverent behaviour during services and forcing them into symbolically yielding precedence to the dean and chapter within the cathedral.[44] Wren, likewise, demanded only minor changes.[45] It is certainly true that the 'Laudian' changes of the 1630s affected cathedrals less than parish churches, for Wren's aim was to bring all parishes into uniformity with the cathedral.[46] Cathedral worship had always been more elaborate than parish worship: the dramatic change of the 1630s was the attempt to make cathedrals the model for all parishes. This was certainly true at Norwich where the reformed cathedral was intended to be the beacon and guide for all the churches in the diocese.[47] The cathedral was used to test the conformity of at least one cleric; he was set to officiate there for trial of his orthodoxy but objected to wearing a cope, refused to bow in the right place and failed.[48] Wren was supported by the dean, three prebendaries and four minor canons, but beyond the cathedral he was probably the most unpopular bishop the diocese has ever had.[49] 'Little Pope Regulus', as his enemies dubbed him, spent eighteen years in the Tower of London (1642–60) largely for what he had done during his three-year episcopate at Norwich.[50]

Other circumstances contributed to mounting antagonism between city and church hierarchies and each time the cathedral found itself the focus of conflict between established lay practice and a new assertive clericalism; between two intimate neighbours ever conscious of their respective corporate dignities. In 1637 Charles I ordered the whole corporation to attend the cathedral every Sunday for the *entire* service rather than just the sermon as had previously been the case. Despite complaints about the winter cold and the exceeding length of the service (three-and-a-half or four hours), this became the constant practice of the corporation.[51] But it hardly made for harmony between the corporation and the cathedral. Civic ceremonies at the cathedral helped to reinforce the government of the city corporation, but they

44. The swordbearer of the corporation, the symbolic embodiment of the city's authority, was ordered no longer to wear the cap of maintenance on his head during services but to remove it on entering the cathedral. Bodleian Library, MS Tanner 68, fos 82r, 88–89.

45. Bodleian Library, MS Rawlinson C. 368, fos 2r, 3r, MS Tanner 68, fo. 167r.

46. P. King, 'Matthew Wren, Bishop of Hereford, Norwich and Ely, 1585–1667' (unpublished Bristol University Ph. D. thesis, 1969), p. 225.

47. Bodleian Library, MS Rawlinson C. 368, fo. 2r.

48. Bodleian Library, MS Tanner 68, fos 82r, 336v.

49. Bodleian Library, MS Tanner 68, fos 86r, 164r, 167r, 309, 336v; Roberts, *Gods Holy Hovse*, sig. *2v.

50. King, 'Wren'; C. Wren, *Parentalia: or Memoirs of the Family of the Wrens* (London, 1750), pp. 73–114; W. Prynne, *Newes from Ipswich* (Ipswich [?London], 1636); Bodleian Library, MS Tanner 220, fos 44–48, 116–27.

51. Bodleian Library, MSS Tanner 220, fos 147–151, Tanner 68, fo. 316r; Browne, *Works*, vi, pp. 10, 12. The common councilmen, however, had ceased attending by 1707: NRO, DCN 115/2, pp. 208–10.

also reminded the aldermen of an alternative vision of order, one where the clergy came before the laity. There was repeated sniping between city and cathedral over the seating in the choir and the corporation's rights and privileges.[52] Moreover, despite the stress on order and decorum, the city dignitaries were subjected to considerable humiliation. The congregation in the 'closets', the two-tier galleries above the corporation's seats across the ends of the transepts, did not always behave as they should. On occasion the gowns and cloaks of citizens were cut and mangled by those sitting behind them. All manner of items were dropped or thrown from the galleries at the corporation. One mayor had his spectacles broken by a large Bible dropped from above; shoes and hats were thrown down; and the mayor and aldermen and their wives had to endure people spitting, urinating and defecating on their heads while they were at prayer.[53]

Much of this ill behaviour may have resulted from the overcrowding caused by cramming a large Sunday congregation into the choir and presbytery. Layfolk tried to clamber into any empty prebendal stalls, treading on the legs of the dean and prebendaries present as they knelt at prayers. Lack of seats meant that substantial citizens often had to take their place among the crowd.[54] In the 1630s the problems of unruliness may have been exacerbated by the novelty of the very solution designed to solve the problem of congestion, the insertion of the galleries or closets across the ends of the transepts. To judge from the drawing of *c.* 1630 (fig. 199) these look as if there were only recently erected, perhaps when Harsnett suppressed all Sunday sermons except that at the cathedral. The desire to enforce the new conformity upon the citizens of Norwich had an adverse effect on the architectural beauty and orderliness which was at the very heart of that orthodoxy.[55]

Religious differences between the city and the cathedral were exacerbated by the running sore of jurisdictional and property disputes. Almost since the day that the cathedral priory's precincts were carved out of medieval Norwich, the citizens and the monks disputed the boundaries of their respective jurisdictions. Such quarrels continued after the priory was dissolved.[56] Successive attempts to define the boundary between the jurisdictions of city and cathedral, particularly concerning rights over Ratton Row, Holme Street and Spiteland, dragged on into the 1630s, without

---

52. NRO, DCN 115/2, pp. 206, 208–10, 239–40; Bodleian Library, MS Tanner 220, fo. 148r.

53. Bodleian Library, MS Tanner 220, fos 149r–150r. These events took place in the 1630s and 1640s, a time of heightened tensions when feelings against some in the city corporation ran high. The galleries were removed *c.* 1848: NRO, DCN 125/1.

54. NRO, DCN 115/1, pp. 220, 234; DCN 115/2, pp. 208–10.

55. Such galleries were not unknown elsewhere, at least in the early nineteenth century, when they also existed at Chichester and Winchester cathedrals: Hobbs, *Chichester Cathedral*, p. 120 and pl. xviii.

56. See above, pp. 524–26.

conclusive resolution.[57] Moreover, the squabbles were aggravated when Charles I tried to impose a rate of two shillings in the pound on house rents in Norwich for the maintenance of the city's clergy.[58] Had it been implemented (and there were further attempts to enact a similar levy later in the century)[59] this measure would have made the clergy more independent of their erstwhile civic patrons and it would have subsidised some individuals whose main offices were in the cathedral.

Reading the chapter books it is easy to forget that the dean and prebendaries did anything more than grant leases. Yet the heart of a cathedral's function was and is the worship of God, and in the 1630s liturgical practices in all churches, but particularly cathedrals, were at the centre of public debate. The attempt by king, archbishop, diocesan and senior cathedral clergy to put Norwich Cathedral back at the heart of worship, liturgy and preaching merged with long-standing jurisdictional and property disputes to produce dangerous levels of antagonism between the city and the dean and chapter. That this was as true of Norwich as of other cathedrals and dioceses does much to explain the fortunes of Norwich Cathedral in the 1640s and 1650s. While undoubtedly the broad direction of events was dictated by national affairs, some of the particular vicissitudes of Norwich Cathedral were determined by the local experiences of the preceding decades. Without these, any understanding of our story over the next generation would be incomplete.

Civil War, Interregnum and Abolition, 1640–60

From the moment the Long Parliament met in November 1640, religious issues were at the heart of the debate. Again it was to be events at the centre of national politics that were to determine the fate of the cathedral in Norwich over the succeeding two decades, but now those events were to take the history of the cathedral in a very different direction from that which it traced in the 1630s. First episcopacy and then the whole church hierarchy, including deans, prebendaries and cathedrals came under attack in a call for 'root and branch' reform.[60] In June 1641, the Commons debated whether to allocate the wealth of the cathedrals to the maintenance of the clergy in general.[61] Looked at from the perspective of a diocese like Norwich, the attractions of this proposal must have been very great. The very institution that had been the site of the humiliation of the burghers of Norwich was to be dismembered in order to provide financial support for the type of religious

---

57. See fig. 116 above. J. T. Evans, *Seventeenth-Century Norwich* (Oxford, 1979), p. 88.

58. *CSPD, 1637–38*, pp. 167, 177; H. Prideaux, *An Award of King Charles* (London, 1707).

59. NRO, DCN 24/3, fos 146v–147r; Bodleian Library, MS Tanner 39, fo. 64r.

60. A. Fletcher, *The Outbreak of the English Civil War* (London, 1981), pp. 91–124; Morrill, *English Revolution*, pp. 45–90.

61. Fletcher, *Outbreak*, p. 105.

provision that they and their like had been creating piecemeal from their own resources.

Although legislation for the abolition of bishops and cathedrals had stalled by the autumn of 1641, the parliamentary debate had the effect of liberating sentiment in Norwich. As the cathedral authorities well understood, the more riotous elements might be keen to take any occasion to express their antagonism. The most likely time was Shrove Tuesday, 1642, traditionally a day of licensed 'misrule'. The rumour spread that the apprentices intended to storm the cathedral and destroy the altar rails and the organs. The dean and chapter took precautions. The rails were removed, the gates of the close closed and a motley crew of clerics and armed guards stood ready. The apprentices stayed at home. Whatever their intentions, the significant thing is the fear that was engendered and the antagonism towards the close underlying that fear.[62]

The sequestration ordinance passed by parliament on 27 March 1643 branded the new bishop of Norwich, Joseph Hall (1641–56), as a delinquent, his goods subject to seizure to pay for the parliament's armies.[63] Hall has left an eloquent testimony of his sufferings over these years in his tract, *Hard Measure*. His palace was searched by armed troopers; his property, corporate and personal, was sequestered; and, probably in the summer of 1644, he was ejected from his palace. For a time one of the residents of the close, Mr Gostlin, took him into his house, before he retreated to what is now the Dolphin Inn at Heigham, just beyond the city walls.[64]

Between 1642 and 1645, acting sometimes with the authority of parliamentary ordinances, sometimes without, the parliament's troops and supporters purged a number of cathedrals of what one puritan manifesto called 'the trash and trumpery of massing ceremonies'.[65] Norwich Cathedral could not long escape once its opponents controlled the city government and its protectors and supporters were subdued. Bishop Hall, in a famous and much-quoted passage, recalled the city's triumph on 12 May 1643:[66]

> It is no other than tragical to relate the carriage of that furious sacrilege, whereof our eyes and ears were the sad witnesses, under the presence of

62. T. L., *True Newes from Norwich*, p. 7. This story is otherwise unconfirmed and so must be treated with some caution.
63. C. H. Firth and R. S. Rait, eds, *Acts and Ordinances of the Interregnum, 1642–1660*, 3 vols (London, 1911), i, pp. 106–17.
64. *DNB*; R. W. Ketton-Cremer, *Norfolk in the Civil War* (London, 1969), pp. 225–31.
65. Firth and Rait, *Acts and Ordinances*, i, pp. 265–66, 425–26; Oxford, Corpus Christi

College, MS 206, fo. 12r. For the desecration of other cathedrals see B. Ryves, *Angliae Ruina* ([London], 1647), pp. 202–4, 231, 247–48, 250.
66. J. Hall, *Hard Measure*, in P. Hall, ed., *The Works of Joseph Hall*, 12 vols (revised edition, Oxford, 1837), i, p. lv. There has long been confusion over the exact date of these events. An anonymous chronicle puts them in 1644, but Benjamin Mackerell places

Linsey, Toftes the sheriff, and Greenwood.[67] Lord what work was here! what clattering of glass! what beating down of walls! what tearing up of monuments! what pulling down of seats! what wresting out of irons and brass from the windows and graves! what defacing of arms! what demolishing of curious stone-work, that had not any representation in the world, but only of the cost of the founder, and skill of the mason![68]

Not many years earlier the cathedral had seemed to be the spearhead of the innovatory liturgical practices that had come to challenge the religious observance that over the years had grown up piecemeal in the city. Now, with crowbar and hammer, its enemies smashed, tore up and ripped out the material signs and signifiers of the religious culture to which they were opposed.[69]

Not content with the destruction wrought within the cathedral, the Norwich radicals organised a symbolic *auto-da-fé* and what amounted to a ritual inversion of the hated ceremonial practices to which they had been subjected in the previous decade. Hall described the event as a 'hideous triumph' performed 'before all the country'. This 'sacrilegious and profane procession' proceeded to the market place with 'a lewd wretch walking before the train, in his cope trailing in the dirt, with a service book in his hand, imitating in an impious scorn the tune, usurping the words of the litany used formerly in the church'. Sir Thomas Browne recalled that the procession was preceded by some who blew upon organ pipes. In the market place, near the market cross, 'with shouting and rejoicing', the organ pipes, vestments,

note 66 continued
them in 1643: NRO, COL 5/19, fo. 48r, MS 453, MS 79, p. 246. Ketton-Cremer, *Norfolk in the Civil War*, pp. 232–33 implies a date after 23 September 1643. However, a note of the payments to four workmen 'for taking down the organ' dated 25 May 1643 in the receiver's and treasurer's accounts fixes the date: NRO, DCN 10/2/1, extraordinary payments, 2 December 1642 to 30 August 1643, bound between 1632 and 1641. See also B. Matthews, 'Thomas Dallam at Norwich Cathedral', *BIOS*, 10 (1986), p. 110.

67. Matthew Linsey, alderman and clavor, became mayor in 1650. Thomas Toft was one of the city's two sheriffs in 1643, becoming alderman in 1644 and mayor in 1654; an Independent of extreme views he was dismissed from his aldermanship in 1662. John Greenwood had been sheriff in 1642 and

served as an alderman between 1643 and 1649. T. Hawes, ed., *An Index to Norwich City Officers, 1453–1835* (NRS, 52, 1986); B. Cozens-Hardy and E. A. Kent, eds, *The Mayors of Norwich 1403 to 1835: Being Biographical Notes on the Mayors of the Old Corporation* (Norwich, 1938).

68. In 1680 Sir Thomas Browne estimated that around a hundred brass inscriptions were removed: *Repertorium*, in Browne, *Works*, v, p. 147. See also above, pp. 474–76.

69. 'Scandalous pictures' at the cathedral remained a problem for the city government nevertheless. Pictures of the four evangelists from the cathedral were burnt in the market, on 9 March 1644, and a year later the dean and chapter were required 'to pull down all pictures and crucifixes yet undemolished in the cathedral church'. NRO, NCR, mayors' court book, 1634–46, case 16a/20, fos 415r, 445v.

the leaden cross from the green yard, the service books and the singing books, 'all these monuments of idolatry [were] sacrificed to the fire'. The conflagration was accompanied with the 'ostentation of a zealous joy' of those who 'professed how much they had longed to see that day'. At the end of this day of symbolic triumph the cathedral stood forlorn, some of its windows gone, its entrails ripped out, and left to the ungentle mercy of the musketeers, 'drinking and tobacconing as freely as if it had turned ale-house'.[70]

The bishop was expelled from his palace (although episcopacy itself was not formally abolished until 9 October 1646),[71] but the cathedral clergy were not immediately excluded from the close. The dean and chapter, still a legal corporation but cowed and emasculated, entered a grey half life. Their presentation rights were eroded, some of their property invaded.[72] Problems arose in extracting customary rents from their tenants; by 1644 money was so short that it was impossible to pay stipends in full, despite the realisation of capital assets through the wholesale selling of timber.[73] The end came on 29 May 1649 with the abolition of deans and chapters and all minor cathedral offices. The chapter's lands were sold by parliamentary trustees. The piecemeal dismantling of the church of England over the previous nine years seemed finally complete.[74]

In the past most attention has concentrated on the fate of the dean and the prebendaries. However, it was not them but the members of the choir who constituted the daily 'working core' of the cathedral. Just as we know relatively little about the circumstances of these individuals in quieter times so also we know very little of their fate at this critical juncture. Some had already been affected by the radical upheavals they saw around them: insubordination in the choir seems to have increased in the 1640s while others, left with few or no duties after the dismantling of the organ, simply wandered off.[75] With the final abolition of the chapter and its staff poverty struck many of the minor officers. Two former minor canons and seven former lay clerks received a share of the meagre £20 granted by the trustees for the maintenance of ministers to the poor officers of the cathedral

---

70. Hall, *Hard Measure*, p. lv; Browne, *Works*, v, p. 167.
71. Firth and Rait, *Acts and Ordinances*, i, pp. 879–83.
72. London, Lambeth Palace Library, MS 1104, no. 94, fo. 260; W. A. Shaw, *A History of the English Church during the Civil Wars and under the Commonwealth, 1640–1660*, 2 vols (London, 1900), i, pp. 204–10, 213, 273.
73. NRO, DCN 24/2, fo. 168. In this period some of the dean and chapter records appear

to have been removed for safe-keeping by Prebendary Howlett: NRO, DCN 115/2, pp. 190–91, 197.
74. Firth and Rait, *Acts and Ordinances*, ii, pp. 81–104, 200–5. The last chapter meeting was on 8 May 1649: NRO, DCN 24/2, fo. 179r. The dispersal of the properties belonging to the cathedral is examined below, p. 673.
75. NRO, DCN 24/2, fos 159v, 161v, 164r, 167v, 169v–170r.

in 1657,[76] while Thomas Searle, the chapter clerk, was reduced to sending begging letters to friends and relatives.[77]

Neither the dean nor most of the prebendaries fared much better. Deprived of their cathedral income and status, most of them had also been ejected from their parochial livings. Only two former prebendaries lived in any ease. According to one story, possibly apocryphal, the daughter of Dean John Hassall ended up on parish relief. True or not, the story indicates the perception of the deprivations inflicted upon the Anglican clergy in these years.[78]

Although the institutional framework for the support of the cathedral was dissolved and those responsible for its use and maintenance expelled, the cathedral was not entirely abandoned. In some respects it could be said to have been 'municipalised'. There was good precedent for this and the corporation of the 1640s would not have been ignorant of what their predecessors had done a hundred years earlier, after the Dissolution. Then they had taken over the Blackfriars (now known as St Andrew's Hall), and converted it to civic purposes. The implied parallel of circumstances and the opportunity at long last to consummate a reformation, hitherto only partly completed, must have been a forceful consideration in their minds.

The unacceptable trappings of the old religious dispensation having been forcibly erased from the cathedral, the corporation started to rearrange the furniture to their own liking. In November 1643 they obtained permission from the House of Commons to nominate and appoint ministers to preach in the cathedral on Sunday mornings.[79] Now at last they were able to hear the sweet tune of a doctrine to their own liking. They did so in surroundings in the cathedral rearranged in order to reflect the power of a city triumphant. The pulpit was moved to a more prominent position, adjacent to Bishop Overall's monument. The seating for the aldermen was moved to the east end, into the sanctuary. The ultimate symbolic displacements were the seating of the mayor at the high altar and the lowering of the founder's table-top tomb to a mere floor slab.[80] This was the visible triumph of the laity, the apotheosis of the city government. In February 1644 further order was taken for the accommodation of the city's hierarchy, when seating in the cathedral was reserved for members of the common council.[81]

76. A. G. Matthews, *Walker Revised* (Oxford, 1948), p. 12.

77. London, Lambeth Palace Library, MS 593 [pp. 259–288]; Cambridge University Library, Additional MS 151 and MS Dd. 8. 40, fos 23–28; Bodleian Library, MS Tanner 115, fo. 69.

78. *DNB*; Matthews, *Walker Revised*, pp. 170– 71, 268, 271–73; Blomefield, *Norfolk*, iii, pp. 622–23, 663.

79. *Commons Journal*, iii, p. 298 (1 November 1643).

80. See p. 484. Browne, *Works*, v, p. 153. The former order was restored after the Restoration.

81. NRO, NCR, assembly book, 1642–68, fo. 14 (20 February 1644).

We can catch only glimpses of what happened to the cathedral building after this. There is still a bullet embedded in the decoration of Bishop Goldwell's monument in the choir and, according to one post-Restoration account, troops were exercised in the building on Christmas Day while a company of city volunteers one Sunday marched up to the altar and turned their backs upon it 'in great derision lifting up their bums and holding down their heads against it . . .'[82] Beyond this, it is clear that the cathedral and the close became pawns in the playing out of the ancient rivalries between the city and the county and between the city and the cathedral.

What to do with cathedral buildings after the abolition of dean and chapters was a national problem, but no one answer was reached. Three times the Rump Parliament debated pulling down all cathedrals, though not one was in fact completely demolished. Many, like York Minster, became preaching centres; others became barracks or gaols. The cloister of St Paul's Cathedral was turned into a shopping precinct and St Asaph's into a wine shop and cattle shed.[83] As for Norwich, in 1650 the corporation of Yarmouth unsuccessfully sought the demolition of what it termed 'that vast and altogether useless cathedral' so that the materials could be used to strengthen the town's harbour walls and build a workhouse.[84] The corporation of Norwich also sought to turn the cathedral into a workhouse.[85] The bishop's palace, described in 1638 as 'a poor, deformed, ill-contrived house', was sold off to Captain John Blackwell, who stripped the roof of its lead and left the rest to decay before the elements.[86]

None the less, for some the very stones of the cathedral continued to have a symbolic resonance. One beggar chose to make his home in the old candle room at the cathedral. For his pillow he adopted a piece of a defaced episcopal monument; calling it his 'Jacob's pillow . . . he desired [it] might be laid under his head in his grave which 'tis said was done in the cloister green where he was buried'. Based thus in the old cathedral, he wandered the city streets proclaiming 'God save King Charles and the bishop of Norwich' and exhorting the townsfolk to 'Be of good cheer [for] God will restore your king and the church to you again'.[87]

82. Ketton-Cremer, *Norfolk in the Civil War*, pp. 234–35; NRO, DCN 107/3.
83. Morrill, *English Revolution*, pp. 154–55.
84. Historical Manuscripts Commission, *Ninth Report: Part I*, p. 320. There might be a certain vengefulness in the request, given the disputes between the town and the dean and chapter in recent years over the nomination of the curate of Yarmouth: J. Browne, *History of Congregationalism and Memorials of Churches in Norfolk and Suffolk* (London, 1877), pp. 122–36. Yarmouth re-

claimed the right in 1642: NRO, DCN 24/2, fo. 160r; DCN 115/9 (1641). The dispute rumbled on throughout the eighteenth century: NRO, DCN 29/2, p. 286; DCN 24/5, fos 201–204; DCN 120/2C/52.
85. BL, Additional MS 22620, fo. 170r.
86. H. R. Trevor-Roper, *Archbishop Laud* (London, 1940), p. 201; *A Compleat History of the Famous City of Norwich* (Norwich, 1728), p. 49; Browne, *Works*, v, p. 160; NRO, DN/MSC 1/39.
87. NRO, DCN 107/3.

The building continued to be used for services until at least November 1649 and possibly throughout the 1650s, since the parish church for the close was in one of the cathedral chapels.[88] There seems to have been at least one attempt, in 1658, to turn the cathedral into a preaching house, but there is no suggestion that this succeeded.[89]

The abolition of the dean and chapter meant that authority within the close was a prize to be fought over in a three-way tussle between the city, the county and the close's inhabitants themselves. The county took its stand on Cardinal Wolsey's judgement in 1524 that the precincts were part of Blofield Hundred, and therefore in Norfolk, not Norwich. The city argued that peculiar (i.e. exempt) jurisdictions such as the cathedral close were 'the occasion of many tumults and disorders to the breach of the peace and hindrance of justice', making the close a refuge for unregulated traders, criminals and the poor. The tenants in the close in response stood on the injustice of reversing 400 years of history should the jurisdiction of the city and close be united.[90] The struggle raged throughout the Interregnum with first one side and then the other gaining the upper hand.[91] No side won victory outright, even though the city acquired the rights to the precinct manor and court leet.[92] The restoration of dean and chapter in 1660 resolved some of the issues but left Tombland and taxation for future generations of lawyers to argue over and grow fat on the proceeds.[93]

The Restoration, 1660–80

'the late most heathenish and tyrannical oppression and persecution begun here AD 1641 and ended 8 May 1660. *Gloria Deo in excelsis*'.
Thomas Searle, 'A Catalogue of All the Deans of the Cathedral Church of Norwich', 1660.[94]

This quotation from Thomas Searle's history of Norwich Cathedral neatly encapsulates the despair of two decades giving way to profound rejoicing at the

88. Bodleian Library, MS Rawlinson D. 1104, fo. 6v; BL, Additional MS 22620, fo. 135r. Choral services, however, would have ceased with the dismantling of the organ and sack of the cathedral in May 1643.

89. *CSPD, 1657–58*, p. 372; Bodleian Library, MS Tanner 133, fo. 52r.

90. Bodleian Library, MSS Tanner 133, fo. 14, Tanner 311, fos 4–5, 49–50; PRO, SP18/69/51 and 51i, fos 136–139.

91. BL, Additional MSS 22619, fo. 23r, 22620, fos 111r, 115r, 119r, 121r, 131r, 135r, 144r, 146r, 170r; *CSPD, 1653–54*, p. 404; *CSPD,*

1654, p. 97; *CSPD, 1657–58*, pp. 287, 291, 372.

92. Bodleian Library, MS Tanner 311, fos 258–268; NRO, DCN 29/4/20.

93. See especially NRO, DCN 24/3, fos 60–61, 104v, 111, 130, 133; DCN 11/6 (1713, 1715); DCN 115/1, pp. 142–50, 186–87, 241–48; DCN 115/2, pp. 206–10, 220, 239–40, 247–50; DCN 115/3, pp. 5–8, 12, 23–24, 32, 40, 58–59; DCN 57/2.

94. London, Lambeth Palace Library, MS 593 [p. 285].

proclamation of King Charles II on 8 May 1660. When Searle first put pen to paper late in 1659 he recorded disconsolately that it was 'the tenth long winter since the Edomites plundered me and our poor church'. He had been chapter clerk at Norwich where the abolition of the cathedral chapter had left him, he lamented, 'irreparably undone'. He filled his account with invective against the 'profane' and 'heathenish Edomites' (great enemies and quondam conquerors of the Israelites), with self pity at his own destitution, and with sorrow both for his five motherless children and for Norwich Cathedral itself, 'poor plundered Zion'. Yet even while he wallowed in self-pity and before he had finished his story, the king returned; he ended by describing England as 'then sorrowing, but now singing'. Having styled himself *tristissimum* ('the saddest of all') on the title page he put a line through the word as the final stroke of his labours.[95]

Searle's rejoicing was matched across England. In Norwich the city government only called a halt to the festivities after they had continued for almost a week.[96] Although the legal settlement of the church did not come until 1662 many people regarded the reestablishment of the forms and hierarchy of the old church of England as the twin sister of the restoration of the monarchy; the twelve months after May 1660 saw their reimposition across England as public pressure (not exclusively from episcopalian clergy) led royal policy.[97] Prominent among the landmarks of the Anglican scene to be reestablished were the cathedrals.

Dean John Hassall and three prebendaries did not live to see the restoration of the chapter. Their successors were all appointed by the king in the middle of July 1660 and the first chapter was held on 7 August.[98] The timing of events at Norwich was similar to those elsewhere: only two cathedral chapters had convened by mid July, while others did not meet until September.[99] The situation facing the restored chapter at Norwich, though daunting, was by no means as difficult as that before other cathedrals. Although none of the newcomers, not even the dean (John Croftes, 1660–70), had any previous cathedral experience, the three surviving prebendaries had between them well over eight decades of experience of Norwich chapter business; the three key lay officers, the chapter clerk, the understeward and the auditor, had all been appointed before the chapter's abolition in

95. London, Lambeth Palace Library, MS 593 [pp. 259–88]. Another copy of Searle's history is in Cambridge University Library, divided between Additional MS 151 (the bishops) and MS Dd. 8. 40, fos 23–28 (the deans).

96. R. Hutton, *The Restoration* (Oxford, 1987), pp. 125–26; NRO, NCR 16b, mayors' court book, 1654–66, fo. 120r.

97. I. M. Green, *The Re-Establishment of the Church of England, 1660–1663* (Oxford, 1978), pp. 61–79.

98. J. Le Neve, *Fasti Ecclesiae Anglicanae, 1541– 1857*, viii, *Ely, Norwich, Westminster and Worcester Dioceses*, rev. J. M. Horn (London, 1992), pp. 51, 53, 58; NRO, DCN 24/3, fos 1–3, 7v.

99. Green, *Re-Establishment*, p. 72.

1649.[100] Moreover, while the problems facing the chapter in its three immediate tasks – the restoration of the services and music, the repair of the fabric and the recovery of its lands and rights – should not be underestimated, it was able to tackle these issues with a large measure of public support and goodwill for the restoration of the old church.

The reestablishment of the cathedral's liturgy with its accompanying ceremony and music was no simple process, since the 1640s had seen the destruction of the organ and the loss of most if not all of the vestments, plate, service and music books.[101] The next decade and beyond saw the piecemeal replacement of these losses, some by purchase and some by donation. Even the city corporation, largely antagonistic to the cathedral service in the 1630s, gave an alms dish and silver candlesticks. The cathedral inventories of 1667 and 1669 show that within a decade of the Restoration the altar was fully furnished and the choir extensively adorned.[102]

Experienced manpower was more valuable and harder to replace. Here the cathedral was fortunate that only three of its eight former lay clerks were dead. More of the minor canons had died and it took longer to replace them, possibly because the dean and chapter had to wait until its Norwich livings, by which minor canons supplemented their meagre stipends, became vacant. Little is known about the recruitment of new choir boys but in November 1661 Peter Sandley, one of the surviving lay clerks, was paid for teaching the singing boys for the past year.[103] Replacing the organ which had been torn down in 1643 presented a greater problem. The gap was temporarily filled by the purchase of a small organ from Richard Plum of Bury St Edmunds for £50 while a public appeal was launched for a new great organ.[104] Over £340 was promised and the dean and chapter contributed a further £100; the new organ, 'fair' and 'well tuned' according to Browne, was complete by 1664.[105] Overall, Norwich Cathedral in the 1660s was musically much better off than York Minster where there were still gaps in the choir in the 1670s.[106] The reestablishment of choral services at Norwich thus proved an early success for the new chapter. The corporation attended on Sundays from

100. Of the prebendaries John Spendlove had been appointed in 1616, Edmund Porter and Edward Young in 1628. Thomas Searle, chapter clerk, and auditor Jeffery Spendlove were appointed in 1643, the understeward Augustine Reeve in 1645.

101. One set of music part books may have survived: see p. 694. Manning, 'Church Plate', pp. 67–75. Of the pre-Civil War plate only the flagon given by Dean Suckling in 1615 survived.

102. Manning, 'Church Plate', pp. 68–70; NRO, DCN 12/29; NRO, NCR, assembly book, 1642–68, fo. 223.

103. NRO, DCN 24/3, fo. 37v.

104. NRO, DCN 29/4/21.

105. Bodleian Library, MS Tanner 134, fos 202–203, 207; NRO, DCN 24/3, fo. 50r; N. Boston, *The Musical History of Norwich Cathedral* (Norwich, 1963), pp. 8–11; Browne, *Works*, v, p. 167.

106. G. E. Aylmer and R. Cant, eds, *A History of York Minster* (Oxford, 1977), p. 409.

September 1660 and by the end of 1661 the congregations were described by Sir Thomas Browne as 'very numerous'.[107]

The fabric of Norwich Cathedral had fared much better in the 1650s than that of many others, particularly Exeter and Lichfield. Some friends of the cathedral, as at Winchester, had attempted to collect money to carry out essential repairs. Under the supervision of Alderman Christopher Jay (easily the most generous benefactor) £182 in labour and materials had been spent on Norwich Cathedral.[108] Consequently, when the chapter returned, the cathedral fabric was in a relatively good condition. Indeed, a great storm in the spring of 1662 may have done more damage than the previous fifteen years put together, for the cost of these repairs was reported to be nearly £1000.[109] Within seven weeks of the chapter's first meeting in 1660 workmen were busy mending the church, some of them even paid by the city corporation. By the end of the year other public donations were coming in. About a hundred contributors raised at least £870: donors included many of the leading families of East Anglia, not least Lord Horatio Townshend, Baron Thomas Richardson of Cramond and the L'Estranges.[110] Such was the speed of the restoration work that in October 1662 a Dutch tourist commented that the cathedral and cloisters had been 'restored as new'.[111] The buildings in the close took longer to renew. Repairs to the deanery (costing over £300) and to the organist's house continued into 1664.[112] The bishop's chapel, which had been completely destroyed in the civil wars, and which was rebuilt by Bishop Reynolds, was not completed until 1672.[113] (See fig. 201 for a view of this new chapel.)

By 1670 the chapter claimed to have spent £2800 on repairs and refurnishing the cathedral over and above what had been received in donations, together with a further £1542 renovating houses in the close. Such extraordinary sums (sufficient, for example, to employ one hundred building labourers for approximately five years) were only possible because of the windfall profits totalling £6206 from the fines of

107. NRO, NCR 16b, mayors' court book, 1654–66, fos 129v–130r; Browne, *Works*, vi, pp. 9, 11–12, 16.

108. Bodleian Library, MS Tanner 133, fo. 53; NRO, DCN 12/28 gives a slightly different figure. B. C. Turner, '"The Return of the Church"; Cathedral and Close, 1660–1662', *Winchester Cathedral Record*, 29 (1960), p. 17.

109. John Collinges's letter of 6 April 1662, A. G. Matthews, 'A Norfolk Dissenter's Letter, 1662', *NA*, 24 (1932), p. 231. The chapter voted £500 towards the repairs on 27 March 1662: NRO, DCN 24/3, fo. 41r.

110. NRO, NCR case 16b, mayors' court book, 1654–66, fo. 129v, DCN 107/2; DCN 29/4/21; Bodleian Library, MS Tanner 138, fo. 156.

111. M. Exwood and H. L. Lehmann, eds, *The Journal of William Schellinks' Travels in England, 1661–1663* (Camden Society, fifth series, I, 1993), p. 159.

112. NRO, DCN 24/3, fo. 40r; DCN 11/1, 1664; Bodleian Library, MS Tanner 133, fo. 105r.

113. Cambridge University Library, MS Mm. I. 51, pp. 96–98.

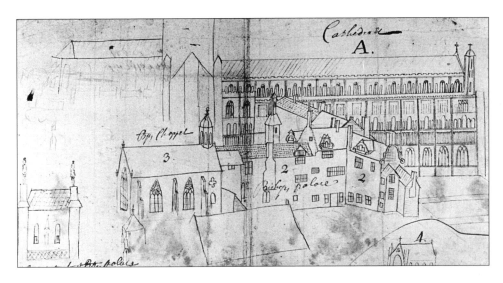

Fig. 201. Undated drawing of the bishop's palace, Bishop Reynolds's new chapel and the cathedral from the north, by John Kirkpatrick (*c.* 1686–1728). Note that of the two northern buttress-turrets of the west front, one is shown uncapped and one with a cupola, replacing the pinnacles shown in Daniel King's engraving of *c.* 1655 (fig. 91). (Norwich Castle Museum, Fitch Collection 1698.76.94.)

leases.[114] Of all the tasks facing the chapter the question of restoring its lands and rights was the most complicated and the most important, not only because they were needed to finance all the other tasks but also because the land question was potentially the most politically charged issue. Fortunately, most of those holding dean and chapter lands in 1660 were eager to pay a fine to the chapter in order to procure a new lease and secure their tenancy. Once again public support helped in the cathedral's restoration. The chapter's greatest problems came from Christopher Jay, someone they described as 'our good friend', who not only wanted the return of the money he claimed to have spent repairing the cathedral in the 1650s but who also expected to be granted a lease of one of the chapter's best manors. Four years of arguing left him with the former but not the latter.[115]

The restoration of cathedral chapters has been described by a leading authority as 'remarkably smooth and rapid'.[116] None the less, the wounds of the 1640s and 1650s did not heal for several generations. For a dozen years the chapter refused to confirm the patent of the office of chancellor to John Mills because of his former office in the parliamentary army: 'his hand had been in blood' explained Dean

114. NRO, DCN 29/4/29.

115. Bodleian Library, MSS Tanner 133, fo. 52, Tanner 134, fos 106r, 140; NRO, DCN 29/4/29; DCN 12/28; PRO, C5/36/45;

CSPD, 1661–62, pp. 54, 181, 234–35, 316–17.

116. Green, *Re-Establishment*, p. 79.

Herbert Astley (1670–81).[117] In 1683 Prebendary William Smyth reminded his congregation at the cathedral of the horrors perpetrated forty years earlier when the building had been sacked.[118] Even in 1707 the dean was still fruitlessly seeking some of the chapter's records lost in 1649.[119]

Nationally, the rush to reestablish the church of England and harry its opponents meant that few of its former problems were addressed; the same was true, in microcosm, of Norwich Cathedral. Bishop Wren's suggestion that the unmanageably large diocese be split in two by making Suffolk a new see was ignored for a further two centuries.[120] The chapter's windfall of £6000 in fines masked the underlying financial weakness of the cathedral which continued to meet large extraordinary expenses only by extraordinary means.[121] Little was done to revise the statutes despite the prewar experience which had shown the cathedral's management structure to be seriously flawed. The only structural change to the running of the cathedral after 1660 was that the dean, of his own accord, ceased to appoint a butler, a caterer and cooks in a tacit admission that the statutes' attempt to create a common dining-table was a dead letter.

Problems surrounding the dean's powers continued after the Restoration. Between 1603 and 1724 only one of the eight deans avoided serious antagonism or resentment from within the cathedral.[122] Herbert Astley, having protested that Dean Croftes acted in an authoritarian manner, proceeded in much the same way when he succeeded to the deanery.[123] Indeed, protests about the dean's exercise of his office continued throughout the eighteenth century: they were inherent in a set of statutes

117. Blomefield, *Norfolk*, iii, pp. 634–35; Bodleian Library, MSS Tanner 133, fo. 129r, Tanner 134, fo. 144r.
118. W. Smyth, *A Sermon Preached in the Cathedral Church of Norwich, on the Ninth of September, 1683* (London, 1683), p. 9.
119. NRO, DCN 115/2, pp. 190–91, 197.
120. C. Wren, *Parentalia*, pp. 51–52. The archdeaconry of Sudbury was transferred to Ely diocese in 1837; in 1914 the new diocese of St Edmundsbury and Ipswich was created for Suffolk: F. A. Youngs, *Guide to the Local Administrative Units of England*, 2 vols (London, 1979–91), i, pp. 781–82, 784.
121. The chapter had to borrow £250 in 1704: NRO, DCN 115/2, p. 32. The chapter continued to hold a totally inadequate cash reserve of only £100.
122. For complaints about George Montgomery (1603–14) and Edmund Suckling (1614–28) see above, pp. 513–14, 532; about John

Hassall (1628–49) see NRO, DCN 86/29; about John Croftes (1660–70) see Bodleian Library, MS Tanner 133, fos 50–51; about Herbert Astley (1670–81) see NRO, DCN 39/37; about Henry Fairfax (1689–1702) see E. M. Thompson, *Letters of Humphrey Prideaux* (Camden Society, new series, 15, 1875), pp. 157, 160–61, 164; about Humphrey Prideaux (1702–24) see NRO, DCN 115/2, p. 294. John Sharpe (1681–89) seems to have escaped serious criticism from within the cathedral.
123. Bodleian Library, MS Tanner 133, fos 50–51; NRO, DCN 39/37. Astley was also lampooned, probably from outside the cathedral, as the 'Dunstable Dean', advanced far beyond his abilities and under the thumb of his brazen-faced wife, 'a bouncing virago': Bodleian Library, MS Tanner 95*, fo. 121r.

(drawn up by a dean in 1620) which concentrated great power in the dean's hands but were sufficiently ambiguous on key points (such as the definition of the minor offices in the gift of the dean) to raise doubts and allow objections.

In the stampede to reassert orthodoxy in 1660 an opportunity was missed to deal with some long-standing constitutional and economic problems facing the cathedral chapter. Moreover, the Restoration created new ones for the cathedral. The problem of religious nonconformity, which had already touched the cathedral before the Civil War, was exacerbated. On the one hand, there were various minor incidents such as when the Quaker, Thomas Morford, disturbed the cathedral preacher in 1668.[124] On the other hand, there were the serious disputes that raged over the next six decades with dissenters, Catholics and nonjurors. And with the church of England's loss of religious monopoly came the creation of parties within and without the church – high and low, Tory and Whig. By and large, the story of the cathedral in the period from the 1670s to the 1720s is of the penetration of parties and party issues into every aspect of its life.

Prideaux and Party Rage, 1680–1720

For forty-three years from his appointment as a prebendary in 1681 to his death in 1724 (he was elevated to the deanery in 1702) the figure of Humphrey Prideaux dominated Norwich Cathedral (fig. 202). His influence is inescapable. He was a forceful administrator and disciplinarian, often with a short temper,[125] who yet tried to steer the cathedral on a middle course through the turbulent and violent waters of Norwich city politics. Moreover, the history of the cathedral is often refracted through his eyes. He was a prodigious annalist and a curt commentator. He reorganised the chapter archives, investigated the cathedral's history, instituted new and improved means of record keeping and began a business diary that allows a unique insight, unparalleled before or for more than a century after, into the affairs of the cathedral.[126] He was a man of pithy, often caustic judgements on others: a Victorian biographer called him 'a man of more frankness than refinement of mind'.[127] If we see the cathedral more clearly for the five decades after 1680, we must remember that it is Prideaux's spectacles we have donned.

---

124. Bodleian Library, MS Tanner 134, fos 120r, 125.
125. T. Newcome, *The Life of John Sharp*, 2 vols (London, 1825), ii, p. 48.
126. P. Mussett, 'Norwich Cathedral under Dean Prideaux, 1702–24', in D. Marcombe and C. S. Knighton, eds, *Close Encounters: English* *Cathedrals and Society since 1540* (Nottingham, 1991), p. 99; *The Life of the Reverend Humphrey Prideaux* (London, 1748), pp. 20–23; Prideaux, *Letters*, p. 121; NRO, DCN 115/1–3, 5–6, 7–11; DCN 24/3, fos 170v–171r, 176v–177r.
127. *DNB*, *sub* Humphrey Prideaux.

Fig. 202. Humphrey Prideaux (1648–1724), prebendary of Norwich from 1681 and dean from 1702 until his death.

The second theme that runs through the story of the cathedral from the later years of Charles II's reign is the intrusion of party strife into so many aspects of cathedral life. Prideaux and party politics, twisted together, form the warp of the story: all other developments are woven across them.

The emergence of political parties, Tory and Whig (the former high church, the latter an alliance of low church and nonconformist dissent), influenced the choice of deans and prebendaries by the crown to such an extent that the composition of the cathedral chapter looked like a fossilised record of government changes. Ideological party differences could easily affect relationships within the cathedral as well as between the cathedral and the outside world; they certainly split the city itself.

After his first visit to Norwich Prideaux described the city as divided into three parties: the violent Tories, the violent Whigs and the moderates. No other city, he believed, had such vicious votaries of either extreme. He railed particularly against Dr John Hildeyard, who was chaplain to the earl and countess of Yarmouth, the leaders of the extreme Tories within the county. He considered Hildeyard, who was not above brawling, to be 'the greatest disturber of the public peace that is in the county', and one whose antics had raised the odium of the people against all the clergy.[128] Imagine, then, poor Prideaux's horror when, in 1683, Yarmouth and the Tories secured Hildeyard's promotion to a Norwich prebend Six years later Prideaux could still be found protesting about Hildeyard who, 'with very indecent violence', and with Tory support, had secured his own election as the chapter's proctor in convocation.[129]

While ideological and personal differences divided the chapter, the rage of party

128. *CSPD, 1682*, pp. 54–56; PRO, SP29/418/ 67. For Prideaux as the author of this report see R. W. Ketton-Cremer, 'Norfolk Politics in 1681–2', *NA*, 28 (1945), pp. 76–77. Prideaux, *Letters*, pp. 90, 123–24; Historical Manuscripts Commission, *Sixth Report* (London, 1877), p. 382a.

129. London, Lambeth Palace Library, MS 934, no. 72; NRO, DCN 24/3, fo. 236r.

and national events impinged on the cathedral from the outside. Extreme Whigs and dissenters viewed the cathedral with suspicion, even outright hostility, while extreme Tories cast those cathedral clergy who failed to support their line as apostates and renegades. Once again, in Norwich and beyond, the cathedral became a political football. Just as there had been an alleged plot to assassinate Bishop Wren in the 1630s, so there were similar allegations in 1678, allowing the Tories to arrest their enemies as the suspected ringleaders. A death-threat directed against Bishop Anthony Sparrow (1676–85) and signed 'S. Blood' was found beside the bishop's stall in the cathedral: 'Your days are very short and narrow, your proceedings very sharp. I will kill you . . . it seems you are grown a viper not fit to live; you limb of Satan farewell; you sparrow, you living Satan'.[130] While dissenters allegedly plotted to kill the bishop, extreme Tories attempted to rouse the people against him for being too moderate.[131] Norwich politics in the late seventeenth and early eighteenth centuries were as heated and violent as in the decade before the Civil War. That the cathedral prospered in the testing times of the 1680s was in large part thanks to the tenure of three remarkable men, possibly the most outstanding chapter members at Norwich in the early modern period: John Sharpe (prebendary 1675–81; dean 1681–89), Richard Kidder (prebendary 1681–91) and Humphrey Prideaux (prebendary 1681–1702; dean 1702–24). And in Anthony Sparrow and his successor William Lloyd (1685–91), Norwich had two of its most able, active and spirited bishops who, unlike so many others, made Norwich (rather than London) their home. The cooperation between an active bishop and an energetic chapter revealed the true potential of Norwich Cathedral.

The accession of the Roman Catholic James II in 1685 posed grave problems for loyal churchmen. Roman Catholics across the country took heart and launched a campaign of evangelism and conversion. In the diocese of Norwich the defence of the church of England, opposition to the church of Rome and to the extreme Tories ('very hot men . . . drunk or mad' with 'such extravagant notions of loyalty as extinguished their regard to law', as Kidder regarded them), were all led from the cathedral and bishop's palace.[132] Kidder and Prideaux published their own defences of the church of England and distributed other controversial works across the diocese; they preached against popery and encouraged others to follow their lead; they steadied waverers in the faith. In the diocese Prideaux coordinated the campaign

---

130. G. J. A. Guth, 'Croakers, Tackers, and Other Citizens: Norwich Voters in the Early Eighteenth Century', 2 vols (unpublished Stanford University Ph. D. thesis, 1985), i, p. 86 n. 108; King, 'Wren', p. 100; *CSPD, 1678*, p. 306; Bodleian Library, MS Tanner 39, fo. 39r.

131. Bodleian Library, MS Tanner 35, fo. 170.

132. A. E. Robinson, ed., *The Life of Richard Kidder, DD Bishop of Bath and Wells, Written by Himself* (Somerset Record Society, 37, 1924), p. 38. See also Sparrow's criticisms of 'hot and eager' loyalists in Bodleian Library, MS Tanner 35, fo. 170.

against the reading of James II's declaration of indulgence, ensuring that very few clergy read the grant of toleration to Catholics and dissenters despite the king's order that it be proclaimed from every pulpit. Prideaux, Sharpe and Lloyd held a disputation with two Catholic clergy.[133] The cathedral became a focus of the struggle, the Catholics well aware of the propaganda value of scoring a victory against the mother church of the diocese and its clergy. When an attempt was made to bury a convert to Rome in the cathedral Prideaux forestalled plans for 'a solemn procession by way of triumph'. When Prebendary William Smyth wobbled and was widely expected to convert to Rome he was persuaded to hold fast.[134] These were indeed 'dangerous times'; Dean Sharpe was suspended by the king for preaching against popery.[135] Amid the turmoil Kidder singled out the efforts of his friend Prideaux for special commendation: 'what he did in this evil time ought never to be forgotten'.[136]

The church of England needed not only defending but strengthening also. Once again, bishop and cathedral in concert led the way. Bishop Lloyd built on the strong links forged with the chapter by his predecessor, particularly on Sparrow's work in setting up catechising and weekly communions in the cathedral.[137] Norwich Cathedral became the religious powerhouse for city and diocese. Abuses were penalised, negligent archdeacons chastised. The laxity of the mayor and aldermen in not receiving communion was corrected. Alms were collected outside the cathedral doors and people instructed within (with over 7000 candidates for confirmations in Lent 1686). Cathedral sermons were supervised by the bishop. Good Friday was kept as a holy day, free from profanity.[138] With bishop and chapter acting together (though not without complaints from the lay clerks who found the discipline of the bishop no more congenial than the rule of the dean),[139] the potential of the cathedral was realised for a clear and definite purpose. For a few brief years in the

133. Kidder, *Life*, pp. 37–39; Prideaux, *Life*, pp. 23–45; H. Prideaux, *The Validity of the Orders of the Church of England* (London, 1688).
134. Prideaux, *Life*, pp. 26–29, 44–45.
135. Kidder, *Life*, p. 37; Historical Manuscripts Commission, *Downshire Volume I*, i, pp. 185–86, 188, 207, 216; Historical Manuscripts Commission, *Report on the Manuscripts of the Earl of Verulam* (London, 1906), pp. 87–94. The fame Sharpe won by opposing the king later brought him rich rewards: the deanery of Canterbury in 1689 and the archbishopric of York in 1691. He was replaced at Norwich by someone else who had made his name standing up to James, Henry Fair-

fax, who had opposed the king's attempts to foist a Catholic head on Magadalen College Oxford.
136. Kidder, *Life*, p. 39. Prideaux recalled that for two years, 1687–89, he continually expected to be turned out of all his preferments: Historical Manuscripts Commission, *Fifth Report* (London, 1876), p. 375.
137. Bodleian Library, MS Tanner 39, fos 64r, 117r. See above, pp. 545.
138. A. C. Miller, 'William Lloyd, Bishop of Norwich, "A Very Able and Worthy Pastor"', *NA*, 39 (1985), pp. 151–55.
139. NRO, DCN 24/3, fos 220–222.

1680s Norwich Cathedral became the flourishing diocesan centre it had for so long failed to be. It did not last long.

James II's flight and his replacement by William and Mary undid all the previous work at a stroke. Bishop Lloyd's refusal to sanction the invasion of Prince William of Orange in November 1688 encouraged the mob, which had already sacked a Catholic chapel in Norwich, to threaten the bishop's palace and the cathedral.[140] In March 1689 the palace was again threatened when a rumour spread that James II was hiding there. 'The clouds are thick and the storm ready to fall upon us', lamented Lloyd.[141] A month later the bill passed through parliament requiring all clergy to swear an oath of allegiance to King William and Queen Mary. Many (the 'nonjurors') refused, believing that their former oath to King James must hold so long as he lived. Norwich Cathedral and diocese were thrown into turmoil. Bishop Lloyd and two of his chaplains refused the oaths and were deprived; so did two minor canons (Gawen Nash and John Shaw) who were expelled, as was a third (John Connould) for refusing to pray for the new king.[142]

For over a year the bishopric lay vacant. The next bishop, John Moore, was not appointed until spring 1691.[143] Even those who accepted the new regime had often to swallow hard. The confusion was visited upon Norwich Cathedral too. The disputes over taking oaths to William and Mary cut through it, leaving those who remained uncertain and disheartened. Prideaux was one of those who only took the oaths after much soul-searching and predictions that 'nothing but a long series of confusion [was] like to come upon this land'.[144] He determined not to seek further preferment (a resolution he soon broke) for in 'troublesome times' it was better to be in a lowly station.[145] The Act of Toleration of 1690 cast the cathedral adrift, once more lacking a clear purpose. For the few previous years the cathedral had found a cause, defending the church of England and resisting the claims of other churches; now that the other Protestant churches and sects had been granted legal toleration, what was the cathedral to do? Prideaux, like many, feared that the act would lead straight to atheism, as the licentious took advantage of their new right to worship in any church as a pretext to worship in none save the tavern. Throughout the 1690s his letters are full of laments and warnings that the Act of Toleration 'has almost undone us', that liberty of conscience 'is the mother of confusion', that 'the whole world is grown corrupt; this nation is like to rue it for ages to come . . . there is scarce any religion, honour, or common integrity left in

---

140. Miller, 'Lloyd', p. 160; Prideaux, *Life*, pp. 47–48; NRO, DCN 11/3 (1689).

141. Bodleian Library, MS Tanner 28, fo. 377r.

142. J. H. Overton, *The Nonjurors* (London, 1902), pp. 484–85, 487, 492–93; NRO, DCN 24/3, fos 249–251r.

143. Le Neve, *Fasti, Norwich*, p. 39.

144. Historical Manuscripts Commission, *Fifth Report*, pp. 375–76.

145. Historical Manuscripts Commission, *Fifth Report*, p. 377 (August 1695).

the land, and God is going, I fear, to punish us in the severest manner for it'. He concluded that the 'genius of the age is run into libertinism'.[146]

Cast adrift in the sea of 'vice and irreligion, that like a pestilence . . . now rages among us' the cathedral degenerated into petty squabbling.[147] Prideaux and Hodges fought over the order of seating in the choir.[148] The old arguments about the dean's power resurfaced.[149] These contests were exacerbated by a failure of leadership from Bishop Moore (1691–1707) and Dean Henry Fairfax (1689–1702), who seem not to have viewed their roles in terms other than those of personal and family aggrandizement. Prideaux castigated Moore as 'a close designing man' who would 'fain grasp everything for his brood', sacrificing the diocese to his own secular interest.[150] Prideaux saved his sharpest darts for Dean Fairfax. His invective against 'our brutish dean' and 'this horrid sot' entertained Prideaux's correspondents for many years:

> He cannot sleep at night till dosed with drink . . . he acts by no rules of justice, honesty, civility, or good manners towards any one, but after an obstinate, self-willed, irrational manner in all sorts of businesses, whereby he disobliges every one that has anything to do with him . . . He comes little to church and never to the sacrament . . . and as for a book, he looks not into any from the beginning of the year to the end. His whole life is the pot and the pipe, and, go to him when you will, you will find him walking about his room with a pipe in his mouth and a bottle of claret and a bottle of old strong beer (which in this country they call nog) upon the table, and every other turn he takes a glass of one or the other of them.[151]

Yet there was more to Prideaux's hatred than a personal animosity and the belief that Fairfax had been promoted beyond his abilities. First, there were important ideological differences, for Fairfax was suspected of courting the extreme Whigs, having allegedly imbibed his politics from the republican hero, the earl of Shaftesbury.[152] Secondly, Prideaux believed that Fairfax put personal gain above the greater good of the cathedral, seeking only a quick profit for himself and minimising expenditure on repairs, thereby mortgaging the future for present

---

146. Prideaux, *Letters*, p. 154; Historical Manuscripts Commission, *Fifth Report*, pp. 374, 376–77.

147. The phrase is from a sermon by Prebendary Charles Trimnell, *A Sermon Preached before the Honourable House of Commons . . .*, Jan. 14. 1707/8 (London, 1708), p. 25.

148. Bodleian Library, MS Tanner 134, fos 3–11, 13–15, 37–39, 118–119, 149–150.

149. Bodleian Library, MS Tanner 134, fos 61–67; NRO, DCN 24/4, fos 17v–18r; DCN 25/1.

150. Prideaux, *Letters*, p. 149; NRO, DCN 115/2, p. 139.

151. Prideaux, *Letters*, pp. 150–51, 160–61, 164.

152. Prideaux, *Letters*, pp. 157, 159, 161. Nathaniel Hodges, Fairfax's one friend in the chapter, had been Shaftesbury's chaplain.

benefit.[153] With a dean who cared for his pocket and his pot and a bishop whose only interest in the diocese lay in providing for his own family, the cathedral turned in on itself in the 1690s, its disheartened prebendaries expending their energy in squabbles. It was all a long way from the vision of the previous decade.

When, therefore, Prideaux was made dean in May 1702 Norwich Cathedral faced four main problems: the finances were mismanaged; the buildings were in need of repair; discipline was lax; and party strife raged on. The first three were Fairfax's chickens coming home to roost, the last a hang-over from the previous twenty years. The solution, Prideaux determined, was strong leadership.

The first problem was the easiest to remedy for, as Prideaux had pointed out back in 1697, over the next two decades the church's financial position would be steadily improved by the addition of corn rents to old leases as they fell in.[154] But first, the storm had to be weathered. The cathedral was actually in debt in the years 1702–4, while there was no surplus on the current account in the years 1706–8.[155] There were hard financial decisions for the chapter to make. There would be jam tomorrow but none today. Timber was sold, £250 borrowed from Prideaux's mother-in-law and arrears exacted from tenants.[156] Although no great building works were undertaken, repairs were carried out, the system of surveying the fabric every March was refined and a more efficient surveyor appointed.[157] Under Prideaux's direction the estates were better managed too, not only because the end of a poor series of harvests in the 1690s meant that tenants were better able to pay their rents, but also because he relieved the prebendaries of some of the burdens of office by appointing a lay deputy for the receiver and treasurer.[158]

Yet Prideaux was only tinkering with a flawed system. The central contradiction remained, that every year the chapter had to decide whether to spend any surplus on repairs to the buildings and improvements to the estates, or whether to divide the money among themselves. There was no long-term financial planning, while the temptation to cut and run, making a quick profit for themselves, was always strong. This was a dilemma that many chapter members would have been familiar

---

153. Mussett, 'Prideaux', pp. 95, 107–8. See also NRO, DCN 26/10/8. Dean Astley had earlier been accused of a similar 'jam today' policy.

154. London, Lambeth Palace Library, MS 930, no. 80. See also below, pp. 671–72.

155. NRO, DCN 11/5. The *exitus anni* showed no dividend for the dean and prebendaries in the years 1706, 1707 and 1708, but there was a profit from corn rents to be divided.

156. NRO, DCN 11/5 (1704); DCN 24/4, fos 111v, 119r; DCN 115/2, p. 32.

157. Prideaux, *Life*, p. 146. A 'supervisor of the works' is first recorded in 1685; his annual £10 salary becomes a regular feature of the accounts from the 1690s: NRO, DCN 24/3, fo. 206v; DCN 11/4. In 1712 Captain Jonathan Symonds replaced the aged and forgetful William Ferrer as surveyor: NRO, DCN 115/2, pp. 351–52.

158. Mussett, 'Prideaux', p. 108.

with in similar institutional circumstances as fellows of colleges.[159] The cost of repairs continued to be met by temporary expedients – borrowings, windfall profits and the sale of timber – or by redirecting money from other purposes: for most of the 1690s and again under Prideaux the places of gospeller and epistoler were frozen, their salaries diverted to pay for repairs or other pressing needs.[160] Prideaux put the finances back on an even keel but he neither overhauled nor improved the basic system. Likewise, while he carried out essential repairs and patched up the church, he undertook no major building campaigns. It is, thus, partly his legacy that no substantial structural improvements took place until 1739–40, by which time the fabric was 'not only in a nasty, but ruinous condition'.[161] Prideaux was an able, but not an imaginative, administrator whose best reforms were limited to methods of record-keeping.

The early eighteenth century saw further intensification of party conflict in Norwich. Contemporaries agreed that the city was 'distracted with party rage, Whig and Tory, high church and low church', that 'all the excess of party fury [is] run up to seed . . . never was city in this miserable kingdom so wretchedly divided as this. Never were such divisions carried on with such feud, such malice, such magisterial tyranny'.[162] The cathedral was affected in two ways. First, cathedral staff involved themselves in Norwich politics. Prideaux used his influence in elections on behalf of his friends and relatives, while the minor officers, Tories almost to a man, voted in parliamentary elections and became embroiled in rowdy celebrations with the winning candidate.[163] Secondly, both parties in Norwich were interested in what went on inside the cathedral. One prebendary, for example, was threatened with a blanket-tossing by a crowd of 'Tory blades' if he did not vote in a chapter meeting according to their wishes.[164] Politically, as in so much else, cathedral and city were intertwined.

Prideaux's determination to steer a middle course opened him and the cathedral to criticism from both sides. Whigs could view the cathedral with suspicion, tending to see a natural alliance between the church of England and the Tories. It was a view reinforced by the political preferences of the inhabitants of the close, especially

159. V. Morgan, 'Country, Court and Cambridge University: A Study in the Emergence of a Political Culture, 1558–1640' (unpublished University of East Anglia Ph. D. thesis, 1983), pp. 319–48.
160. NRO, DCN 11/4; DCN 115/2, p. 61. The *Statutes* (chap. xxvii) reserved only £100 as an emergency fund for the year, a wholly inadequate figure even in 1620.
161. Blomefield, *Norfolk*, iii, p. 630. NRO, DCN

27/1, pp. 493, 495.
162. The first quotation is from the arch-Tory Henry Crossgrove in 1714, the second from the *London Post* in 1705: quoted in Guth, 'Croakers', ii, p. 491, i, p. 411.
163. NRO, DCN 115/1, p. 241; DCN 115/2, pp. 14, 16, 294; BL, Additional MS 29588, fo. 115.
164. London, Lambeth Palace Library, MS 934, no. 72.

those of the cathedral's minor officers.[165] In city government, the greatest opponents of the close, those most likely to levy punitive rates of taxation on the cathedral precincts tended to be Whigs.[166] When, however, after 1703 Prideaux switched his electoral support from the moderate Tories to the moderate Whigs, he was exposed to considerable public criticism in Norwich.[167] At a time when the Tory cry was that the church was in danger, particularly from false brethren within, and when the Tory crowd at elections shouted the name and carried the picture of Dr Sacheverell, Prideaux's support for the Whigs brought odium upon his head. According to Henry Crossgrove, proprietor of the arch-Tory *Norwich Gazette*, he had joined the 'Oliverian club', a phrase recalling the republicanism and extremism of Oliver Cromwell and the Interregnum. To Crossgrove, the Tories were 'true churchmen and loyalists' while the Whigs were 'a strange compound body of false churchmen and sectaries'.[168] Such criticism was also to be found within the cathedral. In 1710, after recommending the election of a Whig as MP for Norwich (his kinsman Waller Bacon), Prideaux had to defend himself from rumours circulating in the cathedral that, as he put it, 'I am not for the church'. That Dean Prideaux, Prebendary (and later Bishop) Charles Trimnell and Lord Charles Townshend, the high steward, were all Whig leaders in Norfolk can only have increased the sense of separation between them and the Tory minor canons and lay clerks.

Prideaux feared what the Tory mob might do to the cathedral. In 1703 he ordered

165. The close was a more Tory area than the city overall: *The Alphabetical Draft of the Poll of Robert Bene Esq.; and Richard Berney Esq.; Taken the 18th of October, 1710* ([Norwich, 1710]), pp. 18–19; *An Alphabetical Draught of the Polls of Sir Edward Ward, Bart, Miles Branthwayt, Esq.; and of Horatio Walpole, Waller Bacon, Esqs . . . Taken May the 15th, 1734* (Norwich, 1735), pp. iv, 80–81.

166. Prideaux singled out Alderman Thomas Cook who always 'expresses a bitter spite against the close', and Alderman John Hall, his son Captain William Hall and Mr Pitts who 'look on us as an enemy's country and treat us accordingly'. The first four were all Whigs. None the less, he also mentioned two Tories, Aldermen Francis Gardiner and Philip Stebbing, who opposed Prideaux's appeal to reduce the taxation of the close, while he described Edward Clarke, a Whig, as 'the worthiest alderman of the city'. NRO, DCN 115/1, pp. 186–87; DCN 115/2, p. 262; DCN 115/3, p. 58; Guth,

'Croakers', i, pp. 197, 232–33, 253, 312, 335, 433, 489.

167. His greatest patrons were the Finch family, earls of Nottingham and Tories. Prideaux, *Life*, pp. 7–9; Prideaux, *The Old and New Testament Connected*, 3 parts in 2 vols (London 1716–18), i, sig. A2. In 1679 and 1702 Prideaux worked for the election of Tories to parliament, but in 1710 and 1715 he supported the Whigs in Norwich: L. S. Sutherland and L. G. Mitchell, eds, *The History of the University of Oxford*, v, *The Eighteenth Century* (Oxford, 1986), p. 15; H. Horwitz, *Revolution Politicks: The Career of Daniel Finch, Second Earl of Nottingham, 1647–1730* (Cambridge, 1968), p. 184; Guth, 'Croakers', i, pp. 208 n. 125, 327; BL, Additional MS 29588, fo. 115.

168. Guth, 'Croakers', i, pp. 40, 212, 411–12, ii, pp. 498, 779. Henry Sacheverell achieved national fame when he was impeached in 1710 for preaching up the Tory cause and the dangers to the church.

the inscription on Dean Fairfax's new tomb to be covered and defaced, in part because it seemed to justify the civil wars against Charles I: should the inscription stand, he wrote 'it would provoke the rabble to break in upon us and tear it down and be a handle for them perchance to execute other violences upon us'.[169] At the time of the Sacheverell trial Prideaux felt that everyone but arch-Tories had to act and speak circumspectly for fear of the Tory mob, while a few years later he still feared the 'mutinous temper' of the 'rude and insolent' citizens of Norwich.[170]

The violence of party rage not only limited the dean's actions, it sometimes undermined his authority. Even cases of immorality became a party issue. On at least two occasions cathedral members facing the dean's power of disciplining and expulsion appealed to the Norwich Tories and received their support even though one, the minor canon John Stukeley, faced dismissal for sexual harassment and exposing himself to women, while the other, chapter clerk Stephen Searle, son of the suffering Thomas, had been arrested in a brothel.[171] Party politics and discipline became entangled. The dean's power to admonish those who had committed abuses and to expel the recalcitrant on the third warning may have been a means of controlling the largely Tory minor officers of the cathedral, but it risked driving the punished into further extremes: John Stukeley was embraced by the Jacobites and thus became even more of a nuisance to the dean (but perhaps not to the women of the close) after his expulsion.[172] Moreover, in the nation at large in the early eighteenth century the prosecution of immorality threatened to become a party issue as Tory high churchmen frowned on the mushrooming societies for the reformation of manners that brought private prosecutions against the licentious. The lamentations about vice and the action taken by Prideaux, the moderate Whig, need to be seen in this context.

Known since his days as an Oxford tutor as a disciplinarian, Prideaux was convinced that Fairfax had been a lax dean who allowed and even encouraged abuses.[173] He was determined to enforce a stricter rule, preventing abuses, punishing the negligent and the immoral, and defending the cathedral's rights.[174] Though he had a reputation for severity, he did recognise the limits of the possible and could act with tact. He

169. NRO, DCN 115/1, pp. 222–24. See also above, pp. 477–78.

170. Guth, 'Croakers', ii, p. 501; NRO, DCN 115/3, p. 23.

171. NRO, DCN 33/22; DCN 115/1, p. 173; DCN 115/2, pp. 139–40; DCN 24/4, fo. 130v. See above, pp. 555, 558, for Thomas Searle.

172. NRO, DCN 115/1, pp. 173–74. *CSPD, 1702–3*, p. 237.

173. Prideaux, *Life*, p. 14; NRO, DCN 24/3, fo. 172v; London, Lambeth Palace Library, MS 930, no. 80. He believed that Fairfax had refused to expel an insufficient and immoral lay clerk, had not regulated the seating in the choir nor building in the close, and had accepted a bribe in granting the portership: NRO, DCN 115/1, pp. 170–71, 213–16, 219–20; DCN 115/2, pp. 8–10.

174. Mussett, 'Prideaux', pp. 100–1, 106.

drew back from a lawsuit with the bishop, admonished even the notorious privately rather than before the whole cathedral, if he saw hope of amendment, and showed a care for those he had disciplined.[175]

Thanks to Prideaux's meticulous record-keeping, we know much more about the misdemeanours during his period of office than about those which occurred under other deans. Often, it makes for sorry reading. John Stukeley, as we have seen, was expelled for

> a very abominable practice of lust and beastly lasciviousness: that is, frequently for several years past, at the sight of women to have taken out his yard or privy part and to have rubbed it up and down, in order unnaturally and wickedly to pollute himself and to tempt and corrupt the said women, sometimes doing it openly in their view . . .

His defence, that his hand was so often to be seen in his codpiece because he suffered from crab lice, was rejected.[176] Another minor canon, John Blagrave, was expelled for repeated drunkenness, his drinking having led him to the debtors' gaol. A third, Philip Burrough, fell off his horse in a drunken stupor and died.[177] To the contemporary mind, atheism and immorality were inextricably linked.[178] One lay clerk was charged with saying 'that there was no hell but the grave and that the clergy did preach up hell only to fright the people'; he was also accused of groping in the codpiece of a chorister.[179] The chapter clerk was admonished as 'a drunkard and a sot': he was too inebriated to carry out his duties, living 'in an atheistical and stupid neglect of all manner of religion', neither saying his prayers nor receiving communion.[180] A further two minor canons resigned rather than face expulsion, one for adultery, the other for fornication.[181] Prideaux remained surprisingly philosophical: 'here men will always be sinners, and as long as clergymen are men, they will be so too . . . As the present circumstances are, it is the great mercy of God if there are not more clergymen wicked than otherwise'.[182]

175. Prideaux, *Life*, p. 150; Mussett, 'Prideaux', pp. 108–9; NRO, DCN 27/1, p. 287; DCN 115/1, p. 170; DCN 115/2, p. 307. Stukeley was allowed to keep his cathedral house for eighteen months after his expulsion; rather than expelling the dissolute Stephen Searle, he was moved from the chapter clerk's place to the portership so that he would still have an income to live on: NRO, DCN 115/1, pp. 173–74; DCN 115/2, p. 162.

176. NRO, DCN 33/22, especially sentence, 22 August 1702, and deposition by Burgess, 12 August 1702.

177. Blagrave: NRO, DCN 115/2, pp. 186–87, 307, 322, 334, 337; DCN 24/2, fos 158v–159r. Burrough: NRO, DCN 115/3, p. 61.

178. NRO, DCN 115/2, pp. 186–87, 307, 322, 334, 337; DCN 24/2, fos 158v–159r.

179. NRO, DCN 115/2, pp. 40–42; DCN 24/4, fo. 120.

180. NRO, DCN 115/2, pp. 156–61.

181. NRO, DCN 115/3, pp. 9, 27–32, 37; DCN 24/4, fos 164v, 174r.

182. Historical Manuscripts Commission, *Fifth Report*, p. 378.

In his first twelve years Prideaux is recorded as having punished more men than any previous dean. After 1714 the admonitions cease. Immorality had not suddenly been cured; rather, Prideaux was slowly losing his grip. As early as 1707 he had professed himself too old to seek the bishopric of Norwich. In 1710, when he was already sixty-two, a botched operation for the stone forced him to give up preaching for ever.[183] His last fourteen years saw a slow decline. By 1717 he was housebound. A year later he described himself as 'broken by age . . . superannuated . . . in an useless state of life' and 'past labouring any further'.[184] After January 1719 he could no longer write his diary himself; deputed to a secretary, the entries grow shorter.[185] Retirement was unheard of, not only for the ancient lay clerks whose voices deteriorated with age but also for deans. Prideaux lingered on, and on, until his death in November 1724. By then many of his earlier achievements had been undone. Squabbling returned to the chapter; the minor officers became inadequately supervised and disciplined.[186] Yet Prideaux was remembered favourably as a man of 'honour and integrity', a 'great and good man' who had 'religion truly at heart'.[187]

In the close the dean and chapter tried to create and manage their own ordered space in the midst of a tumultuous city, just as the dean did with the seating in the choir. It is no surprise that their efforts peaked in the 1690s and 1700s when party rage was at its height.[188] The comparison between the two sides of the precinct wall is implicit in some of Prideaux's correspondence. 'Our close is as it were a town of itself apart from the city', he wrote in 1696, adding that he rarely had dealing with the townsfolk, 'and indeed I very seldom go among them'.[189] As we have emphasised above, the chapter was turning in on itself, especially in the 1690s, almost as an admission of its failure in the wider world. In attempting to build and shape its surroundings and achieve serenity within its environs the chapter was, in

183. *DNB*; Prideaux, *Life*, p. 117; Prideaux, *Letters*, p. 204.
184. Prideaux, *Life*, pp. 117–21, 130, 136–37, 141–42; Prideaux, *Letters*, p. 205; Prideaux, *Old and New Testament Connected*, i, sig. A3r and p. xxviii; ii, part 1, p. xxiv.
185. NRO, DCN 115/3, especially p. 63.
186. London, Lambeth Palace Library, MS 1741, fos 12v–13r, 14r; NRO, DCN 115/3, p. 100.
187. NRO, MS 453, chronicle, sub 1724; T. Hearne, *Remarks and Collections*, ed. C. E.

Doble *et al.*, 11 vols (Oxford Historical Society, 1885–1918), viii, p. 292; see also NRO, Rye MS 18 (i), p. 59, a reference I owe to Nick White. Overton, in the nineteenth century, considered that Prideaux 'passed a life which was most useful, but would not be very interesting if described in detail': J. H. Overton, *Life in the English Church, 1660–1714* (London, 1885), p. 88.
188. See pp. 639–41.
189. Prideaux, *Letters*, p. 170.

a sense, foreshadowing the century after 1720.[190] After two centuries of almost continual disruption since the translation, when the very survival of the cathedral was almost an achievement in itself, it settled down to a comfortable routine where dramatic occurrences were rare. Having overseen the fashioning of the upper green and many of the houses, that peace and quiet liberated the energy and the money for the chapter finally to turn in 1739, for the first time in 200 years, to the task of constructively and substantially improving the cathedral fabric itself.

190. The years between 1690 and 1730 saw many cathedral precincts and houses improved. G. Holmes, *Augustan England: Professions, State and Society, 1680–1730* (London, 1982), pp. 93–94.

28

The Cathedral in the Georgian Period, 1720–1840

R. G. Wilson

Despite the volume of the surviving record, it is not much easier to recreate the life of the cathedral in the Georgian period than it is during its more distant, monastic phase.* For the chief difficulty in the exercise of our imaginations across 900 years of history is to peel back the layers of the recent past – the surge of tourism and the present good order of both the services and the building itself. These aspects of the modern cathedral, like our post-imperial monarchy, are a legacy of the past 150 years at the outside. Before 1840 we enter a remote, unreformed world. Its key, at least after 1660, was the manipulation of a highly complex pattern of national and local patronage to secure the familial advancement of the dean and prebendaries. Enjoying increased incomes, their conduct of the services and their maintenance of the cathedral and close came second in this scheme. How distant they were from later, post-1850s, practices is a matter of some dispute amongst historians.

The most immediate glimpses of the Georgian cathedral are provided by that select band of eighteenth-century tourists who busily scribbled accounts of their journeys into diaries and pocket books. Revelling in distant prospects and modern architecture, they enjoyed planned space and the evidence of burgeoning secular wealth around them. Unlike most tourists now, they were not put off by the bustle of cities and the throb of trade and industry. Norwich, England's second city, was therefore a great draw to them. And they were just as eager to view its famous worsted industry and the prosperity associated with it as they were its celebrated churches, cathedral and castle. In fact, the cathedral often seems to have disappointed them. Some possibly had anticipated the towering presence of those in Durham,

---

* I am most grateful to Dr Ian Atherton, for exemplary research assistance with this chapter, and to Dr W. M. Mathew and Dr Carole Rawcliffe for their comments on the text.

Lincoln or Salisbury. Others, eager to press on to Houghton and Holkham – those temples to Georgian riches and Palladian good taste – were generally dismissive of Gothic architecture. The Honourable Philip Yorke (later second earl of Hardwicke) in 1750 noted, 'the cathedral is large and in very good repair, but there is nothing magnificent or beautiful in the structure itself'. His wife (the Marchioness Gray) recorded similar opinions: 'the cathedral itself is large but I think not fine, though there has been a great deal done towards cleaning and sprucing it up by the present dean [Bullock, 1739–60]; the west end particularly has been new-built'.[1] At least their comments were better informed than those of an anonymous visitor seven years later: 'the cathedral is Saxon built, but has nothing extraordinary either in its structure or ornaments'.[2]

What most visitors drew attention to was the fact that it was difficult to get an uninterrupted view of the cathedral, and that its exterior stonework was friable and discoloured. The Reverend Philip Parsons in 1796 found its elevations 'very confined' with only the west front being seen to advantage, although in the evening from the distance of the Castle Mound he pronounced it 'noble'.[3] Fifty years earlier Philip Yorke's impressions had been much the same: the two closes were 'small'; the bishop's palace adjoining the cathedral was 'a rambling unpleasant house' (a common opinion), and even the two great gates to the upper close though 'tolerable Gothic architecture . . . suffered to be hid by shabby buildings run up about them within side'.[4] Comments on the interior could be equally unflattering. Some thought it heavy; some, such as a tourist in 1735, found 'the inside of the church . . . dark, and not at all answerable to the outside either in beauty or stateliness'.[5] A decision to whitewash the entire interior of the cathedral in 1739–40 fully answered this critic, but the consensus of the Georgian tourists was that, although the cathedral possessed fine features (the cloister being universally admired) and was usually in good repair, its overall impact was weakened by the clutter of buildings surrounding

1. Yorke's journal is published in J. Godber, 'The Marchioness Grey of Wrest Park', *Publications of the Bedfordshire Historical Record Society*, 47 (1968), p. 142; letter of Jemima, Marchioness Gray, 31 July 1750, Bedfordshire Record Office, MS L30/94/6, pp. 10–11 (I am grateful to Lord Lucas of Crudwell for permission to quote the latter).

2. Quoted in R. Gard, ed., *The Observant Traveller: Diaries of Travel in England, Wales and Scotland in the County Record Offices of England and Wales* (London, 1989), p. 17. The Reverend Townley Clarkson in 1804 also pronounced the cathedral 'not handsome in the Saxon style': Cambridgeshire Record Office, MS R58/11/1.

3. Parsons (1729–1812) was rector of Snave and Eastwell (Kent). See *Gentleman's Magazine*, 82 (July-December 1812), pp. 291–92; his travel diary is printed in volumes 87 (July-December 1817), pp. 305–8, and 89 (July-December 1819), pp. 25–27, 111–13.

4. See note 1 above.

5. See the travel diary of the Reverend Jeremiah Miller (August 1735), BL, Additional MS 15776; for comments on the heaviness of the interior, 'A Journal of a Tour from Cambridge through East Anglia to Yorkshire', 1741, BL, Additional MS 38488, fo. 27v.

it and an unimpressive west front. Even as late as 1840 these views persisted, at least amongst critics uninfluenced by the Gothic Revival. R. B. Winkles, still making the point about the cathedral's confined prospects, thought that 'were it altogether disencumbered, isolated, and set in the middle of a spacious lawn, its external appearance either as a whole or in detail, if we except the tower and spire, would be found to possess few if any attractions at all'.[6]

If these opinions, expressed by the scribbling classes, tell us a good deal about their perceptions of a great medieval building in the Georgian period, they tell us nothing of the individuals who made up the cathedral community in these years. For them we have to rely upon the voluminous papers of the dean and chapter and the comments contemporaries made about its principal members. The first consist chiefly of the working papers and records of decisions made about the multifarious activities of the dean and chapter and are inevitably, since they largely deal with property transactions, building matters and the disputes which arose from them, more secular than sacred in tone. The second source offers stray judgements about the capabilities of the cathedral's chief officers in matters of business and ecclesiastical politics. They are difficult sources from which to obtain a balanced view of the spiritual life of this community of some one hundred families. It is all too easy to concentrate upon a dispute or a flagrant piece of patronage and to ignore the contribution of this community to the real purpose of the cathedral. That it was imperfect is not in dispute, but when in the rest of this chapter I concentrate upon personalities, incomes and business, and the repair of the cathedral, this aspect, more fully discussed in the section on the provision and conduct of services, should not be forgotten.

The cathedral community in the Georgian period remained a tightly-knit one. Undoubtedly clerical marriage and the failure to establish a common table for the minor canons, lay clerks and choristers as laid down in the statutes of 1620 demonstrated a growing secularisation at every level of office. Nevertheless shared duties and business transactions in the cathedral, and the fact that the majority of its three dozen officers named in the statutes lived in snug proximity (increased by the boundary walls of the close, by the locking of the Ethelbert and Erpingham Gates into the city at night, and by the precinct's separate jurisdiction), combined to draw together the 130 or so households residing within the cathedral precincts.[7]

6. R. B. Winkles, *History and Description of the Cathedral Church in Norwich* (Norwich, 1842), p. 86.

7. In 1693 the precinct of the close contained 650 people; in 1752, 129 houses and 700 souls: *A Parochial List of the Number of Houses within the City of Norwich* (Norwich, 1752). The Reverend James Wilkins, curate of St Mary in the Marsh, reckoned 'the precinct of the cathedral church of Norwich . . . contains upwards of 100 homes I suppose including small tenements': NRO, DN/VIS

Yet, like eighteenth-century society at large, this segregated community was divided into well-defined ranks. There were three divisions. At the top, the bishop, the dean and the prebendaries ruled the roost. Under them the six minor canons, the gospeller, the epistoler and the organist, and those attorneys who in effect ran the offices of the bishop, the dean and chapter, and the Norfolk and Norwich arch-deaconries stood well apart from the eight lay clerks (often respectable city tradesmen), the six poor men or alms-men, the two vergers, the two under-sacristans and the ferryman. This segregation was as marked in 1830 as it had been a century earlier. In 1725 when Bishop John Leng had carried out the only visitation of the cathedral in our period, the epistoler, organist, lay clerks and lesser officers could make only in-complete answers to the thirty questions he posed because they were 'not privy to what the dean and prebendaries do'.[8] In 1830 when the dean, the Honourable George Pellew, read the statutes, as was required each year, he kept the lay clerks standing for two hours whilst he and the prebendaries sat. While presumably this was usual practice, in this year of rev-olutions and seething unrest in Norfolk, it drew sharp comment about such evi-dent social distinctions.[9]

Fig. 203. Robert Potter (1721–1804), from an etching after A. Payne. Formerly master of Scarning School and busy translator of the Greek tragedies, he never published a word after he became prebendary in 1788 and began to enjoy an income of around £800 a year from his office and the living of Lowestoft granted to him by the bishop a year later.

Yet this tripartite division was never completely watertight. Francis Frank for example, chapter clerk from 1724 to 1773 and a brother-in-law of Edward Bacon of Earlham (one of the Norwich MPs), was on easy social terms with successive bishops, deans and prebendaries. And Robert Potter (fig. 203) found his relationships with the

note 7 continued

29a/7, visitation at the cathedral church in Norwich, 7 June 1784. Dean Prideaux described it in the late seventeenth century: 'Our close is as it were a town of itself apart from the city, separated from it by walls and gates'. Quoted in R. W. Ketton-Cremer, *Norfolk Assembly* (London, 1957), p. 68.

8. NRO, DN/VIS 14/2. The replies of the dean and prebendaries and of the epistoler, organist, etc. survive. Presumably the minor canons also answered the same set of questions.

9. NRO, DCN 120/2D/30.

minor canons warmer than with those of his fellow prebendaries.[10] Moreover, other families than those tied by office to the cathedral resided in the close. Lists of residents before the 1841 census are rare and invariably incomplete: Chase's *Norwich Directory* (1783) included rather fewer than half of the heads of households (sixty-one in total). Besides twenty-two clergymen, five were attorneys and two were land agents chiefly engaged in ecclesiastical business, and seven were gentlewomen, mostly the widows and daughters of prebendaries. But in addition the close provided the Norwich residence of three Norfolk landowners, as well as accommodation for two inn-keepers, a tailor, a baker, a silk throwster, a dentist, a brandy merchant and two builders. Seventy years later, the census enumerator listed ninety-nine houses – suggesting that some thirty had been demolished since 1750 – in St Mary in the Marsh parish (the cathedral precincts). As before, its inhabitants were a mixture of clergy, an increasing number of professional men and some manual workers. Although the community in the close was therefore both more varied and sizeable than might at first sight be expected, it was throughout the Georgian period essentially a Barchester-like world of clerics – vaguely listed in 1784 as 'about twenty or thirty families of note' – widows and spinsters, and a small army of female servants. In 1851 the cathedral parish comprised a highly-skewed sex ratio of 170 males to 348 females.[11]

Authority in this community was essentially wielded by the dean and his chapter of six prebendaries, who shared the rich spoils of the cathedral's estates. Who was admitted to this tight caucus in the Georgian period? The answer in Norwich, as in every cathedral in England, is that it was drawn increasingly from the 'aristocratic' sector of society. As prebendal incomes burgeoned with mounting agricultural prosperity, the patronage system ensured that the landed classes fully shared these ecclesiastical pickings. The advancing social status of bishops, deans and prebendaries in Norwich between 1720 and 1840 exemplifies a well-defined national trend. As in most observations about social movements, the mechanism of advance was never totally precise, for to some degree the Georgian church remained a means of mobility for the presentable, well-educated young man of modest social background. But when the prizes increased in size after 1780 the competition stiffened, and in this

10. Frank was the father of Bacon Frank of Campsall (1739–1812), a West Yorkshire landowner. See J. B. Burke, *Burke's Genealogical and Heraldic History of the Landed Gentry*, ed. H. Pirie-Gordon (15th edn, London, 1937), 'Frank of Campsall'. The latter's long correspondence with his Norwich-based parents is in Sheffield Archives, Bacon Frank MSS, BFM 1309–23. Aberystwyth, National Library of Wales, 12433 D, letter dated 10 June 1796. See notes 33 and 36 below.

11. The 1784 quotation comes from Wilkins' return for St Mary in the Marsh; see note 7 above. A good view of life in the close is provided in J. W. Clark and T. W. Hughes, eds, *The Life and Letters of the Reverend Adam Sedgwick*, 2 vols (Cambridge, 1890), ii, pp. 564–90, where C. K. Robinson, master of St Catharine's College and a Norwich canon, provides a chapter on Sedgwick's life at Norwich.

climate those best-connected, those best able to manipulate the strings of patronage, succeeded.

Recruitment to the office of bishop and dean illustrates the system clearly. The see of Norwich, although it encompassed close on 1100 East Anglian parishes, was not amongst the richest in England.[12] Georgian bishops of Norwich were migratory figures typically *en route* from a Welsh bishopric or Bristol (the poorest English see) to Ely. Two, early in the period, were advanced to London; one, Manners Sutton (at Norwich 1792–1805), was translated to Canterbury. Only half of the fourteen bishops enthroned between 1720 and 1840 died whilst still holding their Norwich appointments. The Reverend William Jacob represented the backgrounds of these bishops as being not unlike that of their clergy in general before the episcopates of Lewis Bagot (1783–1790) and Manners Sutton, the former being the brother of the first Lord Bagot, the latter the grandson of the third duke of Rutland.[13] This upward mobility evident in the late eighteenth century continued into the nineteenth: Henry Bathurst (1805–37; see fig. 204) was a cousin of Earl Bathurst; Edward Stanley (1837–49), a younger brother of the first Baron Stanley of Alderley.

Surprisingly, the presence of the

Fig. 204. Bishop Henry Bathurst (1744–1837) from his statue in the north transept by Sir Francis Chantrey, R.A. Over sixty when appointed to the see, he survived for thirty-two years to become the only nonagenarian bishop of Norwich. He was famed as the sole bishop to support the 1832 Reform Act, as the idlest occupant of the bench of bishops, and as a compulsive whist player.

12. See N. Sykes, *Church and State in England in the XVIIIth Century* (Cambridge, 1934), p. 61. Norwich was worth £2140 a year at the beginning of George III's reign: A. Hartshorne, ed., *Memoirs of a Royal Chaplain, 1729–1763* (London, 1905), p. 358.
13. W. M. Jacob, 'Clergy and Society in Norfolk, 1707–1806' (unpublished University of Exeter Ph. D. thesis, 1982), chap. 4. See also N. Ravitch, 'The Social Origins of French and English Bishops in the Eighteenth Century', *Historical Journal*, 8 (1965), pp. 309–25.

bishop does not seem to have impinged too deeply upon the concerns of the dean and prebendaries. Of course both parties nourished a regular diet of gossip about clerical preferments and peccadilloes. There was a constant exchange of dinners when the bishop was in residence. Yet the spheres of the cathedral and the diocese in fact remained largely separate. Naturally, deference was paid to the bishop as a spiritual and temporal lord, but this was a formal observance: except in nominating his clergy to preach on Sundays in the cathedral (he himself preached only three times each year: at Christmas, Easter and Whitsun), the affairs and finances of the cathedral were beyond his purview. Cathedrals became diocesan centres only in the railway age. True, the bishop had powers of visitation, although after Leng's controversial exercise of this prerogative in 1725 each subsequent bishop before 1840 seems to have thought it politic to let sleeping dogs lie, at least on their own doorstep. There were no more visitations of the cathedral by the bishop. Moreover, their periods of office were often brief: only two held the see for more than twelve years. Frequently they were absent from the diocese: spending seven months in London as members of the House of Lords, taking the waters with their families in summer, or attending to their other preferments. In no fewer than twelve years between 1707 and 1806 the bishop never came to Norwich at all.[14] Continuity in diocesan administration was maintained by a more regular bureaucracy of chancellors, archdeacons and registrars.

Many of these fourteen bishops were not distinguished men. Advancement was a result of political patronage: from the king, from the senior episcopate, from key politicians. Some bishops had seen long service in the universities, like Thomas Gooch (1738–48) the wily master of Gonville and Caius College from 1716 to 1754; others had served as royal chaplains. Leng (1723–27), Bagot and Stanley seem to have been able reformers, genuinely 'good men' as their contemporaries evaluated them.[15] But the two who held office longest, Philip Yonge (1761–83) and Bathurst (1805–37) were famously idle. Bagot (1783–90) complained that, 'much . . . of the state of his diocese is in many respects owing to the easiness and inactivity of his predecessor'.[16] Bathurst was notorious even amongst Regency bishops. Holding office until his death at the age of ninety-two (he declined the archbishopric of Dublin when he was eighty-seven) he was a shockingly bad administrator, greatly addicted to whist, and to long sojourns at Bath and Malvern. 'They blame me for playing cards', he wrote, 'but I can't see to read or write and I can see the spots

14. Jacob, 'Clergy and Society in Norfolk', p. 196.
15. Bishop George Horne (1790–92), previously dean of Canterbury, fell into the same category. President of Magdalen College, Oxford, a good preacher, friend of Lord North and Hannah More, he is best known for his *Commentary on the Psalms* (Oxford, 1771); already in poor health before his preferment to Norwich, he made little impact during his eighteen months' tenure of the see.
16. J. Nichols, *Literary Anecdotes of the Eighteenth Century*, 9 vols (New York, 1966), v, p. 188.

on the cards, so I may without sin amuse myself in this way'.[17] On Prebendary Adam Sedgwick's first visit to dinner at the bishop's palace he was invited, as was customary, to play a rubber of whist. When he declined, through ignorance of the rules, Bathurst lamented to his guest: 'I have consistently supported the Whigs all my life – I believe I am called the only liberal bishop – and now in my old age they [Lord Melbourne's Whig government] have sent me a canon who does not know spades from clubs'.[18] Bathurst was genial, with a fund of common sense; it was during his long tenure at Norwich that some wit dubbed it 'the Dead See'. Perhaps only Robert Butts (1733–38) was infamous. His elevation rested entirely upon his vociferous promotion of the Hervey–Walpole interest. At Cambridge he was noted as a pugilist and footballer; at Norwich his predilection was for the bowling green. Foul-mouthed, he was 'universally hated, not to say detested'. No effort was made to disguise the joy when he was translated to Ely in 1738.[19]

The deans of Norwich in the Georgian period remain essentially more shadowy figures than the bishops. For none of the nine deans in our period, with the flagrant exception of Butts (dean, 1731–33 and unusually advanced to bishop) enjoyed further preferment. None besides Humphrey Prideaux – and his claim is controversial – were notable scholars. It is not that they were local men of blunted ambition, although their average period of office (eighteen years, two months) was almost twice as long as that of the bishops (ten years). Fewer than half of them were born within the diocese.[20] They simply appear to have reached either the limit of their abilities or, more likely, the barriers of their patronage networks. For on any reckoning the deanship of Norwich was a fine preferment: all but the most ambitious patron could rest, knowing that in this exercise of his political clout he had served his nominee splendidly. In terms of education all the deans inevitably possessed the right Oxbridge connections: four were from Oxford, five from Cambridge. Like the bishops, their backgrounds were similar to the rest of the Georgian clergy: they

17. NRO, MS 4257, 'Suffolk Worthies and Persons of Note in East Anglia, no. 68, Bishop Bathurst'. For Bathurst see *DNB*; H. Bathurst, *Memoirs of the Late Dr Henry Bathurst*, 2 vols (London, 1837); T. Thistlethwayte, *Memoirs and Correspondence of Dr Henry Bathurst, Lord Bishop of Norwich* (London, 1853); C. L. S. Linnell, *Some East Anglian Clergy* (London, 1961); and J. C. Hanekamp, *An Appeal for Justice: The Life of Dr Henry Bathurst, Lord Bishop of Norwich, 1744–1837* (Utrecht, 1992). Hanekamp writes (p. 261), 'in later years Bishop Bathurst was perhaps the worst diocesan administrator the diocese had ever had and so it happened that for want of guidance and discipline, the diocese of Norwich became a by-word for disorder'.

18. Clark and Hughes, *Adam Sedgwick*, i, p. 485.

19. *DNB*, sub Robert Butts.

20. Butts was the son of the rector of Hartest (Suffolk); for Baron see note 21; Townshend's Norfolk connections were impeccable; Turner was from a well-known Great Yarmouth family: see H. Turner and F. Johnson, *The Turner Family of Mulbarton and Great Yarmouth* (London, 1907), pp. 81–85.

came from good middling backgrounds or lower gentry stock, with the exceptions of the Honourable Edward Townshend (1761–65) and the Honourable George Pellew (1826–66) whose aristocratic connections are immediately obvious. Their average age at appointment by the king (in effect the lord chancellor) was almost forty-six: two, Lloyd (1765–90) and Pellew managed to secure preferment before they were forty; only Baron (1733–39) at sixty-six was way above average. The essential element in their advancement was that they had been brought early to the attention of great men.[21] The key to the promotion of Thomas Cole (1724–31) was the patronage of the all-powerful Townshend family – preeminent in Norfolk in the first quarter of the eighteenth century. Cole was chaplain to Lord Townshend during his ambassadorship at the Hague; he was vicar of Wisbech in 1714, rector of Raynham – the Townshends' seat – in 1721.[22]

The career of the Honourable Edward Townshend, the fourth son of the second viscount, epitomises that of a cleric on the top rung of the ecclesiastical ladder. Educated at Eton and Trinity College, Cambridge, he was provided with a good Norfolk living in 1745, made deputy clerk of the closet and prebendary at Wells in successive years, and given a stall at Westminster in 1749. All this had been achieved by the time Townshend was thirty. The 1750s were a barren decade for him before his preferment to the deanery of Norwich, 'pressed by all the Townshend and Walpole families . . . all the nobility and MPs of Norfolk'.[23] And even at the end of the period, when the Anglican church was forced to put its house in order, Pellew, a timid reformer, held a number of select preferments. Securing a stall at Canterbury in 1820 (the year in which he married the daughter of Lord Sidmouth, the one-time prime minister), he was nominated prebendary at York in 1824 and given a London parish in 1828 before being advanced to Norwich in the same year.[24]

Clearly family connections ensured that the choicest plums were easily picked. In truth, none of the deans in this period found the tree of ecclesiastical preferment stubborn in shedding its fruits once they had the assistance of a determined bishop

21. The exception was John Baron (1733–39). Born in 1677, he held three south Norfolk livings (Brome, Chedgrave and Saxlingham Nethergate) before becoming archdeacon of Norfolk in 1732 and dean of Norwich the following year.
22. Cole had no obvious Norfolk connections. Born *c.* 1681 in Shropshire he was a scholar at King's College, Cambridge (B.A. 1702–3, M.A. 1706) after schooling at Eton.
23. The duke of Newcastle quoted in Sykes, *Church and State*, pp. 160–61.
24. He was vicar of Nazeing (Essex) in 1819; and of Sutton-on-Forest (Yorkshire) in the following year. He gave up his Canterbury stall in 1828 (and his Canterbury parish) but he held the York stall and the London living (St Dionis Backchurch) until 1852. He provides a further example of the way well-connected, meritorious clergy defeated the aims of the more rabid church reformers in the early Victorian period by hanging on to the key parishes and offices and advancing like-minded men by their patronage networks. See C. Dewey, *The Passing of Barchester* (London, 1991), pp. 2–6.

or, better still, a leading politician. Timing was crucial, and in their day the Herveys, Robert and Horatio Walpole, the duke of Newcastle, and the younger Pitt (Dean Turner was his tutor at Cambridge) had the surest of touches in detaching the riper clerical rewards from its Norwich branches.

In their social origins and in their patronage-dependency the incumbents of the six Norwich prebendal stalls in the Georgian period were no different from those of the bishops and deans. Indeed it would have been odd if they had been, for they relied upon exactly the same preferment networks. Therefore again, at first sight somewhat surprisingly, few of the thirty-four prebendaries whose tenure stretched across the years 1720 to 1840 were of Norfolk origin. Preferment came from the crown, and therefore all governments of whatever creed or composition, were battered by a nation-wide clamour of patrons craving clerical office for their protégés, familial and otherwise. Only one prebendary, Edward South Thurlow (with an incumbency of fifty-nine years from 1788 to 1847, the longest-serving of all in our period), had unambiguous Norwich roots as the son of a city alderman.[25] Inevitably, there were a scattering who were drawn from that segment of the Norfolk gentry with access to the national patronage labyrinth: Philip Wodehouse (1778–1811) was a younger son of Sir Armine Wodehouse Bt of Kimberley; Horace Hammond (1756–86) was a first cousin of Horace Walpole; George Anguish (1790–1820) eventually succeeded to a major Norfolk estate (Somerleyton). But the majority of prebendaries were born outside the diocese, were educated at Cambridge and had held various livings before they were preferred to a Norwich stall. All had the ability to manipulate essential patronage connections. Charles Plumptre (1749–51), sub-sequently archdeacon of Ely, and his brother Robert (1756–88), also president of Queens' College, Cambridge, after 1760, depended upon the interest of Lord Chancellor Hardwicke for their advancement. The poet Thomas Gray mischievously mistranslated the Plumptre motto, *Non magna loquimus sed vivimus*, as 'we don't say much, but we hold good livings'.[26]

Since the prebendaries' required period of residence at Norwich was only for two months each year they could and did hold other appointments. Often these were livings in the Norwich diocese, but the better-connected prebendaries also held stalls elsewhere. Edward Bankes, the son of a leading Dorset landowner and married to Lord Chancellor Eldon's daughter, notoriously held a succession: Norwich (1820–32), Gloucester (1821–57), Bristol (1832–67), as well as a variety of livings (not all simultaneously) in Dorset, Herefordshire and Kent, although he appears to

25. Thurlow (1764–1847) was well-connected and well-to-do; one uncle was lord chancellor (the first Baron Thurlow, 1731–1806), another bishop of Lincoln (1779–87) and then Durham (1787–91).

26. *DNB*; J. Twigg, *A History of Queens' College, Cambridge, 1448–1986* (Woodbridge, 1987), pp. 158, 163, 180–81, 203–4. No fewer than two of Robert's sons and a nephew were fellows of Queens' during his presidency.

have resided principally in Flintshire.[27] John Pretyman (1786–1817) was also prebendary at Lincoln (1793–1809) and archdeacon there (1793–1817); clearly he relied
upon the support of his elder brother, George Pretyman Tomline, who was bishop
of Lincoln (1787–1820) and a close friend of William Pitt the younger.[28] Nicholas
Penny (1722–45) was also prebendary (1725–30) and dean of Lichfield for the last
fifteen years of his life (1730–45); whilst Henry Gally (1731–69), also prebendary at
Gloucester and a chaplain to the king, was writing regularly to the duke of Newcastle
over a period of twenty years for deaneries at Worcester, Bristol (three times),
Gloucester (twice), Norwich and Wells. Gally was a master at detecting decanal
'last gasps', although not at employing the language of plea and service to move
the much-petitioned duke.[29]

The firmest connection between the chapter at Norwich and the university of
Cambridge was maintained in all these years. Indeed, after 1714 (1719 in effect) it
was institutionalised by the annexation of the fourth stall to the mastership of St
Catharine's College to augment the master's income. Bishop Gooch believed that
the arrangement 'did the college more harm than good, as it made the masters
negligent of their duty'. The mid twentieth-century historian of the college went
further, dismissing the four masters who held the stall between 1719 and 1798 as 'all
men of mediocre ability'.[30] Yet often with two masters of colleges as members of
the Norwich chapter, and with others having served periods as fellows, it must to
outsiders have seemed to be an extension of the Cambridge collegiate system.[31]

The salient point to emerge from this prosopography of the Norwich prebendaries
is the sheer length of their periods of office. Of the thirty-four who occupied the
six stalls across the years 1720–1840, each on average served a quarter of a century.
They varied from John Sawyer, also master of St Catharine's College, who myste-
riously resigned from both preferments after a tenure of a mere six weeks, to Edward
Thurlow who served the cathedral for fifty-nine years.[32] No fewer than twenty-three
(68 per cent) reached their biblical allotted span of seventy years, four of them dying

27. J. and J. A. Venn, *Alumni Cantabrigienses: A Biographical List of All Known Students, Graduates and Holders of Office at the University of Cambridge*, 10 vols in 2 parts (Cambridge, 1922–54), part 2, i, p. 140.

28. Venn, *Alumni Cantabrigienses*, part 2, v, pp. 190–91.

29. BL, Additional MSS 32708, fos 286–287; 32874, fos 230–231; 32876, fos 497–498; 32878, fos 114–115, 158–159; 32883, fos 345–346; 32900, fos 47–48; 32901, fos 69–70; 32906, fos 395–396, 472–473; 32921, fos 418–419; 32973, fos 170–171.

30. W. H. S. Jones, *The Story of St Catharine's College, Cambridge* (Cambridge, 1951), pp. 192–195.

31. Beside the masters of St Catharine's, Dean Joseph Turner (1790–1828) was master of Pembroke, Cambridge, 1784–1828, and Charles Plumptre (1756–88) was president of Queens' College, Cambridge, 1760–88. In addition Samuel Salter the younger (1745–78) was master of Charterhouse, 1761–78, as was Philip Fisher (1814–42) from 1803 to 1842.

32. Jones, *St Catharine's*, p. 98.

as octogenarians, while Philip Fisher (1814–42) survived a record ninety-two years. Contemporaries must have mused whether this quite remarkable longevity, far exceeding average Georgian life expectancies, was attributable to the power of prayer, or to unhurried good living and the peace of residence in the close and county.

Although a mere five resigned their stalls at Norwich, it would be misleading to represent the prebendaries as blinkered old men who seldom saw beyond the walls of the close for decades. As we have seen, they frequently held office in other cathedrals, were active in the life of the University of Cambridge or were archdeacons in the Norwich and Ely dioceses. Almost all without exception, if they did not hold these middling-rank preferments, were in occupation of a brace of good livings. Few of them were scholars of distinction besides Robert Potter (1788–1804) and Adam Sedgwick (1834–73).[33] Nevertheless, they were wise in the ways of the clerical world, were well-versed in politics and were seasoned travellers. They were welcome at the tables of the neighbouring county gentry and of the worsted manufacturers and merchants, the attorneys, medical men and brewers who formed the elite of the bustling city beyond the cathedral's gates.[34] And in the close itself, as the letters of Edmund Pyle, Robert Potter and Adam Sedgwick disclose, they were the linchpins of a smaller, yet equally hierarchical community which was awash with good neighbourliness and good food.[35]

Prebendal duties and rewards at Norwich in the Georgian period are brought most vividly to life in a series of letters written by the Reverend Robert Potter.[36] Potter, who successfully ran Scarning School (he sat to Romney for his portrait in 1778) and translated the tragedies of Aeschylus, Euripides and Sophocles, was prebendary from 1788 until his death at the age of eighty-three in 1804. Already

33. For Potter see *DNB*; H. G. Wright, 'Robert Potter as a Critic of Dr Johnson', *Review of English Studies*, 12 (1936), pp. 305–21; D. Stoker, 'Greek Tragedy with a Happy Ending: The Publication of Robert Potter's Translation of Aeschylus, Euripedes and Sophocles', *Studies in Bibliography*, 46 (1993), pp. 282–302. All these were completed before Lord Thurlow procured the second stall at Norwich for Potter. For the geologist, Adam Sedgwick, see *DNB*; and Clark and Hughes, *Adam Sedgwick*. Others with more modest literary pretensions were Samuel Salter the younger (1745–78) and Henry Gally (1731–69).

34. For an account of the composition of Norwich's elite during its 'urban renaissance',

see C. Branford, 'Powers of Association: Aspects of Elite Social, Cultural and Political Life in Norwich *c.* 1680–1760' (unpublished University of East Anglia Ph. D. thesis, 1993).

35. See note 36 and pp. 588–89, 605–6. below, and for Edmund Pyle, Hartshorne, *Memoirs of a Royal Chaplain*. See also the essay on the Reverend Patrick St Clair in R. W. Ketton-Cremer, *Country Neighbourhood* (London, 1951).

36. Aberystwyth, National Library of Wales, 12433 D. Fifty-eight letters written to the Reverend John Conway Potter by the Reverend Robert Potter between 1788 and 1804.

in constant ill-health, his elevation came late and – this was rare – unsolicited. Indeed his letter of appointment from the lord chancellor, acknowledging his 'merit with the literary world', seemed genuinely to surprise him. Potter's prospects were immediately transformed: the preferment was worth 'more than £300 a year' and, as he put it, 'removes me from nothing only I must be resident two months in the year'; the rigours of schoolmastering and translation could be abandoned; his house in the close was 'neat, convenient and pleasant'. Inevitably, residence somewhat eroded this elysium: his nerves 'were shattered to pieces with one oratorio' at the 1788 music festival; his home, fronting full south, was 'as hot as Nebuchadnezzar's burning fiery furnace'; his peace was threatened by 'the daily visits of my neighbours'. But the trials of life in the close – later encapsulated by Potter as 'the laudable vocation of looking for the ace of trumps' – were soon compensated by an additional preferment. In 1789 Bishop Bagot, with whom Potter struck up an immediate warm friendship, was as generous (and unexpected in his kindness) as the lord chancellor had been in the previous year.[37] His reward, the living of Lowestoft with Kessingland (soon served by Potter's son as curate) was worth £470 'and increasing under an act of enclosure of a large extent'.[38] Since there was no vicarage at Lowestoft, the bishop 'under the building act' purchased him a 'princely' house, albeit bleakly sited on a sixty-foot cliff and rather too exposed to the German Ocean for Potter's precarious health. Indeed, in winter the newly-enriched prebendary was crucified between Lowestoft's gales and the cathedral's raw cold. After five months in Norwich in early 1793 he reported, 'I had nothing to do, and did nothing yet I found that the nothing-ism of the day engrossed all my time; I had scarce leisure to do that'. Three years later he wrote in similar vein:

> I go out but little, very, very seldom to church, then I always take cold. I dare not attempt to read. At Lowestoft my curate will not let me, and here the minor canons very readily take my part among them, they are all very worthy men; and I live on more social terms with them than the prebendaries in general.

Potter's blameless career underlines three features of prebendal life in the late eighteenth century: the lightness of cathedral duties; the conviviality and affluence

---

37. Bagot was translated to Bangor from Norwich in 1790. In a letter dated 23 April 1790 Potter wrote of him: 'Some of our clergy hated him, but they are wretches who had first renounced their Saviour: by all good men he was respected and beloved: it was a very agreeable circumstance in my life to have such a man, such a family, within one hundred yards of one for two months in the year; he very often called upon me; he is gentle, very learned, and communicative; a better man does not live; I have lost him'.

38. Lowestoft enjoyed a boom in the early 1790s. Potter reported the town 'full of gentry', the streets being paved and houses 'new built and refronted'. In 1792 it was 'so full of bathers, that every room as big as a bird cage is occupied'.

of life in the close (he enjoyed the ministrations of four servants); and the glaring shortcomings of a system in which retirement was never enforced, however old and decrepit the incumbent. In this world, skill at whist appears to have been rated as high on the scale of clerical competence as liturgical proficiency. Certainly, although these letters were written to a fellow cleric, little mention is made in them of either God or his Saviour.

When we turn to the six minor canons, the gospeller and the epistoler (here collectively referred to as the minor canons), it is clear that there was a marked division between them and the dean and prebendaries.[39] The latter were crown appointees who solely administered the cathedral statutes and estates and with their superior preferments enjoyed superior incomes. In the cathedral and close, in spite of the discontinuities of the 'residence' system, it was they who wielded political, economic and social power. In a word they were the masters, the minor canons the servants. Although responsible for the conduct of twice-daily prayers, the latter seem to have failed from the outset of their careers to secure those patrons who would obtain for them a comfortable cathedral stall or rectory. Their cathedral stipends were a derisory £10 a year. To keep body and soul together they relied upon holding a number – usually two or three – of the dean and chapter's three dozen livings which were invariably poor incumbencies in Norwich's tiny central parishes or ones of little greater value in the immediate county.[40] The patronage network of the minor canons, who were appointed when relatively young, consisted almost entirely of that manipulated by the dean and chapter. They pressed the chapter for additional (or the exchange of) livings, they jockeyed for accommodation in the close. Of course these preferments, since they admitted their incumbents to the civilized life of the close, were in themselves sought after, especially with the general oversupply of clergy by the last quarter of the eighteenth century. But it is significant that the minor canons, in spite of acquiring – minus the easily-purchased doctorates of the prebendaries – similar degrees from Oxford or Cambridge, once jogging along this track of preferment never crossed to the broader and faster prebendal track of either Norwich or any other cathedral. Lack of birth, lack of college connection, lack of first-class patrons dogged their steps. Almost without

39. The status of the epistoler is confusing: sometimes he is listed and paid together with the lay clerks in the audit book, sometimes amongst the minor canons. Both this and the office of gospeller were 'junior' appointments, the bottom two rungs of the minor canons' ladder which they invariably ascended when a vacancy arose.

40. NRO, DN/VSM 1/7, list of clergy and patrons, Norwich diocese (mid eighteenth century); DN/VSM 3, religious census of Norwich archdeaconry (c. 1783): ANW 4/88, Norwich archdeaconry general book, 1785–86; DN/VSM 5, Norwich diocese book compiled from Bishop Bathurst's primary visitation, 1806; DCN 33/32, list of minor canons and their preferments from the dean and chapter, 1829.

exception they died in office, having served the cathedral and their nearby livings often for more than half a lifetime. Even when they were buried, they merited no more than a ledger stone in the south transept or cloister. Not for them the ostentatious wall memorials to the departed deans and prebendaries, alive with armorials, cherubs and urns.

Detailed biographical information about the forty minor canons whose office stretched across the years 1720–1840 is much sparser than for the bishops, deans and prebendaries at Norwich, particularly in the first half of the period. It seems that a greater proportion were Norfolk born, although by no means all of them, since initial preferment depended upon the interest of individual members of the chapter (especially the dean) – the majority of whom were not natives of the county. With those about whom more is known the features which stand out are their youth, since they were often straight from university at first appointment – a good singing voice was an obvious requirement – the consequent length of their period of office (on average about thirty years), and the way in which they had meted out to them the poorer dean and chapter livings on the usual principles of patronage. The chapter retained the few plums in its gift for its own members; the minor canons were allotted the others, chiefly livings within a dozen miles of the cathedral so that they could plausibly serve both.

The brief biographies of half a dozen of the minor canons are instructive, both about cathedral life and the middle ranks of the late-Georgian clergy. Peter Hansell boasted the longest service of all in our period (1786–1841). Born in Reading, he was a mere twenty-three years old when admitted minor canon. Since he had been a chorister at Magdalen College, Oxford, before graduating there it is likely he was selected for his voice (he was precentor, 1811–31). Preferment came slowly: he held two impoverished Norwich perpetual curacies (St John Sepulchre and St Martin at Oak) for about a quarter of a century before being given in addition the country living of Worstead (1811–41). The impression is gained that Hansell was a cathedral workhorse who was relatively unrewarded. The chapter marked his fifty years of service with the purchase of a theological work to the value of about £10. On his death five years later, Canon Wodehouse proclaimed him a pillar of moderation, faith, duty, kindness and humility – the perfect minor canon.[41]

George Day (1817–58) was the son of a Norwich worsted manufacturer, again he was advanced when very young (about twenty-three) and held a combination

---

41. NRO, DCN 24/7, fos 26v–27r; C. N. Wodehouse, *A Sermon, Preached in the Cathedral Church of Norwich, January 17, 1841, being the Sunday after the Funeral of the Reverend Peter Hansell, Senior Minor Canon* (Norwich, 1841), pp. 5–7. Further details about Hansell and the other minor canons referred to have come from the dean and chapter minute books (NRO, DCN 24) not individually noted.

of perpetual curacies and the vicarage of Eaton (1817–65), from the dean and chapter, and the rectory of Barton Bendish concurrently.[42] Only one minor canon, the scholarly Francis Howes (1814–44), had obvious gentry connections, coming from a long line of bookish Norfolk squarsons at Morningthorpe. With nine children to support, he again assembled a good range of poorish livings in the city and county – three from the dean and chapter, one from the bishop and another (Buckenham Ferry) from Sir Thomas Beauchamp Proctor.[43] Only one of the minor canons brought a whiff of the wider world into the close: the thoroughly eccentric Ozias Linley (1790–1815), later fellow and organist of Dulwich College, who was a member of the celebrated Linley-Sheridan clan.[44]

Perhaps it is the careers of the two Millards, Charles (1771–1814) and his son Charles Freeman (1807–47), which best epitomises those of the minor canons in the later Georgian period. That son followed father was otherwise unknown in the years 1720–1840, but their long service was not. The elder Millard was Gloucester-born, again a chorister and graduate of Magdalen College, Oxford, and again appointed to a minor canonry at Norwich at the tender age of twenty-three. He owed his advance to Dr Samuel Salter the younger, the powerful incumbent of the first stall and holder of another at Gloucester. Sensibly and soon, Millard married Salter's daughter, and he is recorded a decade later as holding by far the best income of those listed for the minor canons.[45] In 1793 he was given the living of Taverham; in 1809 at the age of sixty-one he became chancellor of the diocese. His son, Charles Freeman (born 1774–75), was educated in the close at Norwich Grammar School (where he was usher, 1802–7) and Pembroke College, Cambridge, of which Dean Turner (fig. 205) was master. He held two Norfolk livings, Didlington with Colveston (1802–7) and Hickling (1807–49). After his election as gospeller in 1807, he was quickly presented with three dean and chapter livings: the perpetual curacies of two Norwich churches, St Martin at Palace (1807–49) and St Giles (1811–49), and Henley in Suffolk (1807–31). In 1831 he was presented to one of the chapter's best Norfolk livings, Sedgeford (where he built a new parsonage ten years later) and, in the following year, Aldeby.[46] By the minor canons' standards, and through favour with both the chapter and Bishop Bathurst, Millard's income by the early

42. Venn, *Alumni Cantabrigienses*, part 2, ii, p. 259.

43. NRO, MC 340/1, 'Genealogical Notes of the Howes Family', p. 52; BEA 362/3; Venn, *Alumni Cantabrigienses*, part 2, iii, p. 465.

44. C. Black, *The Linleys of Bath* (London, 1911), pp. 207–13, 324–32; [G. Waterfield], *A Nest of Nightingales: Thomas Gainsborough, the Linley Sisters* (London, 1988), pp. 90–91; *DNB*.

45. NRO, DCN 33/21. Millard was listed as being paid £249. The stipends of the other seven ranged from £100 to £190, averaging £145 in 1783.

46. The biographies of the two Millards have been reconstructed from references scattered in NRO, DCN 11/12, 11/16 and 24/5–7, and Venn, *Alumni Cantabrigienses*, part 2, iv, p. 412.

1830s was generous.[47] Even so, by this date, collections of livings on this scale were meeting increasing criticism even in Bathurst's 'Dead See'. Of course, defenders of the system pointed out how it was impossible for clerics to make ends meet by holding poor benefices singly. The fundamental question of how well the Millards and the rest of the minor canons exercised their duties in the cathedral, together with those of their benefices, is discussed in the section on services.[48]

Fig. 205. Joseph Turner (1745–1828) from his portrait at Pembroke College, Cambridge, of which he was master for forty-four years. A member of a well-known Great Yarmouth family whose interests he was always zealous to promote, he held the office of dean, 1790–1828. He frequently absented himself from dean and chapter business, preferring to send written instructions across from Cambridge.

Yet exactly why the Millards were routed throughout their long lives along the minor canons' track, unlike the elder's patron, Samuel Salter the younger (who enjoyed the profits of two prebendal stalls, the great parish church of St Nicholas, Yarmouth, St Bartholomew's in London and the mastership of Charterhouse) is not immediately apparent. The answer seems to lie in Salter's having had the important patronage of Lord Hardwicke – he was his chaplain and the tutor to his son. The Millards, who did well enough for themselves, clearly signalled from the outset (by their acceptance of minor canonries) that they were content with the lesser prizes in the cathedrals and Oxford and Cambridge draws. Such clear career distinctions make dubious the claims of those who maintain that the Georgian Anglican church was open to men of talent and education. Certainly, the minor canonries at Norwich were invariably presented to young men who could vigorously conduct the cathedral services (as well as turning the heads of the female members of the congregation and the close). They were not the rewards for those who had served their East Anglian parishes for decades. Yet the best efforts of the chapter to secure young men of energy was largely negated because the majority of them stayed so long in office and, with retirement

47. Perhaps it recognised Millard's social needs; he married the daughter of Sir Edward

Berry, KCB, RN.

48. See below, pp. 602–6.

unknown, often far beyond the age at which they could effectively discharge of their duties.

It is more difficult to form an impression of the lesser members of the cathedral community – the eight lay clerks, the eight choir boys, the two vergers, the couple of subsacristans, the doorkeeper, the ferryman and the half-dozen poor men supported by the chapter on condition that they attended daily services – because they appear only as a list of names against their remuneration, or sometimes after 1790 as petitioners for an increase in it. Occasionally they are marked out as the subject of disciplinary action by the dean (taking the form, at least before the 1760s, of public admonition after morning prayer). For example John Pleasants, a lay clerk, was denounced for 'rude and insolent behaviour' towards one or more of the city aldermen and 'speaking rude and abusive words' of the dean, both in Norwich and in South Walsham.[49] Although the monetary rewards of these members of the cathedral's workforce seem meagre, even at this level patronage was necessary to secure nomination to what were sought-after posts in an age of low wages, small profits and irregular work. Even the respectable tradesmen who formed the ranks of the lay clerks were anxious to obtain the annual stipend of £8 (in 1808 increased to £20) plus a daily attendance allowance of 6d.[50] Clearly, participation in the twice-daily services, with the odd absence connived at, could be combined with, say, shop-keeping or weaving, and the salary (that of a living-in servant) used to augment vulnerable domestic incomes. Moreover, membership of the cathedral choir gave the lay clerks status in the city. Not only did they form glee or catch clubs at the Gate House Tavern in the upper close with the minor canons and organist, they also led the singing at those interminable, drunken club and patriotic dinners which were such a feature of Georgian city life.[51] Often their service to the cathedral was as extended as that of the prebendaries and minor canons and their faces, performances and eccentricities as well known. But, as in the nation as a whole, the lesser officers who formed the basis of the cathedral's pyramidical social structure, remain, beyond the barest detail, faceless men.

49. Chapter book, 1691–1732, NRO, DCN 24/4, fo. 273r.

50. Chapter book, 1795–1833, NRO, DCN 24/6, fo. 72v. In fact, after 1773 the lay clerks appear to have been paid an additional gratuity of £5 each year at Christmas 'for their diligent attendance in the choir'. Their petition for a salary increase was rejected in 1790. In 1829 they complained that they were worse paid than their peers in other cathedrals and produced evidence from

Carlisle, Exeter, Rochester and York to prove their point: NRO, DCN 120/2B/26–30. A system of modest fines, enforced more rigorously by Dean Pellew, was introduced for non-attendance after 1828.

51. See NRO, DCN 39/54 for rules and accounts of the Harmonic Society (1784–98) and the Cathedral Club (1815–22). The latter in February 1818 put on a concert of glees, duets, songs and catches to which they invited the prebendaries and their families.

Although it is possible to represent the dean and prebendaries as an elite band of itinerant whist players whose lives centred upon a crowded timetable of dinners and patronage squabbles, their careers and stewardship have to be judged against the defined reasons for their existence – the conduct of daily services, the good repair of the cathedral and the management of the chapter's estates which allowed the maintenance of both. The running of the estates is discussed in chapter 31. Here it is necessary to consider only the profits the dean and prebendaries shared from them and that portion they set aside each year to keep the cathedral and close in tolerable order.

In effect the dean and prebendaries were the life directors of a large and flourishing private property company, in which the cathedral and its services and salaries were major cost items, and their estates and ecclesiastical livings a source of considerable profit. Their princely emoluments consisted of a division of these profits (the dean's or managing director's rewards being twice that of the prebendaries) after expenditures had been met. Clearly, the less the chapter spent on these latter, the larger its income for distribution amongst the seven shareholders would be. There was therefore an obvious conflict of interest between their religious and secular responsibilities.

Directors are judged against their achievements. How well did the dean and prebendaries perform in these years? The summary of their balance sheets is set out in the Appendix (see p. 612). There are three salient points: first, the profits (columns 3 and 4) shared by them increased by six times between the 1720s and a century later – well in advance of inflation; secondly, expenditure on the cathedral grew over eight-and-a-half times in the same years; and lastly, the ratio of profits to expenditure on salaries and repairs at least doubled after the 1770s. Yet, impressive as these figures may seem as indicators of prebendal performance, several qualifications are necessary. First, a six-fold increase in income was not unique to members of the Norwich chapter.[52] Peter Virgin reckoned clerical incomes rose by an average of some 700 per cent between 1704 and the 1830s (prices doubled between 1700 and 1840, he maintains).[53] The basis of this increase was rising agricultural prosperity and the benefits of enclosure for the large landowner. Both were marked after the 1750s and accelerated fast during the French Wars. In England's premier arable county, the dean and chapter enjoyed this prosperity to the full.

Secondly, their record of achievement, in spite of its vast detail, is opaque. Their

52. The figure is smaller when the 'corps' money, which remained unchanged across the period, is added to the share of the profits of the dean and prebendaries, i.e. 4.4 times for the dean and 5.3 for the

prebendaries between the annual average for the years 1720–39 compared with that of 1820–39.

53. P. Virgin, *The Church in an Age of Negligence* (Cambridge, 1989), pp. 71–73.

auditor presented the dean and chapter each December with a superb set of accounts. Running to sixty or seventy pages each year, they would warm the heart of the least numerate business or agrarian historian. But of course they need to be placed against the decision-making processes of the chapter, and these are more difficult to reconstruct. The chapter books, minuting every meeting of the dean and prebendaries, tend to be brief records. The *decisions* taken at the end of a long meeting, sometimes extending to several days, are summarised with brevity. *Discussions* went unnoted. It is, therefore, difficult to establish the precise role of the dean and prebendaries in everyday business. Prideaux's was omnipresent, but not all deans possessed his capacity and drive. Besides, the dean was not required to perform his duties for more than four months in any year, the prebendaries for no more than two. Of course at the general chapters in June and December members made more effort to attend. Even so, travel was difficult in the pre-railway age, and ancient prebendaries were often in indifferent health. Although a quorum of four was necessary to conduct business (in the dean's absence three prebendaries sufficed), it was unusual for more to be present. At the majority of chapter meetings it was the dean and three prebendaries in their academic robes who assembled in the chapter house, audit room or, less frequently, the deanery. Comparing chapter meetings in the 1720s, 1780s and 1830s, those at the end of our period were little more regularly held than at the beginning (between three and four a year on average), whilst in the 1780s meetings were sparser – never more than three a year and in 1784 and 1786–89 only the two statutory general chapters were held. Dean Lloyd (1765–90) gave a poor lead. On a European grand tour, he attended no meetings for two years after December 1786. His successor, Dean Turner (1790–1828), was often content to send his written instructions across from Cambridge, presumably being immersed in Pembroke College business. Another noticeable feature is that the long sessions of the general chapter in the 1720s – in 1725 the December session stretched out across eight days – had disappeared by the 1780s.

These lax arrangements, evident in every eighteenth-century public body whether corporate or charitable in purpose, meant that a great deal of routine business, especially in details of estate administration, was processed by the chapter's permanent bureaucracy. This was a trio of men, invariably possessing a legal training, consisting of a chapter clerk, the understeward (the high steward was a decorative nobleman) and the auditor. Their experience was impressive, for their terms of office often exceeded those of the dean and prebendaries (see table 1). There were only two chapter clerks between 1724 and 1812; and Richard Moss served as auditor for sixty-one years between 1761 and 1822.

A large number of Francis Frank's letters survive. Although they are virtually silent about his role as chapter clerk (they dwell more frequently on his visitational role as deputy chancellor of the diocese), they reveal that after 1760 he was racked by ill-health. In 1768 it was taking him five days to write a letter.[54] Of course deputies were employed, in the usual Georgian fashion, and Frank was still in regular contact with the dean. But again the surviving record is deceptive, for all these officers and their deputies shifted mountains of unrecorded business at first hand with members of the chapter. Communication was easy, for all lived cheek by jowl in the close. Therefore it is difficult to gauge managerial leadership. In estate business, particularly in the key area of lease renewal, the understeward probably took the lead. In matters of patronage and cathedral repair, initiatives were jealously guarded by the dean and the more committed prebendaries. Of course most business was highly routinised. Prebendaries took turns to act as vice-dean, treasurer and receiver each year. The splendid audit accounts are unvarying across 120 years; they provided the chapter and its officers with a wonderful historic view of their economic position. Dean Prideaux would have felt as comfortable with chapter procedures in the 1830s as he had been at the height of his authority a century and a quarter earlier. The only difference was that the sums the chapter and their officers dealt with were far larger, their finances far healthier.

But routine and tradition and the endless sleep-inducing reading of leases at meetings did not necessarily guarantee harmony amongst chapter members.[55] As in a family, disputes could be sharp and prolonged amongst the seven members, in areas such as the arrangement of the prebendaries' period of residence and the dean's apportionment of residences within the close. Moreover, there was inherent tension in the system whereby the dean nominated minor canons, who were then dependent for their livelihood upon benefices to which presentation was made by the dean *and* prebendaries in general chapter. Even amongst men who warmly approved of the system, some deans were thought to push family interests too hard. For example, in 1813, Dean Turner and Prebendary Thurlow squabbled over the living of Ormesby St Margaret. Turner attempted to rush his brother's presentation through a hastily convened chapter meeting. Thurlow, seeking the benefice for his son, thought Turner's conduct, both in the manipulation of the chapter and bearing in mind that his brother already held the dean and chapter living of Great Yarmouth, 'unreasonable and unhandsome'. When Bishop Bathurst, to whom Thurlow appealed, ruled that under the statutes he was incompetent to judge the matter, the latter sought legal counsel.[56] And some prebendaries were more avaricious than others. A dispute

---

54. Sheffield Archives, Bacon Frank MSS, BFM 1323/1, 4 January 1769, Elizabeth Frank to Bacon Frank. In March he could at best hold a pen for two minutes. In the following year he was so ill with gout he was scarcely able to read or write: BFM 1325/12, 62, 79.

55. The general observation in this paragraph are based upon a reading of the chapter books covering the period 1720–1840, NRO, DCN 24/4–7.

56. NRO, DN/VSM 7/7, unnumbered bundle of letters from Edward South Thurlow to Bishop Bathurst.

amongst chapter members about augmenting the living of Hindringham, which could have cost each prebendary £25 from his share of the audit profit, dragged on for several years from 1756 to 1763. But it is easy to stress dispute; accord goes largely unnoted. Again, by eighteenth-century standards, the chapter, given its potential seeds for discord, was not unduly disputatious. Mostly, its business was effectively conducted.

One of the chief concerns of the dean and chapter was their repair of the cathedral. By its good maintenance (and the conduct of its services) their stewardship was publicly judged. Much of their responsibility in this area was routine work carried out at the chapter's direction each year by a band of Norwich's leading craftsmen – stonemasons, carpenters, blacksmiths, plumbers, painters, glaziers and, occasionally, upholsterers. Masonry and lead work needed constant repair, windows required reglazing, and alterations and improvements were regularly made both in the cathedral and to the houses in the close. Bishop Leng's 1725 visitation revealed the yearly cycle: that the church be kept in good and decent repair; that the church houses and other buildings belonging to it be viewed at the feast of the Annunciation (25 March) in every year carefully; that any defects be rectified and amended by the feast of St Michael (29 September) next following.[57] Certainly, in many years as much was spent on the houses as on the cathedral itself.

Although this annual pattern of expenditure was maintained there were major items of repair which the regular cycle could not accommodate. In some respects, especially before 1800, large-scale refurbishment was dependent upon the dean persuading the prebendaries of its necessity. This is clearly brought out by the person who compiled tables 2 and 3 (see p. 614). The message is simple. Prideaux and Bullock kept the fabric of the cathedral in good repair; the rest did not. In the 1720s and 1730s there was a real hesitancy to spend on the scale of the past. When Bishop Leng recommended repairing and cleaning the cloister which, on the dean and chapter's own admission, was in a poor state in 1725, Prebendary Francis Barnard believed it to be gross interference at an unnecessary cost of some £70 which the chapter could not afford.[58] Two factors therefore were critical to the rhythm of repair and refurbishment: the dean's determination to push his plans through chapter and the state of its finances. When income was sticky in the 1720s and 1730s as a result of low agricultural rents and prices, and there was a quick succession of three deans following Prideaux's years of ill-health, the cycle of repairs reached its lowest point. Indeed, it never quite fell to this level again, although Dean Bullock's exertions in the 1740s and 1750s were not matched until after 1800. The twenty years after 1775 were mostly years of minimal expenditure, members of the chapter being

57. NRO, DN/VIS 14/2.
58. NRO, DCN 116/1/1–2, Francis Barnard

to Dean Cole at Raynham, 2 and 13 August 1726.

content to enjoy their mounting profits to the full. It was only after 1800 that this alternation of relative neglect and activity was broken, with mounting expenditure upon the cathedral in every decade (see the Appendix).

In this brief account of the state of the cathedral's fabric the hero is Dean Bullock (1739–60). Inheriting two decades of neglect, he set to work with a rare determination. True, the value of the deanery had increased since Prideaux's tenure (by some 54 per cent), and presumably he could thereby more easily persuade the prebendaries to meet at least three years of vastly increased expenditure. Even so, Bullock's task was a hard one. The deplorable state of the building was there for all to see, and he was 'thoroughly sensible, that in pushing on the repairs of a long neglected church, it is a very easy matter to give offence'. He complained bitterly that 'the treacherous designing conduct which so glaringly appeared through all the proceedings in our last chapter has made an impression on me which will not easily be worn out'.[59] The crux of the criticisms was that he had appointed Matthew Brettingham to supervise the work of his elder brother Robert, the mason-cum-architect. The prebendaries believed that such supervision was an unnecessary expenditure.[60]. Nevertheless Bullock persisted in the full implementation of his plans. The interior of the cathedral was whitewashed, the nave was scraped and repainted, the paving in the nave, aisles and transepts reset and where necessary renewed, the two staircase turrets repaired, 145 windows repointed, reglazed and painted, extensive repairs (£770 for the stonework alone) made to the central tower and the steeple releaded.

Bullock continued the work throughout his twenty-one year deanship. The roof of the cathedral was almost entirely releaded; substantial work was carried out to the west end in 1749 (£400); more work on the spire seven years later (£235); and 5794 feet (1766 m.) of Purbeck paving, at a halfpenny per foot were laid in the cloister and forty-nine of its arches cleaned (£341) in 1758–59. The Erpingham Gate was spruced up in 1753; and finally, in a triumphant conclusion to two decades of continuous labour, the organ was repaired and regilded (£277).[61] It was the first stages of these improvements that led the Honourable Philip Yorke to pronounce the cathedral in 1750 as being in 'very good repair'. A decade later he would have had to employ superlatives.

59. NRO, DCN 117/1/17, Dean Bullock to [?], n. d., but mentioning Dr Hubbard (fourth stall, 1736–41).
60. H. M. Colvin, *A Biographical Dictionary of English Architects, 1660–1840* (London, 1954), pp. 91–95. It is significant that Matthew Brettingham was retained as surveyor and soon replaced his less competent brother as contractor. NRO, DCN 24/5, fo. 26v, DCN 11/8–9. Similarly, in the mid 1750s, Robert was replaced by Thomas Ivory in the design and building of Norwich's famous Octagon Chapel.
61. NRO, DCN 107/12, summary list of cathedral repairs, 1740–63, n. d. (*c.* 1763).

Fig. 206. The choir of Norwich Cathedral looking east in 1781, from a painting in the deanery by Joseph Browne. The picture shows the elaborate canopies of the chancellor's stall on the north and the bishop's throne opposite, and the northern cross gallery above the seated figure. The choir had been extensively improved between 1766 and 1768.

Subsequent deans and prebendaries benefited from Bullock's exertions for almost two generations. There were only two major undertakings beyond the routine round: extensive repairs and improvements to the choir (£987) in 1766–68 (fig. 206), entailing the closure of the main body of the cathedral from 25 March 1767 to 12 January 1768, and in 1794–95 restoration work on the spire (£667).[62] Only in

62. Two sets of drawings were made for the choir, one 'from London' costing three guineas, the other, 'two drafts of the choir', made by Thomas Stafford (£11 5s. 4d.). Thomas Ivory, listed in the accounts as 'stonemason' and stone cutter', was paid £171 11s.; William Wilkins, a plasterer and stuccoist, was paid £83 7s., see Colvin, *Biographical Dictionary*, pp. 310–11, 673. The specifications were set down in the chapter book, 3 June 1766, NRO, DCN 24/5. Other work carried out in these years was the early installation of a lightning conductor to the spire in 1770 and the repair of and reglazing of the east window (1776–80), which included new stained glass painted by the dean's wife, Mrs Lloyd (replaced by S. C. Yarrington in the mid-1820s). See NRO, DCN 118/1, Dean Philip

1806–7 (again requiring the closure of the cathedral for nine months) was a massive £1800 spent on the thorough cleaning of the whole building.

In undertaking these renovations the chapter relied for advice about the fabric upon a changing band of Norwich's most skilled craftsmen who, as the architectural profession emerged, often themselves ended up as members of it. These included the two Brettingham brothers, Thomas Ivory and his nephew, John (stone cutter, carver and monumental mason), the two William Wilkins, father and son, and a carpenter called Dove who helped install the lightning conductor in 1770 and who was still regularly engaged forty years later. In 1795 he was, exceptionally, awarded a £10 gratuity by the chapter in recognition of 'his long services and great attention to the repair of the church'.[63] On the chapter's side, day-to-day responsibility for the execution of its specifications devolved upon the chapter clerk. William Utten (clerk, 1773–1813) enjoyed the title of 'surveyor of the repairs of the cathedral', a style assumed by his successor, another attorney, John Kitson. After 1813, however, an annual fabric report was drawn up by the Norwich architect and county surveyor, Francis Stone (1775–1835). He was paid a retainer of £30 a year to produce his report, draw up specifications and supervise the work. Under his direction, a major overhaul of the nave and both transept roofs was carried out between 1813 and 1820.[64] In addition, other architects were consulted: William Wilkins (1749–1819), about the west front in 1806–7; Anthony Salvin (1799–1881), who was paid £50 a year between 1830 and 1834 for the execution of his plans to improve the south transept and choir; and Edward Blore (1787–1879), who remodelled the west front in 1839–40.[65]

By contemporary standards Norwich Cathedral was in good repair in the century after 1740.[66] There was no major catastrophe, for the fire which destroyed 45 feet (14 m.) of the nave roof on 25 June 1801 (through the carelessness of plumbers) was extinguished by the soldiers of the barracks and many other citizens.[67] Yet the

note 62 continued
Lloyd's memoranda book, 1767–80, and B. Haward, *Nineteenth-Century Norfolk Stained Glass* (Norwich, 1984), pp. 193–94. See also pp. 426–30, 705–27.

63. NRO, DCN 24/6, fo. 5r.
64. Colvin, *Biographical Dictionary*, p. 573, and Stone's annual surveyor's reports (1813–21), NRO, DCN 26/9/106–114. His successor (and also surveyor of Norfolk) was another Norfolk architect, John Brown, who held his cathedral post for over thirty years. He was the first of three successive members of a family who occupied the position of surveyor to the cathedral for almost a century: John Brown (1834–69), John H. Brown (1869–91)

and Charles J. Brown (1891–1932).
65. See J. P. McAleer, 'The Façade of Norwich Cathedral: The Nineteenth-Century Restorations', *NA*, 41 (1993), pp. 381–409.
66. At Hereford the west tower collapsed in 1786; at Chichester the central tower in 1861. Durham, Worcester, Winchester and even Canterbury were all considered to be in a poor state in the early nineteenth century. P. Barrett, *Barchester: English Cathedral Life in the Nineteenth Century* (London, 1993).
67. Gratuities of £21 were paid to Mr Browne, £21 to the soldiers and £86 to 'sundry other persons for assistance at the fire': NRO, DCN 22/11. Repairs cost around £600.

friability and decay of the exterior stonework, and the way 'irrelevant and comparatively mean buildings . . . [had] been suffered to encroach injuriously upon the close precincts of the pile', detracted from the cathedral's appearance, at least until the 1830s.[68] And at times reports on the tower and spire, on frequent roof leaks and on the inner turret on the north side of the west front, which fell down in 1815, made thoroughly alarming reading. Essentially, the efforts of members of the chapter, their surveyors and their craftsmen were a response to demonstrable defects revealed each year. There was no pro-active programme of long-term restoration beyond perhaps that undertaken by Dean Bullock after 1739. Repairs and improvements were made as the need arose. Mercifully, however, the Norwich chapter was not a poor one. Even while jealously guarding the major portion of its profits for themselves, the dean and prebendaries could undertake the regular repair of their properties and, when they were so moved, improve the cathedral and close according to the canons of contemporary taste. The choir after its restoration in 1766–68 must have been considered a fine place for the daily worship of the inhabitants of mid Georgian Norwich. In the close Dean Lloyd fenced the lower part and formed a 'handsome garden' and 'fashionable mall', called the prebendaries' walk, which ran down to the River Wensum.[69] In 1825 the upper close lawn was enclosed with iron palisades. Throughout, the houses in the close, with a few exceptions, were kept in good repair.

To make any major improvements the chapter relied principally upon the sale of its estate timber. This device in itself must have fixed the timing of major repairs. Fines upon the renewal of leases were also applied to these purposes, but the prebendaries objected to this more direct distribution of their incomes. Of course, just as marriage portions were public knowledge in the eighteenth century, so were prebendal incomes. Therefore the chapter realised that it had to spend a proportion of this increase on the cathedral and their properties in the close, especially after the 1810s, when there was mounting public criticism about the finance and management of English cathedrals. Moreover, the dean and prebendaries were themselves deeply involved in the entire process of building, repair and improvement. In 1766, for example, they formed a standing committee to make contracts and oversee the choir alterations.[70] The more agile members must have scrambled up ladders and across scaffolding with their workmen to view at first hand their vast, endless responsibility. All had to be able to read a lease expertly, to understand fully the complexities of ecclesiastical patronage rights and clerical incomes; and to discuss building technicalities with authority. Given this brief of their responsibilities, it is

68. C. Mackie, *Norfolk Annals*, 2 vols (Norwich, 1901), ii, p. 1035.

69. *The Norwich Directory* (Norwich, 1783), p. v.

70. NRO, DCN 24/5, fos 104–105.

not surprising that the members of Georgian cathedral chapters appear as much men of business as men of God.

There is no better guide to the England of the 1780s and 1790s than the Honourable John Byng (later Viscount Torrington). Usually deploring change, he had opinions on most things including cathedrals, their clerics and services. Sadly, the surviving diaries of the tours he made each summer do not include East Anglia. Would a chance visit to a service in Norwich Cathedral have echoed his strictures about services elsewhere – at Winchester, Salisbury, Oxford, Canterbury (one service 'well performed', the other 'sadly slurred') and Worcester?[71] At Christ Church, Oxford, evening prayers were 'miserably performed! Our church is terribly upon the decline, which as a gentleman, and a churchman I grieve for; some management, or teaching we should have for our money'.[72] Only at Lincoln and Southwell could he applaud the arrangements without reservation. Elsewhere the impression Byng gives is that the world of cathedrals and closes was one in terminal decline. It was a theme vigorously voiced abroad by William Cobbett thirty years later. In Norwich, similar sentiments were expressed in a letter to Dean Turner by the Reverend Joseph Kinghorn (1766–1832), a well-known dissenting minister. Writing just before Christmas in 1799 he was (it is difficult to know quite why) apprehensive about the way the ill-conducted celebration of the great festivals in the cathedral reflected so badly upon the church of England generally. Although he conceded, sycophantically, that the bishop and dean performed their roles well, Millard (the precentor) rushed through the litany 'in a gutteral rattling', and the speed at which the psalms were chanted was only exceeded by that at which the lesson was read. Indeed, if the Reverend Mr Smith read it, 'I defy any person to know what he says'. 'In short', Kinghorn concluded, 'your conduct in the government of your choir bespeaks your total disbelief of revelation, or a criminal neglect of duty'.[73]

With Byng, Cobbett and Kinghorn it is difficult to disentangle their opinion of the services they took part in from their censure of cathedral chapters and idle clerics generally. In fact, evidence about the conduct of services at Norwich is almost totally lacking before 1800. What we do know are the arrangements made for them. Divine service was held twice daily, at ten o'clock and four o'clock; an anthem was sung at both; the prayers were chanted. Holy communion appears to have been celebrated every Sunday – but not on holy days falling during the week, excepting

71. C. B. Andrews, ed., *The Torrington Diaries: A Selection from the Tours of the Hon. John Byng (Later Fifth Viscount Torrington) between the Years 1781 and 1794* (London, 1954), pp.

51, 70, 84, 161, 316–17, 343, 370, 462.

72. Andrews, *Torrington Diaries*, p. 462.

73. NRO, DCN 33/16, J. Kinghorn to the dean, 23 December 1799.

Christmas Day. The dean, when in Norwich, and the prebendary in residence seem to have attended both services each day, but neither preached frequently. A rota of Sunday morning preachers (John Wesley on 17 October 1790 commented that of Norwich's thirty-six churches only at the cathedral and St Peter Mancroft were sermons preached that Sunday morning) was fixed by the bishop twice yearly and published in the Norwich press.[74] The arrangements for 1766–67 are not untypical. From the last Sunday in May to the last Sunday of October, when the roads were tolerable, the preachers were drawn from the Suffolk clergy. In the other seven months they were selected from the two archdeaconries of Norwich and Norfolk. Even though some of the 1100 benefices in the diocese were held in plurality (there were some 800 clergy in the 1830s), the rota for individual clerics was not burdensome. For most, it was a once-in-a-lifetime occasion. Parson Woodforde managed to escape the ordeal altogether, although he was rector of Weston Longville for twenty-eight years. The dignitaries of the diocese also made sparse appearances in the cathedral's pulpit: at the three great festivals the bishop himself preached; during Advent, the four archdeacons; in Lent, the six prebendaries, each in turn; on Low and Trinity Sundays, the dean. And there were additional services to swell the preaching calendar: for the charity schools and, after 1772, the hospital, and to commemorate Charles King and Martyr (30 January), King Charles II's Restoration (29 May), the king's birthday, the inauguration of his reign and his coronation, Gunpowder Treason (5 November) and the corporation's annual guild service in June. On all these special occasions the corporation paraded in their robes and, similarly attired, attended on most Sunday mornings in summer when the weather was clement. While the cathedral congregation could certainly not complain of lack of variety of preachers, how well the minor canons on duty, the lay clerks and choristers performed the services each day is less clear.

Obviously they varied from dean to dean, from year to year, as organist, minor canons and lay clerks came and went. A good deal depended upon the view of the commentator. Kinghorn gives the impression that services, even at the great festivals, were perfunctorily performed in Dean Turner's time and hints that things were different during Dean Lloyd's tenure (1765–90). Sylas Nevile, however, commenting about two big services held in assize week for the benefit of the newly-established Norfolk and Norwich Hospital, suggests that the chapter could mount an impressive service. At the first, in 1772, he was rather diverted by the appearance of Bishop Yonge ('this fat blown-up fellow') though not by 'his inanimate sermon'. Of the second he wrote, 'a very fine service for a Protestant church; the music well

74. N. Curnock, ed., *The Journal of John Wesley*, 8 vols (London, 1909–16), viii, p. 107. See *Norwich Mercury*, 8 February, 19 April, 7, 14 June, 13 September, 1, 8 November, 6 December 1766. I am grateful to David Cubitt for the newspaper references.

performed by a full band; a temporary orchestra erected before the organ in the stile of church concerts abroad. A very brilliant and crowded audience . . .'[75] When the Reverend Philip Parsons, a Kentish cleric, attended morning service one quiet Saturday morning in early July 1796, his professional appraisal was warm: 'the anthem, the 23rd psalm, set beautifully by Dr Hayes, and sung divinely; the chanting of the psalms superior to what is usually met with in cathedrals, because not chanted in a hurry, but so slow as to be easily followed'.[76] By 1812 matters appear to have deteriorated, for in two rambling letters to the *Gentleman's Magazine* a minor canon, C. J. Smyth, implied that the instruction of choristers was inadequate because the lay clerks and organists were so badly paid.[77] But it is only when Dean Pellew was appointed in 1828 that the reforms he made suggest that the services had been lax in the latter years of Dean Turner's long tenure of office.[78]

Like Dean Bullock, Pellew (1828–66) faced a formidable agenda both in tackling the restoration of the south transept and the approach to it (as well as modernising the deanery) and in bringing the cathedral's services up to scratch. There were two considerations which appear to have driven Pellew along: the clamour for the reform of every traditional institution in the late 1820s and his knowledge of procedures at Canterbury.[79] He quickly drew up (and altered) a system of fines to obtain the better attendance of the lay clerks; he constructed a vestry off the south transept so that a procession could be formed before each service (previously the lay clerks, choristers, the almsmen and minor canons, the dean and residentiary prebendary – both often late – had assembled in the choir stalls); he installed a large clock in the south transept to instil punctuality.[80] In despair, he read Prideaux's diaries and revived the latter's practice of summoning the choir once a week to examine the absence book; he, turning a deaf ear to the clamour for democracy everywhere around him, stopped the custom whereby one of the lay clerks read the first lesson at morning

75. B. Cozens-Hardy, ed., *The Diary of Sylas Nevile, 1767–1788* (London, 1950), pp. 175, 312.

76. *Gentleman's Magazine*, 87 (1817), p. 306.

77. *Gentleman's Magazine*, 82 (1812), pp. 222–23, 324–26. Two even stranger letters to Lord Liverpool survive: BL, Additional MS 38576, fos 22–25, 214.

78. But see *Gentleman's Magazine*, 97 (1827), p. 589, where M. H. found the weekday services were 'performed with gravity and seriousness; and the responses, which in many choirs are gabbled over in the most indecorous manner, are particularly well set and sung'. See also the anonymous diary of a resident of Catton, 1826–38, who, on 25

February 1827, attended evening service at the cathedral 'where I heard a very good anthem', although he was critical of the organ: NRO, MC 580 T131C.

79. Bishop Bathurst wrote in June 1829, 'The new dean promises to be an accession to the society of Norwich. He is busy in making reforms; and if he do not mistake restlessness for activity, he will be of great use': Thistlethwayte, *Memoirs and Correspondence of Bathurst*, p. 358.

80. This paragraph is based upon the voluminous papers and correspondence of Dean Pellew and his diary of chapter business, all in NRO, DCN 120/2.

and evening prayer; he suppressed the practice of the vergers and sub-sacrists extracting tips for opening pews in the galleries of the two transepts at Sunday morning services; he noted with horror in 1835 (his action is unrecorded) 'the grossly indecorous' conduct of a couple of prostitutes sitting in the front row of the new gallery; he installed a heating system (which did not work very well) and refurbished the choir; he improved the organ; he introduced sermons at evensong on Sundays.

Effort exceeded results. Pellew had to admit that the voices of three of the eight lay clerks were useless: since his comment concerned their advanced years it was one he might have extended, at least in a similar ratio, to the minor canons and prebendaries. In 1837 he requested Charles Freeman Millard 'to make some change in [his] present forte piano mode of chanting and reading in the cathedral', and to reconsider his habit of putting in 'pauses at the end of each syllable'. Both usages, Pellew believed, 'excite the less serious portion of the cathedral congregation to feelings quite different from those he would hope for'.[81] Since Millard had been a minor canon for thirty years, his vocal routines were presumably impervious to the dean's criticisms. Nevertheless, the impression is that by the 1830s with Pellew's reforms, Peter Hansell's real efforts to secure minor canons with good voices, and the famous choir-training qualities of Zechariah Buck (organist, 1819–77), the tide of laxity had turned and services in Norwich were as well conducted as in any English cathedral in the second quarter of the nineteenth century.[82]

How many Norwich citizens attended the cathedral services? Were these a beacon in their spiritual lives? The record before 1830 is, again, almost non-existent. One visitor in 1825 lamented that 'there was scarcely a dozen persons beside the ecclesiastics who officiated'.[83] But this was Monday morning prayer. Nevertheless, the average attendance at the weekday services probably averaged no more than the dozen or so, Mr Marten recorded. Adam Sedgwick, the Cambridge geologist and prebendary after 1834, summed up the feeling of many of his predecessors when he wrote three years later:

These long services cut my time to shreds, and destroy the spirit of labour. We have the shadow of Catholicism without a grain of its substance, for not one of the chapter thinks himself better for these heartless formalities, or nearer heaven. A cold empty cathedral, and a set of unwilling hirelings singing prayers

81. NRO, DCN 120/2J/5, draft letter of Dean Pellew to the Reverend Charles Millard, May 1837. For Millard, see above, pp. 591–92
82. For Buck, see F. G. Kitton, *Zechariah Buck* (London, 1899); N. Boston, *The Musical*

History of Norwich Cathedral (Norwich, 1963); and chapter 32 below.
83. 'Journal of an Excursion to Yarmouth, Norwich and Cromer, Sept. 1825 by Mr Marten of Plaistow', NRO, MC 26/1, p. 37, entry for 12 September.

for an hour together. The bell tells me I must be off . . . I am just returned, after a full hour and a half of shivering. And what the congregation? One single old woman in addition to the officials.[84]

Was it any wonder that octogenarian prebendaries, men far less robust than Sedgwick, could not face this arctic ordeal? For six months of the year these conditions prevailed, and at evensong the church was so poorly lit that 'a person must grope his way in the dark, through the nave of the church and is fortunate if he can make his exit at the west door without having previously run his head against a pillar'.[85]

Attendances on Sunday mornings and at the special services in the calendar were a different matter. Dean Pellew made observations about them from Trinity to the second Sunday in Advent, 1830.[86] On the Sunday after Trinity he recorded it in full: 714 persons, including 177 in the choir and 210 'military' and many school children in the galleries and 'cross seats' (the nave not being used for services during our period). On the following Sunday about 300 persons were present and on many others he reported 'seats all full' with as many as 100–150 'unseated'. 'The greatest number of persons', he commented, 'who have no accommodation are those who attend the sermon only of which there are a great number from out the city, principally tradespeople'. On most Sundays between the first Sunday in May and the first Sunday in October the corporation attended. The military were fractionally more robust than the aldermen but, careful of their uniforms, 'never attend when the day is wet'. These Sunday attendances were a far cry from the great crowded services in the nave in the later nineteenth century, when preaching and hymn singing were at their zenith. Eight thousand people attended the Good Friday service in 1880.[87] Yet for the later Georgian period, the congregations noted by Pellew were good ones, contrasting sharply with the weekly ones Sedgwick dreaded.

The Dean and Chapter Act of 1840 did not transform life in the cathedral closes of England and Wales overnight. Peter Virgin represented it as lopping 'a little deadwood from some of the branches'; at York, Owen Chadwick reckoned it 'brought the world of Barchester to a lingering death'.[88] But these evaluations, underlining that 'the Whig reform of the church of England was not a revolution', should not minimise the real threat reform made to every aspect of the church's

84. Clark and Hughes, *Adam Sedgwick*, i, p. 439, letter to R. I. Murchison, 25 January 1837.
85. *Gentleman's Magazine*, 82 (1812), p. 223.
86. NRO, DCN 120/26/1. Pellew made these notes probably with an eye to improving and extending seating in the cathedral.
87. Barrett, *English Cathedral Life*, p. 184.
88. Virgin, *Age of Negligence*, p. 102; G. E. Aylmer and R. Cant, eds, *A History of York Minster* (Oxford, 1977), p. 289.

affairs in the 1830s.[89] For Dean Pellew and his prebendaries it was a decade in which their world often seemed on the point of being turned upside down. Philip Fisher, the octogenarian holder of the first stall, wrote to the dean in 1835 that he was too ill to walk, to eat and to sleep. Wearily, he concluded that the church was in no better condition. A year later he was even less sanguine, assuring the dean, 'he had no doubt but sooner or later the church will be completely overturned'.[90]

Fisher's gloom was universal, for from the mid 1820s the church of England was assailed with a mounting clamour for reform. Not all the difficult issues it faced were of its own immediate creation. The two largest were certainly not. One was the rapid growth of population in manufacturing districts, exposing the totally inadequate provision of the church in those areas. The other was the shifting role of the state, forcing governments to meet the demands of Roman Catholics (and indirectly dissenters) after the union with Ireland and to confront the claims for parliamentary reform. When both were conceded in 1828–32, against the wishes of the large majority of bishops in the House of Lords, and the surge for reform extended to other institutions such as the poor law and municipal corporations, it was inevitable that it should encompass a blatantly unreformed church of England. How was a more representative government compatible with an established church? How far, given the alarming growth of dissent, should the church be forced to respond to the changes, wrought by the industrial revolution? To what extent should the state impose reform upon it, or was it necessary for each institution to buttress the other?

These great questions troubled Whig and, briefly, Tory governments alike in the 1830s. Given the close alliance of church and state their ramifications were endless, embracing reform of the church of Ireland, church rates, church leases, church tithes, dissenting disabilities, the provision of funds to build and to staff more churches, as well as the question of non-residence and poor livings. Cathedrals, the rotten boroughs of the church, were drawn centrally into the debates about reform. Attention was focused on their sinecure preferments, their estates and their patronage. Essentially, well-endowed cathedrals, whose entire purpose was unclear, needed slimming down both to augment impoverished benefices generally and to provide funds for church expansion in urban and industrial areas.

The government tackled the reform of the church of England both more leisurely and less radically than clerics conceded. In June 1832 the Ecclesiastical Revenues Commission was formed to examine the church's income. Two and a half years later with the statistics compiled, Peel, very briefly prime minister in 1834–35, set

---

89. The quotation is from O. Chadwick, *The Victorian Church*, 2 vols (2nd edn, London, 1971–72), i, p. 137.

90. NRO, DCN 120/2H/33, letter dated 27 August 1835; DCN 120/2I/12, letter dated 10 August 1836.

up the Ecclesiastical Commission (with five senior bishops and seven conservative churchmen) to make recommendations for the reform of bishoprics, cathedral and parochial livings. The commission, whose lay membership changed on the formation of Melbourne's ministry in April 1835, rapidly published four reports.[91] The second, appearing in 1836, came to grips with the cathedral and collegiate churches. Concerned with the lack of churches and clerics in 'populous districts', it advocated the use of surplus cathedral revenues (to be achieved by the suppression of prebendal stalls) to augment big, poor benefices and to provide additional clergy.

Norwich was far from the centre of industrial change and already possessed of a surplus of impoverished city churches. Moreover, the see itself was almost entirely rural with a relatively slow-growing population. Therefore many of the concerns of Bishop Blomfield, the prime mover in the commission, must have seemed irrelevant to the cathedral chapter of Norwich. Certainly, few others can have been less well-equipped to face change. The holders of its first four stalls were at least in their late sixties, essentially men of an eighteenth-century outlook. Edward Thurlow had held office since 1788; Joseph Proctor, master of St Catharine's College, almost as long. The much younger Edward Bankes, the incumbent of the fifth stall, was one of the most notorious and idle pluralists in the business. Only C. N. Wodehouse had any claims as a reformer. Admittedly Dean Pellew had set out with some vigour to improve both the services and fabric of the cathedral after his appointment in 1828. But, a man of intensely hierarchical views, he was no progressive when it came to the wider issues of ecclesiastical reform. At times he found himself in serious disagreement with Wodehouse.[92] Of course, no lead was given from the palace. Bishop Bathurst, although a life-long Whig, was incapacitated by age and temperament from serving Grey and Melbourne in any active way.

The evidence from the surviving record is that the dean and chapter faced criticism on two fronts. On the one hand, they were simply part and parcel of that animus directed against cathedral chapters generally. In terms of their cupidity and their management of the cathedral's estates and fabric their record was neither worse nor

91. For an account see O. J. Brose, *Church and Parliament: The Reshaping of the Church of England, 1828–1860* (London, 1959), pp. 120–56; and Chadwick, *Victorian Church*, i, pp. 126–41. A fifth 'draft' report addressed some of the objections the commission received about the previous reports, and published the memorials and correspondence relating to cathedrals. *Parliamentary Papers* (1837–38), xxviii, pp. 9–24.
92. For example, in 1833 about repairs to the cathedral and Wodehouse's accusation that

Pellew lacked zeal: NRO, DCN 120/2F/1–2, 15, September 1833. There was also a straight clash of personalities. Pellew was high-handed; Wodehouse, meddlesome according to his detractors. There was also social rivalry: although Pellew was married to Lord Sidmouth's daughter and was the son of a recently created viscount himself, Wodehouse belonged to one of Norfolk's leading families; his wife was the daughter of the earl of Erroll. This was pure Barchester.

better than that elsewhere. On the other, in Norwich itself, the chapter, especially in the early 1830s, was increasingly criticised about the services in the cathedral and its patronage in the diocese. Some of the obloquy was hurled at the high-handed conduct of the dean, who appeared to make alterations to services and fabric at will.[93] Yet a perusal of *The Life and Letters of the Reverend Adam Sedgwick* suggests that the daily round in the close after 1834 went on much as it ever had. A Whig by label, he was essentially apolitical, bringing together Quakers, dissenters and high churchmen at his table.[94] His two months in Norwich were entirely filled with geological research (Wodehouse censuring him that there was more geology than theology in his sermons), taking duty and recreation, and giving public lectures. But, perhaps because he tacitly approved of moderate Whig reform, no mention is made of the prebendaries' reactions to the reports, circulars and questionnaires of the Ecclesiastical Commissioners which regularly landed on their study tables after 1835. Defence of the chapter's position and the role of cathedral chapters in general seems to have rested with Dean Pellew.

When the first two reports of the commission were published, the comments about Norwich Cathedral and the statistics about its revenues and patronage made unsurprising reading. The fabric was pronounced in a 'sound state', the result of 'much [money] laid out of late years in the repairs of various parts'. In terms of the dean's and prebendaries' incomes for the seven years ending 1834, the Norwich chapter did well, coming fourth in a table of fourteen cathedrals and collegiate churches in the better-endowed new foundation section. Indeed only four deans in England and Wales were better paid than Pellew.[95] The chapter protested that the negotiations of the Sedgeford lease for £12,000 in 1831 gave a quite untypical impression of their profits in other years, and registered 'unanimous disapproval' of the recommendations of the commissioners in their second report. Already, in a long personal and curiously ambivalent memorandum, Dean Pellew had defended the status quo, maintaining that prebendal stalls were 'fair prizes in the church, intended to excite energies and reward the services of a crowded and meritorious

93. The correspondence of Dean Pellew, arranged in bundles by years, is in NRO, DCN 120/2. See especially the years 1830–34. In October 1831 he even received a 'Swing' letter after employing craftsmen directly, seemingly having set up a cathedral works' department. See also the claim that the dean and chapter's wealth and patronage 'have been used to the injury of the character of that body, and to the detriment of the interest of the established religion', citing their conduct at Worstead. See *Norwich*

Mercury, 6 February 1841, and Canon Sedgwick's belated defence in the *Norfolk Chronicle and Norwich Gazette*, 1, 8, 15 May 1841.

94. Clark and Hughes, *Adam Sedgwick*, i, p. 437.

95. The annual incomes of the dean and prebendaries at Norwich for the seven years ending 1834 were £1682 and £813 respectively: *Parliamentary Papers* (1836), xxxvi, second report of the church commission, appendix 7.

profession'.[96] This was a highly-blinkered view of capitular preferment, cutting little ice in 1835, especially as he conceded later in his paper that prebendal rotas detracted from the efficiency of chapters. Pellew was not averse to the suppression of stalls, but any reform introduced by a Whig commission was anathema. It is clear that what Pellew really wanted was the enhancement of the authority of deans within cathedrals and also (given his experience of Bishop Bathurst who can blame him?) in relation to diocesan bishops and their archdeacons. He always felt his talents and dignity could not flourish fully when restricted to the cathedral alone. In a later memorial presented on behalf of the dean and chapter to the commissioners, he underlined its opposition to a disposal of their revenues, envisaging no more than the creation of a repair fund and a scheme to retire superannuated lay clerks (another Norwich problem he had encountered) from any savings made by the commission's reform of cathedral incomes. Again, it was a document which testified to Pellew's insularity. Neither paper was well-calculated to catch Bishop Blomfield's eye.

Although Lord Melbourne's government held no brief for radical reform of the church, and was by and large content to leave it to the ecclesiastical members of the commission, the cabinet was not willing to let it run up against the buffers of Dean Pellew and his like. The proposals made in the commission's second report (March 1836) sought to achieve the well-established objectives of improving poor benefices in populous areas and increasing the number of churches and clerics within them. To these ends the surplus endowments of cathedrals and collegiate churches would be utilised. Their recommendations therefore envisaged that in future the staff of cathedrals should consist of a dean and four canons (with their periods of office extended to nine and three months respectively); that the number of minor canons should be reduced and their stipends increased to £150 each; that bishops should gradually nominate up to twenty-four honorary canons to reward the more diligent clergymen in their dioceses; and that dean and chapter patronage should be transferred in general to the diocesan bishops. But in the next few years, before the Dean and Chapter Act was eventually passed in 1840, these proposals were modified, particularly in relation to the diminution of capitular patronage and the immediate suppression of stalls.[97] The life interest of every existing office holder was protected. Change therefore came slowly.

96. *Parliamentary Papers* (1837), xli, pp. 56–59, memorandum, dated 16 February 1835; memorial of the dean and chapter, 13 December 1836. See also Pellew's *Letter to the Right Honourable Sir Robert Peel, Bart. MP on the Means of 'Rendering Cathedral Churches Most Conducive to the Efficiency of the Established Church'* (London, 1837), and 'Suggestions From the Honourable and Very Reverend the Dean of Norwich', 1853, to the cathedral commission, *Parliamentary Papers* (1854), xxv, pp. 844–46.

97. W. L. Mathieson, *English Church Reform, 1815–1840* (London, 1923), p. 149, described the proposals 'mellowing with age' in the four years between 1836 and 1840.

At Norwich, as the return to the Cathedral Commissioners in 1854 detailed, the requirement of Dean Pellew's residence was still only 122 days and his two senior canons two months each.[98] Admittedly there were now only four canons (the two junior ones serving for three months each as the 1840 act directed) and four minor canons. But the dean and chapter's patronage in the city and county was largely unchanged, as were its list of statutable offices. No reform of the education of the choristers had been made; there was no training college 'in connection with the cathedral', although the chapter made an annual subscription of ten guineas a year and provided a house worth £30 per annum to the clerical superintendent of one founded in Norwich by the National Society. Charitable effort in support of schools and aid in the construction of parsonages was modest indeed. A conservative dean of twenty-five years standing defied the centralizing tendencies of a permanent commission with vigour.

Of course, there was reform from within the church itself after 1830. The old sloppy standards of services and attendance, and the worst aspects of prebendal patronage and cupidity diminished. The cathedral fabric was in far better shape in 1850 than it had been twenty years earlier. A new sense of mission was evident. Yet, as at York and elsewhere, the world of Barchester passed away very slowly in the cathedral close at Norwich. Dean Turner and Robert Potter would still essentially have felt at home in it at the time of the Great Exhibition. Only Bishop Bathurst would have had to enjoy his rubber of whist more discreetly.

98. *Parliamentary Papers* (1854), xxv, appendix to the first report of the cathedral commissioners, appointed November 10, 1852. The Norwich returns and correspondence are printed on pp. 529, 772–73, 844–45, 875–77, 962–63.

Appendix

The Expenditure and Income of the Dean and Chapter of Norwich Cathedral, 1720–1839 (annual averages to nearest £)

	Expenditure			Income[101]		
	1[99]	2[100]		3	4	5
Year ending 30 November	'ordinaries'	'extraordinaries'		profits received by the dean[102]	profits received by each prebendary	total profits as a percentage of columns 1 and 2 (excluding the timber fund proceeds (1790–1839)
	(£)	(£)		(£)	(£)	%
1720–29	639	206		191	95	90
1730–39	640	175		246	123	121
1740–49	639	481		252	125	90
1750–59	636	359		286	143	115
1760–69	638	308		436	218	184
1770–79	638	483		557	278	198
1780–89	636	292		562	281	242
1790–99	634	411[103]	(528)[104]	749	374	257
1800–09	647	544	(1076)	1234	617	287
1810–19	728	1206	(1417)	1304	652	243
1820–29	826	1550	(1736)	1254	627	211
1830–39	856	1656	(2272)	1382[105]	691	220

Source: NRO, DCN 11/6–18

99. 'Ordinaries' were the total salaries paid to the cathedral staff as laid down in the cathedral statutes. From the 1770s gratuities were additionally paid: in the 1810s these were amalgamated with additional salary increases. In this total is included the 'corps' money paid each year to the dean (£102 5s.) and the prebendaries (£20 each). This remained unchanged and should be added to columns 3 and 4 respectively when reckoning their total income.

100. 'Extraordinaries' were the expenses of repairing the cathedral and its properties in the close, of running services and of maintaining the chapter's jurisdiction in the ca-

thedral precincts. They do not include the costs of maintaining other dean and chapter properties.

101. This is the total of the fines paid on the renewal of chapter leases, of money rent arrears (which notably diminished across the period), of money rents (static), of manor court incomes and of cash rents (these increased from £849 per annum in the 1720s to £1676 in the 1790s). The fines income varied considerably from year to year, although the trend was clearly upwards (averaging £346 in the 1720s to £3202 in the 1800s, a nine-fold increase). Income from manorial courts and cash rents

Table 1
Lay Officers of the Dean and Chapter, 1720–1840

Year	Auditor	Chapter Clerk	Understeward
1720	Nicholas Vipond	William Yallop	Edmund Prideaux
1724		Francis Frank	
1731			John Jermy
1744	Henry Field		
1745			John Fowle
1761	Richard Moss		
1773		William Utten	Charles Buckle
1784			John Chambers
1789			Charles Cooper
1796			Charles Harvey
1812		John Kitson	Francis Turner
1822	Matthew Rackham		

Source: NRO, DCN 11/6–18

note 101 continued
also showed considerable fluctuations from year to year.

102. The actual sums received by the dean and prebendaries (available only from the 1760s in NRO, DCN 18) do not exactly square with those entered in the audit books (NRO, DCN 11) and shown in columns 3 and 4. From the seventeenth century additional small sums, divided in the usual ratio between the dean and prebendaries, were recovered from the close rents, the precinct and Thorpe St Andrew meadows, and the hen or provision rents (NRO, DCN 13/4). These sums, not entered in the audit books, explain the small discrepancies between the two sets of figures. Those in columns 3 and 4 (plus the 'corps' money, see note 99) give a fair indication of the growth of decanal and prebendal incomes in these years. They certainly square with Potter's statement of his income (see p. 588).

103. To the 'extraordinaries' after 1790 should be added sums 'expended from the timber fund'. The timber fund appears to have been established in 1779 and consisted of money raised by the sale of timber. It was largely invested in 3 per cent consols, £7400 worth being purchased between 1779 and 1814. These stocks were realised in 1807 (£2000) and between 1825 and 1834. Smaller sums were loaned to individuals. The money was expended chiefly upon repairs to the cathedral and properties in the close. It also met other expenses including the dean and prebendaries' income tax (1797–1815) and the enclosing of the upper close with iron palisades in 1825 (£575). The largest sum expended was one of £1870 in 1806 for 'painting choir etc'. See NRO, DCN 22/11 and 23/38, list of sums taken from the timber fund, 1791–1826.

104. The total in brackets shows the extraordinaries plus the sums expended from the timber fund.

105. The profits of the dean and chapter were inflated by the massive £12,000 fine paid on the renewal of the Sedgeford estate lease in 1833, a point the chapter was not slow in representing to the ecclesiastical commissioners when they enquired into cathedral incomes in the mid 1830s.

Table 2

'Expenses for the Church', 1701–65

(average annual expenditure in £ s. d.)

	£	s.	d.
1701–10	130	14	0½
1711–20	141	5	9½
1721–30	48	12	5
1731–40	95	16	0
1741–50	264	19	8
1751–60	196	4	2
1761–65	60	19	11

Source: NRO, DCN 57/5, 'summary account of extraordinaries and money spent on cathedral repairs with the value of the deanery, 1671–65', n.d. [1765?]. The calculations are those of 'Mr Smith'.

Table 3

Money Spent on the Cathedral Compared with the Value of the Deanery, 1702–65

Dean	Annual average of money spent on church			Annual value of deanery		
	£	s.	d.	£	s.	d.
Humphrey Prideaux (1702–24)	124	19	3	189	4	6¾
Thomas Cole (1724–31)	34	5	7¼	289	14	11½
Robert Butts (1731–33)	11	17	3	305	2	10
John Baron (1733–39)	28	19	0½	299	15	0
Thomas Bullock (1739–60)	255	14	2¾	291	5	3
Edward Townshend (1761–65)	79	3	6	no figures given		

Source: see table 2. Again the calculations are those of 'Mr Smith'.

29

The Cathedral, 1840–1945

Dorothy Owen

The bishopric of Edward Stanley (1837–49) is an appropriate introduction to this next chapter of the cathedral's history. Stanley was a Whig and a reformer, ardent in the causes of popular education and temperance, and an effective administrator in an age of good administrators. Above all he was a lively and humane pastor. As his niece Henrietta Maria Stanley wrote at his death, 'a kinder and better man never lived and now death will have obliterated his small peculiarities people will do justice to his enlarged philanthropy and universal charity'.[1] Bishop Stanley entertained many of his family and connections, some of the Cambridge dons who had links with the chapter and many of the important figures of the day. The summer of 1847 was particularly gay and lively for the inhabitants of the palace: the great Swedish soprano Jenny Lind had come to Norwich to give a series of concerts in aid of the Norwich children's hospital; Bishop Stanley and his wife became her faithful admirers. At much the same time the impassioned supporter of temperance, Father Theobald Mathew, was holding meetings in the town, and Mrs Augustus Hare, and her adopted son Augustus Hare, who were connections of Mrs Stanley, were at the palace along with the articulate and progressive registrary of the University of Cambridge, Joseph Romilly. Romilly's journal of his professional life records that the master of Trinity College (William Whewell) and the vice-master (Adam Sedgwick, a canon of Norwich) had been at the palace, hurrying back to Cambridge for an election to the Trinity seniority, but returning in time to see two hospitals and a jacquard loom, before the bishop's illustrious guests accompanied them to Whewell's house at Lowestoft.[2] The Hares went back with Romilly for more sightseeing in Cambridge, and the host recorded drawing expeditions there

1. N. Mitford, *The Ladies of Alderley* (London, 1938), p. 257.
2. M. E. Bury and J. D. Pickles, eds, *Romilly's Cambridge Diary, 1842–47* (Cambridgeshire Record Society 10, 1994), pp. 219, 221–22, 224–25; A. M. W. Stirling, *The Letter Bag of Lady Elizabeth Spencer-Stanhope*, 2 vols (London, 1913) ii, pp. 208–11.

and at Norwich, with the young man. Later, Augustus was himself to recall some of the bishop's more amusing statements. When Dean George Pellew (1828–66) objected to a plan to affix a cross on the outside of the cathedral he said very emphatically, 'Never be ashamed of the cross, Mr Dean, never be ashamed of the cross'; and when he was preparing to preach in the cathedral to a congregation of soldiers who did not attend because it was raining, being unwilling to waste his sermon, he delivered it to those present with the preface, 'Now this is the sermon I should have preached if the soldiers had been here'.[3]

This animated and cultivated group, which travelled by second-class train through Norfolk in 1847, signals a new epoch in the cathedral's history. It is the tentative beginning, marked by the hesitant revisions to the 1620 statutes in 1840,[4] but even more by the coming of the railway and its corollary, the tourist and excursionist, which would transform the cathedral and its congregation into a great parish church for the whole of eastern England. The cathedral community itself was slow to move. The changes to the statutes had made little difference to the predominant position of the dean; this is particularly obvious in these early years when Dean Pellew made all important decisions and settled all matters of dispute regardless of the rest of the chapter. It was he, for example, who wrote to the directors of the railway company in 1844, protesting against Sunday excursion trains to Thorpe:

> his [the excursionist's] ride could only be paid for by the sacrifice of his and his family's Sunday dinner or of some other claim equally essential to their well-being, to say nothing of the temptation to drinking and to excesses of even worse kinds to which the directors expose numbers unnecessarily every Sunday, by taking them to such sinks of iniquity.[5]

Even so late in his service as 1859 Pellew was dealing personally with disputes about the time of cathedral sermons, the scandal of male visitors who came into the building wearing their hats and the difficulties experienced by Mr Torris's daughter in finding a seat. Minor breezes were caused by the bedesmen's petition for an increase of salary; by Zechariah Buck, organist and choirmaster, who made difficulties about the times of Sunday morning services; and by the resistance of close residents to the continuance of the chapter policy of locking the close gates at nightfall.[6]

3. A. Hare, *The Years with Mother*, ed. M. Barnes (London, 1952), p. 51.
4. Following the first four reports of the Ecclesiastical Commissioners and the statute 3 and 4 Vict. c. 113, two stalls were suppressed at Norwich between 1836 and 1847, reducing the number of canons from six to four; the terms of residence increased to eight months for the dean and three months for the canons. Other changes in the light of these reports were the creation of honorary canons and the reduction of the number of minor canons.
5. NRO, DCN 120/2Q.
6. NRO, DCN 120/2, bundles CC, FF, JJ.

The petty differences suggest no change, yet despite them much solid progress was made in the two decades after 1840 and a good deal of it can certainly be put to Dean Pellew's credit. He was faced first, in 1841, with the need to oppose the obnoxious line proposed by Mr Stephenson, for the Norwich to Yarmouth railway.[7] This would cut through various sections of chapter property. In the following year, although his preliminary opposition had been successful, he was nevertheless obliged to agree to sell land in Trowse and Thorpe to the railway company, and by 1845 the chapter's meadows lying between the Foundry and the Carrow Road were also surrendered.[8] Much detailed tidying of the arrangements of the cathedral took place in these early years: in 1842 it was agreed that an evening service should in future be held each Sunday at 3 pm, to be followed, between March and September, by a service in St Luke's Chapel for the parishioners of the close parish of St Mary in the Marsh. For the other half of the year the parishioners would attend the 3 o'clock service. The chapter, led by the dean, and with the help of the Norwich district visiting society, took firm decisions about the destination of the cathedral alms and, with eager concern for the environment, decided to set out a public walk eighteen feet wide on the river bank across the common and meadows from the railway terminus to the Carrow Road.[9] Activity continued in all branches of chapter administration for the rest of Pellew's time. The seating in the cathedral was improved. Pellew had given two oak chairs for the chancel in 1845. Bishop Stanley was offered 'the old episcopal chair and faldstool' – he evidently accepted them. In 1847 the chapter resolved to buy four new benches in each year until the congregation was accommodated; and to lay down new coconut matting. The piecemeal reorganization continued with a search of the plumbery to find unwanted pieces of stained glass, which could be sold to form a fund for the purchase of new glass.[10] This tidying culminated in 1864, when the chapter decided to surrender to the corporation of Norwich the unenclosed portion of Mousehold Heath which was to be used to form a 'people's park' in the spirit of the recent act of parliament.[11] In general, Pellew's period of office saw much rather uncoordinated activity, carried out by him without much regard for the views of other members of the chapter: Bishop Stanley's reported rebuke, 'Never be ashamed of the cross, Mr Dean', suggests a certain inflexibility of outlook, coupled with recourse to ad hoc, pragmatic decisions. There is at no time a suggestion that he had any coherent plan of reform.

7.   NRO, DCN 120/1/5, 7 December 1841.   120/1/5, 6 December 1842.
8.   NRO, DCN 120/1/5, 7 December 1844.   10.   NRO, DCN 120/1/6, 7 December 1847.
9.   NRO, DCN 120/1/5, 18 December 1844;   11.   NRO, DCN 120/1/7, 1 June 1864.
     DCN 120/6, 1 December 1845; DCN

By the time Edward Meyrick Goulburn had been installed as dean in 1866, the pace of change had markedly accelerated and the personality and experience of the new dean were of the utmost importance. Goulburn had come immediately from a London parish, where his success as a preacher was very marked. His experience of men and affairs, as dean of Merton College, Oxford, and as headmaster of Rugby (in succession to the future Archbishop Archibald Campbell Tait), gave him great wisdom and made him on the whole an effective and influential dean.[12] In 1884, more than midway through his term of office, the Cathedral Commissioners reported on the statutes of 1620 by which, with minor changes, the affairs of the chapter were still controlled. The report proposed a number of changes which would be marked improvements, it was believed. It more clearly defined the episcopal powers over the chapter and slightly diminished the powers and patronage of the dean. It lengthened the time of residence of the canons to eight months and, perhaps most importantly, it recognized the need to create a class of non-residentiary canons, paving the way for a 'greater chapter' to include them. It seems clear that these reforms did not realise Goulburn's ideals and that the offered changes were not likely, in his view at least, to create a new and effective chapter. He vigorously counter-attacked with a minority report, which was printed along with the commissioners' proposals and which was directed essentially to the *means* by which the chapter could be improved. 'It is not', he wrote, 'to be effected by statutes, however ably framed, but by the appointment of men qualified by natural character and by habits of study and devotion for life under the shadow of a cathedral . . .' He objected, too, to the enforcement of a total period of residence of eight months since this made it impossible for a man holding a living to keep such a residence. Most serious of all, the proposed statutes 'ignored the claims of sacred learning . . . Not sacred study but diocesan business seems to have been the ruling idea in the tracing out the duties of the dean and canons of the future . . .' The very terms of this protest, and the record of his activities, leave no doubt of the energetic way in which Goulburn approached his duties.[13]

The chapter, as it emerged in 1884, left the dean still very firmly in control. The dean himself continued to be appointed by the crown and was to reside perpetually. He was able to select all officers of the chapter except minor canons and lay clerks. He took precedence in chapter and was to be obeyed by all officers. The income of the chapter was to be divided into six portions, of which the dean received two. He was to preach on the first Sunday after Christmas, on Low Sunday, Ascension Day and Trinity Sunday, and should conduct the services on Easter Day, Christmas Day, and Whitsunday, unless the bishop expressed a wish to do so. In fact he

12. W. O. Chadwick, *The Victorian Church*, 2   *DNB*.
     vols (London, 1966–70), ii, pp. 373, 380;   13. *Parliamentary Papers* (1884–85), xxi, p. 54.

controlled all services in the cathedral apart from the special events requested or arranged by the bishop.

The pattern which Goulburn had already set, heralded by a chapter order of 4 June 1867, was of two services: at 8 am and 5 pm in the eight 'summer' months (March to October); and 9 am and 5 pm between November and February. This left Sunday afternoons for a variety of special services which would be agreed on between the dean and the bishop. These had become, before the end of the century, a major part of the cathedral's activities.[14] It was arranged that instead of leaving a single minor canon to bear the full burden of singing the services, two men should always be present so that the duties could be shared. Goulburn seems also to have tried, in the face of opposition from the precentor, to have at least one Sunday service in the month at which the congregation's capacities were regarded,

Fig. 207. Part of the chapter in 1927. Dean J. Wakefield Willink, Canon W. Hay M. H. Aitken and Canon Edward A. Parr.

with the hymns and chants made simple. The royal jubilee of 1887 was celebrated very elaborately, and special services for the military garrison seem to have increased and multiplied, apparently in response to popular demand.[15] On the other hand, attempts by some diocesan clergy to alter the balance of the services were resented by Goulburn. As early as 1866 Dean Pellew had circulated a memorial which he had received from sixty-seven diocesan clergy urging more frequent communion services: 'the dean and chapter thought it an unauthorised and not quite respectful interference; they recommended a polite but respectful reply, of which the bishop approves'. No additional communion services would be introduced for some time to come. There was clearly a limit to Goulburn's liberalizing programme.[16]

The chapter was not easily distinguishable from that of earlier years. Four canons, one of whom was still the master of St Catharine's College, Cambridge, each resided

14. NRO, DCN 121/9, 7 June 1867, DCN 121/4, 15 March 1886.

15. NRO, DCN 121/5, 13 March 1887.

16. NRO, DCN 120/1/2, 4 April 1866.

for periods amounting to eight months in each year.[17] There was some modification for the master: of the eight months three were to consist of 'close' residence. One of the other four canons was nominated vice-dean by the dean; they, together with the dean, formed the chapter, which met at least twice in the year. The dean and chapter appointed three minor canons for periods of not longer than ten years; the minor canons themselves elected from their number a precentor, whose business it was to decide on music for the services. In addition the dean and chapter were to choose at least eight lay clerks and twelve choristers, for whose education, clothing and future training generous provision was made.

The statutes declared that the members of the chapter would be prepared to give instruction in sound learning and religious education in the diocese and help in the preparation of ordinands. No one could have been more suitable for this task than Goulburn, ably assisted by two at least of his colleagues. Goulburn had, as we saw, been at first fellow, tutor and then dean of Merton. By upbringing an evangelical, after ordination, and under the influence of William George Ward of Balliol, he was known to be a moderate high churchman.[18] While headmaster of Rugby, and as a London incumbent, he had been a vigorous and highly successful preacher; his sermons were published and widely disseminated, and he had already published *An Introduction to the Devotional Study of the Holy Scriptures*, which reached its tenth edition by 1878. Of the other canons who were already active in Norwich before Goulburn became dean, the two most congenial to him and readiest to engage in educational work were James Heaviside, who was in almost continuous residence and became Goulburn's vice-dean, and Charles Robinson, master of St Catharine's College. He also had much help and sympathy from Henry Symonds, who had been precentor and minor canon since 1844. With Symonds he catalogued and examined the chapter library and arranged for the photography and detailed inspection of the cathedral vault bosses in a major publication devoted to 'the ancient sculptures of the cathedral'; to this was appended a history of the see of Norwich, which he prepared in conjunction with the antiquary Edward Hailstone.[19] Goulburn followed up this work by an edition of the life and writings of the first bishop of the see, Herbert de Losinga, which he and Symonds prepared together and which

17. The fourth stall was finally divided from the mastership of St Catharine's in 1927 and annexed instead to the archdeaconry of Norfolk, an episcopal appointment. In 1934 another stall was suspended, temporarily at first, leaving only three canons: NRO, DCN 24/12, fos 222v, 227–228, 246v, 247v, 249r, 294v–295r.

18. Ward was prominent in the early Oxford or High Church Movement before converting to Roman Catholicism.

19. E. M. Goulburn, H. Symonds and E. Hailstone, *The Ancient Sculptures in the Roof of Norwich Cathedral . . . To Which is Added a History of the See of Norwich from its Foundation to the Dissolution of the Monasteries* (Norwich, 1876).

was published in 1878.[20] As if this literary activity were not enough, Goulburn was for many years putting together notes of the life and activities of his later mentor, whom he favoured after W.G. Ward had left for Rome, the old-fashioned high churchman John W. Burgon, dean of Chichester. These notes were eventually put together and published as a major study in 1892, three years after Goulburn's retirement.

It is clear from the surviving volumes of Goulburn's diary that his mental activity was incessant, matched only by his endless and apparently tireless walks about the city.[21] This intense physical activity in no way diminished his vigorous and continual attention to the affairs of the cathedral and chapter and also those of the diocese and city. There was, for example, a serious attempt to improve conditions for the choir boys and, at the same time, to restore order and dignity to their part of the service. In this Goulburn, in conjunction with his friend Symonds, played a prominent part. Noise coming from the choir boys and the scholars of the grammar school was a regular cause for complaint from inhabitants of the close. Then, too, the awkward question of when, and for how long, the choir was to take its holiday consumed much time and energy in the chapter, especially after increasing numbers of visitors and tourists expected fully musical services throughout the summer months. Shrinking revenues from chapter resources led to other problems: it was thought that two choristers who sang alto parts could be dispensed with, but this was vigorously challenged by Symonds's successor as precentor. It is characteristic of Goulburn's methods that he was able to resolve the difficulty by including two boys not as regular choir members but as supernumeraries. Goulburn was also much exercised about the future careers of the choir boys. Early in 1867 he had made the 'Norman chamber' (the locutory),[22] and the room over it, into school rooms for them; his policy was completed by the provision in 1900 of a shorthand teacher for them. One of his cherished schemes had been an ex-choristers' guild. It languished for a while after his retirement, but was revived in 1894 and proved to be a successful way of attaching past members of the choir to the cause of the cathedral. The growing significance of the musical part of the services is reflected in the chapter orders of Goulburn's last few years: these saw very elaborate provision, for example, for the 1887 jubilee celebrations. The thanksgiving service on 21 June was held in the nave, using a platform devised for musical services to seat the lay congregation, along with the mayor and corporation, parochial clergy and nonconformist ministers.

20. E. M. Goulburn and H. Symonds, *The Life, Letters and Sermons of Bishop Herbert de Losinga*, 2 vols (London, 1878).

21. The diaries, which are not a continuous series, and are often no more than a list of engagements, are preserved in the cathedral library. The Reverend Noel Henderson has been working on a transcript and edition for publication.

22. See above, fig. 114.

Regular troops and volunteers were to sit in the nave gallery, while the singers and the band (of the Nineteenth Hussars) were accommodated in the presbytery. Appropriate gratuities were provided for the lay clerks, choir boys and bandsmen; books of words were bought for the singers; and illuminations were to be set up, on the night of 21 June, outside the gates of the close. This was much appreciated by the authorities and the public. The precentor, aided by the dean, hoped to capitalize on this by launching a regular series of Sunday evening musical services in the nave.[23]

Dean Goulburn had been equally earnest in his efforts to revive and exploit the cathedral library. In 1864 Henry Symonds, the precentor, had been appointed as chapter librarian; as we have seen, he and the dean collaborated in publicising the resources of the library. The first surviving library accounts, for the year 1887, show a rather miserly annual budget of £14. Of this, £6 was expended on regular subscriptions for the publications of the Camden, Early English Text and Wycliffe societies, the *Quarterly Review* and *Notes and Queries*, leaving £8 for purchases of new books. These included in 1887 such predictable accessions as volumes of Grove's *Musical Directory* and Smith's *Dictionary of Christian Biography*, as well as Augustus Jessopp's *Autobiography of Roger North* and *The Heraldry of Norfolk*.[24] Goulburn himself substantially increased the resources of the library by bequests to it of volumes of Ducange, Baronius and Chrysostom which his parishioners at Paddington had given to him when he left for Norwich.[25]

The choir and library were only part of Goulburn's incessant activity, for he was faced with a number of difficult practical decisions which inevitably affected the relations of the chapter with the town and the diocese. Most important, perhaps, was the disputed line of the Lynn and Fakenham railway. An original proposal, in 1881, would have taken the line through the close and required the demolition of the Erpingham Gate. Although the Norwich petitions against this apparently succeeded, in 1882 a second and only slightly altered line was proposed, the bill embodying it reaching a second reading in the House of Commons. Goulburn organised a further campaign of opposition, by letter and personal approach in London and Norfolk, but final success did not come until January 1883, when the Lynn and Fakenham Company relinquished all proposals to take their line through any part of the close. The victory had involved Goulburn, and to a lesser extent his fellow canons, in two years of incessant campaigning, in the course of which approaches were made to all leading national politicians, local members of parliament, some of whom were said to be hostile to the chapter's case, and to the *Times* newspaper.[26]

---

23. NRO, DCN 121/5, 21 January 1887 to 14 July 1887; DCN 121/4, notes of chapter discussions made by Goulburn.

24. NRO, DCN 121/5, 6 December 1887.

25. NRO, DCN 124/11, 17 September 1897.

26. Drawn from Goulburn's diary for 1882.

Fig. 208. Dean Cranage in part of the processions at the service of thanksgiving marking the 1300th anniversary of the diocese of East Anglia, 1930.

Even more time and energy were expended on what became the distinctive feature of Goulburn's deanery, the gradual organisation of the restoration of the cathedral fabric. The details of this restoration are discussed elsewhere,[27] but it must be emphasised how completely the dean was identified with the work. It is true that the initial steps of installing gas lighting, and improving the heating in the building, were taken just before his time of office began, but they made possible the increasing use of the cathedral and its services in the life of the city and the diocese which he was able to initiate.[28] The financial arrangement for restoration involved him in much detailed administration and, what is more, it is clear from the chapter minutes that he and his wife themselves contributed very liberally to the costs.

Throughout the restoration Goulburn took an active interest in the archaeological and historical questions raised by the work. He can be seen, for instance, consulting experts at the Victoria and Albert Museum about the altarpiece of the Jesus Chapel, and attending meetings of local and national antiquarian societies to discuss the problems raised by the work.[29] Much of the period covered by his term of office unfortunately coincided with the onset of agricultural depression, so he was called

27. See pp. 718–27.
28. NRO, DCN 120/1/7, 4 December 1860; 4 June 1861.
29. NRO, DCN 121/9, various dates.

on not only to raise money for restoration but also to deal with recurrent shortfalls of cash in the regular income of the chapter. After 1884 the income of the chapter, apart from a capital sum of £12,000 set aside by order of the Ecclesiastical Commissioners as a fabric fund, consisted mainly of rack rents and tithe rentcharges. It is clear that the sums available to the chapter shrank very markedly during the last two decades of the century.[30] By 1887 the chapter clerk was reporting to a meeting of the chapter that the income of individual canons had shrunk to no more than £560 per annum. (It had been around £800 per annum sixty years earlier.) There were then proposals for economies in fabric repairs, and expenditure on the maintenance of the precinct was halted for six months before Christmas 1886. At the same time it was resolved to keep the cathedral bills for lighting and heating below £350 per annum, to dispense with the services of bedesmen as additional vergers, no longer to employ music copyists and to cease to maintain a cathedral fire brigade.[31]

This was unfortunate, but there is no doubt that every effort was made by the chapter to minimise the hardship to schools on chapter benefices; and to institutions like the diocesan training college for teachers, which had been partly founded by the dean and chapter and had relied very much on their continued support. At the height of the financial crisis the chapter was arranging, persuaded by Goulburn, to find furnishings for an infant nursery, mothers' meeting and class rooms, proposed by Mother Adèle for St James Pockthorpe in the inner city. For efforts of this sort, private charity, much of it from Goulburn and his wife, became essential. They were both indefatigable organisers of working parties and meetings in the deanery to aid, for example, bodies which would later become the Girls' Friendly Society and the Mothers' Union. The deanery was a centre of hospitality for those engaged in such charitable enterprises. It also seems to have served as a place to entertain the judges on circuit, visiting preachers, scholars consulting library manuscripts or studying sculpture in the cathedral, and candidates for lay clerkships coming to the cathedral for interview.[32]

It is not so obvious that there were any very close social relations between the deanery and the town authorities. This was of course a period when the commercial interests of the town, represented for instance by the Lynn and Fakenham Railway Company, or the Norwich Tramway Company (which the chapter opposed in 1886), were scarcely compatible with those of the chapter. It is true that the chapter's common land on Mousehold Heath had become a municipal park, that the opening times of the close gates were adjusted to allow easier access from the

30. See also below, pp. 684–85, 687
31. NRO, DCN 121/4, 18 January 1886; 7 September 1886; DCN 121/5, 21 January 1887; 6 December 1887; *Parliamentary Papers* (1836), xxxvi, p. 38.
32. NRO, DCN 121/4, 18 January 1886; DCN 121/1, fo. 7r.

inner town to the railway station, and for the grammar school scholars, and that the chapter collaborated with the town in the construction on chapter land of a new road from the railway station to Bishopbridge. Moreover, the cathedral building was made more accessible to the townspeople after 1886: on Sundays it was no longer locked between the services; lay sidesmen, who did not rely upon fees for their livelihood, were introduced; and after 1875 pews were allotted to the regular cathedral congregation. It is true that these arrangements on occasion led to disputes, but unseemly incidents were for the most part avoided. Seemly order, however, could not always be maintained in the precinct, the choir boys and other boisterous children being branded a continual nuisance by the more staid members of the chapter and close.[33]

Perhaps Goulburn's principal significance to the county and the diocese, apart from his gallant battle to protect the close from the Lynn and Fakenham Railway, must have seemed his role as a preacher on every conceivable occasion, his part in modernising and popularising the services of the cathedral, and his encouragement to the widespread introduction of popular, and especially diocesan services. His time in office began just after the church congress of 1865, which Bishop John Thomas Pelham (1857–93) had opposed, and his whole deanship was passed in Pelham's episcopate. It is plain that he had occasionally to tread carefully (*Hymns Ancient and Modern* were not to the bishop's taste) but there is not much other evidence of disagreement between them. Goulburn's choice of preachers and plans for courses of sermons went unopposed.[34]

The dean had, as we have seen, paid increasing attention to the development of the choir, greatly enhancing its place in the life and worship of the cathedral. His foundation of the guild of choir boys was symptomatic of the attempts made throughout the last two decades of the century to involve the laity, especially those living in Norwich, in the affairs of the cathedral. Goulburn's method of publicity, apart from his participation in the governing bodies of the diocesan training school and of the Jenny Lind children's hospital fund, was the publication in the local press of the text of his many sermons. Towards the end of his term of office he was increasingly involved in great public services. These functions brought him into touch with the people of the diocese and especially with the resident landed gentry. His farewell to the cathedral took the characteristic form of seven lectures on the seven words of Christ on the cross; these were delivered in Holy Week in 1889 and published, at London and Norwich, in 1891. The general feeling of the chapter and the diocese about Goulburn's term of office is admirably summed up in the entry in the chapter orders of 1889 about the installation of the new nave pulpit as

33. NRO, DCN 121/9, 16 August 1876.

34. Communicated by the Reverend N. Henderson.

a memorial to him: 'the chapter record sincere and grateful thanks for his invariable kindness, consideration and courtesy, which have conduced to the good feeling and harmony which have prevailed in the chapter'.[35]

It seems that this was, indeed, the end of a golden age: with the accession to power of William Lefroy, who was dean from 1889 to 1909, an entirely different atmosphere prevailed. The chapter minutes reflect a series of differences, not in themselves very great, but contributing to produce a feeling of unease. There had been, from 1886, a long dispute about the siting of a dustbin in the close and this was followed by a heartfelt complaint from Archdeacon Henry Ralph Neville about the 'groaning' which hailed the monthly 'read' service; by trouble about replacing a sliding door in the residentiary's stall with a curtain; and over covering the seat with cushions of velvet.[36] The precentor added to the uneasy atmosphere by objecting to a second reduction in the number of choir boys in the interests of economy and the suggestion that the gap they left should be filled by two lay clerks who could sing alto parts. Somewhat reluctantly the chapter responded to the precentor's demand for further seating for the popular nave service by authorising the purchase of a hundred chairs; and to his proposal in 1893 to remove fixed kneeling boards from the lay clerks' seats and to replace them with hassocks. Other measures of economy for which Archdeacon Neville was primarily responsible were the abolition of the office of chapter surveyor in 1896 and the use of volunteer sidesmen to replace an extra subsacrist. It was Neville too who sold unwanted musical instruments from the song school, using the proceeds to buy a mattress for gymnastic exercises for the boys.[37]

Dean Lefroy's early years were also marred by trouble about the bells. This had begun in 1888, with a complaint from the vicar of Hockwold about the unsatisfactory chiming for services. It was alleged that this resulted from a defect in the steel rope which worked the mechanism. The advice of Lord Grimthorpe (of Westminster's Big Ben fame) was sought, and that of the Norwich Association of Bell Ringers. The bell ringers reported that 'the sound was horrible'. Eventually Goulburn had paid £15 out of his own pocket for work recommended by Grimthorpe, but complaints did not cease, and later there were calls for an entirely new peal of bells.[38] Meanwhile fresh difficulties stemmed from economies in the employment of bedesmen as additional subsacrists; these culminated in 1898 in an attempt by a bedesman named Arthur Whiles to recover the post of porter, from which he had

35. NRO, DCN 121/7, 20 April 1889.

36. NRO, DCN 121/6, 5 June 1888; 2 August 1888; 14 September 1888.

37. NRO DCN, 121/A/7, 12 February 1889.

38. NRO, DCN 121/6, 14 February 1888; 11 May 1888.

been dismissed. There were complaints, too, about insubordinate choir boys and some boys were in fact dismissed in 1900.[39] In all this period a series of repairs and restorations launched before Goulburn's time was coming to an end. In 1899 the cost of the restoration of the nave, consisting of 'unflaking', that is, careful removing of the plaster from the walls, was met by Samuel Hoare, the MP for Norwich, and his wife, as a celebration of their wedding anniversary. Although electric power was introduced to the close, there is no evidence of its immediate employment, except for supplying light. When a new organ was ordered in 1898, a gas engine, to be combined with hydraulic power, was acquired for it. By 1900 this was causing a nuisance by 'puffing', to which the bishop took exception. Meanwhile the new organ, a 'Celestial', built by Norman and Beard Limited of Norwich and London, had been installed, at the expense of Mr H.J. Barclay: recitals to display its powers were being held before the end of 1899.[40]

Dean Lefroy had other domestic difficulties which may well have embittered his tenure of office. There seem to have been attempts by speculators to acquire chapter property near to, but not inside, the close for development. Thorpe Hamlet, in particular, was finally surrendered in 1889, and in 1891 it was suggested that part of Browne's meadow in Ferry Road should be let for building. Later, in 1906, there was a dispute in which the city council opposed a proposal, because it represented a threat to open spaces in the town, to allow the sale of the late dean's kitchen garden in the lower close for building.[41] In 1891 the close had a population of 490, slightly fewer than in 1841; it had only eighty-eight inhabited houses, in contrast to ninety-six in 1841, and no houses were being built.[42] It was nevertheless being invaded by the outer world. Vagrants and noisy children had been the problems of the 1870s; in 1900 horses were being trained in the precinct by a horse-broker who had leased one of the chapter's stables. This was creating a serious nuisance. The almost completed restoration of the cathedral and, perhaps, the increasing numbers of popular nave services, brought large numbers of visitors and sightseers into the close. Some, at least, came from the growing resorts on the north-east coast of the county which were served by the railways; day excursions brought them into Thorpe station. Between the wars the cathedral authorities were to welcome, and exploit, such visitors, but in 1898 a more hostile attitude seems to have prevailed. It was then reported that visitors were defacing the walls of the cloister and other parts of the building; and that it had proved necessary to put up warning notices in the threatened areas.[43]

39. NRO, DCN 124/11, 20 October 1898, 27 October 1900.
40. NRO, DCN 124/11, 13 April 1898; 7 June 1898; 7 July 1898; 28 October 1898; 27 May 1899; 6 June 1899; 26 October 1899.
41. NRO, DCN 121/7, 12 February 1887; DCN 122/1, 22 February 1892.
42. NRO, DCN 122/2, unpaginated.
43. NRO DCN 124/11, 24 July 1900; 7 June 1898.

Perhaps the most disagreeable domestic difficulty faced by Dean Lefroy was a claim made in 1898 by the archdeacon of Norwich (who was not a member of the chapter) to precedence in the cathedral processions. This apparently small domestic squabble grew during the next year, with the claim being taken up by other archdeacons, who appealed to the bishop to intervene. Advice was taken by Lefroy, who early in 1900 was able to announce that the right to order processions belonged to him as dean; that no appeal could lie to the bishop; because the archdeacons were outside the cathedral foundation.[44]

The gifts made to the cathedral by the Hoares and Barclays symbolise the growing identification of the people of Norwich and Norfolk with the cathedral and its affairs. Although this had been noticeable in Goulburn's time, and was to reach even greater heights after 1914, it was certainly helped by Lefroy and his successors before 1914. The chapter minutes and the newspaper cuttings which record, for example, the opening of the newly-restored nave, and the launching of the recitals which displayed the powers of the new organ, illustrate this admirably. A number of public, county-wide, functions reinforce the same theme, from the special service of supplication on 3 December 1901 for the war in South Africa, through the charity festival service of June 1900, which raised £1015 for the Jenny Lind endowment for sick children, to the unveiling of a soldiers' memorial on 19 November 1904. The coronation of Edward VII on 9 August 1902, perhaps because of his residence in the county, was marked by a special musical service, a coronation dinner for all the members of the foundation and the cathedral staff, and a treat for the choristers.[45]

Lefroy's successors as dean had much shorter terms of office than most of their predecessors; three deans followed him in the next eighteen years, before the long term of D. H. S. Cranage. Russell Wakefield, dean from 1909 to 1911 and afterwards bishop of Birmingham, has left almost no mark on the chapter records. Bishop Bertram Pollock (1910–42) recorded that his London life was of more interest to him than anything in Norwich; he was a moderate high churchman, who had been deeply involved in ritual controversies but whose real concern was social questions.[46] The next dean, H. C. Beeching, who was in office from 1911 to 1919, was a well-known man of letters, a contemporary and friend of Archbishop Cosmo

44. NRO, DCN 124/11, 6 December 1898; 10 January 1900.
45. NRO, DCN 124/11, 13 April 1898; 16 December 1901; 3 June 1902.
46. B. Pollock, *A Twentieth-Century Bishop: Recollections and Reflections* (London, 1944), p. 80.

Gordon Lang, perhaps best known then and after for his poem 'Going Down Hill on a Bicycle':

> God who created me
> Nimble and light of limb,
> With lifted feet, hands still,
> I am poised and down the hill.[47]

Beeching had learned something of Lefroy's troubles before he arrived in Norwich, recording at the outset of his term: 'in December 1911 I decided to hold my tongue for a month, and my hand for a year'. There were, in fact, very few changes in his time: apart from Archdeacon Brooke Westcott, his colleagues in the chapter were in Norwich only in the months of residence, and he met with little opposition in his plans to introduce greater dignity into the services. Copes and mitres were accepted apparently without question. He recorded that when the executors of John Sheepshanks (bishop of Norwich from 1893 to 1909) had offered a gift of altar frontals, his predecessor's wife had declined them without consulting the chapter. Despite this, Beeching was able to equip the chancel afresh, with the help of the Gurney family who gave altar frontals and candlesticks. Not surprisingly, he appreciated some of the trials of juvenile behaviour: 'the fidgetiness of the choristers was abnormal even for boys, because', he commented perceptively, 'they could not lean back with comfort'. It is characteristic of his time and type that he devised a scheme of boy monitors, improved the seats and eventually incorporated choir boys and monitors in a boy scout troop.[48]

The First World War had made it impossible for Beeching to carry out his cherished scheme to return the ancient episcopal seat, which had been given to the bishop sixty years before, but some of his other efforts were more positive. They range from schemes to insure the houses in the close against damage by hostile aircraft to the imposition of a fee of £50 to be given to the fabric fund, for monuments erected in the cathedral to anyone other than members of the foundation. In 1916 a war bonus was arranged for cathedral servants on active service, and the advice of the Westminster Abbey authorities was sought about the protection of the buildings.[49] There had been some activity at Norwich, inspired, it seems, by the antiquary St John Hope, in the sorting and arranging of the medieval muniments. It seems to have been Beeching's suggestion, to which the chapter agreed, that any account rolls from other cathedrals found at Norwich should be returned to their original owners. Evidence of this exchange has been found in several cathedral

---

47. A. Quiller-Couch, *Oxford Book of English Verse* (Oxford, 1930), no. 855.

48. NRO, DCN 124/1.

49. NRO, DCN 124/12, 1 June 1915; 7 December 1915; 3 April 1916.

collections. It was noted by Beeching that reciprocal action did not always occur; the dean of Windsor declined to send back the pre-Reformation documents from Norwich which were held in his archives.[50] Bishop Pollock had little more to say about Beeching than that he made difficulties (unspecified) about the installation of honorary canons, but that he always read the lessons in service very impressively: 'his rendering of the second lesson on Christmas morning ['In the beginning was the Word'] is something to remember'.[51]

All that Pollock could find to say about the next dean, John Wakefield Willink (1919–27), is that he came from Great Yarmouth via Birmingham and that he was a very acceptable minister to families living in the close. There is little mention in any source of other activities and he seems to have died suddenly early in 1927. In the chapter minutes the announcement of his death was followed by an emergency agreement that the canon in residence should be responsible for services, should give out all notices and dismiss the congregation.[52]

Willink had been in office less than eight years but the next dean, D. H. S. Cranage, was destined to hold the post for eighteen years (1927–45). These were years of turmoil and change sufficient completely to alter the nature of the cathedral institution and especially the office of dean. Cranage was a man of immense vitality, who seems to have been able to work incessantly without exhausting himself, and who had wide and varied interests. His original experience had been at Cambridge, as secretary from 1902 to 1924 of the scheme for local lectures. One of the products of this scheme had been the great ecclesiastical historian, Alexander Hamilton Thompson. Cranage belonged to a similar group of antiquarian-minded medievalists who were to reshape local and regional history in the first half of the twentieth century. When the Cambridge board of extra-mural studies replaced the local lectures scheme, Cranage acted as its first secretary from 1924 to 1928; he then moved to the deanery of Norwich. His antiquarian interests were apparent from the start, and he soon became a vice-president of the London Society of Antiquaries. Early in his time he proposed, on 3 April 1930, the publication of an illustrated guide book to the cathedral. This was soon followed by a proposal for the Norwich Players to put on a cathedral pageant. The rest of the chapter did not see their way to agree to this but did not interfere with the next scheme, which was a great festival to mark the 1300th anniversary of the introduction of Christianity. This was celebrated with a garden party, luncheon and choral celebration. All incumbents of livings in the diocese were invited to this celebration which seems to have been a great

50. D. M. Owen, 'Bringing Home the Archives', *Archives*, 8 (1968) pp. 123–29.

51. Pollock, *Twentieth-Century Bishop*, p. 80.
52. *Who Was Who*, v, p. 252.

success. Also in the celebratory year, building began on the Regimental Chapel to the designs of Sir Charles Nicholson, on the site of the former Lady Chapel. An important agent in Cranage's schemes to popularise the cathedral's image and to exploit its general appeal was his proposal in 1929, immediately realised, for an association of the Friends of Norwich Cathedral, which was to play an important part in future schemes for restoration. In 1938, for instance, the Friends were offering to defray the costs of cleaning the cloister and were discussing proposals for a new organ. The intention of Cranage to appeal to tourists visiting the city and the county was quite unabashed.[53] Bishop Pollock recorded that twice at least on summer Bank Holidays the dean lectured in the cathedral to parties of visitors from the coastal resorts.[54] The influx of visitors to the cathedral in this last decade before the outbreak of the war was, in fact, very marked. Some members of the chapter were concerned enough to discuss officially the noise and disturbance they created, and in particular 'their very unsuitable costume'.

There were, of course, other and more dignified activities in the cathedral: a new high altar was planned in 1932 and Queen Mary came to visit this and related projects during the year. A year later, on 13 July 1933, the centenary of the Oxford Movement was celebrated with a sermon from the dean and appropriate music. In 1935 the jubilee of King George V was marked by a service at which the collection was to be given to King George's fund for the unemployed. Finally, on 29 January 1936, a memorial service was held for the king, who had died at Sandringham early in the year.[55]

Cranage was thus well established at the outbreak of the war as an earnest upholder of historical tradition, and of the role of the cathedral in the life of the diocese of Norwich. At the same time he was earning a sound reputation as prolocutor of the clergy in the convocation of Canterbury, a place he filled from 1936 until he retired in 1945, and in which he gained the approval of Archbishop Lang. His predecessor had been a difficult man, who created trouble, but Lang recorded that 'the atmosphere was better under the very capable management of Cranage dean of Norwich'.[56] It was indeed Cranage's powers of management which saw him through the last difficult six years of his time in Norwich. He started well, employing Professor Tristram to clean the effigy (then thought by many to be that of Herbert de Losinga) on the outer wall of the north transept, and with plans, slow to be realised, for a new organ case, as well as a series of minor alterations to the statutes. There was also a proposal to install a series of gates in the close to minimise the risk from

53. NRO, DCN 124/1, 4 June 1929; 7 November 1929; 3 April 1930.
54. Pollock, *Twentieth-Century Bishop*, p. 80.
55. NRO, DCN 124/1, 1 February 1932; 13 July 1933; 29 January 1936; 6 April 1938.
56. J. G. Lockhart, *Cosmo Gordon Lang* (London, 1949), p. 334.

speeding cycles (chiefly those ridden by schoolboys attending the technical school and speeding through Gooseberry Green).[57] As 1939 went on and war loomed, such considerations were obscured by preparations for the emergency which was threatening. An air raid protection scheme for the district probate registry at 69 The Close was initiated in July. At the beginning of September more ominous steps were taken: the Ethelbert Gate was to remain unlocked; the level of cathedral heating was to be restricted; and, as the electricity supply was overloaded and the 'blackout' became urgent, nave services were transferred to afternoons. Later in the same year Cranage, on his own responsibility, hired the Stewart Hall (in Charing Cross in the centre of Norwich) for evening services. Tenants living close to the back gates of the close were allowed to have keys to them, in case of fire. The organ chamber had been poorly ventilated thus causing a fire in April 1938, which destroyed the organ: insurance paid for it was used to improve ventilation and rebuild the organ. Meanwhile it was decided to leave all the gates unlocked until 7 pm to allow access for fire engines.[58]

Preoccupation with air raid precautions inevitably continued: on 4 June 1940 a first-aid point was established in the deanery, business premises in the close organised fire-watching rotas, and access to the cathedral roofs was improved. It was decided, however, on the advice of the RAF, not to attempt to camouflage the cathedral. On the other hand a professional report on fire precautions recommended the installation of fire doors at the base of the cathedral tower, the blocking of the tower louvres and the removal to safety of the library and the diocesan records. At the same time a water tank was constructed and additional ladders provided. Despite all the precautions the cathedral and the close suffered from two air raids in May and June 1942. Incendiary devices caused serious fires in the roofs of the transepts, destroyed three houses in the close (nos 63, 66 and 67) and badly damaged a fourth (no. 68); a high explosive bomb fell between the palace and the north transept but did not explode. In the same year, Dean Cranage recorded, there had been blitzes on the city on 27 and 29 April which resulted in the death of 200 people.[59]

As the war continued, pressures on the chapter intensified. Dwellers in the close now had to endure black smoke emitted by the Bally shoe factory. They and others had listened to the king's Christmas Day broadcast in the cathedral in 1939. Troops

---

57. This refers to Gooseberry Walk which runs from the bottom of Hook's Walk to Bishopgate. The green probably developed from the medieval great chequer garden. See figs 114, 209, pp. 235, 636.

58. This paragraph is based on entries in the unpaginated chapter clerk's chapter book 13, 1939–56, kept at the cathedral. I am grateful

to Mr Colin Pordham and the dean for facilitating access to this material.

59. D. H. S. Cranage, *Not Only a Dean: Being the Reminiscences of the Very Reverend D. H. S. Cranage* (London, 1952); E. C. Le Grice, *Norwich: The Ordeal of 1942* (Norwich, 1942). I am grateful to the dean for sending me a copy of this item. NRO, DCN 107/39.

were allowed to drill in the close. The dean decided to agree to this in order to avoid the exercise of compulsory powers, but not all the chapter approved and the vice-dean in particular objected to the decision. Demands intensified: in December 1940 a government office had requisitioned number 75 The Close, public shelters were installed at numbers 12 and 14. By March 1943 the officials of the American Red Cross were installed in the palace and were demanding that they should have access to the close through the western gates. Numbers 8 and 10 were requisitioned by the military authorities for auxiliary territorial use, and the chapter felt obliged at the same time to offer Dial House (number 53, on the lower green) as a temporary judges' lodging.

At the beginning of the war the chapter clerk had been reasonably optimistic; the only decline in revenue would be, he thought, from the loss of visitors' fees, but it is clear from the chapter minutes that the pinch was very soon felt. In December 1941 the Friends of the cathedral lent their investment fund to discharge the debt on the organ. A year earlier the stipends of precentor and organist were cut, service papers were to be no longer printed but typed and no money was to be paid into the library fund. Such non-local appeals as one for the protection of Monte Cassino were turned down. More ominously, repeated attempts were made by the dean to persuade the Ecclesiastical Commissioners to allow him to sell surplus or duplicate books from the library, to house which a chamber had been prepared in the Erpingham Gate. When finally the dean was successful, he reported that a small selection of books (one incunable, several early atlases and geographies) was offered to the Cambridge University Library, but not, apparently, accepted.

The principal effect of war on the cathedral, apart of course from the raids of 1942, was one of dislocation of its life. In 1941 the three-hour service was omitted on Good Friday, although the *Messiah* was still performed. A philharmonic society carol service took place just before Christmas. There were many visitors and the local photographer Mr E.C. Le Grice was invited by the chapter to produce a guide book for them. In double-summer time the cathedral remained open until 9 pm and the close gates until 10 pm. Most disturbingly, perhaps, the amount of heavy traffic in the city centre increased inexorably. As early as 1941 the chapter was beginning to protest about this and to demand, without effect, that the city engineer should make Tombland and Cathedral Street one way to traffic, and 'to exclude' traffic from St Faith's Lane. Dean Cranage retired at the end of the war, tired, but relatively undefeated, leaving for his successors a considerable work of reconstruction.[60]

60. Norwich Cathedral, chapter book 13, various dates.

30

The Close

Ian Atherton

In 1096 Bishop Herbert de Losinga founded not only a cathedral, priory and episcopal palace in Norwich, he also carved out precincts for the monastery and grounds for the palace.[1] These were to serve many of the needs of the monks and the bishop's household: separation from the laity and a degree of retreat and security; ground for grazing and growing foodstuffs and medicinal plants; access to the river for transport; a setting for the cathedral, marking out the land inside the walls as distinctively different from that beyond, with the gateways as symbolic crossing-points;[2] and lordship over the soil, making the monks territorial landlords over part of the great city of Norwich. The creation of the close also set up tensions which have informed its history over the succeeding nine centuries, in particular between the desire of its inhabitants for the close to be a place of peace, quite literally 'closed', and its siting within a bustling city. This conflict between seclusion and exposure has been perhaps the greatest determinant in shaping its history and topography.

Although the social world of the present-day close is in many ways the creation of the later seventeenth and eighteenth centuries, the main topographical features of the close were laid out during the middle ages, particularly the division of the precincts into three separate areas around the cathedral: the episcopal palace to the north; the upper close to the west and south west; and the lower close to the east and south east (see fig. 114). At the heart of the upper and lower closes stood two greens, Almary or Upper Green, also later known as Upper Square, and Brewer's or Lower Green, also later known as Lower Square. The main monastic buildings and obedientiaries' offices were gathered around these two greens, the more important ones closest to the cathedral church. In the upper close, the chambers of

1. See pp. 73–115. In addition to those noticed separately, I am indebted to various people for their help. Jonathan Finch supplied references and Jane Tillier ideas; Jeff Atherton,

    Hassell Smith, Nigel Tringham and Richard Wilson kindly read the chapter in draft, supplying comments and corrections.

2. See pp. 199, 201–2.

the communar, cellarer and master of the cellar, all important officials, stood on the east side of Almary Green, near the cloister, while the house, barn and offices of the less important almoner were in the south-west corner, furthest away from the church. The pattern was repeated in the lower close, with the prior's hall at the north-west corner (adjoining the east range of the cloister), the great granary along the north side of the green, and the bakery and brewery on the east side (where any noxious smells they produced were least likely to trouble the monks).[3] The building of separate houses first for the prior and later for the senior obedientiaries reflected the decline of the Benedictine ideals of a common life.

The topographical arrangement of the precincts also reflected the needs of the laity to gain access. A dichotomy is sometimes portrayed between the close in the middle ages as the preserve of the monks, and the 'invasion' of the laity after the Reformation. In fact, the laity were in evidence in the medieval precincts at Norwich, as at other cathedrals and abbeys. Just as the distinction between the nave for the laity and the choir for the monks was not maintained, so the close was never exclusively the preserve of the monks. None the less, the separation between monks and laity was preserved symbolically. For example, the 200 or so lay guests, servants and officials who were fed by the monastery every day ate in their own guest hall.[4] Many of the laity, however, were relegated to the margins. The site of the almonry in the south-west corner of the upper close reflected not only the relative lowliness of the almoner, it allowed the poor to gain access for alms without disturbing bishop, prior or services.

There were, at least by the later fifteenth century, shops in the precincts, but again at the margins – between the clocher next to the Erpingham Gate and the west door to the cathedral.[5] Norwich was by no means unique in this. There were shops around the clocher at Salisbury Cathedral and around the edge of the precincts of Westminster Abbey.[6] Moreover, some important laity did live within the close – the corrodians, for instance, while William Bauchun, lay officer of the granary (*granarius*), and his wife Magdalen probably resided in the precincts in the

3. Topographical details are based on the work of A. B. Whittingham published in: *Arch. J.*, 106 (1949); G. A. Metters, ed., *The Parliamentary Survey of Dean and Chapter Properties in and around Norwich in 1649* (NRS, 51, 1985), pp. 102–20; and *Communar Rolls*. Our understanding of the close will be greatly enhanced by a research project into its archaeology by Dr Roberta Gilchrist of the Centre of East Anglian Studies at the University of East Anglia. Until its completion all topographical judgements in this essay must be regarded as provisional.

4. See pp. 232, 235.

5. NRO, sacrists' rolls, 1490s; *NA*, 19 (1917), pp. xii–xiv.

6. Royal Commission on the Historical Monuments of England, *Salisbury: The Houses of the Close* (London, 1993), p. 24; B. Harvey, *Living and Dying in England, 1100–1540: The Monastic Experience* (Oxford, 1993), pp. xvii, 5.

Fig. 209. Hook's Walk, the lane running from Lower Green to Gooseberry or the Great Chequer Garden, one of the medieval 'ends' and still an area of smaller housing.

1290s.[7] By far the greatest concentration of laity, however, were the priory servants who lived along the ways to the Great Chequer Garden (this path is now known as Hook's Walk) and to Bishopgate, and at the head of the canal which ran down from Brewer's Green to the ferry. Thus, before 1500 we have the development of 'ends', areas of poorer housing tucked away from the cathedral and the two greens, just as in nucleated villages the areas of poorer housing were often away from the main streets and village green.[8] Although physically within the precincts, their separation from cathedral and priory was marked by the placing of three gates to the lower close barring the ways from Bishopgate, the Great Chequer Garden and the ferry. The 'ends' stood outside these gates.

Most of this topographical arrangement has been preserved in modern times. Although the three eastern gates have gone,[9] the houses in the 'ends' remain smaller

7. B. Dodwell, 'William Bauchun and his Connection with the Cathedral Priory at Norwich', *NA*, 36 (1975), p. 114.
8. I owe this point to Professor Hassell Smith.
9. The gate at the north-eastern corner of Lower Green was taken down in 1805: L. G. Bolingbroke, 'A Perambulation of a Part of the Cathedral Precinct with Notes on its Domestic Buildings and Some of their Inmates' (unpublished lecture, 1922), p. 23; there are copies in the Norfolk and Norwich Archaeological Society Library and the Local Studies Library of the Norwich City Library.

than the grand dwellings fronting the two greens (fig. 209). Many of the monastic buildings were converted to domestic use after 1538. Apart from the new houses built along Bishopgate at the beginning of the twentieth century, new building since the Reformation has not departed greatly from the areas already developed by 1500. Topographically, the Reformation marked no dramatic break in the history of the close.

The dissolution of the priory and changes over the following sixty years did, however, see an increase in the numbers of laity living in the close.[10] This was due to three main factors. First, there were simply more buildings available for rent. The ending of a common table (despite the abortive attempt to revive it under the 1620 statutes) left buildings such as the monastic granary free to be converted into houses. Secondly, the sudden steep decline in building operations at the cathedral after 1538 also freed space previously occupied by masons, glaziers and other craftsmen.[11] Thirdly, very many of the deans, prebendaries and cathedral officers were granted houses by the terms of the statutes but were, unlike the monks, resident in the close for only short periods, if at all. They often sublet their houses to supplement their incomes.[12] Prebendal houses might be sublet on condition that the tenants vacated the premises during the prebendary's period of residence, leaving the furniture for the prebendary's use.[13]

The dissolution of the priory and the influx of laity into the close brought a number of problems. The legal and governmental status of the precincts was muddied. The continuing jurisdictional disputes between the city and cathedral led to the chapter's desire to govern its own physical environs. The most significant stage in this battle was the royal grant in 1610 of the cathedral's own commission of the peace for the close.[14] For most of the next three centuries the dean and chapter would be masters of their own backyard.

A further problem was the number of alehouses which were established in the close. Prebendary George Gardiner admitted in 1569 that the brewhouse on the east side of Lower Green had become an unlicensed tippling house, the resort of 'all evil and naughty persons'. At the precinct sessions in 1611 the jury presented four people for selling beer without licence, and a fifth, William Goodwyn, was imprisoned for

10. Norwich's experience parallels that of other cathedrals. At Salisbury (a secular cathedral), although the Reformation saw many laity move into the close, surplus canonry housing had been rented out to layfolk in the fifteenth century: Royal Commission, *Salisbury*, p. 23.

11. The last major construction project at the cathedral before the nineteenth century was the vaulting of both transepts in the years after 1509.

12. In the 1712 land tax assessment for the close the dean was listed as resident but the six prebendaries had all sublet their houses to undertenants: NRO, NCR case 23/28. The extent of subletting can also be judged from Metters, *Parliamentary Survey*.

13. For example, NRO, DCN 26/9/77, agreement of 1814.

14. See above, p. 526.

three days on this account. In 1613 and again in 1615 the jury presented six people for this offence.[15] The widow Alice Wright was notorious for running an unlicensed alehouse in the close, regularly allowing a houseful to drink and play at cards and bowls during service times. On one Sunday in 1620 she was twice visited by the constables: the first time they found six men drinking there; the second there were twenty. The justices' response was to license her premises, but only on condition that she closed during service and sermon times. They were powerless to do much else, such was the magnitude of the problem. At the visitation of 1596 the dean and chapter had been ordered to suppress 'the many alehouses' in the close, but to no avail.[16] The problems of tippling houses diminished only as the close became the fashionable residence of county gentry later in the seventeenth century.

These developments meant that by the early seventeenth century the precincts, packed with tenements, shops and alehouses, can have looked little different from the rest of the city. The inhabitants and others complained of tippling, 'necessary houses', blocked drains and rubbish, the sorts of complaints to be found in any early-modern community.[17]

The chapter, like the priory, managed its own physical space. Indeed, the close was the only one of its estates in which it took a direct interest.[18] In the later Tudor period this meant realising a quick profit by tearing down those parts of the fabric deemed no longer necessary to sell the building materials. The clocher, Lady Chapel, chapter house and the church of St Mary in the Marsh (on the south side of Brewer's Green) were all demolished.[19] A more constructive attitude evolved from the 1620s (although it was interrupted by the Civil War and abolition). Three factors were involved. Gradually, deans and chapters became more certain about their own survival. Secondly, the 'great rebuilding' of England at this time saw very many houses rebuilt in a grander vernacular style. Thirdly, the rising status of the clergy as a whole led many clerics to expect better housing. Accordingly, the chapter began to provide more substantial houses for its members. One such house in the upper close (now number 71), just to the south of the Erpingham Gate and on the site of the monastic clocher, was built by Prebendaries John Hassall and Fulk Robartes in the 1620s. Like many other prebendal houses it was later let to lay tenants: improved by William Burleigh, cathedral understeward, in the 1670s, it became known as Burleigh's tenement.[20]

The 1650s saw a spurt of uncontrolled building after the dean and chapter were abolished. With no effective controls to curb them, several speculators erected small

15. Bolingbroke, 'Perambulation', p. 21; NRO, DCN 81/3–5.

16. NRO, DCN 81/7; Bolingbroke, 'Perambulation', p. 21.

17. NRO, DCN 82/12; *CSPD, 1635*, p. xxx.

18. For their other estates, see chapter 31.

19. See pp. 502–3, 529.

20. NRO, DCN 86/29; J. F. Williams and B. Cozens-Hardy, eds, *Extracts from the Two Earliest Minute Books of the Dean and Chapter*

Fig. 210. Numbers 3 and 4 The Close, built by Jeremy Vynn, alderman and mayor of Norwich, and his wife Susan in 1701 on the site of the almonry granary.

tenements for letting to the poor at rack rents.[21] After 1660 the restored chapter embarked on a policy of controlled building, allowing little extra housing but encouraging tenants (by abatement of fines) to rebuild existing houses in grander fashion. A number of these late seventeenth- or early eighteenth-century improved houses can still be seen in the close (fig. 210). Usually the dean and chapter stipulated that they had to be of a certain rentable value (typically between £10 and £16) and 'fit for gentlemen to live in'.[22] In 1703 Thornhaugh Gurdon was granted a lease of the former almonry which by then had become a storehouse and stables ('a long range of thatched building, an eye sore in the Upper Green') on condition that he built 'a fair house for a gentleman to live in of the value of at least £12 per annum'; this, the chapter hoped, would be 'a great ornament to the Upper Green'. In spite of these directions, it was ill-built and had to be partially reconstructed in 1758.[23]

note 20 continued
of Norwich Cathedral, 1566–1649 (NRS, 24, 1953), pp. 63–66, 68; Metters, *Parliamentary Survey*, p. 105. The houses in the close were not numbered until 1909 after reluctance from the chapter: NRO, DCN 24/11, fos 24r, 173v–174r, 271, 277. Previously all properties had individual and changeable names based on the last or a previous tenant.

21. NRO, DCN 115/1, p. 229.
22. NRO, DCN 27/1, p. 143; DCN 115/1, p. 24.
23. NRO, DCN 115/1, p. 249. Now number 2 The Close: Metters, *Parliamentary Survey*, p. 107.

From the later seventeenth century the dean and chapter also spent their own money on improving the close. Gravel paths were laid, lime trees planted in Upper and Lower Greens, and a gardener employed.[24] The dean and chapter, aware of fashion in London and Bath, realised these improvements fifty years before commercial pleasure gardens were set out along the Wensum south of the close. Certainly, other cathedral precincts such as Lichfield, Salisbury and Gloucester were not landscaped until the mid or late eighteenth century.[25] The precincts at Norwich were transformed from a shambles into the theatre of the polite. They became a fashionable place for the better sort to promenade, where 'the young ladies of the town (and at public times the county too)' strove 'to out do [one] another in showing airs and graces to inspirit and warm the devotion of the beaux'.[26] Both cathedral and close were integral to the development of Norwich as a provincial centre with a 'season' for the county's gentry, the former with its assize service, the latter providing one of the main arenas for display. A visitor to Norwich in 1712 was much less impressed with the cathedral and bishop's palace (both described as 'not very handsome') than with the close, which he thought 'very pleasant, many gentleman living in it in very pretty houses'.[27]

The improvement of the physical surroundings was only part of the scheme to create an environment for polite society; the dean and chapter also wanted to manage those who occupied that space. Partly this was pragmatism, partly an expression of the cathedral's mission to the world. In erecting houses for the gentry, the chapter attracted powerful friends for the cathedral. The close became 'the place which most of the gentry of the country that come to live in this city desire to dwell in'.[28] As in other cathedral precincts, lesser traders were discouraged, particularly by comparison with the pre-Civil War period. Humphrey Prideaux (prebendary 1681–1702 and dean 1702–24), himself a member of a Cornish gentry family, described the close as 'not a place of trade but where persons of better quality on their widowhood, declining age or on other motives choose to reside for their more convenient attendance on God's worship at the cathedral church' and as 'so convenient a place

24. NRO, DCN 115/1, pp. 61, 215; DCN 24/4, fos 79–80r; DCN 29/4/37; DCN 11/2 (1680); DCN 11/3 (1688–89); DCN 11/4 (1698–1700); DCN 11/5 (1702, 1705, 1708); DCN 11/6 (1711); DCN 11/7 (1724); MS 78, p. 61. Bodleian Library, MS Tanner 133, fo. 54. Alderman Jeremy Vynn also paid towards the trees in the upper close.

25. N. J. Tringham, 'The Cathedral and the Close', *VCH Staffordshire*, xiv, Lichfield, ed. M. W. Greenslade (Oxford, 1990), p. 59;

Royal Commission, *Salisbury*, p. 34; S. J. Evans, 'Cathedral Life at Gloucester in the Early Seventeenth Century', *Bristol and Gloucestershire Archaeological Society Transactions*, 80 (1961), pp. 6–7.

26. Bodleian Library, MS Tanner 311, fo. 117r.

27. Thomas Major's diary, Gloucester Record Office, MS D421/F32, 8 August 1712. I am indebted to Mr P. R. Evans for a transcript of this entry.

28. NRO, DCN 29/4/37.

of retirement' for 'the gentry of the county'.[29] It had become like a miniature Bath beside the Wensum. Some traders, however, remained in the close, but they tended to provide luxuries for the gentlefolk who lived there. At the beginning of the eighteenth century the close housed William Holland, a London hatmaker, who advertised 'fine beavers, beaverets, casters, beaver-carolinas' for gentlemen, 'and fine cloth hats of the newest fashion, as cheap as can be bought in London'.[30] There was also John Oslin, who could 'furnish all gentlemen and others with all sorts of July flower plants, auriculas, and others'; he also had a mourning chariot for sale.[31]

The chapter wished positively to exclude three classes of people from the close: nonconformists, Roman Catholics and the poor. All were seen as a threat to the cathedral, or at the very least disadvantageous, and leases were supposed to contain covenants against the subletting of houses to such undesirables.[32] In fact, the chapter never managed wholly to exclude all three categories. At the time of Bishop Compton's census of 1676 the close contained 382 adult conformists, two adult nonconformists and thirteen adult papists, the greatest concentration of Roman Catholics in Norwich and over a quarter of the recorded total for the whole city.[33]

The chapter complained most bitterly about the numbers of poor in the precincts. The close was a separate jurisdiction with its own poor rate levied upon its wealthier inhabitants, particularly the dean and prebendaries. The rate increased markedly: the dean paid sixteen shillings in 1618; he was paying £3 a year in the 1680s and £9 by 1713.[34] One tenant who threatened to subdivide her house and rent it to the indigent was warned that it would be 'very prejudicial to the close in filling it with the poor', while the actions of another, who converted the tenements where sixteen families lived into three good houses, were described as 'very ornamental to the place, as well as advantageous to the church'.[35] There is a certain irony in the contrast between the cathedral's Christian mission to the poor and its statutory provision for six poor men on the one hand, and the chapter's zeal in seeking to exclude all other poor persons from the close on the other. Yet, as Dean Prideaux

29. NRO, DCN 115/1, pp. 145–46; DCN 115/2, pp. 247–50. The chapters of Salisbury and Lichfield tried to restrict the numbers of traders in their precincts, but with only limited success: Royal Commission, *Salisbury*, p. 24; Tringham, 'Cathedral and Close', p. 58.

30. His advertisement appeared regularly in the *Norwich Gazette* from 1707 to 1710; see, for example, no. 21, 26–29 March 1707, and no. 186, 22–29 April 1710. NRO, DCN 115/2, pp. 247–50.

31. *Norwich Gazette*, no. 131, 12–19 March 1709; no. 186, 22–29 April 1710.

32. NRO, DCN 115/1, p. 2; DCN 27/1, pp. 143, 145, 163, 169.

33. A. Whiteman, ed., *The Compton Census of 1676* (Records of Social and Economic History, new series, 10, 1986), pp. 190–94, 216–17. In 1697 Prideaux calculated that the close had 620 inhabitants: London, Lambeth Palace Library, MS 930, no. 80.

34. NRO, DCN 82/17; DCN 115/3, p. 3.

35. NRO, DCN 24/4, fo. 55; DCN 27/1, pp. 86–87.

lamented, 'there are already in the close abundance of poor which we cannot get rid of'.[36]

Manipulation of space and occupiers was insufficient for the dean and chapter; they desired to control the activities of persons in the close. Control of exit and entry was regulated by the locking of the precinct gates at night.[37] The conversion of houses into shops or taverns was forbidden and the chapter attempted to regulate the number of alehouses in and even around the close.[38] One tenant, engaged in a battle with the chapter, deliberately installed a mason in her house: he awoke everyone at 4 am when he started chipping and chiselling – 'the knocking of his hammer would from that time suffer none that dwell in the Upper Green to take their rest and the grating of his saw was very unpleasant music to them all the day'. His workshop was closed down.[39] Walking and talking in the church and disorderly behaviour in the precincts during services were punished.[40] Resident gentry were less easily controlled. They wished to build their own coach houses but Prideaux thought the close 'too much built already'. Some went ahead and built them anyway, much to the annoyance of the largely impotent dean and chapter who could rarely get the offending buildings taken down.[41] One hundred years later such difficulties could still recur. In 1830 George Morse, a member of a well-known Norwich family, violently obstructed the chapter's workmen digging a drain outside his house in the close, sending his own man to fill in the trench and shouting at the labourers that he was as good a gentleman as the dean (the Hon. George Pellew, son-in-law of Lord Sidmouth).[42]

There were long-running problems between the chapter and the officials of St Mary in the Marsh, the parish which was practically coterminous with the close. Disputes occurred over who should pay for the repair of the highways and over the setting of the poor rate. The dean and prebendaries felt that the parish assessments were arbitrary and punitive. When the chapter complained, the inhabitants, according to Prideaux, were whipped up into what he called a 'mutiny' (and 'mutiny' was the word Prideaux always used when the parish disagreed with the chapter) against him and the prebendaries by John Richardson, the minister of St Luke's Chapel. In 1709 Richardson allegedly fulminated, 'what have we been these twenty years making war against the king of France to defend ourselves from arbitrary government and must we now submit to the arbitrary government of a company of little fellows?'.[43]

36. NRO, DCN 115/1, p. 231.
37. NRO, DCN 24/4, fos 103v–104r; W. Laud, *Works*, ed. W. Scott and P. Bliss, 7 vols (Oxford, 1847–60), v, p. 483.
38. NRO, DCN 27/1, p. 143; DCN 115/1, pp. 216–17.
39. NRO, DCN 29/4/37.
40. NRO, DCN 115/2, pp. 240, 283; Bodleian Library, MS Tanner 133, fo. 182.
41. NRO, DCN 24/4, fos 79–80r; DCN 115/1, pp. 213–16; DCN 115/3, p. 43; DCN 29/4/37.
42. NRO, DCN 120/2C/44–47.
43. NRO, DCN 115/1, pp. 47–50, 56–58; DCN 115/2, pp. 149, 211, 251.

The dean and chapter were by no means always successful in their aims of creating and controlling their own environment. Indeed, criticisms about the lack of government in the close persisted from the city's complaints in the early years of the seventeenth century to Prideaux's claim in 1697 that 'the close is grown the most disorderly part of the whole city, and more lewd things are done in it than in all Norwich besides'.[44] There seems to be a paradox, between those who saw the close as the fashionable place to live, full of 'all sorts of conveniences to recommend it',[45] and those who represented it as the worst governed part of the city, teeming with poor and overflowing with alehouses. In part, it is necessary to set the complaints in context. Most came from writers trying to prove a point, whether it be from the city maintaining that the close should come under its jurisdiction, or from Prideaux that Dean Fairfax was grossly incompetent. Prideaux's views need to be set alongside his strictures against vice and immorality in general and his convictions about the debauchery of the minor officers of the cathedral.[46] Moreover, there was a rudimentary social separation in the close, with the larger houses and their wealthier occupants fronting onto the greens, and the smaller and poorer houses clustered behind, especially along the ways to the ferry and Bishopgate – the medieval 'ends'.[47] That the two worlds of rich and poor could remain substantially separate is suggested by the depositions taken at the trial of John Stukeley. The maids, minor canons and some of the tradesmen knew Stukeley and one another well. There were few secrets among this group, as they watched and gossiped with one another from their garrets, along the lanes and in the back yards, but they were reticent about revealing much to chapter members who seemed unaware of many of the goings on in the close.[48] The prebendaries were, after all, usually only resident in the close for two months in the year and this limited presence made their control of the close more difficult.[49]

By the mid eighteenth century the close had settled down to a comfortable and easy-going rhythm, much of which was to persist for the next two centuries, with strong echoes surviving today. The large houses fronting the two greens were among the most fashionable in Norwich. Unlicensed alehouses had been suppressed and the remaining five inns (the Ferry House, the Gate House, the Black Jack, the Three Cranes and the Garden House or Golden Horse Shoes) were respectable

44. See above, pp. 525–26; BL, Additional MS 22620, fo. 111r; Bodleian Library, MS Tanner 133, fo. 14r; MS Tanner 311, fos 4, 49–50; London, Lambeth Palace Library, MS 930, no. 80.

45. E. M. Thompson, ed., *The Letters of Humphrey Prideaux* (Camden Society, new series, 15, 1875), pp. 147–48.

46. See above, pp. 567–68, 573.

47. See, for example, the 1649 survey of the close: Metters, *Parliamentary Survey*, pp. 29–51.

48. NRO, DCN 33/22 (1702).

49. Attendance at the cathedral service by the dean and prebendaries is recorded in the three surviving chanter's or precentor's books, for 1629–30, 1635–36 and 1637–38: NRO, DCN 39/30–32.

enough to be used by the chapter and polite society. A coffee house for gentlemen was opened at the Gate House in 1758, while in 1773 the Garden House held a flower festival.[50] The poorer sort tended to be servants in the greater houses or confined to the smaller tenements away from the two greens. The close had a highly-skewed sex ratio, with far more women than men, particularly young servants, and a high proportion of wealthy widows as heads of households.

What changes there were in the late eighteenth century to the physical environment of the close tended to reinforce the hold of polite society. The canal from the ferry was filled in around 1780 and laid out as 'Prebends' Walk'. In 1782 Dean Philip Lloyd had Lower Green enclosed with iron railings and laid out as a private garden. Soil from the cloister garth (used as the close's graveyard) was used to level the ground, provoking a number of skits against the dean and earning his new 'Lower Square' or 'Dean Square' the alternative name of 'Skeleton Square'.[51] The laying out of the upper close in a similar fashion, with a private garden in the middle, had to wait until 1825, principally because of opposition from the grammar school (which occupied the Carnary College), whose boys used it as their playground.[52] Large parts of the meadows which ran down from Lower Green to the river were also laid out as gardens, as some had been since the Restoration.[53] An account in 1819 described the precinct as 'chiefly distributed into gardens'.[54] The derelict former infirmary was pulled down in 1804 to improve the vista from the deanery.

It was the idea of opening up vistas which lay behind several of the changes to the physical environment of the close in the nineteenth century. For the first time since the middle ages the close was considered as the visual setting for the cathedral. Such a development depended on the rediscovery of the architecture of the Romanesque. Popular appreciation of the cathedral, except for the cloister and spire, was low before the end of the Georgian period. Tourists found little to remark upon in the fabric. 'Nothing curious' was the verdict of Mary Martin Leake in 1796;

50. NRO, DCN 83/1; *Norwich Mercury*, 16 September 1758; H. W. Saunders, *A History of the Norwich Grammar School* (Norwich, 1932), p. 127.
51. W. Chase, *The Norwich Directory* (Norwich, 1783), pp. iv–v. See NRO, MC 186/346 650x4, for a copy of one such skit.
52. H. Turner and F. Johnson, *The Turner Family of Mulbarton and Great Yarmouth* (London, 1907), p. 82; Chase, *Norwich Directory*, p. v. E. C. Le Grice's 1938 film, *The Glory that is Norwich Cathedral*, shows the railings in both the upper and lower closes, Upper Square laid out as a garden with low hedges, flower beds, grass and trees, and grass,

shrubs, beds and trees in Lower Square: East Anglian Film Archive, University of East Anglia, Norwich, cat. no. 632. I am grateful to Cathy Terry for her help in locating this and other films.
53. A. Hochstetter, *Plan of the City of Norwich* (1789). Sir Thomas Browne is reputed to have had a herb garden in the lower close.
54. J. Stacy, *A Topographical and Historical Account of the City and County of Norwich* (Norwich and London, 1819), p. 142. There were eight gardeners or nurserymen living in the close in 1841 and six in 1891: PRO, HO 107/789; RG 12/1522.

'not either striking or imposing' wrote a resident of Catton in 1827.[55] It was perhaps fortunate that views of the cathedral were obscured by the buildings in the close which pressed up against it – the houses that partially hid the west and east fronts or backed up against the cloisters. The *North-East Prospect of Norwich* by Samuel and Nathaniel Buck (1742), for example, shows the cathedral set in a sea of houses and lesser buildings.[56] As late as 1842 R. B. Winkles thought that the cathedral was 'better concealed than exposed'; its 'present inclosed condition' was, therefore, 'not at all to be regretted'.[57]

In part, such comments were the result of a lack of understanding of Romanesque architecture. At least two unimpressed Georgian tourists dismissed the cathedral as 'Saxon' built.[58] Appreciation of the Romanesque grew only slowly in the early nineteenth century, rather later than the first stirrings of the Gothic Revival. As taste for the architecture of the cathedral developed, the houses which stood before it were seen as a hindrance, not a help. Tourists were impractically advised that the best views were to be had from Prebendary Joseph Proctor's drawing-room.[59] Three tenements at the west end of the cathedral were therefore demolished in 1827, 1831 and 1842, and a further house lowered in 1836, to improve the view of and approaches to the cathedral.[60] The greatest change, however, came in 1829–32 when the crowd of buildings that huddled in front of the south transept and around the south-east corner of the cloister was swept away. A new roadway was constructed and Anthony Salvin remodelled the façade of the south transept in Neo-Romanesque style. Dean Pellew proudly recorded the creation of this new 'open vista' and the 'very nice view of the cathedral' from the lower close.[61]

In 1696 Prideaux described the close as 'a town of itself apart from the city', adding that only infrequently had he cause to concern himself with the citizens of Norwich, 'and indeed I very seldom go among them'.[62] For 140 years subsequent deans could have repeated this claim, but from the 1830s the outside world began to intrude

55. Hertfordshire Record Office, MS 84630; NRO, MS 80 T 131 C.
56. It is reproduced in Fernie, *NC*, pl. 13.
57. R. B. Winkles, *History and Description of the Cathedral Church in Norwich* (Norwich, 1842), p. 86.
58. An anonymous tourist of 1757, quoted in R. Gard, ed., *The Observant Traveller: Diaries of Travel in England, Wales and Scotland in the County Record Offices of England and Wales* (London, 1989), p. 17, and the Reverend Townley Clarkson in 1804: Cambridgeshire Record Office, MS R58/11/1.
59. Winkles, *Norwich Cathedral*, p. 89.
60. Metters, *Parliamentary Survey*, pp. 105, 114–15; NRO, DCN 24/6, fos 223–224; DCN 120/21/9. In 1907 one tourist still lamented the houses which hid the cathedral: J. E. Vincent, *Through East Anglia in a Motor Car* (London, 1907), p. 114.
61. NRO, DCN 120/1/2, fos 3, 15v; see also pp. 714–15 and plate VI. The buildings obscuring the south transept are shown in David Hodgson's watercolour, NRO, DCN 128.
62. Prideaux, *Letters*, p. 170.

into the life of the close in ways that were new and, to the dean and chapter, usually unwelcome.

None was so intrusive as the plans of the Lynn and Fakenham Railway Company which wanted to knock down one of the gates and drive a line through the southern half of the close. The chapter clerk recorded Dean Edward Goulburn's reaction to the engineer who came in 1880 to explain the company's ideas:

> The dean denounced the scheme of a railway passing through any part of the cathedral precinct in such vigorous terms, and his determination to spend his last farthing in opposing it, that the engineer quailed before him. At the conclusion of the interview the dean, suddenly rising, said to him, 'And now, Sir, if thine enemy hunger, feed him: if he thirst, give him drink – will you join us at luncheon?' The engineer, much disconcerted, declined and withdrew.[63]

The scheme was defeated after more than two years of campaigning.

Change in the close was invariably less dramatic than this scheme. The reduction in staffing of the cathedral since 1840 has freed houses for rent or demolition. Moreover, the dramatically increasing income of dean and chapter between 1800 and 1870 created a demand for yet grander prebendal housing, 'of a class . . . suitable for a country rectory of £600 or £800 a year', exemplified in the demolition of Canon Charles Wodehouse's house, which stood against the cloister, and its replacement with a large new canonry to the east of the cathedral in 1862. This was designed by John Henry Brown, the cathedral architect, in 'Venetian Gothic' (fig. 211). On completion its ornamentation and polychromatic bricks ('piebald brick walls' Pellew disdainfully called them) divided public and chapter opinion. Canon Adam Sedgwick complained to the dean: 'You know that I much disliked the new canon's house. Now that it is finished I dislike it more than ever'. Canon James Heaviside, however, who had to live in it, was 'well pleased' and an architect friend pronounced it 'the best specimen of the modern style he had seen'.[64] Later opinion has been as divided. Nikolaus Pevsner considered it a *faux-pas* and 'completely insensitive to the demands of the east view of the cathedral'. John Betjeman, on the other hand, thought it the finest Victorian house in existence, earning it the name 'Betjeman's Delight' while, because it became number 57 when the close was numbered, it has jokingly been known as 'Heinz Hall'.[65]

63. Norwich, Dean and Chapter Library, press-mark E1, 'Notes from Chapter Books', 27 November 1880, a reference I owe to Tom Mollard.

64. NRO, DCN 120/2GG/1; DCN 120/2JJ/3, 6–8, 10; W. White, *History, Gazeteer, and Directory of Norfolk* (4th edn, Sheffield and London, 1883), p. 452. J. C. Buckler was called in to advise the chapter.

65. N. Pevsner, *North-East Norfolk and Norwich* (London, 1988; first published 1962), p. 234; information from Alan Webster; press cutting dated 11 August 1977 from unidentified newspaper, courtesy of Ivan Cresswell.

Fig. 211. Number 57 The Close, J.H. Brown's controversial new canonry house of 1862.

Nineteenth- and early twentieth-century reforms also meant the gradual disappearance of the jurisdictional independence of the cathedral precincts. Cathedrals petitioned vigorously against the Municipal Reform Bill of 1835.[66] The final act, as it related to cathedral precincts, was a complicated compromise. Separate commissions of the peace were retained for cathedral closes, but precincts were also to be subject to the justices of the city.[67] At Norwich, effective execution of the chapter's commission of the peace soon withered. The surviving records suggest that the quarter sessions for the close were last held in 1844. They had for several years been concerned usually with little more than the licensing of alehouses.[68] The dean and chapter had previously decided, in 1826, to close their own gaol (inconveniently sited in the south transept of the cathedral), to dispense with the services of their

66. NRO, DCN 24/7, fo. 10v; DCN 120/2H/31.
67. 5 and 6 William IV c. 76 sect. 138.
68. NRO, DCN 81/8; DCN 82/1, 3, 8. It was reported as early as 1819 that the exercise of the dean and chapter's power to hold sessions of the peace was 'discontinued':

Stacy, *Topographical and Historical Account of Norwich*, p. 144. The Three Cranes became a minor canon's house in 1827; the Gate House Inn was rebuilt as committee rooms in 1832; John Pull (d. 1841) was the last ferrykeeper to run an inn at the ferry: Metters, *Parliamentary Survey*, pp. 109, 111.

own gaoler – his duties had never been taxing – and to send any prisoners to the county gaol in Norwich.[69]

Other aspects of the jurisdictional independence of the close slowly dissolved between the 1870s and the 1930s as the city council acquired further authority over the lives of its citizens. The dean and chapter sometimes fought a half-hearted rear-guard action. They appointed their own constable for the close, but had to ask the mayor to swear him in first as a non-stipendiary constable for the city to ensure that he would be recognised by the police authorities.[70] The controversy concerning planning controls over the close (discussed below) was the most bitter and certainly the longest dispute between chapter and city in this period.

Not all changes, however, were resisted by the dean and chapter. Sometimes they eagerly divested themselves of powers which they found expensive and onerous to maintain. This tendency was accelerated by the financial problems which beset the cathedral after the 1870s.[71] In 1887 the dean and chapter dispensed with the services of their own fire brigade. In a further attempt to save money, the chapter tried for several years to persuade the city corporation to take over responsibility for the roads and grounds in the close; agreement was finally sealed in 1938.[72]

Other powers ebbed away with hardly anyone noticing. The dean and chapter continued regularly to appoint their own JPs for the close until 1904, though they had little to do.[73] Exactly when this legal right was extinguished was never made clear. The 1882 Municipal Corporations Act, which superseded that of 1835, made no reference to separate commissions of the peace for cathedrals. It was a power which none but the cathedrals themselves remembered. Consequently, in 1915 the Home Office was surprised by Dean Beeching's claims to appoint justices and coroners. The former the government thought impractical and (wrongly) 'entirely novel'; the latter it could not ignore, since there was still a Norwich solicitor bearing the chapter's patent as coroner.[74] All future rights to appoint independent coroners were abolished in 1926 but the last coroner of the dean and chapter of Norwich did not resign until 1947, finally extinguishing the last vestige of the once mighty fee of the prior of Norwich.[75] It was an obscure end to a chapter in the cathedral's

69. NRO, DCN 24/6, fo. 208v; DCN 26/9/10. There were only three commitments to the chapter's prison between 1809 and 1819, one for felony and two for vagrancy.

70. NRO, DCN 24/9, fo. 116r (1882); DCN 39/79 (1889).

71. See pp. 624, 684–85.

72. NRO, DCN 24/9, fo. 294r; DCN 24/12, fos 259r, 285r, 288r, 292r, 294v–296r (inserts), 301v–302r, 311v, 330r.

73. NRO, DCN 24/11, fo. 185r.

74. NRO, DCN 82/16.

75. NRO, DCN 39/97. The coroners' (amendment) act of 1926, 16 and 17 George V c. 59 sect. 4, abolished all rights in the future to appoint a franchise coroner, on the retirement or death of the present coroner. I am indebted to Keith Arrowsmith for his advice on the finer points of English law.

history which had once provoked riots and bloodshed in the jurisdictional battles between city and cathedral.

The reduction in the chapter's income, the loss of all its estates except the close between the 1870s and 1930s,[76] and the gradual peeling away of the chapter's jurisdiction produced a change of attitude towards the close. The dean and chapter began to look at it more in financial terms than as a social world of their own making. Their first response to the cash crisis facing the cathedral was to seek to build more houses in the close to supplement their rent roll. Discussions began in 1889 about granting building leases on several sites. Suggestions were put forward for eleven new houses near the ferry, forty-two along Bishopgate and seven on St Faith's Lane.[77] Few bore fruit. An architect (Arthur Lacey) was appointed to develop Browne's Meadow (in the lower close) and plots were advertised in the *Eastern Daily Press* before plans had to be abandoned after difficulties in draining the site.[78] A small number of individual houses were built in the lower close, such as that on the site of Dale's tenement.[79] The scheme for Bishopgate was slimmed down and finally, after fourteen years of debate, fifteen new houses were built by Charles Harrison in 1903.[80] This has been the only substantial virgin site in the close to be built upon since the fifteenth century.

The schemes for building in the close met considerable opposition from the city corporation, the residents of the close (thirty-five of whom petitioned the dean and chapter against further building in 1891) and others. Walter Rye, the Norfolk antiquary, lamented that a substantial part of the medieval precinct wall along Bishopgate had been demolished and a view of the spire obscured, only 'to make room for some vulgar little cottages'.[81] It became clear that new building was not the answer to the chapter's financial problems. This was reinforced by the chapter's loss of building control over the close as the city corporation's planning regulations were extended to it. The idea that the dean and chapter could no longer build as they wished to exploit the close as their last economic asset was resented by chapter members. As the chapter clerk wrote to the town clerk:

The dean and chapter are no longer to have power to adapt the property in

76. See pp. 683–86.
77. NRO, DCN 24/10, fos 64, 66v, 70, 78v–79r, 91r, 113, 127, 150, 269, 287, 297, 301, 305, 335; DCN 24/11, fos 120v, 124v–125r.
78. NRO, DCN 24/10, fo. 133.
79. Now number 19; designed by Arthur Lacey and built by W. A. Brewster in 1892: NRO,

DCN 24/10, fos 91r, 110r, 118, 149–150.
80. NRO, DCN 24/10, fo. 297; DCN 24/11, fos 125r, 153r.
81. NRO, DCN 24/10, fos 133–134; DCN 57/15; W. Rye, 'The Precincts of Norwich Cathedral', *Norfolk Antiquarian Miscellany*, second series, 1 (1906), pp. 48–49.

such a manner as they think fit or to develop it as any other landlord would be able to do, but to preserve it as an amenity for the city . . . The result of the scheme would therefore be the complete sterilisation of the close from an economic point of view.

No more would they be masters in their own backyard.[82] The negotiations over the incorporation of the close into the city's town planning scheme lasted from 1926 until 1938, the main point at issue being the city's designation of part of the close as 'public open space'.[83] The dean and chapter feared the effects of an influx of tourists destroying their tranquillity.

Restricted in what and where it could build, the chapter turned to the grammar school for financial assistance. Confined since 1551 to the Carnary Chapel and a few contiguous buildings, the grammar school has expanded dramatically across the close since the 1890s. It has taken over several buildings and plots in the upper close and, gradually since 1860, leased all of the meadow land in the eastern half of the precincts for playing fields. At the beginning of the twentieth century this land was still also used for grazing. One headmaster complained that 'the presence of a number of sheep' posed a 'serious inconvenience to the games': uncharacteristically bold, they even attacked boys fielding at cricket.[84] The extension of Norwich School throughout the close has been one of the greatest changes of use in the precincts since the dissolution of the priory.

The changes of the nineteenth and early twentieth century fundamentally recast the role of the dean and chapter in the precincts, yet they altered the social world of the close little. It is a paradox that, at the same time as the outside world, particularly in the shape of the city and its government, was increasingly intruding into the affairs of the close, the latter was becoming socially more exclusive than ever. Prideaux had complained of the numbers of poor and the chapter had tried to rid the close of them, but the task was only accomplished in the later nineteenth century. Long-term social trends were as important as capitular action. The fate of the poorest of the inhabitants of the close is indicative of these changes. Between 1744 and 1756 the close's own workhouse was situated in the former monastic infirmary, in the heart of the close, next to the cloister and opposite the deanery. It was moved to the north-east corner of the precincts in 1795, away from most

82. NRO, DCN 24/12, fos 295v–296r (insert).
83. NRO, N/TC 24/1, pp. 81, 137, 172, 179–80, 191–92, 195, 225; DCN 57/33; DCN 24/12, fos 208r, 215r, 295v–296r, 330r.
84. R. Harries, P. Cattermole and P. Mac-

kintosh, *A History of Norwich School* (Norwich, 1991), pp. 82, 95–98, 114–115, 120–121, 130, 132–33, 139, 147, 157, 159. In 1937 the dean and chapter banned games on a Sunday; NRO, DCN 24/12, fo. 323.

of the grander housing. Many paupers were removed from the close entirely when, in the early nineteenth century, the precincts were incorporated into St Faith's poor-law union.[85] This was part of a trend to remove the poor out of sight: the workhouses in Norwich were amalgamated and, in 1858–59, moved to Heigham on the outskirts of the city.[86] The cathedral precincts had, however, to be seen as an outward expression of the Christian life and as such were the obvious site for the Norfolk and Norwich Magdalen or female penitentiary, founded in 1827. Its object was 'to afford an asylum to females who, having deviated from the paths of virtue, may be desirous of being restored to their station in society, by religious instruction and the formation of moral and industrious habits'. Most of its inmates were teenage girls.[87] Dean Pellew, newly appointed in 1828, was not keen to observe this example of Christian salvation in action, and transplanted a chestnut tree in his garden to shut the Magdalen out of his sight. The institution was moved out of the close to Chapelfield Road and the house it had occupied demolished for J.H. Brown's new canonry in 1862.[88]

As the institutionalised poor were expelled from the close, so the 'respectable poor', labourers and artisans such as soapboilers, bootmakers and carpenters with their families, became more scarce.[89] The dean and chapter periodically acted to bar tenants from converting properties to manufactures.[90] Only the numbers of servants remained constant.[91] As the close became more exclusive, with wealthier families moving into what had been the poorer 'ends', some of the smaller tenements and houses were amalgamated or demolished. In 1752 there were 129 houses in the close; in 1801, 118; and in 1881 only eighty-eight.[92] The population became smaller and

85. F. Sayers, 'Notices Concerning the Dormitory of the Cathedral-Monastery of Norwich', *Archaeologia*, 15 (1806), p. 314; P. Browne, *An Account and Description of the Cathedral Church of the Holy Trinity, Norwich, and its Precincts* (London, 1807), p. 59; Metters, *Parliamentary Survey*, p. 115; G. K. Blyth, *The Norwich Guide and Directory* (London, 1842), p. 103.

86. W. White, *Directory of Norfolk* (1883), p. 485.

87. W. White, *History, Gazeteer, and Directory of Norfolk* (2nd edn, Sheffield, 1845), pp. 99, 132; censuses of 1841 and 1851: PRO, HO 107/789, 1811.

88. NRO, DCN 120/1/2, fo. 6v; W. White, *History, Gazeteer, and Directory of Norfolk* (3rd edn, Sheffield and London, 1864), p. 232; Metters, *Parliamentary Survey*, p. 110.

89. Occupations can be identified from the St

Mary in the Marsh baptism register, 1813–73, NRO, PD 299/5, and the census returns: compare 1841 with 1891, PRO, HO 107/789 and RG 12/1522.

90. NRO, DCN 24/6, fo. 130 (1804: feltmonger's works at the ferry to be demolished); DCN 26/9/80 (1812: soapboiler allowed to rent the boat yard); DCN 26/9/20 (1818: manufactury in the Black Jack tenement to be closed down); DCN 26/9/28 (1822: lease offered provided no trade, business or manufactury carried on).

91. In 1841 there were 134 servants employed in the close; fifty years later there were 136: PRO, HO 107/789 and RG 12/1522.

92. Chase; *Norwich Directory*; T. Peck, *The Norwich Directory* (Norwich, [c. 1803]); PRO, RG 11/1941.

older. In 1693 there were 650 persons living in the close; in 1752, 700; in 1810, 616; in 1841, 498; in 1901, 451; and in 1931, only 358. At the same time the population of Norwich as a whole grew from nearly 29,000 to over 120,000.[93]

Social life centred on the chapter and particularly the more frequently resident cathedral officers. The letters of Francis Frank (chapter clerk 1724–73) show a world of dinners and social engagements with the dean, prebendaries and understeward, as well as contacts with the city elite and county gentry.[94] A century later 'hospitality' remained a key duty of the chapter members: Canon Sedgwick remarked that 'giving and receiving dinners' constituted 'a formidable service in a city like this'.[95] The reforms of the cathedral after 1840 increased the social role of the clergy by making their periods of residence longer. Dean Goulburn's evening parties – their highlight a reading by the dean of Tennyson's *Dora* – were fondly remembered fifty years later, as were the many tea parties in the precincts and a later dean's description of the close as an 'ecclesiastical hen coop'.[96] Herbert Leeds, looking back on the 1880s from thirty years later, described the close as an 'ecclesiastical elysium', 'charmingly exclusive', where 'things slipped by leisurely for all'.[97]

Nevertheless, social life in the close was not isolated from the outside world. As befitted a gateway, the rooms in the Ethelbert Gate were a place where close and city mixed. These were used for a variety of purposes at different times: the Cathedral Catch Club met there between 1784 and 1832; a century later the rooms were used by a Sunday Bible class, the Institute for Telegraph Messengers, the Deaf and Dumb Mission, the Norfolk and Norwich Incorporated Law Society Library and the Philharmonic Society.[98] By 1878 a military band played in the upper close in summer for the entertainment of close and city; in 1905 the open-air concerts had moved to the lower close.[99] Although the chapter prevented the playing of croquet on the Upper Green in 1900 for fear that 'it would disturb the quietude of the close', it was happy for a clock-golf course to be laid out there in 1934. There were also a croquet lawn and tennis courts down by the river.[100] The close has been a place of

93. W. White, *Directory of Norfolk* (1845), p. 52; F. White, *History, Gazeteer, and Directory of Norfolk* (Sheffield, 1854), p. 53; *Kelly's Directory of Norfolk* (London, 1937), p. 308. The numbers of baptisms recorded in the register of St Mary in the Marsh (NRO, PD 499/5) dropped dramatically as the population grew older: there were only seven between 1913 and 1926.

94. Sheffield Archives, BFM 1309–23.

95. J. W. Clark and T. Hughes, *The Life and Letters of the Reverend Adam Sedgwick*, 2 vols (Cambridge, 1890), i, pp. 434, 436–37; ii, pp. 572–79.

96. *Eastern Daily Press*, 15 November 1921.

97. H. Leeds, *The Life of Dean Lefroy* (London, 1909), p. 24.

98. NRO, DCN 39/54; DCN 24/10, fo. 212; DCN 24/11, fos 89v, 204r; DCN 24/12, fos 4v, 102r, 111r, 140v.

99. NRO, DCN 39/81; DCN 24/11, fo. 189r.

100. NRO, DCN 24/11, fo. 91v; DCN 24/12, fo. 256v; Ordnance Survey map, 1:2500, Norfolk, sheet LXIII. 11 (1914).

Fig. 212. Pull's Ferry, showing the ruins of the water gate (restored in 1948) and the ferry, *c.* 1900–15.

recreation for the citizens of Norwich since the chapter laid out gravel walks at the end of the seventeenth century.

The Second World War brought few changes to the close. Air raid shelters were dug under the school playground. A few houses were damaged by bombs and three (numbers 63, 66 and 67) were destroyed (fig. 216).[101] The ferry across the Wensum (fig. 212) was closed permanently in 1942. Here the final blow was not so much the war as the removal of Norwich City's football ground from the Nest, on the opposite bank of the river from the close, to Carrow Road further downstream in 1935; until then, football supporters had provided good trade for the ferry on match days.[102] Nor did the war greatly alter the social world of the close, what Dean Paul Burbridge later called 'a very limited, enclosed and somewhat conservative community'.[103] Tenants who moved into the close in the 1950s remember a world

101. Metters, *Parliamentary Survey*, pp. 114–15; Harries, Cattermole and Mackintosh, *Norwich School*, p. 125. Dean Cranage had offered to sandbag part of the cathedral itself as a shelter.

102. *Eastern Daily Press*, 5 May 1976; NRO, DCN 24/12, fos 264v–265r; E. Bell, *On the*

Ball City: An Illustrated History of the Norwich City Football Club (Norwich, 1972), p. 39, a reference I owe to Jon Finch.

103. Friends of Norwich Cathedral, *Sixty-Fifth Annual Report, 1994* (Norwich, 1995), p. 4. All statements in this and succeeding paragraphs, except those separately noted,

where residents were either 'in' or 'out' and where connections were deemed all important – what one resident described as 'that feudal system in the close'.

After the war, financial pressures forced structural changes in the estate management of the close but, as in the case of governmental changes in the preceding century, these had little effect on the daily experience of life there. Since the 1880s the rising expectations of the sanitary authorities and the tenants themselves had required the chapter to spend considerable sums improving their housing stock.[104] At a time of falling income, this was something it could ill afford, but difficulties over letting the larger houses forced the chapter to act.[105] Other repairs were often not undertaken at all.[106] The housing stock deteriorated, a trend made worse by the Second World War.

It was in response to this physical decline of the housing that the dean and chapter changed its letting policy in the early 1950s on three counts. First, the management of all the properties in the close was transferred to a firm of land agents, Percy Howes and Co.[107] Secondly, an increased number of properties were let as offices on high, commercial rents. This move accelerated an existing trend: in 1896 three properties had been let as offices; in 1937 the figure was twenty; and by 1995 there were thirty-one commercial tenancies.[108] One new office-block, Holland House, was constructed in 1960–61. Thirdly, residential properties, which previously had been let at low rents with the chapter incurring the repairs, were now let on condition that the tenants put their houses into good repair and kept them in that state. This meant seeking out tenants prepared to invest money in improving the cathedral's housing. Between 1945 and 1970, £250,000 was spent to this end.

These changes were not without their critics. One correspondent to the *Eastern Daily Press* complained of 'the harm done to Norwich, when the dean and chapter allowed commerce and law to enter the close'.[109] Yet the policies have been a notable success. Unlike some cathedrals (such as Salisbury) the dean and chapter have not sold any of their property and retain the freehold of virtually the entire

note 103 continued
are based on interviews with a number of people who have lived and worked in the close: Tom Carr; David Cleveland; Ivan and Olive Cresswell; Doreen Green; Christopher Howes; Bob Molster; Colin Pordham; Alan and Margaret Webster. Their time and assistance is very gratefully acknowledged.

104. NRO, DCN 24/10, fo. 67r; DCN 24/11, fos 198r, 231r, 233, 243v; DCN 24/12, fos 39v, 98r, 103v, 130v, 175v, 206r, 207v.
105. NRO, DCN 24/12, fos 294v–295r (insert).
106. In June 1904 long-term lack of repairs led

to the collapse of Dial House (number 53) in the lower close. It was rebuilt the following year at a cost of £1783 (fig. 213): NRO, DCN 24/11, fos 172–173, 175, 178v–179r, 181v, 190v.
107. This policy had first been mooted in 1938: NRO, DCN 24/12, fo. 335r.
108. *Kelly's Directory of Norfolk* (London, 1896 and 1937 editions); information from Tom Carr of Percy Howes and Co.
109. *Eastern Daily Press*, 1 March 1948. See also W. Harrod and C. L. S. Linnell, *The Shell Guide to Norfolk* (3rd edn, London, 1966), p. 56.

Fig. 213. Part of the great granary, converted into houses after the Reformation. Number 53 (Dial House) collapsed in 1904 during negotiations about its repair and was rebuilt the following year with large dormer windows.

close.[110] Its popularity has increased as the properties have been improved. Whereas in the 1950s some tenants moved into the close because of the ready availability of housing, albeit dilapidated, in 1995 there was a five- to eight-year waiting list for residential lettings.[111]

The policy of repairing leases tended to mean a wealthier and older generation of tenants, reinforcing the impression of the close as an exclusive enclave. This was something that, in the 1970s, Dean Alan Webster and rest of the chapter, along with the steward, Christopher Howes, were keen to reduce. The dean was quoted in the press: 'we have ideas for a greater social use of the close. We want it as a centre for quiet rather than as a place for upper-class Anglicans to retire to'.[112] A

---

110. There are three exceptions: some of the tenants of those Bishopgate properties constructed on ninety-nine year building leases have been entitled to enfranchise and buy the freehold; the grounds of the bishop's palace belong to the Church Commissioners; Norwich School holds part of the close from the dean and chapter on a 999-year lease.

111. *The Times Weekend*, 8 April 1995, p. 13. The waiting list at Norwich in 1974 was 300 applicants long: Friends of Norwich Cathedral, *Annual Report, 1974*, p. 15.

112. Press cutting in possession of Ivan Cresswell.

greater stress was laid on the close as an expression of the cathedral's ministry. Opening up the close and encouraging a broader social mix of tenants were the new policies. In fact, the need to maintain the close as the cathedral's main economic asset tended to cut across the operation of these programmes.[113] A number of symbolic steps were taken. Number 57 (J. H. Brown's new canonry) was converted into an Abbeyfield house for the elderly in 1973. An ecumenical study centre, a visitors' centre, buffet and shop were all opened. The section of the riverside walk through the close, along the right bank of the Wensum from Bishop Bridge to the ferry, projected fifty years earlier by the city council, was finally opened in 1972. The close, it was said, had become 'the open'.[114]

For nine centuries the close has served diverse needs of the cathedral and its residents. How these often conflicting needs have been understood has determined the physical and social topography of the close. Its history has mirrored the aims and objectives of the prior and convent, the dean and chapter, and those who worship at the cathedral. Their concerns, and the outside pressures to which close and cathedral have been subject, have determined the close's threefold role: economic, topographical and religious. It has provided revenue and residence for the chapter, a role which has increased in importance since the Cathedrals' Measure of 1931 left it as the dean and chapter's sole estate. The close has provided the setting for the cathedral. Once this meant security and lordship for the monks; now it is understood in aesthetic terms, with the close as a conservation area and tourist attraction. The close has demonstrated the cathedral's social and religious responsibilities. From the seventeenth century until recent times this meant attempting to exclude the poor, nonconformists and Roman Catholics, and welding alliances with the social and political elite who were encouraged to live in the close and befriend the cathedral. Today, by contrast, it means expressing the church's mission for society. It remains to be seen how these roles will be understood in future, in particular how tourism, conservation and the need to provide revenue for the cathedral can be developed alongside the church's mission, taking account of the wishes of the residents, yet still preserving the close as 'a fine village in a fine city'.[115]

113. 'The Dean's Letter', September 1973; there is a copy in Norwich, Dean and Chapter Library, pressmark L5. In 1995 the precincts rent roll was £660,000.

114. NRO, N/TC 24/1, pp. 179–80, 191–92; DCN 57/33; DCN 24/12, fo. 329r; 'The Dean's Letter', Easter 1972 (copy in Norwich, Dean and Chapter Library,

pressmark L5).

115. 'The Dean's Letter', June 1976 (copy in Norwich, Dean and Chapter Library, pressmark L5). See also C. K. Howes, 'A Consideration of the Role of the Close', Friends of Norwich Cathedral, *Annual Report, 1974*, pp. 14–16.

The Deanery

The translation of the prior and convent into a dean and chapter in 1538 entailed no change of residence for William Castleton, last prior and first dean. The prior's hall, built in 1284, became part of the deanery. It was a very suitable residence, having been extended only recently by Prior Robert Catton, Castleton's predecessor.[116] While we know comparatively little about the deanery, we can infer from heraldic evidence that Tudor and Stuart deans took more care of their house than they did of the cathedral fabric. The initials or arms of four deans – William Castleton (prior 1529/30–38 and dean 1538–39), George Gardiner (1573–89), George Montgomery (1603–14) and Edmund Suckling (1614–28) – can be found on glass, fireplaces and surrounds, even a doorway, from the deanery.[117] Suckling added a passageway from the deanery to the dark entry of the cloister.

In the 1649 parliamentary survey of the close the deanery is described as being a fair stone-built two-frame house with a leaden roof and adjoining tile-covered out buildings. It was estimated to be worth £14 a year, making it, fittingly, one of the grandest houses in the close.[118] Unlike the bishop's palace, it did not suffer much harm in the 1650s. Over £300 was spent in 1660–64 by the new dean, John Croftes (1660–70). He divided the room above the prior's hall in two and added the distinctive brick-and-flint stepped gables (fig. 214).[119]

Expenditure on the deanery in the eighteenth and early nineteenth centuries tended to be high. Each new dean wanted to remodel the house to his own wishes. Moreover, rising chapter profits meant that no dean before Edward Goulburn (1866–89) had to consider whether such repairs and improvements could be afforded. Dean Thomas Bullock (1739–60), a great restorer of the cathedral fabric, spent an average £24 a year on the deanery, compared with a yearly average of £256 on the cathedral itself. His short-lived successor Edward Townshend (1761–65) managed to spend £49 a year on the deanery and only £79 a year on the church. Despite Townshend's high expenditure, his successor Philip Lloyd (1765–90) found it desirous to add new stairs and an orangery, making the deanery 'a very elegant and complete habitation' in the judgement of Philip Browne.[120]

Dean Joseph Turner (1790–1828) cannot be accused of lavish expenditure on the deanery: George Pellew (1828–66) received £750 in dilapidations from his executors,

116. A. B. Whittingham, 'The Deanery, Norwich', *Arch. J.*, 137 (1980), p. 314.

117. Metters, *Parliamentary Survey*, p. 104. See also above, pp. 418, 423.

118. Metters, *Parliamentary Survey*, p. 29.

119. Above, p. 560; Metters, *Parliamentary Survey*, p. 104.

120. NRO, DCN 57/4–5; Whittingham, 'The Deanery', p. 314; Browne, *Cathedral Church of Norwich*, p. 58. See also above, p. 614.

Fig. 214. The deanery, from the south west.

but then Turner had always preferred the master's lodge at Pembroke College to Norwich.[121] On his installation Pellew set about the most drastic redevelopment of the deanery since the Restoration as part of his wider plans to remodel the south transept. In 1829 Suckling's passageway from the deanery to the cloister was swept away along with all the other buildings abutting the east walk. Severed of its physical connection with the cathedral, the deanery turned its back on the church. The front door, which had been on the west since the prior's hall was built, was moved to the east and a new drive to Lower Green constructed. The deanery was turned around. The north-east wing was demolished and the prior's hall divided into a kitchen and scullery.[122] These alterations created a substantial house of forty or so rooms suitable for entertaining, including a wine cellar stocked with 455 bottles (the Pellews and their guests were partial to port – 233 bottles – and sherry – 102 bottles) plus fifty-three pints of champagne.[123]

The reduction in chapter income effected the deanery, as it did all aspects of the cathedral's life. Less was spent on repairs, so much less that when Cranage was

121. NRO, DCN 120/1/2, fos 4–5r. For Turner, see above, p. 592.
122. The alterations are described in detail in

NRO, DCN 120/1/2, fos 3–9r.
123. NRO, DCN 57/22.

offered the deanery in 1927 he was disinclined to accept the office given the great amount of work that needed to be done to the house, including the complete rebuilding of the drains. Expectations of lavish entertaining had been reduced, and the Cranages turned Pellew's 'sordid' kitchen and scullery in the prior's hall into a sitting-room.[124] The size of the deanery, especially the prior's hall, became a problem given the more modest establishments kept by twentieth-century deans.[125] After the Second World War Dean Holland (1947–52) moved out of the deanery into number 26 The Close; the deanery was turned into offices. The feeling that the dean should live in the old deanery persisted, however. Dean Norman Hook (1952–69) moved back into a more compact deanery. Three flats had been carved out of the west part, while the prior's hall was made into a meeting and function room which could be closed off from the deanery, or used as a large dining room for entertaining by the dean.[126] As the policy has become to make the close more open, so the prior's hall now plays its part in that ministry.

The Bishop's Palace

Bishop Herbert de Losinga (1091–1119) built the episcopal palace and chapel to the north of his cathedral church, connecting palace and cathedral with a two-storey passageway. A hall was added in the mid twelfth century, probably by Bishop William Turbe (1146/47–74). Bishop John Salmon (1299–1325) added a further great hall to the north of the palace and extended Losinga's chapel. A covered walkway from the north transept to the palace was added in the early fifteenth century, probably by Bishop John Wakering (1415–25). This supplemented the entrance to the nave at gallery level built by Losinga, and perhaps marked a decline in the use of the chapels in the gallery. The last substantial medieval addition to the palace complex was the new gate to Palace Plain constructed by Bishop Walter Lyhart (1446–72), the latest of the three great gates to the precincts.[127] Although it has been constantly repaired and altered, with parts added and parts demolished, the basic Romanesque L-shaped plan of Losinga's palace, aligned north-south with an east-west chapel, has remained ever since, making the palace one of the most significant, but least-studied, Norman buildings in Norfolk.

From the 1530s to the 1950s the episcopal palace has been subjected to cycles of dilapidation and restoration. There are two principal reasons for this: absence and finance. Unlike the dean and prebendaries, bishops were not subject to periods of

124. D. H. S. Cranage, *Not Only a Dean* (London, 1952), pp. 159–60, 162.

125. Pellew had employed ten servants in 1841; in 1881 Dean Goulburn and Bishop Pelham had seven servants each: PRO, HO 107/789; RG 11/1941.

126. Metters, *Parliamentary Survey*, p. 104.

127. See above, pp. 109–11, 178–79, 185.

residence, and could come and go almost as they pleased, at least until the mid nineteenth century. Many bishops preferred life elsewhere – London for the season, court for the ambitious or, like Henry Bathurst (1805–37), spa towns for their waters and the opportunity to play whist untroubled by diocesan affairs. Harder-working prelates travelled round their huge diocese, staying outside Norwich – at their house at Ludham, for example. Consequently, many rarely stayed at the palace and some never. When, in the middle ages, Norwich was a wealthy see, absence had no deleterious effect on the fabric of the palace, for the bishops could afford to maintain an empty house; it was a sign of their power and wealth. The disastrous episcopate of Richard Nix (1501–35/36) changed this. Henry VIII forced him to exchange most of the episcopal estates for less profitable lands. Henceforth, Norwich would be a much poorer preferment with a palace too large for the episcopal income.[128]

Nix started divesting himself of responsibility for parts of the palace. In 1535 he leased Salmon's great hall to the city corporation for its guild-day feasts. Thirteen years later, however, the city transferred its feasts to Blackfriars' Hall, which it had recently acquired. In response, Bishop Thomas Thirlby (1550–54) pulled down the great hall. His predecessor, William Repps (1536–50), had tried an even more drastic solution. He obtained royal licence in 1548 to alienate the whole palace to Sir Francis Bryan, but the bargain was never completed. John Parkhurst (1560–75) found a use for the chapel in 1565, by which time (so it was alleged sixty years later) it was more like a dovecote than a church, full of debris and filth, the roof decayed and the windows broken. He leased it to the Walloon congregation in Norwich for use as their church.[129]

The rest of the palace, however, was well cared for by the post-Reformation Tudor bishops. Repps wainscotted parts of it with oak panelling from St Benet at Holme – the abbey had been granted to the bishopric by Henry VIII.[130] A survey of the palace in October 1594 reveals a substantial house with around forty rooms, including 'the Lord Cromwell's chamber', 'the green parlour', 'the great chamber', 'the bishop's chamber', an armoury and two studies, plus outbuildings. It was, the survey concluded, 'generally . . . all in good and sufficient reparation'.[131]

After the death of Edmund Scambler (1585–94) the palace seems to have fared

128. F. Heal, *Of Prelates and Princes: A Study of the Economic and Social Position of the Tudor Episcopate* (Cambridge, 1980), pp. 111, 114–15.

129. H. Harrod, 'Excavations Made in the Gardens of the Bishop's Palace, Norwich', *NA*, 6 (1864), p. 33; PRO, E178/1607; *CPR, 1548–49*, p. 67; C. M. Calthrop, 'The Palace of Norwich', in *English Episcopal Palaces (Province of Canterbury)*, ed. R. S. Rait

(London, 1910), pp. 221–27; *CSPD, 1637–38*, p. 356.

130. Calthrop, 'Palace of Norwich', p. 225.

131. PRO, E178/1607. 'Lord Cromwell's chamber' was where Thomas Cromwell allegedly slept when he arranged for the estates of St Benet's Abbey to be transferred to the bishopric: D. E. Muir, *Lift the Curtain* (London, 1953), p. 44.

less well. Each succeeding bishop sued his predecessor or his predecessor's executors for an ever greater amount in dilapidations. John Jegon (1603–18) claimed £194 from the estate of William Redman (1591–1602); Samuel Harsnett (1619–28) engaged in a long suit with Jegon's executrix. Harsnett himself claimed to have spent £2000 on the palaces at Norwich and Ludham (most of it probably at the latter), but after his translation to York he in turn was sued by his successor Francis White (1629–31) for £220. By 1635 the estimated cost of the repairs needed had risen to £600.[132] Much of the problem was that few bishops made Norwich their permanent home. The palace was given over instead to a keeper, who generally discharged the office through a deputy.[133] It was said of Jegon that, as a Cambridge man ('where the air is thick and gross') he preferred Ludham on the Norfolk Broads to Norwich, where the air was 'too thin and sharp for him'.[134] A more likely reason was that, as a strict conformist, he found the Walloons in the palace uncongenial neighbours.[135] To the high-church episcopate which came to power under Charles I it was intolerable that a nonconforming congregation should inhabit the heart of the diocese. The Walloons were ordered to quit in December 1634 but proved difficult to dislodge, not leaving until 1637.[136]

Bishops Richard Mountagu (1638–41) and Joseph Hall (1641–46) had little time to enjoy or alter the palace before the political and religious troubles of the Civil War. The palace was searched and Hall forced to remove much of the glass from the chapel. He himself was ejected from the palace. After the abolition of episcopacy in October 1646 the palace was sequestered and leased to James Scambler before being sold to Captain John Blackwell. The lead was stripped from the roof and the fabric allowed to decay. The hall was turned into a meeting house for sectaries and the remainder divided into small tenements for poor families.[137] This was a common fate for episcopal palaces in the 1640s and 1650s: Salisbury was similarly subdivided; Lichfield was so badly damaged that a new palace was built after the Restoration and the old used as a stone quarry.[138]

The work of repair was undertaken by Bishop Edward Reynolds (1660–76), who

132. Bodleian Library, MS Tanner 228, fo. 9r; MS Tanner 135, fos 93–95; PRO, SP16/270, fos 169–179.
133. In 1628 Thomas Litton was granted the office of palace keeper for life; in January 1647, he was still living but the patent had come 'by several assignments' to Sir Thomas Hoogan, although the palace keeper's house was actually occupied by Robert Randalfe: D. J. Stewart, 'Notes on Norwich Cathedral: The Cloisters', *Arch. J.*, 32 (1875), p. 186. The house of the keeper of the palace was mentioned in 1603: Bodleian Library, MS Tanner 228, fo. 90r.
134. Bodleian Library, MS Tanner 228, fo. 88v.
135. See *DNB* for Jegon's conformist rigour.
136. Calthrop, 'Palace of Norwich', pp. 236–37; *CSPD, 1637–38*, p. 356.
137. See above, p. 552. See also Stewart, 'Notes', pp. 184–86; Calthrop, 'Palace of Norwich', p. 245; Browne, *Cathedral Church of Norwich*, p. 52.
138. Royal Commission, *Salisbury*, p. 26; Tringham, 'Cathedral and Close', p. 61.

made Norwich his home. The connecting passage to the north transept was lost forever, but he did build a new, smaller chapel, reusing stone and the windows from the old chapel (fig. 201). The result has not pleased everyone: John Chambers pronounced it 'destitute of all architectural interest'.[139] Thereafter, until the mid nineteenth century, little beyond minor and essential repairs were undertaken.[140]

In the Georgian period opinion over the palace was divided. Philip Yorke thought it 'rambling' and 'unpleasant', Tom Martin 'surprisingly beautiful', Philip Browne 'elegant'. To many observers, used to the classical symmetry of an eighteenth-century mansion, it must have appeared irregular, as it did to John Chambers.[141] Such irregularity was perhaps less displeasing to the Victorians, encouraged to appreciate their Gothic inheritance. The first impressions of Arthur, son of Bishop Edward Stanley (1837–49) were, he wrote to a friend, 'most favourable':

> as I entered the gate for the first time, I was more struck with the size than
> the ugliness of the palace . . . the inside I do not object to, but I cannot
> compare it to anything, for I never saw any house like it; it is among houses,
> I should think, what Moscow is among towns – rooms which we may really
> call very fine side by side with the meanest of passages and staircases.[142]

Stanley's first impressions were made in August; a more common nineteenth-century reaction concentrated on the cold and drafts. Expectations of domestic warmth and comfort increased faster than improvements made to the interior of the palace. The son of Bishop Henry Bathurst (1805–37) defended his father's frequent absence from the diocese on the grounds that the palace at Norwich was too large and too cold for an old man.[143] More than a century later Dorothy Muir, youngest daughter of Bishop John Sheepshanks (1893–1910), remembered her childhood at the palace. The extensive garden of over six acres had been a delight but her memories of the house itself were not good. The dining room was 'an icy purgatory'. Her overall verdict was scathing: 'it was, on the whole, an ugly house. Vast, bare staircases, long, dark corridors, very little sun, and in winter the most piercing cold were its main characteristics'. Despite the gold panelling, pale yellow brocade paper and

139. Bodleian Library, MS Tanner 137, fos 179–180; J. Chambers, *A General History of the County of Norfolk*, 2 vols (London and Norwich, 1829), ii, p. 1044.
140. Bishops Charles Trimnell (1708–21), Thomas Gooch (1738–48), Thomas Hayter (1749–61) and Philip Yonge (1761–83) were all said to have improved the palace: BL, Additional MS 5828, fo. 125r; Browne, *Cathedral Church of Norwich*, pp. 52–53.
141. J. Godber, 'The Marchioness Grey of Wrest Park', *Publications of the Bedfordshire Historical Record Society*, 47 (1968), p. 142; Calthrop, 'Palace of Norwich', p. 248; Browne, *Cathedral Church of Norwich*, p. 53; Chambers, *History of Norfolk*, ii, p. 1043.
142. R. E. Prothero and G. G. Bradley, *The Life and Correspondence of Arthur Penrhyn Stanley*, 2 vols (London, 1893), i, p. 186.
143. H. Bathurst, *Memoirs of the Late Dr Henry Bathurst*, 2 vols (London, 1837), ii, p. 13.

Fig. 215. The east face of the bishop's palace, showing Ewan Christian's alterations of 1858–59.

suitable Gothic-letter texts in the drawing-room, it was a fitting home for the ascetic Sheepshanks. Having spent several years in the Canadian wilderness, he had an abhorrence of luxury, choosing linoleum not carpet to cover the stairs.[144]

Before Sheepshanks, the palace had undergone its first major remodelling since the Restoration. Not only had the reforms of the early Victorian Ecclesiastical Commissioners a greater revivifying effect on the episcopate than on cathedrals, but also the long-serving Bishop John Pelham of Norwich (1857–93) was a zealous evangelical and great builder of churches, parsonages and schools.[145] His enthusiasms spilled over to the palace, where he employed Ewan Christian, the Ecclesiastical Commissioners' own architect, to remodel the palace in 1858–59. The north-west corner was rebuilt. The bishop's chapel, used as a lumber room, was restored; for the next eighteen years it, and not St Luke's Chapel, served as the church for the parish of St Mary in the Marsh. The 750-year-old passage to the cathedral, containing a kitchen, brewhouse and other service rooms, was cut by the removal of its southern end (fig. 215).[146]

144. Muir, *Lift the Curtain*, pp. 35–49, 102–4.
145. *DNB*.

146. Calthrop, 'Palace of Norwich', p. 252; Chambers, *History of Norfolk*, ii, p. 1044; Pevsner, *Norwich*, p. 229.

Nevertheless, the palace remained too large, too dark and too cold. These were not the ideal attributes of an episcopal residence, especially in the changed climate after the Second World War, when greater home comforts and smaller houses were thought appropriate for bishops. They were, however, still thought suitable for an English public school. Consequently, in 1959–60 the old palace was transferred to Norwich School and a new much smaller, Neo-Georgian residence for the bishop, designed by Fletcher Watson, was built adjacent to the gate to Palace Plain. The chapel, having been used for the diocesan records, was also transferred to the school as a library.[147]

The building history of the palace, at least from the Reformation to the 1950s, parallels that of the cathedral. Like the cathedral fabric, the century from the Translation to the Restoration proved to be a turbulent one for the palace. The 1640s and 1650s proved even more destructive for the palace than for the cathedral, the latter suffering no permanent damage. The Restoration was a time of renewal. As the palace was in a more ruined state, so it benefitted from more refurbishment: Bishop Reynolds's new chapel was the only new ecclesiastical (as opposed to domestic or school) building in the precinct from the Reformation until Sir Charles Nicholson's Regimental Chapel of 1930–32. As with the cathedral, the eighteenth century saw only limited work. Significant change did not come until the Victorian remodelling of 1858–59. It is only since the 1950s that the parallel courses of palace and cathedral have parted company, with the removal of the bishops from the old palace to the new bishop's house. That two institutions should follow the broad lines of each other's building history is noteworthy because, since the Reformation, no bishop of Norwich has had a significant role to play in the cathedral fabric.[148]

147. D. Lindsay, *Friends for Life: A Portrait of Launcelot Fleming* (Seaford, 1981), p. 188; Pevsner, *Norwich*, p. 230; Harries, Cattermole and Mackintosh, *Norwich School*, pp. 133, 145. The palace had been used as a hospital during the First World War:

G. Gliddon, ed., *Norfolk and Suffolk in the Great War* (Norwich, 1988), p. 68.

148. This in itself has been a great contrast with the medieval period, when the bishops were usually the key figures in building operations in the church and priory.

31

The Dean and Chapter Estates
since the Reformation

Ian Atherton and B. A. Holderness

With the dissolution of Norwich Cathedral Priory in 1538 and the translation of its prior and monks into the dean and chapter began five generations of uncertainty and instability in the history of the estates.[*] Portions of the estates were lost to a predatory crown, to rapacious lay people and to grasping tenants as lands were nibbled at the edges or swallowed whole. For nearly a century and a half the threat that the cathedral might lose all its property was never far away. It was the most dramatic phase in the history of the cathedral's estates and a time when their fate conditioned many of the roles the cathedral assumed, or did not assume, within the diocese. Only gradually, from the later seventeenth and early eighteenth centuries, did the estates, and therefore the dean and chapter, recover from these shocks and blows. The century or so between 1720 and 1830 saw the consolidation of the cathedral's lands accompanied by the growth of the chapter's income. The reforms of the Ecclesiastical Commissioners from the 1830s then changed the way that cathedrals were funded and the manner in which deans and chapters owned and administered estates.

At the Dissolution the crown seized the lands of all monasteries except the cathedral priories, which kept their estates as endowments essential to the running of those cathedrals. The medieval heritage of property thus passed intact to the new dean and chapter of Norwich Cathedral in 1538. None the less, the dean and chapter began life heavily in debt. Arranging the translation itself was costly, and the unrequited debts of the now abolished priory were to be borne by the new body. They were forced to sell all their sheep, marking a significant change from the later

---

[*] The writers would like to thank Professor Hassell Smith, Dr Richard Wilson, Dr Jane Tillier and Jeff Atherton for their comments on earlier drafts of this chapter.

middle ages when the priory had one of the largest flocks in East Anglia.[1] Moreover, the fledgeling chapter alienated some of its property over the next nine years, losing estates like the priory of St Leonard, in an attempt to pay its debts and win powerful friends.[2]

King Edward VI's refoundation of the cathedral in 1547 was an even more hazardous experience for the dean and chapter. All the estates were surrendered to the crown in June, and Protector Somerset appeared intent on acquiring the choicest plums for his own use, but when the dean and chapter were refounded in November they received back most of their property. The crown however retained five of the most valuable manors (Hemsby, Martham, Lakenham, Plumstead and Wicklewood) and two parsonages (Hemsby and Wicklewood). Subsequent attempts throughout the remainder of the century to regain these lands always failed. The annual value of the estates, set at £895 14s. 6¼d. in 1538, was reduced to £798 6s. 3d., a fall of nearly 11 per cent. In return the crown gave the dean and chapter the rectory of Scalby, Yorkshire, supposedly as full compensation. In fact, the true value of the impropriation was set at no more than £10 10s. per annum by the new owners.[3] The chapter had incurred significant losses since 1538, but far less than those endured by the bishop. Through an exchange forced by the crown the episcopal rental had fallen by one-third between 1535 and 1543.[4]

Between 1538 and 1547 the dean and chapter had maintained the medieval system of assigning properties to individual members, just as each obedientiary or departmental officer had had his own block of the priory's estates. In this sense the stall holders were properly termed prebendaries, for each did have his own prebend or block of the capitular estates nominally under his control. How far the estates really were administered by each prebendary, rather than corporately, is not clear, although each had his own account roll.[5] The system also meant that the income was unequally divided between the prebendaries. At the refoundation the court of augmentations (the crown's body for administering the estates of the dissolved monasteries) prescribed a reorganisation in the management of the estates. Prebends were abolished (although the six canons continued to be called prebendaries, henceforth, technically a misnomer) and all the lands were to be administered collegially. Quite how the

1. See above, pp. 355, 508.
2. NRO, DCN 29/1; DCN 115/9, 'Annals' (1542, 1544); *Letters and Papers, Foreign and Domestic, of the Reign of Henry VIII*, 21 vols in 35 (London, 1880–91), xiii (i), nos 652, 1256. The priory had been granted licence to alienate lands to the annual value of £48, including its cell at Hoxne, only weeks before the translation.
3. NRO, DCN 41/107; DCN 29/3, fos 144–

149; DCN 29/1, fos 7–23; BL, Lansdowne MS 50, fo. 148, Lansdowne MS 58, fo. 20; J. Caley and J. Hunter, eds, *Valor Ecclesiasticus*, 6 vols (London, 1810–34), iii, pp. 489–94.
4. F. Heal, *Of Prelates and Princes: A Study of the Economic and Social Position of the Tudor Episcopate* (Cambridge, 1980), pp. 111, 114–15.
5. NRO, DCN 10/1/2–10, rolls of the chancellor, succentor and treasurer.

system worked in practice for the next seventy-three years, before the new statutes of 1620, is not entirely clear; in the absence of any legally binding constitution,[6] we have to infer the proper practice from the frequent complaints by prebendaries about abuses. Our main surviving records, therefore, are the original leases and the copies entered into the lease books, the chapter minutes (from 1566) and the surviving account rolls, which often conceal as much as they reveal.[7]

From the start, the dean and chapter leased out most of its property, as the priory had done from the later 1420s,[8] while the sale of the priory's large sheep flocks meant that the dean and chapter were rentiers, uninvolved themselves in farming. This situation pertained throughout the modern period. After the translation, leasing long was preferred.[9] Although the custom is difficult to justify on economic grounds, certain factors probably combined to make sixty and even ninety-nine year leases the norm. First, the desire to make a quick profit from substantial fines (taken by the chapter from the lessee every time a lease was granted or renewed) may have swayed some chapter members, since longer leases presumably meant larger fines. This, however, is hard to substantiate as entry fines do not seem to have been systematically recorded before 1660.[10] None the less, from the seventeenth to the mid nineteenth centuries, entry fines grew dramatically in importance as a part of chapter income. The resulting pressures to seize an inflated and immediate profit at the expense of the future bedevilled estate policy (if such an ad hoc procedure can be graced by so grand a term) for three centuries. Lack of long-term planning can only have been exacerbated by the uncertain future cathedrals had as institutions. Finally, the influence of powerful families may also have been decisive. Having eagerly gobbled up the confiscated property of the dissolved monasteries, the laity turned its greedy eyes to the estates of the surviving ecclesiastical corporations. The political importance of favouring certain dominant magnates to obtain protection or to deflect their hostility was probably paramount in most decisions to issue beneficial leases or to adjust the fines.

The terms agreed in most leases further reinforce the impression that the chapter was not looking to the future. Manors tended to be leased not only with their lands but also with all their manorial rights. This saved the chapter the inconvenience of enforcing these but denied the clergy the profits due from them, such as fines from unruly tenants or the payments for new leases from copyholders (tenants who held

6. See above, pp. 530–31.
7. NRO, DCN 113/1, pp. 41–43. Original leases, NRO, DCN 48–49; ledger books, DCN 47; chapter books, DCN 24; account rolls, DCN 10/1.
8. See above, pp. 355.
9. For all matters regarding the leases, see the

lease registers, NRO, DCN 47.
10. The receivers' rolls show only small sums received in fines before 1576 (for example £1 in 1558–59) but it is possible that fines were generally taken and not recorded: NRO, DCN 10/1/11–29.

lands from the manor not by an ordinary lease but by a copy agreement entered in the rolls of the manorial court). Impropriate rectories (those where the chapter held the great tithes which would otherwise have gone to the minister) tended to be leased along with the right to present the vicar to the benefice. The chapter's woods were leased without safeguarding the trees, so that there was nothing to stop the tenant from cutting them all down – which they frequently did.[11] Rents remained fixed at the level of the later fifteenth or early sixteenth centuries. Money rents which were already fixed below rack valuations in the mid sixteenth century became ossified. They remained so not simply for the duration of a forty or ninety-nine year term but, in almost every case, for subsequent terms spanning centuries. Consequently the aggregate 'money' rents of the dean and chapter's estates remained fairly constant (between £760 p.a. and £800 p.a.) from 1547 until the Ecclesiastical Commission took over in 1869.

Most serious of all, the majority of leases were for very long terms. Between 1538 and 1571 the chapter granted 223 leases: forty-two of these were for forty years, fifty-nine were for ninety-nine years, four were for 500 years and one was for 700 years.[12] The chapter very soon reached a point where all of its best properties were let on long leases and would remain so for years, often generations ahead. So it began to grant leases in reversion, in other words, leases that would only come into effect when the present lease expired. Some of these were for only a few years hence, but others would not take effect for decades. The manor and rectory of Sedgeford, for example, was let in August 1538 for ninety-nine years to Sir Thomas L'Estrange. A new lease in reversion on the same terms for a further ninety-nine years was agreed with Sir Nicholas L'Estrange in 1562; this came into effect seventy-five years later. The net result was that the estate was out of the dean and chapter's hands for 198 years. The worst effect of long leases was the confusion of boundaries that occurred, especially when the tenants were also landowners in the neighbourhood. When the Sedgeford estate finally reverted to the dean and chapter in 1736 Sir Thomas L'Estrange claimed it was too difficult to determine the exact bounds of their property. The ensuing case in chancery cost the chapter at least £177 11s. 9d. in legal and administrative fees.[13]

In 1562–67 new leases for ninety-nine years or longer were granted upon many of the chapter's properties, including Aldeby manor and rectory, Foldholme and Skeetholme marshes, Arminghall manor and rectory, Newton, Pockthorpe and some of the tenements in the close. Substantial portions of the estates were virtually

11. For example, NRO, DCN 90/12, 15.
12. NRO, DCN 47. See also NRO, DCN 29/4/19; G. A. Metters, ed., *The Parliamentary Survey of Dean and Chapter Properties in and around Norwich in 1649* (NRS, 51, 1985),

pp. 43, 50, 59–60, 63, 67, 70–71, 80, 82, 86, 96, 98.
13. NRO, DCN 90/9, 11–12; DCN 11/8 (1736–38); DCN 27/1, pp. 80–82, 493–95.

Fig. 216. Numbers 64 and 63 The Close, taken *c.* 1935–40. No. 64 was a prebendal house from 1611 to 1933. Number 63 contained remains of the monastic infirmary. It was destroyed by incendiary bombs in 1942, and a car park now occupies the site.

amortised. The practice was outlawed by an act of parliament of 1571 which banned all ecclesiastical landowners from granting leases longer than twenty-one years or three lives. Another act the following year allowed tenements and small parcels of land within towns to be let for a maximum of forty years.[14] The Norwich chapter complied. For the future most of its Norwich properties were let for forty years, while properties beyond were almost always granted in twenty-one year leases rather than the less certain term of three named lives. But the damage was already done and the problem of long leases continued to vex the cathedral authorities until well into the eighteenth century.

The 1560s and 1570s saw several allegations of dubious dealing by deans and chapter officials seeking to capitalise on their position for an instant profit. Dean John Salisbury, for instance, sold exemptions from 'knowledge money' (payments due to the dean from copyhold tenants on his installation),[15] thereby lining his

14. 13 Eliz. I c. 10; 14 Eliz. I c. 11. An act of 1575, 18 Eliz. I c. 11, banned reversions until the previous lease was within three years of expiring.

15. NRO, DCN 115/9, pp. 11–12; DCN 47/2, fos 97–115; DCN 47/1, fos 364v–368r; J. F. Williams and B. Cozens-Hardy, *Ex-* *tracts from the Two Earliest Minute Books of the Dean and Chapter of Norwich Cathedral, 1566–1649* (NRS, 24, 1953), pp. 16–17. Prideaux levied a small amount of knowledge money (£5 15s.) on his elevation to the deanery in 1702: NRO, DCN 115/1, p. 174.

pockets but reducing the income of future deans. There was inadequate supervision by the chapter of its officials, who acted on their own behalf. In part this was the fault of underhand dealing by the dean. Salisbury conspired with John Hoo, a layman whom he appointed receiver-general: together they fraudulently manipulated fines, leases and the accounts. Hoo was the last lay person appointed to this important position, the statutes of 1620 ordaining that only a prebendary could be receiver-general. The chapter clerk Thomas Hopkins used the chapter seal to validate a quire of blank sheets which he then employed to draw up secret leases to himself. These he sold to third parties causing immense difficulties as late as the 1620s, when their authenticity was challenged.[16] The chapter was not without blame. Scalby rectory was leased five times between 1570 and 1590, leading to divers lawsuits between various claimants to the property. Part of the motivation for these actions was to satisfy the demands of competing interests in the estates; part was sheer greed, since it was alleged that the dean and chapter issued a 'multitude of fraudulent leases' in order to receive the fees for entry and sealing; part may have been to create confusion among those who wished to seize on capitular property for themselves.[17]

The deliberate spinning of confused webs of leasing and releasing may well have seemed an expedient policy in the 1570s and 1580s, for these were the days of the 'land hunters' and professional searchers. The crown was convinced that institutions and individuals were concealing large estates which were its by right. Searchers who exposed such concealed lands were spurred on by the handsome profits they could make for themselves. In fright, many landholders resorted to various expedients to protect their estates, from subletting them several times (not unlike the ways that strings of holding companies can be used today in an attempt to evade paying tax) to surrendering whole estates to the crown in the hope that they would be granted back. It is probably this which lies behind the three one hundred-year leases made by Dean Gardiner to the crown in 1579–81 of most or all of the Norwich chapter's property.[18] It is also possible that he sought personal gain, as there is evidence of a £100 fine paid for at least one of these leases.[19] Whatever the motivation, the chapter's estates were immediately plunged into a long and bitter controversy over

16. NRO, DCN 29/4/9; DCN 115/9 (1570, 1615) and pp. 11–12; DCN 47/3, fos 168v–169v, 217v–218v; PRO, C2/James I/N1/50; Metters, *Parliamentary Survey*, p. 112.
17. BL, Lansdowne MS 51, fo. 49r.
18. NRO, DCN 47A/1–2; DCN 41/111; DCN 47/3, fos 124–127r, 133–134r; DCN 24/1, fos 56r, 61r, 66r. The second lease is known only from a note in the lease book where its full contents are not recorded. Demises to the crown were exempt from the legislation limiting the maximum length of leases.
19. NRO, DCN 10/1/31, receiver's accounts for 1579–80, show, among the 'foreign receipts', £100 from Cuthbert Brierton for a fine of divers lands and tenements demised to the queen.

concealed lands which, for the rest of the century, sucked in most of Norfolk's political elite and paralysed the cathedral, threatening its very existence as the action widened to consider whether the cathedral had been legally constituted in 1547. This is perhaps the most obscure period in the history of Norwich Cathedral's estates; it has already been treated fully by Dr Houlbrooke.[20]

Here it is sufficient to note that, after numerous twists and turns, the case was largely resolved by 1598, with the dean and chapter of Norwich retaining all the lands granted by the refoundation in November 1547. As Sir Edward Coke, the most eminent lawyer of the day, argued, the dean and chapter could not be illegally constituted. Not only did the mere suggestion of invalidity prejudice their tenants, but without a duly constituted chapter there could have been no bishops elected legally since the Reformation. That would have meant no diocesan jurisdiction nor valid ordinations nor institutions to benefices, 'and so many other mischiefs, inconveniences and ill consequences . . . as are too long to be rehearsed'.[21]

Even as late as 1613 the chapter confessed that 'we are scandalous for our misordered estates', yet the long concealment case had emphasised the need for longer-term planning by the dean and prebendaries, for the importance of an estate policy rather than an attitude of exploitation of their medieval inheritance.[22] Two moves arising out of the aftermath of the concealment case (both later enacted in the new statutes of 1620) began this process. The first concerned the letting of manors. From about 1600 the chapter ceased granting manorial rights (such as the right to hold the manor court and take the profits of that court) with leases of the manorial lands. Instead they were exploited by the chapter itself, becoming an important source of income. The 1620 statutes took this a step further, not only forbidding the leasing of the manor courts but also appointing an understeward who, in the absence of the dean, was to preside at these courts.[23] The second was the imposition of corn rents. One of the suggestions raised during the concealment case was that the dean and chapter should be recompensed by the imposition of a provision rent on all its tenants.[24] Though it came to nothing, the dean and chapter began after 1600 to levy a corn rent in some new leases; by the statutes of 1620 the practice was fixed as a regular obligation in all new leases where the annual rent exceeded £1. One third of the value of the money rent was added to the rent in wheat and malt at 1578 prices. Farmers could pay in cash using a prescribed formula and most seem to have done so from the beginning. The tenant was then reimbursed for the wheat and malt, but at the price of grain prevailing in 1578; the

20. See above, pp. 528–29.
21. NRO, DCN 29/2, p. 215.
22. NRO, DCN 115/9, pp. 45–46.
23. NRO, DCN 47/3, fos 90–91r, 257–258, 390v–392v. *The Statutes of the Cathedral Church of Norwich* (n. p., n. d.); there is a copy at NRO, DCN 28/1.
24. BL, Lansdowne MS 51, fo. 152v.

income of the chapter consisted in the profits accruing from the intervening rise of prices. Smaller tenements, where the annual rental value was below £1, were subject to an additional 'hen rent' or the payment of one shilling per hen in cash. Initially, provision rents were enforceable with difficulty. The chapter had to take a reduced fine to induce lessees to accept the new levy, or in some cases they were forced to convert a lease for years into a lease for lives (widely regarded by lessors as a retrograde step). The loss of immediate income antagonised some prebendaries even though the plan was prudent: for the first time in eighty years the present was sacrificed to the future and immediate consumption to long-term profitability.

Both of these new developments, the exploitation of manorial rights and the imposition of corn rents, proved significant innovations. The effect of the latter was felt immediately. Between 1622 and 1629 corn rents brought in some £90 a year to the cathedral coffers, an increase of over 11 per cent on the money rent income.[25] The full benefits, however, were not realised until new leases could be granted which, for the chapter's best manors, was often not until the early eighteenth century. The new statutes included a number of further provisions intended to put the cathedral on a sounder footing, particularly financially (though it is not always clear what was new in the statutes and what was a codifying of existing practice). Advowsons, the right to present the minister to a parish, were no longer to be let or granted away, whereas previously they had tended to be included in leases of impropriate rectories. This gave the chapter greater control over its minor canons, who could henceforth be appointed to the livings within its gift. The woods were no longer to be demised, ensuring that the chapter always had a stock of timber, not only for repairs but also as a cash reserve.[26] Finally, the issuing of the new statutes marked a greater sense of financial realism in marked contrast to the maladministration of a decade earlier.[27] In 1613 the chapter was said to owe £1600;[28] by contrast the account rolls after 1620 suggest a more managed attitude to the revenue, especially the 'foreign' receipts. Under this heading in the accounts comes a diverse collection of revenues such as fines, profits from the sales of wood and other commodities (particularly lead, stone and glass during the years under Elizabeth when parts of the cathedral and precinct buildings were dismantled and the materials sold), fees for burial and the passing of leases, the goods of felons taken in the

25. NRO, DCN 10/1/56–67. The profits from the manor courts were initially modest, less than £5 a year in the 1620s.

26. The statutes also ordained a limited return to the old system of prebends, assigning the profits of the manor of Trowse solely to the dean, but this scheme soon broke down amid conflict within the chapter and was abandoned in 1629. Henceforward all estates (bar some meadow in the close) were once again to be held in common by the dean and six prebendaries.

27. See above, pp. 514, 529.

28. NRO, DCN 29/2, pp. 129–31.

cathedral liberties and alms received from the guild of St George.[29] After 1620 the recorded profits from fines increase considerably, the beginnings of a development by which they were to become, within 150 years, the major source of revenue for Norwich and, indeed, all cathedrals.

In their essential features the statutes were to set the guidelines and parameters of estate practice (and in much else besides) for the next two centuries. Although modified by the reforms of the Victorian Ecclesiastical Commission, they were not fully superseded until 1941. Yet they had hardly had time to take effect before the political troubles of the English Civil War intervened. It may have been political and economic uncertainties which persuaded the dean and chapter to sell much of their timber in the early 1640s. Moreover, the worsening situation, and in particular the threat to the very future of all cathedrals,[30] meant that by 1644 devious or hard-pressed tenants were withholding their rents. Receipts became insufficient to meet expenses.[31] An air of normality prevailed in chapter, nevertheless, with the granting of leases continuing to be recorded in the chapter book. Some of these were precautionary measures as the chapter granted property to people it trusted, such as Christopher Jay.[32] With the abolition of deans and chapters on 30 April 1649 came the confiscation of all the estates. Ownership of all capitular lands passed to the trustees for the sale of dean and chapter estates, who began the process of selling them to raise money for the government.[33]

The property of the cathedral was surveyed as part of the process of dispersion. (So detailed were these surveys that they were still being used by the chapter well into the eighteenth century.)[34] It is difficult to discover much about the fate of the sequestered property: those who acquired cathedral property in the 1650s, except as agents for third parties, are largely unknown. Certainly, however, some of the lands were bought by local landowners, others even by the tenants. It seems possible that, as with the confiscated episcopal and royalist lands, many estates had been regained by their original lessees before 1660. The list of tenants does show that most of the families who held Norwich Cathedral lands in the 1640s were still in possession, as tenants of the restored dean and chapter, in the 1660s.[35]

29. For example, 19s. 8d. received from goods taken about Andrew Gobbett at the Popinjay, an inn in the cathedral's liberty, 1598–99, NRO, DCN 10/1/43; £117 10s. from sales of oaks from the manors of Eaton and Hindolveston; £1 1s. 8d. from sales of paving stone; and £3 6s. 8d. from the sale of the east window of the chapter house, 1568–69, DCN 10/1/26. For the dismantling of buildings see also pp. 502–3, 529.
30. See above, pp. 551–54.
31. NRO, DCN 10/2/1 (1643); DCN 24/2, fos 160–61, 165, 168.
32. NRO, DCN 24/2, fos 176–179; PRO, C5/36/45.
33. Metters, *Parliamentary Survey*, pp. 11–13.
34. Metters, *Parliamentary Survey*, pp. 12–23.
35. NRO, DCN 10/2/1; DCN 11/1. Sales of capitular lands were recorded centrally, on the dorse of the close rolls, but in such a way as to make the purchasers hard to trace: PRO, C54.

With the restoration of the king, the chapter reconvened speedily, appointing a receiver-general on 7 August 1660 as one of its first acts. Some of the chapter's most pressing concerns were the reassertion of authority over its estates and the collection of its revenues. In both it was assisted by the eagerness of possessors and lessees to secure their tenancy with new leases: some even demonstrated their willingness by paying arrears from the 1650s. By Christmas 1660 business was already routine and several new leases were sealed. The Norwich chapter had awaited government approval for this activity and took care to reoccupy their lands with some solicitude for tenants and even for 'pretended' purchasers.[36] Only in regaining control over its livings did the dean and chapter show disregard for the present possessors, hounding out nonconformist interjectors to make way for more conformable 'Anglican' clergy.[37]

Their resumption of authority produced a financial boom for the dean and chapter, as new leases were issued and old ones surrendered on properties where the tenants were uneasy about their security. Between 1661 and 1664 the chapter sealed sixty-one leases, compared with forty-eight in the more typical years between 1611 and 1620. The fines were unprecedented in volume, so much so that, in spite of abatements amounting to £6000 for all the leases agreed in the 1660s, the chapter still received over £6200 in fines between 1660 and 1670.[38] In summary the Restoration was navigated with little turbulence. The dean and chapter regained all their estates (although small parts of some of the larger properties were almost certainly lost owing to continued confusion over boundaries) and there was little disruption to the tenants. This episode in the history of the dean and chapter's estates was perhaps less profound in its consequences than might have been foreseen, particularly in the 1650s.

The forty years after the Restoration saw a number of innovations in record-keeping which improved the administration of the estates. The most significant of these were achieved by Humphrey Prideaux, appointed prebendary in 1681 and dean from 1702 until his death in 1724. Shortly after his arrival in Norwich he repaired the muniment room, rearranged the records, began a new series of rentals and instituted the private register.[39] This last summarised the details of each lease

36. NRO, DCN 24/3, fos 1–26; DCN 11/1; Bodleian Library, MS Tanner 133, fos 3, 28r–29r.
37. A. G. Matthews, 'A Norfolk Dissenter's Letter, 1662', *NA*, 24 (1932), pp. 229–32.
38. NRO, DCN 29/4/29. At the Restoration, all cathedral chapters granted substantial abatements to ease the process of the recovery of their estates and to deflect criticism of their windfall profits. See I. M. Green, *The Re-Establishment of the Church of England, 1660–1663* (Oxford, 1978), chap. 5.
39. P. Mussett, 'Norwich Cathedral under Dean Prideaux, 1702–24', in D. Marcombe and C. S. Knighton, eds, *Close Encounters: English Cathedrals and Society since 1540* (Nottingham, 1991), pp. 91, 99; NRO, DCN 27/1.

granted (the full text was copied into the ledger books or lease registers) and, more importantly, noted the true value of the estate and the fine taken, information not systematically recorded elsewhere. The private register was therefore of great value to the chapter when leases came to be renewed. Prideaux's other archival innovation was the keeping of his 'diary', a personal record from 1694 of chapter business, lease negotiation and estate business, in fact almost anything that he thought might be useful in the future running of the cathedral.[40] Unfortunately, neither the private register nor the diaries outlived Prideaux by long, but they are of enormous value in illuminating what would otherwise be dark corners of the cathedral's affairs.

The other change in archival practice was the most long-lasting. With the Restoration begins the continuous series of audit books, though the survival of the record of the 1638 audit shows that these were not entirely a Restoration innovation. At first the audit books run parallel with the earlier series of receivers' and treasurers' rolls and books, but finally supersede them in 1687. The series of audit books continues into the twentieth century: before the 1860s the only change was the substitution of English for Latin in 1733. Cast at the audit on 30 November each year and drawn up by the auditor, a lay servant of the dean and chapter, they detailed the rent arrears, the receipts from all the chapter's properties let to farm, the corn rents, the profits from the fines, manor courts and sales of timber, and the other foreign receipts, along with all the expenditure – the stipends of the cathedral officers and sums spent on 'extraordinaries' such as repairs. All that is missing is a statement of 'hen rents' and the profits of the meadows in Thorpe and in the close, the only properties the chapter let at 'rack rents' (i.e. the full yearly value of the land) rather than on long, beneficial leases. In practice, these never amounted to large sums.

The audit books were designed to show the chapter's annual profit, helpfully summarised at the foot of the account, which was then divided up among the dean and prebendaries, the former receiving one quarter, the latter an eighth each. Again they reinforced the tendency to take a quick profit. Such a 'jam today' attitude could influence the running of the estates. For instance, at least two prebendaries insisted on their shares in the £200 fine of Hindringham received in 1756 rather than using the money to augment the vicarage there.[41] Chapter members were easily tempted, especially if they feared dying or hoped for promotion elsewhere, to realise their profits today rather than wait for a greater, future sum. In 1680 Barbara Astley, as her husband the dean lay dying, procured the hasty renewal of a number of leases at low premiums rather than lose her share in the fines if they were not renewed until after his death. In 1697, when Dean Fairfax was short of cash, and again in 1700 when he thought he was dying, similar hasty renewals were entered into.[42]

40. NRO, DCN 115/1–3.
41. NRO, DCN 24/5, fos 71v, 96v.

42. Mussett, 'Prideaux', p. 95.

Nevertheless, this is only part of the picture. More usually, the management reflected the requirements of an undying corporation in which personal interests were perhaps less motivated by profit maximisation than by the desire to maintain incomes. Clearly, the estates were rarely viewed simply in economic terms. There were other factors which worked against any desire to maximise profits. A prebendary was *homo clericus*, not *homo economicus*. The dignitaries of the cathedral were not expected to be ostentatious consumers, but they were obliged by social convention to maintain a figure of respectable affluence in the world. Too much wealth was likely to incur the jealousy of a greedy and anticlerical laity.

Especially until the second quarter of the eighteenth century, when the cathedral existed in a turbulent world,[43] the estates were a means to win friends and influence people, as well as a resource for building up the church militant on earth. These attitudes affected the way the estates were managed, particularly in the choice of tenants and the calculation of fines. Once the cathedral had attained a measure of financial stability after the Restoration, the dean and chapter began to prefer clerical rather than lay tenants for its rectories and started inserting covenants in these leases requiring the performance of divine service on a Sunday.[44]

Hard bargaining by clergymen was discouraged and the dean and chapter frequently recoiled from applying the full rigour of the law: rent arrears, for example, could mount up for several years before the chapter sought legal redress or reentered the property. This tolerant and lenient attitude particularly affected the negotiations over fines for leases. In principle this was a matter of mechanical routine, using published tables of fines (in the years immediately after 1711 most usually those in Edward Hatton's *An Index to Interest*). The gross annual value of the property was ascertained and the rent payable to the chapter deducted to give a net annual value. The length of the new lease and the number of years remaining in the old would be taken into account, and the fine calculated. For a new tenant taking out a twenty-one year lease the fine would be just over seven and three quarter years' net value of the property. If, as was customary, the tenant then renewed the lease after seven years of the old had expired the fine would be one year's net value of the estate.[45] Rarely, however, did the tenant pay the full fine. Abatements were granted to men and women known to be in want, to clergymen and servants of the church, and to those who had done or might do favours for the dean and chapter. Mr Roberts, a former ship's chaplain, had his fine reduced because he had been awarded the king's medal for bravery against Algerian pirates. Lady Pratt's fine was reduced, not only 'to avoid clamour and further trouble', but also because her husband was Sigismund Trafford, formerly the MP for King's Lynn and 'a gentleman

43. See above, pp. 563–75.   45. Mussett, 'Prideaux', pp. 91–92.
44. NRO, DCN 24/4, fos 13v–14.

of interest in the country'.[46] Powerful individuals were also able to beat down the price by direct negotiation. In 1681 John Norris received an abatement of £50 of his fine, to allow for the imposition of corn rents, and £80 'out of consideration of the eminency of his person in the profession of the law and the hope we had that he might be serviceable therein to us'. Yet the grasping lawyer, who was recorder of Norwich and so not a man the chapter could afford to cross, was still not satisfied with the level of his fine, a mere £20: 'he called us Jews and gave us besides very reproachful language, telling us that no church in England would deal so with him but us, and that he was worthy us all and knew things better than us all, and that we dealt unworthily and Jewishly with him'.[47]

One other factor further reduced the fines taken. Until the later eighteenth century the chapter often allowed the tenants themselves to declare the true valuations of the property upon which the fines were to be fixed. In part this was the result of the lack of adequate supervision by the chapter over its own estates. The 1620 statutes envisaged that the dean would travel around the diocese, preaching, inspecting the estates and holding manor courts as he went, but in practice none of this happened. The understeward or his deputy presided at the manor courts but his only other role in the management of the estates seems to have been as a legal adviser. The chapter employed bailiffs of their woodlands, but no other officials solely to administer their estates. When someone was needed to execute a legal entry, for example, it usually fell to one of the minor canons or a cathedral officer, or perhaps a trusted friend or tenant, armed with appropriate letters of attorney. In 1702 Dean Prideaux appointed Isaac Miller keeper of the precinct's gaol, not for any past experience as a turnkey, but because the cathedral lacked a servant 'fit to be . . . employed in any business' and Miller appeared to be 'a person very fit to serve the church on any occasion that may happen'. He was then used to survey the woods.[48]

The chapter depended heavily on its own tenants for information about its estates. The chapter's most far-flung property was Scalby rectory near Scarborough. Here the chapter relied on the vicar to keep an eye on the tenant and the tenant to keep a watch on the vicar. All leases contained covenants that the tenant should return a full terrier every ten or so years, but these covenants were rarely, if ever, enforced. Since most capitular tenants assigned their leases to third parties, or sublet at rack rents (it was the opportunity to do this which made dean and chapter properties so desirable), they were no more in a position to survey the lands than the dean and chapter.

When a survey was required the chapter had to rely on old ones, usually the parliamentary surveys of 1649–50. In the case of Bawburgh rectory in 1694, the

46. NRO, DCN 115/1, pp. 1–3, 16–17, 39, 91.
47. Mussett, 'Prideaux', pp. 101–2.

48. NRO, DCN 23/42/2; DCN 115/1, pp. 181–82; DCN 115/2, pp. 189–90.

chapter relied on a survey conducted two centuries earlier. Only occasionally did the dean and chapter commission a survey, and then usually from one of their number or one of their minor officers. Thomas Martin, a lay clerk, undertook some surveying in the 1680s, a task which fell to Thomas Church, the sub-sacrist, between 1725 and 1742. Clearly, the chapter often neither knew the exact bounds of their lands nor their true value.[49]

The picture outlined above of the chapter's management began to change in the middle of the eighteenth century. The impetus seems to have come from the falling in during the 1730s of a number of properties, such as Sedgeford, which had been out of chapter control on long leases since the early years of the new foundation. The process of surveying these estates (in the case of Sedgeford, for the first time in two centuries), reestablishing boundaries, gaining control of the manor courts and reletting the properties on stricter terms with corn rents included was a complex one, even necessitating separate accounting procedures.[50] From mid century, although the system of beneficial leases remained, the chapter appears to have exercised a firmer grip over its estates. The chapter clerk emerges as the effective steward of the cathedral's properties, handling most of the routine matters of estate business and negotiating with tenants, although final decisions always rested with the chapter.[51] Gradually, the chapter grew better informed about its estates as it built up a series of surveys and terriers – after the 1760s most estates seem to have been mapped or surveyed by a professional surveyor every decade or so.[52] All this meant that the dean and prebendaries were less likely to be duped by devious or duplicitous tenants.[53] Even so, they were neither harsh nor rapacious landlords. In the 1770s and 1780s they were frequently generous over the setting of a fine or the terms for its payment, erring towards slight undervaluation or allowing liberal deductions from the gross value. Moreover, they might still defer to the powerful. For example, they allowed Edmund Rolfe (high sheriff of Norfolk in 1769–70) an abatement of his fine on his promise to send in a true survey of Sedgeford estate, even though they could have enforced this against him as one of the covenants in his lease or sent their own surveyor to compile a terrier.[54]

There is a further change in management style in the early nineteenth century, by which time calculating the fine seems an almost totally mechanical, mathematical matter. Long gone are the abatements of Prideaux's day to those whom the chapter

49. Mussett, 'Prideaux', pp. 99–100; London, Lambeth Palace Library, MS 930, no. 80; NRO, DCN 39/37.
50. NRO, DCN 22/10.
51. NRO, DCN 118/5.

52. NRO, DCN 51–52.
53. For example, see the arguing over the extent of their estate at Ormesby: NRO, DCN 118/5, fos 4v–5v.
54. NRO, DCN 118/5, fo. 4r; see also fo. 8.

feared or hoped might prove useful. No longer could the prospective lessee wear the chapter down by being obstreperous and obstructive. 'No alteration can be made in Mr Wright's valuation' is a phrase repeated time after time in the correspondence of the chapter clerk, John Kitson.[55] The innovation seems to have been the employment of a professional land agent (for many years Robert Wright) to conduct the negotiations with tenants over fines. A layman in such a position probably found it easier to impose a more strictly economic fine.

The chapter remained very much a landlord at arm's length. Its leases did not usually contain clauses about how the land was to be farmed, save that the timber was to be preserved. What the chapter never took was an agricultural survey: it is therefore difficult to obtain a satisfactory view of the estates as agricultural enterprises. For the agricultural historian the long series of chapter records is disappointing.

After the mid eighteenth century, however, it should not be assumed that the chapter was lax or negligent in the administration of its estates. Leases were supervised keenly – indeed, the main business of chapter meetings was the reading of new leases. Improvements were encouraged and rewarded by abatements on the fine – the chapter generally did not take notice of the improvement on the next renewal of a lease.[56] Detail, however, was left to the tenants' discretion. As William Utten, the chapter clerk, wrote to Edmund Rolfe in 1775, the dean and chapter 'have no objection to any improvement that can be made to the West Hall Farm House, and . . . they leave the management of that building to your care and judgement, not doubting but you will do everything therein, as well for their interest as your own'.[57]

What the chapter generally did not do was take any initiative or positive action in the farming of its property. They were reactive, not proactive landlords. Public enclosure affected approximately one third of the capitular landed estates between 1770 and 1820; many estates had been enclosed earlier.[58] In no case does the chapter seem to have taken the initiative yet, once consulted, it could be enthusiastic. In one instance, at Hopton in east Suffolk, it promised to surrender its rights to 'shack over the land' (that is for its tenants to turn animals into stubble fields to graze), to encourage the rest of the village to consent to an enclosure; but the chapter clerk made it perfectly plain that it was the responsibility of their tenant Mr Meek, whose initiative it was, to organise the enclosure.[59]

Only in two fields did the chapter actively seek change: its urban property and its woodland. It deliberately developed the close as a fashionable area for the gentry to reside in Norwich, repairing and improving some of the houses at its own cost

55. NRO, DCN 14/2–3.
56. For example, NRO, DCN 118/5, fos 3v–4r.
57. NRO, DCN 118/5, fo. 2r.
58. NRO, DCN 53; DCN 59/1–53; DCN 24/6, fos 1–3.
59. NRO, DCN 118/5, fo. 2.

while encouraging its tenants to do likewise.[60] While timber represented a good investment for the future, the chapter's woods were carefully conserved as stock against unforeseen expenditure. In 1779, however, the chapter began felling its trees and selling its timber on a wide scale, investing the money in 3 per cent consols (government bonds) and creating a special account, the timber fund, for the proceeds – this was not divided annually among the chapter as the other profits were.[61] While the price of timber was high during the French Wars (1793–1815) virtually all the cathedral's woods were felled (and no new trees were planted) raising £8800.[62] The expedient paid for substantial repairs and improvements to the cathedral, particularly by Anthony Salvin in the 1830s, but after this the woods, and the fund, were exhausted.[63]

The general lack of close capitular involvement in the daily running of their estates was no doubt deliberate policy. Clergymen could not be seen to be too grasping.[64] Moreover, the dean and chapter could afford to take a relatively relaxed attitude because, from the later seventeenth century to the third quarter of the nineteenth, increasing agricultural prosperity in Norfolk meant that their own incomes burgeoned. Rising grain prices meant that income from corn rents increased dramatically, while growing agricultural prosperity pushed up land values which, although not reflected in the rent roll, meant larger fines (see table 1). These changes affected the relative significance of the different sources of the chapter's income; in particular, the fines grew in importance until they became by far the chapter's most vital source of money (see table 2).

Table 1

Increase in Revenue from Selected Sources, 1671–1840

	Annual Average Receipts		
Decade	Manor Courts	Corn Rents	Fines
1671–80	£77	£490	£401
1831–40	£567	£1661	£5297
Increase	736%	339%	1321%

Source: NRO, DCN 26/10/8, DCN 11/17–18.

60. See above, pp. 639–40.
61. NRO, DCN 24/5, fo. 211r.
62. NRO, DCN 23/42/3.
63. NRO, DCN 22/11; DCN 23/28.

64. The earl of Chichester, the First Church Estates Commissioner, said in 1862 that 'it is not desirable for a bishop to have the management of a rack-rent estate': *Parliamentary Papers* (1862), viii, p. 7.

Table 2
Main Derivation of Capitular Income, 1622–1840

Income	1622–29	1671–80	1751–60	1791–1800	1831–40
	%	%	%	%	%
Money Rents	73	43	33	16	16[65]
Corn Rents	9	27	31	36	19
Fines	18[66]	22	31	41	59
Manor Courts	0	4	5	7	6
Wood Sales	0	4	0	0	0

Source: NRO, DCN 10/1/55–67, DCN 11/1–18, DCN 26/10/8.

Overall, the average annual gross capitular income increased almost five fold in the same period, from an annual average of £1937 in the 1670s to £8914 per annum in the 1830s. Table 3 shows the growth of the chapter's income. Even with the hiatus of the mid seventeenth century, it is clear how important were the changes associated with the 1620 statutes. The chapter's income trebled in the seventeenth century, increased only slowly in the first half of the eighteenth century before shooting up dramatically, especially in the first four decades of the nineteenth century: between the 1750s and the 1830s income grew by more than 300 per cent.

The great spurt in chapter profits in the first four decades of the nineteenth century, and the development of the system of taking fines for beneficial leases into an almost mechanical process, coincided with the mounting calls for reform in all walks of public life. The church was not exempt. Attention was focused on two aspects of the church's estates. The first was the great inequalities in their distribution, with large numbers of poorly beneficed clergy contrasting with a few extremely wealthy figures, especially bishops, deans and prebendaries. This situation seemed even more glaring since the growth of manufacturing cities like Manchester and Birmingham, with their large populous parishes and poor, overworked curates. The second aspect was the perceived inefficiencies in the system of church leasing with its low, fixed rents. The solution seemed simple to many reformers. The great estates of cathedrals and bishops should be managed more efficiently to produce an even greater income,

65. After 1800 the money rents were increased by the chapter's exploitation of a change in the law to allow the redemption of land tax.
66. All 'foreign receipts'.

which could then be used to augment poor benefices, especially in the northern industrial cities.[67]

A parliamentary select committee was set up in 1837 to look into the mode of granting and renewing church leases. It reported that the system of beneficial leases and raising revenue by fines was 'always improvident' and 'particularly disadvantageous to the church lessor'. 'The system tends to prevent the investment of capital in the permanent improvement of the estate', it declared, despite the assertion of Robert Wright, land agent to the Norwich dean and chapter, who gave evidence to the committee that, barring the planting of timber (which neither tenant nor chapter would undertake), there was little difference between chapter land and private land in terms of improvements. The committee's reports suggest that the Norwich chapter was perhaps one of the better ecclesiastical land-managers. The one example in England which the MPs established of an estate improvement directly paid for by an ecclesiastical body was a drainage scheme on some woodland, partly funded by the dean and chapter of Norwich.[68]

The slogan of the reformers was 'enfranchisement', by which they meant either the lessee's purchase of the freehold of the land or the lessor's purchase, on the expiry of the lease, of the lessee's residual interest in it.[69] This did not find favour with the chapter at Norwich, who refused to cooperate with the committee, rebuffing its inquiries 'inasmuch as they consider that the committee . . . is exercising a power unknown to the laws of England . . . tending ultimately to interfere with the rights of private property'.[70]

Nevertheless, the dean and chapter's management of their estates began to change in the 1840s. Enfranchisement came, but in a different garb, leaving the system of beneficial leases intact: the chapter began selling enfranchisements to its copyhold tenants only, allowing them to buy the conversion of their tenure to freehold.[71] The chapter also sold some lands to railway companies as the great railway-building age came to Norfolk. Rather than simply dividing the proceeds of these two sorts of sales among themselves, the dean and chapter applied £8200 of the profits to the purchase of an estate of 303 acres at Woodham Walter in Essex in 1847.[72] This was the first innovation – the first new estate to come to the dean and chapter

67. G. F. A. Best, *Temporal Pillars: Queen Anne's Bounty, the Ecclesiastical Commissioners and the Church of England* (Cambridge, 1964), especially chaps vii–viii; O. J. Brose, *Church and Parliament: The Reshaping of the Church of England, 1828–1860* (Stanford and London, 1959).

68. *Parliamentary Papers* (1837), vi, p. 626; (1839), viii, pp. 249–50; (1837–38), ix, pp. 55–68.

69. Best, *Temporal Pillars*, p. 372.

70. *Parliamentary Papers* (1839), viii, p. 309.

71. See, for example, NRO, DCN 24/7, fos 200, 202v, 205r, 207r, 219r, 231; DCN 24/8, fos 1, 23, 31, 40, 44, 54, 64, 67, 116, 119, 140.

72. NRO, DCN 24/7, fos 92–127, 135, 141r, 179, 211.

since the refoundation of 1547 had brought Scalby rectory in North Yorkshire. The second was that the Essex property was let not on a beneficial lease but at rack (i.e. economic) rents — the first time the chapter had done so (excepting some of its Norwich urban properties) since the middle ages. Through the 1850s and 1860s other estates were to follow, as the dean and chapter slowly divested themselves of some of their inherited estates and estate practices, converting some beneficial leases to rack rents, purchasing other lands and investing in dividends and shares.[73] In 1880 they gave the unenclosed 184 acres of Mousehold Heath to the city corporation of Norwich to make a 'people's park'.[74] These changes altered the chapter's sources of income and increased its profits. In the two years 1867–68, the chapter obtained 11 per cent of its wealth from corn rents, 8 per cent from money rents, 2 per cent from dividends and interest, 3 per cent from its manor courts, 42 per cent from fines and 34 per cent from rack rents. Over these two years its annual receipts averaged £10,652.[75]

This was a high point; it was also a time of radical change. Since 1852 chapters had begun commuting their estates with the Ecclesiastical Commissioners. The principle was that chapters transferred all their lands in return for cash payments until such time as they could be reendowed by the Commissioners with a convenient estate sufficient to produce the same annual revenue. Centralised administration, it was hoped, would produce an increased return for the whole church which could be applied to poor livings.[76] The dean and chapter of Norwich, however, resisted, largely thanks to the opposition of Dean Pellew. They sent a counterblast to the Cathedrals' Commission in 1853, denouncing the changes as a 'desecration of ecclesiastical revenue', seeing the weakening of the church in every twist of public debate, and defending their present management of the estates:

> Communication with different tenants . . . bring[s] us usefully in contact with the various classes of society . . . showing us their grievances, necessities, and defects . . . [enabling] us the better to remedy and relieve them, whilst our possession of lands in various parishes . . . [gives] us an interest in the inhabitants, enlist[ing] our sympathies in their favour, and to a certain extent authoriz[ing] our interference in promoting their welfare.[77]

73. In 1857 the chapter bought a portion of Plumstead Hall estate in Norfolk; two years earlier they had been thwarted in their attempts to buy an estate at Holbeach in Lincolnshire by an Ecclesiastical Commissioners' resolution restricting capitular purchases to their respective dioceses: NRO, DCN 24/7, fos 223v, 233.

74. P. Cooper, *The Mousehold Study*, i, *A Dis-* cussion Paper (Norwich, 1978), p. 2. Negotiations for the transfer had begun in 1864: NRO, DCN 24/8, fos 101v, 105r.

75. NRO, DCN 11/20.

76. P. Barrett, *Barchester: English Cathedral Life in the Nineteenth Century* (London, 1993), p. 220.

77. *Parliamentary Papers* (1854), xxv, pp. 875–77; Best, *Temporal Pillars*, pp. 458–59.

The Ecclesiastical Commission could not, however, be resisted for long. Pellew died in 1866 and was succeeded as dean by Edward Goulburn. Parliament ruled against beneficial church leases in 1868.[78] The following year the dean and chapter agreed a commutation with the commissioners. Almost all the dean and chapter's lands and properties were transferred to the Ecclesiastical Commissioners.[79] In return the dean and chapter were granted lands in Middleton, Wormegay, Setchey and Tilney cum Islington in Norfolk and Wingfield in Suffolk. In addition they received a payment from the commissioners of £2600 a year which continued until 1878. Then it was replaced by the transfer from the commissioners of rack rents and tithe rentcharges to the value of £2000 a year.[80]

After two and a half centuries of almost constant growth of capitular income, the commutations brought a decline in receipts to around £8900 a year in the early 1870s.[81] On top of this, agricultural depression hit Britain badly after the late 1870s. Nearly all cathedrals, their revenues still dependent on land rentals, were severely affected. Their incomes had been arranged by the Ecclesiastical Commissioners just before the depression, when Victorian rentals were almost at their peak. They proved unequal to the promises made in those negotiations.[82] Norwich was no exception. Agricultural distress meant that many tenants fell into arrears while others pleaded for rent reductions; the chapter was forced, sometimes, to accede.[83] Total receipts fell, from an annual average of £7555 between 1882 and 1888 to an average of £6606 a year from 1896 to 1902, a drop of more than 12 per cent.[84] It is no surprise that the Norwich chapter felt itself hard done by at the hands of the Ecclesiastical Commissioners, but theirs was a fate by no means worse than that of most large landowners in the east of England after 1880.

Encouraged by the fall in property values and agricultural rents, in the 1880s and 1890s the chapter continued to divest itself of lands. Some appear to have been sold and the profits invested in stocks and shares. Others were transferred to the Ecclesiastical Commissioners by two further agreements, of 1887 and 1894, in return

78. The Ecclesiastical Commission Act, 1868 (31 and 32 Vict. c. 114), section 9, forbade the taking of fines and the granting of beneficial leases and enforced the levying of economic rent on any dean and chapter once they had commuted any of their estates with the Ecclesiastical Commissioners.

79. The dean and chapter retained Arminghall, Eaton, Foldholme and Skeetholme marshes, Great and Little Plumstead, Surlingham marshes, Field Dalling and Thorpe meadows in Norfolk, and Woodham Walter in Essex, together with the cathedral precincts and all rights of patronage. Compare the list above

of medieval cathedral property, fig. 121.

80. NRO, DCN 24/8, fos 135v, 138r; *Parliamentary Papers* (1870), xxi, pp. 644–47; (1871), lv, p. 246; (1884), xxii, p. 87. The lands passed to the commissioners in 1869 were estimated to be worth £380,000 freehold.

81. NRO, DCN 11/20.

82. Barrett, *Barchester*, pp. 220–21; O. Chadwick, *The Victorian Church*, 2 vols (London, 1966–70), ii, p. 367.

83. NRO, DCN 24/9, fos 42v, 51v, 53v–54r, 70r, 130r.

84. NRO, DCN 11/20–21.

for more tithe rentcharges.[85] By 1902 the chapter possessed only two estates – the precinct, let at rack for £1136 a year, and Surlingham Marsh, let for only £4 os. 5¾ d. per annum. The rest of its income came from tithe rentcharges (worth £3876 that year) and dividends and interest (£1798 in 1902).[86]

In his chapter on the cathedral between 1538 and 1628, Dr Houlbrooke raised the question of when the chapter achieved the goal of financial security.[87] There are, in effect, three aspects to this (see table 3). First, the addition of corn rents, the exploitation of the manor courts and the more systematic taking of fines, especially after the 1620 statutes, meant that the chapter no longer suffered the severe debt and financial insecurity of the preceding seventy years. However, as in other areas of the cathedral's life, the intervention of the Civil War and abolition meant that the prolonged enjoyment of the financial benefits arising from these reforms was postponed until later in the century. Secondly, even though the chapter's income rose faster than prices for two centuries after the Restoration, the flaws in the system of capitular finance, particularly the holding of an inadequate cash reserve of only £100 and the annual distribution of profits for the immediate benefit of the dean and prebendaries, meant that chapter finances were by no means copper-bottomed. Finally, expenditure on the fabric tended to increase as the income grew, and often outstripped the immediate ability to pay. Despite increased income, repairs to the spire in 1634 and to the whole church in the 1660s were part-funded by appeals to tenants and the diocese. Salvin's work on the south transept and choir was achieved by the almost total felling of the chapter's woodlands. The £12,000 fabric fund, created in the mid nineteenth century by order of the Ecclesiastical Commissioners, was soon overspent: later nineteenth- and twentieth-century work and embellishments were increasingly undertaken with gifts from individual deans and public appeals.[88] Financial security has, in this sense, been elusive. It remains to be seen whether the application of state aid in the 1990s will finally achieve the goal that Dean Gardiner sought more than four centuries before.

The history of the cathedral's estates fall approximately into three phases. From 1101 to the early fifteenth century was the period of acquisition as the estates were built up, especially at the beginning of the period. The early fifteenth century to the middle of the nineteenth forms virtually a continuous phase, uninterrupted by the Reformation, and with the 1650s as only a caesura. This was the long period of

85. NRO, DCN 50/1–18.
86. NRO, DCN 11/21.
87. See above, p. 530.

88. See above, pp. 624, 627, and below, pp. 719, 726.

beneficial leases and the development of the system of manipulated fines. The estates were slowly eroded throughout the period but, after the mid seventeenth century, inflation was more than compensated by increasing annual revenues. Finally, the mid nineteenth century to the mid twentieth witnessed the heyday of the Ecclesiastical Commissioners and the gradual loss of all the cathedral's estates, finally endorsed by the Cathedrals' Measure of 1931 which transferred all remaining capitular property to the commissioners, bar the tiny island of the cathedral's precincts, the close.[89]

The donations of Roger de Munteny and Eudo the steward, of Hubert de Rye and Godric the steward, given to Norwich Priory in piety and in perpetuity for the salvation of their souls, have been lost to the cathedral. Their only epitaph is the survival of the building itself over nine centuries and the lives and continuing prayers of the unbroken chain of monks and canons who grew fat or preached the gospel with the proceeds. Yet most of the estates remain the property of the wider church and their profits still support the church militant. As the scribe who penned the donation of Eaton Manor from Alan, son of Flaald, to the monks early in the twelfth century wrote, 'our goods are gifts from God and their continuance is established by divine grace . . . Possessions perish through men, and men because of possessions, but the things of God abide for ever in God'.[90]

89. *Parliamentary Papers* (1930–31), x, pp. 482–83, 497, 501. The Ecclesiastical Commissioners became the Church Commissioners in 1948.

90. *First Register*, pp. 43–45.

Table 3
The Income of the Dean and Chapter, 1554–1902

	Annual Receipts	Index 1554–60 = 100	Price of a Composite Unit of Consumables 1554–60 = 100
1554–60	£ 746	100.0	100.0
1561–69	£ 716	95.9	94.7
1573–80	£ 857	114.9	112.7
1581–90	£ 799	107.1	120.4
1595–1600	£ 790	105.9	180.9
1612–16	£ 832	111.5	186.4
1622–29	£1130	151.5	177.6
1638	£1312	175.9	238.5
1671–80	£1937	259.7	207.1
1681–90	£1895	254.0	192.7
1691–1700	£2489	333.6	223.5
1701–10	£2656	356.0	203.6
1711–20	£2519	337.7	218.2
1721–30	£2368	317.4	203.9
1731–40	£2555	342.5	296.4
1741–50	£2736	366.8	200.2
1751–60	£2910	390.0	213.7
1791–1800	£4789	642.0	360.1
1831–40	£8914	1194.9	391.3
1850–56	£8876	1189.9	378.2
1867–68	£10,652	1427.9	444.8
1869–75	£8934	1197.6	450.8
1882–88	£7555	1012.8	349.7
1889–95	£6999	938.2	325.5
1896–1902	£6606	885.5	327.0

Sources: NRO, DCN 10/1/13–44, 52–67; DCN 11/1, 14, 17–21; DCN 26/10/8; E. H. P. Brown and S. V. Hopkins, 'Seven Centuries of the Price of Consumables Compared with Builders' Wage-Rates', in E. M. Carus-Wilson, *Essays in Economic History*, 3 vols (London, 1954–62), ii, pp. 179–96.

32

Music in the Cathedral

Peter Aston and Tom Roast

In common with other Benedictine houses of the middle ages, the cathedral priory of Norwich had music as an integral part of the daily *Opus Dei* from the time of its foundation. The earliest surviving documentation of this is in the Customary, which dates from the late thirteenth century, though the book certainly reflects much of the practice which had gone before.[1] The Customary gives indications of the chants which were to be sung and of the ritual which accompanied them.[2] There is mention of the solo singers who, for example, acted as 'beginners' for certain chants; reference is made to the place which the postulants (*pueri* or *iuvenes*) had in certain services.[3] For services with exceptional richness of ritual – those for Ash Wednesday and Holy Week are good examples – the musical component is described in considerable detail, though here as elsewhere in the manuscript no actual musical notation is given. The Customary also suggests that part-music (probably simple polyphony to be improvised against a plainchant tenor) was allowed for respond-verses on the feast of St Stephen, and for the Alleluia sung on the Sunday after Easter.[4]

It is impossible to establish when professional singing men were first brought into the choir to supplement the routine singing of the monks. The precentors' rolls record payments to singers on special feast days from the middle of the fourteenth century onwards, though it is not clear whether these were laymen or monks. An entry in 1352–53 refers to 'the expenses of singers, viz. at the feast of All Saints, Christmas, Easter and at other times'.[5] While these singers may well have been

1. Cambridge, Corpus Christi College, MS 465. For a description and transcription of the manuscript, see J. B. L. Tolhurst, ed., *The Customary of the Cathedral Priory Church of Norwich* (Henry Bradshaw Society, 82, 1948).
2. See above, pp. 314–24.
3. Since puberty did not occur at such an early age as it does now, it is likely that the postulants (candidates for admission to the priory) included some unbroken voices.
4. F. Ll. Harrison, *Music in Medieval Britain* (London, 1958), pp. 113–14.
5. NRO, DCN 1/9/6. The authors are indebted to Barbara Dodwell for placing details of her research at their disposal and for supplying the references shown in notes 5 to 16.

laymen, payments made in the late 1370s were, variously, 'to our brothers singing at Christmas'[6] and 'to our fellows [*socii*] singing'.[7] Lay musicians were certainly employed by the middle of the fifteenth century. John Scarlet, a minstrel, was paid a stipend during 1441–42,[8] and entries in subsequent years refer to his responsibility for training the choir and organising music for the mass.[9] In 1445 he was put in charge of the song schools in the city. Other lay musicians are mentioned during the last quarter of the fifteenth century. In 1477–78, a small sum was paid for the refreshment of Thomas Borell 'and other singers of the Lord Suffolk',[10] while in 1480–81 a payment of two shillings was made to William of Gloucester 'for singing in the choir for the Mass of the Blessed Mary at the feast of her nativity.[11]

The first Norwich Cathedral musician whose name is known is Adam the organist, for whom a robe was purchased in 1333.[12] The rolls of the master of cellar record a payment of twenty shillings for mending the organs during the year 1313–14.[13] From the mid fourteenth century onwards there are numerous references to repairs to the organs and to payment of an organ-blower on the principal feast days. An entry for the year 1379–80 is of particular interest, for it refers to expenses 'for the great organ and for the little organ in the chapel of St Mary'.[14] The latter would have been used for the daily Lady Mass, which was sung polyphonically from the fourteenth century onwards and may well have required the services of professional lay musicians. An organ was repaired in 1469 following damage by fire.[15] Further fire damage occurred in 1510, resulting in a new organ being placed in the chancel.[16]

From the Reformation to the Interregnum: The New Foundation

When the priory was dissolved in 1538, the entire foundation was taken over, with the prior and convent becoming the dean and chapter.[17] The draft statutes of Henry VIII set down the required number of persons to sing in the choir. There were to be eight minor canons (or vicars choral), six lay clerks and eight choristers, 'boys of tender age and tuneful voice, skilled in singing'.[18] It may be assumed that the choir had been similarly constituted during the period immediately before the Dissolution. The statutes also prescribed that there should be a master of the choristers

6. NRO, DCN 1/9/16.
7. NRO, DCN 1/9/17, 1/9/18, 1/9/25.
8. NRO, DCN 1/6/66.
9. NRO, DCN 1/6/68, 1/12/58.
10. NRO, DCN 1/9/78.
11. NRO, DCN 1/9/79.
12. NRO, DCN 1/4/28.
13. NRO, DCN 1/1/23.
14. NRO, DCN 1/9/18.
15. NRO, DCN 1/4/91.

16. NRO, DCN 1/4/110.
17. P. le Huray, *Music and the Reformation in England, 1549–1660* (London, 1967), p. 14.
18. NRO, DCN 29/2, pp. 23–55. For a translation of the items relevant to the musical establishment, see A. Cornall, 'The Practice of Music at Norwich Cathedral, *c.* 1558–1649' (unpublished University of East Anglia M. Mus. thesis, 1976), pp. 135–37.

who was skilled in playing the organ. In 1542 Thomas Grew from Windsor became the first holder of that office; he received a grant to keep and feed the children and to train them in singing and organ-playing.[19] In 1555 Edmund Inglott was appointed in place of Grew; and in 1580 there is the first account for the full choir, showing that by then it comprised eight minor canons and eight lay clerks, with Inglott as organist and master of the choristers.[20] The statutes of 1620 formalised the musical establishment at six minor canons, one gospeller, one epistoler, eight lay clerks, eight choir boys and an organist,[21] an arrangement kept (barring occasional vacancies and the hiring of supernumerary lay clerks) until the number of minor canons was reduced in the mid nineteenth century.

The senior lay clerk in 1580 was Osbert Parsley, whose surviving compositions provide the first examples of polyphonic music written for Norwich Cathedral. He died in 1585: a memorial tablet in the north aisle of the cathedral records that he was a singing man 'full fifty years'. If this is to be believed, he was singing at the time of the Dissolution and continued as a member of the choir during the years of the Reformation, through the reverses under Mary Tudor and well into the reign of Elizabeth I. His music reflects the changing practices of the times, with works for both Latin and English rites. Like his contemporary Thomas Tallis, Parsley composed a five-part setting of the Lamentations of Jeremiah and some Latin motets, as well as English service music and a quantity of consort music for viols. His setting of the Lamentations is unusual in having the plainsong *cantus firmus* in the highest voice throughout, which may be taken to indicate that it is a pre-Elizabethan composition. His five-part motet *Conserva me, Domine* makes enterprising use of canonic imitation, while his instrumental ensemble music shows considerable contrapuntal ingenuity.

For the visit of Queen Elizabeth to the city in 1578, a new organ was installed at a cost of £16 12s. It took eight weeks to build and involved the use of water to stabilise the wind.[22] The instrument lasted until it was damaged in 1601, when the spire was struck by lightning, causing part of it to fall. Another organ was built in 1607;[23] this instrument remained in use until the cathedral was looted in 1643.[24]

During Edmund Inglott's time in office, the dean and chapter granted reversions

19. W. Shaw, *The Succession of Organists of the Chapel Royal and the Cathedrals of England and Wales from c. 1538* (Oxford, 1991), p. 197.

20. N. Boston, *The Musical History of Norwich Cathedral* (Norwich, 1963), p. 38.

21. NRO, DCN 28/1.

22. H. W. Saunders, 'Gloriana', Friends of Norwich Cathedral, *Third Annual Report* (1932), p. 15.

23. T. Browne, *Repertorium: or, Some Account of the Tombs and Monuments in the Cathedral Church of Norwich* (London, 1712), p. 31.

24. J. Hall, *Hard Measure* (1647), p. 63, quoted in K. R. Long, *The Music of the English Church* (London, 1972), p. 205.

Fig. 217. John Byfield's organ of 1759, replaced in 1834 by one built by Bishop.

of his post to a number of different people, among them Thomas Morley (who was to become the leading English composer of his generation) and William Inglott, Edmund's son.[25] Morley was probably a chorister at Norwich: he succeeded to the position of master of the choristers in 1583, a post he held until 1587.[26] He was subsequently appointed organist at St Paul's Cathedral and became a gentleman of the Chapel Royal in 1592. In his theoretical treatise *A Plain and Easy Introduction to Practical Music* (1597), Morley quoted a three-part instrumental canon by Parsley to show how a plainsong melody could be 'broken' (i.e. elaborated) and used as the basis for a polyphonic composition.[27]

William Inglott held office during two periods, the first as organist and master of the choristers between 1587 and 1591. Later, following the separation of the

25. Shaw, *Succession*, p. 198.

26. W. Shaw, 'Thomas Morley of Norwich', *Musical Times*, 106 (1965), p. 669.

27. T. Morley, *A Plain and Easy Introduction to Practical Music* (London, 1597); modern edition by A. Harman (London, 1952), pp. 177–79.

duties of the organist from those of the master of the choristers, he returned to Norwich, and from 1611 until his death in 1621 he held the post of organist.[28] His sacred compositions, comprising a service setting and at least three anthems, survive only in incomplete form, but there are two extensive keyboard pieces by him in the Fitzwilliam Virginal Book.[29]

In the intervening years between Inglott's appointments (during which time he may have been organist at Hereford Cathedral),[30] two other composers held official posts at Norwich. William Cobbold, a contemporary of Morley, became organist in 1594,[31] by which time some of his compositions were already in print. In 1592 Thomas East published *The Whole Book of Psalms*, a collection of metrical versions of the psalms with four-part harmonisations of common melodies by various contemporary composers. Eleven of the psalms have settings by Cobbold, some of which were reprinted in subsequent collections as late as 1712. Only one church anthem by Cobbold survives,[32] though Morley included a madrigal by him in his collection *The Triumphs of Oriana* (1601).[33]

The other Norwich composer of this period was Richard Carlton, a minor canon of the cathedral from 1591 until at least 1609 and master of the choristers between 1591 and 1605.[34] He, too, contributed to Morley's *Triumphs*,[35] and in the same year he published his own collection of twenty-one pieces under the title *Madrigals to Five Voices*. Since the late 1580s the Italian madrigal had become extremely popular in England, largely as a result of Morley's interest in its lighter forms, the *canzonetta* and *balletta*. From these Morley evolved his own madrigalian style, his various publications exerting a powerful influence on other English composers, Carlton among them. However, most of the pieces in Carlton's collection are in the pre-madrigalian English tradition, being stylistically closer to the polyphonic songs of William Byrd than to the madrigals of Morley. In the preface to the collection Carlton stated: 'I have laboured somewhat to imitate the Italian . . . yet may I not nor cannot forget that I am an Englishman'. The comment is an interesting one, for it reveals that Carlton was aware that his music was in a style that had by then passed out of fashion. An inability to come to terms with recent musical developments was to be a characteristic of virtually every Norwich composer from the early seventeenth century onwards, an indication perhaps of the provincial spirit of the cathedral's

28. Cornall, 'Practice', pp. 119–20.
29. Cambridge, Fitzwilliam Museum, Mus. MS 168; modern edition by J. A. Fuller Maitland and W. Barclay Squire (London and Leipzig, 1894–99). The titles of the compositions by Inglott are *A Galliard Ground* and *The Leaves be Green*.
30. Shaw, *Succession*, p. 135.

31. NRO, MS 431, fo. 31.
32. *In Bethlehem Town*, London, Royal College of Music, MSS 1045–51 and Durham Cathedral, MS A2.
33. *With wreaths of rose and laurel*, no. 12 in the collection.
34. Cornall, 'Practice', p. 112.
35. *Calm was the air*, no. 7 in the collection.

musicians. Like Cobbold, Carlton appears to have spent most of his life in Norfolk. Surprisingly, only the fragments of two anthems by Carlton have survived.

The last organist before the Interregnum was Richard Gibbs. During his time the posts of organist and master of the choristers were once again united.[36] He was still being employed as late as 1649 even though choral services were discontinued in 1643 following the ransacking of the cathedral by puritans and destruction of the organ.[37] One of Gibbs's compositions – the short full anthem *Have mercy upon me* – was sufficiently well regarded by Thomas Tudway for him to include it in the large manuscript collection of cathedral music he prepared during the early years of the eighteenth century under the patronage of Robert, Lord Harley (later earl of Oxford).[38] A two-part version of this piece had already been published in John Playford's 1663 collection, *Catch that Catch Can*. Gibbs also composed a large-scale verse anthem, *See sinful soul*, for performance on Good Friday, but the work is incomplete in the manuscript sources.

The century following the Reformation saw the development of a new order for cathedral music, emanating from the Act of Uniformity of 1549 which required strict adherence to the Book of Common Prayer in worship. New orders of services were created, while the appearance of a number of set canticles within the order for matins and evening prayer provided composers with an opportunity to make musical settings of these invariable texts. Norwich Cathedral had its own composers during this time, but the music of their better-known contemporaries – Tallis, Byrd, Gibbons and others – would, without doubt, have featured in the worship. A pattern of choral services was thus established which became the basis of the cathedral musical tradition which has lasted to the present day.

From the Restoration to 1720

The audit books for 1661 show that the minor canons and lay clerks were reappointed in similar numbers to those in office before the Interregnum, and that Richard Gibbs had been replaced as organist by Richard Ayleward.[39] With the resumption of choral services at the Restoration, choristers appear to have been recruited immediately: on 30 November 1661, Peter Sandley, an experienced lay clerk, was ordered by the chapter to be paid £5 'for teaching the singing boys for one year last past'.[40] In 1665 a new organ was installed,[41] replacing a temporary instrument which had been acquired in 1661. A list of moneys disbursed upon the reparations

36. Shaw, *Succession*, p. 202.
37. Boston, *Musical History*, p. 70.
38. BL, Harleian MS 7340, fo. 42.
39. Boston, *Musical History*, pp. 60–61.
40. NRO, DCN 24/3, fo. 37v.

41. R. M. Wilson, 'Music and Musicians of Norwich Cathedral' (supplementary notes, not dated, to unpublished University of Illinois Ph. D. thesis, 1988), p. 34.

of the church in 1661–62 includes a payment of £45 to 'Richard Plumm of Bury for the organ'; a separate payment of £5 is listed 'for taking down the organ, packing it, carriage etc.'.[42]

Another aspect of the musical revival was the provision of music books for the choir. These were either purchased or copied out by lay clerks. By 1666 there were more than fifty bound volumes of services and anthems in the custody of the precentor.[43] While most of the books from this period have been lost, there is a surviving set of partbooks and an accompanying organ book compiled during the seventeenth and early eighteenth centuries.[44] These books provide a unique source of compositions by Norwich composers, including three service settings and twenty anthems by Ayleward.

Ayleward had been a chorister at Winchester, where his father was a minor canon,[45] and he held office at Norwich between 1661 and 1669, with a break from 1664 to 1666 when Thomas Gibbs (possibly the son of Richard Gibbs) was organist.[46] During Ayleward's time at Winchester, Christopher Gibbons, the son of Orlando Gibbons, was in charge of the music. Ayleward's compositions show signs of Gibbons's influence, with large-scale works for divided choir and some occasional chromatic word-painting of a madrigalian nature. The responses from his morning and evening service in D now have an established place in the repertoire of many cathedral and parish church choirs, but it is his anthems which, though uneven in quality, deserve the greater attention. Some of the solos in his verse anthems reflect his interest in the Italian declamatory style; others demonstrate a lyrical gift unusual among Norwich composers of the post-Restoration period.

The next organist at Norwich was Thomas Pleasants, who held office for twenty years from 1669.[47] No compositions by him survive, though there are fragments of some anthems by his son, William, who was a lay clerk.[48] The task of providing

42. NRO, DCN 29/4, fo. 21.
43. Bodleian Library, MS Tanner, 133, fo. 187v.
44. Cambridge, Rowe Music Library, MSS 9–17. R. T. Daniel and P. le Huray, 'The Sources of English Church Music 1549–1660', *Early English Church Music*, supp. vol. I (London, 1972), date these books *c.* 1660 (i, p. 1); le Huray, *Music and the Reformation in England*, p. 92, dates them *c.* 1640 or very early Restoration. However, since the collection contains music by Norwich composers active during the period 1660–1720, the books cannot have been completed until well into the eighteenth century, though they may well have been begun some years before the Interregnum.

45. P. R. Granger, 'Richard Ayleward', in S. Sadie, ed., *The New Grove Dictionary of Music and Musicians*, 20 vols (London, 1980), i, p. 755.
46. NRO, MS 431, fo. 133.
47. NRO, MS 432, fo. 124.
48. NRO, MS 432, fo. 128. The organ part to *Bring unto the Lord* by William Pleasants is in Cambridge, Rowe Music Library, MS 9, fo. 108. There are voice parts of a service by him in Norwich Cathedral, Mus. MS 4, fo. 40, MS 6, fo. 44v, MS 7, fo. 43, MS 8, fo. 46v, MS 9, fo. 41, and MS 10, fo. 47. A treble part of his anthem *O praise the Lord* is in Norwich Cathedral, Mus. MS 15, fo. 95v.

new works for the choir at this time seems to have shifted to others on the musical staff, most notably Anthony Beck, John Jackson and John Connould.

Anthony Beck had been a lay clerk in the years before the Restoration;[49] in 1663 he became a minor canon and was appointed precentor.[50] His two surviving anthems, *Behold how good and joyful*[51] and *Who can tell how oft he offendeth?*,[52] show him to have been a competent if unadventurous composer. On the other hand, the one anthem by his contemporary, Braithwaite Souter, who was a lay clerk from 1661 to 1680 and one of the copyists involved in compiling the new choir books,[53] is amateurish in the extreme. By his will, Souter left one hundred sets of partbooks to the dean and chapter for the choir's use.[54] The books have been lost but an inventory of them shows that they included music by Byrd, Morley, Wilbye, Nicholas Yonge and Peter Philips, as well as motets by various continental composers, among them Lassus, Sebastian Ertl, Girolamo Boschetti and Giuliano Cartari.[55] The collection may be taken to indicate Souter's antiquarian tastes and his interest in continental music of the sixteenth and early seventeenth centuries. It is impossible to know whether any of the pieces were used in services at Norwich.

John Jackson, who was admitted a lay clerk and appointed master of the choristers in 1669,[56] appears to have been a considerably more prolific composer than Beck or Souter. He had come to Norwich from Ely Cathedral, where he had been instructor in music; he subsequently moved to Wells Cathedral, where he was organist from 1674.[57] Jackson wrote at least twelve anthems and three services; two three-part devotional songs by him were included in Playford's *Cantica sacra* of 1674. Much of his music is now lost, but one anthem, *The Lord said*, occurs in numerous contemporary manuscript sources, differently arranged by Jackson for the three cathedrals he served. The affective declamatory style pervades the solo parts in this anthem, and there is a chorus of Hallelujahs in dance-rhythm, a typical feature of Restoration church music. The anthems of John Connould, who served the cathedral

49. Beck was admitted a lay clerk on 3 September 1639: NRO, DCN 24/2, fo. 161v.
50. NRO, DCN 24/3, fo. 47r.
51. Cambridge, Rowe Music Library, MSS 10–17.
52. Cambridge, Peterhouse Library, MSS 35–37 and 43–44.
53. Wilson, 'Music and Musicians', pp. 4 and 34. Wilson gives 1660 as the year of Souter's appointment. In fact, he was admitted on 27 December 1661: NRO, DCN 24/3, fo. 38r.
54. NRO (Shirehall), MF 475, dean and chapter

peculiar, register of wills, vol. iii, fos 210v–212r, with a copy of an extract in NRO, DCN 29/2, p. 348.
55. NRO, DCN 29/2, pp. 388–90.
56. NRO, DCN 24/3, fo. 89.
57. W. Shaw, 'John Jackson', in S. Sadie, ed., *The New Grove*, xix, p. 438. Jackson appears to have left Norwich in 1672. On 5 October in that year Thomas Pleasants, the organist, was also admitted master of the choristers in place of John Jackson, 'lately gone from the cathedral church': NRO, DCN 24/3, fo. 113v.

in various capacities between 1670 and 1687,[58] show a marked difference in complexity between the elaborate verse sections for solo voices and the sections for full choir, which are much shorter and are generally in a simple chordal style. This suggests that the choir consisted of a few highly competent singers and a majority of lesser ability.

In 1689 James Cooper replaced Pleasants as organist, having been a lay clerk from 1679;[59] he continued as organist until 1720.[60] Cooper was a prolific composer and his verse anthems, like Connould's, contrast simple passages for the full choir with elaborate solos in the declamatory style. Some of these solos are for bass voice and have a range exceeding two octaves. This particular feature may have been in vogue at the time as a result of the virtuoso parts written by Purcell for the celebrated bass singer, John Gostling; but Cooper is unlikely to have written such demanding solos unless he had an accomplished bass at his disposal. Only one of Cooper's anthems seems to have been known outside Norwich: *I waited patiently* joined the earlier composition by Richard Gibbs in Tudway's collection of cathedral music.[61]

A minor musical figure from this period was Richard Blagrave, one of a family of Norwich musicians and a lay clerk from 1684.[62] Not a note of music by Blagrave appears to have survived, but in 1690 he compiled a collection of anthem texts entitled 'Cantica Sacra: or Divine Anthems Usually Sung in the Cathedral Church of Norwich'.[63] As might be expected, Norwich composers feature prominently in the collection, with anthems by Ayleward, Jackson, Cooper and Blagrave himself alongside pieces by some of their better-known contemporaries, including Purcell and Michael Wise.

In the year of Cooper's appointment the organ was rebuilt by Renatus Harris with three manuals, 1375 pipes and twenty stops.[64] Later, a trumpet stop was added at Cooper's expense.[65]

From 1720 to 1819

The death of James Cooper in 1720 represented something of a watershed in the cathedral's musical history. From the time of the Reformation each organist and master of the choristers had been trained in the cathedral tradition; with the possible exception only of Thomas Pleasants, they had all written music for the choir to

58. NRO, DCN 24/3, fos 92v, 97r, 100v, 108v, 122v, 129v, 136r, 143r and 145v. Connould was admitted a lay clerk in 1670 and became a minor canon later the same year. He was at various times epistoler and gospeller, and served as sacrist from 1681 to 1687: NRO, DCN 11/3.

59. NRO, DCN 11/2.
60. Shaw, *Succession*, p. 203.
61. BL, Harleian MS 7341, fo. 127.
62. NRO, DCN 11/2.
63. Bodleian Library, MS Tanner 401.
64. Boston, *Musical History*, p. 12.
65. NRO, MS 431, fo. 55.

perform, as had other members of the musical staff. Humphrey Cotton, who was organist from 1721 to 1749,[66] was not from a cathedral background. He appears to have written little music for the choir, becoming increasingly involved in the musical life of the city. Cotton, whose father was a Norwich freeman, had been organist at the church of St Peter Mancroft from 1717 until his appointment at the cathedral.[67] He, too, was granted the freedom of the city in 1722.[68] The practice of copying anthems into choir and organ books, for which numerous payments were made during the latter part of the seventeenth century, continued into the eighteenth century and included payments to Cotton himself (though the only pieces by Cotton to have survived are one service and one anthem). As well as playing the organ, Cotton seems to have taken over responsibility for its maintenance: between 1726 and 1748 he received an annual payment of £5 'for keeping the organ'.[69] The 1720s and 1730s saw the formation of a number of music societies in the city and the introduction of benefit concerts, at which Cotton was a regular performer.[70]

Cotton's successor as organist was Thomas Garland, who was appointed in 1749 at the age of eighteen and who died in office in 1808 after a tenure of fifty-nine years.[71] Garland, like Cotton, gave many concerts in the city. He was a pupil of Maurice Greene, though since little of his music has survived it is difficult to judge the extent of Greene's influence on him as a composer.[72] The second half of the eighteenth century saw the publication of various collections of church music in score, beginning with the collection compiled by William Boyce and issued in three volumes between 1760 and 1778 under the title *Cathedral Music*. This collection, which included anthems and services by English composers from the sixteenth century to the time of Boyce, was acquired by the cathedral along with another collection compiled by Philip Hayes.[73] From this point onwards, payments for pricking (i.e. copying) music became less frequent and, as further collections were acquired, the repertory of the choir was gradually enlarged.

The organ built by Harris in 1689 was rebuilt by John Byfield in 1759 (fig. 217), when Garland composed an anthem for the occasion of its opening.[74] As music became

66. NRO, MS 431, fo. 63.
67. F. Newman, *Two Centuries of Mancroft Music* (Norwich, 1932), p. 4.
68. Shaw, *Succession*, p. 203.
69. Wilson, 'Music and Musicians', pp. 38–39.
70. T. Fawcett, *Music in Eighteenth-Century Norwich and Norfolk* (Norwich, 1979), frontispiece.
71. Shaw, *Succession*, p. 204.
72. Incomplete parts of Garland's *Sing unto the Lord* are in Norwich Cathedral, Mus. MS

2, fo. 43v, MS 3, fo. 48, and MS 4, fo. 28v. An incomplete part of his *Save me, O God* is in Mus. MS 12, fo. 5v. Parts of three further anthems by him, *Like as the hart*, *Behold now praise* and *Sing ye merrily*, are in unnumbered MSS at Norwich Cathedral.
73. Wilson, 'Music and Musicians', pp. 42–45 passim.
74. J. E. West, *Cathedral Organists Past and Present* (London, 1921), p. 81. The anthem by Garland is not named.

associated increasingly with fund-raising in the city, the cathedral hosted annual charity concerts from 1773, donating substantial sums for the benefit of the recently-opened Norfolk and Norwich Hospital. The music of Handel featured prominently at these concerts, particularly his *Dettingen Te Deum* and his coronation anthem *Zadok the Priest*.[75]

A musical force of particular significance during Garland's time as organist was the Beckwith family. Edward Beckwith was master of the choristers from 1759 while simultaneously holding the post of organist at St Peter Mancroft.[76] His son, John 'Christmas' Beckwith (so called because he was born on Christmas Day), succeeded to both posts at his father's death in 1793; he eventually replaced Garland as cathedral organist in 1808, a position he occupied for only one year until his own death.[77] His elder son, John Charles Beckwith, in turn became organist until 1819.[78] Of the three generations, John 'Christmas' achieved the greatest recognition outside Norwich both as a performer and a composer. Contemporary reports speak highly of his organ playing, praising in particular his abilities as an extemporiser.[79] In 1785 the cathedral subscribed to 'Mr Beckwith's anthems',[80] and in 1789 the stationer was paid £3 4s. 6d. for 'Mr Beckwith's anthem books'.[81] These books were, no doubt, Beckwith's *Six Anthems in Score* which he dedicated to the dean and chapter.[82] He also composed and published pieces for organ and harpsichord, and in 1808 he brought out *The First Verse of Every Psalm . . . with an Ancient and Modern Chant*, a forerunner of the pointed psalter.[83] His music, like that of most English composers of his day, reflects the influence of Handel.

Two clergy composers were attached to the cathedral at this time. James Williams Newton, who became a minor canon in 1776, published a collection of psalm tunes and anthems entitled *Psalmody Improved*.[84] Ozias Thurston Linley, son of the stage composer Thomas Linley, was appointed a minor canon in 1790.[85] Some service music of his survives both at Norwich and at Dulwich College, where he became an organist-fellow in 1816.[86]

75. Fawcett, *Music in Eighteenth-Century Norwich*, p. 15.
76. Boston, *Musical History*, p. 85.
77. Shaw, *Succession*, p. 204.
78. Shaw, *Succession*, p. 205.
79. *Gentleman's Magazine*, 79 (1809), p. 589.
80. Wilson, 'Music and Musicians', p. 43.
81. Wilson, 'Music and Musicians', p. 44.
82. J. Beckwith, *Six Anthems in Score: Dedicated with the Utmost Respect and Gratitude to the Revd. the Dean and Chapter of Norwich*

(Norwich, not dated).
83. J. Beckwith, *The First Verse of Every Psalm of David* (London, 1808).
84. J. W. Newton, *Psalmody Improved: A Collection of Psalm Tunes and Anthems for Two, Three and Four Voices, to Which is Added a Celebrated Anthem by G. F. Handel* (Ipswich, 1775).
85. NRO, MS 431, fo. 221.
86. G. Beechey, 'Ozias Thurston Linley', in S. Sadie, ed., *The New Grove*, xi, p. 10.

From 1819 to 1928

The dominant figure in the musical life of Norwich Cathedral during the nineteenth century was Zechariah Buck. He became a chorister in 1807, having reputedly been singing in the street when he was overheard by Thomas Garland. A few years later he was articled to John Charles Beckwith. When Beckwith became incapacitated through illness Buck assumed many of his duties.[87] On Beckwith's death in 1819 Buck was appointed organist and master of the choristers. When he retired in 1877 he had given the cathedral seventy years of unbroken service.[88]

During the fifty-eight years he was in charge of the music, Buck raised the choir to a standard of excellence at a time when the general standard of cathedral singing in England was extremely low.[89] His reputation as a choir-trainer became legendary. There are recollections by former choristers of his exacting rehearsals and the eccentric techniques he sometimes employed.[90] The quality of the boys' singing was acclaimed by many visitors to the city, including Jenny Lind who heard the choir in 1847.[91] During the latter part of his tenure of office, Buck rarely played the organ, these duties being carried out by one of his pupils, Edward Bunnett.[92]

Buck composed a number of hymns and anthems for the choir, some of which were included by Bunnett in his collection *Sacred Harmony*.[93] Though neither a composer nor organist of the first rank, Buck was an outstanding teacher. Among the large number of his articled pupils who went on to make significant contributions in Norwich and elsewhere were W. R. Bexfield and A. R. Gaul, both of whom achieved some distinction as composers in their day. Another pupil, A. H. Mann, an eminent scholar and historian of musical life in East Anglia, became organist at King's College, Cambridge.[94]

During the 1840s the number of minor canons was reduced from six to three, this number being maintained for the rest of the century. In 1862 there were eleven lay clerks, of whom three were supernumerary, and twelve choristers, four of them supernumerary; in the following year two boy altos first appear in the accounts.[95] The practice of employing boys to supplement the adult altos continued until at least 1886; the account for the year 1885–86 shows that there were still two alto

87. F. G. Kitton, *Zechariah Buck: A Centenary Memoir* (London, 1899), p. 2.
88. Shaw, *Succession*, p. 205.
89. The poor state of English cathedral music at this time was described by S. S. Wesley in his tract *A Few Words on Cathedral Music and the Musical System of the Church, with a Plan of Reform* (London, 1849).
90. Kitton, *Memoir*, p. 9.
91. Kitton, *Memoir*, p. 13.
92. Shaw, *Succession*, p. 359.
93. E. Bunnett, *Sacred Harmony: Consisting of Chants, Sanctuses, Kyries, Doxologies, Anthems, Hymns and Voluntaries for the Organ* (Norwich, 1865).
94. Shaw, *Succession*, p. 359.
95. NRO, DCN 11/20.

boys but only eight choristers and one supernumerary chorister.[96] The audit books suggest that between 1862 and the early 1880s the number of lay clerks was reduced from eight to seven, and eventually to six. This continued to be their number until the early years of the twentieth century, though the regular lay clerks were supplemented by supernumerary singers. The number of supernumeraries fluctuated from year to year: during 1897–98, for example, there were three; during 1901–2 there were five.[97]

Buck's successor as organist was F. E. Gladstone, who held office from 1877 to 1881. He was followed by another of Buck's pupils, F. C. Atkinson, who returned to Norwich from a post in Bradford. Atkinson, a minor composer, left for Cheltenham in 1885.[98] During these years, the choir's library of music was much enlarged. Cheaper methods of printing made sheet music more readily available. Several bound collections of anthems were assembled, most of the music being by Victorian composers.

When Frank Bates was appointed organist in 1885, one of his first concerns was the state of the organ.[99] Byfield's instrument of 1759 had been extensively altered by Bishop in 1834 (fig. 218).[100] The cathedral now turned to the local firm of Norman and Beard, who rebuilt the organ with five manuals and 4148 pipes.[101] For the service of dedication, in 1899, the cathedral choir was augmented by choirs from Ely Cathedral and King's College, Cambridge; A. H. Mann was at the organ.[102] Bates inaugurated a series of popular concerts in the cathedral, called 'Music for the People'. For the cathedral's 800th anniversary celebrations in 1896 he brought together massed choirs, soloists and an orchestra for a performance of Mendelssohn's *Hymn of Praise*.[103] Bates composed a number of modest pieces for the cathedral choir, several of which were published. He retired in 1928.[104]

From 1928 to 1994

Ever since the time of Humphrey Cotton, the Norwich Cathedral organist had been involved, to a greater or lesser extent, in the musical life of the city. Heathcote Statham was another long-serving organist who, between 1928 and 1966, took a leading role in concert activities outside the cathedral. Like F. E. Gladstone and Frank Bates, he served as conductor of the Norwich Philharmonic Society, succeeding

96. NRO, DCN 11/21.
97. NRO, DCN 11/21.
98. Kitton, *Memoir*, p. 56.
99. F. Bates, *Reminiscences and Autobiography of a Musician in Retirement* (Norwich, 1930), p. 40.
100. Boston, *Musical History*, p. 14.
101. Boston, *Musical History*, pp. 18–21.
102. Bates, *Reminiscences*, p. 58.
103. Bates, *Reminiscences*, p. 54.
104. Boston, *Musical History*, p. 90.

Bates in 1928 and continuing for a period of thirty-two years, during which time he greatly extended the scope of the society's programmes, introducing many new works including some of his own compositions.[105] He also shared in the conducting of the Norfolk and Norwich triennial festivals between 1936 and 1961 and, during the mid 1940s, he conducted the London Symphony Orchestra for three seasons of concerts in London. He composed choral and organ music, much of it published, and edited a collection of anthems by John Blow.[106] He retired from the cathedral in 1966 with the title of organist emeritus; the following year he was appointed CBE for services to music.

During Statham's tenure of office the cathedral hosted many diocesan choral festivals in which large numbers of singers took part.[107] It was also during his time that the choir school, after eight centuries of independence, became part of Norwich School; the absorption was marked by a service in the cathedral in July 1951.[108]

Statham was at the organ at evensong on 9 April 1938 when the instrument was badly damaged by fire.[109] The organ was rebuilt by Hill, Norman and Beard to a specification drawn up by Statham and, despite the difficulties of the times, the new instrument was ready by 1942, though the new case, designed by Stephen Dykes Bower, was not built until 1950. The new organ, which is essentially the instrument still in use today, had 105 stops, of which thirty-three remained from the 1899 instrument, and 6655 pipes. A feature of Statham's scheme was the inclusion of six manual divisions, playable from four keyboards, with rocking tablets to enable most divisions to be transferred from one keyboard to another. Two divisions are on the east side of the case, three are on the west, while the remaining pipework is in the north and south triforium galleries. The rocking tablets enable the instrument to speak either to the choir, where most services are held, or to the nave, where larger services, concerts and recitals take place. The scheme is an ingenious means of reconciling the conflicting purposes of an organ built on the pulpitum screen.[110]

Statham's successor was Brian Runnett, who had previously been lecturer in music and organist at the University of Manchester.[111] He was appointed organist and master of the choristers at Norwich in 1967, but held the post for only three years; his tenure of office was brought to a tragic end on 20 August 1970 when he

---

105. N. Miller, 'The Norwich Philharmonic Society: A Brief History', in *Norwich Philharmonic Society: 150th Anniversary Concert Programme Book* (Norwich, 23 March 1991), p. 20.

106. *Fourteen Full Anthems by John Blow* (London, 1925).

107. Boston, *Musical History*, p. 90.

108. Boston, *Musical History*, p. 91.

109. Boston, *Musical History*, p. 24.

110. The original specification is given in Boston, *Musical History*, pp. 29–33. For a description of the instrument and details of the present specification, see *The Organ in Norwich Cathedral* (undated pamphlet published by Norwich Cathedral, author not named).

111. Shaw, *Succession*, p. 207.

was killed in a road accident at Lichfield. During the short time he was at the cathedral, Runnett prompted a number of important tonal changes to the organ. Additionally, in 1969 he added at his own expense the cymbalstern, a set of six bells and rotating star, mounted on the west side of the case. He also founded the Cathedral Recitals Society, quickly establishing it as one of the principal concert-promoting bodies in Norwich.

One of the most significant developments during the 1960s was the contact made between the music department of the cathedral and the music school of the newly-established University of East Anglia at Norwich. On his appointment at the cathedral, Runnett also became a part-time lecturer at the university, thus establishing a link between the two institutions which has continued to the present day. In the same year, the dean and chapter founded an organ scholarship tenable by a student reading music at the university. This was followed in the late 1960s by the institution of an informal scheme of choral scholarships, a scheme which was eventually formalised in 1975. Since that time, the adult section of the cathedral choir has been composed of lay clerks and choral scholars in roughly equal proportions, normally six of each. The existence of choral scholarships has attracted several outstanding young singers to Norwich, some of whom have gone on to achieve international distinction in opera and on the concert platform. The statutes of 1966 allowed some degree of flexibility in the size and composition of the choir, requiring that 'there shall be as many lay clerks as the administrative chapter consider suitable, after consultation with the organist', and that 'wherever possible there shall be not fewer than twenty choristers, including probationers'.[112] In recent years there have been twelve men, six of them choral scholars, and between sixteen and twenty-two choristers, including probationers.

Runnett was greatly admired in Norwich as a choir-trainer; his reputation as an organ recitalist was an international one. In 1968 he was invited by the BBC to play at a Promenade Concert. He made several recordings as an organist and also as a harpsichordist and conductor. After his death, his parents donated his books and music scores to the cathedral, where they form the Runnett Memorial Library.

Following Runnett's death in 1970, Philip Ledger, director of music at the University of East Anglia from 1965 to 1974 and a former organist of Chelmsford Cathedral, took charge of music at the cathedral until Runnett's successor was appointed in 1971. The new organist was Michael Nicholas, who came to Norwich from St Matthew's Church, Northampton. He continued in office until 1994, when he was appointed chief executive of the Royal College of Organists.

During the twenty-three years he was in Norwich, Nicholas made important

---

112. Statutes of 1966 (NRO, DCN 28/3), p. 14 (statute xiii).

contributions to various aspects of the musical life of the East Anglian region.[113] He succeeded Runnett as a part-time lecturer at the university, where he was instrumental in introducing a specialist M.Mus. degree in English church music. In 1972 he was appointed choral conductor of the Norwich Philharmonic Society, a post he held for the next twenty-two years. He was a key figure in the Norfolk and Norwich Festival, serving as chorus-master for two festivals in the 1970s and again for the festival in 1988, and he frequently appeared as an organ recitalist and choral conductor in concerts organised by the Cathedral Recitals Society.

In both the cathedral and the city, Nicholas was best known as a champion of twentieth-century music. His enthusiasm for the work of living composers was reflected in the concerts he gave with the Philharmonic Society and in the music he introduced into services at the cathedral. He himself composed numerous pieces for the cathedral choir, some of them published, others of an occasional nature, but his most important contribution to cathedral music in Norwich and elsewhere was made by commissioning anthems and services from leading contemporary composers, many of them with no organ-loft connections.

It was to provide a focus for the work of such composers and to encourage wider use of their music that Nicholas established the Norwich Festival of Contemporary Church Music as a joint venture by the cathedral and the university.[114] The first festival, in 1981, was held over a single weekend and was attended mainly by local people. Subsequent festivals grew in size and scope, the 1992 festival running for a full week and attracting many visitors from overseas. In the space of eleven years the festival had established itself as a major international event, known by church musicians world-wide.

Though each of these festivals has featured concerts, workshops, lectures and discussion seminars, the core of the programme has always been the daily services sung by the cathedral choir, when anthems and services by such composers as Jonathan Harvey, John Tavener, Arvo Pärt, Stephen Oliver, Giles Swayne and Robert Walker have been given particular prominence. However, it is not only during the festival that music by leading contemporary composers can be heard in the cathedral. During the past two decades, new music reflecting innovations made by composers outside the church has featured regularly in the cathedral's worship alongside works from the established repertoire.

With the departure of Michael Nicholas in 1994, a new chapter in the musical

113. For an account of Nicholas's activities in East Anglia 1971–94, see P. Aston, 'Michael Nicholas: Music-Maker', in C. Smith, ed., *Echoes, Mainly Musical, from Norwich and Around* (Norwich, 1994), pp. 9–11.

114. For an account of the first four festivals, see P. Aston, 'A Festival of Contemporary Church Music', *Musical Times*, 130 (1989), pp. 369–71.

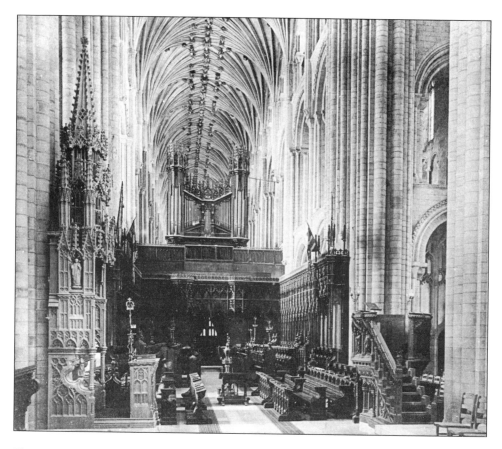

Fig. 218. The choir, looking west, *c.* 1893–94, showing Bishop's organ of 1834.

history of Norwich Cathedral will begin. Organists of the future will follow a long line of musicians stretching back to the Reformation and beyond. During nine centuries of worship at Norwich, the contribution has been, and continues to be, a vital one.

33

Change Not Decay: An Account of the Post-Medieval Fabric

Thomas Cocke

This chapter attempts to sketch the outlines of the long and complex building history of Norwich Cathedral since 1600. There is space only to deal with the church, rather than include the associated buildings in the close. Much research remains to be done. Philip McAleer's pioneering analysis of the successive stages of the west front needs to be followed by similar studies of the rest of the building,[1] in particular of the tower and spire and of the choir. But first of all the subject needs to be accepted as of interest in its own right.

In 1898 the author of the *Bell's Guide to Norwich Cathedral* could dismiss the post-medieval treatment of the building as unbroken vandalism. 'The history of the architecture . . . might safely stop at the Dissolution, since when it is a mere recapitulation of the doings . . . of more or less deeply incriminated fanatics and restorers'.[2] Even the recent authoritative account by Professor Fernie treats these elements in the building as 'additions and alterations' and devotes just three pages to them.[3] The former quotation illustrates well both the devotion of the Victorians to the medieval and their loathing of their more immediate predecessors. That negative view is particularly inappropriate and insensitive in the case of Norwich. More than most cathedrals in England it has been radically refashioned both inside and out. The west front has changed its appearance almost once a century; the south transept was totally transformed in the 1830s. The tower and spire have inevitably needed extensive repair. Inside, the choir, although remaining in its original position under the crossing, has been recast at regular intervals since the Dissolution.

It can be argued that the major 'cause' of these continuous interventions was the

---

1. J. P. McAleer, 'The Façade of Norwich Cathedral: The Nineteenth-Century Restoration', *NA*, 41 (1993), pp. 381–409.

2. C. H. B. Quennell, *The Cathedral Church of Norwich* (London, 1898), p. 19.

3. Fernie, *NC*, pp. 196–99.

Perpendicular reconstruction of the Romanesque building. The west front was given a grand window and portal but the Romanesque framework remained and the two elements were not bound together, either structurally or aesthetically (fig. 219). The spire was raised with the same concern for visual effect rather than for stability. Thus, succeeding generations were faced with fundamental problems to which their answer varied according to the concerns of their own times.

Another general characteristic of the post-medieval restorations at Norwich is that they were inspired and directed almost exclusively by the deans. Although constitutionally deans are the leading figures in cathedrals, significant restoration work has often been inspired by others, notably by diocesan bishops and sometimes prominent laymen. An obvious case is that of Bishop Shute Barrington and the work of James Wyatt which he inspired at both Salisbury and Durham cathedrals during the closing decades of the eighteenth century. The lack of architectural patronage by bishops of Norwich after the Reformation may be due to the relative modesty of the episcopal revenues, as compared for instance with neighbouring Ely. As regards the laity, there may have been some lingering lack of sympathy between the county and the cathedral. There is little evidence of a general appeal to the county until the 1890s – and even then it was cautiously announced – unlike other cathedrals where appeals to the gentry are found from the late seventeenth century onwards.[4]

The seventeenth-century work on the cathedral is a confusing mixture of a few major events, for which no supporting documents survive; and some detailed accounts, which are not easily attributed to any specific part of the building. In the former category comes the damage to the spire by lightning in 1601 and by strong winds in 1629. It was repaired four years later, exactly contemporary with the rebuilding of the spire at Higham Ferrers in Northamptonshire.[5] Frustrating as it is to know so little of the fund-raising and technology involved in these important interventions, it is equally frustrating to have a full sheaf of papers for repairs to the cathedral in 1660–61, starting in September and continuing into January, which is divided between a day-book recording the names of workmen who were mostly carpenters and plumbers, and lists of materials ordered, mostly timber and every form of metalwork, but which rarely mentions whereabouts in the building the work was to be done.[6] Presumably the major need was for expenditure on roofs and windows.

---

4. There are some exceptions to this rule. There was an appeal to tenants for the repair of the spire in 1634 - the circular letter from the dean and chapter of 10 March 1634 was printed in *NA*, 5 (1859), pp. 122–23; and a further appeal for a new organ after the Restoration (Bodleian Library, MS Tanner 134, fo. 207). At the same period £874 was contributed by the public to general repairs (NRO, DCN 29/4/21). I owe these references to the kindness of Ian Atherton.

5. NRO, DCN 107/4.

6. NRO, DCN 107/2.

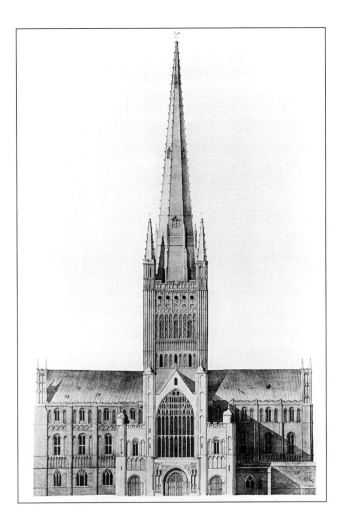

Fig. 219. West elevation of the cathedral, by J. A. Repton, *c.* 1800, showing the west front and transept turrets before the nineteenth-century alterations.

Although puritan Norfolk had not loved its Laudian bishops, the cathedral had not suffered overmuch in the Civil War. Bishop Joseph Hall understandably felt bitterly about the treatment of his cathedral and wrote a vivid and much quoted account of 'clattering of glasses, beating down of walls, tearing up of monuments, demolishing of curious stonework'.[7] Yet, as at Chichester or Winchester, this episode in 1643 was a brief interval of destructiveness, aimed at the trappings of prelatical worship, not at serious damage to the fabric. This is confirmed by a curious post-Restoration account by Mr Woafe of the same sacrilege, which can only cite as grievous damage the riding of horses in the cathedral on Christmas day and the exposure of buttocks to the high altar.[8] Perhaps the most notable casualty was the

7. J. Hall, *Hard Measure as it was Written by Himself* (London 1710), pp. 15–16.

8. NRO, DCN 107/3.

late medieval version of the Losinga tomb, which seems to have suffered the same treatment as the effigy of Robert of Normandy at Gloucester Cathedral.[9]

After 1660 the dean and chapter could set about putting the building and, in particular, the choir to rights. By 1670 the dean and chapter claimed to have spent £2800 on cathedral repairs and furnishings in the past decade, over and above the £900 odd raised from public donations, and a further £1542 on renovating houses in the close.[10] Significantly, a replacement tomb of Losinga the founder was 'built new by Mr Brigstock' in front of the high altar, so reasserting the rights and the legality of the cathedral establishment after the Interregnum.[11] In 1683 the dean and chapter spent the not inconsiderable sum of £30 on this venture. (The inscription around the border dates the setting up of the tomb to 1682 but payment was made in 1683).

With the turn of the eighteenth century, more extensive structural work begins to be recorded. In 1713 and again in 1714 pinnacles were blown down, causing damage particularly in the north aisle. Five bays of the south aisle roof were also repaired, with the timberwork costing over £60 and the lead £150.[12] The collapse of the north-west pinnacle of the west front and the prudent lowering of its south-west pair presumably led to their capping with the ogee cupolas known in the past and again today.[13] This seems on balance a more likely date for the alteration than those proposed of *c*. 1600 or 1678–79 by McAleer (see also above, fig. 201).[14]

The two major campaigns of work on the cathedral in the eighteenth century were much more substantial. The earlier was that conducted by Robert and Matthew Brettingham from 1739.[15] It was strictly practical, concentrating on the structure, in contrast to that in the 1760s which dealt chiefly with the arrangement and appearance of the choir and of the whole east end.

Matthew Brettingham's involvement began with a survey of the building, for which he received £30.[16] The major task was to repair the central tower, excluding

9. J. Alexander and P. Binski, eds, *Age of Chivalry: Art in Plantagenet England, 1200–1400* (London 1987), p. 371. See also p. 484

10. NRO, DCN 29/4/29 for money spent, DCN 29/4/21 and Bodleian Library, MS Tanner 138, fo. 156 for public donations. I owe this information to the kindness of Ian Atherton.

11. NRO, DCN 107/8. N. Boston, 'The Founder's Tomb in Norwich Cathedral', *NA*, 32 (1961), p. 3.

12. NRO, DCN 107/6 and 107/8.

13. NRO, DCN 107/5.

14. McAleer, 'Façade of Norwich Cathedral',

pp. 382–403. The comments by Charles Lyttelton and Dean Bullock cited below (pp. 709–10) indicate that the turrets flanking the gable were not reduced in height until the time of Brettingham's restoration in *c*. 1750.

15. For the first couple of years Matthew Brettingham worked in conjunction with his brother Robert (who was in fact the main contractor), but then Matthew worked alone: NRO, DCN 24/5, fo. 26v; DCN 11/8 (1740).

16. NRO, DCN 11/8.

the spire, the turn of which came later in the 1750s. Work on the building over the three years, 1739–41, cost about £2260, of which half was spent on the tower stonework. Careful preparation beforehand had involved the construction of an 'engine' at the crossing between the walls of the choir – presumably a kind of windlass to help raise materials up into the tower – as well as a model of the scaffolding. In 1742 Brettingham was also involved with the delicate work of reinforcing the foundations on the north side of the church, for which some years later he received a special gratuity.[17]

At the end of the 1740s Brettingham was employed at the cathedral again, this time for work on the west end, including the west window, which was restored thanks to a bequest of £160 by Dean Baron (1733–39). Whereas before Brettingham had been paid simply the conventional consultant's fee of £30 or £35 and the actual labour had been done by the various master craftsmen regularly employed by the cathedral, on this occasion he must have received the building contract himself, since he was paid the large sum of £420 without any further details being given.[18] The experiment, if it was such, was not repeated when the spire was repaired in 1756 under the direction of John Parsons.[19] On the west façade, 'round balls [meaning perhaps the orbs crowning the ogee caps to the turrets depicted in contemporary views: see fig. 215] and other such vile ornaments' were substituted for the original 'fine Gothic of the front', to the disgust of the discriminating medievalist Charles Lyttelton. As will be seen later, it was the dean and chapter rather than Brettingham who should bear the major responsibility for any deficiencies in the design.[20]

Brettingham was qualified for the job not by particular skill or interest in Gothic architecture but by a county-wide reputation for competent surveying. The cathedral was another of the public works on which he was consulted, such as bridges or Norwich Castle. The sparse references to the detailing of his repairs suggests a brisk approach to the fabric. In 1741 there was a payment of £17 for 'cutting down' plinths and bases as well as repairing breaches and burying rubble.[21] But the experience Brettingham gained at the cathedral may have given him a more sympathetic view of medieval buildings. His rebuilding of St Margaret's church at King's Lynn, of which the Norwich dean and chapter held the rectory, after the spire of the

17. NRO, DCN 11/8 and 11/9.
18. NRO, DCN 11/9.
19. NRO, DCN 11/10.
20. Letter of 1750 from Lyttelton to Browne Willis, BL, Additional MS 5841, p. 57. Lyttelton, the dean of Exeter and afterwards bishop of Carlisle, as well as president of the Society of Antiquaries, was a pioneer in the study of medieval architecture, particularly of the Romanesque. See T. Cocke, 'Rediscovery of the Romanesque', in G. Zarnecki, J. Holt and T. Holland, eds, *English Romanesque Art, 1066–1200* (London, 1984), p. 362.
21. NRO, DCN 11/9.

south-west tower had fallen in 1741, is in a respectable if not inspired East Anglian Perpendicular. Equally his repairs to Norwich Castle, including his new battlements, did not compromise the bold Romanesque detail. The elder William Wilkins specifically noted that until a 'recent' (*c.* 1795) rebuilding, 'in all former repairs and changes the original elevation of the structure had been constantly attended to'.[22] Brettingham even designed the new Shire House in Gothic, perhaps with some thought of retaining a stylistic congruity with the two other great public buildings of the city, the castle and the cathedral.

In Brettingham's work concern for the practical was matched by a concern for economy. This typical aspect of eighteenth-century restoration projects is so well illustrated by an (undated) letter from Dean Bullock (1739–60), defending Brettingham from charges of extravagance, that it is worth quoting at length.[23] The dean admitted that he was 'thoroughly sensible that in pushing on the repairs of a long-neglected church, it is very easy to give offence'. He put the words into the mouths of his opponents in chapter, saying that 'this Brettingham is a grievous burden to us and we pay him needlessly for what we could do as well and as cheap without him'. He went on:

> but the truth is that he [Brettingham] has too much skill in forwarding a work which we have no inclination to and therefore we are sick of him. For my own part I had not the least acquaintance with Brettingham, until I first asked Dean Penny's[24] and your consent to consult him about the church and since then I have been thoroughly satisfied that we have had things done in a better manner and at a cheaper rate by his assistance . . . I should wrong my own judgement if I did not support him as far as I am able.

The dean admitted that the proposed pavement was 'a plain job that could be done without a surveyor' but, even there, Brettingham's proposals were cheaper by a penny per foot than those of his rival contractor, Stafford. It had been alleged that Brettingham 'takes money on both sides' but, even if true, he still saved the cathedral expense. For instance, if Brettingham would charge the chapter £20 for a job no one else would have done under £50 and he then arranged matters so that he made £40 out of the contract, then that was still a bargain for the chapter.

The dean claimed that he was not easily persuaded to speak 'thus hardly of his brethren' but 'the treacherous designing conduct which so glaringly appeared through all the proceedings in our last chapter has made an impression on me which will

22. W. Wilkins, 'An Essay towards a History of the Venta Icenorum of the Romans and of Norwich Castle', *Archaeologia*, 12 (1795), p. 155.

23. NRO, DCN 117/1/17.

24. Nicholas Penny held the first stall at Norwich from 1722 to 1745; he was also prebendary (1725–30) and then dean of Lichfield (1730–45).

not easily be worn out'. His final sally was that the bishop not only consented to but approved the taking down of the turrets which, according to Mr Stafford's computation, will 'save us £500 in our pockets'.

Another significant work of the mid eighteenth century was the dismantling and rebuilding of the top of the spire and three of the flanking pinnacles in 1756 (fig. 220). The man responsible was John Parsons, who was obviously more than a run-of-the-mill craftsman, since he was paid for making a model of the upper part of the spire to show how the ironwork was fixed and the scaffolding arranged.[25] The work as described in the accounts seems admirably conservationist with, for instance, 697 ft (212 m.) charged for 'piecing, pointing and mending' the stonework of the flanking pinnacles. William Wilkins senior claimed that the timber framing within the spire (see above, fig. 33) dated from the time of Dean Lloyd (1765–90), but it is perhaps more likely to have been inserted earlier by Parsons.[26] Also probably of this date was the coved ceiling to the tower lantern, apparently removed *c.* 1886 (fig. 221). Its classical design with rosettes and medallions might appear to have been executed in plaster: the Winkles' account describes it as 'a flat ceiling of stucco work, with cornice and panels, adorned with

Fig. 220. The weathercock of 1756, the time of John Parsons's rebuilding of the top of the spire, photographed in 1899 (NRO, DCN 131/49).

wreaths and medallions, very good in its way; but we need hardly say totally out of place here, spoiling the whole effect of the lantern'.[27] Nineteenth-century photographs suggest that it was painted in a 'trompe l'oeil' design on the boarding. The uncertainty as to its form illustrates the difficulty of judging work of this period, since later writers and draughtsmen have been so unsympathetic that proper records have rarely been made even of such major features as the lantern ceiling.

25. NRO, DCN 107/9. Parsons' bill for 1756.
26. S. R. Pierce, ed., *John Adey Repton: Norwich Cathedral at the End of the Eighteenth Century* (Farnborough, 1965), p. 20.

27. H. and B. Winkles, *Architectural and Picturesque Illustrations of the Cathedral Churches of England and Wales*, 3 vols (London, 1838–42), ii, p. 93.

Fig. 221. The tower lantern ceiling in the second half of the nineteenth century, showing the eighteenth-century treatment of panelled rosettes (NRO, DCN 131/36).

The restoration works conducted under Dean Lloyd in the 1760s comprised both structural work, similar to Brettingham's, and a new and different perception of how the interior of the cathedral should look (for a view of the choir after Dean Lloyd's restorations, see fig. 206). In 1766 the choir was repaved under the direction of John Ivory. In 1767 the cathedral was closed for repairs and alterations which lasted until the beginning of 1768.[28]

Before the repair of 1767, the lower arches of the presbytery were in 'utter ruin' and one of the pillars between them so weakened as to endanger the whole east end. Dean Lloyd recognised that the screen wall then running across the apse behind the high altar was an insertion and he had it removed to make the apse a 'beautiful termination' to the choir.[29] The 'ornamental pillars' were newly built in stone but their capitals were executed in plaster. (All evidence of this was carefully removed one hundred years later by Dean Goulburn.) The decorative 'fluting' and the communion rails were designed by Thomas Pitt of Camelford, the noble amateur who had assisted Horace Walpole at Strawberry Hill, Lord Temple with the Corinthian

28. Dean Lloyd's 'Memoranda', NRO, DCN 118/1, pp. 5–7.
29. NRO, DCN 118/1, pp. 38–40. Eighteenth-century sources use the term 'choir' to cover both the choir proper and the eastern arm in general, sometimes also described as the 'chancel'.

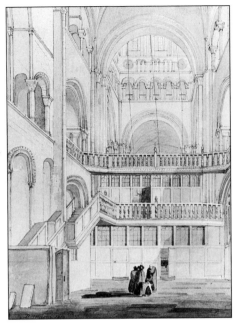

Fig. 222. David Hodgson's watercolour of the front of the gallery across the north transept, with the 'closets' above, in 1832, shortly before Anthony Salvin's alterations. In this form they were probably the work of Thomas Ivory (NRO, DCN 128/3).

Fig. 223. The back view of the 'closets' in the north transept, by David Hodgson, 1832 (NRO, DCN 128/4).

arch at Stowe and Charles Lyttelton with the contemporary choir furnishings at Carlisle Cathedral. However, the new bishop's stall which was installed at this time, thanks to the generosity of Bishop Yonge, and the balancing though simpler chancellor's stall opposite on the north side of the choir, were the work of the local man, Thomas Ivory (John Ivory's uncle) rather than the metropolitan Pitt. Judging from contemporary drawings, it was also Ivory who had designed the boxes and the ornamental cresting above them, thus reshaping the double galleries or 'closets' which ran across the ends of the transepts at the crossing (pl. Vb, c and figs 222, 223). Most of this was lost in the refashioning of the choir in the 1830s, but the bishop's stall survived until displaced in the 1890s to the Bauchun Chapel: it is now in store. The large window at the east end at gallery level was reopened and glazed, in part to obtain a draught through from the west which the dean was acute enough to realise 'keeps the church free from damp'. The five-light window above in the clerestory was altered to give more scope to a painted window, supplied by the dean's wife in 1777. Mrs Lloyd repeated her success in 1780 with an ambitious design in the lower window based on Raphael's *Transfiguration*.

In 1770 a lightning conductor was installed on the spire according to advice given by the Royal Society, with 'metallic communications' to the ground. A lightning strike in 1760 had luckily hit the weathercock and not split the spire as it had done in 1601. The dean used the occasion to repeat the experiment with a plummet to fix the centre of the spire which had been conducted in Salisbury Cathedral in 1737 under Francis Price and Bishop Sherlock. At the same time, timberwork within the spire was replaced and weatherboarding was set in the openings. The roundels were glazed.[30]

In the early nineteenth century the fabric of Norwich Cathedral was treated with a mixture of sensible repair and utilitarian neglect, characteristic of the age. In June 1801 the west end of the nave roof had been damaged by a dangerous fire, which luckily did not spread through the rest of the building; the roof was soon put right.[31] In 1806 the elder William Wilkins superintended repairs and 'many improvements in the appearance of the interior', including the vault 'washed over with one light colour'.[32] Ten years later Britton summed up the situation thus: 'although the interior has been repeatedly repaired and beautified . . . the exterior architecture and masonry have been much neglected and nearly the whole surface displays a ragged, crumbled and decayed appearance'. Only on the west front were some 'very judicious repairs and restorations in progress, by Mr Stone, an architect of Norwich'.[33] However, at the same period, the great infirmary to the south of the cloister was taken down since it no longer served any useful purpose.

It was in a similar spirit that radical alterations to the cathedral were made around 1830 when the huddle of buildings to the east of the cloister (plate VI) was swept away and replaced by a roadway to give public access direct into the south transept. A suitable entrance front thus had to be created for it. Anthony Salvin went back to the Romanesque style of the original, removing the late medieval tracery in the windows (so creating a dangerous precedent for later 'authentic' restoration) and forming new openings in sympathy.[34] His symmetrical entrance, complete with ornamental clockface, marks in its municipal overtones a clear change from the

30. NRO, DCN 57/1, DCN 24/5, fo. 117r, DCN 118/1, pp. 18–20, 26–29, 32–33.
31. P. Browne, *The History of Norwich* (Norwich, 1814), p. 13; P. Browne, *An Account and Description of the Cathedral Church of the Holy Trinity, Norwich and its Precincts* (Norwich, 1807), p. 9.
32. William Wilkins the elder (1749–1819) was a Norwich architect who restored Norwich Castle and built the museum of the Philiosophical Scoiety at York; his more famous

son William (1778–1839) was an important classical architect.
33. J. Britton, 'The History and Antiquities of the See and Cathedral Church of Norwich', in *Cathedral Antiquities* (London, 1836), ii, p. 46. Though not published until 1836, the account is dated 1817.
34. Anthony Salvin (1799–1881) undertook restorations at the Tower of London, Windsor and many other castles and country seats.

inward-looking nature of the medieval cathedral to the concern with the wider public typical of the nineteenth century. (There had been an elaborate clock housed within the south transept, with a dial visible externally on the south gable.)

Inside the cathedral Salvin also had to combine archaeology with utility (plate VII). The main problem was, as always since the Reformation, how to obtain congregational participation in a service in the choir despite the pulpitum to the west, which effectively cuts off the choir from the rest of the building (fig. 224). Ironically, Salvin's work on the choir brought endless complex correspondence and almost led to a rupture between architect and dean;[35] whereas the destructive remodelling of the south transept seems to have caused little controversy either at the time or later and has endured virtually untouched. At this period cathedral chapters were still giving priority to those concerns which had inspired the Wyatt restorations of the later eighteenth century: convenience and comfort. The liturgical and archaeological requirements, though not ignored, had to be balanced with practicalities.

Salvin claimed that in making his 'sketches' for the choir he had two objects in view, 'the ancient arrangement and an increased accommodation'.[36] He resisted attempts to move the bishop's throne and to throw open the transepts into the choir on the grounds that these would destroy the conformity of Norwich with other cathedrals. He also had to contend with conservative doubts that the removal of the Ivory galleries across the transepts would make the choir colder and reduce the number of seats from which the congregation could see and hear the service clearly. Despite his resistance in these matters, he was no reformer in the spirit of the ecclesiological movement of the next decade. He 'admired the effect of the crimson curtains' hung to hinder draughts: 'their colour destroys the usual monotony and as long as they last they are highly decorative'.[37] Even more seriously to later Victorian eyes, he could propose using composition, a form of hard plaster, for the choir stall canopies, on the grounds that it was 'quite as hard as oak' but 'infinitely cheaper'.[38] Again he could suggest using iron columns to support a gallery.[39] There was one innovation however which later ecclesiastical and technological thinking did not despise. The introduction of heating in 'so large a space' as the choir and transepts was 'a novelty' in March 1833.[40]

Despite work by Francis Stone on the west front only twenty years before, it was considered necessary for Edward Blore to undertake a major campaign there in the early 1840s.[41] Philip McAleer has recently demonstrated the extent of Blore's

35. NRO, DCN 102/1/24.
36. NRO, DCN 107/1/7.
37. NRO, DCN 102/1/7.
38. NRO, DCN 102/1/7 and 10.
39. NRO, DCN 102/1/22.

40. NRO, DCN 102/1/29.
41. Edward Blore (1787–1879), artist, employed on the illustrations to John Britton's *English Cathedrals*, and architect to William IV, Queen Victoria and Westminster Abbey.

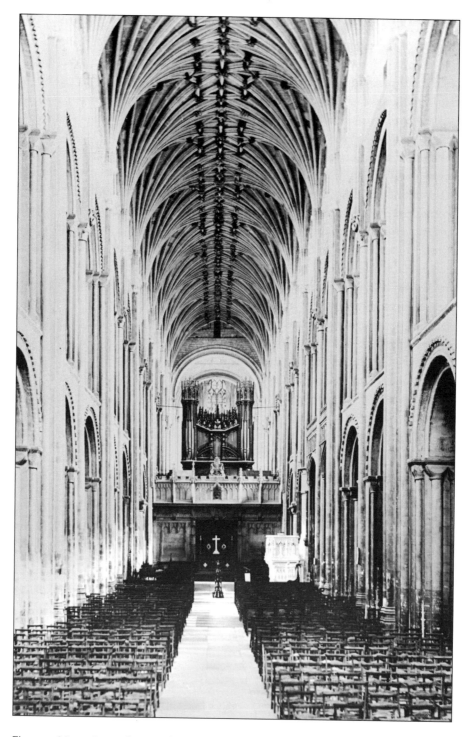

Fig. 224. Nave: view to the east of *c.* 1925, with the upper parts of Salvin's pulpitum still *in situ*.

Fig. 225. The west front *c.*
1870, after the remodelling
by Edward Blore.

involvement.[42] In terms of design it was radical, comprising the refacing and rebuilding of the upper parts of the façade, including the gable and all four turrets (fig. 225). Blore was obviously encouraged to stress the Romanesque at the expense of other periods. The late medieval tracery in the aisle west windows was removed, as were the panelled buttresses, in favour of oculi copied from the centre tower and a straight parapet. The ogee cupolas (see fig. 219) were inevitably condemned and were succeeded by tall, Romanesque pyramids, not following Salvin's design on the south transept but derived perhaps from French models. The only place where later styles were employed was the gable. The former modest single-light window and cross were replaced by a more flamboyant niche and floreated cross. As John Adey Repton commented, 'The new cross . . . over the great west window . . . has a prettiness about it to suit the taste of the present times'.[43] Blore seems to

42. McAleer, 'Façade of Norwich Cathedral', pp. 382–84.

43. J. A. Repton, 'Elevations, Plans, Section and

Details of Norwich Cathedral', *Archaeologia*, 32 (1847), p. 406.

have had no responsibility for the execution of the alterations he designed, so he was not to blame for the lack of structural sense which brought the whole front to ruin within a mere thirty years.

Blore also seems to have been asked to make further alterations to the choir, which, while minor in themselves, are worth mentioning for the comments they elicited from Robert Willis, the great church archaeologist of Cambridge, who was consulted by Dean Pellew (1828–66).[44] Willis agreed that it was 'very desirable' to reduce the level of the pavement in the choir and under the tower to the same level as the transepts. He also approved of the introduction of moveable screens, presumably to allow the limited space available to the congregation on a weekday to be extended on a Sunday. Willis firmly stated that he had 'no desire to interfere in any way with the proper functions of our clever friend Blore' but he was willing to sketch an idea of his proposed platform and screens. Willis admitted then that he felt 'the greatest interest in the matter' and offered help in any way, a kindness obviously taken up, for a letter from Willis to Dean Pellew survives of 4 June 1849.[45] In it he spoke out firmly against overenthusiastic restoration, in particular the removal of the late medieval tracery from the Romanesque windows. To attempt to restore the Norman character of the building could only be done by removing the west window and spire, the clerestory of the presbytery and the vaults and, even for the 1840s, that was 'quite out of the question'. Willis recommended 'simply to repair' the windows in their present style and 'above all to do as little as possible to them'. He added: 'I fear this will appear a very strange opinion to you'.

Salvin and Blore were the last architects of national eminence both to design and to direct any extensive programme of work at Norwich until Sir Charles Nicholson built the Regimental Chapel after the First World War.[46] Unlike Lichfield, Salisbury or Ely, to name only a few, there was no comprehensive restoration of Norwich Cathedral by one architect. The pattern for almost a century was for the dean and chapter to consult the great names, obtain a report or design, execute whatever they could manage and move on to another authority for the next job. George Gilbert Scott made a report on the whole church in the 1860s.[47] Ewan Christian inspected particular parts on a number of occasions.[48] John P. Seddon and James Fergusson

---

44. Cambridge University Library, Additional MS 8170.
45. NRO, DCN 120/2B/11.
46. Sir Charles Nicholson (1867–1949) was consulting architect to seven cathedrals and diocesan architect to four sees. He was famous for his memorial chapels, as at Rugby.
47. Sir George Gilbert Scott (1811–78) was the most famous Victorian architect and church

restorer. His buildings included the Albert Memorial and St Pancras Station in London. He was architect to the cathedrals of Ely, Hereford, Lichfield, Ripon and Salisbury and to Westminster Abbey.
48. Ewan Christian (1814–95) had trained in the office of John Brown of Norwich and became architect to the Ecclesiastical Commision in 1851.

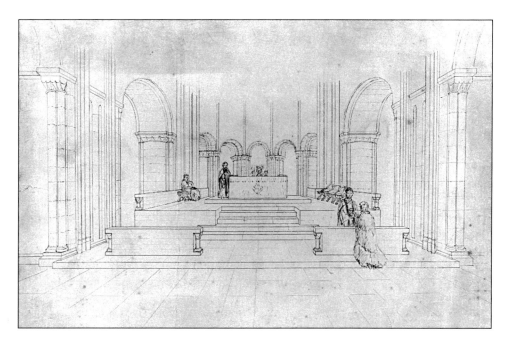

Fig. 226. Proposed rearrangement of the sanctuary, *c.* 1875: a precocious revival of early medieval models (NRO, DCN 131/128).

gave their views on the west front in 1874.[49] Arthur Blomfield was given the commission for the high altar and altar-rails (compare fig. 226), but twenty years later it was John Loughborough Pearson who designed yet another layout for the choir and a new bishop's throne.[50] This inconstancy may partly have been due to a shortage of money, as Norfolk was badly hit by the collapse of agricultural prices in the late nineteenth century: McAleer quotes Dean Goulburn's admission to Scott when paying the bill in 1872 that 'nothing had been done towards a general restoration, because in truth the funds cannot be raised'.[51] The desire by Deans Goulburn (1866–89) and Lefroy (1889–1909) to conduct their own show may also be to blame. Goulburn and his wife, who were childless, were generous in their personal gifts, reckoned to have mounted up to £5000, but this generosity encouraged piecemeal

49. J. P. Seddon (1827–1906) was later diocesan and cathedral architect to Llandaff. James Fergusson (1808–86) was a writer on architectural matters rather than a practising architect.

50. J. L. Pearson (1817–97) had worked with Anthony Salvin before becoming architect to Lincoln Cathedral, advising on restorations at several others and designing the new cathedral of Truro (1879–87). Sir Arthur Blomfield (1829–99), knighted 1889; his works included Sion College Library, London, and important restorations in the cathedrals of Canterbury, Chichester, Lincoln and Salisbury.

51. McAleer, 'Façade of Norwich Cathedral', p. 405 n. 52.

work, rather than comprehensive schemes. Perhaps, however, the principal reason was the establishment of a Norwich architect called John Brown as the regular man on the spot. He remained, together with his successors, concerned with the cathedral for many decades to come. Although involved from the 1830s, his first major work was the refacing of the central tower in the 1850s. There were clearly small-scale restorations of windows and other openings going on all the time, despite Willis's disapproval. In the 1870s much more ambitious work had to be undertaken at the west front and Brown was relegated to the role of executant.

Scott's report of April 1867, soon after Goulburn's appointment to the deanery, gives a valuable overview of the cathedral at this date. He had been asked two specific questions: to estimate how much should be demanded of the Ecclesiastical Commissioners for substantial works of repair; and to give suggestions for the improvement of the interior. On the former he advised requesting between £12,000 and £14,000. Scott reckoned that Ewan Christian, the commissioners' own architect, would fully confirm such an estimate.[52] The question of the interior was less easily settled. Scott reckoned it 'is sadly wanting in all that gives warmth and sentiment to the internal effect of a cathedral'. He accepted that much had been done in the last fifty years to make the place more comfortable but, despite Salvin's efforts, he considered a new and efficient heating system necessary which would allow the unblocking of arches and openings. He would have recommended opening the choir into the nave, as he had done at Ely, but both the fabric of the choir and stalls and their arrangement were ancient and so should be retained. Open screens could be thrown across the transept arches to prevent the appearance of a gap at the crossing but fixed seats should be replaced with chairs. The altar should be moved forward to the chord of the apse and a detached, rich reredos introduced behind it, with the altar steps rearranged and fine paving laid. A new pulpit and bishop's throne 'of worthy character' should also be incorporated.

Scott considered the arrangement of the organ and gallery 'exceedingly objection-able'. It was quite wrong to allow in a cathedral a custom 'nearly banished even from parish churches in placing singers in front of a gallery'. Scott preferred to house as much as possible of the organ in the gallery. As to colour, as well as a rich reredos, screens and paving, Scott suggested the introduction of stained glass in the clerestory and in the windows of the lantern, and also of gilding and some colour on the vaults. He estimated the various improvements at a rough £3000 but the dean and chapter were not to be tempted. (In the years from 1864 to 1873, £4150 was spent on the cathedral, with the yearly sums varying between £336 and £559).[53]

---

52. NRO, DCN 131/4.   53. NRO, DCN 131/6.

Fig. 227. View from the south west, 1874.

Their restraint was fortunate: in 1874 there was a major crisis as regards the west front. The architect John P. Seddon was consulted by the dean and chapter. His report of 5 October 1874 was emphatic that the masonry was 'in a most alarming and critical condition'.[54] The problems were complex and related to all parts. The Norman remains were 'only tolerably sound because some had been 'seriously fractured through settlement' probably soon after building. The Perpendicular alterations, in particular the introduction of the great window, had been carried out in a 'reckless, unscientific and unworkmanlike manner'. The jambs of the window were too slight and insufficiently bonded. The stained glass put up in 1854 in memory of Bishop Stanley had made matters worse by the 'insertion of large iron bars' when the glazing was fixed. Seddon reserved his worst condemnation for the mid eighteenth-century and even more the mid nineteenth-century repairs to the west front. He considered that 'these were of a character that as for folly and bad taste it would be difficult to find any parallel'. According to Seddon, it was in *c.*

54. NRO, DCN 103/1.

Fig. 228. J. H. Brown's drawing for the west front, June 1879, with giant shafts flanking the west window, surmounted by spired pinnacles (NRO, DCN 131/130/2).

1750 (i.e. in Matthew Brettingham's restoration) that the external casing of the lower part of the west front and aisles was taken down and they were recased in new masonry 'more or less in imitation of the previous Norman details'. The work was done in coursed ashlar but indifferently bonded to the core. A century later the remainder of the Romanesque facing was replaced and the upper part of the west front recased, together with new pinnacles and west gable, but the whole rested solely on the eighteenth-century casing below. The work was executed in thin slabs of Portland stone, set on edge, with sham horizontal joints to appear more substantial. The four great pinnacles were built in the same materials and with equal inefficiency so that they and the west gable, having no bond, only supported each other.

The next five years after Seddon's report were filled with earnest debate as to how to rectify the situation. Not only was there a structural problem but also a stylistic issue to resolve. Although it was tempting to remove all evidence of the Perpendicular work and to return to the original Romanesque, James Fergusson

Fig. 229. The west front in its unresolved state, *c.* 1900. The giant shafts date from *c.* 1880, the angle turrets from the 1840s. The turrets flanking the gable have been dismantled.

and 'other persons of eminence' all agreed that, 'whatever restoration might be abstractedly desirable, the dean and chapter are laid under conditions which make it impossible for them to do anything else than faithfully restore the Perpendicular work'.[55]

This stylistic indecision was aggravated by a severe shortage of funds, to cover which the fabric fund was deliberately overspent, with unfortunate consequences for later work.[56] The result, whereby the pinnacles flanking the gable were cropped but the piers below rebuilt with Neo-Romanesque shafts, gave satisfaction to no one. Only twenty years afterwards, Quennell could refer to the west front as 'the most unsatisfactory part of the whole' and even admitted that its early nineteenth-century appearance 'was better far than now' (figs 227, 228, 229, 230).[57]

55. Book containing chapter orders concerning the west front, 1874–83, NRO, DCN 103/22.

56. NRO, DCN 131/13/1, p. 15.

57. Quennell, *Cathedral Church of Norwich*, pp. 30–31.

A firmer attitude prevailed in the other debatable area, the choir and sanctuary. Dean Lefroy, on his appointment in 1889, set about changing the floor level and the arrangements of the stalls yet again. This time they endured, though modified by the bold restoration of the bishop's cathedra in the apse *c.* 1960. (There had been a proposal even in the late nineteenth century for redesigning the sanctuary in the apse in a more early Christian style although elevating the altar, rather than the bishop's throne.)[58]

Fig. 230. Restoration of the flying buttresses on the south side of the presbytery, *c.* 1860(?) (NRO, DCN 131/46).

Pearson successfully recommended the laying of a uniform floor from the crossing eastwards. The floor at the far east end had been lowered by Dean Goulburn in 1873, exposing bases that, since they lacked any evidence of fire damage, must have already been covered by the late middle ages or, according to some modern scholars, in time for the consecration of Bishop Eborard in 1121. The resulting gap between the fifteenth-century screens and the floor was left exposed, perhaps a gesture towards the new thinking of the Society for the Protection of Ancient Buildings. A less sympathetic attempt at putting the stylistic clock back was the introduction of Neo-Romanesque shafts to the chord of the apse and of a further pair of shafts resting on clearly Victorian angel corbels one bay to the west.

Pearson's solution to the perennial problem of the choir seating was to move two rows of fifteenth-century stalls, complete with misericords, into the transept and to create two rows of sub-stalls below the canons to his own design. Such was the technical expertise of the period, it is now difficult to distinguish Pearson's work from the original, with the paradoxical result that the whole choir resembles strongly Pearson's own work, for instance at All Saints, Hove.

The report which Pearson made in March 1893 did however contain more contentious sections.[59] Efforts had been made 'in the last two or three years' to clean off whitewash and to restore lost features, but he considered that much

58. NRO, DCN 131/127/8, p. 18; A. B. Whit-
     tingham, 'Norwich Saxon Throne', *Arch. J.*,

136 (1979), pp. 60–61.
59. NRO, DCN 131/13.

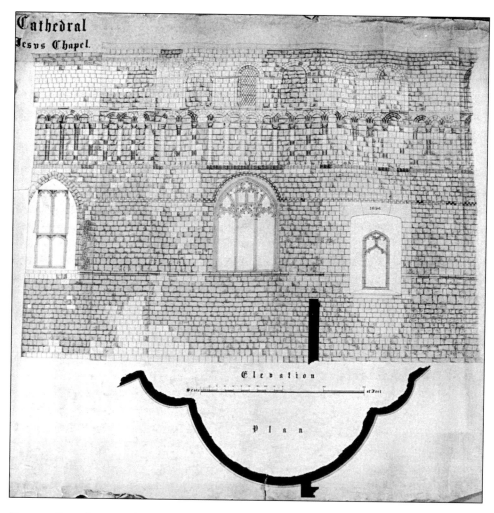

Fig. 231. Stone-by-stone elevation of the Jesus Chapel, 1894. Each element of the masonry was precisely shown and coloured (NRO, DCN 131/154).

remained to be done. Despite the painstaking work by Dean Goulburn on the nave vault bosses, it was not until 1899 that the nave was 'restored to its ancient beauty'.[60] Cleaning should reveal a 'thin coat of plaster', perhaps with evidence of colour. With hindsight he might have been more cautious, especially as the restoration of the polychromy in the Jesus Chapel in the time of Dean Goulburn was 'not altogether satisfactory' (fig. 231). In the fabric itself Pearson recommended reopening further windows in the south transept and north aisle. He hankered after the restoration of those windows 'of particularly poor character [i.e. late in date] so the design could

60. Inscription on brass tablet in south aisle.

be improved'. On the exterior he favoured rebuilding the Lady Chapel on its old foundations but was critical of the erection of the cathedral offices some decades before in the angle between the Bauchun Chapel and the south transept: 'though convenient they add nothing to the dignity or effect of the cathedral'. He noted that the gable and turrets of the north transept were 'miserable in the extreme', the south transept was 'as poor and as foreign to the ancient work in the cathedral as can well be conceived' and the west front was 'wholly unworthy'.

William St John Hope (then assistant secretary of the Society of Antiquaries) took up the cudgels in opposition to such a thoroughgoing approach. He congratulated Pearson on his opposition to the removal of the pulpitum and the canopied screens but was otherwise unenthusiastic concerning Pearson's proposals.[61] In particular, he objected to the reproduction Norman tooling on those stones replaced in the lower parts of the tower piers; and to the over-violent removal of the whitewash by the use of hammer and chisel; to the opening of windows in the south transept, which had been blocked ever since the erection of the present cloister. This last alteration would entail moving fine seventeenth-century monuments and the introduction of imitation Norman mouldings. Hope also doubted the wisdom of interfering further with the floor levels in the choir and with its furnishings. On the exterior he also advocated leaving well alone, for instance in not disturbing the current use of the former chapel of St Anne as a heating chamber.

Dean Lefroy prudently adopted only some of Pearson's recommendations.[62] The whitewash could come off the choir but no further for the moment. Only one window would be opened. On the exterior the authorities would only work according to the 'one broad principle': 'we ought with all speed to rectify whatever endangers the strength or stability of the fabric'. In his restoration appeal he intended to ask for £12,000, of which £3000 would go to the organ, £2000 to the restoration of the choir but the rest would be devoted to the fabric. In the event Lefroy only asked for half of that sum, even though he claimed that the dean and chapter were giving £2000 from their own resources. It is interesting to note that one of the sources of revenue was an admission charge of six pence per visitor.

The financial crises did not preclude further thought about the west front. In 1899 chapter records provide evidence of a proposed study tour of the north of France by Dean Lefroy and the chapter clerk to consider possible models.[63] Some years later, in 1908, Harold Brakspear produced a design which (although the accompanying drawings were lost) was generally of Perpendicular character. He was willing to retain the west ends of both aisles – 'although modern like the rest, they were harmless' – but he would then have added large buttresses in a fifteenth-century

61. NRO, DCN 131/16/1.
62. NRO, DCN 131/11.

63. McAleer, 'Façade of Norwich Cathedral', p. 391.

style, 'to give light and shade' to the façade.[64] The half-century of relentless Neo-Romanesque at Norwich was over. Brakspear considered that his design was 'harmonious and had no pretension to restoring what we can only surmise was the original Norman termination'. The sudden death of the dean on holiday in the Alps and, presumably, lack of finance prevented all such schemes, save a modest making-good of the aisle fronts in 1915.

There is no space to continue the story into the present century, although that is fully as interesting. The design and construction of St Saviour's Chapel (also known as the Regimental Chapel) after the First World War by Sir Charles Nicholson, the war damage in the cloister, the surveyorships of Stephen Dykes Bower and of Bernard Feilden, both men of strong and sometimes controversial views, are no insignificant details. Much of what has been done is hidden from the casual visitor within the fabric or above the vaults, but no one can ignore the creation of the vertiginous bishop's throne in the apse and the reroofing of the aisles. Some of the nineteenth-century contributions have already been reversed, notably on the west front and in the window glazing schemes. What is urgently needed to aid the sensitive treatment of the fabric and its furnishings, as well as to advance academic research, is detailed local study into the achievements of the last three centuries, which for both good and ill have shaped the present character of the cathedral.

---

64. NRO, DCN 131/20/8.

34

Restorations and Repairs after World War II

Bernard M. Feilden

Compared with most other cathedrals, the fabric of Norwich is in a good state of repair due to the unremitting efforts of the Friends, guided by the high steward's committee. Founded in 1929 by Dean Cranage, for the first twenty-three years the Friends' efforts were directed to embellishing the cathedral while the dean and chapter struggled to pay off the cost of the new organ after the destruction of the old one by fire on 9 April 1938.

In 1951 Dean Holland called a conference of the laity and explained the desperate financial state of the cathedral. As a result, the management of the properties in the close was handed to Percy Howes and the responsibility for the fabric to the high steward's committee under Lord Hastings: this was to act as the 'dean and chapter *in extenso*'. Such delegation to lay persons had far-reaching and beneficial consequences. An appeal was launched with an initial target of £20,000 (later raised to £35,000) to which the Friends contributed generously.[1] Work was begun on the presbytery and cloister roofs and on strengthening the tower, but it soon became apparent that the appeal funds were insufficient. Dean Norman Hook presented the critical state of affairs in his report of 1953 with the concluding words:

> Let me express my own deep gratitude and encouragement for all that is being done. You and I, in difficult days, face a hard and colossal task. We have in our trust one of the loveliest cathedrals of our English heritage, and it is a privilege indeed to serve it. But if we are to do our full duty, we must get far more help, and we must ask for heroic service and heroic giving. Gone

1. For some details of the appeal including an appeal leaflet, see the case file inappropriately marked 'Norwich Cathedral: East Apse & N. Transept', in the archives of the Society for the Protection of Ancient Buildings, London.

are the days when we could depend upon wealthy individuals to give substantial monies; we must now rely on the many who can give their little. Please, everyone, give a helping hand towards building up the many, who, by God's help, will bring near the day when we can say that our lovely cathedral is sound and safe. Only then shall we be entitled to claim that we have done our duty to the past and to the future.[2]

It was clear that a lot of money would be needed in the future.[3] Lord Hastings died suddenly in 1955. He was succeeded as high steward by Sir Edmund Bacon, who joined Dean Hook in facing and solving the daunting task of putting the fabric in a sound state.[4]

Although cathedrals, by custom, had come to depend on appeals for major repairs to their fabric, another appeal so soon after 1952 was out of the question, so the high steward's committee began a policy of continuous fund-raising through the Friends. Money was raised in conventional ways such as coffee mornings, wine and cheese parties, the sale of Christmas cards and minutes of history, and by exceptional events such as *son et lumière* and flowers in splendour and the antique fair. These events were coordinated by the appointment of an organising secretary to the Friends; first, in 1959, Group Captain Montgomery, followed in 1962 by Rear Admiral Powlett.

Fund-raising was augmented by many bequests, some quite large, and by generous gifts for specific projects such as the spire. Based on the funds available, projects

2. Friends of Norwich Cathedral, *Twenty-Fourth Annual Report 1953* (Norwich, 1954), p. 4.

3. In 1934 Arthur Whittingham had reported that 'in recent years the cathedral has been maintained on the conservative principle of not doing anything till it was essential'. Advocating a change in policy to one of preventative management and arguing that 'the cathedral buildings need a regular sum spending on their structure annually', Whittingham thought that perhaps £450 a year (the value of a poorish Norfolk benefice, or the annual income of five Norfolk agricultural labourers) 'would keep the building permanently sound', while the suggestion that £5000 should be spent immediately on the fabric was 'unnecessarily drastic' (NRO, DCN 107/38). Whittingham's annual estimate was only £200 a year more than the annual average expended by Dean Bullock

on the fabric two centuries earlier (see above, pp. 614, 708–11). Today the annual average repair bill for the cathedral fabric is around £100,000. This dramatic increase is a measure of a number of factors: inflation; the damage done to the stonework by the old gas works on Palace Plain, just to the north of the close; the change in attitudes to the conservation of cathedrals; and the development of more adequate and organised fund-raising techniques.

4. Both Hastings and Bacon took a very personal interest in the repairs. It was said of Lord Hastings that 'no contract was ever signed which did not receive his most careful and critical scrutiny': Friends of Norwich Cathedral, *Twenty-Sixth Annual Report, 1955*, p. 1. For the work of his successor, Sir Edmund Bacon, high steward 1956–79, see D. Lindsay, *Sir Edmund Bacon: A Norfolk Life* (Maldon, 1988), pp. 101–9.

were authorised and a programme of major repairs to the tower and roofs was
put in hand. Completion of this phase was celebrated in 1975 with a visit by the
Queen, who met the foreman and craftsmen who had carried out the restoration
work.

With continuous fund-raising it was possible to initiate a rolling programme of
masonry maintenance. The concept behind this programme was that the Friends,
as trustees to future generations, should hand on the cathedral to the next
generation in as good a condition as they received it, or if possible an even better
one. So, a thirty-year programme was begun. This involved maintenance of two
bays of the exterior walls each year. By and large this strategy has been followed,
modified if necessary by the regular quinquennial reports of the cathedral architect.
This procedure is much the most efficient way of working, as it keeps a team of
skilled craftsmen in regular employment and avoids the heavy overheads of major
contracts.

Norwich was one of the first cathedrals to have regular quinquennial inspections
which are now mandatory under the Cathedrals Measure of 1990. These inspections
guide the application of available funds where they are most needed, but constant
surveillance of the fabric is necessary because some decay, which is latent, may
suddenly become the subject of urgent action as happened with the pinnacles on
the west front, the presbytery parapets and now the cracked roundels on the tower.

Some of the main restoration projects of the last forty years will now be described.
Inevitably, my account will be somewhat personal but I hope it will interest the
reader and be a useful historical record.

The Spire

Spires are mortal. The first was destroyed by fire in 1272. In 1297 a new leaded
spire costing £248 0s. 1¼ d. was built, but in 1361/62 this blew down. In 1463 the
third spire was struck by lightning and was replaced by Bishop Goldwell. This fourth
spire, of brick and stone, was probably designed by Robert Everard; at 315 feet
(96 m.) is possibly the highest point in Norfolk. The Norman tower may have been
lowered some 15 ft (4.5 m.) to compensate for the 500 tons of masonry in the spire
as the inner sides of the corner turrets are in rough work or faced with brick.
Incidentally these corner turrets are surmounted by pentagonal spirelets which are
unique in form.

Everard's design was economical in two ways. First, it was most likely built from
internal platforms until the top window was reached, so avoiding an expensive
external scaffold. Then sturdy cross members were placed on the sill and the top
section built from an external scaffolding. The masons would lay four or five courses
of brick and then, working overhand, place a course of stone and fill the gap with

mortar. Salisbury spire was built in a like manner and the original oak timbers still exist. At Norwich the internal framing and platforms were renewed in pine at the end of the eighteenth century.

Secondly, instead of using 9 inches (23 cm.) of expensive stone, as at Salisbury, Norwich's spire is faced with only 3 inches (8 cm.) of stone. It is, in fact, an amazing brick structure. The top 130 feet (40 m.) are, in effect, only 4½ to 5 inch (11.4 to 12.7 cm.) brickwork. This is increased in the lowest 50 feet (15 m.) to 13 inches (33 cm.). Although irregular, the bricks are hard and tough with a high clay content.

In time, the spire began to show the defects of Everard's economical design. Gaps developed between the stone facing and the brickwork. In 1756 two wrought iron bands were applied to tie the outer face to the brick core. Square plates were added in 1845, along with a new finial in Darley Dale sandstone – the hardest and most durable of all, but it weathered to an incompatible black. Three more bands were added in 1929 and a further two by Arthur Whittingham in 1952 making seven in all. Moreover, the internal timber frame, independent of the brick lining, suffered from dry rot during the Second World War when all the windows were closed, reducing ventilation.

The spire was very sick. Meanwhile, using the 1952 appeal funds, the tower was strengthened by Mr Haslop of Rattee and Kett. His design was an ingenious system of bronze ties that would act to pull the sides of the tower together should it begin to fail.[5] His report of 1954 surprisingly omitted any mention of the condition of the spire. It had vertical cracks in each of its eight faces, which meant that it no longer worked as a structure.

In 1960, having been instructed to repair the top of one of the spirelets, I climbed up the spire. As a result, I reported that all was not well with the structure and was duly instructed to make an inspection and prepare a project. Naturally I turned to Mr Haslop to learn from his experience. When we met, I pointed out that his report had led the dean and chapter together with the high steward's committee to assume that all was well with the spire. Mr Haslop stated bluntly that this was not the case, and that all one could do was to take the spire down and rebuild it. I was surprised and determined to explore the alternatives.

First, I had to make a detailed inspection, but this was not too easy because one could only view the spire either in acute perspective from the tower parapet or from the four points of the compass from the lower roofs, which was inadequate. I bought a telescope and tripod, with which I was able to study the whole spire stone by stone from ground level. It was in poor condition.

I wanted engineering advice. The first distinguished engineer I approached said

5.   W. F. Haslop. 'Norwich Cathedral Tower   Friends of Norwich Cathedral, *Annual Re-*
     and Spire: The 1952–54 Restoration', in   *port, 1954*, pp. 5–6.

that it would be necessary to install a steel frame to stabilize the spire. I did not like this proposal. The steel frame would transfer all its loads onto a weak central tower; it was structurally incompatible and would have ultimately destroyed the tower and the spire. So I went to another engineer, who proposed a concrete frame: this was not much better and also heavier. Again, I rejected this and realised that I would have to solve the problem myself. Several alternatives were considered and I gave drawings of the spire to a friendly local engineer asking him only to calculate the wind loadings. These calculations were vital in that they showed that the second stage of the spire, just where the brickwork was thinner, was the most vulnerable to 'uplift' in a strong wind. It is worth remembering that the late thirteenth-century spire had blown down in a storm in 1361/62.

The gap between the stone casing and the brick lining was caused by wind vibration combined with thermal movement. A small crack might form, then a speck of dust would drop down into the crack and cause it to widen. No force on earth could push the dust back so gradually the cracks were wedged wider and wider, reaching a maximum of four inches (10 cm.). To fill these cracks I proposed grouting with a hydraulic lime mortar. Then, to counter the vertical cracks, I proposed ties and in some cases rings of concrete to pull all the faces together. The brickwork was decayed in many places and a large amount of external stone was due for replacement. The timber frame and staging inside the spire had also to be repaired.

I devised a safety system to support the second stage which was, as already shown, the weakest. In fact, there was more decayed brickwork here than elsewhere. The system consisted of a central ring with triple ties to each angle where an external channel of bronze would hold it all together. Each tie was tensioned against a twelve tonne railway spring that so all forces were equalised. The workmen christened this octagonal ring the 'threepenny bit', as that strange multifaceted coin had just been introduced.

When my proposals were ready I reported to the dean and chapter that I would like a second opinion on my scheme. I was told (like a revelation), 'Get the best man in Europe'. In 1962 European contacts were minimal; how could I find the best man? Banister Fletcher's *A History of Architecture*, that great compendium, came to my help. I looked up all the cathedrals with spires and wrote to the bishops. The bishop of Chartres replied and gave me the name of Bertrand Monnet, *architecte en chef des monuments historiques*. The dean and chapter invited him to come and advise (luckily he was great anglophile). His first question was very professional: did I want his advice? He cross-questioned me with rigour like a hostile barrister for a day and a half. Then, he changed his tone and said that he liked my proposals but had one suggestion to add – to include stainless steel wire in the horizontal joints of the external stone. Naturally, I adopted this and since then, with due

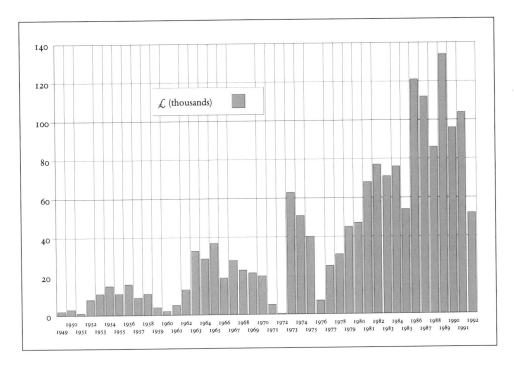

Fig. 232a. Cathedral gifts, 1949–92 (actual pounds).

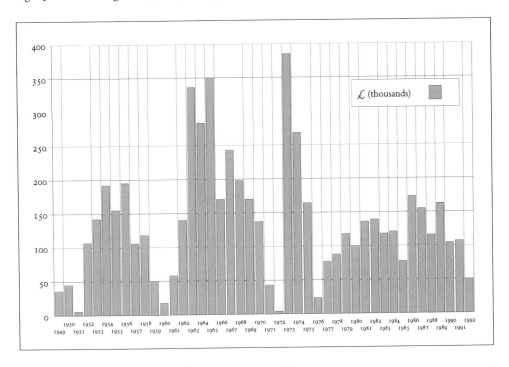

Fig. 232b. Cathedral gifts, 1949–92 (at constant 1992 prices).

acknowledgement, have passed this idea on to hundreds of conservation students.[6]

We met the dean and chapter together with Sir Edmund Bacon, the high steward, for lunch at the Maid's Head Hotel. Bertrand Monnet spoke briefly and said that the spire was in such a critical condition that it could be blown down with a sonic bang. Without estimates of the cost and without delay I was instructed to get on with the project. I chose Messrs Lushers as builder and Messrs A. J. Woods as masons and all the work was executed on a 'cost plus' basis. Cost plus profit means that the contractor is paid the actual cost of labour, plant and materials to which a percentage called profit is added to cover the cost of administration and some real profit. When the difficulties of a project cannot be assessed it is the fairest form of contract and has the advantage that craftsmen can contribute their skill and knowledge; it works in favour of an historic building.

First the spire had to be scaffolded. The scaffolding could rest on the tower but had to be independent of the spire in order to avoid additional wind loads. It gave trouble and had to be strengthened. Then, working upwards, the voids had to be grouted with a creamy mix of mortar at one foot (30 cm.) intervals as the external stone was so tender; then the brickwork had to be repaired and external stone renewed with the stainless steel wire inserted in the horizontal joints. All the stonework was repointed and about 25 per cent renewed.

The threat of autumn gales made me consolidate the top of the spire before the lower portion, as I wanted to reduce the wind load from the scaffolding. This meant that the weak second storey was left until late in the programme. Before lowering the scaffolding, I invited our beloved bishop, Lancelot Fleming, to climb to the top. This he did, so we were able to add a record of this event to the blackened Darley Dale finial.

One morning in June 1963, a pale-faced foreman came to my office, which overlooked the cathedral, and said that the whole spire had rocked. I went to see and found that, contrary to my instructions, too much brickwork in the second lowest stage had been cut away and the remainder could not withstand the weight of the masonry above. As this stage was the weakest I had arranged for eight bronze channels to be clamped on externally and linked together to a central frame as a safety precaution. When the overstressed brickwork was crushed this system took over and fortunately worked. I said no one was to leave the site until all the cutting away had been filled in. At eight o'clock that evening the brickwork was filled in and I inspected, finding all had been made safe. What would I have done if the workmen had left at the first sign of danger?

I learned a vital lesson that day: an architect is nothing without craftsmen. To

6.   B. M. Feilden, *Conservation of Historic Buildings* (London, 1982), p. 67.

express this I put up a plaque giving the names of the whole conservation team in alphabetical order, as we were all equal in the eyes of God. The spire took the best part of two years to restore and cost £33,061. Bertrand Monnet made a second visit, approved the work and said it had been done quickly and at low cost.

On the question of cost I have one regret. I had to rule at which level 'height money', in addition to the hourly rate, would be payable. Strictly I was right to say that the top of the tower was the datum from which height money should be calculated. One day I found a 'Chad' figure drawn on some new stone with the remark, 'Wot no more money'. Realising what we owe to the masons and bricklayers, I regret my ruling.

The Tower

As mentioned above, Rattee and Kett under Mr Haslop had done some strengthening in the lower portion of the tower, visible in the gallery above the main arches. In addition, at some time in the nineteenth century, strong ties had been inserted at about the middle of the bell chamber with external anchor plates.

Patrick Faulkner, chief regional architect in the former ancient monuments section of the ministry of works, was a coassessor with Bertrand Monnet. He commented, 'After you have done the spire look to the tower'. Tell-tales showed continuing movement. Following his advice, I installed more tell-tales and movement in these confirmed the need to consolidate the tower from the foundations upwards. This involved grouting all the piers and the tower masonry. A great deal of lime and fly ash (from power stations) with a small amount of Portland cement was injected under pressure, filling the large voids in the Norman masonry.[7] One face of the tower was worked over each year inserting two reinforced chains of galvanized steel set in concrete as well as replacing defective stone. In the bell chamber the ends of the oak joists carrying the bells, which were bedded in the tower masonry, were found to be rotten and so were strengthened with galvanised channels bolted on to their sides and projecting into the wall.[8]

A cathedral architect always has art historians, antiquaries and archaeologists breathing down his neck and murmuring 'you are doing too much'. I thought I was leaving the masonry in the tower good for sixty years but I was in error, as after thirty years another campaign is now necessary (1993–96).[9] In fact, I was

7. One void ran 20 ft (6 m.) sideways taking 50 gallons (250 litres) of grout.
8. Feilden, *Conservation*, p. 368. B. Feilden, 'Norwich Cathedral: Restoration of the Tower, 1964–1968', in Friends of Norwich Cathedral, *Thirty-Seventh Annual Report, 1966*, pp. 12–17.
9. The cathedral architect at Norwich is no stranger to controversy. In 1948 Stephen Dykes Bower and Arthur Whittingham

reluctant to touch the west face of the tower because it had the last external relics of Caen stone. On the south face I found most of the stone was a replica in mortar which was liable to come off in heavy lumps, so this face was virtually renewed.

Roofs

The Second World War left a great backlog of intensive work to be done on the roofs. Percy Howes and Co. started with releading the cloister roof and then releaded the presbytery roof on a steel frame.

My first project on the cathedral was the reinstatement of the north transept roof in 1956. This meant negotiating with Mr Truman of the War Damage Commission, who queried what had happened to the lead melted by the fire bombs.[10] I designed a reinforced concrete frame to clear the upstanding vaults in such a way that no outward thrust would be transmitted to the side walls, indeed the concept was to hold these walls together. Messrs J. Youngs did the concrete work and Messrs Starling the lead casting and fixing. A year or two later Messrs Carter renewed the south transept roof, this time using precast concrete purlins in place of ones cast *in situ*. Renewing the ambulatory roof followed.

During 1962–63 the spire, and from 1964 to 1968, the tower absorbed all the Friends' resources but in 1969 work on the major tasks of the roofs could restart: first, releading the nave roof in 1970 with concrete frames and wood purlins and boarding all flame-proofed. The work was carried out efficiently by R. G. Carter using a sliding frame covered in tarpaulins to protect the work from rain. The Anglia Lead Casting Company, successors to Mr Starling, laid the lead. The whole work cost £45,978.

Finally, after a pause, the roofs of the north and south galleries were renewed with timber given by various estates in Norfolk. The architect followed the medieval

---

note 9 continued

opposed the dean's desire to remove two of the medieval choir stalls and dismantle a third. Whittingham secretly enlisted the support of the SPAB (the Society for the Protection of Ancient Buildings): one report said that Whittingham wanted 'to get as much opposition against the dean that he can. Mr Whittingham is horrified at what he has been ordered to do and thinks that the dean should be taught a lesson of architectural manners . . . Apparently everybody in Norwich is horrified but are too much cowards to do anything'. None the

less the dean finally had his way, but only after twice facing down the reluctant carpenter, the second time reportedly with the words 'You have not done what I told you. Cut it off!' (London, Society for the Protection of Ancient Buildings, 'Norwich Cathedral, file III, 1940–1955', minute of a telephone conversation from Christopher Perks to the SPAB, 25 October 1948, and Col. Sydney Glendenning to Mrs Dance of the SPAB, 3 November 1948).

10. Fifty-nine incendiaries had fallen on the cathedral in the night of 26–27 June 1942 (NRO, DCN 107/39).

practice and went into the woods to select suitable trees which were then felled and sawn by Messrs Taylors of Wroxham. Unseasoned oak gives off tannic acids as it dries and this is destructive to lead. In the roof design it was therefore necessary to include an effective vapour barrier and a ventilated void under the substrata for the lead.

The nave gallery roofs had to wait several years before they could be renewed. In annual reports to the Friends the architect had stated that the roof was 'beyond repair', a phrase that was to become contentious.[11] As a precaution it had to be propped up. The Society for the Protection of Ancient Buildings intervened and wanted the roof timbers repaired, but this would have cost at least three times as much and it was doubtful if even half the timbers could have been saved, as there was just enough usable salvage to reconstruct one bay at the west end.[12] However, complete record drawings were made and samples of the medieval carpentry joints were preserved, so no knowledge was lost.[13]

The words 'beyond repair' became significant as the chapter, on Percy Howes's advice, decided to challenge the Excise's claim for Value Added Tax. Our appeal, conducted by the chapter clerk, John Mills, went to a tribunal and, to the chagrin of the Excise and joy in the conservation community, we won, saving over £10,000 in tax.[14]

In the meantime the main vaults had been insulated with three inches (8 cm.) of glass wool, sandwiched between polythene to prevent dust and dirt collecting in the glass fibre and reducing its effectiveness. Besides improving the heating in the cathedral, this insulation reduces the problem of pattern staining on the high vaults which was noticeable before the presbytery was cleaned in 1973.

Windows

A great deal of the stained glass in the cathedral had been removed to safety during the Second World War. It was reinstated by Dennis King, the great Norwich glazier

---

11. Friends of Norwich Cathedral, *Annual Report, 1974*, p. 6; London, Society for the Protection of Ancient Buildings, 'Norwich Cathedral, file IV, 1968–1975', Sir Edmund Bacon to Lord Euston, 18 October 1968, and report by Bernard Feilden, 8 October 1974.

12. The duke of Grafton led the criticism of the new roof, but was silenced when Sir Edmund Bacon, the high steward, sent him a sample of the old timbers showing that they were too rotten to be reused. (London, Society for the Protection of

Ancient Buildings, 'Norwich Cathedral, file IV, 1968–1975', Sir Edmund Bacon to the duke of Grafton, 15 October 1974; Lindsay, *Bacon*, p. 104).

13. I had previously described this carpentry as 'medieval jerry-building at its worst'. (London, Society for the Protection of Ancient Buildings, 'Norwich Cathedral, File IV, 1968–1975', Sir Edmund Bacon to Lord Euston, 18 October 1968).

14. The case hinged on whether the gallery roofs were a repair or an alteration.

who also did the war damage repairs. A new window by Moira Forsythe has been put in the Bauchun Chapel and the Barclay window inserted in the east wall of the south transept. Memorial windows were added: to Arnold Kent, treasurer to the Friends for many years, in the presbytery north aisle; and to Sir Edmund Bacon (high steward 1955–79) in the Jesus Chapel, which his friend Mr Baron Ash had done so much to beautify.[15]

Stone Replacement

There were major restorations in the nineteenth century to the south transept in 1830–34, by Salvin, and to the west front in 1874–83. Western pinnacles, as shown in Daniel King's seventeenth-century drawing (fig. 91 above), were rebuilt in *c.* 1840 but they were removed in 1879 and 1973–74. The nineteenth-century restorations used Bath stone of which the individual stones lacked variety. In fact nearly the whole surface of the cathedral has been refaced in a piecemeal fashion using different stones. Ancaster, Barnack, Clipsham, Ketton and Weldon can all be identified by their colour and texture. Some Portland stone has also been used but this is not harmonious as it is too cold and white. If one looks at a square metre (eleven square feet) of masonry one may see as many as six differing stones out of about ten used at one time or another.

Minor Works

Minor works which should be mentioned include the formation of the chapter room (off the west bay of the south aisle of the eastern arm), which was furnished with fine oak panelling from St Benet's Abbey. This gave the opportunity to replace the carved head to Bishop Wakering's door which had been closed. In creating the chapter room one historic feature of the cathedral was lost – namely the prison cell, a small circular feature.

The Jesus Chapel was restored by Stephen Dykes Bower and St Luke's Chapel refurbished with the beautiful Despenser retable conserved by Pauline Plummer. The paintings from the screen in St Michael at Plea were fitted into a fine reredos in St Saviour's Chapel used by the Norfolk Regiment as a chapel, leaving two paintings to be framed separately, which are now in the Visitors' Centre.

Other minor works were completed to the Bauchun Chapel. Its ceiling was cleaned, leaving the original colours untouched. A screen was added to the chapel and John Skelton's Lady of Pity was put into an existing niche in the north wall

---

15. See chapter 20 above for further details of the stained glass in the cathedral.

and Opie's painting of the presentation of Christ, given by Eric and Theo Scott, was hung on the west wall.

Mention should be made that the pulpit in the crossing was moved about two feet closer to the tower pier and that the pelican was taken to pieces and cleaned by Alan Stuart.[16]

Completion of Major Works

To celebrate the completion of the major works, on 11 April 1975 the Queen visited the cathedral for a service of thanksgiving conducted by Dean Alan Webster.[17] I had the honour of introducing the twelve foremen who had each led one of our campaigns and who were supported by their craftsmen. To celebrate this event the high steward authorised the gilding of the finial on top of the spire. This was done by steeplejacks using gold leaf over a background of Canaries' green. The architect had to climb the ladders to inspect the work. After a lightning strike in 1986 a further down-tape was added to the spire, and my successor, David Mawson, also climbed these ladders to the top.

The Rolling Programme

With the major works to the spire, tower and roofs complete it was possible for the Friends to start a rolling programme of preventive maintenance. The plan was to work round the cathedral in a clockwise fashion maintaining two bays each year. First, all the accumulated soot and dirt was washed off, enabling the architect to assess what stone repairs were structurally necessary; superficial decay proceeds but is of no great concern as long as the body of the stone can function for an estimated thirty years.[18]

The rolling programme was divided into two sections: the main one around the

16. In addition, a number of bays of the cloister have been repaired, some with pre-stressed concrete pads connected by a galvanised steel beam to the existing, and defective, foundations of the buttresses. This was a novel technique when it was first used in 1970. (Friends of Norwich Cathedral, *Forty-First Annual Report, 1970*, pp. 14–15). A new sacristy has been constructed to the north of the nave, creating important ancillary accommodation, but not without much public criticism as it involved opening a new doorway through the Norman blind arcade of the aisle wall. (Friends of Norwich

Cathedral, *Fifty-Ninth Annual Report, 1988*, p. 14; Society for the Protection of Ancient Buildings, *Report of the Committee, 1987*, pp. 20–21, 43).

17. After nearly twenty-five years of major works, the roofs of the whole cathedral had been repaired at a cost of over £210,000; and the tower and spire strengthened at a further £128,000.

18. Observations have shown that the exterior stonework on the cathedral erodes by about 0.12–0.16 in. (3–4 mm.) a century. (Feilden, *Conservation*, pp. 160–61).

perimeter as described above; and a secondary programme for the cloister bays. However, there was a hiccup when it was found necessary to renew the parapets of the presbytery and when the two western spirelets (of nineteenth-century design and poor workmanship) showed signs of failure after severe frosts. Nevertheless, the concept of a rolling programme has been maintained by my successor and partner David Mawson and by Keith Darby. We can claim that the cathedral is now one of the best maintained in the country, thanks to the untiring efforts of the Friends.[19]

Future Problems

What of the future? The spire has already withstood two exceptional gales, that in January 1976 gusting up to 105 mph (170 kmh) and another in October 1987.[20] But no restoration is final and in the past work has had to be executed from a full scaffolding every hundred years. The tower needs further stone renewal so perhaps I was not ruthless enough in 1964, or perhaps the causes of decay have become more aggressive.

The great west window in the nave needs conservation. Some might say this provides a chance to commission a work of art to replace an indifferent example of nineteenth-century glazing, but gradually appreciation of Hedgeland's great work is increasing; restoration would win further support for his glass.

There is controversy, as yet unresolved, over the restoration of the cloister bosses. The east and south walks have been restored, by the experienced decorators Messrs Campbell Smith, and the general effect is to enhance the architectural values and bring the spaces to life. Before they were commissioned a conservator prepared a sample which was simply visually unattractive (and expensive). Campbell Smith's work is rather harsh in places but, nevertheless, is toning down more harmoniously. The harshness is due partly to the use of finely ground modern pigments, which do not have the wide range of particles found in medieval paints, and partly to the lack of glazes which make pigments more luminous.

Differing assessments of the work may develop into a conflict between the Friends' council (successor to the high steward's committee), which pays for the work and naturally wants something that improves the cloister, and the new fabric advisory committee (orientated to art history and archaeology), which has statutory powers under the Care of Cathedrals Measure of 1990. In the opinion of some conservators, Professor Tristram's restoration of the cloister bosses, completed in the 1930s, is now 'historic' and the most that should be permitted is cleaning of the already faded

---

19. The first circuit of the cathedral was completed in 1989. (Friends of Norwich Cathedral, *Sixtieth Annual Report, 1989*, p. 25).

20. In a high wind the top of the spire moves about 3 in. (8 cm.) to and fro. (Feilden, *Conservation*, p. 108).

colours. Diplomatic sensitivity and good will are going to be needed if the continuing generosity of the Friends is not to be prejudiced.

There is also the difficult problem of decay in the Purbeck marble capitals and shafts in the cloister. Other cathedrals have similar problems, so a working party, together with English Heritage and some money from the Getty Grant Program, is trying to solve the causes and recommend the most suitable treatment.

The era of the dean and chapter exercising complete autonomy, guided by professionals as necessary yet sensitive to public opinion, is now over. New rules apply under the Care of Cathedrals Measure. It is inconceivable that a project such as the conservation of the spire could be undertaken so efficiently; but equally it must be said that with regular inspections by a cathedral architect such a crisis should not reoccur. Furthermore, English Heritage can now support the efforts of the Friends, without whose funding nothing could be achieved. Projects for repair work to the external faces of the tower, costing £769,000 over three years, have been authorized with a 60 per cent grant from English Heritage.[21]

Under the Cathedrals Measure of 1990 regular reports on the fabric are now mandatory. The fabric advisory committee consists of expert advisers in architecture, archaeology and art history representing local and amenity society interests. All projects submitted by the dean and chapter must receive its approval but those which materially affect the character and setting of the cathedral and its archaeology, or items of outstanding artistic or historical value, are referred to the Cathedrals' Fabric Commission (England). The fabric committee can advise the dean and chapter on projects; before these are approved three weeks' public notice has to be given to enable objectors to register disapproval and have their views considered by the committee. This procedure is necessary to justify the application of public funds to cathedrals, but without the funding provided by the Friends the system would fail. I have prepared a record of expenditure on the fabric of the cathedral showing the actual money spent, adjusting the figures for inflation to show the cost in real terms (figs 232a and 232b).[22] This shows that the works on the spire and tower between

21. With the annual average donation by the Friends to the fabric running at £95,000, the dean and chapter saw no alternative but to apply for state aid in December 1992 for the very first time. (Friends of Norwich Cathedral, *Sixty-Third Annual Report, 1992*, p. 7).

22. Figures derived from Friends of Norwich Cathedral, *Annual Reports*, especially *Forty-Second Annual Report, 1971*, pp. 12–13, and *Forty-Ninth Annual Report, 1977*, pp. 16–17; NRO, DCN 12A, audited accounts, 1946–

1972; Norwich Cathedral, Cathedral Office, dean and chapter accounts, 1966–1977, 1979–1982, seen through the kindness of Colin Pordham, chapter clerk. The graphs were prepared through the kind assistance of Dr Mike Prior and Mrs Chris Clark at the University of East Anglia. Figures for the dean and chapter's contribution to the fabric expenditure were unavailable for the years 1978, 1983–90, so these totals must be regarded as incomplete.

1962 and 1970 were, in real terms, more expensive than the work on the tower now underway (1993–96).

The half century since 1945 has, thus, seen two great changes in the care of the fabric at Norwich. First, in the 1950s, came the systematic management of fabric and fund-raising. Rather than merely reacting to crises, repair work would follow a planned programme, a 'stitch in time'. The culmination of this came with the introduction of quinquennial inspections at Norwich in the 1970s.[23] Moreover, the laity, through the high steward's committee (later superseded by the Friends' council), were involved in the care of the fabric, while responsibility for raising the money to pay for restoration and improvement was given to the Friends. Now, in the 1990s, we see another change, with statutory external controls on the fabric and the grant-aiding of projects by English Heritage. None the less, the work of the Friends will remain essential to the care of the building. It is largely through their efforts that, in the words of Eric Fernie, 'the fabric of the cathedral is now in better condition than it has been at any time in its post-medieval history, and possibly, even, since the year when Eborard completed the façade in the second quarter of the twelfth century'.[24]

Table 1

Schedule of Works and Costs, 1946–92

ROOFS	£
Upper presbytery 1954–56	7992
Cloister 1954–57	8609
North transept 1956–58	9791
Ambulatory 1962–63	9793
South transept 1962–63	11,888
Bauchun Chapel 1963–68	5259
Nave roof 1968–71	45,978
Nave aisles 1973–75	111,891
Choir school 1982	5008
Servers' vestry 1983	2362
SPIRE	
1961–65	33,061

23. For such matters see also I. Hume, 'The Maintenance Problem', and S. D. Stevens, 'Maintenance Management', in M. Jackson, ed., *Engineering a Cathedral* (London, 1993), pp. 180–87 and 188–91 respectively.

24. Fernie, *NC*, p. 199.

TOWER

1953–55	11,950
1964–71	83,975

WINDOWS

1946–69 (including war damage)	21,715

MASONRY REPAIRS

St Luke's Chapel	9559
Repairs 1956–65	11,396
Clerestory walls and buttresses 1959	1922
Cloister 1970	4058
Presbytery repairs	65,606
Tower pinnacles 1982	1512
Old chapter house entry 1985–86	11,704
Spire repairs (lightning) 1986–87	21,151
Tower 1992	6701

ROLLING PROGRAMME

1976	3383	north aisle
1977	7779	presbytery parapet
1978	9232	north transept west face
1979	19,838	north transept west face
1980	38,142	north transept, west face and nave south wall
1981	33,330	
1982	22,867	
1983	46,735	
1984	41,677	
1985	33,535	
1986	47,862	
1987	55,293	
1988	50,107	
1989	52,669	
1990	1968	
1991	—	
1992	6493	

CLOISTER PROGRAMME
INCLUDING LIBRARY AND REFECTORY

1978	2183	1986	7231
1979	1479	1987	16,535
1980	2307	1988	22,682
1981	5733	1989	43,156
1982	—	1990	42,494
1983	17,225	1991	23,690
1984	26,170	1992	7486
1985	6628		

INTERNAL WORKS

Jesus Chapel 1966–67	5000
Cleaning presbytery 1973–75	6789
Lighting 1975–84	22,040
Vault insulation 1975	1773
Dean's vestry 1981–82	40,484
Crossing floor 1981	2445
St Saviour's Chapel 1981	3923
Sir Edmund Bacon memorial window 1984	5750

CONSERVATION WORK

South aisle paintings 1975	2300
Gilding finial 1975	4209
West front pinnacles 1975	10,219
Prior's door 1990–91	10,991

MISCELLANEOUS GRANTS BY THE FRIENDS
TO DEAN AND CHAPTER

Heating system 1975	4500
Visitors' centre 1975	4000
Heating system 1980	47,000
Organ repairs 1986	45,000
Ancillary buildings 1989–92	180,000
Fire precautions 1985–89	71,229

35

Epilogue

Paul Burbridge

The preamble to the 1966 statutes states unequivocally that 'the first and supreme objects of this cathedral church . . . are the offering of continuous and reverent worship . . . and the faithful preaching of the Gospel of Christ'.[1] It therefore seems appropriate to begin this epilogue with a glance at the nature of worship in the cathedral during the postwar period.

Broadly speaking, the pattern has remained constant, marked only by changes of hour, an increase in the number of weekly celebrations of holy communion and, more recently, changes in the liturgy employed. The one constant factor throughout the whole period has been the celebration of holy communion at 8 am daily throughout the year. On a Sunday, choral matins and sermon remained unchallenged until the 1950s; but in the light of the new thinking of the Liturgical Movement, Dean Norman Hook (1953–69) was anxious to see it replaced by a sung eucharist. He began discreetly by introducing it only on the third Sunday in the month. By October 1962 the old and new arrangements were alternating weekly. Finally, from Whitsunday 1967 the 11 am sung eucharist became the norm at Norwich Cathedral.

At that time the ministry of the word was conducted from the lectern in the crossing, whilst the second half of the service was offered at the high altar. As the congregations grew consistently, this presented real problems since the high altar was out of sight of those sitting in both the transepts. In 1974 a new sanctuary was established by Dean Alan Webster (1970–78) in the crossing. This was in regular use until 1988, when the main Sunday eucharist during the summer months was removed to the nave.

Evensong, according to the Book of Common Prayer, has been sung at 3.30 pm on Sundays throughout this period; until autumn 1967 it was graced by a sermon in addition. A 7 pm Sunday evening nave service with sermon at one time attracted very large crowds but, over the years, became markedly less popular; by Lent 1973

---

1. Norwich Cathedral statutes (1966), p. 2: NRO, DCN 28/3.

it was removed to St Saviour's Chapel. More recently it has taken place in the choir at a revised hour of 6.30 pm.

As far as weekday worship was concerned, at the beginning of the postwar period matins was at the late hour of 10 am on all weekdays, on three of them including an element of plainsong and a hymn. In 1955 morning prayer was brought forward to 9.45 am; and in January 1971 it moved again to its present position immediately before the 8 am eucharist. On weekdays holy communion was offered at 8 am daily. This remained the only weekday eucharist until September 1962, when an additional celebration was instituted at 11 am on Thursdays. This was followed in Lent 1976 by a 12.30 pm eucharist on Wednesdays and in July 1977 by a 12.30 pm service on Fridays. In September 1980 a service of holy communion following the Book of Common Prayer of 1662 was added on Tuesdays at 11 am. Evensong was sung daily at 5 pm from Monday to Friday and on Saturday was said at 3.15 pm until 1960, when both services were moved a quarter of an hour later to their present times.[2]

Following the Alternative Services Measure of 1965, Series II Rite was used at holy communion on Mondays, Wednesdays and Fridays from Advent 1967. This was also extended to cover Thursdays in 1968. It was used for the 11 am sung eucharist on Sundays from Advent Sunday 1968. On Saturdays the 1662 rite continued to be used until January 1973. Although series III came into use early in the time of Dean Alan Webster, there is no documentary evidence of the exact date of change from Series II to Series III. The remaining major liturgical change during this period was the adoption of the Alternative Service Book (ASB) as from the first Sunday in Advent 1980, under Dean David Edwards (1978–83). Current practice involves the use of ASB Rite A for most communion services in the cathedral. Rite B is used on one weekday and on the third and fifth Sundays of each month. The Prayer Book rite is used only on Sundays at 8 am and Tuesdays at 11 am. It has been the definite policy of the dean and chapter to ensure that all three legal rites are currently used in the cathedral.

In addition to the 'continuous worship' of which the statutes speak, the cathedral is also host to a whole series of non-liturgical acts of worship, and on occasions is used by Christians of other traditions: for example, every year the Dutch Reformed Church has a service on a Sunday in May. In particular, the cathedral is used by Christians of all traditions at a plethora of Christmas carol services, also on Good Friday, Civic Sunday, Battle of Britain and Remembrance Sundays, and the Royal Norfolk Agricultural Association harvest thanksgiving, to mention but a few.

The cathedral vestry book records that reservation of the sacrament for the sick was revived on 17 March 1966, a practice which still continues. An aumbry to house it is located in the wall of St Andrew's Chapel in the north transept. Two

---

2.   Norwich Cathedral Combination Papers, Norwich Cathedral Library, pressmark L5.

further chapels have been restored. The Bauchun Chapel of Our Lady of Pity (off the south presbytery aisle) was restored as the chapel of the Friends, and rededicated on 6 October 1968, having been used for many years as a consistory court. For many years the chapel of St Catherine of Alexandria (off the east side of the south transept) had been the dean and chapter's vestry; recognizing an increasing need for a place of quiet, for meditation and silent prayer, this chapel was restored to its former use and rededicated by the dean on 24 August 1988. This has proved to be an exceptionally worthwhile project and has clearly met a widely-felt need.

In 1988 a general rearrangement of the nave sanctuary took place. The Dykes Bower sanctuary had hitherto blocked the formal great entrance into the choir. The altar was also needlessly far removed from the congregation. The altar was therefore removed two bays west, to the west of the choir stalls, where it more nearly approximates to the position of the medieval altar of the Holy Cross which was west of the pulpitum. The central altar beneath the spire was finally removed when the main eucharist was transferred to the nave for the summer period. Further development of the nave sanctuary area, designed to give a greater feeling of space, is currently under consideration.

The dean and chapter give a high priority to the daily office, in this they are joined each day by a number of lay people so that the historic ongoing worship of the community remains a reality, as well as being 'the first and supreme object of this cathedral church'.

Staffing

The cathedral is currently administered by the dean and three residentiary canons who, together with the administrator/chapter clerk and two honorary canons, form the administrative committee (or governing body), to whom the various officers and agents regularly report. Whilst there has been a marked increase in the number of officers and professional agents in recent years, there has been a notable decrease in the number of clergy resident at the cathedral (at a time when tourism has increased tenfold). The dean continues to head the team, but although the number of residentiary canons allowed by statute is four, this number has not been achieved during the postwar period, and has been subsequently reduced further in effect by combining the archdeaconry of Norwich (the present holder also has two other diocesan posts) with a residentiary canonry. This office is currently held by the Venerable Clifford Offer.

In 1974 the number of minor canons was also reduced from three to one when the last clerical sacrist, the Reverend Philip Morgan, moved to St Albans Cathedral. This office has since been held by a succession of laymen, of whom George Allison is the present holder.

In common with all cathedrals of the new foundation (those that were formerly monasteries), the office of precentor was traditionally held by a minor canon. Such was the case at Norwich where the last minor canon, Claude Palfrey, held this position for twenty-six years until his resignation in 1984. In that year the precentorship was annexed to a residentiary canonry, as permitted by the statutes of 1966. Worship being the primary function of a cathedral, it is clearly appropriate that the precentor shall be a member of chapter – more particularly in these days of rapid liturgical renewal and revision. Canon Colin Beswick, formerly precentor of Worcester Cathedral, was the first residentiary canon in postwar times to hold this office. By the earliest statutes of the cathedral the precentor was to be a member of the chapter, but this provision was subsequently dropped; it was only revived in the 1920s when Canon Alan Bell, and in the 1930s when Canon Roland Grant, held this office. In recent years the primary formal duty of minor canons (and the precentor in particular) has been to sing the daily office. This is currently carried out by Canon Michael Perham, the present precentor, or else by the dean who was formerly canon precentor of York Minster. On occasions the office has been sung by the lay sacrist or a lay clerk.

In 1992 the administration of the cathedral was carefully scrutinised and placed on a more businesslike basis. The part-time chapter clerk, Colin Pordham, was appointed to the full-time post of cathedral administrator. In addition, the vacant office accommodation at No. 12 The Close was taken over by the dean and chapter to become a more adequate cathedral office. The office of the Friends was also moved into this building in 1993. The advent of office mechanisation and computerisation has resulted in a considerable amount of accountancy, together with the rent roll, being done 'in house'. Outside specialist advisers continue to be involved in the management of close properties and in financial, legal and investment matters.

In 1977 Norwich Cathedral pioneered the provision for the first time of a full-time visitors' officer (Deaconess Joan Diment) to be concerned with the half million or so visitors who pass through the cathedral doors each year. As far as is known, Joan Diment was the first deaconess to have been appointed to the staff of any English cathedral: she ministered and occasionally preached at the Sunday eucharist. The visitors' officer is currently Lucy Sitwell. In 1989, following the example of a number of other cathedrals, Norwich broke new ground with the appointment of a member of a religious order as pastoral assistant. Sister Violet of the Community of All Hallows, Ditchingham, was seconded to the cathedral and now helps with the pastoral ministry to the increasing number of visitors.

Organists of Norwich Cathedral have been noted for their length of tenure of office. Over a period of 109 years there have been only four organists. The current holder of that office is David Cooper, who was organist of Blackburn Cathedral for eleven years before coming to Norwich.[3] The opening of the University of East Anglia to undergraduates in 1963 was an important event for the city and county, and not least for the cathedral. The former half dozen lay clerks have been supplemented by a further six choral scholars from the university, together with an organ scholar. The cathedral organist is a part-time lecturer at the university. Links with the university are cordial and continue to grow.

A Wider Community

If the preamble to the statutes makes worship its first priority, its second relates to the cathedral as 'a centre of work for the religious life of the people of the diocese, and as the home of religious learning, music and art'. It is a simple fact that at no time in history have our medieval cathedrals been more visited. People of all faiths and of none flock to them for a variety of reasons. It is therefore vital to ensure that they feel positively welcomed rather than merely tolerated. To this end, over the years successive deans and chapters have tried to improve the amenities offered to visitors. This has been done most notably by the provision of guides (*c.* 1975) and chaplains (1959) to assist in the ministry of welcome, and by the development of a visitors' and exhibition centre, opened by the queen in 1973. In addition to the full-time staff of dean, canons, organists, vergers, shop and buffet managers and office staff, there is a veritable army of helpers who come in on a voluntary basis to help with this ministry to people. Some indication of the numbers involved is the fact that each year the dean and chapter send out 600 Christmas cards to the voluntary helpers from over a wide area of Norfolk, thanking them for their services. Canon Peter Bradshaw (1974–83), who had served as a parish priest in Norfolk, warm hearted and humorous, exercised a unique pastoral ministry during his years as canon and vice-dean.

One of the most vital ministries of the cathedral is to people who, for one reason or another, want help and yet wish to remain anonymous. Many people come seeking to unburden themselves to somebody whom they know they will never have to meet again unless they wish to do so. A cathedral like this, simply because it is there, is often able to act like a magnet. Chaplains, the pastoral assistant, vergers, guides and welcome-desk helpers, sometimes even flower arrangers, will find themselves lending a listening ear. In addition, there is a ministry of Christian Listeners attached to the cathedral sponsored by the Acorn Christian Healing Trust.

This wider community is not limited to the helpers already mentioned. There are many people who are strong supporters of Norwich Cathedral, even though for various reasons they are unable to give their practical services on a regular basis.

3.   See also above, pp. 700–4.

These are the Friends of Norwich Cathedral. There is nothing particularly unusual about having Friends as such. Most cathedrals have similar organisations. However, we believe that the Friends of Norwich Cathedral are in one particular respect unique. The more usual function of Friends' organisations is to provide 'the icing on the cake' – those embellishments that give that little extra which might not always be provided by hard-pressed deans and chapters. For reasons which are explained below, the Friends of Norwich Cathedral found themselves compelled to take on a somewhat different role following the financial crisis of 1950. At that time the Friends determined to take on the responsibility for maintaining the fabric of the cathedral entirely; and for financing the thirty-year rolling programme, which endeavours to ensure that the cathedral will never again be faced with such a crisis. Over recent years they have contributed an average of £100,000 per annum towards the fabric of the cathedral. The Friends, with their worldwide membership, are an important and invaluable asset to the cathedral.

The statutes also state that the cathedral ought to be 'a home of religious learning and music'. Since an earlier chapter in this volume is devoted to music in the cathedral and brings the story down to 1996, the reader is referred to it.[4] The staff of cathedrals, like the staff of universities, find there are many pressures against being 'homes of learning'. In the period under review Norwich was fortunate in attracting to the chapter a number of clergy who were both scholars and committed to the work of the church in the community. Among those who served the cathedral and succeeded in researching their own specialities – New Testament criticism, theology, history, liturgy, apologetics and antiquarian studies – were Frank Colquhoun, John Drury, David Edwards, Frederick Green, Norman Hook, John Poulton, Gilbert Thurlow and Alan Webster. They all wrote and published while in Norwich. John Drury, now dean of Christ Church, Oxford, dedicated his original work on St Luke, *A Study in Early Christian Historiography*, to the dean and chapter of Norwich Cathedral and expressed gratitude for the time and patience which the cathedral secretary spent on his typescript. Naturally, the preaching of the cathedral gained in thoughtfulness and originality from the chapter being a group of friends who could discuss their faith together.

Others contributed to Norfolk life by helping to found valuable voluntary bodies, including the Association for Mental Health, the Night Shelter, the Theological Society, and the Industrial Mission (Michael Mann). Some served on the city council and the Norfolk Education Committee, or appeared regularly on Anglia TV. The Friday Forum in the prior's hall continues to discuss ethical and political affairs. The imaginative and popular 'Thousand Norfolk Poets' exhibition was staged by Norfolk schools and the cathedral visitors' officer (Margaret Webster). Bishop Kenneth and

4.   Above, pp. 688–704.

Mrs Ethelreda Sansbury came to Norwich in 1973 to care for St Mary in the Marsh, and inspired over many years ecumenical understanding. In 1971 the dean and chapter together with Bishop Launcelot Fleming and other church leaders instituted an ecumenical conference centre within the close called Centre 71. This was intended to be a pastoral and teaching centre for the cathedral and the city. For twelve years it was also an important social centre for the cathedral and beyond. The measure of its teaching ministry was limited however. It fell on hard times and had to be closed in 1983 when the building was taken over by Norwich School.

In 1984 as the new dean I was anxious to set up a study centre to replace Centre 71, but determined this time to start with its teaching role. With the help of Derek Bishop, a former education officer in Norfolk, and premises in the basement of a canonry house, it embarked upon an important teaching ministry using the limited premises available. In 1988 No. 65 The Close became available when the local probate office closed and, on 7 June 1989, it was taken over by a joint partnership of the Christian Study Centre and the Diocesan Training Centre. The dean and chapter have made, and continue to make, a substantial subvention to support the centre in addition to providing help with teaching and management. The new centre is managed jointly under the wardenship of the present Diocesan Director of Training, Canon Maurice Burrell, and is called Emmaus House. The much-used library is largely the gift of Canon Martin Kaye and Bishop Launcelot Fleming, with Canon Hugh Melinsky as librarian.

Although the cathedral does not possess a parish as such, there is a regular core congregation. Therefore, a limited number of parochial-type organisations exist such as discussion groups, a contemplative prayer group, a healing prayer group and a youth group. The cathedral close is approximately coterminous with the ancient parish of St Mary in the Marsh – a parish without a church of its own but which uses St Luke's Chapel within the cathedral once a month. Canon Richard Hanmer cares for this parish in addition to his role as canon treasurer with special responsibility for pastoral matters. The cathedral does, therefore, exercise a local pastoral and caring ministry of its own.

Finance and Property

In his address to the general chapter on 22 July 1949, Dean Holland put his finger on the most pressing immediate postwar problems. The minutes report him as saying 'the War had made it impossible to maintain effectively the fabric of the cathedral and the houses in the precinct, and [that] the arrears of repair work were proving to be a heavy charge on capitular funds'.[5]

5. Norwich Cathedral, first general chapter book, pp. 38–39.

Shortage of money and arrears of repairs were to be the overriding problems during the decanates of Bishop H. St B. Holland (1947–52) and Dean Norman Hook (1952–69). Writing in the Friends' *Report* for 1949 Dean Holland wrote:

> It is only during this past year that the disastrous collapse in the value of money since the days before the war has struck the cathedral with its full blast. The immediate cause has been the necessity for overtaking the wartime arrears of repairs to the cathedral's freehold property from which a large part of the cathedral's income is drawn . . . Added to this was the fact that the normal expenses for the maintenance of the services and worship of the cathedral have risen . . . the fact which is well illustrated by the staggering discovery that the whole of the cathedral collections during the year were not adequate to meet one item of essential expenditure, that of heating the cathedral, which last year reached the figure of £540. Meanwhile, the revenues of the cathedral stand where they did before the war – a static income with an ever-rising expenditure.[6]

Doubtless there would have been many who questioned the wisdom of the chapter in their abolition of entrance fees to the choir and east end only the previous year. In practice, the new visitors' collection boxes produced a sum only £50 short of the average for three previous years from fees. Sales from publications and postcards made up the deficit. (In any case, it should be added that the Friends of Norwich Cathedral had already agreed to underwrite any deficit for two years up to £500 per annum). With this serious state of affairs the Friends' Council felt compelled to ask whether they were really justified in 'embellishing' a building which was no longer financially viable to fulfil its primary purpose. This constituted the starting-point for what was to become the Friends' unique role of being financially responsible for the fabric as a whole.

Writing in the 1950 Friends' *Report*, Dean Holland was able to say that the tide had suddenly turned. Not only had there been a number of windfall gifts but, far more importantly, 'a very representative and influential body of laymen from both city and county volunteered to launch an appeal for £20,000 . . . to cope with the heavy arrears of structural repair to the fabric of the cathedral, and to ensure its stability for the next fifteen years'.[7] However, it was soon recognised that both the extent and the cost of repairs would require a substantially larger sum. The appeal committee, under the chairmanship of Sir Richard Barrett-Lennard, raised the target to £35,000. This appeal reached its climax in the 1951, the year of the Festival of

---

6. Friends of Norwich Cathedral, *Twentieth Annual Report, 1949*, p. 5.

7. Friends of Norwich Cathedral, *Twenty-First Annual Report, 1950*. p. 6.

Britain and was closed later that year. The repairs and restoration to the cathedral during this period are described in detail by Sir Bernard Feilden.[8]

The state of the cathedral itself was, however, not the only cause for concern. At the general chapter on 22 July 1950 Dean Holland reported 'the anxiety caused through [the cathedral choir school's] inability to meet the educational requirements of the present day'.[9] For some years the locutory – the area presently occupied by the cathedral shop – had been the school where the choristers received their education. The dean reported that negotiations were in train with the King Edward VI Grammar School in the close; at the subsequent meeting of the general chapter in 1951 he was able to announce that they had been brought to a successful conclusion, chiefly through the work of Canon R. A. Edwards.[10] To this day twenty choristers continue to be educated at Norwich School on 50 per cent bursaries. The dean and chapter have only been able to maintain this arrangement through the successful appeal for a choir endowment fund, administered by lay trustees under the chairmanship of Lord Edward FitzRoy.

A further area of concern lay with the buildings in the close. In the early 1950s the dean and chapter were actually losing money on the close properties. Wartime rent regulations, coupled with a serious backlog in maintenance, were compounded by the fact that a number of rents appear to have been on a 'grace and favour' basis, and therefore quite unrealistic. Here was something of a vicious circle. Realistic rents could not be demanded on substandard property, yet the necessary repairs could not be carried out without substantial capital investment, which was not available. In 1950 the management of the estate, which had hitherto been the responsibility of the dean and chapter through the chapter clerk, was handed over to a firm of chartered surveyors in the close, Messrs Percy Howes and Co.[11] Percy Howes himself negotiated the Riverside Walk, a boon to Norwich citizens; Christopher Howes (now responsible for the crown estates) enabled the chapter to create an Abbeyfield House in the close, and also provided emergency accommodation for Ugandan-Asian and Chilean refugees, earning the quip that 'the close had become the open'.

The consequent financial upturn came about after it was agreed with the local authority that a number of properties in the upper close, which were too large ever again to be suitable for domestic use, might be let out to commercial firms paying higher rents. However, in order to maintain the proper residential nature of the close, a proportion of properties remains in residential rather than commercial use.

8. Above, pp. 728–45.
9. Norwich Cathedral, first general chapter book, p. 42.
10. Norwich Cathedral, first general chapter book, p. 51.
11. Norwich Cathedral, first general chapter book, pp. 42–43.

This is vital if the close is to retain its character and not to be wholly deserted between the hours of 5 pm and 9 am. During the 1950s and 1960s the dean and chapter were advised to embark on a far-reaching scheme which has continued until the recent present. When properties have required large capital injection, they have been let to tenants willing to apply their own capital in restoring these premises in return for partially abated rents during the initial lease. This has resulted in very substantial improvements in the maintenance and amenity of these properties and their surroundings. The close has been revitalised. With the exception of the old palace and bishop's house (which are the property of the Church Commissioners), and parts of Norwich School, the dean and chapter retain the freehold of all the property within the close.

The result of this policy has led to a £30,000 annual deficit being converted into a £350,000 surplus – although, for many years now, it has been the dean and chapter's policy to reinvest annually about one third of this sum in repairs and essential maintenance. Since the close is a conservation area, and rather more than half the buildings are Grade II listed buildings, its properties are naturally expensive to maintain.

Of the close properties only ten are occupied by members of the cathedral staff; the rest are leased to private residents or commercial firms. There is a substantial waiting-list for properties.

The Cathedral and State Aid

Until 1993 the cathedral gift boxes stated truthfully and unequivocally that the cathedral received no state aid. In 1990 a government white paper announced the possibility of limited state aid for cathedrals. This news was received initially with a measure of scepticism, and there was a certain local resistance lest there should be hidden strings attached. Until 1992 the chapter had been able to finance the cathedral repairs through the good offices of the Friends. In that year it was planned that the west face of the tower would receive attention, together with the restoration of the George Hedgeland great west window of 1854. An estimated £250,000 had been set aside for this purpose. However, a fall of stone on to the presbytery roof from the east face of the tower resulted in closer examination of both the east and north faces, indicating that they both also needed urgent attention. The resulting estimate of £670,600 for the work meant that there was no alternative but to apply for state aid. In April 1993 we successfully applied for an anticipated series of three grants covering 60 per cent of the work.

One of the anxieties concerning accepting state aid hinged on the thinly-veiled warning that grants might be conditional upon the chapter's reintroduction of an admission charge. The examples of the cathedrals of Ely and St Paul have been held up before us, but the chapter of the day was adamant that it could only contemplate admission charges as a very last resort. The question is clearly one that will not go away, and it is one that is repeatedly put.

Why do we look this particular gift horse in the mouth? Basically, because it fundamentally alters people's perceptions of the cathedral. There is a real danger that instead of opening its arms to all and sundry, and being a living place of worship, it may be thought of as a museum or yet another stately home. There is all the difference between being a paid-up sight-seer and going into our parental home. Many of us believe that it would be a seriously retrograde step were charges to be imposed, that is, unless all else failed.

The Future

Perhaps the greatest single change in recent years has been the greater breadth of welcome extended by the cathedral, not only to the city, but to all comers. Even if the war had ended the worst aspects of 'Barchester', a somewhat enclosed atmosphere still survived until the 1970s. That exclusiveness is now a thing of the past – and visitors are no longer regarded as an occupational hazard. When Norwich Cathedral pioneered its shop and visitors' centre in 1972 and 1975 respectively this wider concern was given tangible expression. Its example was rapidly emulated by many other cathedrals. Twenty years on the dean and chapter are very conscious of the need to improve these facilities and to extend them. The inadequacy of toilet provision and the limited space in the long narrow buffet over the west walk of the cloisters at the head of a flight of twenty-five steps, coupled with a shop which is too small for today's needs, are currently receiving careful attention from the dean and chapter.

Speaking to the general chapter as long ago as 1968 Dean Hook said:

looking into the crystal ball I can see two things. (1) I can see the ruined refectory restored, providing a hall big enough to house a diocesan synod. I can see it functioning as an eating place – where parties and groups visiting the cathedral can have a meal. (2) Hard by the refectory, on the site of the ancient guest house, I can see a splendid church house, with rooms where educational work can be done, rooms where people can meet socially, rooms which could house such things as a religious enquiry centre . . .[12]

Quite independently, on 1 August 1985, Dean Paul Burbridge (1983–95) outlined to his colleagues a similar vision of building visitor amenities of this sort. He wrote:

12. Norwich Cathedral, first general chapter book, pp. 190–91 insert.

I would strongly recommend that we pursue the possibility of developing the strip of ground running north/south immediately to the west of the west walk of the cloisters, including the ruins of the doorway leading into the monastic guest hall. Archaeological problems permitting, it seems to me that this site has a number of obvious advantages:

(i), The great majority of visitors approach the cathedral from the Erpingham or Ethelbert gateways. I could envisage visitors being channelled through the new centre via the west walk of the cloister and entering the cathedral by the monks' door.

(ii), A doorway already exists, although at present unused, halfway along the west cloister walk. No further piercing of the medieval walls would therefore be required.

(iii), A single-storey building on this site, although adjacent to the main route into the cathedral, would not in any way compete with the cathedral building itself. This would be a vital consideration as far as securing planning consent is concerned.

(iv), Last, but not least, we should be restoring a centre for the use of our visitors on the very site of the medieval guest hall. Clearly, our medieval predecessors chose this site for the very reasons that we are considering it now.[13]

At that time the scheme could not be pursued, but it is now hoped that such a building may indeed be erected to minister to people's needs before the new millennium.

If there has been a great increase in visitors since the war, this has also been matched by a great loss of independence as far as the dean and chapter are concerned. Until the 1960s deans and chapters enjoyed an almost total freedom to govern themselves and their assets. This they will never have again. They were then at liberty to apply their finances very much as they saw fit. Today all their major financial dealings are closely scrutinized by the Church Commissioners in London, who may give or withhold their consent.

Again, in those days, cathedrals enjoyed all the benefits of the ecclesiastical exemption (from local planning controls) as far as their buildings were concerned – wholly unhindered by any system of faculty jurisdiction that applied to parish churches. When the dean and chapter of Hereford saw fit to put their wrought iron choir screen (designed by Gilbert Scott) into store in 1966, or when the dean and chapter of Salisbury in 1967 no longer cared overmuch for their chapter house glass, they acted without let or hindrance. Following those events that total freedom

13. MS letter from Dean Paul Burbridge to the administrative chapter.

was gradually eroded as deans and chapters were requested to enter an agreement always to consult the Cathedrals Advisory Committee (later Commission) on all significant matters. Later still this became mandatory with the coming of the Care of Cathedrals Measure in 1990. From that time onwards all changes have been subject to widespread consultation and a complex system of bureaucratic controls. Whilst this restriction of liberty may be understandable on grounds of public accountability, only time will reveal whether ultimately it turns out to be in the best interests of any living, developing cathedral. There is a real danger that certain entrenched minority interests may all too easily inhibit natural growth, resulting in cathedrals becoming 'set in aspic', and that would be tragic. One of the glories of our historic cathedral heritage has been its rich degree of diversity coupled with local idiosyncrasies. No one cathedral has been quite like another either in appearance or governance. However, such things do not commend themselves to the tidy modern bureaucratic mind. It remains to be seen therefore whether the findings of the 1994 Howe Report of the archbishops' commission on cathedrals will succeed in imposing a drab uniformity on these institutions that have survived so long in all their variety.[14]

Perhaps that aspect of cathedral life most at risk is the choral tradition – a tradition peculiar to England. There have been periodic anxieties on this score going back to the 1850s when Sir Frederick Ousely felt it essential to safeguard the cathedral musical tradition by founding St Michael's College, Tenbury. In the event the tradition has survived whereas the college he founded has not. In more recent times there was anxiety that the Cathedrals Commission in the 1960s would require the abolition of cathedral choirs. Dean Hook, speaking to the general chapter in 1964, said:

> when the idea of a cathedral commission was first mooted, the permanent officials at Millbank [the Church Commissioners] threatened us with reforms of a most radical nature. We were to dispense with our expensive choirs and put up with a weekend choir. That would have put an end to the great tradition of cathedral music. Fortunately we had an archbishop [Geoffrey Fisher] who said bluntly 'you will do these things over my dead body', and that silenced the aforesaid officials.[15]

Today cathedral music is probably more widely valued than ever before, and we are unlikely to encounter any frontal attack upon it. There remains a potential hazard of a more oblique nature. Most cathedral choirs with boy choristers are

14. *Heritage and Renewal: The Report of the Arch-bishops' Commission on Cathedrals* (London, 1994).

15. Norwich Cathedral, first general chapter book, p. 156, insert p. 3.

strongly dependent on a cooperative local school for their education – a school which is geographically so placed that the boys may fulfil their daily cathedral duties. With only two exceptions, such schools are all in the independent sector. If at some future date the politicians were to inhibit private education, one of the casualties might well prove to be the cathedral choral tradition as we have known it.

One of the undoubted changes in the future is likely to be a much greater lay involvement in the running of our cathedrals. It is now over thirty years since Norwich Cathedral pioneered its high steward's committee of leading lay people. Under the wise and strategic leadership successively of Sir Edmund Bacon (1956–79) and the present high steward, Earl Ferrers, the cathedral has established a far wider support base than was previously the case. This has been to the cathedral's great advantage, and Norwich's example has been followed by other cathedrals. Whilst there has hitherto been no formally elected cathedral council, none the less successive chapters have listened with increasing attention to the expression of lay opinion. Amongst the provisions recommended by the Howe Commission are the addition of up to three persons to join the dean and canons on the administrative chapter, together with a greater council consisting of the bishop, the administrative chapter, two honorary canons, up to four members of the cathedral community, six representatives from the wider diocese, two members of the local community, two regional or national representatives and two independent members.[16] All this is very much in accord with the thinking of a society that pays much lip-service to democracy. Whether or not it will reduce the function of deans and canons to what Dean Eric Evans described in the General Synod debate as 'nondescript, mediocre, bureaucratic clones' remains to be seen.[17] Despite the proposals for these far-reaching changes, the dean and chapter firmly believe that our primary commitment to 'continuous and reverent worship' will remain as much the distinguishing mark of our second 900 years as it was of our first. That certainly is our hope and prayer.

16. *Heritage and Renewal*, chapter 6.
17. Proceedings of General Synod debate on the archbishops' report on cathedrals, November 1994.

Bishops, Priors and Deans

Bishops of Norwich	From	To
Herbert de Losinga[1]	1091	1119
Eborard	1121	1145
William Turbe	1146–47	1174
John of Oxford	1175	1200
John de Gray	1200	1214
Pandulf	1215	1226
Thomas Blundeville	1226	1236
Simon Elmham[2]	*1236*	*1239*
William Raleigh	1239	1243
Walter Suffield	1244	1257
Simon Wauton	1257	1266
Roger Scarning	1266	1278
William Middleton	1278	1288
Ralph Walpole	1288	1299
John Salmon	1299	1325
Robert Baldock[3]	*1325*	*1325*
William Ayremynne	1325	1336
Thomas Hempnall[4]	*1336*	*1337*
Anthony Bek	1337	1343
William Bateman	1344	1355
Thomas Percy	1355	1369
Henry Despenser	1369	1406
Alexander Tottington	1406	1413
Richard Courtenay	1413	1415
John Wakering	1415	1425
William Alnwick	1426	1436
Thomas Brouns	1436	1445
John Stanbury[5]	*1445*	*1446*
Walter Lyhart	1446	1472
James Goldwell	1472	1499
Thomas Jane	1499	1500
Richard Nix	1501	1535–36
William Repps	1536	1550
Thomas Thirlby	1550	1554
John Hopton	1554	1558
Richard Cox[6]	*1559*	*1559*
John Parkhurst	1560	1575
Edmund Freake	1575	1584
Edmund Scambler	1585	1594
William Redman	1595	1602
John Jegon	1603	1618
John Overall	1618	1619
Samuel Harsnett	1619	1628
Francis White	1629	1631
Richard Corbett	1632	1635
Matthew Wren	1635	1638
Richard Mountagu	1638	1641
Joseph Hall	1641	1646
EPISCOPACY ABOLISHED	1646	1660
Edward Reynolds	1660	1676
Anthony Sparrow	1676	1685
William Lloyd	1685	1690
John Moore	1691	1707
Charles Trimnell	1708	1721
Thomas Green	1721	1723
John Leng	1723	1727
William Baker	1727	1732
Robert Butts	1733	1738
Thomas Gooch	1738	1748
Samuel Lisle	1748	1749
Thomas Hayter	1749	1761
Philip Yonge	1761	1783
Lewis Bagot	1783	1790
George Horne	1790	1792
Charles Manners Sutton	1792	1805
Henry Bathurst	1805	1837
Edward Stanley	1837	1849
Samuel Hinds	1849	1857
John Thomas Pelham	1857	1893
John Sheepshanks	1893	1910
Bertram Pollock	1910	1942
Percy Herbert	1942	1959
Launcelot Fleming	1959	1971
Maurice Wood	1971	1985
Peter Nott	1985	

1. Bishop of Thetford and then Norwich.
2. Elected by the monks but election overturned by the pope.
3. Election overturned by the pope.
4. Elected by the monks but election overturned by the pope.
5. Elected but set aside.
6. Elected but translated to Ely before his consecration.

Priors	From	To	Deans	From	To
Ingulph	by 1106–7	after 1136	William Castleton	1538	1539
William Turbe	after 1136	1146–47	John Salisbury	1539	1554
Elias	after 1146–47	1150	John Christopherson	1554	1557
Richard de Ferrarriis	1150	1158	John Boxall	1557	1558
Ranulph	1161–74	1161–74	John Harpsfield	1558	1559
John[7]	1153–74	1153–74	John Salisbury (restored)	1559	1573
Elric	?	1172	George Gardiner	1573	1589
Tancred	1172	1175	Thomas Dove	1589	1601
Gerard	1175	1202–5	John Jegon	1601	1603
William Walsham	1202–5	1217	George Montgomery	1603	1614
Ranulph Wareham	1217	1217	Edmund Suckling	1614	1628
William son of Odo of Norwich	1219	1235	John Hassall	1628	1649
Simon Elmham	1235	1257	DEANS AND CHAPTERS ABOLISHED	1649	1660
Roger Scarning	1257	1266	John Croftes	1660	1670
Nicholas Bramertone	1266	1269	Herbert Astley	1670	1681
William Burnham	1269	1272	John Sharpe	1681	1689
William Kirby	1272	1289	Henry Fairfax	1689	1702
Henry Lakenham	1289	1310	Humphrey Prideaux	1702	1724
Robert Langley	1310	1326	Thomas Cole	1724	1731
William Claxton	1326	1344	Robert Butts	1731	1733
Simon Bouzon	1344	1352	John Baron	1733	1739
Laurence Leck	1352	1357	Thomas Bullock	1739	1760
Nicholas Hoo	1357	1382	Edward Townshend	1761	1765
Alexander Tottington	1382	1406	Philip Lloyd	1765	1790
Robert Burnham	1407	1427	Joseph Turner	1790	1828
William Worsted	1427	1436	George Pellew	1828	1866
John Heverlond	1436	1454	Edward Meyrick Goulburn	1866	1889
John Molet	1454	1471	William Lefroy	1889	1909
Thomas Bouzon	1471	1480	Russell Wakefield	1909	1911
James Bonewell	1480	1488	Henry Charles Beeching	1911	1919
William Spynke	1488	1503	John Wakefield Willink	1919	1927
William Baconthorpe	1503	1504	David Herbert Somerset Cranage	1927	1945
Robert Catton or Bronde	1504	1529–30	Herbert St Barbe Holland	1947	1952
William Castleton	1529–30	1538	Norman Hook	1952	1969
			Alan Webster	1970	1978
			David Edwards	1978	1982
			Paul Burbridge	1983	1995
			Stephen Platten	1995	

7.   Blomefield, *Norfolk*, iii, p. 600, lists them in this order but John could have preceded Ranulph.

Glossary

Abacus (plural **abaci**): slab on top of a capital providing a level surface for an arch or beam.

Advowson: the right to choose the minister appointed to a church benefice.

Aedicule: architectural surround, the framing of a window, door or other opening by columns or pilasters.

Alb: a long, white vestment with tight-fitting sleeves for a priest.

Ambulatory: aisle around the presbytery and apse. Sometimes the term is restricted to the aisle around the apse only, the remainder being called presbytery aisles or choir aisles.

Amice: a white cloth worn by clerics around the neck and shoulders.

Antiphon: church music sung by two parties each responding to the other.

Appropriation: the making over of a benefice, its tithes and endowments to a monastery or bishop. Compare '**impropriation**'.

Apse: semicircular space, as at the east end of a church.

——, **apse echelon design**: a main apse terminating the sanctuary, flanked by apses at the ends of the side aisles and in some cases apses off the transept arms.

Arcade, arcading, arcature: row of arches. The **main arcade** is the ground floor of an elevation.

——, **blind arcade**: row of arches set against a wall.

——, **interlaced arcade**: blind arcade where the arches are woven together, as if two rows are laid on top of one another.

Archdeacon: a diocesan official who, under the bishop, has chief supervision of part of a diocese or **archdeaconry**.

Ashlar: masonry blocks dressed with even faces and square edges.

Baldacchino: a freestanding canopy supported on columns and placed over an altar.

Basilica: a longitudinal hall.

Bays: divisions of a building not by walls but by regular vertical features such as arches, piers or windows.

Benefice: a church living.

Billet: moulding consisting or discontinuous rolls or strips set so that the sections and spaces alternate in alternate rows, forming a chequer-board pattern. **Single billet** is one row of such moulding; **double billet**, is two such rows. **Keeled billet** is formed by discontinuous rolls whose sectional outline is pointed like that of the keel of a ship.

Boss: a carved block of stone at a point where the ribs of a vault meet.

Buttress: a projecting wall support. A **flying buttress** stands free of the wall, connected at the top by an arch or half arch.

Canon: in music, a polyphonic composition in which one part is imitated by one or more other parts entering subsequently in such a way that successive statements of the melody overlap. **Canonic** means in the manner of a canon.

Cantus firmus: literally, 'fixed song'. A pre-existing melody, usually plainsong, used as the basis for polyphonic composition.

Capital: the head of a column.

——, **cushion capital**: one which is spherical in its lower half and square in its upper, providing a transition from the cylindrical shape of the shaft to the rectangular section of the arch. Also called a **block capital**.

——, **foliate capital**: one carved with leaf shapes.

——, **moulded capital**: a capital with a profile formed as if by turning on a lathe.

——, **scallop capital**: a cushion capital with the semicircular shape on one or more of its faces subdivided into two or more semicircles.

——, **tectonic capital**: a less geometric version of the cushion capital.

——, **volute capital**: a capital with a spiral scroll or volute at each corner.

Cavetto: concave moulding with a quarter-round section.

Centering: temporary wood or wicker framework to support an arch or vault during construction.

Chamfer: surface made by cutting off a square edge, usually at forty-five degrees.

——, **double chamfer**: applied to each of two related edges.

Chasuble: a sleeveless garment worn over an alb by a priest when celebrating mass.

Cheese moulding:

——, **double cheese**: two rows of the single variety.

——, **single cheese**: row of sections of cylinders, arranged side by side.

Chevron: moulding in the form of a zigzag.

Choir: where the choir and choir stalls are located, with the presbytery to the east and choir screen or pulpitum to the west. Often loosely, and confusingly, used for the presbytery or eastern arm of the church also.

Chord: the line from which the curve of the apse springs.

Chromatic: derived from the Greek '*chroma*', meaning 'colour', used to describe the introduction of notes which do not belong to the mode or key in which the music is written.

Cinquefoil: a shape like a five-petalled flower.

Claustral: pertaining to the cloister.

Clerestory: uppermost storey of the nave walls, pierced by windows.

Clocher: a freestanding bell tower.

Collar beam: horizontal beam linking the rafters of a roof above the level of the eaves.

Colonnette: a small column or shaft.

Column: member consisting of a cylindrical shaft carrying a capital, and normally resting on a base. Its cylindrical shape distinguishes it from a pier, which is seen as a section of wall and hence must have a rectangular core. Cylindrical supports in Romanesque buildings are, however, often termed piers by architectural historians.

Common: in liturgical terms, a service common to a class of festivals (the opposite of 'proper').

Compline: the last of the services of the day, said before retiring for the night.

Contrapuntal: the adjective from counterpoint,

the combination in a harmonious texture of two or more rhythmically independent parts of equal melodic interest.

Corbel: a support projecting from a wall. A series of corbels is known as a **corbel table**.

Cornice: moulded ledge projecting along the top of a building or wall.

Crockets: projecting leaves or flowers decorating the angles of spires, pinnacles, canopies and the like in Gothic architecture.

Crypt: vaulted room or rooms subsidiary to the sanctuary, usually at least partially underground.

——, **outer crypt**: one lying outside the apse wall.

Curate: an assistant parish cleric.

Curvilinear: see **Tracery**.

Decorated: see **Tracery**.

Dado: decorative finishing of the lower part of a wall.

Diaper: repetitive decorative pattern of squares, half-squares or lozenges.

Diaphragm wall: an arch across a longitudinal space, not carrying a vault.

Easter sepulchre: recess, usually in the sanctuary wall, for a tomb chest to receive an effigy of Christ for Easter celebrations.

Embrasure: opening in a battlement or splay of a window.

Encaustic tile: glazed and decorated earthenware tile.

Epistoler: one who reads the epistle in the church service. Compare **Gospeller**.

Feretory: place behind the high altar where the chief shrine of a church is kept.

Fillet: narrow flat band running along a roll moulding or down a shaft.

Flamboyant: late phase of Gothic architecture where the window tracery is formed of flowing curves; French equivalent of Decorated tracery.

Flushwork: knapped flint used decoratively to form patterns with dressed stone.

Four-centred arch: a pointed arch formed by describing four arcs from four points, producing a more depressed profile than a two-centred arch.

Four doctors: the four theologians acknowledged in the middle ages to be the most outstanding – Gregory the Great, Ambrose, Augustine and Jerome.

Four evangelists: the writers of the four Gospels, SS Matthew, Mark, Luke and John.

Gable: triangular-shaped section of wall supporting the end of a roof; the same shape applied decoratively, as over a niche; also, the kind of decoration on such a shape, as in **gabled billet**. A **gablet** is a small gable.

Galilee: vestibule or chapel at the west end forming a porch.

Gallery: storey above the aisle and of the same width as the aisle (and hence wider than a '**passage**') with openings into the nave; also called a '**tribune**'. In everyday usage also called a **triforium** (technically an arcaded wall passage or blank arcading facing the nave at the height of the aisle roof and below the clerestory windows).

Garth: the square area within the walks of the cloister.

Geometric: see **Tracery**.

Gospeller: one who reads the Gospel in the church service. Compare **Epistoler**.

Gothic: period of medieval architecture characterized by the use of pointed arches, rib vaults and, from the thirteenth century, by tracery; subdivided by types of tracery into different phases such as Early English, Geometric, Decorated, Perpendicular, Flamboyant.

Groin: see **Vault**.

Half shaft: semicylindrical form attached to a pier or a wall, distinguished from a half column by its greater height in relation to its thickness.

Hexafoil: a shape like a six-petalled flower.

History: liturgically speaking, a series of lessons from scripture.

Hood mould: projecting moulding above an arch or lintel to throw off water.

Impost: horizontal moulding at the springing of an arch.

——, **impost block**: a second capital or abacus above the regular one.

Impropriation: the making over of a benefice, its greater tithes and endowments to a lay person. Compare **Appropriation**.

Indult: a papal licence, authorising something to be done which the common law of the church does not sanction.

Jamb: the vertical side of a doorway or window.

Knapped flint: flints broken and laid to form a flat, black surface.

Lancet window: a slender single-light pointed-arched window.

Lantern: windowed stage of the crossing tower. Its ceiling forms the floor of the bell chamber in the crossing tower.

Lauds: night prayers, for which monastic orders rose early in the morning.

Lierne: an extra, decorative rib in a vault, not linked to any of the springing points, as distinct from 'tiercerons' which are decorative ribs springing from the corners of a bay.

Lights: see **Mullions**.

Lintel: horizontal stone or beam across an opening.

Living: in ecclesiastical terms, a benefice, a position in the church such as a parish.

Locutory: room for meetings between monks and outsiders.

Lombardic lettering: style of lettering common in northern Italy in the later part of the middle ages; forerunner to Gothic black letter.

Long-and-short work: quoins with their long side laid alternately horizontally and vertically.

Madrigal: a type of secular polyphonic vocal music which flourished in the sixteenth and seventeenth centuries. A common feature of madrigalian composition of this period is the realistic representation of the text being set, a practice usually referred to as 'word-painting'.

Matins: i) in the medieval church, the night office, followed immediately by lauds; ii) in the church of England since the Reformation, the name for morning prayer.

Merlon: the raised solid portions of battlements or crenellations.

Metropolitan: in ecclesiastical terms, an archbishop.

Motet: a polyphonic choral composition which, until the middle of the fifteenth century, could be sacred or secular. During the late Renaissance the term denoted a setting for unaccompanied voices of a sacred Latin text. Since *c.* 1600 the term has described a setting of a sacred text for solo voices and/or a choir, with or without accompaniment.

Mouchette: a tracery motif like a curved dagger.

Mullion: vertical bar dividing windows into 'lights'.

Neo-Classical: the enthusiasm for forms derived from Ancient Greece and Ancient Rome, which dominated western European design between the mid eighteenth and the early nineteenth centuries.

Nine orders of angels: angels were classified into three hierarchies, each containing three choirs or orders: seraphim, cherubim and thrones; dominations, virtues and powers; principalities, archangels and angels.

Nocturnes: the night office, divided into three.

Nook shaft: shaft set into a nook between two orders on a pier or jamb.

Obedientiary: one of the heads of a department in a monastery.

Official: in church terms, the judge or presiding officer of an archbishop's, bishop's or archdeacon's court.

Ogee: a double curve, bending first one way and then the other.

——, **flip-top ogee**: a small ogee restricted to the apex of an arch.

Opus Dei: the yearly round of liturgical worship.

Order:

——, **of a doorway, window or arch**: a series of steps receding towards the opening. A simple arch has one order, while a second, narrower arch under the first forms an arch of two orders. Each side of a pilaster on a pier forms an order.

——, **giant order**: an elevation in which columns, piers or shafts rise unbroken through more than one storey to support an arch.

Orphrey: an embroidery band on an ecclesiastical vestment.

Overarch: an arch containing other arches.

Perpendicular: see **Tracery**.

Palimpsest: a document in which an older layer has been erased to make room for a new one.

Pier: a support with a rectangular core, as opposed to a column which is cylindrical. Additional elements attached to the pier such as pilasters, half shafts and nook shafts form a **compound pier**.

Pilaster: shallow member attached to a wall or pier, frequently to support the inner order of an arch.

Plainchant: see **Plainsong**.

Plainsong: unmeasured, unaccompanied song, following speech rhythm and consisting of a single line of notes. The term is most commonly applied to the large body of traditional ritual melody of the Latin church.

Plinth: projecting base of a wall, column or pier.

Polyphony: literally meaning 'many sounds', the term is often used as an alternative to 'counterpoint', but is generally reserved for unaccompanied choral music, particularly from the sixteenth and earlier centuries, in which the parts are rhythmically independent.

Prebend: the portion of the property of the cathedral granted to a **prebendary** for his maintenance.

Prime: the first service of the day.

Profession: in monastic terms, the act of reception into a religious order.

Proper: in liturgical terms, an office or part thereof (such as a psalm) appointed for a particular occasion or season. The opposite of 'common'.

Pulpitum: screen shutting off the choir from the nave: also known as the 'choir screen'.

Putlog: scaffolding pole.

Quadrant pilaster: pilaster in the shape of part of a cylinder.

Quarry: a small piece of glass leaded into a window, usually square or diamond-shaped.

Quatrefoil: a shape like a four-petalled flower.

Quincunx: an arrangement of five objects so that four are in the corners and the fifth in the middle, as in the representation of five on dice.

Quirk: a sharp groove in a moulding, which is then said to be 'quirked'.

Quoins: dressed stones forming the angle of a building.

Rebus: an artistic or heraldic pun, as in the representation of Bishop Goldwell by means of a 'gold well' on the bosses of the presbytery vault.

Rector: cleric holding a parish and all the tithes. Compare **Vicar**.

——, **rectory**: the residence of a rector; the lands belonging to a rector.

Reredorter: medieval euphemism for a monastic latrine.

Reredos: decorated screen behind and above an altar.

Respond: half pier or half column bonded into a wall and carrying one end of an arch.

Responsory: a liturgical chant, sung usually at the conclusion of a lesson-reading, with alternate lines of sentences (**respond-verses**) sung by a soloist (or group of soloists) and the whole choir.

Retardataire: behind the times, the style of an earlier period.

Reticulated: see **Tracery**.

Retrochoir: a vague term sometimes applied to the space 'behind', that is west of, the choir, or 'behind', that is east of, the high altar.

Return stalls: the stalls at the western end of the choir placed at right angles to the main stalls.

Reveal: the inward plane of a jamb, lying between the outer surface of the wall and the frame of the door and window set in it.

Roll: a cylindrical moulding defined by its shape (half roll, double roll, hollow roll) or by its position:
——, **angle roll**: roll on the angle between the face of an arch and its soffit.
——, **face roll**: roll on the face of an arch.
——, **soffit roll**: roll on the soffit of an arch.

Romanesque: the architectural style prevalent in the territory of the Latin church between the late tenth century and the twelfth, often in England called 'Norman'.

Sacramentary: a book containing all the prayers and ceremonies used at the celebration of the sacraments.

Scrollwork: decoration composed of rolled up, undulating curves.

Slype: passage from the east walk of the cloister through the east range between the transept and the chapter house.

Soffit: the underside of an arch, also called 'intrados'.

Sole piece: in a roof truss with a triangular base to the rafters, the short horizontal timber connecting the rafter foot to the vertical ashlar piece and jointed to the wall plates on which it rests.

Soulace: a timber in a roof truss connecting the rafter and the underside of the collar.

Spandrel: one of the two roughly triangular shaped sections of wall between an arch and the base of the storey above it.

Splay: angled reveal or embrasure, usually of a window. **Double splayed** means angled on both the interior and exterior faces of the wall.

Springers: the first stones of a vault rib or arch above the springing point (the level at which a vault or arch rises from its supports).

Squinch: arch or arches across an angle between two walls to support a differently-shaped structure such as a spire.

Stair vice: a spiral stair.

Stripwork: decorative masonry made up of strips of stone.

Stole: a long narrow ecclesiastical vestment worn over the shoulders and hanging down in front.

String course: a projecting horizontal course of stone or moulding along a wall, often marking a division in an elevation.

Sub-arcuation: the construction of two or more subordinate arches under a main arch.

Terce: prayers said at the third hour, one of the daily services of the church.

Tie beam: the main connecting transverse timber laid across the space at wall-plate level, to prevent the roof from spreading.

Tierceron: an extra, decorative rib in a vault, springing from the corner of a bay, as distinct from 'liernes' which are decorative ribs not linked to any of the springing points.

Tithe: a tax for church purposes, divided into greater tithes (on major crops such as wheat and oats) and smaller tithes (on produce regarded as minor and more difficult to collect, such as lambs and eggs).

Tonsure: the shaving of part of the head (typically the crown) on entering the priesthood or a monastic order.

Tracery: linear patterns formed in stone in windows or on vaults. It is classified into various types (which can also be used to cover the associated architectural styles) including:
——, **Geometric**: the earliest tracery type, 1240s to 1290s: windows are subdivided by mullions into lights, the upper parts of which are filled with trefoils, quatrefoils, cinquefoils and hexafoils.
——, **Curvilinear**, **Decorated** or **Reticulated**: 1290s to 1340s; the single curves of the Geometric type are continued into reverse curves (ogees) with patterns of undulating lines and curved-dagger types (mouchettes) producing a net-like appearance. (The term Decorated can also, confusingly, be used to encompass Geometric types as well, covering the whole period from the mid thirteenth century to the mid fourteenth).
——, **Perpendicular**: 1330s to the sixteenth century; mullions form numerous lights within the tracery and run straight into the soffit of the containing arch.

Transom: horizontal bar across the lights of a window.

Transubstantiation: the doctrine that, in the consecration of the eucharist, the substance of bread and wine is converted into Christ's body and blood, only the appearance of bread and wine remaining.

Transverse arch: one running across the main axis of an interior space.

Trefoil: a shape like a three-petalled flower.

Trumeau: a pier in the centre of a doorway supporting the tympanum.

Truss: rigid timber framework laid laterally across the building to carry the longitudinal roof timbers.

Two-centred arch: a pointed arch formed by describing two arcs from two points, producing a more pointed profile than a four-centred arch.

Tympanum: arched area above a lintel.

Use of Sarum: the order of divine service used in the diocese of Salisbury from the eleventh century to the Reformation, and widely copied or adapted elsewhere.

Vair: an heraldic fur, represented by bell- or cup-shaped spaces of two colours, usually azure and argent, disposed alternately, in imitation of small squirrel skins arranged similarly and sewn together.

Vault: masonry cover over an architectural space.

——, **barrel vault**: a semicylindrical vault, in effect a continuous semicircular arch.

——, **fan vault**: a late medieval form which is the most complicated form of rib vault, with webbing in the shape of halved concave cones, and a flat area in the centre of each bay, the whole covered in a pattern of decorative blind tracery. All the ribs springing from one springer are of the same length and curvature and are equally spaced.

——, **groin vault**: a vault shape formed, in theory, by the intersection of two barrel vaults. A **groin** is the sharp edge at the meeting of two parts of a groin vault.

——, **intrados vault**: a vault on the underside or soffit of an arch.

——, **lierne vault**: a vault containing liernes.

——, **quadripartite vault**: a vault divided into four parts by two diagonal ribs.

——, **rib vault**: a groin vault with ribs marking the groins.

——, **tierceron vault**: a vault containing tiercerons.

Vespers: the penultimate service of the day.

Vicar: parson of a parish where the tithes had been appropriated or impropriated so that he received only the smaller tithes. Compare **Rector**.

Vicar general: an official representing the bishop.

Voussoir: one of the wedge-shaped blocks forming an arch.

Wall plate: timber laid longitudinally on top of a wall to receive the rafters.

Webbing: the surface of a vault; the form of barrel and groin vaults, and what lies behind the ribs in a rib vault.

Index

Page numbers in **bold** = an illustration; **pl.** = colour plate